READINGS IN MODERN CHINESE HISTORY

READINGS IN

MODERN CHINESE HISTORY

Edited by IMMANUEL C. Y. HSÜ

New York

OXFORD UNIVERSITY PRESS

London   1971   Toronto

PREFACE

This book of readings is designed as the companion volume to the text, *The Rise of Modern China*. It consists of articles, sections of books, and documents that are, in my view, of the highest quality and of seminal importance. They represent a cross-section of the finest scholarship on Modern China. While most of the material is available at major libraries, some is not easily found in college collections. With this compilation, a wealth of information is conveniently placed at the disposal of the reader, wherever he may be.

Obviously, in a work of broad coverage such as this, exhaustiveness is well nigh impossible; selectivity must be the ultimate guide. Of the mountains of material initially assembled, only a fraction has been retained—the criteria have been originality, insight, and brilliance of scholarship, and where the documents are concerned, basic importance. Used in conjunction with the text, this volume will give the reader a broader historical perspective and a deeper understanding of the modern transformation of China.

My organizational scheme for the history of Modern China has been set forth in the text, and there is little reason for repetition here. Suffice it to say that the format of this volume follows that of the text, with the single exception that Part II of the reader corresponds with Parts II and III of the text. Chinese characters are omitted in all the selections, and occasional minor editing is always clearly indicated.

I gratefully acknowledge my indebtedness to the following authors and publishers for permission to reprint their works:

Professor Kung-ch'uan Hsiao for his article, "Weng T'ung-ho and the Reform Movement of 1898," *Tsing Hua Journal of Chinese Studies*, New Series 1, No. 2, April 1957.

Professor Pei Huang for his article, "Aspects of Ch'ing Autocracy: An Institutional Study, 1644-1735," *Tsing Hua Journal of Chinese Studies*, New Series 4, Nos. 1 and 2 (combined issue), December 1967.

Professors Harold L. Kahn and K. C. Liu and the University of California Press for the articles, "The Education of a Prince: The Emperor Learns His Roles," and "Li Hung-chang in Chihli: The Emergence of a Policy, 1870-1875," in *Approaches to Modern Chinese History*, edited by Albert Feuerwerker,

Rhoads Murphey, and Mary C. Wright, University of California Press, 1967.

Slavic Review for my article, "Russia's Special Position in China during the Early Ch'ing Period" (December 1964).

Harvard University Press for selections from my books, *China's Entrance into the Family of Nations: The Diplomatic Phase, 1858-1880,* Harvard University Press, 1960, and *Intellectual Trends in the Ch'ing Period,* Harvard University Press, 1959.

Harvard Journal of Asiatic Studies for my article, "The Great Policy Debate in China, 1874: Maritime Defense vs. Frontier Defense," vol. 25 (1965).

Asian Survey and Professors Kang Chao and Gene T. Hsiao for the articles "Economic Aftermath of the Great Leap in Communist China" (May 1964) and "The Background and Development of 'The Proletarian Cultural Revolution'" (June 1967).

Pacific Coast Philology and Dr. Wen-shun Chi for the article, "The Ideological Source of the People's Communes in Communist China" (April 1967).

Orbis and Dr. Chu-yuan Cheng for the article, "The Root of China's Cultural Revolution: The Feud between Mao Tse-tung and Liu Shao-ch'i" (Winter 1968).

I.C.Y.H.

Santa Barbara, California
January 1971

CONTENTS

PART FOUR. INTELLECTUAL REVOLUTION, IDEOLOGICAL AWAKENING, AND INTERNATIONAL DEVELOPMENTS, 1917-1945

PART FIVE. THE RISE OF THE CHINESE PEOPLE'S REPUBLIC

PART ONE

CH'ING INSTITUTIONS, 1600-1800

INTRODUCTION

Although it is well known that the Manchu dynasty achieved a remarkable degree of autocracy, the inner workings of Ch'ing absolutism have not been examined until recently. Selection 1 by Professors Pei Huang reveals that Ch'ing rulers not only drew inspiration from Chinese precedents and the Confucian and Legalist ideologies but also created means of their own to centralize control. By two ingenious devices—the personal memorial system and the Grand Council —Emperor Yung-cheng (1723-35) succeeded in concentrating powers in his own hands at the expense of the bureaucracy, the princes, and the nobles. The Grand Councillors functioned within the palaces to assist him with confidential decisions while personal memorialists furnished him with key information from all over the empire. The first organ dealt a severe blow to the Grand Secretariat, the traditional bureaucratic stronghold, and the second, to the censorial system. The two innovations reinforced each other, forestalling divisive tendencies and secret opposition and generating the highest form of autocracy.

With so much power vested in the person of the emperor, how did he learn to exercise it judiciously and effectively; when and where did he learn his role? Recent research shows that at an early age Manchu princes began their education at the palace school, where a team of Chinese and Manchu tutors eagerly coached them in the classics, history, philosophy, calligraphy, administrative art, as well as archery and riding. In selection 2 Professor Harold L. Kahn examines how a prospective ruler, later to become Emperor Ch'ien-lung, learned his roles.

The question has often been raised as to how a small minority race such as the Manchus could rule China for so long. Partial answer may be found in the combined use of Chinese and Manchu (as well as Mongol) talent in the government, both central and local. In Selection 3 Dr. Lawrence D. Kessler examines the ethnic composition of provincial leadership, and boldly suggests that the Manchu leadership actually started to decline not after the Taiping Revolution (1850-64) as many have suggested but after the White Lotus Rebellion one-half century earlier.

China's self-image as the Middle Kingdom on earth and the unexcelled universal empire strongly conditioned her confrontation with the West in the 19th century, while the tributary system proved to be a bone of contention in early Chinese-Western intercourse. Selections 4 and 5 study China's position in the East Asian family of nations and her relations with the chief tributary state of Korea, while Selection 6 investigates why her northern neighbor, Russia, neither a regular tributary nor a maritime nation, was given preferential treatment. Russia's privileged position in Peking gave her an unique opportunity to observe the Chinese state and society from within as no other Western power could.

I. POLITICAL INNOVATIONS

1. Aspects of Ch'ing Autocracy:

An Institutional Study, 1644-1735[*]

PEI HUANG

Autocracy took root early in mankind's history. In China it probably began to acquire a foothold with establishment of the imperial system.[1] Historians have agreed that Chinese autocracy made great strides in the Sung dynasty (960-1279). The Yüan and Ming dynasties (1279-1368; 1368-1644) followed in the Sung track and made further progress.[2] The Ch'ing dynasty (1644-1911) was no less autocratic than the Ming.

Ch'ing autocracy presented new aspects in Chinese dynastic history. Ideologically it drew force from the same sources, Confucian and Legalist, as its predecessors, but it was carried out through new machines created for the special needs of Manchu emperors. In the early Ch'ing rulers steadily consolidated their power with changes in the governmental structure. To study autocracy of the Ch'ing one should take account of Manchu political institutions.

The Yung-chêng period (1723-1735),

the reign of Emperor Shih-tsung, saw the height of Ch'ing autocracy. Before it Manchu rulers did not enjoy their absolute power, which was in fact affected by influential princes and other nobles in the Banners. In its early years the Manchu regime was marked by power struggles within the ruling hierarchy. To achieve their purpose Manchu emperors were willing to make contributions to Chinese autocracy. They devised new institutions staffed with personal confidants to strengthen their power. The final solution came with formation of the personal-memorial system and the Grand Council during the Yung-chêng period. They worked side by side for Ch'ing autocracy. Personal memorials crippled the censorial system while the Grand Council weakened the position of the Grand Secretariat. The new institutions were so effective that the soverign power became ultimate both in theory and in practice.

I. DEGRADATION OF THE CENSORIAL SYSTEM

A. Combination of the Censorate and the Offices of Scrutiny

The Yung-chêng period witnessed the degradation of the censorial system. This

From *Tsing Hua Journal of Chinese Studies*, New Series VI, Nos. 1-2 (combined issue), Dec. 1967, pp. 105-48. Reprinted by permission of the author, who is associate professor of history, Youngstown State University, Ohio.

[*] This paper is a revised version of Chapters IV and V of the author's doctoral dissertation written in 1963.

epitomized the effort of the Manchu ruler to increase his authority. As an institution armed with the weapons of remonstrance and impeachment, the censorial system was more or less a check in despotism and other political evils.[3] Autocratic rulers or arbitrary officials found it necessary to reduce its power to attain their goals. The rise of Chinese despotism caused the decline of the censorial system and gave rise to even further despotism. Together, they formed a vicious circle.

The censorial system of the Ch'ing dynasty was copied from that of the Ming.[4] At the suggestion of some Chinese Bannermen the Censorate (*Tu-ch'a-yüan*) was founded by Abahai (reigned 1627-44) in 1636. It seems that not until the Shun-chih period (1644-1661) was this office consolidated. It had two Senior Presidents (*Tso tu-yü shih*) and four Senior Vice-Presidents (*Tso fu-tu-yü shih*). The appointments were given to the Chinese and the Manchu with exact numerical equality. Besides, there were fifty-six provincial censors (*Yü-shih*), distributed over 15 circuits based on geographical divisions.[5] The Six Offices of Scrutiny (*Liu-k'o chi-shih chung*), which evolved behind a scrim, were a body consolidated in the beginning years of the K'ang-hsi period (1662-1722). Staffed by supervising secretaries (*Chi-shih chung*), the Six Offices were paired with the Six Boards (*Liu-pu*). After some changes in the number of personnel each of the Six Offices comprised two senior supervising secretaries and two supervising secretaries—half of which were the Manchus and half Chinese.[6]

An analysis of the two organs—the Censorate and the Six Offices of Scrutiny —shows that their duties were originally very broad. The censors could supervise the offices and officials in both the central and the local government about their performance of official affairs and personal conduct. They supervised provincial and metropolitan examinations and leading events of the day such as the salt monopoly, grain tribute, and state granaries. They had a voice in state assemblies and a seat in the highest tribunal to review important cases. They watched the attendance of general audiences, impeached the absentees without excuse, and corrected officials who did not observe proper propriety on all formal occasions. All municipal affairs, especially judicial, were unavoidably under their supervision. In short, their functions covered all works and affairs of nationwide nature. The supervising secretaries could transmit all decrees and endorsed memorials to the Six Boards, make a copy of each, except secret matters, check and reverse them if they were found impossible to be carried out. They could audit the accounts of the central government and provincial ones as well, and they paid attention to government properties. As a whole, the censors and supervising secretaries, though without the power to enact, execute, annul, or amend laws, could inform the emperor about state affairs, and urge him to do something, or to stop action. They exercised their power through the weapons of impeachment and remonstrance.[7]

As the "ears and eyes of the emperor" the censors and supervising secretaries were in theory given some privileges. They had freedom of speech and the right to petition, and were free from punishment, because of the undaunted performance of their official duties. Their petitions and recommendations for impeachments could be made on hearsay. To avoid incurring the enmity of the impeached the emperor usually kept the accuser's name secret, and exempted him from cross-examination to answer the countercharges of the one to be impeached.

Since the Chinese censorial system had weaknesses in itself, it was destined to be powerless in the face of autocratic rulers. As members of officialdom the censors and supervising secretaries depended upon the favor of the ruler. They could be transferred, dismissed, or even punished as he saw fit. Their right and privileges faded into obscurity in the presence of autocratic masters. Like other bureaucrats, they had subjective considerations or committed malpractice. Some accepted graft, oppressed the people, or curried favor with influential officials. They made criticism and impeachments on trivial matters or simply because of personal enmity. The evils, though individual cases, made them lose their dignity as a whole and also added force to sovereigns who were looking for a chance to concentrate more power into their hands. Adopted from the Ming, the Ch'ing censorial system shared the above weaknesses.[8]

Under the Manchus the censorial system had more difficulties than had its predecessors. Since the Manchu sovereigns were conscious of their alienage, they were suspicious of both the Chinese officials and the common people. The censors and supervising secretaries were the first victims because of their functions.[9] Chinese officials lived a life of humiliation under Manchu rulers. Although Abahai tried to improve the situation of the Chinese officials, the Manchus looked down upon their Chinese colleagues, who were ignorant of their language and were even given corporal punishment for minor errors.[10] Emperor Shêng-tsu was usually considered broad-minded and lenient, but the Chinese officials had to suppress their temper and

refrain from saying anything before their Manchu colleagues. This was the reason why Chang Po-hsing (1652-1725), a Chinese governor noted for his honesty, had to control his anger at the insult of a covetous Manchu colleague, Gali (d. 1714).[11] This was also the reason why Chinese officials, including the censors and supervising secretaries, kept silent in discussion of state affairs, and followed the opinions of the Manchu officials.[12] As a result the censorial system sank into degeneration.

Besides the above factors, the Ch'ing censorial system was further weakened by the early Manchu rulers. As an institution based on the ideologies of Confucianism and Legalism, the Chinese censorial system had no authority beyond its ideological nature. Its impeachment and remonstrance were not binding to the ultimate power of the Son of Heaven. In the early Shun-chih period censors were reproached, dismissed, and forced to face the countercharge by the impeached in a cross-examination, and some were even sentenced to death.[13] This caused Chi Chên-i (b. 1630), a fearless Chinese censor, to petition the emperor to give the supervising secretaries the power to reverse decrees.[14] Naturally his appeal met with a deaf ear. As stated previously, the censors could traditionally make petitions and impeachments based on hearsay, but this privilege was removed in 1661.[15]

During the K'ang-hsi period the situation of the censorial system was even worse. The contemporaries complained that Emperor Shêng-tsu disregarded the censors' power.[16] In 1721 he banished thirteen censors who were moved by the Confucian ruler-minister relationship to remonstrate with him to restore the heir-apparent deposed for evil conduct.[17] Though noted for patronizing scholarship, the emperor was no less than a despotic ruler. In the last years of his reign he charged many officials, central and local, with censorial duties.[18] Now the censorial system was deprived not only of its privileged status but of its traditional functions.

Emperor Shih-tsung struck a deadly blow to the censorial system. At a time when the Censorate and the Six Offices of Scrutiny were losing their last stand he combined them into one office. This great change in the censorial history took place in 1723.[19] After suffering degradation the Censorate probably meant to recover part of its power by taking care of the affairs concerning the Six Offices of Scrutiny. That same year it memorialized the throne concerning the promotion and transfer of the provincial censors and supervising secretaries, and in response, the emperor ordered that their promotion and transfer should not be limited by their salaries and length of service.[20] This decree, no matter how inadequate, is generally considered the beginning of the change in the censorial system. It is said that the emperor sanctioned the proposal and put the Six Offices of Scrutiny under the Censorate. When three supervising secretaries filed a protest against this combination, they were transferred to another office by him.[21] From that time the supervising secretaries lost their traditional independent status.

The amalgamation of these two organs manifested the mentality of autocratic rulers, who disliked and disregarded any checks on their ultimate power. Their power, though omnipotent and self-sufficient at the legal level, was not a constant before political realities.[22] At the operational level bureaucrats had considerable strength to dilute the imperial power. In the case of the censorial system, censors and supervising secretaries

played a specific part in this regard. The censors and supervising secretaries exercised functions in a general sense, but as functionaries independent of each other they had their respective territories. In a certain sense the supervising secretaries were even more important. All state documents had to pass through their offices. For example, they could check and copy imperial decrees to the Six Boards. Although they could not do the same with the secret imperial decrees, they were allowed first to register them according to the indications shown in their envelopes and then to dispatch them to the boards concerned. As document inspectors they put "a kind of editorial veto" on state papers to and from the Six Boards, on memorials to the throne, and on decrees from the monarch.[23] Relatively they exercised a sort of procedural check over imperial orders, but autocratic rulers tolerated no obstruction in the way. After being deprived of their independent status the supervising secretaries were charged with the functions of the censors in addition to their own. As they busied themselves with double duties, they could neither fulfill their original responsibilities nor perform those of the censors.[24] In the Shun-chih period a censor complained that the secret decrees occasionally bypassed the regular channel, but the supervising secretaries could still read them some months later.[25] After the amalgamation of the two censorial organs an official revealed that the supervising secretaries were completely kept away from the secret decrees. Furthermore, they lost their "editorial veto" on ordinary decrees. In operation all decrees had to pass through the Grand Secretariat, in which the supervising secretaries checked and copied them. Now the Grand Secretariat was able to delay showing the supervising secretaries the ordinary decrees. Instead of checking and copying them immediately they could read the contents only from the Peking Gazette about ten days later.[26] The supervising secretaries were no longer document inspectors.

B. Enforcement of the Personal-Memorial System*

The personal-memorial system rendered a most serious blow to the Ch'ing censorial system. If the combination of the Censorate and the Six Offices of Scrutiny took away the document-inspecting functions of the supervising secretaries, the personal-memorial system was designed to divide the authority of the censors. Personal memorials (*tsouchê*) operated in the form of personal reports secret in nature. Selected by the emperor, the reporters were mainly provincial officials scattering over the country. Under the authorization of imperial orders they could expose, criticize, and impeach lawless officials for their personal conduct and administrative performance. Though without censorial title, they functioned as censors. Transmitted through special channel composed of the Grand Secretaries, Grand Councillors, and a few others, personal memorials went directly to the imperial desk. Imperial orders were sent out in the form of court letters or included in the vermilion-ink endorsements, and went straight to the reporters. Like the censorial system, the personal-memorial system formed a network extended across the whole country.

Personal memorials were considered a

* This section is mainly based on the author's article, "Yung-chêng shih-tai ti mi-tsou chih-tu" (The secret-report system during the Yung-chêng period, 1723-1735), *Tsing Hua Journal of Chinese Studies*, New Series 3, No. 1 (May, 1962), pp. 17-52.

special "avenue of criticism," as early as the Former Han dynasty (206 B.C.-23 A.D.), but it was not until the Ch'ing dynasty that they became a system. They took their form in the years 1627-1643. In a letter to the ten princes of the second degree, Abahai asked them to report to him about his and the princes' faults and the sufferings of the subjects.[27] What Abahai asked the princes to do was exactly the same as included in the personal memorials of the Yung-chêng period. Still, at the end of the letter Abahai added that if the information was worthy, they might report to him openly. This wording suggested that if matters are not suitable to make public in the court, they could be reported secretly. In fact Abahai encouraged the officials to submit personal reports.[28] Emperor Shih-tsu had more than one set of regulations about personal memorials. He ordered them transmit through the Three Inner Courts (*Nei san-yüan*), and demanded that they should be sealed. Later, he required the Transmission Office (*T'ung-chêng ssŭ*) to submit personal reports directly to him, and not through the Grand Secretariat.[29] This became a practice in the K'ang-hsi period. In 1712 Emperor Shêng-tsu ordered higher courtiers to submit personal memorials.[30]

Emperor Shih-tsung's effort proved to be a great contribution to systematization of the personal memorials. It was made to meet a special situation which confronted him after his succession to the throne. Coming to power through a bitter court struggle with his ambitious brothers, he was still challenged by his old enemies and their followers. The clique activities were another factor that caused trouble.[31] Moreover, evil practices in officialdom presented a regrettable situation in the Manchu administration, central and local as well. There was a deficit in the state accounting list.[32] Public affairs were delayed.[33] Clerks and runners in offices, especially local governments, became oppressors of the people, and servants of high provincial officials behaved the same way.[34] Manchu officials, the core of the Ch'ing regime, feathered their own nests.[35] This was a situation that demanded rectification.

Emperor Shih-tsung's character had a profound influence on systematization of the personal memorials. He could not allow the existence of corrupt officials and the prevalence of the evil practices because they would harm the power of sovereign. It was intolerable to him to see his sacred Mandate of Heaven be injured by any elements. To consolidate his power he had to recruit able, loyal supporters to follow him and enforce his orders. To suppress opponents, or even political enemies, he had to keep himself informed of their plots and schemes. To be a good sovereign, respected and supported by his subjects, he had to understand the situation of the whole country. Thus to him the operation of the personal-memorial system meant the extension of his eyes and ears. To the censors the activities of the personal memorialists equaled a division of their authority.

Personal memorials were informal reports. The Manchu rulers gave more freedom to the memorialists. The length of these reports seems to be shorter than the formal ones in general, and the number of words could vary from six or seven thousand to only a few words. No official stamps were required on informal reports. Personal memorialists were given the privilege to write their reports in a cursive way.[36]

In general the personal reports of the Yung-chêng period bear the character *Mi* or confidential, appearing either at the beginning and end, or just in the beginning, or only at the end, or in the middle of the text. Some personal memorials, though never bearing this character, are still considered confidential.[37]

Theoretically, the contents of personal memorials cover only important state affairs. Practically, they include matters about the personal conduct, ability, and performance of the officials and also information regarding farmers' harvests, rainfall, manners, and customs of localities collected through personal observation or based on hearsay. Even trivial things about the reporters themselves were put down in personal memorials.[38] In this sense one may conclude that a personal memorial is a report submitted secretly and directly by a special individual to the throne.

Some of the personal memorials were made by the officials serving in Peking, and may be called metropolitan personal memorials, while a large number of others, submitted by the individual officials serving out of the capital, may be labelled provincial personal memorials.

The contents of personal memorials may be divided into six kinds. The first, general memorials, provides such information as the harvest, price of rice, rainfall, customs, security, and local religious affairs. The second consists of replies to secret inquiries from the throne. The third one is exposing the weak points of personal behavior, or administrative performances, of certain officials. The fourth includes secret suggestions by the reporters. The fifth category includes secret requests for imperial suggestions or approval of the memorialist's ideas. The last, grateful personal memorials, expresses the reporter's gratitude for imperial favors they have received.[39] The above classification, though arbitrary, is perhaps helpful for study.

Personal reporters were individuals selected by the ruler from the bureaucrats. A few were chosen by spoken order, while most of them by written order.[40] In the capital the grand secretaries, presidents and vice-presidents of the six boards, vice-presidents of the censorate, sub-chancellors of the grand secretariat, chamberlains of the imperial body-guards, lieutenant and deputy-lieutenant generals of the Eight Banners stationed in Peking, were all qualified for writing personal reports.[41] Imperial commissioners, central government officials from the members of the Hanlin Academy, and department directors up to the censors, chief ministers of the Nine Departments, and secretaries of the Boards and Courts, were all eligible personal reporters.[42]

In provinces governors-general, governors, Tartar generals, provincial commanders-in-chief, and brigadier-generals were given the right to submit personal reports during the K'ang-hsi period and remained to be the personal reporters during the reign of Emperor Shih-tsung.[43] Some lieutenant-generals and judicial commissioners had this right, too. Most of them obtained it through an imperial order in 1728. Among the provincial directors of education, intendants, prefects, and even subprefects many were also selected as personal memorialists.[44] Some special officials like Director-General of the Conservation of the Yellow River and the Grand Canal (Ho-tao tsung-tu), Director-General of Grain Transport (Ts'ao-yün tsung-tu), Salt Controller of Liang-huai (Liang-huai yen-yün shih), and the three Superintendents of the Imperial Manufactories (chih-tsao) at Nanking, Soochow, and Hangchow were also on the list of personal reporters.[45] Deputy lieutenant-generals and colonels of the Banners stationed in various places were also eligible personal memorialists. Colonels of the Green Standard also had this honor.[46] Most of the aforesaid personal memorialists were authorized by written imperial orders. A few of them, however, became personal reporters through their own requests.[47] In short, the personal reporters, appointed by imperial orders or by their own requests, were all officials who filed personal memorials as an additional duty.

Sometimes the personal reporters were given special assignments.[48] To fulfill the missions they had to present the information honestly and in detail, otherwise, they would be punished.[49] As the main purpose of the personal memorials was to supply the ruler with information, the personal reporters were not allowed to conceal the true facts nor to perform their duties perfunctorily.[50] They were also permitted to make no reports if nothing of importance happened. Being the officials of imperial trust, they should not give improper protection to their friends.[51] Secrecy was their severest discipline. They could expose to nobody either the contents of their personal memorials or those of imperial orders or endorsements.[52] They could not leave the drafts of their personal reports unprotected or consult anybody about them in advance.[53] If they violated these rules, they met with a harsh punishment either by a fine or by discharge from office.[54] To maintain secrecy the reporters had to write the memorials in their own hands. Although they could ask their clerks to do this for them, they were held responsible for any leakage of the contents.[55] Their last obligation was to make a report not only of the time they were in office but even after their retirement.[56]

In return personal memorialists, though loaded with responsibilities, enjoyed some rights. Their inclusion in the list of personal reporters was considered an imperial favor. After their choice by the ruler, they had to thank him for his kindness.[57] The personal reports were a means for the ruler to obtain information and also an instrument for the reporters to expose and impeach other officials or to present their opinions about certain affairs.[58] If they faced embarrassing situations, they might ask for imperial help through personal memorials.[59] If they made worthy reports, they might have imperial commendations. Some of them might even get promotions.[60] As a matter of fact, officials not selected as personal memorialists were not powerful bureaucrats.

Personal reporters, no matter how low their rank, might send their reports directly to the monarch without going through the ordinary official channel.[61] To keep safe and secret the personal memorials had to be put in a special leather box given to them by the ruler, and each box had attachments such as locks, keys, and wrapping cloths.[62] Sometimes, though given more, they kept only four boxes.[63] As the boxes and their accessories were given by the ruler, the reporters were obliged to keep them. They could not make a box or its attachments if they lost the original.[64] Put in the box, the personal memorial was sent to Peking by private messengers. During the course of delivery the memorialists were not allowed to use military post stations to dispatch their personal reports, except very important ones. Ordinary personal memorials could also be transmitted by the reporters' superiors or sent together with other officials' personal reports.[65]

The personal memorials were brought to the imperial desk through two special channels operating according to the official ranks of the personal reporters. One of the channels was composed of two offices—the Outer Chancery of Memorials

(*Wai tsou-shih ch'u*), and the Inner Chancery of Memorials (*Nei tsou-shih ch'u*). Situated outside the *Ch'ien-ch'ing* gate, established perhaps in the Shun-chih period, and staffed by chancellors for memorials, the Outer Chancery of Memorials was responsible for the reception of memorials from those officials serving in the central government and governors-general, governors, and lower provincial reporters who sent their first personal memorials.[66] This office, however, had to transmit the memorials it received to the Inner Chancery of Memorials, which was filled with eunuchs, and was responsible for dispatching all memorials to the imperial desk.[67] Thus these two offices formed a channel of transmission, and reduced the authority of the Transmission Office which originally had been charged with the same duty.

The other channel was formed by a few special individuals. They were usually chosen from the Grand Secretaries or other confidants of Emperor Shih-tsung.[68] Each of them was held responsible for the reception of personal memorials from a certain number of reporters. Those provincial personal reporters below the rank of governor, though asked to send their first memorials to the Outer Chancery of Memorials as mentioned above, had to deliver their other personal memorials to one of the special individuals as ordered in the imperial endorsements. If they were promoted to the rank of governor, they could then send their personal reports directly through the Outer Chancery of Memorials to the emperor, as did the governors-general and governors.[69] These special individuals, though receiving some personal reports for the ruler, were not the people who took the memorials to the emperor personally. They transmitted these reports to the eunuchs of the Inner Chancery of Memorials.[70] The personal reporters observed this procedure of transmission. Otherwise, they would meet with the ruler's rebuff.

Emperor Shih-tsung dealt with these memorials personally. A hard working monarch, he read and checked them carefully and thoroughly. He also made endorsements on them. As they came to the court daily one after another, he had to work from night to the next morning, a heavy load indeed.

A study of the endorsements he made on the personal memorials will throw light on some of his principles by which he handled them. As they served him only as a source of information his first principle is likely that he treated them just as a consultative source. He never made a quick decision. He held an inquisitive attitude toward them, especially those reports that exposed the weaknesses of officials. His second principle seems to be a policy flexible to the nature of the personal reports. If they were suggestive in nature, he considered first their applicability and then the proper Boards to put them into effect. If they were grateful memorials, he marked them with the characters "lan" or seen, or "chih-tao liao" or noted. If they were general reports to state good harvests in certain places, he wrote endorsements of his delight and commendation. If a calamity was stated in the personal reports, believing in the interaction between Heaven and man, he scolded the local officials concerned and asked them to improve their acts and personal conduct.[71]

Emperor Shih-tsung used the personal reports also as an instrument of his political orientation to the memorialists. His vermilion endorsements on the personal memorials were instructive in nature. To attain this aim he held the third principle, a policy flexible to the characters of the reporters. If a personal reporter conducted his office work satisfactorily, he encouraged him. If not, he warned him. His last principle was to maintain a harmonious relationship between the public and the personal memorial. Though extending and strengthening the personal-memorial system, he tried to keep the legal status of the open memorials. He allowed no one to misuse the personal reports when the open ones were used. To maintain this rule he permitted no personal memorialists of lower ranks to encroach on the authority of the governors-general and governors.[72]

After being endorsed by Emperor Shih-tsung the personal reports had to go back to their authors. As he did not keep any duplicates of them, the personal memorials were ordered to be sent back after the reporters had read the endorsements.

C. Political Significance of the Personal-memorial System

The rise of the personal-memorial system reduced the traditional Chinese censorial system to a mere existence. Since every personal reporter was given the privilege of censorship, the activities of the personal memorialists were no less than those of the censors. After losing their inherited functions censors and supervising secretaries were but ordinary members of the bureaucracy. Occasionally a few undaunted censors tried to fulfill their original obligation or right of impeachment and remonstrance, but they met with a harsh punishment. The case of Hsieh Chi-shih (1689-1756) afforded a good example of this situation.[73] A few days after his appointment as a censor in 1726, he impeached T'ien Wên-ching (1662-1732), then governor of Honan and one of the most favored officials of

Emperor Shih-tsung, of harsh, corrupt, and unjust administration. Although the case involved a struggle between the officials holding the *chin-shih* degree and those without that degree, it was fundamentally an effort to resume the traditional functions of the censors. Naturally it was considered a great offense by the emperor who was devoted to consolidation of his power. Hsieh Chi-shih was banished to Mongolia as an example to others. He was released from prison in 1730 but still served forced labor in exile until 1736. At the risk of severe punishment no censors dared to exercise their power. Like other bureaucrats, they were obedient servants of the despotic ruler.

The personal-memorial system served as a means of imperial control over bureaucrats. While the web of the personal-memorial system spread to every corner of the country, not only were the ordinary officials subject to the surveillance of the personal reporters but the personal memorialists themselves were also the targets of their fellow-reporters.[74] In this sense the personal reporters, informing the ruler of everything that happened, and exposing others' faults, were not only censors but spies. Even the contemporaries of Emperor Shih-tsung held this opinion.[75] Encircled in the network of the personal reporters, the officials of the Yung-chêng period were constantly afraid of being impeached, and dared not infringe upon the imperial power. They were frightened into submission. Since the emperor aimed at the correction of administrative evils, most officials tended to demand too much from their subordinates and people in order to avoid criticism. It seems that severity became the political current of the time. None was courageous enough to remonstrate with Emperor Shih-tsung about this actual political situation, which was

presented only after his death.[76] All officials followed the will of the emperor. This is the reason why he could successfully remove his offending brothers and their followers and suppress Nien Kêng-yao (d. 1726) and Lungkodo (d. 1728) no matter how influential and powerful they were.

The personal-memorial system signifies the realization of Emperor Shih-tsung's autocratic ideas. As the personal memorials were submitted and handled privately, the impeached had no chance to defend themselves before a formal cross-examination was held.[77] Officials were not only at the disposition of the ruler but also at the mercy of personal reporters. Trembling before the personal-memorial system, each official threw suspicion upon others. Some reporters, in spite of the risk of betrayal of secrecy, used their privilege of submitting personal memorials as weapons to frighten other officials.[78] As a result the officialdom of the Yung-chêng period was divided due to mutual suspicion between officials. Whatever be the reasons for the division of officials, a divided bureaucracy was unable to take any concerted action against imperial despotism.[79] Perhaps one may say that the personal-memorial system was a means of divide and rule. With its help Emperor Shih-tsung exercised his imperial power without checks. Officials followed his likes and dislikes.

II. A NEW INSTRUMENT OF AUTOCRATIC RULE—THE *CHÜN-CHI CH'U*

A. Formation of the *Chün-chi Ch's*

The *Chün-chi ch'u* or Grand Council greatly contributed to the autocracy of the early Ch'ing. It took over the important functions of the Grand Secretariat and completed the change in the Manchu censorial system. Students of Ch'ing history have tended to believe that it was founded mainly for preparing the campaign against the Dzungars, a Mongolian tribe.[80] However, military necessity explains only one of the factors for its formation. The question should be examined in terms of the political climate in which the Grand Council was established, and also in the light of the past Manchu practices in relation to its organization.

Organization of the Grand Council was largely a result of the political development in the early years of the Yung-chêng period. The factors for the enforcement of the personal-memorial system also dominated the establishment of the Grand Council. In a certain sense Emperor Shih-tsung may be considered an "organizing-type" ruler who was gifted with administrative ability, emphasized political reality, and concentrated into his hands both ultimate and executive power for effective use.[81] While he recruited personal reporters from the bureaucracy to keep him informed of the state affairs, he needed a few confidants to carry out his decisions. This group of confidants was eventually institutionalized as the Grand Council.

The Grand Council was primarily an office resulting from the past administrative practices. The early Manchu rulers became used to requiring the assistance of a small, informal, and carefully selected group of scholars.[82] Even before establishment of the Six Boards in 1631, Abahai had founded the Literary Office (Wên-kuan) comprising Chinese scholars and military officers from the Ming turncoats.[83] Though small and informal, it was independent of the Six Boards under princes who were concurrently Banner Commanders. Members of the office were not high officials, but they were imperial favorites. As personal staff of the ruler they offered Abahai suggestions on military strategy and political affairs.[84] They worked for the cause of Abahai, who fought not only for conquest of China but for his supremacy over other Manchu princes. In 1636 the Literary Office developed into the Three Inner Courts from which later came the Grand Secretariat, the center of the Manchu administration before formation of the Grand Council.

The Literary Office marked a milestone in the Manchu evolution from a feudal group to a despotic polity. During the formative period of the Manchu dynasty, kinship was the first concern in choice of officials. Nurhaci (1559-1626), founder of the Manchu dynasty, made his sons and nephews princes (Beile) who commanded Banners and shared inter-Banner matters, namely, state affairs. Under the strong influence of kinship Abahai was but a nominal ruler in the early years of his reign. Moreover, supported by their Banner forces, princes enjoyed both military and political authority. The Banners revolved around kinship and made no difference between military and civilian affairs. The Five Councillors and Ten Associates were appointed to take charge of civilian business, but they were subordinate to the princes, or to all the princes collectively rather than directly to the ruler.[85] To concentrate power Abahai had to fight on both fronts. The Literary Office served him as a double-edged sword. Since it recruited members according to their ability and capacity, it meant the rise of bureaucracy at the cost of the kinship influence, the basis of the princes' power. As bureaucrats depended on the favor of their master, members of the of-

bureau

fice helped Abahai wrestle power from the princes. The suggestions of the officials in the Literary Office were more influential than those of the princes. At a court assembly they even suggested punishment for the guilt of Manggultai (1587-1633), one of the most powerful senior princes.[86] Because the office was civilian in nature, its formation started to distinguish military from civil authority. Its independence of military authority meant its freedom from the influence of the princes. Actually it overshadowed the Six Boards. Although the influence of the princes lingered in the Six Boards until 1652, the Literary Office was an important tool for the promotion of the Manchu ruler's absolute authority. The practice established by Abahai became a model for his successors.

In its early years Ch'ing autocracy followed a winding course. Before 1644 it grew chiefly at the expense of the princes who shared the same origin with the ruler. The power struggle went on within the Aisin Gioro clan, the ruling house of the Manchu dynasty. Abahai founded the Literary Office, a compact group of bureaucrats, to consolidate his rulership. After 1644 the Ch'ing power was based on its bureaucratic structure subordinate to the ruler. The Banners, though preserving a great deal of their feudal vestiges, were at least in name part of the bureaucracy which enjoyed to a certain extent the executive power. Strong bureaucrats demonstrated not only executive ability but initiative and tended to be factional leaders. Dorgon (1612-1650), prince regent in the early years of the Shun-chih period, and Oboi (d. 1669), one of the four regents in the years 1662-1669, belonged to this category of bureaucrats. Autocratic rulers needed bureaucrats but were fearful of their encroachment on the sovereign

power. The rise of imperial confidants after Abahai was at the cost of the bureaucrats, Manchu and Chinese.

Emperor Shih-tsu had a different group of confidants including religious men and eunuchs. Considering the political climate of the Shun-chih period, his contacts with the Jesuits and Buddhists were perhaps not purely religious. Father Adam Schall Von Bell (1591-1666) was a life friend of the emperor and gave him extensive advice from religious to political affairs.[87] Although their relation was largely established on the Father's personal qualifications, his official capacity as director of the Imperial Board of Astronomy (Ch'in-t'ien chien) was probably more important to his prestige in the Manchu court. To give the emperor moral teaching the Jesuit interpreted the natural phenomena in traditional Chinese version. The tasks of the Board of Astronomy in Chinese history provided moral support, and at the same time was a solvent to the absolute power of rulers.[88] Besides, the strict Catholic doctrine and discipline might also have lent a spiritual force to the imperial authority. The Father was the "actual regent of China" in the years 1651-1660.[89]

In the meantime Emperor Shih-tsu's interest in Ch'an Buddhism increased with time. Buddhist priests such as Hsing-ts'ung (1610-1666), T'ung-hsiu (1614-1675), Hsing-sên (1614-1677), and in particular Tao-min (1596-1674) became his entrusted friends and advisors.[90] His interest in Buddhism was not necessarily for political purpose, but Ch'ing rulers respected Buddhists, as they did Lamas, largely for political purposes. Emperor Shih-tsung, for example, secretly ordered an official to protect Buddhism and Taoism on the ground that together with Confucianism they were important to the governing of the people.[91] In the last years of the Shun-chih period the Buddhist influence dominated the Manchu court. It is said that Yu T'ung (1618-1704), a famous man of letters but an unsuccessful graduate student, owed his official appointment to Tao-min's advice.[92] No matter who Emperor Shih-tsu's intimate aides were, Jesuit or Buddhist, or what the nature of their advice, his close contact with them was made at the expense of the bureaucrats who were legally his assistants. This practice was fundamentally despotic and was not different from what Abahai had done before.

In the Shun-chih era eunuchs, another group of imperial confidants, acquired influence after the death of Dorgon in 1650. The eunuch institution had played a significant role in advancing autocracy in Chinese history, notably the Ming dynasty. The eunuchs helped Emperor Shih-tsu eliminate Dorgon's henchmen from the central administration. The emperor organized the eunuchs into the Thirteen Offices (*Shih-san ya-men*) under the leadership of Wu Liang-fu (d. 1661). As they enjoyed the imperial favor, they took charge of court affairs, provided suggestions on the state administration, and led him to abusive conduct.[93] Since he sought advice from private assistants but not from his bureaucrats, a prince submitted a memorial to the effect that the ruler should turn to regular officials for help.[94]

The Imperial Study (*Nan shu-fang*) was a very influential office in the K'ang-hsi period. Originally a reading place of Emperor Shêng-tsu, it was made into an office of his personal advisors in 1677.[95] Most of its staff were holders of the *chin-shih* degree from the Hanlin Academy, and later also from the Grand Secretariat and the Supervisorate of Imperial Instruction (*Chan-shih fu*). Some staff were

holders of the *chü-jên* degree.[96] The licentiate, mathematician, and even holder of a military degree were also qualified for appointment in the office under the imperial favor.[97] As a whole, the selection was made by the emperor personally on their capacity as scholars, calligraphers, poets, or painters. Since the office was informal and personal, the size of its staff was not fixed. At the beginning it had two members, Chang Ying (1638-1708) and Kao Shih-ch'i (1645-1703), but finally expanded to include more. The regular members had to work in the office daily. From 1694 on high officials of the Hanlin Academy, Imperial University, and Supervisorate of Imperial Instruction took turn attending the office as temporary staff.[98]

Members of the Imperial Study acted upon the ruler's wishes. Since their original function was literary in nature, they served as copyists, proofreaders, secretaries, and expositors of Chinese classics, mathematics, or astronomy at imperial whim. However, as time went on, their work expanded to the political sphere. They were ordered to draw up edicts or consulted about state affairs. Sometimes they transmitted imperial oral orders to local officials and even sat with Grand Secretaries to perform special assignment.[99] When the ruler was on trips, they always found themselves among the imperial attendants. Also, they were usually the recipients of special imperial favor. Their personal qualifications and easy access to the throne were the sources of their influence. As a result, they were more powerful than those officials not in the office. If they did not overshadow the Grand Secretaries, they enjoyed the same prestige with them. After successful service in the office they were put in key positions. Many high officials had worked in this office before they received important appointments. A large number of Grand Councilors also started their career as members of the Imperial Study.

The importance of the Imperial Study came from a few factors. Although it borrowed significance from the prestige and talent of its staff, it had advantages of its own. As the office was small, its staff also had to take care of clerical work. Unlike other offices of the time, it was free from the evil practices of clerks. Since literary accomplishment was a basic requirement for appointment in the Imperial Study, its staff were mostly Chinese. It was different from other offices in the central government in which Manchu and Chinese were appointed on an equal numerical basis. Thus it got rid of the limitation to numerical equality. Chinese scholars were in general interested in scholarship and official service more than in racial problems. Under the direct supervision of the emperor they worked diligently and carefully. The Imperial Study was marked by efficiency. As it was located inside the *Ch'ien-ch'ing* Gate, isolated from ordinary bureaucrats, it carried on its work in a secret manner. This was the reason why Wang Hung-hsü (1645-1723), a devoted personal reporter, submitted his memorials to and received secret imperial orders from the office.[100] For the same reason, in later years, it became the waiting room of Grand Councillors and their Secretaries before receiving assignments from the ruler.[101] Efficient and secret, it was an informal political center prevailing over the Grand Secretariat, roughly, after the middle of the K'ang-hsi period.

The influence of the Imperial Study substantially stopped with the death of Emperor Shêng-tsu in 1722. Although it lasted to the end of the dynasty, its main work and practices were taken over by the Grand Council. It was the predecessor of the latter. However, it is interesting to know why Emperor Shih-tsung should found a new office instead of charging the old one with the important work as his father had done. One may find out reasons from the personality of the emperor and the situation of his accession to the throne. A political realist, the emperor did not respect literary achievements of officials as much as the late ruler. In a decree he warned members of the Hanlin Academy not to indulge themselves in writing elegant and refined essays. On the contrary, he encouraged them to write things of practical usefulness.[102] On another occasion he warned Li Fu (1675-1750), a scholar-official of distinction:

If you [Li] are proud of your ability for having memorialized a number of ancient essays and selected a few sentences from history books and thus cherished a contemptuous attitude toward me, I am afraid that it will be too late for you to regret.[103]

The above quotation reflects his autocratic mentality. To him authority was more important than literary accomplishments. Actually the Yung-chêng period saw less publications of literary and philosophical works than during the K'ang-hsi or Ch'ien-lung period. The *Synthesis of Books and Illustrations of Ancient and Modern Times* (*Ku-chin t'u-shu chi-ch'eng*), though printed in the Yung-chêng period, was in fact finished in the K'ang-hsi era. Although his reign was too short for any major literary enterprise, his personality was mainly responsible for this result. An office with staff of literary fame, the Imperial Study naturally lost appeal to the new monarch.

A second factor, which influenced his decision about the Imperial Study, was the factional strift, a struggle involving almost the entire central political hierarchy and a contest for succession starting from the latter half of the K'ang-hsi reign. Obviously the Imperial Study was also involved in the struggle. Ho Ch'o (1661-1722), for example, a member of the office, had intimate contact with Yin-ssǔ (1681-1726), the archenemy of Emperor Shih-tsung. Besides, scholar-officials tended to practise factional contention based on philosophical affiliation, geographical consideration, or personal interest. After succession Emperor Shih-tsung repeatedly attacked the factional practices of bureaucrats.[104] He had no confidence in the officialdom left by his father. To him the Imperial Study was no longer serviceable. As a ruler he would have his own following after the practices provided by his predecessors, and the result was the Grand Council.

B. Problems Concerning the *Chün-chi ch'u*

In study of the Grand Council one is confronted with some of its problems. The first and most controversial problem perhaps concerns the date of its establishment. The problem comes from a lack of reputable sources. Documents of the Ch'ing dynasty do not give reliable information about it. Neither do any private works of the Yung-chêng period. Opinions about its founding date vary. They may be divided into two broader categories, and the year 1959 is a demarcation line between them. Before that year scholars put the date in or after 1729. Their dates range from 1729 to 1732. A closer examination of the sources available shows that none of the dates is definite. In recent years the problem has invited new interest of some scholars.[105] Though without agreement among themselves, they have considered that the Grand Council was founded before 1729.

Professor Li Tsung-tung of National Taiwan University triggered a revisionist gun in 1959. He regards the latter half of 1726 as a possible date of the formation of the office.[106] In the light of historical evidence the date is not definite either but more logical. I supported his argument with more evidence included in my M.A. thesis submitted in 1959.[107] In a long article another student of Ch'ing studies also puts the date in 1729, but he seems to have picked up others' points without acknowledgment.[108] Fang Tu Lien-che, an expert in Ch'ing history, affords a new possibility for consideration. She argues that the year 1727 was most likely the right date.[109] The controversies are now confusing enough. In general, all disputants have overemphasized the military origin of the Grand Council, and thus they missed the point.

As stated the Grand Council resulted primarily from the political development of the Yung-chêng period. One should seek possible solution to the question of its beginning date from the political background. While the censorial system underwent a change, the Grand Council took a rudiment form. Both were a political adjustment to meet the needs of Emperor Shih-tsung. Soon after his enthronement he acquired the assistance of a special, but informal group, which developed a set of practices not only related to the personal-memorial system but connected with the rise of the Grand Council. When personal memorials became the most frequent and important instruments of communication from officials to the throne, imperial orders were more often transmitted in the type of court letters (*t'ing-chi*), a practice beginning at least from the K'ang-hsi period.[110] Court letters came to the officials through private channels composed of a few special individuals. Officials ordered to transmit court letters to the addresses identified themselves mostly with those individuals charged with the duty to transmit personal memorials to the emperor.

As far as sources are concerned, the earliest court letters of the Yung-chêng period appeared in 1724.[111] They could be transmitted under name of the Court or under personal names. The Grand Secretariat often transmitted the emperor's orders in the form of a letter to provincial officials.[112] Certainly Grand Secretaries had this special charge, too. They did this transmission individually or jointly. Joint transmission went on in many ways. It might be done by two, three, or four people with their names indicated together in the letter, or just with one name mentioned in it.[113] Sometimes the court letters were transmitted jointly by Grand Secretaries and Yin-hsiang (1686-1730), the most favorite brother of Emperor Shih-tsung.[114] Almost all Grand Secretaries had been transmitters individually or jointly. They were Chang T'ing-yü (1672-1775), Chu Shih (1665-1736), Chiang T'ing-hsi (1669-1732), Sun Chu (d. 1733), Fu-ninggan (d. 1728), Cha-pi-na (d. 1731), Marsai (d. 1733); and O-êr-t'ai (1680-1745).[115] Grand Secretaries, though having more chance to transmit court letters, were not the only officials charged with this duty. Presidents of the Board of Revenue (*Hu-pu*), Chamberlains of the Imperial Bodyguard (*Ling shih-wei nei ta-ch'ên*) and their senior assistants, and Commissioner of the Imperial Equipage Department (*Luan-i wei*), also took part in this transmission work.[116]

From the above discussion about these political practices of Emperor Shih-tsung one may draw a conclusion. The court letters, a form of the emperor's communication to the officials, are confidential letters transmitted through some special individuals, instead of through the Grand Secretariat, to the men concerned. Formally a court letter or not, this type of communication had been considered a court letter. No matter who transmitted them, they went to the addressees through private channels. Either Grand Secretaries or others, men authorized to do such transmissions were the emperor's favorites or had close access to the throne. As Grand Councillors were later selected out of this group, after appointment they did the same job. Containing imperial instructions, inquiries, and answers, the court letters are the counterpart of personal memorials. Both are closely related. Informed through personal memorials or through other sources or faced with certain unexpected situations, the emperor issued court letters. Having received instructions from court letters or comments from the endorsed memorials, or confronted with problems about their service, officials in places other than Peking submitted their personal memorials. Thus the issuing of court letters and the sending of personal memorials formed an unbroken chain of interaction. To deal with these matters the emperor entrusted some individuals to receive personal memorials and transmit his instructions. Serving the throne, these individuals became an informal group. Though against the legal procedures of communication through the Grand Secretariat, these practices became formal and even legal with the formation of the Grand Council. When the emperor was busy in preparation of a campaign against the Dzungars, he needed more services and suggestions.[117] Direct communication between him and local officials inevitably increased. To insure that the preparation work was secret and efficient he selected a few courtiers of high ability, credit, loyalty, and mastery of management of court letters and personal memorials as his assistants or advisers. Therefore the Grand Council appeared, though secretly, on the scene. Thus the new office was wrapped in informality and secrecy.

The second problem concerning the Grand Council is about its nominal evolution. Though sharing the same opinion that the *Chün-chi ch'u* was its last name, scholars have disputed about its earlier name or names. Opinions fall into three categories. First comes the point that at the beginning the office appeared under name of the "Office of Military Supplies" (*Chün-hsü fang*), then was referred to as the "Office of Military Strategy" (*Chün-chi fang*), and finally became the Grand Council. A second category maintains that the earliest name of the Grand Council had been the Office of Military Supplies. The third opinion is that at first the Grand Council was called the Office of Military Strategy. Each of the above points has its basis.[118] To solve the problem one should understand the viewpoints of Emperor Shih-tsung and Chang T'ing-yü. In decrees the emperor used the terms, *Chün-hsü* (Military Supplies) and *Chün-chi* (Military Strategy) almost interchangeably.[119] When these terms were interpreted as the same, the nominal evolution of the Grand Council becomes meaningless. However, the office did experience a nominal evolution. In consideration of the interchangeable names of these terms, it is safe to say that the evolution did not follow a course as strict as the first category suggests. Then, what would be the possible course? Chang T'ing-yü, a contemporary of Emperor Shih-tsung and one of the first Grand Councillors, afforded a strong clue in his essay in which he states that the Office of Military Strategy had been the name of the Grand Council.[120]

The third problem about the Grand Council is concerning its staff, especially the Grand Councillors. Like the Imperial Study, the new office had no clerks and their duties were carried out by secretaries called the *Chün-chi chang-ching,* sometimes also known as *Hsiao chün-chi.* The secretaries were recruited from the lower ranks of the officials of the Grand Secretariat and the Six Boards and were appointed on the basis of recommendation.[121] In consideration of the evolutional process of the office they appeared on the scene later than the Grand Councillors. At the beginning their number was not fixed and they functioned just as clerks. Since the Ch'ien-lung period they had been influential bureaucrats.

Appointments of the Grand Councillors went without exception to the most favored and entrusted confidants of the emperor. They had worked as the Grand Councillors before establishment of the Grand Office. Yin-hsiang, Chang T'ing-yü, and Chiang T'ing-hsi were the earliest Grand Councillors. According to the list afforded by the *Ch'ing-shih* (History of the Ch'ing dynasty) Emperor Shih-tsung had appointed ten Grand Councillors during his reign.[122] This list seems, however, not without imperfection. The first difficulty concerns the tenure of Chiang T'ing-hsi. The list indicates his tenure from 1729 to 1732.[123] In a decree to the Three Superior Banners (*Shang san-ch'i*) in 1731 Emperor Shih-tsung mentioned Chiang T'ing-hsi's title only as Grand Secretary, independent of the Grand Councillors whom he spoke of at the same time.[124] This means, perhaps, that at that time Chiang T'ing-hsi was not a Grand Councillor.

Another difficulty concerns those Grand Secretaries who were busy in transmitting court letters and receiving personal memorials for the emperor, but who were not included in the list of Grand Councillors. An analysis of the past positions the Grand Councillors had held before their new service will show that four of the ten Grand Councillors had been and were still Grand Secretaries.[125] Two of the rest were Manchu princes, two had served either as Chamberlain of the Imperial Bodyguards or as Commissioner of the Imperial Equipage Department, one had been Sub-chancellor of the Grand Secretariat, and the last had served as provincial Commander-in-Chief.[126] In fact the Grand Council drew its Grand Councillors mostly from the ranks of Grand Secretaries and presidents and vice-presidents of the Six Boards. Moreover, five of these ten Grand Councillors were still active in transmitting court letters and forwarding personal memorials for the emperor.

Bearing this analysis in mind, one has to turn to those who, though qualified candidates for the Grand Councillors, were left out of the list. Chu Shih, though not included in the list of Grand Councillors of the *Ch'ing-shih* and neglected by hisotrians, was mentioned by Liang Chang-chü (1775-1849) and some others as a Grand Councillor under the Ch'ien-lung period.[127] That is impossible, because the office was abolished immediately after Emperor Kao-tsung's accession to the throne, and Chu Shih died in 1736. He seems to have been a Grand Councillor during the Yung-chêng period. A scholar and favorite official of Emperor Shih-tsung, he had served in the Imperial Study early in 1723, and later he obtained promotion from presidency of the Board of Revenue to Grand Secretaryship in 1725. He was not only one of the emperor's confidants but an able and entrusted assistant of Yin-hsiang. Furthermore, he was also one of the transmitters of court letters and personal memorials. In this connection he was probably a Grand Councillor of the Yung-chêng period.

Cha-pi-na presented another case similar to that of Chu Shih. Although no sources mention him as a Grand Councillor, possibly he was one. A Manchu noble of the Plain Yellow Banner, he had been involved in the struggle for the heirdom during the last years of the K'ang-hsi period. However, he was later made president of the Board of War (*Ping-pu*), a position closely connected with the Grand Councillors in the work of military preparation. During his presidency he was also one of the individuals responsible for transmission of court letters.[128] Still, when the emperor launched the campaign against the Dzungars in 1729, Cha-pi-na was sent to Kansu province, where he took charge of military supplies for the western route of troops. This service was also part of the work of the Grand Council. Therefore, he might have been one of the Grand Councillors.[129]

The last problem is about the organization and functions of the Grand Council. Since it developed out of informality and expediency, it was different from regular offices. At its early stage it had no accessory office, but most likely it acquired two subordinate institutes, Military Archives Office (*Fang-lüeh kuan*) and Manchu-Chinese Translation Office (*Nei fan-shu fang*), during the Ch'ien-lung period. While Emperor Kao-tsung was devoted to military exploits, Grand Councillors were busy drawing plans, forwarding court letters, and receiving memorials from commanders. He founded the Military Archives Office to keep documents of the Grand Council. As the Imperial Study had long lost its importance, the new office also took charge of editing and publishing books of military and literary nature. It may have stopped operating after finishing its work. At the same time he established the Manchu-Chinese Translation Office to translate state papers from Manchu to Chinese, or Chinese to Manchu. Since translation was a daily work, this office became permanent.

Functions of the Grand Council identified themselves with responsibilities of its staffs. Basing on an equal footing, the Grand Councillors were at first responsible to the ruler individually, but as a result of accumulated practices a chief Grand Councillor emerged from among the staff during the reign of Emperor Kao-tsung.[130] Obligations of the Grand Councillors were almost all-inclusive. Military affairs such as strategy, supplies, and recruits and training of troops were but part of their responsibilities. They were summoned to the imperial presence when the throne needed them, no matter where they were. When asked, they had to supply information and suggestions. As early as the Yung-chêng period they took an active part in discussion about matters concerning Mongols and Tibetans and affairs regarding other minority groups.[131] Handling important judicial cases was also one of their functions. For example, in 1732 a Manchu general was punished according to their suggestions. Contrary to punishment was reward, another of their duties. When officials deserved commendations, the emperor often ordered the Grand Councillors to suggest a reward, and their suggestions were generally accepted without reservation.[132] As entrusted officials of the ruler, they might suggest changes in official appointments.[133] Their last and most important function was writing decrees and transmitting imperial orders and memorials. Naturally they were most likely to be editors of books for the emperor.

In short, their accessibility to the throne made all these responsibilities inevitable. They served the emperor as personal secretaries and a sort of "brain trust."

C. Political and Cultural Role of the *Chün-chi ch'u*

a. Its Political Role

Establishment of the Grand Council marked the climax of sovereign control over the bureaucrats. While the personal-memorial system weakened the opinion power traditionally given to the censors and supervising secretaries, the Grand Council crippled the executive power nearly enjoyed by the bureaucrats with administrative responsibilities. Consequently both the Manchu and the Chinese bureaucrats were affected by the Grand Council.

The Grand Council rendered a final blow to the princes and other Manchu nobles, who had been struggling for power but had gradually lost it to the ruler since the reign of Abahai. Their power was reduced with the degradation of the Banners.[134] Toward the end of the K'ang-hsi period, though enjoying some privileges, they were in fact members of the bureaucrats. They maintained only one stronghold, the Office for Administrative Deliberations (I-chêng ch'u) through which they had a voice in state affairs. Founded by Abahai, this office consisted of Manchu nobles charged with some advisory and administrative responsibility.[135] It had a strong influence in state affairs. Fundamentally it served Abahai as a tool for weakening the hereditary power of princes, but it became a new power center of the Manchu nobles as time went on. Its position rose higher and higher with the decline of the princes' influence based on the Banners.

Its members always met to discuss state policies and sometimes they drew up edicts for the emperor.[136] Therefore it took over part of the functions of the Grand Secretariat. After formation of the Grand Council the ruler relied on the service of the Grand Councillors but not of the Manchu nobles in the Office for Administrative Deliberations, which became nominal and was finally abolished in 1791. Without the title of the Grand Councillor the Manchu nobles had no voice in state affairs and shared no state secrecy with the ruler. Few lucky princes might be made Grand Councillors, but their appointments were based on their talent and loyalty. They were no more than the ruler's entrusted officials. During the rest of the Ch'ing dynasty there were only nine princes who served in the Grand Council.[137] It was a small number. Most of the princes were not given such posts and were even prohibited from hearing and talking about the affairs carried on by the Grand Councillors.

The Grand Secretaries were another group of bureaucrats influenced by the Grand Council. As members of the Grand Secretariat they had a legal status and were the highest ranking functionaries in the Manchu political hierarchy. Their responsibilities were mainly to draw up edicts, register them, and send them to the Board of War for delivery to the recipients through the postal system. Besides, they had the obligations to transmit, preserve, and review memorials. From these functions the Grand Secretariat derived its power. If the Imperial Study undermined it, the Grand Council decisively devitalized it. Now important edicts and memorials bypassed it and were dealt with by the Grand Council. From then on the Grand Secretariat became an office for routine affairs. Without the title of the Grand Councillor the

Grand Secretaries were but ordinary bureaucrats.

The shift of major functions from the Grand Secretariat to the Grand Council resulted in two lasting impacts on the Manchu central administration. In the first place, this shift strengthened and systematized direct communication between sovereign and local officials. The Grand Councillors recorded important imperial orders in form of court letters and passed them without registration in the Grand Secretariat to the Board of War, or sometimes to the Board of Revenue, for dispatch to the addressees by the postal system. Special deliveries were sent by express.[138] Through this direct communication local officials were brought under direct imperial supervision.

In the second place, the Grand Council militarized the whole civil administration of the Manchu empire. As it dealt with imperial orders secretly and accurately and relayed them fast, the court letters were no less than military messages to the front. Like the commander-in-chief who, sitting in headquarters, ordered generals in the field, the ruler in Peking directed local affairs through the Grand Council and commanded all other organs. This meant concentration of power in the hand of the ruler, who became almost almighty in theory, and in practice.

The Grand Council overshadowed the Grand Secretariat but did not replace it. They existed concurrently and functioned at the highest level of the political structure. There was a delicate relationship between them which insured the successful shift of major functions from the Grand Secretariat to the Grand Council, and made their co-existence possible. Such a relationship was largely the result of personal factors. Since the Grand

Councillors received more imperial trust, they were charged with more important assignments. With the shift of imperial trust the Grand Secretariat lost its importance. As a dynastic institution it maintained a legal but titular status. By imperial favor many Grand Secretaries were selected as Grand Councillors. They served in both offices at the same time. Although they spent more time in the Grand Council, their dual capacity reduced functional conflicts and rationalized the relations between these two offices. During the years 1729-1911 the number of officials concurrently serving in both organs averaged 2.35 of the total number of Grand Secretaries and Grand Councillors.[139] Because both of them owed their appointments to imperial favor, the work in either office made no difference to them.[140] They were both tools of the same owner, the emperor. This is the reason why the Grand Councillors, even after being appointed, transmitted court letters for the ruler, sometimes still under the title of Grand Secretaries.[141]

A division of labor between the Grand Council and the Grand Secretariat provided another reason for avoidance of functional conflicts between these two offices and justified the necessity of their co-existence. During the last three years of the Yung-chêng period a functional line developed between them. Among many assignments the Grand Council was focused on military affairs. To clearly separate this function from that of the Grand Secretariat, the Grand Council stamped all its military documents with a special seal given to it in 1732.[142] In case a matter concerned both institutes, they dealt with it in common. Therefore some decrees, though the same in content, were made public under the name of Grand Secretaries and at the same time also under the name of Grand Councillors.[143] A strict division of labor was a later development.

As a means of autocratic control the Grand Council had a great impact on the Manchu censorial system. The censors and supervising secretaries were theoretically able to watch every office of the state. The Grand Council was, however, not under the authority of the censorial system. In 1801 Emperor Jên-tsung (reigned 1796-1820) assigned a censor to supervise the Grand Council to assure no leakage of information, but he was not permitted to get in the office. In 1820 the emperor withdrew this order.[144] The freedom of the office from any censorship marked the high tide of autocracy.

The Grand Council also overshadowed the personal-memorial system, which weakened the influence of the censors and supervising secretaries. During the Yung-chêng period the Grand Councillors, though without the right to know the contents of the personal reports, were responsible for the transmission of the court letters for the ruler and the reception of the personal memorials from the officials outside Peking. As the Grand Councillors were selected from imperial confidants, it is very possible that Emperor Shih-tsung, especially during the last years of his reign when his physical condition declined, consulted with them about some of the personal reports. Later it seems that they were given the right to read those reports. During the Ch'ien-lung period the Manchu Grand Councillors were given the right to read endorsed Manchu personal memorials.[145] From the Tao-kuang period (1821-1850) they even had the right to see endorsed Chinese personal reports.[146] During the last decade of the eighteenth century Ho-shên (1750-1799), close in Emperor

Kao-tsung's confidence and a very powerful Grand Councillor of the period, dared to ask the personal reporters to send to the Grand Council a copy of each of their personal memorials.[147] Although this practice was stopped by Emperor Jên-tsung, later the Grand Councillors tended to be the ruler's personal assistants in his dealing with the personal memorials.[148] Thus the Grand Council, while free from the supervision of the traditional censorial system, had some authority over the personal-memorial system. Establishment of the Grand Council means, one may say, the completion of the change of the censorial system during the Yung-chêng period.

b. Its Cultural Role

The Grand Council played a cultural role, which also contributed to the autocracy of the Yung-chêng period. As conquerors the Manchus enjoyed political, financial, and legal privileges. There had been a racial line between Manchu and Chinese officials since the time of Abahai. Racial tension developed into mutual distrust and hostilities between them. During the K'ang-hsi period Chinese officials usually placed confidence in their Chinese subordinates and even covered up their faults, while Manchu officials did the same for their Manchu subordinates.[149] Since they were hostile to each other, the Manchu officials were impeached by their Chinese subordinates and vice versa.[150] Some extreme Manchus even suggested that appointments from lieutenant-colonel to lieutenant in the Green Standard in Peking should not be made for the Chinese only.[151]

This inharmonious relationship between Manchu and Chinese proved a ticklish problem to the Manchu rulers. Abahai and his two successors—Emperors Shih-tsu and Shêng-tsu—did recruit their personal confidants mainly from the Chinese, but they failed to do anything positive to change this racial situation. Emperor Shih-tsung exerted himself to treat the Chinese as equal to the Manchu. However, it would be a mistake to consider his aim to be the improving of the status of the Chinese. His chief concern was to increase his authority by removing racial problems which developed at the cost of the sovereign power. To him all officials, Manchu and Chinese, were servants. He emphasized personal qualifications of officials more than their racial origins. Princes Yin-ssu, Yin-t'ang (1683-1726), and Yin-t'i (1688-1755), who offended him, received harsh punishment. Chinese officials, Chang T'ing-yü, Chiang T'ing-hsi, and Li Wei (1687?-1738), who worked diligently and loyally, received his favor. He went beyond racial boundaries.

To delete the racial demarcation between Manchu and Chinese Emperor Shih-tsung took many measures. He started with the legal aspect of the problem. During the years 1726-1729 he made an effort to put Manchu criminals under the same law as Chinese.[152] When he made law the final resort, he permitted responsible local Chinese officials to punish Manchus who were found guilty.[153] He also did his best to make more openings available for the Chinese. In 1727 he combined vacancies for the Chinese Bannermen, and those for the Chinese scholars, into composite posts filled either by Chinese or by Chinese Bannermen.[154] Although this new rule increased the chances for Chinese Bannermen, the Chinese did not lose anything to it. Before him the appointments in the Five Boards of Fêng-t'ien (covering present-day Liaoning and part of Jehol provinces) were available to Manchus or

Chinese Bannermen only. The emperor opened them to the Chinese.[155] Sometimes he even let a Chinese take a job which was originally for the Manchu.[156] To avoid criticism by his tribesmen he had to observe some Manchu traditional attitudes toward the Chinese, but he also showed tenderness to them. He frequently compromised in dealing with problems concerning the relations between the Manchu and the Chinese. According to practice, in audience all Manchu Grand Secretaries stood ahead of all Chinese. Emperor Shih-tsung made a departure from that tradition and regulated that, except the senior Manchu Grand Secretary, the other Grand Secretaries, no matter Chinese or Manchu, stood according to the dates on which they were appointed.[157] He meant to unite the Manchu and Chinese under his leadership.

The *Chün-chi ch'u* was a place for Emperor Shih-tsung to put his ideas into practice. As indicated above, the personnel of the Grand Council was composed of his confidants. He was free from any restriction to appoint his own men to serve in the office. Among the first three Grand Councillors Chang T'ing-yü and Chiang T'ing-hsi were Chinese while Yin-hsiang was a Manchu. This practice was against the principle of appointments, according to which the Grand Secretaries and presidents and vice-presidents in the central government were Manchus and Chinese in equal number. The *Ch'ing-shih* gives ten Grand Councillors during the period from July, 1729, to September, 1735. Of this number only three were Chinese while seven were Manchus, but each of their names appeared several times. A statistical table based on the number of names as they appeared and on their chronological distribution shows the proportion between Manchu and Chinese:

TABLE I

Year	1729		1730		1731		1732		1733		1734		1735	
C or M	C	M	C	M	C	M	C	M	C	M	C	M	C	M
Number of names	2	1	2	2	2	1	3	1	1	5	1	3	2	8

[1] For source, see *Ch'ing-shih*, v. 4, pp. 2486-2487.

[2] The letters C and M as appear in the table stand for Chinese and Manchu, respectively.

During the first four years the Chinese and Manchu Grand Councillors were at a ratio of 9:5, while in the last three years they formed a ratio of 4:16. However, among the Grand Councillors of 1735 many were appointed after the death of Emperor Shih-tsung. As sources fail to show the exact dates of their appointments, it is difficult to pick them out of the list. If one adds Chu Shih to this table, the ratio will be more favorable to the Chinese Grand Councillors.[158] During the years from its establishment (say in 1729) to the end of the dynasty, there were 145 Grand Councillors.[159] Of this number 72 were Manchus, 64 Chinese, 6 Mongols, and 3 Chinese Bannermen.[160] If they are counted on a periodic basis, the proportion will be as follows:

In the Yung-chêng and Ch'ien-lung periods, from 1723 to 1796, the Manchus on the average made up 56% of the personnel, and the Chinese 37%. But in the Chia-ch'ing and Hsien-feng periods, from 1796-1862, the Manchus made up 38% and the Chinese 53%. This was probably due to the full operation of the examination system under which many capable Chinese rose to high positions. After the Taiping Rebellion, from 1862 to 1908, the Manchus made up 52% and the Chinese 47%. This was probably due to the fact the Manchus wanted to increase their power in the central government to counterbalance the increase of power of the Chinese in provincial governments. The average participation of the Manchus and the Chinese through the entire history of the Grand Council was half and half following the pattern of half Manchus and half Chinese distribution in the Grand Secretariat and the Boards.[161]

No matter what the ratio between the Manchu and the Chinese Grand Councillors, the sovereign's trust was always given to his confidants. Imperial favor was the source of authority and power of the Grand Councillors. In the case of the late Yung-chêng period nobody, except O-êr-t'ai, could challenge Chang T'ing-yü with the imperial favor he received. Finally these two became leaders of their cliques, respectively, during the beginning years of the Ch'ien-lung period. This was a situation which had never happened before.

Moreover, as the Grand Council was the office which concentrated functions from the Grand Secretariat and the Office for Administrative Deliberations, it was all-powerful. Its influence penetrated into the Banners. Subject, if not subordinate, to the same authority, both the Grand Secretariat and the Banner system shared the same fate. Establishment of the Grand Council if not meaning promotion of the Chinese status, signifies really the further degradation of the Banners. As the decrease of influence of the Banners resulted in reduction of pride on the part of the Manchus, formation of the Grand Council led to improvement of relations between the Manchu and the Chinese. Only with harmonious relations could the Manchu sovereign consolidate his power and impose tighter control over the country.

Ch'ing autocracy presented the last phase of autocratic development in Chinese dynastic history. In a technical sense it may be considered the height of such a development. Although formation of the personal-memorial system and the Grand Council was a historical repetition of the rise of extra institutions at the cost of regular offices, they were systematized and vitalized as a polity of the Manchu dynasty. As this polity proved highly workable, it lasted until the end of that dynasty.

The serviceability of the personal-memorial system and the Grand council depended upon their staff, who were selected out of qualified officials by the throne personally. Grand Councillors functioned at the central government, and personal memorialits were largely scattered throughout localities. They were at different levels, but worked for the same autocratic cause of the ruler. The Grand Council provided the ruler with special assistance while the personal-memorial system supervised the bulk of bureaucrats, mainly local officials, and kept the throne informed of the situation in different places of the empire. As a whole, they formed a polity, which discouraged intrigues and factional activities within and without the capital, and enforced the order of the ruler.

The workability of the polity also lay in the fact that it was completely under the control of the throne. Its members received assignments directly from the ruler and were responsible to him in the same way. They were required to carry out their tasks fast and secretly. As it operated differently from the regular administrative procedure, the ruler was free from the traditional bureaucratic practices which more or less formed a check on his authority. In the case of Ch'ing the Manchu nobles were additional limitations on the sovereign power. Establishment of the Literary Office and the Imperial Study aimed to do away with these limitations, bureaucratic and aristocratic. The personal-memorial system and the Grand Council were founded for the same purpose.

Functionaries of the personal-memorial system and the Grand Council carried out the will of the ruler, but they did not share his authority. In performance of their duties they were prohibited from claiming personal credit, which naturally belonged to the autocratic ruler. Chang T'ing-yü, for example, the most influential Grand Councillor of the Yung-chêng period, was only an efficient clerk of the ruler. He owed his rise in importance, in no small measure, to his ability to memorize imperial oral orders and put them into written form.[162] Staffed by qualified individuals, controlled by the ruler, and operating according to a special procedure, these two institutions formed a highly centralized polity, through which the Manchu rulers monopolized the final decisions on state affairs.

Abbreviations Used in the Notes

Ch.   *Chüan*, the basic unit of old Chinese books

CPYC   *Chu-p'i yü-chih* (Vermilion endorsements and Edicts of the Yung-Chêng period), (n. p., n. d., 60 v.)

CSL   *Ta-Ch'ing li-ch'ao shih-lu* (Veritable records of successive reigns of the Ch'ing dynasty), (Tokyo, Ōkura Shuppan Kabushiki Kaisha, 1937-1938, 4485 *chüan*.)

SYNK   *Shang-yü nei-ko* (Edicts and decrees to the Grand Secretariat), (Palace ed., 159 *chüan*, 30 v.)

YC   Yung-chêng period (1723-1735)

Notes

1. For a detailed treatment of this matter, see Lei Hai-tsung, "*Huang-ti chih-tu chih ch'eng-li*" (The establishment of the imperial system), *Tsing Hua Journal*, vol. 9, no. 4 (Oct., 1934), pp. 853-71. For a theoretical but disputable discussion on Chinese despotism, see Karl A. Wittfogel, *Oriental Despotism: A Comparative Study of Total Power* (New Haven, 1964, paperback), p. 20 and *passim*. For a critical article on Chinese despotism, see Frederick W. Mote, "The Growth of Chinese Despotism," *Oriens Extremus*, vol. 8, no. 1 (Aug., 1961), pp. 1-41.

2. For Sung despotism, see James T. C. Liu, "An Administrative Cycle in Chinese History," *Journal of Asian Studies*, vol. 21, no. 2 (Feb., 1962), pp. 137-152; Mote, *loc. cit.*, pp. 8-17. For Yüan and Ming despotism, see *ibid.*, pp. 17-31; for a small but useful book in relation to Ming despotism, see Charles O. Hucker, *The Traditional Chinese State in Ming Times* (1368-1644), (Tucson, 1961), especially pp. 38-60.

3. There are many works and articles on the censorial system. For a short but general work, see Kao I-han, *Chung-kuo yü-shih chih-tu ti yen-kê* (A history of the Chinese censorial system), (Shanghai, 1934). For a critical article in English, see Charles O. Hucker, "Confucianism and the Chinese Censorial System," in *Confucianism and Chinese Civilization* ed. by Arthur F. Wright (New York, 1964, paperback), pp. 50-76.

4. For an English treatment of the Ming censorial system, see Charles O. Hucker, "Governmental Organization of the Ming Dynasty," *Harvard Journal of Asiatic Studies*, vol. 21 (Dec., 1958), pp. 48-55; and his recent publication, *The Censorial System of Ming China* (Stanford University Press, 1966), pp. 30-65.

5. For the staff members of the Censorate, see *Li-tai chih-kuan piao* (Official titles and functions of all dynasties), compiled by Chi Yün *et al.*, in *Ssǔ-pu pei-yao*, ch. 18, pp. 4-6. The number of censors was fixed in the Ch'ien-lung period. A recent scholar prepared a chart to indicate the organization of the Ch'ing censorial system. For source, see Richard L. Walker, "The Control System of the Chinese Government," *Far Eastern Quarterly*, vol. 7, no. 1 (Nov., 1947), p. 13.

6. In 1665 each of the six offices had only two supervising secretaries. For information,

see *CSL*, K'ang-hsi period, ch. 14, pp. 5-6, Feb. 26 & March 2, 1665. By the next year two senior supervising secretaries, one Manchu and one Chinese, were added to each section. For reference, see *ibid.*, ch. 19, p. 9, July 11, 1666.

7. For all these functions, see *Ch'ing-ch'ao wên-hsien t'ung-k'ao* (Encyclopedia of the Ch'ing Dynasty), compiled under the imperial auspices of Ch'ing Kao-tsung, in *Shih-t'ung*, v. 1, pp. 5603-5605. For a detailed article, see T'ang Chi-ho, "Ch'ing-tai k'o-tao chih chih-chang" (The functions of the censors and supervising secretaries of the Ch'ing), *Tung-fang tsa-chih* (Eastern Miscellany), vol. 33, no. 1 (Jan., 1936), pp. 343-351. For an English work, see Hsieh Pao-chao, *The Government of China* (1644-1911), (Baltimore, 1925), pp, 90-92.

8. For some evil cases concerning the Ch'ing censors and supervising secretaries, see, *CSL*, Shun-chih period, ch. 97, pp. 8-9, Feb. 13, 1656; ch. 103, pp. 12-13. Oct. 6, 1656; K'ang-hsi period, ch. 14, p. 5, Feb. 26, 1665. Cf. Walker, *loc. cit.* pp. 12-15.

9. For example, see *Chang-ku ts'ung-pien* (Collected historical documents), compiled and published by the Palace Museum (Peiping, 1928-1930), v. 6, Memorials of Wang Shou-lü, p. 29.

10. For instance. see *CSL*, T'ai-tsung, ch. 10, pp. 35-36, Feb. 13, 1632.

11. For the conflict between them, see Liang Chang-chü, *Kuei-t'ien so-chi* (Miscellaneous notes after retirement), in *Liang Chang-chü pi-chi* (A collection of Liang Chang-chü's notes), by the same author, (Shanghai, 1918), ch. 2, pp. 1-2. For their short biographies in English, see Arthur W. Hummel, ed., *Eminent Chinese of the Ch'ing Period* (1644-1912), (Washington, D.C., 1943), I, pp. 51-52 & 268.

12. *CSL*, K'ang-hsi period, ch. 127, pp. 21-22, Nov, 3, 1686.

13. For these cases, see *Chang-ku ts'ung-pien*, v. 3, Memorials of Chuang Hsien-tsu pp. 3-5; Memorials of Li Shên-hsien, pp. 11-13; v. 4, Memorials of Wu Ta, pp. 10-11. For a list of names of censors punished, see Wei Hsiang-shu, *Han-sung t'ang chi* (Works of the Winter-pine studio), in *Ts'ung-shu chi-ch'êng, First Series*, ch. 2, pp. 25-26 & 29-31; *Chang-ku ts'ung-pien*, v. 4, Memorials of Tu Li-tê, p. 15. Cf. Hsieh Pao-chao, *op. cit.*, p. 95.

14. For the text of his memorial, see Ch'in-ch'üan chü-shih, ed., *Huang-Ch'ing tsou-i* or

Huang-Ch'ing ming-ch'ên tsou-i (A collection of memorials of eminent officials during the Ch'ing dynasty), (Tu-ch'êng Kuo-shih Kuan ed.), ch. 14, pp. 15-16.

15. *CSL*, K'ang-hsi period, ch. 1, pp. 12 & 15, Feb. 18 & 25, 1661; ch. 2, p. 20, May 21, 1661.

16. *SYNK*, v. 1, p. 11, March 22, 1723.

17. *CSL*, K'ang-hsi period, ch. 291, pp. 28 & 29-30, April 11 & 21, 1721; Ch'ien I-chi, *K'an-shih chai chi-shih kao* (Notes of the K'an-shih studio), (1880 ed.), "Hsü-kao," ch. 5, p. 5; *Wên-hsien ts'ung-pien* (Collectanea from the historical records), compiled and published by the Palace Museum, (Peiping, 1930-1934), v. 4, "K'ang-hsi chien-ch'u an" pp. 7-8. Cf. Hummel, *op. cit.*, II, p. 830.

18. This will be discussed in the next section.

19. The date for this change is disputable. There are two different dates. Some sources hold that it began in 1723. For reference, see Hsiao Shih, *Yung-hsien lu* (A record for permanent illustration), (Peking, 1959), p. 166; *Li-tai chih-kuan piao*, ch. 18. p. 4; *Ch'ing-ch'ao wên-hsien t'ung-k'ao*, v. 1, p. 5605; Ts'ao I-shih, *Ssŭ-yen chai chi'üan-chi* (Works of the Ssŭ-yen studio), Hsüan-t'ung ed.), "tsou-shu," ch. 2, p. 13; Tai Lu and Wang Chia-hsiang, *Kuo-ch'ao liu-k'o han chi-shih chung t'i-ming lu* (A list of the Chinese supervising secretaries in the Ch'ing Dynasty), (Kuang-hsü ed.), p. 23; T'ang Chi-ho, *loc. cit.*, p. 62; etc. Some sources maintain that it took place in 1724. For reference, see *Ch'in-ting ta-Ch'ing hui-tien shih-li* (Cases of the collected statutes of the Ch'ing), compiled under the imperial auspices of Ch'ing Jên-tsung (Chia-ch'ing ed.), ch. 754, p. 11; Huang Yü-pu *et al.*, *Kuo-ch'ao yü-shih t'i-ming lu* (A list of names of censors in the Ch'ing Dynasty), (Ching-Chi Tao ed., 1904), v. 1, YC, p. 2; *Chi-fu t'ung-chih* (Gazetteer of the metropolitan area), (Shanghai, 1934), ch. 12, p. 503.

20. *CSL*, YC, ch. 4, pp. 13-14, March 19, 1723.

21. Hsiao Shih, *op cit.*, pp. 166-167.

22. Liu, *loc. cit.*, p. 138.

23. "Confucianism and the Chinese Censorial System," p. 55. For a case study of document control by the Ming censorial system, see *The Censorial System of Ming China*, pp. 100-107.

24. Ts'ao I-shih, *op. cit.*, ch. 2, p. 14.

25. See Ch'in-ch'üan Chü-shih, *op. cit.*, ch. 14, p. 16.

26. For the status of the supervising secretaries after the amalgamation, see n. 24 above.

27. *CSL,* T'ai-tsung, ch. 8, pp. 18-19, April 2, 1631.

28. See Lo Chên-yü, ed. *Shih-liao ts'ung-k'an ch'u-pien* (Miscellaneous historical materials, first series), (Tung-fang hsüeh-hui, 1924), "Memorials of the officials during the T'ien-ts'ung period," Part I, p. 29. Cf. Têng Chih-ch'êng, *Ku-tung so-chi ch'üan-pien* (Miscellanea of historical materials), (Peking, 1955), ch. 6, p. 601.

29. *Ch'in-ting ta-Ch'ing hui-t'ien shih-li,* ch. 10, pp. 2-3.

30. *CSL,* K'ang-hsi period, ch. 249, pp. 5-6, March 5, 1712.

31. For instance, Yin-ssŭ, one of his old competitors for the throne, still challenged him in the first four years of the Yung-chêng period. Besides, the clique led by Nien Kêng-yao and that under Lungkodo were very powerful factions.

32. For example, an investigation made by Emperor Shih-tsung showed that the people of Kiangsu province owed taxes in the years 1712-1726 amounting to more than five million taels of silver while about the same amount went to the purse of local officials and bullies (see *CSL, YC,* ch. 115, pp. 3-4, Feb. 27, 1732). For a thoughtful account, see Iwami Hiroshi, "Yōsei Nenkan no minketsu ni tsuite" ('On the policies to clean up the tax-arrears (mien-ch'en) for the Yung-chêng period'), *The Tōyōshi Kenkyū* ("The Journal of Oriental Researches'), v. XVIII, No. 3 (Dec., 1959), pp. 61-84.

33. See *SYNK,* v. 2, p. 5, April 18, 1723.

34. For the abuses of clerks and servants, see *ibid.,* v. 1, pp. 10 & 13, March 22, 1723.

35. After their military conquest of China most Manchus lapsed into a corrupt life. For instance, see *ibid.,* v. 30, p. 1, Oct. 27, 1733. Consequently the emperor could not even trust them. For reference, see *CPYC,* v. 38, Memorials of Ko-shên, p. 11, Sept. 30, 1727; v. 54, Memorials of Mai-chu, p. 73, July 3, 1733.

36. For discussion of these physical aspects of personal memorials, see Huang Pei, "Yung-chêng shih-tai ti mi-tsou chih-tu" (The secret-report system during the Yung-chêng period, 1723-1735), *Tsing Hua Journal of Chinese Studies,* New Series 3, No. 1 (May, 1962), p. 24. For the shortest ones, see *CPYC,* v. 23,

Memorials of Wei Ching-kuo, p. 72, April 24, 1723.

37. For discussion and examples, see "Yung-chêng shih-tai ti mi-tsou chih-tu," pp. 24-25.

38. *SYNK,* v. 6, p. 2, March 21, 1725. Cf. *CPYC,* v. 48, Memorials of O-ch'ang, p. 87, July 13, 1729; v. 47, Memorials of Hsing-kuei, p. 2, Sept. 5, 1728.

39. For discussion on the classifications of the personal memorials, see "Yung-chêng shih-tai ti mi-tsou chih-tu," pp. 26-29.

40. For the case of oral selection, see *CPYC,* v. 47, Memorials of Hsing-kuei, p. 2, Sept. 5, 1728.

41. See n. 30 above.

42. For the case of imperial commissioners, see *CPYC,* v. 44, Memorials of Chi Tsêng-yün, p. 5, May 1, 1724. For the case of the bachelors of the Hanlin Academy, censors, department directors (*lang-chung*) and other central government officials above them, see *SYNK,* v. 17, p. 5, Jan. 16, 1728. Therefore ministers of the *T'ai-ch'ang ssŭ* (Court of Sacrificial Worship), *Kuang-lu ssŭ* (Court of Banqueting), *Hung-lu ssŭ* (Court of State Ceremonial), *T'ai-p'u ssŭ* (Court of the Imperial Stud), *Luan-i wei* (Imperial Equipage Department), *Ta-li ssŭ* (Supreme Court of Justice), *T'ung-chêng ssŭ* (Transmission Office), and *Chan-shih fu* (Supervisorate of Imperial Instruction) should be included in the number. For the case of the secretaries of the departments and boards, see *SYNK,* v. 6, pp. 12-13, April 28, 1725.

43. See n. 30 above. Emperor Shih-tsung confirmed this right for the brigadier-generals in 1723 (see *CSL, YC,* ch. 6, p. 27, June 1, 1723).

44. For the case of lieutenant-generals and judicial commissioners, see *CPYC,* v. 38, Memorials of Chao Ch'êng, p. 100, Nov. 12, 1728. But some of them had not been given this right (see *SYNK,* v. 18, p. 5, May 19, 1728). For the case of the first three, see *CPYC,* v. 47, Memorials of Wu Kuan-chieh, p. 98ff.; v. 52, Memorials of Ch'êng Yüan-chang, p. 49ff. For the case of the sub-prefect, see *ibid.,* v. 48, Memorials of Liao K'un, p. 50ff.

45. For the case of the first three, see *ibid.,* v. 1, Memorials of Ch'i-su-lê, p. 61ff.; v. 16, Memorials of Chang Ta-yu, p. 50ff.; v. 15, Memorials of Chang T'an-lin, p. 69ff. For the case of *Chih-tsao,* see *ibid.,* v. 47, Memorials of Li Ping-chung, p. 37ff.

46. For the case of Banner officers, see *CSL,*

YC, ch. 64, pp. 6-7, Jan. 16, 1738. For the case of colonels of the Green Standard, see *CPYC*, v. 23, Memorials of Yang P'êng, p. 24ff.

47. For instance, see *ibid.*, v. 35, Memorials of K'ung Yu-p'o, p. 33, Oct. 31, 1727.

48. These special tasks were charged by imperial orders. For instance, Han Liang-fu, a personal reporter, was ordered in 1727 to investigate an official, who was to be punished (see *ibid.*, v. 11, Memorials of Han Liang-fu, pp. 38-39, Jan. 27 & Feb. 22, 1727).

49. *SYNK*, v. 16, pp. 8-9, Oct. 26, 1727.

50. For instance, I Chao-hsiung, governor-general of Chihli, who failed to report to the throne a flood occurring in the area under his jurisdiction, was scolded by the emperor (see *CPYC*, v. 14, Memorials of I Chao-hsiung, p. 92, Sept. 21, 1727).

51. *Ibid.*, v. 53, Memorials of Hsü Jung, p. 10. Aug. 2, 1727.

52. For instance, see *SYNK*, v. 23, pp. 13-14, Sept. 10, 1729.

53. *Ibid.*, Chu Chih-jên, *Pên-ch'ao chêng-chih ch'üan-shu* (A complete work of political administration of the Ch'ing Dynasty), (Ch'êng-ên T'ang ed.), v. 21, pp. 60-61.

54. For the case of fine, see *SYNK*, v. 23, pp. 13-14, Sept. 10, 1729. For the cases of discharging the capacity of submitting personal reports, see Ch'ing-shih Kuan, *Man-han ming-ch'ên ch'uan* (Biographies of eminent Manchu and Chinese officials), (Chin-hsiang ed.), "*Han-ming-ch'ên ch'uan*," ch. 17, biography of Yang Ming-shih, pp. 14-15.

55. For their obligations of writing memorials by their own hands, see *CPYC*, v. 24, Memorials of Chi Ch'êng-pin, p. 87, Mar. 14, 1725. For their responsibility for any leakage of secret, see *ibid.*, v. 51, Memorials of Chao Kuo-lin, p. 6, Oct. 17, 1730.

56. The case of Yang T'ien-tsung may serve as example (see *ibid.*, v. 20, Memorials of Yang T'ien-tsung, p. 20, Jan. 14, 1732).

57. *Ibid.*, v. 23, Memorials of Yang Ch'ang-ch'un, p. 90, July 11, 1723.

58. The first four categories of personal reports mentioned above had these functions.

59. Ch'i-su-lê's case may serve as a good example (see *CPYC*, v. 1, Memorials of Ch'i-su-lê, p. 71, Dec. 6, 1724).

60. For rewards for worthy reports, see *ibid.*, v. 24, Memorials of Yen Kuang-wu, p. 28, May 26, 1728. Sun Chi-tsung, a personal reporter, exposed the mistake made by an official. As his report was regarded as valuable, he got promoted (see *ibid.*, v. 24, Memorials of Sun Chi-tsung, pp. 18-19, Sept. 9, 1725).

61. According to the regulations, only governors-general, governors, Tartar generals, and lieutenant-generals had the right to submit memorials directly to the ruler. Other officials below these ranks such as lieutenant-governors, judicial commissioners and intendants and lower officials of the central government should ask their superiors to transmit their memorials to the throne.

62. Before being given the boxes, reporters might use substitutes (see *CPYC*, v. 57, Memorials of Chao Hung-ên, p. 59, July 10, 1734). For attachments to the box, see *ibid.*, v. 47, Memorials of Chao Hsiang-k'uei, p. 82.

63. *Ibid.*, v. 24, Memorials of Chang Yao-tsu, p. 84, Feb. 9, 1731. For discussion about the reason why they kept just four boxes, see "Yung-chêng shih-tai ti mi-tsou chih-tu," p. 37.

64. Ch'ang-lai, governor of Kwangtung, made locks and keys by himself because he lost them. He escaped death sentence only out of his family background (see *Man-han ming-ch'ên ch'uan*, "Man ming-ch'ên ch'uan," ch. 29, biography of Mach'i, p. 23). The boxes should be given back when their users were degraded or passed away. For reference, see *Ch'in-ting ta-Ch'ing hui-tien shih-li*, ch. 599, p. 22.

65. For regulations of delivery through military post stations, see *CPYC*, v. 49, Memorials of Kuo Kung, p. 61, Dec. 10, 1728. For delivery of ordinary personal reports, see *ibid.*, v. 35, Memorials of Sun Kuo-hsi, p, 61, May 8, 1729.

66. For information about this office, see Chao-lien, *Hsiao-t'ing tsa-lu* (A miscellaneous record of Hsiao-t'ing), (Shanghai, 1901) ch. 1, p. 8. For its location, see *CSL*, Chia-ch'ing period, ch. 315, pp. 4-6, Feb. 4, 1816. As early as 1656 Emperor Shih-tsu ordered that memorials of the censors, supervising secretaries, and other officials serving in Peking should be sent to the door of the *Ch'ien-ch'ing* gate (see *Ch'in-ting ta-Ch'ing hui-tien shih-li*, ch. 10, p. 3). For this reason this office might be founded in the Shun-chih period. For its reception of the memorials from the officials serving in Peking, see *ibid.* For its reception of memorials from governors-general and governors, see *CPYC*, v. 13, Memorials of Ch'ang-lai, p. 66, Oct. 16, 1727. For its reception of the personal reports from the lower provincial officials,

see *ibid.*, v. 18, Memorials of Chang Yüan-huai, p. 39, Oct. 17, 1728.

67. For its transmission of memorials to the imperial desk, see Chên-chün, *T'ien-chih ou-wên* (Randoms about the court), Kan-t'ang chuan-shê ed.), ch. 1, p. 3.

68. These individuals were Chang T'ing-yü, Chiang T'ing-hsi, Yin-hsiang, and Lungkodo. For discussion, see the section on the Grand Council below. In addition to them, Sê-er-t'u was also charged with this duty (see *CPYC*, v. 34, Memorials of Hsien-tê, p. 65, July 7, 1726).

69. For transmission of provincial personal memorials, see *ibid.*, v. 18, Memorials of Chang Yüan-huai, p. 39, Oct. 17, 1728; v, 52, Memorials of Yang Yung-pin, p. 6, April 25, 1732.

70. In an endorsement Emperor Shih-tsung told a memorialist that Sê-er-t'u, though ordered to receive the personal reports for him, was not the person to take them personally to the imperial desk (see *ibid.*, v. 34, Memorials of Hsien-tê, p. 65, July 7, 1726). In this regard these special individuals should forward the reports to the eunuchs.

71. For the emperor's principles to handle personal reports, se "Yung-chêng shih-tai ti mi-tsou chih-tu," pp. 41-42.

72. For the emperor's third and fourth principles, see *ibid.*, pp. 42-43.

73. For his English biography, see Hummel, *op. cit.*, I, pp. 306-307.

74. For example, Liu T'ing-ch'ên, a personal memorialist was reminded by the emperor of his faults. Obviously this was a result of other memorialists' reports. For reference, see *CPYC*, v. 48, Memorials of Liu T'ing-ch'ên, p. 46. May 20, 1724.

75. *Lettres édifiantes et curieuses: Écrites des Missions étrangères, Memories de la Chine*, (Toulouse, 1811), v. 20, Du Père Parennin, p. 9. Consequently there are many stories about the emperor's employment of spies to watch over officials. For instance, see Chao-lien, *op. cit.*, ch. 1, pp. 4-5.

76. For example, Shih I-chih (1682-1763), a high official of the Yung-chêng period, advised Emperor Kao-tsung to change some practices of the late ruler. For reference, see *Ch'ing-ju lieh-ch'uan* (Biographies of the Ch'ing Scholars), (n. d., unpaged), v. 3, biography of Shih I-chih.

77. For instance, Ho Shih-chi, governor of Kueichow, rejected a personal request of an influential official who consequently trumped up in a personal memorial a false charge on the former. The governor was removed from office and summoned to Peking for trial. He was released only after a cross-examination. For information, see Chang T'ing-yü, *Ch'êng-huai yüan wên-ts'un* (An anthology of the Ch'êng-huai studio), (1891 ed.), ch. 11, pp. 18-19.

78. See *CPYC*, v. 18, Memorials of Ts'ai Shih-shan, pp. 69-70, May 22, 1730; v. 19, Memorials of Wang Shih-chün, p. 47, May 27, 1730.

79. For cases of the Northern Sung and Ming dynasties, see Liu, *loc. cit.*, p. 146; *The Traditional Chinese State in Ming Times*, p. 49.

80. For instance, Wang Ch'ang, *Ch'un-yung t'ang chi* (A collection of the Ch'un-yung studio), (Shu-nan shu-shê, 1892), ch. 47, p. 1; Chao I, *Yen-pao tsa-chi* (Miscellaneous notes), in *Ou-pei ch'üan-chi* (A complete work of Chao I), (Yunnan, 1877), ch. 1, p. 1; Ch'ing-shih Pien-tsuan Wei-yüan Hui, *Ch'ing shih* (History of the Ch'ing dynasty), (Taipei, Kuo-fang Yen-ch'iu Yüan, 1961), v. 4, p. 2486. Hsiao I-shan, *Ch'ing-tai t'ung-shih* (A general history of the Ch'ing dynasty), (Taipei, 1963), I, pp. 501-2; Fang Tu Lien-che, *Kuan-yü chün-chi ch'u ti chien-chih* ('On the establishment of the Chün-chi ch'u), (Canberra, 1963), pp. 1 & 24; Hummel, *op. cit.*, I, p. 55 & II, pp. 917-918; and John K. Fairbank and Ssŭ-yü Teng, *Ch'ing Administration: Three Studies*, (Cambridge, 1960), p. 55.

81. Liu, *loc. cit.*, pp. 142 & 151.

82. Fairbank and Teng, *op. cit.*, p. 56; for an analytic discussion on the relations among the ruler, bureaucrats, and aristocrats, see Joseph R. Levenson, *Confucian China and Its Modern Fate* (Berkeley, 1964), v. II, pp. 35-50, especially 39-44.

83. For establishment of the office, see *CSL*, T'ai-tsung, ch. 5, pp. 11-12, April 23, 1629; For its staff, see Shih-liang, *Yeh-t'ang hsuan chih-yen* (Collected notes of the Yeh-t'ang studio), in *Yeh-t'ang hsuan wên-chi* (A collection of the work of the Yeh-t'ang studio), by the same author, (Peiping, 1929), ch. 1, p. 3.

84. For instance, see *Shih-liao ts'ung-k'an ch'u-pien.* v. 2, Memorials of Kao Shih-chün, pp. 6-7 & 23-24; Memorials of Wang Wên-k'uei, pp. 18-21 & 24-26 and *passim.;* v. 3, Memorial of Ma Kuo-chu, pp. 1-4 and *passim.*

85. For their appointments, see *CSL*, T'ai-tsu, ch. 4, p. 21, Dec. 20, 1615. For an analytic

discussion of them, see P. Corradini, "Civil Administration at the Beginning of the Manchu Dynasty: A Note on the Establishment of the Six Ministries (Liu-pu)," *Oriens Extremus,* v. 9, no. 2 (Dec., 1962), p. 134.

86. See Fu Tsung-mao, "Ch'ing-ch'u i-chêng t'i-chih chih yen-ch'iu" ('A study on the deliberative body in early Ch'ing'), *The National Chengchi University Journal,* v. 11 (May, 1965), p. 271.

87. For information on their relationship, see Alfons Väth, S.J., *Johann Adam Schall Von Bell S.J.,* trans. into Chinese by Yang Ping-ch'ên, (Taipei, 1950), II, pp. 259-325. For a critical discussion of the same subject, see Ch'ên Yüan, "T'ang Jo-wang yü Mu-ch'ên Min" ('Father John A. Schall von Bell and the Bronze Mu-ch'en Wen'), *Fu-jên Hsüeh-chih,* v. 7, nos. 1-2 (Dec., 1938), pp. 1-27, especially pp. 15-25; Hummel, *op. cit.,* I, p. 256.

88. For the political importance of the board, see Wolfram Eberhard, "The Political Function of Astronomy and Astronomers in Han China," in John K. Fairbank, ed., *Chinese Thought and Institutions,* (Chicago, 1957), pp. 33-70, particulary pp. 62-66 & 68-70.

89. Väth, *op. cit.,* II, p. 294.

90. Hummel, *op. cit.,* I, p. 257; Ch'ên Yüan supplies reasons why the Ch'an Buddhist influence overshadowed that of the Jesuits. For reference, see "T'ang Jo-wang yü Mu-ch'ên) Min," pp. 3-4.

91. *CPYC,* v. 13, Memorials of Li Fu, pp. 41-42, July 19, 1723.

92. Tao-min, "Tsou-tui chi-yüan" (Replies to imperial inquiries) in *Chao-tai t'ung-shu i-chi,* (The Chao-tai series, B), ed. by Chang Ch'ao, (Sao-yeh shan-fang ed.), ch. 19, pp. 14-15.

93. Hummel, *op. cit.,* I, pp. 256-257.

94. Ch'ien I-chi, *Pei-ch'uan chi* (A collection of epitaphs and biographies), (1893 ed.), ch. 1, Part 1, pp. 14-15.

95. Chang Ying, *Tu-su t'ang wên-chi* (Collected essays of the Tu-su studio), (T'ung-ch'êng Chang Family ed., 1897), ch. 5, p. 4, Hummel, *op. cit.,* I, p. 64.

96. For instance, Ho Ch'o (1661-1722), a holder of the *chü-jên* degree, served in the Imperial Study (see *ibid.,* p. 284).

97. Chang T'ang-jung, *Ch'ing-kung shu-wên* (Miscellaneous accounts about the Ch'ing court), (Palace Museum, 1941), ch. 4, p. 24; Hummel, *op. cit.,* I, p. 491.

98. Chiang Liang-chi, *Tung-hua lu* (Tung-hua records), (Shan-ch'êng T'ang ed.), ch. 16, p. 12.

99. For their political functions, see Chao-lien, *op. cit.,* "hsü-lu," ch. 1, p. 12; *CSL,* K'ang-hsi period, ch. 254, p. 6, April 5, 1713; ch. 260, p. 18, Nov. 27, 1714.

100. *Wên-hsien ts'ung-pien,* v. 2, preface to "Secret Memorials of Wang Hung-hsü," pp. 1-2; v. 3, "Secret Memorials of Wang Hung-hsü," p. 36.

101. Chi-ch'ang, *Hsing-so chai tsa-chi* (Miscellaneous notes of the Hsing-so studio), (1901 ed.), ch. 1, p. 8.

102. Ch'ing Shih-tsung, *Shih-tsung hsien huang-ti yü-chih wên-chi* (Collection of Emperor Shih-tsung's essays and poems), (Palace ed., 1897), ch. 3, pp. 23-24.

103. *CPYC,* v. 8, Memorials of Li Fu, p. 97, Dec. 18, 1726.

104. For instance, he published a long essay entitled the *P'êng-tang lun* (On factions) in 1724 (see *CSL, YC,* ch. 22, pp. 17-19, Sept. 3, 1724).

105. In 1959 I submitted to National Taiwan University an M.A. thesis entitled: "Yung-chêng shih-tai chung-yang t'ung-chih t'i-hsi ti kai-pien" (Reorganization of the central governmental system during the Yung-chêng period), which has discussed the problem in detail. In 1963 I included the discussion into chapter IV of my doctoral dissertation, "A Study of the Yung-chêng Period, 1723-1735: A Political Phase," submitted to Indiana University. In the meantime Fang Tu Lien-che independently made a thorough discussion of the subject (see Fang Tu Lien-che, *op. cit.*). Last year Fu Tsung-mao, a young scholar, published "Ch'ing-tai chün-chi ch'u shê-chih chih yen-chiu" ('The study on the establishment of the Council of State in Ch'ing dynasty'), *The National Chengchi University Journal,* v. 12 (Dec., 1965), pp. 229-263, particularly pp. 240-247. Fu's discussion is thorough, but his source is questionable. In his notes he cites neither Fang's work nor my M.A. thesis. However, one of the five scholars who gave me oral examination for the M.A. degree was later an advisor of Fu's doctoral committee. Moreover, Fu's approach to the subject and his conclusion are actually the same as presented in my M.A. thesis.

106. Li Tsung-t'ung, "Pan-li chün-chi ch'u lüeh-k'ao" (A brief study of the Chün-chi ch'u), *Yu-shih Hsüeh-pao* ('The Youth Journal'), v. 1, no. 2 (1959), pp. 1-19.

107. See n. 105 above.

108. Fu Tsung-mao, *"Ch'ing-tai chün-chi ch'u shê-chih . . . ,"* p. 246. Cf. n. 105 above.

109. Fang Tu Lien-che, *op.cit.*, pp. 1, 11 & 23.

110. A photo-copy of this imperial order dated Oct. 31, 1716 appears in Antonio Sisto Rosso, *Apostolic Legations to China of the Eighteenth Century* (South Pasadena, 1948), p. 308.

111. Yin-hsiang (1686-1730) and Lungkodo transmitted a decree through the Board of War to a provincial official. For reference, see *CPYC*, v. 45, Memorials of Kao Ch'i-cho, p. 11. Jan. 15, 1724.

112. For reference to the transmission under name of the Court, see *ibid.*, v. 40. Memorials of Li Wei, p. 40, Nov. 18, 1726. For the transmission done by the Grand Secretariat, see *ibid.*, v. 16, Memorials of Chang Ta-yu, p. 76. June 10, 1727; v. 14. Memorials of I Chao-hsiung, p. 79, May 24, 1727.

113. For the transmission done individually, see *ibid.*, v. 10, Memorials of Fu-t'ai p. 94, June 12, 1730. For joint transmission by two people, see *ibid.*, v. 34, Memorials of Sung K'o-chin, p. 62, Aug. 8, 1732. For joint transmission by three people, see *ibid.*, v. 32; Memorials of T'ien Wên-ching, p. 42, July 29, 1729. For joint transmission by four people, see *ibid.*, v. 5, Memorials of Ch'ên Shih-hsia, p. 105, Jan. 5, 1728. For joint transmission but under one name, see *ibid.*, v. 15, Memorials of Shên T'ing-chêng, p. 43. Jan. 25, 1729.

114. This type of transmission divided into many ways. For the joint transmission by Yin-hsiang and one Grand Secretary, see *ibid.*, v. 13, Memorials of Ch'ang-lai, p. 72, Jan. 3, 1728. For his transmission with two or three Grand Secretaries, see *ibid.*, v. 58, Memorials of Shih-lin, p. 29, Oct. 8, 1728.

115. For the transmission done by Chang, Chiang, Sun, Funinggan, Cha-pi-na, and Marsai, check notes 112-114 above. Chu Shih's name appeared very seldom in the court letters. For reference, see *ibid.*, v. 58, Memorials of Shih-lin, p. 18, Mar. 2, 1728. After his appointment as Grand Secretary in 1732 O-êr-t'ai became one of the transmitters (see the second reference of n. 113 above).

116. Even as a president of the Board of Revenue Chiang T'ing-hsi transmitted court letters (see *ibid.*, v. 38, Memorials of T'ien Wên-ching, p. 52, Mar. 13, 1728). Fêng-shêng-ê had this duty when he was Chamber-lain of the Imperial Bodyguard and Senior Assistant Chamberlain of the Imperial Bodyguard. For reference, see *ibid.*, v. 34, Memorials of Sung K'o-chin, p. 62, Dec. 29, 1731; v. 58, Memorials of Shih-lin, p. 67, April 30, 1732. For the case of the Commissioner of the Imperial Equipage Department, see *ibid.*, v. 54, Memorials of Mai-chu, p. 95, Dec. 28, 1734.

117. *Ibid.*, v. 12, Memorials of Chu Kang, p. 86.

118. For a detailed discussion of the three categories, see "Yung-chêng shih tai chung-yang t'ung-chih . . . ," pp. 228-231; Fu Tsung-mao also supplies a discussion which is almost a repetition of what I did in my thesis. For information, see Fu Tsung-mao, *"Ch'ing-tai chün-chi ch'u shê-chih . . . ,"* pp. 247-48.

119. "Yung-chêng shih-tai chung-yang t'ung-chih . . . ," pp. 228-231.

120. Chang T'ing-yü, *op. cit.*, ch. 15, p. 31.

121. Chao-lien, *op. cit.*, ch. 2, p. 4. From 1813 on they were chosen first through recommendation and then by examination (see *CSL*, Chia-ch'ing period, ch. 271, pp. 16-17, Aug. 5, 1813).

122. Besides these three, the seven others were Marsai, O-êr-t'ai, Ha Yüan-shêng (d. 1738), Ma-lan-t'ai (only two months), Fu-p'êng (designated as Prince P'ing, d. 1748), No-ch'in (d. 1749), and Bandi (d. 1755). For the list, see *Ch'ing-shih*, v. 4, pp. 2486-2487.

123. See *ibid.*, p. 2486. Wang Ch'ang even maintained that Chiang was still in his office as a Grand Councillor during the Ch'ien-lung period (see Wang Ch'ang, *op. cit.*, ch. 47, p. 1). It is a mistake because Chiang died in 1732.

124. *Shang-yü ch'i-wu i-fu* (Edicts on the memorials of the Banner affairs), (Palace ed.), v. 6, p. 8, 1731.

125. Among these four Chiang T'ing-hsi was perhaps an exception. If the new office was created in 1726, Chiang was then but a president of the Board of Revenue. If it was founded in 1729, he had been a Grand Secretary since 1728. For his English biography, see Hummel, *op. cit.*, I. pp. 142-143.

126. This analysis is made according to the notes afforded in the *Chün-chi ta-ch'ên nien-piao* (see *Ch'ing-shih*, v. 4, pp. 2486-2487). Emperor Jên-tsung said that since the creation of the office no princes had been made Grand Councillors. For reference, see *CSL*, Chia-ch'ing period, ch. 53, p. 22, Nov. 19, 1799; Liang Chang-chü, *Shu-yüan chi lüeh* (Brief

Notes on the Central Administration), (1875 ed.), ch. 2, p. 10.

127. *Shu-yüan chi-lüeh*, ch. 15, p. 5; Hsiao I-shan, *op. cit.*, v. 5, pp. 76-77.

128. For his humiliation, see Hsiao Shih, *op. cit.*, pp. 279-280. For his service in the presidency, see *Ch'ing-shih*, v. 5, p. 4105. For his transmission of court letters, see n. 115 above and *CPYC*, v. 34, Memorials of Wang Shao-hsü, p. 26, Aug. 14, 1727.

129. As for Sun Chu and Funinggan, it seems that their exclusion from the list of Grand Councillors is reasonable. The former, though a Grand Secretary entrusted for the work of transmitting court letters, was not so favorite as were Chang T'ing-yü, Chiang T'ing-hsi, and Chu Shih. Furthermore, a compact and secret office, the *Chün-chi ch'u* could not include so many people. Funinggan, though a qualified person for the position, was recalled to Peking from the front in Sinkiang in late 1726 and after a short time of stay he was sent to Sian as the Tartar General. If he had served in the office, it might have been a short term during his stay in the capital. He died in Sian in 1728.

130. In 1771 there even began to have two chief Grand Councillors, one Chinese and one Manchu. For reference, see *Shu-yüan chi-lüeh*, ch. 13, p. 13.

131. For example, see *CSL*, YC, ch. 122, pp. 12-13, Oct. 4, 1732; ch. 131, pp. 8-9, July 3, 1733; ch. 155, p. 4, May 29, 1735. But another expert believes that during the Yung-chêng period its daily functions were limited to the military campaigns in the northwest. For reference, see Fang Tu Lien-che, *op. cit.*, p. 17.

132. For their suggestions about punishment and reward, se *CSL*, YC, ch. 120, pp. 11-12 & 15 Aug. 6 & 16, 1732.

133. *Ibid.*, ch. 150, p. 4, Dec. 28, 1734.

134. For a thorough discussion of the subject, see Mêng Shên, *Ch'ing-tai shih* (History of the Ch'ing dynasty), (Taipei, 1960), pp. 29-100.

135. *CSL*, T'ai-tsung, ch. 34, pp. 23-24, May 22, 1637.

136. *Ibid.*, K'ang-hsi period, ch. 99, pp. 4-5, Jan. 17, 1682; Lo Chên-yü, ed., *Shih-liao ts'ung-pien* (Miscellaneous historical materials), (Port Arthur, 1935), "Shêng-tsu ch'in-chêng shuo-mo jih-lu," p. 20, Nov. 13, 1696.

137. The nine princes were Yin-hsiang, Fu-p'êng, Yung-hsin, I-hsin, I-k'uang, Shih-to,

Tsai-fêng, Tsai-i, and Yü-lang. For these names, see *Ch'ing-shih*, v. 4, pp. 2486-2497, 2504-2508, & 2510-2512.

138. For information of this communication through the Board of Revenue, see *CPYC*, v. 44, Memorials of Chi Tsêng-yün, p. 36, Jan. 16, 1732. For express court letters, see *ibid.*, v. 14, Memorials of Liu Shih-ming, p. 38, July 18, 1731.

139. According to John K. Fairbank and Ssŭ-yü Teng, during these years there were approximately 1140 names of Grand Councillors and 1310 names of Grand Secretaries (see *Ch'ing Administration*, p. 57). For the average cited, see *ibid.*, p. 58.

140. Hsieh Pao-chao, *op. cit.*, p. 80.

141. See *CPYC*, v. 10, Memorials of Fu-t'ai, p. 94, June 12, 1730; v. 32, Memorials of T'ien Wên-ching, p. 42, July 29, 1729.

142. *Shang-yü pa-chi* (Edicts and decrees for the Eight Banners), (Palace ed.), v. 9, p. 5, May 17, 1732.

143. For example, an imperial order appears in the *CSL* as a decree made public through Grand Secretaries (see *ibid.*, YC, ch. 109, p. 24, Sept. 25, 1731). But it appears in the *SYNK* as an order made public by Grand Councillors (see *ibid.*, v. 28, p. 6, Sept. 24, 1731).

144. For his appointment of the censor, see *CSL*, Chia-ch'ing period, ch. 76, pp. 21-22, Jan. 2, 1801. For his withdrawal, see *Shu-yüan chi-lüeh*, ch. 14, p. 10.

145. *Ibid.*, ch. 13, pp. 2-3.

146. *Ibid.*, p. 3.

147. *CSL*, Chia-ch'ing period, ch. 38, p. 9, Feb. 23, 1799. For discussion on the case of Ho-shên, see David S. Nivison, "Ho-shen and His Accusers: Ideology and Political Behavior in the Eighteenth Century," in *Confucianism in Action*, ed. by the same author, (Stanford, 1959), pp. 209-243.

148. *Shu-yüan chi-lüeh*, ch. 13, pp. 14-15.

149. *SYNK*, v. 10, pp. 1 & 3, May 31 & June 1, 1726.

150. *CSL*, K'ang-hsi period, ch. 251, p. 16, Nov. 4, 1712.

151. *SYNK*, v. 20, pp. 3-4, Nov. 7, 1728.

152. *Ibid.*, v. 11, p. 31, Nov. 12, 1726; v. 21, p. 5, March 6, 1729.

153. *CPYC*, v. 57, Memorials of Chao Hung-ên, p. 76, Dec. 1, 1734; *Shang-yü pa-ch'i*, v. 6, p. 9, April 11, 1728.

154. *Pa-ch'i t'ung-chih ch'u-chi* (A preliminary record concerning the Eight Banners),

compiled under the imperial auspices of Ch'ing Kao-tsung, (Palace ed., 1739), ch. 144, *"Chih-kuan chih,"* Part II, pp. 5, 10, 11, & 19.

155. Hsiao Shih, *op. cit.,* p. 10.

156. Chao-lien, *op. cit.,* ch. 5, p. 11.

157. *CSL, YC,* ch. 61, p. 23, Nov. 5, 1727.

158. For the case of Chu Shih, see the discussions appearing in Part B: "Problems concerning the *Chiin-chi ch'u."* Cha-pi-na, though another possible Grand Councillor, was sent out to the front in 1729. The table in the *Ch'ing-shih* begins from 1729, so he could not be included.

159. This statistic is cited from Alfred Kuo-liang Ho, "The Grand Council in the Ch'ing Dynasty," *The Far Eastern Quarterly,* v. XI, no. 2 (Feb., 1952), p. 175. According to another scholar, during the years, 1730-1875, there were 115 Grand Councillors, among whom 59 were Manchu, 9 Mongols, and 47 Chinese (see Hsieh Pao-chao, *op. cit.,* p. 81).

160. See Ho, *loc. cit.,* p. 175.

161. *Ibid.*

162. See *CSL,* YC., ch. 87, p. 26, Dec. 14, 1729.

II. INDOCTRINATION OF IMPERIAL SCIONS

2. THE EDUCATION OF A PRINCE:

THE EMPEROR LEARNS HIS ROLES

HAROLD L. KAHN

The Chinese emperor, it has been observed, was the supreme executive in history: "He was conqueror and patriarch, theocratic ritualist, ethical exemplar, lawgiver and judge, commander-in-chief and patron of arts and letters, and all the time administrator of the empire. . . ."[1] He was, to put it mildly, a man of many parts and his office one of heroic complexity. It is surprising then that so little attention has been given to his preparation for the throne. The emperor, after all, did not spring full grown from some miraculous mechanism of omnicompetence. He was not born to rule. He was taught to. As a prince he was taught a set of values and expectations which defined the ideals and limits of imperial action and which were meant to prepare him, however imperfectly, for the realities of the power that he would one day wield.

The imperial ground was carefully laid, the self-image seriously cultivated. There was nothing particularly glamorous or mysterious about the process. It was a

hard, demanding, comprehensive course of indoctrination, a blend of classroom lessons, court manners, familial obligations, ritual responsibilities, and straightforward administrative assignments. It catered neither to that larger-than-life creature, the *wunderkind* of traditional Chinese emperor lore, nor to that abstraction of more recent analytical literature, the Confucianist-Legalist despot. These were the *personae* of a mythmaking process that began in earnest, at least in the Ch'ing period, only after the prince assumed the throne. Before that he still had an unvarnished job to do—lessons to learn, others to obey, and a workable image of the emperorship to form. If the history of the monarchy is ever to move beyond stereotypes to a real emperor, historians will have to take that job seriously. Even exceptional sovereigns, after all, rarely had more than modest beginnings. The Ch'ien-lung emperor (1711-1799; r. 1736-1795) is a case in point.

From Albert Feuerwerker, Rhodes Murphey, and Mary C. Wright (eds.), *Approaches to Modern Chinese History* (University of California Press, 1967), pp. 15-64. Reprinted by permission. The author teaches in the history department of Stanford University.

TWO BROTHERS: LESSONS IN THE PUBLIC LIFE

Ch'ien-lung[2] did not know that he was going to be emperor; he knew only that he was eligible for consideration. For starting in the late K'ang-hsi reign, after that monarch's disastrous attempt to nominate an heir, Ch'ing monarchs selected their successors in secret, and, in theory at least, revealed the names only on their death beds. Educated guesses were of course made in circles close to the court[3] and signs of imperial prejudice or preference carefully noted. There is no concrete evidence, however, that the naming of Ch'ien-lung as heir apparent in September, 1723, was ever prematurely revealed or obviously flaunted by the emperor. For thirteen years Ch'ien-lung shared the honors and responsibilities of an untitled heir with the only other possible candidate, his half-brother and junior by three months, Hung-chou (1712-1770). Two other brothers, Hung-shih (1704-1727) and Hung-yen (1733-1765), were not in any real sense eligible. The first had been read out of the family for dissolute behavior; the second was born too late to count. And so it fell to the two favorites to prepare themselves for public life.

Hung-chou and Ch'ien-lung, it must be emphasized, were not rivals for power; they were equals before it. In fact the only major public note of discrimination between them during the entire course of their princedom occurred before their father took the throne. In the last year of his reign, the aged K'ang-hsi emperor had personally bade Ch'ien-lung, then only ten and a half years old, to come live and be educated at court. It was a mark of high esteem, to be sure, and one that traditional historians insisted was prophetic of Ch'ien-lung's inevitable rise to fame. Yung-cheng, of course, may have been influenced in his choice of an heir by this act of favoritism, but there is no proof of this nor any indication of bias on his own part once he succeeded K'ang-hsi.

The two princes were raised as companions and friends. From the start they shared their meals, their lessons, and their beds,[4] and later, in his will, Yung-cheng congratulated them on the close fraternal bonds that they had developed over the years and that he himself had so consciously fostered.[5] They received the same instruction from the same sources, made their literary debuts simultaneously,[6] were awarded equal honors on the same date—being created first-degree princes together on March 22, 1733[7]—and were given similar duties in their introduction to the public life of ritual and administrative responsibility. They expressed equally ardent fraternal affection for each other, which, despite the demands of good taste, seems to have been both genuine and sincere.[8] Even after they parted ways, Ch'ien-lung to the throne and Hung-chou to a life of wonderful eccentricity where he rehearsed his own funeral rites, Hamlet-like, at home, appalled dinner guests with idiosyncratic and thoroughly irreverent renditions of classical opera, and struck the august person of a grand secretary at court, the brothers remained on excellent, if not always intimate, terms.[9]

The radical divergence of their later careers, in fact, tends to obscure their earlier parity as princes. Privately they discovered the world of the gentleman-aesthete, learning apparently with equal facility to ride and shoot, compose, exchange and match verses, paint, and write. Publicly they learned to serve and second their father. Yung-cheng trained and assigned both brothers to perform rites and eventually to plan policy. With few exceptions, the public duties executed by the princes were sacerdotal in nature rather than political. Ch'ien-lung and Hung-chou were commissioned to perform, sometimes in conjunction with but more often in place of the emperor, some of the ritual and ceremonial acts associated with the sovereign as head of state and head of the imperial family. These included mourning rites, sacrifices at imperial and subimperial tombs, holiday rites and celebrations, and sacrifices to culture heroes and select deities whose propitiation was meant to assure dynastic equanimity.[10] As princes, in other words, they were trained first in the charismatic functions of the throne. Only later were they asked to participate in its administrative functions too.

In the last year of Yung-cheng's reign, Ch'ien-lung and Hung-chou finally entered active administrative service. They began at the top. On July 15, 1735, together with the two most powerful ministers in the realm, the grand secretaries O-er-t'ai (1680-1745) and Chang T'ing-yü (1672-1755), and nine other high officials, they were appointed to the newly created Council of Miao Control (Pan-li Miao-chiang shih-wu wang ta-ch'en), a high level military policy-planning board in charge of the southwest border areas.[11] This council was specifically established in the summer of 1735 to undertake the suppression of a serious Miao uprising in Kweichow province, the latest in a series of such disorders which had plagued the southwest on and off for ten years. It operated only for several months and was abolished by Ch'ien-lung shortly after he ascended the throne, its functions and those of the Grand Council being subsumed in another specially created office, the General Control Council (Tsung-li shih-wu wang ta-ch'en), the empire's highest policy-planning board during the mourning period for Yung-cheng. During its existence, however, the Council of Miao Control seems to have enjoyed a status equal to that of the nascent Grand Council.

Later in the same year when Ch'ien-lung was himself sovereign, he recalled his service on the council with pride: it had given him the experience necessary to continue the pacification campaign with confidence and purpose and to fulfill his father's posthumous command to put the realm aright. This, on the basis of his prior training, he felt well prepared to do.[12]

SOURCES OF THE SELF-IMAGE: THE INSTITUTIONAL SETTING

In 1737, a year and a half after he took the throne, Ch'ien-lung reminisced about the classroom: "Prior to ascending the throne I had thoroughly got by heart the six classics and the various histories. Since assuming the responsibilities of state I have had less free time but have not stopped examining the classics and studying the rites."[13] The first part of this statement was no idle boast. His introduction to classical learning was rigorous and thorough, though not, as noted, exclusive. It began early and continued through his princedom, first at home under his father's tuition, then, from the age of nine *sui*, under the Manchu scholar, Fu-min (1673-1756), specially engaged by Yung-cheng to instruct his sons, and finally, from 1723 on, in the Palace School for Princes (Shang shu-fang) with his peers.

The Palace School was Yung-cheng's invention, inspired by the need to keep the name of the heir unpublicized in the study halls as well as at court. Thus, upon his accession, Yung-cheng created an institution which would provide for the instruction of all the imperial sons, grandsons, and other princes who were of an age for schooling and whose education inside the palace would minimize the threat of factions outside forming around them as potential claimants to the throne.[14] It was in this school that Ch'ien-lung learned the rigors of an orthodox education. Class hours were long, from the 5:00-7:00 A.M. watch to the 3:00-5:00 P.M. watch, and the school operated throughout the year.[15] When the princes were at the Summer Palace they continued their lessons in another study, the Ch'in-cheng Tien, set aside for that purpose. The curriculum was comprehensive, embracing both the civil and military arts, and protocol was strict. As their tutors entered the classroom the princes faced north and bowed to them, thus reversing the roles which status alone would have prescribed and giving expression thereby to the superior claim of ideological over institutional and hereditary authority.[16]

To educate the emperor's offspring was an honor, no doubt, but it was still a working honor—a bureaucrat's job, not his titular reward. It was not necessarily assigned to the most highly placed or the most intellectually gifted. Intellectual conservatism, competence, and promise had something to do with the choice. So did imperial preference and favor. Thus one of Ch'ien-lung's tutors, Ku Ch'eng-t'ien, about whom little else is known, was selected for service in the school on the basis of an investigation originally intended to prove him a subversive. A poem by Ku, demed insulting to the throne, came to light in 1729, and during the investigation another of Ku's verses, a lament on the death of K'ang-hsi, was discovered and passed on to Yung-cheng. The emperor was reportedly so moved that he quashed the charge of *lèse majesté* and brought Ku into the Hanlin Academy as a compiler and into the Palace School as a tutor.[17] Before that Ku had languished for twelve years as an unemployed *chü-jen*. Quite obviously, in this case academic and bureaucratic qualifications took second place to the imperial whim, and Ch'ien-lung got an untried, if poetically agile, teacher.

Ku Ch'eng-t'ien's success story is admittedly exceptional. Of the fourteen others[18] that I have been able to identify as having had either functional or formal roles in Ch'ien-lung's education, all but two, both members of the imperial family, had some prior claim to scholarly experience, either as expositors or compilers in the Hanlin, as editors or consultants in the Imperial Study (Nan shu-fang), the emperor's personal literary advisorate,[19] as writers in their own right, or simply as instructors or directors in private academies. And the royal tutors, uncles of the prince, had little need for such claims. They were teachers not in the school but in the field, Yin-lu, a mathematician and musicologist, being designated Ch'ien-lung's instructor in firearms, and Yin-hsi, a classmate and exact contemporary of his nephew, his archery master.[20] Neither, however, had any discernible qualification as experts in arms, and their functions appear to have been largely nominal: to personify through their appointments the imperial family's direct concern and involvement with the indoctrination of a potential heir. The sovereign's brothers were tied by a formal martial curriculum to the sovereign's sons: it bespoke unity, caution, and familial pride in the fading memory that once upon a time all the princes—brothers and sons alike—had to know as a matter of course how to ride, shoot, and kill.

Whatever their qualifications, all of the tutors were caught in a common dilemma. As instructors they were expected to set high scholarly and ethical standards for the princes; as fallible and ambitious officials they often failed to meet those standards themselves. Through their teaching they provided the future emperor (as well as the current one) with the scriptural arguments and principles on which he could act to control them and, when necessary, to condemn them. They were vulnerable before their own lessons—honored but not privileged characters. Thus O-er-t'ai posthumously and Chang T'ing-yü at the end of his career were punished by their former pupil for the excesses of their power; Hsü-yüan-meng and Hu Hsü were reprimanded and demoted by their patron, Yung-cheng, for minor bureaucratic offenses after they had already become tutors to his sons; Shao Chi was rebuked for the more serious crime of favoritism and official toadying to the mighty; even Fu-min, the favorite tutor of all and later remembered as a perfect paragon, was not above reproach and twice under Yung-cheng was reprimanded or degraded for minor administrative infractions.

Of Ch'ien-lung's fifteen tutors, five were Manchu, ten Chinese, but, with the exception of the two members of the imperial family, the distinction was irrelevant. They were officials first and representatives of their races second. There is no indication that the Manchus were engaged exclusively as linguists, and O-er-t'ai, Hsü-yüan-meng, and Fu-min were all capable of holding their own against any of the others as claimants to the Confucian heritage. Likewise, geographical distinctions were meaningless. Of the non-banner tutors, four were from Kiangsu, two from Chekiang, and one each from Anhwei, Kiangsi, Fukien, and Honan, a distribution which spoke more of the normal mid-Ch'ing examination quotas than of cliques. There was, in fact, no discernible political or scholastic clique in the Palace School. Several lines of the Chu Hsi tradition were represented, from the more conservative school of Chang Po-hsing as represented by Ts'ai Shih-yüan, to the more sceptical and pragmatic approach of the Yen-Li school as represented briefly by Wang Mou-hung.[21] There was nothing experimental about the palace curriculum or its manipulators. Reliability, not eccentricity or experimentalism, was most prized and in the characters and careers of these men was most apparent. And, with the exception of Liang Shih-cheng, who in 1734 was appointed to the school at the age of thirty-seven long after the prince's lessons had been learned, and Yin-lu and Yin-hsi, who were anomalies at best and anyway marginal to Ch'ienlung's education, there were no tyros among the schoolmasters. The average age in 1730 of those for whom the dates are available (excluding those mentioned above) was sixty-one, a good safe distance from youthful and quixotic dreams. Ch'ien-lung was unquestionably in dependable and venerable hands.

SOURCES OF THE SELF-IMAGE: THE CURRICULUM

It is neither possible nor necessary here to enumerate and analyze all of the books to which Ch'ien-lung was exposed as a student prince. Rather, a brief selection of titles should adequately suggest the range of interests imposed upon him and the strength of expectations held for him.

Ch'ien-lung's encounter with the Confucian canon appears to have been correct but decidedly perfunctory. It was sufficient to make him, appropriately, not a philosopher but an ideologue perfectly capable of drawing on the philosophers for the sanctions he needed to operate effectively as monarch. Like all schoolboys he began by knowing his classics before understanding them. By the time he entered the Palace School he was familiar wtih the texts and had memorized large portions of the *Four Books* and *Five Classics*. This was an exercise in discipline, not interpretation. Interpretation, that is, orthodox understanding, rested on a knowledge of neo-Confucian exegetics and this he got in packaged form, largely through the well-known anthology *Hsing-li ching-i*, [*The Essential Metaphysics*], a work compiled during the K'ang-hsi reign and printed in 1715 as a manageable digest of the massive and disorderly *Hsing-li ta-ch'üan-shu*, a scissors-and-paste symposium of Sung neo-Confucian doctrines compiled in the Ming dynasty. The *Ching-i* represented the ultimate distillation of Sung Confucianist wisdom as sanctioned and approved by the "later sage," K'ang-hsi, and apparently proofread in final draft by him.[22] It comprised summary versions of the seminal texts of the Sung school and anthologized writings grouped under such headings as "spirits," "sages," "Confucians," "the prince's way," and the like, and gave Ch'ien-lung his first and probably only close brush with the writings of Chou Tun-i (1017-1073), Shao Yung (1011-1077), Chang Tsai (1021-1077), and Ts'ai Yüan-ting (1135-1198), all of whose works he singled out for special mention in a colophon on the *Ching-i*.[23]

There were other doctrinal texts as well—the *Ta-hsüeh yen-i*, for example, a forty-three *chüan* cautionary guide for rulers to the ethical imperatives of the *Great Learning* as interpreted by a late Sung adherent of the Chu Hsi school, Chen Te-hsiu (1178-1235);[24] or the writings of Chu Hsi himself;[25] or the *Ku-*

wen yüan-chien, a collection of annotated essays in sixty-four *chüan*, ordered compiled and personally selected by K'ang-hsi and running the gamut of literature from the *Ch'un-ch'iu* and *Tso-chuan* to the writings of the Sung period.[26] Metaphysics and classical literature, however, were not Chien-lung's strong points, and he seems to have been content at this stage to make the requisite polite noises about them and then run for cover to history, a subject he both loved and understood.

Ch'ien-lung's readings in history were both extensive and intensive, covering the broad spectrum of Chinese history in the great synthetic works for which Chinese historiography is famous and probing more specific problems or persons in lesser works and selected excerpts and documents which focused on a specific time or a concrete question. For him, as for most post-Sung students of the past, history was a cumulative, though rarely integrated, chronicle of moral signposts indicating the good and the bad, the praiseworthy and blameworthy. It was a veritable mirror of revealed truth, reflecting past choices as measures for current actions.

It was the chronicle form of history, best exemplified by the *Ch'un-ch'iu, Tzu-chih t'ung-chien*, and Chu Hsi's abridgement, *T'ung-chien kang-mu*, that most appealed to the prince. Bare fact, he argued, was enshrined in this form as moral judgement. Bad men and wicked trembled before the accusing thrust of the chronicler's brush; they thought twice about their reputations and gave up their usurpations and rebellions as a bad thing. History, that is, became a preventive weapon against the future, as well as a corrective one against the past. In Ch'ien-lung's eyes, however, the weaponry was dulled after the fall of the Chou dynasty and not again honed to perfection until the appearance of the *T'ung-chien kang-mu*. Then Chu Hsi took up where Confucius left off, sorted out the good from the bad, the right from the wrong, judged the past, and warned the future. The would-be regicide and power-seeker, the self-seeking official who would serve two dynastic houses—all were given notice: desist or live in history forever condemned. They desisted. And thus, he argued, was worked a qualitative change in post-Sung political history, marked by the expression of new and stronger dynastic loyalties. It was a didactic triumph for the *Kang-mu*. Chu Hsi had, as it were, polished the *Mirror* until it no longer could be ignored.[27]

A prince's job was to know all of Chinese history, but this did not prevent him from developing particular interests. For Ch'ien-lung, the history of the T'ang dynasty held an almost irresistible attraction. Time and again, both as prince and sovereign, he turned back to the high years of the T'ang and its archetypal dynastic accomplishments. The reign of T'ai-tsung (r. 627-649) became almost an obsession with him, as if the very act of reading its record would enhance his own with some of the heroic qualities of that remote age.

A text of signal importance in this respect was the *Chen-kuan cheng-yao* or *Important Deliberations on Government of the Chen-kuan [T'ai-tsung] Period*, written less than a century after the T'ai-tsung era by the censor and state historiographer, Wu Ching (d. 749).[28] The book, comprising some forty pieces in ten *chüan*, is still extant. Annotations to the text were added during the Yuan dynasty and additional comments by twenty-two noted T'ang experts appended. Thus by the time Ch'ien-lung had the text it was a repository of highly reputable observations on early T'ang government and politics, and in the eyes of later critics it remained one of the most reliable early expositions of T'ai-tsung's greatness. This surely was its appeal for Ch'ien-lung. To him it portrayed the quintessential T'ai-tsung, the model king whose record was required reading for all who aspired to rule. And if we can believe his expression of youthful ardor, reading it was an intensely moving experience, transporting him back into a heroic age and filling him with admiration for the abundance of a truly great reign.

Immediately relevant to the T'ang, as well as to the interregnum between the T'ang and Sung, were the writings of Ou-yang Hsiu, compiler of the *New T'ang History* and author of the *History of the Five Dynasties*. Ch'ien-lung was exposed to these and wrote an essay, "On Reading the Collected Works of Ou-yang Hsiu."[29] In it he expressed a commonly held historiographical principle that the state of literature is directly related to the state of the nation. The quality and abundance of the first followed the vitality and fortunes of the second; letters were circumscribed perfectly by politics. Thus in periods of instability the "civilizing lessons of learning" (*wen-chiao*) went unspoken and unheeded. They had to wait for the reappearance of a literary savior who could restate them again boldly and clearly in an age amenable to the task. Thus the literary-moral vacuum of the Six Dynasties period was filled finally in the T'ang by Han Yü and that of the Five Dynasties period by Ou-yang Hsiu some seventy years after the founding of the Sung. Not only did they revive learning but through their inspiration assured its continuance. Their contemporaries and disciples carried forward the good work in a kind of intellectual chain reaction, and in doing so added lustre to their times.

As a prince Ch'ien-lung was required to learn more than the contents of history. He was also expected to be familiar with the methods of state historiography over which he might some day preside. Specifically, he was introduced to the mechanics of the self-glorifying compilation. On January 17, 1732 he witnessed the devout and solemn reception by the throne of the *Veritable Records* and *Sacred Instructions* of the *K'ang-hsi* reign. In a poem commemorating the occasion, he showed his familiarity with the suprahistorical or ideological function of such literature and with the process of compilation, from the day-to-day diarial notations to the final, revised, and perfected edition which was to stand forever as the embodiment of the imperial accomplishment and will.[30]

It is uncertain whether Ch'ien-lung actually had access to these collections during his princehood. While it is reasonable to assume he did—as testaments of dynastic continuity they were meant above all for the eyes of the royal heirs— the record is mute, and we cannot legitimately assign to his curriculum a course in Ch'ing documents. Later, of course, as emperor, he did make use of them, supposedly reading one *chüan* of the *Veritable Records* daily, before bathing, except when on tour, at the hunt, or fasting.[31]

If Ch'ien-lung learned something about the methodology and a great deal about the ideals of history, he also learned about the practical politics and personalities of the past. He read, for example, Yang Lien's (1571-1625) celebrated memorial enumerating the "twenty-four crimes of Wei Chung-hsien" (1568-1627), the infamous eunuch of late Ming times, and was well acquainted with the details

of Wei's reign of terror.[32] He also read the brief collected writings of another courageous Ming official, Yang Chi-sheng (1516-1555), best known for his dogged opposition to the establishment of horse markets on the Ming frontier and for his courageous criticism of the powerful grand secretary, Yen Sung (1480-1568), one of the "Six Wicked Ministers" of the Ming, which led ultimately to his imprisonment and murder.[33]

Thus by the time Ch'ien-lung came to the throne he was well versed in the record of the darker side of court politics. Long before the advent of Ho-shen, he was aware of the crude facts of favoritism and clique machinations. If old age dulled that awareness in the end, during most of his career he was hypersensitive to these problems and their precedents and accordingly kept a tight reign on his court. His lessons in history had prepared him well.

This being so, it is surprising to note one glaring omission in Ch'ien-lung's early writings. There is no single essay or poem devoted expressly to the problem of political cliques. As noted, he was familiar with the works of Ou-yang Hsiu and thus can be presumed to have seen the famous memorial, "On Parties." And recently his father had launched a virulent public attack on this classic justification for group politics with a similarly entitled essay of his own specifically aimed at quashing any bureaucratic notions that factions, however dedicated to the good of the realm, would be tolerated.[34] Certainly Ch'ien-lung was familiar with Yung-cheng's arguments, for this was a major issue of the day and one that could hardly escape the notice of a prince being tutored daily in the principles of power. Moreover, since Yung-cheng's essay was made required reading in all government schools, it surely must also have found its way into the curriculum of the Palace School. Yet Ch'ien-lung did not join the debate. He praised Ou-yang Hsiu for his history while his father was damning him for his politics. He was content to recount the orthodox horror tales of baneful cliques and factions rather than to synthesize his views in a princely echo of the emperor's words. Only after he inherited the throne did he speak out, and then it was to re-iterate and to reinforce what Yung-cheng had said so emphatically in 1724.[35]

Two other aspects of the prince's curriculum must be briefly treated—his training in the arts and in warfare. There is no need at this remove to disturb Ch'ien-lung's very secure reputation as an indifferent painter, poet, and calligrapher, and I intend simply to point to the origins of his later image of himself as a universal patron and connoisseur.

Ch'ien-lung began to paint in earnest in 1729 at the age of nineteen *sui;* presumably his training in calligraphy began earlier, when he began his lessons in composition at the age of fourteen *sui.*[36] His models in both were impeccable—the great masters of bird and flower painting, Pien Luan (fl. ca. 785-802), Lin Ch'un (fl. ca. 1174-1189), Huang Ch'üan (ca. 900-965), and Hsü Hsi (d. before 975), and two of history's greatest calligraphers, Wang Hsi-chih (321-379) and the Ming master, Tung Ch'i-ch'ang (1555-1636). Except for Tung's works, however, and possibly some of Wang's, it is unlikely that Ch'ien-lung ever saw an original of any of these artists. Current criticism argues that none of their works survive, and while early eighteenth-century attributions may have convinced the prince of their authenticity, it is almost certain that he was in fact working from copies or later specimens in the same stylistic tradition.[37]

Mediocre talent and false attributions could not combine to stop the prince any more than they could later stop the emperor from putting his skills to work. Long before he became emperor Ch'ien-lung began that practice, so annoying to later critics, of cluttering up palace treasures with his own brush and seals. In his years as a prince he inscribed over forty paintings and album leaves from almost every important period of Chinese painting.[38] It was a well-meaning effort, no doubt, to continue the honored tradition of expressing admiration and pride of ownership directly on the cherished work itself. Yet the incongruity of indifferent calligraphy often tastelessly misplaced on master paintings and the obscuring of works by obtrusive seal imprints have not endeared him to the world of art.[39] And when it is recalled that he wrote 54 inscriptions on one handscroll alone and eventually possessed at least 195 seals of which he used as many as 13 on a single painting,[40] the charge of bad taste becomes serious.

The charge, however, does not take into consideration the extra-aesthetic function of such exercises. It was not so much the royal prerogative as the royal duty to remain at the head of the arts even if, in the process, the art was destroyed. The paintings, after all, were the private possessions of the throne; the imperial script and seals were the possessions of the realm. Their appearance was an assertion not only of artistic sensibility (however warped) but of dynastic grandeur. And since the dynasty consisted of the royal house as a whole, a prince as well as a sovereign could legitimately participate in that simultaneous function of enhancing the imperial ego and enhancing the riches of the realm. It could only be hoped that the prince and emperor had taste; it had, however, to be expected that they would leave their marks—preferably, as in earlier ages, with discretion—on the treasures that defined the glory of their reign.

Ch'ien-lung was educated to be both a scholar and soldier. The emphasis, of course, was on the first, for by mid-dynasty it was more important for the emperor to be a practicing gentleman than a practicing general. After K'ang-hsi, there was little need for a Manchu warrior-king, and now, on the edge of an age of peace, a passing acquaintance with weaponry was enough. That is what Ch'ien-lung got. He received instruction, of a sort, in both archery and firearms and read just enough military history to gain a rudimentary (and idealized) knowledge of the T'ang militia system and through it an understanding of the evanescence of imperfect military institutions.[41]

Ch'ien-lung's expertise with arms is a matter of conjecture. One story, almost certainly apocryphal, puts him in the expert class with a bow. It recounts how, on a balmy morning in 1749, the young emperor picked up a bow in one of those spur-of-the-moment inspirations so useful to historical fiction and hit the bull's-eye with nineteen of his twenty shots.[42] By making him slightly fallible the story gains in verisimilitude but not necessarily in truth. We simply do not know how good he was. The same may be said about his use of firearms, a more important and more complicated matter by far.

The term "firearms," huo-ch'i, was used generically to describe all armaments which employed gunpowder in any form. It thus included the whole range of individual arms, field pieces, and explosives, such as land and water mines, then known in China. In fact, a contemporary mid-Ch'ing illustrated guide shows twenty-three different pieces of ordnance and forty-nine types of musket,[43] but many of these were useless for anything but ceremonial firing, most were already long obsolete, and almost all were difficult if not impossible or dangerous to fire. It would be misleading then to suppose that Ch'ien-lung learned to handle anything larger or more complicated than the standard musket, the niuo-ch'iang or fowling piece, a derivative of the late Ming long gun and Portuguese snapping matchlock musket, employed both for military and hunting purposes.[44] Until the nineteenth century, the Ch'ing court remained remarkably aloof to the strategic possibilities of modern firepower, and with few exceptions interest in the development and use of arms remained at a minimum in the mid-Ch'ing period. The arsenal was little developed beyond the technical level achieved at the end of the Ming dynasty,[45] and this undoubtedly told on the prince's weapons training. It was confined largely to the single weapon and to the limited tactical context of the hunt.

Throughout his career, Ch'ien-lung was to be ruled by a tension between a poetic self and a practical self, and his training in the hunt was no exception. On numerous occasions he joined a mounted hunting party or one bound for archery practice, but for him getting there was half the fun and he has left heroic stanzas describing the beauty of the morning forests, the nobility of the ride, and the heartiness of the companionship.[46] He was enthralled with the romance of the hunt and the garlanded warrior, not with the brutality or practicality of the shot and the kill. Nevertheless, he did learn the paramilitary purposes of these expeditions, often participated in them, and knew the methods of taking game long before he organized his own autumn extravaganzas in Jehol after 1741.

The most common technique in the hunt was that of surrounding (*hsing-wei*), whereby a large number of beaters would form a ring and drive the game into a confined clearing where the royal hunters could shoot at will. On a large scale this had the makings of a military exercise and often served both as imperial sport and martial maneuver. Another method learned by Ch'ien-lung was the use of large game traps or barriers (*hsiao-lieh*). These were constructed of interwoven lengths of wood and placed in the path of the fleeing game. Thus trapped, the animals presented an easy target to the hunter. A third ruse, not specifically mentioned by the prince but later known to him and to succeeding imperial sportsmen and almost certainly learned in his youth, was that known as "calling the deer" (*shao-lu*).[47] This was a stalking procedure of intriguing proportions. A man was clad in deer skins and antlers and sent into the hills with a whistle which imitated the call of an expiring buck. This would apparently lure the does in the area out of the forest in expectation of meeting their stricken mate and thus provide a fair bag to the waiting marksmen. The lure technique was based on dubious zoological principles. According to the argument, a buck was a virile and libidinous beast who would have at one go up to a hundred of the opposite sex. Thereupon, in understandable exhaustion, he would lie down to die. His last call—that produced by the whistle—supposedly brought to his side his satisfied mates who would attempt to revive him by feeding him grass which they first chewed for him. And so, by attending a fallen buck, they became themselves, as

it were, sitting ducks. With this Ch'ien-lung's education in the field was complete.

THE SELF-IMAGE: PREPARATION FOR REALITY

In 1730 all of this education—in the classroom, in the field, at court—came to a head. Late in the autumn Ch'ien-lung presented to the court the distilled product of seven years of formal learning, the manuscript version of his collected student essays, examination exercises, prefaces and colophons, verse, letters, and historical notes, entitled *Lo-shan t'ang wen-ch'ao* or *A Literary Selection from the Lo-shan Hall*.[48] It was in this work that he began to define his own and his age's understanding of the role of the emperor in history and in politics. It was first printed a year and a half after Ch'ien-lung came to the throne, in 1737, much expanded in forty *chüan*, under the title *Lo-shan t'ang ch'üan-chi* and again in 1758 in a definitive (*ting-pen*) edition of thirty *chüan*.[49]

What we have then is a highly polished version sanctioned by the orthodox considerations of the court and sensitive to the reputation of its imperial author. Nevertheless it remains a useful guide to contemporary opinion. Its views represent the prescribed commitment to what was good and bad in history, to what was admirable and what contemptible. In sum they add up to an impressive accumulation of historical precedent and cliché which serves as the young prince's (and later young emperor's) testament of faith. As he asserts in his 1730 preface, "'It is not the knowing that is difficult, but the doing.' I often refer to the words I have written as a mirror for my actions. Were I incapable of self-examination to the point where words and action had no relevance to each other, were I capable of knowing but not of acting—would this not be to my shame?"[50] To insure against such ignominy, he says, he has placed the collection on a table within easy reach for instant reference, consultation, and guidance.

Appended to the *Ch'üan-chi* is a companion volume in four *chüan*, the *Jih-chih hui-shuo* or *Knowledge Accumulated Day by Day*, a collection of 260 study notes compiled in 1736 as a kind of addendum to the *Ch'üan-chi*.[51] The notes appear to be the residue of Ch'ien-lung's apprentice scholarship, the footnotes and italics, as it were, of the lessons learned. Together the *Ch'üan-chi* and *Hui-shuo* constitute the "complete works" of the prince.

After the author became emperor, his private testament became imperial writ: The "Works" were wrapped in the mantle of infallibility and sent on their way to inspire officials and educate students much in the manner of the sacred edicts of K'ang-hsi and Yung-cheng. Palace officials, provincial governors, and former tutors received copies as gifts or on petition to the throne;[52] others urged that they be distributed throughout the realm in the manner of the sanctioned editions of the classics and histories.[53] Ch'ien-lung wondered only briefly about the propriety of this equation of his own words with those of the ancient canon, managed to overcome his modest evaluation of their didactic and sagely value, and delighted in the new popular demand.[54] In time the *Ch'üan-chi* passed into the folklore of imperial erudition; it became a latter-day classic by a later sage. In 1748 a precocious child of seven was discovered in Shantung who had already committed to memory the five classics and the poems from the *Ch'üan-chi*. He was made a *chü-jen* on the spot, was celebrated as the "child prodigy,"

and fortunately died prematurely to carry his reputation unscathed into popular history.[55]

The title of the *Ch'üan-chi*, taken from the name of Ch'ien-lung's private studio, Lo-shan t'ang or Hall of Delight in Doing Good, expressed an ideal of imperial perfection, one that insisted on a leaven of humility in the exercise of ultimate power. It meant, in Ch'ien-lung's eyes, what Mencius meant when he spoke of "the great Shun . . . delighting to learn from others to practice what was good."[56] The critical words here are those that disappear in the *lo-shan* elision—"to learn from others"—for they point to one of the loftiest of the monarchical ideals: modesty. Institutionally this was expressed by the ruler's willingness to accept remonstrance with good grace—with humility and an open mind: *hsü-huai na-chien* or *t'ing-yen na chien*—phrases that, with other variants, occur frequently in Ch'ien-lung's essays on the monarchy.[57]

For a prince who could hope one day to be sovereign, the ideal of imperial modesty stood as an imperative, for without the ability to listen as well as to act, the monarch could be only a despot, never a sage. And the claim to sage-hood was the key to imperial as well as intellectual greatness. Without it the ruler would remain just another mark of imperfection in the long line of descent from idealized antiquity; with it he stood a good chance before posterity where, in a world hypersensitive to the judgments of history, the experience of his reign really counted. In a very real sense the genius of the Chinese monarchy was precisely that it held the ruler himself responsible for limiting his essentially unlimited sanction to rule, for putting sagely restraint on despotic tendencies. He might fail to do so in practice, but he knew long before he ascended the throne the consequences of failure. History might admire him as a despot but would not praise him. That it reserved for the sage, or for the man who at least sought to be one.

Lo-shan, then, was for the prince a practical, concrete formula for success. It was a direct, specific charge to be filial, respectful and submissive, human-hearted, and righteous.[58]

Ch'ien-lung's model ruler, however, was more than modest. He was also "cautious and circumspect, respectful of both heaven and the people, constantly diligent, and never for a moment presumptuous enough to be lax."[59] He was lenient and broad-minded, magnanimous in his treatment of others and indulgent of men's petty faults. In this way he established his own great virtue and thereby inspired gratitude from the people, contentment in their hearts, and submissiveness to his rule. Harsh and impetuous behavior, on the other hand, led inevitably to ruin. He saw in this the reasons for the fate of the short-lived Ch'in and Sui dynasties. Their founders were admittedly diligent administrators: Shih Huang-ti (r. 221-210 B.C.), according to tradition, wading studiously through 120 catties of state documents each day; and Sui Wen-ti (r. A.D. 589-604) personally attending to the details of daily administrative life. "Yet," asked Ch'ien-lung, "to what avail?" Without compassion and tolerance, the minds and hearts of men were lost and with them the dynasties.[60]

Of all the attributes that went to make up the ideal ruler, the most important in Ch'ien-lung's mind was the ability and desire to discover, select, and use ministers of high talent. To get the right man at the right time, to exhaust his talent in the service of the state—this was the most difficult yet most crucial task facing the sovereign. If he succeeded, all else followed: "Though the realm be vast it is not then difficult to regulate."[61] If he failed, either out of jealousy or contempt of the worthy or from an inability or unwillingness to use them fully, his reputation and his reign would be fatally weakened. His human-heartedness, if he possessed it, his frugality, another requisite monarchical virtue, would be wasted, for without an administration staffed by gifted, outspoken men, he would be cut off from reality—a king with a kingdom that he neither knew nor could hope even vaguely to understand.[62]

Ch'ien-lung's case for correct ministerial employment was compounded of practical, historical, and moralistic considerations. The argument begins in heaven.[63] There the recipient of the mandate is charged with creating a lustrous reign, a prosperous realm, a reasoned and ordered society; with bestowing benefits and benevolence on all. "But," notes the prince realistically, "man's individual capacity is limited," and even the sage kings, Yao and Shun, accomplished their great works only with the assistance of talented councillors. "How much the more," he adds, "is it imperative for those not equal to Yao and Shun to employ talent." It was precisely such employment that gave to high antiquity its greatness, order, prosperity, and contentment. From the highest minister to the lowest functionary, all were worthy of their posts and were justly and appropriately used. In a rueful, almost modern, aside, however, Ch'ien-lung admits that it was easier then than now: "The difficulty in appreciating men's worth today is ten times greater than in ancient times. The reason is that official positions are daily increasing in number and human nature is becoming more devious."[64]

Ch'ien-lung continues to explore this less perfect world. Like K'ang-hsi before him and modern analysts today,[65] he recognizes several emperor-types. He distinguishes between founding and innovating emperors—those who "sought to establish order" (*yüan-chih chih chün*) or, like Han Kuang-wu (r. A.D. 25-57), reestablished it—and successor emperors —those who "succeeded to the throne" (*chi-shih chih chün*). Each type required councillors whose talents were appropriate to the age. Few in either group found them, but those that did were marked for greatness: among the founders, Han Kao-tsu (r. 206-195 B.C.), Han Kuang-wu (restorer of the Later Han, legitimately considered a new dynasty), T'ang T'ai-tsung, and Sung T'ai-tsu (r. 960-975); and Han Wen-ti (r. 179-157 B.C.) and Sung Jen-tsung (r. 1023-1065) among the successors.

Even among these most estimable of emperors, however, Ch'ien-lung discerns critical differences in the use of available talent. T'ang T'ai-tsung in this and other respects is the paragon *par excellence,* not without his faults perhaps—notably his inability to soothe the people sufficiently in an age given to military exploits[66]—but good enough all the same. In his ability to appreciate talent, employ the meritorious, and accept their advice he was without peer. Han Wen-ti, in most other respects a model ruler, was by comparison "insufficient in his appreciation of talent."[67] And Han Kuang-wu, who was comparable to T'ai-tsung in diligence, receptivity to remonstrance, courtesy to the worthy, and sponsorship of learning, nevertheless failed to exploit *fully* the talents of his ministers. Sung Jen-tsung fell short for the same reason. So, outside the list, did Han Wu-ti (r. 140-87 B.C.).[68]

With lesser rulers the shortcomings were more serious. They were guilty not only of a fickle use of competent ministers but of a suffocating reliance on only a few favorites, men whose pettiness and self-interest assured that the emperor would be unable to rule impartially: "He who uses the whole realm as his source of wisdom possesses the public spirit of the sage king; he who uses one or two favorites as his eyes and ears possesses the partial wisdom of the commonplace ruler." Or again: "Since the wisdom in the world is diverse . . . reliance on one man's intelligence as the sum total of wisdom is no match for reliance on the wisdom of many in concert."[69]

Ch'ien-lung cites T'ang Te-tsung (r. A.D. 780-804) as an invidious example. What led to disaster during Te-tsung's reign, he argues, was *not* the three faults historically attributed to him—excessive lenience, tolerance of eunuchs, and avariciousness—but rather the use of mean and petty men and the suspicious, inconsistent use of the accomplished. He wavered between wisdom and foolishness, and his reign wavered accordingly between brilliance and disaster. It began brilliantly, due to his reliance on the accomplished Ts'ui Yu-fu (d. 780). It turned to disorder with his trust in Lu Ch'i (d. 785), a scoundrel. Again it recovered some lustre with his turn to the counsels of Lu Chih (754-805), one of the most courageous of his ministers, and finally it reverted once more to chaos when he withdrew his support of Lu Chih and fell prey to the slanders of palace courtiers and eunuchs. Te-tsung, like Duke Hsiang of Sung in the Warring States period and Ch'in-tsung (r. 1126), last of the Northern Sung emperors, failed out of inconsistency. From this, Ch'ien-lung concluded that all three were capable of heeding advice in times of crisis but foolishly discarded it and the men who gave it when crisis seemed past.[70]

The case of the Southern Sung was even more instructive. There, argues the prince, a whole dynasty, not just a reign, was doomed by injudicious use of talent. Admittedly this was not the only reason for failure, but in combination with a dreary succession of pedestrian rulers, a powerful enemy to the north, a debilitated army, and an impoverished people, it proved fatal.[71] That it was able to last as long as it did was due in fact to the presence of those loyal, upstanding ministers and scholar-officials, filial sons and chaste wives who, despite the lack of encouragement, still "loved their ruler and would die for their commanders."[72]

All of this is, to be sure, oversimplified history, but it tells us something important about Ch'ien-lung's image of the emperorship. Insistently, both here and in many other of his essays, he emphasizes the personal factor in history. It was *people*—their perfection or lack of it—rather than institutions and their possible suitability or perfectability which held the key to success or failure. The worthy man made the emperor great by informing him; the wise ruler made the man whole by employing him in his true vocation, politics.

This did not, of course, mean that they were equals. The Confucian canon, and thus the prince paraphrasing it, preserved the emperor's preeminence. Ruler and minister are seen bound in a relationship as fixed and immutable as that between heaven and earth. Just as heaven is high and the earth low, so there is a gulf between sovereign and subject. The ruler is lofty, superior, the minister lowly and inferior. What bridges the gap is their oneness of heart, their mutuality of principle. And the happy result of this mutual interest, meeting

like two halves of a tally, is ". . . social harmony; those in high places show favor to the lowly and the lowly and inferior in their turn are well disposed toward the highly placed. There is an end to all feuds."[73] If the gulf is not bridged, however, the results are dire: the ruler is smitten with willfulness and overbearing pride so that the loyal utterances of his ministers fail to reach him; the "great treasure," the State, is abandoned; the mean and petty insinuate themselves around the throne; and toadying and favoritism flourish.

To prevent this, the ruler must treat the lowly according to their merits. In the case of those with superior talent, he should approach them with the respect that he would show a teacher, provide them with generous salaries or emoluments, trust them with sincerity, and concentrate their abilities in suitable posts. In other words, he should give effect to their ministerial vocation and thus assure that their talent will be fully used. In the case of those with only moderate abilities, he was to treat them with propriety, exhort them with sincerity (thus, you trust the best, exhort the second best), and encourage them to exert their utmost efforts in the execution of their duties. Talent thus graded would assure a stable, harmonious reign.[74]

Ch'ien-lung concludes his examination of the ruler-minister relationship with an argument and a suggestion. He argues strongly against the hypothesis that "it is easy to employ the meritorious but difficult to find them." This, he says, is nonsense. The ruler's influence and power are such that the people will follow his desires as the shadow follows the body. If the ruler wants to obtain precious and rare birds and beasts from far-off lands he will get them. How much simpler is it to obtain the services of the meritorious, who, after all, exist *within* the realm, in the commonplace walks of everyday life. It is up to the emperor to get them: "If you want to build a great house you obviously seek out an artisan; if you want to refine jade from the rough block, you obviously seek out a craftsman; if you want to rule and yet fail to seek out the worthy, this is like trying to go forward by walking backwards."[75]

The suggestion is that talent may be made to beget talent. If, he says, a ruler appreciates the worthy as he thirsts for water, gathers them about him and implicitly trusts them, *and* has them all recommend those of like worth with whom they are acquainted, then all the posts in the administration will be appropriately filled and all the incumbents will emulate one another. A nice balance will be created both at court and in the provinces and then, even if there are some mean and low types who filter into office, their deceit will be changed into directness and honesty. Imperial attractiveness, that is, will breed ministerial attraction; repulsion will breed repugnance. The ruler's role is to consent to be advised. So consenting, he will attract advice: "Good words will nowhere lie hidden."[76] The minister's role, like the artisan's, is to build a wall against heterodoxy, to shore up the fallible structure of the throne.

It is ironic, perhaps, that Ch'ien-lung was reciting these platitudes just at a time when Yung-cheng, from the throne, was making a mockery of them. Later Ch'ien-lung would follow in his father's steps and stress the hierarchical nature of the ruler-minister relationship to the detriment of nicer ethical considerations. But before he could break the rules he had to know them. To say that a prince's view of the throne was largely idealistic is not to say that it was either dishonest or wrong. As a prince he could

afford the luxury of perfect expectations. As emperor he could not, though even then he just as surely could not ignore them. The monarch might be a realist, but he could not be a Confucianist Jekyll and Legalist Hyde, changing form to suit the needs of the occasion. He was a whole man, imperfect and fallible and hence historical, a prisoner as much of precedent and ideology as of current exigency. This Ch'ien-lung realized even as a prince. He was profoundly aware of the imperfections of the real—the historical—ruler in contrast to the timeless perfections of the ahistorical sage king. In other words, he distinguished between norms and deeds, and while committed of necessity to the former, he was more at home with the latter.

In this world of deeds, one of the most important criteria of excellence was success. All the piety in the world would not help a ruler who failed before reality. Thus Han Wen-ti, moral perfection personified and eminently successful in his own right, took second place in the prince's eyes to T'ang T'ai-tsung, who was even more successful in the immediate matter of making a reign glorious and prosperous.[77] Even in failure Ch'ien-lung discerned priorities. The "hard" ruler—the tyrant—might, in a time of administrative decline, have less consequential effects on dynastic fate than the "soft" ruler—the weakling. The "hard," he argued, might induce swift retribution and restoration by inciting men to assassination or rebellion; the "soft," such as Han Yüan-ti (r. 48-31 B.C.), were less obviously anathema and might live on undisturbed while passing on to their heirs the seeds of doom they sowed.

Imperial success was measurable both by personal and political standards. The emperor could change and so could his historical fortunes; neither was a static quantity. Thus Han Wu-ti moved from tyrant to hero, in Ch'ien-lung's view, by a conscious and highly personal effort to reform his faults. This, he said, was the most difficult and most admirable thing a man could do. T'ang Ming-huang (r. 713-755), on the other hand, went from good to bad, broken objectively by rebellion and personally by a loss in self-confidence. He began his long reign with vigorous determination and caution. He burned pearls and jade as a warning against extravagance, conferred upon the barbarians copies of the classics as a gesture of graciousness to the outlander. So peaceful was his rule that punishments were almost completely abolished. His own forcefulness in the planning and execution of policy was in large part responsible for this early success. But he was unable to sustain the spirit and drive of those years. He became less diligent, less committed to the need first to succor the people and only then to consider his own rewards. And so after the year 742, success turned to failure. The people were squeezed dry of their earnings, the great families gorged themselves on meat and wine, the roads were lined with the starving and the dead. Reason gave way to desire, public interest to private acquisitiveness, compassion for the people to a willful fleecing of them.[78]

Human failure, institutional weakness, and deterioration through time: these, Ch'ien-lung learned, were the constituents of real history. They made the image of the emperorship less pleasing to the idealistic eye, but they prepared a prince for reality. Ch'ien-lung came to the throne sensitive both to the lessons of ethics and to those of history. He was ready, ideologically as well as aesthetically and administratively, to rule. The roles had all been learned. And during his reign they would for the last time be played out when they really mattered. For after Ch'ien-lung new realities would render preparations for the old ones obsolete. Never again would a prince be made so thoroughly aware of what, as sovereign, he would have to do. Never again would the emperor, and hence his education, be at the center of Chinese history.

Notes

1. John K. Fairbank, "Proleptical Prolegomena on the Emperor of China, Etc." (unpublished conference paper [Laconia, N.H., 1959]), p. 6.

2. I prefer, and use throughout, the convenient, if incorrect label, Ch'ien-lung, to the technically more accurate Kao-tsung, Hung-li, or Fourth Imperial Son.

3. See, for example, the "stakes" placed on Chia-ch'ing and his half-brother, Yung-hsing, by the ex-Jesuits in Peking in 1790, five years before the former was officially proclaimed heir. E. H. Pritchard, "Letters from Missionaries at Peking Relating to the Macartney Embassy (1793-1803)," *T'oung Pao*, XXXI, 1-2 (1934), 5.

4. *Lo-shan t'ang ch'üan-chi* [Collected Writings from the Lo-shan Hall], 40 *chüan*, by Ch'ien-lung (1737 ed.; hereafter cited as *LSTCC*), prefaces, pp. 12-13b; 8. 1-3.

5. *Ta-Ch'ing li-ch'ao shih-lu* [Veritable Records of the Ch'ing Dynasty], 4485 *chüan* (Tokyo, 1937-1938; hereafter cited as *CSL: STJ* for the K'ang-hsi reign, *CSL:STH* for the Yung-cheng reign, and *CSL:KTC* for the Ch'ien-lung reign), *CSL:STH*, 159. 23b.

6. In October-November, 1730, Ch'ien-lung with the *Lo-shan t'ang wen-ch'ao* [Selections from the Lo-shan Hall], 14 *chüan*, forerunner of *LSTCC*, and Hung-chou with *Chi-ku chai wen-ch'ao* [Selections from the Chi-ku Studio], forerunner of *Chi-ku chai ch'üan-chi* [Collected Writings from the Chi-ku Studio], 8 *chüan* (printed 1746).

7. *CSL:STH*, 128. 3b.

8. See, for example, *LSTCC*, prefaces, pp. 12-13b, and *Chi-ku chai ch'üan-chi*, prefaces, pp. 32-33b, both by Hung-chou; and *LSTCC*, 7. 10-11; 8. 1-3; 21. 4-4b, 7b-8; 27. 11; 30. 18b; 37. 9, all reminiscences by Ch'ien-lung of his companionship with Hung-chou.

9. See Chi-hsiu chu-jen [Chao-lien], *Hsiao-t'ing tsa-lu* [Miscellaneous Notes from the Hsiao Pavilion], 10 *chüan* (preface, 1880; hereafter cited as *HTTL*), 6. 37b-38; *Ch'ing shih* [The Ch'ing History], 8 vols. (Taipei, 1961), V, 3565; Arthur W. Hummel, ed., *Eminent Chinese of the Ch'ing Period, 1644-1912*, 2 vols. (Washington, D.C., 1943, 1944), II, 99. Cf. also Ch'ien-lung's laudatory second preface, dated June 3, 1746, to *Chi-ku chai ch'üan-chi.*

10. For Ch'ien-lung's services, see *CSL:STH*, 13. 11-11b; 26. 11b; 44. 47b; 50. 20; 51. 13b-14b, 19b-20; 54. 19b; 109. 19; 114. 1b; 128. 9b; 134. 9; 138. 17; 139. 4b; 142. 1-1b, 9b-10; 143. 8b; 151. 2; 153. 6b; 154. 1b; 156. 1b; 159. 1b. For Hung-chou's, see *CSL:STH*, 99. 24; 109. 4b; 115. 14b-15; 122. 2b; 142. 9b-10; 146. 4; 159. 1-1b. This count is based on a cursory survey which necessarily favors Ch'ien-lung as his tabooed personal name, Hung-li, is conveniently and obviously shaded in the text. A more careful count might redress the balance. In any case it would be unwise to take the discrepancy as evidence in itself of paternal favoritism and Ch'ien-lung's prior selection as heir.

11. *CSL:STH*, 156. 15-16, 20b-21. This reference and other related information was kindly supplied by Mrs. Lienche Tu Fang. See also the same scholar's *Kuan-yü Chün-chi ch'u ti chien-chih* [On the Establishment of the Chün-chi Ch'u] (Canberra, 1963), pp. 17-19.

12. *Ta-Ch'ing Kao-tsung ch'un-huang-ti sheng hsün* [Sacred Instructions of the Emperor Kao-tsung], 300 *chüan* (preface, 1807; hereafter cited as *SCSH:KT*), 295. 1.

13. *SCSH:KT*, 13. 1-1b.

14. Hummel, II, 917; *LSTCC*, 8. 21b.

15. For this and the following data, see Chi-hsiu chu-jen [Chao-lien], *Hsiao-t'ing hsü-lu* [Additional Notes from the Hsiao Pavilion], 3 *chüan* (preface, 1880; hereafter cited as *HTHL*), 1. 13-13b, and *Ch'ing-pai lei-ch'ao* [Unofficial Sources on the Ch'ing Arranged by Categories], 48 *ts'e* (Shanghai, last preface 1917), *li-chih lei* [Ritual], p. 2.

16. This was also standard practice in T'ang times. See Robert des Rotours, transl. *Traité des Fonctionnaires et Traité de l'Armée*, 2 vols. (Leiden, 1947-1948), II, 570-571. Cf. also James T. C. Liu, "An Early Sung Reformer: Fan Chung-yen" in *Chinese Thought and Institutions*, ed. John K. Fairbank (Chicago, 1957), p. 123.

.17. *Kuo-ch'ao ch'i-hsien lei-cheng* [Biographies of Ch'ing Venerables and Worthies Arranged by Categories], 720 *chüan*, comp. Li Huan (Hsiang-yin Li-shih ed., 1890), 126. 8-9. Also, *LSTCC*, prefaces, p. 46.

18. Yin-lu (1695-1767), Yin-hsi (1711-1758), O-er-t'ai, Chang T'ing-yü, Chu Shih (1665-1736), Chiang T'ing-hsi (1699-1732), Fu-min, Ts'ai Shih-yüan (1682-1734), Shao Chi (d. 1737), Hu Hsü (1655-1736)—for whom see *LSTCC*, prefaces, pp. 3-5, 8-11, 18-45; and Liang Shih-cheng (1697-1763), Chi Tseng-yün (1671-1739), Hsü-yüan-meng (1655-1741), and Wang Mou-hung (1668-1741), for whom see, respectively, *LSTCC*, colophons, p. 16; *SCSH:KT*, 58. 1-1b; and *Ch'ing-shih lieh-chuan* [Biographies for the Ch'ing History], 80 *chüan* (Shanghai, 1928), 14. 10b-11 and 67. 21b.

19. Established as a palace office by K'ang-hsi. See Hummel, I, 64.

20. *Ch'ing-shih*, I, 128.

21. On Ts'ai's connection with Chang Po-hsing's Ao-feng academy, see *Ch'ing-shih*, V, 4049-4050; *Ch'ing-shih lieh-chuan*, 14. 5b-6b; *Kuo-ch'ao pei-chuan chi* [Ch'ing Epitaphs and Biographies], 160 *chüan*, comp. Ch'ien I-chi (1893 ed.), 23. 15-17b; Hummel, I, 51-52. On Wang's career and adherence to the work of Yen Yüan (1635-1704) and Li Kung (1659-1733), see *Ch'ing-pai lei-ch'ao, chüeh-chih lei* [Rank], p. 42; *Ch'ing-shih*, VII, 5153-5154; Hummel, II, 914.

22. See *LSTCC*, 9. 8b-10; *Ssu-k'u ch'üan-shu tsung-mu t'i-yao* [Summaries of the Contents of the *Ssu-k'u ch'üan-shu*], 4 vols. (Shanghai: Commercial Press, 1933; hereafter cited as *SKCS*), p. 1925; Hummel, I, 474, II, 913.

23. *LSTCC*, 9. 7b-10.

24. See *SKCS*, pp. 1912-1913, 1926-1927; *LSTCC*, 9. 12-13, 7. 8b-9b.

25. See, for example, *LSTCC*, 9. 10-12.

26. See Hummel, I, 310-311; *SKCS*, pp. 4216-4217.

27. *LSTCC*, 7. 7-8b.

28. For this and the following, see *LSTCC*, 7. 1-2b; *SKCS*, pp. 1129-1130; E. G. Pulleyblank, "Chinese Historical Criticism: Liu Chih-chi and Ssu-ma Kuang" in *Historians of China and Japan*, ed. W. G. Beasley and E. G. Pulleyblank (London, 1961), p. 139; and Robert des Rotours, transl., *Le Traité des Examens* (Paris, 1932), pp. 261-262.

29. *LSTCC*, 10. 14-15. The following remarks are based on this essay. For a relevant

discussion of dynamic and cultural correlation, see Lien-sheng Yang, "Toward a Study of Dynastic Configurations in Chinese History" in the same author's *Studies in Chinese Institutional History* (Cambridge, Mass., 1961), pp. 7-10.

30. *LSTCC*, 31. 15b-17b; also *CSL:STH*, 113. 17-18. Cf. Harold L. Kahn, "Some Mid-Ch'ing Views of the Monarchy," *Journal of Asian Studies*, XXIV, 2 (February, 1965), 232.

31. *HTHL*, 1. 11.

32. *LSTCC*, 10. 16-17.

33. *LSTCC*, 31. 9b-10; Hummel, I, 398, II, 864; E-tu Zen Sun and John de Francis, eds. and transls., *Chinese Social History* (Washington, D.C., 1956), pp. 315-318; and Nelson I. Wu, "Tung Ch'i-ch'ang (1555-1636): Apathy in Government and Fervor in Art" in *Confucian Personalities*, eds. Arthur F. Wright and Denis Twitchett (Stanford, 1962), pp. 264-266.

34. David S. Nivison, "Ho-shen and His Accusers" in *Confucianism in Action*, eds. David S. Nivison and Arthur F. Wright (Stanford, 1959), pp. 225-228. For a translation of Ou-yang's memorial, see Wm. Theodore DeBary, Wing-tsit Chan, and Burton Watson, comps., *Sources of Chinese Tradition* (New York, 1960), pp. 446-448.

35. Nivison, "Ho-shen and his Accusers," pp. 228-232. Hummel, II, 917, gives the date as 1725.

36. See, respectively, Sugimura Yūzō, *Kenryū kōtei* [The Ch'ien-lung Emperor] (Tokyo, 1961), p. 27, and *LSTCC*, prefaces, p. 1. The following, on his models, is from Sugimura, pp. 26-27.

37. See Michael Sullivan, *An Introduction to Chinese Art* (London, 1961), pp. 150-151; Laurence Sickman and Alexander Soper, *The Art and Architecture of China* (Baltimore, 1956), p. 125; R. H. van Gulick, *Chinese Pictorial Art, as Viewed by the Connoisseur* (Rome, 1958), pp. 394-395. A more conservative view is Osvald Siren, *Chinese Painting, Leading Masters and Principles,* 7 vols. (London, 1956-1958), II, "Annotated Lists of Paintings . . . ," 20, 27, 28, 66. On the authenticity of Wang's surviving specimens, see Michael Sullivan, *The Birth of Landscape Painting in China* (London, 1962), pp. 85, 197-198, note 35. I am indebted to Sandra Kahn for many of the references here and below in notes 39, 40.

38. See *LSTCC*, *chüan* 19-40, under entries

beginning with the word, *t'i* (superscription).

. 39. See *Chinese Art Treasures, A Selected Group of Objects from the National Palace Museum and the Chinese National Central Museum, Taichung, Taiwan* (Geneva, 1961-1962), p. 18; *Chinese Calligraphy and Painting in the Collection of John M. Crawford, Jr.* (New York, 1962), pp. 24-25;; Sullivan, *Introduction,* p. 168; and Roger Goepper, *The Essence of Chinese Painting* (London, 1963), p. 100 and plate 6. Ch'ien-lung was not, of course, always unsuccessful; see Goepper, p. 109.

40. Sullivan, *Introduction,* p. 169, note 1; *Chinese Calligraphy and Painting,* p. 28, note 11; and Hsien-chi Tseng, "A Study of the Nine Dragons Scroll," *Archives of the Chinese Art Society of America,* XI (1957), 27-29, 30-31 (nos. 16-28). This scroll is in the Boston Museum of Fine Arts.

41. *LSTCC*, 9. 17b-19.

42. *HTTL*, 1. 6b.

43. *Huang-ch'ao li-ch'i t'u-shih* [Illustrated Guide to the Instruments, Utensils, and Paraphernalia of the Ch'ing Dynasty], 18 *chüan* (1759 ed.), 16. 1-75b.

44. See Chou Wei, *Chung-kuo ping-ch'i shih-kao* [Draft History of Chinese Weapons] (Peking, 1957), pp. 270, 311-312.

45. Chou, *Ping-ch'i shih-kao,* pp. 311-313, 320. For the few innovations made—under K'ang-hsi, an artillery and musketry division, Huo-ch'i ying, formed within the banner system, and an elite corps of marksmen, Hu-ch'iang ying, equipped with tiger guns; under Ch'ien-lung, a scouts division supplied with firearms—see *Ch'ing-ch'ao t'ung-tien* [Encyclopedia of Ch'ing Statutes], 100 *chüan* (Taipei, 1959 ed.), 69. 2533, and *Ch'ing-ch'ao hsü wen-hsien t'ung-k'ao* [Continuation of the Encyclopedia of the Historical Records of the Ch'ing Dynasty] 400 *chüan* (Taipei, 1959 ed.), 130. 8904; also *HTHL*, 1. 12.

46. See, for example, *LSTCC*, 21. 18-19, 30. 22-22b.

47. See Yao Yüan-chih, *Chu-yeh t'ing tsa-chi* [Miscellanea from the Bamboo Leaf Pavilion], 18 *chüan* (preface, 1893), 3. 4b, and *HTTL*, 1. 12. Both authors were active in the Chia-ch'ing reign (1796-1820). For a similarly named technique in the Liao dynasty, see Karl A. Wittfogel and Feng Chia-sheng, *History of Chinese Society, Liao (907-1125)* (Philadelphia, 1949), p. 133.

48. See *LSTCC*, 1737 facsimile handwritten preface, pp. 2b-3, and prefaces, p. 36. Also note 6 above.

49. Hummel, I, 370. On the question of its reliability as a source of the self-image, see Kahn, "Some Mid-Ch'ing Views," p. 230.

50. *LSTCC*, prefaces, p. 2. The quotation is from the *Shu-ching*. See James Legge, transl., *The Chinese Classics*, 5 vols. (Hong Kong, 1960), III, 258.

51. *Jih-chih hui-shuo* [Knowledge Accumulated Day by Day], 4 *chüan*, by Ch'ien-lung (printed 1736; hereafter cited as *JCHS*), preface, pp. 2-2b.

52. *SCSH:KT*, 1. 7, 9b; *CSL:KTC*, 64. 6.

53. *SCSH:KT*, 1. 9.

54. *SCSH:KT*, 1. 9-9b.

55. *HTTL*, 9. 47-47b.

56. *LSTCC*, 8. 18, and Legge, *Chinese Classics*, II, 205.

57. See for example, *JCHS*, 1. 13b, 4. 6b; *LSTCC*, 2. 2, an entire essay devoted to the subject, and 5. 19b.

58. *LSTCC*, 8. 18-18b.

59. *JCHS*, 4. 5.

60. *LSTCC*, 1. 13-13b.

61. *JCHS*, 1. 5, 14b-15.

62. *LSTCC*, 3. 11, 16-16b; 2. 7, 9. Cf. Legge, *Chinese Classics*, III, 41-42, esp. note, p. 42.

63. Unless otherwise indicated the following represents a summary of his essay, "Proper Rule Lies in the Selection of Talent," *LSTCC*, 3. 9-11b.

64. *JCHS*, 1. 5b-6.

65. Cf. *CSL:STJ*, 154.6b; Arthur F. Wright, "Sui Yang-ti: Personality and Stereotype" in *The Confucian Persuasion*, ed. Arthur F. Wright (Stanford, 1960), pp. 59 ff; and James T. C. Liu, "An Administrative Cycle in Chinese History, The Case of Northern Sung Emperors," *Journal of Asian Studies*, XXI, 2 (February, 1962), *passim*.

66. *JCHS*, 1. 13b, 21-21b.

67. *JCHS*, 1. 21.

68. See, respectively, *JCHS*, 4. 5b-6; *LSTCC*, 2. 9; *JCHS*, 1. 14b.

69. Respectively, *JCHS*, 1. 11b; *LSTC*, 2. 8. Cf. also *LSTCC*, 3. 10.

70. See, respectively, *LSTCC*, 5. 5-6b, 3. 16-16b; *JCHS*, 1. 14b.

71. See *LSTCC*, 6. 13b-14b, 16-18.

72. *LSTCC*, 6. 16b, alluding to Mencius. See Legge, *Chinese Classics*, II, 174.

73. Richard Wilhelm, transl., *The I Ching or Book of Changes*, one-vol. ed. (New York, 1961), p. 50. This passage provides the inspiration for Ch'ien-lung's essay, *LSTCC*, 1. 20b-23b, from which the summary here is made.

74. *LSTCC*, 3. 10. The following remarks continue from this, pp. 10b-11b.

75. *LSTCC*, 3. 10b-11.

76. *LSTCC*, 2. 7, 8. The phrase, from the *Shu-ching*, continues, ". . . no men of virtue and talents will be neglected away from the court." See Legge, *Chinese Classics*, III, 53.

77. For this, and the following on "hard" and "soft" rulers and Han Wu-ti, see, respectively, *LSTCC*, 5. 2, 4. 2-3, 4. 1-1b. Cf. also Kahn, "Some Mid-Ch'ing Views," p. 231.

78. *JCHS*, 4. 9-10.

III. MANCHU-CHINESE DYARCHY

3. ETHNIC COMPOSITION OF PROVINCIAL LEADERSHIP
DURING THE CH'ING DYNASTY

LAWRENCE D. KESSLER

The Ch'ing dynasty (1644-1911) was the last and most successful of the dynasties of alien rule in China. "The key to its success," noted Professor Ping-ti Ho, "was the adoption by early Manchu rulers of a policy of systematic sinicization."[1] The integration of the Manchu ruling class with their Chinese subjects was most striking in staffing the bureaucracy. Unlike preceding alien dynasties, the Manchus over the course of 268 years of rule shared a good proportion of key offices with Chinese. The system of dual appointments of Manchus and Chinese operated in the capital,[2] while Chinese dominated the local officialdom.[3]

Between these two poles of the Ch'ing bureaucracy, central and local, came a very important intermediate group, the provincial governors-general and governors (*tsung-tu* and *hsün-fu* respectively, or *tu-fu* collectively). As the chief agents of imperial authority outside the capital, they were vital instruments of Manchu control over the Chinese empire. An analysis of Ch'ing *tu-fu* personnel according to politico-ethnic affiliation would yield valuable insights into the nature of alien rule in China.[4]

General estimates have been offered,[5] and a few limited statistical studies have been made,[6] but no one has yet successfully examined the changing composition of *tu-fu* personnel from period to period over the entire life of the dynasty.[7] By using such an approach and by suggesting how the statistical shifts in *tu-fu* composition can be related to broader dynastic policies, we can present a more dynamic picture of Sino-Manchu dyarchy than previously offered. Before presenting statistics on *tu-fu* composition and possible interpretations of this data, I will first treat briefly the historical evolution of the *tu-fu* institution and Manchu ethnic policies in government.

The Manchus were following Ming practice in establishing governors-general and governors in the provinces.[8] Not only institutional arrangements but personnel as well were carried over from one dynasty to the next. Six Ming *tu-fu* came to serve the Ch'ing dynasty in the same posts. The most famous holdover was Hung Ch'eng-ch'ou, who held a number of *tsung-tu* posts under the Ming and

Reprinted from *The Journal of Asian Studies*, Volume XXVIII, Number 3, May 1969, pp. 489-511. By permission.

Lawrence D. Kessler is an Instructor in the Department of History at the University of North Carolina, Chapel Hill.

was specially selected by the Manchu government in 1653 as governor-general of the five provinces of Hukuang, Kwangtung, Kwangsi, Yunnan, and Kweichow.[9]

Initially, the geographical distribution of Ch'ing *tu-fu* for the most part followed the Ming pattern. Gradually, however, all the Ming governorships of subprovincial units were eliminated, and by 1667 there was only one governor in each of the eighteen provinces.[10] The Manchus experiment more with the post of governor-general,[11] and it was not until 1748 that a permanent arrangement was found. Thereafter and until the closing days of the dynasty, there were *tsung-tu* for river conservancy (the number varied from one to three), grain tribute, and the following eight provincial groupings: Chihli, Kiangsu-Kiangsi-Anhwei, Shensi-Kansu, Szechwan, Fukien-Chekiang, Hupei-Hunan, Kwangtung-Kwangsi, and Yunnan-Kweichow.

Ch'ing *tu-fu* held substantive appointments in the central government and drew their ranking from it. As with geographical arrangement, the early Ch'ing rulers experimented freely with the concurrent titles of *tu-fu*. In 1661 a decision was made to divorce governors from the direction of military affairs in the provinces,[12] and this fact was reflected in a 1662 decision to give governors concurrent titles in the Board of Works, whereas governors-general received theirs in the Board of War.[13] This arrangement lasted for only slightly more than a decade, or until the outbreak of the rebellion of the three feudatories in 1673. When news of the revolt of Wu San-kuei, the most powerful of the three feudatories, reached Peking, the government immediately returned to its pre-1661 policy. Governors once more took charge of the military establishment in their provinces,[14] and their concurrent titles were correspond-

ingly changed from the Board of Works to the Board of War.[15]

From the Yung-cheng period on, governor posts in provinces without a resident governor-general even carried with them the concurrent title of *t'i-tu* (provincial commander-in-chief), for convenience in bandit-suppression.[16] The system of concurrent appointments in the central government reached its final form in 1749. A governor-general was given the concurrent titles of president of the Censorate and president of the Board of War, while a governor was given the concurrent titles of vice-president of the same two bodies.[17] With ministerial and censorial titles, and the access to the emperor these positions provided, *tu-fu* had enormous power and prestige.

The formalization of *tu-fu* posts, ranking, and responsibility was accompanied by the institutionalization of *tu-fu* primacy in the provinces. The Ch'ing dynasty at the outset continued a Ming practice of appointing one regional inspector (*hsün-an chien-ch'a yü-shih*) to every province to act as the emperor's "eyes and ears." Here was an official with far-reaching censorial powers who might have provided a check on the power of *tu-fu*. But regional inspectors did not become a permanent feature of the Ch'ing political structure. In a series of decisions in 1661-62 regional inspectors were abolished, and their duties and functions were turned over to the *tu-fu* and the provincial judge (*an-ch'a-shih*).[18]

Another institutional change of importance was the relegation of the provincial financial commissioner (*pu-cheng-shih*) and the provincial judge to secondary rank among provincial officials. The changing English translation of *pu-cheng-shih* in itself reflects the new power structure of provincial officials. In the Ming dynasty, the *pu-cheng-shih* was in charge of general civil administration of a province, and this fact is acknowledged by translating his titles as "administrative commissioner."[19] The same official is known to students of Ch'ing history as "financial commissioner" because he relinquished his position as chief civil official of the province to the newly institutionalized *tu-fu,* and was concerned primarily with economic and fiscal management. Formal recognition of *tu-fu* primacy in the provinces came at the same time as the jurisdictional arrangement and the ranking system of *tu-fu* reached their final form. In 1748 the emperor approved a court decision to designate the financial commissioner and provincial judge as "provincial officials of the second order," and the governor-general and governor as "provincial officials of the first order" with overall supervision of the provincial and local officialdom.[20] Even the financial commissioner's privilege of directly memorializing the throne was being circumscribed in practice by the mid-Ch'ienlung period, as we know from the complaint of a former holder of that post.[21]

The Ch'ing dynasty with one exception did not reserve any *tu-fu* posts for Manchus or bannermen. Appointments of governors-general and governors (and other posts as well) were to be made without regard to politico-ethnic affiliation. Successive emperors in the seventeenth and eighteenth centuries embraced this idea and propagated it as basic dynastic policy.

The Shun-chih emperor several times denied showing any favoritism toward Manchus. Once, in exasperation, he harangued his officials on how much the Manchus had suffered in founding the dynasty and how completely justified he would be to reward his Manchu compatriots with special favors. Still, he protested, he had not done so, but had treated Chinese and Manchus alike.[22] Shun-chih's fairness, in fact, evoked a bitter response from Manchu leaders after the emperor's death. His deathbed will was destroyed by the four regents appointed to take charge of government during the new emperor's minority. The regents issued a new will in which Shun-chih repented for fourteen errors of his reign. The fifth error to which he confessed was his failure to entrust more Manchus with administrative responsibility.[23]

K'ang-hsi at various times reproached both Manchu and Chinese officials for undermining imperial efforts to remain impartial.[24] Yung-cheng made a classic defense of dynastic policy in 1728 in response to a suggestion that more Manchus be employed in minor posts. Not only were there not enough Manchus to go around, Yung-cheng argued, but many of them were incompetent and unworthy of office. The fact that they were Manchus was no basis for appointment. Yung-cheng summed up his policy as follows:

In employing men, I think only of the good of the nation, and the welfare of the people. If a man be honest and just and sincere in his work I will employ him even if he is no intimate of mine. But if a man strives for private gain, is unlawful, or disrupts government, then I will dismiss him even if he is a close favorite. Therefore, I do not make a distinction between Manchus and Chinese, but maintain only the strictest impartiality toward all my subjects. . . . This is the way to assure everlasting peace and good government.[25]

Finally, the Ch'ien-lung emperor summed up the imperial case by saying, "all the emperors of this reigning dynasty, from my grandfather, my father, and on down to me, have all held fast to the principle of impartiality, without a trace of favoritism."[26]

Such was the image and the ideal of Manchu ethnic policy in government, as expounded by successive emperors of the early and middle Ch'ing periods. Certain phrases emerge as their favorite slogans, notably *Man-Han i-chia* ("Manchus and Chinese are all of the same family") and *Man-Han i-t'i hsiang-shih* ("Manchus and Chinese are given the same consideration"). On a number of occasions, however, Chinese officials questioned the validity of the image, and with justification.

After Dorgon's death in 1651, Wei I-chieh, a metropolitan censor at the time but later to become a grand secretary, urged Shun-chih to choose his governors and governors-general carefully and not to rely exclusively on "old supporters from Liaotung."[27] He was not referring to Manchus but to Chinese bannermen, whom many Chinese considered racial renegades and no better than Manchus. Wei's counsel was appropriate and timely because at that time every single *tsung-tu* and seventeen of the twenty-two *hsün-fu* were Chinese bannermen. The other five governors were Han Chinese (used in this study to indicate non-bannermen Chinese).

While K'ang-hsi was reigning (but not ruling),[28] two *chin-shih* candidates complained of the continuing distinction being made between Manchus and Chinese. One of the candidates, writing in 1667, claimed that between 20 and 30 per cent of current *tu-fu* were Chinese, the rest all being Manchus.[29] If we again assume that the writer included Chinese bannermen in the "Manchu" category, then he was more than justified to register his complaint. In fact, he understated his case, because in 1667 Chinese bannermen held twenty-eight of the twenty-nine *tu-fu* posts. Only the single post of Yunnan governor was filled with a Han Chinese.

Finally, let us examine the case of Hang Shih-chün, a censor in the Ch'ienlung period. His 1743 essay on current affairs contained this passage: "The [Manchu-Chinese] distinction should not be too finely drawn. The number of capable Manchus is only about thirty to forty per cent of the number of capable Chinese. And yet at the moment Chinese [only] occupy about half of the govenorships and not a single governor-general post. Why are Chinese excluded [from these posts]?" Hang stated further that in the use of Chinese there was discrimination in favor of Chinese from border provinces and against Chinese from the Liangkiang (Kiangsu, Kiangsi, and Anhwei) and Chekiang areas.[30] The latter charge was completely groundless, as Ch'ien-lung was quick to point out. The emperor checked over his top officials and noted that of the three Chinese grand secretaries, two were from Chekiang and one from Kiangnan, and of the six Chinese board presidents, three were from Kiangnan (a fourth not mentioned by Ch'ien-lung was from Chekiang). Ch'ien-lung did not cite any *tu-fu* figures, but was content to reiterate the dynasty's policy of selecting these officials according to merit and not according to their ethnic affiliation.[31] If the emperor had counted up *tu-fu* he would have discovered that Hang Shih-chün was nearly correct: nine of the seventeen governors but only one of the twelve governors-general at the time were Han Chinese.

These examples of politico-ethnic imbalance in favor of Manchus and bannermen in the appointment of *tu-fu* certainly tarnish the imperially propagated image of impartiality. As I will point out later, however, political rather than ethnic considerations guided Manchu emperors in the selection of *tu-fu*. The Manchu court just once ordered the exclusive use of Manchus in *tu-fu* posts. An imperial decision in 1668 reserved *tu-fu* positions in the Shensi-Shansi area for Manchus only.[32] Thereafter, and until the beginning of Yung-cheng's reign (1723), when this policy was abandoned,[33] all appointments of governors and governors-general in the Shensi-Shansi region were Manchus.

We can conclude, then, that with the exception of the Shansi-Shensi region for a period of fifty-four years (1668-1722), ethnic affiliation was no bar to the holding of power in high provincial posts. Bannermen and non-bannermen alike could be chosen as *tu-fu* "according to their capabilities, the locality, the circumstances, and the time"[34]—in short, according to the dictates of dynastic policy.

A number of sources can be checked in compiling statistics on Ch'ing *tu-fu* but no single work combines both accuracy and completeness. The most basic source is the chronological listing of *hsün-fu* and *tsung-tu* in the dynastic history.[35] These tables have been copied out and arranged according to provinces by Hsiao I-shan in his five volume *History of the Ch'ing dynasty*, (V, 181-396). Neither work, however, gives any information on the official's educational, ethnic, or career backgrounds. They both record the date and type of appointment (regular, acting, temporary) and nothing more.

Information needed for determining the politico-ethnic affiliation of *tu-fu* is available in three sources. Yen Mao-kung in 1931 presented chronological tables of *tu-fu* for the entire dynasty in his compilation, *Ch'ing-tai cheng-hsien lei-pien*.[36] After the first occurrence of any official, he has listed the man's provincial registration (for Chinese) or his banner registration (for any Manchu, Mongol, or Chinese bannerman). Unfortunately, registration information provided in these tables is not trustworthy. This is especially so in the crucial early years of the dynasty. *Tu-fu* listed as registrants of Fengtien and presumably Han Chinese have almost invariably turned out to be Chinese bannermen. Their banner affiliation, so scrupulously avoided in local and dynastic histories, becomes apparent after checking *Pa-ch'i t'ung-chih*, the official banner history.[37] Banner historians were not always correct either,[38] but their access to banner records and their proximity to the times of which they wrote makes their history a surer guide to bannermen serving as officials than any other source. Unless evidence from other sources was overwhelmingly at odds with the banner history, its information was accepted in this study for the period it covers (1644 to about 1795). For the last century of Ch'ing rule, tables of high officials compiled by Ch'ien Shih-fu, a mainland historian, can replace Yen Mao-kung's tables for reliability.[39] Ch'ien's work gives the same type of background information as Yen's but only for the period of 1830-1911.

I have compiled my statistics on *tu-fu* politico-ethnic affiliation, then, from three main sources: Yen Mao-kung's tables are used for the period 1644-1830 except as corrected by information in *Pa-ch'i t'ung-chih* for the period 1644-1795, and Ch'ien Shih-fu's tables are used for the period 1830-1911. At all times, I have checked biographical collections[40] for clarifying information if the main sources were

TABLE 1—Composition of Ch'ing "Tu-fu" Personnel

| | Tu-fu | | Tsung-tu | | Hsün-fu | |
	Number	Per cent of total	Number	Per cent of total	Number	Per cent of total
Chinese bannermen	287	22.0	115	20.8	252	22.4
Manchus	342	26.3	187	33.7	270	24.1
Mongols	26	2.0	14	2.5	21	1.9
Bannermen (total)	655	50.3	316	57.0	543	48.4
Han Chinese	646	49.7	238	43.0	579	51.6
Total	1301	100.0	554	100.0	1122	100.0

in conflict or if there was any reason to doubt the conclusion of the main sources.[41]

Over the life of the dynasty, *tu-fu* positions were shared fairly equally by bannermen (Manchu, Mongol, and Chinese) and by non-bannermen Chinese (see Table 1). If these totals are divided into separate figures for governors-general and governors, the bannermen held a clear majority of the *tsung-tu* posts, while Han Chinese held a slight majority of the *hsün-fu* posts.[42] These proportions, however, do not tell the whole story. A

good percentage of the bannermen totals in each case consists of Chinese bannermen (36 per cent of governors-general, 46 per cent of governors, or 44 per cent of *tu-fu* as a whole). Chinese bannermen were Chinese by ethnic standards but bannermen by political standards. This is a point that seems too obvious to be worth mentioning, but most previous studies on *tu-fu* composition have not given Chinese bannermen the attention they deserve. Their ethnic origins were forgotten but not their political status. Chinese bannermen were lumped to-

TABLE 2—Changing Composition of Ch'ing "Tsung-tu"

| | Total new personnel | Han Chinese | | Chinese bannermen | | Manchus | | Mongols | |
		Number	Per cent of total	Number	Per cent of total	Number	Per cent of total	Number	Per cent of total
1644-1661	49	10	20.4	38	77.6	1	2.0	—	—
1662-1683	30	3	10.0	18	60.0	9	30.0	—	—
1684-1703	35	7	20.0	18	51.4	10	28.6	—	—
1704-1722	29	6	20.7	9	31.0	14	48.3	—	—
1723-1735	39	17	43.6	12	30.8	10	25.6	—	—
1736-1755	32	6	18.8	3	9.4	22	68.7	1	3.1
1756-1775	40	15	37.5	4	10.0	21	52.5	—	—
1776-1795	37	13	35.1	1	2.7	20	54.1	3	8.1
1796-1820	63	34	54.0	5	7.9	22	34.9	2	3.2
1821-1838	39	23	59.0	1	2.5	14	36.0	1	2.5
1839-1850	31	19	61.3	1	3.2	9	29.0	2	6.5
1851-1861	39	23	59.0	1	2.6	13	33.3	2	5.1
1862-1874	31	23	74.2	1	3.2	6	19.4	1	3.2
1875-1884	16	13	81.2	—	—	3	18.8	—	—
1885-1900	20	13	65.0	1	5.0	6	30.0	—	—
1901-1911	24	13	54.2	2	8.3	7	29.2	2	8.3
Ch'ing (total)	554	238	43.0	115	20.8	187	33.7	14	2.5

GRAPH 1—CHANGING COMPOSITION OF CH'ING "TSUNG-TU" (In per cent; based on Table 2)

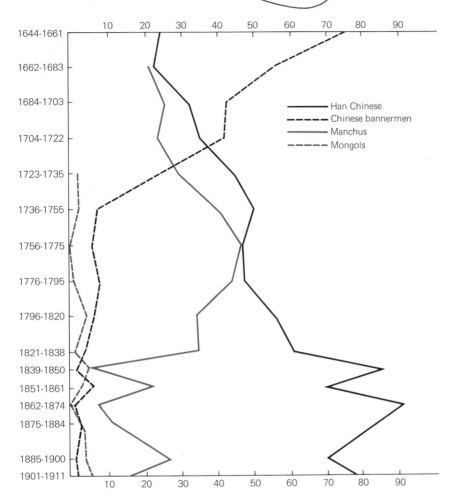

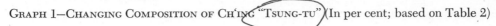

gether with Manchus and Mongols and designated not even as bannermen but as "Manchus." By describing Ch'ing administrative practices only in terms of a Manchu-Chinese duality (expressed in Chinese by the term *Man-Han*), we lose sight of the unique role of Chinese bannermen and sacrifice a dynamic view of Manchu policy.

The fact is that Chinese bannermen were a pivotal group in the early years of the dynasty, when Han Chinese were not to be trusted and Manchus did not have the necessary language and governmental skills to head the provincial administration.[43] Chinese bannermen, on the other hand, suffered neither disability—they could be trusted and they were familiar with the Chinese system of government. Naturally, no language

GRAPH 2—CHANGING COMPOSITION OF CH'ING "HSÜN-FU" (In per cent; based on Table 3)

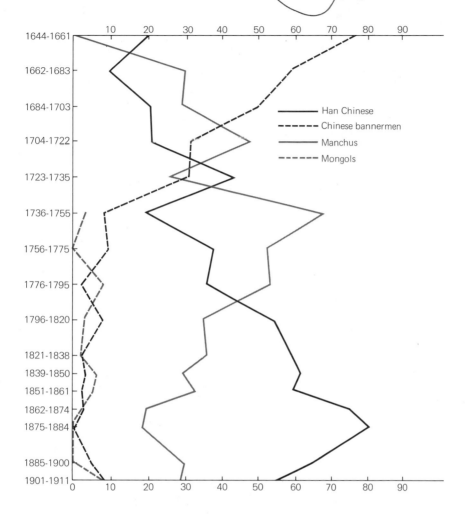

problem existed. The early Manchu rulers were aware of the unique position of Chinese bannermen and appointed them to *tu-fu* posts with great frequency. The heavy reliance on Chinese bannermen at the outset and the rapidly declining use of them after Yung-cheng's reign can be seen in the data given in Tables 2 and 3 and in Graphs 1 and 2.[44] During Shun-chih's reign, 77.6 per cent of the gov-

ernors-general and 75.5 per cent of the governors were Chinese bannermen. In K'ang-hsi's early years (1662-83, a period of consolidation of Manchu power) this group accounted for 60 and 56.1 per cent of new *tsung-tu* and *hsün-fu*, respectively. The respective percentages fell to 51.4 and 42.2 in K'ang-hsi's middle years (1684-1703) and to 31.0 and 41.9 in his later years (1704-22). Chinese banner-

TABLE 3—Changing Composition of Ch'ing "Hsün-fu"

		Han Chinese		Chinese bannermen		Manchus		Mongols	
	Total new personnel	Number	Per cent of total	Number	Per cent of total	Number	Per cent of total	Number	Per cent of total
1644-1661	124	30	24.2	94	75.8	—	—	—	—
1662-1683	66	15	22.7	37	56.1	14	21.2	—	—
1684-1703	90	29	32.2	38	42.2	23	25.6	—	—
1704-1722	74	26	35.1	31	41.9	17	23.0	—	—
1723-1735	81	36	44.4	19	23.5	24	29.6	2	2.5
1736-1755	80	40	50.0	6	7.5	32	40.0	2	2.5
1756-1775	66	31	47.0	4	6.1	31	46.9	—	—
1776-1795	76	36	47.4	6	7.9	33	43.4	1	1.3
1796-1820	91	51	56.0	6	6.6	30	33.0	4	4.4
1821-1838	58	35	60.3	2	3.5	20	34.5	1	1.7
1839-1850	50	43	86.0	1	2.0	3	6.0	3	6.0
1851-1861	64	44	68.7	4	6.3	14	21.9	2	3.1
1862-1874	60	55	91.6	1	1.7	4	6.7	—	—
1875-1884	36	30	83.3	1	2.8	4	11.1	1	2.8
1885-1900	55	38	69.1	1	1.8	14	25.5	2	3.6
1901-1911	51	40	78.5	1	1.9	7	13.7	3	5.9
Ch'ing (total)	1122	579	51.6	252	22.4	270	24.1	21	1.9

men still accounted for a respectable portion of new *tu-fu* in Yung-cheng's reign (30.8 per cent of *tsung-tu* and 23.5 per cent of *hsün-fu*), but thereafter they never accounted for more than 10 per cent of new personnel, and usually much less.

Another look at Tables 2 and 3 and Graphs 1 and 2 will clearly show who replaced Chinese bannermen as *tu-fu*. An increase in the use of both Han Chinese and Manchus in the first three reigns of the dynasty (1644-1735) paralleled the steady decline in the use of Chinese bannermen. This vividly testifies to the changing relations between the Manchu ruling class and its Chinese subjects. Intermarriage and other forms of sinicization were beginning to blunt Manchu-Chinese cultural differences.[45] Manchus now possessed the necessary linguistic and administrative skills to be appointed *tu-fu*. Even more significant, the dynasty had firmly established its

TABLE 4—Composition of "Tu-fu" Personnel in Pre- and Post-Taiping Periods

	1644-1850				1851-1911			
	Tsung-tu		Hsün-fu		Tsung-tu		Hsün-fu	
	Number	Per cent of total	Number	Per cent of total	Number	Per cent of total	Number	Per cent of total
Chinese bannermen	110	25.9	244	28.5	5	3.8	8	3.0
Manchus	152	35.9	227	26.5	35	27.0	43	16.2
Mongols	9	2.1	13	1.5	5	3.8	8	3.0
Bannermen (total)	271	63.9	484	56.5	45	34.6	59	22.2
Han Chinese	153	36.1	372	43.5	85	65.4	207	77.8
Total	424	100.0	856	100.0	130	100.0	266	100.0

rule (with the suppression of the rebellion of the three feudatories in 1681
and the subjugation of Taiwan in 1683)
and no longer feared sharing high governmental responsibility with Han Chinese.

Following Graphs 1 and 2 further
along in time, a very significant development emerges. Manchus and Han Chinese, after generally rising together
throughout the eighteenth century to
offset the declining use of Chinese bannermen (the progression is neater in the
case of *hsün-fu* than *tsung-tu*), followed
diverging paths in the nineteenth century
as far as sharing *tu-fu* posts. Note, however, that the wide divergence in the use
of Han Chinese and Manchus began
around the turn of the century and not
after the Taiping rebellion as is commonly thought. Among both governors-
general and governors, the Han Chinese
held an increasing majority of posts from
Chia-ching's reign on. This fact perhaps
ought to lead Ch'ing historians to give
some attention to early nineteenth century developments and their impact on
dynastic policy. At the least, we need to
scale down our claims for the Taiping
rebellion as marking such a definitive
break in the sharing of power. The immediate post-Taiping period did, of course,
witness a startling increase in the number of Han Chinese serving as *tu-fu* but

it was in the nature of a second spurt. It
is suggestive, but nothing more, that
these two significant shifts in *tu-fu* composition were consequent to major attacks on Ch'ing authority, the White
Lotus and Taiping rebellions.

At this point it might be useful to
check the figures given in Table 4 to
see what sort of generalization can be
made about the use of Manchus and
Chinese before and after the Taiping
Rebellion. Taking "Manchu" to mean
just ethnic Manchus (and not all bannermen), then 35.9 per cent of *tsung-tu* and
26.5 per cent of *hsün-fu* before the Taiping Rebellion were Manchus. After the
Taiping Rebellion, Manchus accounted
for only 27 per cent of *tsung-tu* and 16.2
per cent of *hsün-fu*, about a 10 per cent
drop in each case from the earlier period.
The Han Chinese share of *tu-fu* personnel, however, rose about 30 per cent
after the mid-nineteenth century crisis,
from 36.1 to 65.4 per cent of the governors-general, and from 43.5 to 77.8
per cent of the governors. The great rise
in the use of Han Chinese is not matched
by a correspondingly great decline in the
use of Manchus, because Manchus alone
never had a great share of *tu-fu* posts,
even before 1850. It was the Chinese
bannermen group that suffered a great
decline, from providing about a quarter
of both *tsung-tu* and *hsün-fu* before 1850

TABLE 5—Composition of "Tsung-tu" by Major Phases of the Ch'ing Dynasty

	Total new personnel	Han Chinese		Chinese bannermen		Manchus		Mongols	
		Number	Per cent of total	Number	Per cent of total	Number	Per cent of total	Number	Per cent of total
1644-1683	79	13	16.4	56	70.9	10	12.7	—	—
1684-1735	103	30	29.1	39	37.9	34	33.0	—	—
1736-1795	109	34	31.2	8	7.3	63	57.8	4	3.7
1796-1850	133	76	57.1	7	5.3	45	33.8	5	3.8
1851-1911	130	85	65.4	5	3.8	35	27.0	5	3.8
Ch'ing (total)	554	238	43.0	115	20.8	187	33.7	14	2.5

TABLE 6—Composition of "Hsün-fu" by Major Phases of the Ch'ing Dynasty

	Total new personnel	Han Chinese		Chinese bannermen		Manchus		Mongols	
		Number	Per cent of total	Number	Per cent of total	Number	Per cent of total	Number	Per cent of total
1644-1683	190	45	23.7	131	68.9	14	7.4	—	—
1684-1735	245	91	37.2	88	35.9	64	26.1	2	.8
1736-1795	222	107	48.2	16	7.2	96	43.2	3	1.4
1796-1850	199	129	64.8	9	4.5	53	26.7	8	4.0
1851-1911	266	207	77.8	8	3.0	43	16.2	8	3.0
Ch'ing (total)	1122	579	51.6	252	22.4	270	24.1	21	1.9

to providing less than 4 per cent in each case after that date. So no easy generalization can be made.

I believe a more meaningful configuration of Manchu personnel policy can be obtained if the Ch'ing dynasty is divided into five major phases: (1) a period of conquest and consolidation, 1644-83; (2) a period of stability, 1684-1735; (3) a

TABLE 7—Provincial Registration of Han Chinese "Tu-fu"

Province	Tu-fu[1]	Tsung-tu	Hsün-fu
Kiangsu	94	32	87
Chekiang	77	24	67
Shantung	67	20	61
Chihli	54	18	48
Hunan	51	26	48
Anhwei	43	17	39
Shansi	36	14	31
Honan	35	15	31
Kiangsi	33	13	29
Hupei	31	11	29
Fukien	24	10	22
Shensi	23	7	17
Kwangtung	20	10	17
Szechwan	15	6	13
Yunnan	14	2	13
Kweichow	11	6	11
Kansu	9	4	7
Kwangsi	6	3	6
Chilin	2	—	2
Unknown	1	—	1
Total	646	238	579

[1] Officials serving in both tsung-tu and hsün-fu posts during their careers were counted only once in calculating tu-fu.

period of stagnation, 1736-95; (4) a period of decline (facing the twin disasters of internal disorder and foreign aggression), 1796-1850; and (5) a period of collapse, 1850-1911. The politico-ethnic affiliation of tu-fu personnel for each of these five phases is given in Tables 5 and 6. Considering first the governors-general (Table 5), Chinese bannermen were the predominant group in the period of conquest, no single group was predominant in the period of stability, Manchus held the majority of posts during the period of stagnation, but Han Chinese were in the majority during the last two periods of decline and collapse. The same is virtually true for governors (Table 6), except that Manchus were not the dominant group in the third period. Instead, the balance of Manchus and Han Chinese in the previous period continued.

Among Han Chinese tu-fu certain provinces stand out as the leading producers (Table 7). Taking both posts together, the five most productive provinces over the whole dynasty were Kiangsu, Chekiang, Shantung, Chihli, and Hunan, in descending order. The same ranking holds true for governors but not for governors-general. Hunan was second only to Kiangsu in providing tsung-tu personnel. But Hunan is a special case, because 73 per cent (35 of 48) of all Hunanese governors and 65 per cent (17 of 26) of all Hunanese governors-general served in the post-Taiping period. If Hunan's high ranking is discounted as being too heavily grounded in a short span of time, then the top provinces can be grouped into two areas that between them produced over two-thirds of all *tu-fu*. The rich southeastern provinces of Kiangsu, Kiangsi, Anhwei, and Chekiang together provided 247 *tu-fu* (slightly over 38 per cent), while the capital province of Chihli and its immediate neighbors, Shantung, Honan, and Shansi accounted for another 192 (or almost 30 per cent).[46]

If the geographical distribution of *tu-fu* given in Table 7 is compared with that of metropolitan graduates in Ch'ing times, a striking correlation is obtained. The four provinces of Kiangsu, Kiangsi, Anhwei, and Chekiang ranked first, fifth, tenth, and second, respectively, and to-

gether accounted for 34.6 per cent of all Ch'ing *chin-shih*. The northern provinces of Chihli, Shantung, Honan, and Shansi ranked third, fourth, sixth, and seventh, respectively, and accounted for 31.8 per cent.[47] Hunan only ranked fourteenth in the number of metropolitan graduates, and this fact confirms my conclusion above that the central Yangtze province's high ranking as a producer of provincial leaders was an anomaly created by the special conditions consequent to the Taiping rebellion. With the exception of Hunan, then, the leading producers of *chin-shih* also contributed the greatest number of *tu-fu*, and in roughly the same proportions.

In both areas, however, the political and academic prominence of provinces was not always commensurate with their population and cultural development. Kiangsu (first in both *tu-fu* and *chin-*

TABLE 8—Composition of Ch'ing "Tsung-tu" by Area

Area	Total new appoint-ments	Han Chinese		Chinese bannermen		Manchus		Mongols	
		Number	Per cent of total	Number	Per cent of total	Number	Per cent of total	Number	Per cent of total
Chihli[1]	70	43	61.5	12	17.1	12	17.1	3	4.3
Liangkiang[2]	98	42	42.8	19	19.4	34	34.7	3	3.1
Shen-kan[3]	108	20	18.5	20	18.5	56	51.9	12	11.1
Szechwan	66	21	31.8	12	18.2	29	43.9	4	6.1
Min-che[4]	103	36	34.9	35	34.0	32	31.1	—	—
Hukuang	106	37	34.9	20	18.9	47	44.3	2	1.9
Liangkuang	89	37	41.6	22	24.7	27	30.3	3	3.4
Yun-kuei	86	30	34.9	16	18.6	37	43.0	3	3.5
Special[5]	7	2	28.6	4	57.1	—	—	1	14.3
Grain	107	54	50.5	13	12.2	39	36.4	1	.9
River	150	83	55.3	44	29.3	22	14.7	1	.7
Empire (total)	990	405	40.9	217	21.9	335	33.9	33	3.3

[1] Included in the Chihli totals are the early Ch'ing *tsung-tu* posts of Tientsin and of the Chihli-Shantung-Honan area.

[2] The Kiangsu-Kiangsi-Anhwei area.

[3] The Shensi-Shansi-Kansu area.

[4] The Fukien-Chekiang area.

[5] These totals include special *tsung-tu* posts created for Wang Lai-yung and Hung Ch'eng-ch'ou in Shun-chih's reign and for T'ien Wen-ching in Yung-cheng's reign, and the Three Eastern Provinces *tsung-tu* post in the last decade of the dynasty.

shih) was only tenth in the number of *chin-shih* in relation to her population, while Anhwei (sixth in *tu-fu*, tenth in *chin-shih*) fell to eighteenth place. On the other hand, provinces such as Fukien, Chihli, Yunnan, and Kweichow achieved academic-political success far out of proportion to their economic, cultural, or demographic importance.[48]

There is another question we can ask of the data that will produce some interesting answers. That question would be, "who served where?" Actually the question in that form will not produce a discrete answer because many *tu-fu* served in several provinces during their careers. We need to turn the question around and ask what percentage of the *tu-fu* serving in each province or area were Manchus, Mongols, Chinese bannermen, and Han Chinese. Were there some areas to which Manchus were appointed more frequently than others? What provinces, if any, became the monopoly of Han Chinese or Chinese bannermen?

Dynastic totals are given in Table 8 (governors-general) and Table 9 (governors). Manchus served most frequently as governors-general in the Shensi-Shansi-Kansu area (51.9 per cent) and least frequently in the Chihli area (17.1 per cent) and as directors-general of river conservation (14.7 per cent). Other areas where Manchus served more often than any other group were Hukuang (44.3 per cent), Szechwan (43.9 per cent), and Yunnan-Kweichow (43 per cent). It is just the reverse for Han Chinese governors-general. They were most likely to

TABLE 9—Composition of Ch'ing "Hsün-fu" by Province

Province	Total new appoint- ments	Han Chinese		Chinese bannermen		Manchus		Mongols	
		Number	Per cent of total	Number	Per cent of total	Number	Per cent of total	Number	Per cent of total
Chihli	34	13	38.2	19	55.9	2	5.9	—	—
Kiangsu	122	78	63.9	13	10.7	29	23.8	2	1.6
Anhwei	130	72	55.4	32	24.6	22	16.9	4	3.1
Shantung	129	52	40.3	28	21.7	41	31.8	8	6.2
Shansi	126	47	37.3	8	6.3	67	53.2	4	3.2
Honan	117	56	47.8	27	23.1	29	24.8	5	4.3
Shensi	127	58	45.7	16	12.6	50	39.4	3	2.3
Kansu	53	12	22.7	14	26.4	27	50.9	—	—
Fukien	104	65	62.5	22	21.2	17	16.3	—	—
Chekiang	117	70	59.8	22	18.8	24	20.5	1	.9
Kiangsi	120	58	48.3	27	22.5	33	27.5	2	1.7
Hupei	145	81	55.9	32	22.1	27	18.6	5	3.4
Hunan	125	79	63.2	20	16.0	24	19.2	2	1.6
Szechwan	29	4	13.8	12	41.2	11	37.9	2	6.9
Kwangtung	108	52	48.1	22	20.4	33	30.6	1	.9
Kwangsi	119	80	67.2	20	16.8	18	15.1	1	.9
Yunnan	92	52	56.5	17	18.5	23	25.0	—	—
Kweichow	112	61	54.5	22	19.6	29	25.9	—	—
Special[1]	16	14	87.5	—	—	2	22.5	—	—
Empire (total)	1925	1004	52.1	373	19.4	508	26.4	40	2.1

[1] These totals include the *hsün-fu* posts of Sinkiang and of the Manchurian provinces in the last days of the dynasty.

be serving in Chihli (61.9 per cent) and as director-general of river conservation (55.3 per cent), and least likely to be serving in the Shensi-Shansi-Kansu area (18.5 per cent). The breakdown in Table

9 indicates that much the same situation existed in governor posts. Manchus held a majority of the posts in two of the northern and western frontier provinces (Shansi and Kansu) and served fre-

TABLE 10—Composition of "Tsung-tu" by Area in the Period 1644-1683

Area	Total new appointments[1]	Han Chinese		Chinese bannermen		Manchus	
		Number	Per cent of total	Number	Per cent of total	Number	Per cent of total
Chihli[2]	10	2	20.0	8	80.0	—	—
Liangkiang[2]	9	1	11.1	6	66.7	2	22.2
Shen-kan[2]	22	3	13.7	14	63.6	5	22.7
Szechwan	5	—	—	5	100.0	—	—
Min-che[2]	18	1	5.6	17	94.4	—	—
Hukuang	7	1	14.3	6	85.7	—	—
Liangkuang	11	—	—	11	100.0	—	—
Yun-kuei	8	1	12.5	6	75.0	1	12.5
Special[2]	2	—	—	2	100.0	—	—
Grain	12	4	33.3	5	41.7	3	25.0
River	10	2	20.0	7	70.0	1	10.0
Empire (total)	114	15	13.2	87	76.3	12	10.5

[1] There were no Mongols appointed as *tsung-tu* in this period.
[2] See explanatory notes 1-5 of Table 8.

TABLE 11—Composition of "Hsün-fu" by Province in the Period 1644-1683

Province	Total new appointments[1]	Han Chinese		Chinese bannermen		Manchus	
		Number	Per cent of total	Number	Per cent of total	Number	Per cent of total
Chihli	24	9	37.5	14	58.3	1	4.2
Kiangsu	11	5	45.4	5	45.4	1	9.2
Anhwei	19	4	21.1	15	78.9	—	—
Shantung	19	5	26.3	14	73.7	—	—
Shansi	11	—	—	7	63.6	4	36.4
Honan	11	2	18.2	9	81.8	—	—
Shensi	18	4	22.2	10	55.6	4	22.2
Kansu	18	6	33.3	8	44.5	4	22.2
Fukien	12	1	8.3	11	91.7	—	—
Chekiang	12	2	16.7	10	83.3	—	—
Kiangsi	21	1	4.8	20	95.2	—	—
Hupei	20	4	20.0	16	80.0	—	—
Hunan	9	3	33.3	6	66.7	—	—
Szechwan	8	1	12.5	6	75.0	1	12.5
Kwangtung	8	—	—	8	100.0	—	—
Kwangsi	12	2	16.7	9	75.0	1	8.3
Yunnan	7	2	28.6	5	71.4	—	—
Kweichow	6	2	33.3	4	66.7	—	—
Empire (total)	246	53	21.5	177	72.0	16	6.5

[1] There were no Mongols appointed as *hsün-fu* in this period.

quently in the other two (Shensi and Szechwan). This fact is consistent with the persistent personal attention Manchu rulers gave their Central Asian policy.

It is of interest that Manchus did not very often appear in Canton as governor-general or governor in the critical pre-Taiping period of Sino-western relations. In the period 1796-1850 Manchus accounted for only about 26 per cent of the Kwangtung governors (8 of 31 appointments) and about 37 per cent of the Liangkuang governors-general (7 of 19 appointments). These percentages vary only slightly from the Manchus' share of all *tu-fu* appointments in that period (27 per cent of the governors and 36 per cent of the governors-general). In terms of aggregate service in these two Canton posts, the Manchu share is even less. Manchus served in the Kwangtung governor post only 20 per cent of the time in the period 1796-1850, and in the Liangkuang governor-general post about 25 per cent.

Chinese bannermen do not fare well in dynastic totals. Excluding special arrangements, not a single *tsung-tu* post and only the *hsün-fu* posts of Chihli and Szechwan were filled more often with Chinese bannermen than any other group. The picture changes drastically, however, if we look at *tu-fu* statistics for the first major phase of the Ch'ing dynasty (1644-83). Tables 10 and 11 show just how complete was the dominance of Chinese bannermen during the early years of the dynasty. In the period from 1644 to 1683, there was not a single *tsung-tu* or *hsün-fu* post in which Chinese bannermen did not account for the greatest number of appointments.

Up to this point, I have examined the sharing of power mostly in terms of numbers of people. If length of service of *tu-fu* personnel is also considered, a more complete picture can be drawn. From the summaries of Ch'ing *tsung-tu* and *hsün-fu* in Tables 12 and 13, respectively, it is apparent that the average length of term and the average length of total service varied significantly according to ethnic-political affiliation.

Chinese bannermen were the most favored group while Han Chinese were the least favored (if we exclude the statistically insignificant Mongols). On the average, a Chinese bannerman would serve in a particular governor-general post for three and a half years and have a total length of service as governor-general (in two or more posts) of six years and seven months. A Han Chinese official, on the other hand, would on the average serve for only two years and eight months in any single *tsung-tu* post or a total of four and a half years in his career, more than two years less than the average career service of Chinese bannermen. Among governors, the same situation existed: Chinese bannermen served, on the average, nine months longer than Han Chinese in any single post and eight months longer in terms of overall career service as a governor. Manchus generally fell between the high and low averages of service in both *tsung-tu* and *hsün-fu* posts. Only in the average length of term as governors did Manchus fare worse than Han Chinese.

It might be supposed that Chinese bannermen emerged with better average length of term in dynastic statistics because the bulk of their service came in the early years of the dynasty, when perhaps a lack of talent and the unsettled conditions resulted in longer terms of office for all *tu-fu*. Would not, then, Manchus and Han Chinese serve in *tu-fu* posts just as long as Chinese bannermen in the period of conquest and consolidation (1644-83)? The statistics for this

TABLE 12—Ch'ing "Tsung-tu" Summaries

	Aggregate service		Appointments		Average length of term	Personnel		Average length of total service
	Years/ months	Per cent of total	Number	Per cent of total	Years/ months	Number	Per cent of total	Years/ months
Chinese bannermen	760/3	27.3	217	21.9	3/6	115	20.8	6/7
Manchus	907/9	32.5	335	33.9	2/9	187	33.7	4/10
Mongols	50/1	1.8	33	3.3	1/6	14	2.5	3/7
Bannermen (total)	1718/1	61.6	585	59.1	2/11	316	57.0	5/5
Han Chinese	1072/11	38.4	405	40.9	2/8	238	43.0	4/6
Total	2791/0	100.0	990	100.0	2/10	554	100.0	5/0

TABLE 13—Ch'ing "Hsün-fu" Summaries

	Aggregate service		Appointments		Average length of term	Personnel		Average length of total service
	Years/ months	Per cent of total	Number	Per cent of total	Years/ months	Number	Per cent of total	Years/ months
Chinese bannermen	1097/10	25.1	373	19.4	2/11	252	22.4	4/4
Manchus	1051/4	24.1	508	26.4	2/1	270	24.1	3/11
Mongols	80/3	1.8	40	2.1	2/0	21	1.9	3/10
Bannermen (total)	2229/5	51.0	921	47.9	2/5	543	48.4	4/1
Han Chinese	2140/11	49.0	1004	52.1	2/2	579	51.6	3/8
Total	4370/4	100.0	1925	100.0	2/3	1122	100.0	3/11

TABLE 14—Average Length of "Tu-fu" Appointments in the Period 1644-1683

	Aggregate service (Years/months)	Appointments (Number)	Average length of term (Years/months)
Tsung-tu			
Chinese bannermen	307/11	87	3/6
Manchus	49/3	12	4/1
Han Chinese	36/11	15	2/6
Hsün-fu			
Chinese bannermen	572/—	177	3/3
Manchus	56/10	16	3/7
Han Chinese	135/8	53	2/7

period, given in Table 14, provide an answer. Han Chinese even then served on the average a year less than Chinese bannermen in governor-general posts and eight months less in governor posts.[49] The averages of these two groups for 1644-83 are roughly comparable to dynastic averages (Tables 12 and 13). Manchus, on the other hand, did serve significantly longer during the period of conquest and consolidation than they did over the whole dynastic span. In fact, Manchus outdistanced both Chinese groups in the early reigns. I think this fact bears out my earlier contention that few Manchus in the beginning of the dynasty had the requisite skills to head the provincial administration. Those who did stayed in their posts longer. In contrast, Chinese talent, when the Manchus felt secure enough to tap it, was plentiful. Perhaps this helps explain their generally shorter terms of office throughout the Ch'ing dynasty. Frequent shifting would also prevent Chinese from establishing roots in any one area.

Enough has been said about the evolution and composition of Ch'ing dynasty *tu-fu* to indicate the dynamic nature of Manchu institutional and personnel policies. Basic institutional arrangements, such as the rank, responsibility, and jurisdiction of *tu-fu*, changed freely in the early years of the dynasty according to the exigencies of the time. Final formalization of these institutional features came only after a century of Manchu rule, in a series of decrees in 1748-49. Politico-ethnic composition of *tu-fu* personnel was not a static arrangement either. In the early years between 1644 and 1683, the language barrier of the Manchus made it necessary for the dynasty to entrust the provincial administration mainly to Chinese bannermen (a unique group whose importance has been overlooked). After the pacification of the three feudatories (1681), and the conquest of Taiwan (1683), significant shifts in *tu-fu* composition occurred at least three times. The first shift marked a decline in the use of Chinese bannermen, the second shift around the turn into the nineteenth century left Han Cinese with an increasing proportion of *tu-fu* posts, and the third shift (the only one noticed previously) augmented this trend in the post-Taiping period. I have suggested that these shifts can be associated with specific crises, such as the White Lotus and Taiping rebellions, and also with general trends, such as the consolidation of Manchu rule and the sinicization of the Manchu ruling group. Perhaps further research will bring these relationships into sharper focus.

Notes

1. Ping-ti Ho, "The Significance of the Ch'ing Period in Chinese History," *JAS*, XXVI (February 1967), 191.

2. John K. Fairbank, "The Manchu-Chinese Dyarchy in the 1840's and 50's," *FEQ*, XII (May 1953), 268-270; Alfred Kuo-liang Ho, "The Grand Council in the Ch'ing Dynasty," *FEQ*, XI (February 1952), 175.

3. T'ung-tsu Ch'ü, *Local Government in China under the Ch'ing* (Cambridge, 1962), p. 22, Table 5; Anon., "The Share Taken by Chinese and Bannermen Respectively in the Government of China," *China Review*, VI (1877-78), 137; Fred S. A. Bourne, "Historical Table of the High Officials Composing the Central and Provincial Governments of China," *ibid.*, VII (1878-79), 315.

4. Some of the leading literature on the nature of alien rule in Chinese history is: *Iminzoku no Shina tochi gaisetsu* [Outline of the Rule of Alien Peoples over China] (Tokyo, 1945), which represented a collaborative effort of 16 Japanese scholars; John K. Fairbank, "Synarchy under the Treaties," in *Chinese Thought and Institutions*, ed. John K. Fairbank (Chicago, 1957), pp. 204-231, which summarized the findings of scholars in this field (including the Japanese group just mentioned), and related the historical pattern of alien rule to western participation in China's government under the unequal treaty system; Karl A. Wittfogel and Feng Chia-sheng, *History of Chinese Society: Liao (907-1125)* (Philadelphia, 1949), which presented a comparative analysis of the patterns of alien rule during the Liao, Chin, Yuan, and Ch'ing dynasties.

5. See, for example, Edwin O. Reischauer, John K. Fairbank, and Albert M. Craig, *A History of East Asian Civilization*, Vol. II: *East Asia, the Modern Transformation* (Boston, 1965), p. 328; Hsieh Pao-chao, *The Government of China, 1644-1911* (Baltimore, 1925), p. 297.

6. Fairbank, "Dyarchy" pp. 272-273, for the period 1837-1862; Franz Michael, "Military Organization and Power Structure of China During the Taiping Rebellion," *Pacific Historical Review*, XVIII (1949), 482-483, for the period 1850-1890.

7. The first attempt that I know of to use this approach was made by a Taiwan scholar, Fu Tsung-mao, in his recent study of the *tu-fu*

institution during the Ch'ing dynasty (*Ch'ing-tai tu-fu chih-tu* [Taipei, 1963], pp. 167-168). His statistics, though, are based on a sample that represents only about one half of the total number of *tu-fu*, because he gathered his information from the biographical sections of the *Ch'ing-shih kao* [Draft History of the Ch'ing Dynasty]. Only the more important *tu-fu* would rate a biographical entry in the dynastic history.

8. For an account of Ming provincial institutions, see Charles O. Hucker, "Governmental Organization of the Ming Dynasty," *HJAS*, XXI (1958), 38-43; Fu Tsung-mao, *Tu-fu*, pp. 5-8.

9. Arthur W. Hummel, (ed.), *Eminent Chinese of the Ch'ing Period* (Washington, 1943), I, 358-360. Other holdovers were Sung Ch'üan (*ibid.*, II, 688-689), Li Chien, Li Ch'i-feng, Miao Tso-t'u, and Kao T'ou-kuang.

10. The Yün-yang governorship was reestablished in 1676 as a temporary measure after the outbreak of the rebellion of the three feudatories and then abolished in 1679 when the incumbent governor was shifted to Szechwan; the Kiangsu governorship was called Kiangning until 1689, while the Hupei governorship was called Hukuang and the Hunan governorship was called P'ien-yuan until 1723; the Chihli governorship was abolished in 1724, the Szechwan governorship in 1754, and the Kansu governorship in 1764. There were no further changes in governorships until very late in the Ch'ing period.

11. For example, from 1661 to 1665 there was one governor-general in each provincial capital (*Sheng-tsu Jen-huang-ti* [*K'ang-hsi*] *shih-lu* [Veritable Records of the K'ang-hsi Emperor] [Taipei, 1964], pp. 92 [ch. 4.11a] and 239 [*ch.* 15.14a]). Also, in the short period of 1727-38, there were a bewildering number of changes in the personnel and jurisdictions of *tu-fu* posts in the Fukien-Chekiang and Kwangsi-Yunnan-Kweichow areas. Some of the personnel involved were such favorites of the Yung-cheng emperor as O-erh-t'ai, Li Wei, Shih I-chih, Chi Tseng-yun, Yin-chi-shan, and Chang Kuang-ssu (*Ta-Ch'ing hui-tien shih-li* [Administrative Statutes and Precedents of the Ch'ing Empire], Kuang-hsü edition [Taipei, 1963], pp. 5352-53 [*ch.* 23.12a-13b]).

12. *K'ang-hsi shih-lu*, pp. 100 (*ch.* 5.3b) and 1361 (*ch.* 102.13a); see also *Huang-Ch'ing ming-ch'en tsou-i* [Memorials of Famous Ch'ing Officials] (Chia-ch'ing edition), 17.72.

13. *K'ang-hsi shih-lu*, p. 119 (*ch.* 6.18a).

14. *Ibid.*, p. 617 (*ch.* 44.17b-18a); *Hui-tien shih-li*, p. 5351 (*ch.* 23.9a).

15. *K'ang-hsi shih-lu*, p. 623 (*ch.* 45.6a). The changing responsibilities of governors in the early Ch'ing period can be seen in the imperial instructions (*ch'ih-yü*) given to new appointees. Over 2000 of these *ch'ih-yü* can still be found in the Nei-ko archives housed in Academia Sinica's Institute of History and Philology in Taiwan. For the first two emperors of the dynasty, with whom I am especially concerned, there are a total of 441 pieces (128 from Shun-chih's reign and 313 from K'ang-hsi's reign), and among these pieces can be found a few imperial instructions to *tu-fu*. The earliest extant *ch'ih-yü* to any governor after the 1661 decision to take military control out of the governor's hands was issued to Lin T'ien-ching, who was sent to Yensui (in Shensi) in 1662 (*lieh-tzu* 16, K'ang-hsi 1/8/21). Lin was told that all military matters were under control of the provincial commander-in-chief and he should not interfere. The emperor continued to issue identical instructions to other governor appointees until 1674. In that year, however, Hang-ai was appointed governor of Shensi and told to work with the governor-general and *t'i-tu* in all military matters (*chang-tzu* 5, K'ang-hsi 13/8/26).

16. *Hui-tien shih-li*, pp. 5352-55 (*ch.* 23.12a-18b). This arrangement was approved for Shansi in 1734, Honan in 1739, Shantung in 1742, Kweichow in 1747, Kiangsi in 1749, and Anhwei in 1803. There was no governor-general with jurisdiction over Shansi, Honan, or Shantung; the governor-general for Yunnan and Kweichow was stationed at Yunnan-fu (Kunming), and the governor-general for the Kiangsi-Kiangsu-Anhwei area was stationed at Kiangning (Nanking).

17. *Hui-tien shih-li*, p. 5354 (*ch.* 23.15b).

18. *K'ang-hsi shih-lu*, pp. 68 (*ch.* 2.24a), 75 (*ch.* 3.1b-2a), 77-78 (*ch.* 3.5a-7a), and 79 (*ch.* 3.9b). The post had been abolished and reestablished several times earlier (*Shih-tsu Chang-huang-ti* [Shun-chih] *shih-lu* [Veritable Records of the Shun-chih Emperor] [Taipei, 1964], pp. 647-48 [*ch.* 55.13a-15b], 886 [*ch.* 75.7b-8a], 990 [*ch.* 83.24a], 1062 [*ch.* 89.3b-4a], 1639 [*ch.* 138.17a], and 1679 [*ch.* 142.13b-14b]).

19. Hucker, "Governmental Organization," pp. 42-43.

20. *Hui-tien shih-li*, pp. 5353-54, (*ch.* 23.14b-15a).

21. Fu Tsung-mao, *Tu-fu*, p. 176.

22. *Shun-chih shih-lu*, p. 854 (*ch.* 72.3b-4a); for similar remarks, see *ibid.*, pp. 1021 (*ch.* 86.1b-2b) and 1070 (*ch.* 90.4a-5b).

23. *Ibid.*, p. 1696 (*ch.* 144.3b); Hummel, *Eminent Chinese*, I, 258.

24. *K'ang-hsi shih-lu*, pp. 1122-23 (*ch.* 83.24b-25a), 1528 (*ch.* 114.24a), and 3356-57 (*ch.* 251.15b-18b).

25. *Shih-tsung Hsien-huang-ti* [Yung-cheng] *shih-lu* [Veritable Records of the Yung-cheng Emperor] (Taipei, 1964), pp. 1131-32 (*ch.* 74.5b-7b.).

26. Hsiao I-shan, *Ch'ing-tai t'ung-shih* [General History of the Ch'ing Dynasty] (Taipei, 1962-63), II, 24.

27. *Ch'ing-shih* [History of the Ch'ing Dynasty] (Taipei, 1961), p. 3889, col. 7.

28. K'ang-hsi reigned from 1661 to 1722 but did not actually control the government until he arrested and imprisoned his chief regent (Oboi) in 1669.

29. Hsiao I-shan, *Ch'ing-tai t'ung-shih*, II, 24.

30. *Kao-tsung Ch'un-huang-ti* [Ch'ien-lung] *shih-lu* [Veritable Records of the Ch'ien-lung Emperor] (Taipei, 1964), p. 2734 (*ch.* 184.7b-8a).

31. *Ibid.*, pp. 2734-35 (*ch.* 184.8a-9a).

32. *Hui-tien shih-li*, p. 5350 (*ch.* 23.8b). I have been unable to locate this decree in *K'ang-hsi shih-lu*. This decision of 1668 must be the one cited by Ch'ien Mu, *Kuo-shih ta-kang* [Outline of Chinese History] (Taipei, 1960), p. 603, as being made after the suppression of the rebellion of the three feudatories.

33. *Hui-tien shih-li*, p. 5351 (*ch.* 23.10a).

34. *Pa-ch'i t'ung-chih* [General History of the Eight Banner System] (1799 edition), 339.1a.

35. *Ch'ing-shih*, pp. 2846-3288 (*ch.* 189-209).

36. Taipei, 1961 (a reprint of the original 1931 edition). Appendices to Yen's *tu-fu* tables arranged all Ch'ing governors-general and governors (if not listed as a governor-general) according to their politico-ethnic affiliation. These lists formed the basis of the dynastic totals of *tu-fu* affiliation given in P'an Kuang-t'an, "Chin-tai Su-chou ti jen-ts'ai" [Soochow as an

Aristogenic Center], *She-hui k'o-hsueh,* I (1935), 70-71. Pan's figures, in turn, were cited by Mary C. Wright, *The Last Stand of Chinese Conservatism: the T'ung-chih Restoration, 1862-74,* 2nd printing with additional notes (Stanford, 1962), p. 55, note k.

37. *Ch.* 339-340. I am indebted to Jonathan Spence for first calling my attention to the correlation between Fengtien registration and banner affiliation of prominent Ch'ing officials. Prof. Spence's own findings on this problem are found in his book, *Ts'ao Yin and the K'ang-hsi Emperor* (New Haven, 1966), pp. 71-72, n. 119. A similar correlation between Liaotung registration and banner affiliation can also be hypothesized for the same reasons. A quick glance at the *Sheng-ching t'ung-chih* list of "men of distinction" (*jen-wu*) yields innumerable examples of Chinese bannermen *tu-fu* identified as "Liaotung jen" (Taipei, 1965 reprint of 1736 edition, *ch.* 34). Even a few men with registrations in central provinces have turned out to be bannermen. To cite one case, Shih Wei-han of the Chinese bordered yellow banner is listed as a Shanghai native in *Ch'ing-shih,* p. 3951, col. 9, in *Kuo-ch'ao ch'i-hsien lei-cheng* [Classified Biographies of Famous Ch'ing Men], comp. Li Huan (Hunan, 1884-90), 154.33a, and in the gazetteers of Fukien, Chekiang, and Shantung. None of those works mention his banner affiliation.

38. There are at least 27 *tu-fu* who are not listed in *Pa-ch'i t'ung-chih* when the evidence of other sources clearly indicates they were bannermen. The most notable omissions were Hung Ch'eng-ch'ou and Chang Kuang-ssu. Some of these omissions occur in the 1790's when the editors were compiling the banner history, and they may not have had completely up-to-date records on bannermen serving as officials. The compilers of *Pa-ch'i t'ung-chih* have also confused the two governors of Chihli named Yü Ch'eng-lung (with identical characters). The earlier governor (1680-81) was listed as a Chinese bordered red bannerman although Hummel, *Eminent Chinese,* II, 937, *Ch'ing-shih,* p. 3968, col. 1, and *Ch'ing-shih lieh-chuan* [Biographies for Compiling a Ch'ing History] (Taipei, 1962), 8.20a, all give his registration as Shansi. The second governor (1686-90 and again in 1698) is not to be found in *Pa-ch'i t'ung-chih,* although both *Ch'ing-shih,* p. 3985, col. 0, and *Ch'ing-shih lieh-chuan,* 8.43a, state that he was a Chinese bor-

dered yellow bannerman (Hummel, *Eminent Chinese,* II, 938, says bordered red).

39. *Ch'ing-chi chung-yao chih-kuan nien-piao* (Peking, 1959).

40. The collections I consulted were Hummel, *Eminent Chinese, Kuo-ch'ao ch'i-hsien lei-cheng, Ch'ing-shih lieh-chuan, Ch'ing-shih,* and local gazetteers.

41. There is still a chance for error in identifying the ethnic origin of bannermen, because some Chinese were enlisted in Manchu banners and adopted Manchu names. In addition, some Manchus adopted typically Chinese names. Kao Pin and his nephew Kao Chin were two notable examples of Chinese who were enrolled in Manchu banners (Hummel, *Eminent Chinese,* I, 411-12). In such cases, I have counted them as Chinese bannermen.

42. The total number of *tu-fu* (1301) in Table 1 does not match the added totals of *tsung-tu* (554) and *hsün-fu* (1122) because 375 (or two-thirds) of the *tsung-tu* had previously served as *hsün-fu.* Such officials serving in both posts during their careers were counted only once in calculating *tu-fu.* I have included in my calculations all *tsung-tu* and *hsün-fu,* even if they served for brief periods only. Acting service, however, was not counted.

43. The importance of Chinese bannermen in the early Ch'ing period has also been noted by Jonathan Spence (*Ts'ao Yin,* p. 4 and n. 11). We both reached this conclusion independently.

44. I have subdivided the Ch'ing dynasty into 16 periods as follows: (1) Shun-chih, 1644-61; (2) Early K'ang-hsi, 1662-83; (3) Middle K'ang-hsi, 1684-1702; ;(4) Late K'ang-hsi, 1703-22; (5) Yung-cheng, 1723-35; (6) Early Ch'ien-lung, 1736-55; (7) Middle Ch'ien-lung, 1756-75; (8) Late Ch'ien-lung, 1776-95; (9) Chia-ching, 1796-1820; (10) Early Tao-kuang, 1820-38; (11) Late Tao-kuang, 1839-60; (12) Hsien-feng, 1851-61; (13) T'ung-chih, 1862-74; (14) Early Kuang-hsü, 1875-84; (15) Middle Kuang-hsü, 1885-1900; (16) Late Kuang-hsü and Hsuan-t'ung, 1901-11.

Because of their length, the reigns of K'ang-hsi and Ch'ien-lung are each broken down into three even segments; 1683 is used to end K'ang-hsi's early period because the final Manchu conquest of China (the subjugation of Taiwan) came at that time. The Opium War is used to divide the Tao-kuang period. The last four decades of the dynasty are broken down into smaller segments than usual in order to detect any significant shifts in *tu-fu* composition as China faced increasingly urgent foreign and domestic problems.

45. Ho, "Significance of the Ch'ing period," pp. 191-93.

46. The situation in Anhwei was somewhat comparable to that in Hunan: most Anhwei natives who became *tu-fu* served in the post-Taiping period, but not to the same extent as Hunanese.

47. These rankings are based on figures published by Ping-ti Ho in *The Ladder of Success in Imperial China* (New York: Columbia University Press, 1962), p. 228 (Table 28). I have disregarded the figures for bannermen and separated the figures for Shensi and Kansu in determining provincial rankings and percentages.

48. *Ibid.*, pp. 229 (Table 29) and 233-37.

49. A comparable difference in tenure according to ethnic affiliation also existed in local posts in the early Ch'ing period, if Soochow can be taken as a representative case. During the entire K'ang-hsi period, bannermen served an average of 4.3 years as prefect and 3 years as district magistrate, whereas Han Chinese only averaged 2.7 years in each post (Spence, *Ts'ao Yin*, p. 74).

IV. THE TRIBUTARY SYSTEM

4. THE MEETING OF THE WESTERN AND EASTERN FAMILIES OF NATIONS

IMMANUEL C. Y. HSÜ

A. THE EAST ASIAN FAMILY OF NATIONS

Relations between the states in the Far East were much like those between members of a family, far more so than the relations between the Western nations. It is literally correct to describe them as constituting their own family of nations in East Asia. China, as the Middle Kingdom, took the position of family head, and the smaller states on her periphery—Korea, Annam, Siam, Burma, and Japan for a time—assumed the position of junior members, paying homage to her in the form of periodic tribute. This was an extension to the interstate level of the Confucian idea of the proper relation between individuals. Just as every person in a Confucian society had an assigned status as the basis of his relations with others, so the state in an "international" society must have a properly defined status. By virtue of her cultural, political, economic and military preeminence, China unhesitatingly assumed the

From Immanuel C. Y. Hsü, *China's Entrance into the Family of Nations: The Diplomatic Phase, 1858-1880* (Harvard University Press 1960) pp. 109-118, 236-237. Copyright 1960 by the President and Fellows of Harvard College. Reprinted by permission.

role of family head, while others acknowledged her leadership by willingly accepting their junior status as tribute-paying members. In Korean records, relations with China were described as *sadae*, or serving the senior, whereas those with Japan were known as *kyorin*, or relations with a neighbor.[1] This distinction illustrates well the basic spirit of the East Asian family of nations.

Tributary relations involved both rights and duties. China had the responsibility of maintaining proper order in this family. She recognized the junior members by sending special emissaries to officiate at the investiture of new tributary kings and to confer on them the imperial patent of appointment. China also went to their aid in time of trouble; one of the causes for the downfall of the Ming dynasty was said to be its extensive military aid to Korea in her defense against the Japanese invasion under Hideyoshi at the end of the sixteenth century. Relief missions from China, with messages of sympathy and commiseration from the emperor, were often sent to the tributary states in the wake of such natural calamities as famines, floods, droughts, and typhoons.

Tributary states, as junior members of

the family, accepted China's calendar as theirs and paid homage to the head by sending periodic *ad hoc* tribute-bearers to Peking via an assigned route under Chinese escort. The closer the relation between the tributary state and China, the more frequent the tribute. In the Ch'ing period, Korea paid tribute four times a year, presented all at once at the end of each year; Liu-ch'iu twice every three years, Annam every two years, Siam every three years, and Burma every ten years.[2] The size of each tributary mission was fixed by the Chinese, who also underwrote all the expenses of the mission while in China. The tributary envoy was lodged in the official hostel in the Chinese capital and presented his credentials (*piao*) and tribute to the emperor through the Board of Ceremonies. A felicitous day was then selected for the Son of Heaven to receive him and, in the full assemblage of the Chinese court, the envoy performed the celebrated three kneelings and nine knockings of the head on the ground— the *kowtow*. In return, the emperor showed his appreciation of the homage and his benevolence toward men from afar by bestowing on the envoy, his suite, and the tributary king liberal gifts, which usually far exceeded the tribute in value. Following the audience, the tributary mission was allowed to open a market at the hostel for three to five days to sell the local products of its country, which had been brought in tax-free. The mission was then feted several times by the Board of Ceremonies before departing from Peking over the same assigned route and under the same escort until it left Chinese territory. This system of "international relations" was known as the tributary system; its basis was not the recognition of equality among sovereign states as in the West,

but a father-son or senior-junior relationship. In contrast with the relations between Western imperialist nations and their colonies, the tributary relations were primarily ceremonial and ritualistic, rather than exploitative.[3] Economically, the tributary practice was a loss to China, yet its prestige value could not be overlooked. The Chinese emperor may be said to have been not so much an "economic man" as a "political animal" in the Aristotelian sense.

It was this system that the Western family of nations encountered when it intruded into the Far East in the early and middle nineteenth century. Conflict arose when neither the Western nor the Eastern system could accommodate the other without radical sacrifice. The Western nations could not accept the Chinese tributary system without sacrificing valued principals of state sovereignty and diplomatic intercourse based on international law. The Chinese empire could not accept the Western idea of equality of states without changing radically its traditional thinking and the age-old institutions of "foreign" relations as recorded in the *Collected Statutes of the Great Ch'ing Empire*.[4] Hence the arrival of each Western mission in China invariably marked an occasion for quarrel because the Chinese insisted that such missions be treated as tributary missions. Unsupported by military forces and anxious to achieve trade benefits, early Western envoys usually yielded grudgingly to the Chinese practice. Of the seventeen missions between 1655 and 1795—six from Russia, four from Portugal, three from Holland, three from the Papacy, and one from Britain—all but the last, under Lord Macartney, performed the *kowtow*.[5] It was not until after the Napoleonic Wars that Western nations, notably Britain, with vastly increased surplus energies resulting from the Industrial Revolution, resolved to alter this situation by force.

Needless to say, the Chinese attitude on "foreign" affairs was the product of traditions and a political philosophy that had been in effect since time immemorial. It is therefore imperative to study the nature of the Chinese state and the traditional Chinese views on and approaches to "foreign" affairs, in order to understand the seemingly strange mentality and baffling behavior of Ch'ing officials in their dealings with the West.

B. THE UNIVERSAL CHINESE STATE AND ITS RELATIONS WITH THE BARBARIANS

The unique political philosophy of the Chinese considered the ultimate objective of government to be the setting in order of the whole known world, rather than the state. The emperor claimed to be the Son of Heaven, who ruled supreme over all mankind with the Mandate of Heaven. The *Book of Odes* expressed this sentiment in the following words: "Under the wide heaven, there is no land that is not the Emperor's, and within the sea-boundaries of the land, there is none who is not a subject of the Emperor."[6] The emperor's ministers considered world statesmanship (*p'ing t'ien-hsia*) their highest objective, and *The Great Learning* held that only by first rectifying his mind, cultivating his person, regulating his family, and governing his state could a man reach the goal of setting the world in order. Confucius envisaged a "Universal Commonwealth" (*Ta-t'ung*) as the ultimate stage of human development.

The world as known to the Chinese in earliest times was the Yellow River valley in what is now North China. By the time of the Chou dynasty (1122 B.C.-255 B.C.) it had expanded southward to include the Yangtze River area. The Ch'in unification (221 B.C.) and the subsequent expansions in the Han (206 B.C.-220 A.D.) and T'ang (618 A.D.-907 A.D.) periods virtually pushed the Chinese frontiers to the edge of the Far East, and China became in fact a world in itself, with a group of tributary states clustered on its borders.[7]

Since the emperor claimed to rule over all under heaven, his domain naturally included the barbarian tribes, whose existence was early recognized in ancient records. The test of barbarity was not so much race or religion or national origin as it was cultural achievement; this suggests the Greek standard of regarding a foreign tongue as a sign of barbarity. He was barbarian who did not accept Chinese civilization and who knew not the refinement of ceremony, music, and culture. In their utter ignorance of the beauty of the Chinese way of life and in their lack of sufficient intellect to appreciate reason and ethics, the barbarians were considered no different from the lower animals. Nothing expresses these sentiments so well as the ideographic Chinese characters used to designate the barbarians. The designation for southern barbarians, *Man,* is written with an "insect" (*ch'ung*) radical, and that for the northern barbarians, *Ti,* is written with a "dog" (*ch'üan*) radical. Ch'iang, a Western tribe, is written with the "sheep" (*yang*) radical. Not only the Chinese language, but the Chinese people in their attitude toward the barbarians, often compared them to animals. Pan Ku, author of the *History of Han,* described the Huns (*Hsiung-nu*) in the following terms: "The Sage-King [of China] treated them as animals, not entering into oaths with them or fighting or chastising them. Their land cannot be used for the cultivation of food, and their people cannot be treated as subjects."[8] Su Shih, a famous poet and statesman of the Sung, made a statement which has since become famous: "The barbarians cannot be governed in the same way as China is governed. That is to say, to seek good government among animals will inevitably lead to great confusion."[9] The Ch'ing officials, therefore, did not lack historical foundation when they described Western barbarians as having the disposition of "dogs and sheep."

Barbarians, in a strict sense, were not foreigners, for they were not outside the domain of the universal Chinese empire. They were but "uncivilized and outlandish" peoples awaiting assimilation into the Chinese orbit through a cultural transformation. It was indeed the duty of the emperor, as mediator between Heaven and Man, to effect such a transformation and confer the boon of civilization upon those who had unfortunately been born barbarian. The *Book of History* is replete with advice to the emperor on the importance of winning the hearts of the barbarians through a virtuous rule. The "Canon of Shun" in the Book of Yu states:

Be kind to the distant, and cultivate the ability of the near. Give honor to the virtuous and your confidence to the good, while you discountenance the artful:—so shall the barbarous tribes lead on one another to make their submission.[10]

"The Counsels of the Great Yü" enjoins:

Do not fail in due attention to the laws and ordinances. . . . Do not oppose the people to follow your own desires. Attend to these things without idleness or omission, and from the four quarters the barbarous

tribes will come and acknowledge your sovereignty.[11]

Furthermore, the "Hounds of Leu [Lu]" of the Book of Chou observes that:

The intelligent kings have paid careful attention to their virtues, and the wild tribes on every side have willingly acknowledged subjection to them. The nearer and the more remote have all made offerings of the productions of their countries.[12]

From these quotations one gathers the inevitable impression that the wise emperor was one who won the admiration of barbarians by his irresistible virtue, and in return the barbarians expressed their gratitude by offering their local products to the Son of Heaven. Herein lay the basic spirit of the tributary system.

Since the test of barbarity was primarily one of cultural standards, barbarians could become Chinese when they advanced to the Chinese level of civilization and conformed to the higher Chinese standards of living. Conversely, the Chinese became barbarians when they debased themselves through uncivil practices. In other words, elevated barbarians could be superior to debased Chinese.[13] Confucius once said: "The rude tribes of the East and North have their princes, and are not like the states of our great land which are without them."[14]

However, if the barbarians refused to accept the benefits of civilization and continued to disturb China, then, and only then, a policy of chastisement must be followed. The *Book of Odes* states: "Our prince's chariots are a thousand. . . . His footmen are thirty thousand . . . to deal with the tribes of the West and North, and to punish [those of] King and Shoo [Ching and Shu] so that none of them will dare to withstand us."[15]

It is these ideas and admonitions in the classical canons, which every scholar-statesman studied, that became in time the cornerstone of Chinese policy toward outlandish peoples. The basic tenet of such a policy was that the Chinese emperor should be virtuous and benevolent so that the barbarians, through spontaneous admiration, might voluntarily seek assimilation. It was not an active and aggressive policy of going out to convert the outlandish tribes, but rather a passive, "laissez-faire" policy of expecting them to come to obtain transformation of their own accord.

Exceptions, of course, may be found in especially ambitious emperors or powerful ministers. For instance, Chang Ch'ien and Pan Ch'ao of the Han period were sent by Emperor Wu in 138 B.C. and Emperor Ming in 73 A.D., respectively, to the Western Region, which included the Indoscythians in Central Asia, and the Hsiung-nu and Scythians in Eastern Turkestan. Through their efforts these areas came under Chinese control or influence. There was also the case of the powerful Ming eunuch Cheng Ho, who led a large fleet to the South Seas seven times between 1405 and 1430, bringing Cambodia, Siam, Java, Burma, and other countries into the Chinese tributary system. But these were exceptions to the general Chinese approach to the outside tribes. By and large, the Chinese believed that if the barbarians did not aspire to a higher life, there was no need to force them to do so. The fundamental spirit of the traditional approach to the barbarian problem, therefore, was nongoverning and nonintervening. As Ho Hsiu (129-182 A.D.,), the great Han scholar of the Modern Text school of classical learning, expressed it: "The Emperor does not govern the barbarians. Those who come will not be rejected, and those who leave will not be pursued."[16] The lack of a tradition of positive policy toward the barbarians predisposed China to a state of unpreparedness in case of emergency, new challenge, or new trouble. This may have been one of the basic causes of China's unreadiness to meet the new Western "barbarians" in the nineteenth century.

A corollary of the philosophy of nonintervention was the doctrine of nonexploitation of the barbarians. The Confucianists advocated China's not wearing herself out in endless warfare with the outer tribes, but winning their submission through a benevolent concern for their welfare. During the reign of Emperor Hsüan-tsung (73-49 B.C.) of the Han dynasty, disorder arose in the Hsiung-nu (Huns) tribe. The emperor, tempted to exploit the situation to China's favor, was advised by his minister Hsiao Wang-chih to avoid such opportunistic inclinations and instead to send a mission of commiseration to the Huns tendering his sympathy, so that the barbarians might be moved to gratitude and so to transformation.[17]

On the other hand, barbarians, not being Chinese until assimilation was complete, were watched with vigilance. Meticulous care was taken to prevent their infiltration into the heartland of China and their mixing with the Chinese populace, acts which threatened to adulterate the established way of life.[18] The great Sung statesman and poet Su Shih emphatically pointed out that one of Confucius' purposes in writing the *Spring and Autumn Annals* was to guard against the mixing of barbarians and Chinese. This policy of separate existence stemmed from the fear that barbarians residing in China would breed mischief and intrigue, or learn the ingenious methods of the Chinese whereby they might make trouble with China when they returned home. Thus Empress Wu (reign: 684-704 A.D.) of the T'ang was advised by her ministers against letting barbarian tributary envoys tarry long in the Chinese capital or allowing barbarian princes to serve in the Chinese court.[19] During the Yung-lo (1403-1424) and Hsüan-te (1426-1435) periods of the Ming, Li Hsien, a secretary of the Board of Civil Office, expressed alarm at the increasing migration into the capital area of Tartars, toward whom the court was kindly disposed. He urged the court to expel them, on the ground that treatment of men must be based on degrees of intimacy:

I have heard the Way of the Kings is [to treat Chinese] people as infants, and barbarians as animals. To treat people as infants means to endear them; to treat barbarians as animals means to keep them distant. While the sages looked upon all with equal benevolence, their favor nevertheless started from the near [and proceeded] to the far. There should not be anything like giving favor to the animals before giving the infants their just share. Furthermore, could the sages bear to feed animals with the food of the infants?[20]

The mistrust with which the barbarians were viewed crystallized into a policy of segregation and of constant watchfulness and precaution when they had to be admitted into China. Thus the tributary envoys were escorted by Chinese guards over an assigned route to and from Peking and were not allowed to purchase Chinese guns or books while in the capital, lest they make trouble or become too wise. They were not allowed to roam about freely in the streets without first securing permission from the proper Chinese authority, who would then specially guard the streets they were to pass through. Westerners who came to China for trade were carefully quarantined in Macao and in the thirteen factories outside the city of Canton. Certainly at the bottom of all these precautions was the traditional policy of segregation, which also explains the unusually strong Chinese opposition to the Western demands for diplomatic residence in Peking and free travel in the interior.

The policy of benevolent nonintervention and its corollary, the policy of dissociation, were possible only when China was strong enough to maintain its control over the barbarians. When the barbarians became too powerful and could no longer be controlled, China had to devise new methods to deal with them. Such methods often took the form of appeasement, through the creation of some new personal relationship between the emperor and the chieftain of the trouble-making barbarian tribe, by marriage or some other form of personal diplomacy. For instance, when the Han Emperor Kao-tsu (reign years: 206-193 B.C.) lost the battle to the Huns at Paiteng, he adopted the suggestion of a minister, Liu Ching, that peace be bought at the price of marrying a Chinese princess to the chieftain of the Huns. The future chieftains of the Huns would thus be his grandson and great grandson and hence less likely to be rebellious. This policy of diplomacy by marriage placed the Huns on a more or less equal footing with China. Emperor Wu of the Han dynasty made an even more deft use of the marriage policy by marrying a Chinese princess to the chieftain of the Wu-sun tribe, who were enemies of the Huns, thereby effecting an alliance against the Huns. The celebrated policy of using one barbarian to check another barbarian (*i-i chih-i*) was born.[21]

A more remarkable example of equal and "personal" relationship existed between the Sung dynasty and the Liao nation. After twenty-five years of futile warfare with Liao, the Sung Emperor Chen-tsung (reign years: 993-1022) made an agreement with the Liao king at Shan-yüan (in modern Hopei Province) by which he consented to treat the Liao Empress Dowager as "an aunt," and the Liao king agreed to treat the Sung Emperor as an "elder brother." The Sung was also to subsidize the Liao with 100,000 taels and 200,000 rolls of silk annually. For 160 years *ad hoc* envoys were exchanged between the two on an equal footing on such occasions as New Year's Day, royal birthdays and deaths, and the ascension to the throne of new emperors and kings. The functions of the envoys were primarily ceremonial and ritualistic, rather than diplomatic, and they all performed the *kowtow* before their accredited rulers.[22]

The policy of diplomacy by marriage in the Han dynasty, and the brotherly relations between the Sung and the Liao reflected the Confucian emphasis on the importance of human relations in solving problems. Such precedents throw light on the diplomatic behavior of Ch'i-ying, the famous barbarian manager in the 1840's. His eargerness to befriend Sir Henry Pottinger and his insistence on adopting the latter's son as his godson, if viewed in a historic light, were but latter-day variations of the traditional "personal diplomacy" with the barbarians.

In passing, mention must also be made of the interstate intercourse in the Warring States period of the late Chou dynasty. Numerous *ad hoc* envoys were exchanged between the states, the most famous being Su Ch'in and Chang I. The relations here were not strictly "diplomatic," however, for theoretically all these "states" were feudal principalities still under the nominal rule of the Chou emperor. Because of the decline of the Chou power, they had become independent states in all but theory. Since such interstate intercourse was conducted among the Chinese themselves within the universal empire, rather than between the Chinese and the outlandish barbarian tribes, it is beyond the scope of this study.

Cursory as is the above account, it nevertheless indicates some of the stereotyped Chinese thinking and practices vis-à-vis the barbarians. It is from this heritage that Ch'ing officials of the nineteenth century drew their guidance and inspiration in dealing with the advancing Western states. Needless to say, the lack of a traditional positive approach to the barbarian problem predisposed the Ch'ing government to a state of unpreparedness in meeting the new challenge. The Ch'ing officials' description of foreigners as unreasonable, fickle, unfathomable, and violent, like dogs and sheep, and their stubborn resistance to foreigners' mixing with the Chinese through diplomatic residence in the capital and trade and travel in the interior, all manifested the influence of the past. Yet the past was a poor guide, for the industrial West was as different from the traditional ephemeral barbarian tribes as day is from night. China blundered time and again in her foreign transactions largely because she had no better sources to draw guidance from. Knowledge of history had not been flexibly used to China's advantage; in fact it had limited her response.

C. CHINESE INSTITUTIONS OF "FOREIGN" INTERCOURSE

The existence of a foreign office in a state presupposes an awareness of the necessity for relations with other more or less equal states. Such an awareness was lacking in the universal Chinese state, where there was recognition only of barbarian, and not foreign, affairs. Hence a foreign office did not exist. Parallel to the absence of a foreign office was the absence of any national sentiment; there was no national flag in Imperial China; there were only dynastic or royal banners. It is amusingly reported that before the Opium War in 1839 the British Superintendent of Trade in China, Charles Elliot, urged the Viceroy of Canton, Teng T'ing-tseng, to settle the differences between the "two nations" peacefully. Teng is said to have been puzzled by the term "two nations," which he mistook for England and the United States.[23] A bold sinologist has asserted that China of old was not so much a state as a cultural entity.[24] Doubtless, Imperial China was not a nation-state.[25]

The absence of a foreign office, however, need not imply the absence of institutions and officials in charge of "foreign" affairs. During the Warring States period in Ancient China, the feudal principalities of the Chou dynasty appointed Directors of State Ceremonies and Emissary Affairs (*Ta-hsing-jen, Hsiao-hsing-jen*) to take charge of the reception of envoys from other princely kingdoms. The Ch'in unification saw the creation of the Commissioner of Guests, known as *Tien-k'o*, which office later metamorphosed into the Court of State Ceremonial (*Ta-hung-lu*) under the Han Emperor Wu. The Commissioner of Guests was assisted by an interpreter and reception-secretary known as *I-kuan lin-ch'en*, the forefather of the *Hui-t'ung-kuan* (Common Residence for Envoys) of the Yüan and Ming periods. The Ming dynasty created in addition the *Ssu-i-kuan*, or Residence for Barbarian Envoys, under the Court of Sacrificial Worship.

The early Ch'ing emperors, having inherited the *Hui-t'ung-kuan* and *Ssu-i-kuan* from the Ming, placed the former under the Hanlin Academy to take charge of receptions, and the latter under the Board of Ceremonies to specialize in translation. In 1748 the Emperor Ch'ien-lung combined these two *kuan* into a single organization known as *Hui-t'ung ssu-i kuan*, or Common Residence for Tributary Envoys, superintended by a senior secretary of the Board of Ceremonies. The main functions of this combined organization were reception and lodging of tributary envoys, while leaving matters of ceremony to the Court of State Ceremonial (*Hung-lu Ssu*). There was, in addition, a third organ, the *Li-fan-yüan*, or Court of Colonial Affairs, in charge of Mongolian, Mohammedan, and Russian affairs. Presumably Russia was included because it was an Asiatic state bordering on Mongolia and had trade relations with Mongolia and Manchuria.[26]

Sino-Russian relations rested on a somewhat peculiar ground. China's first equal treaty with a foreign power, the Treaty of Nerchinsk, was signed with Russia in 1689, and after the Treaty of Kiakhta of 1727 the Russians were allowed to maintain a religious mission in Peking, with a language school attached to it. On the other hand, Russian envoys to China accepted the tributary practices and performed the *kowtow* to the Son of Heaven, while the Chinese envoys to Russia in 1729 and 1731 also performed the *kowtow* to the Russian ruler. The relations were thus more or less equal, although on the Chinese side it was the Court of Colonial Affairs that was responsible for the conduct of relations with Russia.

Western maritime nations actually did not fit into the Chinese pattern of "foreign" relations. They were neither regular tributary states, nor like Russia located in Asia, with an overland border trade relationship. But the Ch'ing dynasty insisted that if Western nations cames to China on their own, they must come as tributaries. The various editions of the *Collected Statutes* from K'ang-hsi (1662-1722) to Chia-ch'ing (1796-1820) proudly listed Western nations alongside other regular tributaries, with an explanatory note that these Western nations were too distant from China to fix definite tribute periods. The Chinese were remarkably successful in inducing the Westerners to accept the Chinese practice when they did come to China. As has already been noted, of the seventeen early Western missions to China from 1655 to 1795, sixteen yielded to the Chinese demand for the *kowtow*. While the Ch'ing court was uncompromising in its relations with Western officials, it was far less adamant with private Western traders, who were allowed to reside in Macao and Canton as a special imperial favor toward men from afar, in contravention of the tributary system, which allowed no tributary personnel to dwell permanently in China. But they were allowed no direct communication with Chinese officials; they could only "petition" through the Chinese monopolistic merchants and the Customs Superintendent, known as the Hoppo.

The Ch'ing government appears early to have realized the importance of Western barbarian affairs. They were re-ported directly to the court in great detail by local officials and received careful examination by the emperor in conjunction with members of the all-important Grand Council. A brilliant and resourceful emperor was practically his own "foreign" minister. For instance, Emperor K'ang-hsi, in sending T'u-li-shen on a special mission to the Turgut khan, Ayüki, in southern Russia, in 1712, personally gave such detailed instructions that he practically told his envoy: "Should they ask you such and such a question, you should answer in such and such a way. . . ."[27] A less resourceful emperor was more likely to follow the advice of his Grand Councillors. Emperor Tao-kuang accepted the Treaty of Nanking and supported Ch'i-ying's conciliatory policy in the 1840's largely on the recommendation of the powerful councillor, Mu-chang-a.

When the barbarian problem grew to unusual proportions in a province, the emperor's confidence in the ability of the local officials to manage it was sometimes diminished, and he would appoint a specially deputed Imperial Commissioner to investigate the situation. In 1838 Lin Tse-hsü, viceory of Hu-Kuang, was dispatched to Canton as imperial commissioner specifically to investigate the opium problem. This novel practice of appointing an imperial commissioner to take charge of barbarian affairs continued after the Opium War and became part of the institutions of "foreign" intercourse. During the Opium War, viceroys and governors in coastal provinces were authorized to receive foreign communications, and the old practice of limiting such authority to the viceroy of Canton was ended. Ch'i-shan, viceroy of Chihli, could thus receive and negotiate with Captain Elliot. In 1844 Ch'i-ying, signer of China's first treaties with the West, was appointed viceroy of Canton and imperial commissioner in charge of trade in the ports and of other affairs relative to foreign nations. Since the imperial commissioner had his office in the yamen of the viceroy of Canton and deposited his files there, the Canton viceroyalty became a modified foreign office in all but name during the Opium War-Arrow War period of 1842-1856. This was a makeshift arrangement in deference to the new demands of the time. Viewed historically and institutionally, it was an intermediary development in the transition from the tributary system to the creation of a more modern foreign service. The device of using Canton as China's center for foreign affairs is known as the Canton Viceroy System.[28]

This system worked rather well in the years immediately after the Opium War when Ch'i-ying was the imperial commissioner. But foreigners became increasingly discontented over the fact that Peking was still inaccessible. Neither foreign diplomats nor private individuals were allowed to go to the Chinese capital, and their representations were either sidetracked or sent back to the viceroy of Canton. Foreigners entertained misgivings that the Chinese had no intention of fulfilling Article Eleven of the Treaty of Nanking, which authorized foreign diplomats to have direct correspondence, on an equal footing, with high Chinese officials in the capital.

The conviction grew that Peking was using the Canton viceroy as a breakwater to keep foreigners from direct contact with the court and that the Canton system was a subtle device to slight the Westerners. This the Westerners could not endure. They were convinced that the diplomatic opening of China must be the logical consequence of the commercial opening that had been brought about by the Opium War and the Treaty of Nanking.

Abbreviations Used in the Notes

BPP: British Parliamentary Papers.
CSL: Ta-Ch'ing li-ch'ao shih-lu (Veritable records of successive reigns of the Ch'ing dynasty).
CSK: Ch'ing-shih kao (Draft history of the Ch'ing).
CSPSR: The Chinese Social and Political Science Review.
HJAS: Harvard Journal of Asiatic Studies.
IWSM: Ch'ou-pan i-wu shih-mo (The complete account of the management of barbarian affairs).
Sen. Exec. Doc.: The Executive Documents, the Senate of the United States.
THL: Tung-hua lu (Tung-hua records).
THHL: Tung-hua hsü-lu (Tung-hua records continued).
USFR: Foreign Relations of the United States.
WCSL: Ch'ing-chi wai-chiao shih-liao (Historical materials concerning foreign relations in the late Ch'ing period; 1875-1911).

Unless otherwise indicated, all translations from the Chinese are mine.

Notes

1. George McCune, "The Exchange of Envoys between Korea and Japan during the Tokugawa Period," *The Far Eastern Quarterly*, 5:308 (May 1946). Both terms may be found in *Mencius*.

2. J. K. Fairbank and S. Y. Teng, "On the Ch'ing Tributary System," *HJAS*, 6.2:175-176 (June 1941).

3. Lo Meng-ts'e, *Chung-kuo lun* (On China; Chungking, 1943), pp. 84-85. See also Ch'en Fang-chih, *Ch'ing-tai pien-chih shu-lüeh* (A brief account of the border institutions in the Ch'ing period), *Yen-ching hsüeh-pao* ("Yenching Journal of Chinese Studies"), 34:134 (June 1947).

4. Ueda Tōshio, *Tōyō gaikōshi gaisetsu* (A

survey of Far Eastern diplomatic history; Tokyo, 1948), pp. 217-218.

5. John King Fairbank, *Trade and Diplomacy on the China Coast: The Opening of the Treaty Ports, 1842-1854* (Cambridge, Mass., 1953), I, 14.

6. *Book of Odes*, "Hsiao-ya: Pei-shan" chapter II. James Legge's translation of these passages is somewhat different and probably less literal than mine. Cf. J. Legge, *The Chinese Classics*, IV, Part II, p. 360.

7. Lo Meng-ts'e, p. 52.

8. Pan Ku, The *History of Han*, "Chapter on the Hsiung-nu," quoted in Shigematsu Toshiaki, "Kanjin no gaikō shisō ni tsuite" (On the Chinese idea of diplomacy), *Rekishi chiri* (History and geography), 29.2:162 (February 1917).

9. *Ibid.*, p. 165.

10. Translation taken from Legge, *Chinese Classics*, III, *The Shoo King*, p. 42.

11. *Ibid.*, p. 55.

12. Legge, *Chinese Classics,* IV, 346.

13. Hsiao Kung-ch'üan, *Chung-kuo cheng-chih ssu-hsiang shih* (A history of Chinese political thought; Shanghai, 1947), I, 56.

14. Translation taken from Legge, *Chinese Classics*, I, *The Confucian Analects*, p. 156.

15. Legge, *Chinese Classics*, IV, Part II, "The She King," p. 626.

16. Quoted in Shigematsu, p. 159.

17. *Ibid.*, p. 161. Exxceptions of course can readily be found to this ideal of nonintervention and nonexploitation: such as Chinese "colonization" in Mongolia and pressing the Miao tribes into uplands.

18. In practice, there was much barbarian mixture with the Chinese.

19. Shigematsu, p. 163.

20. *Ibid.*, p. 167.

21. Wang T'ung-ling, *Han-T'ang chih ho-ch'in cheng-ts'e* (The policy of diplomacy by marriage during the Han and T'ang periods), *Shih-hsüeh nien-pao* ("Historical Annual"), No. 1 (July 1929), pp. 9-10.

22. Nieh Ch'ung-ch'i, *Sung-Liao chiao-p'ing k'ao* ("Embassies between Liao and Sung"), *Yen-ching hsüeh-pao* ("Yenching Journal of Chinese Studies"), No. 27 (June 1940), pp. 3-5, 24, 37-38.

23. Yano Jinichi, *Kindai Shina ron* (On modern China; Tokyo, 1927), pp. 24-25.

24. *Ibid., passim*, pp. 3, 4, 24-26, 114.

25. John King Fairbank, "Synarchy under the Treaties," in Fairbank, ed., *Chinese Thought and Institutions* (Chicago, 1957), p. 208.

26. Information in the above two paragraphs is drawn from Ch'en T'i-ch'iang, *Chung-kuo wai-chiao hsing-cheng* (China's administration of foreign affairs; Chungking, 1943), pp. 16-17.

27. Ch'en Fu-kuang, *Yu-Ch'ing i-tai chih Chung-O kuan-hsi* (Sino-Russian relations during the Ch'ing period exclusively; Yunnan, 1947), pp. 43-44.

28. Information on China's administration of foreign affairs before and after the Opium War is drawn from two succinct articles by Chang Chung-fu: "Ya-p'ien-chan ch'ien Ch'ing-t'ing pan-li wai-chiao chih chi-kuan yü shou-hsü" ("The office and procedure for dealing with diplomatic affairs of the Ch'ing dynasty before the Opium War"), *Wai-chiao yüeh-pao* ("Foreign Affairs"), 2.2:1-7 (1933); and "Tzu Ya-p'ien chan-cheng chih Ying-Fa lien-chün ch'i-chung Ch'ing-t'ing pan-li wai-chiao chih chi-kuan yü shou-hsü" ("The office and procedure for dealing with diplomatic affairs of the Ch'ing dynasty during the period between the First and Second Anglo-Chinese Wars"), *Wai-chiao yüeh-pao*, 2.5:43-51 (1933).

5. SINO-KOREAN TRIBUTARY RELATIONS

IN THE CH'ING PERIOD *

HAE-JONG CHUN

Tributary relations with China had developed from the earliest stages of Ko-

Copyright 1968 by the President and Fellows of Harvard College.

* From John K. Fairbank (ed.), *The Chinese World Order: Traditional China's Foreign Relations* (Cambridge, Mass., Harvard University Press, 1968), pp. 90-111, 301-11. Reprinted by permission.

Hao-jong Chun is Professor of East Asian History at Seoul National University, Korea. He studied political science at Tokyo Imperial University, received his B.A. (1947) and M.A. (1952) in East Asian history from Seoul National University, and studied East Asian history at Harvard University (1953-1955). His major interest is modern Chinese history and Sino-Korean relations, and his publications include *Ilbon-sa* (An outline history of Japan; Seoul, 1964, with T. K. Min) and *Han'guk gunse taewe kwan'gye munhŏn biyo* (A manual of Korean foreign relations, 1876-1910; Seoul, 1966).

Abbreviations Used in the Notes

CCJN: *Chich'ik jŏngnye* (see note 42)
CSJGC: *Ch'iksa jŭnggŭp-ch'aek*
HTSL: *Ta-Ch'ing hui-tien shih-li*
MGYR:CY *Man'gi yoram:Chaeyong p'yŏn*
TCJJ: *T'akchi junjŏl* (see note 45)
TMGJ: *T'ongmun-gwan ji*
TMGH: *Tongmum hwigo*
YHNSJ: *Yŏnhaengnok sŏnjip*

rean history,[1] and by the early Ch'ing period they were highly systematized. Korea was the model tributary, and during the Ch'ing era official Sino-Korean relations, mainly concerned with the sending and receiving of embassies and the conduct of trade between the two countries, provided an example of the relations expected or desired between China and other peripheral states. Although the Ch'ing-Korean tributary system was largely an elaboration of the Ming system, this paper concentrates on the Ch'ing in order to present a detailed picture of how the system actually operated.[2]

KOREAN EMBASSIES TO CHINA

We can best begin this examination of the Korean embassies to Ch'ing China by noting the regulations and practices concerning: the kinds of embassies and the business they transacted, their appointment and composition, their preparation for departure to China, the routes they took, the ceremonies and activities in Peking, their reports after they returned to Korea, and their frequency. The economic aspects of the embassies will be described in a later section.

a. The Kinds of Embassies and Their Duties

In the late fourteenth century (the early Ming period) under the Yi dynasty (1392-1910) the rulers of Korea had annually sent three regular embassies to China:[3] on the occasions of (1) New Year's Day, (2) imperial birthdays, and (3) the birthdays of imperial heirs apparent. These embassies bore the title respectively of (1) *chŏngjo* (in Chinese romanization *cheng-ch'ao*), (2) *sŏngjŏl* (*sheng-chieh*), and (3) *ch'ŏnch'u* (*ch'ien-ch'iu*). Besides these there were occasional embassies of thanks for imperial grace (*saun*; Chinese *hsieh-en*), congratulations (*chinha; chin-ho*), condolence (*chinwi; ch'en-wei*), offering incense (*chinhyang; chin-hsiang*), presenting obituary notices (*kobu; kao-fu*), conveying tributary horses (*amma; ya-ma*), memorializing (*chumun; tsou-wen*), and so on.

By late Ming times, in the early seventeenth century, the titles of the Korean embassies still remained the same, except that the embassy for the winter solstice (*tongji; tung-chih*) had replaced all of the three regular embassies mentioned above. This new kind of embassy was usually given concurrently one or both of the titles of the embassies for the imperial birthday and the birthday of the heir apparent. Some of the titles of the occasional embassies also had been changed slightly, although the actual duties of each of them did not change fundamentally.

In the early days of Manchu rule,

when Korea had become tributary to the new Manchu state in South Manchuria, namely from 1637 through 1644, Korea annually sent four regular embassies. These were the embassies on the Manchu ruler's birthday, New Year's Day, winter solstice, and the embassy for annual tribute (*yŏn'gong; nien-kung*). However, in practice one of the first three embassies actually was given the title of annual tribute embassy concurrently every year.[4] In 1645 all of the four regular embassies to the Ch'ing, whose capital was now at Peking, were put together under the title of the winter solstice, which was also called yearly tribute (*sep'ye; sui-pi*). These new regular embassies together with the occasional ones, which were slightly different from those of earlier times, continued to be sent without any significant change up to the very end of Sino-Korean tribute relations in 1894.

The titles of the various kinds of embassies in the Ch'ing period were as follows: the winter solstice, thanking for imperial grace, memorializing (*chuch'ŏng; tsou-ch'ing*), congratulating, responding to accusations (*pyŏnmu; pien-wu*),[5] offering condolence, offering incense, and presenting obituary notices. Envoys were also sent for courtesy visits (*munan; wen-an*) during Ch'ing imperial tours in Manchuria, and for conducting joint investigations of criminals (*ch'amhaek; ts'an-ho*). Again, envoys were frequently sent to transfer memorials (*cheju; chi-tsou*) and other communications (*cheja; chi-tzu*) to the Board of Rites, or to provincial governors or others.[6]

The duties of the various embassies were naturally manifold. Every embassy carried memorials, other communications, and tribute objects. Fortunately for historians, most of the memorials and other communications and the lists of the tributary goods during the Ch'ing period were compiled and published under the title of "Collection of Documents Exchanged between Korea and China, and Korea and Japan" (*Tongmun hwigo;* Chinese, *T'ung-wen hui-k'ao*). According to parts 1 and 5 of this collection,[7] the embassies were classified as follows:

TABLE 1. Korean tribute missions to China.

Categories of missions according to their purpose or function, with chüan numbers	Activities of missions according to the documentation they used
1. Investiture (1-4)	Presenting petition and receiving imperial patent for the adoption of a Korean heir apparent, for appointment of a royal consort, or enthronement, or adoption of posthumous honors.
2. Expression of grief (5-6)	Presenting obituary notices from Korea, receiving funeral odes given by the emperor and others, and presenting thanks for the odes.
3. Congratulations (7-15)	Presented on occasions of imperial enthronement, the adoption of imperial reign titles and posthumous titles, adoption of an imperial heir apparent, appointment of an imperial consort, and suppression of rebellions in China.
4. Condolence (16)	Offering incense on the occasions of the death of the emperor or one of his family members and condolence on the occasions of conflagration in the Ch'ing court.
5. Courtesy visit (17)	Presented on the occasions of imperial visits to Shen-yang (Mukden) and other places.
6. Seasonal embassy (18-32)	In the early Ch'ing period four regular embassies went annually, but after 1645 all of them were put together into this one.
7. Explanation (33-34)	Offering explanations concerning disturbances in Korea, or misunderstanding or false accusation on the part of the Ch'ing—particularly unreasonable statements about Korea in Chinese historical works.
8. Style of memorial (35)	Inquiring about the style of various memorials and, in addition, inquiry into the date of the emperor's birthday.
9. Requests (36)	Requests by China for a supply of rice, falcons, rifles or for presenting Korean books to China.
10. Bestowal of gifts (37)	For bestowal of rice, writing brushes, Chinese books, minerals for medical use, etc.
11. Remission of and exemption from taxes (38-40)	Remission of taxes on tributary goods, exemption from ceremonials in receiving imperial embassies, mitigation of punishment of Korean criminals, or reduction of the retinue and suspension of private trade of Chinese embassy members.
12. Conveying imperial orders (41)	Concerning the return of the Korean hostage, Prince Sohyŏn; discharge of anti-Manchu Koreans from government service and their delivery to China; and improprieties in memorialization and tributary embassies.
13. Calendar (42)	Requesting the imperial calendar every year after 1644.
14. Solar and lunar eclipses (43-44)	Communications from the Peking Board of Rites on eclipses and replies to them.

Categories of missions according to their purpose or function, with chüan numbers	Activities of missions according to the documentation they used
15. Trade (45-47)	Concerning trade in Peking and on the tributary route by Korean embassies, prohibitions, local trade, trade in drugs, and fines accruing from suspending local trade.
16. Border affairs (48)	Fixing border lines and setting up military posts and colonies in the border area.
17. Border trespassers (49-62)	Koreans (chüan 49-59); Chinese (chüan 60-62).
18. Smuggling (63-64)	Smuggling niter (potassium nitrate, used in gunpowder), sulphur, copper, horses, books, maps, ginseng, etc.
19. Extradition (65)	Extradition of runaways, especially from embassies.
20. Castaways (66-73)	Koreans (chüan 66-69); Chinese (chüan 70-73).
21. Indemnification (74-75)	Repayment for private debts and lost properties.
22. Military affairs (76)	Frontier and maritime defense.
23. Relief (77)	Conveying pecuniary assistance from the Ch'ing at the funerals of Korean royal family members, embassy members, and the like.
24. Information on Japan (78)	Incidental reports on Japan and Japanese castaways.
25. Miscellanea (79)	Intermarriage between the two courts, the change of the place name of Shen-yang, and amnesties in time of drought.
26. Information on Western affairs (Pt. 5, all in 1 chüan)	Reports on Western intrusions into Korea from 1866 to 1879.

Note: Items 1-25 are in part 1 of TMHG; item 26 in part 5.

The above classification may be rearranged for our analytic purposes into several categories roughly as follows (those consisting of more than three chüan are italicized).

Highly ritualistic: classifications *1, 2, 3, 4,* and 8.

Semiritualistic and semidiplomatic: 5 and 23.

Tribute: *6,* 9, 10, and *11.*

Trade: *15* and 18.

Border affairs: 16, *17,* 19, *20,* and 22.

Calendar and astronomy: 13 and 14.

Foreign affairs: 24 and 26.

Political and miscellaneous: 7, 12, 21, and 25.

Judging from this rearrangement it may be said that, although more than two thirds of the twenty-six classifications of missions by purpose or function are explicitly characteristic of tributary relations, those numbered from 15 through 22 are not so characteristic but instead are functions which figure also in modern international relations.

b. Appointment and Composition of an Embassy

An embassy was usually composed of one envoy, one associate envoy, one attendant secretary, a certain number of

TABLE 2. Membership of various embassies.

Position	Winter solstice	Presenting thanks	Obituary notice	Courtesy visit	Joint investigation	Presenting memorials or other communications
Envoy	1	1	1	1	1	1
Associate envoy	1	1	0	0	0	0
Attendant secretary	1	1	1	1	0	0
First-class chief interpreter	2[a]	1	1	1 or 2	2 or 3	0
Second-class chief interpreter	2	2	2	0	0	0
Guards of various kinds	14	9	5	3 or 4	2 or 3	0
Minor interpreter	1	1	1	1	0	1
Physician	1	1	1	0	1	0
Writer	1[b]	1	1	0	0	0
Painter	1	0	0	0	0	0
Court physician	0	2	0	1	0	0
Additional minor official	0	1[d]	0	0	0	0
Additional guard	0	2[e]	0	0	0	0
Military officer	7	8	4	5	2	0 or 1
Language student	1	1	1	0	0	0
Military officer from Ŭiju	1	2	2	2	2	0
Astronomer	1[c]	0	0	0	0	0
Total	35	34	20	15-17	10-12	2-3

Source: Table based on *T'ongmun-gwan ji*, 3:2-5b, 57-59. The rest of the embassies, which are not listed here, mostly follow the case of the embassy presenting thanks for imperial grace.

a. Prior to 1765, one.
b. Prior to 1720 accompanied by another minor writer.
c. Prior to 1741 occasionally, after 1741 every year, and after 1763 once every three years.
d. At times two.
e. Abolished in 1697 and restored in 1707.

interpreters, tribute guards, and minor officials; the total membership of an embassy was about thirty persons,[8] although the composition and number varied according to the kind of embassy. Details of the composition of various embassies are given in Table 2.

The envoy and the associate envoy were nominated from among the Korean princes and officials of rank higher than 3A (Korea had the same nine ranks as China, each divided into A and B grades); and the attendant secretary among those higher than 6B. The rank of each was temporarily raised by one or two grades upon his nomination as a member of an embassy. The envoy, the associate envoy, and the attendant secretary were called the "three envoys." The attendant secretary recorded everyday occurrences during the mission and reported them to the Korean king. He was also competent to inspect all the members of the embassy and sometimes acted for the envoys despite the presence of other high-ranking officials or interpreters.[9]

Whereas the "three envoys" were chosen from among royal family members and, in most cases, among officials of various offices, most of the other embassy members were recommended from among the personnel of the Office of Interpretors or Sayŏk won (Ssu-i yüan). The envoys were usually nominated well ahead of their departure. In the case of the winter solstice embassy, they were supposed to be nominated in the sixth month and depart in the tenth or eleventh month.[10]

Many of the embassy members were ordinarily persons who had often been to China. Prince Inp'yong, for example, headed almost a dozen embassies in the seventeenth century. In the case of an embassy in 1787, sixteen members out of twenty-six had been to China before, and seven members more than five times.[11] Indeed, one member had been on twenty-seven embassies, and another on twenty-five—real "China hands"!

Most of the members were accompanied by various retainers such as minor secretaries, horse drivers, umbrella holders, ushers, sedan-chair bearers, heralds, henchmen, and so on, and these were mostly chosen by the members themselves. Thus the whole corps of an embassy usually numbered from 200 to 300 persons.[12]

c. Preparation for Departure

Preceding the departure of an embassy, various memorials and communications[13] as well as tributary goods[14] were prepared, examined, and carefully packed.[15] The documents an embassy carried with it numbered, in most cases, more than ten.[16] And when an embassy was given another title concurrently, the number of documents naturally increased. The embassy was given its travel expenses in kind and in money, and local governments were asked by official letters to support its transportation and provide lodging.[17] An embassy carried an enormous volume of goods,

besides tributary goods, such as the funds for travel expenses mentioned above, goods for private trade, food, fodder, and so on; the whole amount numbered at times more than 350 sacks.[18]

After the envoys had audience of the king, the embassy left Seoul for Peking on the same day.

d. The Route

Although various sea and land routes had been taken during the Ming period,[19] a land route was used during the Ch'ing, and it was considered much shorter and more convenient than any sea route. Main places on the route were, with minor changes during the Ch'ing: Seoul, P'yŏngyang (Chinese, P'ing-jang), Ŭiju (I-chou), the Yalu River, Fenghuang ch'eng, Lien-shan kuan, Liaotung, Shen-yang, Kuang-ning, Sha-ho, Shan-hai kuan, T'ung-chou, and Peking.[20] The route was about 3,000 li, or about 750 miles long and travel over it took forty to sixty days.[21] In some cases the embassy stayed in Ŭiju for several days before crossing the river, and the journey *to* Peking took several days longer than the journey home, which usually took between forty and fifty days.[22]

Before crossing the Yalu the embassy memorialized the king as to its membership, followers, horses, tributary goods, and other goods,[23] and these were also reported to the Manchu local officials on arrival at Ts'e-men.[24] At Shen-yang (Mukden) the embassy presented a part of the local tributary products to the Manchu local authorities and the latter, memorializing the emperor, transmitted them to Peking. At first they also dispatched an escort for the embassy, but this was stopped after 1677.[25] In the meantime the embassy gave presents as a kind of commission to Manchu local officials at several places.[26] This was done en route both to and from Peking.

e. Ceremonies and Activities in Peking

When the embassy entered Peking, its arrival was made known to the Residence for Tributary Envoys (Hui-t'ung kuan) and its members were received by interpreters from that organ.[27]

During their stay in Peking, and during their travel in China, the Banqueting Court (Kuang-lu ssu) of the Ch'ing supplied them with food.[28]

On the day following their arrival they presented the memorials and communications to a minister of the Board of Rites. In the case of a New Year's embassy the envoy, after having practiced the ceremonies, was received in audience with other Manchu officials and tributary envoys from other countries.[29]

In the meantime the annual tribute and "local products" were received, after the Board of Rites had memorialized and subsequently received an imperial endorsement of approval.[30] The Korean envoy was banqueted by the Board of Rites and received an imperial audience and imperial gifts.[31] Included were gifts to the king and embassy members and to only thirty of the embassy's retainers.[32] At its departure the embassy was again banqueted and, after having notified the Court of State Ceremonial (Hung-lu ssu), the embassy left Peking and was escorted as far as Shan-hai kuan by some officials of the Board of War.[33]

In the Ming period the sojourn in Peking was limited to forty days, but in the Ch'ing there was no limitation and embassies could stay for about two months.[34] Many of the embassy members had contact with Chinese officials and scholars and also visited book stores and other places,[35] besides discharging their official duties.

f. Reports to the King

On their arrival at Seoul the "three envoys" had audience of the king, and the attendant secretary presented a written official report of the embassy. Chief interpreters also sometimes presented written reports. Although many of them were superficial and evasive, some showed a profound insight into Chinese society and culture.[36]

g. Frequency of Embassies

Table 3 shows the number and frequency of the various Korean embassies to China in the Ch'ing period. Examining this table, we may note several significant points. Every year until 1894 an embassy for the winter solstice was sent to China, and every year roughly two other embassies, including those for presenting communications and memorials, went to Peking. This number was the average throughout the Ch'ing period; if all these embassies are counted together, almost three embassies went to China every year.

The highest frequency of any year was the thirteen embassies in 1638 and again in 1639, but this was the time of the Manchu invasion of Korea and subsequent Manchu domination. After 1645 the highest was six embassies a year in 1657, 1723, 1757, 1850, and 1875. This frequency, together with the fact that the payment of tributary goods was considerably remitted, would suggest that the originally oppressive attitude of the Manchu rulers toward Korea had been ameliorated. After the latter half of the K'ang-hsi reign there was no significant change in the frequency of embassies. The embassy for the imperial birthday

TABLE 3. Number and frequency of Korean embassies.

		Type of embassy																			
Period	Number of years	Winter solstice	Thanks	Memorializing	Congratulations	Responding to accusations	Condolence	Obituary notice	Courtesy visit	Joint investigation	Imperial birthday	New Year's Day	Annual tribute	Falcon conveying	Escort	Total	Average of above per year	Presenting memorial	Presenting communication	Total including memorial and communication	Average per year, over all
1637-1644	8	2/6	10	1	4	3	1	0	4	0	5	6	/8	0	0	36	4.50	1	24	61	7.26
1645-1661	17	9/8	20	0	10	0	3	2	0	0	0	0	0	11	1	56	3.29	1	15	72	4.23
1662-1692	31	14/17	20	1	16	2	7	3	2	0	0	0	0	0	0	65	2.09	3	24	92	2.96
1693-1722	30	19/11	18	3	3	2	1	2	1	2	0	0	0	0	0	51	1.70	1	27	79	2.63
1723-1735	13	5/8	11	0	5	2	4	2	0	0	0	0	0	0	0	29	2.23	0	16	45	3.46
1736-1765	30	15/15	13	0	12	2	2	2	2	4	0	0	0	0	0	52	1.73	0	30	82	2.73
1766-1795	30	23/7	9	0	9	1	1	1	1	0	1	0	0	0	0	46	1.53	0	12	58	1.93
1796-1820	25	17/8	8	1	7	2	2	2	2	0	2	0	0	0	0	43	1.72	0	17	60	2.40
1821-1850	30	22/8	8	2	14	1	4	4	1	0	0	0	0	0	0	56	1.86	0	10	66	2.20
1851-1874	24	13/11	8	0	11	2	2	2	1	0	1	1	0	0	0	40	1.66	1	8	49	2.04
Total 1637-1874	238	139/99	125	8	91	17	27	20	14	6	9	6	/8	11	1	474	1.59	7	183	664	2.78
1875-1894	20	12/7	3	0	9	4	3	2	0	0	0	0	0	0	0	33	1.65	-	-	-	-

Sources: Data for 1637 to 1881 are based on TMHG, ts'e 43, which gives, in most cases, the title of the embassy, the names of the three envoys, and dates of departure and return. Data for 1882 to 1894 are from Chosen shi (History of Korea; Seoul, 1938), Ser. 6, Vol. 4. In both cases data are arranged by the year of departure. TMHG seems to be the most accurate record of frequency, whereas Chosen shi is not inclusive. The Kuang-hsü period is, therefore, separated in the table on the bottom line.

NB: The whole period has been divided mainly according to the reign periods of emperors. A figure after / (slant) shows the number of times the "winter solstice" title was held concurrently by other embassies. In other words, in 139 years out of 238 there were winter solstice embassies, but in 99 years this title was added to the title of one of the other kinds of embassies. The title of "incense offering" was in every case held concurrently by an embassy of condolence.

was revived in the Ch'ien-lung period to glorify the aged emperor; and embassies for conveying falcons were sent only in the Shun-chih period. We also find a single case of an embassy of escort with which a Korean princess went to China to become an imperial consort.

CHINESE EMBASSIES TO KOREA

Imperial edicts, commands, and other utterances were conveyed to Korea not only by imperial envoys but also by Korean envoys returning from China. Table 4 shows the frequency with which Korea received edicts and commands during the Ch'ing period.

Korea received imperial edicts and commands once every year on the average, and about two thirds of them were conveyed by imperial envoys. It is interesting to find that they were conveyed solely by imperial embassies during the reigns of K'ang-hsi and Yung-cheng, but in the later Ch'ing period more than half

of them were carried by returning Korean embassies. This change might also be taken as evidence that the originally oppressive attitude of the Manchu rulers had been mitigated and had become more friendly toward Korea. During the later period of the reign of Ch'ien-lung he sent only four imperial embassies to Korea in spite of his sending frequent expeditions into peripheral areas.

Although imperial Chinese envoys bore no particular titles, their duties concerned the matters described in my section above on the kinds of embassies and their duties. In Table 1, except for items 3-6, 24, and 26, which were unilateral duties of Korea, most of the other items also concerned the duties of Chinese envoys.

An imperial Ch'ing embassy usually consisted of an envoy, an associate envoy, two chief interpreters, two minor interpreters, and eighteen followers.[37] In the earlier period some of the imperial envoys were men of Korean origin.

TABLE 4. Frequency of Chinese embassies and imperial commands.

Period	Number of years	Number of imperial embassies	Number of times commands carried by Korean embassies	Total number of conveyances of imperial commands	Average number of imperial embassies per year	Average number of commands per year	Percentage of commands carried by imperial embassies
1636-1644	9	18	22	40	2.00	4.44	45.0
1645-1661	17	37	3	40	2.17	2.35	92.5
1662-1692	31	39	0	39	1.25	1.25	100.0
1693-1722	30	15	0	15	0.50	0.50	100.0
1723-1735	13	15	0	15	1.15	1.15	100.0
1736-1765	30	14	2	16	0.46	0.53	87.5
1766-1795	30	4	2	6	0.13	0.20	66.
1796-1820	25	8	7	15	0.32	0.60	53.
1821-1850	30	10	18	28	0.33	0.93	35.7
1851-1874	24	5	17	22	0.20	0.91	22.7
1875-1880	6	4	7	11	0.66	1.83	36.3
1636-1880	245	169	78	247	0.68	1.00	68.4

Source: TMHG, ts'e 44.

NB: Embassies are counted by the year of departure from Peking. Even though an embassy may have conveyed more than one edict or command, still it has been counted as only one.

Chinese embassies took the same route as Korean embassies to Peking except for the visit to Shen-yang.[38]

The reception of imperial embassies was one of the most important affairs of Korea, not least because it was a heavy financial burden. As soon as the notice of an embassy's departure was received, a temporary office was set up for receiving the envoy.[39] During the embassy's travel from the Yalu to Seoul, at least five groups of Korean officials and their retinues were sent out to receive the embassy.[40] The embassy was sumptuously banqueted at several places en route.[41] Local governments also played their parts in receiving the embassy.[42] The reception in Seoul was even more luxurious and ceremonial. The envoy was received in audience by the king and banqueted several times during his comparatively short stay in Seoul.[43]

ECONOMIC ASPECTS OF THE TRIBUTARY RELATIONSHIP

The economic aspects of Sino-Korean tributary relations must be examined if we are to understand and evaluate the whole relationship. But each of the aspects—tributary goods, travel expenses of embassies, and gifts as well as trade—requires further comprehensive study. My discussion is limited to two questions, whether the tributary relationship was profitable to the respective countries and whether or how far the tributary system was maintained for economic purposes.

a. Tributary Goods and Imperial Gifts

By comparing the various editions of *Ta-Ch'ing hui-tien* (Collected statutes of the Ch'ing) one easily discovers that the tributary goods to be sent from Korea to the Ch'ing court differ in kind and in volume according to the various editions of the statutes and that a significant part of the enormous amount and value of the goods required in the early Ch'ing era had been remitted by the Yung-cheng period (1723-1735). The annual tributary goods stipulated in the Ch'ing period are shown in Table 5.[44]

The value of the annual tributary goods in about 1808 was roughly 80,000 copper taels.[45]

Besides the annual tributary goods the envoy presented "local products" or *pang-mul (fang-wu)* to the emperor, the empress dowager, and the heir apparent. These varied slightly in kind and amount according to the occasion. A significant part of the local products had been remitted by the end of the K'ang-hsi period, and the kinds and amounts of them presented on the winter solstice in the late Ch'ing period were as follows:[46]

Item	To the emperor	To the heir apparent
Fine yellow ramie	10 pieces	0
Fine white ramie	20 pieces	15 pieces
Yellow thin silk	20 pieces	0
White thin silk	20 pieces	10 pieces
Mats with dragon pattern	2	0
Mats with yellow pattern	20	10
Mats with full pattern	20	10
Square mats with full pattern	20	0
Mats with variegated pattern	20	10
White cottton-paper	2,000 rolls	500 rolls

TABLE 5. Korean tributary goods required in the Ch'ing period.

Item	Amount required (1637-1640)	Amount remitted and date of remittance (1641-1728)	Amount required (1729-1894)
Gold	100 *liang* (weight)	100 *liang* (1692)	0
Silver	1,000 taels	1,000 taels (1711)	0
Parts of bows	200	100 (1647), 100 (1655)	0
Large-size paper	1,000 rolls	1,000 (1655) *added*	2,000 rolls
Small-size paper	1,500 rolls	1,500 (1655) *added*	3,000 rolls
Leopard skins	100 pieces	100 (1711)	0
Otter skins	400 pieces	100 (1723)	300 pieces
Deer skins	100 pieces	—	100 pieces
Black squirrel skins	300 pieces	300 (1723)	0
Tea	1,000 sacks	1,000 (1645)	0
Pepper	10 catties	10 (1647)	0
Sapan wood	200 catties	200 (1647)	0
Girdle knives	26	6 (1643), 10 (1645)	10
Multi-edged knives	20	10 (1645, 10 (1647)	0
Mats with dragon pattern	4 pieces	2 (1643)	2 pieces
Mats with variegated pattern	40 pieces	20 (1643)	20 pieces
Ramie fiber	200 pieces	—	200 pieces
White thin silk	1,500 pieces	500 (1643), 500 (1645), 100 (1647), 200 (1651)	200 pieces
Red thin silk	250 pieces	50 (1643), 100 (1645)	100 pieces
Green thin silk	250 pieces	50 (1643), 100 (1645)	100 pieces
Various cotton goods	10,000 pieces	200 (1643), 500 (1645), 2,200 (1645), 2,100 (1647), 600 (1651), 600 (1692), 800 (1723)	1,000 pieces (fine) 2,000 pieces (raw)
Various hemp goods	1,800 pieces	300 (1643), 1,500 (1645)	0
Rice	10,000 sacks	9,000 (1641), 900 (1647), 60 (1728)	40 sacks

Source: TMGJ, 3:28–29b.

Local products for the empress were slightly fewer than those for the emperor, and so also were those for the empress dowager, and possibly those for the imperial grandmother. Thus the whole amount of the local products presented on the winter solstice may be estimated as at least three times the amount for the emperor alone. Those presented on New Year's Day were the same, and so were those on the imperial birthday. Since an embassy on the winter solstice presented all of the local products for the three occasions, they must have totaled almost ten times as much as those presented to the emperor solely on the winter solstice. The values of the local products presented by the various Korean embassies in the early nineteenth century were thus as follows:[47]

TABLE 6. Value of Korean local products presented by embassies (in copper taels).

Type of embassy	Value
Winter solstice (to emperor alone, on three occasions)	26,004
Presenting thanks (to emperor, empress, empress dowager, and heir apparent)	10,135
Memorializing (to all the above)	About the same as above
Responding to accusations (to all the above)	About the same as above
Courtesy visit (to all the above)	6,800
Offering incense (to emperor, empress, or empress dowager)	27,008

Thus the total of Korea's annual tributary goods and local products was far more than 100,000 copper taels. This was not by any means compensated by the annual imperial gifts to the Korean king which were as follows:[48]

TABLE 7. Gifts from the Ch'ing emperor to the king of Korea

Type of embassy	Satin (costumes)	Marten (pelts)	Various satins (pieces)	Saddle-horses
Winter solstice	5	100	8	0
New Year's Day	5	100	8	1
Imperial birthday	5	100	8	1
Annual tribute	5	100	8	1
Total	20	400	32	3

The value of these gifts was approximately 7,000 copper taels.[49] There were also imperial bestowals, though trivial, upon the king and his family on the occasion of other Korean embassies to Peking and imperial embassies to Korea. Nevertheless we must conclude that the value of the imperial gifts was about one tenth of that of the Korean tributary goods.

b. Gifts to Embassy Members

Table 8 shows the total amount of the imperial gifts to the embassy members on a winter solstice including the portions due to the embassies for New Year's Day, the imperial birthday, and annual tribute.[50] In the case of the other embassies the amounts were about one fourth.

TABLE 8. Imperial gifts to members of Korean embassies.

Recipients	Large-size satin goods (costumes)	Small-size satin goods (pieces)	Silver (taels)	Silk (pieces)	Horses	Blue cotton cloth (pieces)
2 envoys	20	0	400	12	4	0
1 attendant secretary	6	0	180	4	0	0
3 chief interpreters	9	0	300	12	0	0
24 tribute guards	0	96	1,680	48	0	192
30 retainers	0	0	540	0	0	0
Total	35	96	3,100	76	4	192

The value of these objects in the early nineteenth century was about 22,000 copper taels.[51]

At the other end of this exchange, Korean gifts to Chinese embassy members had decreased significantly in amount by the middle of the Ch'ing period. But still their amount and value were really enormous. A Ch'ing embassy was given several thousand pieces of silk, hemp, ramie, and cotton stuffs, more than 20,000 taels of silver, various skins, various kinds of mats and paper, a voluminous amount of tobacco and pipes, various knives, fans, medicines, food, art objects, books, stationery, and so forth.[52] It may suffice to say that the value of silver, not to speak of other things, given to a Chinese embassy was about four times that of the imperial gifts to a Korean embassy.[53]

c. Travel Expenses of Embassies

Every Korean embassy to Peking seems to have spent an enormous amount for travel costs during their four months or more of travel. Not only the members and their retinue but also the horses consumed a great deal of rice, soybean, and other supplies which were very costly, even though they were supplied by China during their stay in Peking and their travel in China.[54]

But what really tortured Korea was the burden of the expenditure for Chinese embassies.[55] It is really surprising to note that the single province of Hwanghae spent 47,431 copper taels in receiving and sending off an imperial embassy in a period of about two weeks, one week each way to and from Seoul;[56] and Korea's total expenditure for a Ch'ing embassy was more than 230,000 taels,[57] about one sixth of the annual total expenditure of all her central government organs. Chinese embassy members may have enjoyed their travel in Korea, but the Koreans suffered heavily from the burden.

China also spent a large amount on travel expenses. China supplied at the least about 40,000 copper taels worth of food and wood[58] for a Korean embassy, and accordingly spent 80,000 taels a year on the average. This amount does not include other expenses for Korean embassies supported by China or expenses for Chinese embassies. Even though the central government's yearly quota of land tax receipts in nineteenth-century China was about 30 million silver taels,[59] these travel expenses should not be regarded as trivial.

d. Trade

For a deeper understanding of Sino-Korean tributary relations it is important to investigate the subject of trade, but this is another large topic for further study and here I can give only a general outline. Trade between the two countries was conducted in connection with the embassies and also in border areas.

Korean embassy members carried with them a certain amount of private investment in the form of silver or ginseng at their own expense, in addition to the travel expenses supplied by the Korean government.[60] Every member of an embassy was allowed to carry 2,000 taels of silver or ginseng.[61] The total for one embassy, in 1787, amounted to more than 80,000 taels in silver.[62] This private investment was originally designed to make up for the insufficiency of the official travel funds, but actually it became a means of private trade.

About ten per cent of the 80,000 taels mentioned above was for official trade on behalf of the Korean court.[63] This trade was conducted in the area of the residence at Peking of the Korean embassy and was also officially permitted by the Ch'ing.[64] The goods traded there were various: luxuries, daily necessities, goods for commercial purposes, books, and so on.[65] For the use of the Korean court various satins, silks, medicinal herbs, and luxuries were purchased.[66] Merchants and sometimes smugglers, participating in the embassy in disguise as followers or retainers, took advantage of this opportunity.

The Ch'ing banned to trade certain special goods, such as niter and other materials for military use, history books, maps, and a few other things, and also forbade bringing Chinese people out of the Chinese territory.[67] Chinese envoys also conducted trade in Seoul. Although the amount of this trade was usually small, the Chinese often did not pay enough for the goods they acquired and thereby annoyed the Korean government.

In connection with Korean embassies there were two other opportunities for illegal trade: When the Korean embassies arrived at Ts'e-men on the way to and from Peking, local people, and especially certain Chinese licensed carriers accompanying the embassy on its way home, took the opportunity to conduct unauthorized trade.[68] The other opportunity was connected with a special inspector called tallyŏn sa (t'uan-lien shih).[69] The inspector and his followers conducted unauthorized trade quite contrary to their duty. Local Chinese and Koreans joined in.[70] The amount of goods traded in this unauthorized way was apparently enormous. On each occasion almost 100,000 taels of silver flowed out from Korea to China, and, if the legal and illegal trades are added together, more than half a million taels of silver went out every year.[71]

Furthermore, border trade between the two countries was conducted at Chunggang (Chung-chiang), a small island in the estuary of the Yalu, Hoeryŏng (Hui-ning), and Kyŏng'wŏn (Ch'ing-yüan). The last two places are in the lower Tumen valley. Hoeryŏng, Kyŏng'-wŏn, and some other places in the area had been market places where local Manchu tribes had been accustomed to acquiring necessary goods from Korea ever since the early Ming period.

The trade at these three places had started in early Ch'ing times, and the markets were officially set up to be open twice a year in Chunggang, once a year in Hoeryŏng, and once every two years in Kyŏng'wŏn.[72] The fixed items and amounts that could be traded, with a rough estimate of the value of the goods sold to the Manchus at each border market, are as follows:[73]

TABLE 9. Markets for the Manchus on the Korean border.

Item traded	Amount permitted	Value (copper taels)
At Chunggang		
Cows	200	4,000
Sea-tangle	15,795 catties	5,420
Sea cucumbers	2,200 catties	2,200
Cotton cloth	548 pieces	1,096
White paper	8,400 rolls	2,540
Thick paper	600 rolls	2,700
Salt	310 piculs	775
Ploughshares	194	97
Pottery	3,300	330
Total		19,158
At Hoeryŏng		
Cows	114	2,280
Ploughshares	2,600	1,300
Salt	855 piculs	2,138
Total		5,718
At Kyŏng'wŏn		
Cows	50	1,000
Ploughshares	48	24
Iron pots	55	55
Total		1,079

We may note that the Manchus procured at these markets a reasonable amount of necessary goods, whereas Korea received blue cotton cloth, deer skins, and sheep skins, which were comparatively useless.[74] Because these markets were conducted officially, both governments had to pay the necessary expenses. Korea spent about 30,000 copper taels for the trade at Hoeryong, and about 15,000 taels for that at Kyŏng'wŏn, besides the cost of goods in both cases.[75]

The opening of these officially authorized border markets was of course exploited for illegal trade, just as in the case of the trade at Ts'e-men and that by the special inspectors.[76]

In the earliest stage of Manchu-Korean relations, the Manchus had eagerly wanted Korea to trade or to present as tributary goods those things that were lacking in Manchuria. But Korea often rejected these requests on the plea that Korea had been used to getting such goods from China but now they were banned. After the Manchus became the rulers of China their requests were naturally less importunate. But the limitation on the amount of private trade and the bans by both sides were often disregarded, and illegal trade flourished in connection with tributary embassies and in border areas. This illegal trade was a constant problem for both Korea and China.[77]

A BRIEF EVALUATION OF THE TRIBUTARY RELATIONSHIP

Although each aspect of Ch'ing-Korean tributary relations might be further pursued in detail, a general evaluation of the tributary relationship may now be attempted.

Some scholars, particularly those of the tributary state—not only historians but also political scientists and economists—have argued that the major role played by the embassies between the two countries was commercial.

But judging from the above examination of the values of tributary goods, of imperial gifts to the Korean royal family, and the gifts to Chinese and Korean embassies, plus their travel expenses, and the legal and illegal trades, one may make the following points: (1) Through the imperial bestowals and the legal trade Korea could get certain luxuries and necessary medicines, whereas China could also acquire some goods that were badly needed. (2) But the value of the tributary goods from Korea and the Korean gifts to Chinese embassies far exceeded what Korea received. (3) Some Chinese embassy members and the smugglers who conducted illegal trade may no doubt have profited. But it is hardly believable that the Ch'ing government itself profited much from the economic aspect of Sino-Korean tributary relations. (4) Through the trade, both legal and illegal, a large amount of silver, which was an important part of the total income of the Korean government, flowed out to China. Thus the tributary system brought the Korean government an enormous financial loss and net disadvantage. (5) If travel expenses are also taken into considerations, even the Chinese government can hardly have gained financially from these tributary relations.

It seems evident therefore that there was no sound economic reason for the Chinese rulers to work out and maintain such a magnificent system.

Some scholars have emphasized the cultural aspects of the embassies. It is true that many of the embassy members were scholars. They became acquainted with Ch'ing scholarship, and by bringing back important scholarly works they contributed highly to the development of Korean culture. The cultural efflorescence of the late eighteenth and early nineteenth centuries in Korea, which the Koreans of that period enjoyed and of which twentieth-century Koreans are still proud, was much indebted to the scholars who had been in China as embassy members. Granting that this cultural development deserves to be appreciated, it was still the achievement of the Korean scholars, not of the tributary system itself. Instead, the system hindered a general cultural influx from China, and from other countries as well. If the two countries had left their borders open and had freely communicated with each other, Korea might have enjoyed Chinese culture much more widely, and thus Korea might also have become much more sinicized. China naturally welcomed those who wanted to be sinicized, insofar as they were under direct Chinese political control. But Korea was in a tributary relationship with China, not under her direct political control; therefore, China did not exercise intentionally any purely cultural influence on Korea. It may be said that the tributary system was not designed for direct cultural influence, although one should not disregard the fact that tribute missions played an important role in Korea's cultural development.

Thus the nature of the Sino-Korean tributary system can best be explained from the point of view of politics. China only wanted Korea to remain gentle and ritualistic, not to say obedient, and Korea was so; so long as Korea sent tribute, received imperial patents concerning matters of adoption, marriage, and the like in the royal family and remained peaceful both at home and toward China, the Ch'ing did not interfere in Korea's internal affairs.

Korea was not fully devoted to the Ch'ing dynasty, whereas she had highly respected the Ming, not only because the Ming had given help during the Japanese invasions of the late sixteenth century but also because Confucian culture had flourished in Ming China. Even in the late eighteenth century many Korean scholars who had been in Ch'ing China asserted that Korea might properly "respect the great [Ch'ing]" not because it was strong politically or militarily, but because it had "become the successor of the great [Confucian] culture." Here we find that exerting a cultural influence was not an intrinsic aim of the tributary system for China, as the suzerain state, but, ironically, Chinese culture did in fact exert an influence upon the psychology of the people of Korea, the tributary state, and helped them preserve the tributary relationship. To put it another way, the tributary system may have been closely related to the Confucian Chinese culture, but the Ch'ing, knowing consciously or unconsciously that Korea had already been fully sinicized, felt no need to exert further cultural influence on Korea.

Finally, for the rulers and upper class of Korea, the tributary relationship with China helped to preserve their status and power. This relationship seems to have been one reason for the comparatively long duration of dynasties in Korea. In other words, among other factors, the tributary system was politically acceptable to the rulers of Korea as well as of China.

Notes

1. For a comprehensive approach to the long history of Sino-Korean tributary relations, the following materials are good starting points for research, even though not lacking in grandiloquence, literary embellishment and empty or purely statutory false fronts: The "biographies"

of Korea in the dynastic histories of China; the major Chinese encyclopedic works or *San-t'ung* and *Hsü-san-t'ung*, using the index to them, *Shih-t'ung so-yin* (Taipei, 1959); *Ts'e-fu yüan-kuei* and the Japanese index to its foreign relations aspects, *Sappu genki hōshibu gaishinbu sakuin* (Tokyo, 1938); *Chŭngbo munhŏn bigo* (Chinese: *Tseng-pu wen-hsien pei-k'ao*) (The revised encyclopedia of the historical records of Korea), *chüan* 171-177.

For the Ch'ing period: Various editions of *Ta-Ch'ing hui-tien* (Collected statutes of the Ch'ing dynasty) and its *Tse-li* or *Shih-li* (Precedents); *Yukchŏn jorye* (*Liu-tien t'iao-li*) (Regulations of the Six Boards of Korea; Seoul, 1865); *T'ongmun-gwan ji* (*T'ung-wen-kuan chih*) (Records of the Office of Interpreters; Seoul, preface 1720, rev. ed. 1888); *Man'gi yoram: Chaeyong p'yon* (*Wan-chi yao-lan: Ts'ai-yung pien*) (Essentials on state affairs: Finance; Seoul, 1937).

2. John King Fairbank and Ssu-yu Teng, "On the Ch'ing Tributary System," *Ch'ing Administration: Three Studies* (Cambridge, Mass., 1960), describes the general aspects of Ming-Korean, as well as Ch'ing-Korean, tributary relations. The present paper owes much to it and many of the points made here are based on it. Suematsu Yasukazu, "Raimatsu Sensho ni okeru tai-Min kankei" (Ming-Korean relations in the late Koryŏ and early Yi period), in *Keijo teikoku daigaku bungakukai ronshū* (Tokyo, 1941), Vol. 10, is a detailed study of early Ming-Korean relations, but does not give us a clear-cut understanding of the Ming-Korean tributary relationship from a historical point of view.

3. During the early Ming period, the Ming sometimes wanted to receive tribute once every three years, whereas Korea wished to send missions three times a year. See *Chosŏn wangjo sillok* (*Ch'ao-hsien wang-ch'ao shih-lu*) (Veritable records of the Yi dynasty): *Yi T'aejo* (*Li T'ai-tsu*), 4:7.

4. *TMGJ*, 3:1a-b.

5. The word *chinju* (*ch'en-tsou*) was actually used instead of *pyŏnmu*.

6. The embassies for *cheja* and *cheju* had the same duties. See *TMGJ*, 3:58.

7. The first edition of *Tongmun hwigo* was published in 1787 and successive additions were made until 1881. The whole set of the voluminous compilation is divided into ten parts as follows:

Part	Ordinal sequence of Ts'e	Number of Chüan	Contents
1	1-37	79	Correspondence with China
2	38-39	4	Correspondence with China in the Ch'ung-te period
3	40-44	10	Embassies and their reports on China
4	45-60	36	Correspondence with Japan
5	61	1	Reports to China on Western affairs
6	62-78	17	Continuation of Pt. 1 up to 1855
7	79	1	Continuation of Pt. 3 up to 1881
8	80-85	6	Continuation of Pt. 4
9	86-94	9	Continuation of Pt. 6 up to 1881
10	95-96	2	Continuation of Pt. 8

8. *TMGJ*, 3:2.

9. *TMGJ*, 3:32a-b.

10. *TMGJ*, 3:3b.

11. *Yŏnhaengnok sŭnjip* (*Yen-hsing-lu hsüan-chi*) (Collectanea of travel records to Peking; Seoul, 1960 and 1962), 2:1155-59. This table shows the number of embassies in which each member of the 1787 embassy had participated:

Number of members	Number of embassies participated in (including that of 1787)
1	27
1	25
1	17
1	10
1	8
2	6 by 2 persons
1	4
4	3 by 4 persons
4	2 by 4 persons
10	1 by 10 persons
26 (total)	133 (5.1 average)

12. On the number of retainers and horses, see *TMGJ*, 3:12b-14b. *YHNSJ* includes about

30 travel records written by various embassy members mainly during the Ch'ing period. Some examples of the numbers of embassy members, including retainers, and of horses are as follows:

Year	Men	Horses	Source in YHNSJ
1711	225	139	2:319
1765	?	210	1:367-371
1787	324	235	2:1155-59
1801	296	209	2:718
1803	253	196	1:787-788

13. On their types and forms, see *TMGJ*, 3:14b-21b.

14. Tributary goods will be discussed in a section below.

15. *TMGJ*, 3:20-22.

16. For the details, see *TMGJ*, 3:22-23b. For example, documents prepared in the case of the winter solstice embassy included: Memorial to the emperor, 1 original and 1 duplicate; memorial submitting "local products" to the emperor, 1 original and 1 duplicate; communication to the Board of Rites to accompany the above-mentioned memorial, 1; memorial to the empress dowager, 1; communication accompanying it, 1; memorials to the heir apparent, 4 in all; communication accompanying

them, 1. Total: 12 documents. The number of documents in a case in 1832 was forty-eight (*YHNSJ*, 1:934).

17. Official letters were sent to twenty-four local governments located between Seoul and the Yalu River. Until 1762 official letters had been sent by the embassy itself; but after 1762 they were sent by the government; see *TMGJ*, 3:12-14b.

18. An embassy in 1803 carried articles as follows (*YHNSJ*, 1:788): Annual tributary goods, 151 sacks; tributary rice, 68; other objects, 134. Total: 353 sacks.

19. The land route in the Ming was similar to that in the Ch'ing. On the sea route, see *TMGJ*, 3:36-37. On the actual cases by sea in 1624 and 1636, see *YHNSJ*, 1:127-200 and 201-230, respectively.

20. *TMGJ*, 3:12, 34b-35b.

21. From Seoul to the Yalu: the mileage is about 1,050 li (roughly 260 miles), and it took 13 days; see *Kosa ch'waryo* (*K'ao-shih ts'o-yao*) (Concise manual for officials; Seoul, 1613), 2:84. From the Yalu to Peking: 2,049 li (roughly 510 miles), 28 days; see *TMGJ*, 3:35b.

22. Most of the travel records of Korean embassies give their itinerary in detail; the following examples are based on *YHNSJ*. (Month/day by lunar calendar.)

Year of embassy	Leave Seoul	Crossing Yalu	Arrive Peking	Leave Peking	Crossing Yalu	Arrive Seoul	Total days
1574	5/11	6/16	8/1	9/8	10/10	11/3	170
1790	5/27	6/22	–	–	10/10	10/22	142
1803	10/21	11/24	12/24	2/2	3/11	3/25	152
1832	10/20	11/21	12/19	2/7	3/14	4/2	159
1876	5/16	5a/12	6/10	8/7	9/6	9/24	155
						(average:	155.6)

a intercalary month

23. *TMGJ*, 3:29b-33.

24. *TMGJ*, 3:37-38b.

25. *TMGJ*, 3:39b-40.

26. *TMGJ*, 3:52b-57.

27. *TMGJ*, 3:40a-b.

28. *TMGJ*, 3:41-42. A travel record of an embassy in 1765-1766 gives a statistical list of the Ch'ing supplies during a stay in Peking of sixty days. To quote some of the thirty-four items of the list (*YHNSJ*, 1:355): meat, 14,640 catties; 1,920 chickens; bean-curd,

2,040 catties; flour, 2,880 catties; pickles, 6,495 catties; yellow wine, 3,600 jugs; soybean jam, 2,535 catties; 3,300 apples; salt, 1,256.4 catties; rice, 2,022 pecks.

29. *TMGJ*, 3:42b-46; *HTSL: Kuang-hsü, chüan* 505.

30. *TMGJ*, 3:46a-b.

31. *TMGJ*, 3:47b-48b.

32. *TMGJ*, 3:48b-50. For the details of the imperial gifts, see *HTSL:Kuang-hsü, chüan* 506-509.

33. *TMGJ*, 3:51b-52; *HTSL:Kuang-hsü*, 510: 1-16.

34. *TMGJ*, 3:52; cf. note 22 above.

35. To quote an example from a diary in *YHNSJ*, 1:297-298 (month/day by lunar calendar in 1765-1766): 12/27, arrived Peking; 12/28, to Board of Rites; 12/29, to Court of State Ceremonial; 1/1, imperial audience; 1/4, to theater; 1/5, to National Academy and Yung-ho Palace; 1/9, to Catholic church; 1/11, saw lantern procession and firecrackers; 1/17, to T'ai-i Lake; 1/18, to bookstores; 1/20, met Mr. Wu P'eng; 1/22, to residence of Liu-ch'iu envoys; 1/23, saw Wu P'eng; 1/24, to residence of Mongol envoys and Catholic church; 1/25, sightseeing; 1/26, visited bookstores and met Mr. Chiang Chou; 1/28, to Lung-fu Temple; 1/30, visited bookstores and met Mr. Chang Ching; 2/2, visited Catholic church and saw apparatuses on astronomy; 2/3, visited Mr. Yen Fan; 2/6, to T'ai-ho Palace and bookstores; 2/8, visited Yen Fan; 2/11, to Hsi shan (Western Hills); 2/12, visited Yen Fan; 2/17, visited Yen Fan; 2/23, visited Yen Fan and met Mr. Hsiao Yin; 2/24, visited National Academy and met Mr. Chang Yüan-kuan; 2/24, visited Yen Fan and took farewell. It is interesting to find that the author of this travel record visited Catholic churches several times.

36. Official reports and private travel records of Korean embassy members may suggest some of the good points of Sino-Korean relations, although they have been left almost untouched in this paper. About 370 official reports are included in *TMHG* (see note 7 above). Each seems to be the whole text of the original. There are also many travel records which are not included in *YHNSJ*. Again, many other records may have keen kept by descendants of the writers but remain still unknown to historians who might be interested in them.

37. *TMGJ*, 4:1-2. In actual cases the number of interpreters was usually five.

38. Some examples of itineraries of Chinese embassies are shown below (based on *TMHG*, ts'e 44; lunar month/day).

Year	Imperial edict issued	Notice arr. Seoul	Leave Peking	Crossing Yalu	Arrive Seoul	Leave Seoul	Crossing Yalu
1654	5/13	6/8	5/25	6/25	7/15	7/29	8/16
1750	8/4	9/14	8/28	9/26	10/9	10/12	10/24
1800	10/15	10/27	10/15	11/14	11/27	12/9	–

39. On the organization of the office, see *TMGJ*, 4:9b-11. Each of the six sections of the office left voluminous records of its own, of which only those from the early seventeenth century are still extant.

40. See *TMGJ*, 4:5b-6b.

41. On the rules and ceremonies, see *TMGJ*, 4:4-5b, 7-9b.

42. Each of the four local governments, i.e. Uiju prefecture, P'yŏng'an province, Hwanghae province, and Kyŏnggi province, left detailed rules. They are, respectively, *Chich'ik jŏngnye* (*Chih-ch'ih ting-li*) of *Manbu* (abbr. *MB;* Chinese, *Wan-fu*), *Kwansŏ* (*KS; Kuan-hsi*), *Haesŏ* (*HS; Hai-hsi*), and *Kyŏnggi* (*KG; Ching-chi*).

43. *TMGJ*, 4:11-25, esp. pp. 15b-17. Several official records on the reception of imperial embassies are extant:

a. *Ch'iksa dŭngnok* (*Ch'ih-shih teng-lu*) (Records on imperial embassies), by the Reception Department of the Korean Board of Rites, 13 ts'e.

b. *Ch'iksa ilgi* (*Ch'ih-shih jih-chi*) (Daily record on imperial embassies), by the Royal Secretariat, 19 ts'e.

c. *Ch'iksa yŏllye dŭngnok* (*Ch'ih-shih yen-li teng-lu*) (Records of banquets for imperial embassies), by the Banqueting Department, 2 ts'e.

d. *Yŏngch'ik ŭiju dŭngnok* (*Ying-ch'ih i-chu teng-lu*) (Records of ceremonies at the reception of imperial embassies), 3 ts'e.

e. *Ch'iksa jŭnggŭp-ch'aek* (*Ch'ih-shih tseng-chi ts'e*) (Records of gifts to imperial embassies), 8 ts'e.

44. *TMGJ* is the most detailed and reliable source for the kinds and amounts of the tributary goods and changes in them. *K'ang-hsi hui-tien*, 72:7b-8, gives, in accordance with *TMGJ*, the kinds and amounts of the tributary

goods still required in the early K'ang-hsi period, but merely the kinds (not amounts) of goods that had been remitted in the Ch'ung-te and Shun-chih periods. *HTSL:Kuang-hsü* 503:1, also gives (erroneously as stipulated in the second year of Ch'ung-te, 1637) the kind and amount of the tributary goods in the early K'ang-hsi period. (The number of leopard skins should have been 100 instead of 142.) Cf. table 5, esp. "Amount remitted."

45. *MGYR:CY*, pp. 674-676; for details see the tables presented herewith. *T'akcht junjol* (*To-chih chun-che*) (Standard commutation of goods), gives detailed lists of prices of various goods in the Chŏngjo (*CJ*, 1777-1800), and Sunjo (*SJ*, 1801-1834) periods, *TCJJ: CJ and TCJJ:SJ* are both divided into two parts: Part 1 includes lists of prices of 56 categories of goods, such as wood, metals, paper, skins, silk, cloth, colors, grain, cattle, fish, meat, fruits, vegetables, utensils, etc., and Part 2 gives mostly the expenses for various activities, such as official expenses for collecting taxes, transportation fees, expenses for civil examinations, for supporting Chinese envoys, for tributary goods, and for some other purposes. *TCJJ:CJ* was edited and published in *Yonsei Historical Bulletin*, Nos. 8, 9, and 10 (Seoul, 1965).

On the prices of various kinds of goods, the sources listed below give useful information. Following are examples of prices in copper taels:

Source	Date	Price of 1 peck of rice	Price of 1 catty of meat	Price of 1 egg	Price of 1 chicken
CCJN:KG	c. 1785	–	0.24	0.02	–
CCJN:HS	c. 1788	0.4	0.12	0.01	0.2
CCJN:KS	c. 1790	–	0.12	0.01	0.3
TCJJ:CJ	c. 1790	0.4	0.25	0.014	0.35
Retail price in *won* in 1965:		400	160	10	300

Following is a comparison of the prices in *MGYR:CY* (of goods for the use of the royal family) and *TCJJ:CJ* (of goods of best quality), in copper taels:

Article	MGYR:CY Price c. 1808	TCJJ:CJ Price c. 1790
Otter skin	18	14
Leopard skin	102 to 120	90
Tiger skin	78 to 80	30
White ramie fiber, 1 piece	16	16
Rice of better quality, 1 peck	1	0.8
Pear, 1	0.52	0.32
Salt, 1 peck	0.53	0.4
White cotton-paper, 1 roll	2.8	2

By comparing the sources mentioned above one notes that prices were higher in Seoul than in local areas, that prices rose steadily in the course of time, and that tributary goods and goods for the use of the royal family were of the best quality.

Following are prices in copper taels of annual tributary goods around 1808:

Article	Price	Source
Large-size paper	12,000	*MGYR:CY*, pp. 674-676
Small-size paper	10,200	*Ibid.*
Otter skin	7,200	*Ibid.*
Deer skin	3,400	*Ibid.*
Girdle knife	100	Estimate based on *TCJJ:CJ*, Pt. 1, sec. 2
Mat with dragon pattern	72	*MGYR:CY*, pp. 674-676
Mat with variegated pattern	140	*Ibid.*
Ramie fiber	3,200	*Ibid.*
Various thin silks	7,200	*Ibid.*
Various cotton goods	36,000	*Ibid.*
Rice	300	*CCJN:HS*, sec. 19
Total	79,812	

It should also be noted that the value of one silver tael corresponded to two copper taels in the Yŏngjo period (1725-1776) and three copper taels in the early Sunjo period (1801-1834); see *Chŭngbo munhŏn bigo*, 160:16b; and *MGYR:CY*, p. 695.

46. *TMGJ*, 3:23b-28; *MGYR:CY*, pp. 681-690; *Kuang-hsü hui-tien*, 39:4b-5b. For the precedents concerning the tributary goods and "local products" in the Ch'ing period, see *HTSL:Kuang-hsü, chüan* 503 and 504.

47. *MGYR:CY*, pp. 681-690.

48. *TMGJ*, 3:48b-50; *Kuang-hsü hui-tien*, 39:7. For the precedents, see *HTSL:Kuang-hsü, chüan* 506-509.

49. The details of this evaluation are as follows:

Item	Evaluation	Source
Satin costumes	1 costume=2 pieces	*YHNSJ*, 2:611
		TCJJ:CJ, Pt. 1, sec. 32
	1 piece=30 feet	*Ibid.*, Pt. 1, sec. 10
	1 foot=1 silver tael[a]	*Ibid.*
	20 costumes=40 pieces= 1,200 feet=1,200 silver taels	
Marten pelts	1=1.5 silver taels (1 marten-tail=0.6 copper taels)	*TMGJ*, 3:50
		TCJJ:CJ, Pt. 1, sec. 7
	400=600 silver taels	*TMGJ*, 3:50
Various satins	8 pieces=100 silver taels	*Ibid.*
	32 pieces=400 silver taels	
Horses	1=20 to 24 silver taels (1 cow=30 copper taels)	*Yukchŏn jorye*, 8:6b
		TCJJ:CJ, Pt. 1, sec. 23
	3=60 to 72 silver taels	
Saddles	1=20 silver taels	High estimate, cf.
	3=60 silver taels	*Yukchŏn jorye*, 8:19b
Total	2,332 silver taels=6,996 copper taels	

[a] On the value of the silver tael, see the last part of note 45 above.

50. *TMGJ*, 3:48b-50; *Kuang-hsü hui-tien*, 39:7-8b. See also *HTSL:Kuang-hsü, chüan* 506-509.

51. This estimate is derived from the following data:

Item and amount	Value in silver taels	Value in copper taels	Source
Large satin (*ta-tuan*) 35 costumes	2,100	6,300	See note 49
Small satin (*hsiao-tuan*) 96 pieces	1,440	4,320	Cf. *p'eng-tuan*, in *TCJJ:CJ*, Pt. 1, sec. 10
Silver	3,100	9,300	
Silk, 76 pieces	342	1,026	Cf. *ch'ou*, in *ibid.*
Horses with saddles, 4	176	528	See note 49
Blue cotton cloth, 192 pieces	–	516.48	*TCJJ:CJ*, Pt. 1, sec. 11
Total		21,990.48	

52. *CSJGC* gives the details of most of the gifts to the imperial embassies between 1643 and 1786. *TMGJ*, 4:28-32.

53. The amount of silver given to a Chinese embassy around 1800 was as follows:

Place	Amount in silver taels	Source
Ŭiju (to interpreters only)	170	CCJN:MB, sec. 11
P'yŏng'an province (to envoys and interpreters only)	8,618	CCJN:KS, sec. 13
Hwanghae province (to envoys and interpreters only)	10,589	CCJN:HS, sec. 18
Kyŏnggi province	726	CCJN:KG, sec. 13
Seoul	6,640	TCJJ:SJ, Pt. 2, sec. 30
Total	26,743 (=80,229 copper taels)	

For the amount of silver given in Seoul, see also *MGYR:CY*, pp. 694-695.

54. According to *MGYR:CY*, pp. 701-710, the central government of Korea had to pay more than 13,000 copper taels, moderately estimated, of incidental expenses for an embassy, whereas its transportation and lodging were provided by the postal system and local governments. See also *TMGJ*, 3:7b-12. The amount of the Ch'ing supply to an embassy during its travel in China was "no less than" that during their stay in Peking (*YHNSJ*, 1:355; see note 28 above).

55. A memorial to the king, to quote one of the most typical evidences, discusses the serious condition of the financial deficit in connection with the reception of Chinese embassies see *CCJN:HS*, sec. 1.

56. *Ibid.*, sec. 21.

57. This total does not include the ordinary expenditures in Ŭiju and Hwanghae province nor the value of silver (except for that cited in note 53 above). Cf. *CCJN:KS*, sec. 18; *CCJN:HS*, sec. 20; *TCJJ:SJ*, Pt. 2, sec. 30; *MGYR:CY*, pp. 694-695; and *TMGJ*, 4:25b-32. Finally, this total corresponded to one sixth of the expenditure of all the central government organs for a year, which was about 1,300,000 copper taels (1 picul of rice=6 taels). See *MGYR:CY*, pp. 163-166.

58. To quote only a few items among 34 items listed in *YHNSJ*, 1:355, and show the value in copper taels based on *TCJJ:CJ*, Pt. 1:

Item	Amount	Value
Meat	14,640 catties	3,660
Chickens	1,920	672
Geese	180	720
Apples	3,300	182
"White rice"	2,020 pecks	1,616
Sheep	80	3,200
Wood	92,880 catties	1,114
Total		11,164

If other items are included, the total should be more than 20,000 taels. Note that these costs were only for food and wood during the embassy's stay in Peking, and China received two missions besides those presenting communications every year on the average. The expense per diem for meals and refreshments for Chinese embassies was 975.42 taels; see *CCJN:KS*, sec. 18. For the items and amounts of the Ch'ing supply, see *Kuang-hsü hui-tien*, 39:9b, 14b-15; *HTSL:Kuang-hsü*, 501:1-16; *TMGJ*, 3:41-42b.

59. *HTSL:Kuang-hsü*, 169:1-3b; 170:1-4b.

60. The government supply could not cover the whole of the travel expenses. See note 54 above.

61. Everyone was allowed to carry eight sacks (*p'alp'o*; hence the term "*p'alp'o* system") of ginseng, which were sometimes substituted by silver. See *TMGJ*, 3:33-34b; *MGYR:CY*, pp. 711-715. Changes in the kind and amount of investment were as follows:

Period	Kind of investment	Amount
In early Yi period	Ginseng	10 catties
In Ch'ung-chen period (1628-1643)	Ginseng	80 catties
1644	Silver	50 taels
1653	Ginseng	80 catties
In early K'ang-hsi period (1662-?)	Silver	2,000 taels (to those higher than rank 3A, 1,000 taels was added)

62. *YHNSJ*, 2:1159.

63. *Ibid.* For general information on the official trade, see *MGYR:CY*, pp. 717-721.

64. *TMGJ*, 3:50b-51b; *Kuang-hsü hui-tien* 39:13.

65. For the actual examples of goods, see *YHNSJ*, 1:359-361. Korean embassy members also received various gifts from Chinese friends; see *ibid.*, 1:361-362.

66. *YHNSJ*, 2:1159.

67. *TMGJ*, 3:50b-51b; *Kuang-hsü hui-tien*, 39:13-14; *Shih-li*, *chüan* 511, 512. Cf. Fairbank and Teng, p. 139. Korea also forbade trade in certain literary works from China.

68. *TMGJ*, 3:62b-63b; particularly on the licensed carriers called *lan-t'ou*, see *ibid.*, 7:27a-b; *MGYR:CY*, pp. 725-729; *Chŭngbo munhŏn bigo*, 164:5-6b; on *lan-t'ou*, see *ibid.*, 176:2-3.

69. On the *tallyŏn sa* (*t'uan-lien shih*), see *TMGJ*, 3:31b, 37b-38, 39b-40; and *MGYR: CY*, p. 726. A part of the tributary goods and "local products" which had been carried by horses from Korea was unloaded at a place in south Manchuria and thence transmitted by Manchu local officials to Peking. The duty of the inspector in question, who was nominally concerned with local militia organization, was to bring back the horses to Korea and prevent any misdeeds, especially unauthorized trade, by his followers on the way home.

70. On the trade, see *TMGJ*, 3: 61b-62b; *MGYR:CY*, p. 726.

71. *Ibid.*, p. 727.

72. For the details of the border trade see the following materials: *TMGJ*, 3:61-64b; *Kuang-hsü hui-tien*, 39:12b-13; *Shih-li*, 510: 16-22b; *MGYR:CY*, pp. 723-725, 729-735; *Chŭngbo munhŏn bigo*, 164:5-12.

73. See note 72 above, particularly *TMGJ*, 3:64a-b; *MGYR:CY*, pp. 724-725, 733-734. According to *ibid.*, p. 724, the price of a piece of blue cotton cloth, with which the Manchus paid for part of the goods they acquired in these markets, was 0.35 silver taels; and, accordingly, the price of a cow of medium size was only 2.8 silver taels (*ibid.*, p. 733). Since this seems to be incorrect, I have based the prices in these lists mainly on *TCJJ:CJ*, Pt. 1.

74. The goods, especially the blue cotton cloth, that Korea received in these markets were almost useless; see *MGYR:CY*, pp. 724-725; *TMGJ*, 3:63a-b.

75. *MGYR:CY*, pp. 734-735.

76. *Ibid.*, pp. 723-724.

77. *TMGJ*, 3:33-34b, 50b-51b, *et passim*.

V. UNIQUENESS OF RUSSIA'S POSITION

6. RUSSIA'S SPECIAL POSITION IN CHINA

DURING THE EARLY CH'ING PERIOD

IMMANUEL C. Y. HSÜ

During the K'ang-hsi (1662-1722) and Yung-cheng (1723-35) periods, Russia was the only foreign country with which China maintained treaty relations, the only "Western" state to which China sent diplomatic missions, and the only foreign power granted religious, commercial, and educational privileges in Peking. These were most unusual phenomena in Chinese foreign relations in view of China's claim to universal overlordship. As the Celestial Empire and the Middle Kingdom, China normally maintained no treaty relations with other states, sent no diplomatic missions abroad, and allowed no foreign country to keep permanent establishments in the capital city of Peking. It may therefore be asked, what differentiated Russia from the other foreign states in Chinese eyes and what prompted the Chinese to accord Russia preferential treatment?

Russia, as an immediate northern neighbor of considerable military strength, was

From the *Slavic Review* Volume XXIII, Number 4, December 1964, pp. 688-700. Reprinted by permission. Mr. Hsü is professor of history and chairman of the department at the University of California, Santa Barbara. Research on this article was partially made possible by a Guggenheim fellowship in 1962-63.

in a strategic position to invade Manchuria or to ally with the tribes of Mongolia and Turkestan to block China's control of her northern and northwestern frontier areas. Chinese political wisdom recognized that such a state could not be ignored with impunity. The early Ch'ing rulers realistically accepted Russia as a potential enemy,[1] whose good will had to be cultivated before they could consolidate the dynastic hold on Outer Mongolia and Eastern Turkestan. It was therefore necessary to conciliate Russia with favors and humor her with preferential treatment.

The Ch'ing policy was largely a product of premodern military concepts and political practices. For nearly two thousand years before the advent of firearms, barbarians from the north and mounted archers from the Central Asian steppes periodically disturbed North China. The Chinese resisted or conquered them whenever possible and humored them with special favors whenever necessary. The existence of the threat from the north and northwest led the Chinese to regard Sinkiang, Mongolia, and Manchuria as an outer defensive perimeter essential to China's security. The Ch'ing rulers, coming from Manchuria themselves, were particularly aware of the importance of frontier areas. They were determined that Manchuria be kept safe from foreign threat and that Sinkiang and Outer Mongolia be brought under their control. Since Russia bordered on all three vital areas, it was necessary to examine her potential realistically. Thus, Russia had already entered into the strategic considerations of the Ch'ing dynasty a century and a half before the maritime nations of Europe and America became a factor in Chinese foreign relations.

Russia posed a threat to Manchuria at almost the same time that the Manchus established the Ch'ing dynasty in China (1644). Cossacks from Siberia, tempted by the rumored riches of the Amur Region, the "Eldorado of Eastern Asia," where gold, silver, cattle, and grain were said to abound, pillaged the area continually.[2] V. Poiarkov raided the Amur Region from 1643 to 1646, E. Khabarov from 1647 to 1652, and O. Stepanov from 1652 to 1661.[3] Troubled by these incursions and plunder, Emperor K'ang-hsi, who inherited the throne in 1662 at the age of seven, absorbed himself in the Russian problem as soon as he began personal rule in 1668 at the age of thirteen.[4] The Cossacks in 1669 founded Albazin (Ya-k'e-sa or Yacsa) as an advance base, and intensified their activities in the decade that followed.[5] K'ang-hsi, though determined to check the Russian advance, had to postpone action because of his preoccupation with the suppression of the Revolt of the Three Feudatories (*San-fan*) in southern China, which lasted from 1673 to 1681.

Simultaneously with the Russian threat in Manchuria loomed the menace from the Oirats (Ölöd), also known as the Kalmuks or Western Mongols. Galdan (1644?-1697),[6] the khan of the Dzungar in northern Sinkiang, a tribe of the Oirats, rose to power in the 1670's and began to build a Central Asian empire in 1676. He conquered Eastern Turkestan in 1679 and invaded Outer Mongolia in 1687 with thirty thousand men, completely routing the Khalkhas (Qalqa or Eastern Mongols) and penetrating as far as the Kerulen River. Not only did he block the Ch'ing conquest of Eastern Turkestan and Outer Mongolia, but also he threatened Peking itself. Since the Russians and the Oirats had maintained relations for several decades, it was possible that an alliance might be formed between them. In fact, Galdan's emissaries went to Russia in 1674-75 to seek military aid, and his various agents visited Russia continually in 1676-79, 1681, and 1683.[7] Galdan was known to have sought formal alliance with Russia during his war with the Khalkhas; he was also said to have told the Russians that if they gave him cannons and two or three thousand Cossacks he would ravage all the borders of China outside the Great Wall.[8] Although the Russians did not grant Galdan his wishes, they cleverly maintained a benevolent attitude toward him and always took care not to ignore the Oirat "half-advances."[9] The possibility of Russian aid to Galdan or an Oirat-Russian alliance could therefore not be discounted.[10] Russia thus became an important factor in China's relation with the Oirats. K'ang-hsi was determined to isolate the Oirats from the Russians and prevent any union between them.

As soon as the Revolt of the Three Feudatories was suppressed in 1681, K'ang-hsi ordered General Langtan and Pengcun to organize an expedition against the Russians in Albazin. After several years of elaborate preparation, Pengcun marched from Tsitsihar in 1685 with 10,000 soldiers, 5,000 sailors, and

200 pieces of artillery, and by sheer weight of numbers overpowered the 450 Cossack defenders under Aleksei Tolbuzin. Albazin was reduced to ashes and some forty-five Russians were taken prisoners, although Tolbuzin himself escaped to Nerchinsk.[11] At the news of this total victory, K'ang-hsi proudly announced: "Many considered the Russian campaign too difficult because of the great distance, but I alone decided that an expedition must be sent. By the grace of Heaven, we have now conquered."[12] Thereupon he issued an edict to explain the necessity of the expedition:

The aim of government is enduring peace and order, not temporary expediency. . . . The present campaign against the Russians, for example, does not look very important on the surface but it is actually of the greatest significance. For more than thirty years the Russians have disturbed our Amur and Sungari rivers and have stolen an outpost which is very close to the original home of our imperial dynasty. If we do not eradicate them, I am afraid that there will be no place for our people on the frontiers. Ever since I personally assumed power at thirteen *sui*, I have always been alert to this problem, carefully examining [the enemy's] topography, the distance of the [Russian] position, their people and their customs, in order that I might take the necessary steps, moving ahead with ammunition at the opportune moment; and in the face of opposition by many people, I determinedly sent my generals on an expedition, striking deeply [into their positions].[13]

How important Russian affairs were in the minds of the Ch'ing rulers may be seen in the fact that K'ang-hsi considered his victory at Albazin as crucial as his subjugation of the three internal feudatories; the one triumph relieved him of a foreign threat, and the other, of a domestic one.[14]

After having destroyed Albazin, Peng-

cun returned home. Tolbuzin, with the help of 336 Cossacks, soon re-established himself on the ruins of Albazin. New fortifications were erected under the direction of an experienced German engineer, Afanase Baiton (Beiton), and Tolbuzin renewed his raids on the Amur Region in March, 1686.[15] K'ang-hsi once again dispatched an expedition to Albazin. The Russians resisted the Chinese siege boldly for more than a year; Tolbuzin was killed in action, and many of his men died of disease. At last, in mid-1687, when only sixty-six Cossack defenders were left and when one more powerful attack would have enabled the Chinese to take Albuzin, K'ang-hsi suddenly ordered the siege lifted and his general Sabsu even offered provisions to the starving Cossacks.[16]

K'ang-hsi acted ostensibly in deference to the request of the tsar, who was then sending a diplomatic mission to China to settle the differences between the two countries, but actually he wanted to use this occasion to show his magnanimity and win Russian good will. It may seem paradoxical that he fought the Russians and at the same time wanted to cultivate their friendship. The fact was that he wanted to avoid goading them into uniting with the still unpacified Oirats against China. To the Ch'ing dynasty, the Oirats represented a far greater threat than the Russians. By lifting the siege and providing the Cossacks with food, K'ang-hsi hoped to win Russian good will, and by negotiating a "generous" treaty of peace to ensure Russian neutrality in his war against the Oirats.

The Russian delegation was led by Fedor A. Golovin, son of the Tobolsk governor. He knew, if the Chinese did not, that Russia was in no position to make war at this point. Peter, not yet "the Great," was a youngster in his early teens sharing a shaky throne with his invalid brother. Russia was preoccupied with military affairs in the Baltic, and the treasury was depleted by military expenses and internal economic depression.[17] It was therefore necessary to maintain peace with China. Diplomatic negotiations led to the conclusion of the Treaty of Nerchinsk in 1689, China's first agreement with a "Western" power.[18] Under its terms, Russia agreed to demolish the fortresses in Albazin and repatriate all her subjects there. China accepted the ridge of the Stanovoi Mountains and the Argun River as the boundaries between the two countries; in doing so she conceded to Russia some 93,000 square miles of undecided frontier, including the city of Nerchinsk.[19] Russian traders won the right to enter China under passport. However, the Mongolian-Siberian border remained unsettled, since Golovin insisted that he had no authority to negotiate the issue. It was apparent that the Russians declined to settle the border because the Ch'ing dynasty was not yet in full control of Outer Mongolia. On the whole the treaty was satisfactory to both parties: Russia won territorial and commercial concessions from China, and China solved the Russian problem at Albazin and gained the secure feeling that Russia would likely remain neutral in China's war against the Oirats.

K'ang-hsi demonstrated farsighted statesmanship in this diplomatic exchange, for Galdan did in fact send agents to Russia in search of aid or alliance. One of them met Golovin in Irkutsk in March, 1690, another went to Tolbolsk in August of the same year, and still another went to Nerchinsk. Russia, having just concluded a treaty of peace with China, was in no mood for an alliance with the Oirats.[20] While it is questionable whether the Russians would have given Galdan assistance if K'ang-hsi had not lifted the Albazin siege and signed the Treaty of Nerchinsk, and whether such Russian assistance, if given, could have altered the course of events, there is little doubt that K'ang-hsi's clever maneuver killed any such possibility before it arose. When the news of the Russian rejection of the proposed alliance with Galdan came, K'ang-hsi announced with satisfaction: "In regard to the pacification of the Russians, I was advised by all the Manchu and Chinese ministers that it could not succeed because of the great distance between China and Russia. But I declared that this matter could not be allowed to stand interrupted midway. Therewith I ordered my high officials to move ahead according to plan, and as a result the Russians were pacified."[21]

K'ang-hsi now turned to Galdan, who had grown stronger and bolder than ever before. In 1690 the ambitious Oirat chieftain again invaded Outer Mongolia and penetrated as far as the Kerulen River. Then he turned south toward Inner Mongolia, apparently with the intention of taking Peking. Although K'ang-hsi was able to frustrate him at Ulan Butung, within 700 *li* or 80 leagues of Peking, Galdan's power was not destroyed. Several years of inconclusive warfare followed, in which the imperial forces sustained considerable losses. K'ang-hsi was now convinced that nothing less than a grand expedition could defeat the Oirats. Galdan once again sought Russian aid by dispatching an envoy to Moscow in 1693-94, but to no avail.[22] The Ch'ing imperial expedition, 80,000 men strong, set out in three columns in 1696, with the emperor himself commanding the central army, General Fiyanggu the western one, and General Sabsu guarding the eastern borders of Mongolia. The imperial forces advanced with great difficulty in the deserts of Mongolia; logistic problems seemed insuperable. Under conditions of extreme hardship, the Ch'ing forces heard the disquieting rumor that 60,000 Russians were allied with Galdan, but K'ang-hsi discounted the news. Finally, on June 12, 1696, Galdan was enticed to face Fiyanggu at Jau Modo (Jao Modo), where the Ch'ing artillery and musketeers dealt a crushing blow to the Oirat horsemen. Without Russian aid, Galdan was soundly defeated. Too proud to surrender, he fled with a small following. The next year, 1697, he died of a sudden illness—possibly he took his own life by poison. K'ang-hsi thus extended his rule to Outer Mongolia and Hami.[23] Wei Yüan, the celebrated author of the late Ch'ing period, praised K'ang-hsi for his sagacity in keeping Russia peaceful and neutral, and stated that this policy not only ensured his victory over Galdan but also facilitated Emperor Ch'ien-lung's later expansion into the heart of the Western Region (*Hsi-yü*) in the 1750's, which added thousands of *li* of territory to the empire.[24]

Within twenty-five years of the Treaty of Nerchinsk, Russia again figured in the plans of the Ch'ing dynasty, this time in connection with the Torgut question. The Torguts were an Oirat tribe which had originally lived in the Tarbagatai area but had migrated to Russia in 1630.[25] By 1654 they had become Russian vassals, although their chieftains continued to send periodic tribute to China. In 1712 a Torgut tributary mission came to Peking from the chief Ayüki, whose daughter was married to the new Oirat leader, Cewang Arabdan, Galdan's nephew.[26] K'ang-hsi sent a return mission to the Torguts, ostensibly to express his appreciation of Ayüki's loyalty but ac-

tually to strengthen China's tie with the Torguts and to forestall any alliance between Ayüki and Cewang Arabdan.[27] It is also possible that K'ang-hsi wanted to persuade the Torgut tribe to return to China.[28]

The mission was put under the charge of Tulisen, an assistant reader of the Grand Secretariat.[29] He set out in 1712, traveling by way of Mongolia and Siberia, and was well received by Prince Gagarin, governor of Siberia.[30] In June, 1714, the mission reached the Volga, and Tulisen met with Ayüki. Except that there was a friendly exchange of expressions of good will and discussion of returning Ayüki's nephew from China, little is known of their meeting.[31] Presumably Ayüki secretly pledged his friendship with China and nonalliance with Cewang Arabdan. Tulisen returned with an account of his travels entitled *I-yü lu* ("Description of a Foreign Land"), which was probably the first authentic Chinese work on Russia in the Ch'ing period.[32]

In sending the mission, K'ang-hsi was obviously interested in establishing closer relations with Russia, as evidenced in his instructions to Tulisen: if the tsar would receive him he should go to the Russian capital for an audience. However, Peter the Great, then engaged in an expedition to Sweden, had not been in St. Petersburg to receive him.[33]

Tulisen's mission succeeded in strengthening China's tie with the Torguts and possibly prevented an alliance between Ayüki and Cewang Arabdan, but the Oirat threat to the Ch'ing dynasty was still present. In view of the traffic between Cewang Arabdan and the Russians, there was renewed Chinese fear of secret plotting between them. In this light, the question of fixing the boundary between Outer Mongolia and Siberia—

an issue unresolved by the Treaty of Nerchinsk—became doubly important. In 1720 K'ang-hsi repeatedly impressed upon the Russian envoy Leon V. Izmailov the need for delimiting the Mongolian-Siberian frontier.[34] K'ang-hsi's concern was not unwarranted, for the Russians did entertain hopes of exploiting China's trouble with the Oirats. A mission under Ivan Unkovsky was sent to Cewang Arabdan in 1722, proposing that if the latter accepted the status of a vassal, Russia would take a strong stand toward China and might even make a military demonstration against her.[35] However, the death of K'ang-hsi in that year made the Oirats less anxious for Russian aid. The new emperor in China, Yung-cheng, carrying on his father's policy of isolating Mongolia from Russia, decided to settle all pending issues with Russia in a new treaty, so as to remove any excuse she might use for aiding the Oirats or entering into an alliance with them.[36] The resultant Treaty of Kiakhta of 1727 secured for China a clear delineation of the Mongolian-Siberian frontier at a cost of nearly 40,000 square miles between the Upper Irtysh and the Sayan Mountains, as well as south and southwest of Lake Baikal.[37] Russia was also granted favorable terms of trade and the right to establish a religious mission with a language school in Peking.[38] With this treaty, which was clearly favorable to Russia, China felt assured of Russian neutrality in her struggle against the Oirats.[39] A Chinese expedition was then dispatched to Dzungaria against the new Oirat leader, Galdan Cereng, son of Cewang Arabdan, who had died in 1727.

Although the Treaty of Kiakhta settled many important issues, it also created new problems through increased contacts between the subjects of the two countries. There were constant Russian complaints of border raids by Mongolian bandits, who stole horses, camels, oxen, and sheep, and of debts to Russian traders owed by Chinese merchants.[40] Emperor Yung-cheng, not wishing to see Sino-Russian relations impaired and desirous of reassurance of Russian neutrality, decided, during his campaign against Galdan Cereng, to dispatch a diplomatic mission to Russia in 1729—the first ever sent by China to a "Western" state.[41]

The mission, led by T'o-shih, a vice-president of a board, went on the pretext of congratulating Peter the Second on his coronation. However, upon his arrival in St. Petersburg, T'o-shih found that the tsar had died and that the new ruler was Anna Ivanovna, a niece of Peter the Great. His credentials had to be changed, necessitating a return to China. In 1731, T'o-shih was sent on a second mission. To the Russians he suggested that if the Chinese attack drove the Oirats into refuge in Russia, the Russian government should extradite their rulers and nobles to China but keep their tribesmen under strict control so as to prevent them from troubling China in the future. In return for this cooperation, China would give Russia part of the land seized from the Oirats. The Russian government expressed willingness to discuss the question of extradition in a friendly manner when it arose, but refused to make other commitments.[42] In any case, Russia was then engaged in the war of the Polish succession, and was in no position to aid the Oirats. Galdan Cereng, without Russian help, was defeated by the Chinese in 1733 and agreed to a peace settlement.[43]

These episodes indicate that Russia occupied a crucial position in Ch'ing policy toward the Oirats during the K'ang-hsi and Yung-cheng periods. A peaceful and neutral Russia was essential to China's consolidation of her northern and north-western frontiers. The Ch'ing rulers therefore found it expedient to make exceptions in their treatment of Russia, according her special considerations and granting her many privileges denied to other foreign states.

Although the Ch'ing dynasty claimed universal overlordship and insisted that all foreign envoys kowtow to the Chinese emperor, and although Chinese records always described Russian emissaries as tribute-bearers, Russia was not officially listed as a tributary state in any of the five editions of the *Ta-Ch'ing hui-tien* ("Collected Statutes of the Great Ch'ing Empire").[44] In fact, K'ang-hsi himself explicitly explained why Russia should not be classified as such: "Although tribute from a foreign country (Russia) would be a magnificent thing, I am afraid that when it is carried on into later generations it may become a source of trouble."[45] K'ang-hsi was much more liberal toward foreigners and foreign states than the Chinese in general. Most Chinese of his time still considered Russia an outlandish barbarian state on the northern frontier, a sort of *wai-fan* (outer tribe) though not a *shu-kuo* (vassal state).[46] But K'ang-hsi was willing on many occasions to grant Russia the consideration due an independent state. When he sent Tulisen to Russia in 1712, he ordered the envoy "to act in accordance with the ceremonies of that state."[47] No such instructions had ever been given any Chinese emissary to tributary states; on the contrary, all tributary kings were required to conform to Chinese etiquette and kneel when receiving a Chinese envoy. K'ang-hsi's liberal attitude manifested itself again in his exchange with the Russian envoy, Izmailov, in 1720. He told the latter that if he complied with Chinese court cere-monies and performed the kowtow, the Ch'ing government would see to it that future Chinese envoys to Russia would follow Russian ceremonies and perform whatever ritual required of them. Izmailov accepted this fair exchange and performed the kowtow.[48] K'ang-hsi then favored him with a dozen audiences in three months and announced that Peter the Great was "his [K'ang-hsi's] equal" and "his good neighbor."[49] The message he asked Izmailov to bring to the tsar was remarkable for its earnestness and egalitarian tone:

I have a few words for you which you need not answer but remember well to tell your sovereign. First, your emperor is a most great and honorable ruler in possession of a vast territory. He has often led expeditions to enemy states in person, but the seas are wide and unfathomable, and frequently there are dangerous, rolling waves. With all his fine soldiers and loyal ministers, he should not lack men to send out, and he himself should stay in a safe place. Secondly, although there are some twenty or thirty Russians who have fled to China, there are also Chinese who have escaped to Russia. The relationship of the two states should not be impaired by these rascals. I truly want to maintain a firm and lasting peace with the great emperor of your state.

Furthermore, there is no reason why our two countries should come into conflict. Russia is an extremely cold and remote country. If I send an expedition (to her), it will doubtless end in a complete fiasco. Even if I should gain something, how would it profit me? The same is true of the Russian emperor. If he should send officers and soldiers to fight in my warm country, to which they are not accustomed, would they not be annihilated for no good reason? What then is the benefit of war to either country? Indeed, we both have enough territory to live by ourselves.[50]

When K'ang-hsi described the Russian ruler as "great" and "honorable," he must have been thinking of him as an independent sovereign and a potential enemy of more or less equal status. No such expressions had ever been applied to China's tributary kings or to any other foreign rulers. China's special consideration for Russia was again shown in 1731 when Emperor Yung-cheng sent T'o-shih to Russia. The Chinese envoy actually knelt before the tsarina,[51] as no Chinese envoy had done before a tributary king, although in all likelihood he did not perform the full kowtow—kneeling three times and knocking his head on the ground nine times—that the Chinese required of Russian envoys in the court at Peking.

In addition to special consideration for Russian honor and dignity, K'ang-hsi and Yung-cheng also granted Russia a number of privileges usually not given to foreign states. Russian prisoners of war, about one hundred in all, taken in the several battles of Albazin, were pardoned and organized into a unit of the Ch'ing army—the Eleventh Company of the Fourth Regiment of the Manchu Bordered Yellow Banner.[52] As bannermen, they were given rank and the privilege of living in quarters by themselves. They received annual pensions and were allowed complete religious freedom. Emperor K'ang-hsi even gave them a Buddhist temple, on the site of which they built an Orthodox church known as the Church of St. Nicholas, later renamed the Church of the Assumption. To the Chinese it was known as the *Lo-ch'a miao* (Temple of the Lo-ch'a); more often it was incorrectly called the Northern Russian Hostel.[53]

The Russian traders were also well treated. During the Isbrants Ides mission in 1693, the Chinese granted Russian traders the right to come to Peking every three years in groups of two hundred, and although they paid their own way, their goods were exempt from duty. While in Peking they were lodged in the Southern Russian Hostel, which was the old Hui-t'ung kuan of the Ming dynasty.[54] Officially they were supposed to conclude their business and leave Peking within eighty days, but the regulations were not strictly enforced.[55] The caravan under Liangusov and Savatiev in 1698 consisted of 289 travelers, secretaries, and domestic servants, and 189 salesmen and workmen, a total of 478 men.[56] Between 1698 and 1718, ten such caravans came to Peking, averaging one every two years instead of every three as officially stipulated, and they were often permitted to remain in the Chinese capital longer than eighty days.[57] At times the Chinese court even advanced loans to distressed Russian merchants.[58]

After the Treaty of Kiakhta of 1727, groups of Russian priests were allowed to come every ten years to minister to the Russians in Peking, and the Chinese government paid their traveling and living expenses.[59] From 1729 to 1859 thirteen such missions came.[60] These priests lived in the Southern Russian Hostel, where they maintained a church called the Convent of Candlemas. Its construction was begun in late 1727 and it was consecrated in 1732. This church was later renamed the Church of the Purification of the Virgin.[61] After 1729 the priests of the religious mission also conducted services at the Church of St. Nicholas.[62]

The Treaty of Kiakhta permitted Russia to send students to Peking to learn Chinese and Manchu. In 1728 a language school for Russians was inaugurated within the Southern Russian Hostel as a separate institution.[63] The students came for a ten-year period under Chinese subsidy for traveling and living expenses. They were required to wear Chinese clothes supplied by the Court of Colonial Affairs. The Board of Rites provided them with adequate food, and the Imperial Academy (*Kuo-tzu chien*) assigned a Chinese and a Manchu instructor to teach them the languages; there were also private tutors attached to the school.[64]

By virtue of these religious, educational, and commercial privileges, Russia, alone among nations, enjoyed a foothold in the Chinese capital. These privileges were not revoked even after China's subjugation of the Oirats in the 1750's. It was not until China was opened to the West in the mid-nineteenth century that Russia's monopoly was broken.

In summary, we see that the early Ch'ing rulers strove to win Russian friendship and neutrality, and their policy in the end produced handsome results. Throughout China's long struggle with the Oirats—from K'ang-hsi's campaigns against Galdan in the 1690's to Ch'ien-lung's final conquest of Sinkiang in the 1750's—Russia never once swerved from her position of neutrality. China was thus able to solve the Oirat problem and extend her rule far into Central Asia. The exertions of K'ang-hsi, Yung-cheng, and Ch'ien-lung laid the foundation of peace and security for the dynasty for a century until the Western powers came in the middle of the nineteenth century.

On her side, Russia also gained substantially from her special position in China. Not only did she receive territorial and commercial concessions in the two treaty settlements, but also she won the unique privilege of maintaining a permanent establishment in the Chinese capital. Members of the Russian religious mission and the language school in Peking were able to see China from within and study Chinese language, politics, and social and economic structure at first

hand.[65] They learned about the Chinese mentality and way of life. They detected the strength and weakness of the Ch'ing dynasty long before other Westerners could. They witnessed the progressive decline of the Manchu power, and their reports to the home government helped guide Russia's policy toward China. They assisted Russian diplomats who had come to China.[66] When they returned home, they introduced sinological studies into Russia, and were frequently called upon to work with the Foreign Ministry. Against this background, is it any wonder that Russian policy in China during the nineteenth century was far more cleverly conceived and implemented than were those of the Western powers?

Notes

1. In reviewing the early Ch'ing relations with Russia, Tseng Kuo-fan, the eminent statesman of the late Ch'ing period, remarked in 1867: "When we negotiated on boundaries and trade with Russia (in 1689 and 1727), we actually treated her with the etiquette due an enemy state, which was entirely different from that accorded dependencies like Korea." See *Ch'ou-pan i-wu shih-mo* ("The Complete Account of the Management of Barbarian Affairs"), T'ung-chih period, 54:2b-3.

2. E. G. Ravenstein, *The Russians on the Amur: Its Discovery, Conquest, and Colonisation* (London, 1861), pp. 26-27.

3. For the activities of Poiarkov, Khabarov, and Stepanov, see *ibid.*, pp. 9-33; F. A. Golder, *Russian Expansion on the Pacific, 1641-1850* (Cleveland, 1914), pp. 33-66; John F. Baddeley, *Russia, Mongolia, China* (London, 1919), II, 195 ff.

4. "Ch'in-ting p'ing-ting Lo-ch'a fang-lüeh, erh" ("The Imperial Edition of the Outline of Pacifying the Russians, Part II"), in *Shuo-fang pei-sheng* ("A Manual of Northern Places"), ed. Ho Ch'iu-t'ao, opening section, 6:16b-17 (hereafter cited as *SFPS*).

5. For the founding of Albazin, see Joseph Sebes, S.J., *The Jesuits and the Sino-Russian*

Treaty of Nerchinsk (1689) (Rome, 1961), pp. 24-25; also Ravenstein, *op. cit.*, p. 38. However, John F. Baddeley, in his *Russia, Mongolia, China,* quoted above, stated that Fort Albazin was built in 1666 (p. 195).

6. For a brief account of Galdan, see Arthur W. Hummel, *Eminent Chinese of the Ch'ing Period* (Washington, D.C., 1943-44), I, 265-68.

7. Gaston Cahen, *Histoire des relations de la Russie avec la Chine, 1689-1730* (Paris, 1912), p. 137; Baddeley, *op. cit.*, II, 42-43, 177.

8. Henry H. Howorth, *History of the Mongols* (London, 1876), I, 627-28; Sebes, *op. cit.*, p. 74.

9. Cahen, *op. cit.*, pp. 136, 139, 140, 149.

10. *Ibid.*, pp. 26-27.

11. Sebes, *op. cit.*, pp. 69-70.

12. *SFPS*, 6:16b-17.

13. *Ibid.*

14. *Ibid.*, opening section, 5:1.

15. Golder, *op. cit.*, p. 61.

16. *Ibid.*, p. 63; Ravenstein, *op. cit.*, p. 52.

17. Sebes, *op. cit.*, pp. 70-71, 75.

18. For the negotiations of the Treaty of Nerchinsk, see two recent works: Joseph Sebes, *op. cit.*, especially chaps. 3-9; P. T. Iakovleva, *Pervyi Russko-Kitaiskii dogovor 1689 goda* (Moscow, 1958). For text of the Treaty of Nerchinsk, see P. E. Skachkov and V. S. Miasnikov, *Russko-Kitaiskie otnosheniia, 1689-1916: Ofitsialinye dokumenty* (Moscow, 1958), pp. 9-11.

19. W. A. Douglas Jackson, *The Russo-Chinese Borderlands* (Princeton, 1962), p. 112.

20. Cahen, *op. cit.*, pp. 51, 79 (note 1), 138-39.

21. *SFPS*, opening section, 1:23, imperial edict, K'ang-hsi twenty-ninth year.

22. Cahen, *op. cit.*, p. 138.

23. For the story of K'ang-hsi's expedition and Galdan's defeat, see *Sheng-chia ch'in-cheng Ko-erh-tan fang-lüeh* ("A Brief Account of His Imperial Highness's Personal Expedition against Galdan"), 1696; Howorth, *op. cit.*, I, 622-40.

24. Wei Yüan, *Hai-kuo t'u-chih* ("An Illustrated Gazetteer of the Maritime Countries"), 54:1.

25. Hsiao I-shan, *Ch'ing-tai t'ung-shih* ("A General History of the Ch'ing Dynasty") (rev. ed.; Taipei, 1962), I, 82; II, 159.

26. *Ibid.*, II, 160.

27. *Ku-kung O-wen shih-liao* ("Documents in Russian Preserved in the National Palace Museum of Peiping"), ed. Wang Chih-hsiang and Liu Tse-jung (Peiping, 1936), Introduction, pp. 12-13 (hereafter cited as *OWSL*). See also Chang Wei-hua, "T'u-erh-hu-t'e hsi-hsi yü T'u-li-ch'en chih ch'u-shih" ("The Westward Migration of the Torguts and the Mission of Tulisen"), *Pien-cheng kung-lun* ("Frontier Affairs"), II, Nos. 3-4-5, pp. 30-31 (June, 1943).

28. Cahen, *op. cit.*, p. 131. The Torguts eventually returned to China in 1768. For a complete account of their return, see "T'u-erh-hu-t'e ch'üan-pu kuei-shun chi" ("The Submission and Return of the Entire Torgut Tribe"), in *Yü-chih-wen* ("Imperial Writings"), Series II, 11:6b-10b.

29. For details of Tulisen's mission, see Cahen, *op. cit.*, pp. 115-33; Sir G. T. Staunton, *Narrative of the Chinese Embassy to the Khan of the Tourgouth Tartars, in the Years 1712, 13, 14, and 15, by the Chinese Ambassador, and Published by the Emperor's Authority, at Pekin* (London, 1821).

30. For allowing the Chinese mission to visit Ayüki, the Russians were blamed by the Oirat leader, Cewang Arabdan, who insisted that the objective of Tulisen was to negotiate a Chinese-Torgut alliance against him. See Cahen, *op. cit.*, p. 147.

31. Cahen, *op. cit.*, pp. 127-28, 130.

32. For a study of this work, see Imanishi Shunjū, "Explanatory Notes on Tulisen's I-yü-lu," *Studia Serica,* Vol. IX, Part I (Sept., 1950), 1-17.

33. *OWSL*, pp. 12-13.

34. Cahen, *op. cit.*, pp. 165-66, 168.

35. *Ibid.*, p. 149.

36. *Ibid.*, p. 191.

37. Jackson, *op. cit.*, p. 112.

38. For a study of the Treaty of Kiakhta, see Agnes Fang-chih Ch'en, "Chinese Frontier Diplomacy: Kiakhta Boundary Treaties and Agreements," *The Yenching Journal of Social Studies,* Vol. IV, No. 2 (Feb., 1949), 151-205. For texts of the various agreements pertaining to the Treaty of Kiakhta, see Skachkov and Miasnikov, *op. cit.*, pp. 11-22.

39. Cahen, *op. cit.*, p. 271.

40. *OWSL*, p. 11 of the Introduction; pp. 299-303, document 21.

41. For a study of the mission, see Mark Mancall, "China's First Missions to Russia, 1729-1731," *Papers on China,* Vol. IX (1956), East Asia Regional Studies Seminar, Harvard University.

42. *OWSL,* p. 13 of the Introduction; pp. 307, 312, document 23.

43. For the story of the Ch'ing campaign against Galdan Cereng, see Hsiao I-shan, *op. cit.,* I, 836-43; also Ch'en Fu-kuang, *Yu-Ch'ing i-tai chih Chung-O kuan-hsi* ("Sino-Russian Relations during the Ch'ing Period Exclusively") (Kunming, 1947), p. 58.

44. Wein Yüan, "O-lo-ssu meng-p'in chi" ("A Record of Diplomatic Relations with Russia"), *SFPS,* 52:10b.

45. *SFPS,* opening section, 1:23b-24.

46. For a discussion of the Chinese concepts of *wai-fan* and *shu-kuo, see* Fu Lo-shu, "Sino-Western Relations during the K'ang-hsi Period, 1661-1722," unpubl. Ph.D. diss. (University of Chicago, 1952), pp. 10-12. Miss Fu's statement on page 130 that "some Chinese regarded the Russians as a kind of Mongol" is open to question.

47. Tulisen, "I-yüeh lu," *SFPS,* 43:7.

48. Hsiao I-shan, *op. cit.,* I, 764-65.

49. Cahen, *op. cit.,* p. 165.

50. *OWSL,* pp. 9-10 of the Introduction.

51. Mancall, *op. cit.,* p. 93.

52. Yü Cheng-hsi, "O-lo-ssu tso-ling" ("On the Russian Company"), *SFPS,* 47:1b-2, 4b.

53. Meng Ssu-ming, "The E-lo-ssu Kuan (Russian Hostel) in Peking," *Harvard Journal of Asiatic Studies,* XXIII (1960-61), 29-34.

54. *Ibid.,* p. 20.

55. *SFPS,* 12:5.

56. Cahen, *op. cit.,* pp. 97-98. Figures given by the Russian governor of Nerchinsk, Ivan Nikolev, July 25/Aug. 4, 1698.

57. Liu Hsüan-min, "Chung-O tsao-ch'i mao-i k'ao" ("A Study of Early Russo-Chinese Commercial Relations"), *Yen-ching hsüeh-pao* ("Yenching Journal of Chinese Studies"), XXV (1939), 165.

58. Agnes Fang-chih Ch'en, *op. cit.,* pp. 155-56, 172.

59. *SFPS,* 12:3-4.

60. Meng Ssu-ming, *op. cit.,* p. 33.

61. *Ibid.,* p. 28.

62. *Ibid.,* p. 32.

63. *Ibid.,* pp. 34-39; *SFPS,* 12:5b.

64. *SFPS,* 12:3-5. It cost China more than 1,000 rubles and 9,000 pounds of rice annually to support these Russian students and the religious mission in Peking. See George Timkowski (E. F. Timkovskii), *Travels of the Russian Mission through Mongolia to China, and Residence in Peking, in the Years 1820-1821,* trans. H. E. Lloyd (London, 1827), I, 4.

65. For the works of the Russian religious mission, see *Trudy Chlenov: Rossiiskoi dukhovnoi missii v Pekinie* (4 vols.; Petersburg, 1952-66).

66. From its establishment in 1728 until 1861, the Russian Orthodox mission in Peking was officially described as "religious and diplomatic." see Cahen, *op. cit.,* p. 264.

PART TWO

CONFRONTATION WITH THE OUTSIDE WORLD, 1800-1900

INTRODUCTION

Released from the Napoleonic Wars, Britain, aggressive and powerful from the Industrial Revolution, took the lead in intensifying her bid to open China to greater trade and diplomatic relations. The Ch'ing dynasty, however, though weakened by internal decay and rebellion, still clung to the age-old myth that China was the universal overlord and that all nations desiring relations must acknowledge her superiority and accept the tributary practice. China's behavior during this phase of confrontation was in many ways baffling: on the one hand rejecting peaceful expansion of trade and the establishment of normal diplomatic relations, while on the other agreeing to give up such basic sovereign rights as tariff autonomy, extraterritoriality, and unilateral most-favored-nation treatment. Much criticism has been leveled against Ch'ing blindness to the realities of international politics and the abject surrender of Chinese national interests. Doubtless, Manchu diplomats, groping in the dark and unaware of the nature of the Western advance, were guilty of ignorance and shortsightedness. Yet the real cause of their behavior went far beyond these superficial explanations, as Selections 7 and 8 by Dr. T. F. Tsiang endeavor to reveal.

Dr. Tsiang was the foremost among Chinese historians to examine in depth the problem of China's confrontation with the West. Having obtained his B.A. from Oberlin College in 1918 and his doctorate from Columbia University in 1923, he returned to China to teach and became chairman of the history department of Tsing-hua University in 1929. This was the time of the opening of the Ch'ing diplomatic archives, and Tsiang with his Western historical training was able to pioneer a new approach to modern Chinese studies through the application of the multi-archival and multilingual methods. The result was a heightened level of scholarship and a new trend in modern Chinese historical scholarship. Though somewhat dated, his writings are still amazingly instructive, and as such are something of a modern classic.

Selections 9 and 10 are mine and seek to explain China's difficult adjustment to the diplomatic requirements of the modern world in the light of her institutional impediment (*t'i-chih*) and psychological inertia. There was no recognition in the universal Confucian empire of the principle of equality of states, and men of learning and ambitions shuddered to think of living outside China. Envoyship came to mean exile from the land of Confucius. So strong was this Sinocentrism that every step in China's transition to a modern state encountered strong resistance.

Simultaneous with the challenge from abroad was the great domestic upheaval, the Taiping Revolution (1850-64), which swept over sixteen provinces and nearly toppled the Manchu dynasty. The outbreak was the result of a number of domestic and foreign problems which had long plagued the country. In Selection 11 Professor Franz Michael interprets the background of this unprecedented social and political outburst.

With the suppression of the Taiping Revolution in 1864 and the signing of peace treaties with the Western powers earlier in 1860, the Ch'ing dynasty took a new lease on life. During the period that followed, the court and the leading provincial authorities promoted the Self-strengthening Movement, which constitutes a most important aspect of Chinese history in the second half of the nineteenth century. Biographies of three leaders, Tseng Kuo-fan, Tso Tsung-t'ang, and Li Hung-chang, are presented in Selection 12.

Selection 13, a report by American minister Frederick F. Low, recounts the T'ung-chih audience of 1873. As the first audience granted to foreign diplomats, it represents a major concession to the West during China's transition from a universal empire to a nation-state. Selection 14 by John K. Fairbank, Francis Lee Higginson Professor of History at Harvard and director of its East Asian Research Center, is a ground-breaking article which perceptively delineates the emergence of a Manchu-Chinese-foreign *synarchy* under the treaty system.

Selection 15 is a study of Li Hung-chang's role in the Self-strengthening movement by Professor K. C. Liu. Li, as

is well known, was the main spirit of modernization in China for the quarter of a century since 1870. Though a provincial official, he performed a number of functions for the central government, and through his close relationship with the Empress Dowager Tz'u-hsi he was able to exert an influence far beyond that indicated by his titles.

Selection 16, by me, centers on the grand debate on national priorities in 1874. The country was beset on the one hand, by Moslem rebellions in the Northwest and Russian occupation of Ili and on the other by the rising threat of Japan and the Western powers on the coast. The question arose as to whether the country should devote its limited resources to coastal defense or to inner frontier defense. The debate resulted in the decision that both should be conducted simultaneously and that one should not be made at the expense of the other. The decision imposed an extremely heavy financial burden on an already strained economy.

Selection 17 by Dr. T. C. Lin is a study of the Sino-Japanese conflict in Korea during 1870-85. It was a period of growing Japanese challenge of Chinese suzerainty in Korea, which sowed the seed of war in 1894-95. China's disastrous defeat all but sealed the fate of the Ch'ing dynasty. The postwar period witnessed the intensification of the foreign drive to cut up the China "melon"—a development which prompted the United States to deliver its famous Open Door Notes. The first, issued September 6, 1899, emphasized equal commercial opportunity and non-discriminatory treatment of foreign nationals in the various spheres of influence or interest, and the second, issued March 20, 1900, called for the territorial and administrative entity of China (Selection 18).

I. CHINA VIS À VIS THE WEST

7. CHINA AND EUROPEAN EXPANSION

T. F. TSIANG

No movement born inside or outside China has affected the destinies of the Chinese people to the same extent as that movement, which, beginning at the end of the 15th century, has gradually extended European domination, political or cultural or both, to all the continents of the world. It was in reference to this movement that back in 1874 Li Hung-chang, urging the Peking government to launch big projects of modernization, characterized the situation in which China found herself as one unprecedented in all her history. The expansion of Europe to the Far East has fundamentally altered the nature of China's historical curve, if we could reduce history to statistical curves. The revolutions which have already occurred in Chinese political, economic, and cultural life, momentous as they have been, will dwindle into insignificance when compared with the changes which the future has in store for us.

The history of the impact of the West upon China has already attracted the attention of many able scholars. Some have

From *Politica*, Vol. 2, No. 5 (March 1936), pp. 1-18. Reprinted by permission. The author was professor and chairman of the history department, National Tsing-hua University, Peiping. This essay was originally delivered as a lecture at the London School of Economics and Political Science, on May 13th, 1935.

devoted years of labor to the diplomacy involved; their results have been embodied in numerous treatises and monographs. Others have been interested in the commercial aspect; though systematic treatises are fewer, learned articles and monographs on China's trade probably fill a good many library shelves. Still others have studied the cultural aspect, especially the influence of Chinese culture on Europe in the 18th, and that of European culture on China in the past century. Within the hour at my disposal it is obvious that I cannot treat with any degree of adequacy any one of the above aspects. I have chosen to limit myself to a line of thought which has not hitherto received as much attention as it seems to me it should have: I mean China's efforts or lack of efforts at meeting the expansion of Europe. When did China realize that something must be done; why did she realize it just then; what did she propose to do with herself when she awakened to this unprecedented situation, and how have her proposals at an adjustment evolved in the course of time—these are the questions with which I hope to occupy myself. In other words, I wish to discuss the interplay between China's diplomatic history and her internal history.

When the Portuguese first appeared off the Chinese coast in 1516, China had already had many centuries of dealing with alien peoples, or barbarians as they were called. The original China at the beginning of authentic history was composed of a relatively small region along the middle course of the Yellow River. It expanded and in the course of expansion absorbed both land and people of alien races. The process was so gradual and so natural that it is almost impossible to say at what date such and such a province came within the Chinese dominion, but the result has been so solid that it is very unlikely that China will ever have trouble from racial minorities within China Proper.

With the barbarians beyond the northern frontier, China's experience has been most varied. In some cases the process of assimilation worked to China's advantage, just as with peoples within China Proper. In other cases all possible methods of dealing with alien peoples were tried and found insufficient. In the 3rd century B.C. there was the attempt to guard the northern frontier from nomadic invasion by completing a continuous wall stretching from the sea in the East to Central Asia in the West. The Great Wall did not prove effective. We find the emperors of the Han Dynasty at first trying to preserve peace by according equality to the ruler of the Huns, calling him brother monarch and giving him a Chinese princess in marriage. When this policy failed, conquest was resorted to. In the second century of our era the Chinese name was both feared and respected in the northern and northwestern regions of China. But the further the Chinese frontier was extended to the West, the more necessary it was found to extend still further. If this policy had been carried out to its logical conclusion, the end would have been universal dominion. Short of that no scientific frontier could have been found. As it was, the glory of imperial expansion was often purchased at the price of internal exhaustion. If the nomads would adopt a sedentary life or if their lands had been more attractive to Chinese farmers, the problem might have been solved. The efforts to seek peace through relations of equality or through relations of conquest were later repeated in the T'ang Dynasty, resulting in the same indecisiveness. Chinese literature is full of disillusionment in regard to relations with alien peoples even under the Han and the T'ang Dynasties when Chinese power was at its height.

Curiously, in the 11th and 12th centuries, when China, pressed again by the northern barbarians, was at her weakest, Chinese nationalism had its first period of bloom. European slogans popular in the last century, some popular even to-day, such as "révanche," "la guerre à l'outrance," "recovery of lost children," were the current coin of the litterateurs and politicians of the Southern Sung Dynasty. Out of this period of intense struggle and bitter humiliation, the neo-Confucian philosophy, which began then to dominate China, worked out a dogma in regard to international relations, to hold sway in China right to the middle of the 19th century. The Chinese *literati* held on to that dogma in face of all new facts and repeated disasters, until British representatives in the Far East from Lord Macartney to Lord Elgin pronounced that dogma to be *the* enemy of England in China.

That dogma asserts that national security could only be found in isolation and stipulates that whoever wished to enter into relations with China must do so as China's vassal, acknowledging the supremacy of the Chinese emperor and obeying his commands, thus ruling out all possibility of international intercourse on terms of equality. It must not be construed to be a dogma of conquest or universal dominion, for it imposed nothing on foreign peoples who chose to remain outside the Chinese world. It sought peace and security, with both of which international relations were held incompatible. If relations there had to be, they must be of the suzerain-vassal type, acceptance of which meant to the Chinese acceptance of the Chinese ethic on the part of the barbarian.

This dogma was inherited by the Ming emperors, who ruled China from the end of the 14th to the middle of the 17th century. In their hands it became a political system. All who wished to enter into relations with China—and there were many from the mouth of the Amur River to the mouth of the Red Sea—must acknowledge the suzerainty of the Chinese emperor. The sign of such acknowledgment was the periodic tribute. It must not be assumed that the Chinese Court made a profit out of such tributes. The imperial gifts bestowed in return were usually more valuable than the tribute. The latter was a symbol, signifying the submissiveness of the tributary state, which obtained in return, besides the imperial gifts, the much-coveted permission to do a limited trade. Thus every tributary mission was accompanied by merchants who traded partly at Canton, Amoy, Foochow, or Ningpo, and partly at Peking. As China had only tributary relations with other states and no international relations, so she had only tributary trade and no international trade. Chinese statesmen before the latter part of the 19th century would have ridiculed the notion that national finance and wealth should be or could be promoted by means of international trade. On China's part the permission to trade was in-

tended to be a mark of imperial bounty and a means of keeping the barbarians in the proper state of submissiveness. Any violation of the elaborate code governing tribute mission and trade was penalized by the breaking of relations, including the stoppage of trade.

Facts of actual life did not always fit tributary system. No matter what the *literati* might think and emperors might decree, the craftsmen and merchants at the marts were eager for the profit they could make from trade with foreigners. Local officials were glad at the increase of customs revenue which trade with foreigners promoted and at the private fortune which they derived from concealed participation in the trade and from illegal exactions. On the other hand cessation of trade brought economic difficulties to the local population and loss to the local officials both in their public and private capacities; furthermore, it might drive the barbarians to war. It was therefore to the interest of the local officials and population to wink at irregularities of the foreigner so long as the emperor did not get wind of them.

When the Portuguese first arrived at Canton in 1516, they had previously learned from the peoples around the Indian Ocean the peculiar nature of China's relations with alien peoples and were ready to enter into compromises. They professed themselves to be tributary agents of their sovereign and conformed with the established regulations and the wishes of the local officials. Although they had not formally obtained the tributary status, they had no difficulty in doing the trade they desired. But beginning with 1518, conflicts developed, lasting almost four decades. The main causes were two. In the first place individual Portuguese could not forgo chances to indulge in lawlessness so common among traders in the 16th century in far-off seas. Secondly the Portuguese had in 1510 occupied Malacca, which had been one of China's tributaries since 1403. The prince of Malacca appealed to the suzerain for protection. The emperor ordered the Portuguese to restore Malacca to its prince. The refusal to submit was taken to mean rebellion. The desultory fighting was indecisive: it spread to the coast of Fukien and Chekiang; it got mixed [up] with the Japanese raiders and the Chinese pirates. The Portuguese found the mixture of war with trade unprofitable; the Chinese learned that the new enemy was really a new kind of nomad, equipped with guns superior to what China possessed and using the sea as the northern nomads used the steppe. In the shifting fortunes of war the Portuguese eventually came to side with the Chinese authorities against pirates and mutinous soldiers. In return for this service and in order to effect a permanent settlement, a modified tributary system was devised for the Portuguese.

The compromise, which China and Portugal eventually accepted, was of fundamental importance, because it regulated not only Sino-Portuguese relations but also Sino-Western relations in general till the middle of the 19th century. China allowed the Portuguese to settle at Macao and to trade at Canton. The Portuguese, while not bearing periodic tribute to Peking, sent at long intervals missions to the imperial court, which observed the etiquette of tribute missions. The settlers at Macao adopted forms of intercourse with the local Chinese officials as humble as those observed by China's other tributary peoples. Their settling on land on the small peninsula of Macao was equivalent to giving up their nomadism and placed them more in the control of China, removing there-

by China's sense of insecurity. On their part the Portuguese devoted themselves to maintaining the monopoly of the Chinese trade, to the exclusion of the Dutch and the English, which they succeeded in doing for a century.

This modified tributary sytem worked smoothly; it even won the acquiescence of the later comers, chief among whom were the English. As decades and centuries rolled by, it persisted and persisting it became an unshakable tradition in the Chinese state. The causes of the smooth working of the sytem were hidden from China and gave her a false sense of security. It was due in the first place to the fact that the position of the Portuguese at Macao, though dishonourable, was highly profitable; then, the rapid decline of Portuguese power made revision by the Portuguese impossible. Secondly, it was due to the concentration of interest on the part of the Dutch and the English on India, the Malay Peninsula, and the South Sea Islands. Before the 19th century the West regarded China as a side-show; it was busy elsewhere. The Chinese government and people had no idea of all this. They imagined that the West had been tamed and would never pretend to break through the tributary system which with some gloss seemed to regulate successfully such relations as existed. For this reason European ships and guns, though admittedly superior to those of China in the 17th and 18th centuries, left China indifferent. The learning of the Jesuits made no deep impression, for reasons too complicated to be explained here. If Sino-European relations had not had the development of the last century, those of the preceding three centuries would have been a mere episode, to be of interest only to the antiquarian.

When we come to the 19th century,

we find certain titanic forces at work, which swept away the modified tributary sytem. The conflict between China and England, which broke out in 1839, was inevitable. The new manufacturers and the new shipping interests of England, accompanied by the development of the new dogma of free trade, demanded that the restrictions on trade which the old system imposed should be abolished. The sense of power and pride which the West acquired from the same industrial revolution made the inequality and its dishonour, inseparable from the old system, intolerable in the new times. The tragedy was that while the West had changed, China had not. Indeed the evil of the spread of the opium habit in China was forcing her to consider tightening the bonds of the old system. British writers have always called that conflict one of trade and equality; China, on the other hand, has always regarded it as the Opium War. Let me offer a revision of both opinions: it was a war for trade, with trade in opium included. England wished for greater opportunities for her new economic forces and at the same time to maintain the opium trade, profitable beyond measure and necessary to the general trade. China on her part wished to get rid of opium and at the same time to maintain the old system of trade. Britain took the offensive on the trade system and maintained a stubborn defence for opium: China launched a bold offensive on opium and put up a heartbreaking defence for the old system of trade, as if that system meant to her both honour and life. It is for these reasons that I consider that conflict inevitable.

From the point of view of China's internal history, the most interesting aspect of the war of 1839-42 was the course of its development. The principal actor on China's side was Lin Tse-hsu, special commissioner for the suppression of the opium trade at Canton. He did not seek that appointment, for he and his fellow anti-opium enthusiasts thought that opium could be got rid of by inflicting the death penalty on the smoker who failed to reform within a year and a half of the promulgation of the new law of total prohibition; they argued that if nobody smoked opium there would be no buyer of and therefore no trader in opium. The moderates, with Keshen and Kiying in the lead, objected to the severity of the death penalty and argued that if trading in opium were stopped smoking would be *ipso facto* stopped. The emperor decided to apply pressure on both trading and smoking. Since the center of the trade was at Canton, where corruption had stimulated its development, Lin was appointed to that vital post. The choice could not have been better. Lin's origin as scholar and as a man of integrity, his previous record as administrator and faithful servant of state and crown, and his intimate association with the literary and political circle of Viceroy Tao at Nanking all pointed him out as the man for the difficult task. He carried to Canton in the spring of 1839 not only the confidence of Peking but the hopes of the best elements of China of that day. If China must play a match with England, Lin without question should captain China's team.

Shortly after his arrival at Canton in the spring of 1839 Commissioner Lin shot a straight goal and scored for China. He succeeded in getting hold of all the opium in the hands of the foreign importers, amounting in all to one thousand five hundred tons. That victory was cheered all over China. The Emperor showered upon him both approval and honor, and for reward promoted him to the viceroyalty at Nanking. He refused the promotion so as to remain at Canton to prevent future imports. That gesture of public-spiritedness won him further fame.

Meanwhile Captain Elliot laid his case before Lord Palmerston, who sent out land and naval forces to enforce certain demands on China, with Admiral George Elliot as commander and Chief Plenipotentiary and Captain Charles Elliot as the second member of the mission. These forces arrived in the southern waters of China in the summer of 1840. Lin had been preparing for this and fully expected the Elliots to try strength with him. But they did nothing of the kind; instead, in obedience to Palmerston's instructions, they declared a blockade of Canton and proceeded north to occupy the island of Chusan on the coast of Chekiang. The blockade was meaningless to China; in fact, many a Chinese then thought that the prohibition of all maritime trade was the only way to rid China of opium and of troublesome foreigners. Chusan was beyond Lin's jurisdiction and was undefended; in taking it instead of attacking Canton the British appeared to the Chinese to be afraid of Lin.

After doing these incomprehensible things, the Elliots went to Taku at the mouth of Peiho. There they requested Viceroy Keshen, leader of the moderate party, to transmit to "The Minister of The Emperor of China" a letter from Palmerston. That document is most astounding. The first two-thirds of it were devoted to the activities of Commissioner Lin without however mentioning his name, and the last third detailed the redress which England expected. It complained that China should not suddenly enforce laws which had not hitherto been strictly enforced: the Chinese reader did

not feel that any government should warn its subjects that a law was about to be strictly enforced. It complained that in enforcing the law China had been severer on the foreigner than on the Chinese: this was untrue, for many a Chinese had lost his life for connections with opium whereas the British merchant had lost only his property. It complained of the virtual imprisonment of foreign merchants in their Canton factories, with food supplies cut off: in doing this Lin had only applied the traditions of the old trade system; food supplies, though officially stopped, were really continued. It complained finally that "in violation of the Law of Nations, and in utter disregard of the respect which was due by him [Lin] to an officer of the British Crown, he imprisoned the Superintendent as well as the merchants"; in fact Captain Elliot's official character had never been recognized by China and Lin issued the order to surround the factories before Elliot entered them, whose coming was unexpected and unasked. The Chinese translation furnished by the British accentuated the personal nature of the document, so that the Chinese government understood it to mean that the British were bringing a suit before the Chinese Crown against one of its officers.

The Peking government appointed Keshen to "manage the barbarians." He took for granted that the British representatives, accompanied by a considerable force, came with no peaceful intentions; and war near Tientsin would endanger the capital. He began with a twofold task: on the one hand he hurried up his own military preparations; on the other he made a thorough investigation of British ships and their armament. The Elliots were only too glad to let him know that the forces at their disposal were overwhelming and afforded his agents every facility for seeing things with their own eyes. Keshen was at once convinced that war was out of the question. He sent to the Court vivid descriptions of British fighting machines. There was a "fire ship" which could sail with or against wind and current. The guns were mounted on a thing which directed the firing upwards or downwards, to the right or to the left at man's pleasure. China had nothing like these. The Elliots visited Shanhaikwan and were surprised that China had placed no guns on such an important point. Keshen tried to fool the Elliots by saying that Chinese guns were so placed as to be invisible to the enemy, but he explained to the Emperor that really at Shanhaikwan there were only a few pieces left by the Ming Dynasty, which he had had hurriedly brushed up. These descriptions and contrasts were calculated to persuade the Emperor to accept a policy of peace. In carrying out this set purpose he was marvellously aided by Palmerston's letter. He told the Elliots that the Emperor regarded all humanity with equal passion and that if Commissioner Lin had committed excesses against the English, who had come so far from their homeland, His Majesty would see to it that justice was done to men from afar. In other words, since the British brought suit against Lin, his punishment must satisfy them. As to the demands for redress, Keshen told the Elliots that not a single one would be accepted by China, with the possible exception of a sum of money, so that the Elliots "would not have to return to their sovereign empty-handed." He reasoned that the British, being a mercantile people, would insist on recovering their financial losses. To his surprise and to that of the Emperor these tactics succeeded: the Elliots agreed to take their ships away and to settle the details with him at the comfortable distance of Canton. China thought the war was over and that the British had been soothed. The Emperor, being parsimonious, ordered immediate demobilization; soldiers who had started on their march from the interior to the coast were all turned back. The stocks of Keshen went up, while those of Lin went down. The Emperor degraded Lin and appointed Keshen to be Special Commissioner at Canton.

It is unnecessary for me to say that all this was a misunderstanding. The Elliots had only consented to transfer negotiations from Tientsin to Canton; they had not given up any of their demands or agreed to forgo enforcement by arms. When Keshen arrived at Canton, he discovered to his dismay the real state of things. The English would only sign peace on their own terms, which the Emperor could not possibly accept. Keshen knew that even on English terms peace was preferable to war. He strove to convince the Court and the public. For this he was denounced for being a fool and a traitor, for did he not allow himself to be used by the English as a tool to get rid of Lin the patriot and the invincible? With Lin degraded the English had nothing more to fear and therefore resorted to war. Would Keshen serve the purposes of the English without being bribed? Unfortunately his previous reputation for corruption fitted in too well with the hypothesis.

After the Emperor had decided on rejecting the English terms and on war to the end, he should have recalled Lin to the chief command. He was reluctant to do this because of court intrigue and also because he would not admit that he had done wrong in degrading Lin. The war party called for Lin insistingly, so that the Court finally had to reappoint him, but only to a subordinate post in Chekiang. The English spent the winter of 1840-41 in war against Canton, which was defended by the "defeatist" Keshen. In spring of 1841 they moved northwards. Just as they were about to meet in the field the "invincible" Lin, the orders of the Emperor arrived, exiling him to Turkestan. After all Lin had no opportunity to show what he could do. China lost the war, but the Chinese did not admit defeat, for they reasoned that the best of old China had not been tried. They explained the unfavorable score by saying that the coach for some reason kept their best player out of the game. I repeat: if China and England must play a match, Lin should have been China's captain throughout. If he had been he undoubtedly would have lost the war just the same, for the material means of war were too unequal. If this had occurred the *literati* of China would have had no excuse for not reforming, that is, for not westernizing China's army at least. Lin himself in the course of his two years at Canton realized the necessity of using "barbarian's weapons to fight the barbarian," and made a modest beginning of westernization. If his leadership had been continued during and after the war, westernization of China could have made some progress, for in China, as in Japan, only men who had the confidence of men of the old culture could have furnished effective leadership in the new culture. As things actually turned out, China slept on for another twenty years, which I call the lost twenty years of China's modern history. For the fate of all non-European nations in the last century has been decided by the degree and the time of the westernization of their fighting forces. I know the latter alone is insufficient to meet the expansion of Europe, but no country can really westernize its fighting forces without in some degree westernizing its economy and its polity: the one inevitably involves the other.

With England leading the way in "opening up" China, the United States and France immediately followed in demanding the same rights and privileges of trade. China was dragged to the high seas of world politics, but her heart yearned for the return of the old system of trade. The traditional mentality in regard to international relations, coupled with the same old defenselessness, brought on the second conflict of 1858-60. Although fundamentally the same in its causes, the second war had a course of development entirely different from that of the first war. This time the best that old China could produce got a chance to show what it could do. The commander guarding the approaches to Peking was Prince Sengkolintsin, the bravest in the Emperor's service. His army crumbled before the Anglo-French Expedition. After the Emperor fled to Jehol, Peking was left in the charge of his brother, Prince Kung, and Wensiang. The former was then twenty-seven, hotheaded, contemptuous of the foreigner, but patriotic and honorable. It was he who opposed most strongly the opening of ports on the Yangtze; it was he also who first suggested that to strike at the dragon's head one must arrest the British and French negotiators. Wensiang's origin, character, and record in public service were a replica of those of Lin. Here facing the foreigner were two men who had the confidence of old China.

From their experiences of 1860, Prince Kung and Wensiang learned several fundamental lessons. First they learned that the Westerners kept their plighted word; treaties, once signed, were something to rely upon. Secondly they learned that without a shadow of doubt western arms were far superior to Chinese arms, a fact which they regarded as both a danger and a shame. Thirdly—this was the most important lesson—they learned that the Westerners were eager to sell to China their arms and to supply instructors who would teach the Chinese how to use and make these arms. Russia, afraid that England might make a second India out of China, was the first to press such offers on China. England, anxious to see China restored to peace so that her merchants could enjoy the newly-won commercial privileges, lent men and arms to suppress the Taiping rebellion. France, not to be outdone, also made generous offers. From these lessons Prince Kung and Wensiang constructed a policy, which called for strict adherence to the letter of the treaties so as to avoid fresh conflicts and for the westernization of China's army.

Circumstances of the time favoured the two men. In the war against the Taipings Tseng Kuo-fan had risen to a position of political and moral leadership. Both as man and as statesman he was the finest flower of Confucian culture, whose life is even to-day an inspiration to many. Fighting on the banks of the Yangtze he came in contact with foreign-made steamers, and realized at once the possibilities of machines. He commissioned the first Chinese who had had a foreign university education to go abroad to get him machines that could make machines. But his schemes of modernization did not go so far as those of his pupil Li Hung-chang. Li was in Tseng's secretariat, which was deliberately enlarged and used as a training school for politicians. After serving such an apprenticeship, Li was recommended for the governorship of Kiangsu, in which

capacity he came into contact with British consuls and officers at Shanghai. He had been trained in the traditional way and knew no more about the West than his contemporaries. In the bewilderment of foreign complications at Shanghai he wrote to his master for guidance. Tseng replied that he too knew nothing about foreigners and their ways, but that Confucius once said, "Let your words be true and your conduct sincere, then you can even get along in barbarian countries." From this sage saying Li drew a rule of conduct: he would never allow his performance to fall short of his promise. In the military campaign in eastern Kiangsu he co-operated first with the American Ward, then with Gordon, and in such co-operation he saw to it that his own army should bear as much of the brunt of battle as his foreign helpers. As the foreigners showed more confidence in him, he reciprocated. In those few years at Shanghai he learned the same lessons which Prince Kung and Wensiang had learned in Peking.

The combination of Prince Kung and Wensiang in Peking and of Tseng, Li, and other lesser men in the provinces ushered in that period in modern Chinese history, from 1861 to 1894, which might be called the Period of Self-Strengthening. At first their program was limited to the westernization of the army. But this humble beginning led to many developments. These men soon found that it was better to establish arsenals and shipyards in China, which in turn created the demand for educated Chinese engineers and scientists. Schools teaching western languages and sciences were established in China, graduates from which were sent abroad. Modern armament and modern education involved larger expenditure, which in turn led these men, especially Li Hung-chang, to start cotton mills, to organize the China Merchants' Navigation Company, to build telegraphs and railways, and to open coal mines.

It is not to be supposed that Commissioner Lin could or would alone have accomplished this program of self-strengthening after the first war and that the entire time schedule of modern Chinese history could have been integrally advanced twenty years. What is contended is that if the course of development of the first war had been different, Lin would have attempted similar things and the beginning of China's westernization could have been made twenty years earlier.

While China was trying to make up for lost time in the period 1861-94, Japan was enacting the same program, with a political revolution thrown in. The latter gave her the needed unity; the island basis of her existence afforded her less room for retreat from the Westerner. Therefore, once she began the task of westernization, she proceeded with greater rapidity and thoroughness. But she owed part of her initial impulse to the Chinese example; even in the latest phase of Japan's history she is indebted to China. The earliest Japanese books on western countries were translations from Chinese. One of the Japanese editors wrote in the preface to such a translated work the following passage:

With these Chinese books on western countries at our disposal it is unnecessary for Japanese to learn western languages, which are indeed too difficult for the Japanese to learn.[1]

1. I owe this quotation to Professor Nakayama, formerly of the Tokyo Normal University.

But in return the Japanese effort stimulated China. It was dimly realized in both countries that the question of su-

premacy in the Far East was to be decided by the race in modernization between the two Far Eastern nations.

Westernization in China suffered from political decentralization and further enhanced it. Under the programme the provincial governors did more things than ever before, and in doing more attracted more power into their hands. The provinces were never made a team pulling together. The new army and navy, the new arsenals and dockyards, the new merchant marine, and even the new education suffered from provincial jealousies and conflicts of jurisdiction. Wensiang and Tseng Kuo-fan went to their graves in the 'seventies; Prince Kung declined in initiative and suffered from family intrigue. Li Hung-chang became *the* leader. His abilities were recognized, but his personality could not dominate the situation as that of his master did. He could not overcome the evil of provincialism.

Another evil, greater in importance, was the intrigue within the imperial family. Emperor Kuangsu, who ascended the throne in 1874, owed it entirely to his aunt, the later famous Empress Dowager, who acted as regent during his minority. When he came of age ten years later, he and his father, Prince Chün, were anxious to get into his hands real power. To achieve this object without a conflict with the Empress Dowager was the question. Prince Chün hit upon the idea of rebuilding the Summer Palace to please the Empress, as a gift from nephew to aunt. It was hoped that the Empress would spend her days in luxurious leisure and gradually forget politics. The woman did nothing of the kind; but the Summer Palace cost millions, money borrowed in the name of the navy. From 1886 to 1894, not a single ship was added to the young navy, because funds earmarked for the navy had been spent on the palace. It was this starved navy which met the Japanese navy on September 17th, 1894. That battle decided that henceforth Japan and not China should be the Far Eastern naval power.

Just as the crisis in 1860 ushered in a new period in China's modern history, so did the Sino-Japanese War of 1894-95. In pointing this out I am not leaving my subject, for modern Japan is westernized Japan, a by-product of that historic movement—the expansion of Europe.

The internal changes after the defeat of 1895, followed soon after by the so-called partition of China, took a sharp turn from those of the previous period. After 1895 it was thought that the measures of modernization undertaken in the earlier period failed because they did not go deep enough. What China needed was a fundamental reform of the state. Japan's victory was attributed partly to her constitutionalism, which was also then the vogue in Europe. Hence we have the reforms of the constitutional monarchists of 1898. These reforms again came to grief because of the conflict between Emperor and Empress Dowager. The former was for reform; the latter, for the *status quo*. The reformers in their eagerness to achieve measures in weeks and months, which under all conditions should be allowed years and decades, injured too many vested interests at once. The discontented elements flocked to the banner of the Empress Dowager. The reformers saw in her the nest of reaction and were ready to destroy it at one stroke. They invited Yüan Shih-k'ai to lead his army to surround the Summer Palace and imprison her. Yüan betrayed reform, and the Emperor became a prisoner on an island in the Central Lake in Peking.

Besides imprisoning the Emperor and sweeping away all reforms the Empress Dowager wished to depose him and put another in his place. The plot was opposed by some powerful provincial governors; it was frowned upon by the diplomatic corps in Peking. For this foreign opposition to her plans the Empress swore revenge. Just then rose the Boxer Movement, in which she thought she saw a weapon to use against the foreigner. The result was great humiliation for the dynasty and heavy financial burden on the people. These fresh disasters gave birth to the revolutionary movement.

In the 19th century it was mainly what Europe and Europeanized Japan did in the Far East which influenced China's internal development. In the 20th century what was thought and done in Europe and the United States exercised even greater influence upon China; for by this time large numbers of China's young men went abroad as students or as political refugees. We can see most clearly this influence at work in the development of Dr. Sun Yat-sen's thought.

The official historians of the Kuomintang would have us believe that Dr. Sun was born a revolutionary. The tendency to assign very early dates to his various ideas of social and political reconstruction has been carried to such an extent that it amounts to virtual denial of all development. That Dr. Sun in his student days came into contact with members of the secret societies is an undoubted fact. These societies have a long history and are a pure Chinese product. But besides the determination to overthrow the Manchus they had no other political program. It was not until the first decade of the 20th century when Dr. Sun was a political refugee and revolutionary agitator among Chinese in foreign lands, that he acquired his republican and socialistic ideas. He thought he saw in the West a democratic revolution, followed on its heels by a social revolution. He decided that China might as well have both at the same time. In fact he wished to improve upon western experience; for, thinking that social discontent in Europe was fundamentally caused by misdirection or lack of direction of the Industrial Revolution, he insisted that the coming Industrial Revolution in China should be directed from the very beginning into forms that would benefit society at large and not private capitalists only. If we take Dr. Sun's life and work as a whole, this is his real testament to his followers.

In regard to recent developments in China there have been much misunderstanding and loose talk. It is sometimes forgotten that Dr. Sun's socialistic ideas antedated the Soviet Revolution by at least ten years and that to the end of his life he never accepted communism of the Marxist type. Intellectually he owed much to foreign thinkers and political leaders, but only of Western Europe and the United States and not of Soviet Russia. It is also sometimes forgotten that the nationalism of Kuomintang cannot be attributed to Soviet influence. As I have said, in the Chinese revolutionary movement nationalism originally meant nothing more than the overthrow of the Manchus and the restoration of Chinese rule in China. This type of nationalism was indigenous in China and owed nothing whatever to foreign influence. After 1911, especially during the years of the World War, it gradually took on a different meaning; it came to stand for recovery of full sovereignty and equality among the nations. The change had become complete by the time of the Paris Peace Conference. Chinese nationalism of the later type was a child of "the war for democracy" and of Wilson's fourteen points. What the Russians did in 1925-26 was to utilize and further excite the already existing nationalism for the purpose of the world revolution.

In a contribution to the *Cambridge Historical Review,* which I made seven years ago, I pointed out certain persisting tendencies in Sino-Russian relations. I called attention to the fact that in the past century China turned three times to Russia for aid, once in 1860, once in 1896 by Li Hung-chang, and the third time by Dr. Sun in 1924. In all three cases China took the road to Russia as the last resort, pressed by overwhelming necessities. Dr. Sun was convinced that China could only be saved by his revolution, which in turn depended on some measure of foreign aid. If Dr. Sun could have found the aid in the United States or in Great Britain, he would not have turned to Moscow. His alliance with Lenin was a *mariage de convenance.*

While this was true of the past, it will not necessarily be true of the future. For in the meantime two vital facts have intervened. One is the communistic philosophy of life, embodied in the Soviet Union, which is proving attractive to the most determined elements of the young in China. Communism as a military movement against the Nanking government may fail, but communism as a dream of a new mode of life may live in the hearts of the young until favorable material circumstances come to give it political and military strength. The other important fact is the overwhelming pressure of Japan, in face of which the ruling classes in China know only submission. The pent-up national hatred is a source of power which communism might some day exploit. When that day comes, it would be a strange denouncement to the expansion of Europe in the Far East. Or would it be only the most natural thing?

8. The Extension of Equal Commercial Privileges to Other Nations than the British after the Treaty of Nanking

T. F. TSIANG

Before the Opium War there existed a system of commercial intercourse between China and the Western maritime nations. It was not based on treaty; it did not conform to practices prevailing among the Western nations, but it was not only definite, but rigid, almost sanctified. How rigid that system had become by the end of the eighteenth century, both the Macartney and Amherst missions demonstrated to the world without leaving any room for doubt. The main features of that system were: (1) trade at the one port of Canton; (2) monopoly of co-hong; (3) a Chinese national tariff, which was never made known to Western merchants, with very low official rates but increased enormously by extra extractions; (4) question of jurisdiction undecided and liable to lead to great conflicts and (5) restrictions on personal freedom of Western merchants. The

From *The Chinese Social and Political Science Review*, Vol. 15, No. 3, Oct. 1931, pp. 422-44. Reprinted by permission.

elaboration of the system began at the end of the seventeenth century; it had already acquired definiteness by the middle of the eighteenth, and became almost sanctified by the end of that century. There can be no doubt that nothing but war could induce China to accept any change. That war came in 1840, and the resulting Treaty of Nanking with the Supplementary Treaty of Hoomun Chai swept away the *ancien régime* as thoroughly as great national changes could be made. Under the circumstances, it can be easily seen that China regarded the new commercial privileges granted to England as a necessary evil, as a great national humiliation and calamity. Even to-day one can see the tears of bitterness shed by Emperor, Mandarin, and Literati, as one reads the documents of that day.

The question then arises: how did it happen that China extended the same commercial privileges to other nations, notably America and France, without a war? What motives led Chinese states-men to make that extension? Who among Western negotiators was especially re-sponsible for leading China to take such a step, if leading there was? How should the claims for such honor on the part of Sir Henry Pottinger, Commodore Law-rence Kearny, and Caleb Cushing be ad-judged? All these are questions of great historical interest. The attempt will be made here, not to answer these questions definitely, but to contribute the Chinese documentary evidence which must be taken into consideration.

The old commercial system, peculiar as it was, had one feature in common with the later system, namely, equal treatment of the all foreign nations trad-ing at Canton. In the sixteenth and first half of the seventeenth century, China and Portugal together upheld the mo-noply of the latter. Then the East India Companies of England and Holland could not establish any regular trade at a Chinese port. But after the unification of China under the Manchu dynasty around 1680, the Dutch and the English, the one supporter of Manchu and the other supporter of Koxinga, traded al-most alike. The coming of the French, the Danish, the Swede, the Prussian, the Ostend Company, and last the American, all involved no special negotiation, all traded as a matter of course. The Chinese emperors, as they expressed it in their decrees, regarded the outer barbarians all as of one humanity. Privileges, exac-tions, restrictions were shared all alike. In fact, the geographical and ethnological knowledge then prevailing among the Chinese was very limited. The finer dis-tinctions among the Westerners were al-most non-existent for the Chinese. By the end of eighteenth century, England and America were the predominant trading nations at Canton. Chinese statesmen

often remarked on the proud and trouble-some spirit of the English and the obe-dient and respectful spirit of the Amer-icans, but no differential treatment was attempted. When we remember the background of the eighteenth century, half of our problem is solved.

During the Opium War the other Western nations simply watched events. Soon after the signature of the Treaty of Nanking, the United States of America, through the voice of Commodore Law-rence Kearny, requested of China com-mercial privileges equal to that of Eng-land. The request was reported to the Emperor by the Viceroy at Canton, Ke-kung, in a Memorial to the Throne which reached Peking on December 12th, 1842.[1] The pertinent passage reads as follows:

> On the tenth day of the ninth moon (Oc-tober 13th) the American chieftain Kearny presented a dispatch to me, urgently re-questing me to memorialize the Throne, that His Imperial Majesty may grant the mer-chants of his country the same conditions of trade as those granted to the English mer-chants. After consulting together with the Barbarian-Pacificating General Yishan and the Governor Liang Pao-ch'ang, I replied that he should wait till the arrival of the Special Imperial Commissioner at Canton. Then the matter will be taken up together and decided upon.

The Imperial Commissioner referred to was Ilipoo, who was then sent by the Emperor to Canton to negotiate the de-tailed commercial treaty with Sir Henry Pottinger. The request of Commodore Kearny was presented on October 13th and the report of it only reached the Throne on December 12th. This shows that provincial officials did not regard it as a matter of urgency or importance. The Imperial Decree[2] in reply thereto was rendered on the same day, Decem-ber 12th:

. . . Let Ilipoo, after his arrival at Canton, deliberate carefully, together with Kekung, on the matter of trade as presented by the barbarian chieftain Kearny. Old regulations should all be followed; no change or addition is permissible. If the hong merchants should make unreasonable exactions on the Americans, let Ilipoo investigate and prohibit, to show our sympathy. If however the Americans should dare to claim ports of trade and such things, Ilipoo must earnestly put stop to such claims. No compromise is to be allowed.

On December 15th a report[3] from Kiying, the Viceroy at Nanking, who shared with Ilipoo the management of foreign affairs, reached Peking, that on November 27th an American merchant ship dropped anchor at Ningpo, loaded with foreign cloths and asking to be permitted to trade. The Taotai at Ningpo had told the Americans that although the English had been permitted by Imperial Decree to trade there, regulations for trade had not been settled and the port had not been declared open; that as to the Americans, as they had always traded at Canton, they should return there. After such persuasions, the Americans appeared quite respectful and obedient and left the port days afterwards. The Emperor, after repeating to Kiying the instructions which he had given to Ilipoo, added:[4]

Now, since those barbarians had already come to Chekiang, it is very likely that they will proceed to Kiangsu to present their requests. Let the Viceroy (Kiying) order his subordinates to examine carefully the purpose of their coming, and manage them properly. Let it be said to them that since they had always traded at Canton, since it has long been so, they should still return to Canton and trade there in the old way. The laws of the Heavenly Dynasty have naturally their fixity and cannot be changed in the least. All this is to show that there is a limit to things.

Ten days later (December 25th) a similar report came to Peking from the Governor of Chekiang and the Imperial rescript, though briefer, was couched in similar terms.

It is clear that up to the end of the year 1842 there was no intention on the part of the Peking Government to extend the benefits of the new commercial regime to other nations than the British. On the contrary, it was the declared purpose of the Court to keep the other nations to the old regime.

Ilipoo on his way to Canton, that is, *before he could get in touch with Kearny*, sent in a Memorial[5] which put the matter in an entirely new light for the Emperor. It reached Peking on January 17th, 1843; it was written near Nan-hsiung-chow on the northern border of Kwangtung, probably near the end of the previous December. As it is a document of great importance for our question, it merits attention:

I have previously received the Imperial Decree of the eleventh day of the eleventh moon (December 12th, 1842), commanding me to take into joint deliberation the matter of trade presented by the American chieftain Kearny. In regard to this question of foreign merchants coming together (with the English) to trade at the additional ports (additional to Canton), the barbarian Chieftain Pottinger, while at Nanking, declared that in case merchants of the various countries should come to Fukien, Chekiang, and Kiangsu to trade, if only China is willing, England would not try to prevent, in order to set up a monopoly. It appears then that England has already secretly agreed with the other countries to come together to trade. Furthermore, the Americans made request for trade first at Chekiang and now again at Canton in an official dispatch. The

French were at Nanking, most likely also with commercial purposes in view. If we allow only the English to have additional ports and not allow the other nations to go there together for trade, it is to be feared that in the appearance of their ships and clothes there is little difference, so little that it would be hard to distinguish one from the other. Furthermore, it is to be feared that any attempt to prevent such trade would create unnecessary trouble, the other nations using the English example as excuse. England may also effect some combination with them, allowing them to trade together with the English. In that case, it would also be hard for us to prevent. Then the benefit of trade will be conferred by England on the other nations, who will feel grateful to England and resentful towards us. That would bespeak bad calculation on our part. This matter must wait my arrival at Canton and joint deliberation with the Viceroy and Governor there. It would also be necessary to consult Pottinger. Then we can have this matter settled and reported to Throne for final decision.

Imperial opinion was immediately changed by the Memorial. The Rescript[6] in reply to Ilipoo recognized it as a real bad policy to allow the other nations to feel grateful to England and resentful towards China on account of trade in the new ports.

. . . what Elipoo said in his Memorial is not without acumen. But if we allow the other nations right away to come to trade, the English may resent the division of profits by the other nations and thus create new trouble. Let Elipoo in his forthcoming conferences with Pottinger talk this matter over with him at length and settle it carefully. Our main aim is a long peace, without fresh conflicts.

On January 19th, two days after the arrival of Ilipoo's Memorial and the issuance of the above Decree, Kiying's Memorial[7] on the same subject reached Peking. We give the document in its entirety, omitting only the introductory paragraph:

In August, while I was negotiating with English (at Nanking), I already thought of the possibility of all barbarians demanding the same privileges (as the English). I then made inquiries of the English and their reply was that if the trade of the other maritime nations should still be confined to Canton, they (the English) will not proffer demands on the behalf of the others, but that if the Great Emperor should permit the others to resort to Fukien, Chekiang, and Kiangsu for trade, the English would not be small-minded about it; that they would not mind if the ships of other nations frequented Hongkong. At that time Ilipoo and I agreed that we should wait till we examine the question at Canton before we come to a decision, and report to the Throne. Now, since the Americans have requested for trade, once at Canton and once at Chekiang, permit me to present to Your Majesty the favorable and unfavorable aspects of the question.

Where there is profit to be gained, there men will gather. In the reign of Kanghsi, the English had a factory at Tinghai. Because of the multiplicity and heaviness of duties collected, merchants, finding the trade profitless, became fewer, but went continually to Canton. For a hundred years, Canton administration was pure and the barbarians were quiet, never showing any rebellious spirit. But with elapse of time, corruption crept in: the barbarians found the burden unbearable and harbored resentment in their hearts. The English then precipitated trouble, going even to the last extremity (of war.) The other barbarians, although respectful and quiet on the outside, were really watching the outcome of the conflict. If we could defeat the English (and get rid of them), the others would take over the former's profits (market); if otherwise, the others, being of similar sentiments as the English, will join them and still reap the usual profit. So, for example, when the English started the war, their fighting ships were few; later they were increased until they numbered one hundred and several tens. These barbarians are several tens of thousands of li from home; the assembling and dispatch of such a large fleet must have been a matter of great difficulty. I can scarcely believe that the other barbarians did not combine to offer aid to the English. Now, since the English have obtained what they wished, if the others should still be confined to Canton, we can easily by placing ourselves in their position, see that they will feel the injustice. Since they had helped the English, why would not the latter help them? Isn't this dictated by the reason and nature of things? Suppose the other barbarians would not openly declare war but secretly go to the other ports to trade under the aegis of the English, how can that be detected? In the case, the English can make a show of generosity to the other barbarians and secretly control our national economic valve; and the others, failing to obtain grace from the Heavenly Dynasty, will cling to the English. Ever afterwards barbarian and barbarian will draw closer while barbarian and Chinese will be more and more at enmity. One English nation has proven sufficient to violate our frontier, all the barbarians, driven to form one unit, would be more than sufficient. This is a matter which deserves our deep thought and mature deliberation.

Some say that if all the corrupt practices at Canton should be swept away and a new era begun, the barbarians would then trade quietly at Canton and not harbor undue expectations. This would indeed be a thorough method. But the roots of evil, being deep, cannot suddenly be pulled up. It is further to be feared that after the old corruption had been done away with, the bureaucracy, feeling the exactions to be its due, would impose new extra charges. Take for example the case of Amoy. It was once a resort of numerous Chinese merchant ships. Later, because of the numerous and heavy exactions which, though often prohibited, only increased with every prohibi-

tion, the firms doing an overseas trade closed their doors. Fortunately, being Chinese merchants they could resort to other ports and so no trouble came. In case of foreign merchants, if limited strictly to one port, will not endure such things, human as they are. This is another aspect of the question which has troubled my thought a great deal.

After careful deliberation, it appears to me that if America and the other countries should demand other ports (other than these opened to the British) in the provinces of Fukien, Chekiang, and Kiangsu, we ought to refuse in dignified words. If the English claimed the ports as exclusively theirs and refused to allow other nations to trade therein, they will then start a quarrel among themselves and we can meet plan with plan. But now both the English and the other barbarians are willing to share with each other. As the old saying goes, laws after reaching the stage of exhaustion must change. Rather than adhere strictly to the old regulations and arouse thereby trouble, it would be much better to suit policy to circumstance and regard them all as of one humanity. If America and the other countries really wish to trade in Fukien, Chekiang, and Kiangsu, it seems they should be allowed to go where they wish, after settling with us the tariff, but they should not be allowed to entertain hopes beyond the provinces of Fukien, Chekiang, and Kiangsu, nor should they be allowed separate exclusive port areas in these provinces. Although the customs revenue at Canton will decrease, the income at Fukien, Chekiang and Kiangsu will increase: altogether, the national revenue will suffer no less.

Furthermore, since we already allow the English to trade in Fukien, Chekiang, and Kiangsu, it does not seem that any harm will ensue if other barbarians are to be added. By separating the foreign ships into five ports instead of concentrating them in one, their positions will be scattered and their union loosened. Such a development will not be impolitic to us in the management of the outer barbarians.

The Emperor replied[8] that Kiying and Ilipoo should negotiate along the lines that they themselves had proposed.

Ilipoo arrived at Canton in the middle of January, 1843. He got immediately in touch with Sir Henry Pottinger and until his death on March 4th was busy with the English negotiations. During his brief term of office at Canton as Imperial Commissioner, he had no occasion to deal with the American request for equal commercial privileges at all. His Memorial[9] written in the middle of February contained this passage:

As to America and France: since my arrival here at Canton, they have not asked to be permitted to trade at all the ports. This is naturally due to the fact that since commercial regulations for the English have not been settled, they are simply watching events.

Ilipoo was succeeded in the Commissionership by Kiying, who left Nanking on April 17th and reached Canton in the middle of June. On the 26th of June, he exchanged with Sir Henry Pottinger the ratifications of the Treaty of Nanking. In his Memorial[10] reporting that event, he made a passing mention of the other countries.

America and France now also request that they should be treated according to the new regulations. Permit me, in consultation with the Viceroy and Governor, to treat their request as a separate question and to try to arrive at a clear understanding with them after the new regulations have been settled.

This proposal of Kiying was accepted by the Emperor in a Decree[11] rendered on July 30th.

In the beginning of September, the question of the trading privileges of the other nations was taken up in earnest by Kiying. His report[12] to the Emperor follows:

I, upon examination, find that of the foreign ships frequenting Canton, the English and their dependents, the Indians, have the most; the Americans come next, not far behind; then Holland sends every year three or four to about ten ships; France, Luçon (Spain), Denmark, Sweden, Prussia, Austria, and Jen-po-li (Naples?) send some years some ships and some years none at all, generally one or two in a year and never more than five or six. Now, since the trade regulations with the English are settled, since they do not monopolize the port of Shanghai and others, and since at Tinghai and other places American ships are anchored with the English, eager for the opening of trade, we ought to of course arrive at some understanding with the Americans in regard to trade. But the chieftain Kearny had already returned to his own country in the middle of February before my arrival here. There is only an Acting Consul by the name of King, supervising trade at Canton. He has requested of me to be permitted to trade according to the new regulations. I, suiting policy to convenience, in the name of Imperial Grace, gave the permission to pay customs and trade according to the new regulations in all of the five ports, thus showing kindness to the men from afar. He expressed his gratitude, but stated that of the imports, two things, ginseng and lead, products of his country, were formerly much smuggled in because of the heavy duties, and that now although the extra charges were abolished, the new tariff still imposed a duty of 38 taels on every hundred catties of first-class ginseng, 3 taels and half on second-class, and four-tenths of a tael on every hundred catties of lead. He says the duties amount to forty, even fifty per cent. on the sales price. The merchants not only failed to get any profit but actually suffered losses. He requested that five per cent. be made the standard, making first-class ginseng pay 4 taels per hundred catties, second-class 2 taels 7/10 and lead 2 mace per hundred catties. We felt that since the new tariff had already been submitted to Throne, and since the first change at the request of the barbarian will be followed by similar requests in future, it would not do at all and we immediately refused the request. The barbarian also stated that there had not been any classification of ginseng, the first-class and the second-class being usually mixed in equal proportions; and that ginseng and lead might pay duties for the time being according to the new rates till all the ships have arrived and the barbarian chieftain had come to settle the matter in negotiation. Fearing that he might not have told the truth or all the truth, we sent trusty men to the market to buy samples. They found that one catty of first-class ginseng cost 1 tael 4 mace per catty, making 140 taels per hundred catties. Upon further inquiry, they found that prices varied according to the quantity imported, the lowest price within 1 tael per catty. Thus it appears that the barbarian's request was not unreasonable. The annual import of first-class ginseng never exceeded four hundred piculs and second-class one thousand piculs, and lead two hundred piculs. Even if the duties were lowered according to his request annual customs income will be only reduced by several thousand taels. Rather than impose heavy duties and arouse smuggling and give pretense for grievance, it is much better to show generosity and get the duties really paid and avoid trouble. But at present since France and other countries have not come to any settlement, the precedent of changing the tarriff should be avoided. Permit us to take time to consider the question as a whole and report later to Your Majesty.

The Memorial goes on to detail the difficulty of negotiating with the French since nobody knows whether Jancigny or Ratti-Menton is the real Consul for the French. The report was approved by the Emperor in Decree[13] of September 23rd.

Therefore by September of 1843, it was virtually decided that the new commercial privileges obtained by England should be extended to all other Western maritime nations. The question was not whether the new régime should be applied or not to other nations than the British; it was what changes will be demanded by the other nations and what changes should be permitted by China. The formal decree declaring the new ports open to all nations had not yet been rendered but American merchant ships had on July 27th already begun to trade under the new régime.

The documents show that after the signing of the Treaty of Nanking, the Emperor and his advisors wished to confine the nations other than the British to the old port of Canton. The change came with the Memorials of Ilipoo and Kiying, which reached the Throne on January 17th and January 19th, 1843, respectively. Both before and after submitting the Memorials, neither Ilipoo nor Kiying got in touch with Commodore Lawrence Kearny, whose representations to Viceroy Kekung at Canton did not make much of an impression on the latter. No doubt, Kekung communicated Kearny's notes to both Ilipoo and Kiying, who were then responsible for the foreign affairs of China, but Ilipoo and Kiying used arguments which could hardly come from the notes or verbal statements of Kearny. When we read the Memorials of the two statesmen carefully, noting particularly how they piled argument on argument for the extension of equal commercial privileges to all Western maritime nations, we must assign to them the chief credit for putting at the basis of all China's foreign policy the grant of most-favored-nation treatment to all foreign nations. What Commodore Lawrence Kearny did was to put the question of equal commercial privileges for American merchants on the agenda of the Chinese government. He formally brought the question up for action. But it must be remembered that he received no reply from any responsible statesman in China that his request would be granted. Furthermore, as we have stated, his representations did not exercise much influence, if any, on Ilipoo and Kiying whose opinions decided the question. So far as the Chinese documentary evidence is concerned, there can be no other conclusion than the one given above. Any correction of the above conclusion can only be based on the documents of other governments.

The part of the English, that is, of Sir Henry Pottinger, in bringing about equal privileges for all is considerable, but of a peculiar kind. Both Ilipoo and Kiying thought that the attitude of the English was an important factor. They felt free to propose their policy of equality because Sir Henry Pottinger had declared at Nanking that if China should grant equal privileges to other nations England would not object. Ilipoo even went so far as to say that although he favored equality for all and had heard Sir Henry's declaration he must consult the latter again at Canton before he came to any agreement with America. The Emperor felt that this point must be made doubly sure. Kiying too failed to understand the grounds of British policy. If the other nations should be allowed to trade at Shanghai, Ningpo, Amoy, and Foochow, would they not divide the profits of the English merchants? In spite of this, the British are willing! Well, then should not China allow the merchants of other nations to share in British profits? All this shows the psychology of military defeat. If England's attitude had been for exclusive privileges, it would indeed place China in a difficult position, and nobody to-day

can surmise the consequences. However, the English attitude *permitted* China to adopt the policy of equality for all. Sir Henry did not urge China to adopt that policy. In fact, Kiying understood from him that England was not to negotiate on behalf of the other nations. This permissive character of the English attitude is shown clearly by Article VIII of the Supplementary Treaty of Hoomun Chai, signed on October 8th, 1843. The wording of the article in Chinese has indeed been variously given, but the text as given in *Treaties, Conventions, Etc.,* published by the Maritime Customs of China, gives the meaning as understood by Chinese statesmen of that day. The Chinese version, translated literally, reads [as follows]:*

Formerly merchants of all foreign countries traded at the one port of Canton. Last year, at Nanking, it was agreed that if the Great Emperor should permit the merchants of the various Western nations to go to Foochow, Amoy, Ningpo, and Shanghai to trade, England would not be small-minded about it and regret. But since the various nations do not differ (in treatment), if in future the Great Emperor should confer new benefits on the various nations, He should allow the English to share in them, in order to show equity. However, the English and the various nations may not, on pretense of this article, capariciously make requests, so as to keep faith.

The Supplementary Treaty of Hoomun Chai was submitted by Kiying to the Emperor for approval, who, before doing so, in accordance with Chinese constitutional practice, asked the Privy [Grand] Council to examine and report. The report was in turn submitted to the Throne on November 15th. It summarized and explained the treaty article by

* Chinese text omitted [Ed.].

article. Concerning Article VIII, the report said:[14]

The enclosed (treaty as submitted by Kiying) has an article to the effect that merchants of the various Western (foreign) nations, if permitted to trade at the various ports, (in this respect) in no way differ from the English, in future if new benefits are conferred on the various nations, the English should be permitted to share alike. Formerly, all foreign merchants were permitted to trade in Kwangtung only. Now, the permission to trade at Foochow, Amoy, Ningpo, and Shanghai, is in itself new Imperial grace, shared alike by England and the various nations. . . .

In other words, the English case for most-favored-nation treatment was presented to the Emperor as follows: what China originally granted to England alone is now granted to all other nations, therefore what China will grant in future to the other nations will also be granted to England. Both the Chinese version of Article VIII and the report on it do two things: one, the acquisition of most-favored-nation treatment by England, and two, the reason for it. The article in itself cannot be used by America or France to claim equal privileges, but it does indicate that equal treatment of all foreign nations is the policy of China.

The most-favored-nation clause in the Treaty Hoomun Chai merits a little further attention. China then knew not the existence of international law or the usual practices of Western diplomacy. China gave to the clause a common-sense interpretation, that is, equality of foreign nations in the privileges of trade in China if and when China grants such privileges. All technicalities connected with the clause were ignored by China. This view

of the matter had some advantages and also some disadvantages. It related to commerce alone; and commerce by its very nature demands ever wider and wider markets. Furthermore, the very first applications of the clause in China led to the acquisition of equal commercial privileges by the Western nations in the same ports. In other words, no exclusive or superior *commercial* rights for any one foreign nation *in any particular region of China* is consistent with the most-favored-nation clause in China's treaties. Some division of land in the ports is permissible, for evidently only one house can be built on one lot; but if any one nation should claim a series of lots so as to make conditions of trade in any one port unequal for the participating nations, such would constitute a violation of the clause. From this point of view, John Hay's open door doctrine is only a new application of old treaties. One should even go further and say that Hay's doctrine aimed at the preservation of the historic status quo. But when the early treaties were signed, nobody foresaw the question of foreign loans, especially loans for railways. The nature of investment, unlike that of commerce, tended towards spheres of interest or influence. This defect in the old treaty stipulations as well as in the Hay doctrine was, however, made good by the Washington Conference. The other disadvantages of the most-favored-nation clause were its liability to abuse by the foreign nations and its tendency towards international control.

To return to our narrative: the report of the Privy [Grand] Council on the Supplementary Treaty of Hoomun Chai was submitted, as stated above, on November 15th, 1843; it was entirely favorable; and the Emperor immediately approved it. On the same day, a Memorial concerning American and French affairs reached Peking, sent by the officials at Canton, with Kiying at their head. We give here the translation of the whole document:[15]

We previously reported to Your Majesty the general conditions of the request of America and other countries for trade according to the new regulations. Then the American chieftain Kearny had already returned to his country, there was at Canton only an Acting Consul by the name of King, supervising trade here. The French chieftain Jancigny was accused by another French chieftain Ratti-Menton of being a pretender. We could not tell the truth or falsity of the accusation; we felt it inconvenient to begin vain negotiations. Since then, our deputies have reported after inquiry that the new American chieftain Forbes had already arrived at Canton; that Ratti-Menton was the true French chieftain and that Jancigny had already gone back. All the barbarian merchants at Canton, who have been here long, upon being asked, say the same thing. We find, after re-examination on our part, that the report of the deputies is true.

Forbes and Ratti-Menton have one after another asked for an interview. Formerly, when barbarian chieftains of all countries had something to communicate to us, it was always the hong merchants who conveyed our instructions to them for guidance; personal interview was not allowed. Sentiments and conditions were often in this way misunderstood and all the barbarians resented the lack of a means of direct communication. At the present time when regulations are being changed, if we do not grant an interview and conclude things face to face, there will be left many suspicions and uncertainties. This is not the proper way of barbarian management. Therefore we told Huang En-tung and Hsien-lin to receive Forbes and Ratti-Menton first: The sentiments and words of the latter two were quite proper. At that particular time, I, Cheng Yu-chai (the Governor) had to superintend the literary examinations and I, Wen-feng (the "Hoppo") had to attend to customs matters; we, Kiying and Kekung, taking with us Huang En-tung and others, met Forbes and Ratti-Menton separately at public places outside of the city.

The American chieftain Forbes said to us that the merchants of his country, being graciously permitted to trade and pay customs at the five ports according to the new regulations, appreciated greatly this benefit conferred on men from afar; that he was sent by his national chief to reside at Canton in order to superintend (American) trade at the various ports; that he only asked the high officials of the Heavenly Dynasty to show special sympathy and to accord proper treatment; that his national chief had appointed an Envoy to proceed to Canton, to ask for credentials to go to Peking, to pay his respects to his Imperial Majesty, thus expressing his sentiments of admiration; and that conditions of ocean travel being uncertain, he (Forbes) could not tell when the Envoy would arrive. We told him that his countrymen came so far for the sole purpose of trade. Canton had long ago begun trade operations, and the other ports had also successively been declared open to trade. All matters connected therewith were settled by the Imperial Commissioner at Canton, together with the Viceroy, the Governor, and the Customs Superintendent. If he had something to say, he should communicate sincerely with them and wait for their decision. Furthermore, his country had always been respectfully obedient, and this fact had been long known by the Great Emperor, who would not fail in showing sympathy. From his country to Canton was a distance of more than seventy thousand li, and from Canton to Peking, the journeys both ways again exceeded ten thousand li. His Majesty would certainly not bear to allow the Envoy to travel such long distances in order to get to Peking and to incur such great labor and expense. If the Envoy came on account of commercial matters, he would undoubtedly be told by the Great Emperor to return (to Canton) for the negotiations; thus the difficult journey would be to no purpose. Forbes ought to stop the Envoy as soon as possible, and we would report the fact to the Emperor for him. As to the barbarian chieftain's living in China and superintending the trade at the various ports, if he could control the merchants, making them trade fairly and pay customs according to official tariff, we would naturally communicate with the authorities of the other ports, telling them to accord proper treatment, never allowing any injustice. The chieftain replied that he dared not put forth unnecessary demands; that he would report to the Envoy and prevent him from going to Peking; but that since he could not get an immediate reply from the Envoy, he could not give the final answer. If in future the Envoy should nevertheless arrive at Canton and the Imperial Commissioner should have left, he would report to the provincial officials at Canton and await their decision.

A supplementary Memorial[16] of the same day considered the question of the American Envoy's going to Peking. Kiying saw in it some intrigue on the part of the English. England had previously raised the point of appointing some representative to reside in Peking. Then in the Treaty of Hoomun Chai, England inserted the article granting most-favored-nation treatment to her. Kiying had inquired of the English whether England had not been satisfied with the commercial privileges she had obtained and England had replied in the affirmative. Therefore England was not aiming at further commercial privileges. The demand of America for sending an Envoy to Peking was evidently instigated by England so that she might claim the same privilege. Such a development was to be prevented at all costs. This was the

thought of Kiying, the most enlightened statesman in the Emperor's service of that day.

It is clear from the above document that in fact Kiying had taken upon himself [to extend] to the other nations the same commercial privileges that England had obtained. On this point, neither King nor Forbes had any difficulty. The great question raised up by America was the sending of an Envoy to Peking. On the same day, (November 15th, 1843) the Emperor gave his formal approval of the extension of commercial privileges to the other nations, although it was really only a mere formality. The Emperor at the same time told the Canton officials to prevent Caleb Cushing's going to Peking at all costs and by all means.

The significance of Cushing's mission was to put American commercial privileges, already enjoyed *de facto,* on a treaty basis. Furthermore, the Treaty of Wanghia was the first treaty signed by China with a Western maritime power, which was not preceded by a war. From this point of view, it was of considerable historical significance. But looked at as a personal diplomatic achievement for Cushing, it was but a matter of minor importance. From all the existing Chinese documents relating to Cushing's mission, we have not been able to find any evidence that China needed any persuasion for concluding a treaty. Cushing's semi-bluff that he must see the Emperor was taken seriously by the Chinese officials. The question of an audience with the Emperor aroused then and till much later difficulties which are incomprehensible not only to Westerners but to present-day Chinese. The initial difficulties that Cushing experienced were of his own creation. As soon as he declared that he might give up the intention of going to Peking, the negotiations proceeded smoothly and rapidly. The modifications which he wished to introduce into the American treaty were accepted readily by Kiying. Even his famous declaration in regard to extraterritoriality met with no protest from China because Chinese statesmen were ignorant of its import.

To sum up: the extension of equal commercial privileges to other Western nations than the British after the conclusion of the Treaty of Nanking, which extension meant in treaty phraseology the most-favored-nation treatment, was due primarily to the ideas and actions of two Chinese (or rather two Manchu) statesmen, Ilipoo and Kiying, who however, only continued the Chinese tradition of the eighteenth century. The attitude of Great Britain, as declared by Sir Henry Pottinger at Nanking, made the Chinese statesmen feel free to carry out their policy of equality. The diplomacy of Commodore Lawrence Kearny put the question of America's claim for equality on the agenda of the Chinese Government so that it was taken up and decided at that particular time, so soon after the Treaty of Nanking. And Caleb Cushing simply put the previous developments into a treaty.

Whatever modifications must be introduced into the above conclusions must be based on other than Chinese documentary evidence. As in all questions of diplomatic history, so in this one, sources of one country should be supplemented by sources of other countries, and the final truth can only be reached after a study of the sources of all countries. We claim for our conclusions no finality.

Notes

1. YWSM Series I, Bk. LXIII, p. 17
Note: In the last issue of this Review, I proposed PMDCD (Palace Museum Documents of Chinese Diplomacy) as a footnote title for the collection of documents, the title of which means *The Beginning and End of the Management of Barbarian Affairs*. Mr. T. K. Kuo, of the Metropolitan Library at Peiping, wrote me that since librarians of the world have decided on romanization of titles of serial publications in oriental languages for reference purposes, he proposed YWSM as the foot-note title for this important collection, being derived from Yi Wu Shih Mo. I accept his proposal.
The present article is entirely based on YWSM, as a thorough search of the Privy Council Records having failed to reveal any new material.
2. Ibid., p. 18
3. Ibid., p. 29
4. Ibid., p. 30
5. YWSM Series I, Bk. LXIV, p. 37
6. Ibid., pp. 38-39
7. Ibid., pp. 43-45
8. Ibid., p. 46
9. YWSM Series I, Bk. LXV, p. 27
10. YWSM Series I, Bk., LXVII, p. 3
11. Ibid., p. 8
12. YWSM Series I, Bk., LXVIII, pp. 25-26
13. Ibid., p. 29
14. YWSM Series I, BK, LXIX, p. 29
15. Ibid., pp. 34-36
16. Ibid., pp. 37-38

9. DIPLOMATIC REPRESENTATION VS. T'I-CHIH

IMMANUEL C. Y. HSÜ

The forcible imposition of foreign legations on China raises the inevitable question of whether a state, under the law of nations, has the right to compel another state into diplomatic intercourse. Students of international law and diplomacy for the most part agree that no state is bound to receive permanent envoys from other states.[1] However, R. R. Foulke, a writer on jurisprudence, while condemning compulsory diplomatic relations as "a plain act of aggression," concedes that the phrase "right of legation" in the final analysis signifies the "power of legation." When a state has developed its resources and power to a certain extent, it is bound to expand its influence and contact with other states. The necessities of commerce, civilization, and self-interest compel states into relationships with one another.[2] The question of compulsory diplomatic representation is therefore one of national power as well as one of legality. On the one hand it

From Immanuel C. Y. Hsü, *China's Entrance into the Family of Nations: The Diplomatic Phase, 1858-1880* (Harvard University Press, 1960), pp. 109-118, 236-237.

portrays an inevitable and even progressive trend in international living, and on the other it points up the ugly phenomenon of imperialism.

The "unequal" Treaties of Tientsin and Peking left an indelible mark of injustice on the Chinese mind. Nationalist writers for decades angrily denounced the Western record in China as nothing but imperialism and exploitation at the expense of the poor Chinese, but they generally refrained from attacking the British for imposing diplomatic relations on China. Rather, they assailed the stupidity and blindness of the corrupt Manchu rulers in resisting this innocuous issue while readily giving away such important sovereign rights as extraterritoriality, tariff autonomy, and the most-favored-nation treatment. Communist writers today, however, not only attack the British imposition of diplomatic residence as a naked act of imperialism, but go farther still to assail the Manchu ruling class for accepting this arrangement. Fan Wen-lan, a leading Communist historian, denounces the Treaty of Tientsin as a "sell-out of the Chinese people by the Manchu overlords."[3] Hu Sheng, a propagandist writer, portrays the acceptance of foreign envoys in Peking as an act of Manchu surrender to the imperialist world order and of affording imperialist nations a commanding position in China. "Foreign envoys who forced their way into the (Chinese) capital were not to be ordinary diplomatic representatives, but masters of China. The reason that foreign ministers insisted on the right to apply their own ceremony in the audience with the Chinese emperor was to consolidate their position in Peking."[4]

The propriety of these views is a moot point, but the fact remains that Elgin's action was imperialistic by any standard; it left behind bitter memories which have lasted even until today. When the price for resident ministers was so high, one wonders whether the gain was worth the effort. Judging by the nature of the modern world, it appears that no nation could live long in isolation, but had sooner or later to come into relationship with others. Compulsory diplomatic intercourse forced the pace of progress in international living and impeded the growth of harmonious relationships among states. It could not be justified by the principle of sovereignty, upon which the modern community of nations is founded. Thus, while diplomatic representation was an accepted practice in international law, compulsory diplomatic representation was not sanctioned by it.

Probably because of this, the London government was not too anxious to force a resident minister on China. Lord Elgin, although led by his China experiences to believe it the sovereign cure for all the troubles in China, was nevertheless conscious of its precipitant and illegal nature. Hence he was willing to tone it down in Shanghai. However, such Britons on the local scene as Lay and Parkes and other Old China Hands, who had no idea or intention of applying inter-

national law or justice to China, were intent upon humiliating the Chinese emperor by demanding exactly what he feared most: residence in the capital. Three levels of attitude toward the resident minister issue could therefore be observed on the British side: London was not too anxious about it; Elgin was willing to hold this right in abeyance; while the Old China Hands pressed for its immediate realization. Distance from the China scene and position in the British official hierarchy seemed to constitute the two overriding factors in determining attitudes.

If compulsory diplomatic representation ran counter to the principle of sovereignty in international law, it contradicted even more drastically the political and social systems of Imperial China. The expression "incompatibility with the *t'i-chih*" inevitably appeared in all Chinese rejections of foreign demands. What did it mean? Literally, *t'i* means "base," "essence," "form," or "prestige," and *chih* "institution," "system," or "polity." The combination *t'i-chih*, in a narrow sense, meant "basic institution," with the implication that its maintenance was a matter of prestige and face. The larger meaning of this term, however, went far beyond the above description to include virtually the Chinese way of life and the proper manner of doing things from the Chinese standpoint. It was in essence the Chinese counterpart of the English unwritten constitution: both being the sum total of all tangible and intangible traditions, beliefs, codes, statutes, governmental systems, and religious observances. To demand of the Chinese a change in their *t'i-chih* would be tantamount to demanding of the English a change in their common law or Magna Carta. The Western practice of exchanging resident ministers was alien to the Chinese mind and totally incompatible with the Chinese institutions of foreign intercourse as recorded in the Collected Statutes of the Great Ch'ing Empire (*Ta-Ch'ing hui-tien*). It was impossible to accede to this foreign demand without amending the *Ta-Ch'ing hui-tien,* and any such amendment would be an acknowledgement of the impropriety of the Chinese system that had proved adequate for the past two thousand years.

The underlying spirit of *t'i-chih* was the concept of *li,* or propriety, which, together with *jen,* or benevolence, formed the two basic tenets of Confucianism. *Li* in a narrow sense meant ritual ceremonies, or court formalities; in a broader sense, the whole corpus of governmental laws, regulations, social institutions, and proper human relationships.[5] The aim of *li* was to achieve social stability, and the means to such an end was to make a distinction between men. Everyone had an assigned station in this society, including the barbarians, and the highest was that of the emperor, to whom everyone must bow. To demand equality and to refuse to *kowtow* to him was a worse crime than *lèse majesté. Li* was the deepest bond betwen the members of the Confucian patriarchal society, and the censors were entrusted with its guardianship.

The international relations of the Far East were regulated by a product of *li,* the tributary system. No foreign resident ministers were ever received in the Chinese capital, and no Chinese resident ministers were ever sent abroad.[6] To demand a resident minister at the capital was to disrupt the tributary system externally and to preempt the concept of *li* internally, thereby shaking the very foundations of Chinese society. The question involved was not ritual formality, as it might appear on the surface, but the basic fabric of Chinese society and government. Therefore, the demand had to be resisted to the bitter end.

Filial piety was another cause for the strong imperial resistance to diplomatic representation. The emperor was head of the state, but not head of the imperial family. He could say: *"L'état, c'est moi;"* but not: *"La famille, c'est moi."* This was especially true during the Ch'ing dynasty, when imperial "family laws" reigned supreme. The emperor, although above state laws, was under ancestral instructions. Filial piety demanded that he preserve the institutions set up by his forefathers, and that he place his duty to the family above all else. Since childhood he had been taught to "revere Heaven and emulate ancestors" (*ching-t'ien fa-tsu*). Ancestral admonitions, edicts, decrees and practices were presented to him as sacred and inviolable, as the constitution was in a Western state. Constantly he was reminded that the dynasty was the property of the founding fathers and that the chief function of later emperors was to preserve the dynasty for their ancestors. The founding fathers of a dynasty far exceeded their offspring in greatness and foresight; for later emperors to try to change ancestral practices was to invite confusion, disorder, chaos, and even extinction of the dynasty. Thus, the basic principle of ancestral laws must be kept by later emperors at all times; only minor adjustment could be allowed after careful consideration.[7] Shackled by this kind of imperial familial system, only the extremely strong-willed emperors dared to challenge the established practices: K'ang-hsi introduced Europeans into the Chinese bureaucracy, and Yung-cheng allowed the establishment of a Russian religious mission with a language school in Peking. Lesser emperors dared not deviate but strove to preserve the established order; Hsien-feng belonged to this category, and the hand of the past lay heavily on him. The double demands of *li* and filial piety left him no alternative but to resist the foreign demand of diplomatic residence in Peking. *T'i-chih* was a two-edged sword; it served strong emperors and enslaved weak ones.

It is indeed unfortunate that in her hours of great need China had no great emperors like K'ang-hsi or Ch'ien-lung. Yet a mediocre emperor might still have been rescued from the tragedy of history had there existed a galaxy of able and perceptive advisors like the Meiji statesmen in Japan. Unhappily such was not the case with the Ch'ing empire during the Hsien-feng period. The Grand Council, which usually assisted the emperor in deciding national policies, had declined greatly in power during the latter part of Hsien-feng's reign. The emperor took personal direction of the vexatious, pressing barbarian affairs and was virtually his own foreign minister.[8] Selections and dismissals of imperial commissioners as negotiators with the barbarians were made by himself. He gave them instructions during the negotiations and read their memorials in detail with marginal or interlinear comments; occasionally he even wrote edicts himself with the vermilion pen. The proud dualistic approach to the barbarian problem was formulated by the emperor, who also took the initiative in calling the June 23 grand conference to mollify the belligerent feelings of the advocates of war. It was he also who sponsored the secret plan.

Emperor Hsien-feng's personal direction of foreign affairs could not but prove a disaster for China. His refusal of Lord Elgin's initial request for negotiations in Shanghai was a grave tactical error. It not only deprived China of a golden chance to keep the scene of negotiations, and hence barbarian pressure, far from Peking, but in fact precipitated Elgin's northern thrust. It goaded him into the demand for direct contact with the court as a punitive measure to offset the slight he had received. If the Ch'ing court had accepted his proposal, he would probably have been pleased by the Chinese cooperative response and in all likelihood would have been less belligerent and insistent upon a resident minister in the Chinese capital. Moreover, without the experience of storming the Taku Forts and occupying Tientsin with only limited forces, Elgin could not so easily have discovered China's weakness. Peking, on its part, would also have enjoyed a much stronger bargaining position when it was not under the direct threat of the enemy. Thus, hindsight reveals that insofar as China was concerned, Shanghai was by far preferable to Tientsin as a site for negotiations. Kuei-liang realized this, as he repeatedly complained to the court that the successive mismanagement of barbarian affairs in Canton and Shanghai had left him no basis for bargaining with Elgin in Tientsin. Ho Kuei-ch'ing also discovered this tactical error when he expressed regret to the court over his failure to persuade Huang Tsung-han, viceroy of Canton who succeeded Viceroy Yeh, to open negotiations with Elgin in Shanghai.[9] Later, when reflecting on the course of Chinese foreign affairs in 1867, Prince Kung, head of the Tsungli Yamen, remarked: "We should never [repeat] the old mistake of passing the responsibility from Canton to Shanghai and from Shanghai to Tientsin. When trouble began, people watched from the side and congratulated themselves that they were luckily not involved."[10] For this tactical error China paid dearly.

This tactical error was followed by the even greater strategic mistake of having no definite overall policy toward the barbarians. The emperor's vacillation between the course of war and peace was, in the opinion of both Marxist and non-Marxist writers, the basic weakness of Chinese diplomacy.[11] His inability to take a definite stand had a demoralizing effect on the nation, and while he talked in stern tones his secret hope was to make peace through appeasement. It was not until the very last moment, when Elgin was marching on Peking in 1860, that he determined to give up this wavering attitude in favor of fighting. All during the negotiations of 1858-1860 he took no definite position as to whether he would fight the barbarians to the end or accept their peace terms, but he repeatedly warned Kuei-liang of severe punishment if he failed in the management. No comprehensive, definite instructions were ever given to Kuei-liang as a guide in his negotiations; there was only piecemeal approval or disapproval of his intercession for the barbarians at each point in the negotiations. Edicts to Kuei-liang abounded in such expressions as "watch for his [Elgin's] reaction and then quickly memorialize me for instructions."[12] The imperial commissioner was consequently in an impossible position. Not infrequently, before Kuei-liang had received the anticipated instructions from the emperor, a new situation had come into existence, in which he could only put off the barbarians with vague promises while waiting for new instructions. These, when they arrived, might order him to reverse completely his stand of the previous day and the barbarians would then accuse him of bad faith. He had either to think up new excuses to muddle along, or accept the barbarian demand in order to prevent the break-down of the negotiations, and then confront the emperor with a *fait accompli* so as to force him to approve it.

It has been suggested that the emperor's vacillation stemmed from the indecision of Su-shun, president of the Li-fan-yüan and a powerful personality whom the emperor had taken into his confidence.[13] Although usually assertive and articulate in his views, Su-shun was divided on the barbarian problem, caught as he was between the opposite views of his two most trusted friends and advisors: the one, Censor Yin Keng-yün, who strongly urged war to resist foreign residence in Peking, and the other, Kuo Sung-tao, later first minister to England, who advocated peace.[14] The emperor, used to having Su-shun's advice, suffered from the lack of it during this period, and was therefore hampered in making up his mind. No doubt he was also a victim of China's traditional attitude toward the barbarians.

Historically, China never had a positive long-term policy toward the barbarians, except the vague principle of playing them off against one another known as *i-i chih-i*. She dreamed of getting nothing from them but peaceful co-existence. As a result she developed toward them only a negative attitude of watchfulness and *ad hoc* "management" when troubles arose. This traditional attitude was sufficient to cope with her border tribes but proved inadequate for the well organized new nation-states of the West. The emperor in particular and the Chinese in general suffered from this tradition.

In the larger context of social and cultural backgrounds, Sinic ethnocentrism accounted for the general xenophobia so clearly exhibited by the censors and Han-lin scholars, who formed the most articulate sector of Chinese society. While all nations exhibit pride in their culture and a certain degree of ethnocentrism, the Chinese version went far beyond a mere state of mind or sense of pride. It became, in fact, an established philosophy toward foreign countries. It has been asserted by an able modern historian that since the Southern Sung (1127-1280 A.D.) Chinese xenophobia has been intensified and transformed by Neo-Confucian philosophers into a national policy of self-defense. The realization of China's inability to cope with constant foreign incursions prompted them to develop a defensive dogma, which asserted that "national security could only be found in isolation, and stipulated (that) whoever wished to enter into relations with China must do so as China's vassal, acknowledging the supremacy of the Chinese emperor and obeying his commands, thus ruling out all possibility of international intercourse on terms of equality."[15]

Although Ch'ing intellectual trends on the whole rejected metaphysical Neo-Confucianism,[16] this defensive dogma remained embedded deep in the minds of the literati. In fact, anti-foreignism was sensitized by the alien rule of the Manchus. The Chinese became more appreciative of their culture and traditions, and the extensive research on ancient classical texts (*k'ao-cheng hsüeh*) reflected their ardent interest in their cultural past. They were ever ready to defend their way of life against foreign infiltration. The Manchu overloards won Chinese cooperation by identifying the dynastic interest with the Confucian order. But Western nations made no such commitment. Their demands for diplomatic residence and inland trade exceeded the bounds of propriety, challenged the established order, and threatened the basic Three Bonds and Five Relationships of the Confucian society. It was only natural that the censors and Hanlin scholars, whose duty it was to safeguard social order and the principle of *li*, should react violently against foreign contravention of the Chinese way of life and time-tested institutions. Here we discern the delicate difference between Chinese and Manchu motives in resisting the foreign challenge; the Chinese literati were basically against foreign pollution of their culture in order to preserve the old way of life; the Manchu officials were against the foreign threat to the dynasty in order to preserve their political interest. But this does not mean that the Chinese did not care at all for the dynasty or that the Manchus did not care for the Chinese way of life. The Chinese scholar-official class, inextricably intertwined with the government bureaucracy, did have a vital interest in the continuance of the Manchu dynasty. It would be hard to believe that men like T'an T'ing-hsiang and Ho Kuei-ch'ing, both viceroys, did not have a vested interest in the existing political order. Among the Chinese themselves, those who were in the government were probably more identified with the dynastic interest than the literati who were not in the government. The Manchu overlords, on the other hand, having committed themselves to the Confucian order, also wanted to maintain the Chinese culture which, though alien to them, was infinitely preferable to Western ways. Yet these considerations were far less *basic* than culturalism for the Chinese and dynastic interest for the Manchus. However, when threatened by the more fundamental problem of immediate extinction, the Manchus and the Chinese, regardless of the differences in their ethnic backgrounds, alike gave in to foreign pressure. As we have seen, Kuei-liang, a Manchu, Hua-sha-na, a Mongol, and T'an T'ing-hsiang and Ho Kuei-ch'ing, both Chinese, all advocated peace in order to avert a barbarian march on Peking.

While the alien rule served as a stimulus to Chinese ethnocentrism, it was also a constant reminder to the Manchu rulers of their insecure position. The maintenance of dignity before the Chinese subjects was essential to effective control of their teeming millions; any concession to foreign demands under the threat of force was a blatant admission of weakness. It lowered the Chinese esteem for the Manchu ruling class and exposed its inability to defend the established order. This was tantamount to an invitation to Chinese rebellion, which certainly could not be allowed to happen. At a time when Tseng Kuo-fan and Chinese scholars rallied under the slogan of preserving the traditional order to save the almost-lost imperialist cause from the Taipings, what alternative did the Manchu rulers have but to do their part in upholding the old order? They had to reject foreign demands on the grounds of "incompatibility with the established institutions."

Moreover, domestic disorder was believed to be directly or indirectly related to external trouble. The Manchus, having entered China themselves when the Ming was troubled by internal disorder, were well aware of the lurking dangers from the Taipings within and the barbarians without. Only by reasserting the Confucian moral order could they renew their spiritual strength, and this order could not coexist with the foreign demands for residence in Peking, which must therefore be resisted to the bitter end. On the other hand, commercial interests and trade profits were trivial matters of far less importance than the basic problems of ceremony and dignity, and could therefore be sacrificed more easily under the euphemistic pretext of "benev-

olence toward men from afar." Hence the secret plan of 1858.

Thus a multitude of factors—institutions, filial piety, imperial familial law, Neo-Confucian ethnocentrism, Chinese culturalism, and the alien Manchu rule—were operating on the Chinese scene during the 1858-1860 negotiations. Only by taking them into account can one understand why Peking resisted so stubbornly what seemed to be a more innocuous issue, diplomatic representation.

The establishment of foreign legations in Peking signified the victory of the expanding Western family of nations in the East. China was brought half-way into this family. Her complete entrance into it was achieved after she developed a due regard for international law as the basis of state relationships and established her legations in foreign nations in the 1870's.

Notes

[For complete titles of works cited, see the editor's *China's Entrance into the Family of Nations: The Diplomatic Phase, 1858-1880,* in the Bibliography.]

1. Oppenheim, I, 700.

2. R. R. Foulke, *A Treatise on International Law* (Philadelphia, 1920), I, 184-185.

3. Fan Wen-lan, I, 197.

4. Hu Sheng, *Ti-kuo chu-i yü Chung-kuo cheng-chih* (Imperialism and Chinese politics; Peking, 1952), p. 47.

5. Hsiao Kung-ch'üan, I, 75 and 77.

6. On the tributary system, see J. K. Fairbank and S. Y. Teng, "On the Ch'ing Tributary System," *HJAS,* 6.2:135-246 (June 1941).

7. Ch'en Ch'iu, "Wu-hsü cheng-pien shih fan-pien-fa jen-wu chih cheng-chih ssu-hsiang" (Political thought of anti-reformers during the coup d'état of 1898), *Yen-ching hsü-pao* ("Yenching Journal of Chinese Studies"), 25:88 (June 1939); see also *Ch'ing-kung shih-lüeh* (Historical sketches of the Ch'ing palaces), p. 1. Upon the death of the Emperor Hsien-feng, his biographer praised him for "perfect reverence and emulation of his ancestors." See *CSL,* 356:19b-20.

8. Swisher, p. 13.

9. *IWSM*, 29:32b, received at court Aug. 2, 1858.

10. *IWSM*, Tung-chih period, 50:26.

11. Hua Kang, *Chung-hua min-tsu chieh-fang yün-tung-shih* (A history of the Chinese people's liberation movement; Shanghai, 1951), pp. 264-265.

12. *CSL*, 314:8a-b, 322:27b.

13. Wu Hsiang-hsiang, *Wan-Ch'ing kung-t'ing shih-chi* (Veritable accounts of the palaces in the late Ch'ing; Taipei, 1952), p. 15; Lo Tun-yung, "Ping-tui sui-pi" (Random notes after the guests are gone), *Yung-yen* ("The Justice"; Tientsin), 2.5:1.

14. Wu Hsiang-hsiang, p. 15.

15. T. F. Tsiang, "China and European Expansion," *Politica*, 2.5:3 (March 1936).

16. Ch'ing intellectual activities are discussed in Liang Ch'i-ch'ao, *Ch'ing-tai hsüeh-shu kai-lun* (A general survey of Ch'ing intellectual trends; Shanghai, 1921). This work has been translated by Immanuel C. Y. Hsü under the title *Intellectual Trends in the Ch'ing Period* (Cambridge, Mass., 1959).

10. The Imperial Chinese Tradition

in the Modern World

IMMANUEL C. Y. HSÜ

Fifteen years elapsed after the establishment of foreign legations in Peking before China sent diplomatic missions abroad. Why did she delay so long? The stock explanation given by the mandarins was the unavailability of suitable men and concern over the expenses involved. Yet the facts belied these explanations. Early envoys were readily chosen from the existing officialdom without special training in foreign affairs, and the early legation funds far exceeded the expenditures. The mandarin's explanations could only be accepted as excuses for inaction.

From Immanuel C. Y. Hsü, *China's Entrance into the Family of Nations: The Diplomatic Phase, 1858-1880* (Harvard University Press, 1960), pp. 199-210, 246-47. Copyright 1960 by the President and Fellows of Harvard College. Reprinted by permission.

What they really meant was that suitable men were not willing to be envoys, and the court was not willing to spend money in that way. The disinclination to accept diplomacy as a normal function of the state was rooted in Chinese institution and psychology. While closely interrelated, these two aspects may be usefully distinguished. The institutional barrier was the *t'i-chih*, which has been discussed in a previous chapter; the psychological barrier is studied here.

A. THE IDEOLOGICAL OPPOSITION TO LEGATIONS ABROAD

A state seldom initiates a new policy until it has recognized its necessity. It took the mandarins some fifteen years to appreciate the benefit of diplomatic representation abroad. This process involved a fundamental psychological transformation which by its very nature was slow and gradual. Several stages can be observed. The initial reaction to the idea of diplomatic representation was rejection, and the recommendations of Hart and Wade in 1865-1866 were regarded by the mandarins as veiled threats. The success of the Burlingame mission could not have failed to impress them with the usefulness of foreign missions, and the Formosa Incident of 1874 literally shocked the mandarins into realizing the stupidity of further delay. They came to see that diplomatic representation abroad would benefit China more than anyone else, and Wade's demand for a mission of apology in 1875 set off the long delayed move and brought China out of her shell. That this reorientation was so long delayed is attributable to the unfavorable intellectual milieu in which it was taking place.

The intellectual world of Imperial China was dominated by the literati, composed largely of censors, courtiers, writers, and gentry. Their utterances constituted "public opinion," which even the court dared not ignore. This type of "public opinion" was very different from that of the West. It was not *vox populi*, but the prevailing opinion of the educated few who were the articulate section of the society. It was not expressed through newspapers or public speaking, but through such media as official impeachments, social gatherings, poems, folk songs, scrolls, ballads, and gossip. In Chinese it is known as the *ch-ing-i*, meaning roughly "pure discussion" or "gossipy criticism," and implying an irresponsible attitude on the part of the critics. While it is hard to describe precisely this fluid term *ch'ing-i*, what eludes definition need not pass understanding. For the sake of simplicity, *ch'ing-i* may well be accepted as the Chinese counterpart of Western public opinion.

Ch'ing-i in the late Ch'ing period was molded by three main forces: the noisy accusations of the censors, the murmured gossip in the court, and the casual expressions of the literati. The censors were particularly vociferous. Known as the *yen-kuan,* or speech officials, they were first appointed by the Emperor Wu of the Liang dynasty (502-557 A.D.). During the T'ang (618-907) they were merely subordinates of the prime minister, but during the Sung they were promoted and became independent officials. In the wake of foreign incursions during the Southern Sung (1127-1280) they became unusually assertive and led the attacks on the prime ministers for having failed to take revenge on the enemy. Gradually they acquired a reputation as leaders of public sentiment. During the Ming and Ch'ing (1368-1911) they were made the "eyes and ears" of the court in order to ferret out secret opposition, and were given the privilege of attacking, impeaching, criticizing, or praising a man or a policy, openly or secretly as they saw fit, under no pain of penalty. Even high officials dreaded them. Robert Hart, in his memorandum of 1865 on modernization, sarcastically remarked that the censors were "the wrong eyes and ears for the throne, men who contributed to the corruption of officials and did not hear the people's anger."[1]

The Ch'ing censorate, headquarters of die-hards and ultra-conservatives, consisted of two Left Grand Censors, four Left Associate Censors and a large number of departmental and circuit censors.[2] Right Grand Censor was usually a brevet title to be conferred on worthy and meritorious viceroys and governors. The censors' institutional functions were to detect derelictions of duty by any official and to keep the emperor informed on all important matters. Although they were not supposed to concern themselves with governmental policies, yet through their watchful supervision of the execution of such policies and their constant readiness to impeach the officials in charge, they actually exerted a considerable influence on both the administration of current policies and the formulation of future ones. Moreover, they considered themselves loyal defenders of the Chinese heritage and jealous guardians of the principle of *li,* which was "the unwritten constitution of the state and the moral code of society."[3] Any un-Chinese activity was condemned by them as traitorous to the national tradition and unfilial to the ancestors. They freely described the actions of members of the Tsungli Yamen, advocates of Westernization, and envoys to the West, in such offensive terms as "ingratiating themselves with foreigners," "serving the barbarians," or "having clandestine relations with the enemy."[4] Their fierce accusations usually produced quick results. A typical example was the destruction of Kuo Sung-tao's diary.

In parallel existence with the censorate were the conservative courtiers, the Hanlin scholars, and the headstrong literati. Steeped in tradition and secure in vested interests, they spent their days in political maneuvering or reading old books, and their nights in idyllic idleness or metaphysical contemplation. Externally they advocated a get-tough policy toward foreigners, and internally they adopted an attitude of *quieta non movere,* opposing any changes that threatened their comfortable and privileged position. They announced that they had heard of transforming the barbarians by the Chinese way of life, but never of changing the Chinese with barbarian ways. Texts from the classics were carefully chosen to disarm opposition, and the failures of Shang Yang and Wang An-shih were often cited as proofs of the evils of reform. Boldly they dared anyone to try to change China; those who accepted their challenge were quickly condemned as "sinners against the Confucian heritage."[5] Kuo Sung-tao, for one, was ruined by their defamatory campaign against him. They ridiculed him for having left his fatherland to serve the foreign devils, and his diary was derided by the great Hunanese scholar Wang K'ai-yün as a product of "foreign poison."[6] Wang also offered a piece of advice to the Marquis Tseng in 1877 on foreign affairs: "To advocate war is good for you both from the private and public standpoints."[7]

The literati had extensive roots in both the metropolis and the countryside. Local gentry usually echoed their views, and opportunists and social climbers, craving fame at all costs, were anxious to be associated with them. They also found a ready following in disgruntled men who had themselves failed to find positions in foreign affairs and, out of jealousy, attacked those who had succeeded.[8] The censors, courtiers, literati, gentry, opportunists, and petty men together created a powerful anti-foreign atmosphere, which was most unfavorable to the growth of progressive ideas and novel undertakings. Their anti-foreignism, in the view of Communist writers today, did not stem from a realization of the dangers of foreign imperialism, but from a feeling of insecurity about their privileged position in a society under the disrupting influence of foreign forces.[9]

These anti-foreign elements successfully created the impression that foreign affairs was a dangerous subject and to associate with it was to betray one's decency. When Grand Secretary Yen Ching-ming was asked, "Who among men of rectitude today excel in foreign affairs?", he snapped back: "Do men of rectitude care to engage in foreign affairs?"[10] To serve as an envoy was described by the obscurantists as particularly degrading because it implied begging peace from barbarian rulers. No man would volunteer to exile himself to a far, outlandish nation. Li Hung-chang continually declined Yamen's requests for recommendations of competent men to serve as envoys, mainly because he was afraid of offending the men he thus recommended. He wrote: "Men all seek after governmental positions, but not envoyships. I am afraid that those who are willing to be envoys are not too reliable."[11] Liu Hsi-hung told Li: "The envoy of today is the hostage of the past."[12] Even a liberal like Kuo Sung-tao could not help conceding: "Being an envoy abroad is looked down upon by men today. It is what people do not care to be."[13]

A general impression prevailed over the nation that to be an envoy was even worse than to be banished, for it meant a term of exile in a foreign land plus a dark future after returning to China. People recalled that one of Burlingame's associates, Chih-kang, spent his life on the frontier of Mongolia, and the other, Sun Chia-ku, in an obscure part of West China.[14] Such was the misfortune of the early envoys that no man could think of foreign missions without a shudder; all wanted to avoid this fate. Even Kuo Sung-tao did not accept his foreign assignment willingly.

The principal targets of the censors and literati were the advocates of Westernization, better known as the *yang-wu* group. This group adopted "foreign matters" not out of love or admiration but out of a cold realization that it was the only way to survive. They understood, if the majority of the literati, censors, and Hanlin scholars did not, that the traditional view of foreign affairs must be rectified in the light of current circumstances and necessities. Alone in the sprawling hierarchy of the state, they saw in international living a way to survival in the new world that had been so rudely thrust upon China recently. In this they were at once very un-Confucian and very Confucian: un-Confucian in their willingness to adapt themselves to foreign ways, Confucian in their practical approach to the facts of life. Progressives by the standards of their time, they have been scorned in recent decades by many as forerunners of the compradores. Communist writers take the stand that these *yang-wu* men did not really want to create a progressive force in China but wanted merely to maintain the old, decadent social order with foreign help.[15]

The die-hard obscurantists spared no one. A man of Tseng Kuo-fan's stature enjoyed no exemption. His impartial report on the Tientsin Massacre in 1870 was vehemently attacked by the old guard and young politicians, some of whom made high-flown attacks in order to hurl themselves into national prominence overnight. The thought of their selfishness and misguidance of state affairs drove Tseng into "bitter cries and gushing tears." Unable to withstand the powerful force of "public opinion," he bowed out of the Tientsin scene.

Li Hung-chang succeeded Tseng as viceroy of Chihli. As the central spirit of the modernization program, he was branded by the obscurantists as a traitor to traditionalism. Li in return ridiculed them as blind "bookworms," who wanted to cure all diseases with the same ancient prescription. He proudly announced:

"Now is the right time to discuss 'foreign matters.' People fear and are loath to talk about them. When incidents occur, they become either lost or rash, and it is seldom that they do not misguide the nation. It may be all right for you people not to take an interest in [foreign matters], but if I too do not talk about them, by what method is the ship of state to be steered?"[16]

The one that suffered most at the hands of the censors and literati was also the one that criticized them the most. Kuo Sung-tao declared publicly that his study of history had revealed the amazing fact that censors were more harmful than beneficial to the state.[17] The institution of censors was not bad in itself, he stated, but when the censors became a privileged class after the Southern Sung and meddled in politics in attempts to influence national policies, they became a nuisance. "The trouble is not censors *per se*," he wrote, "but rather their unbridled interference in things outside their jurisdiction."[18] In the Southern Sung, when barbarian incursions were frequent, the generals and soldiers urged war against foreign tribes to efface the national humiliation, but during the Ming period, when the generals had become timid and dared not fight, the censors forced them into war. Thereafter the censors took on the new role of voicing "public opinion" and attempted to impose their will on policy makers. They had become so powerful that opportunists flocked to them as a sure way to win imperial attention and subsequent appointment. The court was thus led into the belief that it had the support of the public, when in fact the "support" consisted merely of empty arguments and verbal assurances. Kuo insisted that good government was impossible with these men in power.[19]

Caught between the horns of die-hard obscurantists and progressive modernizers was the court, which, in the last analysis, was the Empress Dowager Tz'u-hsi herself. Her miserable flight to Jehol in 1860 in the face of the advancing enemy under Lord Elgin was too painful an experience to forget. No less violently antiforeign at heart than the censors and the literati, the Dowager nevertheless was bold enough to side with the progressive *yang-wu* group in many respects, as the price for building up defenses with which to erase the humiliation of 1860. In aim, she was at one with the conservatives. In method, she was with the modernizers.

The Dowager's political acumen was highest when she played the intricate game of the balance of weakness in domestic politics. She was so deeply apprehensive of things Western that she secretly feared the *yang-wu* advocates, especially when they were Chinese and not Manchu. Her attitude toward the powerful Li Hung-chang is a good case in point. She respected Li's unusual abilities as she feared his vast powers. Yet she was too clever to dismiss a man who had behind him a Huai army, a Peiyang navy, and a coterie of enterprising compradores and able foreign advisers.[20] He must be humored by high positions but kept in check by some force. A balancing force was found in the violent accusations of the censors and the literati. The meaninglessness of the censors' hue and cry was only too obvious, yet she secretly fostered it, under the appealing pretexts of "opening the way for opinions" and "getting the benefits of collective thinking," thus creating a powerful force to checkmate the progressive *yang-wu* group. She dignified the nonsense of the old guard as "pure discussion" and "public opinion." In 1874 Li urged the construction of a railway, running from north to south, to facilitate transportation. Prince Kung approved the plan but hesitated to sponsor it. "I repeatedly requested him to speak to the two Dowagers at an opportune moment," Li wrote, "he said that even the two Dowagers could not decide upon such an important policy. Henceforth, I shut my mouth and spoke no more."[21] Undoubtedly the Dowager Tz'u-hsi pretended that she had to listen to the "public opinion" of the literati; it was her ingenious device to restrict Li's aggrandizement. Years later, when visiting Bismarck in Germany, Li asked him for the secrets of statesmanship, to which Bismarck replied that the first essential was to win control over the sovereign, but if the sovereign was a woman, it would be a different matter.[22] Li accepted the implication of the statement in deep silence.

By playing both sides the Dowager cleverly established a delicate balance, taking constant precaution that it not be tipped. She allowed Wo-jen and his associates to remain in high posts, despite their vicious attack on Western learning, while at the same time she allowed Prince Kung to launch the self-strengthening movement and expand the T'ung-wen kuan. When a magistrate of an independent department, Yang T'ing-hsi, suggested the abolition of the T'ung-wen kuan as a way to avert natural calamity, she reprimanded him for "murmuring a few thousand words" of nonsense.[23] On the other hand she acceded to the popular demand for the destruction of Kuo Sung tao's diary.

The subject of diplomatic missions abroad was personally unpleasant to the Dowager, who understood the functions of envoys only from the past history of China. When China was strong, her envoys spread the prestige of the Son of Heaven to distant lands; when China was weak, they begged peace from foreign tribes. During the 1860's and 1870's China was undoubtedly weak. To send envoys would be humiliating, and to be forced to send them was even worse. Time and again she procrastinated, hoping to put off the evil day by delaying its coming. High officials joined her in the feeling that envoys should not be sent until China was relatively strong. Li Hung-chang felt it unwise to send envoys without an accompanying naval force, impressed as he was with the close coordination between the Western diplomats and their gunboats.[24] Pride and vanity thus were also deterrents.

In conclusion, one cannot escape the impression that under the secret patronage of the court an anti-foreign, anti-modernizing atmosphere prevailed over the nation. The feeble efforts of the *yang-wu* men met opposition everywhere, and the idea of permanent legations abroad lacked a fertile soil in which to grow. The Dowager feared for the future, and the future confirmed her fear. Ironically, the first permanent Chinese legation abroad had its origin in a mission of apology.

B. TRADITION WITHIN CHANGE: CHINA AMONG THE NATIONS

China had no sooner firmly established her legations in the Western world than she was invited to participate in the sixth meeting of the Association for the Reform and Codification of the Law of Nations in 1878. This association, founded in Brussels in 1873, had exhibited a strong interest in extending international law to the Far East during its fourth and fifth meetings in 1876 and 1877, and a motion had been passed to invite China and Japan to participate in its future meetings. Kuo Sung-tao, China's first minister to England, accepted the invitation on China's behalf, and Ueno Kagenori, Japanese minister in London, accepted for his government. The presence of the two Far Eastern representatives lent much interest and color to the meeting of 1878, and the honorary international secretary of the association enthusiastically characterized their attendance as "a novel feature in the history of the Association and, indeed, in the history of European Congresses."[25] Kuo, on his part, paid high tribute to the association for its efforts to improve the law of nations "for the benefit of all governments and peoples." Politely he explained that although his country had not completely subscribed to the rules of international law because of her different cultural and political background, he was "very desirous of attaining a knowledge of the science, in the hope that it will be beneficial to my country."[26] In appreciation of China's new membership, the association elected Kuo honorary vice-president, and his name, for some mysterious reason, remained in every issue of the association's *Report* until 1922, some forty-five years after his retirement from his London post and some thirty-five years after his death!

Kuo's successor in London, the famous Marquis Tseng Chi-tse, was also elected to the same honorary post in the association. Versatile and familiar with Western diplomacy, while retaining the fundamental Confucian touch, Tseng attempted to blend the requirements of international law with the established Chinese practices of foreign intercourse. In a conversation with an English international jurist in 1879 he made it clear that in a country like China, where traditions and old standards abounded, time was needed to assimilate new ideas and values. Nonetheless, despite disagreements and divergent views on international law

among Western writers themselves, which confounded its ready understanding by China, she had striven to make frequent references to it in her dealing with foreign powers. China was willing to take into consideration the Western methods of international relations without totally and unconditionally surrendering her own traditional practices, some of which, like the treatment of tributary states, Tseng pointed out, were far more benevolent than Western colonial practices.[27]

By 1880 China's international position had reached a point where she maintained legations in most of the leading Western states and Japan, kept membership in the leading international law association, and indicated her willingness to learn more about the new science of international law and make reference to it in conducting her foreign relations. So inextricably was she drawn into the stream of world affairs that it was a foregone conclusion that the age of her universal empire was far spent and the day of nation-statehood was at hand. Through increased contact with the outside world the statesmen of the T'ung-chih and Kuang-hsü periods discovered the stark fact that in a world of contending states, where social Darwinism was a dominant force, the only way to survive was to struggle for survival like anyone else. A universal state had no place in a family of nation-states. The myth of universal overlordship became untenable, especially when foreign diplomats in Peking did not *kowtow* to the T'ung-chih Emperor during the audience of 1873, and when China had to send missions of apology to France and Britain in 1870 and 1876 to ward off foreign punitive expeditions. The Son of Heaven had to descend from the apex of the Confucian world order to bow to foreign countries not one-tenth the size of China. Was there any doubt that the universal state was a sweet dream of yesteryear, a glory of the past, and a luxury that China could no longer afford? Adjustment had to be made to metamorphose the Confucian universal empire into a modern nationstate in order to survive in the new world.

To be sure, the metamorphosis was long, hard, and painful. Every step in the process was a struggle, and in the final analysis, an intellectual one. Strangely enough, the diplomatic phase of the battle was among the first to be won. As early as 1864, in a preface to W. A. P. Martin's translation of Wheaton, Chang Ssu-kuei, a member of the Tsungli Yamen and later associate envoy to Japan, risked the accusation of "heresy" by comparing the leading Western states—England, France, Russia, the United States, Austria, Prussia, and Italy—to the seven contending nations of the Warring States Period in ancient China. The comparison amounted to a brave admission of the existence of strong and independent states beyond China; it was in fact an indirect disavowal of the Chinese claim to universal overlordship.

There was an increasing sense of urgency among the more enlightened elements in Confucian officialdom with respect to China's greatly changed position vis-à-vis the rest of the world. Li Hung-chang cogently told his countrymen that China's precarious status was such as she had never known in the past three thousand years. His powerful advocacy of diplomatic representation abroad had a decisive effect on the court, and once the missions were sent, increased understanding of the outside world followed. From Kuo Sung-tao came the daring revelation that the West had a civilization of two thousand years, and from the Marquis Tseng came the open admission that the modern Western nations were

truly different from the historical barbarian tribes that had disturbed China from time to time. There was no mistake that the fictitious belief of China's unrivalled excellence and universal overlordship was disintegrating into the oblivion of history.

By 1880 China had realistically, if also painfully, assumed her place in the world community of nations. Forty years had elapsed since the Opium War and the opening of China, and some twenty years had passed since the appearance of the foreign diplomatic corps in Peking. Yet the diplomatic phase of China's response to the Western challenge, slow as it was, was much faster than many of the other phases. It came about in the wake of military modernization and was among the first measures adopted in the self-strengthening movement, probably because of its immediately discernible beneficial effects on China. A modernized foreign service enabled China not only to get along better with foreign diplomats, but also to bypass them when they proved headstrong and unyielding. With her own legations abroad, China could present her views directly to the foreign governments, which, far away from the China scene and hence less likely to be excited over local occurrences, could receive Chinese representations with broader perspective and greater objectivity. They were therefore more prone to peaceful settlement of disputes than their overseas servants.

The awareness of these tangible advantages to be gained from entering the Western world, added to the fact that such an awareness could be translated into reality by a few powerful officials from above without the support of the masses, largely accounted for the early completion of the diplomatic metamorphosis. Nationalism was not involved in the process. But after China's entrance into the family of nations, her new position gave rise to a new sense of national entity; hence it helped to stimulate the growth of nationalism in the long run.

When China accepted the fact that it was more profitable to act like a nation-state than a universal empire, she in fact subscribed to what had been the Western view since before the Opium War. The Western nations had always approached China as an incipient nation-state, and treaties with her were all drawn up on a bilateral nation-to-nation basis.[28] To the Westerner it was only a matter of time until China would accept this fact and emerge as a modern sovereign state in the family of nations. This wish was realized around 1880. The world community was enriched by the addition of the hitherto unaccounted one-fifth humanity, and China stood to gain new experiences and an enlarged world view from international living. Chinese history began to merge with world history.

But it was only through necessity, not free choice, that China had entered the world community. The old dream of universal empire, the glory of being the Middle Kingdom in East Asia, and the prestige of the tributary system still lingered in the Chinese mind, and their residual effects were clearly discernible. The nostalgia for the past generated a burning hope and even a strong conviction that some day China would again become strong and reassert her rightful place under the sun. If universal Confucianism could not attain such an objective, perhaps some other system could. A century of trial and error, and decades of groping in the dark led to the discovery that international communism, which envisages an ultimate universal classless society, might be the new vehicle for the fulfillment of the old dream. With the rise of Communist China as the most

powerful nation in East Asia, with its growing influence in northern Korea, northern Vietnam and other peripheral states, and with the constant flow of peace delegations to Peking from East European and Asian states, one wonders whether the "universal" state and the tributary system of the past have not been revived in a modern form.

Notes

[For complete titles of works cited, see the editor's *China's Entrance into the Family of Nations: The Diplomatic Phase, 1858-1880,* in the Bibliography.]

1. Mary Wright, p. 264.
2. Edgar C. Tang, "The Censorial Institution in China, 1644-1911," Ph.D. thesis (Harvard, 1932), pp. 35, 69-72.
3. *Ibid.,* pp. 82-83.
4. Ch'en T'i-ch'iang, p. 26.
5. Wang Chih-ch'un, 19:6.
6. Wang K'ai-yün, 6:18.
7. *Ibid.,* 6:18.
8. Tseng Chi-tse, Series IV, "Diary," 1:15b.
9. Hu Sheng, pp. 61-63.
10. Quoted in Ch'en Kung-lu, p. 255.
11. Li Hung-chang, *Ch'üan-chi,* II, 16:2.
12. *Ibid.,* III, 8:6b.
13. Ch'en Kung-lu, pp. 252-253.
14. *THHL,* 1:7; Martin, *Cycle,* p. 379.
15. Hu Sheng, p. 63.
16. Li Hung-chang, *Ch'üan-chi,* II, 16:30a-b; I, 24:2b.
17. *San-hsing-shih shu-tu* (Correspondence of the three envoys; Shanghai, 1910), 1:8, 1:52.
18. Kuo Sung-tao, *Yang-chih,* I, 12:42.
19. *Ibid.,* 12:44a-b; 12:46.
20. Fan Wen-lan, p. 257.
21. Li Hung-chang, *Ch'üan-chi,* II, 17:13.
22. Liang Ch'i-ch'ao, "Chung-kuo ssu-shih-nien ta-shih-chi" (Major events in China during the last forty years), in *Yin-ping-shih ho-chih* (Collected works of the Ice-drinker's Study), *Chuan-chi* (Monographs), No. 3, p. 3.
23. *CSL,* T'ung-chih period, 204:30b.
24. Li Hung-chang, *Ch'üan-chi,* III, 4:24b.
25. *Reports of Sixth Annual Conference, 1878* (Association for the Reform and Codification of the Law of Nations), Preface.
26. *Ibid.,* p. 40.
27. Tseng chi-tse, Series IV, "Diary," 2:22b-23.
28. Fairbank, "Synarchy under the Treaties," p. 224.

II. THE TAIPING REVOLUTION

11. THE SETTING OF THE REBELLION

FRANZ MICHAEL

One may well say that modern Chinese history begins with the Taiping Rebellion. The great tradition of China's two thousand years of imperial history came to an end in the political, social, and intellectual turmoil that prevailed in Chinese affairs from the latter half of the last century to the Revolution of 1911. In this period of crisis the first major break with the past was brought on in the middle of the nineteenth century by the Taiping Rebellion, a vast uprising that, though unsuccessful in the end, contained, in the beliefs it propagated and the organization it established, elements so alien to China's tradition that they indicate to us in retrospect the first internal manifestation of the effect of an outer and inner crisis in Chinese traditional society.

Even the name given the rebellious movement by its leaders had its special appeal in the expression of a new slogan that differed basically from the dynastic titles assumed by the founders of new dynasties in the past. *T'aip'ing T'ien-kuo,* "The Heavenly Kingdom of Great Peace," as it is usually translated, was to

From Franz Michael, *The Taiping Rebellion, History and Documents* (University of Washington Press, Seattle, 1966), pp. 3-20. Reprinted by permission. The author is professor of Chinese history at George Washington University.

be a kingdom that secured a new kind of "peace"—the everlasting fulfillment of God's will on earth, and—in an implied meaning of the word "Taiping"—of justice and equality for all.[1]

An extraordinary combination of individual and general factors characterizes the Taiping Rebellion and sets it off from the past: a fanatical religious faith derived from Christianity, which clashed with traditional Chinese culture; a system that combined primitive equality of the members of a revolutionary sect supported by a common treasury with the absolute power of a ruthless, self-indulgent leadership, and that combined equality and separation of the sexes and complete chastity among the followers with the possession of large harems by the rulers; a leadership headed by a man who was clearly mentally ill and made up of others who used crude religious hoaxes to assert authority—these were new and most unusual characteristics that demonstrated how different the Taipings were from all earlier rebels in Chinese history. If to these special phenomena are added the drama of the shifting fortunes of battle in a major civil war, the savage infighting among the rebel leaders, and the vast destruction and loss of life caused by fourteen years of fighting, the Taiping Rebellion becomes a spectacle of new extremes in China and one of the most extraordinary stories of all history.

If the Taiping Rebellion was a new beginning in Chinese history, it arose in a setting that still contained the familiar elements characteristic of periods of dynastic decline and rebellious uprisings in the past. Grave corruption in government, heavy overtaxation of the farmers, high rent, desertion of the land by the peasants, the increase of a roaming population, banditry and general insecurity, the increasing importance of secret societies, the formation of local self-defense units that took matters into their own hands, and frequent small-scale warfare which led to uprisings against goverment authority—these had been the conditions for dynastic changes by rebellion or foreign conquest throughout imperial history. These same conditions existed under the Ch'ing dynasty in the first part of the nineteenth century, conditions that boded well for the success of any leader who could use them to defeat the government forces and re-establish the political order under a new dynasty.

While the setting was similar to that of earlier rebellions, the Taiping Rebellion itself and its goal were basically different from former dynastic upheavals. The Taipings attacked not only the ruling dynasty—they attacked the traditional social order itself. And this wider attack gave their rebellion a character totally different from that of rebellious movements of the past.

It had been the strength of the Chinese system that its periods of crisis affected the political order only. After the fall of a dynasty and a shorter or longer period of crisis in the battle of contending leaders, a new political beginning was made under a new dynastic rule;

but the social system remained essentially intact throughout. The strength and stability of the Chinese social order was indeed demonstrated by its ability to survive not only the fall of dynasties but even prolonged political disorder.

This system was based on the acceptance of Confucian social and political beliefs, which sanctioned dynastic authority and under which the educated elite, the gentry, who preserved and handed down these beliefs, played a dual role as officials of the government and as the leading stratum of society. Whatever rebel leader from within or military conqueror from without tried in periods of chaos to establish a new dynasty, he needed the services of the educated Chinese gentry to re-establish a functioning administrative system and maintain control over society.

The survival of the social system through the many political crises of Chinese past imperial history and the ever continued success in the rebuilding of the political structure in this traditional Chinese society testify to the strength and relative autonomy of the social order, which the dynastic state affected only to a limited degree. Imperial administration was always limited in scope, just as the government's administrative staff was limited in number. The educated, the gentry, held a monopoly on office, but most of them did not serve the state. Instead of becoming government officials, they remained at home in their own districts and provinces where, on their own responsibility and not under any orders or instructions from the government, they carried on functions of public service that took the place of government administration.[2] Arbitration of conflicts, management of public works, the handling of public welfare problems, the education of the next generation of gentry, these were among the services rendered by that large majority of the gentry who did not hold official position. These services, expected from the gentry as an obligation connected with their privileged positions in society, were also the main source of income for most of them.[3] The government approved of and counted on these services of the gentry, which were not only a necessary counterpart to the administrative actions of the officials but were also in some cases connected with them. The government officials handled the taxes but received some assistance from the gentry in collecting them and sometimes levied additional taxes to reimburse the gentry for some of its services. The government reserved to itself all military authority but in emergencies it tolerated and even encouraged gentry leadership of local military forces. The line between the affairs that the government handled through its officials and those that were handled by the gentry on their own was thus fluid and shifted according to the situation. But the general division between the functions of the government officials and those carried out by the gentry as leaders of society remained characteristic of the relationship of state and society in imperial China.[4]

There was thus in imperial time a distinction between a small number of crucial matters handled by the government and the large number of public affairs handled outside the government structure by the leaders of society. This division of jurisdictional authority no dynasty could have changed without attacking the Confucian system itself and thus undermining the very basis on which the cooperation of the Confucian gentry depended. Though applied in its own autonomous area, the gentry's authority for maintaining order in society

was based on the same beliefs that sanctioned the dynastic authority of the government and was carried on by the same group who as officials served the government.

The beliefs on which this authority was based were not shaken by the downfall of a dynasty. In fact the Confucian code worked as a check on the dynastic government and provided an explanation for the fall and rise of dynasties, while maintaining its claim as the basis for the only possible social order. During all the political upheavals of the past the social order continued and provided the elastic recuperative power that enabled Chinese imperial society to survive many internal and external political crises. In times of political chaos, when the dynastic government no longer functioned, the gentry's management of day-to-day affairs under the moral code not only remained valid, but the prestige which they held enabled the gentry to take over many of the functions of the dynastic government, especially those of tax collection and military defense. Sometimes members of the gentry themselves assumed new military and political leadership, or upstarts, seizing power during a time of crisis, depended on the services of the educated to establish their own political and military organization. It was thus from the social foundation that the Chinese political order was rebuilt after each dynastic change. After the failure of any one dynastic government, the gentry remained the stratum from which the new conqueror could recruit a staff willing to serve as long as the gentry's role in society and the state was accepted. Until the nineteenth century there had been attacks only against a government in power—attacks permitted by the Confucian teachings—but no attacks against these Confucian teachings, the Confucian gentry, and the Confucian society itself.[5]

The first major challenge to this dualistic system came from the Taipings, who sought not only to destroy the dynasty but also to replace the Confucian ethics with their own religious teachings and to end the traditional autonomy of the moral and social order. By their attempt to incorporate the teachings of their beliefs and the management of all public affairs in their governmental structure, the Taipings sought to introduce a monist order in which the state would be all. This set the Taipings not only against the government but against the defenders of the existing social order itself, the gentry, and all those who believed in the Confucian system.

In the nineteenth century, when the Ch'ing government showed all the symptoms of approaching collapse, the social leadership of the gentry was still strong enough to maintain the social order and defend it against attack. In defending the social order against the Taiping attack, the gentry had no choice but to defend the dynasty as well. The hold of the Confucian beliefs over Chinese society and the strength of the gentry's leadership were demonstrated in the defeat of the Taipings, not by the armies of the government but by newly formed forces under gentry leadership which took over when the dynasty failed. It was the resistance of these new armies that defeated the Taiping Rebellion and in so doing saved the dynasty. In fact, had the Taiping Rebellion challenged only the heavenly mandate of the ruling house, it might well have succeeded, for the time seemed ripe for a dynastic change in China, if not yet for the overthrow of traditional beliefs and the traditional social order.

The decline of organization and government, which had contributed to the downfall of previous dynasties and which undermined the position of the Ch'ing dynasty in the nineteenth century, had its reasons in the imperial system itself. Since the dynastic government had to respect the gentry's special position as guardians of the Confucian political philosophy and moral code and as managers of social affairs, the dynasties faced a vital problem of control over the very group on whose services they depended. There was the danger that the officials, who were themselves members of the gentry, could, with the support of this social group, gain an autonomy that might become fatal to the dynastic government. Each dynasty faced, therefore, the problem of controlling the educated elite and preventing it from misusing its power against the interest of dynastic authority. The measures taken by each dynasty to strengthen its authority were more or less the same, and eventually there developed a system that reached its highest point of sophistication under the Ch'ing.

Official control over the gentry's management of social affairs was very limited. It could only be exercised with regard to those gentry functions that were carried out with government approval and cooperation. But in this cooperation between officials and gentry each side depended on the other, and relative strength depended on the given situation. In times of crisis the officials might depend more on the gentry's action in collecting funds and establishing military defense corps than the members of the gentry on official approval. Even in times of peace the government had to depend so much on the gentry's services that it had little direct means of control.

The main means used to maintain government power over the gentry was the imperial examination system, fully developed since Sung times. Through it the government could determine entrance into gentry status, which now depended on the degrees given in the examinations. By limiting the number of candidates that could pass the examinations, the government could limit the number of gentry. In fact the number of degree-holders in each district was about equal to the number needed to carry on the public functions the gentry performed. The group was large enough to handle local affairs and yet not so large as to become dangerous to the government. The control of the examinations, however, permitted the government also to determine the content of the examinations and to emphasize that aspect of Confucian teaching which stressed discipline and loyalty to the dynasty. Through the educational officials the government also maintained a supervision over the gentry in each area. The educational officials were selected from the area in which they were to serve, an exception to the general rule that no official should serve in his home area. It was the very task of the educational officials to maintain close connections with the local gentry and thus form a link between the administration and the social leadership. Through their management of the examinations, their control of stipends, and their disciplinary authority, the educational officials maintained the government's control over the scholar-gentry, and at the same time transmitted the gentry's views and feelings to the government. Through its educational officials and the management of the examination system, the government exercised some control over the gentry, a control which was, however, at best indirect and tenuous.

If its influence over the nonofficial gentry remained indirect, the government established a direct system of control over the officials with the aim of preventing them from building their own power on the basis of cooperation with their fellow gentry. It had become a government practice not to permit any official to serve in his home district or province, where he would have close relations with the local gentry. He came as a stranger to the locale where he held office and did not have enough time to grow roots and establish a working agreement with the local gentry leaders. Officials were not permitted to remain in any such position more than three years at most, so that they could not become too closely identified with the interests of the administrative areas they served.

More important, however, was the system of mutual checks and division of functions and authority that characterized the official system. Each official on the higher regional level and also in the military organization was extraordinarily circumscribed in his authority and handicapped in his activity by a plurality of administrative organizations in which the functions of officials often overlapped and were not always clearly defined, a situation that fostered a spirit of competition and administrative rivalry. Since any false move could be reported to the court by superiors and competitors, the whole system led to a stifling of initiative and personal effort. It aimed at securing the government against ambitious members of the organization and chilled the spirit of all officials. It discouraged initiative, energy, and ambition and created a situation in which each officeholder was concerned with avoiding any risky move and maintaining the good relations with his superiors and other officials so important for promotion and survival in office. In this system there was little room for bold innovation, and each official could only attempt to maintain and improve his position within the existing order. The system, which aimed at protecting government authority and security, stressed the continuation of routine and was not the most propitious form of administration for efficient government.

It was this trend that under each new dynasty led after a period of the full development of given possibilities to stagnation and demoralization. Since advance was possible only within a system that could not expand, officials could only improve their position at the expense of others or by imposing a greater burden on the taxpaying population. To get a larger share one had to take from the funds that were to serve the public and to cover up through one's connections. This practice was always bound to lead to corruption, a corruption in which each member of the government organization had to participate. The phenomena of corruption and vast overtaxation that accompanied the decline of each dynasty can therefore be traced to the limitations of the system itself.

Overtaxation forced many small farmers into debt and eventually caused them to lose their land, while some of the officials and gentry were able to buy up property. This property, privileged as it was, did not have to carry the same tax burden as that of the common farming population. The tax burden on the working farmers was thus further increased, while high rent paid to landlords aggravated the lot of the tenant farmers.

Heavy taxes and high rent and lack of protection from a corrupt officialdom caused many farmers to leave their land and join roving groups of dispossessed people who became bandits. Indeed in each period of dynastic decline, large-scale banditry prevailed in many parts of the country. Sometimes this banditry required military action and appeared in the official records of the dynasty, but beyond these major incidents there was a general state of insecurity. Bandit groups that established themselves in the hills and other less accessible areas were a constant threat to the settled communities.

Against this threat there was insufficient protection from the officials. Only large-scale trouble justified a call for troops by the local officials. And the troops themselves were no longer a protection. Since the military forces had been incorporated into the administrative organization by the dynasty in order to prevent military officials from becoming autonomous in their power, the military organizations were exposed to the same corruptive influences as the rest of the administration. Like other officials, military officers were shifted from post to post, were limited in their authority, and had no clear chain of command. Position and advancement depended on influence and connections; and the natural result of this system was bribery and corruption. In each such crisis the records speak of officers pocketing the pay of the soldiers, and of units vastly under strength and without training. The frequent desertions by soldiers who did not receive their pay were not only ignored by the officers but actually welcomed by some who in this way found it easier to misappropriate the deserters' pay. When inspections were made, the ranks were filled by men hired for the occasion—beggars or coolies or farmers. As a result, the officers were corrupt and the troops demoralized. Each campaign was a new opportunity for graft by the officers and an occasion for the troops to live off the land. In fact the armies were feared by the population, and their coming was dreaded as much as a raid by bandits.

Since the corrupt officialdom and the equally corrupt military forces no longer provided protection, the people of the villages and towns began to establish their own defense units. This development ran counter to the policy of the dynastic government, which considered its monopoly of military organization one of the main safeguards against rebellion. It was the rule that soldiers were professionals and that ordinary people were not permitted to carry arms. But in times of decline, when its own forces had become ineffective, the government had to permit or even encourage the arming of such local forces for defense and maintenance of order. It was a dangerous expedient to surrender the main weapon of power to local forces, and the risk was recognized by the court, which attempted to limit the use of such extra-regular local forces to a specific occasion of desperate need and to dissolve them as soon as the emergency had passed. But once accepted, such local defense units could not easily be abolished, especially when the need for them remained. Once in existence, these local corps became important factors in local politics. To maintain themselves, they had to have financial support to buy weapons and other equipment and to provide for their upkeep, and they had the power to obtain such support. Special contributions changed to regular levies, and special income was derived from levying duties on trade, and, frequently, from illegal activities such as gambling and prostitution. To prevent clashes and difficulties with these units, the officials had to close their eyes to these financial activities and had to permit their development into regular local financial and political enterprises.

These military units thus became the most important political forces of their localities. They took up the fight for local issues in which their communities were involved. From the defense of their villages against banditry they moved on to battles against neighboring forces over local interests. Issues between villages over water rights, over property, over women, over ethnic or religious controversies were settled by arms. In peaceful times, the local magistrate had been the arbiter in these conflicts. If the local gentry leaders had acted as intermediaries, they had done so with the approval and backing of the official. Now the issue was settled by force or the threat of force. Local defense corps and bandit organizations came to fight with each other for local control, and the line between them became ever more difficult to draw. In the small-scale warfare that ensued the officials often remained neutral; or they supported one side and so gave it a mantle of legality, automatically classing the opponent as an outlaw or bandit. As long as local clashes did not lead to large-scale trouble but could be hushed up, the official more often than not was unwilling to interfere and was inclined to accept the dictates of the stronger side or maintain a neutral attitude. Official authority therefore declined, and local leadership arose that controlled its own local forces and collected its own funds to maintain its authority and protection over a submissive area.

Administrative officials could, however, maintain a neutral position only so long as the issues and battles were minor and so long as they themselves retained the major share of the tax revenues and general control and authority in the areas under their jurisdiction. There was a very precarious line between the autonomy of local forces and a challenge to all government authority. A single local corps consisting of some hundred men could not easily attempt open rebellion. It was not strong enough to oppose the troops that the officials could still muster, and it had to guard against the rival local forces that a skillful official could employ as counterforces against it. Such an official policy of "divide and rule" became impossible whenever a number of local corps of one area succeeded in banding together to form a regional force, and a stage of open rebellion was reached.

During such times of crisis, much of the leadership of local organization came from the gentry. But there was also another type of organization and another type of leadership that became important during such periods—the secret societies and their leaders.

Secret societies led many of the uprisings that occurred all through imperial history. Based on the mutual aid and protection of their members, the secret societies had a type of organization that was easily transformed into a military and political structure. The secrecy of their membership and leadership made these societies the ideal vehicle for conspiracy and political uprisings against the government.

What the secret societies had to contribute was their militant political organization. They were formed as brotherhoods of the persecuted and of those who had no voice or power in the existing political and social structure. They formed underground political organizations, rival and potentially hostile to the existing state organization. Their members were sworn to aid each other in distress, to give refuge to members who were in hiding from the officials, and to support each other in conflicts with outsiders as well as with the government. Loyalty to society brothers was the first obligation, but above the brotherhood of equal members was a hierarchy of officials of the society who could enforce absolute authority and discipline. The societies were secret orders of all those who had no other way to defend themselves against the pressures of the state and the privileged social leaders. They flourished especially in the rural villages and among the peasants but frequently included within their membership lower scholar-gentry.

Their jointly held popular beliefs, derived from Taoist and Buddhist tradition, unified the members of the secret societies. From these religious and philosophical schools they took their concepts of brotherhood and equality and a system of rites and magic, which they used to enforce their belief that supernatural powers gave them support. These ideas ran counter to the tenets of state Confucianism, but they formed no clearly defined rival ideology.

Secret societies in China had developed over the last centuries into two differing types of organization. The secret societies in the provinces of North China were called religious societies and placed much more emphasis on religious beliefs and practices derived from Buddhist tenets. There was also a much greater unity of control under a centralized system in which all branches were under the direction of one group of leaders. In south and central China the relations between different local society branches remained much looser. All branch societies belonged to an over-all roof organization called the Triad, but local leadership remained autonomous. There was also less stress on religious beliefs. It was therefore perhaps easier in the south to establish new organizations similar to the existing secret societies, especially if such an organization introduced a strong ideological appeal that the existing societies did not have. In the south as in the north the secret societies provided centers of unrest and a potential framework to unite local armed groups under a larger regional leadership, but the Triad organization in the south lacked the compactness and most of all the ideological appeal necessary for a rebellion. The existing societies therefore provided a model after which a rebellious organization could be patterned instead of being themselves the vehicles through which it could be carried out.[6]

All these elements of crisis and of new beginnings appeared during the nineteenth century and formed a serious threat to the survival of the Ch'ing dynasty. Besides these general phenomena of the cyclical crisis, a number of special factors aggravated the problem for the Ch'ing government. One of these special factors was the pressure of a rapidly growing population on the limited resources of agricultural land. The population, which has been roughly estimated

TABLE 1   Official Census of Population and Cultivated Land, 1661-1833

Year	Population*	Cultivated Land† (in mou)	Land-Population Ratio (mou per capita)
1661	19,137,652‡	549,357,640	—
1685	20,341,738‡	607,843,001	—
1724	25,510,115‡	683,791,427	—
1753	183,678,259	708,114,288	3.8
1766	208,095,796	741,449,550	3.5
1812	333,700,560	791,525,100	2.4
1833	398,942,360	737,512,900	1.8

* From year-end entries in Ch'ing-shih-lu or Tung-hua-lu.

† From sections on land system in Huang-ch'ao wen-hsien t'ung-k'ao and Huang-ch'ao hsü wen-hsien t'ung-k'ao.

‡ Taxable population only (ting).

Note: The reliability of the Chinese official figures on cultivated land and population has been questioned and under each category there are indeed serious doubts about the accuracy of these figures. The most obvious impossibility is the discrepancy between the population figures for the years 1724 and 1753 as given in the chart. This discrepancy is easily understood if one considers the change in the tax system that occurred during this time. In early Ch'ing time one of the major taxes was a head tax, and it was therefore not in the interest of the taxpaying families to admit the existence of more taxable adults than were already registered by the officials. It is quite an indication of the weakness of the governmental authority that it was unable to overcome this resistance to any true recording of the population for tax purposes. When this head tax was amalgamated with the land tax in all the key provinces in the 1720's, there was no longer any reason to conceal the number of members of each family, and the official census figures suddenly swelled to many times its former total. The figures from 1753 on must therefore be regarded as much more reliable than those of the earlier decades. But aside from the break in the figures, the steady increase in population is apparent from both the earlier and later figures.

A different problem exists with regard to the figures on cultivated land. It was in the interest neither of the taxpaying farmers nor of the local officials responsible for the transmission of taxes to admit the existence of all the taxable land under cultivation, and it is generally assumed that these figures remained somewhat below reality. But the steady increase of the land reported indicates that new land brought under cultivation could not be concealed altogether and had eventually to be included in the tax record; and it can actually be assumed that the land record was not too far behind the reality. (See Supplement to Chang, The Income of the Chinese Gentry, pp. 294-95.) But even if both the population and the land figures are, as some suspect, below the reality, these figures indicate quite clearly the growing discrepancy between population increase and cultivated land. Since the existing technique of land cultivation did not change, there was thus a serious problem of overpopulation, which added another element to the cyclical problems in producing the crisis of the nineteenth century.

as 100,000,000 at the start of the dynasty, had increased to about 300,000,000 by the beginning of the nineteenth century. The population thus increased threefold while the square mileage of cultivated land and the quantity of agricultural production grew only very little. This increasing disproportion between population and cultivated land emerges clearly from the records of the Ch'ing dynasty. (See Table 1.)

The reasons for the rapid population growth during the preceding two hundred years or so, which has its parallel in other parts of the world in industrial as well as agricultural countries, remains still a matter of speculation. In China the period of comparative peace and orderly government secured by the Ch'ing dynasty during the first century after the complete conquest of the country has been given as one explanation for the population increase. No rebellions large enough to affect the population figures occurred before the nineteenth century. No epidemics or natural catastrophes caused large loss of life. But there was also no economic change that would have provided the resources to feed so many more people. It has been said that new crops introduced from abroad, such as the sweet potato and the peanut, increased the food available and that such increases could not be deduced from the records of taxable land, since such crops were planted on hilly and mountainous land not used for the main crops and not registered for taxation. But even if these additional food crops made some difference, the over-all problem of a rapid population increase was one of the most critical issues faced by the Ch'ing dynasty, and in effect by all subsequent Chinese governments.

Another new factor that added to the

crisis was the currency and fiscal problem created by the impact of the West. Since the eighteenth century, Western trade had grown considerably through the system of controlled exchange between the foreign merchants and the licensed Chinese firms, the Cohong, at Canton. This trade at first had not had a substantial effect on the over-all Chinese economy. Under the Ch'ing dynasty, trade, including frontier trade, had been favored more than previously, but its total amount had remained negligible in relation to the total substance of the Chinese economy. By the turn of the eighteenth century, however, the Canton trade began to have a serious impact on the Chinese economy, not so much because of the quantity of goods involved as because of the imbalance of the trade. By that time there had been added to the legitimate trade, under which Chinese goods such as tea, silk, and porcelain had been exported and cotton goods from India as well as some other Western products had been imported, a vast illegitimate trade in foreign opium. By the beginning of the nineteenth century, the value of this new import had become much higher than the value of all the legitimate trade. Formerly in the regular trade the value of the exports had been much higher than that of the imports, and the balance had to be covered through an import of silver into China, but the amount was negligible in relation to the total Chinese economy. Through the import of opium the imbalance was not only reversed, but the outflow of Chinese silver that resulted became serious enough to upset the internal Chinese fiscal system.

The Chinese internal currency system was based on silver and copper—silver to be used for tax payment, for the payment of salaries by the government, and for all calculations of the official treasury; copper to be used for local buying and selling, especially in the local agricultural markets. As a result of the outflow of silver, the internal value of silver to copper was changed from 1:2 to 1:3. This greatly aggravated the financial problems of the Chinese farming population, whose tax and rent payments were calculated in silver but whose income was based on devaluated copper.

The general causes of cyclical decline and the special effects of population increase and the economic impact of Western trade and opium smuggling created the conditions that resulted in the crisis of the Ch'ing dynasty in the nineteenth century. The Ch'ing government had become corrupt and inefficient. Overtaxation, high rents, and population pressure had forced people off the land, and banditry had increased. Local defense organizations had taken over in many parts of the country where official protection was no longer available. Secret societies had become active in organizing local unrest. The government was financially weakened through graft and the great costs of military campaigns. The military adventures under the Ch'ien-lung emperor in the second half of the eighteenth century, which had expanded the Chinese position in central Asia, had depleted the treasury reserves; and during the same time the vastly expanded system of presents, bribes, and graft had cut into government revenues. After the death of the Ch'ien-lung emperor, his chief political adviser, Ho Shen, was tried on charges of corruption, sentenced to death, and the immense fortune which he had accumulated was confiscated. But the malaise of the system was not cured. By the turn of the century, local out-

breaks had occurred in several parts of the country. In the first decades of the nineteenth century, the uprising of the White Lotus Society covered much of the territory of central China. In the southwest there had been trouble with the Miao tribes, who reacted against Chinese seizure of their lands and extortion by local officials. In the 1830's small-scale local uprisings occurred in many provinces all over the country, and banditry increased. To deal with the trouble, officials had permitted or actively sponsored local self-defense corps, and in many instances local authority had shifted into the hands of the leaders of these local forces.

This was the necessary result of the decline of the regular Manchu military forces. The Manchu banners had already lost their military value during the eighteenth century. The life of an idle elite had corrupted their morale. Their pay remained the same and could not have easily been increased under the fixed government budget system. In a steady, slow inflation, prices had risen, so that the real pay of the troops had declined. The number of paid soldiers in the banners also remained the same, while the banner population increased. Occasional handouts by the government had not changed the situation, and the banner families had become privileged paupers, whose value as a fighting force, for the most part, had become negligible.[7]

The Chinese professional troops, the *lü-ying* or "green-banner" battalions, had been affected by the general corruption and demoralization. Their salaries, which were low to begin with, were often pocketed by the officers, and the underpaid soldiers lived off the land. Most of the units were considerably under strength, since vacancies created by death or desertion were not filled, and the officers kept the pay of the nonexistent soldiers. When inspections were made, stand-ins were hired for the occasion. Training was negligible and equipment was lacking; the army had become a typical part of the corrupted bureaucratic organization, totally unprepared to deal with any major emergency.

The weakness of the military forces was demonstrated during the time of the great external crisis which the dynasty faced with the first attack from the West. The Opium War (1839-42) had demonstrated the total inadequacy of the Manchu military forces for defense against outside attack. The fighting had been limited to the areas of Canton and the lower Yangtze, and in both regions local corps, led by gentry, had taken part in it. The weakness of the government forces demonstrated during the war and the humiliation of the defeat had done further damage to the prestige of the dynasty in China.

The Opium War and the Treaty of Nanking had had other effects on the internal Chinese development, especially in the south. One of the geographical and political units of China was formed by the area known as Liang-Kuang, the two provinces of Kwangtung and Kwangsi, Eastern and Western Kuang. In this region the Taiping Rebellion originated. Special geographic features set this region apart from other parts of China. Its ethnic, social, economic, and political complexities aggravated the problems created by the general conditions of economic decline and breakdown of political order in all of China. In these special local expressions of overall problems can be found the immediate causes of the Taiping Rebellion.

Canton was the principal city of Kwangtung province. It was the political and military headquarters of the area and its center of communications and commerce. Canton's network of waterways was the outlet for three major rivers, the West River, the North River, and the East River, which bound the area together. The North River and East River connected the hinterland of Kwangtung province itself with the port of Canton; the West River, much longer than the other two, flowed through the province of Kwangsi and gave this province its outlet toward Kwangtung and the city of Canton. The two provinces were separated from other parts of China by natural borders of mountains and formed in themselves an economic unit. Kwangsi province was then the hinterland of Kwangtung and therefore felt all the repercussions of events that occurred in Canton.

During the Opium War, Canton had seen most of the fighting, and the changes brought about by the Treaty of Nanking had destroyed the trade monopoly formerly held by the merchants of the city. The end of the monopoly of trade and the growing competition of the new treaty ports, especially Shanghai, affected the trade routes and upset the existing transportation system. Groups of porters and of boat people were affected. After breaking down official resistance to their demands, the British also attacked the pirates in the delta of Canton who had made regular trade hazardous. The defeated pirates were driven upriver into the hinterland of Kwangtung and Kwangsi and added a further element of insecurity to a region already suffering from economic dislocation and local conflict.

Once internal decline and foreign attack had destroyed the equilibrium that had been maintained by the government, the problems that arose in the two southern provinces were perhaps more complex than in most other parts of China. Kwangtung province, and still more, Kwangsi were settled by a composite population. Most of the Chinese population consisted of two groups, the Punti and the Hakka. The Punti were descendants of the early Chinese settlers who had reached the area first and made up the majority of the population. The Hakka were a later group of Chinese settlers who had migrated to the south as a result of the invasions of north and central China by peoples from central Asia. Each, the Punti and the Hakka, had maintained their special customs and dialects. They were settled in different villages, and their differing customs and traditions often led to communal rivalries and clashes.[8]

In addition to these Chinese population groups, a large number of tribal people lived in the two provinces, especially in Kwangsi. People like the Miao, Yao, and the Lolo who had made up the pre-Chinese population of the area had been pressed back by the Chinese settlement to less desirable land and mountainous regions. These tribal people had a latent hostility against the Chinese officials and farmers who had taken land and imposed taxes. At times, when the pressure had become too harsh or when the Chinese authorities seemed weakened, the tribes attempted to strike back, and Kwangsi province especially had been the scene of a number of Miao rebellions. When Miao strength was in ascendance, their leading families had ruled over and taxed Chinese farmers, and their local military and political tradition had by no means been inferior to that of the Chinese.

In addition to these diverse ethnic groups, there were occupational groupings that created communities with special traditions and interests. The boat people, who lived on their boats and monopolized the traffic on the rivers, formed communities of their own. The miners and the charcoal burners in the mountains formed tight groups organized under their own leadership.

The diversity of ethnic composition and of occupational groupings made the province the favorite ground for the establishment of secret societies. All over the province branches of the secret societies were established which protected the members of the different interest groups and often gave these groups a political coherence. Some of the activities of these societies were as illegal as they were profitable. Kwangtung and Kwangsi were salt-producing areas, and salt was a government monopoly. Salt-smuggling was one of the major activities of such local organizations. The more government authority declined, the stronger these local underground organizations of different kinds became. The provincial accounts of the early part of the nineteenth century are full of reports on smuggling, banditry, piracy, and rebellious activities of secret societies.[9]

This was the setting in which the Taiping uprising took place. When official authority declined and corruption increased, and when the government troops had become demoralized and ineffective, local organizations took over to defend the many legitimate and illegitimate interests of their members. Kwangtung and Kwangsi provinces became the scene of small-scale warfare between rival groups. There was a basic conflict between the Punti and Hakka villages. Both sides were armed, and in the clashes between local corps and other local forces the officials could either side with one group against the other or remain neutral altogether, hoping that the local unrest would not lead to the banding together of larger forces and rebellious outbreaks that would challenge the authority of the officials themselves.[10]

The origin of the Taiping Rebellion can be found in these conditions of decline that characterized the end of a dynastic cycle, aggravated by special factors of population growth and the new Western impact. The rebellion's geographical starting point in the southeast can be explained by the complicated ethnic and social conditions of that area, which sharpened any local conflict. However, both the cause of the rebellion and its goals differed basically from those of the upheavals in earlier periods of crisis. The new faith preached by the Taiping leaders and the system they tried to establish marked a radical departure from the past.

Notes

1. For the translation of T'aip'ing T'ien-kuo as "Heavenly Kingdom of Great Equality," see Lo, Shih-kang, pp. 52-53. For the previous history of the term "Taiping" see Vincent Y. C. Shih, The Taiping Ideology: Its Sources, Interpretations, and Influence (Seattle, 1967).

2. See Chung-li Chang, The Chinese Gentry (Seattle: University of Washington Press, 1955).

3. See Chung-li Chang, The Income of the Chinese Gentry (Seattle: University of Washington Press, 1962).

4. See Franz Michael, "Regionalism in Nineteenth-Century China," introduction to Stanley Spector, Li Hung-chang and the Huai Army (Seattle: University of Washington Press, 1964).

5. Buddhism, which had been a rival educational system in earlier centuries, had been unsuccessful in challenging the Confucian monopoly.

6. At the fall of the Ming dynasty, secret societies caried on the fight for Ming pretenders to the throne against the new Manchu rulers. The secret-society organizations that carried on during the rule of the Manchu dynasty continued to hold a vague allegiance to the idea of a Chinese Ming ruler as against the emperors of the alien Manchu dynasty. There was not much reality in their Ming loyalism, but their continued opposition to the Manchu dynasty could be brought to life through any conditions favoring rebellion. Secret societies played, therefore, a part in the uprisings of the troubled years of the nineteenth century and later became the basis of Sun Yat-sen's revolutionary movement.

7. See Michael, "Regionalism in Nineteenth-Century China."

8. There were villages of people of other Chinese groups, such as the Min; most of these people lived in Fukien province, but some of them had migrated into Kwangtung.

9. See Laai Yi-faai, Franz Michael, and John C. Sherman, "The Use of Maps in Social Research: A Case Study in South China," The Geographical Review, LII, No. 1 (1962), 92-111.

10. A contemporary Western missionary writer dealing with the background of the Taiping Rebellion describes the growing local autonomy, village warfare, and the decline of authority of the officials as follows: "In China, where the distance to the district town or nearest Mandarin office is often very great, perhaps twenty or thirty miles, and where a lawsuit generally results in a mere spending of large sums of money to the benefit of the Mandarins and their servants, the method of settling any disputes between themselves by means of appointed, or generally acknowledged headmen, is in most instances resorted to, and very often war between different villages is resolved upon, carried on for months, and peace finally concluded without any interference on the side of the Mandarins who at the present time have lost a great part of their influence among the native population." Theodore Hamberg, The Visions of Hung-Siu tshuen and Origin of the Kwang-si Insurrection (Hong Kong, 1854), p. 3.

III. ASPECTS OF THE SELF-STRENGTHENING MOVEMENT

12. BIOGRAPHIES OF THREE LEADERS

TSÊNG KUO-FAN*

Teng Ssu-yü

Tsêng Kuo-fan, Nov. 26, 1811-1872, Mar. 12, statesman, general and scholar, the first Marquis I-yung, was a native of Hsiang-hsiang, Hunan. He was born in a poor peasant family and in his youth was much influenced, in his characteristic tendencies and habits of thought, by his grandfather, Tsêng Yü-p'ing (1774-1849). His father, Tsêng Lin-shu (1790-1857), became a *hsiu-ts'ai* in 1832—a year before Tsêng Kuo-fan himself obtained the same degree. Tsêng Kuo-fan was a *chin-shih* of 1838 and in June of the same year became a member of the Hanlin Academy. At the capital, he pursued his studies with great tenacity of purpose and profited by his contacts with noted contemporary scholars. After routine promotions he was appointed, in 1849, junior vice-president of the Board of Ceremonies. At different times he served as acting vice-president on several other Boards and thus gained wide knowledge of state affairs. This experience enabled him, in his later memorials to the throne, to make practical proposals

* From Arthur W. Hummel (ed.), *Eminent Chinese of the Ch'ing Period (1644-1912)* (Washington, D.C., Government Printing Office, 1944), Vol. II, 751-56. [Bibliography omitted—Ed.]. Reprinted by permission.

and to frame them with great clarity and precision. In 1852 he was sent to conduct the provincial examination of Kiangsi, but learning, on his way south, of the death of his mother, he was granted leave to return home to observe the customary mourning period.

From 1850 onward the Taiping Rebellion had spread rapidly from Kwangsi to Hunan, Hupeh and down the Yangtze River to Nanking (see under Hung Hsiuch'üan). For three years the pursuing imperial troops vainly followed the insurgents from Kwangsi to the outskirts of Nanking (see under Hsiang Jung). But the militia, organized in the villages by Chiang Chung-yüan and Lo Tsê-nan [*qq. v.*], proved to be more effective than the regulars—particularly in 1852 in the defense of Changsha (see under Lo Ping-chang). After the Taipings had abandoned the siege of Changsha (November 30, 1852) Tsêng was ordered by the emperor to recruit and drill the Hunan militia. When, after much persuasion, he decided on January 20, 1853 to assume this responsibility he swore to himself that he would not covet wealth nor fear death.

Tsêng Kuo-fan's first task was to organize the Hunan Army (Hsiang-chün), usually referred to as the "Hunan Braves." It comprised, among other troops, Lo Tsê-nan's "Hsiang Yung" and

Chiang Chung-yüan's "Ch'u Yung." These constituted Tsêng's land force. With foresight, characteristic of his later campaigns, he laid careful plans for the training of his troops and initiated methods of discipline and organization which greatly contributed to his ultimate success. He established central training camps at which those troops with previous military experience received further instruction, and opened recruiting stations in each district of Hunan where new recruits received initial preparation. He determined to send his troops first against local bandit groups, to give them experience in fighting before taking them outside the province to war against the Taipings. For this he was severely criticized by those generals who were vainly fighting the Taipings, and even by the Emperor himself, to whom he addressed a long memorial explaining his plan for the campaign. Stubbornly refusing to be moved, either by ridicule or pleas for aid, he kept on with his organization of the poorly disciplined and untrained militia. The success of his plan depended upon funds given by Hunan officials and gentry. They proved lukewarm in their support until a victory by Chiang Chung-yüan and Lo Tsê-nan at Hêng-shan-hsien so impressed the Court that local officials found it expedient to give him the necessary funds. Tsêng was embarrassed in all his campaigns by lack of support of the officials until he finally accepted an official post himself, which placed him in control of the finances of the provinces in which his campaigns were waged. Within a few months he acquiesced in the urgent proposal of Chiang Chung-yüan and Kuo Sung-tao [q. v.] to build gunboats and to train marines under the command of Yang Yüeh-pin (see under P'êng Yü-lin) and others, in the hope of driving the Taipings off the Yangtze.

After the conquest of Nanking in 1853 the Taipings were pressing two major campaigns: one to North China, the other westward to Anhwei, Kiangsi and Hupeh. At that time Tsêng Kuo-fan, though again besieged by requests for aid, had no force which he could spare for the defense of Hupeh. A large part of the Hunan Braves already had been sent to the rescue of Kiangsi, and the rest were occupied in quelling local uprisings in Hunan, while the "navy" was still in process of organization. When, however, a few months later the Taipings from Hupeh pressed upon his forces in Hunan, Tsêng mobilized (February 25, 1854) his new flotilla of 240 boats with 5,000 marines, and a still larger army under the command of T'a-ch'i-pu [q. v.], to stem their advance. But owing to a storm which rendered many boats unfit, and to the inexperience of his troops in fighting, Tsêng was twice defeated in Hunan— once in Yochow and again at Ching-chiang. So mortified was he that he attempted to commit suicide. Fortunately T'a-ch'i-pu and P'êng Yü-lin triumphed over the Taipings at Hsiang-t'an (May 1, 1854), forcing them to retreat to Yochow, which was finally taken on July 25, 1854—a victory which much encouraged Tsêng. On January 12, 1852 the Taipings had taken Wuchang—the first of three occupations—but had lost it to the government forces in February of the same year. They again seized the city on June 26, 1854, and successfully defended it until October 14 when they were overcome by Tsêng's forces under Lo and Chiang—a severe blow to their plan of conquest. On December 2, 1854 Tsêng also won a signal victory over the strong defense which the Taipings made at T'ien-chia-chên. Meanwhile the city of Shanghai, which had been taken by a band of local rebels in 1853, was recovered in February 1855. By the end of May 1855 the northern expedition of the Taipings was finally suppressed.

The victorious advance of Tsêng Kuo-fan's forces was stemmed at Kiukiang, however, by the stubborn resistance of the rebel chief, Lin Ch'i-jung (d. 1858), who had fought for the Taipings from the beginning of their activities. A part of Tsêng's navy was bottled up in Po-yang Lake; that part which was in the Yangtze was defeated, even Tsêng's flagship being captured by the rebels; and a storm damaged many of the remaining boats. The morale of Tsêng's troops, disheartened by these reverses, was now at a low ebb. After making the required adjustments, he went to Nanchang, capital of Kiangsi, to rehabilitate the imprisoned fleet which was on the west shore of Po-yang Lake. The Taipings, on the other hand, hoping to weaken the attack which the government troops were making on Kiukiang, retook Wuchang for the third time on April 3, 1855. Despite this threat, Tsêng ordered T'a-ch'i-pu to keep on assaulting Kiukiang while Lo Tsê-nan and Hu Lin-i [q. v.] were sent to attack Wuchang, he himself remaining at Nanchang. The situation became all the more grave when T'a-ch'i-pu and Lo Tsê-nan both died and Tsêng himself was harassed by the almost invincible Taiping leader, Shih Ta-k'ai [q. v.]. But thanks to Tsêng's farsighted planning, his patience and his perseverance against great odds, coupled with his ability to select and inspire able commanders, Wuchang was recovered for the last time, December 19, 1856, by the forces under Hu Lin-i and Li Hsü-pin [q. v.]. Owing to the help of P'êng Yü-lin and the reinforcements sent to Kiangsi from Hunan by Tsêng's younger brother, Tsêng Kuo-ch'üan [q. v.], Tsêng's difficult position in Nanchang was alleviated.

Though at this time (1856) the Taipings failed in Hupeh and Kiangsi, they succeeded in crushing Hsiang Jung's large army at Nanking. Thereafter their forces were greatly weakened by a series of murders among their leaders (see under Hung Hsiu-ch'üan), and so they failed to press the advantage their victory offered. Tsêng Kuo-fan's father died on February 27, 1857, making it necessary for him to retire temporarily for mourning, but his capable generals were able to carry out his plans and recover Kiukiang on May 19, 1858. He was recalled from retirement before the period of mourning elapsed, and resumed his task —the working out of a careful plan to take Anking as a first step in the final recovery of Nanking. To accomplish these objectives he again declined to go to the relief of other cities still in the hands of the Taipings, although implored to do so. In pursuance of his plan to retake Anking he encamped at Ch'i-mên in southern Anhwei (1860-61). In 1860 he was appointed governor-general of Kiangnan and Kiangsi and Imperial Commissioner for the suppression of the Taipings in South China. He thus was given full power to deal with all matters relating to the campaign, including the levy of funds for this purpose.

In the period 1860-61 Tsêng faced a difficult situation. The Taipings, who had earlier in 1860 crushed the reorganized imperial force near Nanking, again became very strong and active under the leadership of Li Hsiu-ch'êng [q. v.]. A large part of Kiangsu and Chekiang were still in the enemy's hands—only Shanghai was never fully occupied by the rebels, their assaults in that area being repeatedly repulsed (see under Li Hung-chang). At the same time (1860) British and French forces were fighting their way to Peking, while the Court took refuge in Jehol. Appeals for help came to Tsêng from all sides, though after September 1860 he himself was so harried by the Taipings at Ch'i-mên as to be unable, had he wished, to render aid to others. His difficulties reached a climax in April 1861, but by this time he was determined to die rather than retreat. The tide finally turned in his favor when Tso Tsung-t'ang [*q. v.*] and others came to the relief of Ch'i-mên. Moreover, Anking was taken (September 5, 1861) by his brother, Tsêng Kuo-ch'üan, after long and murderous attacks. Tsêng Kuo-fan then made that city his base of operations for the conquest of Nanking. Fearing to concentrate too large an army at Nanking lest the Taipings retake districts already under government control—as had repeatedly happened in the past— he set up three military areas: one in Kiangsu under Li Hung-chang [*q. v.*], another in Chekiang under Tso Tsung-t'ang, and a third in Anhwei under his own command. In all these areas active campaigns were carried out against the Taipings who were gradually encircled as Nanking was being besieged. Tsêng Kuo-ch'üan, who had proved himself an indomitable commander, volunteered for the difficult task of taking Nanking, the Taiping capital since March 19, 1853, where large government armies had several times been crushed, particularly in August 1856, November 1859, and August 1860. Though he was offered the aid of foreigners, he declined their help, and after a long siege and desperate fighting took Nanking on July 19, 1864. The last remnants of the Taipings, however, were not cleared away until the beginning of 1866. The chief credit for the suppression of this long and bloody Rebellion naturally went to Tsêng Kuo-fan who was made a Marquis of the first class with the designation I-yung—the first civil official to obtain such a rank.

After the Taiping Rebellion ended Tsêng Kuo-fan resumed his post as governor-general of Kiangnan and Kiangsi— thus remaining in Nanking for several months. His main objective was to restore peace and order and to promote the rehabilitation of learning in South China after a terribly destructive war lasting fifteen years. At his headquarters at Anking he established, early in 1864, an official printing office to reprint important works, chiefly classics and histories; and he now invited celebrated scholars, such as Wang Shih-to, Mo Yu-chih [*qq. v.*] and others, to be the chief editors. He disbanded a majority of the Hunan army, sending the soldiers home to their farms and employing the officers (many of whom were students) in proofreading. In 1864 he issued regulations for printing establishments in each of the cities of Nanking, Soochow, Yangchow, Hangchow and Wuchang. These were known as "the five official printing offices." At the same time he restored (December 20, 1864) the provincial examinations at Nanking where, owing to the Taiping occupation, they had been for many years discontinued.

In June 1865 Tsêng Kuo-fan was ordered, by hurried mandate, to Shantung where Prince Sêng-ko-lin-ch'in had been killed in battle (May 1865) while fighting the Nien bandits. Tsêng, now in supreme command of military affairs in Shantung, Chihli, and Honan, at once reorganized his forces, distributing them at four points in order to draw a net about the elusive rebels. After more than a year in the north in an unsatisfactory campaign to exterminate these rebels, and increasingly conscious of the criticism of his enemies, he recommended Li Hung-chang as his successor (December 12, 1866), he himself returning to his former post as governor-general at Nanking.

In 1863 Jung Hung [*q. v.*] had recommended to Tsêng the establishment of ironworks at Shanghai—works which later became the Kiangnan Arsenal—and Jung had purchased the machinery for it from abroad. In 1868 the first steamship was built there by Chinese and brought to Nanking for Tsêng's inspection. The opening of these ironworks was one of the most important contributions Tsêng made to the future welfare of China.

In 1867 he was appointed a Grand Secretary, and in September 1868 was made governor-general of Chihli province. In the latter capacity he cleared up a large number of long-pending legal cases, improved administrative efficiency, and set up a plan for a standing army which, however, was not carried out. In 1870 he was ordered to investigate and settle the case of the Tientsin Massacre. Fully conscious of China's military weakness, he pressed for a policy of justice and conciliation toward the Western powers involved, and so incurred the ill-will of many officials in Peking who desired war. The case was nearly settled when, aged and ill, he was transferred (1871) to his old post at Nanking, made vacant through the assassination of Ma Hsin-i [*q. v.*]. He was succeeded in Tientsin by Li Hung-chang. On August 18, 1871 he sent a joint memorial with Li, recommending the dispatch of young students to study abroad. Their plan was put into effect in 1872, but Tsêng died a few months before the students actually set sail. He was given posthumously the title of Grand Tutor, and was canonized as Wên-chêng.

Tsêng was a man of great foresight, as evidenced not only in his preparation for military campaigns but in many other matters as well. Several times the Shanghai and Kiangsi gentry suggested to the Court that foreign troops, who had successfully defended Shanghai against the rebels, be sent inland in an effort to bring the Taiping rebellion to a speedier close. Tsêng, whose opinion in the matter was asked by the Emperor, pointed out that though there was justification for using foreign troops at Shanghai and Ningpo, where in reality they were defending their own interests, the situation in the interior was different. Here, should joint Chinese and foreign troops be victorious, complications would surely arise and the "guest-soldiers" might seize the land and become a danger to the empire. He urged that, even in the use of foreign troops at treaty ports, a careful understanding should be reached before any fighting was undertaken. In addition to being a man of great foresight and indomitable perseverance, he showed an extraordinary ability to select men of promise, to train them for their posts, and to retain their loyalty. He had on his staff more than eighty able men—many of whom, like Li Hung-chang and P'êng Yü-lin, later became famous in history. He learned a great deal from personal experience in drilling soldiers, controlling subordinate officers, and co-ordinating troops from different parts of the country—and so finally was able to develop far-reaching plans which he carried out regardless of obstacles. Sometimes he is criticized for his loyalty to the Manchu dynasty, for conservatism and obstinacy, and for cruelty in his treatment of the rebels. Yet the times in which he lived called for stern action, and however strict he may have been with others, he was even more strict with himself. He sought daily to improve himself by constant examination of his own mistakes and shortcomings, as shown vividly in his diary which he kept from January 1, 1839 to March 11, 1872—the day before he died. The same habits of rigid self-examination are shown in the letters which he wrote to his parents, to his brothers, and to his sons; and in the admonitions he gave to the young to live lives of frugality, diligence, and integrity.

Tsêng was an honest and upright official. We are told in the *nien-p'u* of his youngest daughter, that during the years he lived in Peking, he was always poor; and that even when he held high command in the army, he sent home annually to his family not more than ten to twenty taels silver. It was not until he became governor-general of Chihli that he was able to save 20,000 taels from his salary. Throughout his life, no matter under what stress of war or governmental activity, he seldom passed a day in which he did not seek consolation or self-improvement by reading selections from the classics, history, or poetry. He found in the Sung philosophers, rather than in the writings of the School of Han Learning (see under Ku Yen-wu), the solace and encouragement which the times required. It is therefore no wonder that he was instrumental in reviving Sung philosophy in his day. Like some of the great Neo-Confucianists, he became master of a lucid, emotive style, interspersed with wise mottoes and sententious sayings concerning political, social, military, academic, and family affairs. . . .

TSO TSUNG-T'ANG*

Tu Lien-che

Tso Tsung-t'ang, Nov. 10, 1812-1855, Sept. 5, military leader and statesman, was a native of Hsiang-yin, Hunan. Born in a family of moderate means but with scholarly traditions, his schooling began at an early age, first with his grand-

* From Arthur W. Hummel (ed.), *Eminent Chinese of the Ch'ing Period (1644-1912)* (Washington, D.C., Government Printing Office, 1944), Vol. II, 762-67. [Bibliography omitted—Ed.]

father, Tso Jên-chin (1738-1817), and then with his father, Tso Kuan-lan (1778-1830). When he was eighteen *sui* (1829) he read for the first time the two great geographical works, *T'ien-hsia chün-kuo li-ping shu* by Ku Yen-wu [*q. v.*] and *Tu-shih fang-yü chi-yao* by Ku Tsu-yü [*q. v.*], and evinced a great interest in them. Doubtless the study of these works inspired a life-long interest in the topography of the Chinese Empire and later helped him considerably in military strategy. After his father's death, in 1830, the financial condition of the family became worse, but in the same year he met Ho Ch'ang-ling [*q. v.*], who saw in him great promise and gave him access to his own library. In the following year he studied in the Academy, Ch'êng-nan Shu-yüan, in Shan-hua, Hunan, where Ho Hsi-ling was director. Both he and his older brother, Tso Tsung-chih (d. 1872), became *chü-jên* in 1832. In the same year he married Chou I-tuan (1812-1870) who left a collection of verse, entitled *Shih-hsing chai i-kao*. They made their home with his wife's family in Hsiang-t'an, Hunan, until 1844. In the meantime Tso participated three times (1833, 1835, 1838) in the metropolitan examinations, but failed to qualify for the *chin-shih* degree. In 1837 he lectured in the Lu-chiang Shu-yüan, in Li-ling, Hunan, where he made the acquaintance of T'ao Chu [*q. v.*] who was then viceroy of Liang-Kiang (Kiangsu, Kiangsi and Anhwei). After failing for a third time in the metropolitan examination (1838) he determined not to try again.

Tso then studied seriously works in the fields of history, classics, geography and agriculture—particularly the last two. During this time, too, he familiarized himself with the *Ch'in-ting Huang-yü Hsi-yü t'u-chih*, an official work on Chinese Turkestan compiled during the years 1756-1782. In 1839 he compiled an historical atlas of military strategy which seems not to have been printed. He also promoted the planting of mulberry trees and introduced the members of his family to the art of sericulture. When his friend, T'ao Chu, died (1839) the latter left a request that Tso be the teacher of his son, T'ao Kuang, who later became Tso's son-in-law. Thereupon he taught in the T'ao family in Anhua, Hunan, for eight years (1840-48). During this period there occurred the Anglo-Chinese War (1840-42), and though he took no active part in it, he was deeply concerned over the course of events. In this period, also, he first made the acquaintance of Hu Lin-i [*q. v.*] who had great respect for his talents and did much to bring him to the position and the fame which he later achieved. As Tso's financial condition improved he bought a farm in his native district and moved his family there in 1844. He experimented in ancient methods of agriculture; he cultivated tea; he promoted sericulture; and therefore styled himself, "Husbandman of the River Hsiang." In 1845 he wrote a work on agriculture, entitled *P'u-ts'un ko nung-shu*. In 1848 he was recommended to Lin Tsê-hsü [*q. v.*], but for some reason did not join his staff. Yet when Lin was on his way from Yunnan to Fukien in the following year, Tso had an interview with him in Changsha. During the initial stages of the Taiping Rebellion in Kwangsi Tso and his fellow-townsman, Kuo Sung-tao [*q. v.*], found a place of refuge in the mountains east of Hsiang-yin. By 1851 he was already forty *sui* and that year marks the end of his early years of seclusion and comparative inactivity. From the year 1852 till his death in 1885, he was continuously connected with, or in charge of, military operations—campaigning against the Taipings, the Nien-fei, and the Muslims of the Northwest, or preparing for hostilities with the French on the question of Annam.

In 1852, on the recommendation of Hu Lin-i, Tso Tsung-t'ang was invited to the secretarial staff of Chang Liang-chi (1807-1871) who was then governor of Hunan and later acting governor-general of Hu-Kuang (Hupeh and Hunan). Tso was given full responsibility in all military affairs. The Taiping forces were launching attacks at many points in Central China, with the result that Wuchang, the capital of Hupeh, fell early in 1853. But this city was recovered soon after, and when Tso's merits were reported to the government he was given the rank of a magistrate. In the same year (1853) Nanking fell into the hands of the rebels. Chang Liang-chi was transferred, in the autumn of 1853, to be governor of Shantung, and Tso then retired and went home. In the following year, in consequence of an interview with Tsêng Kuo-fan [*q. v.*], he went to Yochow, Hunan, to serve on the secretarial staff of Lo Ping-chang [*q. v.*], governor of that province. For more than five years he acted as Lo's chief assistant in supervising military affairs in Hunan. But the weight of his influence, and the frankness and self-assurance with which he performed his duties, aroused the jealousy of his colleagues, so that in 1859 charges of corruption and unruliness were lodged against him and he was ordered to Wuchang for inquiry. However, his friend Hu Lin-i came to his rescue and the charges were dropped.

He then decided to participate once more in the metropolitan examination, and early in 1860 set out for Peking. But a letter from Hu Lin-i intercepted him at Hsiang-yang, Hupeh, with the result that he went instead to Tsêng Kuo-fan's headquarters at Su-sung, Anhwei. His abilities as a soldier were brought to the attention of the throne from various sources, and as the pressure of the Taipings was becoming increasingly menacing, he was finally ordered to raise, in Hunan, a volunteer corps of five thousand men for service in Kiangsi and Anhwei. Upon his return to Changsha in June he raised his army and began training it in July. On September 22, 1860 he led his men from Changsha toward Nanchang, Kiangsi. His small force made a good showing, taking Wu-yüan (Anhwei) in December. The rebels then fled toward Chekiang. By October 1861 he had engaged them in more than twenty battles. On December 27, he was appointed commander-in-chief of the government forces in Chekiang. Two days later Hangchow fell in the hands of the Taipings for the second time. On January 23, 1862 he was appointed governor of Chekiang, at a time when virtually the entire province was in the hands of the enemy. But step by step he battled his way into the province to take over the administration. He recovered Ch'ü-chou and Yen-chou in 1862 and, by early 1863, Chin-hua and Shao-hsing. On May 5, 1863 he was promoted to governor-general of Fukien and Chekiang. The siege of Hangchow began in the autumn of 1863 and by April 1, 1864 his forces entered that city. With the recovery of Hangchow the tranquilization of Chekiang was complete and Tso was rewarded with the rank of Junior Guardian of the Heir Apparent, with the coveted Yellow Jacket, and a little later with an earldom of the first rank and the designation K'o-ching. Then he proceeded to Fukien. By February 1866 the last remnants of the rebels were pursued to Chia-ying chou, Kwangtung, and there they were annihilated. This campaign ended the Taiping régime and Tso was given the double-eyed peacock feather. His exploits in Chekiang are recounted in the work, P'ing-Chê chi-lüeh, 16 chüan, compiled by Ch'in Hsiang-yeh and Ch'ên Chung-ying. The preface is dated 1874.

Tso Tsung-t'ang was also an able administrator. In both Chekiang and Fukien he accomplished a great deal for the rehabilitation and reorganization of those provinces—paying special attention to education and to the storage of grain. In Foochow he established a bureau for sericulture and cotton and also a printing office named Chêng-i t'ang Shu-chü. Aroused by recurring international difficulties, he paid special attention to naval matters and, in 1864 when he was in Hangchow, he experimented with small steam-boats on West Lake. In Foochow he selected Ma-wei shan as the site of a small navy yard which was later managed by Shên Pao-chên [q. v.]. But as China was still harassed by troubles in the North, which called for his military skill, his peaceful rehabilitation of the South was unavoidably cut short.

On September 25, 1866 Tso Tsung-t'ang was appointed governor-general of Shensi and Kansu, a portion of the empire then harassed by a serious Mohammedan uprising. He left Foochow in December 1866, arrived at Hankow toward the end of January 1867, and there made preparations for his northwestern campaign. But on his way to Shensi he received an imperial order commanding him first to fight the Nien-fei, or mounted bandits who since 1851 had spread carnage in the provinces of Honan, Anhwei, Hupeh, Shantung and Chihli. These bandits, being mounted, were very mobile; and, unlike the Taipings, made no attempt to settle in one place or to establish a government. Though Tsêng Kuo-fan and Li Hung-chang [*q. v.*] had in turn been made responsible for their suppression, one group of Nien-fei under Chang Tsung-yü began in 1867 a westward movement which caused the government to fear that they might join the Mohammedans. Late in the same year Chang's forces ravaged Shansi, Honan, and Chihli, and even endangered the Metropolitan area of Peking. For their failure to suppress them Tso Tsung-t'ang, Li Hung-chang and others were deprived of their ranks. In 1868 Tso moved his army to Wu-ch'iao, Chihli, and in the summer the Nien-fei were surrounded and annihilated at Ch'ih-p'ing, Shantung, by combined government forces. Tso's rank was restored to him and he was ordered to Peking for audiences with the Emperor (September 25, 30, 1868). By November 26 he was in Sian, the capital of Shensi, and there began to take measures for the suppression of the Mohammedan uprising.

For some eighty years following the north-western campaign of Emperor Kao-tsung the Mohammedans in China, except during the early Tao-kuang period, were fairly peaceful. Then, owing to the progressive weakening of the central government by the Opium War, the Taiping Rebellion, the wars of 1858-60, and the troubles with the Nien-fei, the hold of China on the Northwest steadily relaxed. Finally there broke out a Mohammedan Rebellion that lasted from 1862 to 1877 and devastated most of Shensi and Kansu. The outstanding leader of the Mohammedans in these two provinces was Ma Hua-lung (d. 1871) who took as his base of operations Chin-chi-pu, Kansu. Tso Tsung-t'ang began his campaign by dividing his forces into three units and pressing on to Chin-chi-pu by three routes. By the spring of 1869 Shensi was pacified, and later in the same year Tso moved his headquarters to P'ing-liang, Kansu. However, the northern route army under the very able leader, Sung-shan (1833-1870), suffered a serious reverse around Chin-chi-pu, and Liu died in action. His command was taken over by his nephew, Liu Chin-t'ang, (1844-1894), who proved worthy of the charge. On February 17, 1871 Chin-chi-pu was taken and Ma Hua-lung was executed. Though occupied both in suppressing the rebels and rehabilitating devastated areas, Tso Tsung-t'ang had, by August 1872, moved his headquarters to Lanchow. Meanwhile he had a printing establishment set up in Sian and an arsenal in Lanchow. In October he joined his armies in the attack on Suchow, Kansu. On November 4, 1873 Suchow was taken and the entire province of Kansu was pacified, but about this time Po Yen-hu, another rebel Mohammedan from Shensi, escaped to Hami. Tso was made associate Grand Secretary, but remained at his post as governor-general. In reorganizing his newly-pacified provinces he carried out several important reforms, among them prohibition of opium culture and encouragement of the cotton industry according to methods outlined in his printed booklets. He established factories for weaving both cotton and wool, and utilized the leisure hours of his soldiers in farming unused land—farms which were later transferred to the people. In the autumn of 1874 he was promoted to full Grand Secretary and in the following year was placed in charge of military affairs in Sinkiang.

For carrying on a campaign so far removed from his source of supplies, and in a land so sparsely settled as Chinese Turkestan, the two most pressing needs were food and money. Fortunately Tso Tsung-t'ang had always been interested in farming, and his practice of putting his men to work on the land when they were not otherwise occupied, made it possible for him to meet in part, at least, the first of these needs. In June 1875 the Russian traveller, Sosnowsky, arrived in Lanchow on his way to Russia, and with him Tso contracted for the purchase of Siberian grain to be delivered at Ku-ch'êng, Sinkiang—it being actually cheaper to transport it from there than over the long route from China. By April 1876 the Russians had delivered four million catties of this grain. In order to provide funds for his campaign Tso memorialized the throne, urging that ten million taels be borrowed from foreign banks in Shanghai. This request, however, provoked the opposition of many officials in Peking who regarded the building of an adequate navy and coastal defense more pressing needs than the recovery of territory in far distant Sinkiang. Even those who believed in the prosecution of the campaign were not sufficiently convinced of its importance to advocate a foreign loan. Among those who held this view was the influential Li Hung-chang [q.v.]. But Tso Tsung-t'ang persistently pleaded his case and finally won his point. He argued that the recovery of Sinkiang was necessary for the retention of Mongolia which in turn was essential to the safety of Peking. Unless all the strategic points in Sinkiang were held by China the Mohammedan rulers of that area would sooner or later have to yield, either to Russia or to Britain. In his opinion, the primary reason for the encroachment of Western nations on the sea-board of China was for commercial advantages and not for territorial aggrandizement. This, he believed, was a problem to be solved by diplomacy rather than by force of arms. Moreover, funds had previously been ear-marked for a navy, and therefore the problem of coast

defense had nothing to do with the crisis in Sinkiang. He obtained the loan early in 1876, and having previously made all preparations, moved his headquarters to Suchow with a view to regaining the territory north of the T'ien-shan and then taking the region to the south.

The dominant figure in Sinkiang at this time was Yakoob Beg (c. 1820-1877). Some ten years previously (1864) a Mohammedan leader named Chin Hsiang-yin started a rebellion. Finding himself unable fully to overcome the Chinese government troops stationed in Sinkiang, Chin requested help from Khokand. But as Khokand was then in process of being absorbed by Russia, he could not expect much help from that quarter. Nevertheless Buzurg, a son of Jehangir, and Yakoob were sent to his aid. The two arrived in Kashgaria in January 1865. Yakoob, being the more able and aggressive, emerged by 1873 as master of the entire Tarim Basin from the Pamirs to Lob Nor. In the same year Po Yen-hu escaped from Shensi and Kansu to Sinkiang and paid allegiance to Yakoob who stationed him at Urumchi to guard the region north of T'ien-shan. As soon as Yakoob assumed the leadership of all the Mohammedans in this area he attracted the attention of Delhi, London, St. Petersburg and Constantinople, and in the same year (1873) the Sultan of Turkey conferred upon him the title of Amir of Kashgaria. In that year, too, the British sent to Kashgar the Forsyth Mission to form an estimate of the situation. Yakoob had fought against the Russians for Khokand and he had no friendly feelings toward Russia which in turn feared lest he hold designs on regions farther north. In July 1871 Russia had occupied Kuldja. But in 1872 she signed a treaty of commerce with Yakoob, and in the following year Britain signed a similar treaty with him, thus effectually giving international recognition to his régime.

But Tso Tsung-t'ang, having secured the necessary funds and made his preparations, planned his campaign and started westward. One city after another fell into his hands, and during the year 1876 the north T'ien-shan region was pacified. At this juncture the British government, through Sir Thomas Francis Wade (1818-1895) in Peking and through Kuo Sung-tao in London, proposed that Yakoob Beg would surrender should China allow him to keep his kingdom under Chinese suzerainty. When the offer was reported to Tso he memorialized the throne that the status of Yakoob was purely a domestic question and if Britain wished to create a buffer state in Central Asia she was herself well able to furnish the territory. In the following spring (1877) Tso's victorious forces moved southward. The much heralded Yakoob Beg did not put up a vigorous defense for his régime and, with the fall of Turfan on May 16, 1877, the kingdom of Kashgaria came to an end and Yakoob is reported to have committed suicide by poison. Po Yen-hu and Yakoob's sons struggled along for a short period and later fled across the border to Russia. Early in 1878 all of Turkestan was recovered. Tso Tsung-t'ang was rewarded by being raised to a second class marquis, and Liu Chin-t'ang was made a baron. The official account of Tso's campaign against the Mohammedan rebels, entitled *P'ing-ting Shan, Kan, Hsin-chiang, Hui-fei fang-lüeh* was printed in 1896.

Since Sinkiang had now become tranquilized, negotiations about the Russian evacuation of Ili began. When Russia moved her troops into Ili in 1871, she gave assurances to the Chinese government and to the world that the territory would be restored to China as soon as that country was in a position to assert her authority there. At the close of 1878 Ch'ung-hou [q. v.] was sent to St. Petersburg to demand the return of Ili, and in the following year he concluded with Russia the Treaty of Livadia. When the terms of this Treaty became known in China they met severe opposition, and it was obvious that it would not be recognized. Hence on February 12, 1880 Tsêng Chi-tsê [q. v.] was appointed minister to Russia to negotiate a new one, but as the outcome of the renewed negotiation remained uncertain, China continued her military preparations. In May Tso Tsung-t'ang's forces took up positions in Sinkiang and, in June, he made his headquarters at Hami. At the same time there were troop movements in Tientsin, Mukden and Shantung. If Tsêng Chi-tsê is to be praised for his diplomatic success in concluding the new Treaty of St. Petersburg (February 24, 1881), it must be granted that the achievement of Tso Tsung-t'ang in recovering Chinese Turkestan was an important factor in that success.

From the area in Turkestan recovered by Tso, and the territory of Ili returned by Russia, a new province was created in 1884, and given the name, Hsin-chiang (Sinkiang). Liu Chin-t'ang was the first governor (1884-89), being succeeded by Wei Kuang-tao.

On August 11, 1880 an Imperial order was issued, summoning Tso Tsung-t'ang to Peking for advisory duties. He arrived at the capital on February 24, 1881, on the very day that the Treaty of St. Petersburg was signed. After an Imperial audience he was appointed to serve in the Grand Council and in the Tsungli Yamen, with the honor of being permitted to ride horseback inside the Forbidden City. But his long years of isolation on the wind-swept plains of Central

Asia and his honesty and outspokenness made it difficult for him to fit into the ways of an effete officialdom. He did not feel at home in Peking, and his colleagues felt uneasy in his presence. After taking a month's sick leave in the autumn (1881) he was on October 28 appointed governor-general of Kiangnan and Kiangsi. He assumed his new post on February 12, 1882, after a visit to his native place in Hunan. By the end of the year he was a tired and sick man and had lost the use of his left eye. He begged leave to retire, but in deference to his fame and his position his wish could not be granted. He was given instead three months' leave. In the fall of 1883 he was called to quell an uprising in southern Shantung and before long he had the situation in hand. When trouble with the French over Annam became acute he was once more summoned to Peking. He reached the capital in June 1884 and was put in charge of all military affairs of the Empire. By August conflict with the French along the coast of Fukien became serious and Tso was appointed high commissioner of that province. In September 1884 he left the capital, and in December reached Foochow which he had left some twenty years previously. Before long a settlement with France seemed imminent and negotiations were resumed in the spring of 1885. On June 9 a treaty was signed by Li Hung-chang. On September 5 Tso Tsung-t'ang died in Foochow, age seventy-four (*sui*). He was granted all appropriate posthumous honors and was canonized as Wên-hsiang.

As in the case of most great characters of history, many anecdotes, usually exaggerated and sometimes without foundation, are told about Tso Tsung-t'ang. Some of these relate to alleged misunderstandings between himself and Tsêng Kuo-fan. It is clear that these two great

heroes—natives though they were of the same province—were not good friends. They differed much in tastes, temper, and other characteristics, and their estrangement seems to have grown deeper as the years passed. Nevertheless, they had great respect for each other and they never permitted their differences to degenerate into a feud. Another point frequently mentioned, and as often overemphasized, is the assertion that Tso in suppressing the Mohammedan uprising resorted to unnecessary cruelty and wholesale slaughter of the native population. That there was much killing is certainly true, but it does not follow that Tso himself was a cruel man. Though he was strict he was fair, and when the conflict ended he did what he could to rehabilitate the devastated areas. The great highway in Kansu, lined on both sides with willow trees, still stands as a testimony to his concern to make the land fairer and more habitable. . . .

LI HUNG-CHANG*

William J. Hail

Li Hung-chang, Feb. 15, 1823-1901, Nov. 7, statesman and diplomat, was a native of Ho-fei (Lu-chou), Anhwei. An ancestor eight generations before him was born into a family named Hsü but changed his surname when he was adopted into the Li family. His father, Li Wên-an (1801-1855), was a *chin-shih* of 1838 and therefore a classmate of Tsêng Kuo-fan [*q. v.*]. After Li Hung-chang became a *chü-jên* (1844), he went to Peking where he studied intensively under the direction of Tsêng who became thereafter his patron and close

* From Arthur W. Hummel (ed.), *Eminent Chinese of the Ch'ing Period (1644-1912)* (Washington, D.C., Government Printing Office, 1943), Vol. I, 464-71. [Bibliography omitted—Ed.].

friend. He became a *chin-shih* in 1847, was selected a bachelor in the Hanlin Academy and three years later was made a compiler.

When the Taiping rebels reached Anhwei in 1853 Li Hung-chang and his father returned to their native place to organize the militia to combat them. In the meantime Tsêng Kuo-fan recommended Li Hung-chang to Chiang Chung-yüan [*q. v.*], then governor of Anhwei. Under Chiang's direction, Li led his local recruits and won a battle at Yü-hsi k'ou in the department of Ho-chou, thus gaining the decorations of a sixth grade official. However, Chiang died with the capture of Lu-chou and Li's force was dispersed after serious reverses. Early in 1854 Li joined the staff of the new governor of Anhwei, Fu-chi (d. 1875), and a year later, when Han-shan, Anhwei, was recovered, he won the rank of prefect. On July 6, 1855 his father, Li Wên-an, died, but the exigencies of war made it necessary for Li to remain in camp (unofficially) instead of retiring to observe the period of mourning. In the years 1855-57 the army of Fu-chi recaptured Ho-fei and was successful in other operations around Lake Ch'ao. As a member of the staff Li received due rewards. He was given the rank of a provincial judge (1856) and was registered as prepared for the office of an intendant (1857).

Discontented with Fu-chi's policies, Li left Anhwei in 1858 to join his patron, Tsêng Kuo-fan, who was then encamped at Nanchang. There he had a share in the recapture of Ching-tê-chên (May, 1858) and the rest of Kiangsi province. Tsêng was appointed governor-general of Kiangnan and Kiangsi in 1860, but Li, disagreeing with his policy of operating from Ch'i-mên as being too cautious, and on other matters as well, left his service

early in 1861. After Tsêng Kuo-ch'üan [*q. v.*] captured Anking (September 5, 1861) Li sent Tsêng Kuo-fan a letter of congratulation and in return was invited to rejoin him.

When the Chung-wang (Li Hsiu-ch'êng) by spectacular victories revived the Taiping cause in 1860, the coastal provinces were thrown into panic and merchants and gentry begged for imperial aid to augment the help secured from foreign sources at Shanghai. But troops could not be spared until after the capture of Anking (1861). Then Li was persuaded to recruit a sufficient force in Anhwei and proceed to Shanghai as acting governor of Kiangsu. With his new army (henceforth known as Huai-chün) and a detachment of Tsêng's veterans, he reached Shanghai by steamer in April 1862, prepared to co-operate with Tsêng Kuo-fan at Anking, with Tso Tsung-t'ang [*q. v.*], now viceroy of Fukien and Chekiang, and with Tsêng Kuo-ch'üan at Nanking—the aim being to drive on the Taipings from three directions and hem them in.

Li, at the early age of thirty-nine (*sui*), was thus placed at the head of a normally wealthy province, virtually all of which was in rebel hands. He found foreign forces defending Shanghai, and a foreign-trained and officered Chinese brigade, later known as the Ever Victorious Army, organized by Frederick Townsend Ward, helping the imperialists to drive the insurgents from near-by towns. Ward's brigade was subsidized by the provincial authorities through a merchant known by the firm name of "Ta-kee" who acted as paymaster. The expense of these well-drilled troops and their arrogance made them unpopular, but they had ability to win victories, and Li made it clear that he would continue to employ them. Ward lost his life at

Tzeki in September 1862, and after a short interval Henry Burgevine was installed as commander. But Burgevine, despite his popularity with the men, soon incurred the hostility of Li by failing to go to Nanking when a severe crisis brought a request from Tsêng for aid. This antagonism grew when Burgevine later forcibly collected from "Takee" sums due his army. He was dismissed, and after some delay and negotiations Charles George ("Chinese") Gordon (1833-1885), was released by the British Government to take his place. Gordon won renown by reorganizing the force and by co-operating effectively with Li. This force became the spearhead of Li's campaign, going forward side by side with the Hunan and Anhwei "Braves" in the capture of T'ai-ts'ang, K'un-shan, Chiang-yin, and then Soochow where a number of Taiping chiefs were forced to submit. When these chiefs were put to death on the suspicion that they planned treachery, Gordon was furious and threatened to attack Li.

Early in 1864 the government forces moved towards Ch'ang-chou in three divisions—in close co-operation with each other and with Tso-Tsung-t'ang's Chekiang armies. With the capture of Ch'ang-chou the Ever Victorious Army had completed its task and was disbanded. Tsêng ordered Li to join forces with Tsêng Kuo-ch'üan at Nanking, but fearing that jealousies might be aroused if he shared with Tsêng the honor of Nanking (which fell on July 19, 1864), he refrained on the ground that his forces were needed elsewhere. For his part in crushing the Taiping Rebellion he was made a first class Earl with the designation Su-i.

During the next year (1865), in co-operation with Tsêng, civil government was restored in Kiangsu and steps were taken toward the building of iron works. In May 1865 Tsêng was ordered to take command in Shantung against the Nien bandits, and Li was made acting governor-general at Nanking where he established an arsenal under the direction of Halliday Macartney. But as Tsêng failed to win a swift victory over the bandits and was ordered back to Nanking (late in 1866), Li was made Imperial Commissioner to direct the campaign. Early in 1867 Li was made governor-general of Hunan and Hupeh but did not assume that office until the bandits were suppressed in 1868. For his exploits in this campaign Li was given the minor hereditary rank of *Ch'i-tu-yü* and the title of Grand Guardian of the Heir Apparent and was made concurrently an Associate Grand Secretary. He also secured leave to visit Peking where he was received with great honor. The official account of the campaign against the Nien rebels, entitled *Chiao-p'ing Nien-fei fang-lüeh* was completed in 1872 and published by the Tsungli Yamen with a preface of the same date.

Li Hung-chang took over his duties as governor-general at Wuchang on March 1, 1869. But his routine as a civil official was broken when in July he was sent to investigate charges against the governor-general of Szechwan, Wu T'ang (*chü-jên* of 1835, d. 1876), and to look into disorders arising from quarrels between Christians and the local populace in Yu-yang, Szechwan, and in Tsun-i, Kwei-chow—the last-named cases having been appealed by church authorities through the French minister at Peking. Li was negotiating with the Bishop when word came that the French minister, Roche-chouart, was on his way up the Yangtze to investigate other cases in Hupeh, and Li hastened back to meet him at Wuchang. These negotiations were scarcely completed when Li was again ordered to Kweichow to investigate the failure of the provincial forces of Szechwan, Kwei-chow and Hunan to co-operate in their conflict with the Miao. But when about to assume this duty he was summoned forth to cope with the Mohammedan uprising. Gathering his forces at T'ung-kuan he reached Sian in July 1870. But in the meantime another crisis had arisen which caused him to be summoned to the coast—namely the Tientsin massacre of June 21, 1870. Tsêng Kuo-fan had not reached a complete settlement of this issue and was ill; the French were bringing warships, and panic had seized the authorities in Peking. At first Li seemed inclined to fight, but grew more cautious as he approached Tientsin. His appointment to succeed Tsêng as governor-general reached him en route and Tsêng returned to Nanking after having virtually settled the case.

Hereafter routine administrative duties held Li Hung-chang in Chihli for a quarter of a century. During this period he served concurrently as Grand Secretary (1872-1901) and after 1879 held the honorary title of Grand Tutor of the Heir Apparent. As Superintendent of Trade for the North almost every question involving foreign relations, the adoption of Western techniques, or the dispatch of students abroad came to his attention. To carry out these multifarious duties he at first divided his time between Pao-tingfu and Tientsin, but later spent most of his time in the latter place.

Li's first experience as a diplomat came in 1871 when he was called upon to negotiate a treaty with Japan. China was unwilling to concede 'most favored nation' rights or to permit trade in the interior. The resulting treaty signed on July 29, 1871 between Li and Date Mu-nenari (1818-1892) was highly unsatis-

factory to Japan but she soon obtained a diplomatic victory which resulted in her first seizure of Chinese territory. China had declined in 1871 to assume responsibility for the murder by Formosan savages of a number of shipwrecked Liu-ch'iuan Islanders, on the ground that the issue was a purely Chinese one. However, rather than go to war, for which the country was then unprepared, an indemnity was paid to Japan. Unfortunately, however, in the documents which were drawn up the Chinese government referred to the Liu-ch'iuan Islanders as "people belonging to Japan" and from 1874 onward Japan seized upon this as a sufficient renunciation to organize the islands as a feudal dependency and in 1879 to incorporate them as a Japanese prefecture. When General Grant was in China on his world tour Li requested him to plead in Japan for reconsideration of the annexation issue, intimating that China in return would facilitate the proposed negotiations for limiting the emigration of Chinese to the United States. Grant was instrumental, as a private citizen, in securing a re-study of the case with the result that, early in 1880, Japan sent Takezoe Shinichirō (1842-1917) to negotiate with Li at Tientsin. Li at first agreed to Takezoe's proposal to divide the islands between China and Japan, as suggested by others; but several months later, when opposition in China grew stronger and when it became known that the islands to be ceded were barren, the agreement was allowed to lapse.

The settlement of the stormy issues that the British Minister raised in connection with the Margary case was finally entrusted to Li Hung-chang. As plenipotentiary he reached Chefoo in August 1876, and there he concluded the Chefoo Convention (September 13) which not only settled this case but provided for the opening of new ports, for regulation of the trade between Burma and Yunnan, and for rules of procedure in the reception of foreign envoys.

During this time Korea was steadily slipping legally from the suzerainty of China and the status of that kingdom became problematical when China declined to assume responsibility in a dispute which arose between Korea and Japan in 1875. Since China's relationship was rather that of a patron than a protector she encouraged Japan to negotiate with Korea directly. Japan, therefore, made a treaty in 1876 as though dealing with an independent power. The question of Korea's relationship to China was temporarily deferred, but the ground was steadily being cut from under China's claim. This became apparent a few years later when the United States tried to open trade with Korea. Though Commodore Shufeldt availed himself of Li's aid in negotiating in 1882 a treaty of commerce, and though the terms were actually drawn up by the two men for the Korean envoys to sign, Li was unable to insert in it any recognition that Korea was a dependency of China. The best he could do was to secure consent for an accompanying letter from the King of Korea, recognizing this fact but adding that Korea was free in her internal and foreign relations. Li was only partly responsible for the blunders in diplomacy of this period; some were made without his consent in Peking, and he did the best he could to retrieve what others had lost.

More than most higher officials of his day, Li Hung-chang realized that the backwardness of China in the matter of arms placed her at the mercy of stronger powers and that the lack of swifter communications and modern machinery re-

tarded her economic progress. Hence he became the patron of many new economic enterprises and technical innovations. In 1872 the conservatives complained at the excessive cost of steamers, but in a memorial Li made a spirited defense of his policies on the ground that foreign encroachment was imminent and that China must provide herself with some of the things that made Western nations strong. Hence he supported in 1872 the proposal of Jung Hung for a steamship line, recommending that a government-subsidized company be formed, operating at first with chartered vessels to carry tribute rice from the South. From this developed the China Merchant's Line whose ships ran not only between northern and southern ports, but also to Japan, the Philippines and Singapore. Incidentally, a large part of the company's stock was owned by Li, as was the case with most of the enterprises he sponsored. Unfortunately, an experimental railway built between Shanghai and Woosung in 1876 was discontinued in the following year. But in 1880 Li submitted a memorial vigorously urging resumption of railway building. He proposed four trunk lines: Peking to Ch'ing-chiang-p'u (near Nanking on the Grand Canal), to Hankow, to Mukden, and to distant Kansu, all to be financed by properly safe-guarded loans. But much inertia had to be overcome before a line was authorized, namely, an eighty-one mile railway linking Tientsin with the T'ang-shan coal mines which Li had been instrumental in opening with modern machinery. Other railways were not constructed until years later.

Li Hung-chang likewise sponsored the first permanent telegraph lines in China. Sporadic attempts had been made since 1865 to construct short lines, among them one from Shanghai to Woosung, built under foreign auspices, and one from Tientsin to the Taku forts, built by Chinese. In 1880 Li recommended the construction of a line from Tientsin to Shanghai and this was completed on December 24, 1881. Three years later it was extended to Peking and from then on to the chief cities of the empire. Li sponsored a number of proposals for schools of a technical character to train Chinese to conduct these modern enterprises, including a weaving mill which was installed in Shanghai in 1882. But many of his proposals were not carried out, owing to the conservatism of the officials or to the cost which seemed to them prohibitive. A Military Academy was opened in Tientsin in 1885, and long before this there were the beginnings of a modern navy. But it was a distinct drawback to China that the arsenals and shipbuilding yards—the first of these being established when Li was governor at Shanghai, others being located later at Foochow and Tientsin—were regarded as provincial rather than national enterprises. Up to 1888 Li, as an associate controller of the Board of Admiralty, was able to secure funds to build up a fleet of some twenty-eight vessels, but from then till the out-break of the war with Japan (1894) a series of setbacks crippled the navy, among them the requisition of two million taels to celebrate the Empress Dowager's birthday, the resignation of Captain Lang, formerly of the British Navy, who with Admiral Ting Ju-ch'ang (d. 1895), had built up the navy; and the death of Prince Ch'un, one of its chief friends among the Manchu princes. The provincial authorities who thus saw sums, which they had grudgingly contributed to the navy, diverted to other uses, naturally cut down their appropriations. Other reforms likewise were retarded after 1888.

Owing to the death of his mother in 1882, Li Hung-chang secured a leave of absence, but trouble in Korea forced his recall in the same year. Leave for the burial was curtailed in 1883 because of French aggressions in Annam. Prior to taking his second leave, Li negotiated a treaty with France securing recognition of Chinese suzerainty over Annam and placing a neutral zone between Chinese and French spheres. But this understanding was repudiated in Paris and M. Tricou was sent from Tokyo to negotiate another treaty recognizing the independence of Annam. Tricou awaited Li at Shanghai, but when Li passed through that city in July 1883 Li could not be held there to revise the treaty in conformity with French wishes. He was coldly received by all the foreign officials, except the American Minister, John Russell Young (1840-1899). Li tried in vain to secure mediation on this menacing problem, and M. Tricou followed him to Tientsin where a tentative agreement was reached which would save some vestige of Chinese prestige in Annam. But even this was not drawn into a definite treaty, and an undeclared war ensued. Li did not contribute his northern fleet to this war lest it be needed for defense, but he did inspire the negotiations for selling the China Merchant's steamers to Russell and Company with a verbal understanding that they might be repurchased after the danger of capture was over. France attacked Formosa and in February 1885 declared a state of war to exist. But some Chinese successes on land, together with a French Cabinet crisis, resulted in a new treaty on April 4, 1885, which was signed by Li Hung-chang on June 9. France virtually got what she desired yet without great loss of prestige to China.

The indifferent success regarding Annam led to a determined effort to retrieve China's position in Korea. The riots in July 1882 which forced the Japanese minister, Hanabusa Yoshitada (1842-1917), to flee, and caused Li to hasten north from Anhwei, resulted from a break between pro-Japanese radicals and pro-Chinese conservatives in Korea. The Tai Wŏn Kun was brought to China as a prisoner. But the issues were settled directly (August 29) between Korea and Japan, thus still further damaging Chinese prestige. One faction in China hoped to establish overlordship in Korea by stationing a resident at Seoul, but Li, fearful of foreign complications, contented himself with putting in force a set of trade regulations—to be enforced by commissioners both in Tientsin and in Seoul—granting Chinese greater privileges than those enjoyed by subjects of other nations. He secured the appointment of P. G. Mollendorff (1847-1901) to organize the Korean Customs, and in place of Chinese consuls in Korean ports he appointed deputy trade commissioners who also exercised criminal jurisdiction over Chinese subjects. But Harry Parkes ignored China's plan when he negotiated treaties with the Koreans in 1883, and in the following year various nations pressed Korea for privileges equal to those the Chinese enjoyed. Moreover, Korean radicals supported by Japanese, sought full independence for their country. On December 4, when the newly-established postal system was being celebrated, a pro-Japanese faction staged a riot and, according to a pre-arranged plan, forced the King to summon Japanese Legation guards to the Palace. Two days later the Chinese garrison at Seoul, in an attempt to rescue the King, attacked the Japanese guards in the Palace and compelled them to withdraw from Korea. Japan sent two of her ablest statesmen to settle this case: Inoue Kaoru to Seoul to seek redress from the King, and Itō Hirobumi (1841-1909) to Tientsin to reach an understanding with Li. After several meetings Itō and Li decided upon the following points: mutually to renounce the policy of stationing troops or military advisors in Korea; the modernization of Korea would be effected by advisors from a third power; and in case of further disturbance no troops would be sent without prior notification to the other power.

Despite this virtual acknowledgment of Japan as an equal in Korea, Li spent the ensuing nine years seeking to recover Chinese prestige and control of that country. While Mollendorff administered the Customs under Robert Hart's directions from Peking, Yüan Shih-k'ai was made 'Resident' to assist the King in internal and foreign affairs; and Judge Denny, former consul at Tientsin and a personal friend of Li, was persuaded to take the office of advisor to the King. Denny, however, disappointed Li by taking for granted the independence of Korea. In 1885 the British suddenly occupied Port Hamilton, whereupon Li negotiated a secret treaty of alliance with the Russian Minister. The British were, however, given the necessary guarantee which led to the evacuation of Port Hamilton (1886) and the treaty of alliance with Russia was never ratified.

While matters were proceeding thus in Korea Li managed in 1886 to carry through the long-desired removal of the Catholic church which overlooked the Imperial Palace in Peking. This was effected by direct negotiation in Rome and also with the Bishop in Peking. Direct diplomatic relations with the Vatican were suggested in the hope of settling numerous church cases without the intervention of France, but France vetoed the proposal.

The prestige of Li Hung-chang seems to have reached its highest point early in the 'nineties. On his seventieth birthday in 1892 the Empress Dowager and the Emperor showered him with gifts and honors. A work containing pictures of the celebration and eulogies by his friends, was published in 6 volumes under the title, *Ho-fei hsiang-kuo ch'i-shih tz'u-shou t'u.*

In the meantime affairs in Korea did not become less confusing. The constant struggle between radicals and conservatives, and the unending foreign intrigue, came to a head in 1893 when the reactionary, semi-religious society known as Tong Haks came forward. This group, whose aim it was to cast out all Western innovations, had a special animus against Japan, which in their eyes had proved a renegade to Eastern Civilization and to Confucian teachings. The danger of revolution was not lessened when Kim Ok-kyun (1851-1894), leader of the radical, pro-Japanese faction and a refugee at Shanghai, was murdered (March 29) and his corpse brought to Korea and cut up and distributed through the country as a warning to liberals. The Korean government managed to suppress the disturbance, but called on China for military aid. Japan, who also sent forces, proposed to China reforms in the government, and when China declined to co-operate, made demands on Korea. The sending by China of reinforcements was regarded as a challenge to Japan who commenced hostilities by sinking the chartered troopship, *Kowshing* (July 25, 1894).

It was far from Li's intention to challenge Japan to war, for as stated above his navy was crippled, after 1888, for want of funds. But the Peking government controlled by his political rival, Wêng T'ung-ho [*q. v.*], advocated resistance. The resulting defeat was fatal to Li's prestige. His Korean policy was shattered, his navy was routed, and for both catastrophes he alone was blamed. He was deprived of honors but held at his post, frantically seeking for funds, for munitions, for mediation. He was dejected and at his wit's end. Yet the blame was laid on him for a war which he would have avoided. In November he sent his trusted advisor, Detring, with a personal letter to Ito to negotiate peace, but Detring was not received. Attempts were made through the American minister, Charles Denby (1830-1904), to discuss peace on the basis of Korean independence, but Japan replied that she would make her terms known only to properly accredited plenipotentiaries sent to Japan. Consequently China dispatched Chang Yin-huan [*q. v.*] and Shao Yu-lien to Hiroshima. There they were met early in January by Ito and Mutsu Munemitsu (1844-1897). But Japan rebuffed them on the ground that their credentials were improperly drawn up, nor would she permit them to secure revised credentials by telegraph. Only a man of very high rank would be acceptable, and this pointed to Li himself. Li's cup of bitterness was not yet drained to the dregs, for on February 17 a cablegram from Tokyo stated that no plenipotentiary need come who was not authorized to cede territory and settle outstanding questions, great and small, including demands Japan would later make known. China could only accept the hard terms and Li was appointed. Prior to setting out for Shimonoseki he called on various legations to seek aid. Though no such pledges are definitely known to have been given, some writers profess to believe that Count Cassini of Russia did virtually pledge Russian aid in case Manchurian territory should be demanded, and that Britain intimated she would not be indifferent if her sphere in the South were invaded. The first meeting with the Japanese took place on March 20, when an armistice was refused except on impossible terms. Four days later Li was shot by a fanatic and the incident so stirred public opinion that profuse apologies were made and a generous armistice was granted (March 30) for a limited period. Li's nephew and adopted son, Li Ching-fang (1855?-1934) became the plenipotentiary and continued the negotiations.

The terms of peace confirmed China's worst fears. They included not only the independence of Korea but the cession of the Liaotung Peninsula, Formosa, and the Pescadores. Included also were an indemnity of 300,000,000 Kuping taels, the opening of seven new ports to trade —chiefly in the Yangtze and West River regions—and numerous concessions to Japanese merchants. Though a few slight concessions were granted, China was compelled to accept them virtually as first made on April 1. The last touches were added on April 17, 1895, and the treaty was signed, but China still hoped for modifications before final ratification. The hoped-for intervention came on April 23 when Russia, France and Germany advised Japan to retrocede the Liaotung Peninsula. China suggested that the treaty be rewritten, but Japan insisted on ratification first, and after that bowed to the will of the three European powers.

As reward for her services Russia desired the immediate recognition of Li's alleged promises, but Li had been transferred to a non-political post in Peking and could do nothing. The following year, however (1896), on the occasion of the Tsar's coronation in Moscow, Russia insisted that Li was the most suitable delegate to represent China, and the appointment was made. He left Shanghai on March 28, passed through Odessa on April 27, and reached St. Petersburg on April 30. There he was received with great honor by Lobanoff and Witte, and he negotiated with the latter a secret treaty aimed against Japan and providing for an alliance. Permission was given to Russia to build (through the semi-official Russo-Chinese Bank) the Chinese Eastern Railway across Manchuria. Later a contract was officially made between the Chinese Government and the Railway (organized under the bank) which granted special tariff rates, and set forth the terms under which guards might be placed along the line. It was agreed that the road might be purchased by China at the end of thirty-six years and that it might revert to her without compensation after eighty years.

From Russia Li proceeded round the world visiting the Kaiser and Bismarck in Germany, and making stops at The Hague, Brussels and Paris. On August 5 he had an audience with Queen Victoria, and at the end of that month was introduced to President Cleveland in Washington. Sailing from Vancouver on September 14—but refusing to go ashore in Japan—he returned to Tientsin on October 3, 1896. Many anecdotes are still current about this journey round the world. In sharp contrast with his triumphant progress abroad was the cool welcome he received at home. It was owing to the power of the Empress Dowager alone that his enemies did not reach him; and Chinese writers hint that her protection at this juncture was secured at a round price. So Li remained in office, attached to the Tsungli Yamen. Early in 1898 Russia secured the lease of the Liaotung Peninsula, and in connection with the further right which she received to extend her railway south from Harbin to Port Arthur and Dalny, Count Witte is authority for the statement that he gave bribes both to Li Hung-chang and to Chang Yin-huan.

In the summer of 1898—during the Hundred Days of Reform—Li was dismissed from the Tsungli Yamen, and that autumn was sent to supervise conservancy work along the Yellow River. He retained his position as Superintendent of Trade for the North and in that capacity made, in the autumn of 1899, an extended tour of inspection of the chief northern seaports. Soon thereafter he was appointed acting governor-general of Kwangtung and Kwangsi, the appointment being changed after a few months to full governor-general. In that capacity he sought to curb the gambling which was then widespread, but he did not accomplish much before the Boxer outbreak (1900), and the attendant calamities made it urgent that he return to the capital to negotiate with the angered Western powers. Having managed, along with the other southern governors, to maintain order and protect foreign lives and property during the storm, he was virtually the only acceptable spokesman for the scattered and discredited northern régime. Appointed plenipotentiary and governor-general of Chihli, he came north toward the end of the summer, stopping in Shanghai long enough to explore the situation and hold preliminary conversations. Li strove with all his power to make the indemnities as small as possible and the other conditions free from undue humiliation. But the cards were all in the hands of the triumphant allies and the onerous treaty was finally signed on September 7, 1901. Even while he was thus engaged, Russia was hounding him to sign another treaty granting her a free hand in Manchuria. This last bitterness was evaded, however, when he died on November 7.

During his public career which covered nearly half a century, Li Hung-chang had helped to deliver the dynasty from the Taiping Rebellion and had introduced many reforms, particularly in the years 1870-94. Relying much on the advice of Sir Halliday Macartney, William Pethick (d. 1901), Chester Holcombe (1844-1912), Sir Robert Hart and Detring, not to mention others, he did perhaps all he could for a land where the conservatism of the people, a reactionary officialdom, and unrestrained international rivalry, made each step forward a matter of great difficulty. Always progressive, yet patient and conciliatory, it was his fate to bear the blame for failures which might have been avoided if he had had his way. Nevertheless he bore defeat with composure and dignity. Fateful also is the fact that the triumph of Japan caused such a strong reaction in favor of Russia that the policies Li worked out brought about, not a Far Eastern-balance, but the Russo-Japanese war and a train of consequences that may be attributed to it.

Li Hung-chang was posthumously given the honorary title of Grand Tutor, the name Wên-chung, and the hereditary rank of Marquis of the first class. His name was entered in the Temple of Eminent Statesmen, and in later years special temples were erected to his memory in Peking, Tientsin, Shanghai, Nanking, Soochow and other places. . . .

13. THE T'UNG-CHIH AUDIENCE, JUNE 29, 1873

FREDERICK F. LOW

Sir: On the 29th ultimo the embassador of Japan and the ministers of Russia, the United States, England, France, and Holland were personally presented to the Emperor. Subsequently the French minister had a separate audience, to present a letter from the President of the French Republic addressed to the Emperor of China. This letter was a reply to one from the Emperor to the head of the French government which Chunghow took to France in 1870.

The arrangements for the audience and the ceremonies were in strict accordance with the agreement made with the ministers of the yamên, a memorandum of which had been officially submitted to the foreign ministers by Prince Kung. A translation of this memorandum is herewith inclosed (Inclosure No. 1.)

At 6 o'clock a.m. on the day before mentioned the five foreign ministers assembled at the Fu Hua gate, (one of the gates in the wall that surrounds the for-

Dispatch of United States minister to China, Frederick F. Low, to the Secretary of State, Mr. Fish, dated Peking, July 10, 1873, and received September 3. From *Foreign Relations of the United States*, 1873, Part I, pp. 195-201 (Washington, D.C., 1873).

bidden city,) where they were met by the grand secretary, Wên-Hsiang, and several ministers of the yamên, who conducted them to the Shih Ying Kung, a temple within the forbidden city, which contains the rain god, and where the Emperor goes to offer sacrifices and pray for rain in seasons of drought. Here we found the Japanese embassador, who had arrived before us. We were shown into the imperial robing-rooms attached to the temple, where refreshments, consisting of cakes, sweetmeats, fruits, and tea, were served. The refreshments, the Chinese ministers were particular to inform us, had been prepared in the imperial household. After waiting at the temple an hour and more, we were conducted to a large marquee on the west side of the Tsz-Kuang-Ko—the reception-hall—where Prince Kung and the rest of the ministers of the yamên were waiting to receive us. Here we rested for some time awaiting the arrival of the Emperor. All along the route on either side, from the Fu Hua gate to the temple, and between the temple and the hall of reception, were ranged rows of officials, civil and military; and a few cavalry soldiers, and a still larger number of officials, were assembled in the immediate vicinity of the hall. The officials were chiefly civil mandarins, the military being largely in the minority. All were dressed in their official uniforms.

As soon as the Emperor arrived and had taken his seat in the chair of state within the hall, the Japanese embassador was introduced. He delivered a short address and presented his letter in the manner agreed upon; and the Emperor responded through Prince Kung in substantially the same terms that he did to the foreign ministers.

When he had retired the five foreign ministers entered the hall in the order of the priority of their commissions, and ranged themselves in a line in front of and facing the Emperor, with Mr. Bismarck, the interpreter, immediately behind the dean-general, Vlangaly. The Emperor was seated in his chair of state, which was placed upon a dais about ten or twelve feet square and surrounded by a railing. Upon the dais and near the Emperor's chair stood Prince Kung, two other princes, and two "ministers of the presence." Extending from either front corner of the dais, in oblique line to the front corners of the hall, were double rows of high ministers, including all the ministers of the yamên. Upon the terrace outside the hall and on the grounds in front were hundreds, and probably thousands, of mandarins whose rank would not permit of their entering a building in the presence of the Emperor.

As soon as the foreign ministers had taken their places within the hall the Russian minister proceded to read the French version of the address. (Inclosure No. 2.) When he had concluded, Mr. Bismarck read a Chinese version of it. As soon as the reading of the address was concluded, all the ministers ad-

vanced one step, and placed their credentials on the yellow table, which stood between them and the Emperor, the latter, at the same moment, bowing in token of recognizing their reception. Then Prince Kung, who had been standing at the left of the Emperor, knelt to receive His Majesty's reply. After which he advanced toward us, and said: "His Majesty acknowledges the receipt of the letters presented by the foreign ministers." The prince returned, and again knelt near the Emperor to receive another message, when he advanced as before and delivered it as follows:

"His Majesty expresses the hope that the emperors, kings, and presidents of the states represented by your excellencies are all in good health, and His Majesty trusts that all business between foreign ministers and those of the tsung li yamên (foreign office) will be settled amicably and satisfactorily." All the ministers then retired except M. de Geofroy, who, after his interpreter had been introduced, made a short address and delivered the special letter with which he had been charged by his government, the Emperor acknowledging its receipt the same as before. When the foreign representatives had all re-assembled at the temple, and after again partaking of refreshments, they were conducted by the ministers of the yamên to their chairs at the Fu Hua gate.

It is due to the ministers of the yamên that I should say that all their promises touching the reception were fulfilled honestly and fairly. The arrangements were well ordered, so that there was really nothing to complain of; and the reception was in itself respectable and entirely respectful to foreign governments.

I may remark in this connection that

the hall in which the reception took place is not the great hall where the Emperor usually receives his own officials. It is, however, one of the many reception-halls scattered through the grounds of the forbidden city, and is exclusively used for receptions by His Majesty.

It is not impossible that the effect upon the Chinese would have been better had the reception taken place in the great hall. Upon this point, however, we did not deem it advisable to insist; indeed, it was waived voluntarily early in the discussion. The reasons for not insisting upon the reception taking place in the great hall were:

First. By the usages of nations the sovereign granting an audience can name the time and place; and,

Second. We deemed it policy not to be too exacting on minor points provided the Chinese government would sacrifice all their notions of propriety and consent to receive the representatives of foreign governments without prostration or genuflection.

In addition to these considerations it may be doubted whether any government would sustain its diplomatic representative were he to insist on dictating to the Emperor of China as to the place for a reception, so long as the reception-hall proposed was one usually devoted to that purpose, as was the case in the present instance.

Upon some other points there was disagreement and considerable discussion before they were finally arranged. The Chinese ministers objected to having the secretaries and attachés of the legations accompany the ministers, and, as our discussions had all been carried on through the agency of a single interpreter, they objected to having more than one present at the audience.

These two points were yielded on the condition that they would consent to give the French minister a separate reception for the purpose of delivering his special letter, at which he should be accompanied by the interpreter of his own legation. This was finally agreed to.

By this arrangement the Chinese ministers yielded, at the last moment, one of the positions they had been fighting to maintain all through the discussions; and a precedent is now established which will, it may be presumed, obviate the necessity of discussion or dispute in the future—that a foreign minister coming to China and bringing a letter from the head of his government addressed to the Emperor on any subject is entitled to deliver it in person.

By the programme originally submitted to us we were to lay our letters of credence on a table, from which they would be taken by one of the Chinese ministers and handed to Prince Kung, who would in turn hand them to the Emperor. This was strenuously objected to, for the reason that, although it was not so stated, we suspected (and as it proved rightly so) that when handing the letters to the Emperor the prince would be obliged to kneel. This led to a protracted and animated discussion. We finally proposed as our ultimatum that we would hand our letters to the prince if we could have an assurance that he would stand when handing them to the Emperor; or we would lay the letters on a table placed between us and His Majesty if he would then and there acknowledge their receipt. The latter proposition was finally accepted.

In the programme first submitted it was stated that foreign ministers should, when presented to the Emperor, wear a diplomatic uniform, but without swords.

The impropriety of this was pointed out, and the impossibility of complying with it definitely stated. I said that by the laws of the United States I was prohibited from wearing any kind of uniform; and my colleagues affirmed that a sword was a part and parcel of a diplomatic uniform. The question of uniform was finally erased from the programme; it was also left optional with us to make as many or as few salutations as we chose when entering and retiring from the hall.

Touching one question I was situated differently from any of my colleagues. Following the precedent set by my two predecessors, I delivered to Prince Kung my original letter of credence at my first interview with him. The other ministers had delivered copies of their letters only, retaining the originals until an opportunity should be afforded to present them in person to the sovereign.

This difficulty was arranged by the handing back of my letter of credence. I was by this means enabled to present it in due form with the others.

The result attained after four months of wearisome discussion may, I think, be considered satisfactory. It will, I trust, be viewed in the same light by the governments directly concerned.

Speculations as to the future are generally valueless; hence I prefer to let time determine the value of the recent concession. It is too much to expect or hope that that audience of the Emperor will cure all the ills from which foreign intercourse and trade suffer in China. It is, however, an important step in advance—the most important that the Chinese government has ever taken except when compelled by force of arms—and I shall be much disappointed if it does not lead to a marked improvement in relations between the treaty powers and this government.

Trusting that the Department will take a hopeful view of the situation, and that my action in the premises will meet the approval of the President,

I have, &c.,

Frederick F. Low.

[INCLOSURE 1.—TRANSLATION.]

Memorandum of the etiquette to be observed at the audience.

The foreign ministers will bring with them M. Bismarck as their interpreter in common; M. de Geofroy will bring M. Deveria as his interpreter in particular.

The ministers will alight from their chairs or horses at the Fu Hua gate, and they will then be conducted by ministers of the yamên, who will accompany them, in the first instance, to the Shih Ying Kung,[1] where for a short time they will rest. If His Majesty be pleased to furnish refreshments it is here they will be partaken of.

The escort (foreign) will remain in a tent outside the Fu Hua gate, where there will be persons to attend to them. The retinue (Chinese) will also remain in the same vicinity. Neither escort nor retinue will enter the Fu Hua gate.

As soon as His Majesty, coming from the eastern side of the building, reaches the inner hall of the Tze-Kuang-Ko,[2] the ministers of the yamên will accompany the foreign ministers and the interpreters to a marquee to the west of the Tze-Kuang-Ko, where they will wait a short time, until His Majesty shall have entered the main hall. The ministers of the yamên will accompany the foreign ministers and the interpreter, M. Bismarck, up the western flight of steps into the Tze Kuang-Ko by the western space.

The speech (or speeches) of the foreign

1. "Palace of Seasonableness," a temple to the Dragon King.
2. The violet hall.

ministers ended, they will each spread his letter of credence upon the yellow table. His Majesty will make some special sign of affability (probably a bow) and will say (literal answer) that the letters of credence have now been received; he will also make gracious remarks and put kindly questions. His Majesty's remarks will be interpreted with solemn reverence by Prince Kung.[3]

Foreign ministers, when they enter the hall, when they are speaking or stating their names, as also when questions are addressed them, and when they reply, will, in token of extraordinary respect, make the usual reverences as proposed.

The forms will be settled by rehearsal before the audience.

When the ceremony is ended, the other four ministers and the interpreter, M. Bismarck, will retire by the western flight of steps. The ministers of the yamên will accompany them to the Shih Ying Kung, where they will wait a short time, M. Devéria being meanwhile brought by the ministers of the yamên into the Tze-Kuang-Ko.

M. de Geofroy will then speak, and spread upon the yellow table the answer to the letter of the Chinese government.[4]

His Majesty will, as before, acknowledge the receipt of this letter.

The audience being ended, M. de Geofroy and M. Devéria, the interpreter, will retire, the ministers of the yamên accompanying them to the Shih Ying Kung; thence, the whole party being re-assembled, they will conduct the foreign ministers and the interpreters out of the Fu Hua gate.

The arrangements set forth in this paper are made because the Emperor having to receive letters of credence, a decree has been received from His Majesty according an audience.

Hence the liberality of the ceremonial June 26, 1873.

3. By this it is understood that the Emperor will speak in Manchu, and Prince Kung will interpret it in Chinese.
4. The letter addressed by the Emperor of China to the French Emperor in 1870, and sent to France by Chung Hou.

[INCLOSURE No. 2.]

SIRE: The representatives of Russia, Vlangaly; of the United States of America, Low; of Great Britain, Wade; of France, Geofroy, and of the Netherlands, Ferguson, have the honor to offer, in the name of their governments, their congratulations to your Imperial Majesty on your majority, and pray for a long duration of your reign and for the prosperity of your people.

They hope to see in your Majesty's reign the continuation of the reign of your illustrious forefather, Kang-hi, who, while he raised China to the summit of its glory and power, gave free access to western arts and sciences.

China, sire, will return to these happy days under your Majesty's government, and the fóreign powers who have concluded treaties with your Imperial Majesty will see with pleasure the development of relations and the strengthening of the friendship that exists with your vast empire.

We have the honor, sire, to lay before you the letters that accredit us as envoys extraordinary and ministers plenipotentiary at your Imperial Majesty's court.

[INCLOSURE No. 3.]

Memorandum of the reception of foreign ministers by the Emperor of China, 29th June, 1873.

The foreign ministers, provided with letters of credence, having accepted the programme communicated to them by the yamên on the 25th June, it was agreed that each should proceed from his own residence on the morning of the 29th to the Roman Catholic establishment known as the Pei-Tang, where the bishop, Monseigneur de Laplace, had been so good as to provide accommodation for those who might wish to change their dress. The rendezvous was to be at a quarter before six a.m., at which time the minister, Chunghow, was to meet the foreign ministers at the Pei-Tang for the purpose of conducting them to the gate by which they were to enter the palace grounds.

On his arrival the different ministers, each in his chair, and, if he had a foreign escort, attended by his escort, proceeded toward the marble bridge which spans the pei-hai, the lake in the palace grounds. The bridge is, on ordinary days, a thoroughfare, but by the Emperor's desire a barricade had been thrown across the western end of it. This, with a corresponding barricade a little farther to the west, marked off a space right and left of the Fu-Hua-mun, the gate by which the ministers were to be admitted into the palace grounds, in such wise that room was left for the chairs of the ministers and their escort.

Within the gate there were waiting the grand secretary, Wănsiang, and all the other ministers of the tsung li yamên, with the exception of the presidents, Pao-Tsun and Thăn-Kwei-Făn, who, as it had been intimated upon the 26th June they would be, were with Prince Kung in attendance upon the Emperor.

The grand secretary and his colleagues conducted the foreign ministers to the Shih Ying Kung, where they found the Japanese embassador, Soyisima Tranéomi, who had come from his residence in another part of the city. The Japanese embassador was accompanied by his interpreter. The envoys extraordinary and ministers plenipotentiary of Russia, the United States, England, and France, and the diplomatic agent of the Netherlands, were accompanied by Mr. Bismarck, *sécrétarie interprète* of the German legation, as interpreter of the corps diplomatique. Mr. Devéria, first interpreter of the French legation, accompanied his minister, who, it had been arranged, was to have a second audience for the purpose of delivering the reply of the French government to the letter of explanations carried to France by the minister Chunghow, in 1870, after the massacre of Tien-tsin.

The Shih Ying Kung, or palace of Due Season, is a temple in which prayers are offered by the Emperor for rain or for fair weather, as the case may require. In rear of it are some apartments in which, when about to sacrifice, the Emperor robes and unrobes. Here there were some refreshments from the imperial buttery spread out upon two tables. The foreign ministers seated themselves at these, and, after waiting about an hour and half, were invited to move onward to a large tent pitched on the west side of the Tze-Kwang-Ko, or purple pavilion, the building in which the Emperor had decided to give audience.

Prince Kung, with the ministers Pao and Shen, met the foreign ministers outside the tent, in which, it had been understood, they would have to wait a short time before they were summoned to the presence. The interval here, however, as already in the Shih Ying Kung, proved much longer than had been expected. The Prince and his colleagues explained that the Emperor had received important dispatches from the seat of war in the northwest, and that these had detained His Majesty. His highness and his colleagues went and came, apologizing from time to time for the delay. Thus about another hour and half passed away.

At last, a little after nine o'clock, the Japanese embassador and his interpreter were ushered into the pavilion by some of the ministers of the yamên. They returned in a few minutes, and the representatives of western powers were then called for.

Turning to the left as they quitted the tent, the ministers of the yamên conducted them up a low flight of stone steps on the western side of a large platform lying to the south or in front of the pavilion, and, crossing the angle of this platform, they entered the pavilion, as it had been agreed they should, by the space between the first and second columns to the west of the center division of the pavilion. General Vlangaly, minister of Russia, led the way as doyen of the corps diplomatique, and was followed in the order of their seniority by Mr. Low, Mr. Wade, M. de Geofroy, and Mr. Ferguson, respectively, representing the governments of the United States, Great Britain, France, and the Netherlands.

The interior of the pavilion is divided by

wooden pillars into five sections, running from north to south. The Emperor was seated on a throne at the northernmost end of the center section. The throne itself stood on a dais or platform raised three or four feet above the floor of the hall, access being gained to it by three small flights of steps, one in the center and the other two right and left of the throne. A light balustrade, broken, of course, by these three flights of steps, ran around the wooden platform. Half way down the hall, at some ten or twelve paces from the throne, and directly opposite to it, stood a long, narrow table, covered with yellow.

Beside the throne were a few princes of the highest order. On the Emperor's left stood Prince Kung, Prince Chun, (known to foreigners as the 7th prince,) and Prince Po, son of the famous Sungolinsin; on the right, Prince Li and another. On either side of the hall, in double rank, were arranged officials, apparently of the first rank. They were placed so that the inner flanks of their line touched the platform below the throne, near its outer angles, the reverse flanks extending outward till they reached the limits of the central division of the hall. In rear of them, on either side of the throne, were other officials in groups, without arrangement.

The foreign ministers having filed across the hall, as they came in front of the throne bowed to the Emperor, then advanced a few paces and bowed again, and finally halting bowed a third time. M. Bismarck, who had followed the ministers in his capacity of interpreter, took his place in rear of the doyen. The grand secretary, probably as the officer charged with the introduction of the ministers, took post slightly in advance of their line, at the same time somewhat to the left of it.

The doyen then read the address appended to this memorandum. M. Bismarck read a Chinese translation of it, and, the reading ended, the foreign ministers laid their letters of credence upon the yellow table, bowing once as before.

As the letters were laid upon the table the Emperor bent slightly forward, as in acknowledgment of their reception, and Prince Kung, falling on his knees, was commanded by His Majesty, in a low voice, to inform the foreign ministers that the letters had been received. The prince rose, descended the steps, and advancing a short distance toward the ministers, repeated what had been said to him.

His highness then re-ascended the platform, and again falling on his knees was again addressed by the Emperor. On rising he again came down the steps, and coming up this time to the doyen, he said that his Majesty trusted that the emperors, kings, and presidents of the states represented were in good health, and hoped that foreign affairs would be satisfactorily arranged between the Tsungli-yamên and foreign ministers.

This ended the general audience. The French minister, M. de Geofroy, having, as above mentioned, a second letter to deliver from his government, remained, his interpreter, M. Devéria, being introduced as the rest of the ministers withdrew. This they did *à reculons*, and bowing as is usual in other countries.

The whole party, the Japanese embassador included, was in a few minutes re-assembled in the Shih Ying Kung, and after staying there a short time they were conducted to their chairs by the ministers of the yamên present, the grand secretary joining his colleagues as they approached the gate.

A. Vlangaly
Frederick F. Low
Thomas Francis Wade
L. De Geofroy
J. H. Ferguson

14. SYNARCHY UNDER THE TREATIES

JOHN K. FAIRBANK

1. FOREIGN PARTICIPATION IN THE GOVERNMENT OF CHINA

Alien rule is one of the commonplaces of the Chinese political tradition, but its implications for modern times have been generally disregarded. During the last seven centuries China has been ruled more than half the time by non-Chinese emperors—the Yuan dynasty of the Mongols (1279-1368) and the Ch'ing dynasty of the Manchus (1644-1912). Yet this alien rule was not an utterly new experience in Chinese history (witness the dynasties of the Northern Wei, Liao, and Chin in North China in earlier centuries), and China's sociocultural entity was not basically transformed by it. These "dynasties of conquest" were somehow fitted into the Chinese scheme of things, their emperors ruled, on the whole, in the ancient Confucian tradition, and Chinese life went on with the "barbarian" conquerors playing a specialized military-political role as power-holders within the Chinese state. Indeed, since a million or

From John K. Fairbank (ed.), *Chinese Thought and Institutions* (University of Chicago Press, 1957), pp. 204-31. Reprinted by permission. The author is Francis Lee Higginson Professor of History at Harvard University.

so alien invaders were out-numbered a hundred or more to one by the Chinese populace, they could rule only with Chinese help. We may say that, in effect, the Mongols and Manchus *participated* in the government of China, albeit at the top level.

Inner Asian barbarians had in fact always participated in one way or another in the government of the Chinese empire, because the empire had normally embraced both China and the peripheral areas. In institutional terms we must think of agrarian China and nomadic Inner Asia as a single Sino-barbarian political universe, which in its periods of greatest integration and order could be ruled either by Chinese dynasties (like the Han, T'ang, and Ming) or by non-Chinese dynasties (like the Yuan and Ch'ing) but in either case had to be treated as a single interconnected imperial area.

Throughout East Asian history runs this motif of the marriage of the steppe and the sown, the indissoluble connections—military, political, economic—between China's densely populated farmlands and the sparsely populated grasslands of the peripheral regions. The complex reasons for this long historical relationship are grand subjects for speculation and difficult ones for research. The military superiority of mounted archers over peasant conscripts, the economic dependence of nomads on trade with settled areas, the greater political opportunity afforded to rebels on the periphery of empire (where they could develop effective administrations in comparative peace while rebels within China, obliged to keep fighting, had less chance to learn how to govern), all these are facets of this large problem of Sino-barbarian relations, which form the historical background of modern China's foreign relations.

As a result of this long tradition, the Chinese state came onto the international scene a century ago with a well-developed institution of *foreign participation* in its government. Under strong, expansive Chinese dynasties this had taken the form of vassalage on the part of the Inner Asian tribal chieftains, who maintained a tributary relationship to the Chinese emperor. Under non-Chinese dynasties ruling in China, this participation had taken the form of *joint administration* by a mixed Chinese and non-Chinese bureaucracy.

This phenomenon of joint administration, needless to say, had been extremely variegated. It had covered a wide spectrum, running from tyrannical forms of barbarian domination under the early Mongols to egalitarian forms of Sino-barbarian co-operation under the late Manchus. Many subtle factors had entered into it—cultural elements of language, dress, and custom; social considerations and economic interests; military strategy; political theory. I propose to call this intricate institution of "joint Sino-foreign administration of the government of China under a foreign dynasty" by the special name *synarchy*, not because it is a clearly known quantity but precisely because it is so largely unknown. (Later sections of this paper will attempt to define synarchy more fully; I prefer it to "dyarchy," because the latter term implies that only two parties are involved and already has a special meaning with reference to British India.)

Foreign rule in China under dynasties of conquest has thus far been studied almost entirely within the framework of the Chinese imperial tradition before modern times. Yet reflection suggests that the role played by non-Chinese in the Chinese state during the Northern Wei, Liao, Chin, Yuan, and Ch'ing periods, between the fourth and nineteenth centuries, has had some sort of historical relationship to the roles played in the nineteenth and twentieth centuries by the British and other Western powers under the unequal treaty system, by the Japanese invaders in their "co-prosperity sphere" subsequently, and perhaps by the Russians under communism most recently.

Just as synarchy became a recognizable political institution under the barbarian dynasties of conquest, so, I suggest, the treaty system after 1842 became for a time a major political institution of the Chinese state with certain "synarchic" features.

However, as we shall see, this tendency toward a brief *continuity of institutional practices*, before and after 1842, was not accompanied by a similar continuity of political theory concerning Sino-foreign relations. On the contrary, the *ideological discontinuity* created by Western contact eventually undermined and destroyed China's traditional political order, in its foreign as well as its domestic aspects.

In order to test out this analytic

scheme, we will look first at certain traditional features of synarchy as an institution, both in theory and in practice; then note certain evidences of their persistence in the early years of the treaty system after 1842; and finally touch upon the decline of both the theory and the practice as a result of Western contact. In these speculations it will avail little either to assert the uniqueness of Chinese institutions (as sinologists sometimes do out of ignorance of other regions) or to stress their universal aspects and comparability with institutions elsewhere (which does not necessarily advance our knowledge of China). The problem is rather to formulate hypotheses that will more clearly illuminate the boundary of our ignorance and stimulate concrete research.

2. SYNARCHY AS A TRADITIONAL INSTITUTION

A survey of the dynasties of conquest was attempted by a group of Japanese scholars a decade ago.[1] While their study by its nature was superficial and subject to wartime pressure for haste, it nevertheless brings out a consistent pattern in some detail. In the history of the Northern Wei (A.D. 386-556), Liao (907-1125), and Chin (1115-1234) there had already appeared certain features which recurred in the history of the Mongols and Manchus:

1. The barbarian invaders were able to seize power in North China usually after a period of disorder, at a time when a previous dynasty was collapsing and the need for unity and order was widely felt.

2. In organizing their effort at conquest, the barbarians inevitably enlisted Chinese advice and guidance, which

they got most easily from Chinese of the border region.

3. Chinese army forces were similarly absorbed into the invading horde, even though the superior military striking power of the barbarians continued to be concentrated in their cavalry, which was supplied with more and better horses from the grazing land of the steppe than could be maintained in the cultivated region of China.

4. As they acquired control over Chinese territory, the invaders pursued a policy both of terror and of appeasement of the Chinese local leadership. The alien regime had first to be built on the support of the Chinese upper class, principally the gentry-landlords. Frequently these latter groups had organized local self-defense corps by which to maintain local order and the old structure of social relationships in the village. The first aim of the alien conqueror was to appease these interests and secure their support. Chinese leaders must be used in order to enlist a larger corps of Chinese administrators.

5. Again in general terms, it seems characteristic of all these invaders from the north that they recognized the impossibility of imposing their own culture upon the settled masses of China, which of course was made the more difficult by the invaders' great inferiority in numbers. In varying degree, but to some extent in each case, the dynasties of conquest therefore conducted their administration of Chinese territory in the Chinese tradition of the day: they preserved the traditional forms of administration and of social and cultural life in China, even when, as under the Liao, they divided the region under their rule into two areas—one within North China and one outside the Wall, where the Liao culture and way of life could be preserved.

6. Thus, as a corollary to the principle of ruling China in a Chinese way, the invaders found it most essential to maintain a homeland of their own beyond the Wall whence they had come. In this way they attempted to preserve their own conscious existence as a people and avoid or postpone that "absorption" which a popular but superficial Western tradition used to assign as the ineluctable fate of foreigners who conquer China.

7. The preservation of Chinese ways in the governments of China meant, in effect, that the administration should be conducted, at least on the local level, largely by Chinese under the supervision of the alien conquerors. The use of both types of personnel was an inevitable feature of every alien dynasty.

8. In addition, the invaders found it useful to employ other foreigners. Thus the Liao made use of the Hsi people of Mongolian stock from Jehol. The Chin used the Ch'itan Mongols widely in administration.

9. Once the conquest had been achieved, the barbarians' next task was to insure control through military force held in reserve. A territorial army had to be built up, into which Chinese could be recruited and which would be completely loyal to the new dynasty. Units of this army could then be garrisoned to protect the capital and to hold key spots such as the Yangtze delta.

10. Toward the border peoples who remained behind them on the frontier of Inner Asia, meanwhile, the dynasties of conquest typically developed a divide-and-rule policy, setting tribe off against tribe, so as to insure their rear and prevent the rise of competitors in that quarter.

In addition to these various practices, and underlying them, was another factor which facilitated alien rule, namely, the political theory of the Chinese state—a similarly large and unstudied subject concerning which generalization must also be attempted.

In general, I suggest that the Chinese emperor as a political institution can be discussed most conveniently under the heading of the "Confucian monarchy." (While the monarchy owed much to the ancient, Legalist enemies of Confucius, its use of the ideology enshrined in the Confucian classics would seem to legitimize the adjective "Confucian." Similarly, the Roman Catholic Church may appear to be institutionally far advanced beyond the explicit teachings of Christ, yet it seems not inappropriate to call it "Christian.") The Confucian monarchy exercised the universal rule of the Son of Heaven, who in theory represented all mankind, and set no territorial limits to his sway. The Chinese emperor's role may be better described by calling him simply the Son of Heaven, rather than an emperor of any kind. His influence according to the Confucian-Mencian theory of government was held to emanate from the fact of his virtuous conduct. While his semireligious functions, signalized in the state cult of Confucius of which the emperor was the head, were centered in China, they were held to be valid also for the surrounding peoples. Whenever occasion offered, it was therefore appropriate in theory that the moral supremacy and as far as possible the actual rule of the Son of Heaven should be spread over the barbarians of Inner Asia. This extension of the rule of the Chinese Son of Heaven was often thwarted in practice by the Huns and their non-Chinese successors outside the Wall; yet the example of the universal and inclusive Confucian monarchy seems to have set the political style for barbarian rulers, from the Shan-yü of the Huns down to the unlimited sway of Chinghis Khan himself. At all events, as barbarian conquest became more frequent and thorough, the imperial institutions of China and of Inner Asia tended to coalesce—despite the continuing differences in social base, economy, and culture, barbarian Sons of Heaven came to look very much like Chinese Sons of Heaven both in their administrative functions and in their theoretical position in the political order of East Asia. Thus by early modern times the Manchu rulers of Mongolia and China were able to use, over Mongolia, devices of divide-and-rule administration which they had inherited from the Ming and, over China, devices of centralized control which the Ming had originally inherited from the Mongols.

The result of all this was that the Confucian monarchy became a Sino-Barbarian institution. The Mandate of Heaven (manifested in the tacit acquiescence of the Chinese populace) might be held by either a Chinese or a non-Chinese. Also, contenders for it might come either from within China or from outside.

The practice of joint administration or synarchy under a dynasty of conquest reached its most developed form under the Manchus. While it would be tedious to describe at length the dual system of administration which continued at Peking for well-nigh three centuries, certain bases of power which underlay it may be distinguished briefly in sequence.

A. The External Base

The barbarian power in China was most visibly represented by the military forces which were kept in readiness and in reserve with a demonstrable capacity to overcome any attempt at Chinese armed rebellion. Back of this, however, lay the fact of social and racial cohesion on the part of the barbarian minority group in China. Led by the reigning dynasty, the conquerors took great pains to maintain their identity and the special status and prestige which went with it. For this purpose it was important that they maintain a territorial base external to China proper. As successful rebels from the Manchurian pale, who had got ahead of competing Chinese rebels from within North China, the Manchus owed much to their territorial base outside the Wall. There they had imitated and taken over many features of Chinese economic life and government while retaining certain barbarian features of strength such as their military power. The secret of their success was that their external base gave them an opportunity for institutional development, especially the acquiring of the administrative skills necessary for the civil government of China. This was an opportunity often denied to Chinese domestic rebels—*vide* their competitor Li Tzu-ch'eng, who was strong enough to destroy the Ming in 1644 but not capable of recruiting upper-class scholar-gentry to help him govern in their place.[2]

B. The Use of the Gentry Class

Once in power, the conquerors' first needs were to revive civil administration by Chinese local magistrates and, for this purpose, to secure the co-operation of the local gentry both as a necessary adjunct of government and as a reservoir of potential officials. Whether one regards the key position of the scholar-gentry class as based primarily on land-owning or, more broadly speaking, on its performance of local economic, social, cultural, and administrative functions, it is generally accepted that it was the central element in an elitist government conducted by the special class of literati-bureaucrats, over the politically inert mass of the peasantry. The ruling class of officials interpenetrated the scholar-gentry or literati, and the whole stratum of scholars and bureaucrats had special privileges and prerogatives which set them apart from the peasant mass (their personal connections, their competence in the written language, and their capacity to act in terms of Confucian ideology; also, their exemption from *corvée* labor and corporal punishment). The first task of every ruler was to act as the patron of the literati, maintain the examination system by which they qualified themselves, and choose his officials from among the successful candidates. The Manchu emperors proved extremely competent at this universalistic procedure.[3]

C. The Civil Control System

To keep the civil governments in working order, the barbarian dynasties used a "control system," as we may call it, of administrative practices which had been developed and used also by Chinese rulers and which went with the Confucian monarchy in the Chinese empire regardless of whether the monarch was Chinese or barbarian. In other words, the Manchu conquest consisted of their capture of the Chinese monarchy, leadership of the gentry class, and application of the control system.

To a considerable degree the control system of the Manchus was merely a continuation of that of the Ming. (What features the Ming had inherited from the Mongols is a question which needs further research.) Under it, the populace was held in check not only by military garrisons but mainly by the *pao-chia*

system of mutual guaranty and responsibility among the village households. The literati were caught up in the examination system, which served both to recruit and to indoctrinate human talent that might otherwise become organized against the regime. To this the Manchus added a control of thought and literature. The institution of the censorate gave opportunity for the official schooled in orthodoxy to invoke the Confucian ideology against deviant conduct. Meanwhile the inveterate use of one man in several functions or part-functions, and the performance of every function by several men part-time, produced a situation of collegial or collective responsibility among officials such that one was obliged to check upon another. The administrative procedure by which provincial officials transacted their business through memorials directly to the emperor, rather than through the ministries at the capital, prevented the diffusion of central power. The "law of avoidance," by which a man could not serve in his native locality, checked family influence. At the top the emperor not only dispensed with a prime minister (as the Ming had also done) and retained the decisive position in the administrative procedure but also by custom was able to act as a despot without check or hindrance—promoting and discarding his officials arbitrarily as though his absolutism needed constantly to be demonstrated.[4]

D. Culturalism as the Focus of Loyalty

Without attempting to describe further this enormously complex and variegated governmental system, we may conclude, I think, that it exalted the exercise of central power by the Son of Heaven on a universal and nonnational plane. The Manchu rulers' patronage of the Chinese scholar-gentry exemplified traditional cultural values which also sanctioned their overlordship of the Mongol tribes, Turkestan, and Tibet. Just as the Mongols had used Arabs and other West Asians, Russians and other Europeans, so the Ch'ing had employed the Jesuits and would later hire Western advisers and civil servants. The touchstone of loyalty to the regime was a matter separate from one's origin or race. It was this emphasis upon the personal relationship between the Confucian ruler and his Chinese or foreign vassal which facilitated the use by the monarch of one barbarian against another, corresponding to his playing-off of one clique of Chinese officials against another. All of them were within the embrace of the universal empire.

As a consequence, the Confucian monarchy had a basis more cultural than national. Under it might function all those who had assumed a proper place with reference to the Confucian polity. Since Eastern Asia is the Chinese cultural area, where the Chinese type of writing system, bureaucracy, and intensive agriculture provide a common bond in the settled communities from Korea to Annam, this culturalistic basis of political order was no doubt to be expected. The greatest achievement of the Confucian monarchy, however, lay in its capacity to embrace the fighting nomads of Inner Asia within the same polity, no matter whether they were dominant or dominated. This capacity to bring the nomad into the Confucian state was undoubtedly a great accomplishment. Historically the nomad conquerors had made their contribution to it: for it had been forced upon the sedentary Chinese state through the instances of barbarian conquest.

The foregoing sketch will perhaps make it apparent that synarchy, as the "joint Sino-foreign administration of the government of China under a foreign dynasty," was no fly-by-night phenomenon but an old-established institution which stemmed from the very center of the Sino-barbarian political experience in East Asia, an integral aspect of the imperial Confucian order.

3. THE GENESIS OF THE TREATY SYSTEM

The eventual upshot of British military superiority, as demonstrated in the Opium War of 1840-42, was a nexus of mutually supporting naval, legal, administrative, and commercial arrangements which for brevity we call the "treaty system." Its most conspicuous manifestations, the treaty ports, were produced by the confluence of two traditions—on the foreign side, that of European maritime expansion and, on the Chinese side, that of tribute relations. These two traditions had of course been in contact on the coast of China for several centuries, and their miscegenation had been no sudden act. Let us first note certain features of the Western maritime expansion and then see how it had been fitted into the tradition of tribute relations.

A. The Early European Factory Network in Asia

European adventuring overseas at first combined piratical seizure of goods and people with bartering for them as a less preferred alternative. Portuguese expansion paid its way around Africa largely by the traffic in slaves, and across the Indian Ocean by seizing the entrepôts of the Arab spice trade.[5] Early Portuguese freebooters on the China coast were quite comparable to their more formidable contemporaries, the pirates of Japan. In time, as trade became more profitable than buccaneering, the various joint-stock East India companies of the seventeenth century built up their trading posts (factories) at the focal points of Asian trade. Each Dutch, British, or French factory carried within it the seeds of colonial empire—namely, the company's wide prerogatives to monopolize the home country's trade in Asia, to exercise legal jurisdiction over its citizens there, to protect its goods and persons by naval and military forces, and, in short, to act as a government overseas by fiat of the national sovereign in Europe. These assorted prerogatives of government combined with the acquisitive motives of trade to make the European factories into dangerous nodes of expansion amid the political disunity of South and Southeast Asia. The same explosive danger remained locked within the factories at Canton, ready to burst forth whenever the government of China should lose its local military superiority vis-à-vis the Europeans there.[6]

B. The Factories in China under the Tribute System

From the Chinese point of view, barbarian ships arriving by sea seemed just as much inclined to raid the Middle Kingdom, when they were strong enough, as were nomad horsemen coming from Inner Asia. The early European sea-raiders were even more mobile and their home bases comparatively invulnerable through distance across the ocean. But a greater difference became apparent when they were eventually supplanted by regular traders whose seaborne goods far exceeded the volume which came overland by Inner Asian

caravans. Maritime trade soon became a form of Sino-barbarian contact entirely different from land trade—economically larger and more valuable, strategically less easy to control by the twin tools of military force and Confucian personal relationships (even though the big Ming naval expeditions of the early fifteenth century had made efforts in that direction).

The Chinese solution to this problem of sea trade was to quarantine the European merchants in their factories, restrict their factories to Canton, and control them through the prime motive which had brought them to China, their lust for commercial profit. This solution remained effective until the nineteenth century, because the Ch'ing power remained too formidable on its home soil and too remote from Europe to invite military attack.

The Western network of trading posts and naval bases, flung across the Indian Ocean by Portugal and woven tighter by Holland, France, and Britain, thus frayed out when it came to China. The little outposts like that of the Dutch in seventeenth-century Formosa, which elsewhere in Asia expanded into colonial empires, could not pursue their inveterate tendencies on the mainland of China any more than in Japan. By the late eighteenth century the British East India Company, already restricted to Canton, found that the appearance of His Majesty's naval vessels hurt the trade more than helped it: the dominant incentive of Sino-British relations was mutual profit within the established Ch'ing political order, and the E.I.C. Select Committee could protect itself better by stoppages of trade within this framework than by bringing in British warships to try to change it. As it turned out, this situation was exceptional and temporary, in the history of

Europe's world-wide colonial expansion, but it permitted China to assimilate the Western factories for the time being into the institutional framework of the tribute system, or at least to give the appearance of doing so.

For this purpose the precedents went far back, to the treatment accorded Arab merchants in ports like Canton and Ch'uan-chou (Zayton) as early as the Sung period. Arab traders in these ports had had their own quarter, within which they were expected to reside, and their own headmen, who acted responsibly for their community in its relations with Chinese officials. They also applied their own legal institutions among themselves and had their own mosque and religious practices. As the imperial tribute system developed in succeeding centuries under the Yuan, Ming, and early Ch'ing, it took account in practice of this type of foreign merchant community on the Chinese frontier. While merchants of Inner Asia, including eventually those from Russia, were expected to bring their caravans to certain centers of trade on the land frontier such as Yü-men-kuan or Mai-mai-chen, the maritime traders from Liuch'iu came regularly to Foochow, those of Siam to Canton, and so on for each of the overseas countries which sent tribute as the necessary concomitant of its trade.

When the tribute system was applied to Europeans, the foreign merchants in the Thirteen Factories at Canton, under their own recognized headmen, were left to practice their own legal arrangements and religious observances among themselves. Similarly the early Jesuits had been able to function within the Macao community long before they succeeded in breaking away from this commercial connection and getting Chinese consent for mission posts in the interior.

The aim of the Manchu dynasty was to prevent Chinese contact with the European foreigner except as he entered into the Confucian scheme of things and played a proper tributary role. The early tribute missions from the Portuguese and Dutch served to confirm this principle. Care was taken to make the factories a point of economic contact only and to limit intellectual interchange. Thus there was a ban on teaching the Chinese language to foreigners or letting them secure gazetteers or other writings of strategic importance. By the early nineteenth century the custom was well established for the Ch'ing dynasty to cast the Western barbarians in a traditional role as tributaries of the Confucian monarchy. The chief element of discord which had emerged at Canton was that the Western barbarians, unlike their predecessors of Inner Asia, were not ready to accept the theoretical premises and political practices of this relationship. From this eventually flowed the conflict at Canton over practical matters of diplomacy, law, and trade.[7]

C. The Treaty Ports' Continuity with Tradition

The British after 1834 finally used gunfire to knock down the structure of the tribute system, including the Cohong trade monopoly and other restrictions at the Thirteen Factories of Canton, but, when the smoke of battle and the talk of the treaty negotiations had both subsided, they and their foreign colleagues of other treaty powers were left with the five treaty ports: foreign merchants and missionaries were still restricted to certain areas on the Chinese coast, which were measured by the distance which one might go inland and still return by evening to the treaty ports. These foreign communities were still under their own recognized headmen, who were now called "consuls." Among themselves they observed their own legal procedures, under the terms of what was now called extra-territoriality, as well as their own religious practices. They were in a more aggressive position with power to make further demands. But for the time being, in the 1840's and 1850's, they sought only treaty rights, the fulfilment of which in time would allow them to profit from the Chinese scene without being responsible for it.

On the political level, the institutional continuity of these early treaty ports with the preceding centuries of Sino-foreign relations is certainly very plain—plainer than the Westerners in nineteenth-century China ever realized. The most-favored-nation clause, for example, was not the sole invention of Western diplomats, as some of them believed, but embodied the Son of Heaven's traditional treatment of all barbarians with equal condescension, the better to manipulate them against one another.

If we now try to look at the early treaty system through traditional Confucian eyes (no easy feat), we may glimpse the persistent outlines of certain time-tested Sino-barbarian relationships, certain institutional tendencies which remained half-latent, half-emergent during the two decades after the Opium War of 1840. The essence of these postwar tendencies, I suggest, was for the Western participation in Chinese affairs to shift from the rejected forms of tribute relations toward those of synarchy—toward forms of "joint Sino-foreign administration." This tendency was manifested especially in the treaty ports, where the Western powers participated increasingly in the government of these small but strategic parts of China.

4. SYNARCHIC TENDENCIES UNDER THE EARLY TREATIES

My suggestion in what follows is that inveterate synarchic habits had some influence on Sino-foreign relations under the early treaties on the level of institutional practice. In this period the Ch'ing officialdom was still largely unaffected by the ideas of Western nationalism and clung to the Confucian view of foreign relations which had been coexistent with synarchy. While the Westerners in these two decades remained impervious to Confucian ideas, they found some practical usefulness in the synarchic tendencies in question.

For purposes of this analysis, we must deny any hard-and-fast causal relationship between thought and institutions. They are actually intermixed and interdependent, neither one existing in fact without the other, and the distinction between them is an analytic step taken by the observer on a high level of abstraction. Similarly the customary distinction between economics and politics, while implicit in most modern thinking, has limited usefulness and seems indeed to be breaking down. In the case of nineteenth-century China, economic determinists, by asserting the primary causal importance of economic factors like foreign trade, have persuaded a whole generation to look at the treaty system in mainly economic terms, thereby neglecting the important cognate approach to it in political terms. In what follows we need not deny the corrosive effect of Western trade on China, nor the contrast between the all-transforming industrial power of Britain and the comparatively innocuous influence of traditional invaders like the Manchus—all of which became more evident after the period here discussed.

The British were able after the Opium

War to set forth a new structure of ideas including such elements as free trade and the equality of states, which were all expressed in the words of the treaties. However, the British and other Westerners in the treaty ports were not the only actors in the drama of Sino-foreign relations. Even after they had obtained the treaties on paper and were able to threaten the renewed use of superior force, they were far from dominant in the day-to-day situation and could not dictate Chinese action. In fact, the path of progress for the British often lay in a judicious accommodation of Western ways to those of the Middle Kingdom. As practical men representing their merchant compatriots, the British consuls not infrequently had to compromise with the institutional situation which confronted them.[8] This left the way open, during the interval from 1842 until the early 1860's, for a body of treaty-port practices and institutions to grow up which exhibited certain synarchic features reminiscent of Sino-barbarian relations in the past.

As an intellectual device for looking at these tendencies, let us compare aspects of the British opening of China in the 1840's with the Manchu conquest of the 1640's. If we acknowledge from the start that these invasions represent two very different traditions and social forces, far apart in time and cultural background, the similarities between them may take on added interest. The comparison will at least show more in common on the level of action and practice than on the level of theory and ideology.

The Manchu Conquest and the British Opening of China

1. TERRITORIAL BASES ON THE CHINESE FRONTIER

Unlike domestic rebels, both the Manchus and the British before attacking China had built up their military striking power in territorial bases outside the area controlled by the dynasty then ruling at Peking. In what is now called Manchuria the nascent Ch'ing regime by 1644 had already developed its banner forces (totaling some 169,000 warriors), more than half of whom were Chinese and Mongols.[9]

The British territorial base in 1840 began with India, whence the China expedition was outfitted with a considerable proportion of Indian troops among its landing forces (Bengal and Madras infantry, artillery, sappers, and miners).[10] This base then extended through Singapore, where British administrators were already accustomed to dealing with a growing Chinese population, and Malacca, where British missionaries had first established the Anglo-Chinese College to train Chinese youths in Christianity and, incidentally, in the English language and customs.[11] This British external base was nonetheless territorial for being largely maritime—in it British war vessels dominated an area where the big Chinese junk fleets of Canton and Amoy[12] provided much of the economic activity and Chinese pirates much of the disorder. Operating from this sanctuary inaccessible to the dynasty in China, and with the unusual mobility of their fleet, the British, like the Manchus, were able to appear suddenly upon the Chinese frontier and demonstrate their military superiority, which became most evident when they captured walled cities and defeated imperial garrisons. Where the Manchus had established their border base by expelling the Ming power from Manchuria, the British established their advanced bases on islands like Hong Kong, Kulangsu at Amoy, and Chusan (south of Shanghai near Ningpo on the outer edge of the Hangchow estuary).

2. FORCE IN RESERVE: THE MAINTENANCE OF ORDER

Once they had achieved their immediate ends (which in the case of the Manchu conquest of course went much further than the British), the invaders in each case distributed their military power at strategic spots where it was held ready to defend their position. The garrisons of Manchu bannermen at major cities like Chengtu and Foochow had their later counterparts in the British gunboats stationed at the treaty ports or patrolling the Yangtze. In both cases the military force held in reserve could be dispatched to suppress armed opposition in the areas of interest to the invaders. Where, for the Manchus, this included the entire country, for the British it included the treaty-port centers of residence and the coastal and later riverine routes of water-borne commerce. The British Navy's systematic suppression of Chinese piracy on the South China coast in the late 1840's and 1850's, by convoy and punitive expeditions, was a local police action. It was smaller in scope and aim than the Manchus' extirpation of the rebel Li Tzu-ch'eng after 1644 but similar in requiring the co-operation of the local Chinese populace and officials. During the two decades 1848-69 the British Navy paid 149,000 pounds sterling in bounties while carrying on this policing of the China coast. Usually, "the Viceroys of the maritime provinces . . . sent mandarins with the Queen's ships, who . . . sealed these undertakings with Imperial approval."[13]

3. ENLISTMENT OF CHINESE ASSISTANCE

Neither invasion in practice was a purely military matter. In each case the invader sought to conciliate local Chinese sentiment and secure the aid of the local people as well as the expert help of a body of Chinese collaborators. The British felt little need for domestic military allies like General Wu San-kuei, who let the Manchus enter Shanhaikuan and assisted their subsequent conquest of the provinces. But the preliminary British commercial invasion of Central China, particularly the opium traffic, was carried on for them by their allies in trade, the Cantonese.

As the Manchu forces finally came within the Wall, according to their account, the local officials tendered their submission, which the invaders graciously accepted. On May 30, 1644, for example, when the Manchu invading force was at Fu-ning-hsien on the route to Peking, "the District Magistrate Hou I-kuang and his colleagues at the head of the local populace came out to welcome it. Robes (of office) were bestowed upon them and they were ordered to continue in the discharge of their official duties and to distribute grain from the storehouses for the relief of the populace."[14] The Manchus laid claim to the Mandate of Heaven by announcing that their mission was to save the Chinese people from disorder and bring them peace. Once installed in Peking, they used many of the Chinese members of the existing bureaucracy. As immediate acts indicating legitimate succession, the Manchu regent at Peking kotowed to Heaven and decreed mourning for the recently deceased Ming emperor. Toward the populace he showed the Son of Heaven's compassion by the remission of taxes.

In the case of the Opium War, even without the ceremonial vestments and the guidance supplied by the theory of the Mandate of Heaven and the record of previous dynasties, the British found it expedient to concentrate their attack on the ruling dynasty and announce that they had no quarrel with the common people. Even before the outbreak of hostilities, the British representative of the crown in China, Lord Napier, at Canton in 1834 had issued proclamations, addressed to the Chinese populace, which cast the blame for current difficulties upon "the perversity of their government" and by implication made it plain that Britain was no enemy of the people.[15] In 1841 British naval officers tried "to confine hostilities as much as possible to the servants and property of the Chinese government, leaving the people uninjured." The interpreters, J. R. Morrison and R. Thom, "frequently enlisted in our favour the people of the country, who might have offered great annoyance." They "knew well how to allay their fears, and conciliate even their good offices."

As a result the Canton delta populace even at close quarters seemed often "more moved by curiosity and astonishment" than by fear of the British steamers; they crowded the river banks, housetops, and surrounding hills and even helped clear the river passage, "the Chinese peasantry . . . coming forward to assist and even venturing . . . on board the steamer itself . . . undoubtedly, one of the good results of not having inflicted any injury upon the country people." Learning by experience, the British at Ningpo in October, 1841, after "the Chinese themselves voluntarily assisted to remove the obstructions . . . behind the city gates," called "some of the principal inhabitants" together and assured them that British hostility was directed "against the government, and not against the people." The Chinese of Ningpo thereupon welcomed British "protection," until they found themselves taxed to ransom the city.[16] The British invaders' success in securing co-operation from the local population was evident in their use of a Chinese coolie corps.

A type of Chinese leadership had already been recruited in the form of the "Chinese traitors" who assisted the early British interpreters in their correspondence and acted as go-betweens with local officials. The British merchants already had their compradors,[17] who assisted them in every form of commercial operation, and the opium trade had provided an incentive for both merchants and officials of the Middle Kingdom to collaborate with the foreign commercial invasion. Throughout the first two decades of the treaty system, the foreign establishments on the Chinese coast attracted a mixed body of Chinese collaborators, which ran the gamut from the early Christian converts (or would-be converts like the founder of the Taiping regime, Hung Hsiu-ch'uan) and translators like Dr. James Legge's assistant, Wang T'ao, to the many unknown and less savory characters who handled opium, scouted for coolies, or represented secret societies like the offshoots of the Triad.

Naturally, these points of comparison between the Manchu and British invasions are outnumbered by points of difference which in retrospect now seem to us far more significant. Yet such points of comparison should not for that reason be entirely overlooked, as has been the custom.

4. THE INVADERS' PRIVILEGED AND EXPLOITATIVE POSITION

Extraterritoriality and the special status and immunities enjoyed by Westerners in modern China (which have helped to make the Western experience of life there often very pleasant) were new versions of the conquerors' traditional prerogatives. The Mongols had lived like overlords in the Middle Kingdom. The Manchus required all China to shave their heads and wear the queue, bend the knee and render tribute. Manchu bannermen living on grain stipends in their special quarters of the big cities had become effete and impecunious by 1842, but institutionally they formed a precedent for the inviolable treaty-port communities which grew up after that date. For two centuries before the modern commercial exploitation by the imperialist powers, moreover, China had paid yearly tribute to alien rulers whose entire tribe and race lived off the Chinese surplus. The annual grain shipments from the Yangtze to Peking may well have been a greater economic burden than the opium trade ever became (a detailed comparison would be of interest).[18]

Western privileges under the treaties have been too well advertised as part of Western imperialism to need recounting in detail. Yet it seems valid to note that many, if not most, of these privileges can also be viewed as traditional concomitants of barbarian conquest and synarchy, in modern dress. Thus China's eventual payment of most of her customs revenue to foreign bond-holders, while not termed "tribute" or paid in rice, was nothing new in principle. The exploitative financial power of the treaty-port banks might well be compared with that of the Moslem guilds during the century of Mongol synarchy, when China was drawn involuntarily into the international trade of the Mongol empire.

The modern tendency to stress the economic aspects of the imperialist situation has led us to ignore in retrospect the social and political aspects. Treaty-power nationals in recent decades (even though they have enjoyed the subtle satisfaction of extraterritorial status) have not really experienced the baronial life of the sometimes very ordinary Westerner who became a taipan, or at least managed to live like one, in a nineteenth-century treaty port. The Western superiority suggested by the (apocryphal) notice "Chinese and dogs not allowed" was effective not only in social life but also in politics, where the acceptability of late Ch'ing officials to the foreigners sometimes became a prime factor in their careers.

5. ECONOMIC DEVELOPMENT

After the setting-up of their respective dispensations, both the Manchus and the British sought to make their new order work and fostered its economic prosperity. Where the Manchu emperors became the patrons of agricultural development, especially the reclamation or breaking-in of new land, and gave edifying advice to farmers, the British administrators in the treaty ports, on the contrary, sought to foster international and local free trade. The first consul at Shanghai lent assistance to the Canton broker, Alum, who energetically tried to bring the silk and tea exports of the interior to the new emporium on the Whangpu.[19] Chinese merchants were soon investing capital in foreign firms, just as the Canton hong merchant, Howqua, had put his money to work through Russell and Company of Boston. The British suppression of the piracy which formerly had handicapped coastal trade was only part of a general extension of orderly commerce, ships, telegraphs, and postal communications to China. In a port like Shanghai the consul soon secured the appointment of a harbor master and the establishment of aids to navigation such as channel markings, and eventually helped dredge the Woosung bar. Meanwhile Shanghai's new international settlement, together with the adjoining French concession, entered on that phenomenal period of growth which has made it in a century one of the world's greatest cities. Where Manchu peace and order had been accompanied by the unfortunate doubling, if not the tripling, of China's population, Western trade and enterprise helped produce the giant, if not overgrown, city of Shanghai.[20]

6. JOINT ADMINISTRATION

The development of administrative institutions involving a joint exercise of power by the invaders and the local regime is more fundamental for our purposes than the sometimes superficial similarities noted above. It seems unnecessary to describe the system of Manchu-Chinese rule which had been worked out with such care and balance at Peking, where each of the Six Boards had a Manchu and a Chinese president, two Manchu and two Chinese vice-presidents, and so on. Here it is of interest to notice comparable institutions built up under the treaty system. Since the British never had the slightest intention of themselves becoming the rulers of China, this development is all the more striking. It grew out of the local situation in the treaty ports, and the impetus arose in the field of practice from day to day rather than in the field of theory and policy aims.

First of all, let us note that in both the first and second China wars, whenever the British forces occupied a city, they were obliged to maintain Chinese local officials in office for purposes of local administration. The last occupation of Canton was followed by almost four years (January, 1858–October, 1861) of a so-called allied government over that metropolis, in which British and French officers, under the leadership of the energetic Harry Parkes, established the first puppet regime of modern times. Their chief puppet was the unfortunate governor of Kwangtung, Po-kuei, and the result was a thoroughly synarchic Sino-barbarian administration of the Canton area, using traditional Chinese forms.

The most striking form of joint administration became the Imperial Maritime Customs Service, in which the foreign commissioners of customs were employed by the emperor of China under the administrative supervision of the British Inspector-General, Robert Hart. The commissioners maintained a careful parallel relationship to the Chinese superintendents of customs, who continued during the nineteenth century to administer the "native customs" establishment and to receive the maritime customs duties at each port. In most cases this Chinese superintendent was concurrently a territorial official of considerable rank, like the taotai (intendant) in charge of the Shanghai area.[21] The foreign commissioners were early instructed by Hart to regard themselves as the "brother officers" of the native officials and, "in a sense, the countrymen" of the Chinese people. "The foreign staff," said Hart, "aids the Chinese Superintendent in the collection of the Revenue." The commissioner was "necessarily subordinate" to the latter official; he should act as the "head of the Superintendent's executive . . . be the Superintendent's adviser." A commissioner whose action or advice placed his "Superintendent in a false or untenable position" would lose his post. He should not "arrogate to himself the tone of the Superintendent" nor prejudice the latter's final decisions.[22]

Throughout its career until the end of the dynasty the foreign inspectorate of customs thus functioned in a partnership. The foreign employees of the emperor saw to it that the customs revenue was properly calculated and collected, but before 1911 they did not themselves receive or handle the funds. Their service was paid for by a fixed monthly allowance from the local superintendent of customs, who retained control over the essential operation of receiving the revenue at the customs bank and disposing of it at the order of Peking. This dual arrangement proved to be a great solution for the British problem of establishing optimum and reliable conditions for commercial expansion.

It is significant that the foreign inspectorate was invented at Shanghai and not in London and that the Foreign Office within two years after 1854 decreed the abolition of the system, on account of the fact that it had not yet been extended to the other ports.[23] H. N. Lay and Robert Hart, who created the inspectorate, both began their careers as British vice-consuls and interpreters, but they ceased to represent the British government directly. Both saw themselves as intermediaries between East and West, as indeed they were.

Joint administration also developed at Shanghai, which remained Chinese territory and was not made a "free city," as had been suggested in 1862. Quite aside from the extraterritoriality applied to foreigners, the Chinese authorities' powers over *Chinese* residents became "subject to certain definite restrictions" regarding law courts, police, taxation, and legislation.[24] While not seeking to remove luster from the Anglo-Saxon capacity for pragmatic governmental arrangements, we may well search for the roots of the Shanghai anomaly in Chinese as well as in Western tradition. Even allowing for the well-known historical fact that evidences properly selected will "prove" almost any point, our perspective on the treaty system may be usefully deepened by this exercise of viewing it against its synarchic background.

5. THE ECLIPSE OF SYNARCHY BY NATIONALISM

While the British were drawn part way into the traditional Confucian orbit on the level of practice, they failed to accept Chinese political ideas. Viewed against the age-old synarchic tradition of China's foreign relations, the British invaders of 1840, once their superiority in warfare was evident, might well have been expected to seek imperial power and to try to supplant the Manchu dynasty. This had been the prize available in time past to tributaries who "rebelled" successfully (Ch'ing documents regularly referred to the British in wartime as *ni*, "rebels"). British conquest in India was no secret to Peking; even some Americans, like the anglophobic and overquoted Commissioner Humphrey Marshall,[25] foresaw a British attempt to take over China. But the British did not picture themselves as contenders for the Mandate of Heaven. Where the Manchus had made themselves the new managers of the old system, the British invaders tried to get a new system set up, but without becoming managers of it. They therefore worked with and through the Ch'ing regime, participated in its synarchic administration of China, but did not try to take its place.

The essence of the Western view was to approach China as an incipient nation. This was implicit in the treaties themselves, for they were each drawn up explicitly as between two equal states, one of which agreed to give unilateral privileges to the other. The treaties posited the equality of all nation-states even while creating a situation of inequality.

But these unequal provisions came to be regarded by the West as temporary and transitional, imperfect arrangements along the road to China's eventual emergence as a modern sovereign nation. To the Western mind it was "normal" when Japan, saddled with a similar treaty system in the 1850's, succeeded in throwing it off by the end of the century.[26]

As a prime example of nation-state thinking in the Western approach to China, we may take the American development and expansion of the idea of the "Open Door for trade" into the idea of China's national independence. The conception of the Open Door which eventually caught on with the American public was not the demand for equal opportunity among the capitalist competitors in the commercial exploitation of China (embodied in John Hay's first notes of 1899) but rather the concept of Chinese "territorial and administrative entity" or "integrity" expressed more vaguely in the second set of notes in 1900.[27] We need not deny that the Open Door for equality of trading conditions as espoused by Hart and his deputy, Hippisley, who helped Rockhill draft the first notes, had an appeal for American business interests. The fact remains that the "integrity" of China, her national independence of the imperialist powers, her development as a nation-state, became the actual shibboleth of American policy.

Given these Western expectations, which go far back in Western thinking, it was inevitable that Western contact should bring nationalism to China just as disruptively as it brought industrialism. Sides of the same entering wedge, these cognate developments of nationalism and industrialism not only remade Chinese life but also remade the Western and modern Chinese evaluations of Chinese political institutions, including synarchy.

This process may be seen at work if we look briefly at (a) the increasing foreign participation in the Ch'ing administration and economy under the policy of intra-Western and Sino-foreign "co-operation" after 1860, and (b) the Chinese intellectual response to this foreign influx.

A. Synarchic Aspects of the Co-operative Policy

The tendency toward synarchic practices under the early treaties reached its last significant phase in the period of the "co-operative policy" of the 1860's at Peking, after the treaty system had finally been accepted by the dynasty. Here the British ministers Bruce and Alcock participated in measures which would strengthen the Ch'ing regime in a gradual progress toward stability and the meeting of its problems.[28] With the help of Bruce and Hart, the interpreter's college, or T'ung-wen Kuan, was staffed with foreign professors to train a Chinese body of Western specialists. With the blessing of Bruce and the American minister, Burlingame, the adventurous F. T. Ward of Salem and the British officer of engineers, C. G. Gordon, successively organized and led the "Ever-Victorious Army" which defended Shanghai against the Taipings in the early 1860's. In the same period H. N. Lay and Captain Sherard Osborn, with the support of the Foreign Office and the British Navy, were securing the building and manning of a fleet of powerful modern warships, which actually came to China before the project collapsed over the question of control and jurisdiction.[29] Already the imperial forces in the Yangtze Valley, under Tseng Kuo-fan, had procured Western steamers and the assistance of Western personnel to outmaneuver the rebels. Tseng and Li Hung-chang fostered the Kiangnan

Arsenal at Shanghai to make foreign arms and gunboats, and at it John Fryer translated Western technical works into Chinese. As the climax of this period, Anson Burlingame toured the Western capitals as an envoy of the Ch'ing regime. All these activities, which were more various than is yet realized,[30] involved Sino-foreign co-operation and, specifically, the formal and informal acceptance by the Manchu-Chinese officialdom of Western officials' and private individuals' services and policy proposals.

One result, especially after the opening of the Yangtze to steamer traffic, was to place the major centers of Chinese economic development and so of political control—namely, the treaty ports both on the coast and on the inland waterways—under a mixed foreign and Chinese jurisdiction. The prototype of this development was under the Shanghai Municipal Council, which administered a Chinese city with the help of Chinese employees and eventually had a mixed Chinese and foreign membership. Amoy also developed an International Settlement on the island of Kulangsu.

As time went on, the participation of the foreigner in the Ch'ing administration was extended from the maritime customs to the new post office and salt gabelle. Meanwhile the modern economy was dominated by the foreign treaty-port banks and, after 1896, by foreign industrial establishments. Foreign domination of the carrying trade in Chinese waters was challenged only after the China Merchants Steam Navigation Company, founded in 1872, had purchased the steamship fleet of Russell and Company, which had been built up by Edward Cunningham of Boston with the help of Chinese merchant capital.[31] Education under government auspices was inaugurated with the aid of foreigners like

W. A. P. Martin; eventually, the pace was set by Christian missionary colleges, which began as foreign-managed institutions and gradually "devolved" into the hands of Chinese staffs and trustees.

This Western participation in China's institutional development was so multifarious and varied as to give one the impression of a general influx of Western individuals and influences without, however, any center of political direction and control—much Western "participation" but little "joint rule." This view may be oversimplistic. The institutions of Western Europe and the United States in the latter part of the nineteenth century were highly pluralistic; the governments of the respective Western nations did not play as dominant a role in their foreign activities as did the Ch'ing officialdom in the corresponding lines of Chinese activity. The private enterprises of the mission boards, the trading companies, the treaty-port entrepreneurs, and sundry adventurers far outweighed the official acts and programs of the Western governments. Western participation in the conduct of affairs in late-nineteenth-century China must be seen in this larger context and not merely on the Western official plane. Timothy Richard was a private individual but influenced Ch'ing mandarins. W. A. P. Martin, another private citizen, headed a central government college, although he came from the American educational tradition of private colleges. F. T. Ward was a mere Yankee adventurer but received Ch'ing official rank. Chinese officialdom was corrupted by an opium trade founded by free-enterprise Scotsmen and never controlled by the Foreign Office. It is hard to find in this varied private activity of Westerners in China a tangible entity called "foreign rule" beyond the limits of the ports and foreign concessions, yet from the Chinese side it is plain that Ch'ing rule was greatly affected, circumscribed, and sometimes guided by foreign influences of various kinds. The possibility of "Sino-foreign rule" was thus left standing on one leg—the Manchu-Chinese side often felt forced into it and sometimes was willing, but the Western side never got it formally organized. Synarchy never became full-fledged.

B. The Increasing Nationalism of China's Intellectual Response

Meanwhile, on the side of ideology and political ideals the potentialities of synarchy were gradually snuffed out by the growth of modern Chinese nationalism. This little-known process was first evidenced among the Canton populace and on a different level may also be traced in the writings of scholar-officials. In the 1840's the inauguration of the treaty system had been seen as an application, *faute de mieux*, of the traditional practice of "getting the barbarians under control through concessions" (*chi-mi*).[32] The Chinese reaction had been to attribute this disaster to the ineffectiveness of the Ch'ing regime rather than to emphasize the factor of foreign aggression. This attitude applied the traditional Confucian doctrine that barbarian invasion is inspired by domestic disorder and that domestic disorder results from the regime's lack of sufficient "men of ability" or "human talent" (*jen-ts'ai*). Tseng Kuo-fan's diary in 1862 notes, "If we wish to find a method of self-strengthening, we should begin by considering the reform service and the securing of men of ability." As he wrote to Li Hung-chang in the same year, "Confucius says, 'If you can rule your own country, who dares to insult you?'"[33]

In this period Tseng and his scholar-gentry colleagues were supporting the foreign (Manchu) dynasty and accepting foreign (Western) military aid to suppress the Chinese (Taiping) rebels, all in defense of the Confucian tradition and polity. Stigmatized today as unpatriotic "collaborators," these suppressors of native rebellion were merely demonstrating that Confucian "culturalism" was the focus of their loyalty: while imbued with a strong love of country and identification with "our mountains and rivers," they were yet pre-modern in their concept of the Chinese state. Indeed, its loose, decentralized social structure, the exclusion of the peasant masses from political life, the lack of modern communications and unifying symbols, kept China still below the level of nineteenth-century Western nationalism. Most of all, nationalism in the most developed form of *mass participation* in political life was antithetic to the tradition of the upper-class monopoly of government by emperor, bureaucracy, and gentry. Under the co-operative policy of the 1860's Confucian administrators like Tseng moved briefly in the direction of that community of interest between the Chinese gentry and the foreign invader which we have noted above as a hallmark of synarchy.

To Manchu leadership at Peking, meanwhile, the Taiping rebels were a disease within the Confucian body politic, while the Russians ("aiming to nibble away our territory like silkworms") and the British (seeking trade but "not coveting our territory and people") were lesser external dangers. In 1861 the policy was to "suppress the Taipings . . . first, get the Russians under control next, and attend to the British last."[34]

From this traditional point of view, the British invaders and their Western allies and hangers-on after 1860, having established themselves in a position of strategic, but not ubiquitous, military superiority, could be accorded a status analogous to that of border "allies." Like the Liao and Chin regimes in North China (eleventh and twelfth centuries), they ruled one part of a now divided empire. In the trading centers and on the waterways, their power made them potentially dominant, but they had made their peace with the Son of Heaven at Peking. In traditional terms the co-operative policy of the 1860's meant that the British and their foreign colleagues of other nations had been admitted into the power structure of the universal Confucian state on a basis which, though uncertain for the future, was at least temporarily limited and stabilized. Thus it made sense for the British to co-operate, to the extent that they were permitted, in the suppression of the Taiping Rebellion. As barbarian allies on the maritime frontier who had been "pacified" by concessions, the British could be allowed to participate part way in the affairs of the dynasty without posing an immediate threat to it. This could be tolerated under the assumptions and attitudes connected with synarchy when it would not have been tolerable under the modern theory of nationalism, as indeed proved to be the case in the next century.

The theoretical rationale which was constructed to clothe the fact of British and other Western participation in a diluted form of synarchy was an application of the classical concept of *t'i* and *yung*. First applied to Sino-Western relations by Feng Kuei-fen about 1860, this formula became widely current through Chang Chih-tung's writings in the late 1890's. Stated by Chang as *Chung-hsueh wei t'i, Hsi-hsueh wei yung*, it may be translated, "Chinese studies for the essential principles and Western studies for

the practical application."[35] Under this dichotomy, the continuation of the Confucian rule of the Manchu Son of Heaven, along with the Manchu-Chinese bureaucracy and the Chinese scholar-gentry, represented a basic principle, or *t'i*, while the whole process of modernization in which the Westerner participated, including the treaty-port system of trade regulations through the Maritime Customs and city administration in the foreign concessions, served as a mere "practical application," or *yung*.

The *t'i-yung* bifurcation was an unrealistic one from the beginning. The Western *yung* could not be imported without a considerable bit of Western *t'i* coming with it, and the Chinese *t'i* could not survive once the Chinese *yung* had been abandoned. It would be a mistake, however, to regard this famous dichotomy as a *source* of official action or even of policies; on the contrary, it was a formula which became widespread rather late, after modern contact had begun its inexorable course. The situation which it attempted to rationalize had come into being with the very advent of the treaty system. As described above, this situation was basically the early treaty-period adaptation of synarchy, which let the Westerner participate in the Confucian order. Unfortunately, the acceptance of anything Western proved to be a one-way ratchet which could serve only to draw the Confucian state further off its traditional base. When the British at Canton demanded the abolition of the Cohong monopoly and the inauguration of "free trade," they may have seemed to be introducing into the Chinese scene a mere Western practice (or *yung*), but the implication of the treaty clause which finally abolished the Cohong was that the Son of Heaven should turn his back upon the traditional hierarchy of classes which placed the merchant far below the official and should thus alter the ideological structure (or *t'i*) of the Confucian state. Similarly, when Commissioner Lin Tse-hsü and his literary colleague, Wei Yuan, advocated the use of foreign arms, which were the most obvious form of *yung*, they were in fact suggesting that China must develop an armament industry and embark on that process of industrialization which would inevitably destroy the traditional Confucian state and its agrarian economy administered by tax-gatherers. Once the treaty system and foreign contact had become established, it was already too late to save the old order by a distinction between *t'i* and *yung*. The theory was merely an insecure adjustment to a collapsing situation, a halfway house on the road to modernization.

Continued contact with the Western nation-states enforced the conclusion that nationalism was the only possible form of state organization for meeting the problems of the modern world. Learning by imitation, farsighted Chinese officials as early as 1861 were already holding up the examples of Peter the Great and other nation-builders and the object lesson of Turkey—a theme continued down to 1898 and after. The Western assumption about China's inevitable metamorphosis into a nation-state was thus taken over by modern Chinese themselves. The central theme of China's political history in the first half of the twentieth century, under Sun Yat-sen, Chiang Kai-shek, and even Mao Tse-tung, has been the struggle to create a nation-state which could take its place in the international order.

In retrospect we can see that the sentiments of nationalism were attached to almost every aspect of Westernization or modernization. Early Ch'ing efforts at armament against the West had to become nationalistic, at the very beginning of the modernization process, as soon as it proved impossible either to find Western allies who would fight against the British or to rely on Western mercenaries. Lin Tse-hsü and Wei Yuan in 1840-42, in the use-barbarians-against-barbarians tradition, had hopefully opined that "there is no better method of attacking England than to use France or America." But their successor as a "barbarian specialist," Feng Kuei-fen, was soon declaring, "It is utterly impossible for us outsiders to sow dissension among the closely related barbarians." Similarly his superiors, Tseng Kuo-fan and Li Hung-chang, saw the need of becoming independent of foreign officers to lead modernized Chinese troops.[36] There was no way, in short, for contact to grow between China and the West except on the nation-state assumptions of sovereign independence or else colonialism. China's "semicolonial" echo of synarchy appeared increasingly anomalous.

In this way the treaty system, which began in the 1840's partly as a modified form of the traditional institution of synarchy, steadily, increasingly, and inexorably became a source of "disintegration and demoralization," as Generalissimo Chiang later so aptly phrased it,[37] which in the course of time undermined and destroyed the old Confucian order, including any possibility of permanent Sino-foreign administration of the Chinese state. Where the treaty system had begun by affecting mainly the Chinese economy, it ended by remaking Chinese political thought.

This reinterpretation leads to the final conclusion that synarchy proved to be the Achilles' heel of the universal Confucian empire. Once again, as so often before, the powerful barbarian invader had to be taken into the Chinese scheme of things. The tradition of synarchy made it at first relatively painless to do this. But while the Westerners in the treaty ports were inclined to welcome synarchic practices, which often seemed quaintly convenient, they denied the Confucian ideology which should have accompanied them. The eventual rise of modern Chinese nationalism led to the elimination, first, of the "unequal treaties" as documents, by Chiang Kai-shek in 1943, and, second, of the postwar American participation in the government of mainland China, by Mao Tse-tung in 1949. How far the ideology and institutions of Communist China may still show traces of the ancient synarchic tradition remains a question.

Notes

1. This comprehensive, systematic effort to analyze the dynasties of conquest comparatively was made by a group of fourteen scholars at Kyoto and Tokyo in a wartime research project for the Tōa Kenkyūjo. Some nineteen papers were reduced and revised to form the volume *Iminzoku no Shina Tōchishi* ("History of the Rule of Alien Peoples over China") (Tokyo, 1944; 424 pp.). (The first edition, *Iminzoku no Shina Tōchi Gaisetsu* [1943; 312 pp.], is practically identical.) Contributors included Momose Hiromu, Miyazaki Ichisada, Abe Takeo, Tamura Jitsuzō, and Sudō Yoshiyuki. The chief monographic study in this field (with broad implications) is by Karl A. Wittfogel and Feng Chia-sheng, *History of Chinese Society: Liao (907-1125)* (Philadelphia: American Philosophical Society, 1949; 752 pp.). The important pioneer work is by Owen Lattimore, *Inner Asian Frontiers of China* (New York: American Geographical Society, 1940; 2d ed., 1951; 585 pp.). In revising this paper, I have been much indebted to comments, among others, of James T. C. Liu, Owen Lattimore, and Wolfram Eberhard; note the latter's chapter, "Patterns of Nomadic Rule," in his *Conquerors and Rulers* (Leiden: Brill, 1952).

2. The chief analytic study is by Franz Michael, *The Origin of Manchu Rule in China*

(Baltimore: John Hopkins Press, 1942; 127 pp.). The chief source has been translated by Erich Hauer as *Huang-Ts'ing K'ai-kuo Fanglüeh, Die Gründung des Mandschurischen Kaiserreiches* (Berlin and Leipzig, 1926; 710 pp.).

3. On the relation of gentry to dynasty, suggestive theories have been put forward by Wolfram Eberhard, *A History of China* (Berkeley and Los Angeles: University of California Press, 1950; 374 pp.), *passim*.

4. It is a commentary on political science studies of China in the West that the most thorough work in English on the Ch'ing administration is now thirty years old, that of Pao-chao Hsieh, *The Government of China (1644-1911)* Baltimore: Johns Hopkins Press, 1925; 414 pp., no index), while the chief Japanese work has remained unused, namely, the Taiwan Government-General's eight-volume *Shinkoku Gyōseihō* (Tokyo and Kobe, 1910-14; 3,046 pp.).

5. On the early Portuguese depredations see Richard Thurnwald, *Koloniale Gestaltung: Methoden und Probleme überseeischer Ausdehnung* (Hamburg: Hoffmann und Campe, 1939; 492 pp.), pp. 57-68 and *passim*.

6. On European sea expansion into Asia generally see G. B. Sansom, *The Western World and Japan* (New York: A. A. Knopf, 1950; 504 pp.), Part I, "Europe and Asia."

7. The above developments are dealt with at greater length in J. K. Fairbank, *Trade and Diplomacy on the China Coast* (2 vols.; Cambridge, Mass.: Harvard University Press, 1953; 577 pp.), Part I, "China's Unpreparedness for Western Contact."

8. See *ibid.*, Parts II and III, on the first treaty settlement and its application.

9. See tables in Chao-ying Fang, "A New Technique for Estimating the Numerical Strength of the Early Manchu Military Forces," *Harvard Journal of Asiatic Studies*, XIII (June, 1950), 192-215.

10. References to the sepoys are in, e.g., John Ouchterlony, *The Chinese War* (London, 1844), pp. 39, 92, 152-56 and *passim*.

11. The Anglo-Chinese College was founded in 1818 by the pioneer Protestant missionary Robert Morrison. It was continued under W. C. Milne and remained closely connected with missions in China.

12. The Chinese junk trade played an important economic role in Far Eastern economic history and could be (but has not been) stud-

ied in a variety of gazetteers and special sources. See bibliography in J. K. Fairbank and S. Y. Teng, "On the Ch'ing Tributary System," *Harvard Journal of Asiatic Studies,* VI (June, 1941), 135-246.

13. Grace Fox, *British Admirals and Chinese Pirates, 1832-1869* (London: Kegan Paul, 1940), p. 126 and *passim.*

14. See *Huang-Ch'ing K'ai-kuo Fang-lüeh* (*Kuang-pai-sung-chai* movable type ed.; Shanghai), chap. 32, p. 5*b;* cf. Hauer, *op. cit.,* p. 584.

15. See the British bluebook, *Correspondence and Papers Relating to China* (1840), p. 33, Napier's lithographed statement of August 26, 1834. For this example I am indebted to Mr. Hsin-pao Chang.

16. W. D. Bernard, *Narrative of the Voyages and Services of the Nemesis* . . . (1-vol. ed.; London, 1844), pp. 183, 180, 188, 185, and 331, successively. Cf. Alexander Murray, *Doings in China* (London, 1843), p. 219: "The people, in general, were civil and seemed well-disposed to us, when none of their authorities or soldiers were near . . . readily supplying our men with water or tea."

17. Japanese scholars have gone furthest in study of the comprador system (see Negishi Tadashi, *Baiben Seido no Kenkyū,* and other works described in J. K. Fairbank and Masataka Banno, *Japanese Studies of Modern China* [Tokyo: Tuttle & Co., for the Harvard-Yenching Institute, 1955]).

18. The grain shipments have recently been studied by Harold C. Hinton, "The Grain Tribute System of the Ch'ing Dynasty," *Far Eastern Quarterly,* XI (May, 1952), 339-54.

19. Fairbank, *op. cit.,* p. 220.

20. The latest study of this growth is Rhoads Murphey, *Shanghai, Key to Modern China* (Cambridge, Mass.: Harvard University Press, 1953; 232 pp.).

21. Cf. Stanley F. Wright, *Hart and the Chinese Customs* (Belfast, 1950), p. 220.

22. Inspector-General's circular No. 8 of June 21, 1864. Also in H. B. Morse, *International Relations of the Chinese Empire,* III, 453-60. These sanguine instructions breathed the spirit of the "co-operative policy" then being pursued at Peking (see below).

23. See J. K. Fairbank, "The Definition of the Foreign Inspectors' Status, 1854-55 . . . ," *Nankai Social and Economic Quarterly,* IX (April, 1936), 125-63.

24. See Justice Richard Feetham, *Report of . . . to the Shanghai Municipal Council* (2 vols.; Shanghai, 1931), I, 99-111.

25. Marshall's anglophobia has been widely disseminated through Tyler Dennett's influential volume, *Americans in Eastern Asia* (New York: Macmillan Co., 1922, 725 pp.).

26. On the British and American assistance to Japan in her abolition of extrality see F. C. Jones, *Extraterritoriality in Japan* (New Haven, Conn.: Yale University Press, 1931), p. 155, and Dennett, *op. cit.,* p. 530.

27. As George Kennan (*American Diplomacy, 1900-1950* [Chicago: University of Chicago Press, 1951]) points out, "None of these communications had any perceptible practical effect" at the time. See also Charles S. Campbell, Jr., *Special Business Interests and the Open Door Policy* (New Haven, Conn.: Yale University Press, 1951).

28. This period has been studied by Dr. Mary C. Wright in her manuscript, "The T'ung-chih Restoration," now in process of publication. See also S. Y. Teng and J. K. Fairbank, *China's Response to the West: A Documentary Survey, 1839-1923* (Cambridge, Mass.: Harvard University Press, 1954; 296 pp.).

29. The most recent study is by John L. Rawlinson, "The Lay-Osborn Flotilla," *Papers on China* (Harvard Committee on Regional Studies), IV (April, 1950), 58-93.

30. See the extensive sources described in S. Y. Teng and J. K. Fairbank, *Research Guide for "China's Response to the West"* (Cambridge, Mass.: Harvard University Press, 1954; 84 pp.).

31. Mr. Kwang-ching Liu is making an illuminating study of this Sino-foreign enterprise. See his article, "Financing a Steam-Navigation Company in China, 1861-62," *Business History Review,* XXVIII (June, 1954), 154-81.

32. On this concept (*chi-mi*) see Fairbank, *Trade and Diplomacy,* p. 94.

33. Teng and Fairbank, *China's Response to the West,* pp. 62-63.

34. *Ibid.,* p. 48.

35. *Ibid.,* chaps. v*b* and xvii.

36. *Ibid.,* p. 53 (quoting Feng's *Chiao-pin-lu K'ang-i*) and p. 68 (quoting *Ch'ing Shih-lu,* edict of November, 1862).

37. Chiang Kai-shek, *China's Destiny* (authorized Wang trans.; New York: Macmillan Co., 1947, p. 77.

15. Li Hung-chang in Chihli:

The Emergence of a Policy, 1870-1875

KWANG-CHING LIU

The year 1870, which saw the unifica-tion of Germany and the consolidation of a revolution from above in Japan, saw a major event in China—the appoint-ment of Li Hung-chang (1823-1901) as governor-general of Chihli and as im-perial commissioner for the northern ports. Even while he was absorbed in the task of suppressing internal rebellion in the 1860's, Li had been the foremost advocate of "self-strengthening" (*tzu-ch'iang*)—the policy of building up China's military potential, chiefly by adopting Western technology, so as to meet the challenge of external aggres-sion.[1] In his new position of influence, close to Peking, Li worked to continue and expand this policy.

A reassessment of the self-strengthen-ing movement must include an inquiry into the ideological implications. Did men like Li (there were very few of

From Albert Feuerwerker, Rhoads Murphey, and Mary C. Wright (eds.). *Approaches to Modern Chinese History* (University of Cali-fornia Press, 1967), pp. 68-104. The author is professor of history at University of California, Davis. Reprinted by permission.

them) aim merely at the adoption of Western technology, or did they also pro-pose reform? Did they modify the Con-fucian emphasis on moral government, which relied chiefly on virtue and culture as the sources of power? Inquiry must also be made into the complex factors that frustrated the success of the move-ment—the institutional and intellectual milieu, and the weakness of the new military and economic forces that had arisen after a generation of contact with the West. But first of all, it is necessary to consider the political context. Was the self-strengthening movement initiated by the central government or by the prov-inces? Was it a matter of sporadic efforts by a governor-general here, by a gov-ernor there, or was it a part of Ch'ing national policy?

The self-strengthening movement be-gan in the early T'ung-chih period, origi-nating chiefly in the provinces but enjoy-ing the strong support of the court. It was Li Hung-chang who first proposed the teaching of mathematics and the sci-ences at a government "interpreter's col-lege," and who founded China's earliest modern arsenals; it was Tso Tsung-t'ang who planned a large shipbuilding program. Li and Tso were stoutly backed, however, by the Tsungli Yamen at a time when Prince Kung was at the height of his power and when Wen-hsiang was still in good health. The development of "regionalism"—the administrative leeway which the governors-general and governors enjoyed regarding the temporary imperial armies (*yung*) and the likin—did not handicap the cooperation between Peking and provinces in the new projects.

In 1870, a new page was turned in the history of the self-strengthening movement. Li Hung-chang, in moving so close to Peking, became in effect a metropolitan official. Li performed many central government functions in the fields of diplomacy and military planning, and he made an attempt to coordinate self-strengthening efforts not only in Chihli but in other parts of the empire. It remained to be seen, however, whether on the one hand Li—and for that matter Prince Kung and Wen-hsiang (before his death in 1876)—would continue to have an effective voice in the councils around the throne, and whether on the other hand the measures they proposed could be carried out in the provinces, particularly in the militarily and finacially vital area of the lower Yangtze.

This paper presents aspects of Li's first five years in Tientsin—his functions in the imperial government, his ideas regarding self-strengthening, and the manner in which his proposals were received in Peking and in the provinces. As a senior official who had occupied key positions during the campaigns for the suppression of the Taipings and the Niens, Li had formed many friendships among governors-general, governors, and lesser officials. As the acknowledged but untitled leader of the Anhwei Army, Li also developed a degree of influence in provinces where units of that army were stationed.[2] But in the last analysis, it was the specific imperial sanction for each of Li's proposals, as well as his position as imperial commissioner, that accounted for his role as coordinator of policy. In the early 1870's, we find him taking remarkable initiative in shaping policy, and for a time it appeared that his programs might, at least in part, be carried out on a national scale.

LI'S CENTRAL GOVERNMENT FUNCTIONS

It was a crisis in China's foreign relations that brought Li to Chihli. Under the pressure of the harsh French demands that followed the Tientsin Massacre of June 21, the court on July 26 ordered Li, who had been engaged in operations against the Moslem rebels in Shensi, to move his forces to Chihli and join the twenty-eight battalions of the Anhwei Army (*Huai-chün*) previously brought there by Tseng Kuo-fan. A month later, on August 29, when Li and an army of about 25,000 men arrived at the border of Chihli, he was appointed its governor-general, replacing the ailing Tseng.[3] It was the court's wish that the Anhwei Army, which had proved so effective in fighting the Taipings and the Niens, should now be used for the defense of the metropolitan province against possible invaders.

For one who thinks in terms of twentieth-century Chinese politics it is possible to imagine Li as a proto-warlord, henceforth dominating the area where the capital was situated. This is completely misleading, for although Li's role as leader of the Anhwei Army certainly accounted for his being brought to Chihli, the Anhwei Army itself was by this time an integral part of the dynasty's armed forces. While its status continued to be that of *yung*, or temporary imperial army, Peking had control over the appointment of its higher officers and over its finances. The commanders (*t'ung-ling*) of the Anhwei Army, although normally recommended by Li, were appointed by imperial edict and all had the title of general-in-chief (*t'i-tu*) or brigade general (*tsung-ping*) under the Green Standard system. The subordinate officers, although chosen by the commanders, were also given the titles of Green Standard officers by the Board of War—colonel (*fu-chiang*), lieutenant-colonel (*ts'an-chiang*), and the rest, usually in an "expectant" (*hou-pu*) capacity.[4] There is no question that the troops and officers of the Anhwei Army regarded themselves as serving the dynasty. It was, moreover, from imperially authorized sources that the Anhwei Army was financed—the maritime customs of Shanghai and Hankow, the likin from Kiangsu and Kiangsi, and in smaller amounts the treasuries of Liang-chiang, Hupeh, Chekiang, Shantung, Szechuan, and Shansi. While Li enjoyed close personal relationships with the governors-general of Liang-chiang (Tseng) and of Hu-kuang (Li Han-chang) and was friendly with several governors, the court had the authority and influence to see that the funds were continued or withheld and, indeed, to change the governors-general or governors.[5] Ever since 1864, units of the Anhwei Army had been frequently moved by imperial edict from one province to another. In summoning Anhwei troops to Chihli, the throne was merely calling upon the services of one of its best forces.

On the other hand, thanks to his role as the leader of the Anhwei Army, Li gained a trusted position near the capital itself and was relied on to perform duties that belonged to a central government official. On November 12, 1870, less than three months after his designation as governor-general, he was given the further appointment of imperial commissioner (*ch'in-ch'ai ta-ch'en*), vested with duties even broader than those of the former commissioner of trade for the three northern ports (*san-k'ou t'ung-shang ta-ch'en*).[6] Li was instructed to reside at the strategic port of Tientsin and not at the provincial capital of Paoting. The edict stipulated that Li was to go to Paoting only in the winter months when the port of Tientsin was closed; it was not until December, 1871, that he first visited Paoting. Beginning in 1872, he also went to Peking about once a year for audiences with the throne and consultation with the ministers. Li's letters of 1872-1875 mention his discussions with Prince Kung, Wen-hsiang, Shen Kuei-fen, Pao-yün, and Li Hung-tsao—all five being grand councillors and, except for the last, ministers of the Tsungli Yamen.[7]

Li was responsible, of course, for Chihli provincial affairs. The provincial treasurer at Paoting was authorized to act for him on routine petitions, but important matters were brought to his yamen at Tientsin.[8] Among provincial matters to which Li gave his personal attention was internal policing, for which he used the so-called Trained Troops (*lien-chün*), an army of about 6,000 men selected from the Green Standard forces by previous governors-general.[9] Among questions of civil administration brought up by Li in memorials to the throne were local government finance (particularly the question of how to reduce the burden on *chou* and *hsien* magistrates), the province's financial obligations to

Peking, the salt monopoly, and the transmission of tribute rice to T'ung-chou. Li's most pressing and difficult provincial problems, however, were those created by the breaches in the dikes of the Yünting River. Northern Chihli saw one of its worst floods of the century in the summer of 1871, followed by a more moderate one in 1873. It was Li's responsibility to raise funds for relief and to revive agriculture in the areas affected. He also had to supervise repairs on the dikes—work that was to continue for several years.[10]

Meanwhile, Li was increasingly involved in his duties as imperial commissioner. These entailed first of all the supervision of foreign trade at the ports of Tientsin, Chefoo, and Newchwang through the superintendents of customs at the three ports—the one at Tientsin being a new post created at Li's recommendation.[11] But Li was also relied on by the Tsungli Yamen in questions concerning foreign trade in the empire as a whole. The Yamen often asked Li to study the proposals made to it by Robert Hart—for example, the latter's draft regulations, submitted in the spring of 1872, concerning the customs declaration form, the re-export certificate, and the transit pass. On his authority as imperial commissioner, Li sent "instructions by letter" (*cha-ch'ih*) to the superintendents of customs at Tientsin, Shanghai, and Hankow for their comments. Li added his own ideas and recommended to the Yamen that revisions be made in Hart's draft to make it more difficult for Chinese merchants to evade duties and likin. The final draft was worked out at Tientsin between Li and Hart.[12]

As imperial commissioner, Li had the responsibility of dealing with foreign representatives on local issues—for example, ironing out the final details of the Sino-French settlement regarding the Tientsin Massacre and determining the Russian and British claims.[13] Li's diplomatic activity soon included, however, national issues which the Tsungli Yamen considered it would be more convenient for him to handle at Tientsin. Moreover, the Yamen frequently sought Li's advice on policy and sometimes would entrust policy-making to him.

The first important national issue Li handled was the treaty with Japan. As early as October, 1870, after his first meeting with the Japanese representative who came to China to request a treaty, Li advised the Yamen that it was in the Ch'ing interest to form such ties. Li was impressed by Japan's comparative success in dealing with the West (for example, their ability to manage maritime customs without employing foreigners and to regulate missionary activity) and by the large funds which Japan was reported to have raised for arsenals and steamships. Li felt that China should befriend Japan, perhaps even send officials to reside in that country, with a view to preventing her from siding with the Western nations. On the Yamen's recommendation, the throne entrusted Li and Tseng Kuo-fan, who was the commissioner of trade for the southern ports, with formulating a policy for the treaty. Subsequently, Li was given full powers for the negotiations. The talks took place in the summer of 1871, China being represented by two officials of lower rank under Li's supervision. Eight months later, when the Japanese representative came to China to demand changes in the draft of the treaty, he was again dealt with at Tientsin. In May, 1873, Li was the plenipotentiary who exchanged the ratified texts with the Japanese foreign minister, who came to Tientsin for the purpose. Li discussed various matters with him, including China's concern about Korea.[14]

Similarly, Li was given the authority to meet with the representative of Peru who requested a treaty in October, 1873. Through the intermittent negotiations that lasted until June, 1874, Li's objective was to have the Peruvian representative accept a Chinese mission to investigate the conditions of Chinese labor in that country. The upshot was the Yung Wing mission to Peru in August, 1874.[15]

Beginning in 1872, the Yamen often enlisted Li's assistance in vital matters with which the Yamen itself was dealing. In September of that year, Li took the opportunity of the Russian and German ministers' passing through Tientsin to discuss with them, on the Yamen's behalf, aspects of the "audience question." In April, 1873, when Li himself was in Peking, he supported the compromise solution proposed by Wen-hsiang against those who insisted on kowtow. Li's intervention is said to have been important among the factors that "smoothed away all difficulties," resulting in the modified ceremony adopted at the audience held on June 14.[16]

In May and June, 1874, during the crisis created by the Japanese landing of troops on Taiwan to seek redress for shipwrecked Ryūkyū sailors murdered by the aborigines, Li participated in the search for a solution. Li advised the Yamen on the military measures which would strengthen China's hand in the negotiations—"to prepare for war secretly so that peace may be achieved quickly and be lasting."[17] When the Japanese minister to China arrived in June, 1874, the Yamen hoped that he could remain at Tientsin to negotiate with Li. However, he proceeded immediately to Peking, as did Ōkubo, the special commissioner who came in August. A set-

tlement which involved China paying Tls. 500,000 to Japan was reached on October 31, with Sir Thomas Wade acting as intermediary. But meanwhile Li had been active in seeking the mediation of Benjamin P. Avery, the new American minister who had just come from Japan and was at that moment in Tientsin.[18]

If Li was serving as a central government official in his diplomatic activities, the same may be said of his role in the Ch'ing government's military planning—despite the fact that he played but little part in the great Ch'ing military achievement of the period, namely the suppression of the Moslem rebels in Kansu in 1873 and the reconquest of Sinkiang that followed three years later. It was on Li however, that the court relied for the defense of the capital area and for co-ordination of military preparations in the coastal and Yangtze provinces. It has been shown above that as the Chihli governor-general, Li had control over the 6,000 Trained Troops used primarily for local policing. As imperial commissioner, he had the further duty of supervising the coastal defense of the metropolitan area, including the safeguarding of the Taku estuary and points halfway between Tientsin and Peking.[19] Similar responsibility was formerly borne by the Mongol prince Seng-k'o-lin-ch'in, who was imperial commissioner during the crisis of 1857-1860, and by the Manchu grandee Ch'ung-hou between 1861 and 1870, when he served as commissioner of trade for the three northern ports. Ch'ung-hou had built fortifications in the Taku area and had organized the Foreign Arms and Cannon Corps (*yang ch'iang-p'ao tui*), which grew to 3,200 men, under the command of the Tientsin brigade general.[20] Li was authorized to take charge of the forts and the corps, although his predecessors as governor-general, including Tseng Kuo-fan, were never given this authority. In November, 1870, Li appointed Lo Jung-kuang, the famous Anhwei Army artillery officer, as the Taku regiment colonel in charge of the forts. The Anhwei Army's best artillery, as well as new cannon built at the Nanking Arsenal, was brought to Taku, and new Krupp guns were ordered. Li put the Foreign Arms and Cannon Corps through retraining, particularly in the Anhwei Army's favorite technique of constructing fortified encampments.[21]

In November, 1870, the court directed that the twenty-eight battalions (about 14,000 men) of the Anhwei Army originally under Liu Ming-ch'uan be moved from Chihli to join the nine battalions of the Anhwei Army which Li had left in Shensi. At Li's recommendation, ten battalions of the Anhwei Army under Kuo Sung-lin also went to Shensi and Kuo himself was to bring ten battalions to Hupeh, to help guard against the secret societies of the Hunan-Hupeh area. However, two battalions of Liu's best troops were retained at Paoting, together with two battalions of the Anhwei Army cavalry. Two battalions of Li's personal guards were stationed at Tientsin. In addition, twenty-three battalions (about 11,500 men) under Chou Sheng-ch'uan were stationed in the area south of Tientsin, particularly at Ma-ch'ang, a base which Chou was to build up. In 1873, Chou's troops were used to construct a fortified town between Taku and Tientsin, and later they were put to work repairing dikes and reclaiming salt marshes for farmland. But they were also drilled and given training in the latest types of rifles and artillery. Li described them as a "mobile force for the defense of the metropolitan territory."[22]

Due chiefly to Li's relationship with the Anhwei Army, he also participated at times in the court's military planning for other parts of the empire. His role was passive with regard to the northwest. In 1870-1872, he sent two contingents of 1,000 men each from the Trained Troops of Chihli to Urga, to help guard against possible Russian encroachment on Outer Mongolia.[23] On September 1, 1871, apprized of the Russian occupation of Ili, the court ordered Liu Ming-ch'uan, who had requested a leave of absence on the ground of illness, to take his forces from Shensi to Kansu and thence to Sinkiang. Liu again pleaded illness, and on September 21 the court revised its orders, requiring him only to advance to Su-chou in Kansu. Although Li was not convinced of the value of Sinkiang in China's total strategic picture, he wrote Liu to urge him to comply. Without consulting Li, however, Liu once more begged the throne for a leave and recommended that Ts'ao K'e-chung, a general not of Anhwei Army background replace him and lead his forces to attack Su-chou. The request was granted. Ts'ao was summoned to Peking for an audience in November, 1871, and appointed to the command. Li pledged himself to support Ts'ao with Anhwei Army funds but recommended that only twenty-two of Liu's thirty-seven battalions be transferred to him.[24] In August, 1872, mutiny occurred in certain units of Ts'ao's forces; the throne referred the matter to Li, who recommended that Liu Sheng-tsao, Liu Ming-ch'uan's nephew and a former Anhwei Army officer, should take over. Liu Sheng-tsao came to Tientsin for consultations with Li and was given the appointment by the throne. Li had hoped to suggest that Liu move all the Anhwei forces in Shensi back to the coastal area, but the twenty-two battalions were retained in Shensi at the request of its governor.[25]

Li's own conviction was that the coast, particularly with a restless Japan quickly arming, was far more in need of protection. Ever since the end of the Nien Rebellion, eight battalions of the Anhwei Army, under Wu Ch'ang-ch'ing, had been stationed at several points in Kiangsu; at Li's recommendation, the throne in November, 1870, approved their remaining there. These forces were under the direction of Tseng Kuo-fan, the governor-general of Liang-chiang, but Li often wrote to him to make suggestions on such subjects as the training needed by the artillery corps or the strategic places where troops should be quartered. Tseng, on his part, would inform Li when he ordered the transfer of units from one location to another. In November, 1871, Li took the opportunity of the Anhwei Army in Shensi being transferred to Ts'ao K'e-chung's command to recommend to the throne that fifteen of the thirty-seven battalions be moved to Hsü-chou in northern Kiangsu. In approving the idea, the throne directed that these battalions (led by an Anhwei Army officer named T'ang Ting-k'uei) be put at the disposal of Tseng.[26] After Tseng died in March, 1872, Li continued to give his successors in the Liang-chiang post advice on military affairs—including the organization of a small navy with gunboats built by the Kiangnan Arsenal. Though Tseng's successors were free to direct the Anhwei Army in Kiangsu, they developed the practice of informing Li of their decisions whenever units were reassigned to new locations.[27]

In the summer of 1874, during the crisis created by the Japanese invasion of Taiwan, Li extended his concern to the Fukien-Taiwan area. It was upon Li's advice that the Tsungli Yamen recommended to the throne that Shen Pao-chen, the director-general of the Foochow Navy Yard, be appointed imperial commissioner for the defense of Taiwan. In June, Li suggested to Shen and to the Yamen that thirteen battalions (6,500 men) of the Anhwei Army at Hsü-chou, under T'ang Ting-k'uei, be dispatched to Taiwan to be put under Shen's control. This was approved by the throne in late July, as was Li's further recommendation that the twenty-two battalions of the Anhwei Army in Shensi be transferred to Kiangsu and Shantung, to meet the contingency of a Sino-Japanese conflict.[28]

Meanwhile, Li kept in touch by correspondence with Shen, with Li Tsung-hsi, the governor-general of Liang-chiang, and with Chang Shu-sheng, the governor of Kiangsu, arranging to ship munitions from Kiangsu and Chihli to Taiwan. On July 13, Li was instructed by the throne to "make a general plan for the entire situation" and to "deliberate jointly" (hui-shang) with officials in the provinces concerned regarding defense preparations.[29] Li advised Shen that clashes with the Japanese were to be avoided, while preparations for war must be hastened. Li arranged to have three ships of the China Merchants' Steam Navigation Company and three Foochow-built steamships transport the troops in Kiangsu to Taiwan. Since the six vessels had to make three volages to complete the shipping of 6,500 men, the last contingents did not reach their destinations until October, although the first arrived in mid-August. Li corresponded with officials in Fukien and in Liang-chiang on defense measures. Alarmed by rumors of Japanese intentions, Li Tsung-hsi and Chang Shu-sheng requested that the twenty-two battalions of the Anhwei Army from Shensi come to southern Kiangsu. Li decided, however, that only five should go there, and that the remaining seventeen (including five cavalry battalions) should be stationed at Chi-ning, Shantung, where they could easily be moved either north or south. Li assured his colleagues that even should there be war, given the resources of the Japanese, action was not likely to spread to the coast for a few months. There was, therefore, time to plan coastal fortifications carefully and to order foreign-made guns and rifles.[30] It is difficult to say whether these defense efforts had any actual bearing on Japan's accepting a peaceful settlement in late October. But Li had clearly emerged during the episode as the coordinator of Ch'ing military preparations on Taiwan and on the coast.

The crisis also revealed that Li depended on the throne's support for the continued financing of the Anhwei Army. Beginning in 1872, such provinces as Shantung, Chekiang, Szechuan, and Shansi had been reducing their annual contributions (*hsieh-hsiang*) to the Anhwei Army, if not defaulting entirely, due to Peking's pressure on them to supply funds for other purposes. In 1872, the Anhwei Army still received large sums from the Shanghai and Hankow maritime customs and from Liang-chiang sources (especially from Kiangsu likin and Kiangsi salt likin), but in the eighteen months following January 29, 1873, the annual average received from Kiangsu likin (which was the largest single source of Anhwei Army funds) dropped from Tls. 1,000,019 to Tls. 873,332.[31] There was danger that the trend might continue, for we find Li frequently writing to the governor of Kiangsu and governor-general of Liang-chiang, urging them to see that payments were made

promptly. Li had to remind these officials that the appropriations were backed by the throne itself. He warned Li Tsung-hsi not to withhold the Anhwei Army funds "so that I do not have to appeal to the throne." To Chang Shu-sheng, who had formerly been an Anhwei Army commander but whose interests were now not necessarily identical with its interests, Li wrote bluntly: "I will certainly fight for the funds. Let me swear it by smearing my mouth with blood."[32] On at least one occasion, Li actually did appeal to the throne regarding the Anhwei Army appropriations. He requested in a memorial dated September 1, 1874, that Szechuan province be instructed to pay its arrears of more than Tls. 200,000. In his letters to the governor-general of Szechuan and others, Li stressed that the Anhwei Army was in the service of the state and should be supported by it.[33]

SELF-STRENGTHENING— THE EMERGENCE OF A POLICY

Li's service to the state was not limited to diplomatic work or to advising the throne on the use of the Anhwei Army. As he himself conceived it, his role in the dynasty's military planning should include the enhancement of China's military capability—which alone could insure peaceful relations with the powers. Li assumed that the aim of the Western maritime powers in China was commerce and not aggrandizement. Nevertheless, he feared that an occasion might arise when one or more powers would use force. Moreover, a real threat existed in a rising Japan. "It is only when we can strengthen ourselves every moment," Li exhorted his colleagues, "that peace can be maintained and trouble prevented."[34]

Li found that he had to redefine as

well as to expand his program for self-strengthening. While his primary objective continued to be the building up of an armament industry, experience had shown that arsenals and shipyards were by no means easy to operate. Moreover, innovations in these fields were constantly being made in Western countries, and it was impossible to catch up quickly. To meet China's needs for some time to come, it was necessary to purchase foreign-made weapons of the latest types and to create a navy of foreign-built ships. Li further realized that the capacity of Chinese arsenals and shipyards had been severely restricted by lack of competent personnel and of revenue—the two Chinese words both pronounced *ts'ai*.[35] While seeking a gradual expansion of the armament industry, it was necessary to support new programs of personnel training and to devise means for enlarging the income of the state.

How then could the state best encourage technical personnel or increase its revenue? Although perhaps he was aware that they were not all feasible, Li nevertheless advocated certain institutional reforms—which he had been considering since the mid-1860's. The Taiwan crisis and the discussion on coastal defense that followed gave him the opportunity to present his views to the throne, along with his proposal for a fundamental change in the dynasty's strategic concept: to abandon the plans for reconquering Sinkiang and instead to concentrate the available resources on defense and self-strengthening programs on the coast.

While Li could usually count on the court's approval of his conduct of diplomacy or his advice regarding the disposition of the Anhwei Army, it was not as easy to persuade the throne to accept self-strengthening measures in-

volving innovation. The Tsungli Yamen enthusiastically supported some of Li's recommendations, but it was either indifferent or unable to give support to some others. There was, moreover, the need for coordinated efforts at the provincial level. After Tseng Kuo-fan's death in 1872, Li felt increasingly the need for allies in Liang-chiang and other parts of south China, and we find him using his influence on the court to see that such men as Shen Pao-chen and Ting Jih-ch'ang were appointed to key posts.

Li's Efforts up to November, 1874

Since the mid-1860's, four modern arsenals had been founded, two of them being shipyards as well: the Nanking Arsenal (moved from Soochow to that city in 1865), the Kiangnan Arsenal in Shanghai (founded in 1865), the Foochow Navy Yard (1866), and the Tientsin Arsenal (1867). Except for the Nanking Arsenal which was financed by Anhwei Army funds,[36] all had been authorized by imperial edict. The Nanking and the Kiangnan arsenals had been founded by Li himself, but he was disappointed by the results. The Nanking plant, which was operated by the Scotsman Halliday Macartney, could produce bronze cannon as well as percussion caps and shells. The Kiangnan Arsenal, a much larger establishment, had spent about Tls. 2,500,000 in five years, principally from the Shanghai maritime customs revenue. It did contribute to the Anhwei Army's campaign against the Niens with muskets and carbines, bronze cannon, percussion caps, and shells, but it was not until about 1868 that it succeeded for the first time in producing a rifle—the outdated muzzle-loading type.[37] Li regarded the Kiangnan and Nanking arsenals as no more than "the first beginning." Between 1867 and 1870, the shipyard attached to the Kiangnan Arsenal constructed four small steamships, described by Li as "neither merchant steamers nor warships," and as "useful for warfare on the river but not at sea."[38]

One of Li's earliest acts in Chihli was to expand the Tientsin Arsenal, founded by Ch'ung-hou three years before. Li recommended to the throne that a former manager of the Kiangnan Arsenal be appointed its head and that its equipment be increased. Since Li was, at that juncture, planning to equip his army in Chihli with foreign-made breechloading rifles and Krupp guns, he decided that the best contribution the Tientsin Arsenal could make was to supply the ammunition required by these weapons. Between 1871 and 1874, the arsenal received nearly a million taels allocated by the throne from the maritime customs revenue of Tientsin and Chefoo. Three new plants were added to the one originally in existence, so that by 1874 more than a ton of powder was produced daily, as well as a large quantity of cartridges and shells. Li also planned, however, to manufacture the breechloading rifle itself. Machinery for the production of rifles of the Remington type was ordered and installed in 1874-1875.[39]

Li hoped that the Kiangnan Arsenal, with its larger plant, could devote greater resources to the manufacture of rifles and ordnance. Although the Kiangnan Arsenal was controlled by the governor-general of Liang-chiang, Li often discussed its affairs in his letters to Tseng Kuo-fan. Twice in 1871, Li urged Tseng to check the accuracy of the boastful reports made by Feng Chün-kuang, its chief manager, and to give greater authority to Hsü Shou, the famous mathematician and engineer in the arsenal's service. Li sometimes communicated directly with these managers. It was presumably on his advice that the arsenal acquired additional machinery in 1871 for rifles of the Remington type, some 4,200 of which were produced before the end of 1873.[40] After Tseng died in March, 1872, Li continued to advise his successors regarding the arsenal. He urged that, in addition to breechloading rifles and bronze cannon, it should manufacture cast-iron cannon and torpedoes. The first cast-iron cannon was produced in February, 1874. In the period 1871-1874, 2,000 rifles and 1,100 carbines produced by Kiangnan were sent to Chihli, but the bulk of its products were assigned to the various armies of the Liang-chiang area.[41]

Since the Nanking Arsenal was financed with Anhwei Army funds, Li retained control over its personnel and policies. There was at least one occasion, in 1873, when an order for the change of the arsenal's Chinese director was issued by Li (presumably in his capacity as imperial commissioner for the northern ports), although he acted with the written concurrence of Li Tsung-hsi, the governor-general of Liang-chiang. Until 1874, the bronze mortars built by Macartney were for the exclusive use of the coastal fortifications at Chihli. Beginning in early 1874, however, Li Tsung-hsi ordered the arsenal to make guns and various kinds of ammunition needed by the forces in Kiangsu.[42]

Li's concern for the Chinese armament industry also extended to Fukien. Late in 1871, the Foochow Navy Yard was attacked by a sub-chancellor of the Grand Secretariat as wasteful and ineffective. This official, Sung Ching, recommended to the throne that the shipbuilding programs at both Foochow and Shanghai be discontinued. Instructed by the throne to give his views, Li joined Tso Tsung-t'ang and Shen Pao-chen, the founder and the director of the Foochow Navy Yard, in defending it. Li's memorial of June 20, 1872, made the famous statement that China was encountering "the greatest change of situation (*pien-chü*) in three thousand years." Since Western military power was based on rifles, cannon, and steamships, China must master the secrets of such equipment so as to insure her survival in the long run. Li warned that Japan was ahead of China in these matters and was "viewing China in a threatening manner." Supporting a suggestion made earlier by the Tsungli Yamen, Li proposed that the Foochow and Shanghai shipyards might build freighters as well as gunboats and make the former available for purchase or hire by Chinese merchants. Li added a proposal of his own involving reform of institutions. Since the government-built gunboats could be used for coastal and river patrol by the coast and Yangtze provinces, should they not be financed by the appropriations from the provinces devoted to the old-style navy? Li suggested that the court should issue an edict to the effect that the construction of war junks be discontinued altogether.[43] He was greatly disappointed when this last proposal was not supported by the Tsungli Yamen, although at its recommendation the throne decided to continue shipbuilding at Foochow and Shanghai.[44]

Li attached great importance to the Foochow Navy Yard and its training programs and took it upon himself to assist Shen Pao-chen's work. Li had formed the opinion by 1872 that Shen (who happened to be a *chin-shih* classmate of Li) was one of the very few high officials of the time who had a clear understanding of what self-strengthening required. Several times Li used his influence with Li Ho-nien, governor-general of Fukien and Chekiang, to persuade the latter not to obstruct Shen's work. In May, 1874, during a visit to Peking, Li spoke on Shen Pao-chen's behalf with Shen Kuei-fen, grand councillor and president of the Board of War (who also happened to be a *chin-shih* classmate) and obtained his promise and that of Prince Kung that they would make favorable recommendations on Shen's future requests about the financing of the Foochow yard.[45]

Li realized, more acutely than he had in the early T'ung-chih period, that successful operation or arsenals and shipyards depended on trained technical personnel. The school Li founded in 1863, the Shanghai T'ung-wen Kuan (which was combined with a new translator's school of the Kiangnan Arsenal in 1867 and renamed Kuang Fang-yen Kuan) had been giving instruction in English, mathematics, and sciences to classes of about forty students still in their teens. But few outstanding graduates had been produced; the results, as in the case of the Peking T'ung-wen Kuan, were disappointing.[46] In 1864, Li had suggested to the Tsungli Yamen that a new category (*k'o*) be created under the examination system to accommodate men who specialized in technology. The little interest which the Shanghai and Peking schools had aroused among the literati convinced Li that only some such change could provide the incentive for the pursuit of "Western learning."[47]

Li supported a proposal to send Chinese youths to the United States for education. He was persuaded that a prolonged period of study abroad was the best way to train Chinese who, upon their return to China, could become instructors in the Shanghai and Peking schools or serve in the arsenals and shipyards. The proposal originated with

Yung Wing and Ch'en Lan-pin and was brought to the court's attention in a memorial from Tseng Kuo-fan in October, 1870. However, Tseng merely mentioned the idea casually in connection with another matter, and Li, in a letter dated December 13, 1870, urged him to draft concrete plans to be submitted to the court. "It can never be expected," Li wrote, "that the matter be initated by the court."[48] Li also suggested that the draft regulations include a provision that the students be awarded *chien-sheng* status before going abroad and that upon their return they be assigned official ranks, after being given an examination by the Tsungli Yamen. Li was later satisfied that the regulations merely promised official positions for the returning students. In August, 1871, he joined Tseng in submitting a memorial to the throne on the subject, after having corresponded with the Tsungli Yamen and obtained its concurrence, particularly on the proposal that Tls. 1,200,000 be allocated over a twenty-year period from the Shanghai maritime customs revenue.[49] As authorized by an imperial edict, a bureau was established in Shanghai in 1872 to select students, and the first group of thirty left Shanghai that summer, to be followed by a similar number annually for three years. The boys selected were between eleven and sixteen *sui*. A tutor went along to teach them Chinese subjects, but each student was to spend fifteen years abroad, travelling during the last two years. Since the plan authorized was based on a joint memorial from Tseng and Li, it was regarded as under the supervision of the two commissioners at Nanking and Tientsin. The officials in charge in the United States reported to Li and to the governor-general of Liang-chiang.[50]

In June, 1871, Li had briefly considered sending students to Britain also. His more urgent problem, however, was to find mature personnel in China who could serve at once in managerial or technical capacities in the arsenals, the shipyards, or the customs administration. Li often wrote to colleagues in other provinces inviting nominations of such personnel.[51] In January, 1874, when Shen Pao-chen consulted him about a plan to send the graduates of the Foochow Navy Yard School to Britain and France, Li responded with enthusiasm. He wrote to the Yamen about the plan and brought it to Prince Kung's attention when he was in Peking in May, 1874. Li also considered sending the sons of the Tientsin Arsenal's Chinese technicians to Germany for study.[52] The Taiwan crisis intervened, and it was not until 1876 that further action was taken.

Li was increasingly convinced that Western technology could be used to augment the wealth of the Ch'ing state as well as its military strength. In Kiangsu, in the early T'ung-chih period, he had been impressed by the successful invasion of the carrying trade in Chinese waters by Western steamships, although at that time he was anxious to protect the seagoing junks which carried the tribute rice to Chihli. As early as 1864, Li had proposed to the Tsungli Yamen that Chinese merchants be permitted to own and operate steamships and foreign-style sailing vessels, in competition with Western ships.[53] In the two years after he came to Tientsin, a series of events prompted him to make immediate plans for a Chinese steamship company. During the flood and famine in Chihli in 1871, he deeply resented the exorbitant rates foreign ships demanded for the transport of relief grain. New breaches of the Yellow River dikes that winter convinced him that the Grand Canal was to become useless. He was against investing enormous sums to restore the former course of the Yellow River so as to improve the Grand Canal's navigability. He saw in a fleet of Chinese-owned coastal steamships the solution to the ancient problem of how to carry tribute rice from the south to the north.[54] It was at this juncture that the Tsungli Yamen suggested that ships built by the Foochow Navy Yard might be hired out to Chinese merchants. Li was asked by the Yamen to make arrangements to this purpose, and through the summer of 1872 we find him corresponding on the subject with such officials as the superintendent of customs at Shanghai and the head of the Liang-chiang administration's new naval fleet (which consisted chiefly of Kiangnan-built ships.)[55]

Li found that the Foochow- and Shanghai-built ships were not suitable for the freighting trade, since they were costly to operate and drew too much water for some harbors. Following the advice of Chu Ch'i-ang, a Chekiang official in charge of the junk transport of that province's tribute rice, Li decided that the best plan was for a group of Chinese merchants to buy foreign-built steamships and to operate them for the general carrying trade as well as for the transport of tribute rice; presumably Chinese-built ships could be added to the fleet later. Li approved Chu's plan to establish a bureau (*chü*) in Shanghai and to "invite merchants" (*chao-shang*) to operate steamships. It was understood that the enterprise was to be "supervised by the government and undertaken by the merchants" (*kuan-tu shang-pan*). Li arranged a loan of Tls. 136,000 to the enterprise from Chihli military funds, making it clear, however, that "profits and loss are entirely the responsibility of the merchants and do not involve the government."[56] While the availability of government appropriations for tribute rice transport made the project particularly feasible, Li undoubtedly regarded it as part of a general policy for China's self-strengthening. "The use of the steamship for the transport of tribute rice is but a minor consideration," Li wrote the governor of Kiangsu in December, 1872. "The project will open up new prospects for the dignity of the state (*kuo-t'i*), for commerce, for revenue, for military strength—for the China of centuries to come." Li was also interested in reports of Japan's effort to develop commercial shipping. He wrote in early January to an official whom he had recommended to be a secretary of the Tsungli Yamen: "We let other people move about at will in Chinese waters. Why do we deny the Chinese merchants alone a foothold? Even Japan has sixty or seventy [merchant] steamships of her own; we alone do not have any. How does this look?"[57]

To obtain the tribute rice cargo for the steamships, Li had to enlist the cooperation of officials in the lower Yangtze area. Siding with the vested interests of the junk owners, the Kiangsu officials initially opposed Li's plan. In October, 1871, Shen Ping-ch'eng, the superintendent of customs at Shanghai, and Feng Chün-kuang, the head of the Kiangnan Arsenal, joined in a petition of protest to Ho Ching, the governor-general of Liang-chiang, and their views were supported by Chang Shu-sheng, the Kiangsu governor. Invoking Peking's authority, Li reminded Ho that the proposed steamship company eventually would purchase and hire Chinese-built ships and was in line with the Tsungli Yamen's original proposal which had been approved by the throne in June, 1872; it was therefore a matter with which Ho, as acting commissioner of trade for the southern ports, should be properly concerned. To governor Chang, Li exploded: "I have worked together with you for nearly twenty years. Did you ever see anything I am determined to do discontinued because of unjustful criticism?"[58] Ho and Chang eventually allowed twenty percent of the Kiangsu tribute rice to be shipped annually by steamer. Together with a similar quota from Chekiang, this assured the new enterprise an annual tribute rice freight of 200,000 piculs, or a payment of Tls. 112,000. In December, Li memorialized to request imperial sanction of the entire plan. The memorial was approved on December 26, and on January 14, the Bureau for Inviting Merchants to Operate Steamships (Lun-ch'uan chao-shang chü; known in English as the China Merchants' Steam Navigation Company) was inaugurated in Shanghai.[59] Since it was on the basis of Li's memorial that the project was approved, the Bureau was regarded as under the jurisdiction of the imperial commissioner for the northern ports. Li retained firm control of its personnel and policies. In July, 1873, when two Cantonese compradors, Tong King-sing and Hsü Jun, became the directors (tsung-pan) of the new company, it was Li who issued the appointment. Li found it necessary, however, to appeal to the Kiangsu governor and the Liang-chiang governor-general to help by giving the enterprise larger tribute-rice consignments and by providing it with loans from provincial funds. Thanks to such assistance, as well as to the efforts of its excomprador managers, the company's fleet grew to thirteen ships (8,546 net tons) by 1875 and services were developed on the Yangtze River and on several coastal routes.[60]

The purpose of the Chinese merchant steamers, as Li told the Tsungli Yamen, was to compete with foreign enterprise and restore China's "control of profit" (li-ch'üan).[61] But Li was particularly intrigued by the possibility of opening up a new source of revenue to the state by working mines with Western methods. Early in 1868, when he was still involved in the war against the Niens, Li had proposed in connection with the question of treaty revision that foreign engineers be allowed to work Chinese coal and iron mines. After coming to Chihli, Li became increasingly convinced that the use of pumps and other machines in mining pits not only would provide the Chinese arsenals and shipyards with vital materials and fuel but would profit the state financially. Li was also aware of the fact that the Japanese had been working their mines with Western techniques. In his memorial of June 20, 1872, concerning the Foochow shipyard, he proposed projects "supervised by the government and undertaken by merchants" to work mines with machinery. He also recommended using Western foundry techniques to produce cast iron and steel. Li emphasized that coal and iron could be marketed for profit and were "of great importance to the policy of enriching the state and strengthening military power."[62]

Li was disappointed when the Tsungli Yamen, while favoring the continuation of the Foochow shipyard, failed to make a recommendation to the throne regarding mining projects. He wrote Wang K'ai-t'ai, the governor of Fukien, that the failure indicated that the Yamen thought only of the present and not the future: "What will become of us a few decades hence?"[63] On his own initiative, Li encouraged Feng Chün-kuang, the director of the Kiangnan Arsenal, and others to make plans for working coal and iron mines at Tz'u-chou, in southern Chihli. In 1874, an English merchant, James Henderson, was sent to Britain to buy machinery and hire workmen.[64] Li was not, however, merely concerned with the opportunities for such projects in Chihli. He wrote the governor of Shansi, Pao Yüan-shen, in November, 1873, urging him to open up the rich mineral deposits of that province with new methods. "The earth is not stingy with its treasure," Li wrote, "but few in China are aware of this truth; please give this matter your attention and not worry all the time about poverty." Early in 1874, Li asked Li Tsung-hsi, the governor-general of Liang-chiang, to try to persuade Liu K'un-i, the governor of Kiangsi, to introduce machinery in the coal fields at Lo-p'ing, Kiangsi. Liu refused, however. In August, 1874, at the height of the Taiwan crisis, Li advised Shen Pao-chen to try to work the mines of that island. Assisted by H. E. Hobson, the commissioner of customs at Tamsui, Shen succeeded in 1875 in making arrangements for a coal mine near Keelung.[65]

Li's Proposals of December, 1874

Since the Tientsin Massacre, the initiative for self-strengthening had come chiefly from Li, with some cooperation from the Tsungli Yamen and from Tseng Kuo-fan and Shen Pao-chen in the provinces. The Taiwan affair further stimulated attention to the problem of military preparedness. On November 5, 1874, the Tsungli Yamen, in which the ailing Wen-hsiang was still the dominant spirit, memorialized on the lessons of the incident. The Yamen lamented that although there had been much talk of self-strengthening since 1860, little had actually been done. The Yamen recommended that governors-general, governors, and Manchu commanders-in-chief of the coastal and Yangtze provinces be invited to submit their views on the needs of coastal defense (hai-fang) under five headings: military training, weapons, shipbuilding, revenue, and personnel. In a personal memorial submitted a month later, Wen-hsiang (who had risen from his sickbed to take charge of the negotiations with the Japanese on the Taiwan incident) reminded the throne that there was a real possibility that Japan, "accustomed to break her word," would allow her rebels at home to seek adventure in China. Wen-hsiang recommended that military preparations on Taiwan be continued and that plans be made immediately to buy ironclads and gunboats from abroad.[66]

While it was the Yamen that initiated the policy debate in 1874, Li put forward the boldest proposals. "What is urgently needed today is to abandon established notions and seek practical results," he urged in his memorial of December 10.[67] The two essentials for a successful coastal defense program were, in his view, "the change of institutions (pien-fa) and the proper use of personnel (yung-jen)." Li wrote Wen-hsiang that he was aware that not all his proposals could be adopted, but he had to make them, since "the responsibility is on my shoulders."[68]

Li proposed general military reform for the coastal and Yangtze provinces. In the early T'ung-chih period, when he worked with the British and French forces in Shanghai and with the Ever Victorious Army, he had formed the conviction that the number of troops in the Chinese armies could be much reduced; funds saved thereby could provide better equipment and pay for selected and efficient units. Soon after he became imperial commissioner in 1870, Li had drawn the throne's attention to the uselessness of the Green Standard Army, including the so-called Trained Troops.[69] He now went further and pleaded that "Rather than having a large number that are useless, it is better to have fewer of high quality." Li proposed that all "weak and exhausted" army units, whether Green Standard, Trained Troops, or *yung* forces, should be disbanded altogether, while the best troops, fewer than 100,000 for all the coastal and Yangtze provinces, should be converted into "foreign-arms and cannon corps." Equipped with rifles and cannon of recent model and reinforced by coastal fortifications, the comparatively small number of troops could be relied on at least to defend the two vital areas, Chihli and the lower Yangtze Valley. Li suggested that orders be placed immediately for firearms such as the Martini-Henry and the Snider and for cannon produced by Krupp, Woolwich, Armstrong, and Gatling. China's own arsenals, however, must also be expanded. They must aim at making breechloading rifles and cannon, as well as torpedoes, while further plans could await the day when a steel industry was developed, along with the coal and iron mines. The manufacture of powder, cartridges, and shells needed to be expanded and new plants for this purpose should be established at inland places like Soochow and in the interior provinces.

Li supported Wen-hsiang's proposal for a Chinese naval fleet of foreign-built vessels. Li felt that the navy was not quite as important as the army, but agreed that effective defense required ironclads for the open seas and floating gun-carriages as well as torpedoes for the harbors. H recommended that six ironclads be ordered immediately, two to be stationed in north China (probably at Chefoo and Port Arthur), two close to the Yangtze estuary, and two at Amoy

or Canton. In addition, twenty floating gun-carriages should be ordered for use at the various ports. Li suggested that Chinese students should be sent abroad to the shipyards where the vessels were to be built, to learn shipbuilding and navigation techniques. Meanwhile, the building programs at the Foochow and Kiangnan yards should be strengthened. Li visualized a Chinese naval fleet consisting eventually of sixty vessels.

To finance the new army and navy, Li suggested, first of all, that revenue be saved by disbanding worthless troops and by discontinuing the construction of war junks. The new army and navy were expected, however, to cost more than Tls. 10,000,000, and additional appropriations must be arranged. The most reliable source, Li emphasized, was the "four-tenths quota of the maritime customs revenue" (*ssu-ch'eng yang-shui*).[70] This fund had been allocated at some ports for the use of arsenals and for the Anhwei Army, but a considerable portion remained, particularly if the part reserved for the Board of Revenue at Peking was included. Li proposed that some Tls. 3,000,000 which had been saved by the Board from this source should also be used for coastal defense. He also suggested that loans could be obtained from foreign firms, to be paid in installments out of the four-tenths quota. Li recommended that likin on imported opium could be raised somewhat, while taxes could be levied on native opium, which might as well be legalized until such time as the drug's importation could be stopped altogether. To insure larger revenue for coastal defense, Li proposed, for the first time explicitly, that preparations in coastal provinces be accorded priority over the recovery of Sinkiang. He pointed out that Sinkiang had come under Ch'ing rule only in the

Ch'ien-lung reign, and that it was very difficult to defend, particularly now that the Moslem chieftain at Kashgar had Russian and British support and the Russians had occupied Ili. Given the limited revenue available, the court would have to make a choice between adequate preparations in the coastal area and the recovery of the "wasteland" in the far northwest. Li would draw the defense line at the Kansu border and guard it with military colonies into which some of the present armies there could be converted, while the Moslem leaders at Ili, Urumchi, and Kashgar might be accorded the status of native chieftains (t'u-ssu) or tributaries. Presumably a balance between Russian and British influences would help to insure stability in Sinkiang. Funds saved by cancelling the expedition could be diverted immediately to the coastal provinces.

Undoubtedly with Li in mind, the Tsungli Yamen had proposed in its memorial of November 5, 1874, that there should be a single commander-in-chief (t'ung-shuai) in charge of the coastal and Yangtze provinces, and that under him there should be a system of newly chosen generals-in-chief and brigade generals, to be stationed in different provinces. Li regarded the idea as impractical. Given the existing authority of the governors-general and governors in financial and military affairs, a single command for all the provinces concerned was hardly feasible, particularly since the lack of telegraph and railway prevented rapid communication. Moreover, mere "consultation" (hui-t'ung shang-ch'ou) between the commander-in-chief and the provinces was not likely to lead to effective action. Li, therefore, favored more than one command for the coastal and Yangtze areas—perhaps three "high officials" (ta yüan) exercising su-

pervision over such new projects as the naval fleet. For the supervisory positions in south China, Li recommended Shen Pao-chen and Ting Jih-ch'ang. From Li's correspondence, we know that he had been using his influence with Wen-hsiang and other ministers at court to get Shen appointed as the governor-general of Liang-chiang and Ting to a responsible post in south China.[71] Li obviously hoped that with himself at Tientsin and Shen at Nanking, a high degree of coordination could be achieved in carrying out new programs.

While Li was concerned with the immediate financial and political arrangements, he also put forth proposals of long-range significance. He brought up, for the first time directly to the throne, the need for a change in the examination and civil service systems. Li lamented the continuing apathy among the literati toward Western methods (yang-fa) and pointed out that neither the T'ung-wen Kuan type of school nor sending students abroad would arouse sufficient interest if the criteria for the selection and the advancement of officials remained unchanged. Li attacked the literary examinations, which emphasized calligraphy and the eight-legged essay, as "hollow and ornamental." He pleaded that while this kind of examination could not be "abolished immediately," it was necessary to create "another basis (k'o) of advancement through government activity concerning foreign relations (yang-wu)." Li proposed that a Bureau of Foreign Learning (yang-hsüeh chü) be created in each province involved in coastal defense, where science and technology (including such subjects as chemistry, electricity, and gunnery) would be taught by carefully chosen Western instructors, as well as by qualified Chinese, such as those being trained in the United States.

Advanced students were to be "tested through performance" and were to be assigned posts in arsenals, shipyards, and the armed forces. Moreover, such personnel were to be allowed opportunities for rapid promotion, comparable to those for persons possessing military merits, and were to be awarded "substantive posts, in the same way as officials who advanced through regular channels." Li predicted such a new personnel policy would result in an appreciable advance in armament-making in China in about twenty years.

Li urged the use of Western technology in transport, mining, and manufacturing. He drew the throne's attention to the military and commercial advantages of the railway, and to the military value of the telegraph. Pointing out that British textile imports into China amounted to more than Tls. 30,000,000 per year and were harmful to Chinese handicrafts, Li suggested that the Chinese themselves should establish machine-operated textile mills. He particularly stressed the opportunity that lay in opening up mines—not only coal and iron, but also copper, lead, mercury, and the precious metals. Li compared the failure to exploit such resources to keeping family treasures permanently sealed up while worrying about starvation and cold. He recommended that foreign geologists be invited to prospect the mines in the provinces and that Chinese merchants be encouraged to form companies (*kung-ssu*) to work mines with machines; the government could help the companies with initial loans and thereafter receive ten or twenty percent of their profits. Li expected the benefits from the mines to be apparent in ten years. He realized that new mining projects were opposed by the gentry and the people on grounds of geomancy and by

"incompetent officials" who feared that the concentration of miners might lead to disorderly conduct. Li described such objections as "ridiculous," for the Western nations and Japan were all developing mines: "Why is it that they do not suffer from them and on the contrary have achieved wealth and strength (*fu-ch'iang*) through them?"

Li had thus proposed programs for self-strengthening which were broader and more far-reaching than those presented by him or by others in the 1860's. The question was, of course, whether any or all of the proposals might be accepted. Li received scant help from the governors-general, governors, and Manchu commanders-in-chief who also gave their views on the Tsungli Yamen's original memorial. Stimulated by the recent Taiwan crisis, all the memorialists agreed that coastal defense needed to be strengthened. But, in the view of the Tsungli Yamen, except for Li and Shen Pao-chen (who also made a strong plea for a navy which included foreign-built ironclads and for the development of mines), none put forward proposals that were "concrete and practical." By early January, 1875, replies had been received from twelve officials, in addition to Li and Shen.[72] While all twelve favored new training for the army, only one suggested that the particularly weak units of the Green Standard forces should be disbanded. Six favored forming a new navy with foreign-built ironclads, but only one or two had useful suggestions on how they were to be financed. All twelve assumed that war was to be carried into Sinkiang; two in particular argued eloquently that the Russian threat to the land frontier posed an even more urgent problem than coastal defense. Four favored making some exception in the rules of civil or military service to place competent men where they were needed, but only two vaguely suggested that Western studies should be encouraged. Four realized the importance of mineral resources, but only one (Li's brother Han-chang) supported without reservation the use of machines in mines. Only one (the governor of Kiangsi, Liu K'un-i) agreed with the Tsungli Yamen that there should be a single commander-in-chief for coastal defense, but he qualified the proposal by suggesting that the generals-in-chief and brigade generals chosen by the commander-in-chief should be under the direction of the governors-general and the governors of the provinces concerned. Three recommended that the command of coastal defense be divided between the two commissioners at Tientsin and Nanking —two mentioned Li by name for the supervisory responsibility in north China.

Decision rested, of course, with the court. A meeting of the ministers was to consider the matter on January 2, but it was postponed due to the T'ung-chih emperor's illness and his death on the 12th. In late January, Li went to Peking and was summoned three times to audiences with the dowager empresses. He also talked with Wen-hsiang and Li Wen-tsao and urged that Shen Pao-chen be appointed governor-general of Liang-chiang, a post which had been vacated by Li Tsung-hsi (who was taken ill) and temporarily filled by Liu K'un-i as acting governor-general. Wen-hsiang arranged to have Robert Hart, who had obtained price quotations on British-built gunboats through his agent in London, go to Tientsin and discuss the details with Li.[73]

While in Peking, Li personally urged the court to reconsider the expedition into Sinkiang, and according to Li there were people at court who agreed with him.[74] But due chiefly to reluctance to "abandon territories acquired by an imperial ancestor," the throne abided by its decision (made as early as February, 1874) to encourage Tso Tsung-t'ang to proceed. On March 10, Tso was instructed to formulate plans for the expedition, including arrangements for the supply line. On May 3, Tso was appointed imperial commissioner for military operations in Sinkiang.[75] This effort to reconquer the far northwest was bound to cut into the revenue for the proposed coastal defense plans, although as of 1875 it was still uncertain whether Tso or the dynasty would really persevere in the long and arduous task of recovering Kashgar and Ili.

The court did not entirely neglect coastal defense, however. The Taiwan affair was fresh in its memory and in April, 1875, the murder of A. R. Margary, an interpreter entering Yunnan from Burma, raised the possibility of a threat from the British. The court was willing to see Li in a position to coordinate military preparations on the coast. On May 30, 1875, Shen Pao-chen was appointed governor-general of Liang-chiang and commissioner of trade for the southern ports. At the same time, Li was appointed commissioner of coastal defense for north China and Shen, commissioner of coastal defense for south China, both charged with the responsibility of training troops, establishing "bureaus" (meaning, probably, chiefly arsenals), reorganizing taxes, and other tasks necessary to defense. An edict of the same day declared: "Coastal defense is vitally important, and it is urgently necessary to make preparation before the coming of trouble, so as to strengthen ourselves." The throne noted that ironclads were extremely costly, but authorized Li and Shen to order "one or two to begin with."[76] The Board of Revenue and the Tsungli Yamen subsequently recommended that beginning in August, 1875, an annual appropriation of Tls. 4,000,000 be made for coastal defense, to be expended by the two commissioners. It was specified that the yearly sum was to come from the "four-tenths quota of the maritime customs revenue" at the coastal ports and from the likin revenue of coastal and Yangtze provinces. Since the Board of Revenue did not want to give up that portion of the four-tenths quota reserved for itself (or the sums it had received in the past from this source), and since the board plainly was not giving coastal defense priority over other imperially sanctioned claims on the four-tenths quota, Li feared that only a fraction of this annual fund would be left for him and Shen. Moreover, Li was certain that with the pressure from Peking to raise large sums (at least two or three million taels annually) for the construction of imperial mausoleums and palaces and with the Sinkiang campaign being given priority, probably only one or two coastal and Yangtze provinces would have any surplus in their likin revenue, which was also relied on by the provinces themselves for their own financial needs. Li foresaw that the Tls. 4,000,000 appropriated was to become largely nominal, although he hoped that at least some small portion might be available.[77]

Predictably, the court did not heed Li's counsel concerning the reform of institutions. Admitting the weaknesses of the Green Standard Army, the court, also on May 30, instructed all governors-general and governors concerned with coastal defense to complete, within a year, the reorganization and consolidation of the Green Standard "outposts" (hsün) and to provide the troops with uniform training. No mention was made,

however, of disbanding the inferior units. The throne also passed over the proposed "bureaus of Western learning" and the new civil service category for persons versed in this learning. One of the May 30 edicts states that both proposals had been referred to Prince Li (Shih-to) and to Prince Ch'un (the new child-emperor's father), along with the Tsungli Yamen's recommendation that diplomatic envoys be sent to Japan and the West. While the two princes favored the latter idea, they did not comment on the proposals regarding Western learning. So as to avoid "disagreement," the throne would, therefore, defer decision on these proposals until the diplomatic missions abroad proved successful! In another edict of the same day, the throne encouraged Li and Shen to recommend to it men who were versed in yang-wu, including those qualified to serve as envoys abroad. None of the edicts mentioned Li's proposals regarding railways, telegraphs, and textile mills, but one gave Li and Shen authorization to proceed with the specific mining projects they had mentioned in their memorials—the coal and iron mines in Tz'u-chou, Chihli, and on Taiwan.[78]

Thus only a few of the proposals Li put forward were adopted by the throne, and, in view of the priority it gave to Sinkiang and to the increasing financial needs of the court itself, a major new start in coastal defense and in self-strengthening was hardly to be expected. Yet it may be said that new ground had been broken in Ch'ing policy. Not being able to compete with the arsenals and shipyards of the West, China, it was decided, would have to acquire Western-made armaments through purchase. In the next few years, a spate of orders came from Tientsin and elsewhere for Remingtons, Sniders, Krupp, and Gatling guns.[79] As early as April, 1875, with the Tsungli Yamen's support, Li ordered four gunboats from Armstrong & Co., through Robert Hart's London agent— two 330-ton ships, each carrying a 26.5-ton rifle gun, and two 440-ton ones, each equipped with a 38-ton gun. The ordering of more gunboats and of an ironclad was contemplated, pending the availability of funds. It was planned during 1875-1876 to send graduates of the Foochow Navy Yard School to Britain and France.[80] Both Li and Shen interpreted the imperial sanction for the mines in Chihli and on Taiwan as general approval covering such projects elsewhere. Within the year following May, 1875, Li wrote to the governors of Hupeh, Kiangsi, Fukien, and Shantung, urging them to work mines with machines. Coal and iron fields were planned in Kuang-chi and Hsing-kuo, Hupeh, in late 1875 under the sponsorship of the commissioners at Tientsin and Nanking as well as the Hupeh governor; a similar project was initiated in Kiangsi in 1876, the same year that prospecting was done at K'ai-p'ing, Chihli. During that year, Li and Shen Pao-chen also considered the establishment of a cotton textile mill at Shanghai.[81]

What was particularly gratifying to Li was the fact that at least two like-minded colleagues had been brought, partly on his recommendation, to positions of influence. Shen Pao-chen arrived at his new post in Nanking in November, 1875. In September, Ting Jih-ch'ang, on Li's recommendation, had been appointed director-general of the Foochow Navy Yard, and in January, 1876, he became governor of Fukien with authority over Taiwan.[82] In Chihli, Li pressed forward with plans of long-range significance— the sending of five young officers of the Anhwei Army to German military academies, further expansion of the Tientsin Arsenal, the establishment of a school of Western sciences in connection with the Arsenal's new plant for manufacturing torpedoes.[83] Similar work was being carried on by Shen and Ting in south China. In early 1877, thirty students of the Foochow Navy Yard School were sent to Europe. Meanwhile, Shen did much to strengthen the Nanking and Kiangnan arsenals, adding to the former a torpedo plant and acquiring for the latter machinery for making cast-iron rifle guns of the Armstrong type, the first of which was produced in 1878. A school was set up at the Nanking Arsenal, and an effort was made to improve the school and the translation department at the Kiangnan Arsenal. Although the plan for a textile mill was found not to be immediately feasible, in late 1876 Shen Pao-chen arranged large loans from the Liang-chiang provinces to the China Merchants' Steam Navigation Company, enabling it to buy sixteen ships from the American firm of Russell and Co. and thereby increase its fleet to thirty-one vessels (22,168 net tons).[84] For the first time since Tseng Kuo-fan's death in 1872, Li had an ally at the head of the Liang-chiang administration.

We see, therefore, that only a small part of Li's comprehensive program was put into practice. Nevertheless, as compared with its beginnings in the early T'ung-chih period, the self-strengthening movement had certainly expanded. In the new shipping and mining enterprises, the movement had gained another dimension: to the desire for effective armament was added the desire to augment the state's wealth, again by using Western technology. The plan for a navy of foreign-built vessels represented a realistic appraisal of the capacity of

China's new shipyards, as well as an awareness of the urgent need for preparedness. The sending of students to Europe, in the wake of the educational mission to the United States, was a further acknowledgment of the need for technical personnel. Among the high officials there were very few men who, like Li, wanted to see drastic reform in civil service regulations and in the military system. But under the continued pressure from foreign powers, at least the objective of gaining "wealth and strength" for the state, which Li so eloquently advocated, had won widespread acceptance, if not active support.

With Li as the imperial commissioner at Tientsin, the self-strengthening movement had, moreover, acquired a strategically placed coordinator. It is plain that Li's power was limited. He could get the court to accept only a few of his proposals, and the finacnial and other resources he needed often lay in provinces beyond his jurisdiction. But it may be said that in the 1870's, Li was at least given a good opportunity to expand his efforts. The Anhwei Army in Chihli and elsewhere enjoyed the throne's support, and imperial approval had been given to his program for the arsenals, for studies abroad, for merchant steamships and mines, and for a new navy. Beginning in 1875, men recommended by Li, Shen Pao-chen and Ting Jih-ch'ang, were in the vital posts in Liang-chiang and Fukien, and with sympathetic officials in other provinces, there was at least a chance that self-strengthening might become an empire-wide effort. If by "regionalism" is meant the administrative leeway enjoyed by the governors-general and governors over the armies and the likin of the provinces, this trend had continued since the early T'ung-chih period. But the imperial authority

over armies and revenue anywhere in the empire was never questioned, and Peking's control over provincial appointments, at least at the higher levels, had not diminished. The court's support was plainly still the key to the success of any new policy. To the extent that Li's recommendations on policy and personnel met with imperial approval, he represented, in effect, a centralizing force on behalf of what he considered an urgent national task.

Notes

1. I have dealt with Li's early advocacy of *tzu-ch'iang* in a forthcoming article, "Li Hung-chang and 'Self-strengthening': The Origins of a Policy, 1862-1867."

2. See Stanley Spector, *Li Hung-chang and the Huai Army: A Study in Nineteenth-Century Regionalism* (Seattle, 1964).

3. Li Hung-chang, *Li Wen-chung kung ch'üan-chi* [Complete Works of Li Hung-chang], 100 *ts'e* (Nanking, 1908; hereafter cited as *LWCK*), *Tsou-kao* (hereafter cited as *Memorials*), 16. 34, 48, 50.

4. In 1870, Liu Ming-ch'uan and Kuo Sung-lin had the title of *t'i-tu*, while Wu Ch'ang-ch'ing was a *chi-ming* (designated) *t'i-tu*, and Chou-Sheng-ch'uan a *tsung-ping*. See, for example, *LWCK Memorials*, 17. 6b-7, 12; Chou Sheng-ch'uan, *Chou Wu-chuang kung i-shu* [Works of Chou Sheng-ch'uan], 10 *ts'e* (Nanking, 1905), 2 *hsia*, 1-9.

5. *LWCK Memorials*, 17. 8 and 21. 30-31.

6. *LWCK Memorials*, 17. 10. When Ch'ung-hou was appointed *san-k'ou t'ung-shang ta-ch'en* in 1861, the edict specifically stated that he was not given the title *ch'in-ch'ai*. However, the commissioner of trade for the southern ports (*nan-yang t'ung-shang ta-ch'en*) had been given the title *ch'in-ch'ai* in the early 1860's. Li's office of imperial commissioner at Tientsin was often referred to later as commissioner of trade for the northern ports. See *Ch'ou-pan i-wu shih-mo* [The Complete Account of Our Management of Barbarian Affairs], 260 *chüan* (Peiping, 1930; hereafter cited as *IWSM*), Hsien-feng, 72. 1b-2; T'ung-chih, 18. 25b.

7. *LWCK Memorials*, 18. 76 and 19. 83.

P'eng-liao han-kao (hereafter cited as *Letters*), 12. 26; 13. 3-4, 6b-8, 32b; 15. 16.

8. *LWCK Memorials,* 17. 29b and 18. 76.

9. *LWCK Memorials,* 19. 31b and 20. 46. *Letters,* 11. 12. For the figures on the Green Standard forces in Chihil, see *Memorials,* 20. 39b.

10. *LWCK Memorials, chüan* 17-26, especially 17. 41-43; 18. 88-89, 92-93; 19. 5-6, 20-21, 40; 20. 10-11b, 67; 21. 7-8, 12-13, 51-52; 22. 10-11, 39-41; 24. 36. *Letters,* 10. 33; 11. 6b, 13b-18, 20b-23; 12. 2, 9-10b; 13. 18.

11. *LWCK Memorials,* 17. 10, 14.

12. *LWCK, I-shu han-kao* (hereafter cited as *Tsungli Yamen Letters*), 1. 32-33b; *Letters,* 12. 23b.

13. *LWCK Tsungli Yamen Letters,* 1. 2b-8b, 14-15b, 17b-19, 24b-25b; *Memorials,* 18. 57.

14. *LWCK Tsungli Yamen Letters,* 1. 3b-4, 10-13, 22-24b, 28b-30, 34-35, 40-46, 48b-50. *Memorials,* 17. 53-54b; 18. 11-13, 28, 36, 42-52b; 19. 24, 57-59; 20. 73-74b; 21. 18-19. Cf. T. F. Tsiang, "Sino-Japanese Diplomatic Relations, 1870-1894," *Chinese Social and Political Science Review,* XVII (1933), 4-16.

15. *LWCK Tsungli Yamen Letters,* 1. 51-52; 2. 1-7, 29b, 31-33, 34-35. *Memorials,* 23. 23-25b; 25. 24-25.

16. *LWCK Tsungli Yamen Letters,* 1. 35b-38; *Letters,* 13. 4, 10b; Hosea Ballou Morse, *The International Relations of the Chinese Empire,* 3 vols. (London, 1910-1918), II, 267.

17. *LWCK Tsungli Yamen Letters,* 2. 34; see also 2. 20, 24, 26b-29, 30-31.

18. *LWCK Tsungli Yamen Letters,* 2.35-40, 51b-57. Cf. Tsiang, "Sino-Japanese Diplomatic Relations," pp. 16-34.

19. *LWCK Memorials,* 17. 10b.

20. *LWCK Memorials,* 17. 50b; 21. 40-41. Cf. *IWSM,* T'ung-chih, 10. 16; 61. 22.

21. *LWCK Letters,* 10. 30b, 34b, 35b; 11. 5b; 13. 14b. *Memorials,* 17. 50b; 18. 20, 66, 67b; 20. 36-37; 21. 40-41.

22. *LWCK Memorials,* 16. 42; 17. 1, 6b, 12b, 51; 20. 37; 23. 27b. *Letters,* 11. 2b. Chou Sheng-ch'uan, *Chou Wu-chuang Kung i-shu, chüan-shou,* 32-40.

23. *LWCK Memorials,* 17. 27b; 18. 32, 63.

24. *Tung-hua hsü-lu* [Continuation of the Tung-hua Records] (Taipei reprint, 1963), T'ung-chih, 91. 53, 55-56, 61b, 62b; 92. 1. *LWCK Letters,* 11. 19, 22-25.

25. *LWCK Memorials,* 19. 80-82b; 20. 16. *Letters,* 12. 20, 23; 13. 31b. *Tung-hua hsü-lu,* T'ung-chih, 95. 37, 45.

26. *LWCK Memorials,* 17. 7. *Letters,* 10. 27b, 30b; 11. 7b, 12b-13, 23b. *Tung-hua hsü-lu,* T'ung-chih, 92. 7.

27. *LWCK Letters,* 12. 12b-13, 24; 13. 7, 10b-11, 14b, 27b, 31b, 14. 2b. Tseng's successors as governor-general of Liang-chiang up to early 1875 were Ho Ching (acting, March-November, 1872), Chang Shu-sheng (acting, November, 1872-February, 1873), and Li Tsung-hsi (February, 1873-January, 1875).

28. *LWCK Tsungli Yamen Letters,* 2. 24b, 34b; *Letters,* 14. 6b-7, 9b; *Tung-hua hsü-lu,* T'ung-chih, 98. 39b-40.

29. *LWCK Memorials,* 23. 28b; *Letters,* 14. 7b, 8, 11, 14b-15, 18b, 19b, 24, 31.

30. *LWCK Letters,* 14. 12-13, 16-18, 20b-23.

31. *LWCK Memorials,* 21. 30-31b; 25. 40-41b; 27. 16-17.

32. *LWCK Letters,* 14. 16b, 22. See also 13. 8.

33. *LWCK Memorials,* 23. 37-38; *Letters,* 14. 24b, 26.

34. *LWCK Letters,* 11. 10. See also 10. 22b, 25, 27b-28; 11. 6, 21, 27; 12. 14; 13. 8.

35. *LWCK Letters,* 12. 3b; 14. 28b, 32.

36. Sun Yü-t'ang, ed. *Chung-kuo chin-tai kung-yeh shih tzu-liao, ti-i-chi, 1840-1895 nien* [Materials on the History of Modern Industry in China, First Collection, 1840-1895], 2 vols. (Peking, 1957), I, 263; *LWCK Memorials,* 21. 31b; *Yang-wu yün-tung* [The "Foreign Matters" Movement], comp. by the Institute of Modern History, Chinese Academy of Sciences, and Bureau of Ming and Ch'ing Archives, Central Archives, 8 vols. (Shanghai, 1961), IV, 127.

37. Demetrius C. Boulger, *The Life of Sir Halliday Macartney, K.C.M.G.* (London, 1908), pp. 148-150, 177; *North-China Herald,* August 16, 1867; *Chiang-nan chih-tsao-chü chi* [Records of the Kiangnan Arsenal], 11 *chüan,* comp. Wei Yün-kung (Shanghai, 1905), 3. 2, 58; *Chi-ch'i chü* [Arsenals], 2 vols., in *Hai-fang tang* [Files on Maritime Defense], ed. Kuo T'ing-yi et al. (Taiwan, 1957), I, 27-28, 41.

38. *LWCK Letters,* 11. 7b, 23b, 13. 14b. See also 11. 6b, 27b.

39. *LWCK Memorials,* 17. 16-17, 36; 20. 12-15; 23. 19-22; 24. 16; 28. 1-4.

40. *LWCK Letters,* 10. 28; 11. 23b, 31b; 12. 3. *Chiang-nan chih-tsao-chü chi,* 3. 2.

41. *LWCK Letters,* 13. 7, 11, 14; 14. 38b-39; 15. 13b. Sun Yü-t'ang, *Chung-kuo chin-tai kung-yeh shih tzu-liao,* I, 294, 299; *Chiang-*

nan chih-tsao-chü chi, 5. 3b-4b.

42. Boulger, *Life of Sir Halliday Macartney*, pp. 188, 198, 209, 212. *LWCK Letters*, 13. 11b, 27b; 14. 7a, 10. Sun Yü-t'ang, *Chung-kuo chin-tai kung-yeh shih tzu-liao*, I, 327.

43. *IWSM*, T'ung-chih, 84. 35; *LWCK Memorials*, 19. 44-49.

44. *LWCK Letters*, 12. 21, 26b.

45. *LWCK Letters*, 12. 25b; 13. 2, 13, 28-29, 32b-33.

46. Knight Biggerstaff, *The Earliest Modern Government Schools in China* (Ithaca, 1961), pp. 156-176; *LWCK Letters*, 10. 34.

47. *IWSM*, T'ung-chih, 25. 9-10b; *LWCK Memorials*, 24. 23b; *Letters*, 15. 4.

48. *LWCK Letters*, 10. 28.

49. *LWCK Letters*, 10. 32b; 11. 1b, 4b, 7b, 11; 12. 3. *Tsungli Yamen Letters*, 1. 19b-22. *Memorials*, 19. 7-10. *IWSM*, T'ung-chih, 82. 46b-52.

50. *IWSM*, T'ung-chih, 86. 13-14b. Hsü Jun, *Hsü Yü-chai tzu-hsü nien-p'u* [Chronological Autobiography] (preface dated 1927), pp. 17-23. *LWCK Letters*, 12. 15, 17b; 13. 12; 14. 1b, 8b-9; 15. 12. *Yang-wu yün-tung*, II, 165.

51. *LWCK Tsungli Yamen Letters*, 1. 22. *Letters*, 11. 12, 31b; 13. 6b, 7, 28, 30; 14. 31, 38b; 15. 14b, 16b.

52. *LWCK Letters*, 13. 28b, 32b-33.

53. *Chi-ch'i chü*, I, 3-5. *LWCK Memorials*, 8. 30-31; 9. 67-68.

54. *LWCK Letters*, 11. 22, 30b; 12. 1b-2, 9, 22b; 13. 15b, 17b-18, 22. *Memorials*, 22. 9-18.

55. *Kou-mai ch'uan-p'ao* [Purchase of Ships and Weapons], 3 vols. in *Hai-fang tang*, III, 903-910. *LWCK Letters*, 11. 31b; 12. 2b, 4, 9b.

56. *Kou-mai ch'uan-p'ao*, III, 910-923: *LWCK Tsungli Yamen Letters*, 1. 38-40; *Memorials*, 20. 32-33b.

57. *LWCK Letters*, 12. 31, 34b. See also 12. 36b.

58. *LWCK Letters*, 12. 28b-29, 30b.

59. *Kou-mai ch'uan-p'ao*, III, 925; *Han-cheng pien* [Section on Shipping], 6 vols. in *Chiao-t'ung shih* [History of Communications in China], comp. Ministries of Communications and Railroads (Nanking, 1930 ff.), I, 142.

60. Hsü Jun, *Hsü Yü-chai tzu-hsü nien-p'u*, p. 18. *LWCK Letters*, 13. 13b, 23-24; 14. 1b-2. Kwang-Ching Liu, "British-Chinese Steamship Rivalry in China, 1873-1885," in C. D. Cowan, ed., *Economic Development of China and Japan* (London, 1964), pp. 55-58.

61. *LWCK Tsungli Yamen Letters*, 1. 40; *Memorials*, 20. 33b.

62. *IWSM*, T'ung-chih, 55. 15b-16; Knight Biggerstaff, "The Secret Correspondence of 1867-1868: The Views of Leading Chinese Statesmen Regarding the Further Opening of China to Western Influence," *Journal of Modern History*, XXII (1950), 132; *LWCK Memorials*, 19. 49b-50.

63. *LWCK Letters*, 12. 21, 26b.

64. *LWCK Letters*, 14. 30b, 34b; 15. 14b. Ellsworth C. Carlson, *The Kaiping Mines, 1877-1912* (Cambridge, Mass., 1957), p. 7.

65. *LWCK Letters*, 13. 21b; 14. 2, 19, 30b. *Yang-wu yün-tung*, VII, 70. Morse, *International Relations*, II. 263.

66. *IWSM*, T'ung-chih, 98. 19-21, 40-42.

67. *LWCK Memorials*, 24. 10-25. See also 24. 26-28; *Letters*, 15. 12-15b.

68. *LWCK Letters*, 14. 32; *Tsungli Yamen Letters*, 2. 57b-59.

69. *LWCK Letters*, 3. 16b-17; 5. 28b, 32, 34-35. *Memorials*, 7. 29; 17. 12.

70. See C. John Stanley, *Late Ch'ing Finance: Hu Kuang-yung as an Innovator* (Cambridge, Mass., 1961), pp. 81-84.

71. *LWCK Memorials*, 12. 26; 13. 2; 14. 32; 15. 2b, 6b-7. See also 14. 38; 15. 17.

72. *IWSM*, T'ung-chih, 98. 31-100. 44.

73. *LWCK Letters*, 14. 34, 38b-39; 15. 1b. *Tung-hua hsü-lu*, T'ung-chih, 100. 47-48.

74. *LWCK Letters*, 15. 2b. Strangely enough, Prince Ch'un, who had urged a belligerent stand during the crisis created by the Tientsin Massacre, agreed with Li on Sinkiang; see 16. 17.

75. *LWCK Letters*, 15. 2, 10b; *Ch'ing-chi wai-chiao shih-liao* [Historical Materials on Foreign Relations in the Latter Part of the Ch'ing Dynasty], 243 *chüan* (Peiping, 1932-1935), Kuang-hsü, 1. 4-5; *Tung-hua hsü-lu*, T'ung-chih, 98. 30, 32; Kuang-hsü, 1. 35. Cf. Immanuel C. Y. Hsü, "The Great Policy Debate in China, 1874: Maritime Defense vs. Frontier Defense," *Harvard Journal of Asiatic Studies*, XXV (1965), 217-227; Wen-djang Chu, "Tso Tsung-T'ang's Role in the Recovery of Sinkiang," *Tsing Hua Journal of Chinese Studies*, New Series I. No. 3, pp. 136-145.

76. *Tung-hua hsü-lu*, Kuang-hsü, 1. 33, 56-57.

77. *LWCK Letters*, 15. 19b, 20b, 21b, 22b, 26b, 30b-31, 33b-35. *Tsungli Yamen Letters*, 3. 18; 5. 40.

78. *Tung-hua hsü-lu,* Kuang-hsü, 1. 56-57. According to Li's information when the officials at court held a meeting to discuss the proposals on coastal defense, Wen-hsiang was sympathetically inclined toward Li's recommendations on "bureaus of foreign learning," railways, telegraph, and mines, but two Chinese officials strongly condemned them, and others at the meeting were indifferent. *LWCK Letters,* 17. 13.

79. In a letter to C. Hannen dated October 25, 1875, Robert Hart commented on the Chinese purchase of foreign arms and on the arrangements being made for a modern coal mine on Taiwan: "Forts are bristling all round Tientsin and in many other places, and official talk loves to dwell on the sweet syllables the Chinese mouth makes of the word 'Krupp.' Torpedoes are toys in all the houses, and, as for an 80-ton gun creating astonishment, the wonder is that thousand-tonners have not yet been devised for the Chinese and sent out in cases, and as numerously, as needles and matches! The big giant is really waking up, but what a time it takes to yawn and rub his eyes!" Quoted in Morse, *International Rela-*

tions, II, 263. See also *LWCK Tsungli Yamen Letters,* 3. 17-19; Chou Sheng-ch'uan, *Chou Wu-chuang kung i-shu, chüan-shou.* 40b.

80. *LWCK Tsungli Yamen Letters,* 3. 6-14, 16; 4. 26; 5. 40b; 6. 28-29b. *Letters,* 15. 21b, 31, 33b, 36; 16. 3, 12, 14b, 21b-22, 26b-27. Stanley F. Wright, *Hart and the Chinese Customs* (Belfast, 1950), pp. 469-474.

81. *LWCK Letters,* 15. 14, 16, 22, 24, 27b, 29b-30, 31, 36; 16. 3b, 20. *Yang-wu yün-tung,* VII, 103-106, 113.

82. *LWCK Letters,* 15. 29, 30b, 33, 35; *Memorials,* 29. 1-2; *Tung-hua hsü-lu,* Kuang-hsü, 1. 115, 140.

83. *LWCK Letters,* 16. 12. *Tsungli Yamen Letters,* 4. 39. *Memorials,* 28. 1-4; 33. 25-29.

84. *LWCK Letters,* 15. 35-36b; 16. 1b, 3, 5b, 7-9, 14b, 22, 24, 31b, 34b-36. *Tsungli Yamen Letters,* 6. 47b-38. Shen Pao-chen, *Shen Wen-su kung cheng-shu* [Works of Shen Pao-chen], 8 vols. (1880), *chüan* 6-7. Sun Yü-t'ang, *Chung-kuo chin-tai kung-yeh shih tzu-liao,* I, 282, 299-300, 317-319, 328. *Yang-wu yün-tung,* IV, 37-41. Liu, "British-Chinese Steamship Rivalry," p. 60.

16. THE GREAT POLICY DEBATE IN CHINA, 1874:

MARITIME DEFENSE VS. FRONTIER DEFENSE

IMMANUEL C. Y. HSU

Few government policies in late Ch'ing China received more attention than that

From *Harvard Journal of Asiatic Studies,* Vol. 25 (1964-65), pp. 212-28. The author is grateful to the John Simon Guggenheim Foundation for fellowshi in 1962-1963 which made research for this article possible.

concerning the relative importance of coastal defense and inland defense in 1874. The occasion was highly significant; not only did it decide whether China should try to become a land power or a naval power during the next few decades, but it also reflected the views of leading relations with Russia and Japan, the two neighbors which were to influence her destiny profoundly in the next hundred years. Li Hung-chang, governor-general of Chihli and chief advocate of maritime defense, urged the adoption of a new naval program to strengthen China's coastal defense against future Japanese aggression. Tso Tsung-t'ang, governor-general of Shensi and Kansu and chief advocate of frontier defense, on the other hand, was concerned with the dangers of Russian advance in Sinkiang. Tso's views reflected China's traditional fear of invasion by barbarian hordes from the Central Asian steppes, while Li's indicated a keen awareness of China's new position in the world and the rising threat of Japan. It is noteworthy that the seeds of Li's later anti-Japanese and pro-Russian policy in the 1890's were already discernible in his arguments of 1874.

The question that precipitated this grand debate was whether or not China should send a costly expedition to Sinkiang to suppress a Moslem rebellion in the wake of Japanese aggression in Formosa. It will be recalled, the country had been troubled by a Moslem rebellion, which broke out in Shensi in 1862 and which quickly spread to Kansu and Sinkiang. The entire northwest of China was ablaze.[1] Nearly all of Sinkiang had fallen to a Khokandian adventurer, Yakub Beg, and the rich Ili Valley was occupied by Russia in 1871. The court at Peking appointed Tso Tsung-t'ang, governor-general of Shensi and Kansu in 1966, with the specific assignment of suppressing the rebels in these provinces, but he was unable to assume command until he had suppressed the Nien rebels in the summer of 1868. Then, after five years of hard campaigning, he accom-

plished the earlier mission of clearing Shensi and Kansu of the Moslem rebels in 1873.[2] The government had spent forty million taels on the campaign, and its victorious army was poised to strike into Sinkiang.[3] At this critical juncture, a foreign crisis arose on the coast. Japan invaded Formosa in 1874 on the pretext of punishing the aborigines for killing fifty-three shipwrecked Ryukyuan sailors. China's inability to defend Formosa, to say nothing of winning the war, led to the humiliating decision of buying off, rather than fighting, the aggressor at the price of half a million taels.[4] The court at Peking was shocked by China's lack of preparation and was desperately anxious to strengthen the coastal defense. The question was, could the financially hard-pressed country support a bold naval program while conducting a costly campaign in Sinkiang? Which issue, coastal defense or frontier defense, was more urgent and which should be given a higher priority? A grand debate on national policy followed.

Prince Kung, head of the Tsungli Yamen, sounded the first note of alarm at China's inadequate coastal defenses in a memorial that reached the court on November 5, 1874. China's weakness, as exposed by Japan in the Formosa case, he warned, would encourage Western nations to cast covetous eyes on her, and her future was bleak. "Since the war of 1860 . . . people [in China] have set their minds on self-strengthening and have talked about it, but until today there has been no reality at all to self-strengthening. The [defeat] seems to have become a thing of the past and is long forgotten."[5] He urged a renewal of China's efforts to strengthen herself. On December 6, 1874 Wen-hsiang, a leading minister in the Yamen, felt impelled, in spite of serious illness, to reinforce

Prince Kung's plea for coastal defense with one of his own:

Japan, a small country in the eastern ocean, has only lately adopted Western military methods and bought two ironclads; on the basis of these, she has dared to stir up trouble. Shen Pao-chen and other high officials on the coast were all convinced that we, not having bought ironclads, had better avoid a break with her. Clearly, we have accommodated her in settling this issue, because our preparations have not been completed. If we continue to drift along passively and do not anxiously try to seek improvement to catch up, trouble in the future will be even more difficult to meet.[6]

Ting Jih-ch'ang, ex-governor of Kiangsu, answered the Yamen's call for action and submitted to the court a "Six-Item Naval Proposal" through the good offices of Chang Chao-tung, the governor of Kwangtung. He urged the creation of three squadrons of sixteen ships each, a total of forty-eight ships, for the north, central, and south China coasts, with an admiral in charge of each squadron. The six proposals were: purchase of big gunboats, construction of naval fortresses at key points along the coast, training of the army, selection of able and incorruptible officials on the coast, coordination among the squadrons, and establishment of dockyards and munitions factories. The court referred Ting's proposal and the Yamen's memorial to the leading officials for comment.[7]

Other high mandarins too made similar suggestions for the development of a navy. Wen-pin, the acting governor of Shantung and director-general of grain transport, recommended the creation of three fleets, one to be stationed in Tientsin, one at the mouth of the Yangtze, and one on the coast of Fukien, each to consist of one or two big foreign-built ironclads and several smaller home-built ships.[8] Wang K'ai-t'ai, governor of Fukien, likewise urged the formation of three naval forces: a northern fleet based at Taku to take charge of the defense of Fengt'ien, Chihli, and the Shantung coastal area; a central fleet based at Woosung to defend the Kiangsu and Chekiang coast; and a southern fleet based on Formosa to defend the Fukien and Kwangtung coast. Each fleet was to be commanded by a high commissioner of the navy and would comprise sixteen ships: two ironclads, four large ships, six medium ones, and four small ones. The three fleets would have a combined strength of forty-eight ships.[9]

By far the most powerful proponent of the naval project was Li Hung-chang, the grand secretary and governor-general of Chihli, who energetically defended the importance of maritime defense in a long memorial that reached the court on December 12, 1874. China was facing a totally different world with enemies more powerful than any she had known before, Li argued, and to meet this unprecedented situation with the old measures was like prescribing the same medicine for all kinds of disease. For the new challenge that had been thrust upon her, China had to adopt new measures bravely.[10] Li's key word was "change," and he quoted the famous passage from the *Book of Changes* to support his views: " 'When a series of changes has run its course, another change ensues [which will lead to fruition].' Without changes no war or defensive measure can be undertaken and there can be no lasting peace . . . . In sum, if we want to put our coastal defense in good order, there is no other way to begin than to change our (old) methods and employ (new) talents."[11] He went on to state:

Western nations, no matter how powerful, are more than 70,000 *li* away, but Japan is right on our threshold, capable of spying out our weakness or readiness. She is China's most important permanent problem. Although she has been momentarily restrained to some extent, she still has artfully designed stratagems and plots and is intensely covetous of the riches of our products and people. She hopes to find a pretext for further action at opportune moments before we complete our [programs of] ships and guns. For this reason, things like ironclads, naval fortresses, etc. must be begun at once. But substantial funds are not available, and besides, purchasing orders take time to fill.[12]

It is clear that Li's naval program took Japan, and not the Western states, for the supposed enemy. He realized that the Western states had been building ships and making guns for a long time and would continue to outdo anything that China could expect to achieve in a few years. But Japan had only recently begun to imitate the West and could be overtaken. Li's project called for the purchase of foreign ships and guns, the training of officers and sailors, the recruitment of new talent by a new "foreign affairs" examination, the opening of mines, the manufacture of munitions, and an increase in customs duties on opium imports to help pay for naval expenses. He estimated the total cost at ten million taels annually.[13] Li boldly asked the court to weigh the relative importance of maritime defense and frontier defense and to shift the funds from the Sinkiang campaign to his naval program:

It is common knowledge that our finances of late have been extremely strained. For our own good, we must keep in mind the situation of the entire country before we can decide on a policy. The various cities in

Sinkiang first came under our control in the Ch'ien-lung period (1736-1795). Quite apart from the great difficulty of winning these cities, we spent more than three million taels annually on military expenses in peacetime [just to keep them]. We have taken several thousand *li* of open space at the price of a [pecuniary] drain that will continue hundreds and thousands of years. It is not worthwhile. Moreover, the territory (i.e. Sinkiang) borders on Russia in the west, and British India in the south. Foreign [nations] are increasing in power daily while our internal conditions degenerate daily. The present situation is entirely different from that of the past. Even if we can recover [Sinkiang] we will not be able to hold it for long.

A reading of foreign newspapers and intelligence from the western front from time to time [shows] that the Moslem chieftain in Kashgaria (Yakub Beg) has recently been given a title by the Turkish Sultan and has concluded commercial agreements with Britain and Russia.[14] He has aligned himself with the several great nations and acts in concert with them. Ili is under [Russian] occupation. From all the evidence, it appears that Russia is beginning to nibble, and Britain will soon join her in seeking profit, both of them unwilling to see China gain ascendancy in the Western Region (Sinkiang). From the standpoint of China's present strength, she certainly should not concentrate exclusively on the Western Region and exhaust her troops and money. Tseng Kuo-fan formerly proposed temporary renunciation [of the land] beyond the passes, in order to concentrate on settling affairs within them. His approach to state planning was indeed a careful one.

Today, although we may order our generals to extend the campaign [beyond the passes], our military strength and our funds are absolutely unequal to the task. Can we not secretly order the commanding general on the western front only to guard the existing border vigilantly and use his soldiers for military colonizing and farming, without taking a rashly aggressive stand? At the

same time we can pacify the Moslem chieftains in Ili, Urumchi, and Kashgar by allowing them to form autonomous tribes, as
the Miao and Yao native headmen have
done in Yunnan, Kweichow, and Kwangtung,
while asking them to use the Chinese calendar more or less as Annam and Korea do.
Letting them live is good for us as well as
for them; not only will it block the British
and Russian attempts to annex them, but
it will also save China the trouble of frequent expeditions. This approach looks like
a durable one. Furthermore, nonrecovery of
Sinkiang will not hurt us physically or spiritually, whereas lack of preparedness in
coastal defense renders our basic trouble
even more difficult. Which issue (i.e. maritime defense or border defense) is the more
important is readily seen.

If this proposal is adopted, the armies that
have already been sent beyond the passes
and those which have not yet been sent
should be somehow limited—disbanded or
their movements stopped whenever possible.
The funds saved should be shifted to maritime defense. Otherwise, with our limited
financial resources, is it possible to conduct
coastal defense over [an area of] 10,000 *li*
in the Southeast simultaneously with frontier defense over [an area of] 10,000 *li* in the
Northwest, without thoroughly exhausting
us?[15]

Many other high provincial authorities also grasped the importance of
coastal defense and echoed Li's arguments. Yang Ch'ang-chün, the governor
of Chekiang, argued that naval development was more important than army
training and that, regardless of the vast
expenditures of money that would be
necessary, China had to begin to build
a navy. "When a small and poor country like Japan can invest heavily and unhesitatingly in imitating the West, cannot our big country, China, move ahead
boldly at a time when there are foreign
threats and invasions? Can we procrasti-
nate and lose by default so that for-

eign domination results?"[16] Ying-han,
governor-general of Kwangtung and
Kwangsi, and Yü-lu, the governor of Anhwei, jointly recommended to the court
the creation of a naval fund by establishing new bureaus to collect *likin* on salt
and by increasing the opium duty thirty
per cent. The first measure would yield
several million taels yearly and the second, a possible two and a half million.[17]

In short, the advocates of maritime defense made five points. First, border
defense was not so important and urgent
as maritime defense in view of Peking's
proximity to the coast and Sinkiang's
long distance from the capital. Second,
financial exigency and the uncertainty of
victory compelled re-examination of the
present policy for the Sinkiang campaign.
Third, Sinkiang, a vast piece of barren
land, was of little practical use to China
and was not worth the cost of maintaining it. Fourth, Sinkiang was surrounded
by strong neighbors and could not be
effectively defended for long. Fifth, to
postpone the recovery of Sinkiang was
not unfilial; the withdrawal of troops for
the time being was not renunciation of
territory conquered by Emperor Ch'ien-
lung, but simply a sensible way to preserve China's strength for the future.[18]

The importance of the naval program
was so obvious that few had the temerity
to question it. But many high officials
argued that it should not be undertaken
at the expense of defending the frontiers; the rebels in Sinkiang had to be
suppressed and the lost land recovered,
regardless of the naval program. These
were the border-defense "firsters," as
opposed to Li and Ting who were the
coastal-defense "firsters." For instance,
Wang Wen-shao, governor of Hunan,
while acknowledging the need for buying foreign ships to strengthen coastal
defenses, argued that the peace of China

really hinged on a successful campaign in Sinkiang, because coastal trouble was likely to flare up if China failed in the Northwest:

If our troops fall behind a step, the Russians advance a step. If our troops lose a day, the Russians gain a day. There is nothing more urgent than this affair. The several nations of Britain, France, and the United States also may exploit the situation to their advantage and take action. Any progressive worsening of the Russian affair will inevitably bring on the maritime problem, and our defense will be hard put to meet the double challenge. As a result, the general state of Chinese foreign relations in the future will be unthinkable.

It was therefore necessary, he said, to bring all Chinese power to bear on the Sinkiang campaign, in order to check the Russians first, if only to prevent Western nations from making trouble on the coast. If China should flounder in the naval program, the Sinkiang problem would become increasingly difficult to handle.[19]

A somewhat similar view was expressed by Ting Pao-chen, governor of Shantung, who argued that Russia was a much greater threat than Japan or any Western nation, since Russia and China had common frontiers and therefore Russia could reach China by land as well as by water. Japan, though near, could only reach China by water, and the Western nations, though capable of reaching China by sea, were far away. Therefore neither of these powers was so menacing as Russia. Besides, the Russians repeatedly used the trick of playing both ends against the middle—posing as a mediator between China and the Western states and profiting from both. "In your minister's view," Ting contended, "the trouble of the various [maritime]

nations is like the sickness of the limbs which is distant and light, whereas the trouble of Russia is like the sickness of the heart and stomach, which is near and serious." He feared a Russian back-door thrust to Peking from Manchuria, in which case Japan and the Western states might also take advantage of the situation to stir up trouble on the coast. For this reason, defense of the inland frontier against Russia was a matter of the greatest urgency.[20]

Li Han-chang, governor-general of Hu-Kuang and brother of Li Hung-chang, suggested a compromise between maritime defense and inland defense. The Sinkiang campaign, he said, had to go on to complete the extermination of the Moslem rebels, but expenses might be cut by eliminating the old inefficient troops. The money saved could be used for the naval program, which was important enough to be undertaken regardless of the cost.[21]

Having received all these varied but closely-reasoned memorials, the court solicited Tso Tsung-t'ang's opinion on the issue. On March 10, 1875 it summarized for his comment the memorials of Li Hung-chang and Wang Wen-shao, the chief exponents of the two opposing policies. The court also made this comment of its own: "If the campaign in the west can be delayed to save money for naval defense, it would of course help our finances to some extent. But . . . the Russian soldiers may advance step by step . . . . Moreover, once the defensible line beyond the passes is removed, we cannot be sure that the Moslem bandits will not revive and create trouble again along the frontier. Once the rebel force is rolling, we would be unable to close the door to preserve ourselves, even if we would like to."[22]

Tso responded to the imperial call on

April 12, 1875 with a long masterly memorial. Contrary to his reputation as a diehard advocate of frontier defense, he strongly maintained the importance of both maritime and frontier defense, and chided the devotees of one or the other school for parochial thinking. With aplomb, he told Peking that his former services on the coast as governor-general of Fukien and Chekiang and as founder of the Foochow Dockyard had familiarized him with the importance of coastal defense, and his more recent campaign against the Moslem rebels in the Northwest had instructed him in the importance of frontier defense. Only a man with this dual experience could speak with authority, freedom, and impartiality about the vital problems of maritime defense and frontier defense. From this vantage-point Tso began energetic argument stating that, while certainly not opposed to the naval program, he was convinced that the Sinkiang campaign had to be carried to total victory regardless of what became of the naval program. Western maritime nations, he asserted, driven primarily by the desire for trade profits, fought for harbors and ports, not for territory. The danger from that quarter, therefore, was not immediate. Russia, on the other hand, had territorial as well as commercial designs. "People have suggested that funds for the army which had gone beyond the passes be withdrawn or cut and shifted to coastal defense. If coastal defense were twice as urgent as frontier defense and the budget for the army in the Northwest more substantial than that for coastal defense, the suggestion might be tenable." But his own army, he went on to say, was hard pressed for funds too: it needed eight million taels yearly but had only an annual budget of five million, with the result that his army

received only three months' pay every year. The suggestion to shift his army's funds to maritime defense, Tso insisted, had to be rejected. Moreover, he was convinced that the new naval program would not entail much extra expense, since there was already a standing amount earmarked for that purpose. As the Foochow Dockyard turned out more and more ships, the cost of buying foreign ships would rapidly decrease, and the main expenses of the naval program would be only the training of sailors and soldiers and the construction of forts.

He was adamant in his stand that not only should the Sinkiang campaign go on, but it should not stop even with the recovery of Urumchi. Artfully he pleaded:

Emperor Ch'ien-lung successively conquered Djungaria and Kashgaria, opening up some 20,000 *li* of territory, with Ili as the western military headquarters of the (T'ien-shan) Northern Route and Kashgar as the western military headquarters of the Southern Route. At that time, many court officials doubted [the wisdom] of consuming resources to extend the endless frontiers, but so powerful and deep was His Majesty's conviction that he was not moved by them. Certainly, in laying the foundations of a state, there is a proper approach to the frontier which is appropriate to the occasion.[23]

In these statements is seen Tso's persuasive appeal to the two basic elements of Chinese psychology: filial piety and the lesson of history. He told the court, in effect, that if the wise emperors of the past spared no effort in conquering Mongolia and Sinkiang, they must have had good reasons. They knew that the barbarian horsemen from the steppes of Inner Asia could threaten China through gradual absorption of the frontier areas. Peking's security would be endangered if

Mongolia were lost, and the defense of Mongolia would be impossible if Sinkiang were lost. In the days of the mounted archers, Sinkiang was China's first line of defense, as was clearly demonstrated in the case of the ambitious Ölöd leader, Galdan. Having conquered Chinese Turkestan in 1679, he pillaged the Qalqa (Eastern Mongols) in 1688 and invaded Outer Mongolia in 1690, penetrating all the way to the lower Kerulun River. Then he turned south toward Inner Mongolia, apparently with the intention of taking Peking. But at Ulan Butung, within eighty leagues of Peking, he suffered a defeat by the Ch'ing army. Although his advance was stopped, Galdan's power was not destroyed. It was not until 1696 that Emperor K'ang-hsi (1662-1722), after many years of preparation, was finally able to crush him at Jau Modo. As a result Outer Mongolia and Hami came under Ch'ing control.[24] Emperor Ch'ien-lung (1736-1795) continued the exploits; Djungaria was pacified in 1757 and Kashgaria in 1759, thereby laying the foundation of peace for a century. Tso's argument was in fact a masterful appeal to this strategic tradition, replete with the emotional implication that no dutiful son of these great emperors should ignore the tradition and sacrifice the fruits of their labor.

Tso concluded his powerful arguments with a warning that to stop the Sinkiang campaign now was to invite the rebels to advance. The money saved would not be enough to aid coastal defense but would definitely injure frontier defense. As for the international complications of the Sinkiang campaign arising from Yakub Beg's diplomatic and commercial relations with Turkey, Britain, and Russia, he suggested a policy of cautious watchfulness until Urumchi had been recovered. He predicted that Russia, a large civilized state, quite different from the Moslem countries, would probably not join forces with the rebels against China. But the important thing at this moment was that China must not lose by default.[25]

In short, Tso and the other advocates of frontier defense made these five points:

First, Sinkiang was the first line of defense in the Northwest. It protected Mongolia, which in turn protected Peking. If Sinkiang were lost, Mongolia would be indefensible and Peking itself threatened. Second, there was no immediate danger of invasion from Western nations, which were primarily interested in trade. Third, the funds for frontier defense should not be shifted to coastal defense, which already had its own standing fund; the tight budget for frontier defense allowed no borrowing. Fourth, the land conquered by the former emperors of the dynasty should not lightly be given up. Fifth, such strategic spots as Urumchi and Aksu should be recovered first.[26]

One cannot but be impressed with the cogent, persuasive, and well-reasoned arguments of both Li and Tso. There were elements of truth in each, but there were also exaggerations and distortions. The importance of the coastal area to the defense of Peking was indisputably far greater than that of remote Sinkiang. If Sinkiang was China's first line of defense in the age of the horseman, the coastal area played the same role in the age of sea power. The arrival of Western maritime powers and Peking's proximity to the coast necessitated a total reevaluation of China's defense strategy. Li Hung-chang tried to impress upon his countrymen that China was facing a situation unprecedented in her three thousand years of history.[27] To meet this

challenge, he urged adoption of modernization programs such as the naval project, even at the expense of Sinkiang. Li's
suggestions resulted from objective,
hard-headed calculations of the new
forces in international relations, and his
arguments *for* maritime defense were
basically sound, farsighted, and statesmanlike.

However, his arguments *against* frontier defense were not as praiseworthy.
He was incorrect in asserting that Sinkiang in time of peace represented a financial drain on the treasury; on the
contrary, it had proved financially profitable for China.[28] Although the court
spent considerable sums of money each
year to station troops there, the expenses
were part of the regular army budget.
Emperor Chi'ien-lung had specifically
stated that the expenses of maintaining
these troops would have been incurred
whether they were stationed in Sinkiang
or elsewhere in the empire.[29] Moreover,
many of Li's statements betrayed a spirit
of defeatism designed to discourage the
court from undertaking the frontier defense. Sinkiang was said to be surrounded
by strong neighbors such as Russia and
British India, "both of whom [were]
unwilling to see China gain ascendancy
in the Western Region." "Foreign [na-
tions] are increasing in power daily
while our internal conditions degenerate
daily. . . . Even if we can recover [Sin-
kiang] we will not be able to hold it for
long." Yakub Beg's official relations with
Britain and Russia and his alignment
with Turkey and Britain were stressed
by Li as obstacles to China's reconquest
of Sinkiang. All these statements were
calculated to arouse fear on the part of
the court and to dissuade it from approving the frontier defense.

Li's arguments against the Sinkiang
campaign, though conducted on the high

level of policy debate, were probably not
free of private considerations. A sly politician at heart, he never lost sight of his
personal stake in any major undertaking
of the state. He was concerned over the
effect of the Sinkiang campaign on his
own power. It was evident that the
country had limited resources and that
any appropriations for the campaign
would reduce available funds for his
projects. The Sinkiang campaign might
even bring on a clash with the Russian
forces in Ili. If war broke out, Russia
would likely avoid fighting in Sinkiang
but instead attack directly the key points
in Manchuria and on the coast. The
major burden of defending Peking would
fall on Li's shoulders, and he knew full
well that his nascent navy was no match
for the more experienced Russian fleet
and that his Huai army would probably
disintegrate in a modern war. The inevitable result would be destruction of
his army, his navy, and his numerous
modernization projects. Once they were
gone, his power base in North China
would be lost, and so would his political
influence. He could not see why China
and he, himself, should risk losing so
much for the remote area of Sinkiang.
There may be some validity in the accusation of a Marxist writer that Li
preached "surrenderism" to save his own
army and navy from the clash with Russia.[30] One might say that the motives for
Li's arguments against frontier defense
rested on a lower plane than did the motives for his arguments in favor of maritime defense.

Tso Tsung-t'ang's forceful exposition
of the need for recovering the lost land
from the standpoint of traditional strategy and the urgency of blocking Russian
advance represented a masterly mixture
of reason and emotion. He applied anach-
ronistically the military concepts of

the age of horsemen to the age of gun-boats. China's primary enemies in the nineteenth century were not mounted archers from the steppes—although the danger of Russian advance from Central Asia still existed—but sea-faring West-erners. Though powerfully presented and well-reasoned, Tso's arguments were ba-sically out of date and revealed vestiges of the steppe-oriented mentality. Yet his patriotic utterances stirred the emotions and moved the heart, while Li's argu-ments could at best appeal to the in-tellect. Tso's position was materially strengthened by the fact that there was no foreign war on the coast at the mo-ment while there was a rebellion in Sinkiang which required immediate at-tention and suppression. To stop the Sinkiang campaign was likened to inter-rupting a serious operation midway on grounds of saving the patient's blood.[31]

The court at Peking was ultimately convinced that any interruption of the Sinkiang campaign at this point would only hamper frontier defense without benefiting coastal defense. In coming to this decision, it was undoubtedly influ-enced by the traditional lack of enthu-siasm for maritime affairs on the one hand, and by China's deep historical in-terest in Sinkiang on the other. Although it was well known that China during the Southern Sung, Yüan, and early Ming periods maintained powerful fleets and merchant marine,[32] the Manchus in China had inherited the middle and late Ming attitude of relative indifference to coastal affairs and general disdain for overseas trade.[33] Coming from the Inner Asian frontier of Manchuria, the Man-chus were basically a land-oriented peo-ple, who, like the Chinese, looked to the northern and northwestern frontiers, rather than the sea coast, in devising security measures.[34] The early Ch'ing

rulers spent nearly a century conquering Turkestan in the belief that control of Central Asia was essential to control of China.[35] Such concepts were doubtless the product of pre-modern military tech-nology, not unmixed with China's deep-rooted relations with Sinkiang, histor-ically known as Hsi-yü (the Western Region).

To many Chinese, the very name of Hsi-yü was associated with mystery, ad-venture, and military glory. During the two thousand years since the Han dy-nasty, nearly all ambitious emperors—Wu-ti of the Han period, T'ai-tsung of the T'ang period, and K'ang-hsi and Ch'ien-lung of the Ch'ing period—had sent expeditions to conquer it. Their ac-tions were defended as necessary for dynastic survival, for North China was vulnerable to attacks by the swift-moving barbarian hordes from the Central Asian steppes. In this sense, China's destiny during the age of the mounted archer was linked with the control of the fron-tier areas. So vital were these areas to Chinese planning that a bold if over-simplified historical thesis had emerged, which suggested that China's relations with these areas were a barometer of her dynastic fortunes. During periods of strength and prosperity, China could maintain peace and order internally and also hold the barbarian hordes of Central Asia in check. This ideal state of affairs, described as a "Grand Unification" (ta i-t'ung), was realized under the mighty dynasties of the Han, T'ang, Yüan, and Ch'ing. A less propitious situation, some-times described as a "Minor Unification" (hsiao i-t'ung), prevailed whenever China, though not strong enough to pac-ify the nomadic tribes, was able to de-fend her interior against their incursions, as, for example, during the Northern Sung and Ming dynasties. Yet a third phase developed whenever China was weak and decadent, troubled by internal disorders and foreign invasions. The barbarian invaders were then able to make powerful thrusts into the Yellow River Valley in northern China, driving the Chinese dynasty to take refuge in the Yangtze River Valley in the south. Though under constant threat, the exiled dynasty could still maintain a shaky existence within a shrunken area. Such a state of affairs, typified by the Southern Sung period, was described as "Partial Security" (p'ien-an). These terms suggest that Chinese history, exclusive of the periods of barbarian conquest, was regarded as simply a cyclical alternation of these three dynastic phases.[36]

The validity of this historical thesis is a moot point, but it serves to indicate the importance of frontier areas, especially Sinkiang, in the Chinese mind. Failure to exercise control of these areas came to mean admission of dynastic weakness. It is therefore not surprising that Emperors K'ang-hsi and Ch'ien-lung spent the better part of a century conquering Sinkiang. However, with the advent of the age of sea power and China's opening to the West in the middle of the nineteenth century, such steppe-oriented strategical thinking was decidedly obsolescent; yet in varying degrees it still prevailed among the historically-minded Chinese scholars and officials. Small wonder that the Ch'ing government in the 1870's, despite financial stringency and military limitation, decided in favor of the frontier defense. Nevertheless, maritime defense was not altogether disregarded; it received a second priority and was to be carried out on a more limited scale.

The Sinkiang campaign was formally approved and the court on April 23, 1875 appointed Tso imperial commissioner in charge of military affairs in Sinkiang. With this authorization, Tso established his headquarters in Lanchow, Kansu, and engaged in reorganizing the army, raising funds, and resolving the problem of logistics. By early 1876 his preparations were complete, and his army swept successfully into Sinkiang, pacifying Djungaria in the north by November 1876, and subjugating Yakub Beg's kingdom in Kashgaria in December 1877. By early 1878, Chinese imperial authority was re-established in all Sinkiang except a small pocket in Ili, which was under Russian occupation.[37]

The recovery of Sinkiang was truly a great accomplishment, especially in view of the financial difficulty, military weakness, and political decline of the Manchu dynasty. Tso of course was proud of his record, which he described as "a truly great feat seldom seen since the Ch'in and Han dynasties."[38] The victory was made possible by generous contributions of funds from the provinces, large appropriations from the treasury, and two foreign loans. Military expenses in Sinkiang ran to some twenty-six million taels from the beginning of 1875 to the end of 1877 when the pacification was complete, and some twenty-five million more in the postwar period of 1878-1881, making a total of fifty-one million taels.[39] These expenses strained the finances of the country, and the naval program suffered seriously. Only four million taels were approved annually for the navy, and of this meagre sum barely one-fourth was actually appropriated.[40] It is therefore apparent that there was a definite correlation between the weakness of the nascent Chinese navy and the Sinkiang campaign. In 1882 Li Hung-chang pleaded with the government that full appropriation of the allotted four million taels be made annually, so that a northern and a southern fleet might be developed in five years.[41] The total fund necessary for the building of the two fleets was thus only twenty million taels, which was less than half of the amount spent in Sinkiang. Had the Sinkiang expenses been invested in the naval program instead, China might have been able to build up a powerful navy, with an efficient command, a corps of well-trained officers and sailors, and a plentiful supply of ammunition. If so, one wonders whether she could not have avoided the pathetic fate of losing the naval battle to Japan in the war of 1894. Inasmuch as China's defeat by Japan paved the way for the ultimate downfall of the Manchu dynasty, the far-reaching consequences of the 1874 debate on maritime defense versus frontier defense cannot be overemphasized.

Notes

1. For a study of the Moslem rebellion in Northwestern China, see Wen-djang Chu, "The Policy of the Manchu Government in the Suppression of the Moslem Rebellion in Shensi, Kansu, and Sinkiang from 1862 to 1878" (unpublished doctoral dissertation, University of Washington, 1955).

2. For a biography of Tso Tsung-t'ang and an account of his campaign in Shensi and Kansu, see Arthur W. Hummel, *Eminent Chinese of the Ch'ing Period* (Washington, 1944) II, 762-767; W. L. Bales, *Tso Tsung-t'ang, Soldier and Statesman of Old China* (Shanghai, 1937), 212-293; Ch'in Han-ts'ai, *Tso-wen-hsiang-kung tsai Hsi-pei* [Tso Tsung-t'ang in the Northwest] (Shanghai, 1946), 68-72.

3. Tso Tsung-t'ang, *Tso-wen-hsiang-kung ch'uan-chi* [Complete Works of Tso Tsung-t'ang] (Ch'ang-sha, 1888), "Memorials," 45.38a-39b.

4. Immanuel C. Y. Hsü, *China's Entrance into the Family of Nations: The Diplomatic Phase* (Cambridge, Mass., 1960), 172-174.

5. *Ch'ou-pan i-wu shih-mo* [The Complete Account of the Management of Barbarian Affairs] (Peiping, 1930; hereafter *IWSM*), T'ung-chih period, 98. 19a-21b.

6. *IWSM*, 98.41a.

7. *IWSM*, 98.24a-27a.

8. *IWSM*, 98.31a-34b.

9. *IWSM*, 99.44b-45a.

10. *IWSM*, 99.14ab.

11. *IWSM*, 99.14b-15a.

12. *IWSM*, 99.32b.

13. *IWSM*, 99.15a, 24b.

14. In 1872 Yakub Beg concluded a commercial treaty with Russia, by which he allowed Russian traders freedom of trade in his state and a low import duty of 2.5 per cent *ad valorem* in exchange for Russian recognition of him as leader of Moslem Sinkiang. In 1873 he signed a commercial treaty with Britain, by which the British granted him official recognition in return for the right of legation and consulate, as well as preferential commercial treatment, in his domain. Yakub Beg also established diplomatic relations with Turkey, which he honored as a superior state. The Turkish Sultan, Abdul Aziz, bestowed on him the title of Amir-ul-Mulmin (Commander of the Faithful). See Tsing Yuan, "Yakub Beg (1820-1877) and the Moslem Rebellion in Chinese Turkestan," *Central Asiatic Journal* VI(1961).134-167.

15. *IWSM*, 99.23b-24b.

16. *IWSM*, 99.34bff.

17. *IWSM*, 99.2b-12b.

18. Tseng Wen-wu, *Chung-kuo ching-ying Hsi-yü shih* [A History of China's Management of the Western Region] (Shanghai, 1936), 331-332.

19. *IWSM*, 99.60b-70b.

20. *IWSM*, 100.41ab.

21. *IWSM*, 100.13b, Dec. 22, 1874.

22. *Ch'ing-chi wai-chiao shih-liao* [Historical Materials concerning Foreign Relations in the Late Ch'ing Period] (Peiping, 1932-1935), Kuang-hsü period, 1.4b.

23. Tso Tsung-t'ang, "Memorials," 46.32a-35b.

24. For details of K'ang-hsi's war against Galdan, see *Sheng-chia ch'in-cheng Ko-erh-tan fang-lüeh* [A Brief Account of His Imperial Highness's Personal Expedition against Galdan] (1696); Hsiao I-shan, *Ch'ing-tai t'ung-shih* [A General History of the Ch'ing Period] (revised ed., Taipei, 1962) I, 826-832; Henry H. Howorth, *History of the Mongols* (London, 1876), I, 622-640; Hummel, I, 265-268.

25. Tso Tsung-t'ang, "Memorials," 46.36b-37a.

26. Tseng Wen-wu, 332-333.

27. Li Chien-nung, *Chung-kuo chin pai-nien cheng-chih shih* [A Political History of China in the Last Hundred Years] (3rd ed., Taipei, 1962), I, 134.

28. Wen-djang Chu, 276.

29. *Ibid.*

30. Fan Wen-lan, *Chung-kuo chin-tai shih* [Modern Chinese History] (Peking, 1949) I, 279-280.

31. Wen-djang Chu, 275.

32. See Jung-pang Lo, "The Emergence of China as a Sea Power during the Late Sung and Early Yüan Periods," *FEQ* XIV (1955), 489-503.

33. Edwin O. Reischauer and John K. Fairbank, *East Asia: The Great Tradition* (Boston, 1958), I, 325, 331.

34. Jung-pang Lo, 495.

35. Reischauer and Fairbank, I, 357.

36. Ch'en Fang-chih, "Ch'ing-tai pien-chih shu-lüeh" ("Frontier Governments in the Ch'ing Dynasty"), *YCHP* 34(1948).133. See also Lien-sheng Yang, *Studies in Chinese Institutional History* (Cambridge, Mass., 1961), 2.

37. For details of the Sinkiang campaign, see Wen-djang Chu, "Tso Tsung-t'ang's Role in the Recovery of Sinkiang," *CHHP*, New Series 1.3 (September, 1958).136-165.

38. Tso Tsung-t'ang, "Letters," 20.30a.

39. Tso Tsung-t'ang, 'Memorials," 55.52a-53a; 59.21a-33a.

40. Chiang T'ing-fu, *Chung-kuo chin-tai shih* ta-kang [Outline of Modern Chinese History] (Taipei, 1959), 132.

41. *Ibid.*

IV. CHINA VIS À VIS JAPAN

17. LI HUNG-CHANG: HIS KOREA POLICIES, 1870-1885

T. C. LIN

China's international relations in the last quarter of the nineteenth century, probably the most crucial period in modern times, were inseparably associated with Li Hung-chang. For the handling of the case of Korea, Li was particularly responsible. This short study on his Korea policies is based on his collected writings and such Chinese diplomatic documents as have been published in recent years.[1] With a view to interpreting Li in his own words, lengthy direct quotations are liberally employed.

No attempt is herein made to evaluate Li as a statesman. It would be helpful to suggest, however, that in order to place Li in a correct perspective, one should not fail to bear in mind the following factors: (1) China had just emerged from a most disastrous civil war and was still suffering from the fresh blows of the Anglo-French invasions of 1858-1860. She was, therefore, too impotent, economically and militarily, to face a show-down with any of her external adversaries. (2) China's foreign affairs were officially conducted and ultimately determined by the Tsungli Yamen, though Li's advice and service were constantly called for and, in the case of Korea, his voice was practically final from the eighties onward. (3)

From *The Chinese Social and Political Science Review*, Vol. XIX, No. 2, pp. 202-233 (July 1935).

Li did not always enjoy the full confidence of the Peking Court. He had political foes as well as followers. (4) Li's foreign policies must be judged in connection with his attempt at internal reforms and military and naval reconstruction, for which he deserved credit as well as blame.

I

When Li Hung-chang was made Viceroy of Chihli and Northern Superintendent of Trade in 1870, Korea's external status was that of a vassal state of China and the "Hermit Kingdom" of the world.

Korea's relationship to China, though fundamentally similar to that of the British Self-governing Dominions to the British Crown at present, was alien then to the Western juridicial concept. Just as the British Dominions accept the sovereignty of the Crown, so Korea received investitures from China and recognized the overlordship of the Son of Heaven. As a ritual indication of her vassalage, she paid regular tribute to Peking and observed the "Calendar" of the Chinese Empire. On the other hand, like the British Dominions, she was singularly free in her internal administration and external relations. China would step in only when her suzerainty over the Peninsula was threatened by outside powers, or as was more likely the case, when Korea asked for assistance in the face of external danger of internal strife. There had developed such a cultural affinity and traditional bond between the two that the one characteristically refrained from exercising a superior authority while the other took pride in a willing loyalty. The relationship was in a way ideal as an embodiment of Chinese international ethics expressed in the traditional phrase *tzŭ hsiao shih ta* (loving the small and serving the big.) And on the whole, it had worked smoothly for hundreds of years when there was no third power seriously to dispute the arrangement.

As a nation governed by *literati* ideologies, Korea took no interest in foreign commerce. This indifference toward external commerce and intercourse was further developed into an isolationist complex after the Hideyoshi invasion at the end of the sixteenth century. Aside from maintaining her relationship of vassalage toward China, Korea closed her door fast. So in the eighteen sixties when all the major Western powers and Japan came one by one and asked for the right of trade, Korea was full of apprehension and could see no advantage in getting entangled with the outside world. She was willing to "rescue and protect" foreign shipwrecked sailors as had been her practice. But on the issue of establishing permanent trade relations, her conviction was simple and strong:

As the world is aware, our country comprises only a tiny territory at a secluded corner of the sea. Our people are poor. Our resources are meagre. We do not produce gold or silver, pearls or jade. Nor have we an abundant supply of rice, grain, cloth, and silk. The products of our country hardly meet our own needs. If they be allowed to be exported overseas, it would lead to the eventual depletion of our domain and make the preservation of our feeble country even more difficult.[2]

This interesting bit of isolationist theory of foreign trade is based essentially on a sense of fear and is quite in consonance with the historic and geographic background of Korea.

In fact, in the opinion of the Korean Government, there was no economic basis for a Korean-foreign trade. "The crude handicraft industry of our country does not provide any worthy commodities to meet the needs of the foreigners."[3] On the other hand," commodities brought to our shores by the foreign ships, though ingenius and clever in the extreme, are not necessities from the viewpoint of utility for daily existence. As to their opium, our people have learnt of it and have known it to be a life-impairing drug comparable to the 'falcon poison' or the 'metallid grain' and untouchable to the mouth. . . . Trade exists where there is a mutual supply of wants. When we have nothing to offer to them and they cannot supply us with anything we want, there is no *raison d'être* for trade."[4]

This will to isolation on the part of Korea presented a frontal clash with the persistent demand of the foreign nations for commercial intercourse. The situation was further complicated by the presence of Western missionaries in Korea and their conflict with the tradition and policy of the land. China, as the suzerain of the peninsular state, was inevitably involved from the beginning. She was appealed to by the two contending parties to vindicate their respective causes.

It is out of place here to speculate as to what course the Chinese Government should have taken. The interest of the Chinese Government as conceived and determined by the responsible authorities of the time was twofold. It was, first of all, the preservation of the age-old suzerain-and-vassal relationship between China and Korea in all its traditional aspects. The Chinese Government had no desire to modify its historic relationship with Korea: it did not contemplate any step to change the old suzerainty of *laissez-faire* into one of active interference. This policy of scrupulous maintenance of the *status quo* existing between China and Korea was not only to be taken for granted by the suzerain and the vassal but also to be made known to and appreciated by the outside world.

As a parallel and corollary to this basic policy, it was the interest of the Chinese Government to see that peace be maintained in the Far East. While it did not propose to intervene in behalf of the foreign Powers, the Chinese Government was anxious that the two contending parties settle their disputes by nothing but peaceful means. It was clear from the outset that a war waged by any of the foreign Powers on Korea would eventually lead to an alteration of the *status quo*. For in that case, China would either see her historic vassal state go under the domination of a third party or come to Korea's rescue only to have herself overwhelmed in war for which she was not prepared. The former course would mean a disgraceful failure to execute her historic duty as suzerain. The latter course would probably cost China a price dearer than the loss of Korea. In either case, the traditional relationship between China and her most faithful vassal state would be seriously disturbed or altered.

Thus the preservation of peace between Korea and the foreign Powers was really the means and necessary requisite for the preservation of the historic relationship between China and Korea. The fundamental weakness of China's position was not, as has been generally maintained, her inaptitude to assert a right of active intervention against Korea, but rather her inability to *enforce* peace against the foreign Powers. With an adequate navy to *enforce* peace in the Southern Pacific, Great Britain could safely maintain the thesis of non-interference as regards her Self-governing Dominions and see Australia push through her "White Australia" policy without incurring a Japanese challenge of the Britainnic Unity. Non-interference with Korea was a morally commendable policy and a historically determined course. It would have been a feasible policy if China could effectively enforce the peace. But when China's peace plank was nothing more than a pious wish, her refusal to intervene actively in behalf of the foreign Powers became a course fraught with grave dangers. This the Chinese Government failed to see. Even a man like Li Hung-chang had to go through a decade of diplomatic experience before he came to realize it.

II

The simple truism that for the preservation of Korea and her relationship with China, war must be prevented was understood by all Chinese statesmen. Li Hung-chang was the first man, however, to do anything about it.

He showed his innate political sense the moment he started his diplomatic career in the negotiation of the Sino-Japanese Treaty of 1871—the first "equal and reciprocal" treaty which China had concluded since the Opium War. The desire for concluding such a treaty was first expressed by Japan in 1870. The Tsungli Yamen was favorably disposed to it though some opposition did come forth from the die-hard elements of the officialdom. Among the more enlightened statesmen of the time who urged a favorable response to the Japanese, Li was one of the most outstanding. He took his stand on purely political grounds.[5] His activities in suppressing the Taiping and the Nien rebels had impressed upon him two bitter facts: the utter exhaustion of the nation and the military superiority of the West. The Anglo-French invasion of 1858 and the Russian occupation of the Amur and the Ussuri regions in 1860 were warning enough of the irresistible spread of the "White Peril." Though he expected no immediate danger from Japan, he was quick to recognize the growing strength of Nippon as a result of rapid Westernization and her strategic proximity to the Chinese Empire as a matter of serious importance.[6] In accepting the appointment as the negotiator of the treaty with Japan, he had two ideas in mind in particular: (1) to prevent Japan from attacking the outlying territories of the Chinese Empire or, as he thought to be the more likely, from joining the Occidental nations in attacking the coastal regions of the Chinese Empire; (2) to secure Japanese friendship, if not an alliance, with a view to the eventual establishment of a defensive Oriental front against Occidental aggression.[7]

These were very significant ideas when we judge them against the historical background of Chinese diplomacy. For they were evidence that Li had cast aside the complacent and passive attitude of the old Mandarins and began to think in terms of active diplomacy and *Weltpolitik*. In this sense, Li was really the first *realistic* statesman of China who instinctively caught the spirit of the time and essayed in a half conscious manner the *intricate game* of international politics.

He succeeded in embodying these two ideas in the first two articles of the treaty:[8]

Article 1. Relations of amity shall henceforth be maintained in redoubled force between China and Japan in measure as boundless as Heaven and Earth. In all that regards the nations and territories belonging to either country, the two Governments shall treat each other with proper courtesy without the slightest infringement or encroachment on either side, to the end that there may be forever-more peace between them undisturbed.

Article 2. Friendly intercourse thus existing between the two Governments, it is the duty of each to be concerned with the welfare of the other, and in the event of any other nation acting unjustly or treating either of the two Powers with contempt, on notice being given (by the one to the other), mutual assistance shall be rendered and mediation offered for a satisfactory arrangement of the difficulty, in fulfillment of the duty imposed by relations of friendship.

In his report to the Court regarding the conclusion of the treaty, he specifically stated that the non-aggression clause in the treaty with respect to the nations and territories belonging to either of the Contracting Parties "tacitly implies the protection of Korea and other countries (of similar nature)."[9] It would appear from the words *tacitly implies* that during the course of the negotiation, Li probably did not make any explicit statement to the Japanese envoy on the security of Korea and China's other vassal states. Apparently he thought that such a statement was unnecessary at the time of the negotiation or that it was impolitic. In 1876, however, he was certainly plain-speaking when Mori Yurei came to see him at Pao-ting. Mori had been sent by the Japanese Government to secure China's good offices in the opening up of Korea. He visited Li with a view to soliciting his help to influence the action of the Peking Court. In the course of their conversation, Mori indirectly questioned the status of Korea's vassalage to China. Li immediately referred to Article I of the Treaty of 1871. "The word *territories*," he said, "refers to the provinces, which are our inner domains or inner possessions subject to Imperial taxation and administration. The word *nations* refers to Korea and other similar countries, which are our outer dominions or outer posessions and whose administration and taxation have always been carried on by the natives themselves." When Mori expressed doubt as to the validity of Li's interpretation because no explicit statement about Korea had been made in the treaty, Li reiterated his stand by saying that Korea was obviously implied and that the implication could easily be made explicit by inserting "Korea, the Liuchius, the Eighteen Provinces, etc." as explanatory notes to the wording *nations* and *territories* when occasion should occur for a revision of the treaty.[10]

Against every subsequent aggression on the part of Japan respecting Formosa, the Liuchius, Korea, etc., Li never failed to invoke this article. There is little doubt that by the word *nations* Li meant Korea more than any other tributary states. For he not only considered Korea to be specifically important to the safety of China, but during the negotiation of the treaty he also learned of the Japanese naval demonstration in Korean waters as a result of the latter's refusal to accept the Tsushima mission of 1868. And the news brought to him at that time about the possibility of the United States sending warships to Korea in cooperation with Japan had undoubtedly its effect, too, on his insistence upon the adoption of the two articles cited above.

It is not to be inferred that Li put an implicit naive faith in the efficacy of these provisions. In one of his letters to his friends (1871), he commented on his own policy:. "The idea of forming an Oriental alliance against the Occident is not to be taken too seriously." Treaty provisions had their limitations. "If China cannot devise means to make herself strong, she will be the victim everywhere, let alone the Orient or the Occident."[11]

Korea had rejected the Tsushima mission because the Japanese letter employed the term "His Imperial Majesty" which in the opinion of Korea could be used only by China and because Japan was suspected to be in alliance with France, whose expedition to Korea in 1866 was undertaken by the French garrison at Yokohama. The matter soon became involved in the internal political dissension of Japan and burst into a furious advocacy of the invasion of Korea by the discontented feudal military factions. Aside from a naval demonstration along the Korean coast, the Japanese Government thought it expedient to further appease the opposition by despatching an expedition to Formosa (1874) on the alleged ground of demanding reparations for the murder of a few Liuchiu natives by the Formosans.[12]

Li did not seem to take the report of Japan's Formosan expedition seriously at first. He thought the undertaking was not quite feasible for Japan because the Formosan natives were warlike and the regions they occupied were mountainous. He felt more anxiety for Korea, which he deemed as the real object of Japan. So he wrote to the Tsungli Yamen:[13]

Japan's ambition in Korea is ages old. Korea is important to us as a protective fence for the Eastern Territory [i. e. the Three Eastern Provinces]. Back in the Wan-li period of the Ming Dynasty, Hideyoshi sent huge expeditions to Korea with the ultimate purpose of attacking Yenching [Peking] from the direction of Liaotung. The Ming Government was obliged to come to Korea's rescue with military forces. Japan's army is stronger than her navy, and Korea is closest to her shores. While any [naval] attack on the part of Japan on our Kiangsu and Chekiang Provinces could only be a danger to our coastal regions, her invasion of Korea would constitute a menace to the vital land of Liao-ching [i. e. present-day Liaoning Province]. In concluding the recent treaty [with Japan], I put in the provision that neither of the two States shall encroach upon the territories and nations belonging to the other, for the very purpose of preventing such a design [i.e. the invasion of Korea] on her part.

These remarkable words set forth in a terse manner what may be considered as Li's conception of the basic political and military strategy of East Asia. On the basis of historical precedents and in view of the geographical proximity between Korea and Japan, Li anticipated grave dangers in the Peninsula rather than anywhere in the sea down south. He considered Manchuria, at least the area of present-day Liaoning, as the "fundamental territory," surpassing Kiangsu and Chekiang in importance. Korea, as the "protective fence" for Manchuria, was therefore the first line of defense of the Chinese Empire. So when Japanese envoy Soyeshima came to Tientsin in 1873 to exchange the ratifications of the treaty concluded more than two years before, Li took the chance to warn him against any overt action on the part of "Japan's attack on Korea would be a violation of her treaty agreement with China," said Li.[14] It is altogether probable that Li had learned of Soyeshima's

advocacy of the invasion of Korea before his arrival in China. The warning Li gave must have sounded particularly deliberate to the Japanese envoy.

Although Japan's invasion of Korea—the worst of Li's fears—did not materialize for the time, her expedition to Formosa certainly served to shatter whatever hopes Li had entertained for Japanese friendship. China had to pay a "compensation" of 500,000 taels for the Formosa incident, although Japanese territorial ambition for that island was temporarily thwarted. It had become all too clear now that the dream of a Sino-Japanese cooperation in the interest of peace was a delusion and that treaty pledges could give no check to the *Realpolitik* of Japan. Li realized all the more the importance of military preparedness:

From now on, in all the coastal regions, no effort should be spared in drilling stronger forces and acquiring superior weapons so that we shall be better equipped to handle our foreign relations and to forestall future trouble.[15]

III

If by 1874 Li had definitely abandoned any faith in his idea of Sino-Japanese friendship and alliance, he was as yet unable to see that the rapid development in the international situation demanded a quick adoption of a more positive policy toward Korea: either China must assume the role of an active suzerain and direct the external policy of Korea; or she would inevitably see her position as suzerain denied in principle by the narrow juristic interpretation of the West or altered in face by a war waged by the foreign Powers in reprisal against the seclusionist policy of Korea.

The tradition of Korean autonomy was

too long established for any of the Chinese statesmen to cast aside. As long as Korea's national policy was not incompatible with China's traditional suzerain rights, interference was unthinkable. It must be admitted, too, that China, having just emerged from the Second Opium War, did not particularly relish intercourse with the Occident herself. Nor had her cultural and commercial contact with the same convinced her of its advantage and desirability. To force Korea to open herself to the trade and the missionaries of the foreigners would be imposing on the vassal something which China herself did not care for!

Korea's sentiment on the issue was unmistakable. Thus, in 1871 when the American expedition under Admiral John S. Rogers was sent to Korea to inquire into the fate of the vessel *General Sherman* supposedly destroyed by the Koreans in 1866 and to conclude a commercial treaty if possible, the Korean King memorialized the Board of Rites and expressed definitely his determination to maintain the seclusion policy.[16]

I humbly hope that the Board of Rites will lay before the Throne all the facts connected with this matter and that the Emperor will issue a special edict to exhort and instruct the envoy of the said country [the United States] so as to overcome doubts and dispel his anxiety and thus each of us may be left to himself without trouble.[17]

To the legal-minded Occidentals, the King's letter was the "most profuse acknowledgement of vassalage to the Emperor of China," or as Mr. F. F. Low, American Minister to China, put it, "Korea acknowledges the supremacy of China in a manner amounting almost to servility."[18] All this might be true, but it was beside the point. To the Tsungli Yamen, the King's letter was a practical appeal, announcing that Korea would not in any way have intercourse with the foreigners. In view of this China naturally felt indisposed to exercise her superior authority against the declared will of the vassal.

Viewed in this light, the Chinese announcement to the Powers that "although Korea is a country subordinate to China, nevertheless it is wholly self-determining in government, religion, prohibitions and laws,"[19] becomes perfectly understandable. One may accuse the Chinese Government of being too honest for a world of changed morals or too sentimental toward its old faithful vassal. But to accuse it of evading responsibility is to assign to it a responsibility which was non-existent.

Rogers' expedition ended in a failure as previous expeditions of other Occidental nations did. It was now Japan's turn to take the leading role in the opening of Korea. In 1875, the year following the Formosan expedition, Japan sent a surveying party to the mouth of the Han River, the gateway by sea to the Korean capital. When it was fired upon by the Koreans from the shore, Japan hastened to fit out an expedition in the next year. Preceding the expedition, Mori Yurei was sent to Peking to ask for credentials for a Japanese mission to Korea and to intimate to the Chinese Government the possibility of "incalculable calamity" to Korea if the Japanese mission should not be received with courtesy and their demands should be ignored. The Tsungli Yamen, in view of the foregoing letter of the Korean King and the prevailing anti-Japanese sentiment in Korea, declined to grant the credentials but reiterated the hope that Japan would conform to the non-aggression clause of the Treaty of 1871 by desisting from any measure of force against Korea.[20]

Mori went to Pao-ting to seek the good offices of Li Hung-chang. On learning of the Yamen's decision and the coming of Mori to the provincial capital, Li realized that some compromise must be made and suggested to the Yamen that it confidentially advise the Korean Government to receive the Japanese envoy or to send a mission to Japan to explain the situation. In his letter to the Tsungli Yamen he said:[21]

. . . Japan is sending an envoy to Korea, accompanied by warships, to demand reparations. Korea, having been recently humiliated by the destruction of her forts, is naturally not disposed to receive the envoy in any friendly manner. With resentment and bitterness on both sides, war may easily ensue. Korea, poor and weak, is no match for Japan. In all probability, she would follow the precedent in the Ming Dynasty and ask for assistance from us. How are we going to face the predicament? Although we may point to the treaty and accuse Japan of invading our vassal state, Japan may well meet our charge by arguing that she has referred the matter to us and we have refused to take it up. What control then can we have over the situation? By persisting in our refusal to take a hand in the matter, we might cause disappointment to Korea and arouse the ambition of Japan . . . . And above all, Korea might be harassed or even conquered by Japan, and the all important region of the Three Eastern Provinces would be deprived of its protection and put in constant danger! All these factors should be taken into consideration.

It seems to me, therefore, that whatever be her real intention, Japan has come ostensibly for peace and not war. We should take her words at their face value. Although publicly we have declared it inexpedient to grant to the Japanese envoy the permit to enter Korea or to forward the Japanese letter to the Korean Government, it seems advisable that the Yamen quickly proceed to despatch a confidential communication to the Government in Seoul, counselling it to have forbearance and to receive the Japanese envoy with proper courtesy or to send an envoy to Japan to explain the entire incident, so that resentment and suspicion may be dispelled and peace assured. *As to whether or not Korea should start trade relations with Japan, it is a matter which should be left to her own decision and China is not in a position to intervene.*

When Li received Mori, he on the one hand explained the Korean attitude, suggesting mutual forbearance, and on the other, vigorously reasserted that Korea was China's vassal state and that Japan should not violate Article one of the Treaty of 1871. He even went so far as to hint that any Japanese aggression in Korea would constitute an affront to China.[22]

As a result of Li's letter quoted above, the Yamen sent a message to Korea, counselling it not to go to extremes in dealing with Japan. In the meantime the peace party gained ascendency in Korea. On February 27th, 1876, was signed the first treaty between Korea and Japan, a copy of which was subsequently sent by the Korean Government to the Board of Rites for file. By this treaty, the mutual right of sending envoys was confirmed, two Korean ports in addition to Fusan were to be opened, and the Japanese consuls at these ports were to exercise extraterritoriality in criminal cases, etc. The opening sentence of the first article deserves more than passing notice. It declares, "Korea, being a self-governing (*tzu chu*) nation, enjoys the right of equality with Japan." It is generally believed that by styling Korea as a self-governing nation, Japan was seeking to undermine the centuries-old relationship between China and Korea. The Chinese Government, however, did not see it this way; it took the said sentence as implying no departure from the long established situation or modification of Korea's status as China's vassal. Nor did Korea take it as meaning any break in her traditional relationship with China. Thus in 1878 when Japan asked Korea to deliver from prison some French missionaries, Korea again referred the case to China for instructions. Observing that China employed the term "superior nation" in her answer to Korea, Japan made an inquiry as to China's attitude toward Article one of the Korean-Japanese Treaty. Thereupon the Chinese Government declared: "With respect to the said article about Korea being a self-governing nation, etc., we may say that Korea has long been subordinate to China and has always been self-governing in its administration and laws. That it is a self-governing [*tzu chu*] nation is a fact long known to all under Heaven." This answer of the Tsungli Yamen was both politic and explicit. *Korean autonomy (tzu chu), and Chinese suzerainty (tsung kuo), were not incompatible terms.*[23] On the contrary, they formed an inseparable pair in the announced policy of China. Indeed, in mentioning the one, the Chinese Government never failed to mention the other.[24]

While the recognition of Korea's status as a self-governing nation in the Korean-Japanese Treaty did not in itself necessarily contradict China's position as suzerain, it is to be noted, however, that the omission in the treaty of any allusion to the latter, besides suggesting Japan's possible sinister motives, might in certain contingencies give rise to untoward misunderstandings. Li saw the danger. So later on, when the question of Korean treaties with the Western nations came up, he insisted upon the provision of the "safe-guarding clause," the declaration of the suzerainty of China.

IV

In 1879, Japan prevented the King of the Liuchiu Islands from sending tribute to China and proceeded to formally annex the islands. There was a strong opinion in China in favor of war.[25] Li thought China was not ready to run the risk. He did all he could to secure a diplomatic arrangement. The failure to reach a final agreement despite General Grant's mediation left the Liuchiu question still legally unsettled although Japan has asserted a *de facto* control ever since. The loss of the Liuchius made Li Hung-chang even more anxious for the security of Korea. He realized that China must do something more positive. Hence he wrote to the Yamen:[26]

Korea's relations with Japan have lately been marked by ill-feelings. On the other hand Korea has not receded from her former position of complete seclusion and exclusion with respect to the Occidental nations, and that her old prejudice has not yet abated is evidenced by the repeated arrests of foreign missionaries. Japan, confident in her tricks and strength, is not disposed to maintain peace. As the Liuchius have been annexed, Korea is in a position of imminent danger. In view of this and of the growing interest of the Occidental nations in Korea, *we can no longer refrain from devising ways and means for the security of Korea.*

But the same reluctance still characterized Li's action. For some time he had been keeping in touch with certain of the foremost Korean statesmen, in a personal capacity. In 1875, when Mori Yurei was coming to China for credentials to Korea, Li, in his reply to a complimentary letter from Li Yü-yüan, an influential member of the Korean court, already hinted at the inevitableness of opening trade relations with the outside world as experienced by China.[27] In 1879, after he was entrusted by the Yamen with the task of persuading Korea, he wrote a confidential letter to this official, definitely advising him on two things: (1) military re-organization, (2) negotiation of commercial treaties with the West, both being directed primarily against Japan and secondarily against Russia.

The Korean Government immediately took Li's advice regarding military preparation. And "to follow the ancient precedent of sending students to China," it asked the Board of Rites to select capable Koreans and have them sent to Tientsin for military training. Li promised to acquaint them with "all the secrets so as to give Korea a chance of getting on her own meet."[28] Korea also sent commissioners to consult Li in person and a plan for the re-organization of the Korean army was drawn up.[29]

In the matter of concluding treaties with the Western nations, Li did not find any comment in this regard in Li Yü-yüan's reply. He thought it expedient not to press the matter for a time as he learned then that to the Korean authorities, "trade with Japan is already a concession under duress; trade with the West would be unthinkable."[30]

Ever since the sixties, Japanese policy had been directed toward inducing the Western Powers to deal with Korea through Japan and thus establishing for Japan a position of priority in Korea. Despite the fact that Korea countenanced no mediation except from China, Japan offered vainly her good offices to the United States and Germany in 1867 and 1868 respectively although she herself had been rejected by Korea as an unacceptable neighbor. On the other hand, after the Treaty of 1876, she imposed on Korea a supplementary article that in case any foreigners got shipwrecked on the coast of Korea, they were to be delivered to the Japanese authorities who would assume the responsibility for their repatriation.

In 1880 when the United States commissioned Commodore R. W. Shufeldt to attempt anew to establish treaty relations with Korea, invitation was sent to the Japanese Government for a suitable letter of introduction. Japan, however, seemed to have changed her policy somehow. Foreign Minister Inouye refused the American request and offered only a letter of introduction to the Japanese consul at Fusan. When told by the consul that Korea would not receive him, Shufeldt returned to Tokyo. "With no little reluctance, Inouye was persuaded to send Shufeldt's letter with one of his own to the King of Korea on the condition that Shufeldt would remain at Nagasaki for an answer. . . . The second attempt failed as dismally as the first. . . . It was reasonably clear to Shufeldt that Japan was actuated by no earnest desire to have the trade of Korea open to the world and that the Japanese were manipulating the negotiations to serve their own purpose."[31]

In 1880, Li Hung-chang was given full power to deal with Korean affairs. On being informed that America had approached the Japanese Government, Li grew suspicious of an American-Japanese cooperation in Korea at a time of a possible Russian war in Chinese Turkestan. So he immediately sent a timely invitation to Shufeldt, promising to use his influence to secure a treaty from Korea. Shufeldt immediately came to Tientsin.

Li thus scored a victory over Japan by making the United States deal with Korea through China.[32]

The Korean Government intimated to the Chinese Government that it was prepared to render assistance to distressed foreign vessels; but it showed no intention to conclude a treaty. Ho Ju-chang, Chinese Minister to Japan, who had once advocated despatch of warships to the defense of the Liuchius, suggested now that either a commissioner be sent to Korea to conduct the negotiation on Korea's behalf or an Imperial edict be issued ordering Korea to negotiate treaties with the Western nations, which in his opinion should contain the definite statement: "In accordance with the mandate of the Chinese Government, Korea thereby concludes the treaty, etc." Li, however, was not yet quite so bold. When consulted as to his opinion, he wrote to the Yamen:[33]

There would have been ground for considering such a measure, *had it been proposed to the Court by the Korean King*. But the Korean official opinion, being newly converted, does not appear ready to take up the negotiations. Indeed, it desires to preserve for Korea freedom of action, as the Korean letter to us declares: If they [Western nations] anchored their vessels in our harbors and present us their letters, we shall reply to them in friendly terms. 'If their vessels fall into distress, we shall offer them assistance.' Our action will depend on circumstances. If, therefore, we definitely order the Korean King to enter into treaty negotiations with Western nations, he may turn suspicious and reject our suggestion; whereupon the Western nations would, as you have observed, refer everything to us and hold us responsible.

Moreover, when Korea concluded the treaty with Japan, we only tactfully urged the matter as a by-stander. We did not despatch any commissioners to direct the negotiations. Nor did the consequent treaty contain such a statement as 'In accordance with the mandate of the Chinese Government etc.' Thus, even if Korea acquiesces in our order, the Western nations might not accept the arrangement.

Furthermore, our treaties with the West have been made under duress and many terms therein are contrary to customary international law. We are at present trying to remove them gradually. Since Korea is to conclude her treaties in time of peace, she should be able to avoid such unfavorable terms. Once a Chinese commissioner participates in the negotiations, the Western nations would claim the old Chinese treaties as models. This would be inimical to Korean interests.

Mr. Ho has foresight, to be sure, when he says that in letting Korea conclude the treaties by herself with the West, Korea would be regarded by all as independent and her vassalage to China would eventually pass out of notice. It seems to me, however, that by building up her foreign relations to assure her security, Korea can serve as an effective protection for Feng-t'ien, Kirin and East Chihli. As to her loyalty to China, it will in all probability persist in spite of the conclusion of treaties with the West. Should China be able to make herself a Power by training her armies and re-enforcing her coastal defense, not only would she retain the respect of small nations like Korea but would also inspire the awe of the big European states. If not, there might not be any chance for our own existence, let alone the attitude of our vassal state.

In the meantime, Li sought to exert influence over the sentiment of the Korean Government through informal channels. As soon as the Korean Government decided to negotiate the treaty and asked him (1881) to take the matter up with Shufeldt, he lost no time in taking action. He ordered Ma Chienchung and Tseng Tsao-ju to draw up a tentative treaty "with all precautions for preserving Korean interests against foreign encroachment."[34] At the same time he proceeded immediately to detain Shufeldt at Tientsin while a special commissioner was being sent over by the Korean King to consult Li. Negotiations began in the spring of 1882.

Li's original draft consisted of ten articles. Article I read:[35]

Korea is a vassal state of China, but has always enjoyed autonomy in both its internal and external affairs. After the conclusion of the treaty, the King of Korea and the President of the United States shall treat each other on an equal footing and the peoples of the two nations shall permanently maintain their peaceful relations. In case of any injustice or insult from other nations, mutual assistance or mediation shall be offered so as to assure each other's security.

In other articles, he specified that inland trade was to be reserved for the Koreans; importation of opium was to be prohibited; foreigners were to be permitted to rent land with the explicit understanding that the land could not be alienated from Korea; extraterritoriality was to be granted "temporarily," but Korean officials should be permitted to arrest Koreans in the service of foreigners; no merchant consuls were to be allowed; missionary work was to be excluded; import duties were to be ten *per cent* on necessities and thirty *per cent* on luxuries, and the export duties were to be three *per cent;* the treaty was to come to an end in five years; and the Chinese language was to be used in official intercourse. "The Viceroy's first draft is of peculiar interest, because it reveals the motives of the government of China in encouraging the treaty and also shows the attitude of the Chinese with

reference to their own treaties with foreign Powers."[36]

Shufeldt had made a draft based largely on the Japanese treaty of 1876. He objected strongly to Article I of Li's draft. He thought that the reference to Korea as being a vassal state of China was irrelevant to the conclusion of the treaty between the United States and Korea, that the mediation clause amounted to putting Korea under the joint protection of China and the United States, and that he was not empowered to conclude a treaty of alliance. Li insisted on the first Article because "its omission, if conceded to America, would be claimed as a precedent by other Powers. There would be a time when the Powers would forget that Korea is our vassal state, which situation would necessarily breed future troubles." On the other hand, in order to distinguish Korea from those vassal states which were not autonomous and hence could not conclude treaties with other states, Li deemed it necessary to mention both the vassalage of Korea and its autonomous status. This view met with the full concurrence of the Korean envoy.[37]

Finally a compromise was reached. Korea's vassalage to China was to be acknowledged in two ways: (1) Shufeldt would write a letter to Li officially stating that he had requested the assistance of China in making the treaty, because Korea was a dependency of China; (2) he would also transmit to the President of the United States a letter from the King of Korea in which the latter stated that the treaty had been made by consent of the Chinese Government. In dating the treaty, the Chinese Calendar was to be used alongside with the Western.[38]

The treaty agreed upon was sent to Korea by a Chinese naval vessel and signed on May 22, 1882. Commenting on the treaty, Li said in his letter to the Premier of Korea: "The United States, situated at the other end of the Pacific, has never entertained any territorial ambition. By our concluding a treaty of peace and amity with her, not only will Japan's aggression be checked but also the other nations demanding trade will have a model treaty to base theirs upon."[39]

England and Germany followed the United States in negotiating treaties with Korea, but they soon demanded some modifications of the rates of the duties pending the exchange of the treaties. Li urged the United States to exchange the treaty first, so that the other nations might follow suit. "But as the United States envoy passed Japan," said Li, "he was accompanied by the Japanese directly to Korea, possibly with the purpose of avoiding China's hand in the matter. Fortunately, Korea gave consent to only a few modifications without much material change of the original text."[40]

When the English and German envoys were proceeding to Korea for making some changes in the original treaty drafts, China was involved with France in the Indo-China affair. Li expressed the fear that these two Powers would imitate the tactics of Japan in 1876. In his interview with the British Minister at Tientsin he repeatedly stressed the fact that Korea was a vassal state of China. At the same time, he sent a note to the Korean court permitting its discretion in modifying the regulations regarding commerce but definitely warning it not to assent to any departure from the arrangement made in the preceding year regarding Korea's notification to the Powers of her vassalage to China.[41]

After the exchange of the British and German treaties which were signed in November, 1883, Li observed with satisfaction:[42]

Since separate notes stating Korea's vassalage to China have thus been preserved in the archives of the respective Powers, in case of future attack on Korea by any of these Powers or in case of Korea's disloyalty to us, we can hold either of them responsible.

Italy concluded its treaty with Korea in June, 1884; Russia in July 1884; France in June, 1886; and Austria in June, 1892. Austria attempted to dispense with the note regarding Korea's vassalage, but it was successfully insisted upon by China.[43] The European Powers commissioned their respective envoys at Peking to be also their representatives, under various titles, at Seoul, but the United States followed Japan in commissioning to Korea a minister plenipotentiary independent of the legation at Peking—a procedure highly gratifying to Japan.

The conclusion of the Korean-American Treaty marked the beginning of Li's active policy in Korea. Trade between China and Korea was hitherto limited to the border. Now that Korea had entered into commercial relations with the world, a change in the old conditions was necessary. The matter had been discussed even before the signing of the Shufeldt Treaty, and trade regulations of eight articles were promulgated in September, 1882. The preamble reads as follows:[44]

Korea has long been ranked among the vassal state. All that pertains to the rites has been definitely regulated and no change is required there. But as various countries have now entered into trade relations [with Korea] by water, it becomes necessary to remove at once the maritime prohibitions and let the merchants of both countries enter into commercial relations and share in the profits. The regulations for the frontier trade will also, as required by new circumstances, be accordingly modified; but the regulations for the maritime and overland trade are now decided upon. Be it understood that they are made out of China's favor for the vassal and shall not be subject to equal participation by other nations.

In the following year, twenty-four regulations for the frontier trade were also drawn up with a similar declaration in the preamble. According to Li, for several years after concluding the commercial treaty with Korea in 1876, Japan had refused to pay any duties either for imports or for exports. After the conclusion of the Shufeldt Treaty and the promulgation of the general tariff regulations, Japan found herself compelled to submit to them.[45]

Meanwhile, the signing of the Shufeldt Treaty had alarmed the reactionary party in Korea, and the intrigues of the Japanese added fuel to the fire. On July 23, 1882, a coup d'état was effected against the Court in favor of Tai Wen-kun, father of the King, and the anti-Japanese sentiment led to the burning by a mob of the Japanese legation. The Japanese Government hastened to despatch more troops to Korea, while China, at the direct request of the Korean envoys at Tientsin, sent forces to the scene and quickly restored the Korean King. Tai Wen-kun was captured and sent to Pao-ting.

Japan presented its demands to the Korean Government and intimated through the British Minister to China that "if China despatches troops to suppress the internal strife of Korea, Japan is in no position to interfere. But if China should want to conduct the nego-

tiations with Japan on behalf of Korea, Japan would not consent to it."[46] Japan soon secured the consent of Korea to an indemnity of 500,000 *yuan* (silver dollars) and to the stationing of Japanese troops at their legation, to be withdrawn in one year if order could be effectively maintained by the Korean Government. Li Hung-chang criticized the severity of the Japanese demands; but as the King of Korea was not disposed to re-open negotiations with Japan, Li thought it "inconvenient for China to overturn the agreement."[47]

Korea was in a state of financial bankruptcy. The Japanese negotiators had attempted to have her agree first to a loan of 500,000 *yuan*, and then to some mining concessions in return for a lighter indemnity. The Korean Government refused. Li expressed his worry over the deplorable financial situation in Korea and suggested a loan to be advanced by Chinese merchants on the security of the Korean customs revenue and mining profits.[48] At the same time, two thousand Chinese troops were retained in Korea and Chinese advisors were employed in the Korean armies.

V

The Japanese continued in their attempt to undermine the predominant influence of China. Opportunity came in the latter part of 1884 when China was confronted with a war with France. As soon as hostilities had begun, Takezoye, the Japanese Minister, waited upon the King of Korea, painted the probable fate of China in the darkest of colors and offered to remit the indemnity agreed to two years before if the King would introduce military reform in Korea with a view to eliminating Chinese influence. He promised Japanese support if Korea would assert her independence. At the same time he secured for Japanese merchants the most-favored-nation treatment on the basis of the Chinese trade regulations of September, 1882. On December 4, a conspiracy was brought about under Japanese instigation. The King and the Queen were seized and forced to declare the independence of Korea. Chinese troops in Korea were hurried to the palace and became involved in a conflict with the Japanese soldiers who had occupied the palace.

Order, however, was soon restored by the Chinese troops. Japan, urged on by France, clamored for war with China. But finally she contented herself with an apology and reparation from Korea. At the same time Count Ito Hirobumi was sent to China for a parley on the incident.

Li's Korea policy had by this time taken a fairly definite shape. He was determined to maintain the suzerainty of China over Korea and to preserve the territorial integrity of Korea against Japanese attack. He was prepared to support this policy by force. In 1883 he told the British minister to China that the special historic relations between Korea and China made him regard Korea as different from Annam or the Liuchius. "If Japan attacks Korea, China will have to come to the latter's rescue. . . . If Japan repudiates China's suzerain authority over Korea or attempts to annex Korea, I cannot but take up the issue with her."[49] He does not appear to have ever entertained the idea of annexing Korea or establishing Chinese control over the administration of Korea. He sent military advisors to Korea with the purpose of helping her to organize an effective national defense and indirectly giving security to Manchuria. He stationed troops in Korea partly for the temporary need of insuring peace and order and partly for the purpose of checking Japanese influence. In fact, he considered the maintenance of Chinese troops in Korea as a great burden on the Chinese Government. He objected to sending more troops after the Korean palace conspiracy.[50] When he heard that Ito was coming to China for the settlement of the dispute, he suggested to the Yamen: "If Japan promises to withdraw her troops from Korea, we may temporarily withdraw ours also. I shall recommend to Korea some German experts to train her troops so that she may eventually be able to protect herself."[51]

The conference between Li and Ito began on April the fourth, the very day when the Sino-French war closed. It was opened with Ito's announcement of the two purposes of his mission: (1) to settle the incident at the Korean capital and (2) to agree on the matter of withdrawing troops from Korea. Ito assumed the part of an injured party and demanded punishment of the Chinese military officers and reparations for injured Japanese residents. Li rejected this, as there was no substantial evidence of the alleged misconduct of the Chinese troops; and he proved on the other hand that the Japanese troops were to blame. After three sessions, Ito sent one of his colleagues to Li demanding explicit answers. Li replied that he was prepared to negotiate on the matter of withdrawing troops from Korea which would remove the cause of future conflict, but he could not assent to the demand for the punishment of Chinese officers and for the payment of reparations to Japanese residents. The Japanese threatened to break up the conference, declaring that Japan was not interested in the withdrawal of troops. Thereupon Li announced with indignation that for the Korean incident the blame was on the

Japanese side. "If the conference breaks down on this point, I have only to prepare for war."[52]

Ito came to the next conference with a more conciliatory manner and proceeded to discuss the question of the withdrawal of troops from Korea. Li proposed simultaneous withdrawal of the Chinese and Japanese troops, but he stood firmly upon the traditional right of China to send troops to Korea in case of Korean rebellion or important internal strife, or in case Korea was involved in a war with other states. He was willing to promise that in such cases there should be immediate withdrawal of the Chinese troops as soon as order was restored in Korea. He even consented to Japan's right of sending troops to Korea in case Japanese officers or subjects were attacked by Koreans, provided that notice should be given beforehand to the Chinese Government. But he would not accept Ito's suggestion that both Japan and China might send troops to Korea when so requested by the Korean Government. He insisted on the superiority of the Chinese position over the Japanese because China had her proper duties and rights as the suzerain of Korea.[53]

A deadlock followed. Li referred the case to the Tsung-li Yamen for instructions. The break-up of the Conference would mean war with Japan. The Yamen decided that China was not ready for the duel. And Li signed the convention on April 18, 1885. In Article 1, China agreed to withdraw her troops to Masanpo and Japan her legation guards to Jinsen within four months. In Article 2, China and Japan agreed to urge the Korean King to organize his forces under instructors who should be neither Chinese nor Japanese. In Article 3, the following was provided:

In case any disturbance of a grave nature occurs in Korea which necessitates the respective countries, or either of them, to send troops to Korea, it is hereby understood that they shall give, each to the other, previous notice in writing of their intention so to do, and that after the matter is settled they shall withdraw their troops and not further station them there.

Commenting on this last Article, Li wrote to the Yamen:[54]

With the provision for mutual previous notice, we can send troops to Korea when attacked by Japan, or send troops jointly with Japan to Korea when attacked by any Western nations. It seems that the provision would lead to no embarrassment to the general situation.

In addition to the convention, Li was to issue a note to the Japanese Government stating that he would send "words of caution" to his troops in Korea in connection with the incident of 1884.

With this convention, Japan secured practically an equal footing with China in Korea, though nominally China had not relinquished her suzerain prerogatives and still enjoyed a vague recognition by other powers of her superior position in Korea which was so strenuously won by Li in negotiating the several commercial treaties of Korea just a couple of years previously.

VI

The foregoing survey of Li's Korea policies deserves a few words of interpretation. In this period of fifteen years (1870-1885), four stages can be detected.

1. 1870-1875. *Forecast.* Li was the first among Chinese statesmen to discern the importance of the Korean problem and forecast the coming of the storm. He

started to forestall the issue by providing a safeguard clause of non-aggression in the Treaty of 1871, but he had the bitterness to see in the years immediately following that the sanctity of treaties could by no means protect the Liuchius and Formosa from Japanese aggression.

2. 1875-1879. *Hesitancy and Miscalculation.* Japanese insistence on the opening of Korea made Li realize that China must no longer stand by as a silent observer but should do something on the issue. The tradition of non-interference with Korea, however, held him back. While he was hesitating, he failed to anticipate Japan's tactical step in concluding the Korean-Japanese treaty of 1876. The inactive attitude of the Chinese Government prompted also the Japanese annexation of the Liuchius.

3. 1879-1884. *Assistance and Assertion.* Li began to be interested in Korea in an active way. With the Korean King's request for help, he began to assist Korea in reforming her armies. In conducting the treaty negotiations with Western nations, he asserted Chinese suzerainty in Korea in the best manner then possible. He made further advances through the tariff regulations and through the intervention of 1882.

4. 1884-1885. *Conflict and Retreat.* Then in 1884, armed conflict with Japan, which he had tried his best to avoid since the Formosa and Liuchiu affairs, first took place in Korea. Though he had evolved a fairly positive policy, he again found himself compelled by circumstances and by the decision of the Yamen to make some retreat before the Japanese in the Convention of 1885.

The retreat, however, was only a diplomatic one. The *Realpolitik* continued to develop along its own course. Thus, the story after 1885 was really one of Li's redoubled activity in Korea as against the redoubled activity of the Japanese and the growing complications caused by the participation of Occidental nations. After the signing of the Convention of 1885, Li wrote to the Yamen praising Ito's ability and predicting that within a decade Japan's wealth and power would be considerably increased and Japan would become a menace to China. He implored the Chinese government to pay timely attention to this fact. Prophetically enough, it was exactly within a decade that Li was called upon to face the catastrophe.

Notes

1. (A) *The Collected Writings of Li Hung-chang,* compiled by Wu Ju-lun, 100 vols., Nanking, 1908. The first volume consists of Imperial edicts concerning Li's death and of official memorials and biographical notes about Li's life. The rest of the volumes are divided into: (a) 80 books of Li's *Memorials;* (b) 20 books of Li's *Letters to Friends and Colleagues;* (c) 20 books of Li's *Communications to the Tsungli Yamen;* (d) 1 book of Li's *Letters concerning the Ch'an Ch'ih Church;* (e) 4 books of Li's *Communications to the Navy Department;* (f) 40 books of Li's *Telegraphic and Cable Despatches.*
(B) *Ch'ou Pan Yi-wu Shih-mo,* Series III, (the T'ung-chih Reign), 50 vols., Palace Museum, Peiping, 1931.
(C) Wang, Yen-wei (Compiler), *Sources of the Diplomatic History toward the End of the Ch'ing Dynasty,* (the Kuang-hsü Reign, 1875-1908), 111 vols.
(D) *Documents on Sino-Japanese Relations during the Kuang-hsü Reign;* 44 vols., Palace Museum, Peiping, 1932.
2. Korean King's memorial to the Board of Rites, 1871, *Ch'ou Pan Yi-wu,* bk. 81, p. 11a-b.
3. *Ibid.,* p. 11b.
4. *Ibid.,* bk. 45, p. 24b.
5. For his general opinion on the advisability of entering into treaty relations with Japan, see *Memorials,* bk. 17, pp. 53a-54b; *Communications to the Tsungli Yamen,* bk. i, pp. 10a-12b.
6. *Memorials,* bk. 17, p. 54a-b.
7. *Communications to the Tsungli Yamen,* bk. 1, 10b-11a.

8. For the draft version of the treaty, see *Ch'ou Pan Yi-wu*, bk. 82, pp. 33a-37b. For the English translation of the text, see *Treaties, Conventions, etc., between China and Foreign States* (Chinese Maritime Customs, Shanghai, 1908, 1917), vol. 2, p. 1236.

9. *Memorials*, bk. 18, p. 49b; also *Ch'ou Pan Yi-wu*, bk. 82, p. 31b.

10. *Communications to the Tsungli Yamen*, bk. 4, pp. 35a-37b.

11. *Letters to Friends and Colleagues*, bk. 11, p. 6b.

12. *Communications to the Tsungli Yamen*, bk. 2, 6. 25.

13. *Ibid.*, bk. 1, p. 49.

14. *Ibid.*, bk. 1, p. 45a.

15. *Ibid.*, bk. 2, p. 57.

16. For the memorial of the Korean King, see *Ch'ou Pan Yi-wu*, bk. 81, pp. 8b-12a. Cf. memorial in *ibid.*, bk. 45, pp. 22-25.

17. See translation in Hsü, S., *China and her Political Entity*, (New York, 1926), p. 105.

18. See Dennett, T., *Americans in East Asia*, (New York, 1922), p. 436.

19. See *Ch'ou Pan Yi-wu*, bk. 42, p. 54 ff.; bk. 80, p. 13a.

20. See *Documents on Sino-Japanese Relations during the Kuang-hsü Reign*, bk. 1, pp. 1-6.

21. *Communications to the Tsungli Yamen*, bk. 4, pp. 30-31. (Italics mine).

22. *Ibid.*, bk. 4, p. 34.

23. Cf. the status of the Irish Free State or Canada with respect to the British Commonwealth on the one hand and to other states and the League of Nations on the other.

24. See Wang Yun-sheng, *Sino-Japanese Relations for the Past Sixty Years*, (Tientsin, 1932) Vol. 1, pp. 86-94.

25. *Communications to the Tsungli Yamen*, bk. 8, pp. 1-5.

26. *Ibid.*, bk. 9, p. 34. (Italics mine).

27. *Ibid.*, bk. 4, pp. 31-32.

28. *Ibid.*, bk. 10, p. 16.

29. *Telegraphic and Cable Despatches*, bk. 34, p. 38; bk. 42, p. 44.

30. *Communications to the Tsung-li Yamen*, bk. 10, p. 16.

31. Dennett, *op. cit.*, pp. 456-7.

32. *Ibid.*, pp. 457-8.

33. *Communications to the Tsungli Yamen*, bk. 11, p. 42 (Italics mine).

34. *Ibid.*, bk. 12, p. 6.

35. *Ibid.*, bk. 13, pp. 10-12.

36. Dennett, *op. cit.*, p. 459.

37. *Communications to the Tsungli Yamen*, bk. 13, p. 7.

38. *Ibid.*, bk. 13 p. 31; Dennett, *op. cit.*, p. 460.

39. *Communications to the Tsungli Yamen*, bk. 13, p. 33.

40. *Ibid.*, bk. 15, pp. 12-13.

41. *Ibid.*, p. 13.

42. *Ibid.*, p. 19.

43. *Ibid.*, bk. 20, p. 28.

44. See Hsü, *op. cit.*, pp. 112-3; *Telegraphic and Cable Communications*, bk. 44, p. 40.

45. *Communications to the Tsungli Yamen*, bk. 15, p. 6.

46. *Ibid.*, bk. 13, p. 34.

47. *Ibid.*

48. *Ibid.*, bk. 13, p. 34.

49. *Ibid.*, bk. 15, p. 6.

50. *Ibid.*, bk. 16, p. 14.

51. *Ibid.*, bk. 16, p. 16.

52. *Ibid.*, bk. 16, p. 33.

53. *Ibid.*, bk. 16, pp. 37-42.

54. *Ibid.*, bk. 17, p. 1.

V. SINO-AMERICAN RELATIONS

18. THE OPEN DOOR POLICY

JOHN HAY

THE FIRST NOTE

Secretary Hay to the Ambassador in Great Britain (Choate)[1]

Washington, September 6, 1899

SIR: The Government of Her Britannic Majesty has declared that its policy and its very traditions precluded it from using any privileges which might be granted it in China as a weapon for excluding commercial rivals, and that freedom of trade for Great Britain in that Empire meant freedom of trade for all the world alike. While conceding by formal agreements, first with Germany and then with Russia, the possession of "spheres of influence or interest" in China in which they are to enjoy special rights and privileges, more especially in response of railroads and mining enterprises. Her Britannic Majesty's Government has therefore sought to maintain at the same time what is called the "open door" policy, to insure to the commerce of the world in China equality of treatment within said "spheres" for commerce and navigation. This latter policy is alike urgently demanded by the British mercantile com-

From *United States Relations with China: With Special Reference to the Period 1944-1949* (U.S. Government Printing Office, Washington D.C., 1949), pp. 414-417.

munities and by those of the United States, as it is justly held by them to be the only one which will improve existing conditions, enable them to maintain their positions in the markets of China, and extend their operations in the future. While the Government of the United States will in no way commit itself to a recognition of exclusive rights of any power within or control over any portion of the Chinese Empire under such agreements as have within the last year been made, it can not conceal its apprehension that under existing conditions there is a possibility, even a probability, of complications arising between the treaty powers which may imperil the rights insured to the United States under our treaties with China.

This Government is animated by a sincere desire that the interests of our citizens may not be prejudiced through exclusive treatment by any of the controlling powers within their so-called "spheres of interest" in China, and hopes also to retain there an open market for the commerce of the world, remove dangerous sources of international irritation, and hasten thereby united or concerted action of the powers at Pekin in favor of the administrative reforms so urgently needed for strengthening the Imperial

Government and maintaining the integrity of China in which the whole western world is alike concerned. It believes that such a result may be greatly assisted by a declaration by the various powers claiming "spheres of interest" in China of their intentions as regards treatment of foreign trade therein. The present moment seems a particularly opportune one for informing Her Britannic Majesty's Government of the desire of the United States to see it make a formal declaration and to lend its support in obtaining similar declarations from the various powers claiming "spheres of influence" in China, to the effect that each in its respective spheres of interest or influence.

First. Will in no wise interfere with any treaty port or any vested interest within any so-called "sphere of interest" or leased territory it may have in China.

Second. That the Chinese treaty tariff of the time being shall apply to all merchandise landed or shipped to all such ports as are within said "sphere of interest" (unless they be "free ports"), no matter to what nationality it may belong, and that duties so leviable shall be collected by the Chinese Government.

Third. That it will levy no higher harbor duties on vessels of another nationality frequenting any port in such "sphere" than shall be levied on vessels of its own nationality, and no higher railroad charges over lines built, controlled, or operated within its "sphere" on merchandise belonging to citizens or subjects of other nationalities transported through such "sphere" than shall be levied on similar merchandise belonging to its own nationals transported over equal distances.

The recent ukase of His Majesty the Emperor of Russia, declaring the port of Ta-lien-wan open to the merchant ships of all nations during the whole of the lease under which it is to be held by Russia, removing as it does all uncertainty as to the liberal and conciliatory policy of that power, together with the assurances given this Government by Russia, justifies the expectation that His Majesty will cooperate in such an understanding as is here proposed, and our ambassador at the court of St. Petersburg has been instructed accordingly to submit the propositions above detailed to His Imperial Majesty, and ask their early consideration. Copy of my instruction to Mr. Tower is herewith inclosed for your confidential information.

The action of Germany in declaring the port of Kiaochao a "free port," and the aid the Imperial Government has given China in the establishment there of a Chinese custom-house, coupled with the oral assurance conveyed the United States by Germany that our interests within its "sphere" would in no wise be affected by its occupation of this portion of the province of Shang-tung, tend to show that little opposition may be anticipated from that power to the desired declaration.

The interests of Japan, the next most interested power in the trade of China, will be so clearly served by the proposed arrangement, and the declaration of its statesmen within the last year are so entirely in line with the views here expressed, that its hearty cooperation is confidently counted on.

You will, at as early [a] date as practicable, submit the considerations to Her Britannic Majesty's principal secretary of state for foreign affairs and request their immediate consideration.

I inclose herewith a copy of the instruction sent to our ambassador at Berlin bearing on the above subject.

I have the honor to be [etc.]

John Hay.

THE SECOND NOTE

Secretary Hay to American Diplomatic Representatives at Berlin, Paris, London, Rome, St. Petersburg, Vienna, Brussels, Madrid, Tokyo, The Hague, and Lisbon[2]

Washington, July 3, 1900

In this critical posture of affairs in China it is deemed appropriate to define the attitude of the United States as far as present circumstances permit this to be done. We adhere to the policy initiated by us in 1857 of peace with the Chinese nation, of furtherance of lawful commerce, and of protection of lives and property of our citizens by all means guaranteed under extraterritorial treaty rights and by the law of nations. If wrong be done to our citizens we propose to hold the responsible authors to the uttermost accountability. We regard the condition at Pekin as one of virtual anarchy, whereby power and responsibility are practically devolved upon the local provincial authorities. So long as they are not in overt collusion with rebellion and use their power to protect foreign life and property, we regard them as representing the Chinese people, with whom we seek to remain in peace and friendship. The purpose of the President is, as it has been heretofore, to act concurrently with the other powers; first, in opening up communication with Pekin and rescuing the American officials, missionaries, and other Americans who are in danger; secondly, in affording all possible protection everywhere in China to American life and property; thirdly, in guarding and protecting all legitimate American interests; and fourthly, in aiding to prevent a spread of the disorders to the other provinces of the Empire and a recurrence of such disasters. It is of course too early to forecast the means of attaining this last result; but the policy of the Government of the United States is to seek a solution which may bring about permanent safety and peace to China, preserve Chinese territorial and administrative entity, protect all rights guaranteed to friendly powers by treaty and international law, and safeguard for the world the principle of equal and impartial trade with all parts of the Chinese Empire.

You will communicate the purport of this instruction to the minister for foreign affairs.

JOHN HAY.

Notes

1. *Foreign Relations of the United States,* 1899, p. 131. Similar instructions were sent to American Diplomatic Representatives at Paris, Berlin, St. Petersburg, Rome, and Tokyo.
2. *Foreign Relations,* 1900, p. 299.

PART THREE

REFORM AND REVOLUTION, 1895-1912

INTRODUCTION

Seldom has the nexus between scholarship and politics been more clearly demonstrated than in the late Ch'ing, when the Modern Text School of Classical Learning became a vehicle for political reform. The rise of this school followed the demise of the School of Empirical Research (*K'ao-cheng hsüeh*), which having reached its zenith during the middle Ch'ing began to show signs of decay at the end of the eighteenth century and the beginning of the nineteenth centuries. A shattering blow was dealt it by the Taiping Revolution (1850-64) when its strongholds in Kiangsu and Chekiang were devastated. The intellectual void thus created facilitated the emergence of a new school more in tune with the spirit of the times. The pressing problems of domestic rebellion and foreign invasion agitated scholars not only to produce works relevant to the age but also to be actively involved in discussion of politics and participation in public service. Selections 19 and 20 by Liang Ch'i-ch'ao and Kung-ch'uan Hsiao discuss the Modern Text Movement in the late Ch'ing and the rise of K'ang Yu-wei, who capitalized on the Modern Text idea of "progress" to promote his own program of institutional reform in 1898. When the reform proved abortive after 103 days, the future of the dynasty was doomed.

Amid the hue and cry for institutional modernization and constitutionalism in the 1900's, one man stood out as the symbol of New China—the Western-trained physician Dr. Sun Yat-sen. However, without a traditional education and degrees, he was distrusted by the literati-gentry and could only operate on the fringes of Chinese society. In spite of all odds, his flexible tactics, his deftness in political maneuvering, and his charismatic personality ultimately enabled him to unite the various groups and overthrow the Manchu dynasty. The "enigma" of Dr. Sun forms the main theme of study by Dr. Harold Z. Schiffrin in Selection 21, while Sun's revolutionary philosophy, *The Three Principles of the People* (*San Min Chu I*), constitute Selection 22. The original manuscript of *San Min Chu I* was burned during Ch'en Chiung-ming's mutiny in 1922; reproduced here are excerpts from Dr. Sun's public lectures in 1924.

I. LATE CH'ING INTELLECTUAL TRENDS

19. THE MODERN TEXT MOVEMENT

LIANG CH'I-CH'AO

Why did the Ch'ing school of learning [i.e., empirical research] disintegrate after the Tao-kuang and Hsien-feng periods (1821-1861)? There were causes that originated with the school of learning itself, and others that were precipitated by environmental changes.

What were the internal causes arising out of the school of learning itself? For one thing, although the methodology of the School of Empirical Research was quite excellent, the scope of its studies was nevertheless restricted and rigid. Within this school, the highest distinctions were achieved only in the field of philology, which, however, had been exhaustively developed by the various great masters so that only the dregs were left. The study of the nomenclature of artifacts included investigations of the [Chou] sacrificial hall, royal sleeping chambers, hats and dress, and the system of conveyance, but since the originals [of these things] no longer existed now, disputes could not be finally settled. The topic of government regula-

From Immanuel C. Y. Hsü, *Intellectual Trends in the Ch'ing Period*, a translation of Liang Ch'i-ch'ao's *Ch'ing-tai hsüeh-shu kai-lun* (Harvard University Press, 1959), pp. 83-107, 139-141. Copyright 1959 by the President and Fellows of Harvard College. Reprinted by permission.

tions and institutions mainly covered funeral dress, imperial sacrifice, political feudalism, and the well-field system, but there had always been variations [in these things] in each period since ancient times; no general reconciliation of views could be achieved from the numerous books [on these subjects]. Ch'ing learning had replaced Ming learning and flourished in its stead for no other reason than that it was concrete while [Ming learning] was abstract. Now that [Ch'ing scholars] split over the indefinable technical terms and institutions, it too became abstract; how different were they from the [Ming] exponents of "Mind" and "Nature"? Even though those who studied the *Book of Changes* rejected the "River Chart and Lo Writing" in favor of "breaths of the year and the correlation of the twelve months with the twelve lines of the *ch'ien* and *k'un* hexagrams,"[1] their deceitful pretentions were similar. Cases like this were quite numerous and could not win over men. In short, Ch'ing learning flourished by advocating the one word "concreteness," and declined because of its inability to realize this word. Naturally, one reaps what one sows.

Secondly, when an organism grows to a certain point, it becomes static and does not continue to grow, and from

297

this stagnation comes corruption and decadence; this is the unchanging principle of things. The transformation of political systems follows this law, as do schools of thought. The rise of Ch'ing learning was a revolution against the Ming "intellectual oligarchy"; but after the Ch'ien-lung and Chia-ch'ing periods (1736-1820) it had itself become an imposing "intellectual oligarchy" par excellence. Take, for example, Fang Tung-shu's *Han-hsüeh shang-tui* [Discussions of Han Learning]: although it does frequently evince signs of temper and intolerance, it nevertheless aptly strikes at many of the then-prevailing shortcomings. This the various masters of the Orthodox School could not accept, and their opportunistic followers, riding their coat-tails, even took an arrogant and hostile attitude toward it. The intellectual world was thus turned into a "dictatorship of the Han school." When a school of learning is itself defective and furthermore acts "dictatorially," it portends its own extinction.

Thirdly, Ch'ing scholars on the one hand asked men to honor antiquity, and on the other taught them to be skeptical. If a man reveres antiquity, there is always something more ancient which he ought to revere more; if he is skeptical, why cannot he also doubt what is generally believed by his contemporaries? After its golden period in the Ch'ien-lung and Chia-ch'ing periods, Ch'ing learning [found itself in a position] much like that of the early period of Modern European history when nations enjoyed internal peace and order, and men, like Columbus, looking outward for new lands were bound to appear. Therefore, when there is a sudden offshoot from a certain school, the fate of that school is implicitly doomed; this is in the very nature of things.

In what way did the environment help to induce these changes? First, the early Ch'ing school of "practical statesmanship" suffered a premature death, in part because the prevailing intellectual trend toward the method of inductive research tended to shun abstract generalization, and in part because of the desire to avoid offending official sensibilities and [to secure] self-preservation. After the Chia-ch'ing and Tao-kuang periods (1796-1850), state power and control were increasingly relaxed, and the people's minds thus gradually became liberated. But, when the leisurely inertia of civil officials and the flighty irresponsibility of the military went to extremes, all men of some judgment knew that a great calamity was approaching. Looking for an explanation, they blamed the impracticality of learning, and the dignified "oligarchs of learning" could not but become the first targets of attack.

Secondly, the Ch'ing learning had its birthplace and base in Kiangsu and Chekiang provinces. During the [Taiping] rebellion in the Hsien-feng and T'ung-chih periods (1851-1874) these two provinces suffered the severest blows, and documents and materials were scattered and lost. Younger scholars fled from place to place, having no leisure to revitalize learning. The brilliant and outstanding men of that time were passionately absorbed in public affairs and could hardly pay much attention to learning. The continuity and development of learning require relatively peaceful times, and thus the sudden decline of all branches of learning during the Hsien-feng and T'ung-chih periods was quite understandable.

Thirdly, after the "Opium War" resolute men of purpose [lit., "clenching their fists and grinding their teeth"] considered it a profound humiliation and a singular catastrophe; they sought for ways to redeem themselves. The revival of the conception of practical studies for the service of the state burst forth like an unextinguishable, raging fire. With the lifting of the ban on oceanic communication, so-called "Western learning" gradually came in: first the study of industrial arts and then political institutions. Scholars hitherto had lived as if in a dark room, unaware of what was beyond it; now a window was suddenly opened, through which they peered out and discovered all sorts of radiant objects which they had never seen before. Looking back into their own room, [they saw] only depressing darkness and piled-up dust. Consequently, their yearning for foreign knowledge became stronger daily and their feelings of disgust with internal [developments] daily became more pronounced. To break through the wall and to get out of this darkness, it was necessary first to attempt to fight the existing political system. Therefore, with their very elementary knowledge of "Western learning" they coalesced with the so-called "school of practical statesmanship" of the Formative Period in early Ch'ing to form an independent school of their own, openly raising the rebel's flag against the Orthodox School. These were the main reasons for the disintegration of the Ch'ing school of learning.

MODERN TEXTS VERSUS ANCIENT TEXTS

The spark that set off the disintegration of the Ch'ing school of learning was the dispute between the Modern and Ancient Text schools of classical learning. What are the Modern and Ancient Text [schools]? It [the distinction] had its origin in the book burning of Ch'in Shih-

huang-ti when the Six Classics were destroyed. With the rise of Han the various scholars gradually began to teach on the basis of their [own] knowledge and different schools arose among them. With respect to the *Book of Changes*, there were three schools: Shih (Ts'ou), Meng (Hsi), and Liang-ch'iu (Ho), all of which evolved from T'ien Ho. As to the *Book of History*, there were the three schools of Ou-yang (Sheng), Ta Hsia-hou (Sheng), and Hsiao Hsia-hou (Chien), all evolving from Fu Sheng. With respect to the *Book of Odes*, there were the three schools of Ch'i, Lu, and Han: the *Lu Odes* coming from Shen Kung, the *Ch'i Odes* from Yüan Ku, and the *Han Odes* from Han Ing. In regard to the *Spring and Autumn Annals* there was only the *Kung-yang Commentary* [which was expounded by] the two schools of Yen (P'eng-tsu) and Yen (An-lo), both evolving from Hu-mu Sheng and Tung Chung-shu. Of *Li* there was only the *Yi Li* [Ceremony and Ritual] [expounded by] three schools: Ta-tai (te), Hsiao-tai (sheng), and Ch'ing (P'u), all originating with Kao T'ang-sheng.

These fourteen schools were established with the officials of learning during the times of Emperor Wu (140-86 B.C.) and Emperor Hsüan (73-48 B.C.) of the Han Dynasty, and Erudites were appointed to lecture [on them]. The texts they used were all written in the "seal writing," in use during the Ch'in and Han, and these were known as the Modern Texts. The transmission and teaching of the classical learning as stated in the "Biographies of Scholars" in the *Historical Records* ended here, and these were the so-called Fourteen Erudites.

Toward the end of the Former Han (206 B.C.-25 A.D.) there appeared the so-called Ancient Text classics and commentaries. There was a Fei [version] of the *Book of Changes* which was said to have been transmitted by Fei Chih of Tung-lai; there was also a K'ung [version] of the *Book of History,* which was to have been proffered by a descendant of Confucius, Kung An-kuo, who discovered it stored within a wall. There was a Mao [version] of the *Book of Odes,* which was said to have been transmitted by the Erudite Mao Kung under Prince Hsien of Ho-chien. With respect to the *Spring and Autumn Annals,* there was the *Tso Commentary,* which was said to have been once taught by Chang, Ts'ang. Of *Li* there were the thirty-nine sections of "Dispersed Rituals," which were said to have been obtained by Prince Kung of Lu from the dismantled house of Confucius. There was also the *Officials of Chou,* which was said to have been obtained by Prince Hsien of Ho-chien. As all these classics and commentaries were written in the tadpole characters [of ancient times], they were known as the Ancient Texts.

Most of the classical masters of the Two Han dynasties did not believe in the [authenticity of the] Ancient Texts, which Liu Hsin (ca. 46 B.C.-23 A.D.) repeatedly sought to establish with the officials of learning, but to no avail. He sent a letter to the Erudites of the Court of Sacrifices, accusing them of being "egocentric, hyper-conservative, cliquish, and jealous of the truth." When Wang Mang usurped the Han [throne in 9 A.D.], utilized his [Wang's] power to establish [the Ancient Texts], but the Emperor Kuang-wu (25-58 A.D.) again abolished them. During the early periods of the Eastern Capital [i.e., Late Han], believers [in the Ancient Texts] were very few. Toward the end of Late Han, however, great masters like Fu Ch'ien,

Ma Yung (79-166 A.D.), and Cheng Hsüan (127-200 A.D.), all honored and studied the ancient texts; as a result, the Ancient Text school of learning prospered greatly.

The focal point of the dispute then was the *Kung-yang Commentary* on the *Spring and Autumn Annals.* The great Modern Text scholar, Ho Hsiu (129-182 A.D.), wrote *Tso-shih kao-mang* [The Incurability of Mr. Tso], *Ku-liang fei-chi* [The Disabling Diseases of Ku-liang], and *Kung-yang mo-shou* [The Conservatism of Kung-yang]. On the other hand, the great Ancient Text scholar, Cheng Hsüan, refuted him with Chen kao-huang [Revitalize the Incurable], *Ch'i fei-chi* [Rehabilitate the Disabled], and *Fa mo-shou* [Enlighten the Conservative]. As Cheng Hsüan was very learned, he wrote commentaries extensively on the various classics. Later, Tu Yü (222-284) and Wang Su (195-256) of Chin, furthered his work. Hence the decline of the Modern Text School. This was the *cause célèbre* of the dispute between the Modern and Ancient Texts during the two Han dynasties.

From the period of Southern and Northern Dynasties (420-589 A.D.) on, schools of classical learning and interpretation argued only about Cheng Hsüan and Wang Su; and thus the dispute between the Modern and Ancient Texts came to an end. Lu Te-ming of the T'ang period wrote *Shih-wen* [Explanatory Notes] and Kung Ying-ta (574-648 A.D.) wrote *Cheng-i* [The correct meaning of the *Book of History*], both modeled after Cheng and Wang in a mixed manner. As to the *Shih-san ching chu-shu* [*Commentaries and Sub-Commentaries on the Thirteen Classics*] now in circulation, the Wang (Pi) commentary is used for the *Book of Changes;* the fabricated commentary by K'ung An-kuo is used for the *Book of Odes;* Chen's Sub-Commentary on *Mao's Commentary* is used for the *Book of Odes;* Chen's commentaries are used for the Chou *Rituals, Ceremony and Ritual,* and the *Book of Rites;* and Tu Yü's Commentary is used for *Tso Commentary* on the *Spring and Autumn Annals.*

After the Sung (960-1127 A.D.), Che'ng (Hao and Yi) and Chu (Hsi) and others also extensively annotated the various classics, thereby rendering the commentaries and sub-commentaries of the Han and T'ang obsolete. Coming into the Ch'ing Period, [one sees] the gradual revival of antiquity; men like Ku Yen-wu and Hui Shih-ch'i intensively promoted the subject of annotation and commentary, an occupation which revived [the studies of] the Six Dynasties and T'ang. After Yen Jo-chü attacked the fabricated *Book of History* in the Ancient Text and later proved its forger to be Wang Su, scholars once again opened the famous issue of Cheng (Hsüan) versus Wang (Su) of the Southern and Northern Dynasties, downgrading Wang and upgrading Cheng. This revived [the learning] of Late Han. After the Ch'ien-lung (1736-1795) and Chia-ch'ing (1796-1820) periods, every school [accepted] Hsü (Shen) and Cheng (Hsüan), and everyone [accepted] Chia (K'uei) (30-101 A.D.) and Ma (Yung). The learning of Late Han glowed as the mid-day sun. Like an avalanche which will not stop until it reaches the ground, the old issue of the Modern and Ancient Texts of the Former Han was inevitably reopened once more, as might be expected.[2]

THE KUNG-YANG COMMENTARY

The core of the Modern Text School was the *Kung-yang Commentary.* The language of the *Kung-yang* scholars was aptly characterized as "abounding in unusually bizarre and eccentric ideas,"[3] and no one since the time of Wei (220-265 A.D.) and Chin (265-420) had dared to discuss it. Although the *Commentaries and Sub-Commentaries on the Thirteen Classics* now in circulation used Ho Hsiu's Commentary for the *Kung-yang Commentary,* there was a sub-commentary by Hsü Yen of the T'ang period (618-907), which however did not illuminate Ho's interpretation. The *Kung-yang Commentary* thus became a lost subject for almost two thousand years.

Since Ch'ing scholars were fully engaged in studying old classics, K'ung Kuang-shen, a student of Tai Chen, took the initiative in writing *Kung-yang t'ung-i* [A Comprehensive Interpretation of the *Kung-yang Commentary*], but because he did not understand methodology very thoroughly, it was not considered authoritative by Modern Text scholars.

The great pioneer of the Modern Text School was Chuang Ts'un-yü of Wuchin, who wrote the *Ch'un-ch'iu cheng-tz'u* [Correct Commentary on the *Spring and Autumn Annals*]; he omitted trivial philological points and the nomenclature of artifacts, concentrating only on [elucidating] the so-called "great principles hidden in esoteric language"; thus he took an entirely different route from that of the school of Tai and Tuan. A later scholar of his native country, Liu Feng-lu (1776-1829), followed [his footsteps] and wrote *Ch'un-ch'iu Kung-yang ching-chuan Ho-shih shih-li* [Explanation of the Rules of Mr. Ho in His Study of the *Kung-yang Commentary* on the *Spring and Autumn Classical Annals*], which successively brought to light the meaning of such "unusually bizarre and eccentric ideas," to use an expression of Ho

Hsiu's,[4] as the "Unfolding of the Three Epochs," "Going through the Three Periods of Unity," "Relegating the Chou Dynasty and Entrusting the Kingship to Lu," and "Receiving the Mandate to Reform Institutions."[5] His book employed a scientific, inductive, research method, consistent in reasoning and conclusive in judgment; among the writings of Ch'ing scholars, it is a most valuable creative work.

Tuan Yü-ts'ai's grandson, Kung Tze-chen, had studied philology with Tuan on the one hand and was interested in the Modern Text School on the other; he expounded the classics after the fashion of Chuang Ts'un-yü and Liu Feng-lu. By nature Kung was a lighthearted dilettante, unscrupulous about detailed rules of behavior; in this he was quite similar to Rousseau in France. He had a taste for oversubtle thinking, and employed unrestrained, picturesque, and ambiguous diction, a fact not appreciated by his contemporaries. But this delighted him all the more. He often quoted ideas from the *Kung-yang Commentary* to criticize and satirize current political events and inveigh against despotism. In later life he also studied Buddhism and liked to discuss logic.

All in all, Kung's studies had the defect of lacking depth; no sooner did his thinking reach the outer limits [of any field of learning] than it stopped, and it was also buried under luxuriant diction which made his ideas not easily accessible. Nevertheless, he did contribute to the liberation of thought in the late Ch'ing period. Most of the so-called "Scholars of New Learning" of the Kuang-hsü period (1875-1908) went through a period in which they worshiped him. A reading of his *Ting-an wen-chi* [Literary Collection of Kung Tze-chen] electrifies a man at first, but after a time one gets tired of his shallowness. Nevertheless, the development of the Modern Text School actually began with him. A poem by Hsia Tseng-yu to Liang Ch'i-ch'ao runs as follows:

> Kung and Liu both evolved from Chuang,
>   This line, alone and dim,
> Reached back to Tung Chung-shu.

This was a most lucid statement of the origins of the Modern Text School. To make a comparison with the men of the Orthodox School, Chuang is similar to Ku Yen-wu, and Kung and Liu, to Yen Jo-chü and Hu Wei.

In the early stage of the "Modern Text [Movement]," only the *Kung-yang Commentary* was discussed while other classics were left untouched; however, as a result [of this study] it became known that the approaches of the Ancient and Modern schools of classical masters were entirely different during the Han period. To know Chia K'uei, Ma Yung, Hsü Shen, and Cheng Hsüan was not to exhaust the entire Han learning. At the time, the work of assembling lost texts was highly popular, and no efforts were spared to collect even a single word or phrase of the ancient classics and other interpretations. Thus an increasing number of people studied the legacy of the Modern Text School:

Feng Teng-fu, *San-chia-shih i-wen shu-cheng* [Commentary on the Different Texts of the Three Schools of *Odes*]

Ch'en Shou-ch'i, *San-chia-shih i-shuo k'ao* [A Study of the Legacy of the Three Schools of *Odes*]

Ch'en Ch'iao-ts'ung, *Chin-wen Shang-shu ching-shuo k'ao* [An Examination of the Interpretations of the Classics according to the *Book of History* in the Modern Text]

——, *Shang-shu Ou-yang Hsia-hou i-shuo*

k'ao [An Examination of the *Book of History* according to the Legacy of Ou-yang Hsia-hou]

——, *San-chia-shih i-shuo k'ao* [A Study of the Legacy of the Three Schools of *Odes*]

——, *Ch'i-shih I-shih-hsüeh shu-cheng* [Commentary on Mr. I's Work on the Ch'i *Odes*]

Cha Ho-shou, *Ch'i-shih I-shih hsüeh* [Mr. I's Work on the Ch'i *Odes*]

All of these concentrated solely on the similarities and differences between methodologies [of the Modern and Ancient Text Schools] without questioning their authenticity or spuriousness. By the end of the Tao-kuang period (1821-1850), Wei Yüan (1794-1856) wrote *Shih ku-wei* [The Ancient Hidden Meanings of the *Odes*], launching his first major attack on the *Mao Commentary* [on the *Odes*] and the *Big and Small Prefaces* [of the *Odes*], which he said were forgeries of a later origin. His arguments were erudite and convincing, like Yen Jo-chü's elucidation of the *Book of History*, and he sometimes advanced new interpretations also. He argued that poetry was not written to eulogize or criticize: "It is certainly true that eulogy and criticism are the order of the day with the Mao school of *Odes* . . . but the poet describes his emotions and stops when they are expressed. . . . How can there be genuine joy, sorrow, and happiness for subjects which require no emotion? [lit., "solely for the purpose of groaning for one who is not sick"]. . . ."[6] This view has a deep affinity to the "art for art's sake" approach, and, in fact, breaks the fetters that had bound literature for the previous two thousand years. Again, on the identity of poetry and music, he said: "In ancient times music was based on poetry; Confucius rectified poetry by rectifying music."[7] His ability to advance new interpreta-tions gave new vitality to old books.

Wei Yüan also wrote *Shu ku-wei* [The Ancient Hidden Meanings in the *Book of History*] to state that not only was the *Book of History* in Ancient Text, which appeared late in Eastern Chin (317-420 A.D.) [i.e., the one attacked by Yen], a forgery, but the disquisitions on ancient texts by Ma Yung and Cheng Hsüan of the Later Han (25-221 A.D.) was also not based on [the works of] K'ung An-kuo either. Meanwhile, Shao I-ch'en (1810-1861) also wrote *Li-ching t'ung-lun* [A General Treatise on the Classics on Rituals] to assert that the seventeen chapters of *Ceremony and Ritual* were complete in themselves, and that the thirty-nine chapters of the so-called *Dispersed Rituals* in the Ancient Text were forged by Liu Hsin. Liu Feng-lu had also previously written *Tso-shih Ch'un-ch'iu k'ao-cheng* [The Textual Criticism on the *Tso Commentary* on the *Spring and Autumn Annals*], stating that the original title of that book was Tso-shih Ch'un-ch'iu [Mr. Tso's Spring and Autumn Annals] and not *Ch'un-ch'iu Tso-shih-chuan* [*Spring and Autumn Annals* according to Mr. Tso], and that it was in the same class as *Yen-tzu Ch'un-ch'iu* [Mr. Yen's Spring and Autumn Annals] and *Lü-shih Ch'un-ch'iu* [Mr. Lü's Spring and Autumn Annals], being a chronicle and not interpretation of the classics. Where the interpretations of classics did occur, they had been interpolated by Liu Hsin, who had even forged the title *Tso-shih-chuan*.

After Liu Feng-lu's book appeared, the question of the authenticity or spuriousness of the *Tso Commentary* arose. When Wei's book appeared, the authenticity of the *Mao Odes* was questioned; so was the *Dispersed Rituals* after the appearance of Shao's book. As to the question of the authenticity of the *Rites of Chou*, it had been an issue since the

Sung dynasty (960-1127 A.D.). At first each of the various scholars merely selected a book for a limited study; but later, when they looked for the background of [these books], they found that all of them had appeared simultaneously at the end of the Former Han period (206 B.C.-25 A.D.), that their transmission-process could not be thoroughly investigated, and that Liu Hsin had been the man who sponsored and struggled for their establishment. In fine, the various classics in Ancient Texts were all related to each other; if one were authentic, then all were authentic, and if one were forged, then all were forged. So the whole question of the Ancient and Modern Texts of the Two Hans was reopened for examination, and the man who [undertook] this was K'ang Yu-wei.

The strong advocates of the Modern Text School were perforce Kung and Wei, during whose lives the Ch'ing government was already becoming weak and decadent. The whole nation was drugged by the enjoyment of peace at that time, but these men, as if they alone sensed national dangers and grievances, often came together to discuss [lit., "to point their fingers toward heaven and make designs on the earth"] grandiose plans for their country. Empirical research as a branch of learning had not originally been their specialty, but because everybody else was engaged in it, they too were able to do so, planning to open new frontiers of learning. Therefore, although they studied classics, they did so in a spirit quite different from that of the Orthodox School, which engaged in classical study for its own sake.

Both Kung Tzu-chen and Wei Yüan were fond of discussing governmental affairs and paid great attention to border events. Kung's Hsi-yü chih hsing-sheng i [Suggestion to Make the Western Territory a Province] was put into practice during the Kuang-hsü period (1875-1908), and it is today's Sinkiang Province. He also wrote Meng-ku t'u-chih [An Illustrated Record of Mongolia], dealing with Mongolian politics and customs, and including in it his own comments.[8] Wei, who wrote Yüan-shih [A History of the Yüan Dynasty] and Hai-kuo t'u-chih [An Illustrated Gazetteer of Maritime Countries], was actually a pioneer among specialists in foreign geography. Therefore, it was their legacy that prompted later Modern Text Scholars to discuss politics in classical terms.

K'ANG YU-WEI [1858-1927]

The Modern Text Movement centered around K'ang Yu-wei (1858-1927) of Nan-hai, who however, was not its founder but its synthesizer. During his early life he had been very interested in the Rites of Chou, and after mastering it thoroughly, he wrote the Cheng-hsüeh t'ung-i [A General Discourse on Government and Learning]. Later, when he saw the writings of Liao P'ing (1852-1932), he gave up his old ideas entirely. Liao P'ing was a student of Wang K'ai-yün (1833-1916). Wang achieved fame in his time through his study of the Kung-yang Commentary, although his accomplishments in classical learning were quite superficial since he was fundamentally a belle-lettrist. Wang's work, the Kung-yang ch'ien [Explanation of the Kung-yang Commentary] was even less valuable than that of K'ung Kuang-sen (1752-1786). Liao studied with Wang and wrote the Ssu-i-kuan ching hsüeh ts'ung-shu [Collection of Classical Studies of the Hall of Four Benefits], which contained more than ten pieces of writing, all of them quite firmly based on the methodology of the Modern Text School.

Late in life he was pressured and bribed[9] by Chang Chih-tung into writing a book repudiating his former [beliefs]. As a man, he certainly had little to recommend him, but it is undeniable that he influenced the thinking of K'ang Yu-wei.

The first book K'ang wrote was the *Hsin-hsüeh wei-ching k'ao* [Study of the Classics Forged during the Hsin Period], the "forged classics" being the *Rites of Chou*, the *Dispersed Rituals*, the *Tso Commentary* (*Tso chüan*), and the *Mao Commentary* on the *Book of Odes*, works for which Liu Hsin (ca. 46 B.C.-23 A.D.) had tried hard to appoint Erudites[10] at the end of the Former Han (206 B.C.-46 A.D.). "Hsin learning" referred to the learning of Wang Mang of the Hsin Dynasty (9-23 A.D.). Contemporary Ch'ing scholars who modelled themselves on Hsü Shen (ca. 100 A.D.) and Cheng Hsüan (127-200 A.D.) styled their studies "Han learning," but K'ang considered it the learning of the Hsin Dynasty rather than that of the Han, and so changed its name.

The essential points of the *Hsin-hsüeh wei-ching k'ao* are these: (1) The classical learning of the Former Han had never had anything called the Ancient Texts and all the Ancient Texts had been forged by Liu Hsin. (2) The book-burning by the Ch'in [in 213 B.C.] had not impaired the Six Classics, and the ones transmitted by the Fourteen Erudites of the Han were all complete texts of the Confucian school, with nothing missing or omitted. (3) The written character used at the time of Confucius was the "seal character" of the Ch'in and Han, and moreover, as regards the "texts," there had never been the classifications of "Ancient" and "Modern." (4) Liu Hsin had tried to cover up the traces of his forgery by adding glosses and creating confusion among all the ancient

works, while he was collating books in the imperial library. (5) The reason Liu Hsin had undertaken forgery of the classics was that he wished to help Wang Mang usurp the Han [throne] by conspiring in advance to distort and submerge Confucius' great principles hidden in esoteric language.

Whether these opinions are entirely correct need not be discussed here; what is important is that the appearance of this interpretation had two repercussions: (1) The foundation of the orthodox Ch'ing school of learning was basically shaken; (2) all ancient books had to be examined anew and reappraised. This was certainly a "hurricane" in the intellectual world.

K'ang Yu-wei had two students, Ch'en Ch'ien-ch'iu and Liang Ch'i-ch'ao (1873-1929), who had been following [the methods of] the School of Empirical Research for a long time, and Ch'en was particularly gifted and competent. When [the two of them] heard K'ang's doctrine, they gave up their own work completely and studied with him. [K'ang's] writing of the *Wei-ching k'ao* was accomplished with considerable participation by these two men, and although they were often troubled by their teacher's dogmatism, they could not influence him. Actually this book is quite excellent and competent on the whole, and the points that can be criticized are but minor ones. As to [Kang's] arguments that Liu Hsin had secretly introduced several tens of items into the *Shih-chi* [Historical Records] and the *Ch'u-tz'u* [Elegies of Ch'u] and that he had secretly cast and buried the bells, tripods, and other ritual bronzes that had been excavated, in order to dupe posterity, these were certainly completely untenable even from a commonsense viewpoint, and yet he maintained them stubbornly. Actually, the essential points of his thesis do not require these irrelevant remarks and forced arguments in order to be maintained, but because he was so anxious to be erudite and different, he often went so far as to suppress or distort evidence, thereby committing a serious crime for the scientist. This was his shortcoming.

As a man, K'ang was totally subjective in myriads of things. His self-confidence was extremely strong and he maintained it very stubbornly. As for objective facts, he either ignored them completely or insisted on remolding them to his own views. He was this way in his practical career as well as in scholarship. It is precisely because of this that he was able to found a school of thought and rise to fame with it for a time, and it was precisely for the same reason that he was unable to lay a strong and solid foundation for it. Reading his Study of the Classics Forged during the Hsin Period will readily reveal this. Barely a year after this work appeared, it incurred the displeasure of the Ch'ing court; its printing blocks were destroyed and its circulation was thus much restricted. Later, a certain Ts'ui Shih (1851-1924) wrote Shih-chi t'an-yüan [An Inquiry into the Origins of the Historical Records] and Ch'un-ch'iu fu-shih [The Restoration of the Spring and Autumn Annals in its Original Form]. These two books quoted and developed K'ang's ideas, making them more precise and terse. Ts'ui Shih was a late protagonist of the Modern Text School.

K'ang's second work was the K'ung-tzu kai-chih k'ao [A Study of Confucius on Institutional Reform] and his third, the Ta-t'ung shu [Book of the Universal Commonwealth]. If his Study of the Classic Forged during the Hsin Period is comparable to a cyclone, these two works were a mighty volcanic eruption

and huge earthquake. He studied the Kung-yang Commentary without bothering with the minutiae of the rules of writing composition; he was only looking for the great principles hidden in esoteric language which Ho Hsiu (129-182 A.D.) labelled "the extraordinary and the marvelous." He decided that the Spring and Autumn Annals had been Confucius' creation for the purpose of institutional reforms, and that written words were nothing but symbols, like a secret telegraphic code and the notes of musical scores, which cannot be understood without oral instructions. Moreover, [he said that] not only the Spring and Autumn Annals, but all of the Six Classics had been written by Confucius; men in the past were wrong when they said that Confucius had merely edited them. [He believed that] Confucius wanted to establish an independent criterion by which to promote or demote the men of old and to select or discard the ancient texts. He always [tried to justify] his institutional reforms on the basis of antiquity, relying on Yao (2357?-2256? B.C.) and Shun (2255?-2206? B. C.), although we do not know whether there actually were such men, and even if there were, they must [in all probability] have been very ordinary men; their salient virtues and great accomplishments, depicted in the classical canon, were all figments of Confucius' imagination. Not only was this the case with Confucius, but all the philosophers of the Chou (1122?-256 B.C.) and Ch'in (255-207 B.C.) too advocated institutional reforms on the basis of antiquity. For instance, Lao-tzu relied on the Yellow Emperor; Mo-tzu, on the Great Yü; and Hsü Hsing, on the Divine Husbandman.

More recently, men who have looked to Ho Hsiu (129-182 A.D.) for guidance in the study of the *Kung-yang Commentary* like Liu Feng-lu (1776-1829), Kung Tzu-chen (1792-1841), and Ch'en Li (1809-1869) have all talked of changing institution, but K'ang's doctrine was quite different from theirs. What he called institutional change involved a kind of political revolution and reform of society; for this reason he liked to talk about "going through the three periods of unity." "Three periods" implied that the three dynasties of Hsia (2205?-1766? B.C.), Shang (1766-1123? B.C.), and Chou (1122?-256 B.C.) were different from each other; hence, reforms should be made as time went on. He was also fond of speaking of "the unfolding of the three epochs," the "three epochs" being "the epoch of disorder," "the epoch of rising peace," and "the epoch of universal peace." The more one made changes, the more one would progress. K'ang's advocacy of political "reform and restoration"[11] was indeed based on these ideas. He said that Confucius' institutional reforms had covered a hundred generations before him and a hundred generations after him, and therefore K'ang honored him as the founder of a religion. But since K'ang mistakenly considered Christian worship in Europe as the basis of good government and state power, he frequently attempted to equate Confucius with Christ by quoting a variety of apocryphal prognostications to support [his thesis], and consequently, Confucius, as K'ang saw him, was imbued with a "quality of mystery." These, in brief, are the contents of his Study of Confucius on Institutional Reform. The influence of this work on the intellectual world may be said to have been the following:

(1) It taught men not to study the ancient works with the intention of seeking out the trivialities of commentary on isolated phrases, or philology, or the terms for artifacts, or [minute details] concerning institutions, but [to study them] for their general meaning. On the other hand, their general meaning was not to be found in the discussion of Mind and Human Nature,[12] but rather in the basic ideas with which ancient men initiated laws and established institutions. As a result, both Han and Sung learning were rejected, and this opened up new frontiers to the academic world.

(2) In asserting that Confucius' greatness lay in his establishing a new school of learning [i.e., initiating a religion], it encouraged men's creative spirit.

(3) Since the *Wei-ching k'ao* had already condemned the majority of the classics as Liu Hsin's forgeries, and the *Kai-chih k'ao* had gone further to say that the entire corpus of the true classics had been created by Confucius under the pretense of their antiquity, the classical canon, which had commonly been considered sacrosanct and inviolable for the past several thousand years, was now laid open to question to its very foundations. This prompted scholars to a [more] critical and skeptical attitude.

(4) Although [K'ang] praised Confucius highly, he nevertheless said that Confucius had established a school of learning with the same motives, the same means, and the same objectives as had the other philosophers in establishing theirs. In this way he relegated Confucius to the rank of other philosophers, dissolving the so-called notion of "a black-white demarcation and a fixed orthodoxy" and so leading men into comparative studies.

K'ANG'S *TA-T'UNG SHU*

The two works mentioned above represent K'ang Yu-wei's reinterpretation of the older learning: his own creative work was the *Ta-t'ung shu* [Book of the Universal Commonwealth]. Formerly, when K'ang had completed his studies with Chu Tz'u-ch'i, he had withdrawn into solitude on the Hsi-ch'iao Mountain for two years in order to engage in deep meditation alone, by which he hoped to probe exhaustively the way of Heaven and Man and then create his own school of learning by applying [what he had learned] to practical affairs of the world. He interpreted the *Li Yün* [The Evolution of Li][13] in terms of the "three epochs" of the *Ch'un-ch'iu* and asserted that the "epoch of rising peace" was "partial security" and the "epoch of universal peace" was a "universal commonwealth." As The Evolution of Li has it:

When the Grand Course was pursued, a public and common spirit ruled all under the sky; they chose men of talents, virtue, and ability; their words were sincere, and what they cultivated was harmony. Thus men did not love their parents only, nor treat as children only their own sons. A competent provision was secured for the aged till their death, employment for the able-bodied, and the means for growing up to the young. They showed kindness and compassion to widows, orphans, childless men, and those who were disabled by disease, so that they were all sufficiently maintained. Males had their proper work, and females had their homes. [They accumulated] articles [of value], disliking that they should be thrown away upon the ground, but not wishing to keep them for their own gratification. [They labored] with their strength, disliking that it should not be exerted, but not exciting it [only] with a view to their own advantage. . . . This was [the period of] what we call the Grand Union [Universal Commonwealth]. [14]

If this paragraph is translated into modern terms, it contains the ideas of *democracy* ["a public and common spirit ruled all under the sky; they chose men of talents, and ability"], a *League of Nations* ["their words were sincere and what they cultivated was harmony"], *public upbringing of children* ["men did not treat as children only their own sons"], *sickness and old-age insurance* ["a competent provision was secured for the aged . . ."], *communism* ["they accumulated articles of value . . . but not wishing to keep them for their own gratification"], and the *sanctity of labor* ["they labored . . . but not with a view to their own advantage"].

K'ang held that this was the ideal social system of Confucius and was actually the "epoch of universal peace" mentioned in the *Ch'un-ch'iu*. He developed these ideas into a book, which may be summarized as follows:

(1) No nations; the whole world should set up a single government and be divided into several regions.

(2) Both the central and regional govments should be popularly elected.

(3) No family and clans; a man and a woman should cohabit not more than a year together; upon expiration of this term, there should be a change of mates.

(4) Pregnant women should go to an institution for pre-natal education, and babies after birth should go to nurseries.

(5) Children should enter kindergarten and respective schools according to age.

(6) Upon coming of age they should be assigned by the government to various duties in agricultural, industrial, and other types of productive enterprise.

(7) The sick shall go to hospitals, and the aged to Homes for the Aged.

(8) The establishments for pre-natal

education, the nurseries, the kindergartens, the hospitals, and the homes for the aged should be the highest institutions within the regional [government]; those who enter them should obtain the highest satisfaction.

(9) Adult men and women should as a rule serve in these establishments for a certain number of years, as they do at present in the military.

(10) Establish different classes of public dormitories and dining halls so that each may freely enjoy and use them according to his working income.

(11) Reproach for idleness should be the severest form of punishment.

(12) Those who make new discoveries in learning and those who serve with special distinction in the five establishments of pre-natal education, etc., should receive specific rewards.

(13) There should be cremation of the dead, and fertilizer factories in the neighborhood of the crematoria.

This, briefly, is the outline of the Book of the Universal Commonwealth. The whole work runs to several hundred thousand words, discussing heatedly and minutely the roots of human suffering and happiness and the standards of good and evil, and going on to state the reasons for his [proposed] legislation, the crucial point of which was the destruction of family and clan. K'ang states that since a Buddhist renounces his family in order to find escape from suffering, it would be better to arrange it that he has no family to renounce; that since private property is the source of quarrel and embroilment, who without a family would enjoy having private property? As for nations, they too will follow the family and die out.

K'ang set up these objectives as the ultimate aim of human evolution, but he did not state by what method these could be attained. He does not satisfactorily explain either whether his first objective —a time limit on the cohabitation of a man and a woman—accords with human nature. Nevertheless, when he wrote this book thirty years ago, he relied on nothing and he plagiarized nothing [from others]; yet his ideas correspond in many ways to the internationalism and socialism of today, and in statement of high principle he even surpasses them. Yes, he may certainly be called a spectacular man!

Although K'ang had written this work, he kept it secret from other men and never taught its ideas to his students, averring that the present was but the "disordered" epoch, in which one could speak only of "partial security" and not of the "universal commonwealth." To speak of the latter would be like committing mankind to floods and ravening beasts.[15] Among his students only Ch'en Ch'ien-ch'iu and Liang Ch'i-ch'ao were permitted to read this book at first. They enjoyed reading it tremendously and were bent on making parts of it public. K'ang did not encourage this, but he could not prevent them from doing so either, and from that time forth, students at the *Wan-mu ts'ao-t'ang* ["the grass hut amidst a myriad of trees"] all talked about the universal commonwealth. Nevertheless, K'ang from beginning to end advocated salvation of the present world by the principles of "partial security" alone; in regard to the problems of politics as well as social ethics, he considered it his duty to maintain the status quo. He had formulated a new ideal which he considered most worthy and most perfect, yet he did not desire its realization and even fought with all his might to suppress it. I suppose the strangeness and unpredictability of human nature can hardly exceed this.

Immediately after the Sino-Japanese War (1894-1895), K'ang gathered several thousand young scholars[16] to present a memorial on current affairs, known as the *"Kung-ch'e shang-shu"* ["Memorial Presented by Provincial Candidates"]. This is actually the beginning of the "mass political movement" in China.

Since K'ang wanted to practice his doctrine of "partial security" in the government, he had to look for [patronage] from others, but they steadfastly refused to use him and frequently drove him away. Moreover, the younger generation for the most part disliked his conduct and exchanged criticisms with him, while K'ang, for his part, being overconfident, was contemptuous of these younger man, taking an even more recalcitrant attitude toward them. He is now old and much retired from the world; thus a great thinker of our country does not lend his lustre to his countrymen, which is indeed a pity.

Liang asked him repeatedly to print and distribute his Book of the Universal Commonwealth, but for a long time he would not consent. Finally, it was printed in the *Pu-jen tsa-chih* [Pu-jen Magazine]; but when barely one-third of it was published, the magazine stopped publication and never resumed again.

LIANG CH'I-CH'AO [1873-1929]

One vigorous propagandist of the Modern Text School was Liang Ch'i-ch'ao of Hsin-hui. At thirteen he had studied with his friend Ch'en Ch'ien-ch'iu at the *Hsüeh-hai-t'ang* [School of the Ocean of Knowledge], concentrating on the study of Tai Chen, Tuan Yü-ts'ai, Wang Nien-sun, and Wang Yin-chih; because of this

association [Liang] received considerable help and benefit from Ch'en Ch'ien-ch'iu. Three years later, when K'ang Yu-wei was sent home as a result of his presentation of a memorial while a mere commoner [1888], and at a time when the whole nation regarded him as an eccentric, Ch'en and Liang were curious about this and went to see him. At first sight they were thoroughly taken with him and formally became his students, urging him to open a school and give lectures. The [school] was [later] known as the *Wan-mu ts'ao-t'ang* ["the grass hut amidst a myriad of trees"]. After studying there for several months, the two ardently proclaimed what they had learned [to people] at the *Hsüeh-hai-t'ang,* and severely attacked the old learning; not a day went by that they did not argue with their elders and contemporaries.

K'ang did not lightly impart his knowledge to others. The regular curriculum at the school included, apart from the *Kung-yang Commentary,* punctuation and reading of the *Tzu-chih t'ung-chien* [Comprehensive Mirror for Aid in Government], the *Sung-Yüan hsüeh-an* [Writings of Sung and Yüan Philosophers], the *Chu-tzu yü-lei* [Classified Conversations of Chu Hsi], and others. Frequently old ceremonies were performed too, and since Ch'en and Liang had little taste for this, they changed to the study of the Chou and Ch'in philosophers and the Buddhist scriptures; they also browsed through various political works by Ch'ing scholars as well as translations of Western works, turning to K'ang for solutions to their problems. It was not until a year later that they learned about the idea of the universal commonwealth and, ecstatically delighted as they were, wished very much to publicize it. K'ang felt that the time was not ripe, but he could not stop them. Two years later, Ch'en died [at the age of 22] and Liang felt the more impelled [to continue] single-handed.

Liang studied the *Wei-ching k'ao* [Examination of the Forged Classics], but since he was often unable to bear his teacher's dogmatism, he left it completely, without further ado. His teacher was in the habit of quoting apocryphal works to explain Confucius in mystic terms, and he did not approve of this either. Liang maintained that the Confucian school of learning had evolved in time into two factions of Mencius and Hsün-tzu, the latter expounding [the idea] of partial security [relative order], and the former, that of a universal commonwealth [Great Harmony]. The classical masters of the Han Dynasty, whether of the Modern or Ancient Text Schools, had all evolved from Hsün-tzu [according to Wang Chung]; therefore, over the past two thousand years, even if the schools had often changed, all of them had changed uniformly within the framework of the Hsün-tzu school. The school of Mencius was thus discontinued and hence that of Confucius also declined. [Liang] therefore took upon himself the task of raising the banner: "disregard Hsün-tzu and emphasize Mencius." He drew a number of ideas from *Mencius*—among them, killing and punishing "enemies of the people"; "autocrats"; "having those skilled in making war suffer the highest punishment"; and "distributing land in order to regulate property holdings"—which he felt embodied the fundamental essence of the universal commonwealth idea. He promulgated these daily, and as he was also partial to *Mo-tzu*, he read and proclaimed its ideas of "universal love" and "non-aggression."

Liang often visited the capital and gradually came into contact with leading scholars and officials of the time, among whom his most intimate academic friends were Hsia Tseng-yu (1865-1924) and T'an Ssu-t'ung (1865-1898). Hsia was at that time beginning to study the Modern Text learning of Kung Tzu-chen and Liu Feng-lu, and whenever he developed a [new] idea he shared it with his bosom friends. Later when Liang went into exile in Japan, Hsia presented him with a poem which read in part:

> A nether gloom shrouds the gate of
>   Lan-ling [home of Hsün-tzu],
>   Myriads of ghostly heads [swarm
>   about] like ants;
> A demon [Hsü-tzu] lifts his hand, and
>   The sunlight is blotted out;
> We tuck up our sleeves to attack him,
>   With one blow we fell him like a pig,
> Flushed with drink we throw away our
>   glasses and rise,
>   Laughing and looking about, care-
>   free, and gay:
> Within the universe, only this can give
>   us joy.

From this we can discern with what a spirit of high exuberance the "anti-Hsün" movement of that generation was actually carried on. T'an was then beginning his study of Wang Fu-chih and liked to discuss logic and statesmanship, but upon meeting Liang he became greatly obsessed with the idea of the universal comwealth [Great Harmony] also and promulgated it with even greater vigor [see next section for details]; on the other hand, Liang's views were in turn greatly influenced by Hsia and T'an.

Thereafter, the movement of Liang and his associates took on even stronger political overtones. Liang started a magazine at Shanghai published every ten days, known at the *Shih-wu-pao* [often called "The Chinese Progress"], and wrote *Pien-fa t'ung-i* [A General Discussion of Reform], which criticized the worthless government and proposed to abolish the old examination system and establish modern schools as ways of remedying the crisis. From time to time he also wrote on "popular sovereignty" but he touched on this only very generally, not daring to espouse it too overtly.

Shortly afterwards, T'an Ssu-t'ung, Huang Tsun-hsien, and Hsiung Hsi-ling, among others, established the *Shih-wu hsüeh-t'ang* [School of Current Affairs] at Changsha, inviting Liang to be head lecturer, with T'ang Ts'ai-ch'ang and others as assistant instructors. Liang went there and lectured on the *Kung-yang Commentary* and the *Mencius*, also teaching his students the methods of note-taking. There were only forty students altogether, the most outstanding being Li Ping-huan, Lin Kuei, and Ts'ai Ao. Liang remained in the lecture hall for four hours a day, and at night wrote comments on the students' notes, a single comment sometimes running to several thousand words; it was not unusual for him to spend whole nights at this without sleep. His discussions were concerned, in the main, with the current version of the theory of popular sovereignty, and he also talked of historical events of the Ch'ing dynasty, listing [episodes of] misgovernment and strongly advocating revolution. As for his views on learning, he excoriated pitilessly all the scholars from Hsün-tzu down to those of the Han, T'ang, Sung, Ming, and Ch'ing.

At that time, all the students lived in dormitories and had no contact with the outside world; the atmosphere within the school became more radical day by day, but the outside world had no way of knowing this. Then, when the new

year vacation arrived and the students went home, they showed their notes to relatives and friends, causing a great stir throughout the entire Hunan province.

Prior to this, T'an Ssu-t'ung, T'ang Ts'ai-ch'ang, and others had established a Reform Association of China for group discussions; they also published *Hsiang-pao* [*The Hunan Daily*] and *Hsiang hsüeh-pao* [*The Hunan Journal*] [published every ten days]. Although their writings were not so radical as those of [Liang's] school, these men were in fact secretly acting in concert with it. They also reprinted clandestinely the *Ming-i tai-fang lu* [Plan for the Prince], *Yang-chou shih-jih chi* [Record of Ten Days in Yang-chou], and other books, with editorial comments, for secret distribution as a means of disseminating revolutionary ideas. Their followers increased day by day and a bitter quarrel between the new and old parties of Hunan arose. Yeh Te-hui wrote *I-chiao ts'ung-pien* [Collected Works in Defence of Confucianism] which ran to several hundred thousand words of bitter, item-by-item refutation of K'ang Yu-wei's books, Liang's comments on [his students'] notes, and the various articles in the *Chinese Progress*, the *Hunan Daily*, and the *Hunan Journal*. Chang Chih-tung too wrote the *Ch'üan-hsüeh p'ien* [Exhortation to Learning] with more or less the same intent. Before the *coup d'état* of 1898, a certain censor memorialized the throne to impeach [Liang] by listing several tens of his comments on the [students'] notes, comments criticizing the Ch'ing ruling house and advocating popular sovereignty. This ultimately led to a large-scale inquisition which resulted in the death of T'an, the exile of Liang, the expulsion of T'ang and others, and the dissolution of the school. The academic conflict thus was enlarged to become a political one.

As Liang was living in exile in Japan, eleven of his students, including Li, Lin, and Ts'ai, left their homes to follow him. T'ang also traveled back and forth many times to plan a revolution with them, and after more than a year's [preparation], he started an uprising at Hankow; these eleven men returned [to China] one after another, and six of them died with him [in the attempt]. Liang too hurried back from America, but the rising had already failed when he reached Shanghai, and from that time on he once again devoted himself solely to the task of propaganda, publishing *Hsin-min ts'ung-pao* [New People's Periodical], *Hsin-hsiao-shuo* [New Works of Fiction], and other magazines to expound his [revolutionary] ideas and objectives. His countrymen vied eagerly [for an opportunity] to read them, and although the Ch'ing government strictly prohibited this, it could not be stopped. For each issue that appeared [in Japan], there were usually more than ten reprinted editions in China. The thinking of students for the past twenty years has been much influenced by them.

Liang never liked the ancient-style writing of the T'ung-ch'eng school. His own early writing had been modeled after that of Han, Wei, and Chin, and was quite cogent and skillful, but at this point he liberated himself from it, and made it a rule to be plain, easy, expressive, and fluent of communication. He interlarded his writings with colloquialisms, verses, and foreign expressions fairly frequently, letting his pen flow freely and without restraint. Scholars hastened to imitate his style and it became known as the New-Style Writing; however, the older generation were bitterly resentful of it and condemned it as heretical [lit., "a wild fox"]. Nevertheless, his style had a clear structure and the flow of his pen was often passionate, with a rare magical kind of power for the reader.

CONTRAST BETWEEN K'ANG AND LIANG

While Liang Ch'i-ch'ao daily espoused the revolutionary and republican cause against the Manchus, his teacher K'ang Yu-wei strongly disapproved of it, frequently reprimanding Liang and following this with tactful persuasion. In a period of two years his letters [to Liang] ran to several tens of thousands of words. Liang, on his part, had also become somewhat displeased with the work of the revolutionaries, and in a mood of precaution [lit., "once burned by hot soup, thereafter blowing upon even cold salad"] he slightly altered his stand. Nevertheless, his conservative instincts and his progressive instincts frequently fought against each other within himself whenever his emotions were aroused, and his views of one day often contradicted those of an earlier day. He once spoke thus of himself: "I do not mind criticizing myself of yesterday with myself of today." Since men generally considered this a shortcoming, the effectiveness of his words was often compromised. This [mercurial quality] was probably the result of an inherent weakness of character.

After thirty, Liang never again spoke of the "forged classics," nor did he refer very often to "institutional reforms." On the other hand, his teacher K'ang Yu-wei vigorously advocated the creation of a Confucian Association, the establishment of Confucianism as a state religion, and the worship of Confucius together with Heaven. He did not lack adherents in the nation, but Liang could not agree with him and several times rose to repudiate him as in the following words:

The intellectual world of our nation was never more illustrious, and its personages never greater, than at the time of the Warring States, and this was clearly a result of freedom of thought. When the First Emperor of Ch'in burned the works of the Hundred Schools [of philosophy], thought was stifled for the first time, and when the Han Emperor Wu apotheosized the Six Arts, suppressing the Hundred Schools, thought was stifled once more. Since the Han dynasty, it has been said that Confucianism has prevailed for over two thousand years, and yet the so-called "spirit of apotheosizing this man and deprecating that one" was persistently maintained. Consequently, there were disputes between the orthodox school of learning and the unorthodox and between the Modern Texts and the Ancient Texts. Those who were engaged in empirical research wrangled over the authenticity of interpretation, and those who discussed Human Nature and Rational Principle argued over the Proper Line of Orthodoxy. Each group considered itself the Confucian school, and rejected others as not Confucian. . . . Confucius was gradually metamorphosed into Tung Chung-shu (179?-104? B.C.) and Ho Hsiu (129-182); then into Ma Yung (79-166 A.D.) and Cheng Hsüan (127-200); then he became Han Yü (768-824) and Ou-yang Hsiu (1017-1072); again he became Ch'eng I (1033-1108) and Chu Hsi (1130-1200); then again he became Lu Hsiang-shan (1139-1193) and Wang Yang-ming (1472-1529); and still again he became Ku Yen-wu (1613-1682) and Tai Chen (1723-1777). This all happened because thinking was tied to one fixed point and could not break out into new directions. It was exactly like a band of monkeys, leaping and clutching at some fruit, or a group of old women struggling over a penny and cursing each other. What a pitiful situation it was! This was the result

achieved by the party for the preservation of the [Confucian] cult during the past two thousand years . . .[17]

Again Liang stated:

The advocates of the preservation of the [Confucian] cult today have identified themselves with the new learning and the new principles of modern times and say: "This Confucius already knew and that Confucius already said." . . . But they follow the new learning and the new principles not precisely because these latter are palatable to their minds but because these things secretly coincided with 'their' Confucius. Thus, what they love is still Confucius and not truth. If they search the *Four Books* and the *Six Classics* and still cannot find anything to identify themselves with, then they do not dare maintain [their own ideas], even if they clearly know it is the truth, and if other criticize their ideas as unConfucian, they do not dare not to relinquish them. Because of this, the truth can never be revealed to our countrymen. Therefore I despise the shoddy scholars who toy with words and are ever anxious to engraft Western learning upon Chinese learning under the pretext of introducing new things but who, in fact, want to preserve [the old ones]. They nurture a slavish spirit in the intellectual world.[18]

Liang went on to say:

Snatching single phrases and isolated passages from ancient works and identifying them with modern ideas will very easily produce two kinds of error: (1) It is fine as long as the ideas to be proved analogous correspond with each other in all respects, but if the analogy is forced even slightly, it will most probably lead our people into misconceptions, and explanation of new learning in terms of old sayings will only nurture the growth of errors. For example, not long ago when the advocates of a constitution and a republic happened to see a certain word or phrase in classical canon which was close to the ideas of "constitution" or "republic," they were always ready to fix on it with a self-congratulatory air, claiming these institutions as indigenous to us; whereas in fact the modern republican and constitutional institutions developed a mere one hundred years ago even in the West. It is impossible to find them in ancient Greece and Rome, let alone in our country! Also, when the analogous words have a wide currency, many people will be limited in their thinking to the words and phrases used in the analogy. They will come to regard the so-called 'constitution' and 'republic' as mere commonplaces and will no longer look for the true meaning [of such institutions themselves]. . . . This kind of habit, once formed, will very readily prove to be a devilish stumbling block to our people's pursuit of practical studies. (2) Persuading people to implement a certain institutional reform by telling them that our ancient philosophers did it in the past, and urging them to study a certain subject by telling them that our early philosophers studied it, is of course a relatively easy way of introducing [Western things]. Yet repeated pronouncements of this kind will lead people to suspect that any institutions not initiated by our early philosophers are impracticable and that the pursuit of any studies not engaged in by our ancient philosophers is inadvisable. Unwittingly, this [practice] often strengthens the tendencies toward prejudice and complacency, and blurs one's [power of] discernment necessary in selecting the right thing to follow. . . . I will never pick the tempting and luscious peach and plum blossoms of my next-door neighbor to set off the old trunks of fir and pine around my own house, thereby becoming elated and self-satified. If indeed I love peaches and plums, I should think of transplanting them. Why cause them to be confused with fir and pine in Name and Reality?[19]

Although these discussions were aimed at specific problems, they reveal briefly Liang's general appraisal of our country's traditional thought and his opinions on the proper way in which new thought should develop in the future.

The chronic trouble with Chinese thinking was its "tendency towards reliance on [ancient authority]" and its "confusion of [Name with Reality]." For instance, the introduction of Buddhist elements into Confucianism or the proneness to forge texts all originated in this kind of spirit, or take the case of Ch'ing scholars: Yen Yüan's (1635-1704) thinking was close to Mo-tzu's, and yet he felt impelled to claim Confucius as his source; Tai Chen's (1723-1777) thinking was entirely Western,[20] yet he felt obliged to state that he derived it from Confucius; K'ang Yu-wei's Universal Commonwealth was a creative masterpiece without precedent, yet he had to claim a Confucian origin for it. As to why Confucius had to use antiquity to justify his institutional reforms and why the various philosophers all relied upon antiquity, we scarcely need look beyond these [phrases] "reliance on [ancient authority]" and "confusion of [Name with Reality]." If the root of this disease is not eradicated, there can be no hope for the liberation and independence of thought. Liang tried to re-emphasize this point repeatedly. His opinions often disagreed with those of his teacher, hence the K'ang-Liang school split.

In intellectual circles, Liang's destructive force was far from negligible, while his constructive [contributions] are not evident. He was partly to blame for the superficiality and vulgarity of the late Ch'ing intellectual world. Nevertheless, he frequently quoted the Buddhist saying: "Before being able to save myself, I try to save others. This is the Bodhisattva's motivation." Thus he produced a great many works in the course of his life, for whatever he had to say he published it! He once spoke of himself: "By the time I had read as far as 'Human nature was originally good,' I was already teaching others about 'In the beginning of man.'"[21] He did not think of the fact that he had not mastered the passages after the phrase "By nature they are similar to one another," and possibly he did not even [completely] understand [the phrase] "In the beginning of man." Teaching in this way, how was it possible not to mislead men?[22]

Liang always maintained that all the doctrines of the world should have free entry [into China], and this was quite right. However, unless what were introduced bore authentic resemblance to the respective [schools] of thought and [unless they] contained their complete systems and features, they could not provide our countrymen with material for a well-founded study. This type of work cannot be carried on without a division of labor among a number of specialists.

Liang tended to be extensive and thus superficial, scarcely reaching the outer limits of [a field of] learning when he began to discuss and expound it. For this reason, there are many dubious generalizations in his writings, and in extreme cases there were outright errors. When he discovered this and attempted corrections, he had already lapsed into inconsistency. Nevertheless, speaking objectively and taking into account the isolation and moribundity of the intellectual world of twenty years ago, without this type of crude and wide-ranging approach the pioneer work of opening up new fields would not have been possible. From this point of view, Liang Ch'i-ch'ao may be considered the Ch'en She[23] of the new intellectual world. However, what his countrymen require and expect of him does not end here; with

his innate forcefulness and the qualifications accumulated over a thirty-year period, he ought to try his utmost to lay groundwork for our new intellectual world. If this man lives out his life in the present manner,[24] we cannot but say that it is a great loss insofar as Chinese cultural history is concerned.

The point of greatest contrast between Liang and K'ang is that the latter had too many fixed ideas and the former too few, and this was reflected in the ways they managed their affairs as well as in their methods of study. K'ang often said, "My knowledge was complete by the time I was thirty; from that point on I made no more progress, as indeed there was no need to advance." Liang was different, feeling always that his knowledge was still incomplete and worrying that it might never be complete. For several decades he wandered about seeking [knowledge] daily. Consequently K'ang's knowledge now can be discussed definitely, whereas Liang's cannot. Because Liang had too few convictions, he would often be carried away by events and abandon positions he had held. We can say quite definitely that he had less creative power than K'ang.

Liang had a burning "desire for knowledge" and a great variety of interests. Whenever he took up a task, he immersed himself in it and concentrated his energies on it at the expense of everything else; after some time he would move on to another task and discard the previous one. Thus, because he concentrated his energies [on one point], he often produced results, but because he drifted along and forsook his old [work], he could not go deeply [into any subject]. He once wrote this poem for his daughter Ling-hsien's *Diary in I-heng-kuan*: "The flaw in my learning is my love of extensiveness; therefore it is superficial and discursive. A still greater trouble is my lack of persistence; whatever I won I quickly lost. You may imitate me in a hundred things, but not in these two!" He may be said to have had the wit to know himself.

Although Liang realized his shortcomings, he did not try hard to correct them. Moreover, he was interrupted intermittently by frequent foolish political activities which sapped his energy and caused him to neglect his study. Knowledgeable men say that if Liang can leave politics forever and limit his thirst for knowledge by concentrating on one or two subjects, he will make even greater contributions to the intellectual world of the future. Otherwise he may just be the last representative of the intellectual history of the Ch'ing period.

Notes

For complete titles of citations, see Immanuel C. Y. IIsü (tr.), *Intellectual Trends in the Ch'ing Period* (Harvard University Press, 1959), Notes, pp. 129-42.

1. See Section 2, note 1, and Bodde, II, 8, 89, 106, 118.

2. For a discussion of the controversy over the Modern and Ancient Texts, cf. Levenson, *Liang Ch'i-ch'ao,* Appendix, "The Controversy over the Authenticity of the Confucian Classics," pp. 221-223, which draws largely from P. Pelliot, "Le Chou King en caractères anciens et le Chang Chou Che Wen," *Mémoires concernant l'Asie Orientale* (Paris, 1916), pp. 123-177.

3. Ho Hsiu, *Kung-yang chuan-chu tzu-hsü* [Commentary on the *Kung-yang Commentary,* Preface].

4. Ho Hsiu (129-182 A.D.) was a great classical scholar of the Eastern Han period. His commentary on the *Kung-yang Commentary* on the *Spring and Autumn Annals,* which attaches to it an esoteric meaning, has been accepted as a standard work over the centuries. Cf. Woo Kang, *Les trois théories politiques du Tch'ouen, Ts'ieou, interprétées par Tong Tchong-chou (Tung Chung-shu) d'après les*

principes de l'école de Kong-yang (Paris, 1932).

5. The "Three Epochs" and "Three Periods of Unity" are explained in the next section. The phrase "relegating the Chou Dynasty and entrusting the kingship to Lu" means that the Chou Dynasty had become too decadent to deserve the kingship, which should pass to Lu, the state of the Duke of Chou and Confucius. The phrase "receiving the Mandate to reform institutions" means that Confucius had actually received the Mandate from Heaven "to correct the faults of the decadent Chou dynasty and establish the institutions of a new king and dynasty." Since only a king can receive the Mandate of Heaven, Confucius was canonized by the Modern Text School as the *su-wang,* uncrowned king. Cf. Bodde, II, 71 ff.; Liu Feng-lu, *Ch'un-ch'iu Kung-yang ching-chuan Ho-shih shih-li,* in Juan Yuan, ed., *Huang-Ch'ing ching-chieh* [Exegesis of the Classics in the Imperial Ch'ing Period], *chüan* 1285, p. 1.

6. *Shih ku-wei,* "Ch'i Lu Han Mao i-t'ung lun," *chung* [The Ancient Hidden Meaning of the *Odes,* "On the Similarities and Differences of the Ch'i, Lu, Han, and Mao Schools of Odes," middle section].

7. *Shih ku-wei,* "Fu-tzu cheng-yüeh lun" [The Ancient Hidden Meaning of the *Odes,* "On the Master Rectifying Music"], upper section.

8. Not published.

9. In some versions, the phrase "pressured and bribed" is omitted.

10. *Po-shih* was an official title in the Han period, literally, "erudite scholar." In modern Chinese, *po-shih* denotes the holder of a doctoral degree.

11. It is interesting to note that all the reforms in China before K'ang were reforms within the Confucian framework, whereas K'ang wanted to introduce reform after the fashion of Japan's Meiji Restoration and Russia's westernization by Peter the Great. His attempts led to the *coup d'état* of 1898.

12. Here the word "nature" means "the nature of man and things," and not the "naturalistic world" as understood in the West. Neo-Confucianists spent much time contemplating the nature of bamboo trees.

13. A chapter of the *Book of Rites.*

14. Translation taken from James Legge, *The Sacred Books of China,* Part III, *The Li Ki* (Oxford, 1885), pp. 364-366.

15. This is a Chinese expression for "dis-

order," "calamity," and perhaps even the "state of nature."

16. Actually 1200-1300 scholars.

17. *Hsin-min ts'ung-pao* [New People's Periodical], 1902.

18. *Ibid.*

19. *Kuo-feng pao* [Kuo-feng Newspaper], 1915.

20. This is an overstatement.

21. These phrases are the opening passages of the famous primer for Chinese children, *San-tzu-ching*, the Three-Character-Classic or Trimetrical Classic, composed by Wang Ying-lin (1223-1296), "arranged in 356 alternately rhyming lines of three characters to each, and containing about 500 different characters in all." See Herbert A. Giles' translation: *San Tzu-ching (Elementary Chinese)* (2nd ed.; Shanghai, 1910). Mr. Giles' translation of the opening passages, below, is less literal than mine:

Jen chih ch'u	Men at their birth
Hsing pen shan	are naturally good.
Hsing hsiang chin	Their natures are much the same.
Hsi hsiang yüan	Their habits become widely different.

22. What Liang probably meant to say was: before he himself had mastered a subject in full he already began to teach it to others.

23. Better known as Ch'en Sheng (d. 209 B.C.), who, together with Wu Kuang, rebelled against the Ch'in state. Though supported by a large following, he did not ultimately succeed in overthrowing the Ch'in.

24. Liang's life was marked by frequent excursions into politics, as well as lack of persistence and depth in literary pursuit.

II. THE "HUNDRED-DAY" REFORM

20. WENG T'UNG-HO AND THE REFORM MOVEMENT OF 1898

KUNG-CHUAN HSIAO

INTRODUCTION

This study is undertaken on the assumption that an important development such as the reform movement of 1898 cannot be adequately understood without a knowledge of the historical circumstances under which it arose, and that a convenient way to gain this knowledge is to take a crucial figure of the time as the center of reference and to trace therefrom the pertinent forces and influences that bore on the situation.

That Weng T'ung-ho serves our purpose admirably can be readily seen. As Emperor Te-tsung's tutor for over two decades, Weng had played a decisive role in shaping the mind of the youthful ruler; and later, as one of the active high officials in Peking, he enjoyed the emperor's confidence for a number of years up to the time of his abrupt dismissal in the spring of 1898. Moreover, for about thirty years Weng also had the confidence of the Empress Dowager Tz'u-hsi who, in addition to giving him a number

From *Tsing Hua Journal of Chinese Studies*, New Series I, No. 2, April 1957, pp. 111-98, Footnotes have been omitted. Reprinted by permission of the author, who is professor of Chinese history, emeritus, The Far Eastern and Russian Institute, University of Washington.

This article represents part of the results of research done by the writer in connection with the Modern Chinese History Project, in The Far Eastern and Russian Institute, University of Washington.

of notable assignments, twice appointed him to serve as imperial tutor and entrusted him with the task of helping to make momentous decisions during the troubled days of 1880, when the Sino-Russian treaty negotiations were in progress. Between 1886 and 1898 he rose to great official eminence, holding the posts of the president of the Board of Revenue, grand councillor, member of Tsungli yamen, and associate grand secretary. He was thus in a position to exert considerable influence on important policies of the empire, if not actually to determine them. He was politically important in another way. As one of the two leaders of the so-called southern party among the officials in Peking, he constituted a focal point of high-level factional and personal rivalries that prevailed in the closing decades of the dynasty. A knowledge of Weng's attitudes, activities, and personal relations, therefore, particularly those which he displayed in the 1890's, should serve as a useful introduction to a study of the reform movement of 1898.

The evidence to be presented here, it is hoped, will justify the following tentative conclusions: (1) that the reform movement of 1898 did not materialize merely because a number of well-intentioned and well-informed persons wished to save the empire from destruction, but was brought about by a complex of divergent human motives and various institutional forces; (2) that the movement was, consequently, supported or opposed by men not simply because they were "conservative" or "progressive" in their outlooks but also because they felt that reform would have been conducive or detrimental to their immediate interests; (3) that the movement did not produce the results which its supporters desired, not merely because it met with strong opposition from "conservatives"—those who opposed reform out of personal conviction together with those who wished to preserve their vested interests—but also because it called forth serious objections from persons who refused to go beyond a certain limit in reforming the existing state of affairs; that, in other words, the movement faced insurmountable difficulties because it met opposition from the "moderates" as well as from the "conservatives"; (4) that the advocates of moderate reform in the 1890's, including Weng T'ung-ho, represented the general trend which began in the 1860's, and continued down to the end of the dynasty, whereas K'ang Yu-wei's program constituted a departure from this general trend and that, therefore, the *coup d'état* of 1898 did away with K'ang's program without terminating this trend; (5) that the historical circumstances being such, the reform movement of 1898 could not have saved the tottering dynasty, even if it had been carried out in accordance with the wishes of Weng T'ung-ho and other moderates.

To some extent Weng was a controversial figure. His contemporaries and historians of later times did not hold the same view of him. He was, for instance, sometimes regarded as a promoter of reform but, at other times, identified simply as a conservative. Recent scholars have dealt with some of the divergent interpretations and varying accounts of the man and his historic role. Further inquiries into the matter, however, may still be useful. The present writer makes no pretense to originality but proposes to trace, with special attention to details, some of the promising trails already marked out, hoping thus to present a more or less coherent view of the total situation.

Weng T'ung-ho's monumental diary, reproduced in facsimile in forty volumes, constitutes the most important single source of first-hand information. It may not be a completely accurate or faithful record of events; it certainly does not give all the information that a historian wishes to have. There is no reason, however, to question its general reliability. Assuming that some alterations were made in it by its author, these do not appear to have been extensive. Of course, Weng's diary, like other contemporary writings, such as those of K'ang Yu-wei and Liang Ch'i-ch'ao, must be used with discretion. Allowances must be made for partisan prejudices, personal predilections, and the common failings of human memory. Different accounts must be compared and weighed against the known facts. When these and other precautions are taken, the diary and other pertinent works of the period should furnish much of the vital information necessary for drawing valid conclusions. As, however, a number of sources has not been available to the present writer, the conclusions which will be offered here can be no more than tentative.

I. WENG T'UNG-HO'S INTELLECTUAL OUTLOOK AND PERSONAL ATTITUDES

Weng T'ung-ho was characterized by

some historians in these interesting words:

T'ung-ho served as imperial tutor for a long time and took part in conducting the affairs of state. He sought to make his views prevail on every matter and often fell into disputes with those who were close to him. Many criticized him for presuming on power. In his last years he suffered slander and defamation, and almost met with unfathomable calamity. He died eventually in exile.

This judgment of Weng can hardly be taken as complimentary. A careful reading of his diary, especially those portions which he wrote in the early years of his career, leads one to think that he had given some ground for such a judgment. Unwittingly, in recording some of his most intimate thoughts and sentiments Weng revealed himself as an ambitious official, anxious to "forge ahead" in his career, as well as a serious-minded scholar deeply concerned about the affairs of the troubled empire.

An entry in his diary made on the Chinese New Year's eve, when he was thirty-two *sui* and had passed the examinations for the *chin-shih* only six years before, is particularly revealing:

Sat quietly late in the night; the sound of fire-crackers was very sparse. An insignificant, tiny creature [in the official world], I turned my thought upward to our recently demised emperor, now beyond the fleecy clouds and separated [from his servants], and downward to the conflagration and deluge in the southeastern part [of the empire]—a hundred emotions filled my breast. . . . I made a resolution: to direct my efforts to [the cultivation of] my mind and my personality. For only when all thoughts concerning wealth, honor, advantages, and promotion are completely swept clean, shall I be able to bear true responsibilities and to perceive the true principles.

Two years later, he wrote this on the Chinese New Year's day:

Considering that grey hair begins to show on my head and that enduring fame has not been established, I shall strive hereafter to regard this as my first task: to show sincerity and to do away with all that is vain and false.

When, however, he advanced to the position of a vice-president of the Board of Revenue ten years later, he became confident of his success in officialdom and promptly took steps to prepare himself for the day when further promotion would bring to him the coveted privilege of "riding a horse in the Forbidden City." Thus he confessed in 1876 that he practiced horsemanship partly to attain speed in going about and partly to help cure an ailment, but "actually the purpose lies elsewhere." Barely two years had passed when the anticipated imperial favor came through. Another seemingly unimportant behavior also gives a clue to Weng's ruling passion. He took pains to narrate every bit of consideration or honor shown him by the imperial rulers. On many occasions he described the details of imperial banquets which he was commanded to attend, including the arrangements of the seats, the "guests" present, and the particular seats assigned to him and his colleagues.

When national or personal interests were at stake, Weng often resorted to superstitious practices, just as many of his fellow countrymen were accustomed to do. For instance, he interpreted a divinatory piece circulating in 1871 in some parts of south China as ominously suggestive of the invasion of the empire by foreigners and was greatly disturbed by it. On many occasions he interpreted awesome natural phenomena as omens of impending misfortune. In one instance, when his concubine fell seriously ill, he personally went to a temple of the "god of war" in Peking and resorted to divination. As late as in 1894, when the peace treaty with Japan was in the process of negotiation, he interpreted a dream of his as portending "submissiveness to the barbarians."

Weng's everyday behavior, therefore, did not differ in any appreciable way from that of the average ambitious, serious-minded scholar-official of his time. The same may be said of his intellectual outlook. Like virtually all of his fellow scholar-officials Weng was thoroughly steeped in the Confucian tradition as it was generally accepted. He did not, however, consistently follow the doctrines of Ch'eng-Chu school which was the brand of neo-Confucianism upheld by the imperial government and was represented in his time by a number of high officials in Peking, especially by Wo-jen and Hsü T'ung. For a while Weng was interested in the rival Lu-Wang school, although soon afterwards he also became appreciative of the doctrines of Chu Hsi. His eclectic attitude later persuaded him to subscribe to the tenets of Li Kung, one of the most outspoken and influential critics of neo-Confucianism.

Perhaps it was partly due to the influence of Li Kung who stressed the importance of active engagement to the practical affairs of the world in opposition to the study of the theoretical problems of "reason" and "nature" as posed by the Ch'eng-Chu school, that Weng began to take serious interest in the affairs of the empire. Previously, Weng hardly took notice of the wars with England and France. He merely recorded in his diary that "barbarian troops" invaded the imperial capital, and continued calmly to pursue his scholarly routine, including composing poems and practicing calligraphy, as if nothing of importance had happened to the empire. He showed a similar lack of concern when the imperial government was engaged in a mortal struggle with the T'ai'p'ing and Nien rebellions. As late as in 1862 he appeared to have been still leading the leisurely life of the average scholar-official. By 1870, two years after he expressed his admiration for Li Kung, however, he had begun to show serious concern for the troubled affairs of the empire. Thus, when he heard of the news that mobs in Tientsin murdered the French consul and destroyed missionary churches, he spent a sleepless night in speculating about the consequences of the incident. He was equally concerned about the Korean situation in 1871. Five years later, when he was a vice-president of the Board of Revenue, he studied books that had direct bearing on the economic affairs of the empire. In 1888, then a president of the same Board, he formulated his basic financial policies, namely, "a surplus of ten million taels in the imperial coffers; complete replacement of the regulation cash (coins) in the imperial capital, and full collection of the land and grain taxes in the whole empire." Increased administrative responsibilities, reinforced by Li Kung's intellectual influence, had obviously transformed Weng into a full-fledged man of affairs.

Weng's attitude toward foreigners and foreign policy also underwent changes during his long official career. Essentially a "self-righteous patriot," he placed China above all countries and regarded conciliatory policies toward foreign powers as decidedly shameful. He condemned foreign religions, especially the Catholic, describing the converts in Peking as "jackals and wolves that infested the capitol." He did not conceal his disapproval of Tseng Kuo-fan's conciliatory approach to the Tientsin incident of 1870. His increased interest in the practical affairs of the empire did not bring about any basic change in his anti-foreign attitude. In fact, as late as in 1891 (then a president of Board), he spoke of the anti-foreign riots in various localities of Kiangsu and Anhwei as expressions of "popular indignation," although he was not unaware of their adverse effects on imperial peace. Even in 1900 the news of the Boxer uprising and the occupation of Peking by foreign troops aroused in him more resentment against the intruding "barbarian soldiers" (*i ping*) and the "foreign barbarians" (*wai i*) than against those who misled the empress dowager into the calamitous blunder. His profound contempt for foreigners is best illustrated by a remark which he made in the 1880's. As a member of high officialdom he attended the New Year reception in the Tsungli yamen where the diplomatic corps went to extend their greetings. Weng wrote in his diary that the Western diplomats whom he met there were no better than "a confused flock of geese and ducks." He gave vent to his detestation of foreigners again in 1891 when, as a member of Tsungli yamen, he was present at the sessions in which Li Hung-chang took a leading part in negotiating with the British and French ministers concerning mining and railway construction. He was irritated by the demands of these diplomats and described them as "greedy like wolves and stubborn like goats—truly not of our own kind!" and his meeting with them as tantamount to "associating with dogs and swine—a misfortune in a man's life." As it is well known, Weng's anti-foreign attitude did not remain an idle sentiment. It was translated into action when he urged

war against Japan in 1894, vehemently opposed the ceding of Formosa, and wept bitterly when he realized that his views could not prevail.

Weng, however, did not consistently maintain this hostile attitude. A significant charge occurred in 1880. During the tortuous days of negotiating the treaty with Russia, Weng sided with Prince Kung, against Prince Ch'un and Hsü T'ung who favored war, arguing that "to negotiate peace after waging war would be more disastrous than to maintain peace." Again, in 1883, when the imperial court was making decisions concerning the dispute with France over Yueh-nan, Weng showed a remarkably cautious attitude. "Many claimed," he said, "that our wishes could be fulfilled by sending troops into Yüeh-nan. Why don't these people appraise our own strength?" An even more significant departure came in 1897, in connection with the negotiations with the German minister to settle the Shantung incident. After receiving reports that German warships had entered Kiaochow Bay, Weng issued two telegrams under the emperor's name, instructing the governor of Shantung not to fire the first shot, and the Chinese minister at Berlin to negotiate with the German government. Another telegram sent the following day instructed the governor again "not to speak lightly of war thus bringing calamity to the empire." That Weng was chiefly, if not solely, responsible for this conciliatory policy may be inferred from the fact that he was authorized to negotiate with the German minister in Peking and that Li Hung-chang was not even informed of this matter, although Li was on hand in Tsungli yamen on the same day. Commenting on the terms of settlement which Weng with the assistance of Chang Yin-huan negotiated with the German minister,

Weng said, "I really could not bear to let these words [of concession] come from my mouth; but I wished to avert a great disaster and had to stoop and compromise."

A question naturally arises. Why did Weng change his anti-foreign attitude in 1880 and 1897 in dealing with Russia and Germany?

An obvious explanation is that as Weng came into more and closer contact with Westerners and as he gained more knowledge of Western countries, he was able to take a more "realistic" view concerning foreign affairs. Moreover, when he himself was sharing the direct responsibility of making important decisions, he realized that it was never wise to be rash in dealing with foreign powers. This explanation, however, may be valid without being adequate. It does not satisfactorily explain the fact that many years after 1880 Weng aligned with "the war party" and precipitated the conflict with Japan. It also fails to account for Weng's deliberate exclusion of Li Hung-chang in 1897, a man who was the most experienced in international negotiations, a past master of settlement by concessions, and one most likely to be helpful in the situation. That Li Hung-chang was kept out of the matter and was resentful for being excluded may be gathered from Weng's admission that the preliminary results of negotiations which Weng so laboriously achieved were virtually sabotaged later by Li.

One is naturally led to seek an additional explanation in Weng's involvement in the factional strifes and personal rivalries that prevailed in Peking. His conciliatory attitude toward Russia in 1880 may have been prompted by his desire to place himself in Prince Kung's favor and, at the same time, to frustrate his political rival, Hsü T'ung. We have no direct evidence to support this conjecture, but the general circumstances (with which we shall deal at some length in a later section) lent plausibility to it. Weng's action in 1897, however, can be more definitely traced to the well-known enmity between Weng and Li Hung-chang. The Sino-Japanese war left Li a discredited man, a target of much scholar-official criticism. His official career might have been abruptly ended but for the protecting hand of the empress dowager. Assuming that Weng had the ambition of eventually replacing Li as the most influential official in Peking, the years that immediately followed 1895 would have seemed to Weng the most opportune time for realizing this ambition. One of the best ways to retire Li was to make him no longer indispensable in the service for which he was famous, namely, conducting foreign affairs. It is conceivable that Weng, using the Shantung incident of 1897, tried to steal the diplomatic thunder from Li. Unluckily for Weng, however, he got his fingers badly burned, despite the assistance of Chang Yin-huan who had more knowledge of foreign affairs than Weng. To Weng's chagrin, Li Hung-chang was eventually called upon to clear away the diplomatic mess which resulted from Weng's bungling hand.

It appears, therefore, despite Weng's basically anti-foreign sentiments, he did not maintain a consistent attitude toward foreign affairs but shifted his stand as the immediate situations dictated. He allowed personal considerations to guide his judgment and made decisions not always on the basis of imperial interest. He was, in other words, as much a calculating politician as a sentimental patriot.

The same may be broadly said of his attitude toward reform. Similiar motivations prompted his actions, and changing circumstances swayed his views and attitudes, with the result that at one time he took active interest in reform but at another time he worked against it, so much so that he could not be characterized as "conservative" or "progressive" with any degree of accuracy.

In a certain sense Weng may be regarded as a conservative, namely, as a man determined to conserve the traditional values of imperial China and resolutely opposed Westernization. Being a product of the age-long scholar-official tradition he naturally had no wish to alter China's cultural and institutional system. This explains the fact that he paid no attention to *yang-wu*, "foreign affairs," until 1875, even then he remained unreconciled to the idea that the empire could be benefited by the adoption of "Western methods" as leaders of the "self-strengthening" movement had been advocating since the 1860's. He maintained such a "conservative" attitude as late as in 1888, as the following words which he wrote on the Chinese New Year's eve clearly indicate:

Earthquakes occurred in the fifth moon of this year, a flood in the Western Hills came in the seventh moon, and a fire broke out in the T'ai-ho Gate—all these were premonitions [of evil] revealed through natural phenomena. . . . Moreover, steamboats ply the Lake [in the Summer Palace], a railway runs through the Forbidden City, and, in addition, noisy discussions concerning the construction of railways were heard in the imperial court. The views of the princes begin to change [from disapproval to acceptance of the innovations] and the proposals made by Pei-yang still stand. A survey of the current situation saddens my heart. As a high official can I not but be ashamed and feel remorse [for not being able to remedy the situation]?

There is nothing to distinguish these sentiments from those entertained by the most extreme conservatives. The "proposals made by Pei-yang" Weng mentioned came from Li Hung-chang who wished to see a railway built between Tientsin and T'ung Chou (near Peking). Weng raised strong objections to Li's proposals; he likewise opposed Chang Chih-tung's alternative recommendation that a line be constructed in "the interior" (i.e., between Hankow and Lu-kou-ch'-iao) in lieu of the line suggested by Li. Weng's arguments echoed those of the diehards of the 1860's and 1870's, who brought much frustration to Tseng Kuo-fan and Li Hung-chang.

Strangely, however, Weng exhibited a dramatic change of attitude toward *yang-wu* at about the same time. The sixteen books on "Western learning" (translated under the supervision of Robert Hart) which Tseng Kuo-ch'üan presented to Weng in 1887, probably exerted considerable influence on Weng's thinking. It appears that Weng was soon converted to the cause of reform and undertook to initiate the young emperor into it. In 1889, shortly after he wrote the disheartening passage quoted above, he went with Sun Chia-nai, in their capacity as imperial tutors, to offer New Year's greetings to their pupil and took the occasion to submit to him this important advice: that "it is unnecessary to apply all the methods of government formulated by the sages of the past." On the next day Weng presented to the emperor a copy of Feng Kuei-fen's *Chiao-pin-lu k'ang-i*, a collection of essays on reform. About a month later, Weng brought this book to the attention of the empress dowager also. He wrote in his diary (February 23, 1889):

Favored by the empress dowager and the emperor with an audience. . . . [After other matters were discussed] *yang-wu* came up; replied: "This is the first urgent task which the emperor ought to study. Feng Kuei-fen's *K'ang-i,* a copy of which your servant had presented the other day, is useful in this very connection. . . . Then the railway [question] came up. Strongly asserted that the Tientsin–T'ung Chou [line proposed by Li Hung-chaug] should not be built. . . . As to [Chang Chih-tung's suggestion to build a line in] the interior, it is merely to seek profit; what has it to do with any farsighted plan?"

In the winter of the same year Weng wrote again in his diary concerning Feng's *K'ang-i:*

Went to the [emperor's] study. . . . Read the *K'ang-i.* I said yesterday that this book is most pertinent to current affairs [and suggested that the emperor] select several essays [from the book for special study]. . . . Today his majesty had the six essays which he selected bound in one volume. . . . This is sufficient indication that [the emperor] is giving his attention to the study [of this book]—gratifying indeed!

It may be recalled that Feng Kuei-fen, one of the most outstanding advocates of reform prior to 1898, wrote the *K'ang-i* around 1860. In addition to urging fairly extensive administrative reform (in particular fiscal and economic reform) and changes in the examination-school system, Feng stressed the necessity of adopting what he called "Western learning," manufacturing "foreign implements," and acquiring the knowledge and technique of dealing with "the barbarians." Feng made it clear, however, that "Western learning" should merely supplement but not replace "the moral principles and ethical teachings of China" which should remain the foundation of imperial reconstruction. Feng's book was widely acclaimed as the most judicious and pertinent work on reform; it may have actually sowed the seed of reform thirty

years before 1898, as some writers were inclined to think. There can be little doubt that in presenting this book to the emperor, Weng had taken the first step to indoctrinate his pupil in what he regarded as the correct ideas of reform. By 1889, therefore, Weng had ceased to be a conservative, in the sense that Hsü T'ung or Hsü Ying-k'uei were said to have been.

It appears strange that Weng showed so much antagonism to the railway proposals of Li Hung-chang and Chang Chih-tung—proposals that were definitely in line with modernization and would have been acceptable to men like Feng Kuei-fen—at the same time when he undertook to acquaint the emperor with Feng's *K'ang-i.* Weng's behavior is particularly difficult to understand when we recall that his arguments against the railway proposals ran directly contrary to the substance as well as spirit of the *K'ang-i.* The explanation lies perhaps again in the perennial rivalry between Weng on the one side and Li and Chang on the other side. It is highly probable that just as Weng tried in 1897 to wrest from Li his leadership in conducting the foreign affairs of the empire, he tried to wrest leadership in modernization from Li and Chang in 1889, by hamstringing their efforts in order to leave more room for himself later to assume such leadership.

As a matter of fact, Weng's behavior in later years indicates that he continued to play a two-faced role: to promote and support reform on his own and at the same time to frustrate modernizing undertakings sponsored by his political opponents. Between 1889 and the early days of 1898 Weng increasingly became identified with the cause of reform. In addition to the intellectual influences exerted on him by the sixteen books which Tseng Kuo-ch'üan gave him in 1887 and by Feng Kuei-fen's *K'ang-i* (and a few other works to which we shall refer later), the defeat of 1894 deepened his conviction that the empire could be saved only by timely reform. He completely reversed his stand concerning railway construction in 1895. He joined Prince Kung and others in authorizing railways, Western-style military drill, and modern military schools for Banner soldiers. He received the appointment as director of T'ung-wen College with unconcealed satisfaction and immediately declared his resolve to make that institution a prosperous and efficient one. His active interest in reform became known to many. Chang Chih-tung who himself was actively engaged in modernization on a provincial level, acknowledged Weng as a promoter of reform. In a letter to Weng written in October 1895 Chang said:

Your excellency . . . resolutely leads the world with great counsels of reconstructing [the empire] and repelling [foreign aggressors]. Within [the imperial court] plans attending to what is fundamental are set in motion, while outside [the court] methods of reform are applied. Whatever direction you care to issue to me will be followed with sincere efforts.

Allowance should of course be made for overgenerosity in lip-service customarily practiced by Chinese officials on their colleagues and superiors. It is nevertheless certain that Chang Chih-tung could not have credited Weng with actions which the latter did not actually take. Other writers of the time generally corroborated Chang's view of Weng. For instance, Fei Hsing-chien, a man who had firsthand information, testified to Weng's active role in promoting reform, and Richard Timothy who discussed matters personally with Weng on more than one occasion, stated that Weng was in full sympathy with "the reform party."

Meanwhile, as Weng moved rapidly along the road to reform between 1889 and 1895, he continued to stymie the efforts of Li Hung-chang and Chang Chih-tung, two high-ranking officials who, by virtue of their prestige and knowledge, could challenge Weng's leadership in reform. Chang Chih-tung, who was at the time more actively engaged in modernization than Li, seems to have received the most attention from Weng. In a short work allegedly written by Chang's students but actually by Chang himself it is said:

Between 1889 and 1890 [when Chang was governor-general of Liang-Kuang], a certain president of the Board of Revenue in high central officialdom was determined to make trouble [for Chang]. Every matter drew from him questioning or censure, regardless of fact or reason. Practically each one of the administrative measures of Kwangtung province was reversed or contradicted; each word or sentence in the dispatches sent [from Kwangtung] was subject to minute scrutiny with a view to finding fault.

The "certain president of the Board of Revenue" was none other than Weng T'ung-ho who held that post since 1886 for twelve consecutive years. 1889 and 1890 were the same years in which Chang proposed or undertook a considerable number of modernizing measures in Kwangtung, including the establishment of an arsenal, a mint, a textile factory, an iron foundry, and a naval school—the same years when Weng was earnestly indoctrinating the emperor with Feng Kuei-fen's essays on reform. The contrast between Chang Chih-tung's letter and this statement is indeed glaring.

It may be argued that the letter was written in 1895 when Weng's attitude toward reform had become much more positive than in 1889. The difference in Weng's attitude toward Chang may therefore be explained by a change of convictions on Weng's part. There is, however, some ground for suspecting that during these years Weng had been consistently trying to frustrate Chang and that Weng continued to do so as late as in 1897. In fact, the rivalry between the two men became so patent that it may have induced enemies of Weng to enlist Chang's help to sidetrack the reform movement which Weng undertook to foster. A curious episode in Chang's career deserves notice. After serving at Wuchang for about five years during which time Chang proposed and inaugurated an even larger number of modern enterprises than he did at Canton, he was transferred late in the autumn of 1894 to Nanking as acting governor-general of Liang-Chiang to cope with the situation created by the Sino-Japanese war. In addition to carrying out his mission creditably he pursued with unabated speed the same program of modernization in the region now under his jurisdiction; in fact, he extended his program after the end of the war to include measures that paralleled many of Feng Kuei-fen's suggestions. Chang was, however, not allowed to remain in Nanking long. Liu K'un-i, the original incumbent, was ordered to resume his post, and Chang returned to his own post at Wuchang in 1897. He resumed his modernizing program there. Then, in the spring of 1898, the curious episode occurred. He was summoned to an imperial audience for the purpose of being consulted on some unspecified matter. When he arrived at Shanghai on his way to Peking, however, he was instructed to return to Wuchang, to take care of an anti-foreign incident in Shashi, Hupeh; he was to appear for the audience after the incident was settled. The incident was speedily settled, but the audience never took place.

Su Chi-tsu, a contemporary of Chang, offered an explanation for this rather strange action of the imperial court:

> Governor-general Chang . . . had been singled out for imperial attention for a long time. Even greater confidence was placed in him since he acted as governor-general of Liang-Chiang in *chia-wu* year [1894. The imperial rulers] wished to call him in to assist the administration, but he was prevented [from serving in Peking] by Weng T'ung-ho and Sun Yu-wen . . . In the present spring, after the emperor had resolved to carry out reforms, he summoned Chang to come to the capital, to assist him in the task of reform. Conservative high officials, afraid that Chang would prove incompatible with themselves, resorted to every available means to prevent him [from gaining access to the emperor]. They used the missionary incident of Shashi as a pretext to send Chang back to his post.

This explanation contains two interesting points. First, that between 1894 and 1898 Weng T'ung-ho undertook to prevent Chang from being admitted into the inner circle of central officialdom, and second, that it was "conservative high officials" who spoiled Chang's chance again in 1898. As we shall see presently, both points come near to the actual facts.

Weng T'ung-ho gave an apparently different version of this episode. He made a total of eight entries concerning it in his diary, the first of which, dated KH 24/interc. 3/2, reads as follows:

> Two telegraph-edicts: one in reply to governor-general in Kwangtung . . .; the other ordering governor-general of Hu-

Kuang [i.e., Chang Chih-tung] to come to the capital for imperial audience,—complying with the request of Hsü T'ung. [Hsü's memorial] was submitted to the empress dowager; such is her majesty's wish.

As it is generally recognized, Hsü T'ung was one of the arch conservatives of the time, sometimes identified as a leader of the so-called "northern party" and therefore a political enemy of Weng. The third entry in Weng's diary, written nine days later, is also noteworthy:

One telegram: Chang Chih-tung memorialized that he will not be able to begin his journey [to Peking] until over ten days later; he requested that the matter on which he is to be consulted be made known to him [beforehand].

The remaining six entries concerning the episode indicate in very brief terms the contents of the telegrams exchanged between the central and provincial authorities concerning the Shashi incident, the unrest along the Yangtze Valley, and Chang's return to Wuchang.

According to Weng, it was Hsü T'ung who initiated the move to bring Chang Chih-tung to Peking and the empress dowager who approved of the move. There is no reason to question Weng's veracity here; it is difficult to find a motive on his part to attribute to Hsü T'ung a move which he did not make. Moreover, Weng was in a position to know the facts.

The question is, why did Hsü T'ung, a confirmed hater of innovations and "foreign ways," undertake to bring Chang to Peking?

A recent writer suggested that Hsü T'ung's move was intended to undermine Weng T'ung-ho by bringing one of his major political opponents to the capital. This seems to be a correct surmise, but it does not explain why Chang Chih-tung was made use of for this purpose. From what is known of the situation at the time, it can be safely inferred that Hsü T'ung chose Chang because the latter, as a recognized leader of moderate reform, promised to be the most suitable man to counteract Weng's influence on the emperor and to divert into a different channel the reform movement which Weng helped materially to launch. By calling Chang to the emperor's side there was a chance to install him as his majesty's mentor of reform, replacing at once Weng T'ung-ho and K'ang Yu-wei.

It may be recalled that largely thanks to Weng T'ung-ho's recommendation (a matter which will be examined in detail at a more appropriate place later) K'ang Yu-wei came into the confidence of the emperor and persuaded the latter to adopt a reform program which thoroughly alarmed those who were opposed to "altering the house rules of the ancestors." Two courses of action were open to these men who understandably desired to put a stop to such a development. Some of them offered direct opposition to reform, while others tried to deflect it, but substituting changes of a less drastic and, from their point of view, less objectionable type. Hsü T'ung may have been one of those who were persuaded that the second course was tactically more advantageous than the first. Now, Chang Chih-tung had recently severed his short-lived cordial relation with K'ang Yu-wei. As a matter of fact, his *Ch'üan-hsüeh p'ien* ("Exhortation to Learning") was written for the express purpose of refuting K'ang's reform views and of stating Chang's own theory of moderate reform. Chang was emphatic in affirming the superiority of China's moral tradition and in reiterating that

"Western learning" should merely supplement but not modify "Chinese learning." To the diehards, therefore, Chang's brand of reform was a lesser evil than K'ang Yu-wei's. This may have constituted one of the reasons for Hsü T'ung's choice. Li Hung-chang, as a veteran leader of the self-strengthening movement, was of course eminently qualified to guide the emperor to travel the road of limited reform. Unfortunately, however, Li was discredited since 1895, while Chang was not similarly "tainted" (in fact, Chang was one of those who loudly criticized Li's performance in 1895).

The "audience episode," therefore, appears to have resulted from the convergence of two struggles: the personal strife between Weng and his political enemies, and the conflict among officials holding different views concerning reform. The fact that Chang Chih-tung demanded to be informed of the precise nature of the matter on which his counsel was desired, suggests that he was wary of the action taken by the imperial government. Important provincial officials, it is well known, were accustomed to installing confidential "correspondents" in Peking to keep themselves informed of the doings and intrigues at the imperial court. Chang undoubtedly had such agents; it is likely that he had an inkling of the political background of the summons to audience. He might not be averse to undermining Weng T'ung-ho and K'ang Yu-wei, but it is doubtful that he thought it prudent to involve himself in one of the major factional strifes in Peking, particularly when ultra conservatives who were actually his own enemies, were "pulling the strings." He could not refuse to comply with the imperial order, but he bade his time, purposely delaying his trip for about two weeks. The Shashi incident gave an excuse to those who did not wish to see Chang in Peking, for ordering him to postpone the trip. If Weng T'ung-ho did not actually make use of this excuse, he would certainly have welcomed the postponement. Su Chi-tsu's explanation, quoted a moment ago, is after all not contradicted by Weng's seemingly divergent account but is in reality corroborated by it, especially if we think of Weng as one of the "conservative high officials" (in the sense that he persistently opposed Chang's modernizing enterprises).

The supposition that Chang Chih-tung was regarded by some as an effective agent to undermine Weng' influence on the emperor receives an indirect confirmation by the action of another anti-reform official. The day after the telegraph-edict summoning Chang to audience was issued, Yü Yin-lin, provincial treasurer of Anhwei, submitted a "memorial on current affairs" in which he recommended Hsü T'ung, Chang Chih-tung, Ch'en Pao-chen, and a few others as "upright officials" who could be depended upon to bring the affairs of the empire to a turn for the better and, at the same time, impeached in very strong language, Li Hung-chang, Weng T'ung-ho, and Chang Yin-huan, charging them with bringing the empire to the verge of ruin. It is interesting to note that Yü mentioned in the same breath an ultra conservative and two men widely known for their enthusiastic support of modernization. Yü's action may have been taken independently of Hsü T'ung's. Yet their actions had one effect in common: to bring Chang Chih-tung to a vantage position in the imperial government.

It appears, therefore, that Weng's two-faced role, as patron of reform under his own leadership and as obstructionist of modernizing undertakings promoted by his political opponents, did not always work to his own political advantage. It rendered Weng unwelcome to many modernizers as well as to all conservatives.

The vacillating stand which Weng took on the question of reform induced Ku Hung-ming, Chang Chih-tung's foreign-language secretary, to remark caustically that in a crisis "bigoted ultra conservatives" (of whom Weng was taken as a representative) "might out of sheer despair join hand with ultra radicals" (i.e., K'ang Yu-wei and his associates). A man of strong prejudices and stronger language, Ku Hung-ming was accustomed to making overstatements. The present remark is decidely an exaggeration and an over-simplification, but it underscores the fact that Weng, as a career politician, acted on considerations other than consistency in personal views and attitudes—an aspect of Weng's mental makeup which must be taken into account for a correct interpretation of his behavior. We must, however, supplement Ku's observation by pointing out that Weng sincerely wished to serve the empire as much as he earnestly desired to attain his political ambition. Such a mixed motivation made him a man of accommodating views, ever ready to trade off his convictions as practical situations required. Sometimes he acted as a patriot. He was concerned about the waning fortunes of the dynasty and was dedicated to preserving the empire with all the traditional values and institutions that were inseparably bound up with it. The defeats and humiliations suffered by China from foreign powers in the closing decades of the century awakened Weng to the urgent need of administrative reform. He shed his early complacency and "conservatism," and set about to pre-

pare the young emperor for making the changes which he deemed necessary. At other times, however, he acted as a politician, as a man interested in achieving personal success in officialdom. He undertook to promote reform because he saw in it the prospect of making himself the undisputed leader among his colleagues, safe from the assault of his rivals and opponents. That being the case, he took pains to obstruct the modernizing efforts of men like Li Hung-chang and Chang Chih-tung who could effectively challenge his leadership in reform. He did not seek their cooperation or assistance but instead attempted to develop a reform of his own—to recruit his own assistants and followers. In order to make Peking the exclusive center of reform he opposed the modernizing enterprises of provincial officials, even though these were energetically carried out and with some tangible results. For, having identified his interests with those of the central government he could not tolerate any regional development even if moved in the same general direction toward which his own reform program aimed. Patriotic sentiments and personal ambition thus converged to prompt Weng to behave as he did in the years 1895-98. To label him simply as "conservative" or "progressive" is to miss much of the concrete realities of the man's personal motivation and his political environment.

II. WENG'S RELATIONS WITH SOME OF HIS COLLEAGUES AND CONTEMPORARIES

Behind the facade of studied civilities in the officialdom of imperial China lay a partially exposed maze of personal rivalries, factional strifes, tenacious partisanships, and shifting loyalties among the high officials both in Peking and the provincial capitals. Political principles and moral convictions were not absent in determining personal associations and factional alignments, but these were often overruled by or commingled with purely selfish considerations, especially when one's political survival or advantage was at stake. Apparent friendship might camouflage deep enmity; a worthy cause might serve as a convenient pretext to embarrass or ruin one's opponent, irrespective of the latter's personal merits or service to the empire. Few, if any, could rise above the situation, for the simple reason that in order to succeed in the political arena one must learn and follow the rules of the game.

Weng T'ung-ho's attempts to impede or undermine Li Hung-chang and Chang Chih-tung, already indicated above, are illustrative of the conditions that prevailed in the closing decades of the nineteenth century. Weng, however, was not the most unscrupulous of the politicians of the period. Some of his contemporaries and predecessors treated their rivals in equal, if not in even more dishonorable fashion. It was said, for example, that Ch'i Chün-tsao slandered Tseng Kuo-fan by insinuation so successfully that the latter was hamstrung for a number of years during his campaign against the T'aip'ing rebels. Later, in the 1860's, another high official did the same thing to Tseng who was thus deterred from actively contributing to the tasks of post-campaign rehabilitation. In Weng's own time the rivalries and maneuverings among Li Hung-chang, Chang Chih-tung, Li Hung-tsao, and other high officials were quite notorious. For instance, when Chang Chih-tung sided with Li Hung-chang in the 1870's, he joined others to denounce Liu K'un-i for his criticisms of Li. In 1884,

however, Chang shifted his political alignment and joined another group of partisans to denounce Li for his foreign policies. Li Hung-tsao was ousted from the Grand Council as a result of impeachments instigated by his opponents who used the crisis created by the war with France over Yüeh-nan to undo him. The empress dowager, according to some sources, joined in the game; she took this opportunity to throw out Prince Kung who had by that time fallen out of her grace. A particularly nefarious case involving Li Hung-chang was reported in 1894. Wen T'ing-shih, highly regarded by Li Hung-chang as well as Weng T'ung-ho, chose to join Weng's "war party" and impeached Li for his "cowardly attitude" in dealing with Japan. Naturally, Li was incensed; Wen prudently left Peking upon the advice of a friend. Liu Ch'i-hsiang, intendant of Shanghai, a relative of Li Hung-chang, made a point to entertain Wen in his official residence, secured by ruse the draft of one of Wen's secret memorials to the emperor, and sent a copy of it to Li who promptly showed it to the empress dowager. Meanwhile, Li persuaded Yang Ts'ung-i, a censor, to impeach Wen and thus quickly brought about the latter's dismissal.

Such, in general, was the atmosphere of imperial officialdom in which Weng T'ung-ho moved and by which, in fact, his reactions and behavior were shaped. A man brought up in the established Confucian tradition, he of course shared the basic moral precepts with the bulk of the scholar-officials of the time. But as an astute and ambitious politician he did not adhere rigidly to the "correct principles," in disregard of the realities of the political environment. He was ready to adapt his views and attitudes to the circumstances, in order to secure advantages or avoid damages. Like many of his colleagues, he identified his best interests with those of the dynasty; in that sense he was loyal to the existing regime. He, however, did not hesitate to shift personal friendships or to transfer private loyalties whenever the practical situation demanded. His relations with men were often maintained more on utilitarian considerations than on the basis of genuine sentiment. As a historian put it, Weng "liked to have protégés but insisted that they be useful to himself; widely he made ties of friendship but he could not tolerate anyone who did not comply with his wishes or beliefs." All these factors contributed to making Weng a man of complex motivations, unsteady convictions, and vacillating personal loyalties.

A brief survey of his relations with some of his contemporaries bears out the above observation. Weng apparently was willing to show respect to veteran scholar-officials with whom he had no conflict of interest. Wo-jen and Wen-hsiang afforded the most outstanding instances in this connection. In the early years of his career, Weng took interest in the Lu-Wang school of neo-Confucianism; around 1876, however, he was partially converted to the philosophy of Chu Hsi. This change was probably due to the influence of Wo-jen, a staunch defender of the "orthodox" neo-Confucian tradition and senior imperial tutor with whom Weng associated for a number of years and to whom Weng showed respect. Weng held Wen-hsiang in high regard. Weng was probably impressed by his firm attitude toward foreigners, a stand which Weng took until the 1870's. Meanwhile, Weng showed appreciation of some of the high officials who in various ways contributed to the "self-strengthening" movement of the 1860's.

He admired, for instance, Lin Tse-hsü and discovered the "greatness" of the man upon reading his collected works in 1878. Weng expressed profound regret upon receiving the news of Tso Tsung-t'ang's death in Foochow in 1885. He had a number of intimate contacts with Tso in 1881 when the latter was in Peking serving in the Grand Council.

Weng, however, did not hold Tseng Kuo-fan in such high regard. Scant mention was made of Tseng in his diary. On hearing of Tseng's death in Nanking in 1872 he merely noted that "Grand Secretary Tseng Kuo-fan died in Liang-Chiang," without even following the customary practice of using Tseng's *tzu* ("courtesy name")—a marked contrast to the deferential manner in which he recorded Tso Tsung-t'ang's death. Another mention of Tseng was made fifteen years later, in 1887, when he read Tseng's diary without comment. All these men, Lin Tse-hsü (1785-1850), Wo-jen (d. 1871), Tseng Kuo-fan (1811-1872), Tso Tsung-t'ang (1812-1885), and Wen-hsiang (1818-1876), were Weng's seniors in official service as well as in age (Weng was born in 1830). Probably for two reasons Weng found it difficult to place Tseng on the same level with the rest. One arose from personal grudge. Tseng's accusation of Weng T'ung-shu, Weng T'ung-ho's elder brother who achieved distinction in the campaign against the T'aip'ing rebels, resulted in the latter's dismissal and exile to Ili. The other reason was difference in opinion. As already said, Weng strongly objected to Tseng's conciliatory attitude toward foreigners in dealing with the Tientsin incident of 1870. One is not sure, however, that this objection did not have its roots in the personal grudge which Weng bore against the elderly statesman.

It appears, therefore, that Weng's

judgments of men were not always guided by impartial standards. One gains the same impression in examining his relations with other contemporaries. Perhaps the most revealing was his relation with Li Hung-tsao, who was regarded by some as one of the top leaders of the so-called "northern party" and was therefore one of Weng's chief political opponents. Weng was ostensibly on very cordial and even intimate terms with Li. Weng frequently visited Li, sometimes chatting for hours far into the night. He lamented Li's death in 1897, eulogizing him as "an upright man." It may seem strange that Weng befriended a man who not only belonged to a rival faction but held opposite views on important matters. Li's influential position in Peking officialdom offered a possible explanation of Weng's behavior. By allying himself with Prince Kung, Li attained considerable influence up to the early 1880's when his antagonism to Prince Ch'un incurred the wrath of the empress dowager. In 1885, however, Li began to regain her favor. Obviously, he was a man whose good will would have proved useful to any ambitious official. Weng himself indicated the extent of help he once received from Li. On several occasions in the 1880's, he enjoyed Li's support in his conflict with Hsü T'ung over instructional procedures, in their capacity as imperial tutor to the T'ung-chih emperor. Thanks to Li's strong support, Weng won a decisive victory over Hsü.

Weng's relation with Jung-lu, who was destined to play a decisive role in the *coup d'état* of 1898, is also noteworthy. Weng had been on intimate terms with him since 1876, when both men were vice-presidents of the Board of Revenue. Close personal contacts were frequent. For instance, Weng visited Jung-lu immediately upon learning the latter's dismissal in 1879. On a number of occasions

he accepted Jung-lu's gifts without hesitation; he, however, was accustomed to refusing presents from persons whom he did not consider his intimate friends. This seemingly cordial relation, however, did not last indefinitely. The first clear indication of estrangement came to light in 1898 when Weng refused to accept a gift Jung-lu sent him before he departed from Peking after his dismissal. When Jung-lu died in 1903, Weng disclosed his dissapointment in his one-time friend in the following remarks:

I felt depressed on hearing the news [of his death]. He was an old friend of mine. The Sage [Confucius] did not terminate his friendship with Yüan-jang who stood on the coffin [of his deceased mother and sang].

Some writers alleged that Jung-lu was responsible for Weng's summary dismissal in 1898, a matter which we shall have occasion to investigate. For the moment it suffices to admit that it is difficult to ascertain the reason for Weng's change of attitude toward Jung-lu, and that it is equally difficult to determine the precise ground upon which their previous friendship rested. One may well suppose that their relationship was from the first an alliance for political expediency rather than a comradeship based on mutual affection and understanding.

Weng's relations with men who in various ways were connected with the "self-strengthening" movement or versed in *yang-wu*, throw additional light on Weng's character. His admiration of Wo-jen and high esteem of Li Hung-tsao, both arch conservatives, did not prevent him from coming into friendly contacts with men of entirely different persuasions and experiences. A few of the most notable among the latter group may be mentioned here.

Kuo Sung-tao may well have been one of the first to arouse Weng's interest in reform. Before Kuo set out late in 1876 for London as minister to England, he had several conversations with Weng and presented his views on reform, expressing his "wish to see iron and coal mines opened and railways built in every part of the empire." He gave his "essay on foreign countries" for Weng to read. Weng indicated general approval of Kuo's views and evidently was on very friendly terms with Kuo.

Weng's cold attitude toward Tseng Kuo-fan did not prevent him from appreciating the abilities of Tseng Kuo-ch'üan, the marquis's younger brother who distinguished himself in the T'aip'ing campaigns. When Tseng Kuo-ch'üan was on sick leave in 1875, Weng had a long discussion with him and was convinced of Tseng's "sound scholarship" and "correct understanding" of the problems of administration. Nine years later, when Tseng was called to Peking to serve as an acting president of the Board of Rites, Weng again came into contact with him. Weng was so favorably impressed by the man that he viewed his death in 1890 as having crucial influence on "the entire situation in the southeast." Weng's relation with Tseng Chi-tse, Tseng Kuo-fan's heir, was even more cordial. The two men first met in 1870; Weng took notice of Tseng's "outstanding personality and intelligence." Many years later (1888), Tseng presented Weng with sixteen books on "Western learning" which, as already said, may have helped Weng to crystallize his thoughts on reform. Six months after he received these works, he joined with Sun Chia-nai in introducing the emperor to the idea of reform.

Weng showed interest in Ting Jih-ch'ang, despite the latter's association with Li Hung-chang. Weng had a number of "long chats" with Ting in the spring of 1875, when Ting was called to

Tientsin to assist Li to negotiate the treaties with Japan and Peru. That Weng thought highly of Ting, one of the younger officials of the time noted for his knowledge of "foreign affairs," may be inferred from the fact that Weng was distressed to hear in 1877 a rumor of Ting's death and rejoiced when he found out that the report was false. Similar sentiments were expressed when Weng was informed of Ting's death in 1882. Weng was also friendly to Ma Chien-chung, a protégé of Li Hung-chang who sent him to study in France, and author of a number of essays on reform. Weng met Ma in the summer of 1897 and, after commenting on the latter's "eminent abilities," entered in his diary the names of a number of men (including Yen Fu and Ch'en Chih) who were "versed in Western techniques."

By 1897 Weng had become actively engaged in promoting reform. Naturally, he looked for competent persons to assist him in the important task. Thus, in the few years immediately preceding 1898 Weng brought himself into contact with many younger men among whom (in addition to those already mentioned) were Sung Yü-jen, a Hanlin compiler who served for a time as counselor to the Chinese legation in England and France, T'ang Chen (i.e., T'ang Shou-ch'ien), a magistrate and author of Wei-yen which he wrote in 1890, T'an Ssu-t'ung, destined to be one of the six "martyrs" of 1898; P'eng Kuang-yü, an expectant intendant who for eight years had assisted Chang Yin-huan in his diplomatic mission to the United States; Lo Feng-lu, an intendant who followed Li Hung-chang on various diplomatic missions; and Huang Tsun-hsien, an intendant serving for sometime as consul-general at Singapore and author of the famous work on Japan, Jih-pen kuo-chih. Personal contacts with these men were made by Weng between

1895 and 1897. It was during these years also that Weng made the acquaintance of a few Westerners whom he regarded as friendly and trustworthy, especially Robert Hart and Timothy Richard.

As already said, Weng began to guide the emperor into reform in 1889. The defeat of 1894 persuaded him to quicken his steps in that direction, in order to save the languishing dynasty before it was too late. His interest in reform, however, was not unmixed with ulterior motives. There is reason to believe that he saw in reform a road on which his imperial pupil and he himself might travel together to eminence—provided he could assume unchallenged leadership in the task. It was necessary, therefore, to draw as many qualified persons as he could to rally around himself and, at the same time, to exclude all who by virtue of their prestige or seniority in officialdom could dispute his leadership. This explains Weng's antagonism to Li Hungchang and Chang Chih-tung and his friendship to younger men, some of whom being their junior associates. This explains also Weng's patronage of K'ang Yu-wei, as we shall see, despite wide differences in philosophical outlook and views on reform between the two men.

Weng's attempt to enlist younger men to develop his reform program brought relatively little positive result to him personally. In some instances, the results were decidedly disappointing or disastrous to him. His ability to read human character did not always match his will to lead. Yüan Shih-k'ai and Chang Yin-huan afforded two of the most unfortunate examples. Weng mentioned Yüan for the first time in 1894 when he commented upon Yüan's "fine reputation" as China's emissary to Korea where he served from 1885 until the outbreak of war. Upon meeting Yüan in the summer of 1895 Weng was impressed by Yüan's obvious talent but "lack of sincerity." Further contacts, however, changed Weng's opinion. Less than three months later, Weng felt that Yüan was "not slippery" and "could be relied upon," and that "after all this man is frank and honest." Weng's favorable opinion was strengthened by another interview shortly before the One Hundred Days, when Yüan "pledged with noble words" to dedicate himself to serving the empire. Before three months had passed, Weng was dismissed and returned south by way of Tientsin. Yüan who was still in Tientsin, sent Weng a letter with gifts, but did not see fit to pay Weng a visit as many of Weng's friends did. Weng promptly answered the letter, saying that he decided "absolutely to refuse to accept" the gifts. Apparently, Weng no longer regarded Yüan as a close friend.

Weng's association with Chang Yin-huan was even less gratifying. Chang was seven years younger than Weng and was among the junior members of high officialdom in Peking. As early as in 1890 the two men seem to have already been on rather intimate terms. They were in frequent contact since then, socially as well as in their official capacities. The first indication of Weng's disillusionment occurred in 1897 when the Shantung incident proved a diplomatic hornets' nest for Weng. Commenting on the episode Weng wrote in his diary:

Mr. Chang and I are conducting the same affair, but at one moment he stands close to me, while at another he stands aloof. Each time I went to his place he [chose to] lie in bed, chatting and laughing. I simply cannot understand [his behavior].

This, in reality, is not difficult to understand. It may be recalled that at one point in Chang's career (around 1869) he worked with Li Han-chang, Li Hung-chang's elder brother, then serving as governor-general at Wuchang. Since 1875 Chang had associated with Li Hung-chang on various missions. Although strictly speaking not a protégé of Li's, Chang may have deemed it unwise to align himself with Weng and to act against Li, when Weng was jockeying for diplomatic leadership against the veteran diplomat. Indeed, there is some ground for suspecting that it was Chang who divulged to Li the terms of the negotiation which he ostensibly helped Weng to conduct, and thus place Li in a position to sabotage them.

Whatever cordial feelings that may have previously existed between Weng and Chang must have dissipated themselves before the year 1897 came to an end. In fact, Weng's ill-feeling toward Chang became so evident that the emperor suspected Weng of instigating the impeachments which were brought against Chang in the spring of 1898. By then Weng had definitely regretted his former association with Chang. He wrote in his diary:

Fragrant and fetid plants are placed in the same vase; clear and muddy waters flow in the same stream; the filth of a scoundrel contaminates a good man—isn't this lamentable?

It would be hasty to conclude that the fault was all Weng's. Chang was not necessarily a man of pure motivations. It was reported, for example, that Chang lent vigorous support of K'ang Yu-wei at first but soon turned against him, revealing himself as a Janus-faced double-crosser. Nevertheless, Weng must bear the blame for allowing himself to be "contaminated" by Chang. It appears that Weng made another unhappy choice in his attempt to recruit his own assistants in reform.

In the case of the strained relation between Weng and Li Hung-chang, and that between him and Chang Chih-tung, Weng must be held largely if not solely responsible, as our previous discussion shows. It remains to add here that according to Weng himself, he held Chang in high esteem and was on cordial terms with Chang until at least 1884, when Chang was appointed governor-general at Canton where he initiated a series of modernizing enterprises. And, according to Chang, by 1889 Weng's hostile attitude toward him had become painfully evident. This drastic change of attitude on Weng's part, from friendship to enmity, is somewhat surprising but not inexplicable. It was due not simply to difference in opinion concerning reform, for Weng began to oppose Chang's modernizing activities precisely at the time when he himself undertook to promote reform and, as we shall presently see, the direction and scope of Chang's efforts did not go beyond or contrary to Weng's general idea of reform. Personal jealousy and political rivalry must have played an important part in changing Weng's attitude toward Chang.

It may also be added that Weng was definitely responsible for the conflict between Li Hung-chang and himself, although Li came to despise Weng as much as the other way round. Timothy Richard related that in an interview (September 25, 1895) Li Hung-chang remarked to him "that Weng T'ung-ho was very suspicious and that he had no head and only a half-doubting heart." Weng reciprocated at about the same time (1894) in describing Li as "crooked" and criticizing him for "falling behind at every turn" in managing the affairs of the empire. Meanwhile, Weng "resorted to diverse methods to tie Li's hands," much like he did to Chang Chih-tung. Chang Chien, Weng's favorite protégé, cooperated with Weng in 1895 to work for Li's undoing by charging him with "bringing the empire to the brink of ruin." As in the case of Chang Chih-tung, the relation between Weng and Li deteriorated from cordiality to hostility as Weng advanced in his career. The two men were bound by a tie known in imperial China as *shih-chiao,* "friendship in several generations." A *shih-chiao* relationship was normally maintained with scrupulous care among officials and their families, both for sentimental and utilitarian reasons. Outwardly, Weng and Li did nothing to mar this relationship between themselves. Friction, however, eventually developed and by 1886, when Weng became a president of the Board of Revenue, his dislike for Li had become unmistakable. Differences in view concerning imperial financial matters contributed to their quarrels. An open break occurred in 1888 when Weng opposed Li's railways proposals and Li criticized Weng in very harsh language. The controversy over war and peace with Japan brought their feud to a climax; neither concealed the resentment felt of the other's actions and words.

It would be oversimplification to say that the conflict between Weng and Li was merely a matter of difference in view. There was a deeper and less tangible case. A recent writer has suggested that Weng bore an ancient grudge against Li because the latter had blackmailed the Weng family with damaging information involving it—information which Li happened to come upon during the T'aip'ing campaign when Li was operating in the regions surrounding Weng's home locality. Li may not have been above such practice, but there is no direct evidence

to prove that he actually engaged in it. There is much better evidence to support the view that Weng's political ambition made Li a major target of his maneuverings.

The above discussion strengthens the conclusion suggested in the preceding section: that as a practical politician Weng T'ung-ho often permitted considerations of expediency to outweigh moral principles and that, consequently, he often chose friends or made enemies according as the individuals in question were regarded by him to be useful for his purposes or detrimental to his interests, rather than on the merits of their personal character or convictions. This conclusion, we believe, will prove helpful in explaining some of the important actions which Weng took on the eve and at the beginning of the One Hundred Days of reform.

III. THE IMPERIAL RULERS AND WENG'S RELATION WITH THEM

Historians generally agree that the conflict between Emperor Te-tsung and the empress dowager constituted a major factor that determined the course of events in the closing decades of the nineteenth century. The *coup d'état* of 1898 marked the climax not only of the struggles between reformers and their opponents but also of the clash between Te-tsung and his supporters, *ti tang* ("the emperor faction") and Tz'u-hsi and her supporters, *hou tang* ("the empress faction").

A number of men were identified as members of these rival factions. Outstanding on the side of the empress dowager were Jung-lu, Kang-i, Hsü T'ung, and Sun Yü-wen; and in the opposite camp, Ch'ang-ling, Wang Ming-luan, An Wei-chün, and Wen T'ing-shih. Weng

T'ung-ho was regarded by some as virtually the leader of "the emperor faction," although speaking accurately he was pro-emperor without being anti-empress dowager. Weng was, however, personally concerned about the conflict between the imperial rulers and his course of action during the years immediately preceding the One Hundred Days was influenced considerably by that conflict.

It was a patent fact that the relations among the immediate members of the imperial family had been far from harmonious during the T'ung-chih and Kuang-hsü reigns. The T'ung-chih emperor had incurred the lasting resentment of his own mother, Tz'u-hsi, in failing to comply with her wishes in the choice of his imperial consort. The Kuang-hsü emperor, not being Tz'u-hsi's own son, found himself in a situation even less congenial than what his predecessor faced. Prince Ch'un (I-huan), the emperor's father, must have had foreknowledge of what was in store for his child when he wept and fainted upon hearing Tz'u-hsi's decision to choose Tsai-t'ien to ascend the throne.

Personal traits of the empress dowager contributed much to the unsatisfactory atmosphere in the imperial palaces. Whatever may have been her qualifications as a ruler, it appears certain that a domineering woman with a strong will but weak affections, Tz'u-hsi was too often more shrewd than truly wise. She was, like many "outstanding women" in history, of the "tiger-cat type." To make the situation particularly difficult for the young emperor she was said to have possessed "unquenchable ambition," a "love of power," and "a physical vitality which almost never failed." In addition, she was inordinately vain and fiercely cruel toward those who dared to displease her.

Tz'u-hsi's austere attitude toward the emperor was proverbial. Liang Ch'i-ch'ao charged her with having actually being cruel to him. Quoting the words of K'ou Lien-ts'ai, a eunuch loyal to the emperor, Liang alleged that the emperor was subjected to reprimand and whipping, and was made to kneel for long hours at a time as a disciplinary measure. As a result, "the emperor faced the Western Empress as if she were a lioness or tigress." No one could prove the accuracy of these words, but other sources generally confirm the view that Tz'u-hsi was devoid of motherly tenderness toward the emperor. She may not have been purposely or particularly "cruel" to the emperor. But as she was noted for her ability to inculcate fear into those who surrounded her, it is probable that she made no effort to spare the child emperor of her accustomed treatment of her inferiors.

The strained relation between the aunt and nephew (officially, mother and son) was complicated by the strained relation between the emperor and his imperial wife (Tz'u-hsi's niece) who was chosen by Tz'u-hsi "less with a view to the emperor's felicity than to the furtherance of her own purposes." "From the first," it was said, the young empress "was on bad terms with the emperor. It was no secret at court that they indulged in fierce and protracted quarrels." The emperor developed a marked preference for the society of the imperial concubines, Chin-fei and Chen-fei, who inevitably earned the resentment of the empress dowager, and rendered the entire situation worse than before.

The situation was further aggravated by actions of those officials and eunuchs who willfully or unwittingly sowed discord between the imperial rulers. The officials belonging to the so-called "emperor faction" and "empress faction" must be held partly responsible. But the greatest damage seems to have been done by some of the eunuchs.

Despite "ancestral regulations" which aimed at minimizing the potential influence of eunuchs on imperial affairs, and despite repeated impeachments brought up by officials against the reportedly offensive conduct of palace servants, the power of these men had a tendency to wax as the dynasty went on. Their interference with matters outside of the Forbidden City went unnoticed until it became too flagrant to ignore. Even as early as in Chia-ch'ing times, a eunuch was said to have ruined a high official in the emperor's confidence. With the empress dowager holding the reins of government eunuchs rapidly attained unprecedented importance at the imperial court. The decapitation of the notorious An Te-hai in 1879 did not alter the general trend. In fact, owing to the strategic position which the eunuchs occupied under the empress dowager, some of them acquired immense power and influence. They were persons who had constant and direct contact with Tz'u-hsi; often it was through them that officials gained access to her. In addition to facilities for "peddling influence," a practice in which they were said to have widely indulged, there existed many opportunities for them to speak well or ill of officials as they chose. Moreover, they made themselves indispensable to the suspicious Tz'u-hsi by spying upon officials and getting information (or misinformation) from outside the palaces. This alone would have been enough to make the eunuchs feared even by the most powerful of the officials. It is hardly surprising that Li Lien-ying, Tz'u-hsi's chief eunuch, became widely known as the most powerful person at court, a center of extensive corruption, and a major

influence on the empress dowager. The charges made by K'ang Yu-wei and by Wen Ching were not without corroboration by unbiased, well-informed writers.

Nor is it surprising that Li Lien-ying and many of his associates sided with the empress dowager and "had little respect" for the emperor. In fact, they had no scruples in helping Tz'u-hsi to make the life of the emperor miserable. Li Lien-ying, in particular, was thought by some to have been largely responsible for instigating the enmity between the imperial rulers. His hatred of the emperor may have been "one of the first causes of the *coup d'état* of 1898." We should of course guard against overstressing the importance of the chief eunuch, but there is little doubt that he had done more to worsen the relation between Tz'u-hsi and Kuang-hsü than any official belonging to "the empress faction."

Li Lien-ying, it was said, had more than one reason to dislike the emperor. He was flogged by the emperor's order in 1890 for showing disrespect to his majesty. Even without such an episode the fact that the emperor's increased interest in reforming the administration was bound to bring him into sharp conflict with Li whose corrupt practices could continue only if the *status quo* was maintained. On several occasions the emperor actually undertook to undo the offensive deeds of some of the eunuchs. Finally, when the emperor showed too much consideration for foreigners and too much appreciation of foreign ways to suit the empress dowager, Li Lien-ying added fuel to her xenophobia by spreading anti-foreign rumors, thus indirectly further intensified her suspicion of the emperor. Even without express order from her, Li Lien-ying must have been quite ready to report to her the emperor's supposedly unfilial ways—to set to naught the rules and institutions of the imperial ancestors—by spying upon him. It is conceivable that the emperor's premature demise in 1908 was welcomed by the pro-empress eunuchs, even if they did not hasten it.

Not every eunuch, of course, stood against the emperor. K'ou Lien-ts'ai, a hitherto obscure individual, was "summarily beheaded for venturing to advise the Emperor to select his own staff of personal attendants, so as to avoid the constant espionage of the Empress Dowager." It appears, therefore, that the partisan division among court officials had its counterpart among the eunuchs. Indeed, K'ou Lien-ts'ai may well have been a mouthpiece of officials belonging to "the emperor faction." The support offered by the few eunuchs like K'ou, however, was too feeble to be useful; it merely made the circumstances worse for the emperor.

The root of the trouble, it must be emphasized, lay in the basic conflict of interest between the two rulers. Tz'u-hsi's motive in choosing Tsai-t'ien, a child of six (1875), to succeed the T'ung-chih emperor was none other than to prolong her role as empress dowager, namely, to continue "to listen to reports on affairs of state behind screens." Her reportedly cruel treatment of the child emperor may have been calculated to instill fear in his mind so that he would remain forever obedient to her. She apparently succeeded in this to a remarkable extent, although later developments proved that her success was short of complete. She went through the gesture of *kuei-cheng*, "returning the rulership," to the emperor in 1887. She was, however, "beseeched" to assume the task of *hsün-cheng*, "giving instruction in administration" to the emperor for two years, thus delaying the formal relinquishment of an authority

which she had been wielding more or less freely for over a quarter of a century. She was then (1889) in her middle fifties, while the emperor was a young man of eighteen. Still strong in body and will, she "had no intention of becoming a negligible quantity." Meanwhile, events and circumstances quickly convinced the emperor of the urgency "to do great things" in order to salvage the sinking empire. An inevitable struggle for power between the two rulers developed rapidly, reaching the climax in 1898.

The first crisis came in 1894-5, five years after the empress dowager formally ended the *hsün-cheng* regime. But instead of leaving the emperor (now over twenty-three) to shoulder the responsibilities of a full-fledged ruler, she continued to make important decisions, including those concerning international relations. For instance, early in 1895, when Prince Kung called her attention to the emperor's reluctance to summon Li Hung-chang to Peking for consultation, she said, with apparent displeasure, "I can make one half of the decisions." Her overbearing attitude toward the emperor was too obvious to escape the notice of officials who sympathized with the emperor. Some of these men tried to put a stop to Tz'u-hsi's interference by urging the emperor to assert his independence. Instead of improving the situation, however, they were cashiered by the empress dowager for what they dared to try.

The emperor himself, it appears, was not in a position to take the advice of these men. In an edict (KH 21/10/17) which dismissed Ch'ang-ling, a vice-president of the Board of Revenue, and Wang Ming-luan, a vice-president of the Board of Civil Appointments, and threatened with severe punishment any other official who dared to follow their examples, the emperor is represented as saying:

We have been enjoying the benefit of the empress dowager's motherly instruction. In matters great and small, ranging from military affairs . . . to details in daily living, she has taken meticulous care of Us. But ignorant, uninstructed persons who misconstrued Our intentions, such as vice-presidents of Boards Wang Ming-luan and Ch'angling, uttered indiscreet words while in audience with Us; . . . their action came near to sowing discord [between her majesty and Ourselves]. . . .

But the emperor did not remain docile for long. His mother (Tz'u-hsi's sister) died in 1896, and "the last bond of amity and possible reconciliation" between the nephew and his aunt disappeared. The occupation of Kiaochow Bay by German troops (December 1897) so aroused the emperor that he was reported to have threatened to abdicate unless he was given free hand in conducting the imperial administration. According to one account, his threat was presented to the empress dowager through Prince Ch'ing (I-k'uang). According to others, she consented to let the emperor do things as he chose but reserved the right to have her say when he failed to achieve results. It is difficult to ascertain the accuracy of these reports, but they afforded a reasonable explanation of the fact that despite his lack of authority and habitual fear of the empress dowager, the emperor eventually launched the reforms of 1898.

This did not mean, however, that she had given whole-hearted approval of his reform program or that she had decided to grant him complete freedom of action. Her consent mentioned above could have been only a qualified one grudgingly given. Subsequent events showed that she was ready to resume power at the earliest

opportunity. Moreover, her love of power, her inveterate dislike and suspicion of the emperor, and her unreasoned xenophobia afforded ample opportunity to anti-reformers whose bigotry or selfish interests were affected by reform. These "conservatives" rallied around her and resorted to every available means to undermine the emperor in order to put a complete stop to his reform program. There was some ground, therefore, for the view held by a number of the reformers that to remove the empress dowager or to render her powerless was an indispensable condition of successful reform.

It may also be said that the conflict between the two imperial rulers had some of its roots in difference of temperament and outlook. For one thing, the empress dowager had little confidence in the emperor's abilities as a ruler and did little to cultivate them. During the period of *hsün-cheng* (1887-89) all the dispatches transmitted through the Tsou-shih-ch'u (with eunuchs in charge) went to her; she only "occasionally showed one or two of these documents to the emperor who could not touch any of them without her permission." On the eve of the emperors's "assumption of rulership" in 1889, she tried to tie his hands by extorting from him a promise that he would never "alter the established rules." As late as in 1904, long after the dust of the Boxer uprising had settled, the empress dowager continued to hold a low opinion of her nephew's knowledge and acumen. "Do you know," she said, "I have often thought that I am the most clever woman that ever lived. . . . What does the emperor know?"

Her contemptuous opinion, however, was not shared by all who had come into contact with the emperor. Der Ling thought that "He was a most intelligent man with a wonderful memory and learned very quickly." In contrast, the empress dowager had no aptitude for learning, despite her self-confidence. Weng T'ung-ho, the emperor's tutor for many years, generally confirmed Der Ling's appraisal of the emperor.

The emperor was not exactly an angel. Since his childhood he had been a person of strong emotions and hot temper. When he was about eight years old he impressed Weng T'ung-ho as an intelligent boy with a dislike to being compelled by others and a taste for flattery. Weng found it necessary to speak to him long and earnestly on the undesirability of being headstrong and suspicious. The young emperor frequently became irritated by trivial things and readily gave violent demonstrations of his ire. He was, however, frankly affectionate and sentimental. He wept in front of his tutor when he referred to his father (Prince Ch'un) who was seriously ill but whom he could not visit. He broke into tears when he discussed with court officials the impossible situation which the empire faced in 1895, and when he read the account of the partition of Poland, presented to him by K'ang Yu-wei in the spring of 1898. A man of such disposition could not have found it easy to live in harmony with the empress dowager.

Incompatibility of views further widened the chasm between Kuang-hsü and Tz'u-hsi. It is easy to over-stress the importance of the struggle for power between them, as, for example, K'ang Yu-wei did when he charged that the conflict between them had nothing to do with political principles. Wang Chao held a similar opinion. Chang Ping-lin accused the emperor of the same lack of principles and further alleged that he used the reform movement merely as a means to consolidate his shaky personal position. These were unadorned partisan opinions and cannot be accepted without reservation. For, while it is inaccurate to describe the empress dowager as a "conservative" or the emperor as a "progressive," it would be oversimplifying matters to rule out differences in their views concerning imperial policies or to disregard the differences in general outlook that existed between them as individuals of widely different ages. In the years 1895 to 1898 the emperor was in his middle twenties, whereas Tz'u-hsi was in her early sixties. It would have been unusual, indeed, if this discrepancy in age was not reflected in their ways of looking at things, which in turn influenced their actions.

The empress dowager, it must be pointed out, was not opposed to adopting "Western methods" for the purpose of "self-strengthening." She was adverse only to altering or abandoning the accustomed ways and traditional values of imperial China. She held fast to these not only because she was deeply steeped in them but also because she saw that much of her authority and prestige stemmed from the basic precepts of the traditional ethical code—in particular, the precept of filial piety. As late as in 1903 she declared, "I don't mind owning up that I like old ways the best, and I don't see any reason why we should adopt the foreign style." Another statement made at about the same time is even more significant:

I may be conservative in saying that I admire our custom and will not change it as long as I live. You see our people are taught to be polite from their earliest childhood, and just look back at the oldest teachings and compare them with the new. People seem to like the latter the best. I mean that the new idea is to be Christians, to chop up their Ancestral Tablets and burn them.

Shortly after she made the above statement, she confided to Der Ling: "K'ang Yu-wei . . . tried to make the Emperor believe that [Christian] religion. No one shall believe [it] as long as I live."

The youthful emperor, however, had much less interest in honoring the "ancestral tablets" and less antipathy to "that religion." He became deeply engrossed in books on Western learning, especially during 1895-7 and, thanks to the zeal of some missionaries, he became interested in the New Testament, a fact which lent point to Tz'u-hsi's remark quoted above. He developed a taste for toys made in foreign countries and showed keen interest in learning the English language—a predilection which displeased Weng T'ung-ho. It seems that novelty which usually appeals to youth, was at work here; it may have reenforced the emperor's fervent wish to make China prosperous and strong by fashioning the imperial institution after western models. Psychologically, he was thoroughly conditioned for making the bold moves of 1898, as his aunt was for condemning these very moves. Thus, about a half dozen years before he met K'ang Yu-wei, the emperor had already displayed a tendency toward Westernization.

The differences in outlook between the two rulers were of course not absolute. As already said, the empress dowager was not completely opposed to adopting "Western methods." According to one source, she even told the emperor, sometime before the One Hundred Days of 1898, that reform had been her own wish for a long time. That this statement was not without substance may be seen from the fact that it was she who approved, at the beginning of the T'ung-chih reign,

Tseng Kuo-fan's proposal to send students abroad, to build steamships, and to manufacture Western-style weapons of war, although she warned against "committing sins against the ancestors" by imitating Japan's course of reform. Many years later, when the Kuang-hsü emperor showed her Feng Kuei-fen's *K'ang-i*, she was favorably impressed by the ideas of reform it contains, although again she cautioned the emperor against taking rash steps. It was only then that he and Weng felt free to go ahead with reform. All this points to the fact that Tz'u-hsi stood close to the position of the leaders of the "self-strengthening" movement and of those officials who were in favor of moderate reform. She shared with them the view that "Western methods" should be adopted but at the same time the empire's own cultural heritage must be upheld. She subscribed, in other words, to the theory of reform as summarized in the famous formula, "Chinese learning for the foundation, Western learning for application." She opposed the reform movement of 1898 partly because the emperor and his advisers pushed their reform program too far beyond the limits which she had set, and partly because their moves threatened to relegate her to political oblivion.

As a matter of fact, it appears that before the conflict between the two imperial rulers became irreconcilable, the empress dowager's conditional acceptance of reform gave hope to some officials who saw the possibility to reconcile the emperor to her and to induce them to work together for the cause of saving the dynasty through reform.

Weng T'ung-ho was one of those who saw this possibility and tried actually to exploit it. From the practical point of view, it was evident to anyone who was familiar with the fact that during the years covering the T'ung-chih and the first part of the Kuang-hsü reigns the empress dowager had firmly consolidated her power and occupied an unshakable position at court. It was sheer folly to try to dislodge her. Moreover, from the ideological point of view, it was clear that as the "mother" of the emperor she had the indisputable claim to filial obedience from him. It was a serious breach of one of the most sacred precepts of "imperial Confucianism" for the emperor to question her authority over himself as well as over the affairs of state. The high position of the empress dowager, therefore, resulted from certain essential features of the imperial system, quite apart from "the strength and vigor" of her personality. Assuming on the one hand that the person and authority of Tz'u-hsi were inviolable and, on the other hand, that the emperor's legitimate aspirations should not be ignored, the only sensible way to deal with the misunderstandings and conflicts between the two rulers was to resolve these difficulties through conciliation.

Weng T'ung-ho was of course not alone in correctly interpreting the situation. Others were known to have been in favor of reconciliation. Timothy Richard, for instance, raised this question with K'ang Yu-wei, shortly before the *coup d'état* of 1898: "Is it really impossible to reconcile the two imperial rulers?" An editor of Chih-hsin Pao, "The Reformer China" (organ of K'ang Yu-wei's group, published in Macao), echoed the same view in an editorial entitled "That Today's Reform Must Begin with the Conciliation of the Two Imperial Rulers." Yang Jui, one of the "martyrs" of 1898, was reported to have given the emperor this advice: "The empress dowager personally gave the throne to your majesty; your majesty ought to set an example to

the empire in the performance of filial duty, by paying due respect to her wishes." According to one source, the emperor himself favored conciliation as a condition to bringing prosperity and strength to the empire. He, in fact, tried to live up to this conviction. The reform movement of 1898 was not launched without her knowledge. Before the emperor proclaimed each new measure he invariably reported to the empress dowager, although she sometimes showed her displeasure by remaining silent or indicated her conditional approval by saying: "So long as you keep the ancestral tablets and do not burn them, and so long as you do not cut off your queue, I shall not interfere."

In a few known instances efforts were made by officials to effect the desired conciliation. One of these men was Wang Chao who, in the summer of 1898 and at the height of the reform movement, submitted a memorial proposing, among other things, that the emperor accompany the empress dowager on an inspection tour of neighboring countries. Wang supported his proposal with these words:

Since China's communication with the West, our Empress Dowager has been conducting the affairs of state for thirty years. . . . All the changes and reforms [effected during this period] have been initiated by the Empress Dowager and carried on by the Emperor . . . At present . . . . it seems suitable [for the Emperor] to accompany the Empress Dowager to tour neighboring countries, with a view to studying the merits and shortcomings [of their institutions and practices], and to deciding what to adopt or not to adopt. . . . In this way, the Emperor carries out reforms in compliance with the wishes of the Empress Dowager, attributing every good deed to the Imperial Mother. By this ruling the empire with the principle of filial piety, who dares to voice dissent?

Wang Chao explained in a note that the proposal he made was in reality a pretext for introducing his main point, namely, to bring about conciliation of the imperial rulers. Since, Wang reasoned, the conflict between them was essentially a struggle for power, the path to reform might be made easier by giving satisfaction to Tz'u-hsi's vanity and "will to dominate."

The most sustained effort at conciliation, however, was made by Weng T'ung-ho. He was, in some ways, in an especially favorable position to make the attempt. Prior to his dismissal he had enjoyed simultaneously the confidence of the emperor and the empress dowager. And he had more than one reason for taking the action. He, like the empress dowager, was committed to upholding the traditional moral values. There is some ground for saying, therefore, that Weng "took filial piety as the basis on which a reconciliation of the imperial rulers might be effected." Moreover, he owed much to the empress dowager for his rise in officialdom, perhaps even more than to the emperor. Even in the last years of his career every major imperial favor was granted him only with the knowledge and consent of the empress dowager. Thus, in 1897, when the emperor had nominally assumed full authority, Weng was made an associate grand secretary only after the emperor received her express approval.

By the very nature of the case, Weng's attempt at conciliation must be made unobserved and unobtrusively. A number of actions which he took between the crucial years 1886 (when the empress dowager announced her intention to relinquish authority) and 1894 (when the relation between the imperial rulers took a turn decidedly for the worse) suggest that Weng had been trying to keep the emperor from arousing Tz'u-hsi's suspicion or incurring her displeasure. For example, Weng advised the emperor to entreat the empress dowager to postpone her retirement. The emperor followed his advice, thereby bringing about the *hsün-cheng* regime (1886-8). Weng perhaps intended this move to be a gesture to show Tz'u-hsi that the emperor was not anxious to grab authority and that he regarded her guidance as indispensable. Weng probably did not advise the emperor to entreat her to postpone the termination of the *hsün-cheng* regime in 1889, but he continued to counsel the emperor to respect the feelings of Tz'u-hsi who had by then officially retired from government. One revealing instance occurred in 1894 when the emperor was confronted by the exasperating situation created by the Korean crisis. Weng advised the emperor against issuing an "edict of self-censure" suggested by some officials. He pointed out that to do so would have unavoidably cast unfavorable reflections upon the empress dowager. He argued:

Could matters such as the construction work [i.e., the Summer Palace built in compliance with the empress dowager's undeclared wish] and the eunuchs be mentioned? or should these be left out altogether? To leave them out would be dishonest; and to mention them, improper.

The view, therefore, that Weng was the leader of "the emperor faction" while not entirely groundless, is somewhat misleading. It is true in so far as it points to the fact that since 1889 (namely, after the emperor assumed nominal authority) Weng worked loyally for the cause of the emperor. It would be false, however, if it is interpreted to mean that in serving the emperor Weng worked for the elimination of the empress dowager. It is more accurate to say with a Chinese historian that Weng "gained the favor and confidence of the empress dowager as well as of the emperor, by mediating between them."

This does not imply that Weng urged the emperor to remain content with being "nothing more than a boy" or "being of no consequence at all." That would have made Weng a member of "the empress faction" instead of a mediator between the two contenders for imperial power. The logic of the situation may have convinced Weng of the wisdom of being patient, assuming that in the late 1890's he began to side secretly more and more with the emperor. Tz'u-hsi, after all, was thirty years older than her nephew who could therefore afford to wait. The most prudent course of action, obviously, was to avoid an open break with the empress dowager and, at the same time, to make the conditions favorable for the emperor's eventual assumption of full sovereignty, in fact as well as in name.

The chief means whereby Weng sought to prepare for the emperor's assumption of real authority seems to have been the promotion of administrative reform which promised to serve the emperor's cause in two ways. It would reduce the empress dowager's power and influence by doing away with some of the inept personnel, vested interests, and corrupt practices that existed under her rule; and, at the same time, enhance the emperor's power and prestige by identifying him with a movement which avowedly would give prosperity and strength to the empire. As every astute politician knows, one of the best ways to achieve preeminence is to become the sponsor of a worthwhile cause. In the case of China of Weng's time, a program of reform would command the support of many. Moreover, it was a line of action acceptable to Tz'u-hsi herself. Properly pursued, it should afford a common objective for both the emperor and the empress dowager. Accordingly, during the Chinese New Year season of 1889 when the *hsün-cheng* regime came to an official end, Weng T'ung-ho and Sun Chia-nai introduced the emperor to the concept of reform—the first preparatory step to help him to attain eminence. The emperor proved extremely receptive. Although at times he showed too much zeal in "Westernization" to suit the moderate views of Weng who was no more willing than the empress dowager to see the ancestral tablets burned, his attitude made it possible for Weng to take aggressive measures in promoting reform. Early in 1894, presumably on the advice of Weng, the emperor began to implement minor administrative reforms, with a view to putting a stop to some of the most flagrantly sluggish or corrupt ways of Peking officialdom. For instance, within one month's time, two high officials were punished for taking unduly long leaves of absence. A number of other officials were cashiered or demoted for various offences. All presidents and vice-presidents of Boards were sternly commanded to appear regularly in their offices each day. These actions dealt with some of the malpractices which Weng had previously observed with concern. He understandably remarked with satisfaction "that a new atmosphere now prevails in officialdom," as a result of the emperor's action.

Everything, however, did not turn out as Weng hoped. The emperor's enthusiasm for reform exceeded the bounds which Weng (and Tz'u-hsi) wished to set. And, as we shall explain later, K'ang Yu-wei whom Weng intended to be his chief assistant in reform, worked against Weng's concept of reform as well as contrary to his political interests. The friction and ill-will generated by the One Hundred Days' reform which Weng in a real sense helped to bring about, aggravated the already tense relation between the imperial rulers, instead of easing it. Weng, who had hitherto enjoyed the emperor's confidence, became the prime target of "the empress faction"; and in his eleventh hour attempt to dissociate with K'ang Yu-wei, he discredited himself in the eyes of the reformers.

Weng T'ung-ho's endeavor to reconcile the emperor and the empress dowager through reform thus proved to be an impossible task. The misunderstandings between the imperial rulers grew out of an inherently difficult situation; no amount of statesmanship or political maneuvering could remove them. The temperaments and outlooks of the elderly aunt and the youthful nephew were so incompatible that any action taken by either one beyond the usual routine was likely to arouse the suspicion or resentment of the other. It is not surprising at all that the emperor's resolve to renovate the administration was, according to some sources, interpreted by the empress dowager as a concealed scheme to wrest control from her. Enemies of reform promptly rallied around her, adding strength to the forces that moved inexorably toward the catastrophe of 1898. Ironically, Weng-T'ung-ho who sought to serve the emperor by promoting reform, contributed unknowingly to the emperor's undoing.

Weng's friendship with the emperor, somewhat ironically also, rendered him an unsuitable agent of conciliation. He enjoyed the emperor's confidence to such an extent that he was naturally taken as the emperor's man. As some foreign observers had it, he was "practically the emperor of China," although the sovereign who at the time occupied the throne, did not have much power himself. Between 1894 and 1898 the emperor sought Weng's guidance on practically everything of importance. He was in all probability chiefly responsible for the emperor's decision to wage the disastrous war with Japan, against the counsel of a large number of high officials. In the eyes of Tz'u-hsi (and of all his political opponents), Weng must have appeared to have too much influence over the emperor. Significantly, less than three months after the defeat of 1894, the empress dowager ordered the termination of the services of all imperial tutors; tutors in Chinese studies were allowed to continue on a reduced schedule for a while longer, only upon the earnest entreaty of the emperor and Weng himself. Tz'u-hsi's move, according to some, was an attempt to diminish the opportunities of contact between Weng and his pupil.

The empress dowager seems to have become suspicious of Weng after she dismissed Wang Ming-luan and Ch'ang-ling in 1895. Kang-i alleged that Weng was a member of "the emperor faction" as much as Wang Ming-luan, and that Weng was the leader of a small "anti-empress clique." These allegations may not be completely justifiable. Yet the fact that such allegations were made shows that despite Weng's desire to be a mediator, his personal behavior and his relation with the emperor made him readily an object of partisan suspicion.

The emperor did things that hardly improved the situation. Contrary to his best intentions, he widened the gulf between his aunt and himself. In the summer of 1894 he began to make a few minor decisions without consulting her. The important decision to make war with Japan was reached without her positive support. When he revealed his willingness to modify the accustomed ways of the empire (1896-7), he took a further step that led to the final break with the empress dowager. These moves may have been made without the advice of Weng T'ung-ho. Taking the decision of 1894 as a clue, one is inclined to think that Weng probably was in favor of some of these moves. After all, the *hsün cheng* regime had ended years before and the emperor must at least partially justify his role as a full-fledged sovereign. As the mediator between the imperial rulers, Weng naturally wished to see the contenders of authority meet each other halfway. Meanwhile, he continued to promote reform and was soon to introduce K'ang Yu-wei into the scene, thus supplying the final factor that made the tragedy of 1898.

IV. WENG T'UNG-HO AND K'ANG YU-WEI

(a) Their Views on Reform

We shall now ascertain the role which Weng T'ung-ho played in the reform movement of 1898 and the factors that lead to his dismissal on June 15 of that year. Our inquiry may conveniently begin with his relation with K'ang Yu-wei. Two questions pose themselves: (1) To what extent did Weng accept or support K'ang's ideas of reform? and (2) To what extent was Weng responsible for starting K'ang on his reform career?

The answer to either of these questions is far from simple. Records are relatively meagre and accounts do not always agree. Some of these are obviously biased or possibly colored by partisan feelings; and it is not easy to evaluate the claims or counter-claims of their authors. The first question stated above, however, may be answered with a fair degree of accuracy by comparing the views of the two men in so far as these are ascertainable. K'ang's ideas on reform are well known. Although Weng did not formulate in writing his views in any systematic way, he had given sufficiently clear indications of the general drift of his thinking.

It can safely be assumed that since 1889 when Weng began to indoctrinate the emperor with the concept of reform, he had been in general agreement with K'ang as to the necessity of reform. Agreeing with K'ang also, Weng seems to have believed that reform should go beyond the mere adoption of Western technology and implements and should, as Weng put it, "begin with the fundamentals of internal administration." There was, however, a vital difference between the views of the two men: K'ang had much less respect for the established imperial tradition (both in its ideological and institutional aspects) than Weng who stood quite close to the position maintained by Feng Kuei-fen, Ch'en Chih, T'ang Chen, and Chang Chih-tung. In other words, K'ang was willing to modify the imperial system by taking advantage of modern Western experiences in government, education, and social life in general as well as in science and technology, whereas Weng refused to go beyond the adoption of "Western methods" which should serve merely to supplement "Chinese learning" but not to modify it.

That Weng was in essential agreement with Feng, Ch'en, and T'ang may be inferred from the fact that he presented to the emperor in 1889 Feng's *K'ang-i* and about five years later, Ch'en's *Yung-shu* and T'ang's *Wei-yen*, all these works containing specific recommendations of reform and covering a wide range of topics.

Weng would not have used these works to indoctrinate the emperor in the theory and practice of reform, if he had not approved of the leading ideas outlined in them. A brief survey of these works, therefore, should give us a reliable clue to Weng's own views.

Feng Kuei-fen's *K'ang-i* was published in its entirety in 1884, although portions of it had appeared before that year. After arguing that China was confronted by a completely new situation brought about by the arrival of the Westerners and that, as a consequence, she must adopt the things in which Westerners excelled in order for her to survive, Feng set forth his basic theory of reform in this rhetorical question:

If we let the moral principles and ethical teachings of China serve as the original foundation and let them be supplemented by the methods used by various [Western] countries for the attainment of prosperity and strength, would it not be the best of all procedures?

The ultimate objective of reform as envisaged by Feng, therefore, was to enable the empire to achieve political equality with foreign powers. It was not to alter China's moral tradition or institutional system in order to bring her into a cultural *rapprochement* with the West. As Feng put it:

We must try to discover some means to become their equal. . . . Regarding the present situation there are several major points: in making use of the ability of our manpower, with no one neglected, we are inferior to the barbarians; in securing the benefits of the soil, with nothing wasted, we are inferior to the barbarians; in maintaining a close relationship between the ruler and the people, with no barrier between them we are inferior to the barbarians; and in the necessary accord of word with deed, we are also inferior to the

barbarians. The way to correct these four points lies with ourselves, for they can be changed at once if only our emperor would set the general policy right. . . .

What then we have to learn from the barbarians is only one thing, solid ships and effective guns.

Feng then went on to quote with approval Wei Yüan's well-known formula: "Learn the superior techniques of the barbarians in order to keep them in check." Whatever administrative, economic, and military reforms were required should be effected by China's own efforts and within the frame work of the existing system.

There is little doubt that Weng T'ungho attached great importance to the *K'ang-i*. For a few months after he presented it to the emperor he read it again and commented enthusiastically that Feng's suggestions were "most pertinent to the needs of the time." It is also probable that his statement made in 1898, in reply to the emperor's question concerning reform, namely, it should begin with internal administration, reflected the influence of Feng Kuei-fen.

Ch'en Chih's *Yung-shu*, "Practical Writings," was written probably soon after the war of 1894. Ch'en went somewhat farther than Feng Kuei-fen in his proposals of reform, but he took a general standpoint essentially identical with that of Feng. Ch'en made a sharp distinction between *tao*, "principles," and *ch'i*, "instruments," and asserted that China was anciently in possession of both. She lost the latter as the result of placing exclusive emphasis on the former. Western countries, on the contrary, have never possessed "true principles" that govern human personality and human relationships (*tao*), but have developed the practical arts and sciences (*ch'i*) which latter, he reiterated, had their origins in ancient

China. The increasingly close contact of China with Western countries was an indication that "heaven would return the *ch'i* to China and make *tao* prevail in the West." In practical terms, this meant that China should preserve her moral tradition (i.e., Confucianism) which was eternally valid and unchangeable, but meanwhile should adopt the techniques and instruments that had made Western countries prosperous and strong. With the fundamental principle of reform thus established, Ch'en proceeded to recommend a wide range of changes, educational, administrative, military, economic, and diplomatic—suggestions which foreshadowed many of the *hsin cheng*, "new measures," of 1898.

T'ang Chen's *Wei-yen*, "Words of Warning," is a shorter work than either of the above mentioned books, but it represents substantially the same standpoint and covers similiar topics on reform. T'ang repeated the familiar argument that "the governmental and educational systems of the Westerners were mostly based on the *Chou-li*, The Constitution of Chou," and that their science and technology stemmed from the writings of ancient Chinese philosphers, such as *Kuan-tzu, Mo-tzu, and Huai-nan-tzu.* China succeeded in maintaining *tao*, the basic principles of morality, but allowed *ch'i*, knowledge and skill in material life, to fall into oblivion, leaving Westerners alone to excel in the latter. That being the case, it would not have been shameful for China to adopt "Western methods," for this would in reality amount to receiving back what she had given to the West. In T'ang's own words: "They have built upon what we had invented, why should we not make innovations of what they copied [from us]?" Reform, accordingly, was to be effected in two direction. First, China must modernize herself by freely borrowing Western "instruments" (*ch'i*) but, at the same time, zealously preserve the "principles" (*tao*) that were her own. Second, China must rid herself of the time-worn, useless or harmful practices that beset her educational, administrative, and economic system. This, T'ang made clear, did not mean that Chinese traditional values should be replaced by Western religion. On the contrary, those values should be preserved; and when the empire regained strength and prestige as the result of judicious reform, the way was open to the realization of *ta-t'ung*, "the great harmony," namely, the conversion of the West to Confucianism.

The views of Ch'en and T'ang, we think, should prove equally congenial to Weng T'ung-ho. And there is good reason to suppose that Weng also subscribed to the general views of Chang Chih-tung, although Chang's major work on reform, *Ch'üan-hsüch p'ien,* appeared in 1898, too late to exert formative influence on Weng's thinking.

A Western missionary once characterized Chang Chih-tung as "a Chinese to the backbone" and justified his opinion thus:

To him [Chang] there is no country like China, no people like the Chinese, and no religion to be compared with the Confucian. . . . He rests his hope on two things —namely, the renaissance of Confucianism and the adoption of Western science and methods. The old is to form the moral basis, and the new is to be used for practical purposes.

This, we think, is a remarkably accurate characterization of Chang's intellectual outlook and a precise restatement of his famous formula, *Chung-hsüeh wei t'i, Hsi-hsüeh wei yung.* For, according to Chang, "reform" did not mean the alteration of the established tradition of the empire; it meant, in reality, the preservation of that tradition by wisely selecting and adopting those elements of Western civilization that had proved efficacious in giving Western countries their material resources and military might. Reform, in other words, was not a step toward Westernization but an indispensable means to insure the continuance of the Confucian empire.

It is interesting to note that Ku Hung-ming who associated with Chang for a number of years, underscored Chang's characteristic position by contrasting it with that of Li Hung-chang. According to Ku, one of the basic differences between the two men was that while the former had a profound respect for China's moral heritage, the latter devoted his attention exclusively to matters of immediate, practical advantage. The defeat of 1894 convinced Chang that China could not be preserved unless she adopted what he called "Western learning," but the true purpose of reform always remained the preservation of the Confucian tradition which alone made China "superior" to all other countries. To impair or abandon that tradition was to defeat the very aim of reform.

It appears that, speaking generally, this was also the position taken by Weng T'ung-ho. Weng as much as Chang Chih-tung was a product of the established Confucian tradition, and was equally proud of it. To Weng, therefore, "reform" could have been nothing more than adopting some of the devices and implements of the "barbarians" with which to defend the morally superior Chinese empire against foreign aggression, and refurbishing the administrative practices so as to prevent the benefits of these "Western methods" from being lost in the notoriously inefficient and corrupt officialdom of Peking. His cultural pride, reinforced by his anti-foreign sentiments, prevented him from perceiving anything worthwhile in Western civilization beyond those elements which men like Feng Kuei-fen, Ch'en Chih, T'ang Chen, and Chang Chih-tung had recognized as useful within definite limits. His appreciation of the friendships of a few Westerners did not change his basic attitude toward the West; for he held fast to the assumption that all foreigners were despicable unless they proved themselves to be otherwise.

Furthermore, there was some similarity between the intellectual outlooks of Weng and Chang. Chang was on the whole an eclectic, committing himself to no one single school of Confucian thought. He held the doctrines of Chu Hsi in high esteem, but this was due more to his wish to uphold the orthodox ideology of existing regime than to any desire for doctrinal purity. His eclecticism, however, did not embrace the doctrines of the Kung-yang school, which to him were decidedly unorthodox and therefore unacceptable. As a matter of fact, he detested the Kung-yang doctrines so much that for forty years he had been consistently refuting them, regarding them as "capital for seditious subjects and undutiful sons." From his point of view, to subscribe to these doctrines, especially as they were propounded by contemporary followers of that school, was tantamount to throwing overboard the very ideological tradition which had made China "superior to all barbarian countries." Naturally, therefore, Chang Chih-tung could not remain long on cordial terms with K'ang Yu-wei whose exposition of Kung-yang doctrines ran directly contrary to what Chang thought to have been decent and correct.

The similarity between Weng and Chang in this connection is also remarkable. Weng, too, was essentially an eclectic, although his eclecticism embraced somewhat different elements from that of Chang. For our purpose, it is important to note that in common with Chang, Weng showed appreciation of Chu Hsi and the "imperial Confucianism" that developed from his philosophy, and was repelled by K'ang Yu-wei's "wild-fox" interpretations of the Confucian classics, based on the Kung-yang doctrines as K'ang understood them.

The foregoing discussion, we hope, affords some useful clues to Weng T'ung-ho's views concerning reform. In addition to the persons just mentioned, however, there were a few others who had exerted some influence on Weng or whose ideas proved cogenial to him. One of these was Sung Yü-jen. Before Sung sailed for Europe to take up his duties as secretary of the Chinese legation at London and Paris, he showed Weng his work on current affairs. Weng indicated that he was favorably impressed by Sung's suggestions, but he doubted the praticability of the proposal "to alter the institutions" of the empire. Unfortunately, we have no way to ascertain the contents of this work of Sung's. Some of his ideas on reform, however, may be gathered from his work on the countries of Europe, *T'ai-hsi ko-kuo ts'ai-feng chi*. One of the most important recommendations he made is that China should adopt the parliamentary institutions of European countries. Sung was convinced that among the institutions of the West the parliament and the school were the most useful, for the former gave expression to the wishes of the people and the latter trained scholars to serve as the people's leaders. He admitted that owing to the absence of what he regarded as true moral principles and correct conceptions of social relationships in Western nations, their parliamentary systems were not without some grave shortcomings. The parliamentary institution, however, should work perfectly in China where "the dicta of the sages" would serve as the infallible criterion by which all opinions could be judged.

It may be noted that Ch'en Chih and T'ang Chen also recommended the establishment of *i-hui*, "parliaments," in China. They differed from Sung, however, in their conceptions of "parliament"; Sung was somewhat more radical in this respect than either Ch'en or T'ang. Ch'en Chih's "parliament" for China was to be composed by the gentry on the local level and by the gentry and some of the officials on the central level. T'ang Chen's "parliament" was a bicameral affair composed of officials of various ranks. The "parliaments" envisaged by these men, therefore, remained within the broad conceptual and institutional framework of the imperial system, amounting in reality to little more than institutionalizing the age-old practice of discussing public affairs by the gentry and officials. Sung went one step farther than both men in arguing that "parliaments" of the empire could function properly only when they were composed of persons who had been educated in the modern style schools. The implication of this argument is obvious. To Sung Yü-jen, the parliament and the school constituted the warp and the woof of the social fabric, and, as a result, basic educational reform must precede political reform. This twofold reform was probably the same institutional change to which Weng T'ung-ho raised objections.

Timothy Richard also furnished some information which throws light on Weng's idea of reform. Richard was known as a friend of China and an advocate of reform before he met Weng personally on October 26, 1895. Weng listened to Richard's suggestions with interest, but he did not accept them without reservations. Weng recorded the main points of Richard's conversation and commented upon them as follows:

"The true principles (*tao*) of Yao, Shun, Chou, and K'ung" [Richard said] "are valid everywhere on the globe. . . . When government policies that benefit the people fall into decay, the true principles of the sages will no longer prevail. . . . There are four major policies, namely, educating the people, nourishing them, giving them peace, and renovating them. The method of educating the people consists in making the five constant virtues prevail in all countries; of nourishing the people, in sharing benefits with all countries . . . ; of giving the people peace, in avoiding war; and of renovating the people, in reform. The first task of reform is the construction of railways; the training of troops comes next. China should employ Western personnel along side [of Chinese personnel] and give instruction in Western subjects [in the schools]." I raised objection to the two [last-mentioned suggestions].

Weng's comment implied that he accepted the other points made by Richard. As a president of the Board of Revenue, Weng was naturally interested in fiscal and economical reform, particularly in such matters as currency, railways, mining, manufacturing, etc. That he undertook actively to promote reform in these fields may be seen from the fact that he showed personal attention to men known as experts in industrial or commercial enterprises, among whom Chang Chien seems to have enjoyed his greatest confidence. Weng probably accepted many of Chang's recommendations concerning industrial development. As Weng was aware of the habitually listless, bungling, and corrupt ways of Peking officialdom, he must have come to the conclusion that no economic reform could be successfully carried out without administrative reform. This was probably what he had in mind when he said, on January 18, 1898 in reply to the emperor's question, that reform should begin with the basic task of internal administration. He, however, wished merely to sweep away the malpractices of imperial officialdom; he had no desire to bring about any institutional change in the imperial system, such as the introduction of "parliaments," employment of foreign personnel, and establishment of modern schools would have certainly involved.

There is, therefore, ample evidence to support the statement ventured earlier in the present section, that the reform which Weng T'ung-ho envisaged was of limited scope: he was willing to modernize China in economic and military matters and to introduce a degree of efficiency and honesty into imperial officialdom as a necessary condition of modernization, but he was opposed to modifying institutional structure or abandoning the traditional values of the empire. He could not permit "Westernization," in other words, beyond the adoption of those "methods and implements" which constituted the secret of "the barbarians'" overwhelming material strength. His concept of reform may thus be characterized as "moderate," in contrast to the more "radical" program of K'ang Yu-wei, which called for more extensive changes in the existing system and a higher degree of Westernization.

Weng's basic attitude was made clear in a remark addressed to the emperor on June 11, 1898, the very day on which the edict formally announcing the inauguration of the reform regime was issued.

Upon hearing the emperor's declaration that "from now on undivided attention should be paid to Western learning" Weng retorted that "we cannot do without studying Western methods, but it is even more important not to forget the moral and philosophical teachings of the sages and wise men" of China. The same thought was expressed in this document itself which, as a matter of fact, was drafted by Weng who was still performing his duties as a high court official:

Changes must be made in accord with the necessities of the times. . . . Let this, therefore, be made known to one and all in the four corners of the empire: let us keep in mind the moral and philosophical teachings of our sages and wise men, and make these the foundation [of imperial reconstruction.] We must also select over a wide range such subjects of Western knowledge as are pertinent to the current needs and diligently study and apply them in order to correct the evils of empty, impractical, and deceptive ways [which have hitherto prevailed].

It is noteworthy that the phrase "the moral and philosophical teachings of the sages and wise men" (*sheng hsien i li chih hsieh*) appears both in Weng's oral statement and in the imperial edict. This reflects Weng's firm resolve to uphold the moral tradition of imperial China—an attitude which may have induced some writers to identify him as a "conservative," despite his unmistakable desire to implement reform in the sphere of financial, military, and administrative affairs.

It hardly needs stressing that K'ang Yu-wei's position differed appreciably from that of Weng T'ung-ho. As we shall undertake to show, K'ang was, during the closing decades of the nineteenth century, a "radical" in his views concerning not only the practical affairs of state but also doctrinal and ideological matters. The difference was, of course, largely a matter of degree; in fact, there was an area of agreement between the views of the two men, especially those which concerned reform. It has been pointed out that some of K'ang's ideas of reform coincided with the suggestions made by Ch'en Chih in his *Yung-shu* and by T'ang Chen in his *Wei-yen*. Assuming that Weng also subscribed to some of the views of Ch'en and T'ang, there may have been points of contact between K'ang and Weng even with regard to certain details of reform. In so far, however, as K'ang's ideas went beyond Ch'en and T'ang, and in so far as K'ang revealed his desire to alter the traditional ideology and the imperial system, even though all this was proposed with the avowed intention of showing "the true Confucius" and of "preserving the country," Weng could no longer allow himself to remain in K'ang's intellectual company.

The most important expression of Weng's disagreement with K'ang, already mentioned before, was given in 1894 when Weng read the latter's *Hsin-hsüeh wei-ching k'ao*. The general drift of this book as Weng understood it was as follows:

[K'ang Yu-wei] holds that every bit of the old text of Lui Hsin is spurious—who interpolated and adulterated the six classics—and that all [commentators] after Cheng K'ang-ch'eng had been deceived [by Liu Hsin].

Weng then commented upon K'ang's view:

Truly a wild-fox meditator among the commentators of the classics! No end to my astonishment.

Weng's astonishment is readily understandable. For, although K'ang claimed that his merciless attack on the old-text school was motivated by a desire to rid Confucianism of "false ascriptions," he was impliedly attacking the entire neo-Confucian tradition which since Ming times had served as the foundation of the established imperial ideology. His attack, moreover, amounted to an assault not only on the followers of Chu Hsi but practically on all Confucianists who did not subscribe to the doctrines of the Kung-yang school. These latter would include Weng T'ung-ho and the overwhelming majority of the scholars and officials of the time. Such an assault could hardly remain unnoticed. About two months after Weng read the *Wei-ching k'ao* K'ang was impeached by an official who accused him of "reviling his predecessors and misleading future scholars." The offending book was quickly banned by imperial order.

Differences of opinion between Weng and K'ang concerning the details of administrative reform were also substantial. A full examination of K'ang's views must be reserved for another opportunity, but it is useful to indicate here some of the major disagreements between the two men.

Among the many suggestion which were submitted in his memorials written in the years 1888-98, three were repeatedly stressed by K'ang. The first of these was the proposal that the emperor should follow the examples of Russia's Peter the Great and Japan's Meiji. The earliest mention of the successful reforms of Japan was made by K'ang in his "first memorial" to the emperor, submitted in the autumn of 1888. This, by the way, was the same memorial which Weng refused to transmit to the throne. This "follow Japan" proposal was reiterated

with added emphasis in another memorial submitted early in 1898. In this later document K'ang put forward three alternative courses of action, the first and "best" of which was for the emperor

to adopt the methods of Russia and Japan with which to fix the policies of the empire, to accept the intentions of Peter the Great as "the law of the mind," and to take the Meiji government as the model of administration.

K'ang explained that Russia and Japan were able to emerge from weakness to strength by simply "following the footsteps of the West" and "altering the institutions and laws." Since, however, "Japan is geographically near to us and her governmental form and social customs are similar to ours," it would have been easier for China to imitate Japan than Russia. Substantially the same arguments were repeated by K'ang in subsequent memorials and in his treatises on Russia and Japan.

K'ang's suggestion that in effecting reform China should follow the examples set by Russia and Japan is not without some cogency. It, as a matter of fact, appealed to a considerable number of persons, apparently including the emperor himself. It had, however, certain implications which made it unacceptable to men like Weng T'ung-ho. To begin with, K'ang's unreserved admiration for Peter and Meiji must have readily led Weng and others like him to suspect that K'ang was willing to commit the empire to a program of extensive Westernization, involving drastic changes in the existing institutional and ideological system. K'ang's argument that Japan was close to China culturally as well as geographically, did not mitigate this suspicion, for the Japan which he wished to take as

China's paradigm of reform was not the traditional Japan which indeed had cultural affinity with imperial China, but the post-Tokugawa Japan which had given up much of that affinity and had, in K'ang's own words, followed the footsteps of Western countries. It has been said that

in spite of being an insular people ever zealous to maintain the integrity of their national life, the Japanese have always shown compromise and assimilative attitude toward foreign cultures and religions.

That attitude made it easy for Japan to adopt Western ideas and institutions in the nineteenth century as it had made it easy for her to accept Chinese ethics and philosophy many centuries earlier. It partly explains the fact that Japan was able to modernize herself and transform herself into a powerful nation within a short period of time. From the viewpoint of men like Keng T'ung-ho, however, her readiness to give up her traditional cultural affinity with imperial China and to Westernize herself must have proved definitely distasteful.

That Weng did not favor the idea of "following Japan" may be gathered partly from the fact that he refused to share the emperor's interest in Huang Tsun-hsien's work on Japan, *Jih-pen-kuo chih*, widely esteemed as an authoritative treatise on Japanese history and a standard reference for men interested in *yang-wu*. Weng flatly turned down the emperor's request for a copy of this work—an episode which occurred within a few days after K'ang Yu-wei presented to the emperor his works on Russia and Japan. Weng could not prevent K'ang from sending in his own works but gave a hint of his disapproval of the "follow Japan" approach to reform

by refusing to furnish the desired work of Huang Tsun-hsien. It may be noted that Huang had been cooperating with Liang Ch'i-ch'ao and T'an Ssu-t'ung, two of K'ang's more prominent "disciples," in the reform undertakings sponsored by Ch'en Pao-chen, governor of Hunan. Huang's relationship to K'ang (though a somewhat indirect one) and the fact that he was engaged in reform on a provincial level may have constituted additional reasons for Weng's reluctance to send in the *Jih-pen-kuo chih*.

A second proposal to which K'ang attached much importance was *pien cheng*, "to change the governmental system." Chang Chien, a close friend of Weng's, was so scared of K'ang's views in this connection that he decided to leave Peking, at the hightide of the reform movement. In all probability, Weng shared Chang's misgivings.

K'ang's recommendations concerning political reform went far beyond Weng's idea of administrative reform. This became increasingly clear in the months just before the reform regime was officially announced and during its progress. When K'ang was summoned to appear in Tsungli yamen on January 24, 1898, Liao Shou-heng, a president of the Board of Punishment, asked him, "How to implement reform." In reply K'ang said, "Changing the laws and institutions is to be the first task." Later, in a number of memorials to which reference has already been made, K'ang specified the sort of legal and institutional changes he had in mind. He was highly critical of the existing system which, as he said in his "first memorial" of 1888, was nominally a heritage from the imperial ancestors but in reality "the decayed governmental system" of previous dynasties. This system, evolved in the days when China knew no civilized countries outside herself, was based on the principle of internal security. Political institutions and administrative methods were designed primarily to prevent or forestall rebellion. This basic objective constituted the rationale of the examination system and the system of checks and surveillance in which several officials were appointed to one single position and one official concurrently occupied several administrative posts. With the coming of the Westerners the situation drastically changed. Internal security was no longer the sole concern and, as a consequence, the imperial system became utterly outmoded. The conclusion, according to K'ang, was inevitable: "Unless old practices are all abandoned and a new structure is erected, there is no way to rid of the inveterate evils" that had rendered the empire helpless against the encroachments of Western powers.

It is no surprise, therefore, that K'ang made a number of proposals concerning administrative reform which, if carried out, would have affected some of the vital parts or the operative principles of the imperial system. One of the most important among these was made in his "sixth memorial" (January 29, 1898). He strongly urged the establishment of a *chih-tu chü*, "bureau of government institutions," which was to be a central organ to assist the emperor to plan and decide basic policies of reform. To carry out the policies thus formulated, K'ang suggested the creation of twelve administrative bureaux, each of which resembled a ministry in the cabinet of a European government and was to be charged with a specific administrative function, such as finance, education, military affairs, etc. The adoption of such an administrative structure, obviously, would have rendered the Grand Council, the Six Boards, and a host of other imperial government offices useless. The only important organization which K'ang left untouched was Tsungli yamen which he allowed to stand and to continue to deal with foreign affairs. It is important to note that the underlying principle of K'ang's *chih-tu chü* and the twelve bureaux was administrative efficiency to be achieved through specialization and expert personnel instead of the old principle of security through check and surveillance.

In the same memorial K'ang made another proposal which may have frightened many a conservative official and displeased Weng T'ung-ho. K'ang urged the introduction of embryonic institutions of local self-government and local representation, in the form of a *min-cheng chü*, "bureau of the people's affairs," one for each circuit, and a *min-cheng fen-chü*, branch bureau of the people's affairs, one for each of the districts in the circuit. The district magistrate was to retain authority to deal with lawsuit and revenue collection. All other administrative matters, education, public health, agriculture, police, etc., were to be entrusted to the "bureau" in which the local gentry and government appointees worked together to carry out measures of reform. An even more radical proposal was made in K'ang's "fourth memorial" (1895), in which he urged the establishment of a "parliament" in Peking. He reasoned that one of the chief sources of the strength of Western countries lay in the parliamentary institution which gave expression to the wishes of the people; he was convinced that parliaments facilitated tax collection, the promotion of public welfare, and the prevention of official corruption. And, finally, in the summer of 1898, K'ang went so far as to advocate the establishment of a *kuo-hui*, "national assembly," and the drafting of a constitution for the empire. Parliamentary and constitutional government, according to K'ang, had made European countries strong, whereas *chuan-chih*, autocracy, was the chief cause of China's weakness. The only way to save the empire, therefore, was to put into practice the principle of "the separation of the three powers" so that the legislative, judicial, and executive powers would no longer be concentrated in one man or one organ. In other words, K'ang urged the transformation of the imperial system as it developed during the past two thousand years into a Western-style "constitutional monarchy"—a transformation amounting to a veritable "revolution" in the Aristotelian sense. All this was good political theory, much of which had been put into practice in Western countries. But viewed in the context of the general way of thinking in K'ang's own time, it was nothing short of terrifying to the average scholar-official. The "changes in internal administration" which K'ang recommended, implied a sweeping condemnation of the existing system; it is no surprise that it was regarded as totally unacceptable. Weng T'ung-ho gave no direct indication of his reaction to these ideas of K'ang; the fact, however, that he objected to the much milder proposals of Sung Yü-jen justifies the conjecture that he would have definitely rejected K'ang's *chih-tu chü*, national assembly, and constitutional government.

K'ang made other equally radical proposals, including the introduction of Western learning in the new schools that were to be established throughout the empire, the modification of the examination system, the revision of the imperial legal code, and the adoption of Western-style dress and the cutting off of the queue (a visible symbol of Manchu rule). In proposing legal reform K'ang argued that the only way to removing the "national shame"—the extraterritorial jurisdiction in China by foreign powers —was to adopt appropriate principles of Roman law and the laws of England, France, Germany, the United States, and Japan, and to evolve on the basis of these principles a new legal code for the empire. In order to insure that legal reform was properly carried out, K'ang urged that a foreigner be engaged to work with him, "to revise the laws and the Government administrative departments" of the empire—an idea which reminds us of one of the two unacceptable suggestions made by Timothy Richard to Weng T'ung-ho in 1895.

It can be safely concluded, therefore, that K'ang Yu-wei advocated Westernization beyond the adoption of Western methods" and urged institutional reform beyond the refurbishing of the existing administrative structure, to an extent unmatched by any other leading exponents of reform. It becomes clear also that K'ang's statement that "changing the laws and institutions" was the first task of reform, and that "unless old practices were all abandoned and a new structure erected" the chronic diseases of the empire could not be cured, were no empty rhetoric but expressed his personal convictions and served as guiding principles of his reform efforts.

Such an approach to reform was bound to clash with Weng T'ung-ho's concept of limited reform. It is of course doubtful that Weng had knowledge of the entire range of K'ang's philosophical and reform ideas. But there is no question but that he was sufficiently acquainted with the general drift of K'ang's thinking to reach the final decision to part company with K'ang even before the One Hundred Days had begun. Whatever general agreement that once existed between the two men, was soon dissipated by the wide differences in intellectual outlook, theory of reform, and personal temperament. It was simply impossible for Weng, a shrewd, prudent, "down-to-earth" official, deeply steeped in the established imperial tradition, to tolerate for long a man who wished to amputate the imperial system, who authored the *Wei-ching k'ao* and the *Ta-t'ung shu*, the impact of which on the intellectual world of the time assumed cataclysmic proportions—a man who dreamed of the abolition of the family, marriage, private property (the most characteristic, if not essential, social institutions of imperial China), and who even allowed his "utopian tendencies" to project themselves into "a study of roaming through the heavens."

Weng was prevented from remaining in agreement with K'ang for another reason. As we have seen, Weng strove to effect conciliation between the emperor and the empress dowager. K'ang Yu-wei, however, somewhat like Wang Ming-luan and Ch'ang-ling, sided with the emperor and became increasingly hostile to the empress dowager as the reform movement developed, eventually coming to the view that "the Empress Dowager was the only obstacle to reform" and therefore should be eliminated, by assassination if necessary. Even long before the *coup d'état* of 1898 K'ang was convinced that the hope of realizing reform rested with the emperor alone. Thus, as early as in 1888, K'ang said frankly in his "first memorial" that "the affairs of the empire remained in a sorry state as a result of the evil influences of eunuchs and palace maids," and that, consequently, the emperor should "carefully choose officials who are in immediate contact with him" to assist him to ameliorate the situation. Later, K'ang suggested in his "fourth memorial" (June 30, 1895) that the emperor should take drastic steps to clear the administration of useless, decrepit officials (who were, it may be noted, appointed and retained by the empress dowager) and "to make decisions according to his own sagely wishes alone." And when K'ang realized that the emperor did not possess adequate power to do what he wished, he counseled the emperor "to use whatever authority your majesty now have to do things that reform requires."

The implications of these utterances is clear: K'ang wished to see the emperor assume full sovereignty, by wresting control from Tz'u-hsi. There was, therefore, some basis for the charge that K'ang Yu-wei and his associates plotted against the empress dowager. Understandably, Weng was one among those who lent credence to that charge. Thus, when Weng heard the news of the *coup d'état* of September 20, he remarked with apparent indignation that "the seditious schemes of scoundrels had misled the Sagely One into a pitfall."

A little later, when Weng heard that he was accused of having strongly recommended K'ang to the emperor, he wrote that if he had not left Peking he would have certainly prevented "that scoundrel" from plotting for the empress dowager's downfall. It is of course doubtful that Weng could have changed the course of events even if he had remained in Peking during the One Hundred Days. But we have no reason to question Weng's sincerity in thus indicating that he could not share K'ang's anti-empress attitude despite his loyalty to the emperor.

It may be speculated that if Weng had been allowed to assume full leadership in reform (a possibility precluded by the historical situation), he would have pushed reform in a manner and direction different from what K'ang did in the One Hundred Days. This conjecture finds some support in the fact that two crucial documents, one issued when Weng was still able to exert his influence and the other when K'ang Yu-wei dominated the scene, reflected two theories of reform which corresponded respectively to the viewpoints of Weng and K'ang. In the "reform edict" of June 11, 1898, which came from Weng's hand, the emperor is represented as saying:

Let us keep in mind the moral and philosophical teachings of our sages and wise men and make them the foundation [of imperial reconstruction].

In the edict dated September 12 of the same year, issued many days after Weng left Peking, it is said:

In revitalizing the various administrative departments our government adopts Western methods and principles. For, in a true sense, there is no difference between China and the West in setting up government for the sake of the people. Since, however, Westerners have studied [the science of government] more diligently [than us, their findings] can be used to supplement our deficiencies. Scholars and officials of today whose purview does not go beyond China, [regard Westerners] as practically devoid of precepts or principles. They do not know that the science of government as it exists in Western countries has very rich and varied contents, and that its chief aim is to develop the people's knowledge and intelligence and to make their living commodious. The best part of that science is capable of bringing about improvements in human nature and the prolongation of human life.

It is impossible to ascertain the authorship of this document; one, however, naturally suspects that K'ang Yu-wei had exercised his influence on it as the above passage indicates.

A comparison of these two edicts reveals a vital difference in points of view. The earlier document represents the view that while "Western methods" should be adopted, they should not affect the moral tradition of China, which was not only different from the non-material aspect of Western civilization but in reality superior to it. The later document represents the view that there was no essential difference in the basic principles of government between China and the West and that, therefore, reform was not so much a task of supplementing Chinese tradition with Western science as that of putting into practice methods and principles which were intrinsically and universally valid, the soundness of which had been first demonstrated in Western countries. The distance that separated these two views corresponded roughly to the difference between the positions taken by Weng T'ung-ho and K'ang Yu-wei.

(b) Weng's Attitude toward K'ang

We shall now take up the second of the two questions posed at the beginning of the present section: Did Weng T'ung-ho strongly recommend K'ang Yu-wei to the emperor and was thus chiefly instrumental in starting K'ang on his career as leader of the reform movement?

This question has aroused a good deal of controversy among writers. Some placed the main responsibility on Weng, while others denied that Weng recommended K'ang at all. It is perhaps impossible to find a categorically certain answer to this question. A survey of the available sources, however, compels one to draw the conclusion that although Weng did not make any formal recommendation, he was chiefly responsible for giving K'ang the opportunity to gain the emperor's unreserved confidence.

It will be necessary to examine some of the claims and accounts furnished by writers of the time. In agreement with many of his contemporaries, K'ang Yu-wei himself credited Weng with recommending him to the emperor in the later months of 1897 when Russia was demanding Port Arthur and Dairen. These are K'ang's words:

> When the Empress Dowager decided to give them to Russia and Weng T'ung-ho realized that all my prophecies came true, he strongly recommended me to the Emperor. Kao Hsüeh Tseng, the Supervising Censor, Chen Pao Chen, the Governor of Hunan, Su Chih Ching, of the Hanlin College, and Li Twan Fen, President of the Board of Rites, also recommended me from time to time. When the Emperor asked the members of the Cabinet [concerning my qualifications], Weng T'ung-ho recommended me, saying, "His abilities are a hundred times superior to my own," and prayed the Emperor to listen to me in all matters of reform.

K'ang's statement, made in 1899, about a year after the *coup d'état,* is not entirely clear. It does show, however, that some time before the One Hundred Days Weng "strongly recommended" K'ang to the emperor, presumably orally, when about the same time a few other officials also recommended K'ang, and that Weng strongly supported the recommendations of these officials, in reply to the emperor's inquiry about K'ang.

It is also clear that Weng was not alone in bringing K'ang Yu-wei to the emperor's attention. K'ang himself named four officials besides Weng who recommended him, but his list is not complete. So far as it has been definitely established, the following men had, at different times, requested the emperor to avail himself of K'ang's service: (1) Kao Hsieh-tseng (whom K'ang referred to as Kao Hsüeh Tseng), (2) Sun Chia-nai, (3) Chang Po-hsi (both of whom K'ang failed to mention), (4) Li Tuan-fen (whom K'ang referred to as Li Twan Fen), (5) Ch'en Pao-chen, and (6) Hsü Chih-ch'ing (whom K'ang referred to as Su Chih Ching).

In a statement which K'ang made shortly after the *coup d'état*, he indicated that Kao Hsieh-tseng was the first person to recommend him, meaning apparently that Kao was the first to do so in writing. According to Liang Ch'i-ch'ao, Kao recommended K'ang after reading his "fifth memorial" and requested the emperor to grant K'ang an audience. Prince Kung advised against the audience, but suggested that K'ang be consulted by high officials. This brought about the well-known interview in Tsungli yamen on January 24, 1898. According to Lu Nai-hsiang, one of K'ang's biographers, Kao made the recommendation on the day (December 12, 1897) when Weng T'ung-ho visited K'ang in his hostel and told him that he had personally recommended K'ang to the emperor. These accounts are not as clear and precise as one should like, but they all point to the fact that Kao made the recommendation quite early, probably at about the same time when Weng made his.

Other written recommendations followed in rapid succession. Early in 1898 Sun Chia-nai recommended K'ang for his qualifications for diplomatic service. At about the same time, Chang Po-hsi, then director of studies in Kwangtung, recommended K'ang for his knowledge of practical and foreign affairs. Li Tuan-fen, a vice-president of the Board of Punishment, recommended, both orally and in writing, K'ang Yu-wei and T'an Ssu-t'ung. Ch'en Pao-chen, governor of Hunan, joined the chorus and drew imperial attention to K'ang's abilities in a memorial. And finally Hsü Chih-ch'ing recommended K'ang (together with Huang Tsun-hsien, T'an Ssu-t'ung, Chang Yüan-chi, and Liang Ch'i-ch'ao) in a memorial submitted on June 13, 1898, and helped to bring about the imperial audience three days later.

One cannot deny that these written recommendations contributed materially to bringing K'ang into contact with the emperor. One should not, however, underestimate the force of Weng's oral recommendation, regardless of the precise time it was made. It may well have been the decisive factor which rendered the emperor so favorably predisposed toward K'ang that he readily placed his confidence in the latter upon meeting him for the first time. For, as one of the first two officials to introduce the emperor to the concept of reform and as the emperor's trusted friend for many years, Weng's high opinion of K'ang must have exercised a crucial influence on the emperor's attitude and lent considerable force to the recommendations made by other officials. Thus, even though Weng cannot be identified as one of the "reformers of 1898," one can hardly resist the conclusion that he was largely instrumental in bringing about K'ang's sudden rise to prominence as the leader of the reform movement. Sun Chia-nai, of course, was also in a position to exert a similar influence on the emperor; but the recommendation which he made of K'ang was a limited one and the confidence which he enjoyed was not quite comparable to what Weng was then enjoying. As a result, Sun's recom-

mendation was of secondary importance. This perhaps partly explains the fact that K'ang did not include Sun among those who recommended him.

Weng T'ung-ho, as it is well known, repeatedly denied that he had ever recommended K'ang to the emperor. The first denial was made on October 18, 1898:

Newspapers have always been absurd. The conversation of K'ang, the traitor, published in today's paper, alleging that I had recommended [him to the emperor] is particularly strange. Does he intend to implicate and ruin me because I had rejected him?

A year later, on December 23, 1899, when Weng saw the edict which ordered the apprehension of K'ang and charged him with having "strongly recommended" K'ang to the emperor, he wrote the following in his diary:

Reverentially read [the edict] with trembling fear. Humbly I recall that when K'ang Yu-wei, the traitor, presented himself [to the emperor on June 16, 1898], I had already been dismissed [on the previous day]. Moreover, I had repeatedly said [to the emperor] that this man's intentions are unpredictable and that I dared not associate with him. On several occasions the emperor ordered me to send in K'ang's writings. [I demurred at first but] eventually I had to transmit his order, instructing Chang Yin-huan to ask K'ang for the desired writings. When these were delivered to the Grand Council, my colleagues placed them in an envelope and sent them [to the emperor]. I did not know what was said in these writings. Later, if I had remained with my colleagues [to serve the emperor], I would have never allowed this traitor to become madly perverse to such an extent [as to plot against the empress dowager]. But I was punished for this [attempt to expose K'ang]. I have now only myself to blame.

Weng's denials, despite their firm tone, do not square with the established facts. The statement which he made in 1899 is particularly misleading. It points to the fact that K'ang's audience with the emperor took place one day after Weng's dismissal but suppresses the fact that Weng's comment on K'ang's superlative abilities contributed to the emperor's determination to meet K'ang, i.e., to bringing about that very audience. It calls attention to the fact that Weng voiced his suspicion of K'ang shortly before his dismissal but fails to mention that prior to his attempt to discredit K'ang he was on cordial terms with K'ang for a while. The truth is, as we shall presently show, that Weng changed his attitude toward K'ang more than once between 1888 and 1898, a fact which the statement just quoted does not suggest at all. For the relationship between the two men began with a period of coldness or aversion on the part of Weng, followed by an interval of cordiality, and ended in Weng's attempt openly to discredit and to dissociate himself from K'ang. It is not difficult to understand Weng's denial that he was responsible for bringing K'ang into the emperor's confidence, for after all K'ang was officially branded a "traitor" after the *coup d'état*, and considerations of personal safety alone would have been sufficient to induce Weng to make the denial. His shifting attitude toward K'ang, however, involved motivations and requires explanation.

It may be useful to trace briefly the development of this unstable relationship. K'ang began his efforts to win Weng's patronage in 1888, when for the first time he made his views known to Weng. He, however, found Weng far from receptive or courteous. In the autumn of that year, his request for an interview with Weng was refused. At about the same time, Weng turned down Sheng-yü's request that he transmit K'ang's memorial to the throne; according to Weng's own explanation, K'ang's language was "too blunt and overly frank," making it imprudent to bring the memorial to imperial attention. In the summer of 1894 Weng expressed his astonishment at K'ang's "wild-fox" interpretations of the Confucian classics. In the spring of the following year Weng refused to grant an interview to Liang Ch'i-ch'ao whom he pointedly identified as "K'ang's student." Shortly afterwards, however, Weng changed his attitude toward K'ang, ushering in a brief period of seeming cordiality between the two men which lasted until the early months of 1898. By 1895, we recall, Weng had become known as an active promotor of reform, a role which he continued to play down to the spring of 1898. Thus, significantly, the period of Weng's cordiality toward K'ang coincided with the period of his active promotion of reform. But beginning with K'ang's appearance in Tsungli yamen on January 24, 1898, Weng again became critical of K'ang. His terse comment on K'ang's proposals concerning legal and administrative reform, "unrestrained to the extreme," can hardly be construed as a favorable reaction to them. Presently, Weng began to withdraw his support of K'ang and his reform program (as Weng himself indicated in the statement quoted above). It was this final period of hostility which gave seeming plausibility to Weng's denial that he was instrumental in introducing K'ang to the emperor.

The question is then, why did Weng change his attitude toward K'ang in 1895 and again in 1898?

An obvious explanation of the first

change is that the crisis of 1894-5 prompted Weng to redouble his efforts to bring about administrative reform and to look for competent men to help him in that task. As far back as in 1889, Weng had already undertaken to plant the idea of reform in the young emperor's mind. Despite Weng's increased attention to current affairs and to *yang-wu* during the years that followed, however, he had very little knowledge of those matters that would have enabled him to formulate a practical program of reform. He himself confessed, during the progress of the Sino-Japanese war, that his knowledge fell short of the emperor's enthusiasm:

His majesty . . . invariably consulted me on reading each memorial which I handed him; for he places extreme confidence in me. I regret that my abilities are too meager to render him assistance.

Naturally, therefore, Weng sought to make up for his personal deficiencies by enlisting the help of men who had the necessary knowledge or abilities. He took interest in men who were versed in practical affairs; he extended his patronage to promising young scholars and officials. For instance, in addition to the persons already mentioned in an earlier connection, Weng became particularly friendly to Chang Chien who was destined to be one of China's pioneering industrialists; he recommended to the emperor Tuan-fang, a young Manchu official who later was sent abroad on an investigation trip and upon whose return wrote a book on European and American governments.

Under such circumstances, it should not have been difficult for Weng to waive his objections to K'ang's philosophical views and to regard K'ang as a prospec-

tive assistant in reform, since K'ang was widely known for his zeal for reform. In more ways than one K'ang was an outstanding man among the advocates of reform, a man who could be expected to furnish useful ideas toward formulating a reform program and to support it courageously in face of strong opposition from many quarters. Moreover, being a man younger in years than Weng and far inferior to Weng in official position, K'ang could hardly challenge Weng's leadership. From Weng's point of view, therefore, K'ang promised to be a major asset and could be safely patronized. Weng may have even entertained the hope, as it has been suggested, that "he would become, by virtue of his influence over the emperor, the leader, and K'ang the chief lieutenant, of the reform movement." Thus he could very well dispense with the help or cooperation from men like Li Hung-chang and Chang Chih-tung. Despite Weng's disagreement with K'ang on many matters, therefore, he spoke to the emperor in glowing terms of K'ang's superlative abilities.

There were other reasons for Weng's change of attitude toward K'ang, from dislike to cordiality. The Korean crisis divided the imperial court into two opposing factions, one of which strongly advised a cautious, conciliatory foreign policy, whereas the other urged war against Japan. Weng was one of the leaders of "the war party," in opposition to Li Hung-chang, Sun Yü-wen, and others." When the peace negotiations with Japan reached preliminary agreement, Sun Yü-wen was among those who favored prompt approval, whereas Weng tried to delay it. K'ang Yu-wei submitted a memorial (May 2, 1895), signed by K'ang and a large number of *chü-jen* then gathered in Peking for the metropolitan examinations, petitioned the throne not to conclude peace with Japan. Strong objections were raised in this memorial against the terms of peace (including the ceding of Taiwan, a move which Weng bitterly opposed). It was asserted that

Those who speak in favor of war unite the wills of the people and thus make energetic preparations for the empire's future. This insures survival. Those who speak in favor of peace impair the empire's solidarity and encourage the barbarians' ambitions. This will bring about ruin in an even shorter time [than risking defeat in war].

This memorial did not reach the emperor; the treaty of Shimonoseki was signed. But in all probability Weng was informed of K'ang's action and must have appreciated the latter's moral support of his "war policy." The extent of his appreciation may be seen from the fact that "resentful of the ceding of Taiwan and with the intention to effect reform," Weng paid a personal visit to K'ang and discussed matters with him. After apologizing for his failure to transmit K'ang's memorial of 1888, he conferred with K'ang for several hours and asked to read K'ang's "writings on government."

Another little noticed action taken by K'ang at that time may also have helped to melt away Weng's initial aversion to K'ang. A few months after the signing of the treaty with Japan, Hsü Yung-i, a vice-president of the Board of Civil Appointments, who aligned himself with Sun Yü-wen and Li Hung-chang in opposing Weng's "war policy," was ousted from both the Grand Council and Tsungli yamen (August 6, 1895). Weng wrote in his diary that Hsü was impeached for his factional association with Sun

and Li, and that the emperor, after securing the approval of the empress dowager, relieved Hsü of his duties in these two high offices. Weng did not identify the person who impeached Hsü. This omission was made good by K'ang in the following passage taken from his *nien-p'u:*

Although Sun Yü-wen was removed, Hsü Yung-i was still in the government to obstruct things. Both Prince Kung and [Weng] T'ung-ho wished to get rid of him. Censors had repeatedly impeached him but he still remained, unwilling to give up his posts. On the ninth day of the sixth moon [I] drafted a memorial and asked Tai Hung-tz'u to impeach [Hsü]. Tai hesitated; he dared not submit [the memorial I wrote]. Thereupon, [I] spoke to Censor Wang P'eng-yün. Wang entered the Censorate only recently and was not afraid to speak out. [He] submitted the memorial on the fourteenth day [i.e., August 4, 1895]. The next day, Hsü Yung-i was finally ousted from the Grand Council and Tsungli yamen.

One may of course discount K'ang's claim that it was he who precipitated Hsü's dismissal. One can hardly deny, however, that even if K'ang's claim does not strictly correspond to facts, it shows clearly the extent to which K'ang was willing to go to lend support to Weng in the political arena of Peking.

By the summer of 1895, so it appears, general circumstances and personal actions had rendered K'ang Yu-wei acceptable to Weng both as a welcome political friend and a prospective assistant in reform. For reasons which remain to be ascertained, however, Weng was not as yet ready at that time to bring K'ang into direct contact with the emperor, a step which Weng took only after the Kaiochow incident of 1897 and thereby started the chain of events leading to the

One Hundred Days. Perhaps in 1895 Weng himself was not prepared to push reform openly and actively.

Weng's cordiality toward K'ang did not last long. Between January and May 1898 the situation in Peking changed and so did Weng's attitude toward K'ang. One reason for this change may be surmised by examining the circumstances of the time. The daring views and unguarded behavior of K'ang aroused the worst suspicion and fears of the traditionalists; a large number of diehards among the officials intensified their opposition to reform. Weng who had by now become known as K'ang's patron and the prime mover of reform, rapidly became a major target of the "conservatives"; his political opponents naturally were glad to seize the opportunity thus offered to embarrass or undermine him. By the last days of May the situation had become quite critical for Weng, as witnessed by the impeachments that were brought up against him in rapid succession. It was precisely in these days that Weng began to voice his dislike of K'ang to the emperor. An entry in his diary, dated May 26, 1898, reads:

The emperor ordered me to have another copy made of the writings which K'ang previously presented to his majesty and to send it in [as soon as it was ready]. I replied, "I do not associate with K'ang." The emperor asked, "Why not?" I replied, "This man's intentions are unpredictable." The emperor said, "Why haven't you mentioned this before?" I replied, "Your servant discovered this recently upon reading his K'ung-tzu kai-chih k'ao [Confucius as Reformer"].

Weng appended a significant remark at the end of the day's entry: "Tossed and turned—sleepless." The emperor reiterated his order the following day. Weng made the same reply which drew from the emperor an "angry reprimand." Weng tried to pass the buck to Tsungli yamen, but the emperor insisted that Weng should go to Chang Yin-huan (another of Weng's estranged friends) and personally instruct Chang to transmit this order to K'ang.

Weng, apparently, sought to dissociate himself from K'ang, hoping thus to mitigate the opposition of his enemies. It was a measure of self-preservation not too gracefully taken. It perhaps surprised as much as irritated the emperor, and certainly placed Weng in a most uncomfortable plight—between the opposition of his inveterate political opponents and the displeasure of his hitherto trusting pupil.

Weng's statement that K'ang's intentions were "unpredictable" is highly significant and requires examination. He came to this conclusion, he said, after reading K'ang's K'ung-tzu kai-chih k'ao which was published in Shanghai in the winter of 1897-8. It immediately received wide hostile attention, so much so that two high officials actively interested in reform condemned it openly in no uncertain terms. One of these was Ch'en Pao-chen who submitted a memorial late in June or early in July 1898, in which he acknowledged K'ang's knowledge and abilities but admitted that the Kai-chih k'ao was the cause of the calumnies which were heaped upon the author. Ch'en went on to say:

K'an Yu-wei . . . seeing that European countries honored the popes (chiao-huang, literary, "religious emperors") who held the reins of government, thinks that this [action] constituted the real basis of the prosperity and strength of foreign nations. . . . [He] therefore elevates Confucius to the position of the head of a church (chiao-chu, literally "religious lord"), wishing to put him on the same level with [the heads of] the Catholic and Protestant [churches], in order to enlighten the people and to make Confucius' moral doctrines and political principles prevail. He does not realize that . . . although [a sage like Confucius] possessed his own proper virtues, he dared not exercise the prerogatives of a ruler because he did not occupy the position of a sovereign; nor does K'ang see that the followers of the popes in Europe eventually provoked wars that lasted for decades, as a result of the popes' overbearing conduct in the various countries.

In other words, Ch'en Pao-chen was of the opinion that K'ang's treatment of Confucius as "reformer" went beyond academic interpretations of Confucian philosophical and moral teachings and had political implications that were decidedly dangerous.

Shortly after Ch'en Pao-chen submitted the above-mentioned memorial, Sun Chia-nai presented his views concerning *K'ung-tzu kai-chih k'ao* to the throne (July 17) as follows:

In reading K'ang Yu-wei's writings your servant [has discovered] . . . that in the eighth *chüan* of his *K'ung-tzu kai-chih k'ao* there is a section entitled *"K'ung-tzu chih-fa ch'eng-wang"* ["Confucius formed institutions and assumed the title of king"]. K'ang tries to establish, on questionable grounds, that Confucius assumed the kingly title when he projected his reforms. . . . It is feared that if this view is taught [to scholars], every one [of them] would entertain the idea of altering the institutions, every one would believe that he could be a *"su-wang"* ("uncrowned king"). As a consequence, schools which are established to educate talented men, would instead confuse and poison the minds of the people. That would lead the empire into disorder.

Sun Chia-nai, it appears, came to virtually identical conclusions concerning the

dangerous implications of K'ang's *Kai-chih k'ao*.

The intention of Ch'en Pao-chen and Sun Chia-nai in pointing out the objectionable features of this book and in bringing about its suppression may have been to save K'ang from more serious troubles and thus to make his talents serve the cause of reform. Nevertheless, the very necessity of condemning the book in order to protect its author shows how much resentment it must have aroused among the scholars and officials of the time. As a matter of fact, even before Ch'en and Sun expressed their disapproval, H'ung Chia-yü, a secretary in the Board of Civil Appointments, had already accused K'ang of desiring to become *min-chu chiao-huang*, "the people's lord, religious emperor," the second part of this phrase was employed by K'ang in this very book. Hung, in effect, was accusing K'ang of ideological sedition. It is no suprise that Hung's accusation touched off a flurry of impeachment aiming at K'ang personally and at his Pao-kuo hui, "National Protection Society," which held its first meeting April 12, 1898 and went out of existence in about a month later, as a result of loud protests.

Weng T'ung-ho had read K'ang's book and must have seen all these memorials, including those of Ch'en Pao-chen and Sun Chia-nai. Weng was probably as much shocked, if not more so, by this book as by K'ang's earlier publication, *Hsin-hsüeh wei-ching k'ao*, which Weng read in 1894. Even if Weng could again waive his doctrinal objection to K'ang's views, he could hardly afford to ignore the dangerous implications of the *Kai-chih k'ao* and the ideological furor it caused. To make his own stand clear, the only course open to Weng was to disown K'ang Yu-wei.

There was still another reason for

Weng to reconsider his relationship with K'ang and decide to part company with him. The initial agreement between the two men concerning the need of administrative reform soon gave way to disagreement concerning the direction and extent of such reform after K'ang gained the emperor's ear. Consequently, Weng made some attempts to stem the tide of K'ang's radicalism. For instance, he reminded (June 11) the emperor in unequivocal language that while it was necessary to adopt "Western methods," it was even more important not to forsake "the moral and philosophical teachings of the sages and wise men" of imperial China. He even managed to inject into the edict of the same date his own view concerning reform.

Weng was perhaps alarmed for the first time at K'ang's radical views, when he took part in the interview in Tsungli yamen on January 24, 1898. K'ang's own narrative of the episode is noteworthy:

Jung-lu said: "The institutions of the ancestors cannot be changed." To which I replied: "The institutions of the ancestors are used to govern the realm that had been theirs. Now we cannot preserve the realm of the ancestors; what is the use for their institutions? . . ."

Liao [Shou-heng, a president of the Board of Punishment] asked: "How should the institutions be reformed?" I replied: "We shall change the laws and regulations; the governmental system (kuan-chih) should be the first [to be reformed]."

Li [Hung-chang] said: "Shall we, then, abolish all the Six Boards and throw away all the existing institutions and rules?" I replied him with: "The present is a time in which countries exist side by side; the world is no longer a unified one. The laws and governmental system [as they now exist in China] are institutions of a unified empire. It is these that have made China weak and will ruin her [if they remain un-

changed]. Undoubtedly, they should be done away with. Even if we could not abolish them all at once, we should modify them as circumstances require. Only so can we carry out reform."

Weng asked: "How to finance [the reform]?" I answered with: "The banking system and paper money of Japan, the stamp tax of France, the land tax of India [are ways to raise revenue]. . . ." I also said: "Japan adopted Western ways and institutions to effect reform. Her laws and institutions are now very complete. Being close to China she is the model which is the easiest [for China] to follow. . . ."

The meeting adjourned in the evening.

Weng T'ung-ho's comment on this interview also deserves quoting in this connection:

Summoned K'ang to the yamen. High-flown talk (kao t'an) on current affairs, with reform as the chief theme. Several main points: to establish chih-tu chü, to renovate the administrative system, to drill a conscript army, to build railways, and to make extensive foreign loans. Unrestrained to the extreme. Returned in the evening; very indignant, very tired.

It hardly needs pointing out that K'ang's recommendations made in Tsungli yamen were frighteningly drastic by the standards of the time and that his daring stand proved too much for Weng T'ung-ho whose idea of administrative reform was of a far more limited scope than what K'ang indicated in his answer to Li Hung-chang's question. Moreover, if Weng was able to tolerate K'ang's radical views, he could hardly overlook the likelihood that K'ang's demand for sweeping institutional changes would incite the powerful opposition of the majority of the scholar-officials, thus jeopardizing not only the cause of reform but also Weng's own political position. The remarks, "unrestrained to the extreme" and "very indignant" can be construed only as indications of Weng's keen disappointment in K'ang.

The interview of January 24, therefore, may well have marked a turning point in the relationship between Weng and K'ang. From then on Weng must have found it difficult to lend further support to K'ang. For to do so would have amounted to identifying himself with a program supported by a man who openly committed himself to liquidating the existing imperial system—"to burn the ancestral tablets," as the empress dowager once put it. That would have been incompatible both with Weng's political safety and his personal convictions. The only prudent course left to Weng was to retract, by either making K'ang less "unrestrained" or by shying away from him. Weng, obviously, chose the latter alternative. Chang Chien, his favorite protégé and trusted friend, "did his utmost to urge moderation upon K'ang." When Chang realized that he was preaching to deaf ears, he began to move away from the uncompromising reformer, precisely as Weng did under somewhat different circumstances.

Another important factor that contributed to Weng's change of attitude toward K'ang should not be overlooked. K'ang's opposition to the empress dowager became increasingly noticeable as opposition to the reform movement grew. Up to the time of Weng's dismissal K'ang probably had not gone as far as "to plot against her sacred person." But K'ang's general attitude toward Tz'u-hsi must have been known to Weng who for decades had been trying to conciliate the imperial rulers. The danger of playing the emperor against the empress dowager, a course of action which K'ang was inclined to take, was extremely great;

even if the risk was worth taking, the ideological objections involved were exceedingly grave. This factor alone should have been sufficient to drive Weng away from K'ang.

Personal jealously seems to have influenced Weng's action in disowning K'ang Yu-wei. Weng's interest in reform stemmed from his loyalty to the emperor and the dynasty, but it was not unmixed with selfish motivation. By endeavoring to put the empire on an even keel through reform he hoped to achieve supremacy in Peking officialdom, outranking both Li Hung-chang and Chang Chih-tung as leaders of reform. Unexpectedly, however, K'ang Yu-wei gained almost the exclusive confidence of the emperor. If it was K'ang's "vigorous personality"— his militant and aggressive attitude— which deeply impressed Weng who therefore saw in him an energetic assistant in reform, it was the same personal quality of K'ang that ultimately alienated him from Weng. Weng, naturally, was no more willing to relinquish leadership to K'ang than to Li Hung-chang or Chang Chih-tung.

The situation may have been aggravated by the deteriorating relationship between Weng and Chang Yin-huan. After Sun Yü-wen was ousted in 1895, Weng took Chang Yin-huan into his political circle, intending to make Chang one of his lieutenants. Chang, however, soon enjoyed too much of the emperor's confidence to please Weng. Meanwhile, shortly before the One Hundred Days, Chang Yin-huan and K'ang Yu-wei came into a brief period of *rapprochement,* both having gained the emperor's favor. Weng was alarmed and took steps to curtail their further advance. His sudden change of attitude toward these men irritated the emperor who put Weng in a very uncomfortable situation (June 12,

1898) by compelling Weng to give Chang Yin-huan "strong moral support," and on another occasion (May 26, 1898) showed his displeasure for Weng's unfriendly attitude toward K'ang.

Perhaps Weng was not solely responsible for the deterioration of his relation with K'ang. The latter's aggressiveness must have also contributed to it. We have indirect evidence to support this conjecture. According to K'ang's own statement, his eagerness to place himself in a prominent position in reform turned Sun Chia-nai from an admiring friend into a resentful enemy. Sometime before K'ang came into contact with the emperor Sun was said to have remarked to a colleague that:

Among the court officials K'ang alone is patriotic from his heart and thoroughly understands the affairs of the day. If the emperor charges me with the responsibility of reform, my only recourse would be to recommend K'ang [for the task]. For, how could I shoulder this responsibility?

This early enthusiasm soon cooled. When Sun became minister in charge of the newly authorized Imperial University of Peking and discovered that in the drafted regulations for the university Liang Ch'i-ch'ao ("ghost-writing" for K'ang) "placed all powers in the hands of the dean, leaving the chancellor a figure head," he "thereupon became very angry and criticised" K'ang. Sun's resentment, obviously, stemmed from the fact that he was to be the chancellor while K'ang was recommended for the dean's post. It is interesting to observe that Sun's early opinion of K'ang was almost a repetition of Weng's words when he strongly recommended K'ang to the emperor. It is conceivable that Weng and Sun who had together introduced the emperor to the idea of reform a number of years before, shared their transient friendship with K'ang and became equally disillusioned when K'ang's "vigorous personality" later asserted itself.

The above discussion points to one conclusion: a number of circumstances and a variety of motives led Weng T'ung-ho to discredit K'ang Yu-wei, with the purpose of blocking the latter's further advance. Thus, ironically, Weng who started the emperor on the road to reform in early 1889, ended with playing "the role of an opponent instead of the official leader of the reform movement."

This dramatic shift did not involve any basic change in Weng's personal outlook. As a man of complex motivations, he was at once anxious for personal advancement and concerned about the empire's uncertain future. His ruling passion was political success but his crowning ambition was to become the statemen who saved the tottering dynasty by the administrative reform. When the prospect of realizing this ambition looked good, he patronized men who were qualified for or dedicated to the task of reform. But when that prospect receded, he beat a hasty retreat. Roughly the same considerations which at first led Weng to acclaim K'ang as a man of superlative abilities, later compelled him to denounce him as a man of questionable intentions. As a result, to borrow the words of Liang Ch'i-ch'ao, Weng's attitude toward K'ang was "trust at first but suspicion in the end." The word "trust" is perhaps a little too strong to be accurate. For, in so far as Weng was concerned, his attitude toward K'ang could have never been more than intellectually and emotionally ambivalent. It was an unstable tie that joined together two men of different temperaments and persuasions. Such a tie was readily broken as soon as its usefulness to one of the parties began to disappear. Weng's open repudiation of K'ang in May 1898, so it appears, was in reality not the result of disenchantment; for Weng could not have been charmed by K'ang, on the strength of either the latter's philosphical ideas or personal qualities.

V. WENG'S DISMISSAL AND ITS SIGNIFICANCE

(a) Factors Leading to the Dismissal

Weng T'ung-ho had weathered many a political storm during his forty years in Peking officialdom, but his deftness failed him in 1898. Apparently without warning, a "vermillion edict" was issued June 15, just one day before K'ang Yu-wei was summoned to imperial audience. It reads in part:

Recently, Weng T'ung-ho, associate grand secretary and president of the Board of Revenue, has been managing affairs mostly in an unsatisfactory manner. As a consequence, he has drawn protests from many quarters and has been repeatedly impeached by a number of persons. Moreover, when he was called to audience and consulted [by Us] on various matters, he expressed his approval or disapproval as his whim directed, allowing personal likes or dislikes to show on his face. He has shown signs of a perverse tendency to arrogate power to himself, thus absolutely disqualifying himself for shouldering the responsibilities of [an official] in a pivotal position. He should indeed be thoroughly investigated and severely punished but, considering his many years of service in Yü-ch'ing Palace [as imperial tutor], We cannot bear to inflict severe punishment upon him. To show [Our wish] to preserve him, Weng T'ung-ho is hereby ordered to relinquish his posts and to return to his native place.

Writers differed as to who actually made the decision to dismiss Weng. K'ang Yu-wei and Liang Ch'i-ch'ao placed the entire responsibility on the empress dowager. A number of observers and historians shared this view. Some traced the move to opponents of reform, while others attributed it to Kang-i, Yung-lu, or Prince Kung. All these views imply that the emperor who issued the edict by his own hand, did so only at the command of the empress dowager.

Other writers held a different view. It was believed that the emperor himself made the momentous decision because Weng's cautious approach to reform clashed with the emperor's unbounded enthusiasm. The emperor was ready to get rid of Weng who had by then also fallen out of the empress dowager's grace.

This view, we think, comes closer to the actual facts. A survey of Weng's diary reveals that while Weng did not raise objection to the reform movement led by K'ang, he quickly ceased to support reform with the ardor which he displayed on January 16. The last important task which he performed in behalf of reform was the drafting of the edict of June 11. On more than one occasion, between January 16 and June 15, he incurred the emperor's displeasure; a climax was reached on May 27 when he repeated his derogatory remarks concerning K'ang Yu-wei. Knowingly or unknowingly Weng impaired the trusting, affectionate relationship between himself and the emperor, which took him many years to cultivate. From the emperor's viewpoint, it was bad enough for Weng to be rude to him; but to encourage him to undertake reform at first, to speak highly of K'ang Yu-wei, and, all of a sudden, to renege and retract, was really insufferable. (The charge against Weng made in the vermillion edict that he was whimsical in his opinions and unrestrained in his speech was therefore not trumped up.) Recalling the fact that the emperor was not a person of mild temperament, it is not difficult to imagine that he was eventually incited into decisive action by the cumulative effects of repeated frustration and provocation inflicted on him by his former tutor. He shattered Weng's official career at one stroke even as he had many years ago (1883, aged 12) smashed a tea cup when he was angered by Sun Chia-nai, another of his tutors. If that was the case, the decision to dismiss Weng may have been made even without reference to the empress dowager's wishes.

The edict mentions the repeated impeachments brought up against Weng. These may also have helped the emperor to make the decision or afforded him a convenient pretext for making it. These impeachments, accusing Weng of diverse offenses, are of considerable significance. One of the most damaging was made (May 20, 1898) by Wang P'eng-yün, a censor, charging Weng with taking bribes in collusion with Chang Yin-huan. Another impeachment (June 9) made by Kao Hsieh-tseng, also a censor, accusing the Board of Revenue of unconscionable conduct of business. Kao did not mention Weng by name but it was clear that the impeachment was directed primarily against Weng. Although these "harsh worded" memorials did not bring to Weng any punishment, they must have adversely affected Weng's prestige and may perhaps have impaired the emperor's confidence in him. It is noteworthy that the day after Kao submitted his memorial, Jung-lu was appointed a grand secretary to take control of the Board of Revenue.

A few days later (June 14), Li Sheng-t'o, another censor, submitted a secret memorial urging the emperor "to reward and punish openly" officials who actively supported reform or obstructed it. Li named Ch'en Pao-chen (governor of Hunan), Chang Chih-tung (governor-general of Hu-kuang), and Lu Ch'uan-lin (governor of Kwangtung) as among the former and T'an Chung-lin (governor-general of Liang-Kuang) as among the latter. At the same time, Sung Po-lu, a colleague of Li Sheng-t'o, made a substantially identical request in a memorial. According to Weng, the emperor "temporarily pigeonholed these two memorials," obviously the emperor wished to postpone his decision for a while. That these documents had serious implications may be gathered from the fact that Weng was very much disturbed after seeing them. This item in his diary is revealing: "Sunny; slightly cloudy afternoon. Gazing at the Vast Heaven, my heart was like [being tortured] by pounding."

The personal backgrounds of these memorialists afford some clues to the reason for Weng's mental anguish. Sung Po-lu was one of the most ardent supporters of K'ang Yu-wei's reform movement. Naturally, Sung was cashiered at the end of the One Hundred Days; had he not fled to Shanghai, disguised himself and sought asylum in the British consulate, he might have suffered the same fate as his colleague, Yang Shen-hsiu. Li Sheng-t'o also lent strong, though unsteady, support to K'ang's reform activities. The memorial which Li submitted to the emperor was, in fact, drafted by K'ang Yu-wei himself. In K'ang's own words:

I also drafted for Censor Li Sheng-t'o a memorial concerning the translation of books, travels abroad, open rewards and punishments, and distinguishing between new [i.e., reformers] and old [conservatives]. Li submitted it.

Kao Hsieh-tseng, the third memorialist mentioned above, was the man who strongly recommended K'ang at a crucial moment, and Wang P'eng-yün, the last of the memorialists, was the censor who impeached Hsü Yung-i at K'ang's bidding. These four men, in short, were in diverse ways connected with K'ang and for some time cooperated with him. We have no evidence to support the conjecture that K'ang instigated their impeachments (overt or implied) of Weng. It is safe to assume, however, that words from these men must have had a more disheartening effect on Weng than those from out-and-out conservatives or from his inveterate political enemies. For, in the latter case, while Weng could not count upon the empress dowager's continued favor (one of the two props of his official position), he still could rely on the emperor's trust. But in the former case, namely, when persons associated with K'ang Yu-wei and supported reform attacked him, he faced a two-pronged assault and could depend on the protection of neither of the imperial rulers. Weng had reasons to be particularly disturbed by the impeachments brought up by Li Sheng-t'o and Sung Po-lu. At that moment, "reform" was largely synonymous with the program supported by K'ang and his associates. To oppose K'ang and his program, therefore, was for practical purposes tantamount to opposing reform as such. Thus, in urging the emperor to distinguish between "the new and the old," and to punish officials who hindered reform, Li and Sung hinted the possibility of calling into account all officials who showed too little zeal toward K'ang's proposals to suit the emperor—although they specifically named in their memorials only a few "delinquent" provincial officials. Weng, who had chosen to become hostile to K'ang, could therefore be readily accused

of "obstructing reform" and excluded from the company of "the new," despite his early efforts in initiating the reform movement. It is significant that Weng was ousted the day after Li and Sung submitted their memorials. It is interesting to note also that one day after Weng's dismissal, Sung Po-lu and Yang Shen-hsiu (one of K'ang's close associates and the "martyrs" of 1898) impeached Hsü Ying-k'uei, an arch conservative, for "obstructing reform measures" and brought about Hsü's dismissal. Earnest efforts, so it appears, were made by K'ang's followers to clear the way for his ambitious program, by sweeping away whoever tried to block it. Ironically, therefore, Weng T'ung-ho, the men who introduced the emperor to the cause of reform and who more than anyone else helped K'ang to become the emperor's mentor in reform, was made the first major casualty, sharing the same treatment with an arch conservative.

The death of Prince Kung (May 30, 1898) probably had a crucial bearing on the situation. The prince held moderate views on reform and had sufficient prestige to exert a restraining influence both on the emperor who developed an almost fanatical devotion to the cause of reform, and on the empress dowager who became resolutely opposed to radical changes. Prince Kung's part in the reforms inaugurated in the 1860's is well known. His restraining influence on the emperor was demonstrated in January 1898 when he dissuaded the latter against summoning K'ang to an audience. The prince's demise, therefore, may have encouraged the emperor to take bolder steps toward reform. Somewhat curiously, Weng did not show any sign of alarm or anxiety upon hearing the news of the death. Perhaps Weng felt relief at the disappearance of his perennial, powerful political enemy who had been annoyingly lukewarm toward the reform movement which Weng undertook to foster. Perhaps Weng was blinded by his personal animosity against the prince and was unable to discern the dangerous implications of his death. Whatever may have been the reason for Weng's lack of concern, he was soon forced by the circumstances to do the very same thing which the prince did before with temporary success, namely, to check the advance of K'ang Yu-wei and his reform program. Thus, according to K'ang's own narrative, when he sought to take the advantage of the prince's death to urge Weng to launch extensive reform measures in a hurry, Weng (already sufficiently disillusioned by his would-be "chief lieutenant") simply ignored the suggestion and expressed his wish to see K'ang depart from Peking. Without Prince Kung's prestige, however, Weng did not achieve a temporary success in trying to check K'ang's advance; he was summarily cashiered, for making the attempt. Now with Prince Kung dead and Weng in exile, the last effective restraining influences on the emperor vanished. From that point on the battle line was sharply drawn between "reformers" and "conservatives," between those who demanded changes in the existing ideological and institutional system, and those who opposed not only such changes but also the adoption of Western science and technology. A fierce struggle between the two camps promptly began. The reformers won a transient victory but were soon to be overwhelmed by their opponents who rallied around the powerful empress dowager.

(b) An Evaluation of Weng's Position

Weng T'ung-ho's failure to realize his ambition of saving the dynasty through reform may be more readily explained by his strategical mistakes than by any ideological error that he may have committed. In the context of the practical situation Weng's ideological position was in fact not unreasonable. His view that the traditional values should not be forsaken although "Western methods" should be adopted, was acceptable to a considerable number of influential men in Peking and the provinces, and, what is even more important, to the empress dowager herself. We need not go as far as to say with a recent writer that at the inception of the reform movement of 1898, something like a "unity of mind" existed between the emperor and the empress dowager with regard to reform. But we cannot deny the fact that the movement was not inaugurated without her knowledge and consent and that the emperor took no important step without first securing her understanding or approval, especially before K'ang Yu-wei became chief adviser in reform. In fact, the basic difference in view between the imperial rulers (namely, that the emperor wished to effect a certain degree of Westernization, whereas the empress dowager could not tolerate any tampering with the accustomed ways and institutions) did not develop until K'ang gained the former's confidence. Psychologically speaking, it was easier at that time to continue the line of reform where the "self-strengthening" movement of the 1860's left off, i.e., refurbishing the administration without involving institutional changes, than to effectuate the more ambitious program of K'ang Yu-wei. Weng's conception of reform, substantially identical with that of Chang Chih-tung and others of the same school of thought, thus appears to possess the theoretical advantage of being compatible with the given political situation in the 1890's.

Weng was astute enough to see the

strategical necessity of maintaining a degree of harmony between the emperor and the empress dowager. Even though he was personally more intimate to the former than the latter and even though his political future depended increasingly more on the former as time went on, he could not ignore the fact that the empress dowager occupied an unshakable position in the existing regime and would occupy it as long as she lived and desired. The tremendous power which she acquired during the many years of "listening reports on affairs of state behind screens" and the indisputable prestige she enjoyed as the emperor's "mother"— a prestige accorded her by the accepted Confucian ideology—rendered it unwise to challenge her authority by the emperor or by anyone else. The best policy then was to accept her paramount position in the administration and to do nothing to antagonize her. Meanwhile, the emperor could gradually build up his own power and prestige, by doing worthwhile things. He could afford to take his time; after all, he was Tz'u-hsi's junior by over forty-five years. Weng's attempt to reconcile the imperial rulers, to make them partners in reform, was therefore justified by the practical situation, although he failed to achieve results because his efforts were partly neutralized by some of the unexpected developments brought about by K'ang Yu-wei's activities.

Weng, however, was not consistently shrewd. He committed a number of tactical mistakes which made his apparently reasonable position untenable. One of the most costly mistakes he committed was his unwillingness to seek the cooperation of persons who held views of reform that were substantially similar to his own. His antagonism to Li Hung-chang and Chang Chih-tung not only deprived him of much potentially valuable support but invited actual opposition from quarters where cooperation should have been expected. His political ambition got the better of him; instead of availing himself of the help of like-minded, well-established, and experienced colleagues, he chose to recruit subordinates of his own, to draw around himself men younger than himself in years or inferior to him in official position, so that his leadership in reform could be assured. In so doing he weakened the cause of reform not only by reducing the numerical strength of his own camp but by introducing strife among persons supporting the same cause.

Weng's readiness to compromise personal convictions whenever expediency required led him into another grave mistake. Despite his pride in the moral tradition of imperial China, he did not always take the Confucian precepts as a practical guide of conduct. This explains partly the fact that he was willing to recommend K'ang Yu-wei to the emperor, although he was aware of K'ang's unorthodox interpretations of the Confucian classics, which tended to weaken the very basis of imperial China's moral tradition. His statement that he discovered K'ang's "unpredictable intentions" only after seeing the book on "Confucius as Reformer" in 1898, was poor excuse. Had Weng taken that tradition more seriously than he did, he should have been sufficiently warned by K'ang's "wild fox" propensities when he read the book on "false classics" in 1894, to rely on K'ang as a likely assistant in implementing a program of reform with the purpose of borrowing "Western methods" to preserve Chinese tradition—the same ideological and institutional system which K'ang virtually renounced.

Weng's association with K'ang proved to be the most costly mistake which he ever made in his long career. He counted on K'ang's help to develop a reform movement all his own but only to find out later that K'ang rapidly replaced him as the prophet of reform. Evidently, K'ang who did not respect his theory of limited reform or defer to his leadership in reform, turned out to be an even greater threat to his position than Li Hung-chang or Chang Chih-tung. Moreover, in trying to undo K'ang he quickly brought about his own undoing. With his removal from Peking the last effective link between the imperial rulers disappeared. K'ang Yu-wei was left free to lead the emperor down the path of ruin. By recommending K'ang to the emperor he was to some extent indirectly responsible for this disaster.

It is worth noting that the edict of December 4, 1898, which inflicted heavier punishment on Weng than the lenient treatment accorded him by the vermillion edict of June 15, stressed Weng's responsibility in recommending K'ang. After reiterating the charges that Weng acted "perversely" toward the emperor, that as an imperial tutor he amused his pupil with art objects instead of instructing him in moral principles, and that he held arbitrary views concerning war and peace (referring obviously to 1894), the emperor is represented as further accusing Weng of the following:

Last spring he strongly advocated reform and secretly recommended K'ang Yu-wei, saying that this man's abilities were a hundred times superior to his, with the intention of making K'ang an arbiter of all affairs of state. Considering the difficulties of the time and the urgent need of reform, We did not hesitate to condescend and follow [Weng's advice]. However, K'ang Yu-wei took the opportunity offered him during the days of reform to perpetrate seditious and perverse schemes. Thus in indiscriminately recommending a bad man, the offence committed by Weng T'ung-ho is verily beyond pardon. . . . Previously, [We] ordered him to relinquish his posts and return to his native place. [This treatment] hardly covers his crimes. It is hereby ordered that Weng T'ung-ho be deprived of his ranks and offices, permanently barred from official appointments, and handed over to local officials who shall put him under strict discipline.

This edict is significant, for instead of blaming Weng for promoting reform it accused him of recommending a "bad man." Whatever may have been the fact —whether or not K'ang Yu-wei had actually plotted against the empress dowager —the charge that he did so was repeatedly made against him and constituted a major justification used by the imperial government to put an end to the reform movement of 1898 and to punish (with one single exception) all officials who had recommended K'ang Yu-wei. This fact lends further support to the view that, so far as his personal interests were concerned, Weng made the grave mistake not in advocating reform but in bringing K'ang into the emperor's confidence.

(c) Weng's Reaction to His Dismissal

Although Weng denied categorically his responsibility in recommending K'ang, he accepted the verdict that K'ang indeed was a "traitor." In all probability, he was not merely parroting the official line but was expressing his own personal sentiments. For Weng had good reasons to regard K'ang as a "traitor." From Weng's point of view, in addition to betraying the empire—by openly attacking the traditional ideological and institutional system, and by perpetrating the "seditious schemes" against the empress dowager—K'ang had virtually betrayed Weng himself, the man to whom he owed much of his rise to unprecedented prominence, by pushing reform in a direction toward which Weng could not go and by taking away from Weng the coveted leadership in reform.

Weng appears to have felt some remorse for the part he played in the reform movement. One year after the *coup d'état* (on September 12, 1899) he wrote this in his diary:

Returned; read *Huai-nan-tzu*. . . . The essay entitled *"Ching-shen hsün"* in this book is unadorned, close [to common sense], and easy to put into practice. Having previously read this book, I nevertheless departed from [the teachings which it affords]; this is as good as not having read it. The comment on reforming ways and institutions without knowing how to reform them is particularly germane to the affairs of the present time.

A careful scanning of the essay Weng referred to fails to locate any passage that deals directly with reform. There are, however, a few passages which may have struck Weng as especially meaningful in the light of his experience as a promoter of reform. For instance:

The sage obeys the laws of heaven and complies with the nature of man; he is not bound by custom, nor is he seduced by men.

To stop the bubbling of boiling water by stirring it will not stop the bubbling; but if one knows the real cause, he simply removes the fire.

It is conceivable that after a post-mortem examination of his political life Weng became convinced that he had made too many and too grave mistakes in the 1890's to survive in the stormy officialdom of Peking. Perhaps the passages from *Huai-nan-tzu* quoted here made him regret that in trying to break away from "custom" (i.e., to promote reform) he allowed himself to be "seduced by men," such as K'ang Yu-wei, Chang Yin-huan, and Yüan Shih-k'ai, and that in attacking K'ang Yu-wei in front of the emperor he was committing the folly of trying to stop the bubbling of boiling water by stirring it.

At any rate, it seems clear that Weng bore little grudge toward the emperor or the empress dowager. A considerable number of entries in his diary covering the post-reform years show his unwavering loyalty, especially to the emperor. In fact, on one occasion in 1899 he broke into tears when he expressed his concern for "the sagely sovereign." On another occasion, he expressed gratitude for being permitted to live peacefully near the graves of his ancestors, despite the "crimes" which he committed. Weng, however, did not put all the blame on himself. Although he may have regretted the strategical mistakes he made in promoting reform, he did not feel sorry that he advised the emperor against abandoning the traditional values of imperial China. Referring to a visit to his ancestral graveyard shortly after he returned to his home in 1898, he wrote this in his diary:

What I had presented to my sovereign were the principles of Yao and Shun; there had been no unrighteous words. [My conduct during my career] had not brought disgrace to my forebearers.

This leads one to think that Weng remained unconvinced of the emperor's wisdom in preferring K'ang Yu-wei to himself as his mentor of reform. On one occasion at least, Weng voiced his disappointment in the emperor. Upon reading the edict (December 30, 1899) which ordered the apprehension of K'ang Yu-wei and Liang Ch'i-ch'ao and which laid the blame on Weng for his "strong recommendation" of K'ang, Weng wrote a long comment in his diary. After recalling his repeated efforts to expose K'ang's "unpredictable intentions," he asserted:

Had I remained among my colleagues [at court], I certainly would have prevented this scoundrel from acting in such a mad way. But I was punished on account of this [attempt to expose K'ang].

Weng may also have voiced his disappointment in the emperor on another occasion, although in a very subtle and indirect manner. Less than two months after he wrote the above comment, he recorded in his diary that he read in a dream a poetic composition which contained these lines:

Every care have I exercised in painting
    my moth-eyebrows,
  but utterly unappreciative he remains;
In Ling-ho he plants another willow
    tree lissome and blithe.

Did Weng take the lissome willow tree to symbolize K'ang Yu-wei who gained the emperor's exclusive attention and put to naught Weng's every effort to serve his former pupil? No conclusive answer of course can be given to this question. But as it was a standard literary device in old China to indicate in allegorical poems and to attribute to dreams sentiments that were too intimate to be frankly or directly expressed, one can hardly resist the temptation to read in these lines the hidden meaning as suggested above.

(d) Continuation of Moderate Reform

Contrary to a generally accepted belief, the reaction which set in after the *coup d'état* of 1898, did not stop the movement toward limited modernization. Liang Ch'i-ch'ao, who was understandably inclined to exaggerate the deeds of the anti-reformers, enumerated as many as ten items, among which were the reinstatement of the sinecure posts abolished during the One Hundred Days, the prohibiting of scholars and common people to submit memorials, the halting of the establishment of schools in the provinces, and the restoring of the old examination system. He purposely or unintentionally omitted to mention the various measures of modernization which the imperial government announced after September 21, thus giving a one-sided presentation of the situation.

An edict dated September 26, 1898 which summarized the general official view, merits attention here. It begins by saying that the "new measures" which were adopted from time to time were all calculated to meet the need of the circumstances—"to bring prosperity and strength to the empire and to provide livelihood for the people"—and that they were adopted not with a view to altering the existing institutions for the sake of novelty. The document then goes on to indicate the matters which the government considered as particularly important. One of these was the abolition of sinecure offices and supernumerary officials. The six central offices which were abolished about one month ago were now reinstalled, but provincial authorities were ordered to proceed to abolish or combine superfluous bureaus and other government agencies, and to dismiss officials who had no useful functions to perform.

Another matter regarded as of paramount importance was the establishment of schools. The pertinent portion of the edict reads:

Universities and higher schools are places to develop men of ability. Those which have already been established at different times in Peking and in the provincial capitals [shall be allowed to stand]. The primary and lower schools which have been proposed for the prefectures and districts shall be left to the convenience of the local inhabitants. Local officials are ordered to exercise discretion [in the matter], with due consideration for local conditions.

The edict finally outlines policies concerning other matters, such as industry, commerce, agriculture, military defense, and finance, and declares that these policies "shall be earnestly implemented one by one." It makes clear, however, that the mistakes of the One Hundred Days must be corrected. The reform measures then adopted were not necessarily bad but "the functionaries who carried them out acted in a bad way," with the result that the people were confused and the cause of reform prejudiced. The remedy, logically, was not to give up reform, but to abandon the radical program formulated by K'ang Yu-wei and pursue the line of reform as Weng T'ung-ho and other moderates conceived it. Weng, then in retirement, watched this new development perhaps not without some satisfaction. His interpretation of the basic policy of the imperial government is highly interesting, which, according to him, was "to strike a balance between extremes and not to be bound by previous commitments." This interpretation, it appears, is essentially correct.

Another edict issued on November 3, 1898, less than two months after the

one cited above, is even more significant. It reads in part as follows:

The first principle of governance has always been to break away from preconceptions and to guard strongly against letting matters drift. . . . For laws and institutions are not bad when they are first established, but as time goes on defects accumulate, making it necessary to change them in order to meet the requirements of the time. But if no attention is paid to the actual situation, a set of new defects would then be produced as new laws are enacted. Such a procedure would contribute nothing useful to the affairs of state. Only the most grave defects, therefore, should be remedied; a new law should be enacted only if it promises to be of practical advantage. . . .

Although the customs and governmental systems of Western countries differ in more than one way from those of China, their methods and techniques pertaining to military, agricultural, industrial, and commercial matters are as a rule capable of [helping a country] to attain prosperity and strength; the effectiveness of these methods and technique has been clearly demonstrated. If we can select what are good among these and apply them, putting them into use one by one, we shall be able to achieve the desired results promptly and consistently.

It is feared, however, that persons of shallow thinking interpret Our intentions wrongly, imagining that the Government has decided to follow the beaten path and is no longer concerned with far-sighted plans. This would be entirely contrary to Our intention earnestly and diligently to achieve good administration.

The "persons of shallowing thinking" referred to in this document were none other than the ultra conservative officials who would naturally have wished that every trace of reform be obliterated with the *coup d'état*. They tried hard to carry out their wishes, but even in such cases, such as the petition of the Board of Rites to revive the old examination system and to put an end to the "newstyle schools," the empress dowager refused to go along with the anti-reformers all the way. The "eight-legged essay" indeed was reinstated and the old, imperially sanctioned texts were again made to serve as the official guide for aspiring scholars, but the request to close the schools (*hsüeh-t'ang*) was unequivocally rejected. The portion of the edict (November 3, 1898) which deals with the schools, deserves quoting:

Academies (*shu-yüan*) are established for the pursuit and the acquiring of practical knowledge. Their function is not to honor exclusively the study of the commentaries on the classics and the cultivation of the art of literary composition. All subjects which are indispensable to promoting the country's welfare, such as astronomy, geography, military strategy, and mathematics, fall well within the scholar's proper province.

The same holds true for schools (*hsüeh-t'ang*). Academies and schools differ only in their names, but their functions are in reality the same. . . .

It is a mistake to think that all branches of useful knowledge are outside the scope of the academies.

Despite the obvious difference in emphasis, the conception of the aims of schools as defined in the above passage departs very little in essence from the general principle laid down in the reform edict of June 11, which was drafted by Weng T'ung-ho:

Let us keep in mind the moral and philosophical teachings of our sages and wise men. . . . We must also widely select such subjects of Western knowledge as are pertinent to the requirements of the time and study them with real diligence.

The fact is, then, that the idea of moderate reform—that Western techniques should be adopted to supplement Chinese tradition but not to supplant it—did not die out with the dismissal of Weng T'ung-ho. A number of the officials in Peking who had previously cooperated with Weng or who sympathized with him, were retained by the empress dowager to serve in various important capacities in the years immediately after Weng left the imperial court. Particularly noteworthy were Sun Chia-nai and Wang Wen-shao. The former, then a president of the Board of Civil Appointments, was given the distinction of an associate grand secretary and entrusted with the task of establishing the Imperial University of Peking; the latter was called from Tientsin where he was governor-general, to serve concurrently as a president of the Board of Revenue, minister in Tsungli yamen, and member of the Grand Council—filling the posts left vacant by Weng. One of the most significant moves made by these officials was Sun Chia-nai's request to reprint and distribute copies of Feng Kui-fen's *Chiao-pin-lu k'ang-i*, so that this celebrated book might be used as a basic reference work on reform. Sun's memorial, interestingly, was submitted July 17, 1898, four days after Tsungli yamen refused to make any recommendation on the reform program outlined by K'ang Yu-wei in his "sixth memorial." Feng's *K'ang-i*, to recall, was presented to the emperor by Sun and Weng T'ung-ho back in 1889. By calling attention to it again in 1898, Sun obviously wished to remind the emperor of a line of thought which Sun and other moderates regarded as essentially sound and useful as an effective antidote to the radicalism with which K'ang was feeding the emperor.

Sun of course was not alone in the attempt to check radicalism and at the same time to fight ultra conservatism. A few other officials followed his steps. For instance, Huang Shao-chi, a Hanlin reader, presented a number of copies of Chang Chih-tung's *Ch'üan-hsüeh p'ien,* to the emperor, on July 25, a few days after Sun submitted his memorial. As a result, this well-known book on reform was reprinted and widely distributed to provincial officials. Other efforts were made, prior to and during the One Hundred Days, to substitute for K'ang's reform program an alternative program based on the axiom, "Chinese learning for the fundamental principles and Western learning for practical application," a philosophy of reform to which Feng Kuei-fen, Chang Chih-tung, Weng T'ung-ho, and other moderates subscribed.

This philosophy, as already said, suffered a temporary and partial eclipse during the One Hundred Days when radicalism asserted its influence, and again in the days of the Boxer uprising when a violent reaction against reform set in. But it revived quickly in each case. A lengthy edict issued January 29, 1901, sounded the keynote of the post-Boxer reform movement:

There are in the world constant principles which remain eternally unalterable; there are no methods of government that are not subject to modification after they have been formulated. . . . Now that which do not change are the three basic human relationships and the five constant virtues; they illuminate the world as the sun and the stars. There is, however, no more objection to altering particular laws than there is to putting fresh strings on a musical instrument. . . . Former emperors of the present dynasty established institutions to suit their times. . . . Generally speaking, institutions become defective with the passing

of time; and when they become defective, they are changed. The purpose [of so doing] is none other than to strengthen the empire and to benefit the people.

Since the court left [Peking], the Empress Dowager has been consumed with anxiety day and night. We Ourselves have not ceased from vehement self-reproach, when We reflected profoundly that the accumulated abuses and complacent adherence to the accustomed ways . . . of the last several decades have contributed to bringing about the present grave disaster. Now that peace negotiations have commenced, the entire administrative system must especially be reformed thoroughly in the hope that prosperity and strength may be gradually attained. The Empress Dowager has enjoined upon Us the necessity of appropriating the things in which foreign countries excel, to supplement the shortcomings of China. . . .

Since 1897 and 1898, specious arguments have been rampant, which erroneously draw a line between the new and the old. The calamity brought about by the traitor K'ang was even more serious than that caused by the Red Boxers. . . . The traitor K'ang's talk of "new institutions" amounted to playing havoc with the institutions, not to reforming them. The said traitor and his associates took advantage of Our illness secretly to develop seditious schemes. We therefore earnestly entreated the Empress Dowager to guide the administration. . . . In annihilating the rebels and the traitors, the Empress Dowager has no objection to reform. [At the same time, however,] in modifying laws and regulations We do not intend to sweep away everything old. . . . That mother and son hold one and the same conviction should be seen by all, officials and common people alike. . . .

Recently, those who study Western ways have confined themselves to languages, manufacture, and machinery. These are but the rudiments of Western technique, which do not constitute the fountain source of Western statecraft. To rule liberally and to deal with the people in a simple and direct manner, to speak with sincerity and to act decisively—these are the principles handed down from our sages in the past and form the first foundation of the prosperity and strength of Western countries. . . . Overlooking the foundation and merely copying the superficial elements can never bring prosperity and strength to the empire. In short, without changing the laws and regulations we cannot break the inveterate customs; in order to attain prosperity we must consider reform. . . .

The edict then goes on to require all ranking officials, provincial as well as central, to draw upon the experiences of both China and foreign countries, and to make proposals of reform with respect to administration, education, finance, and military defense.

This edict which virtually ushered in another reform movement, repeated some of the leading ideas of the One Hundred Days with, of course, significant differences. The "foundation and application" (*t'i-yung*) theory of reform which was kept in abeyance (if not expressly rejected) when K'ang Yu-wei represented the dominant influence, was now formally recognized as the guiding principle. K'ang Yu-wei was inclined to question the usefulness of some of the basic features of the imperial system, whereas the leading reformers of the post-Boxer years took that system for granted, even though they were ready to modify some of its characteristic institutional forms. One of such changes introduced was the creation of a system of modern schools, which was intended eventually to replace the old "examination and school" system. This and other institutional changes, it was explained, were made not by simply copying Western patterns or following Western principles, but by putting into practice "the principles handed down from our sages in the past

and forming the foundation of prosperity and strength of Western countries." This, in reality, is a re-statement of the claim that all the useful sciences originated in China and were effectively applied by Westerners—a claim made by some of the advocates of limited reform not only in order to disarm ultra conservatives who objected to making China follow the ways of "the barbarians" but also to counter the argument of those who favored unrestricted Westernization, that truth is universal and China should not cling to her tradition which was far from perfect. The concessions thus made to Western civilization, namely, that it contained valid elements beyond mere technological skill, was calculated to bolster up the belief in China's inherent cultural superiority instead of dispelling it.

It is not surprising that Chang Chih-tung, the chief exponent of the *t'i-yung* theory of reform, became active again and exerted considerable influence on Peking, and that other officials of the same school of thought, such as Sun Chia-nai and Chang Po-hsi, figured also prominently in the post-Boxer reform movement. Chang appeared virtually as the chief spokesman, coming out with perhaps the strongest arguments for reform and the most concrete or far-reaching proposals. His memorial, "to plan and adopt Western methods," covered a wide range of practical reforms. In a letter to Jung-lu, written in the summer of 1901, Chang made his stand clear:

I humbly think that the matter of reform requires great effort at the beginning and involves numerous details in its execution. Unless there is resolute determination to break away from the established routine, I am afraid that reform will be eventually hamstrung, difficult to implement. . . . Now the only move that can hold together the minds of men today lies in reform, in which scholars and common people of the empire still find hope for attaining self-strengthening some day in the future.

The empress dowager herself lent support to reform, showing a somewhat more positive attitude than she did in the 1860's and 1890's, although, at the same time, she echoed the *t'i-yung* theory by reiterating her opposition to changing "any Chinese custom for one which was less civilized." The central thought expressed in the edict of September 12, 1898, asserting essential identity of the principles of governance between China and the West, was thus definitely though only impliedly repudiated. Significantly, Chang Chih-tung also took an occasion in 1901 to repeat his condemnation of K'ang Yu-wei's "unorthodox theories," which were treated by Chang as such because they implied a denial of the validity of the tradition of "imperial Confucianism."

One thus comes to the conclusion that Weng T'ung-ho who advocated a line of reform which was to borrow Western methods without affecting China's moral tradition, was ideologically vindicated by the developments of the post-Boxer years. This, however, serves also to underscore the strategical mistake which he made in antagonizing officials holding compatible views on reform and in relying on a man with a decidedly and widely different intellectual outlook. It may be granted, of course, that Weng might not have developed a successful reform program even if he cooperated with men like Chang Chih-tung; but one can hardly deny that he damaged his own cause of limited reform by patronizing K'ang Yu-wei and frustrating Chang Chih-tung. Since the early 1890's the emperor had already exhibited a tendency to appreciate the non-material aspects of Western civilization—a tendency which was disquieting to Weng T'ung-ho. Weng should have known better than to bring K'ang, a man with a parallel tendency, into the emperor's confidence.

The imperial authorities did not easily forgive Weng for that mistake. To the last days of his life Weng had hoped in vain for receiving the "lenient treatment" which was accorded (1904) to other officials cashiered in 1898. He was not officially exonerated until 1909 when the emperor, the empress dowager, and Weng himself had all died. It appears that the emperor, frustrated but not repentant of his actions taken in 1898, remained unconvinced even of the validity of Weng's philosophy of reform, as the following statement made in 1903 suggests:

I have plenty of ideas regarding the development of this country but . . . I am not able to carry them out as I am not my own master. I don't think the Empress Dowager herself has sufficient power to alter the state of things existing in China at present, and even if she has, she is not willing to. I am afraid it will be a long time before anything can be done toward reform.

As subsequent events showed, the emperor's pessimistic view concerning reform was not entirely unfounded. The political circumstances that prevailed in the closing decade of the nineteenth century and the opening years of the twentieth precluded the possibility of saving the dynasty through reform, not only reform of the radical variety which he and K'ang Yu-wei favored but also the limited variety advocated by moderates like Weng T'ung-ho and Chang Chih-tung. The imperial system, beset with personal and factional strifes, cursed with an inept and decaying administration, and perplexed by recurrent internal and international crises, was in an advanced stage of disintegration. It could not furnish the conditions for accomplishing anything of positive benefit to itself; the elixir of reform could not be administered to a dying regime. The reformers themselves, remarkable men in more ways than one, could not rise above the limitations imposed upon them by the very ways and circumstances which they undertook to change. They fought among themselves, neutralized their own efforts, and brought discredit or suspicion upon their actions. A worthy cause was thus doomed to be a lost cause. Carl Becker was perhaps right when he remarked that "history is a cynical, tough old nut" that frustrates the best aspirations of men.

The above considerations afford a useful basis on which to appraise the respective roles played by Weng T'ung-ho and K'ang Yu-wei as leaders of reform. Both men wished to save the empire from being "partitioned like a melon" by Western powers. They differed in their views as to the proper type of reform that might serve to attain that objective. Weng desired to inject Western science and technology into the traditional foundation and to refurbish the administration, and, at the same time, to preserve intact the ideological and institutional structure of the empire. K'ang, in contrast, sought to reinterpret Chinese tradition in the light of the modern civilization as he understood it and to alter the existing ideological and administrative system in the light of that interpretation. Ideologically speaking, K'ang's position was virtually revolutionary, in the sense that it implied drastic changes in the imperial system. It is to K'ang's credit that he discerned correctly that the established tradition, being largely outmoded, should be

radically reconstructed. But he failed to see that that would have spelled the doom of the imperial system itself. It did not occur to him to raise the question whether or not was it possible to salvage the dynasty (which he intended to do) by doing away with some of its essential features. It did not occur to him, in other words, that the same circumstances which rendered the existing ideological and institutional system obsolete, as he courageously pointed out in the interview with members of Tsungli yamen, took away the rationale of the dynastic system which he wished to save.

It may be argued, of course, that the program of limited reform favored by Weng T'ung-ho, Chang Chih-tung, and others should be easier to implement than K'ang's more advanced program—a program too advanced for the historical circumstances prevailing in 1898. K'ang's frontal assault on the imperial tradition earned for him the fear and hatred of the majority, of the scholar-officials who, under the circumstances, were more than capable of stultifying K'ang's efforts. Thus, as the leaders of the T'aip'ing rebellion made war on the scholar-officials and on what was dear to them, thereby calling forth formidable social and intellectual forces that contributed to their ultimate ruin, K'ang waged war on the traditional scholar-officialdom and on what gave it shape and continued existence, thus causing the reform movement of 1898 to suffer similar consequences. This argument, however, reasonable as it is, does not take into sufficient account of the fact that the imperial system after all had deteriorated beyond repair and was soon to be given the *coup de grace* by a revolutionary movement which was already in the making when the reformers were struggling fruitlessly toward their tantalizing goal. As a means to preserving the dynasty, therefore, the limited program of Weng T'ung-ho was no more useful than the more extensive program of K'ang Yu-wei. There was, speaking from the practical point of view, little choice between the two.

In the larger context of the intellectual history of modern China, however, K'ang Yu-wei occupied a decidedly different place from Weng T'ung-ho. By clinging to the traditional imperial tradition of China Weng made himself a typical example of the patriotic, serious-minded, but tradition-bound scholar-official that dominated the political scene during the critical years when the empire was forced by changing circumstances to make adjustments in its institutional and intellectual life. With the passing of the dynastic system the objective conditions which gave reality to the beliefs and aspirations of men like Weng, disappeared irrevocably. On the other hand, K'ang Yu-wei, in questioning the traditional ideological and institutional system of imperial China and in acknowledging the validity of what he regarded as the best elements of modern Western civilization, was pointing to new intellectual vistas which were soon to unfold themselves after the downfall of the dynasty. These were not necessarily all bright or beneficial; K'ang himself came to look askance at them. But he more than anyone else among his contemporaries had contributed to their emergence. In this way he exerted a more far-reaching historical influence than Weng T'ung-ho.

III. A NEW APPRAISAL OF THE REVOLUTIONARY LEADERSHIP

21. THE ENIGMA OF SUN YAT-SEN

HAROLD Z. SCHIFFRIN

The political style of Sun Yat-sen was the product of the interaction of personal temperament and unique social and historical circumstances. The period 1895-1911 in China had a revolutionary atmosphere about it: growing impotence and financial bankruptcy of the central government, disaffection of intelluctuals, turbulence of the masses, and above all, the inability to resist foreign pressure. Fear and resentment of the foreign presence and power was the major theme of the Chinese political mood.

Sun Yat-sen shared the concern for China's survival, yet his response was affected by factors of social origin and education that set him apart from the great majority of modern Chinese political figures. He was born a peasant and lacked both gentry connections and training in the literary tradition which were part of the inheritance of most modern intellectuals. He was also unique as a product of missionary schooling, treaty port influences, and emigrant communities. No other Chinese leader has ever

From Mary C. Wright (ed.), *China in Revolution: The First Phase, 1900-1913* (New Haven: Yale University Press, 1968), pp. 443-74. Copyright © 1968, by Yale University. Reprinted by permission. The author is Senior Lecturer in Chinese Studies, Hebrew University, Jerusalem.

been so closely identified with foreigners.

His nongentry status cut him off from the only legitimate channels for political recruitment and action in traditional China. Even modern intellectuals were for a long time repelled by his lack of classical scholarship. Yet his social antecedents facilitated collaboration with the lower rungs of Chinese society at home and abroad, and his foreign upbringing made him ambitious. It gave him the assurance that he could contribute to China's modernization and mitigate the pressure of Western power, or even manipulate it to the advantage of revolution.

As for personality, Sun Yat-sen's outstanding trait was his incredible capacity for change and adjustment. Flexible, even impulsive, his style was an enigma of contradiction and improvisation. When is he rhetorical and when is he to be taken literally? The best we can do is to recognize this personality trait and view it as the hallmark of a politician or political entrepreneur.

But Sun's flexibility was not merely a necessity based on his weak personal position and the country's vulnerability. It was also a sign of strength. Improvisation came easily because of his supreme confidence that he could outmaneuver any individual and master any situation. Some of his attempted negotiations were not in keeping with the democratic, nationalist impulse he claimed to represent. But since he felt that he and his goals would somehow come out on top, it is easier to accuse him of overconfidence and naïveté than of insincerity. What was the source of his confidence? It was his faith in his destiny, a faith which seems to have crystalized after the London experience of 1896. It was also rooted in the conviction that despite the submissiveness dictated by her present position, China with her "multitude of 400 millions" would inexorably assert her rights and attain great power status.

The 1911 Revolution was the pivotal event in Sun's career. It ended his political apprenticeship. He had spent eighteen years prior to 1911 working for the Revolution and he spent the thirteen years following it trying to realize its unfinished tasks. Leadership of the renovated Kuomintang in the 1920s gave him more substantial power and influence. It was the Revolution, though, that turned him into a national political figure. This was the event around which the legend of the "Father of the Republic" and architect of China's regeneration was later woven. The Revolution assumed such importance in Sun's mind that he even claimed that it inspired the Russians to overthrow the Tsar.[1]

While the Revolution's positive achievements may be questioned, there is no denying that Sun's presence in Nanking when he held the presidency of the Republic in trust for Yuan Shih-k'ai marked a tremendous personal triumph. The ex-peasant, who eighteen years earlier had dejectedly left Li Hung-chang's yamen, now exchanged telegrams with Li's successor and helped decide the fate of the country. How did Sun get to

Nanking and what did he represent? It is to these questions that this chapter is addressed. I shall attempt a profile of Sun's political personality for the two decades preceding the Revolution and try to determine why and under what conditions his leadership was accepted by the revolutionary movement.

The prerepublican political style of Sun Yat-sen evolved through four stages: reformism, initial activism, adjustment to the mainstream of Chinese nationalism, and conditional leadership of a modern yet not cohesive revolutionary movement.[2]

THE REFORMIST PERIOD: 1890-1894

Sun's earliest manifestations of political interest reflect the composite legacy of his youth. Modern education had detached him from rural mores and the peasant mentality: the story of his smashing the village deity is illustrative. Yet the romantic tradition of peasant militancy continued to intrigue him. While studying in Canton and Hong Kong he is said to have admired Hung Hsiu-ch'üan,[3] castigated the Manchus, showed interest in the Triads, and even experimented with bombs in his medical school laboratory.[4] Although some of the stories may be apocryphal, there is no doubt that Sun was aware of the anti-Manchu tradition in the countryside—he was born only two years after the downfall of the Taipings—and that he even sympathized with it. But the thought of using his modern credentials to enter the privileged ranks of the literati initially proved more seductive. His overture to Li Hung-chang in 1894 is only the best known of these attempts to impress gentry reformers. While in medical school in Hong Kong (1887-92) Sun also submitted two essays to Cheng Kuan-ying,[5] and in 1890 he requested the patronage of Cheng Tsao-ju,[6] both natives of Hsiang-shan, his home district, and prominent in national affairs. In 1893 while practicing medicine in Canton, Sun tried and failed to get an interview with his reformist fellow provincial, K'ang Yu-wei.[7]

There was nothing unique about Sun's reformist proposals. His long statement to Li Hung-chang shows traces of Feng Kuei-fen's influence and close resemblance to arguments in Cheng Kuan-ying's famous *Sheng-shih wei-yen* (Words of Warning to a Prosperous Age).[8] What was unique was the attempt itself. Admitting his inability to write an "eight-legged essay," Sun still claimed a role in China's modernization by virtue of his foreign training. The approach to Li required courage, and after being turned down, it took even more courage to work for the overthrow of the dynasty.

One reformist influence which carried over to Sun's activist stage was that exerted by Ho Kai (Ho Ch'i) (1859-1914), a British-trained physician and barrister who achieved remarkable success in Hong Kong and taught in the medical school Sun attended.[9] Written with the help of a collaborator,[10] his essays were later translated into Chinese; Ho, like Sun, was more proficient in English. The distinctive feature of Ho's reformism was his unequivocal plea for foreign and especially British support. He urged Britain to "Come forward and . . . apply the requisite pressures" for China's reformation.[11] Even a rejuvenated China, he insisted, would pose no threat to the West.[12] This was the type of nationalism inherited by Sun Yat-sen when he first turned his full attention to politics.

The difference between Ho and Sun was the latter's readiness to sacrifice his professional training for the chance of becoming directly involved in China's future. Where Ho was generally content to lambast the mandarins in the Hong Kong press, Sun became a full-time conspirator. He turned to less respectable social elements, the Triads and peasant bandits, with whom Ho in his Hong Kong sanctuary had little affinity. Sun took for granted the latent anti-dynasticism of his native Kwangtung and added some new ingredients to the old formula for peasant rebellion.

INITIAL ACTIVISM: 1895-1900

The merchants, peddlers, planters, laborers, and clerks of Hawaii and Hong Kong were the Chinese Sun knew best and the most likely financial backers of the Revolution. The Society to Restore China's Prosperity, formed by Sun in Hawaii and Hong Kong in 1894-95, consisted chiefly of these overseas supporters and a small leadership group composed of young men like himself: missionary-educated nonliterati from Hong Kong and Canton. (Even some of their internal correspondence was in English.) With a little over 150 members the organization as such was unimpressive,[13] but it was never meant to be a mass movement. The Canton plot of 1895 and the Waichow campaign of 1900 were the only occasions when it functioned, and both times it worked on the assumption that thousands of fighters would enter the field as soon as it made the initial spark. On neither occasion was the name Hsing-Chung-hui publicized. Sun and his friends were not only convinced that China was ripe for revolution but that traditional vehicles of anti-dynasticism—secret societies and bandit gangs (*lü-lin*)—would bear the brunt of the fighting. If a key yamen fell they assumed that the whole province would go and that others would fall in line. Instead of directly recruiting peasants the revolutionaries made temporary alliances with Triad and bandit chiefs or merely hired mercenaries. Primitive rebels[14] directed by a Westernized elite and subsidized by overseas merchants—this was the formula for the Canton and Waichow uprisings.

Sun and his friends also felt that no major political change could be carried out in China without the active assistance or friendly neutrality of foreigners. While respect for foreign power was universal, no group had more reason to seek external approval. Even if their revolutionary plans succeeded, they assumed that the foreign stamp of legitimacy would be needed as a substitute for influential connections at home. It is significant that both the Canton and Waichow plots were timed to exploit critical episodes in foreign affairs—after the sino-Japanese War and while the Boxer settlement was pending—when increased intervention appeared likely.

Furthermore the conspirators were confident that foreigners also needed them. The European powers had been promoting missionary and commercial enterprises for half a century. Who were better equipped to further their interests than the Western-educated and Christian leaders of the Society to Restore China's Prosperity? No other group in China was so closely connected with the compradores and native pastors of Hong Kong and Canton.

This pro-European orientation was personified by Ho Kai. In 1895, while Sun organized his conspiracy in Canton and Yang Ch'ü-yün, his party rival, solicited merchants and mercenaries in Hong Kong, Ho was their foreign spokesman. Though he never joined the society he attended the first conspiratorial sessions. It was probably through him that the British editors of the *China Mail* and *Hongkong Telegraph* became the conspirators' confidants and mouthpieces.[15]

In March 1895, more than six months before the attack on the Canton yamen was scheduled, the *China Mail*, probably briefed by Ho-Kai, disclosed that the reform party was planning to overthrow the Manchus and establish constitutional rule. Foreigners were advised not to repeat the mistake of supporting the dynasty, as they had done against the Taipings, because the new government would at last open China to Western trade and civilization. Printing a highly detailed version of the plotters' program, the *Mail* listed various institutional reforms and intimated that foreign advisers would help reconstitute the government. The collection of inland revenue, it suggested, would be placed in the hands of foreigners "under a similar arrangement to the Maritime Customs, until China is in a position to dispense with all foreign assistance."[16]

According to the *Mail* the rebels planned to replace the Manchus with a Chinese dynasty. What then is the significance of the Society to Restore China's Prosperity membership oath, which called for the establishment of a republic? Republicanism, I believe, represented their ultimate goal.[17] It was the most modern Western form of government and the logical model for avowed modernizers. Yet it was characteristic of Sun to avoid rigid programmatic formulas and to concentrate on the instrumental rather than the terminal aspects of revolution. He wanted to set the anti-dynastic forces into motion and was confident that he could do so. He was less confident of his ability to achieve quick success without catering to foreign preferences or even compromising with venal gentry like Liu Hsüeh-hsün, who toyed with the idea of using Sun to further his own imperial ambitions. What Sun wanted was freedom to maneuver without being tied down to a specific policy beyond that of overthrowing the Manchus and modernizing China's government. He had no audience for explicating ideological nuances at home. The rank and file of his potential fighters were motivated more by hunger and hatred of the authorities than by any programming aims.

For the Europeans, though, he had to show himself as a moderate and reasonable reformer and specify advantages for traders, manufacturers, and missionaries. Instead of insisting on a republic—which most foreigners considered an unrealistic goal—it was preferable to postulate a respectable transition to Chinese monarchical rule under foreign tutelage. Revolution, if it was to be approved of or permitted by foreigners, had to be carried out quickly, with a minimum of disorder and disruption.

In this first attempt Ho was the ideologist and Sun the conspirator. After its failure they temporarily parted. Ho returned to his civic duties in Hong Kong, and Sun, forced to flee from both China and Hong Kong, began a sixteen-year exile by trying to rebuild his network. After a brief stay in Japan, he returned to Hawaii and then went on to the United States.[18]

The campaign abroad was disappointing, and even Sun might have been permanently discouraged had he not been suddenly thrust into the limelight in London in the fall of 1896. The Manchus had taken Sun seriously, and it was their panic—seeing Sun as a Hung Hsiuch'üan marshaling the Overseas Chinese —which turned him into a much more dangerous adversary. His imprisonment in the Chinese legation in London made him famous and confirmed his faith in the Revolution and in himself. If he had not felt so previously, the outcome of the kidnapping episode led him to believe that he was destined to save China. It also reinforced his original conviction concerning the foreign role in the Chinese Revolution. Seeing the British public outraged over the Manchu attempt to spirit him out of London and subject him to the "slicing" punishment at home, Sun conjured up the vision of British support for the Revolution. He wrote letters of thanks to the newspapers and asserted that England represented the enlightened society he wanted to create at home.[19] He took great care to let the press know of his Christian affiliation and it was even reported that he would join a medical missionary venture.[20] Though he had ceased writing in Chinese he suddenly became very prolific in English. With the help of friends, in 1897, he published *Kidnapped in London,* a book that for a long time would remain his best known work, and in March 1897, again aided by a collaborator, Sun made a plea for British "benevolent neutrality" in an article in the *Fortnightly Review.*[21] Boasting that the Chinese army was to "a great extent leavened with sympathizers to the Reform Party," Sun echoed Ho Kai's attack on the mandarin system, which he claimed was buttressed solely by the Manchus. He dangled the promise of increased trade and access to China's mineral wealth. European advisers and administrative assistance would be invited to modernize the new regime. "The benevolent neutrality of Great Britain, and of the other Powers," he asserted, "is all the aid needed to enable us to make the present system give place to one that is not corrupt."[22]

Sun had already shown his ability to

impress individual foreigners. His American missionary teachers helped him in Hawaii[23] and an American chemistry teacher from the Islands had joined the Canton plotters as an expert on explosives.[24] A Danish sailor drilled Sun's recruits in a Hawaiian mission schoolyard.[25] British journalists had backed him in Hong Kong, and Portuguese friends had smuggled him out of Macao when the Manchus were after him.[26] His former teachers in Hong Kong, Dr. Cantlie and Dr. Manson—the latter convinced that Sun was a born Christian and not a convert[27]—had rescued him from the Chinese legation. And now Professor Giles of Cambridge translated his autobiography,[28] a member of Parliament raised a question on his behalf in Parliament,[29] and a British soldier, Rowland Mulkern, volunteered to join the next uprising against the Manchus.[30] More than ever Sun had reason to believe in his ability to win foreign sympathy for the Revolution.

Sun also took time out for intensive reading and study, mostly at the British Museum. Between December 1896 and June 1897, he visited the museum on fifty-nine days, spending hours on each visit.[31] Cantlie, with whom he was in close contact, testifies to Sun's wide range of interests covering scientific and political subjects.[32] Sun later claimed that this study period inspired the formulation of his famous Three Principles. This seems doubtful since it was five or six years before he began expressing these ideas. Though the nine months—not the two years he subsequently claimed—spent in Britain had enabled him to learn more about contemporary political and social movements, Sun still showed no serious concern with political theory.

In the fall of 1897 he established his base in Japan and also looked for signs of Britain's "benevolent neutrality." He wrote to the Hong Kong Colonial Secretary demanding revocation of the banishment order issued against him in March 1896 and threatening to "appeal it to the English public and the civilized world." The reply informed him that the colony could not be used for conspiracies against a "friendly neighbouring Empire" and warned that he would be arrested if he set foot in Hong Kong.[33]

The rebuff was more than balanced by developments in Japan, where he was warmly welcomed by Miyazaki Torazō, Hirayama Amane (Shū), and their influential sponsor, Inukai Tsuyoshi (Ki). Quickly attuning himself to the mood of those pan-Asian Japanese sinophiles, Sun discarded the role he had played in London. Now he was no longer the churchgoing supplicant of Europeans but the would-be redeemer of humiliated Asians. Declaring his republicanism—something he had not done in Britain—he asked for Japanese help in "saving China's four hundred million people" and "wiping away the humiliation of Asia's yellow race."[34]

The Japanese were impressed with Sun, and their joint adventures, including the Philippine episode, are a delight in fanciful conspiracy.[35] They also present a remarkable study of Sino-Japanese comradeship. Yet even the Japanese could not overcome literati ostracism of Sun Yat-sen. K'ang Yu-wei and Liang Ch'i-ch'ao, in exile after 1898, won over the Overseas Chinese, and their friends in the Independent Army successfully competed for the allegiance of the secret societies.[36]

The summer of 1900, with the Boxer troubles, provided an ideal occasion for Sun to display his political style. The foreign powers were pitted against the

Manchus, important governors-general were ignoring Peking, and literati reformers were acting belligerent. Though preparations for his own Waichow uprising were under way, the opportunities for negotiating with these other foci of power were too good to pass up. Sun made a last, futile attempt to conciliate K'ang Yu-wei. He tried to induce Li Hung-chang to establish an independent Kwangtung-Kwangsi government, and calling once more upon Ho Kai, offered Britain and the other foreign powers temporary tutelary rule over China.[37] This too failed as did his fantastic negotiations with Li's lieutenant, Liu Hsüeh-hsün, whom he offered an emperorship or presidency in return for financing the Waichow uprising.[38]

Without receiving orders from Sun, who placed his final hopes on Japanese support from Taiwan, the Waichow fighters struck in early October. Under the leadership of Cheng Shih-liang, the Triads, Hakkas, and mercenaries, supported by peasants in the East River area, engaged the government forces in hard fighting for two weeks. Originally scheduled to attack Canton, where they had a sizable contingent of Christian-led followers, the rebels followed Sun's orders and turned toward Amoy where he was supposed to arrive with Japanese help. But the Japanese changed their minds and Cheng's makeshift army, now numbering about 20,000, was caught in a pocket and forced to disband.[39]

Waichow validated one of Sun's premises, that the Chinese countryside was sympathetic to revolution. It also exposed the weakness of his leadership. He had not prepared a self-contained movement for a sustained revolutionary campaign. What he contributed instead was a flurry of intrigues which left the fighters pursuing a dubious strategy.

The Waichow uprising, supplemented by the martyrdom of Shih Chien-ju,[40] grandson of a Hanlin scholar, was nevertheless impressive and redounded to Sun's fame as an activist precisely at the time when militancy was coming into vogue among the growing body of overseas students.[41] Yet almost five years passed before Sun was accepted by the students, whose gentry prejudices never dissolved completely. Nor was Sun quick to contend for the loyalty of this group. Perhaps he felt uneasy in the presence of Chinese intellectuals. His earlier attempts at reaching literati through elegant essays had failed, and his impatience led him to seek faster ways of asserting himself. He assumed he was playing for higher stakes and scorned what he must have considered the inconsequential theorizing of youngsters who had only recently discovered George Washington and the French Revolution. His experience with Liang Ch'i-ch'ao in 1899-1900 left him with a deep suspicion concerning the reliability of literati even when they espoused revolution.

When his own formula for revolutionary conspiracy led to a dead end in the years following Waichow, Sun nevertheless found a way to reach the students. That he was able to suit his style to this new audience again attests to his versatility. This was not, however, simply a question of converting the students to revolution. Largely inspired by Liang Ch'i-ch'ao, they had been preaching a tough-minded nationalism which envisaged confrontation with a predatory Europe. This was the main current of Chinese nationalism and ran counter to the pro-Western protestations of Ho Kai, who until now had been speaking for Sun Yat-sen.[42]

The mainstream of Chinese nationalism originated with literati whose faith in the traditional system had been eroded in various degrees since 1895, when the system was discredited by Japan's victory. After the Boxer disaster this nationalist consciousness attained a high degree of sophistication among émigré intellectuals and the overseas students. Their anti-Manchuism flowed *directly* from the need for resisting foreign pressure when they became convinced of Manchu inability to perform this role.

As for Sun Yat-sen, anti-Manchuism derived *directly* from the need for a rapprochement with the West and was only *indirectly* concerned with resisting it. Sun's main enemy was outmoded, xenophobic government which he identified with Manchu rule. Why was Chinese sovereignty being violated? The student reply was that a deeply embedded impulse in modern capitalist society—this was their discovery of modern imperialism and its economic mainspring—was encouraged by Manchu appeasement tactics. Sun Yat-sen's reply, as far as we can discern, was that "Tartar" rulers were incapable of conducting civilized relations in the modern world. Western aggression, according to Sun, was a response to Manchu intransigence and obscurantism. Sun attacked the Manchus for blocking the beneficient influences of foreign trade and religion. The students attacked the Manchus for opening China to the imperialist incursions of missionaries and merchants. How were these contrasting attitudes reconciled?

First, it is quite obvious that these two approaches were aimed at different targets. The students were talking to the Chinese and Sun was addressing foreigners, the same missionaries and merchants who were anathema to the young intellectuals. And we know that Sun was quite adept at adjusting to his audiences. That he possessed unique powers of dis-

simulation and rarely hesitated to deceive foreigners is a matter of record. That he cherished more typically Chinese feelings is recorded by Miyazaki.

Nevertheless I feel that unless we consider Sun a complete rogue, it would be a mistake not to credit him with some degree of sincerity in his pro-Western orientation during this early period, and as far as that goes, until the end of his life. His Westernized background and education cannot be so easily dismissed. Though their governments consistently disappointed him, Sun's attitude toward foreigners in general can best be described as ambivalent rather than hypocritical or hostile.

What was required to bring him closer to the mainstream of Chinese nationalism was a mutual adjustment. Student anti-imperialism had to be diverted or softened, while Sun's attitude required a more sophisticated mode of expression and a touch of belligerence.

First, the young intellectuals changed; I think the adjustment was anticipated by Chang Ping-lin, the most traditional of the literati nationalists and an elder and respected figure amidst the student ferment of Tokyo and Shanghai. Heir to the traditional gentry anti-Manchuism of the Eastern Chekiang school, Chang had nevertheless been prepared to accept reformed Manchu rule as long as he saw the possibility of a joint Chinese-Manchu effort to resist the white invaders. By 1901 he despaired of the Manchus as defenders of Chinese sovereignty, and anti-imperialism tipped the balance in favor of militant anti-Manchuism in the pattern previously described.[43] In his famous rebuttal of K'ang Yu-wei in 1903[44]—one of the most significant documents in revolutionary literature—Chang intimated that there was really no immediate solution to the problem of imperialism. When K'ang asserted that revolution would invite further intervention, Chang replied that intervention could not be prevented no matter what China did. The foreign presence was already felt and was a fact which had to be taken into consideration. What was required was a realistic attitude. The revolution, he admitted, would have to go along with the foreigners, but if it enjoyed the massive popular support he anticipated, and if it quickly established effective government, foreigners would have no alternative but to recognize the new regime. Westerners, he asserted, would naturally seek self-aggrandizement should the Revolution be unsuccessful, but faced with a fait accompli they too would be realistic and make the best of the situation. In the crisis of Japan's response to the West, France had wanted to help the Shogun, he asserted, but the pro-imperial movement had had more support, and Japan's Meiji Restoration had succeeded.[45]

In the following years, though he continued to see the foreigners as the main danger to China, Chang became even more reluctant to clash with them. "From a political and social standpoint," he declared, "the West inflicts much more harm upon our race than the Manchus."[46] But contemporary China, he felt, was inadequate to this larger struggle against imperialism. The white race, "the most powerful in the world," would eventually be subdued by the colored people—"the black men and red men"—of the entire world.[47] China alone was too weak, and instead of openly proclaiming their anti-imperialist intentions, Chang argued that the revolutionaries had to remain silent and tread softly. Though "aware of the missionary evil and the merchant evil"[48] Chang insisted that the revolutionary army be restrained

and tolerant. It was imperative not to give the foreigners the slightest provocation. Above all the revolutionaries had to prevent a Manchu-white man coalition.[49] As to the ultimate goal of Chinese nationalism, Chang had no doubts. Its aim was the complete recovery of Chinese sovereignty and elimination of foreigners' special privileges—the return of Weihaiwei and Shanghai's international settlement, abolition of spheres of influence, and so forth. "The foreigners," he cautioned, "had better not know this; otherwise their anger will be kindled . . . We must keep our mouths shut and not say a word."[50]

On the other hand, in 1903 Chang was convinced that any popular uprising— the Boxer uprising, T'ang Ts'ai-ch'ang's plot, the Kwangsi revolt—acted to increase the people's political consciousness and to prepare them for the greater struggle of the future.[51] These two concepts—the need for a temporary reconciliation with the foreign presence and the hope that a revolution would rapidly mature the Chinese political capacity— became crucial to militant nationalist thinking.

What happened was that even while elaborating upon the imperialist danger, the young intellectuals recoiled from the immensity of their task. Overthrowing the Manchus, establishing a republic, and at the same time belligerently redressing the wrongs committed by foreigners—this was too much to contemplate. Their mentor, Liang Ch'i-ch'ao, was convinced that revolution would invite further intervention. By 1903 he had repudiated his brief flirtation with revolution and pressed for institutional reform to strengthen national resistance. But the students shifted their focus to the easier hurdle. Avoiding the social and class implications of revolution, which they had touched upon tangentially in their writings, they elevated anti-Manchuism to the highest priority. Their predilection for heroic assassinations reveals their desperation.[52] They felt impelled to act, yet at least for the time being a collision course with the West had to be avoided.

With anti-Manchu revolution enshrined as the transcendent goal the way was paved for the oldest, most experienced, and most notorious revolutionary of the time. But it was not only that Sun Yat-sen had behind him a decade of revolutionary intrigue and well-publicized activism. More than anyone else he had combined revolutionary conspiracy with solicitation of foreign goodwill. No one else was as confident that he could guarantee the Revolution safe conduct past the foreign gunboats.

This shift in the student mood was matched by a corresponding adjustment on the part of Sun Yat-sen.

TRANSITION AND ADJUSTMENT

The two or three years following Waichow are among the most obscure in Sun's career. Until the fall of 1903 he spent most of his time in Yokohama, except for a short visit to Hong Kong in the beginning of 1902 and a longer trip to Hanoi toward the end of the year. With respect to the nationalist ferment among the Tokyo students and their colleagues in Shanghai, where the *Supao* case became a *cause célèbre*,[53] Sun remained on the periphery. It was mostly through long-standing Cantonese friends like Feng Tzu-yu and Wang Ch'ung-hui that tenuous contact was established. Sun contributed money to student publications like *K'ai-chih lu* (Record of Expanding Wisdom) and *Kuo-min pao* (National Journal) in 1900-01, but there

is no evidence of any ideological contribution.[54] Several non-Cantonese students like Shen Hsiang-yün, Wu Lu-chen, and Ch'i I-hui were said to have been attracted to him as early as 1898-99,[55] but none were interested enough to join the Waichow enterprise and they instead devoted themselves to the Hankow plot of that same year. Among the older non-Cantonese intellectuals, Chang Ping-lin seems to have been one of the first to recognize Sun's talents as an exponent of anti-Manchuism. He had little regard, though, for Sun's attainments in foreign learning.[56] Both Chang and Liang undoubtedly contributed to Sun's knowledge of Chinese history and political thought in general.

Still unsure of the potential and trustworthiness of this new intellectual element, Sun preferred trying to revive the old Society for the Revival of China's Prosperity pattern of conspiracy. In 1902 he solicited French support and went to Hanoi to see representatives of the governor-general of Indochina. When negotiations lapsed he spent a desultory six months agitating among the local Overseas Chinese, and gained a handful of recruits while missing out on the student furor in Japan.[57]

At the same time the old Hong Kong-based combination was revived behind his back. Tse Tsan-tai, always closer to Yang Ch'ü-yün, Sun's early rival in the Society to Restore China's Prosperity (who had been eliminated by Manchu gunmen after Waichow), planned an attack on Canton in the beginning of 1903.[58] This plot, like that of 1895, was abortive but the attempt showed that Sun was drifting or being pushed away from his old base before establishing himself on new ground.

In the same year, with the Yokohama Overseas Chinese showing no more resistance to the K'ang-Liang appeal than Sun's former followers in Hawaii, Sun made his first tentative efforts toward creating a new combination among the overseas students. First was his unsuccessful attempt, backed by the Japanese, to provide students with military training. Though it closed down after several months and attracted only fourteen or fifteen cadets—all Cantonese except for two Fukienese—Sun's Yokohama school foreshadowed his new line of attack. By adding Equal Land Rights (*p'ing-chün ti-ch'üan*) to the principles of the Society to Restore China's Prosperity, he had the basis for an all-embracing political program. The oath administered to these cadets was the same as he would demand of the students in the Revolutionary Alliance two years later.[59]

Also indicative of Sun's new approach was his article in the student journal, *Chiang-su*, in November 1903.[60] The short essay, "On the Preservation or Dismemberment of China," was Sun's first contribution to the influential nationalistic press and his first article in Chinese since the petition to Li Hung-chang nine years earlier. It throbs with a militancy that carries him beyond Ho Kai and closer to the student tenor. Using the metaphors popularized by Liang Ch'i-ch'ao and the Tokyo-Shanghai firebrands, Sun acknowledged the imperialist motif in foreign policies toward China, praised the Boxers, and criticized the late Li Hung-chang's failure to drive out the foreign invaders. After arguing that the Manchus were incapable of defending China, Sun warned foreigners that China would not easily submit to dismemberment: "Even though they may try to dismember, they will never be able to slaughter the majority of the Chinese people."[61] On the other hand,

Sun pointed out that not all foreigners were motivated by imperialism. There were those who admired China's traditional civilization, her moral power, and her abhorrence of war. These men of goodwill wished to preserve China's territorial integrity, but as long as the Manchus remained, Sun argued, aggression would be invited.

It is significant that in this first public expression of his views to a student audience, Sun concentrated upon foreign affairs. His arguments were directed toward foreigners: warning the rapacious element and offering a reasonable approach to the friendlier segment. What he in fact was doing was showing the students that he possessed the expertise required to handle the foreign threat. Although he also hinted at his plan to create a new party, Sun did not remain in Japan. Before making a serious play for student support, he needed funds. Thus it was first necessary to recover his Overseas Chinese base.

The Sun Yat-sen who returned to Hawaii at the end of 1903 responded to Liang Ch'i-ch'ao's challenge with a new polemical style and displayed his mettle as a speaker and publicist.[62] He addressed thousands of Overseas Chinese at mass meetings and wrote newspaper articles defining his revolutionary, republican position. Liang had not only taken over the Overseas Chinese but the concept of revolution, and Sun proceeded to expose the contradiction between Liang's militancy and K'ang Yu-wei's unequivocal declarations of loyalty to the Emperor. He attacked gradualism in politics as comparable to using the earliest locomotive instead of buying the latest models. If a republic was admittedly the latest model of government, why settle for an obsolete constitutional monarchy?[63]

Continuing the approach he had recently taken in Japan Sun also emphasized the external advantages of internal revolution: "If the people . . . could rise and overthrow the worthless . . . Manchu government, every country would respect [us]. . . . Would it then still be possible to carve us up like a melon?" This was the line the students were taking, and in castigating alleged Manchu appeasement policies, Sun no longer sounds like Ho Kai but like Yang Shou-jen (Yang Tu-sheng) and his associates: "The Manchu government not only signs treaties hacking at and mortgaging us, but it pacifies the country for the foreigners and presents them with Kwangtung's Hsin-an district and Kwangchow-wan."[64]

Though he recovered some lost ground Sun did not completely nullify Liang's success. The larger American Overseas Chinese community had likewise fallen under the reformer's spell. Armed with credentials from the Triads, whom he joined in Honolulu, Sun undertook an ambitious coast-to-coast tour of the United States accompanied by the titular leader of the secret society. By the winter of 1904 he had reached New York. Again Sun found himself at a low point. Overseas Chinese audiences turned out to hear him but on the whole remained apathetic and the financial drive failed.[65] The need for a shift in tactics was obvious. While in New York Sun renewed his friendship with Wang Ch'ung-hui, then studying at the Yale Law School. With Wang's assistance Sun composed and privately printed his "True Solution to the Chinese Question."[66] This was his first direct appeal to the Americans.

Though containing the same basic arguments he had used in his article in *Chiang-su,* there were tones reminiscent of the Ho Kai period. Instead of mentioning the recent imperialist conquest of the Philippines, he now recognized America as "one of the nearest neighbors of China," and called for American "Lafayettes" to join the struggle against the Manchus. Now he did not blame the Manchus for appeasing foreigners as he had done in Tokyo and Honolulu but charged them with cutting off the Chinese from foreign intercourse.

The pamphlet, said to have been circulated among influential foreigners, evoked no significant response.[67] However, news from the student front suddenly took a favorable turn. Student nationalists in Europe, mostly from Hupeh, invited Sun for discussions and sent travel expenses. The young militants were looking for a leader and Sun eagerly grasped the opportunity.[68]

LEADERSHIP OF THE REVOLUTIONARY MOVEMENT

As a result of preliminary recruitment in Brussels, Berlin, and Paris, in the summer of 1905, Sun felt strong enough to submit his candidacy for leadership to the Tokyo hotbed of student activism. The resulting establishment of the Revolutionary Alliance in the summer of 1905 finally brought Sun to the forefront of the anti-Manchu revolutionary movement.[69] This predominantly student organization, representing almost every province in China, was actually China's first modern-style political party. It had a rudimentary organization, an ideology, and a program of propaganda and action. What it lacked was the cohesion and long-range staying power of a successful revolutionary movement.

Why was Sun chosen leader? I have already indicated that one of the crucial factors was the overriding concern with the foreign threat and Sun's purported ability to neutralize it. This impression is reinforced by Sung Chiao-jen's recollection of his first conversation with Sun in Tokyo. Sung did not remember all the details of their preliminary talk but he did recall Sun's assurance that China was in no danger of partition and that only an internal power struggle among the Chinese themselves would present foreigners with such an opportunity.[70]

Then too, the Japanese were his enthusiastic sponsors—living proof of his ability to gain foreign support.[71] Sun also had Overseas Chinese connections, which were required to finance revolution. And finally, he had cultivated the secret societies, which he continued to believe would provide the main fighting strength for the Revolution. (In his talk with Sung Chiao-jen, Sun noted the success of the Kwangsi Triads. They had tried to get in touch with him the previous year, he asserted, but were prevented by his absence from Hong Kong.) Given educated leadership, as by the students, Sun insisted that the Triads were capable of overthrowing the dynasty.[72]

The result was purely instrumental or entrepreneurial leadership.[73] Sun was accepted because he appeared to be the most successful practitioner of revolution, and in particular a kind of revolution which could avoid a disaster in foreign relations. This was no ideological leadership. Sun was not accepted as the fountainhead of political wisdom. His appeal to the intellectuals lacked that element of personal authority without which the centralized organizational structure planned in 1905 could never be realized.

This is not to say that Sun did not attempt to assert ideological leadership. His reading and travels, the tutelage of Ho Kai, Japanese intellectuals, Russian revolutionaries, Chinese émigrés, and students all exposed to the latest currents of foreign thinking as well as giving him insight into Chinese history. Now that he finally had an intellectual audience he rose to the challenge and presented a comprehensive program distilled from the fund of world knowledge. The substance of his famous Three Principles of the People (*San-min chu-i*) is too well known to require further elaboration. It is significant however that these principles, outlined in 1905 and given the collective term the following year, are so comprehensive that they include almost everything. "Nationalism, Democracy, and Socialism"—what is left? This much must be said for Sun Yat-sen: When he finally had to define his program, he made it all-inclusive. But its very comprehensiveness turned it into a generalized slogan. The Three Principles represented the universal main political trends, and had in various forms already been suggested by earlier Chinese writers.[74] All Sun was saying was that China was capable of incorporating and realizing these trends in a one-stroke revolution. Although he did suggest some improvements upon Western achievements, such as the "five-power constitution" and "equalization of land rights," he brought few new ideas to the revolutionary movement. It was precisely his innovations mentioned above that were least acceptable to his audience. Above all the striking characteristic of the Three Principles is their relative detachment from China's specific situation. The most pressing social problem—the agrarian question—is left in abeyance, and instead Sun's version of "social revolution" actually points to a way of preventing social injustice in China's future industrialized society. Of the inadequacies of traditional culture and society there is no mention. The essence of his position was that only the Manchu regime stood in the way of China's easy transplantation of the latest Western political institutions. True, Sun's subsequent suggestion of a nine-year hiatus before the final attainment of true representative government indicates recognition of the need for some sort of transition, a recognition perhaps forced upon him by Liang Ch'i-ch'ao's arguments. But the tutelary role of a revolutionary party required tighter control than he or any other party leader exercised; this was another of his innovations that would be forgotten by 1912.[75]

While the substance of Sun's program did not penetrate deeply into the revolutionary consciousness, the mood of his presentation was sufficiently attuned to student mentality to override the sober objections of Liang Ch'i-ch'ao. From 1905 to 1907 Liang, in his *Hsin-min ts'ung-pao* (New People's Miscellany), single-handedly took on a whole platoon of revolutionary scribes who defended the Revolutionary Alliance program in the *Min-pao* (People's Report). The significance of the debate[76] lies in its elaboration of the revolutionary values embodied in Sun's presentation. Among the values shared by Sun and the students was first of all the assertion of Chinese group-superiority. All their interpretations and commitments to action were in consonance with the hope of an early establishment of Chinese preeminence in the world. Secondly, there was a commitment to criteria of universal validity. Whenever possible, examples from the outside world, both past and present, were invoked in order to justify the revolutionary course. Yet their apparent submission to rational, universal criteria was always limited by their Chinese particularism. When Liang Ch'i-ch'ao pointed out that what they were attempting had

no successful precedent in world history, they were quick to postulate a special road for China.

This brings us to the third value—elitism. Sun's frequent references to the interventionist, spearheading role of "men of determination" reflect his faith in a disciplined and enlightened elite. An elite that knew the course of world progress could transcend the social and cultural obstacles described by Liang Ch'i-ch'ao. And finally there was the emphasis upon speed. It was not only that China had to take her place among the major powers but she had to do so quickly. Gradualism was rejected in favor of stage-skipping.

This value complex was implicit in Sun's first major speech to the students in 1905:

Everything can be managed by men of determination. What the ordinary people do not understand will have to be introduced by [such] men. If the thoughts of [these] men are elevated, the people's qualifications will be elevated. . . . It is incumbent upon us . . . to choose the most civilized form of government in the world. . . . If in one transformation we can stir people's hearts, civilization will come in a hurry and in only ten years the world "independence" will be stamped on people's brains. . . . We have decided not to follow evolutionary change [the way the rest of the world changed] but to pursue artificially induced change with its quick progress. I want you gentlemen to save China by choosing from the top. . . .[77]

As a leader, then, I think Sun caught the young nationalist mood, and in catering to it won the battle with Liang even before it began. Yet in promising everything so quickly and easily he was not laying the groundwork for long-term leadership. Sun was in a position where he had to produce tangible success immediately. He could not command the unswerving loyalty of his followers in a prolonged struggle preceded by intensive organization and agitation. The circumstances, as I have indicated, were conducive to the choice of a noncataclysmic but swift revolution. Only a truly Leninist-type leader, one commanding intellectual authority and possessed of extreme hardness of character, could have imposed his will completely upon the impatient band of students. Sun simply did not have such authority. In his speeches he perhaps asserted a demagogic sway over his listeners, but never real intellectual leadership. Compare, for example, Lenin's key editorial role in the Bolshevik organ, *Iskra*, with Sun's passive role in *Min-pao's* comparable internecine struggle with Liang.[78] By 1907 *Min-pao* was actually edited by Sun's party rivals who at that time began disputing his leadership.[79] In effect Sun never really overcame his original handicap. Lack of literary skill weakened his hold over followers who instinctively equated leadership with scholarship. And if the leader remained a functionary, the organization itself was only a temporary arrangement and not a chosen vehicle for the salvation of the country. The Revolutionary Alliance as an organization did not command that feeling of sacredness that characterizes the transcendent party, which is "Raised to the dignity of an end in itself, instead of remaining in the domain of ways and means."[80]

In action the Revolutionary Alliance for the most part extended and intensified the same pattern that Sun had evolved for the Society to Restore China's Prosperity. The difference, and this of course was crucial, was in the size and quality of the leadership echelon. The Revolutionary Alliance's social roots were not in the treaty ports and missionary institutions but in well-placed families from the interior of China. From 1907 to the spring of 1911 the organization sponsored eight unsuccessful uprisings, the first six of which (1907-08) relied chiefly upon secret societies and peasant dissidents. It was only in 1910 that it concentrated on subverting the army, whose ranks had by then been infiltrated by revolutionary sympathizers, many of them young officers trained in Japan.[81] After the failures of 1910 and the spring of 1911, this new strategy finally paid off at Wuchang. Though as with most revolutions, this successful uprising broke out unexpectedly, the Revolutionary Alliance's previous attempts, including the two undertaken by the Society to Restore China's Prosperity, had a cumulative, catalytic effect which weakened dynastic prestige and power and facilitated final victory. Though Sun's tactics failed, his original strategy of responsive revolt—that if one province fell the others would quickly fall in line—was largely validated by the events of 1911. Yet the very ease with which many provinces fell through negotiation with essentially nonrevolutionary elements precluded centralized party control. As Ernest Young points out in Chapter 10 of this volume, by the end of 1911 when they faced Yuan Shih-k'ai's Northern Army the revolutionaries were not in an inferior military position for continuing the struggle and bringing about a complete transfer of power. But it was soon apparent that they lacked the internal cohesion required for such an effort and were quite unprepared for a prolonged conflict. In most revolutions, as well as traditional Chinese rebellions, the crucial stage is the elimination of rivals after the ancien régime has been immobilized. The 1911 Revolution stopped short of this stage. The final transfer of power was less important to the Revolutionary Alliance than a negotiated replacement of traditional government by a third party without risking foreign intervention. Their leader lacked both the authority and the frame of mind required for such an all-out effort.

What exactly, then, was Sun's contribution to the Revolution? First there was his tangible role as fund-raiser, which was partly the result of circumstances. He was expelled from Japan in 1907 and a year later from Hanoi where he had joined the party's military strategists. There is no question, though, that his real milieu was among the overseas communities. He acted as the Revolution's spokesman among the Overseas Chinese, especially those of Southeast Asia and America.[82] The funds that Sun himself collected or which were remitted by others after he had laid the groundwork financed the Revolutionary Alliance's military engagements. It should be noted too that while tens of thousands of dollars flowed through his hands, Sun made no money out of the Revolution. Later, in the corruption ridden republican era, this rectitude in financial matters helped substantiate the image of the patriotic national leader.

Sun's other specialty was his dexterous handling of foreigners. Yet though he tried vigorously, making bids to the Japanese, Americans, French, and again to the British, only a few individuals, not governments, responded.[83] Among these were some French officers at Hanoi,[84] the adventurous American, Homer Lea,[85] the Russian social revolutionaries, Russel and Gershuni,[86] and a hodgepodge of English socialists,[87] Old China Hands,[88] and devout Christians[89] who saw Sun as a Chinese Constantine. The British government hurt him the most, still keeping him out of Hong Kong, and in 1910 de-

claring him *persona non grata* in Penang, by then one of his strongest overseas bases.[90]

In the end, however, Sun's basic contention concerning foreign behavior was validated. By scrupulously respecting foreign privileges, the Revolution suffered no overt interference. It was not, however, that Sun had to restrain his followers. His rise, as we have indicated, was the result rather than the cause of moderation in foreign policy. It is true, nevertheless, that his personal followers, such as Wang Ching-wei and Hu Han-min,[91] showed less concern with the foreign threat than others like Chang Ping-lin, who by 1907 was questioning Sun's leadership on different grounds.[92] We can conclude that if the Revolution already tended to be moderate, Sun's influence strengthened this tendency.

Actually, though foreigners were pleased with the revolutionary restraint, they were also impressed with the Revolution's popular support and the fact that all except two treaty ports were in territory controlled by the rebels. While revolutionary generals were congratulating themselves on having obtained foreign neutrality, European diplomats and statesmen were sighing with relief at having found few signs of Boxerism. The fear of violence, in fact, was mutual rather than one-sided.[93]

Ultimately Sun's major contribution to the Revolution was his optimism. While even stalwarts like Huang Hsing, Hu Han-min, and Wang Ching-wei at times despaired of the Revolution's chances,[94] Sun continued to plug away, boosting the morale of the fighters with promises of funds and luring the Overseas Chinese with talk of imminent victory and promises of investment opportunities. Even with overseas supporters it was necessary to produce quick and tangible results. One gets the impression that military uprisings *had* to be undertaken in order to sell "patriotic bonds" which were to be redeemable at high premiums after the establishment of the Republic.[95] If Sun's unrestrained optimism did not prepare his followers for a decisive struggle in 1911-12, it nevertheless energized their repeated attempts which eventually overthrew the Manchus. And when the Revolution did break out, he was recognized as "undoubtedly its prime mover."[96]

The circumstances that led Sun and his followers to propose Yuan for the presidency only a month after Wuchang are discussed elsewhere in this volume. I would only emphasize that Sun's attitude was based upon three factors: his fear of foreign intervention, his lack of unqualified organizational loyalty, and once more, paradoxically, his naïve confidence. If the Manchus were overthrown and Yuan converted to republicanism, the major revolutionary aims would be achieved. All that seemed to remain of his own program was "mass welfare" (*min-sheng*), which his followers had in any event discarded. The realization of mass welfare was exactly what he concentrated upon after the dust had settled in 1912, trying to convert both Yuan and the public.[97]

What of his personal ambitions? If it was still too early for a peasant to supplant the Son of Heaven, and if Chinese intellectuals still viewed him as the "skillful organizer of secret societies"[98] and not as presidential material, he nevertheless had the satisfaction of seeing his ideas ostensibly realized and himself universally acclaimed as a disinterested patriot. China and the rest of the world never praised him as much as when he exerted his influence for a peaceful solution and gave way to Yuan.[99]

There is some evidence, however, that immediately after Wu chang Sun entertained higher hopes. It is significant that his reactions to news of the uprising while in America had been to take the long way back to China through Europe. He apparently still felt that the foreign attitude would not be decisive for the Revolution but for his personal position. The Revolution could succeed if foreigners remained neutral and refused to advance funds to the Manchus. And active support by foreign governments could very well catapult him into supreme power. By this time he had less faith in the Japanese,[100] and concentrated upon Europe and especially the British.

Homer Lea and Sir Trevor Dawson of Vickers, Sons and Maxim acted on his behalf in London. The contact with the Foreign Secretary, Sir Edward Grey, was actually made through Trevor Dawson, who apparently hoped to obtain orders for munitions and armaments from Sun (who, he was led to believe, would be the "President of the Uunited States of China"). In a statement signed by Sun and Lea and submitted to the Foreign Office by Dawson *after* Sun had left London for Paris, a number of proposals were made. Sun's party wished to make an alliance with Britain and the United States. Senators (sic) Knox and Root were interested, and prepared to lend the revolutionaries one million pounds if Britain agreed. Sun stated that he required Britain's friendship and support and promised to act under the advice of her government, whose nominee he would appoint as political officer. He further agreed that if his party came to power and he assumed the presidency, which he "believed to be a certainty," he would give Britain and the United States favored nation terms over all other countries and would place the navy under the command of British officers subject to his own orders. His attitude toward Japan would be determined by British advice. As for his support in China, Sun declared that no less than 30,000 to 40,000 of the country's "best educated students" had sworn under blood oath to serve him and that several secret societies with 35 million members backed him for the presidency.[101]

Sun Yat-sen's style, it appears, had not really changed very much since 1895-1900. This latest proposal was made at a time when he had already expressed privately extremely realistic and pessimistic views concerning possible support from the West. In 1906 he wrote Dr. Russel, whom he had met in Japan that year, that he did not think much of the Russian's efforts to gain capitalist support for the Chinese Revolution. How could you expect American capitalists to "commit commercial suicide" by helping China attain sovereignty and industrialization? he asked. If China showed the slightest sign of developing her industry, Sun asserted, the entire Western capitalist world would "scream about the so-called Yellow Industrial Peril." As for Russel's remark that China's revival would accelerate Western social revolutions—a prevision of Lenin's argument—Sun replied that the less Western capitalists knew of this, the better. Although he still believed that the "regeneration of one-fourth of the world's population would benefit all mankind" he was afraid that it would be a long time before Westerners had any sympathetic understanding of the Chinese problem.[102]

The British of course were not taken in by Sun's claims, though he actually invited them to check with Knox and Root. In the end all Sun got was permission to stop over briefly in British colonies, including Hong Kong, on his way back to China. Sun learned that the British would remain neutral—this was the result not of his diplomacy but rather of their appraisal of revolutionary strength and fear of great power rivalry—and would oppose making loans to either side. He also learned that the British considered Yuan Shih-k'ai the person best qualified to lead China.

Though this desperate bluff was made several days after Sun had already wired from Paris suggesting Yuan for the presidency,[103] it could be considered Sun's final long-shot gamble for personal success.[104] When Sun returned to Shanghai at the end of 1911 it was without the funds his followers had expected him to bring.[105] Given Sun's evaluation of the situation there was no option but to press for a peaceful settlement with Yuan.[106]

It has been said that there is no better way of bringing a decade or generation into focus than to ask what they were most afraid of and what they did about it. The Chinese of 1911 feared foreign conquest or dismemberment. What they did was to carry out a revolution characterized by unrevolutionary restraint and "sweet reasonableness,"[107] as a British observer so aptly phrased it. It was no accident, moreover, that such a revolution was led by Sun Yat-sen, who at that time was less concerned with seizing power for himself and his party than with the overthrow of the dynasty and preservation of Chinese unity.

That one of the aftereffects of the Revolution was the internal breakup of China into military satrapies is an historical irony, the discussion of which is beyond the scope of this paper. As for Sun Yat-sen, however, it should be pointed out that awareness of the Revolution's shortcomings led to one of his characteristic transformations. What he had learned was the significance and substance of power. After the failure of his "Second Revolution" of 1913, Sun Yat-sen in exile was no longer satisfied with being the entrepreneurial functionary of a loose revolutionary movement. In forming his new organization, the Revolutionary Party in Japan in 1914, he insisted upon a new basis of loyalty, not the four-plank oath of the Revolutionary Alliance or the platform of the defunct Kuomintang, but an oath of loyalty to himself.[108] He now visualized the ideal party as a personally controlled conspiracy, a closed body of select personnel whose uniqueness consisted of its recognition of his personal and undisputed leadership. Less concerned with the foreign threat and fortified by his final attainment of national stature, Sun Yat-sen saw the creation of an instrument for the seizure of power as his main political task. Two years before the Bolshevik Revolution and eight years before his formal alliance with the Soviet Union, Sun was quoting Michels to the Southeast Asian secret societies in order to justify oligarchic party rule:

The Italian, Dr. Michels, in his sociology of political parties, says that even the political parties most dedicated to popular rule have to be obedient to the will of one man in . . . their daily activities. It is apparent that no matter what the party, all must be obedient to the dictates of the party chief. And how much truer this is in the case of a revolutionary party which has to be obedient in carrying out military commands . . .[109]

Sun's style during his period of apprenticeship, however, did not foreshadow a future Chinese Lenin. It did contain the main ingredient of a populist-type leadership recently fashionable in Asia and Africa: a mystical belief that the leader personifies the nation and its aspirations, thus permitting grand improvisation in tactics and fluid generalization in ideology.

Notes

For abbreviations of titles, see Mary C. Wright (ed.), *China in Revolution: The First Phase, 1900-1913* (Yale University Press, 1968), xi-xiii.

1. *KFCC*, 3 (July 17, 1917), 161.

2. Discussion of the first three stages is based largely upon my *Sun Yat-sen and the Origins of the 1911 Revolution*, to be published by the University of California Press.

3. The now legendary leader of the Taiping Rebellion, 1850-64, and like Sun an anti-Manchu South Chinese.

4. *KFNP*, 1, 25, 35, 90; Ch'en Shao-pai, *Hsing-Chung-hui ko-ming shih-yao* (Outline of the Revolutionary History of the Hsing-Chung-hui) (reprinted Taipei, 1956), p. 2.

5. Lo Hsiang-lin, *Kuo-fu chih ta-hsüeh shih-tai* (Sun Yat-sen's University Days) (Taipei, 1954), pp. 61-64. See also Chou Hung-jan, "Kuo-fu 'Shang Li Hung-chang shu' chih shih-tai pei-ching" (Background of Sun Yat-sen's Letter to Li Hung-chang). *KKWH*, 1st series, *Ko-ming chih ch'ang-tao yü fa-chan*, 9, 274.

6. Ch'en Hsi-ch'i, *T'ung-meng-hui ch'eng-li ch'ien ti Sun Chung-shan* (Sun Yat-sen Prior to the Founding of the Revolutionary Alliance) (Canton, 1957), pp. 7, 24-25.

7. Feng, *I-shih*, 1 (Taipei, 1953), 47; Yen-p'ing Hao, "The Abortive Cooperation between Reformers and Revolutionaries," Harvard University, East Asian Research Center, *Papers on China*, 15 (1961), 93.

8. Chou Hung-jan, "Kuo-fu 'Shang Li Hung-chang shu,'" in *KKWH*, 1st series, *Ko-ming chih ch'ang-tao yü fa-chan*, 9, 275-76.

9. For a biographical sketch of Ho, see Lindsay Ride, "The Antecedents," in Brian Harrison, ed., *The University of Hong Kong: The First Fifty Years, 1911-1961* (Hong Kong, 1962), pp. 11-12. See also Arnold Wright, ed., *Twentieth Century Impressions of Hongkong, Shanghai and other Treaty Ports of China* (London, 1908), p. 109; and Lo Hsiang-lin, *Ta-hsüeh shih-tai*, pp. 9-10.

10. Ho's collaborator was Hu Li-yüan, a prosperous Hong Kong merchant. See Lo Hsiang-lin, *Ta-hsüeh shih-tai*, pp. 9, 114, n. 10. For an analysis of their political writings, see Hsiao Kung-ch'üan, *Chung-kuo cheng-chih ssu-hsiang shih* (History of Chinese Political Thought), 6 (Taipei, 1961), 795-803.

11. See the letter by Ho and Wei Tyuk (Wei Yü) in Lord Charles Beresford, *The Break-up of China* (New York and London, 1899), p. 218.

12. See "Sinensis" (Ho's pseudonym), "Open Letter to John Bull" in the *China Mail* (Aug. 22, 1900).

13. Feng Tzu-yu in *KMWH, 3,* 331-72, gives the membership of the Society to Restore China's Prosperity from 1894 to 1903. See also Chün-tu Hsüeh, *Huang Hsing and the Chinese Revolution* (Stanford, 1961), pp. 26-30.

14. I have taken the term "primitive rebels" from E. J. Hobsbawm, *Primitive Rebels: Studies in Archaic Forms of Social Movement in the 19th and 20th Centuries* (Manchester, 1959). Though he deals only with Europe, Hobsbawm's study of social bandits and millenarian movements provides many ideas pertinent to Chinese secret societies and *lü-lin.*

15. See Tse Tsan Tai, *The Chinese Republic: Secret History of the Revolution* (Hong Kong, 1924), p. 9.

16. *China Mail* (March 12, 16, 1895).

17. For evidence of Sun's doubts concerning republicanism at this time, see Hsüeh, *Huang Hsing,* p. 29. I agree, however, with Wu Yü-chang, *Hsin-hai ko-ming* (The Revolution of 1911) (Peking, 1961), p. 15, that the conspirators were thinking of a federated republic based on the United States model.

18. Ch'en Shao-pai, *Hsing-Chung-hui,* p. 12.

19. Sun Yat-sen, *Kidnapped in London* (Bristol, 1897), p. 133.

20. *The Globe* (Oct. 26, 1897).

21. Written with the assistance of one Edwin Collins, Sun's article, "China's Present and Future: The Reform Party's Plea for British Benevolent Neutrality," has not, as far as I know, ever appeared in any collection of Sun's works.

22. *Fortnightly Review, 61* (new series), no. 363 (1897), pp. 424, 440.

23. Chung Kun Ai (Chung Kung-yü), *My Seventy Nine Years in Hawaii* (Hong Kong, 1960), p. 107.

24. Ch'en Shao-pai, *Hsing-Chung-hui,* p. 11.

25. Henry B. Restarick, *Sun Yat Sen, Liberator of China* (New Haven, 1931), p. 49.

26. While in Macao Sun had become friendly with the Fernandes family, and in 1893 contributed articles to the Chinese supplement of *O Eco Macaense,* published by Francisco Fernandes Mr. J. M. Braga of Hong Kong, who knew Fernandes, kindly supplied me with information concerning Sun's relationship with this family, including their help to him in 1895.

27. See Dr. Manson's testimony in the report of the Treasury Solicitor, H. Cuffe, in FO 17/1718, p. 122. Cuffe's report is the authoritative version of Britain's role in the kidnapping episode.

28. *KFNP, 1,* 72.

29. In February 1897, Sir Edward Gourley raised a parliamentary question concerning the Chinese legation's actions. See FO 17/1718, p. 154.

30. Chin P'ing-ou, ed., *San-min chu-i tz'u-tien* (Concordance of the Three Principles of the People) (Taipei, 1956), p. 524, under "Mo-ken."

31. I am indebted to Professor C. Martin Wilbur of Columbia University, who informed me that a detailed account of Sun's visits to the museum can be found in *Chang P'u-ch'üan hsien-sheng ch'üan-chi (pu pien)* (Supplement to the Collected Works of Chang Chi) (Taipei, 1952), pp. 204-06. The appendix to Lo Chia-lun's *Chung-shan hsien-sheng Lun-tun meng-nan shih-liao k'ao-ting* (A Critical Study of the Official Documents Concerning Sun Yat-sen's Kidnapping) (Shanghai, 1930) gives the reports of the detective agency that followed Sun's movements until he left England in the summer of 1897.

32. Quoted in Lyon Sharman, *Sun Yat-sen: His Life and its Meaning* (New York, 1934), p. 58.

33. Sun's letter, undated, and Colonial Secretary Lockhart's reply of October 4, 1897, are enclosed in Black to Chamberlain, May 18, 1898, in CO (Colonial Office) 129/283. The five-year banishment order, later renewed, was issued on March 4, 1896. See Robinson to Chamberlain, March 11, 1896, in CO 129/271.

34. Marius B. Jansen, *The Japanese and Sun Yat-sen* (Cambridge, Mass., 1954), pp. 65-66.

35. Ibid., pp. 68-74.

36. See Hao, "Abortive Cooperation," pp. 91-114.

37. The Chinese version of Ho Kai's proposal to Governor-general Blake of Hong Kong appears in *KFCC, 5,* 16-19. I have not located the original English version.

38. Feng, *I-shih, 1,* 76-80; Chün-tu Hsüeh, "Sun Yat-sen, Yang Ch'ü-yün, and the Early Revolutionary Movement in China," *JAS, 19* (1960), 316.

39. The best sources on the Waichow cam-

paign appear to be Ch'en Ch'un-sheng, "Keng-tzu Hui-chou ch'i-i chi" (An Account of the Waichow Uprising of 1900) in *HHKM, 1,* 235-44; and Miyazaki Tōten (Torazō), *Sanjū-sannen no yume* (The Thirty-three Years' Dream) (Tokyo, 1943), pp. 277-84.

40. On Shih Chien-ju, see Ch'en Ch'un-sheng, *HHKM, 1,* 235-36; Miyazaki, *Sanjū-sannen,* pp. 200-02.

41. See Hu Han-min, *Tzu-chuan* (Autobiography), in *KMWH, 2,* 377.

42. My evaluation of the student mood from 1901 to 1904 is based upon the articles reprinted in *SLHC, 1.* Detailed references can be found in my forthcoming book, *Sun Yat-sen and the Origins of the 1911 Revolution,* chap. 10. For Liang's contribution, see Chang P'eng-yüan, *Liang Ch'i-ch'ao yü Ch'ing-chi ko-ming* (Liang Ch'i-ch'ao and the Revolution in the Late Ch'ing Period) (Taipei, 1964); and Joseph R. Levenson, *Liang Ch'i-ch'ao and the Mind of Modern China* (Cambridge Mass., 1953).

43. For an excellent summary of Chang's thinking, see Hu Sheng-wu and Chin Ch'ung-chi, "Hsin-hai ko-ming shih-ch'i Chang Ping-lin ti cheng-chih ssu-hsiang" (The Political Thought of Chang Ping-lin during the period of the 1911 Revolution), in Hupeh Provincial Philosophical Society and Scientific Society, ed., *Hsin-hai ko-ming wu-shih chou-nien chi-nien lun-wen chi* (Essays in Commemoration of the Fiftieth Anniversary of the 1911 Revolution) (Peking, 1962), ts'e 1, pp. 323-53.

44. "Po K'ang Yu-wei shu" (Letter refuting K'ang Yu-wei), reprinted in *SLHC* (Hong Kong, 1962), *1,* ts'e, 2, 752-64.

45. Ibid., pp. 760-61.

46. *Min-pao, 22* (July 10, 1908), 49.

47. *Min-pao, 16* (Sept. 25, 1907), 29-30.

48. *Min-pao, 22* (July 10, 1908), 49.

49. Ibid., p. 50.

50. Ibid., pp. 130-31.

51. *SLHC, 1,* ts'e 2, 759-60.

52. Infatuation with violence is especially noted in the writings of Tsou Jung, Ch'en T'ien-hua, Yang Shou-jen, Liu Shih-p'ei, and Lin Hsieh. See infra Bernal and Rankin.

53. See Y. C. Wang, "The *Su-pao* Case: A Study of Foreign Pressure, Intellectual Fermentation, and Dynastic Decline," *Monumenta Serica, 24* (1965), 84-129. The draft of this article was first discussed at the Conference on the Revolution of 1911 from which the present volume emerged.

54. Feng Tzu-yu, in *KKWH,* 1st series, *Ko-ming chih ch'ang-tao yü fa-chan, 10,* 665-66.

55. Feng, *I-shih, 1,* 80-81.

56. Ibid., p. 54.

57. Jansen, *Sun Yat-sen,* p. 115; Ch'en Shao-pai, *Hsing-Chung-hui,* pp. 60-61.

58. Tse Tsan Tai, *Secret History,* pp. 20, 22-23.

59. Feng, *I-shih, 1,* 133-34.

60. Reprinted in *SLHC, 1,* ts'e 2, 597-602.

61. Ibid., p. 602.

62. *KFNP, 1,* 125-28.

63. *KFCC, 6,* 230.

64. Ibid., p. 227.

65. Feng, *I-shih, 2,* 123-24. Sharman, *Sun Yat-sen,* pp. 91-93.

66. Feng, *I-shih, 1,* 101; *KFNP, 1,* 134-35. The original English text of the pamphlet appears in *Tang-shih shih-liao ts'ung-k'an* (Serial Publication of Historical Materials on Party History) (Chungking, no date). I am grateful to the late Professor Shelley H. Cheng for lending me his copy.

67. Feng, *I-shih, 2,* 124.

68. *KFNP, 1,* pp. 137-38; Chu Ho-chung, "Ou-chou T'ung-meng-hui chi-shih" (Record of the Revolutionary Alliance in Europe), in *KMWH, 2,* 255.

69. Hsüeh, *Huang Hsing,* chap. 4, gives an informative account of the organization of the Revolutionary Alliance, its composition and leading personalities.

70. Sung Chiao-jen, *Wo chih-li-shih* (My Diary), reprinted in *CHS ts'ung-shu,* p. 68.

71. Ibid., pp. 65-66. Three years previously, Miyazaki's publication of his *Sanjū-sannen no yume* with its glowing tribute to Sun did much to raise Sun's prestige among the young intellectuals. See Chang Shih-chao, "*Su Huang Ti Hun*" (Commentary on *Huang Ti Hum*), *HH-KMHIL, 1,* 243-44. Chang's abridged translation of Miyazaki's book appeared in 1903, a year after publication of the original.

72. Sung Chiao-jen, *Wo chih li-shih,* p. 69. On the Kwangsi uprisings, see Lai Hsin-hsia, "Shih-lun Ch'ing Kuang-hsü mo-nien ti Kuang-hsi jen-min ta ch'i-i" (Inquiry into the Great Popular Risings in Kwangsi during the Last Years of the Kuang-hsü Reign), *Li-shih yen-chiu, 11* (December 1957), 57-77. Some of Sun's followers attempted to establish contact with the Kwangsi Triad leader, Li Li-t'ing, in 1898. See Feng, *I-shih, 1,* 43.

73. On entrepreneurial leadership, see Joseph A. Schumpeter, *The Theory of Economic*

Development (Cambridge, Mass., 1959), p. 88.

74. See Y. C. Wang, "The Influence of Yen Fu and Liang Ch'i-ch'ao on the *San Min Chu I*," *Pacific Historical Review, 34* (1965), 163-84. Yang Shou-jen (Yang Tu-sheng in his *Hsin Hu-nan* (New Hunan), published in 1903, had already listed *ko-jen ch'üan-li* (individual rights and privileges) and *min-tsu chien-kuo chu-i* (nationalism, or the principle of nations creating states) as the two universal principles discovered in the West and necessary for China's regeneration (see *SLHC, 1,* ts'e 2, 631). Another adumbration of Sun's Three Principles can be found in an anonymously written *Hsin-min ts'ung-pao* article of the same year discussing the "Three Great Principles" of modern Europe: "Rights and privileges for majority of the people"; "Benefits from taxation"; and "National states" (see *SLHC, 1,* ts'e 1, 343-48). Furthermore, some of the ideas appearing in Sun's blueprint for democracy in China were expounded by Ho Kai between 1895 and 1900. These include the provision that all candidates for office undergo examination, that the capacity for self-rule was inherent in the Chinese people and could be awakened by stimulating local self-government, and that Yao, Shun, and the rulers of the Three Dynasties (at the dawn of history) were harbingers of democracy (*min-ch'üan*). See Hsiao Kung-ch'üan, *Chung-kuo cheng-chih ssu-hsiang shih, 6,* 795-803.

75. George T. Yu, *Party Politics in Republican China: The Kuomintang, 1912–1924* (Berkeley and Los Angeles, 1966), pp. 25, 80.

76. See infra Gasster. See also R. Scalapino and H. Schiffrin, "Early Socialist Currents in the Chinese Revolutionary Movement," *JAS, 18* (1959), 321-42.

77. *KFCC, 2,* 5-6.

78. On Lenin and *Iskra, see* Bertram Wolfe, *Three Who Made a Revolution* (New York, 1948), p. 251.

79. See infra Bernal.

80. Maurice Duverger, *Political Parties: Their Organization and Activity in the Modern State,* trans. Barbara and Robert North (London and New York, 1959), p. 122.

81. Hsüeh, *Huang Hsing,* chap. 5.

82. See Feng Tzu-yu, *Hua-ch'iao ko-ming k'ai-kuo shih* (History of the Overseas Chinese in the Revolution and the Establishment of the Republic) (reprinted Taipei, 1953); Feng Tzu-yu, *Hua-ch'iao ko-ming tsu-chih shih hua* (Discussion of the History of the Overseas Chinese

Revolutionary Organizations) (Taipei, 1954); Huang Chen-wu, *Hua-ch'iao yü Chung-kuo ko-ming* (The Overseas Chinese and the Chinese Revolution) (Taipei, 1963), pp. 1-221; Huang Fu-luan, *Hua-ch'iao yü Chung-kuo ko-ming* (The Overseas Chinese and the Chinese Revolution) (Hong Kong, 1954), pp. 1-221.

83. Shao Chuan Leng and Norman D. Palmer, *Sun Yat-sen and Communism* (New York, 1960), pp. 29-30.

84. *Ibid.,* p. 29; *KFNP, 1,* 193-94; Sharman, *Sun Yat-sen,* pp. 105-07.

85. Jansen, *Sun Yat-sen,* p. 127.

86. See infra Bernal.

87. See the letter sent by the Norwich branch of the Independent Labour Party to Sir Edward Grey, November 11, 1911, in FO 371/1095, no. 45240. The branch passed a resolution favoring the republican Revolution.

88. See J. Ellis Barker's letter to Asquith on October 13, 1911, in FO 371/1093, no. 40313. Barker, who had met Sun some months previously, strongly warned against British intervention on behalf of the Manchu government. See also the letters of Charles J. H. Halcombe to the *Daily Chronicle,* October 17, 1911, and to Sir Edward Grey on October 18, in FO 371/1093, both no. 4174. Halcombe was an honorary member of the China Reform Party (i.e. Sun's party) and a member of the Friends of China Society, said to have been formed in London in 1898 by Cantlie and Sun (who was not in London in 1898). Halcombe stressed the pro-Christian orientation of the rebels and pointed out that the Boxers too had been originally antidynastic, contending that it was only their realization that foreigners supported the Manchus that turned them against the West. He warned that pro-Manchu intervention would be fatal to continued British supremacy in the trade of West and South China.

89. See for example the letter sent to Grey by an English clergyman on December 30, 1911, in FO 371/1310: "Recognize, get Russia to recognize the super mensch Sun in China, 400 million human lives under a Christian President . . . The Missionary Societies . . . have spent at least one-half million a year to convert the world. In a day Sun has converted 400 million souls."

90. See Anderson to Harcourt, December 29, 1910, in FO 371/1086, no. 4028.

91. See for example Wang's article in *Min-pao, 6* (Jan. 10, 1907), 17-39; and Hu's, *6,* 41-63. See also infra Gasster.

92. Hsüeh, *Huang Hsing*, pp. 52-54.

93. This is based upon my reading of British diplomatic correspondence for 1911-12, available at the Public Record Office, London.

94. Hsüeh, *Huang Hsing*, pp. 75, 100.

95. See Wang Gung-wu, "Sun Yat-sen and Singapore," *Journal of the South Seas Society, 15* (December 1959), 55-68. See also the translated excerpt from Sun's speech in Penang (October 30, 1910), enclosed in Anderson to Harcourt, December 29, 1910, FO 371/1086, no. 4028. Sun declared that Western millionaires like Roosevelt, Rockefeller, and Morgan derived their wealth not from trade but from their "indirect assistance to . . . revolutionaries in the various countries." Instead of investing their money in other ways, the Overseas Chinese, Sun declared, could get one hundred times more profit by supporting the Revolution.

96. This was the opinion of the British minister, Sir John Jordan. See Jordan to Grey, Nov. 6, 1911, in FO 371/1095, no. 46946.

97. See Harold Schniffrin, "Sun Yat-sen's Early Land Policy," *JAS, 16* (1957), 554-57.

98. See the appraisals in the *Chinese Students' Monthly* (Boston), 7 (January 1912), 204; 7 (February 1912), 292; and 7 (June 1912), 655. While Sun is considered a patriotic conspirator, Li Yüan-hung is compared to Garibaldi and Yuan Shih-k'ai to Cavour.

99. For praise of Sun's "self-restraint" see the London *Times* (Feb. 27, 1912); and Li Yüan-hung's letter to Yuan Shih-k'ai and various officials on March 22, 1912, in *Li fu-tsung-t'ung cheng-shu* (Political Correspondence of Vice-president Li), reprinted in CHS *ts'ung-shu*, p. 112.

100. See Jansen, *Sun Yat-sen*, pp. 143-48. Through personal contacts with Mitsui officials and a flagrant disregard for Chinese national interests, Sun nevertheless got three loans from Japan. See Chang Chien's strong criticism in Samuel C. Chu, *Reformer in Modern China: Chang Chien, 1853-1926* (New York and London, 1965), pp. 78-79.

101. See Grey to Jordan, November 14, 1911, in FO 371/1095, no. 45661, and the enclosed memorandum of the previous day submitted by Sir Trevor Dawson.

102. The text I have used is a Chinese translation that appeared in the Hong Kong *Ta Kung Pao* (Nov. 17, 1956), p. 11. I am very grateful to Dr. T. C. Lau of Hong Kong for sending me the clipping. The Russian versions of these letters, originally written in English, are cited in Bernal, infra, n. 136.

103. On November 12 Sun wired from Paris proposing either Li Yüan-hung or Yuan Shih-k'ai for the presidency. See Kuo T'ing-i, *Chin-tai Chung-kuo shih-shih jih-chih* (A Daily Chronology of Modern Chinese History) (Taipei, 1963), ts'e 2, p. 1426.

104. I have no verified knowledge of purported negotiations with the French, including Clemenceau (*KFNP, 1,* 277). There was even a rumor, apparently circulated by Sun via the Japanese, that the Kaiser supported the Revolution. See Grey to MacDonald, Oct. 26, 1911, in FO 371/1094. Sun, according to the Japanese chargé d'affaires in London, had informed Japanese friends that his "special object" in going to Europe was to stimulate Chinese students in Germany. According to the record, however, the only continental country he visited was France.

105. Hsüeh, *Huang Hsing*, p. 131.

106. See Sun's reply to Hu Han-min, who urged him to remain in Canton and fight for complete power, ibid., pp. 125-26, and Hu, *Tzu-chuan, KMWH, 3,* 426.

107. Memorandum of F. A. Aglen in H. B. Morse, *The International Relations of the Chinese Empire* (London, 1910-18), 3, 402.

108. *KFNP, 1,* 370-71.

109. *KFCC, 3,* 177. The letter is dated July 1914 in this collection of Sun's works, but I have seen it dated a year later in other collections. I assume the later date is correct since the English translation of Michel's work, *Political Parties*, only appeared in 1915.

IV. THE "GOSPEL" OF SUN YAT-SEN

22. THE THREE PRINCIPLES OF THE PEOPLE

(SAN MIN CHU I)

SUN YAT-SEN

THE PRINCIPLE OF NATIONALISM

What is the Principle of Nationalism? I would say briefly that the Principle of Nationalism is equivalent to the "doctrine of the state." The Chinese people have shown the greatest loyalty to family and clan with the result that in China there have been family-ism and clan-ism but no real nationalism. Foreign observers say that the Chinese are like a sheet of loose sand. Why? Simply because our people have shown loyalty to family and clan but not to the nation—there has been no nationalism. The family and the clan have been powerful unifying forces; again and again the Chinese have sacrificed themselves, their families, their lives in defense of their clan. But for the nation there has never been an instance of the supreme spirit of sacrifice. The unity of the Chinese people has stopped short at the clan and has not extended to the nation.

Considering the law of survival of an-

From *San Min Chu I: The Three Principles of the People* (Taipei, China Publishing Company, date unknown), pp. 1-2, 4-5, 8-10, 24-25, 28-35, 48-50, 58-59, 63-65, 66, 142-148, 172-184, 187-188, 198. With minor editing by the editor.

cient and modern races, we want to save China and to preserve the Chinese race, we must certainly promote Nationalism. To make this principle luminous for China's salvation, we must first understand it clearly. The Chinese race totals four hundred million people; for the most part, the Chinese people are of the Han or Chinese race with common blood, common language, common religion, and common customs—a single, pure race.

What is the standing of our nation in the world? In comparison with other nations we have the greatest population and the oldest culture, of four thousand years' duration. We ought to be advancing in line with the nations of Europe and America. But the Chinese people have only family and clan groups; there is no national spirit. Consequently, in spite of four hundred million people gathered together in one China, we are in fact but a sheet of loose sand. We are the poorest and weakest state in the world, occupying the lowest position in international affairs; the rest of mankind is the carving knife and the serving dish, while we are the fish and the meat. Our position now is extremely perilous; if we do not earnestly promote nationalism and weld together our four hundred millions into a strong nation, we face a tragedy—the loss of our country and the destruction of our race. To ward off this danger, we must espouse Nationalism and employ the national spirit to save the country.

Now compare the rate of increase of the world's populations during the last century: the United States, 1,000 per cent; England, 300 per cent; Japan, also 300 per cent; Russia, 400 per cent; Germany, 250 per cent; France, 25 per cent. The large gain has been due to the advance of science, the progress of medicine, and yearly improvement of hygienic conditions, all of which tend to reduce the death rate and augment the birth rate. What is the significance for China of this rapid growth of other populations? When I compare their increase with China's, I tremble.

China has been under the political domination of the West for a century. During the past century China has lost a huge amount of territory. The Powers' attitude was formerly something like this: since China would never awaken and could not govern herself, they would occupy the points along the coast like Dairen, Weihaiwei, and Kowloon as bases for "slicing up" China. Then when the Revolution broke out in China, the Powers realized that China still had life, and therefore gave up the idea for partitioning her. When the Powers had their greedy eyes on China, some counter-revolutionists said that Revolution would only invite dismemberment; but the result was just the opposite, for it frustrated foreign designs upon China.

Further back in history, our territorial losses were Korea, Taiwan (Formosa), the Pescadores, and such places, which as a result of the Sino-Japanese War, were ceded to Japan. Still further back in the century, we lost Burma and Annam. China did put up a slight opposition at the time to giving up Annam. In the battle of Chen-Nan-Kuan (Southern Frontier) China was really victorious but was so overawed later by France that she made peace and was compelled to cede Annam to France. Annam and Burma were both formerly Chinese territory; as soon as Annam was ceded to France, England occupied Burma. Still earlier in the history of territorial losses were the Amur and Ussuri river basins and before that the areas north of the Ili, Khohand, and Amur rivers—the territory of the recent Far Eastern Republic —all of which China gave over with folded hands to the foreigner without so much as a question. In addition there are those small countries which at one time or another paid tribute to China— the Loochoo Islands, Siam, Borneo, the Sulu Archipelago, Java, Ceylon, Nepal, Bhutan.

After the Chinese Revolution, the Powers realized that it would be exceedingly difficult to dismember China by political force. A China which had learned how to revolt against the control of the Manchus would be sure some day to oppose the political control of the Powers. As this would put them in a difficult position, they are now reducing their political activities against China and are using economic pressure instead to keep us down. Economic oppression is more severe than political oppression. Political oppression is an apparent thing. The common people are easily provoked by political oppression but are hardly conscious of economic oppression. China has already endured several tens of years of economic domination from the Powers and nobody has felt irritated at all.

The result is that China is everywhere becoming a colony of the Powers. The people of the nation still think we are only a "semi-colony" and comfort themselves with this term, but in reality we are being crushed by the economic strength of the Powers to a greater degree than if we were a full colony. China is not the colony of one nation but of all, and we are not the slaves of one country but of all. I think we ought to be called a "hypo-colony."

Now we want to revive China's lost nationalism and use the strength of our four hundred millions to fight for mankind against injustice; this is our divine mission. The Powers are afraid that we will have such thoughts and are setting forth a specious doctrine. They are now advocating cosmopolitanism to inflame us, declaring that, as the civilization of the world advances and as mankind's vision enlarges, nationalism becomes too narrow, unsuited to the present age, and hence that we should espouse cosmopolitanism. In recent years led astray by this doctrine, some of China's youths, devotees of the new culture, have been opposing nationalism. But it is not a doctrine which wronged races should talk about. We, the wronged races, must first recover our position of national freedom and equality before we are fit to discuss cosmopolitanism. We must understand that cosmopolitanism grows out of nationalism; if we want to extend cosmopolitanism we must first establish strongly our own nationalism. If nationalism cannot become strong, cosmopolitanism certainly cannot prosper.

What means shall we use to revive our nationalism? If we do not find some means to recover our lost nationalism, then China will not only perish as a nation but also perhaps as a race. So, if we want to save China, we must first find a way to revive our nationalism.

To-day I shall discuss two ways by which our nationalism can be revived: the first is by awakening our four hundred millions to see where we stand. We are at a crisis when we must escape misery and seek happiness, escape death and find life. First we must see clearly and then, of course, act. . . .

What are the disasters which threaten us and from what direction do they come? They come from the Great Powers, and they are: first, political oppression; second, economic oppression; and third, the more rapid growth of population among the Powers. These three disasters from without are already upon our heads, and our people are in a most dangerous situation. The first disaster, the destruction of the nation by political force, may happen in a day. China, now under the political yoke of the Powers, may go to smash at any moment; we are not sure we can live from one morning to another. There are two ways in which political force can destroy a nation: through military power and through diplomacy. . . .

Looking at the political forces which threaten a nation, China is now in a position of extreme peril.

The second disaster is the foreign economic domination which is increasing each day.

So, as I see it, if we still do not awake but go on in the way we have been going, even though the foreign diplomatists should sleep on their job, our nation would be ruined in ten years.

Then there is a third disaster which threatens us. The population of China has not increased during the past hundred years, and it will hardly increase during the next hundred years unless we find some way to stimulate the growth.

The three disasters are already upon us. We ourselves must first know the facts, we must understand that these disasters are imminent, we must broadcast them until everyone realizes what a tragedy would be our nation's downfall and with what difficulty China will escape from the perils that encompass her. When we know all these facts, what shall we do? The proverb says, "The desperate beast can yet fight." When we are driven to no place of escape, then we have to rouse our energies to a life and death struggle with our enemies. These calamities are already upon us. Can we fight? Certainly we can fight. But to be able to fight we must realize that our death hour is near. If we want to advance nationalism we must first make our four hundred millions know that their death hour is at hand, then the beset beast will still turn and fight. Do our people on the point of death want to fight? Gentlemen, you are students, officials; you are all men of foresight and vision. You must lead our four hundred millions to see that our race is in dire peril; and if our four hundred millions understand the danger, then it will not be difficult to revive our nationalism.

Foreigners are constantly saying that the Chinese are a "sheet of loose sand"; in the matter of national sentiment it is true. We have never had national unity. Have we had any other kind of unity? As I said before, China has had exceedingly compact family and clan groups and the family and clan sentiment of the Chinese is very deep-rooted. For instance, when two Chinese meet each other on the road, they will chat together and ask each other's "honorable surname" and "great name"; if they happen to find that they are of the same clan, they become wonderfully intimate and cordial and look upon each other as uncle or brother of the same family, If this worthy clan sentiment could be expanded we might develop nationalism out of clanism. If we are to recover our lost nationalism, we must have some kind of group unity, large group unity. An easy and successful way to bring about the unity of a large group is to build upon the foundation of small united groups, and the small units we can build upon in China are the clan groups and also the family groups. The "native place" sentiment of the Chinese is very deep-rooted too; it is especially easy to unite those who are from the same province, prefecture or village.

As I see it, if we take these two fine sentiments as a foundation, it will be easy to bring together the people of the whole country. But to reach the desired end, it will be necessary for all to cooperate; if we can secure this cooperation, it should be easier for the Chinese to revive their nationalism than for people of other countries. For in the West the individual is the unit, and laws regarding the rights of parents and children, brothers and sisters, husbands and wives, aim at the protection of the individual; in lawsuits, no questions are asked about family conditions, only the morals of the individual are considered. The individual expands immediately into the state; between the individual and the state there is no common, firm, social unit. So in welding the citizens together into a state, foreign countries do not have the advantage that China has. Because China lays emphasis upon the family as well as upon the individual, the family head has to be consulted on all matters, a system which some approve and some criticize. But I think that in the relation between the citizens of China and their state, there must first be family loyalty, then clan loyalty, and finally national loyalty. Such a system, expanding step by step, will be orderly and well regulated and the relationship between the small and large groups will be a real one. If we take the clans as our social units and, after improving their internal organization, join them together to form a state, our task will naturally be easier than that of foreign countries which will make the individual the unit. Where the individual is the unit, there will be at least millions of units in a country, four hundred millions in China; the knitting together of such a huge number of separate units would naturally be very difficult. . . .

Let us take the clans as small foundations and work at building up the nation upon these. Suppose China has four hundred clans: it would be just as if we were working with four hundred individual people. We would make use of the original organization that each family name already has, and, in the name of the clan, begin to rally the people together, first in the neighborhood and prefecture, then in the province, and finally throughout the country, until each family name had become a large united group. For instance, if all members bearing the surname of Chen, using the original organization as a basis, would rally together all those who bore the same surname in their neighborhood and prefecture, then in the province, within two or three years, I think, the Chen clan would become a very large body. When every clan was so organized upon a very large scale, we would next unite the clans that had some connection with each other to form larger groups, and we would make every group know that great disasters threaten us, that our death hour is approaching, but that if we all combined, we could become a great national union—the Republic of China—and that with such a union we need not fear outside adversaries or our inability to revive the state. If we start with our four hundred million individual citizens instead of with our four hundred clans, we will not know where to begin in consolidating the sheet of loose sand.

If all our people know that they are oppressed citizens, that we have come to a time when we are simply up against it, that if we combine we must first organize the various clans into clan groups and then these clan groups into a great national union, we will have some positive methods with which to combat the foreigner. As it is, we cannot fight because we have no united groups; if we had, resistance would be easy. China is not at the present moment destroyed; the common people, though they may not easily perform other tasks, can do such things as these—refuse to work for foreigners, refuse to be foreign slaves or to use foreign goods manufactured abroad, push the use of native goods, decline to use foreign bank notes, use only Chinese government money, and sever economic relations with foreigners. The other problem of population growth will be easily solved; China's population has always been large and her resources abundant, and our past oppression can be attributed to the ignorance of the masses, who "live in a stupor and die in a dream." If our whole body of citizens can realize a great national unity upon the basis of our clan groups, no matter what pressure foreign nations bring upon us—military, economic, or population— we will not fear. So the fundamental way to save China from her imminent destruction is for us first to attain unity. If three or four hundred clan groups will take thought for the state, there will be a way out for us and, no matter what nation we face, we will be able to resist.

There are two ways of resisting a foreign Power. The first is the positive way —arousing the national spirit, and seeking solutions for the problems of democracy and livelihood. The second way is the negative way—non-cooperation and passive resistance—whereby foreign imperialistic activity is weakened, the national standing is defended, and national destruction is averted.

If we want to learn from the West, we will have to catch up with the advance line and not chase from behind. In the study of science, for instance, this will mean the saving of two hundred years. We are in such a position to-day that if we should still slumber on, not commence to struggle, and not know how to restore the standing of our state, our country would be lost and our race wiped out forever. But now that we know how, we ought to follow the world currents and study the best features of Western nations; we certainly should go beyond other countries in what we study and cause the "last to be first." Although we went backward for many centuries, yet now it should take us but a few years to catch up with the rest of the world. Japan is a good example. Her culture was formerly copied from China and was much inferior to ours, but recently Japan has studied only European and American civilization and within a few decades has become one of the world's great powers. I do not think that our intellectual powers are below those of the Japanese, and it should be easier for us now than for Japan to learn from the West. So the next ten years is a critical period for us; if we can come to life as the Japanese did and all put forth a very sincere effort to elevate the standing of our nation, within a decade we should be able to get rid of foreign political and economic control, the pressure of foreign population increase, and all the various calamities that are now upon us.

After China reaches that place, what then? A common phrase in ancient China was, "Rescue the weak, lift up the fallen." Because of this noble policy China prospered for thousands of years, and Annam, Burma, Korea, Siam, and other small states were able to maintain their independence. As European influence spread over the East, Annam was overthrown by France, Burma by Great Britain, Korea by Japan. If we want China to rise to power, we must not only restore our national standing, but we must also assume a great responsibility towards the world. If China cannot assume that responsibility, she will be a great disadvantage not an advantage to the world, no matter how strong she may be. What really is our duty to the world? The road which the Great Powers are traveling to-day means the destruction of other states; if China, when she becomes strong, wants to crush other countries, copy the Powers' imperialism, and go their road, we will just be following in their tracks. Let us first of all decide on our policy. Only if we "rescue the weak and lift up the fallen" will we be carrying out the divine obligation of our nation. We must aid the weaker and smaller peoples and oppose the great powers of the world. If all the people of the country resolve upon this purpose, our nation will prosper; otherwise, there is no hope for us. Let us to-day, before China's development begins, pledge ourselves to lift up the fallen and to aid the weak; then when we become strong and look back upon our own sufferings under the political and economic domination of the Powers and see weaker and smaller peoples undergoing similar treatment, we will rise and smite that imperialism. Then will we be truly "governing the state and pacifying the world."

If we want to be able to reach this ideal in the future, we must now revive our national spirit, recover our national standing, unify the world upon the foundation of our ancient morality and love of peace, and bring about a universal rule of equality and fraternity. This is the great responsibility which devolves upon our four hundred millions. You, gentlemen, are a part of our four hundred millions; you must all shoulder this responsibility and manifest the true spirit of our nation.

THE PRINCIPLE OF DEMOCRACY

. . . Confucius and Mencius two thousand years ago spoke for people's rights. Confucius said, "When the Great Doctrine prevails, all under heaven will work for the common good." He was pleading for a free and fraternal world in which the people would rule. He was constantly referring to Yao and Shun simply because they did not try to monopolize the empire. Although their government was autocratic in name, yet in reality they gave the people power and so were highly reverenced by Confucius. Mencius said, "Most precious are the people; next come the land and grain; and last, the princes." Again: "Heaven sees as the people see, Heaven hears as the people hear," and "I have heard of the punishment of the tyrant Chou but never of the assassination of a sovereign." He, in his age, already saw that kings were not absolutely necessary and would not last forever, so he called those who brought happiness to the people holy monarchs, but those who were cruel and unprincipled he called individualists whom all should oppose. Thus China more than two millenniums ago had already considered the idea of democracy, but at that time she could not put it into operation. Democracy was then what foreigners call a Utopia, an ideal which could not be immediately realized.

Thirty years ago, therefore, we fellow revolutionists firmly resolved that, if we wanted China to be strong and our revolution to be effective, we must espouse the cause of democracy. Those Chinese who opposed democracy used to ask what strength there was in our Revolutionary Party to be able to overthrow the Manchu emperor. But in 1911 he fell with one push, another victim of the world tide. This world tendency has flowed from theocracy on to autocracy and from autocracy now on to democracy, and there is no way to stem the current. Autocracy in Europe is on the wane. Great Britain uses a political party rather than a king to govern the country; it may be called a republic with a king. From all this we see that not only theocracy but also autocracy will soon crumble before the on-flowing world current. The present age of democracy is a sequence of the democratic ideas in the Greek and Roman age and, while it has been only one hundred fifty years since the beginnings of democracy, its future will be growing brighter day by day.

So we in our revolution have chosen democracy, first, that we may be following the world current, and second, that we may reduce the period of civil war. From ancient times in China, men of great ambition have all wanted to be king. Thus, when Liu Pang* saw Ch'in Shih Huang riding out, he said, "That is the way for men of valor!" and Hsiang Yu** also said, "Let me usurp his place!" From one generation to another, there has been no end to this unscrupulous greed for power. When I launched the revolution, six or seven out of every ten who came to our support had imperialistic ideas, but after we made it known that our revolutionary principles aimed not only at the overthrow of the Manchus but also at the establishment of a

* The founder of the Han dynasty (204 B.C.-219 A.D.).

** A rival of Liu Pang.

republic, this group gradually got rid of their selfish ambitions. But there are still a few among them who, even in this thirteenth year of the Republic, cling to the old hope of becoming king, and this is the reason why even among our followers there were some who fought against each other. When we first proclaimed our revolution, we lifted up the rights of the people as the basis upon which to build our republic, with the hope that this would prevent the rivalry for imperial power.

To-day I am speaking about the people's sovereignty and I want you all to understand clearly what it really means. Unless we do understand clearly, we can never get rid of imperial ambitions among us, ambitions which will make even brethren in a cause and citizens of the same country fight one another. The whole land will be torn year after year with civil strife and there will be no end to the sufferings of the people. Because I wanted us to avert such calamities, I lifted up the banner of democracy as soon as the revolution began and determined that we should found a republic. When we have a real republic, who will be king? The people, our four hundred millions, will be king. This will prevent everybody from struggling for power and will reduce the war evil in China. The history of China shows that every change of dynasty has meant war. A peaceful period has always been followed by disorder, disorder over the rivalry for kingship. Foreign countries have had wars over religion and wars over freedom, but China in her thousands of years has had but one kind of war, the war for the throne. In order to avert further civil war, we, as soon as we launched our revolution, proclaimed that we wanted a republic and not kings.

What are the newest discoveries in the way of applying democracy? First, there is the suffrage, and it is the only method in operation throughout the so-called modern democracies. Is this one form of popular sovereignty enough in government? This one power by itself may be compared to the early machines which could move forward only but not back. The second of the newly discovered methods is the power of recall. With this power, the people can pull the machine back. These two rights, the right to elect and the right to recall give the people control over their officials and enable them to put all government officials in their positions or to move them out of their positions. The coming and going of officials follows the free will of the people just as modern machines move to and fro by the free action of the engine. Another important thing in a state, in addition to officials, is law; "with men to govern there must also be ways of governing." What power must the people possess in order to control the laws? If all the people think that a certain law would be of great advantage to them, they should have the power to decide upon this law and turn it over to the government for execution. This third kind of popular power is called the initiative. If everybody thinks that an old law is not beneficial to the people, they should have the power to amend it and to ask the government to administer the revised law and do away with the old law. This is called the referendum and is a fourth form of popular sovereignty. Only when the people have these four powers can we say that there is a full measure of democracy, and only where these four powers are effectively applied can we say that there is thoroughgoing, direct, popular sovereignty. Before there was any complete democracy, people elected their officials and representatives and then could not hold them responsible. This was only indirect democracy or a representative system of government. The people could not control the government directly but only through their representatives. For direct control of the government it is necessary that the people practice these four forms of popular sovereignty. Only then can we speak of government by all the people. This means that our four hundred millions shall be king, exerting their kingly authority and controlling the great affairs of state by means of the four powers of the people. These four powers are also called political powers and are powers for control of the government.

The government's own power to transact business may be called the power to work, to work on behalf of the people. If the people are very powerful, whether the government can work or not and what kind of work it does will depend entirely upon the will of the people. If the government is very powerful, as soon as it starts work it can display great strength, and whenever the people want it to stop, it will have to stop. In a nutshell, if the people are really to have direct control over the power of government they must be able to command at any time the actions of the government.

With the people exerting these four great powers to control the government, what methods will the government use in performing its work? In order that the government may have a complete organ through which to do its best work, there must be a quintuple-power constitution. A government is not complete and cannot do its best work for the people unless it is based upon a quintuple-power constitution. I spoke before of an American scholar who advanced the new theory that what a nation fears most is an all-powerful, uncontrollable government,

yet what it most desires is an all-powerful government which the people can use and which will seek the people's welfare. Popular rule cannot really prevail until there is the latter kind of government. We are now making a distinction between sovereignty and ability; we are saying that the people are like the engineer and the government like the machinery. On the one hand, we want government machinery to be all-powerful so that it can do any sort of work; on the other hand, we want the engineer-people to be very strong so that they can control the all-powerful machinery. Now what great powers are the people and the government each to have in order that they may balance each other? I have already discussed the four powers on the people's side—suffrage, recall, initiative, and referendum. On the side of the government there must be five powers—executive, legislative, judicial, civil service examination, and censoring. When the four political powers of the people control the five governing powers of the government, then we will have a completely democratic government organ, and the strength of the people and of the government will be well balanced. This diagram will help us to understand more clearly the relation between these powers:

POLITICAL POWER OF THE PEOPLE

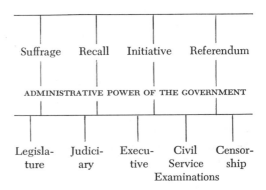

| Suffrage | Recall | Initiative | Referendum |

ADMINISTRATIVE POWER OF THE GOVERNMENT

| Legislature | Judiciary | Executive | Civil Service Examinations | Censorship |

The political power above is in the hands of the people, the administrative power below is in the hands of the government. The people control the government through the suffrage, the recall, the initiative, and the referendum; the government works for the people through its legislative, judicial, executive, civil examination, and censoring departments. With these nine powers in operation and preserving a balance, the problem of democracy will truly be solved and the government will have a definite course to follow. The materials for this new plan have been discovered before now. Switzerland has already applied three of the political powers but does not have the recall. Some of the northwestern states in the United States have taken over the three political rights from Switzerland and have added the right of recall. Suffrage is the people's power most widely exercised in the world to-day. Switzerland is already exercising three of the popular powers and one fourth of the United States is exercising all four. Where the four powers have been exercised in a careful, compact way the results have been excellent. They are facts of experience, not mere hypothetical ideals. We will be safe in using these methods and will not run into any danger.

All governmental powers were formerly monopolized by kings and emperors, but after the revolutions they were divided into three groups: thus the United States, after securing its independence, established a government with three coordinate departments, with splendid results. Other nations followed the example of the United States. But foreign governments have never exercised more than these three powers—legislative, executive, and judicial. What is the source of the two new features in our quintuple-power constitution? They come from old China. China long ago had the independent systems of civil service examination and censorship and they were very effective. The imperial censors or historiographers of the Manchu dynasty and the official advisers of the T'ang dynasty made a fine censoring system. The power of censorship includes the power to impeach, which other governments have but which is placed in the legislative body and is not a separate governmental power. The selection of real talent and ability through examinations has been characteristic of China for thousands of years. Modern foreign scholars who have studied Chinese institutions give high praise to China's old independent examination system, and there have been imitations of the system for the selection of able men in the West. Great Britain's civil service examinations are modeled after the old Chinese system, but only ordinary officials are examined. The British system does not yet possess the spirit of the independent examination system of old China. In Chinese political history, the three governmental powers—judicial, legislative, and executive—were vested in the emperor. The other powers of civil service examination and censorship were separate from the throne. The old autocratic government of China can also be said to have had three departments and so was very different from the autocratic governments of the West in which all power was monopolized by the king or emperor himself. During the period of autocratic government in China, the emperor still did not have sole authority over the power of examination and censorship. So China in a way had three coordinate departments of government, just as the modern democracies of the West have their three departments, with this difference—the Chinese government has exercised the powers of autocracy, censorship, and civil examination for many thousands of years, while Western governments have exercised legislative, judicial, and executive powers for only a little over a century. However, the three governmental powers in the West have been imperfectly applied and the three coordinate powers of ancient China led to many abuses. If we now want to combine the best from China and the best from other countries and guard against all kinds of abuse in the future, we must take the three Western governmental powers—the executive, legislative, and judicial; add to them the old Chinese powers of examination and censorship and make a finished wall, a quintuple-power government. Such a government will be the most complete and the finest in the world, and a state with such a government will indeed be of the people, by the people, and for the people.

THE PRINCIPLE OF PEOPLE'S LIVELIHOOD

The Principle of Livelihood which the Kuomintang advocates is not merely a high ideal; it is also a driving force in society, it is the center of all historical movements. Only as this principle is applied can our social problems be solved, and only as our social problems are solved can mankind enjoy the greatest blessings . . .

All of us have a share in the distressing poverty of the Chinese people. There is no especially rich class, there is only a general poverty. The "inequalities between rich and poor" which the Chinese speak of are only differences within the poor class, differences in degree of poverty. As a matter of fact, the great capitalists of China, in comparison with the great foreign capitalists, are really poor; the rest of the poor people are extremely poor. Since China's largest capitalists are poor men out in the world, then all the Chinese people must be counted as poor. There are no great rich among us, only differences between the fairly poor and the extremely poor. How can we equalize this condition so that there will be no more extreme poverty?

Western books on socialism are full of interesting stories about rise in land values. There was a place in Australia, for instance, where land was very cheap before the building up of a trade center. The government once wanted to sell at auction a piece of land which at the time was simply waste ground, covered with trash piles and of no other use. Nobody was willing to pay a price for the land. Suddenly a drunken fellow broke into the place where the auctioning was going on. The auctioneer was just then calling for bids on the land; there had been bids of one hundred, two hundred, two hundred and fifty dollars. As no one would bid higher, the auctioneer then called, "Who will bid three hundred?" At that moment the drunken fellow, now completely befuddled, yelled out, "I will give three hundred!" The auctioneer then took down his name and assigned him the land. Since the land was sold, the crowd left and the drunken man also walked away. The next day, the auctioneer sent the man a bill for the price of the land, but the man did not remember what he had done in his drunken condition the day before and would not acknowledge the bill against him. When he finally did call to mind what he had done, he was bitterly regretful; but since it was impossible to default to the government, he had to try all sorts of plans and exhaust all his resources in order to pay over three hundred dollars to the auctioneer. For a long time after he acquired the land, he was not able to give it any attention. Over a decade passed; tall buildings and great mansions had been erected all around that piece of land, and the price of land had soared. Some people offered the owner of the empty tract millions of dollars, but he refused to let it go. He simply rented out his land and took the rent money. Finally, when the land was worth tens of millions, the old drunkard became the wealthiest man in Australia. All this wealth came from that first investment in a three-hundred-dollar lot. The owner of the land was of course delighted when he became a millionaire, but what about other people? After paying three hundred dollars for the land, the man did not do a bit of work to improve it; in fact he let it alone. While he slept or sat with folded hands enjoying his success, the millions poured into his lap.

To whom did these millions really belong? In my opinion, they belonged to everybody. For it was because the people in the community chose this section as an industrial and commercial center and made improvements upon it, that this tract of land increased in value and gradually reached such a high price. So foreign scholars speak of the profits which the landowner gets out of the increased price of land as "unearned increment," a very different thing from the profits which industrial and commercial manufacturers get by dint of hard mental and physical labor, by buying cheap and selling dear, by all sorts of business schemes and methods. We have already felt that the profits which the industrial and commercial leaders make by monopolies over materials are not just profits. But these men at least work hard; the landowner, however, simply holds what he has, does not use a bit of mental effort, and reaps

huge profits. Yet, what is it that makes the value of his land rise? The improvements which people make around his land and the competition which they carry on for possession of his land. When the price of land rises, every single commodity in the community also rises in price. So we may truly say that the money which the people in the community earn through their business is indirectly and imperceptibly robbed from them by the landowner. . . .

Western nations have not yet found any satisfactory methods to deal with these evil practices arising out of the land question. If we want to solve the land question we must do it now; if we wait until industry and commerce are fully developed, we will have no way to solve it. Now that Western influences are coming in and our industry and commerce are undergoing such marked transformations, inequalities are arising not only between the rich and poor, but also between common owners of land. The aim of our party's *Min Sheng* Principle is to equalize the financial resources in society. Our first step is to be the solution of the land problem.

The methods for the solution of the land problem are different in various countries, and each country has its own peculiar difficulties. The plan which we are following is simple and easy—the equalization of landownership. . . .

We propose that the government shall buy back the land, if necessary, according to the amount of land tax and the price of the land. How indeed, can the price of the land be determined? I would advocate that the landowner himself should fix the price. The landowner reports the value of his land to the government and the government levies a land tax accordingly. Many people think that if the landowners make their own assessment, they will undervalue the land and the government will lose out. For instance, the landowner might report a piece of land worth a hundred thousand dollars as worth only ten thousand. According to an assessment of a hundred thousand dollars the government would receive a thousand dollars in taxes, but according to an assessment of ten thousand, the government would get only one hundred dollars. The tax office would of course lose nine hundred dollars. But suppose the government makes two regulations: first, that it will collect taxes according to the declared value of the land; second, that it can also buy back the land at the same price. The landowner who assesses his hundred-thousand dollar land at ten thousand dollars fools the government out of nine hundred dollars and naturally gets the best of the bargain; but if the government buys back his land at the price of ten thousand dollars, he loses nine thousand dollars, a tremendous loss. According to my plan, if the landowner makes a low assessment, he will be afraid lest the government buy back his land at that value and make him lose his property; if he makes too high an assessment, he will be afraid of the government taxes according to this value and his loss through heavy taxes. Comparing these two serious possibilities, he will certainly not want to report the value of his land too high or too low; he will strike a mean and report the true market price to the government. As a result, neither landowner nor government will suffer.

After the land values have been fixed, we should have a regulation by law that from that year on, all increase in land values, which in other countries means heavier taxation, shall revert to the community. This is because the increase in land values is due to improvement made by society and to the progress of industry and commerce. China's industry and commerce have made little progress for thousands of years, so land values have scarcely changed through all these generations. But as soon as there is progress and improvement, as in the modern cities of China, land prices change every day, sometimes increasing a thousandfold or ten thousandfold. The credit for the improvement and progress belongs to the energy and business activity of all the people and not merely to a few private individuals. For example: if a landowner now assesses his land at ten thousand dollars and several decades later that land rises in value to a million dollars, this increase of nine hundred and ninety thousand dollars would, in our plan, become a public fund as a reward to all those who had improved the community and who had advanced industry and commerce around the land. This proposal that all future increment shall be given to the community is the "equalization of land ownership" advocated by the Kuomintang; it is the *Min Sheng* Principle. When the landowners clearly understand the principle involved in our plan for equalization of landownership, they will not be apprehensive. Our plan provides that land now fixed in value shall still be privately owned. If the land problem can be solved, one half of the problem of livelihood will be solved.

When modern, enlightened cities levy land taxes, the burdens upon the common people are lightened and many other advantages follow. Although land values in foreign countries have risen very high and the landowners are consequently enjoying large incomes, yet the advance of science and the development of machinery, together with the heavy production on the part of the machine-owning capitalists have made immense incomes which capitalists enjoy a far more serious matter than landowners' incomes. The capitalists in China with the largest incomes are still landowners, not machine owners. So it should be very easy for us now to equalize land ownership, to regulate capital, and to find a way out of the land problem.

Speaking of taxing or buying back land according to its value, we must make clear one important point. Land value refers only to the value of the bare land; it does not include improvements made by human labor or construction work upon the surface. For instance, if land valued at ten thousand dollars has upon it buildings valued at a million dollars, the land tax at the rate of one per cent would be only one hundred dollars. But if the land were bought back by the government, compensation would have to be made for the million dollars' worth of buildings upon the land. Other land with artificial improvements such as trees, embankments, drains, and such would have to be paid for in the same way.

If we want to solve the livelihood problem in China and "by one supreme effort win eternal ease," it will not be enough to depend upon the regulation of capital. The income tax levied in foreign countries is one method of regulating capital. But have these other countries solved the livelihood problem? China cannot be compared to foreign countries; it is not sufficient for us to regulate capital. Other countries are rich while China is poor; other countries have a surplus of production while China is not producing enough. So China must not only regulate private capital, but she must also develop state capital and promote industry. First, we must begin to build means of communication, railroads and waterways, on a large scale. Second, we must open up mines. China is rich in minerals, but alas, they are buried in the earth! Third, we must hasten to foster manufacturing. Although China has a multitude of workers, yet she has no machinery and so cannot compete with other nations. Goods used throughout China depend upon other countries for manufacture and transportation hither, and consequently our economic rights and interests are simply leaking away. If we want to recover these rights and interests, we must quickly employ state power to promote industry, use machinery in production, and give employment to the workers of the whole nation. When all the workers have employment and can use machinery in production, then China will have a great, new source of wealth. If we do not use state power to build up these enterprises but leave them in the hands of private Chinese or of foreign business men, the result will be simply the expansion of private capital and the emergence of a great wealthy class with the consequent inequalities in society. So in working out our Principle of Livelihood, we cannot use or apply in China the methods of Marx. The reason for this is obvious. Russia has been trying to apply Marx's methods since the Revolution until now, yet she wants to change to a new economic policy, because the economic life of her society has not reached the standard of economic life in Great Britain or the United States, and is not ripe for the application of Marx's methods. If Russia's economic standards are below those of Great Britain or the United States, how could China's economic standards possibly be high enough for the application of Marx's methods? Even Marx's disciples says that we cannot use his methods for the solution of all social problems in China.

The youthful scholars to-day who are pinning their faith on Marxism, and who, as soon as socialism is mentioned, advocate Marx's way for the solution of China's social and economic problems. But they fail to realize that China now is suffering from poverty, not from unequal distribution of wealth. In seeking a solution for our livelihood problem, we are not going to propose some impracticable and radical method and then wait until industry is developed. We want a plan which will anticipate dangers and forearm us against emergencies, which will check the growth of large private capital and prevent the social disease of extreme inequality between the rich and the poor. Such a plan will rightly solve our immediate social problems and will not be like first wearing furs and then hoping for the north winds.

As I said a little while ago, the regulations of capital to-day in China will not be enough to solve our livelihood problem. It will also be necessary to build up state capital. What does this mean? Simply the development of state industries. The details of this scheme can be found in the second volume of my *Plans for National Reconstruction,** under the heading "Material Reconstruction or Industrial Measures." In this volume I have given the outline of the plan for building up state capital. As I said before, money was capital in the commerical age, but machinery is capital in the industrial age. The state should lead in business enterprises and set up all kinds of productive machinery which will be the property of the state. During the European War, it was the policy of each country to nationalize its great industries and its factories. But this policy was abandoned soon afterwards. China has never had any great capitalists; if the

* Written in 1918. In three parts: Psychological Reconstruction, Material Reconstruction, Social Reconstruction.

state can control and develop capital and give the benefits to all the people, it will be easy to avoid the conflicts with capitalists. The United States has developed capital in three ways: through railroads, through manufacturing, and through mining. We shall not be able to promote one of these three great industries by our own knowledge and experience with our own capital; we cannot but depend upon the already created capital of other countries. If we wait until we ourselves have enough capital before we start to promote industry, the process of development will be exceedingly slow. China now has no machinery to speak of. We have only six or seven thousand miles of railroad. To meet our needs, we should have a mileage ten times as great. At least sixty or seventy thousand miles are necessary. So we shall certainly have to borrow foreign capital to develop our communication and transportation facilities, and foreign brains and experience to manage them.

As for our mines, we have not even begun to open them. China exceeds the United States in population and in size of territory, yet the United States produces 600,000,000 tons of coal and 90,-000,000 tons of steel every year, while China does not produce a thousandth of that amount. If we want to open up our mines quickly, again we must borrow foreign capital. To construct steamships. to develop a merchant marine and to build up all kinds of manufacturing industries on a large scale, it will be absolutely necessary for us to borrow foreign capital. If these three great industries— communications, mining, and manufacturing—should all begin to thrive in China, our annual income from them would be very great. If the industries are carried on by the state, the rights and privileges which they bring will be enjoyed by all the people. The people of the whole nation will then have a share in the profits of capital and will not be injured by capital. In the solution of the social problem, we have the same object in view as that in foreign countries: to make everybody contented and happy, free from suffering caused by the unequal distribution of wealth and property.

Our Three Principles of the People mean government "of the people, by the people, and for the people"—that is, a state belonging to all the people, a government controlled by all the people, and rights and benefits for the enjoyment of all the people. If this is true, the people will have a share in everything. When the people share everything in the state, then will we truly reach the goal of the *Min Sheng* Principle, which is Confucius' hope of a "great commonwealth."

Since olden times China has been a farming nation. Agriculture has been the great industry for the production of food. By what methods can we increase plant production? Chinese agriculture has always depended entirely upon human labor, yet cultivation has developed to a very high point and all the various products are of a superior and beautiful quality. Foreign scientists have been led to give high praise to Chinese farming. Since the production of food in China depends upon the peasants, and since the peasants have to toil so bitterly, we must have the government make regulations by law for the protection of peasants if we want to increase the production of food. A large majority of the people in China are peasants, at least nine out of ten, yet the food which they raise with such wearisome labor is mostly taken away by the landowners. What they themselves can keep is barely sufficient to keep them alive. This is a most unjust situation. If we are to increase the production of food, we must make laws regarding the rights and interests of the farmers; we must give them encouragement and protection and allow them to keep more of the fruit of their land. The protection of the farmers' rights and the giving to them of a larger share in their harvests are questions related to the equalization of land ownership. When the *Min Sheng* Principle is fully realized and the problems of the farmer are all solved, each tiller of the soil will possess his own fields—that is to be the final fruit of our efforts.

What are the real conditions among Chinese farmers? Although China does not have great landowners, yet nine out of ten farmers do not own their fields. Most of the farming land is in the possession of landlords who do not do the cultivating themselves. It seems only right that the farmer should till his farm for himself and claim its products, yet farmers to-day are tilling for others and over half of the agricultural products from the farms are taken by the landlords. We must immediately use government and law to remedy this grave situation. Unless we can solve the agrarian problem, there will be no solution for the livelihood problem. Of the food produced in the fields, sixty per cent, according to our latest rural surveys, goes to the landlord, while only forty per cent goes to the farmer. If this unjust state of affairs continues, when the farmers become intelligent, who will still be willing to toil and suffer in the fields? But if the food raised in the fields all goes to the farmers, the farmers will be more eager to farm and production will increase.

If we apply the *Min Sheng* Principle we must make the aim of food production not profit but the provision of sustenance for all the people. To do this we must store up the surplus in production every year. Not only must we wait to see if this year's food supply is sufficient, we must wait until the supply next year and the year after is abundant before we ship any food for sale abroad. If after three years the food supply is still short, we will not make any shipments abroad. If we can apply the *Min Sheng* Principle in this way and make the support of the people rather than profit the aim of production, then there will be hope for an abundant food supply in China. The fundamental difference, then, between the Principle of Livelihood and capitalism is this: capitalism makes profit its sole aim, while the Principle of Livelihood makes the nurture of the people its aim. With such a noble principle we can destroy the old, evil capitalistic system.

PART FOUR

INTELLECTUAL REVOLUTION,

IDEOLOGICAL AWAKENING,

AND INTERNATIONAL DEVELOPMENTS 1917-45

INTRODUCTION

The failure of the republic to regenerate the country and to usher in a period of peace and order led many Chinese to search for new ways to revitalize their country. A number of intellectuals came to realize that mere adoption of a republican form of government was not sufficient to save the nation; what China needed was a reconstitution of the minds of men—in short, an intellectual revolution. Westernization, science, and democracy became the creed of the age and a new movement was set in motion to introduce Western thought and methods of learning, as well as to effect a critical re-evaluation and reorganization of traditional learning, as shown by Professor Chow Tse-tsung in Selection 23. Selection 24 by Professor Maurice Meisner reveals the influence of Li Ta-chao, the librarian at the National University of Peking and a co-founder of the Chinese Communist Party, on his young assistant, Mao Tse-tung.

After the Nationalist-Communist split of 1927, a bifurcation took place within the Communist movement in China, with the party's central organization subsisting underground in Shanghai under the leadership of Moscow-trained Communists, and Mao developing his own Soviets in the Hunan-Kiangsi border areas.

Though "in opposition" to the CCP Central Committee, Mao ultimately won out in his bout with the Twenty-eight Bolsheviks. The Maoist strategy, his frustration, and final victory are examined in Selections 25 and 26 by Professors Benjamin I. Schwartz and John E. Rue.

By August 1935 the Comintern had adopted the policy of United Front against Nazism, Fascism, and Japanese militarism—avowed enemies of Marxism-Leninism. In China, the United Front strategy had the added advantage of relieving the CCP of Nationalist attacks. Though ignored by Chiang Kai-shek at first, the United Front began to take shape after the Sian Incident of December 1936 (Selection 27), and the subsequent negotiations between the two parties led to an entente during the war against Japan (Selection 28).

Internationally, a number of important developments affecting China took place during the 1930's and first half of 1940's. On January 7, 1932, in connection with the Japanese invasion of Manchuria, Secretary of State Henry Stimson announced the Non-Recognition Doctrine by which the United States refused to "recognize any situation, treaty, or agreement which may be brought about by means contrary to the covenants and obligations of the Pact of Paris of August 27, 1928, to which Treaty both China and Japan, as well as the United States, are parties" (Selection 29). The non-recognition doctrine has since become a doctrine in international law. By it the United States refused to recognize the Japanese occupation of Manchuria and the puppet state of Manchukuo. On February 24, 1933, the Assembly of the League of Nations also recommended that member states not recognize the regime in Manchuria either *de jure* or *de facto* (Selection 30).

Selection 31 is the treaty between China and the United States signed on January 11, 1943, by which the latter agreed to renounce all extra-territorial rights in China. This, along with a similar Sino-British treaty, ended a century of national stigma for China that began with the Opium War and the Treaty of Nanking in 1842. China was accorded the honorable status as one of the Big Four (later Big Five) in the postwar era.

Selection 32 is the Cairo Declaration by President Roosevelt, Generalissimo Chiang Kai-shek, and Prime Minister Churchill on December 1, 1943, which demanded for the first time "the unconditional surrender of Japan" and restoration to the original states of all territories that Japan had seized by violence and greed. Selections 33 is the Yalta Agreement of February 11, 1945, and Selection 34 the Sino-Soviet Treaty of August 14, 1945, which dealt with the conditions of the Soviet entry into the war against Japan, and a thirty-year Sino-Soviet alliance against future Japanese aggression.

I. THE NEW CULTURAL MOVEMENT

23. THE NEW THOUGHT AND RE-EVALUATION

OF THE TRADITION

CHOW TSE-TSUNG

It is no exaggeration to say that, of all the activities of the new intellectuals, the new thought tide was the most significant. The main aim of the reformers in the May Fourth Movement was the creation of a new China; one method was to be the substitution of new thought for the old and traditional. From the time *New Youth* was established, this had become the major idea of the new reform movement. In a sense, the May Fourth Incident was a result and manifestation of this idea.

Most of the leading new intellectuals during the early period adopted an uncomprising attitude on ideological reform. This attitude is well exemplified in Ch'en Tu-hsiu's and Hu Shih's joint answer to a reader of *New Youth* in 1918: "The old literature, old politics, and the old ethics have always belonged to one family; we cannot abandon one and preserve the others. It is Oriental to compromise and only go half way while reforming, for fear of opposition. This was the most important factor behind the

From Chow Tse-tsung, *The May Fourth Movement: Intellectual Revolution in Modern China* (Harvard University Press, Cambridge, Mass.), pp. 289-313, 443-448. Copyright, 1960 by the President and Fellows of Harvard College. Reprinted by permission. The author is professor of Chinese literature at University of Wisconsin, Madison, Wisconsin.

failures of reform movements during the last several decades."[1]

THE HARD CORE OF THE OLD THOUGHT

To understand what the new thought innovators were fighting, it is necessary to examine briefly the Chinese philosophical tradition in general, and in particular how Confucianism was manipulated by authorities to their own advantage in recent centuries.

For many centuries, China had been dominated by four schools of thought: Confucianism, Legalism, Taoism, and Buddhism. In their popular forms, Confucianism had been for long mixed with Legalist ideas and Taoism and Buddhism had been corrupted by all kinds of superstitions such as spiritualism and divination. These superstitious ideas were further popularized by traditional Chinese operas and stories. In the sphere of systematic philosophy and ethics, the Chinese mind in the last century was greatly influenced by Neo-Confucianism dating from the Sung dynasty and the Han learning developed early in the Ch'ing dynasty.[2]

Neo-Confucianism, which was influenced by Buddhism and Taoism, asserted that everything is governed by *li* (principles, or reason, somewhat similar to Plato's ideas or the Western higher law of nature), and the one great *li*, the Supreme Ultimate, which was sometimes identified with the tao, was regarded as absolute truth, eternal and forever unchanging. According to the orthodox interpretation of the theory, the ideal type of political conduct conformed to *li* or tao. The actual government, if it corresponded to this ideal government, would be considered absolutely good. To achieve this ideal, the ruler should obtain virtue by investigating things to extend his knowledge, making his thought sincere, rectifying his heart to cultivate his character, and regulating his family.[3] By doing this, the ruler might achieve the goal of becoming a sage-king of absolute virtue. In practice, Chinese emperors or usurpers, by claiming that they possessed the "mandate of heaven" and absolute virtue, in accordance with Confucian orthodoxy, easily found justification for their absolute rule, although the people also made appeal to *li* or *tao-li* as a higher law in their struggle against political authority. Early in the Ming dynasty, the Neo-Confucianist interpretation of the classics or Canons by Chu Hsi (1130-1200) was approved by the government as the official interpretation, and it was adopted in 1313 as the standard for the civil service examinations until 1905 when the examination system was abolished. With this orthodox theory and the rising Legalist influence upon practical government, a monarch's power was made absolute.

In the late Ming and the early Ch'ing periods, Neo-Confucianism was opposed by a few enlightened thinkers such as Huang Tsung-hsi, Ku Yen-wu (1613-1682), Yen Yüan (1635-1704), and Li Kung (1659-1733).[4] The stand taken against Neo-Confucianism by these men was based on the argument that its interpretation of Confucianism was not based on Confucius' own teaching, and that the idea of *li* could not be found in the five classics, i.e., the *Book of Odes, Book of History, Book of Changes, Book of Rites,* and *Spring and Autumn Annals,* or any other records of Confucius and Mencius. Ku and Huang even advocated individual liberty and emphasized Mencius' idea that "in a state the people are of first importance, the shrines of the state gods are next, and the ruler is least important." But these thinkers did not develop their theories. Later on, a number of prominent Ch'ing scholars devoted themselves to a careful analysis of classical texts. They studied more or less objectively the earliest commentaries on the classics, commentaries made in the Han dynasty (206 B.C.-A.D. 221), and turned up material which discredited Neo-Confucianism.[5] They criticized the ancient texts, extracted new meanings, and exposed forgeries. This group of classicists was known as the school of "Han learning," while the Neo-Confucianists were called the school of "Sung learning."

The discoveries of the classicists of the Han learning exerted some influence upon the new intelligentsia of the May Fourth Movement when the latter attacked orthodox Neo-Confucianism. In their textual criticisms the earlier scholars had spotted many ancient Chinese philosophers who were not Confucians. The educational philosophy of Yen Yüan and Li Kung was even considered by Liang Ch'i-ch'ao to be similar to John Dewey's.[6] But the influence of the Ch'ing scholars of the Han learning on the criticism of Confucian orthodoxy was limited. Their studies were confined to rather specialized and esoteric subjects such as phonetics, etymology, and semantics. In philosophy, some of them tended in the later years of the Ch'ing to follow the line of the Sung learning. Those who criticized

Neo-Confucianism did so on the basis of a literal acceptance of original Confucianism itself. Their intention had been not to question or revise but to restore true Confucianism as they saw it. Consequently, Confucianism continued to retain its stereotype and predominance in the nineteenth century. Indeed, the most powerful slogan for Tseng Kuo-fan's (1811-1872) suppression of the T'ai-p'ing Rebellion was the need to defend Confucianism, the Sage's teachings, and the traditional ethics. K'ang Yu-wei's reform movement of 1898 was also based on his interpretation of Confucianism, namely, that Confucius himself was a reformer. At the other extreme, the Ch'ing ultraconservatives displayed great enthusiasm in offering sacrifices to Confucius. In December 1906, Tz'u-hsi, the Dowager Empress, decreed that Confucius should receive the highest sacrificial rites.[7]

In the Yüan Shik-k'ai period (1912-1916) of the Republic, the Confucian controversy became more and more intense. In 1912 a Confucian Society (*K'ung-chiao hui*) was established in Shanghai by K'ang Yu-wei's disciple Ch'en Huang-chang and a number of famous old literati such as Sheng Tseng-chih, Chu Tsu-mou, Liang Ting-fen, and Yen Fu. In July 1913 when the Constitutional Commission of Parliament started to draw up a draft constitution for the Republic of China, known as the "Temple-of-Heaven Draft," an article providing for the establishment of Confucianism as a state religion was proposed by members of the Chinputang. It was opposed by the members of the Kuomintang and soon became a heated debating point throughout the country. After long, weary arguments, the issue was temporarily settled by a compromise. Article XIX read "Confucius' principles (*tao*) shall be the basis for the cultivation of character in national education."[8]

Yüan Shih-k'ai, in his monarchical move, leaned heavily on the prop of Confucian orthodoxy. In preparing for his "coronation," he was careful to sacrifice to Confucius.[9] On January 1, 1916, the first day of his monarchy, Yüan decreed that K'ung Ling-i, who claimed descent from Confucius, should be given the title "Holy Duke" (*Yen-sheng-kung*) which was first conferred upon the lineal descendant of Confucius in A.D. 1055 by an Emperor of the Sung dynasty. Yüan went even further, and gave him an additional title of Prince.[10] A few societies and periodicals specializing in Confucianism were also established to support the monarchial movement.*

The struggle over Confucianism did

* The Confucian Society founded the monthly *Journal of the Confucian Society* (*K'ung-chiao hui tsa-chih*) in Peking in Feb. 1913, advocating the establishment of Confucianism as a state religion. The society was one of the most enthusiastic supporters of Yüan's monarchical movement. Paul S. Reinsch recorded: "'The whole Chinese people hold the doctrines of Confucius most sacred,' declared President Yüan Shih-kai in his decree of November 26, 1913, which reintroduced much of the old state religion. He stopped a little short of giving Confucianism the character of an established religion, but ordered that the sacrificial rites and the biennial commemoration exercises be restored. 'I am strongly convinced,' he said, 'of the importance of preserving the traditional beliefs of China.' In this he was upheld by the Confucian Society at Peking, in the organization of which an American [Columbia] University graduate, Dr. Chen Huan-chang, was a leading spirit. Mr. Chen's doctoral dissertation had dealt with the economic principles of Confucius and his school; upon his return to China, his aim had been to make Confucianism the state religion under the Republic."[11] In 1913-1915 similar societies for a Confucian religion and a monarchical movement existed in many provinces, such as the Confucian Association (*K'ung she*) of Chihli, and that of Honan. Others were called *K'ung-tao hui* or *K'ung-chiao kung-hui* as in Hunan, Shantung, and Hehlungchiang (Amur River) Provinces.

not die away with the collapse of Yüan's monarchical movement. In August 1916, while Parliament was in session in Peking, Article XIX of the Temple-of-Heaven Draft Constitution became a crucial issue. Some parliamentary members resumed their efforts to establish Confucianism as a state religion. K'ang Yu-wei, after the failure of Yüan's utilization of Confucianism, wrote a letter to President Li Yüan-hung and Premier Tuan Ch'i-jui with the same suggestion. He even produced his own draft constitution embodying the idea. He asserted that all peoples had religions except the barbarians; that Confucius had been the founder of a religion; that if the people did not read the Confucian classics, they would not know how to behave; that Confucius' *Annals* was actually a traditional Chinese constitution according to which many judicial and other important cases after the Han dynasty had been decided; that the ancient Chinese had advocated the recitation of the *Book of Filial Piety* for the suppression of bandits, and the use of the *Great Learning* for the pacification of evil spirits, and had claimed that the use of even half of the *Analects of Confucius* could govern the whole country.[12] K'ang also argued that, since Confucianism had dominated China for two thousand years, on its abandonment, China would be divided and eliminated. Every country had to have a spiritual base; Confucian teaching was the Chinese one: "No Confucianism, no China."[13] Therefore, he suggested: (1) All officials, from the President down to the local magistrates should sacrifice to Confucius every month and on important occasions. They should kow-tow to the icons of the Sage. (2) All students from the university level down to the elementary school ought to read the Confucian classics. The schools should offer degrees

in such studies, and the state should subsidize them. (3) Confucian "churches" should be established and subsidized by the state.[14] The opinions of the other supporters of Confucianism varied in degree. But all of them argued that Confucianism was the best teaching China had had and should be accepted as a basic code for the nation.

These proposals obtained strong support from the conservatives, who thought only of tradition, but they were furiously opposed by the new reformers. Consequently, after hot debates both within and without Parliament, the article concerning Confucianism in the draft constitution was amended to read: "The people of the Republic of China have freedom to worship Confucius and freedom of religion which shall not be restricted except by law."[15] The situation was such that, on the eve of the May Fourth Movement and in its early years, especially in 1916 and 1917, although Yüan Shih-k'ai was already dead, Ts'ai Yüan-p'ei, Ch'en Tu-hsiu, and many other intellectuals felt that his spirit was still alive; "there were numerous Yüan Shih-k'ais, thinking, talking, and acting in China.*

NEW THOUGHT: REALISM, UTILITARIANISM, LIBERALISM, INDIVIDUALISM, SOCIALISM, AND DARWINISM

While the older generation and the conservatives clung to traditional thought and ethics, the new intellectuals, influenced by Western ideas, were rallying to the support of "Mr. *Te*" (Democracy) and "Mr. *Sai*" (Science), as they conveniently dubbed the new currents. It

* There was a rumor spread by the Chinese and Western newspapers in Shanghai in the winter of 1916 that Yüan had not, in fact, died.[16]

was in the names of these two gentlemen that Confucianism and its followers were attacked. An examination of the ideas of the new intellectuals during the early period of the May Fourth Movement reveals that they were a mélange of post-seventeenth-century Western ones; especially highly regarded were ideas stemming from the American and French Revolutions.

During the two decades before 1919, various Western philosophic ideas had been popularized in China. Utilitarianism, the theory of evolution, and empiricism were introduced by Yen Fu's translations. These included Thomas Huxley's *Evolution and Ethics* (translated in 1894-1895, published in 1895 and April 1898); Adam Smith's *The Wealth of Nations* (translated from late 1897 to the fall of 1900, published late in 1901); John Stuart Mill's *On Liberty* (translated in 1899, published in October 1903) and *System of Logic* (only first half, translated in 1900-1902, published in 1902); Herbert Spencer's *Study of Sociology* (translated in 1898-1902, published in May 1903); Edward Jenks' *A Short History of Politics* (translated in 1903, published in February 1904); Montesquieu's *L'Esprit des lois* (translated in 1900-1905, published in September 1904-1909); and William Stanley Jevons' *Primer of Logic* (translated in the fall of 1908, published in the same year). Those intellectual leaders who were middle-aged at the time of the May Fourth Movement had been influenced mainly by these works. French revolutionary ideas were first introduced by Liang Ch'i-ch'ao at the beginning of this century. Rousseau was popularized by Liang's lucid essays. After 1906, Lamarck's *Philosophie Zoologique,* Kropotkin's *Mutual Assistance,* an other French philosophic works were introduced by Wu Chih-hui, Li Shih-tseng, Ts'ai Yüan-p'ei, Chang Chi, and Wang Ching-wei. Schopenhauer, Nietzsche, and Kant were introduced by Wang Kuo-wei and others. Some of Bertrand Russell's works were translated into Chinese before the May Fourth Incident. They reinforced the influence of British empiricism introduced earlier Russell's work, with John Dewey's introduction of the Cartesian method later, laid a foundation for the study of mathematical logic in China.

At the beginning of the May Fourth period, all these ideas affected in various degrees the critical thinking of the new Chinese intellectual leaders, but realism and utilitarianism were the most widely prevailing principles. In the opening article of the first issue of *New Youth,* Ch'en Tu-hsiu suggested a utilitarian and realistic approach to the problems of life. He expressed his admiration of John Mill and Comte.[17] In Ch'en's opinion, one of the fundamental differences between East and West was that the latter paid more attention to pratical matters while the former paid more to ceremony.[18] Therefore, the rejuvenation of the Chinese people, he advocated the adoption of realism as one of the principles of Chinese education.[19] Utilitarianism was propagated also by many other writers.[20] These ideas were later merged with pragmatism. After the May Fourth Incident, though the young were gripped by fantasy, they still based, or at least pretended to base, their activities on practicality.

Liberalism was a catchword among the intellectuals in those early years. Individual freedom had been propounded by Liang Ch'i-ch'ao and the Kuomintang leaders at the beginning of the twentieth century. In the first issue of *New Youth,* Ch'en Tu-hsiu emphasized individual freedom, and came out in opposition to any kind of slavery.[21] In the second issue, he published his Chinese translation of Samuel F. Smith's "America" (American national hymn).[22] Edmund Burke's speech in the House of Commons supporting the resistance of the American colonists was also translated and published in the monthly.[23] In the main, the concept of freedom current among these Chinese intellectuals was derived from Rousseau's theory of general will and from British utilitarianism.[24] They talked of freedom in terms of human rights, and freedom of speech and the press.[25]

At a time when most people had become aware of the need for national unity and the importance of statehood, some new intellectuals tended to emphasize individualism. They maintained that the defense of a sovereign and independent republic should not be at the expense of individual freedom.[26] Most of the new intellectual leaders rejected the idea that statehood and nationalism should be ultimate ideals. They conceded only that these were temporarily necessary for the betterment of the welfare of the individual.[27] Ch'en Tu-hsiu realized that the most significant difference between East and West was that Western civilization, be it British, American, French, or German, was based on a thoroughgoing individualism, whereas the Eastern variety was based on family or clan units. As he understood them, Western ethics, moral principles, political theories, and law all tended to advocate individual rights and welfare, freedom of thought and speech, as well as the development of individuality. Under the Eastern system, a man was a member of his family or clan, and not an independent individual. This system destroyed individual dignity and self-respect, choked free will and independent

thought, deprived a person of equal rights under the law, and encouraged people to rely on others. Consequently, he suggested the substitution of individualism for the family system.[28] Hu Shih also stimulated the spread of individualism by introducing Ibsen to China. He explained Ibsen's opposition to the conformity imposed by law, religion, and moral principles. Ibsen asserted, so Hu said, that society "destroyed individuality by force and suppressed the spirit of individual freedom and independence."[29] Ibsen's ideal was a life in which an "individual might develop to the full his talent and individuality."[30] Hu, inflenced by Ibsen's plays, such as *A Doll's House, An Enemy of the People,* and *Ghosts,* drew attention to the inferior status of women in Chinese society, and encouraged Chinese women to protest and secure emancipation, as well as exalted independent thinking.

Among the pre-1919 intellectuals there were some who toyed with ideas of socialism or anarchism on the ground that only thus could the freedom of the individual be balanced by the equality of others. These ideas were derived mainly from the early French socialists and anarchists, but also owed something to traditional Chinese ideas. However, most of the vanguard intellectuals were not completely committed to socialism, perhaps because they felt that the same liberal program which would achieve individual freedom would also achieve equality. Therefore, they preferred to advocate the equality of every individual's rights, and to propound the ideas of universal love and mutual assistance.[31] In discussing the French contribution to modern civilization, Ch'en Tu-hsiu hailed the socialist idea of economic and social equality as the latest tendency of modern European culture. Private property could not be abandoned immediately; the rich and the poor would be leveled by social policies.[32] These ideas had been promoted previously by Sun Yat-sen and by many socialists and anarchists. After 1919, they had increasing appeal for the youth of China.

Turning to science, we find that most of the new intellectuals emphasized Darwin's theory of evolution. It was on the basis of this theory that they attacked religion and tradition. Some of them, for example Tai Chi-t'ao, while accepting this theory, advocated mutual assistance. They thought that whereas life was maintained by struggle, mutual assistance was the best way to advance humanity in this struggle. In any case, Darwinism was the first scientific theory to exert a strong influence upon Chinese social thought.

Technology and the control of nature were also recognized as signficant aspects of the scientific civilization of the West. The new intellectual leaders discarded the old idea that the spiritual civilization of the East was superior to the materialistic civilization of the West. Wu-Chih-hui in particular was the champion of the beneficence of a material welfare achieved by the control and improvement of tools, although he himself lived a very simple, stoical life.[33] Wu believed in the "omnipotence of science."[34]

NEW METHODS: PRAGMATIC, SKEPTICAL, AND AGNOSTIC APPROACHES AND THE BEGINNING OF MARXIST INFLUENCE

The fact that the new intellectual leaders had a better training in logical thinking made their arguments against the old gentry more effective. This was true especially in the case of Hu Shih who gave more emphasis to methodology than did other writers. In the re-evaluation of the Chinese tradition, Hu insisted that all inferences must be based on evidence and anything without proof should be held doubtful. As a means of verification, historical evolution or, in Dewey's phrase, the "genetic method." i.e., concentrating attention on the origin and evolution of the subject, was emphasized. This method owed a debt to Huxley's agnosticism, but stemmed immediately from Dewey's pragmatism, As Hu himself said.

My thought is influenced mainly by two persons: one is Huxley and the other is Mr. Dewey. Huxley teaches me how to doubt and teaches me to believe in nothing without sufficient evidence. Mr. Dewey teaches me how to think and teaches me to consider the immediate problems in all cases, to regard all theories and ideals as hypotheses which are in need of verification, and to take into account the effect of thoughts. These two persons make me understand the character and function of scientific method.[35]

In the prevalent climate of agnosticism, an iconoclastic spirit arose among the new intelligentsia. Ch'en Tu-hsiu, Hu Shih, Chih-hui, and Lu Hsün were "laughing lions" who "annihilated with laughter," as Nietzsche said of Voltaire in Europe, and with all their strength called for the destruction of idols.[36] Ch'en said: "Destroy! Destroy idols! Our beliefs must be based on reality and reasonableness. All the fantasies handed down from ancient times, religious, political, and ethical, and other false and unreasonable beliefs are idols which should be destroyed! If these false idols are not destroyed, universal truth cannot be restored to the profound beliefs in our minds."[37] This was the call of the time.

On the whole, it is fair to say that, in the early period of the May Fourth Movement, pragmatism, skepticism, and agnosticism were the principal critical approaches found in the reformers' attack on traditional ethics and ideas. There was no strong competition from either materialism or dialectical materialism until the middle of the twenties.

However, as early as 1915, Ch'en Tu-hsiu had developed some interest in the economic interpretation of history and society.[38] Materialism in a vague sense was also advocated to some extent by a few writers.[39] In 1916 and 1918, Li Ta-chao's writings showed some embryonic traces of dialectics in opposition to the "genetic method."[40] But no genuine Marxist theories could be found in Li's writings in this early stage. Beside Chu Chih-hsin's translation of a part of *The Communist Manifesto* in 1906, as we have mentioned, the earliest Chinese translation of Marx's major work published within China was his *Wage, Labor, and Capital*, which appeared with the title "Labor and Capital" (*Lao-tung yü tzu-pen*) in the Chinputang newspaper, *The Morning Post*, from May 9 to June 1, 1919. In the summer of 1919, following the vogue of pragmatism, dialectical materialism came to the attention of the Chinese intellectual leaders, but they took a more or less critical and skeptical attitude toward it, and did not accept it as a whole. The Society for the Study of Socialism established in about December of 1919 was not dedicated primarily to Marxism, but in the main to guild socialism, syndicalism, and anarchism. Organized study of Marxism did not begin until the spring of 1920.[41]

A notable critical introduction to Marxism was published in May 1919 by Li Ta-chao, who was in fact basically sympathetic to it. He said: "Recently there has appeared in philosophy a neo-idealism which may rectify Marx's materialism and remedy its defects."[42] Li actually took a revisionist view of Marx's

historical materialism: (1) He followed Eugenio Rignano's criticism of Marx that historical materialism was contradictory to the theory of class struggle. He imagined Marx might have replied that class struggle would ultimately be part of the process of economic change; "but," Li remarked, "even though this reply would be true, it would be a forced interpretation and somehow self-contradictory."[43] (2) To Li, historical materialism had the defect of determinism or fatalism; but this was offset by the rallying cry of *The Communist Manifesto*, which called upon the working classes to unite and struggle.[44] (3) Marx overlooked the function of ethics and the humanitarian movement in the course of history. It was here that Li prescribed the remedy of neo-idealism. (4) Li remarked: "Marx's theory was a product of his time; in his time it was indeed a great discovery. However, history should not be interpreted forever by this theory which was formulated at a specific time and under specific circumstances, nor should Marxist theory be accepted as a whole and applied uncritically to modern society. On the other hand, we should not disregard its historical value and specific findings."[45]

It is striking that Li criticism of Marx's materialistic interpretation of history was rejected by one of the Kuomintang leaders, Hu Han-min. His long article "A Criticism of Criticism of Historical Materialism" was almost a direct rebuttal, point by point, of Li's article.* Hu Han-min also seems to have been the first to study Chinese history, philosophy, ethics, and institutions in the light of historical

---

* At this time, Li Ta-chao had quite close relations with the Kuomintang leaders in Shanghai. Li was one of the agents in Peking in charge of selling the Kuomintang organ, *The Construction*.[46]

materialism. His "A Materialistic Study of the History of Chinese Philosophy" was published in October 1919. The Chinese translation of Karl Kautsky's *Karl Marx's ökonomische lehren* (1887) published in *Ch'en pao* from June 2 and that by Tai-Chi-t'ao from November were the first major, systematic introduction of *Das Kapital* into China.[47] Following these, Li Ta-chao published his "Material Change and Ethical Change" in December 1919 and "An Economic Interpretation of the Cause of Changes in Modern Chinese Thought" in January 1920.[48] The latter was the first attempt to explain the new thought movement in terms of materialism. But it must be noted that Tai and Hu approached Marxism differently from Li. The two former emphasized the nationalist implications of the theory, while Li followed the line of class struggle. This factor led to their later split.[49]

Meanwhile, a Chinese translation of the first section of *The Communist Manifesto* was published in the students' monthly, *The Citizens*, on November 1, 1919 (Vol. II, No. 1), and that of Marx's preface to *Das Kapital* on October 1, 1920 in the same magazine (Vol. II, No. 3). The manifesto was translated in full into Chinese by Ch'en Wang-tao and published in April 1920. After these translations, Part III of Engels' *Anti-Dühring* (1877) was translated in *The Construction* in December 1920 (Vol. III, No. 1). Marx's preface to *The Critique of Political Economy* (1859) was translated in *The Eastern Miscellany* in January 1921 (Vol. XVIII, No. 1), and Engels' *Socialism: Utopian and Scientific* was first rendered into Chinese by Shih Jen-yung and published in the *New World* (*Hsin shih-chieh*) fornightly after 1912. A translation of the latter by Cheng Tz'u-ch'uan was published in book form by the Shanghai Ch'ün-i shu-chü in 1921.

The above includes the list of almost all major works of Marx and Engels which Chinese students of Marxism could read in their own language in the years before 1921. It is notable that most of the works were translated by those who were not finally converted into Marxism.[50]

After 1923 dialectical materialism began to be accepted by some Chinese writers and from the latter part of the twenties onwards it had increasing influence on Chinese thinking. However, to pursue it further here would be a diversion from our immediate concern with the May Fourth period.

"DOWN WITH CONFUCIUS AND SONS"

Aided by Mr. *Te* and Mr. *Sai*, the new intellectual leaders set out to attack traditional ethics. They aimed first of all at dethroning what became known in Hu Shih's catch phrase as "Confucius and Sons" (*K'ung-chia-tien*)* from its undisputed sway over ethics and ideas in China which had lasted two thousand years.

There had not been very many people who declared themselves anti-Confucian during these two thousand years. But some thinkers like Wang Ch'ung (A.D. 27-97) and Li Chih (Li Tso-wu, A.D. 1527-1602) had dared to take exception for anti-Confucian opinions had generally been suppressed by government and

---

* A term first used by Hu Yü's selected essays to refer to Confucianism and its followers. It became popular later in the anti-Confucian movement.[51] For a more systematic study of this, see the present author's "The Anti-Confucian Movement in the Early Republic of China" (a paper for the Fourth Conference on Chinese Thought, 1958, to be published in Arthur F. Wright, ed., *The Confucian Persuasion* by Stanford University Press in 1960).

society. At the turn of the nineteenth century a few writers had expressed opinions skeptical or critical of Confucianism. Yen Fu had for a time raised his doubt of the traditional Chinese thinking as a whole, and Chinese anarchists and socialists provided devastating criticism of the general existing orthodoxy. Liang Ch'i-ch'ao had said, "I love Confucius, but I love truth more." Wu Yü** had written a series of essays attacking Confucianism, but had been forbidden to publish them, both by the Ch'ing dynasty and the Re-

** Wu Yü (*tzu*: Yu-ling, *hao*: Ai-chih-lu chu-jen, or the Master of the Hut of Love for Wisdom, 1871-1949) was born in Chengtu, Szechwan. He went to Japan for study in 1905 (some say in 1896) and was influenced there by Western liberal and democratic ideas. Because of its anti-Confucian characteristics, his book, *Discussions of the Intellectual Trends in the Sung and Yüan Dynasties* (*Sung Yüan hsüeh-an ts'ui-yü*), was banned from sale by the Ministry of Education under the Ch'ing government. He escaped to the countryside and avoided the arrest ordered by the government. In 1913 he edited the *Awaken-the-Masses Magazine* (*Hsing ch'ün pao*) in Chengtu. It was also suppressed by the government because of its unconventional opinions. His poems had been published by Ch'en Tu-hsiu in *The Tiger* magazine in July 1915 before his anti-Confucian articles appeared in *New Youth* in 1917. Late in 1916 Wu was impressed by the anti-Confucian stand of *New Youth* and wrote a letter to Ch'en Tu-hsiu. Consequently, a number of Wu's articles were published in the magazine from February 1917 on. In 1919 Wu was invited to teach at Peking University where he remained until his return to Chengtu in the mid-1920's. There he taught at Chengtu University from about 1926 and at the National Szechwan University from 1931. In his last years he retired to the vicinity of Chengtu. Among his published works are *Collected Essays of Wu Yü* (*Wu Yü wen-lu*), *Supplements* (*Wu Yü wen pieh-lu*, Chengtu, 1936; *Wu Yü wen hsü-lu*, Chengtu, 1937), and a collection of poems in the literary language, *The Autumn Water* (*Ch'iu-shui chi*, Chengtu, 1913). Many of his essays were written in the vernacular.

publican government.[52] In 1915 several articles in *New Youth* attacked the whole frame-work of traditional ethics and institutions. Yet they did not specifically point to Confucius' teachings. It was not until the spring of 1916, when Yüan Shih-k'ai's monarchial movement was in the doldrums, that anti-Confucianism began to gain ground.

In the February 1916 issue of *New Youth*, there first appeared an article by Yi Pai-sha (1886-1921), Yi P'ei-chi's younger brother who was a teacher at the Hunan Province First Normal School in Changsha and the Nankai School in Tientsin between 1916 and 1919, and later, as a nationalist with anarchist ideas, committed suicide because of his pessimistic view of the Chinese political outlook. The article, "A Discussion of Confucius," was intended by the author to "expose the secret of Confucian worship" during the previous two thousand years. Yi's analysis went as follows: Confucianism was originally but one of the "nine schools" of thought. Confucius and his disciples upheld the authority of the emperor, but they often joined rebellions against the kings of states. After their suppression by Ch'in Shih-huang-ti (the first emperor of the Ch'in dynasty) Confucians joined the rebellion that overthrew the Ch'in dynasty in 206 B.C. Aware of the causes of the Ch'in failure, the subsequent Han emperors adopted a placatory policy toward the Confucians and set up Confucius as an idol to be worshiped. Consequently, Confucianism became the official dogma, a tool for the suppression of other schools and of freedom of thought. Yi went further and said that the fact that Confucianism could be and was used as a tool by the rulers was Confucius' own fault. First, Confucius advocated, as Yi probably overstated, unlimited authority for the monarch and government by man instead of by law. He identified the emperor with Heaven, a being to be checked by nothing save his own conscience. This would, of course, easily make a ruler an autocrat. Secondly, in his teaching, Confucius often discouraged his disciples from asking questions, thus helping to lay the foundations of ideological orthodoxy. Thirdly, Confucius' advocacy of the "golden mean" was merely a way of evading making decisions in regard to practical problems. His ambiguity invited distortion. Fourthly, Confucius was too enthusiastic an office seeker, and neglected to ensure himself means for an independent livelihood. He visited and entreated seventy-two kings, hoping in vain to obtain an official appointment. He said that he would be in great perturbation if he did not live under the rule of a king for three months. On the other hand, he looked down upon material welfare and the effort of making a living. Therefore, his followers had to depend upon the rulers' financial support, and were utilized as tools. Thus Confucianism itself became the tool of the reigning monarch.[53] In the second part of article, Yi said that Confucianism had no right to claim a monopoly of Chinese thought, because the Chinese intellectual tradition was rich with the ideas of diverse schools. He felt, however, that Confucius and his disciples were in fact political revolutionaries. They themselves wanted to be kings and joined many rebellions.[54]

The author in the above article intended to expose only the reasons why Confucian worship was imposed by rulers. He did not make a concentrated attack on Confucianism as a philosophic or ethical system, or point out why it should not be accepted in modern times as, after the publication of this article, was done by Ch'en Tu-hsiu, Wu Yü, and in a different way, Lu Hsün in their later powerful and influential attacks on Confucianism.

While he saw some value in Confucius' teachings, Ch'en Tu-hsiu opposed the undiscriminating acceptance of Confucianism mainly on the grounds that it was a product of feudal ages, and did not fit the needs of modern society. His arguments which are to be found in various articles may be summarized as follows: (1) The Confucians advocated superfluous ceremonies and preached the morality of meek compliance and a yielding nature, decrying struggle and competition. This made the Chinese people too weak and passive to survive in the modern world.[55] (2) Modern society was composed of individuals acting as independent units, and its laws and ethics tended to protect individual freedom and rights. Confucianism was based on a feudal society composed of family and clan units. The individual was regarded only as a member of the family, and not as an independent unit in the society and state. Confucian ethics imposed on the individual filial piety to the family and loyal duty to the ruler, without providing him with individual rights. All these ethical principles of the feudal ages were highly inappropriate to modern individualistic society.* (3) Confucianism upheld a caste system, and the inequality of status of individuals in the state. This could not be retained in a republic.[57] (4) The ethical concept of the independence of the individual personality was required to sanction the individual's financial independence. In accordance with Confu-

---

* According to the [Han period] Confucian theory of "Three Bonds [duties]," the emperor was the master of his subjects, the father the master of his sons, and the husband the master of his wife.[56]

cian theory grown-up children could not possess private property until their parents died, and women were deprived of all financial rights. This clashed directly with modern economic conceptions.[58] (5) In modern democracies, sons and wives might join political parties other than those of their parents and husbands, But according to Confucianism, sons should accept their parent's beliefs, at least until three years after the latter's death. Furthermore, since women had to obey their fathers, husbands, or sons, women's suffrage was impossible.[59] (6) Confucianism demanded a one-sided female chastity. Widows could not marry again. And many trifling taboos concerning sexual relations were now impractical for everyday life.* (7) To oppose K'ang Yu-wei's proposal for an officially established Confucian religion, Ch'en argued that Confucianism was not a religion at all because Confucius refused to discuss the soul or life after death, and did not advocate religious worship. Therefore, it would be ridiculous to make Confucianism a state religion under the constitution. Even if it were a religion, the adoption of a state

* According to the *Book of Rites* (*Li chi*), which was attributed to Confucius' disciples and edited by a Han Confucian scholar, Tai Sheng, in order to avoid suspicion, widows had to refrain from weeping mournfully at night; and men had to refrain from befriending a widow's sons. In addition, according to the Confucian classics, women should not sit together. Women should not talk with their brothers-in-law; married women should not sit at the same table with their brothers when the former visited their parents' home; things should not be passed directly by hand between men and women; boys and girls of seven years of age or above should not sit at the same table to eat. Ch'en argued that all these teachings were respected by the traditional Confucianists, but could hardly be lived up to in the twentieth century.[60] We must point out here, however, that these teachings had never been carried out completely in Chinese history.

religion would be contrary to the principle of freedom of religious belief which had been accepted in the draft constitution.[61] (8) To enforce Confucianism as an official principle of education militated against freedom of thought and teaching. Ch'en thought that no theory should be regarded as the sole truth, since that would hamper the free development of thought and civilization.[62] (9) Confucius' apologists argued that Confucius' theories had been distorted and utilized for their own purposes by the scholars of the Han and Sung dynasties and that consequently he himself was not responsible for later interpretations. To this Ch'en retorted: why did those scholars not distort and utilize theories other than those of Confucius? Ch'en went further to assert that the Han and Sung scholars did in fact closely follow Confucius' teachings. In the main they only systematized his theories and did not change them in essence. The Neo-Confucianists should not be blamed any more than Confucius himself. Since Confucius' teachings were products of feudalism, their feudal characteristics were inevitable. The question was: after more than two thousand years, how could a feudalistic doctrine still be used for worship and applied to a modern republic?[63]

Ch'en's criticism of Confucianism was very straightforward. But the real champion of the anti-Confucianists was Wu Yü, a scholar who had studied law and political science in Tokyo. Wu criticized Confucianism not only as an abstract philosophic and ethical system, but also in its application to "the teachings of proprieties" (*li-chiao*), the law, institutions, customs, and the evaluation of historical events. For ten years he studied the traditional arguments and briefs in the judicial and ritual cases cited in Chinese historical records—arguments and briefs based on the allegedly Confucian classics or on traditional laws embodying them. He compared these cases and arguments with the theories of the two Taoist philosophers, Lao-tzu and Chuang-tzu, and with those of Montesquieu, Jenks, John Mill, Herbert Spencer, Endō Ryūkichi, and Kubo Tenzui (1875-1934) as well as with the principles of the constitutional, civil, and criminal laws of European countries and the United States.[64] In other words, in his attack on Confucianism Wu concentrated his attention on institutions, customs, and the philosophy of law.

Wu's major arguments against Confucianism were that it upheld the traditional family system; that its advocacy of paternalism had become the basis of despotism; and that its fundamental ethical principle, filial piety (*hsiao*), became the basis of the principle of unquestioning loyalty (*chung*) to the sovereign. Wu traced the development of the idea of filial piety and its relation to the idea of loyalty and to propriety.* In Wu's view, which cannot be completely justi-

* According to the classics, the editorship or authorship of which was at the time attributed to Confucius or his disciples, filial piety was considered the very root of morality, the basis of proper behavior, and the source of education. Filial piety was defined in the classics as a duty "beginning with serving one's parents, developing in serving the emperor, and ending with benefitting one's self." The *Book of Filial Piety*, which has traditionally but erroneously been attributed to Confucius or his disciples, held that "to serve the emperor with filial piety means loyalty," and that "a gentleman who serves his parents with filial piety may transfer it to his loyalty to the emperor; who serves his elder brother with fraternal obedience may transfer it to his obedience to his superiors; since he manages his family well, he will govern well as an official." In this connotation, state was similar to family and emperor to father. The meaning of filial piety expanded in the *Book of Rites:* "One is not filial if one does not respect one's superiors in office."[65]

fied so far as Confucius' own words are concerned, the Confucian idea was to eliminate any desire to protest or rebel on the part of the people. "Because filial piety and fraternal duty are virtues of obedience," a Neo-Confucianist of the Sung dynasty held, "those who possess these virtues will not offend their superiors, and there will be of course no rebellion."[66] In this matter Wu Yü remarked: "The effect of the idea of filial piety has been to turn China into a big factory for the manufacturing of obedient subjects."[67]

This combination or mixture of the idea of filial piety with the idea of loyalty, family with state, was certainly welcomed by all rulers, especially autocrats. Hence the rulers embodied the theory in institutions, laws, and customs. One of the principles of the philosophy of law set by the *Book of Filial Piety* said, "In the application of the three thousand categories of the five classes of punishment, the most severe crime is the committing of an unfilial act. Those who offend the sovereign are disloyal, those who reject the sages are lawbreakers, and those who commit an unfilial act are rejecting their parents: these ways lead to turmoil."[68] In the teachings of propriety, there were numerous trifling regulations for the performance of acts of filial piety.

In the traditional laws of the Manchu dynasty and earlier periods an unfilial act was regarded as one of the "ten vices." And custom encouraged the performance of acts of filial piety to an extreme degree. There were legends of people who buried their infant sons alive in order to save money to feed their parents, and they were honored in history as "filial sons."[69] But, one who had no son was considered, as Mencius said, the most unfilial. As a result, concubinage prevailed, women were despised, and birth control was impossible. Confucius also taught that one should not travel afar when his parents were living; thus the spirit of adventure was discouraged.[70]

After exposing all the defects of the Confucian ethic, Wu Yü said that its principles had been opposed by many ancient Chinese philosophers. Han Fei (?-233 B.C.), one of the leaders of the Legalist School, pointed out the possible contradiction between filial piety and loyalty to the sovereign. He gave as an example a man whose father stole another's sheep. The son tipped off the government. By his act, which was disapproved by Confucius, he was loyal to the sovereign but not to his father.* In another case given by Han Fei there was a soldier who always retreated from battle when fighting in defense of his sovereign, not risking his life because he loved his old father. He was of course very filial, but was he loyal to his sovereign or state?[73]

The fierce attack on filial piety by Wu Yü and Ch'en Tu-hsiu was a great shock to the conservatives. They then accused Ch'en of changing the old proverb,

"Adultery is the first of all sins, and filial piety, the first of all virtues" (*Wan o yin wei shou, po shan hsiao wei hsien*), into a new dictum, "Filial piety is the first of all sins, and adultery, the first of all virtues" (*Wan o hsiao wei shou, po shan yin wei hsien*). While the charge is unfounded, it well indicates the temper both of the attack on and the defense of the old ethical principles.

This attack on the traditional family ethics was carried forward enthusiastically by young students and created a furious reaction in the society. For instance, on November 8, 1919, Shih Ts'unt'ung, a student of the Chekiang Province First Normal School in Hangchow (a school very similar in nature to its Changsha counterpart) with strong anarchist leanings who, though he was later one of the founders of the Chinese Communist Party, soon withdrew from the party and became an economic writer, published in a student magazine an article titled "Oppose Filial Piety." The author, as he conceded later, attempted to arouse a great controversy by severe criticism of filial piety in order to overthrow the traditional family system to prepare the way for the construction of a new society. The article achieved the purpose of creating a controversy. It was soon praised by supporters, including the Kuomintang newspaper, *Min-kuo jih-pao*, as a thunderstorm which would clear the air, but denounced by opponents, led by the Governor and legislature, as heresy and treason. It is interesting to note that in this issue Ch'en Tu-hsiu, Shen Ting-i, and Shen Chung-chiu, an anarchist and former teacher at the school, wrote letters to the students to support Shih, whereas Tai Chi-t'ao wrote one to support those students who opposed Shih. Because of the article, the magazine was immediately suppressed by the Peking govern-

* Herbert Allen Giles translates the story as follows: "One of the feudal princes was boasting to Confucius of the high level of morality which prevailed in his own State. 'Among us here,' he said, 'you will find upright men. If a father has stolen a sheep, his son will give evidence against him.' 'In my part of the country,' replied Confucius, 'there is a different standard from this. A father will shield his son, a son will shield his father. It is thus that uprightness will be found.' " [71] Bertrand Russell, in contrasting the Confucian filial piety to the growth of public spirit in the West commented: "It is interesting to contrast this story with that of the elder Brutus and his son, upon which we in the West were all brought up." [72] Russell here referred to the legend of Junius Brutus who condemned to death his two sons for joining a conspiracy to restore to the throne a banished Roman king. It may be also interesting to compare these with Euthyphro's prosecution of his father for homicide in *The Dialogues of Plato*.

ment. Shih Ts'un-t'ung and his three schoolmates, Yü Hsiu-sung, Chou Po-ti, Yü T'an-fen, withdrew from the school and went to Peking to join the Work-and-Learning Mutual Assistance Corps. Shih was later helped by Ch'en Tu-hsiu to go to Japan. Under the influence of Ōsugi Sakae there, he was converted to anarchism. This episode and other disputes concerning the vernacular literature and classic studies led to a furious struggle between the provincial government and the students and teachers of the school. As a result, the head of the school, Ching Heng-i, was dismissed and the school forcibly closed by the government in the spring of 1920. But subsequently the students won a right to choose their new principal and teachers. On the government's side, the director of the education bureau of the province at that time was Hsia Ching-kuan, a famous poet of the Kiangsi school of the old style. On the other side, leading teachers at the school supporting the new thought included Liu-Ta-pai, a distinguished poet of both the vernacular and literary languages, Hsia Mien-tsun, later a writer and translator, very influential among middle school students, and Ch'en Wang-tao. Among the students were Feng Hsüeh-fang, Wang Ching-chih, P'an Mo-hua, lyric poets, and Ts'ao Chü-jen, later a famous leftist writer and journalist. Shortly after this, Chiang Ch'i succeeded Ching as the principal and Chu Tzu-ch'ing and Yü P'ing-po joined the faculty, all recommended by Chiang Monlin. Thus the school became a center of the new culture and new literature movements in Chekiang.[74]

In addition to the criticism of Confucian filial ethics, Wu Yü attacked Confucius' advocacy of the caste system and social inequality. According to Wu's interpretation, Confucius actually upheld the distinction between the superior and the inferior and it was by analogy with the basic concept of a superior Heaven and an inferior earth that Confucius regarded the sovereign, fathers, husbands, and officials as superior, and the ministers, sons, wives, and people as inferior.[75] Confucius said that such a relation between monarch and subjects could not be abandoned. While Mencius had the idea that in the state people are of most importance and monarch the least, he said, when he criticized Yang Chu (fourth century B.C.) and Mo Ti (fifth century B.C.), that those who rejected their parents and monarch were beasts.[76] The idea of universal harmony, or one world (ta-t'ung) in which there would be equality for all had long been attributed to Confucius. But Wu argued that since the Sung dynasty the Neo-Confucianists had suspected that Confucius was not the author of the paragraph containing this idea. It was, he said, actually borrowed from Lao-tzu. On this question, Ch'en Tu-hsiu held a very definite view. Even if the idea was really held by Confucius, it only meant that in this ideal world the sovereigns might freely choose able men as their successors in substitution for hereditary succession. The sovereign power was still transmitted from ruler to ruler instead of through popular elections. Therefore, such a world should not be accepted by a modern democracy as ideal.[77]

Since Wu's criticism of Confucianism was aimed not only at Confucius' own teachings or the original Confucian doctrine, but also at the application of the theory to Chinese institutions, laws, and customs and their practical effects on Chinese life and society, Hu Shih praised him for his unconscious application of the pragmatic method and for his correct criticism of Confucianism. In a preface to Wu Yü's works Hu called Wu "the old hero from Szechwan Province who beat 'Confucius and Sons single-handed.' "* Chiefly owing to Wu's efforts, "overthrow Confucius and Sons" (*ta-tao K'ung-chia-tien*) became a popular slogan among the Chinese intellectuals during the May Fourth period.

Wu's critical attitude toward Confucianism probably met the needs of the time. The real issue was not merely to re-examine Confucius' own teachings but to expose the falsity and cruelty of all the ethical principles and institutions imposed on the people by rulers and officials down the centuries, i.e., the inequitable principles and institutions which either were based on Confucius' original theories or pretended to adopt them. The vital battle was the fight against a stagnant tradition, of which Confucianism was the core.

Shortly after Wu's criticism there came the fiercer and more effective fighter, Lu Hsün. His attack on Confucian ethics extended to the whole of traditional society and life, and to the Chinese character. His approach was not via theoretical discussion, but by satiric, pungent, and humorous exposure. His excellent style and wit, and occasional flashes of irony, won a great number of readers.

Persuaded by Ch'ien Hsüan-t'ung, Lu Hsün joined the circle of *New Youth* in the summer of 1917. His first short story, "The Diary of a Madman," written in April 1918, and published in the May issue of the monthly, showed the influence of Gogol and Andreyev. It was a furious attack upon the old Chinese civilization and tradition. In the story he said through the madman: "I take a look at history; it is not a record of time but

on each page are confusedly written the characters 'benevolence, righteousness, and morals.' " "Desperately unsleeping, I carefully look it over again and again for half the night, and at last find between the lines that it is full of the same word 'cannibalism!' " "Having unconsciously practiced cannibalism for four thousand years, I am awakening now and feel ashamed to face a genuine human being!" The madman's conclusion was: "There may be some children who haven't yet become cannibals. Save the children. . . ."[79]

In a latter issue the story was interpreted by Wu Yü. He explained: the people who talk etiquette, morality, or ethics most enthusiastically, are literally the most brutal cannibals. Wu supported this proposition with a number of cases recorded in Chinese history and the classics.* He then jumped to the conclusion

---

* Hu's remarks on Wu Yü was an allusion to a fight episode in the Chinese novel *All Men Are Brothers,* which, according to Wu, Hu was studying when he wrote his preface.[78]

* For example, in the Chou dynasty, Duke Huan of Ch'i (*Ch'i Huan-kung*) was regarded as loyal and filial. When the Emperor exempted him from the kowtow on account of his old age, he insisted on performing it in order to affirm his loyalty and ethical principles. But once he told his obsequious courtier Yi Ya that he (the Duke) had enjoyed all the food Yi cooked for him but that he had unfortunately never eaten an infant's head. On learning this, Yi cooked his own son alive for the Duke. So the loyal and filial Duke was actually a cannibal.[80] Another example was: The first Emperor of the Han dynasty, Liu Pang (247-195 B.C.), who was also the first in Chinese history to worship Confucius cooked the flesh of one of his rebel generals and gave it as a reward to his ministers to eat.[81] Chang Hsün (A.D. 709-757), the famous general of the T'ang dynasty, cooked his concubine to feed his soldiers while defending a besieged city for the Emperor. When the soldiers wept and dared not eat, he forced them to. Later, about twenty to thirty thousand women and children in the city were eaten. Subsequently, the general was praised as one of the most loyal and righteous in Chinese history.[82] The story about Yi Ya is actually a fable.

that, in extreme cases, cannibalism was the only means by which the Confucian ethics could be completely observed.

Lu Hsün's short essays and stories directed not so much against ethics as against customs in general. His criticism of these was made largely from a realistic and humanitarian point of view though delivered with a satiric sting. In his re-evaluation of the Chinese tradition, what concerned him most was the well-being of the average Chinese. "What most people fear is that the *term* 'the Chinese race' will disappear, while what I fear is that the *Chinese* will be extinguished from the 'world races.' "[83] The ultraconservative traditionalists often talked of the preservation of the "national quintessence"; Lu Hsün commented that what they wanted to preserve was not national quintessence but "national refuse." Against such people, Lu Hsün argued, "A friend of mine has said, 'the question is not whether we can preserve our national quintessence, but whether the national quintessence can preserve us.' To preserve ourselves is the first thing. We ask only whether it has or has not the power to preserve us, regardless of whether it is our national quintessence or not."[84] Lu Hsün declared that the Chinese should live for themselves instead of for their ancestors. To learn modern science and Western knowledge was more important than to recite the Confucian classics. "Even a cow cannot serve both as a sacrifice animal and as a draught animal, both for beef and for milking; how can a human being survive both for his ancestors and for himself?"[85] Hence Lu Hsün advocated creation instead of preservation. If one could create, one should at least find something better —even a new idol, if it was better than the older one: "Rather than worship Confucius and Kuan Kung [A.D. 160-219]

one should worship Darwin and Ibsen. Rather than sacrifice to the God of Pestilence and the Five Classes of Spirits, one should worship Apollo."[86] Of this argument Lin Yutang, once a colleague and friend of Lu Hsün, remarked two decades later, "This has justified the witticism that the American bug is better than the Chinese bug and the American moon is better than the Chinese moon."[87] Lu Hsün was sincere from his realistic and utilitarian point of view; if the new was more useful than the old, he asked, in effect, why should one bother whether it was Chinese or foreign? In fact, in the same article criticized by Lin Yutang, Lu Hsün had advocated Western iconoclasm against idolatry, but it was ignored by Lin. Nevertheless there is evil inherent in any idol worship, no matter whether the idol is old or new, Eastern or Western—a proposition which was proved tragically true in the case of many Chinese extreme leftist and rightist intellectuals in later decades.*

---

* Lu Hsün himself had never been an idol worshiper. He expressed himself strongly against any excessive praise of authority, either conservative or revolutionary, by men of letters when he came to oppose the "revolutionary literature" proposed by Kuo Mo-jo and other members of the Creation Society in the middle of the twenties. Not a few of the Chinese new intellectuals who joined in the iconoclastic tide in the May Fourth period later became idol worshipers. The unconditional support and praise of Chiang Kai-shek by Wu Chih-hui and Tai Chi-t'ao, exemplify those who abandoned their early ideals and surrendered to nationalist authority. On the other hand, the Marxist poet and historian Kuo Mo-jo provides an example of those who submitted to leftist authority. Kuo wrote a paradoxical poem between May and June 1920 titled "I Am an Idol Worshiper":

O I am an idol worshiper!
I worship the sun, mountains, and oceans;
I worship the water, the fire, volcanoes, and great rivers;

Lu Hsün was a wholehearted supporter of the new learning, ridiculing backward conservatives, both Chinese and foreign, in China. There were many concession authorities and foreign businessmen in China who insisted on the treaty privileges on the ground that traditional Chinese laws and customs were archaic; but at the same time they supported the backward Chinese conservatives who advocated the preservation of the traditional laws, institutions, customs, and ethics. These foreign interests joined in praising the Chinese national heritage and opposing the progressives in order that their own privileges in China might be preserved. In Lu Hsün's opinion, what these people wanted was to subdue China with an invisible knife. "Almost all of those who praise the old Chinese culture," he declared, "are the rich who are residing in the concessions or other safe places. They praise it because they have money and do not suffer from the civil wars."[90] He even pushed his point to an extreme: "Chinese culture is a culture of serving one's masters who are triumphant at the cost of the misery of the multitude. Those who praise Chinese culture, whether they be Chinese or for-

I worship life, death, light, and night;
I worship Suez, Panama, the Great Wall
 of China, and the Pyramids;
I worship the spirit of creation, force,
 blood, and heart;
I worship bombs, sadness, and destruction;
I worship iconoclasts and myself!
O I am also an iconoclast![88]

These lines reveal the romantic pantheism which characterizes Kuo's poetry, as well as his self-contradiction which illuminates for us his later actions. In recent years his idolatry has predominated over his iconoclasm. Now president of the Chinese Academy of Sciences in Peking, he has published a collection of 21 short poems in which Stalin's and Mao Tse-tung's names are praised 55 times and the slogan "long live . . ." occurs 27 times (twice in Russian); 20 times this slogan refers to the two leaders and never to the people.[89]

eigners conceive of themselves as belonging to the ruling class." At the same time he exposed the falsity of the traditionalists by saying, "There is a favorite technique of those who know the old literature. When a new idea is introduced, they call it 'heresy' and bend all their efforts to destroy it. If that new idea, by its struggle against their efforts, wins a place for itself, they then discover that 'it's the same thing as was taught by Confucius.' They object to all imported things, saying that these are 'to convert Chinese into barbarians', but when the barbarians become rulers of China, they discover these 'barbarians' are also descendants of Yellow Emperor(*Huang-ti*)."[91]

Between 1918 and 1925, Lu Hsün wrote twenty-six stories and many short commentaries.[92] The characters in the stories were almost all grotesque, caricatured to represent the shortcomings in character of the Chinese people under the influence of traditional ethics and institutions. "The True Story of Ah Q" (*Ah Q cheng chuan*), a brilliant satire which was published in December 1921 and has since been translated into thirteen different languages, was typical. The weaknesses of the Chinese exposed by Lu Hsün in his writings included intolerance, inertia, hypocrisy, servility toward a superior and arrogance toward a subordinate, opportunism, and hesitation. In his short commentaries, he fiercely attacked conversatism, superstition, and the old ethics. Lu Hsün always described the dark side of life and society. As a writer he was primarily a fighter. His pen was like a rapier. With one sudden stroke it would fatally pierce the very heart of its objective. Heinrich Heine asked in his own epitaph that a sword instead of a pen be laid beside his bier. Lu Hsün might have done the same.

Lu Hsün was undoubtedly one of the most influential and effective attackers of Chinese tradition. A Chinese writer who had been at one time critical of Lu Hsün concluded later that "Lu Hsün's place in the May Fourth Movement of China was like Voltaire's in the Enlightenment of France."[93] Lu Hsün's "The True Story of Ah Q" was compared also by a Western writer with Voltaire's *Candide*.[94]

It should be pointed out that the greater part of the "Confucianism" attacked by the new intellectuals in the early period of the May Fourth Movement was the currently orthodox interpretation of Confucianism. This interpretation and the attacks upon it, although neither was entirely groundless, did not necessarily take into account Confucius' whole theory or spirit. Whether the spirit of Confucius himself is precisely the same as the spirit of the later Confucianism attacked by the intellectuals still remains debatable. Confucius' doctrines are not free from ambiguities and limitations. Varying emphases or distortions will certainly paint a different Confucius. Indeed, he has been arbitrarily painted as a leading revolutionary since the May Fourth period by some Chinese writers such as Kuo-Mo-jo. There are other interpreters including some Western writers, who go so far as to consider him a genuine democrat and maintain that his theories have influenced the Western Enlightenment and French and American democratic ideas.[95]

Very few effective defenses of Confucianism were offered in this early period. It was only after 1920 that some theoretical opposition to the attack was raised. Besides Liang Sou-ming, whose defense of Confucianism and Eastern civilization will be discussed in the next chapter, Bertrand Russell gave a short, rather sympathetic reappraisal of some Confucian principles. After a discussion of the shortcomings of the theory of filial

piety, such as its militating against public spirit, Russell said that "it is certainly less harmful than its Western counterpart, patriotism," which, he thought, "leads much more easily to imperialism and militarism."[96]

Whatever the merits of Russell's argument, it could hardly appeal to the young Chinese intelligentsia during and after the May Fourth period, when a loosely organized China was facing an aggressive modern world dominated by nation-states. That patriotism, nationalism, and anti-imperialism developed in China was mainly due to a reaction against this situation. To many Chinese reformers, the traditional Chinese passive ethics would be ineffective in this struggle for the independence of China, unless the Great Powers and other nations also gave up the idea of the sovereign state and its aggressive policies.

Russell himself pointed out why so many foreign conservatives in China joined their Chinese counterparts in defending the Confucian tradition. He said: "In the present day, when China is confronted with problems requiring a radically new outlook, these features of the Confucian system have made it a barrier to necessary reconstruction, and accordingly we find all those foreigners who wish to exploit China praising the old tradition and deriding the efforts of Young China to construct something more suited to modern needs."[97] To question the motive of all the promoters of Confucianism in China in this way may have been unfair to honest Confucianists, but the "foreign exploiters," as Russell termed them, should themselves have heeded Confucius' teachings of self-restraint, moderation, and altruism. This was probably Russell's original intention when he acknowledged on the one hand that some of the Chinese tradition "has had to be swept away to meet modern needs," on the other hand, that he hoped something of value in the traditional Chinese ethics and institutions would not "have to perish in the struggle to repel the foreign exploiters and the fierce and cruel system which they miscall [Western] civilization."[98] In view of Russell's prestige, it was not strange that his praise of certain aspects of Confucianism and Chinese tradition should have intensified the debate between the reformers and their opponents.

In the task of "overthrowing Confucius and Sons," there were, apart from Ch'en Tu-hsiu, Wu Yü, and Lu Hsün, many other intellectuals who took important roles, men such as Ku Chieh-kang, Ch'ien Hsüan-t'ung, and Hu Shih. Their sober approach was more academic and fairer to the ancient philosophers but no less effective than that of the former writers.

Notes

For Arabic numerals in italic type following an author's or editor's name, see Bibliography in Chow Tse-tsung, *Research Guide to the May Fourth Movement* (Harvard University Press, 1963).

1. Hu Shih and Ch'en Tu-hsiu, "Lun *Hsin ch'ing-nien* chih chu-chang" ("A Discussion on the Advocacies of *New Youth*"), letter in reply to Yi Chung-k'uei, New Youth, V, 4 (Oct. 15, 1918), p. 433.

2. For a summary of the development of Neo-Confucianism and later reaction to it see H. C. Creel *602*, *Chinese Thought: From Confucius to Mao Tse-tung* (Chicago, 1953), pp. 204ff; and W. Theodore de Bary, "A Reappraisal of Neo-Confucianism," in Arthur F. Wright *785*, ed., *Studies in Chinese Thought*, Vol. 55, No. 5, Part 2 of *The American Anthropologist* (Chicago, Dec. 1953), pp. 81-111.

3. James Legge, trans., *The Great Learning*, pp. 357-58. Also Chu Hsi's commentary in the book.

4. See Arthur W. Hummel, ed., *Eminent Chinese of the Ch'ing Period (1644-1912)* (Washington, D.C., 1943-44).

5. See *ibid.*

6. Liang Ch'i-ch'ao, "Yen Li hsüeh-p'ai yü hsien-tai chiao-yü ssu-ch'ao" ("The School of Yen Yüan and Li Kung and Modern Educational Thought"), in *310*, Collected Works of Liang Ch'i-ch'ao, Essays (Shanghai, 1936, 1941), Vol. XIV, Part 41, pp. 3-27.

7. Pan-su [Li Chien-nung], *Chung-shan ch'u-shih hou Chung-kuo liu-shih nien ta-shih chi* (Chronological Records of the Important Events of China in the Sixty Years after Sun Yat-sen's Birth) (enlarged ed.; Shanghai, 1929), p. 86.

8. For this issue see Wu Tsung-tz'u, *Chung-hua min-kuo hsien-fa shih* (A Constitutional History of the Republic of China) (Peking, 1924), Vol. I, Chap. 3, p. 38; Kuo-hsien ch'i-ts'ao wei-yüan-hui (Committee for the Drafting of the National Constitution) *272*, ed., *Ts'ao-hsien pien-lan* (A Guide to Constitutional Drafting) (Peking, 1925), Part 3, pp. 2-4; Part 4, p. 28; Wu Ching-hsiung [John C. H. Wu] and Huang Kung-chüeh, *Chung-kuo chih-hsien shih* (A History of Constitution-making in China) (Shanghai, 1937), Sec. 3, p. 53; Ch'en Ju-hsüan, *Chung-kuo hsien-fa shih* (A History of the Chinese Constitution) (Shanghai, 1933), Chap. V, p. 51.

9. For an interesting description of the ceremony, see Paul S. Reinsch *707*, *An American Diplomat in China* (Garden City, 1922), Chap. III, pp. 26-27. See also Pai Chiao, *Yüan Shih-k'ai yü Chung-hua min-kuo* (Yüan Shih-k'ai and the Republic of China) (Shanghai, 1936), p. 162.

10. Pan-su, Chronological Records of the Important Events of China, p. 162.

11. Reinsch *707*, *An American Diplomat in China*, Chap. III, p. 23.

12. K'ang Yu-wei *249*, A Proposed Draft Constitution for the Republic of China (2nd printing; Shanghai, 1916), pp. 1-5, 134-40; originally published in *Pu-jen* (Compassion), No. 3 (Shanghai, April 1913), pp. 1-54, written in 1898-99. Most of K'ang's writings on Confucian problems may be found in this monthly. Ch'en Tu-hsiu *57*, "Refutation of K'ang Yu-wei's Letter to the President [Li Yüan-hung] and the Premier [Tuan Ch'i-jui]," New Youth, II, 2 (Oct. 1, 1916).

13. K'ang Yu-wei *249*, A Proposed Draft Constitution, pp. 135-36.

14. *Ibid.*, p. 140.

15. Wu Ching-hsiung and Huang Kung-chüeh, A History of Constitution-making in China, Part I, Chap. II, p. 64.

16. See Ch'en Tu-hsiu, "Yüan Shih-k'ai fu-huo" ("The Resurrection of Yüan Shih-k'ai"), New Youth, II, 4 (Dec. 1, 1916).

17. Ch'en Tu-hsiu 49, "Call to Youth," New Youth, I, 1 (Sept. 15, 1915), p. 5.

18. Ch'en-Tu-hsiu 63, "Differences of Basic Thought between the Eastern and Western Peoples," ibid., 4 (Dec. 15, 1915), pp. 2-4.

19. Ch'en Tu-hsiu 48, "The Principles of Education of Today," ibid., 2 (Oct. 15, 1915), pp. 3-4.

20. See Li I-min, "Jen-sheng wei-i chih mu-ti" '("The Sole Aim of Life"), ibid.; and Kao I-han 225, "Utilitarianism and Life," ibid., II, 1 (Sept. 1, 1916).

21. Chen Tu-hsiu 49, "Call to Youth," p. 2.

22. Chen Tu-hsiu, trans., "Ya-mei-li-chia (Mei-kuo kuo-ko)" ("America—the American National Hymn"), ibid., I, 2 (Oct. 15, 1915).

23. Liu Shu-ya, trans., "Mei-kuo-jen chih tzu-yu ching-shen" ("The Spirit of Liberty in the American Colonies") (from Burke's speech "Conciliation with America"), ibid., 6 (Feb. 15, 1916).

24. See Kao I-han 253, "The Republic and the Self-awakening of Youth," ibid., 1 (Sept. 15, 1915); and his 257, "Self-government and Freedom," ibid., 5 (Jan. 15, 1916).

25. Ch'en Tu-hsiu, "Fa-lan-hsi-jen yü chin-tai wen-ming" ("The French and Modern Civilization"), ibid., I, 1 (Sept. 15, 1915); Kao I-han, trans., "Tai-hsüeh Yin-kuo yen-lun tzu-yu chih ch'üan-li lun" ("A. V. Dicey's Discussion on the Right of Freedom of Speech in Great Britain") [from Chap. VI of his The Law of the Constitution], ibid., 6 (Feb. 15, 1916).

26. Kao I-han 253, "The Republic and the Self-awakening of Youth," p. 7.

27. Kao I-han 254, "State Is Not the Final Goal of Life," New Youth, I, 4 (Dec. 15, 1915); also Ch'en Tu-hsiu 48, "The Principles of Education Today," ibid., I, 2 (Oct. 15, 1915), pp. 4-5; and his 54, "The Year 1916," ibid., I, 5 (Jan. 1916), p. 3.

28. Ch'en Tu-hsiu 63, "Differences of Basic Thought between Eastern and Western Peoples," pp. 1-2.

29. Hu Shih 209, "Ibsenism," New Youth, IV, 6 (June 15, 1918), p. 497. Hu conceded that Ibsen's individualism was one of the most fundamental principles of his (Hu's) view of life and his religion. See his 200, "An Introduction to My Own Thought," preface (written on Nov. 27, 1930) to Selected Essays of Hu Shih, pp. 8-10.

30. Ibid., p. 502.

31. See Wang Shu-ch'ien 494, "The Problem of the New and the Old," New Youth, I, 1 (Sept. 1, 1915), p. 3; I Pai-sha, "Shu Mo" ("A Study of Motzu"), ibid., 2 (Oct. 15, 1915) and 5 (Jan. 15, 1916).

32. Ch'en Tu-hsiu, "The French and Modern Civilization," pp. 2-3.

33. Wu Chih-hui, "Ch'ing-nien yü kung-chü" ("Youth and Tools"), New Youth, II, 2 (Oct. 1, 1916); "Tsai lun kung-chü ("Second Essay on Tools"), ibid., 3 (Nov. 1, 1916).

34. Wu Chih-hui 510, "A New Conception of the Universe and of Life, Based Upon a New Belief," in Wu Chih-hui's Academic Works and Other Essays (Shanghai, 1925, 1926), p. 118.

35. Hu Shih 200, "An Introduction to My Own Thought," p. 3.

36. Georg Brandes, Main Currents in Nineteenth Century Literature (New York, 1905), III, 57.

37. Ch'en Tu-hsiu 58, "On Iconoclasm," New Youth, V, 2 (Aug. 15, 1918), p. 91; see also [Chu] Chih-hsin 128, "Inviolable Sacredness and Iconoclasm," Chien-she (The Construction), I, 1 (Shanghai, Aug. 1, 1919), pp. 169-72.

38. Ch'en Tu-hsiu 48, "The Principles of Education Today," p. 5.

39. Li I-min, "The Sole Aim of Life," pp. 2-3.

40. Li Ta-chao 298, "Youth," New Youth, II, 1 (Sept. 1, 1916); "Chin" ("The Present"), ibid., IV, 4 (April 15, 1918), pp. 307-10.

41. Hu Shih's article 219, "Experimentalism [or Pragmatism]," New Youth, VI, 4 (April 1, 1919); the next issue (May 1) was the special one on Marxism; see also above, Chap. IX.

42. Li Ta-chao 303, "My View on Marxism," New Youth, VI, 5 (May 1919), p. 536.

43. Ibid., p. 533.

44. Ibid., p. 534.

45. Ibid., p. 537.

46. Hu Han-min 188, "A Criticism of Criticism of Historical Materialism," The Construction, I, 5 (Dec. 1919), reprinted in Hu Han-min A Study of the Historical Conception of Materialism and Ethics, ed. Huang Ch'ang-ku (Shanghai 1927), pp. 1-61.

47. Hu Han-min 187, "A Materialistic Study of the History of Chinese Philosophy," The Construction, I, 3 (Oct. 1919) and the following issues; also in Hu Han-min 188, A Study of the Historical Conception of Materialism and Ethics, pp. 63-153. Tai Chi-t'ao's retrans-

lation from Japanese of most of Kautsky's book, which was given the Chinese title "Ma-k'e-ssu Tzu-pen-lun chieh-shao" ("Introduction to Marx's *Capital*") appeared in The Construction, I, 4 (Nov. 1, 1919), pp. 811-21, and the following issues. The translation was later completed by Hu Han-min and published in book form in Shanghai in 1927. (Kautsky's book was written before his split with the orthodox Communists).

48. Li Ta-chao *304*, "Material Change and Ethical Change," New Tide, II, 2 (Dec. 1919), pp. 207-24; and his *305*, "An Economic Interpretation of the Cause of Changes in Modern Chinese Thought," New Youth, VII, 2 (Jan. 1, 1920), pp. 47-53. See also Benjamin Schwartz *735*, *Chinese Communism and the Rise of Mao* (Cambridge, Mass., 1951), Chap. I, pp. 17, 23-24. Ho Kan-chih considered Li Ta-chao's latter article as the first by a Chinese to survey intellectual history in the light of Materialism. He did not mention Hu Han-min. See Ho's *170*, History of the Chinese Enlightenment (Shanghai, 1947), Chap. IV, p. 117.

49. Benjamin Schwartz *735*, *Chinese Communism and the Rise of Mao*, Chap. II, pp. 32-33.

50. See above, Chap. IX, n. k.

51. See below, Chap. XII, n. j.

52. Wu Yü, "Letter to Ch'en Tu-hsiu," New Youth, II, 5 (Jan. 1, 1917), pp. 3-4.

53. Yi Pai-sha *554*, "A Discussion of Confucius," Part I, New Youth, I, 6 (Feb. 15, 1916).

54. Part II, *ibid.*, II, 1 (Sept. 1, 1916).

55. Ch'en Tu-hsiu, "Ti-k'ang li" ("The Force of Resistance"), *ibid.*, I, 3 (Nov. 15, 1915), p. 4; also *63*, "Differences of Basic Thought between Eastern and Western Peoples," *ibid.*, 4 (Dec. 15, 1915), p. 1.

56. *Ibid.*, pp. 1-2. Also Ch'en Tu-hsiu *55*, "Confucius' Principles and Modern Life," *ibid.*, II, 4 (Dec. 1, 1916), p 3; and his *54*, "The Year 1916," p. 3.

57. Ch'en Tu-hsiu *67*, "Our Final Awakening," New Youth, I, 6 (Feb. 15, 1916), p. 4.

58. Ch'en Tu-hsiu *55*, "Confucius' Principles and Modern Life," New Youth, II, 4 (Dec. 1, 1916), pp. 3-4.

59. *Ibid.*, p. 4.

60. Ch'en Tu-hsiu *55*, "Confucius' Principles and Modern Life," pp. 3-4.

61. Ch'en Tu-hsiu *57*, "Refutation of K'ang Yu-wei's Letter to the President [Li Yüan-hung] and Premier [Tuan ch'i-jui]," p. 2; also

Ch'en *61*, "One More Discussion of the Problem of Confucianism," New Youth, II, 5 (Jan. 1, 1917), pp. 1-2.

62. Ch'en Tu-hsiu, "Letter in Reply to Wu Yü," *ibid.*, p. 4:

63. Ch'en Tu-hsiu, "Letter in Reply to Ch'ang Nai-te," *ibid.*, 4 (Dec. 1, 1916), pp. 5-6; *ibid.*, 6 (Feb. 1, 1917), p. 10. According to Ch'en a contemporary writer, Ku Shih, was one of the apologists for Confucius at the expense of the Neo-Confucianists of the Sung dynasty. See also Ch'en *51*, "The Constitution and Confucianism," *ibid.*, 3 (Nov. 1, 1916), pp. 3-5.

64. Wu Yü, "Letter to Ch'en Tu-hsiu," *ibid.*, 5 (Jan. 1, 1917), p. 3. For a preliminary study of the early Confucian ethical principle, *li,* see Chow Tse-tsung, "Hsün-tzu li yüeh lun fa-wei" (An Introduction to Hsün-tzu's Theory of *Li* and *Yüeh*), *Hsüeh-shu shih-chieh* (Academic World), II, 3 (Shanghai, Jan. 1937), pp. 69-71; 4 (April 1937), pp. 61-66.

65. See Wu Yü *528*, "The Old Family and Clan System is the Basis of Despotism," New Youth, II, 6 (Feb. 1, 1917), pp. 1-2. For a bibliography concerning the problem of authorship and time of the *Book of Filial Piety* see n. 4 of William Hung, "A Bibliographical controversy at the T'ang Court, A.D. 719," in *Harvard Journal of Asiatic Studies*, XX, 1-2 (June 1957), p. 99.

66. Ch'eng Hao's comment on "Tseng-tzu ta hsiao p'ien" (Tseng-tzu's Inquiry of Filial Piety") of the *Ta-tai chi*, or *Ta-tai li,* a work attributed to the Han dynasty Confucian scholar, Tai Te; see also Wu Yü, "Shuo hsiao" ("On Filial Piety"), in *531*, Collected Essays of Wu Yü (6th printing; Shanghai, 1921, 1929), pp. 15-16.

67. *Ibid.*, pp. 1-2.

68. *Ibid.*, p. 17.

69. *Ibid.*, pp. 19-20.

70. Ibid., pp. 19-23.

71. See Herbert Allen Giles, *Confucianism and Its Rivals* (London, 1915), p. 86. Confucius' remark on the story is in *Analects*, Bk. XIII, Chap. XVIII. See also the translations by James Legge and Arthur Waley.

72. See Bertrand Russell *729*, *The Problem of China* (London, 1922), Chap. II, 40.

73. Wu Yü, "Tao-chia Fa-chia fan-tui chiu tao-te shuo" ("An Explanation of the Fact That the Taoists and Legalists Were All Opposed to the Old Ethics"), in Wu *531*, Collected Essays, pp. 4-41.

74. See Shih Ts'un-t'ung, "Fei hsiao" (Oppose Filial Piety"), *Che-chiang hsin-ch'ao* (The Chekiang New Tide), No. 2 (Hangchow, Nov. 8, 1919); also "Pei-t'ing ch'a-chin *Che-chiang hsin-ch'ao* tien" ("The Peking Government's Telegram to Suppress the *Chekiang New Tide*"), *Min-kuo jih-pao* (Republic Daily) (Shanghai, Dec. 15, 1919); and [Shih] Ts'un-t'ung, "Hui-t'ou k'an erh-shih-erh nien lai ti o" ("A Retrospect of My Past Twenty-two Years"), *ibid.* (Sept. 23, 1920), in its supplementary magazine, *Chüeh-wu* (Awakening), pp. 20-24. See also Ts'ao Chü-jen *469*, Three Recollections of the Literary Circles (Hong Kong, 1954), pp. 9-57.

75. Wu Yü *530*, "Disadvantages of Confucianists' Advocacy of the Caste System," New Youth, III, 4 (June 1, 1917), p. 1.

76. Wu Yü, "Hsiao-chi ke-ming chih Lao Chuang" ("The Passive Revolutionists Lao-tzu and Chuang-tzu"), *ibid.*, 2 (April 1, 1917), p. 1.

77. Wu Yü, "Ju-chia ta-t'ung chih i pen-yü Lao-tzu shuo" ("The Confucian Conception of One World Originated in Lao-tzu"), *ibid.*, 5 (July 1, 1917), pp. 1-3; Wu Yü, "Letter to Ch'en Tu-hsiu" and Ch'en's reply, *ibid.*, pp. 4-5.

78. Hu Shih, "*Wu Yü wen-lu hsü*" ("Preface to the *Collected Essays of Wu Yü*"), written on June 16, 1921, in *531*, The Collected Essays of Wu Yü, pp. 5-7.

79. Lu Hsün *348*, "The Diary of a Madman," New Youth, IV, 5 (May 15, 1918), pp. 414-24, reprinted in *Na-han* (Cries) (Shanghai, 1923), pp. 13-22.

80. From *Tso Chuan*, "Hsi-kung chiu nien" [651 B.C.]; and *Han Fei Tzu*, Vol. II, Chap. VII, "Erh-ping"; Vol. III, Chap. X, "Shih ko"; and Vol. XV Chap. XXXVI, "Nan-i" cited in Wu Yü *529*, "Cannibalism and [the Traditional Chinese] Ethics," New Youth, VI, 6 (Nov. 1, 1919), p. 578.

81. From "Biography of Ching Pu," in Ssu-ma Ch'ien's *Shih-chi* (Historical Records), cited in Wu Yü *529*, "Cannibalism and Ethics," New Youth VI, 6, p. 579.

82. "Biographies of the Loyal and Righteous," in Ou-yang Hsiu and others, comps., *Hsin T'ang-shu* (The New History of the T'ang Dynasty), cited in Wu Yü *529*, "Cannibalism and Ethics," New Youth, VI, 6, p. 580.

83. [T'ang] Ssu (another of Lu Hsün's pen names), "Sui-kan lu" ("Random Thoughts"), No. 36 *ibid.*, V, 5 (Nov. 15, 1918), p. 514.

84. T'ang Ssu, "Random Thoughts," No. 35, *ibid.*, pp. 513-14. Cf. Lin Yutang's English translation in *The Wisdom of China and India* (New York, 1942), p. 1089.

85. T'ang Ssu, "Random Thoughts," No. 46, New Youth, VI, 2 (Feb. 15, 1919), p. 212.

86. *Ibid.*, p. 213, trans. Lin Yutang, *The Wisdom of China and India*, p. 1090.

87. *Ibid.*

88. In *Nü-shen* (The Goddesses), his collected poems, first published in Shanghai, Aug. 1921; reprinted in Peking, 1953.

89. See Kuo Mo-jo, *Hsin-Hua sung* (In Praise of New China [collected poems]) (Peking, 1953).

90. Lu Hsün, "Lao tiao-tzu i-ching ch'ang wan" ("The Old Tune Has Been Sung Enough"), a speech delivered in Hong Kong on Feb. 19, 1927, in *349*, Lu Hsün hsüan-chi (Selected Works of Lu Hsün) (Peking, 1952), p. 666; see also Ho Kan-chih *171*, A Study of Lu Hsün's Thought (rev. ed.; Peking, 1940, 1950), I, 23-24.

91. "The Old Tune Has Been Sung Enough"; cf. the translation by Lin Yutang, *The Wisdom of China and India*, p. 1089.

92. The stories were collected by him into 2 volumes, titled *Na-han* (Cries) (Peking, 1923) and *P'ang-huang* (Hesitation) (Peking, 1926). Most of his short commentaries concerning the period of the May Fourth Movement were reprinted in *Je feng* (Hot Wind) (Peking, 1925) and *Fen* (The Grave) (Peking 1927).

93. Hsü Mou-yung, "Lu Hsün hsien-sheng yü i pi" ("Another Comparison with Lu Hsün), cited in Wang Shih-ching *491*, Biography of Lu Hsün (Shanghai, 1949), Chap. X, p. 504.

94. Edgar Snow, "The Chinese Voltaire," cited *ibid.*, pp. 504-05.

95. Confucius was hailed by Kuo Mo-jo as a revolutionary in his *Shih p'i-p'an shu* (Ten Critiques of Ancient Chinese Thoughts) (Chungking, 1945). We may also note Yi Pai-sha's article in New Youth, cited above. H. C. Creel tried to prove that Confucian theory has influenced Western democratic thinkers such as Voltaire, Leibniz, Quesnay, Franklin, and Jefferson; see his *603*, Confucius, the Man and the Myth (New York, 1949), Chap. XV, pp. 254-78.

96. Bertrand Russell *729*, *The Problem of China*, Chap. II, pp. 38-44, esp. p. 41.

97. *Ibid.*, p. 40.

98. *Ibid.*, p. 47.

II. LI TA-CHAO'S INFLUENCE ON MAO TSE-TUNG

24. LI TA-CHAO AND THE ORIGINS OF CHINESE COMMUNISM

MAURICE MEISNER

Today Li Ta-chao is honored in China as the most heroic of revolutionary martyrs. In Communist historical writings he is treated as the real leader of the May Fourth movement, the pioneer of Marxism in China, and the true founder of the Chinese Communist party. In such writings Li's role in modern Chinese history is magnified beyond its real proportions, although never so much as to dim the luster of Mao Tse-tung in the areas in which the latter was also involved. In the glorification of Li Ta-chao and the vilification of Ch'en Tu-hsiu, there is reflected more than the obvious political need to find heroes and heretics, for Li was the forerunner of those revolutionary voluntaristic tendencies and nationalistic impulses that have since governed the Maoist version of Marxism-Leninism, whereas Ch'en represented the internationalistic and Westernizing Marxist influences that were to perish in the Chinese environment.

There is no way to know for certain

From Maurice Meisner, *Li Ta-chao and the Origins of Chinese Marxism* (Harvard University Press), pp. 261-266, 298. Copyright, 1967 by the President and Fellows of Harvard College. Reprinted by permission. The author is associate professor of history at the University of Wisconsin, Madison, Wisconsin.

how much of the young Mao Tse-tung's intellectual orientation was derived from the ideas and writings of Li Ta-chao, for those who claim to have made historic and universally valid innovations in theory are reluctant to acknowledge intellectual debts, even in the rare cases where they are fully conscious of such debts. Yet it seems highly likely, as Stuart Schram has argued in his excellent study of Mao's intellectual development, that Mao's ideas in his formative years were shaped in large measure by the ideas of Li. Li not only introduced Mao to Marxist theory in the winter of 1918-1919, when Mao served as assistant to the librarian of Peking National University, but he also communicated to Mao his own particular version of Marxism and his chiliastic feelings on the significance of the October Revolution. Nor is it likely that Mao was uninfluenced by the heretical Populist notions intermingled with Li's Marxist ideas, particularly Li's passionate appeals in 1919 for young intellectuals to leave the cities and devote their energies to the liberation of the peasantry in the countryside. Mao did not rediscover the peasantry until 1925, but as Schram has suggested, "Li Ta-chao in 1919 may well have started him on the road to that rediscovery."[1]

The earliest political writings of the young Mao Tse-tung, published in mid-1919, faithfully echoed the nationalist, Populist, and Bolshevik ideas of his teacher. A belief that the whole Chinese nation was essentially united against its external oppressors, a faith in the "intrinsic energy" of the Chinese people, an affirmation of the historic greatness and future glory of the Chinese nation, and a chiliastic feeling that the Bolshevik Revolution was a "great tide" about to sweep over the world—such were the notions that Mao derived from Li in 1919.[2] In the years thereafter Mao's treatment of Marxist theory followed closely the pattern set by Li. In the hands of both the deterministic laws of Marxism were to bend, and eventually break, before an inexhaustible faith in the power of the human will and consciousness to shape historical reality. Neither was willing to allow predetermined levels of social and economic development to restrict opportunities for immediate revolutionary action. In fact, the very absence of the objective prerequisites for socialism seemed to demand that the Chinese exert ever greater energies to achieve those prerequisites, and both treated the situation as an advantage that would enable China to move all the more rapidly to the socialist utopia of the future.

Both Li and Mao felt the need to find objective Marxist correlatives for what was basically a subjective system of revolutionary values, and both drew from the materialist conception of history the assurance of the inevitability of socialism. But their socialist faith was ultimately based not upon confidence in the workings of the objective laws of social development, but rather upon confidence in their abilities to bring forth the powerful subjective forces latent in the present

—the great storehouses of "surplus energy" that Li argued had been accumulating in China over the centuries. The ideas, the wills, and the "self-consciousness" of men would really determine the course of Chinese history.

These activistic and voluntaristic impulses were inspired by and also reinforced even more deeply rooted nationalistic impulses. For Mao, as well as for Li, the salvation and rebirth of the Chinese nation was the major concern, but it was to be a socialist rebirth, China's precapitalist social and economic structure notwithstanding, for China was not to be allowed to fall behind in the progressive march of history. It was to achieve this rebirth that both undertook to transform Marxist doctrine. In the process of the transformation the internationalist and cosmopolitan content of the original doctrine gave way to a messianic nationalism, which saw China not only fully qualified to join the forces of international socialism but destined to play a special role in the world revolution.

The combination of revolutionary voluntarism and Chinese nationalism made for a curious dichotomy in both Li's and Mao's vision of the rebirth of China. Although their confidence in this rebirth was based upon their faith in the energies of the people, particularly the youth, who were to write a new Chinese history in accordance with the new Marxist ideals and values which had come from the West, this very real rejection of the values of old China was accompanied by a nationalistic attachment to Chinese traditions and a feeling of pride in the glories of the Chinese past.

The combination of voluntarism and nationalism was also reflected in their treatment of the concept of class struggle, the theoretical area most directly related to political practice. Both Li and Mao promoted class struggle in theory as well as in practice. However, they drew from Marx's theory more the notion of struggle than the need to analyze political situations upon the basis of objective social class criteria. "Proletarian consciousness" was more important than the proletariat itself. Li was quite explicit in attributing a latent proletarian consciousness to the entire Chinese nation by virtue of China's "proletarian" status in the international capitalist economy, and this idea was implicit in Mao's thesis that the major contest was not so much within China as between the Chinese nation and foreign imperialism. These notions reflected not only the voluntarist's impatience with the economic forces of history and his impulse to carry out the proletarian revolution, even without the actual proletariat if need be, but also the willingness of the Chinese nationalist to abandon the only progressive social class in Chinese society that had been formed in the image of the West and instead look to broader, "national" sources of revolution.

It perhaps matters little how much of his ideology Mao Tse-tung derived directly from Li Ta-chao. Without Li, Mao might have arrived at much the same ideas and followed the same ideological and political path. What is important, however, is that the immersion of Marxism in the Chinese environment gave rise to their particular intellectual and ideological orientations, and that those orientations were intimately related to the political strategies that brought the Chinese Communist party to power.

This close relationship between politics and ideology was apparent in the striking parallels between Li's and Mao's political positions in the years before 1927. Like Li, Mao was an enthusiastic, not a reluctant, supporter of the alliance with the Kuomintang, for he too looked to the revolutionary energies of the whole nation rather than of a single social class, and eventually both Li and Mao abandoned that particular united front to embrace the elemental forces of peasant revolt. In the mid-1920's Mao probably did not look to Li for political leadership as he had looked to him for intellectual guidance in 1919, but their advocacy of similar political strategies followed from similar intellectual and ideological assumptions.

On the basis of these two elements of revolutionary strategy that appeared before 1927—the united front and, especially, peasant revolution—the Chinese Communist party was eventually to triumph. In the application of these very general strategies Mao developed a variety of particular innovations that were essential to the Communist success. Although it may be true, as has often been noted, that Mao's real innovations lay in the realm of political strategy and tactics rather than in the realm of Marxist theory, what is frequently ignored are the intellectual and ideological elements that were the prerequisites for those innovations. It was not predetermined that Communism would come to power in China upon a wave of peasant revolt —or indeed that it would come to power at all. Even if it is assumed that the peasant risings that began in the mid-1920's were entirely spontaneous in character (an historically erroneous assumption), the ability fully to appreciate the forces of peasant revolt and the willingness to build Communist revolutionary strategy upon a purely peasant foundation required certain general but fundamental theoretical perspectives and intellectual orientations. Some Chinese

Communists were able to entertain this possibility; others were not.

The reasons why Li Ta-chao was willing to abandon the Western-influenced cities and the proletariat for the Chinese countryside also applied to Mao Tse-tung. Mao was a better student of Leninist organizational techniques and methods of manipulating mass movements. He was also more concerned than Li had been with maintaining at least the appearance of doctrinal orthodoxy. However, essentially the same voluntaristic interpretation of Marxism, the same nationalistic impulses, and a similar Populist emphasis on the inherent unity of the people governed the thought of Mao Tse-tung as had governed Li Ta-chao's. These ideological factors were essential preconditions for the development of the Maoist strategy of peasant revolution.

There is, of course, that peculiarly deterministic variety of contemporary social science theory that tends to see the Chinese Communists as little more than playthings in the hands of vaster and deeper social forces. To the practitioners of this "science" the ideological tendencies that have been considered in this study will seem of little moment, for they are convinced that history can be analyzed without inquiring into the ideas and emotions of the men who made that history. For such practitioners, the nationalist aspect of Chinese Communism, for example, might appear as no more than the function of the Communist party's inevitable immersion in a rural environment. Yet the Chinese Communists who went to the countryside were profoundly nationalistic long before they left the cities. In fact, a particular kind of nationalistic predisposition drew them to the peasantry. The rural environment no doubt reinforced this nationalism, but no less important was the role played by the Communists in transforming the innate antiforeign feelings of the Chinese peasantry into genuine nationalist feelings. "Mass nationalism" was not something that welled up from the elemental forces of the countryside and eventually reached Mao Tse-tung and his associates. It is more historically accurate to say that nationalism was brought to the peasants from without by an ardently nationalistic elite intent upon shaping history in accordance with its ideals.

Li Ta-chao did not live to see the triumph of the Communist movement that he had founded, but he did much to mold the ideological orientations that guided his successors to that triumph. He could hardly have objected to the unorthodox strategy by which Mao Tse-tung reached power, for he had pioneered in promoting the general outlines of that strategy. He might not have found in Communist China the "truly human life" that he had thought a Marxist revolution would bring, but he would have been more than fully satisfied with the resurgence of the Chinese nation and the power of the Chinese Communist state, for the notion of the rebirth of a "young China" had always been at the emotional core of his entire world view.

Notes

1. Stuart R. Schram, *The Political Thought of Mao Tse-tung* (New York, 1963), pp. 14-19.

2. See the extracts from Mao's essay "The Great Union of the Popular Masses" that appeared in July 1919 in *Hsiang-chiang p'ing-lun*, a journal of which Li was an editor. Schram, pp. 105-106.

III. THE MAOIST STRATEGY

25. Essential Features of the Maoist Strategy

BENJAMIN I. SCHWARTZ

It is not the purpose of this book to treat the history of the Soviet period or of the New Democracy period which followed it. If I nevertheless presume to discuss the essential features of Maoism at this point it is because of my conviction that these features lie not in the sphere of theory but in the sphere of strategy and that the basic elements of this strategy were already formed by the time Mao Tse-tung had achieved a position of leadership within the Chinese Communist movement. While this strategy does indeed have profound implications for Marxist-Leninist doctrine, they are implications which are never made explicit in theory. On the contrary, every effort is made in the theoretical sphere to conceal these implications.

THE MAOIST STRATEGY

Essentially, the Maoist strategy involves the imposition of a political party organized in accordance with Leninist principles and animated by faith in certain basic tenets of Marxism-Leninism onto a purely peasant mass base.

From Benjamin I. Schwartz, *Chinese Communism and the Rise of Mao* (Harvard University Press, Cambridge, Mass.), pp. 188-204, 238. Copyright, 1951 by the President and Fellows of Harvard College. Reprinted by permission. The author is professor of history at Harvard University.

While this is the heart of the strategy, more specific features were evolved in the course of the experiences in Hunan during the 1926-1927 period and the experiences of the autumn harvest uprising. It can, however, be stated that the basic features are already present in a report written by Mao as early as 1928. In his Report of the Chingkanshan Front Committee to the Central Committee,[1] Mao enumerates the conditions necessary for the maintenance and development of "separate armed Soviet bases." The first condition is the existence of "a strong mass base." Although it is not specified, the mass base is, of course, to be a peasant mass base. These peasant masses are to be won by a program of land reform designed to satisfy the basic grievances of the bulk of the peasantry within the areas under Communist control. The second condition is the existence of a strong party, that is, of a party leadership organized along the lines prescribed by Lenin. The third is the existence of a strong Red Army for, in an environment in which military power was decisive, a Soviet base could survive only by possessing its own military force. The fourth condition is the control of a strategically located territorial base, and the fifth condition is that the area in question be self-sufficient enough to maintain its population. Remembering his experiences in the autumn harvest uprising, Mao lays particular stress on the possession of a "central, solid base" and repudiates charges of the Central Committee that the insistence on the maintenance of such a base is an expression of "conservatism."[2]

Another peculiar feature of the Maoist strategy already mentioned in the report is the preference for "border area" bases; that is, bases from which it would be possible "to influence both provinces."[3] "The Red Army must resolve to carry on its battles in border areas where it must have sufficient fortitude to carry on sustained warfare . . . If the Red Army is able to sustain itself in these border areas its reputation will spread throughout the surrounding countryside and even among the troops of the enemy. This will create a favorable atmosphere for its advance into the surrounding areas."[4]

Thus we see that the Maoist strategy was based not only on an insight into the revolutionary potentialities of the peasantry but also on the realization that in a country where centralized authority had been destroyed and only precariously reëstablished, state power was weakest in the vast swamplike countryside, in those areas furthest removed from centers of administrative and military power.

The main tasks of the Red Army within the context of this strategy were succintly summarized by Mao in his interview with Edgar Snow. "The main tasks of the Red Army," he said, "were the recruiting of new troops, the Sovietization of new rural areas, and above all, the consolidation under thorough Soviet power of such areas as already had fallen to the Red Army."[5]

Such, I think, are the main lines of the strategy which, *in conjunction with favorable external circumstances,* was finally to lead the Chinese Communist movement to victory.

What, then, are the implications of this strategy for Marxist-Leninist dogma?

THE MAOIST STRATEGY AND MARXIST-LENINIST DOGMA

Officially, of course, there was no break whatsoever between the Comintern line, as fixed in the November 16 letter of the ECCI and in the Resolutions of the Fourth Plenum, and the theoretical line of the Chinese Communist movement during the whole Soviet period. Actually, however, the gravitation of power into the Soviet areas marked almost the total severance of the Chinese Communist party from its supposed urban proletarian base. It was the beginning of a heresy in act never made explicit in theory. Chinese Communism in its Maoist development demonstrates in fact that a communist party organized along Leninist lines and imbued with a sincere faith in certain basic Marxist-Leninist tenets can exist quite apart from any organic connection with the proletariat. The experience of Chinese Communism thus casts a doubt on the whole organic conception of the relation of party to class.

This is, however, a doubt which neither the Chinese Communist movement nor the Kremlin can tolerate, for it is a doubt which strikes at the very heart of the legitimization of power within the Leninist framework. The extraordinary and total power which the Communist Party arrogates to itself and the infallibility which it ascribes to itself are justified entirely on the ground that it is the head of a social organism the body of which is the proletariat, the class destined by history to inherit the earth as well as to grasp ultimate absolute truth.

In the words of the Hungarian Communist theoretician, Lukacs, the activity of the Communist Party "is not an activity representing the class but the focalization of the activity of the class itself."[6] Elsewhere, he states that the Communists are "the class consciousness of the proletariat which has taken on visible form."[7] It has, however, always been considered a minimum guarantee of the identity of a communist party that it stand in some concrete relationship to a visible proletariat. Otherwise, it might easily lose its identity as a communist party. Most Communist literature suggests in fact, that the Communist Party is a peculiarly sensitive organ highly susceptible to infection from nonproletarian classes, even when its base is secure. The implication is clear that in isolation from the proletariat the Communist Party must lose its very identity.

If the ties between the Communist Party and its proletarian base are weak then it is the first and paramount duty of the party to strengthen these bonds lest the party lose its basis of existence. Nowhere in the whole body of Lenin's writings do we find a hint that the Communist Party can exist as an entity apart from its proletarian base.

We thus find that after 1931 it became one of the basic concerns of the Kremlin as well as of the Chinese Communist Party to conceal by every device possible the actual severance of the Chinese party from its proletarian base.

The process of devising such concealment devices had actually begun before Mao Tse-tung's final victory. While the Comintern and the Chinese leadership were straining every nerve to win back the urban proletariat, the "scissors" between the movement in the city and the movement in the country had of course become a fact long before the final victory of Mao. In his Report on the Third Plenum, Chou En-lai is forced to admit that the party has no more than two thousand proletarian members[8] (probably an exaggerated figure). Seizing upon this fact—and ignoring the intentions of the Comintern—Trotsky had as early as 1928 begun to flay the Comintern for the anomaly of supposedly Communist elements operating in a completely peasant environment in isolation from the urban proletariat.[9] In China, Ch'en Tu-hsiu had taken up the refrain. We have already seen how unhappy the Comintern and the Chinese leadership themselves had been about this state of affairs. They could not, however, allow Trotsky's accusation to go unanswered. Thus we find Manuilsky stating at the Sixteenth Congress of the Soviet Communist Party that "the third perculiarity [of the Chinese revolution] is that the Chinese revolution even before the final victory of the workers has at its disposal a Red Army. It is in possession of a considerable territory. At this very moment it is creating in this territory a Soviet system of workers' and peasants' power in whose government the Communists are in a majority. And this condition permits the proletariat to realize *not only an ideological but also a state hegemony over the peasantry*" (emphasis my own.)[10] This phrase was to be repeated over and over again in subsequent Chinese Communist literature as a defense against the charge that the movement lacked a proletarian base.

What does this phrase mean in essence? It can only mean that since the leaders of the Soviet areas are convinced Communists, since the Soviet areas are under the control of the Communist Party, that is in itself a guarantee of proletarian hegemony. Trotsky answers this claim most incisively from the solid ground of orthodoxy. "In what way," he asks, "can the proletariat realize state hegemony over the peasantry when state power is not in its hands? It is absolutely impossible to understand this. The leading role of isolated Communist groups in the peasant war does not decide the question of power. *Classes decide and not parties*" (emphasis my own).[11] This is the very crux of the matter. Manuilsky's phrase assumes that a political group held together by common convictions and organized as a communist party can initiate fundamental historic changes. Such a proposition strikes at the heart of even the most "sophisticated" versions of Marxism-Leninism. Was this not one of the issues which had divided Marx from the utopian socialists? It was not simply that the utopian socialists thought that socialism could be implemented when objective conditions were not ripe for socialism, but also their belief that small groups of men with benevolent ideas could realize these ideas when actually only economic classes could act as the instruments of history. Neither Marx nor Lenin could in the nature of things deny that well-intentioned men of nonproletarian origin could become identified with the proletariat but both would have strenuously denied that they could become identified simply by an act of faith in the absence of any actual ties to the proletariat. To believe that the "vanguard of the proletariat" can exist without a main force in the rear is to grant political power a role in human history which Marxism-Leninism cannot allow.

Discussing this problem in her book *Inside Red China* Nym Wales remarks that "the Chinese Communists seem to consider their party itself equivalent to direct participation by the proletariat."[12] This, of course, is another version of the Manuilsky formula. Is the subjective conviction of the Chinese Communist leaders that they are the bona fide representatives of the proletariat sufficient proof in terms of Marxist-Leninist doctrine of the validity of their claim? How then are Communist subjective convictions to be weighed against those of Socialist Democrats or Syndicalists? To those standing outside the tradition, it may well seem that it is nothing more than such a subjective conviction (or pretense) which lies at the heart of the Communist faith everywhere. A Marxist-Leninist, however, cannot admit this. Theoretically, he must be able to show at least a minimum relationship between the Communist Party and the urban proletariat and must at all times make every effort to strengthen such relations.

Manuilsky's phrase is, however, not the only concealment device used to disguise the true state of affairs. Another common device is the equation of the "rural proletariat" with the proletariat proper. It has already been pointed out that while Lenin and Trotsky had advocated the absorption of the "rural poor" into the Communist Party, they had advocated it only on the condition that the "rural poor" be tied to a strong urban-based party. "Only the industrial proletariat," Lenin insisted, "led by the Communist Party, can liberate the toiling masses of the countryside from the yoke of capital."[13] The "rural proletariat" in isolation from the urban proletariat is essentially "petty bourgeois" in mentality, bitter against those with land but consumed by the desire to win for itself a foothold in landed property.

The constitution of the Soviet government drawn up at the All-China Soviet Conference in November 1931 contains an imposing series of labor laws, including ordinances regarding working hours, child and female labor, etc.[14] Many of these laws were obviously designed for the industrial proletariat. Under the conditions of the Soviet areas, they could only have a propaganda value by helping to create the impression of a proletarian base where none existed.

The Soviet government did indeed make strenuous efforts to establish labor unions based squarely on the "rural proletariat." In fact, most of the references to labor unions in the Soviet period refer to such unions. The peculiar difficulties which these unions confronted are graphically illustrated in a "Circular of the Standing Committee of the General Labor Federation" which appears in *Red Flag* of November 15, 1932.[15] The circular is essentially an attack on local union organizers who tend to set overstringent qualification requirements for union membership. Many of these organizers had formerly been organizers of industrial labor and were finding it most difficult in terms of their Marxist-Leninist precepts to classify large groups of the "rural poor" as bona fide proletarians. For one thing, many of these rural poor possessed their own tools, while one of the prime marks of the proletarian in the Marxist definition is his alienation from his means of production.[16] Furthermore, most of the rural proletarians worked on an individual basis now with one employer and now with another; in the view of the organizer, "independent laborers who sell their labor from house to house are not qualified to enter a labor union."[17] What was even more serious, the very land reforms effected by the Soviet government had served to "deproletarianize" many of the rural poor. The circular itself admits that 90 per cent of the workers in Hunan and Hupeh were landholding peasants who worked in their spare time.[18]

The Standing Committee of the General Labor Federation is not inclined, however to lose its *raison d'être* without further ado. "To set such requirements for entry into labor unions," it complains, "is simply to liquidate labor unions in the Soviet areas."[19] The mere possession of tools should not disqualify a candidate since the tools are not being used by these men for their own enterprise but in order to perform work for others. (In the view of Marx, the possession of tools by a producer whose labor is exploited by others is actually characteristic of precapitalist modes of production.) While their work may be independent and allotted among several employers, is it still exploited by others. (In the view of Marx, all pre-socialist systems—except of course primitive Communism—are characterized by exploitation.) Finally, workers should not be debarred simply because they own a plot of land. The land will merely serve to measure their loyalty to the revolution![20]

Now, while the labor-union form has been adopted throughout the world by occupations which are not strictly proletarian in the Marxist sense, in Chinese Communist literature the existence of labor unions in the Soviet areas is often cited as proof of the existence of a genuine proletariat in these areas. The factual data adduced in this "Circular" prove quite clearly that the rural workers with their fluid and nondescript economic status possessed few of those attributes which account for the revolutionary potentialities of the proletariat in the Marxist scheme.

Another device of concealment frequently used during the Soviet period was the constant emphasis on the "soviet" as a genuine proletarian political institution. After the abandonment of the soviet form in the "New Democracy" period, this earlier fetishism of the soviet was to prove a source of embarrassment. At the time, however, it was used as yet another proof of "proletarian hegemony" within the Soviet areas. The very fact, it was argued, that the Soviet government operated within the framework of the soviet was a visible sign of proletarian hegemony since the role played by that institution in the Soviet Union, the land of proletarian dictatorship, proved its fundamentally proletarian nature. "The very form of the soviet is a conquest of the Chinese proletariat"[21] states the introduction to the book *Soviets in China*. By focusing the history of the Chinese Communist movement on the institution of the soviet, it is possible to begin with the Canton Commune, an eminently proletarian phenomenon, and to pass imperceptibly as it were to the purely peasant soviets of the 1931-1935 period, thus casting a mist over the actual shift which has taken place. Thus we read in the introduction to *Soviets in China* that "the Soviet power in Canton in the December days of 1927, the Soviet republic in Hailufeng, the Soviets in Liling, and the victorious wave of the Soviet movement occupying the important provinces of south and central China were all organized and led by the Communists."[22]

Actually, of course, Lenin had not always thought of the soviets as an eminently proletarian institution. During the July days of 1917 he had even thought of abandoning the soviets. "The power can be seized henceforth," he declared, "only by armed insurrection. We must obviously rely in this operation not on soviets demoralized by compromisers but on factory committees." It was only after the Bolsheviks had won control of the soviets that they took on their sacred "proletarian" character. We know, however, that even after the revolution Lenin had speculated on the possibility of ap-

plying the form of soviets to "backward" lands of Asia where the proletariat was presumed not to exist at all.[23] The soviet was a form, he felt, which could be adapted to the psychology of a backward peasant society. It is somewhat curious to note that, in his polemics against Trotsky at the Eighth Plenum of the ECCI, Stalin had used this passage from Lenin in a rather sophistical attempt to prove that China did not need soviets. "Lenin," he said, "did not have in mind countries like China and India where a certain minimum of industrial proletariat exists . . . He rather had in mind other backward countries like Persia."[24] It is thus clear that there is no warrant in Communist tradition for considering the soviet form itself a proof of "proletarian hegemony." After the abandonment of the soviet form, of course, the Chinese Communists themselves were to bend every effort to prove that the soviet form was not a necessary vehicle of proletarian hegemony.

One of the most effective devices of all, from the point of view of its appeal to the emotions, is the use of Lenin's own polemical tactic of offense rather than defense. The Trotskyists, Social Democrats, and others who were raising embarrassing questions concerning the Chinese Communist Party's lack of a proletarian base did this, it was maintained, only in order to deliver China over to the bourgeoisie "because they wish to create a rift between the world proletariat and the Chinese proletariat. They wish to hide from the European proletarian the heroic history of the struggle of the Chinese proletariat for hegemony in the national movement of liberation."[25]

Now, however sinister the motives of the Trotskyists and Social Democrats might be, the question they raised still remained unanswered. The fact that the Chinese Communist Party carried on a truly heroic struggle against overwhelming odds in the hinterlands of Hunan and Kiangsi, and later in the northwest areas, might prove its heroic qualities of leadership. It does not, however, prove that the party had an urban proletarian base.

We thus find that the hard fact of the isolation of the Chinese Communist Party from the urban proletariat during all the years of its rise to power emerges, naked and irreducible, from behind all the devices of concealment used to hide it.

At present, of course, the Chinese Communist Party can once more claim a proletarian base. It is once more in contact with the urban industrial proletariat. Yet, the very circumstances under which the Communists finally achieved power throw a glaring light on the lack of relationship between the urban proletariat and the Chinese Communist Party. The Chinese urban proletariat—whatever its sympathies may have been—waited inertly and passively for the peasant troops to occupy the cities. It certainly played a much less active role than the students.

The fact that the Chinese Communist Party has existed for some twenty years without any significant connections with the industrial proletariat, and the fact that the industrial proletariat played no actual role in the consummation of the revolution, are circumstances which cannot be erased by the belated reunion of head and body. It has already been demonstrated that a communist party can exist quite apart from any real connection with the urban proletariat.

If the concealment devices used by the Kremlin and the Chinese Communists cannot bear scrutiny, what can be said of the Trotskyist interpretation of the de-velopment of Chinese Communism? There can be no doubt that from the point of view of Marxist-Leninist orthodoxy the Trotskyist position is unimpeachable. By severing itself from its urban proletarian base and tying itself to the peasantry, the Chinese Communist Party has ceased to be a party of the proletariat, for a political party can have no autonomous life of its own. In the words of Isaacs, "the Communist Party tried to substitute itself for the proletariat as a class. In the process, however, it was transformed into a peasant party."[26]

To what extent, however, does this allegation correspond to fact? Did the Chinese Communist Party indeed become a party of the peasants in the sense in which that word is used by Trotsky, Isaacs, and Ch'en Tu-hsiu? Such a view, I think, falsifies realities no less than the camouflage of the official line. There is no evidence that the aspirations and ambitions of the Communist Party leaders were at any time circumscribed by what Marxist-Leninists consider to be the peasant mentality or that they at any time aspired to achieve the "peasant socialism" advocated by the Russian *narodniki* who were considered the very archetype of the peasant party.

I would suggest that Chinese Communism in its Maoist development can simply not be understood within the narrow framework of Marxist-Leninist premises; that both the official and the Trotskyist interpretations obscure rather than illuminate the nature of the movement since 1931. The Chinese Communist Party under the leadership of Mao Tse-tung has not been the party of the industrial proletariat nor has it been the party of the peasantry in the Marxist-Leninist sense. It has rather been an elite corps of politically articulate leaders organized along Leninist lines but drawn

THE MAOIST STRATEGY   465

on its top levels from various strata of Chinese society. In her study of the background of seventy Chinese Communist leaders in the New Democracy period, Nym Wales finds that only seventeen per cent are proletarians. This percentage is probably obtained by stretching the meaning of the word "proletarian" well beyond its legitimate Marxist limits. She finds, however, that seventy per cent are *hsüeh-sheng* or "students from families of small farmers, professionals, merchants, and even aristocratic official families."[27] Under the leadership of Mao Tse-tung this elite group had come to realize in the face of Marxist-Leninist dogma that the peasantry could itself provide the mass basis and the motive power for a revolutionary transformation. This realization may owe much to the peasant background of such leaders as Mao Tse-tung. It would, however, be a grave error to assume that once having achieved power, the aspirations or intentions of the Communist leaders would necessarily be determined by their peasant background or by the interests of the peasantry. On the contrary, we have every reason to believe that these men had thoroughly absorbed the Leninist abhorrence of "backwardness" as well as the extravagant Marxist-Leninist belief in the potentialities of industrialization even when circumstances forced them to lurk in the hinterlands. Chinese Communism in its Maoist development can only be understood when—to modify Trotsky's phrase—we realize that parties *as well as* classes decide. The Chinese Communist Party under the leadership of Mao Tse-tung has been, I would suggest, neither "the vanguard of the proletariat" in the Marxist-Leninist sense, nor a "peasant party" in the Marxist-Leninist sense, but an elite of professional revolutionaries which has risen to power by basing itself on the dynamic of peasant discontent.

THE MAOIST STRATEGY AND THE PARTY LINE

We have chosen to draw a distinction between vital core pre-suppositions of Marxism-Leninism and the transient superficial elements of the shifting party lines. It has been suggested that the Maoist strategy represents a heresy in act toward one such vital pre-supposition. We should now like to consider briefly the relations of this strategy to the shifting party lines after 1931.

The shift of the center of power from Shanghai to Juichin was not accompanied by any change in party line on the part of the Kremlin. On the contrary, the Kremlin was most concerned to obscure the change which had taken place. Everything was done to maintain the appearance of a smooth continuity. On the other hand, the Mao leadership seemed quite content to pursue its strategy within the framework of the theoretical line formulated at the Fourth Plenum. We find little evidence at this time of any ambition on the part of Mao to create theoretical innovations within the Marxist-Leninist tradition.

The result was, of course, an utter lack of relation between theory and practice. Presumably, the political form of the bourgeois democratic revolution during the whole Soviet period was still the "democratic dictatorship of workers and peasants." We have already noted that this formula had already lost a great deal of its relevance as early as 1928 when it was decided that the proletariat—that is, the Communist Party—would exercise exclusive political hegemony within the dictatorship and that the peasantry would not be represented by a political party of its own.[28] With the establishment of the Soviet Provisional Government, the formula became completely meaningless. We have in the Soviet Republic a "democratic dictatorship of workers and peasants" in which the peasantry is allowed no political expression of its own and in which the party of the proletariat has no mass basis of its own.

While it would go beyond the scope of this book to consider the party line of the New Democracy period, it should nevertheless be pointed out that the shift to the New Democracy line involved no change in the basic Maoist strategy outlined above. I would suggest that the actual strategic shifts made in 1935 were more in the nature of shifts in "foreign policy" than shifts in basic strategy. At no time during the New Democracy period do we find any inclination on the part of the Yenan leadership to renounce its territorial base, its actual control of its own armed forces, or its tendency to infiltrate "border areas." The changes in agrarian policy do not contradict this contention for it has nowhere been implied that a fixed agrarian policy was a basic feature of the Maoist strategy. The change from the "soviet" to the "assembly" with its allotment of representation to other parties is overridden by the basic fact that fundamental decisions of policy were made by neither the "soviets" nor the "assemblies" but by the Communist Party itself. The fact that the New Democracy period is marked by a statesmanlike regard for local initiative and by a marked decline in the use of force as an instrument of policy represents a refinement in strategy rather than a basic modification of it.

While the New Democracy period marks no change in the basic Maoist strategy, it does, however, add many new and significant features. As a result of its role in the war against Japan, the Chinese Communist Party was finally able to harness nationalist sentiment to its own cause. The period also marks a profound change in the psychology of the Communist leadership which may itself spring in no small measure from nationalist sentiment. Having taken the initiative in the field of strategy in the early thirties, having exercised actual state power during the Soviet period, and having led the movement through the vicissitudes of the Long March, Mao was now sufficiently self-confident to take the initiative in the field of theoretical formulation. He was no longer content to explain his strategy in terms of the general theory of the "United Front" as promulgated in Moscow, but was intent on proving that developments in China represented a unique and original development in the course of human history and that he himself was a theoretical innovator in the line of Marx, Lenin, and Stalin. It is here, I think, that we must seek the unique significance of the whole "New Democracy" theory. For a time, at least, Mao Tsetung has received Moscow's acquiescence in this also.

ABIDING ELEMENTS OF MARXISM-LENINISM

How far can a historic movement, based on certain beliefs, drift from basic original premises and still maintain its identity? This is, of course, one of the most perplexing questions in the history of human thought. To some extent this may be a question of semantics, for our ultimate judgment may depend in no small measure on our evaluation of the relative importance of various premises of the movement at its beginnings. What, for instance, are the essential premises of early Marxism? To what extent is Lenin still a true Marxist? To what extent is Stalin a good Marxist-Leninist? To what extent has Mao Tse-tung been a faithful Stalinist? Our answers to each of these questions will depend, of course, on where we seek the crucial elements of Marxism-Leninism-Stalinism respectively. The general view underlying this study is that the general trend of Marxism in its Leninist form has been toward disintegration and not toward "enrichment" and "deepening" as its orthodox adherents would have us believe. Thus we would maintain that the Maoist heresy *in action* on the matter of the relations of party to class represents yet another major step in this process of disintegration. In spite of this movement toward disintegration, however, we would nevertheless maintain that the other core elements of Marxism-Leninism still remain integral living elements of Chinese Communism.

In the first place, we must not overlook the abiding conviction of the Chinese Communists themselves that they are unswerving Marxist-Leninists. Just as Lenin had thought of himself as a monolithic Marxist, so are the Chinese Communists convinced that they are monolithic Marxist-Leninist. Such a subjective conviction is no guarantee against heresy in action, but is a historic force which must be considered in its own right, for the feeling of solidarity of belief is a force which must not be underestimated. At the same time, however, whether such solidarity of belief is as important in the long run as certain factors working in an opposite direction, is open to doubt.

Second, all evidence would indicate that the basic Hegelian faith which underlies and animates Marxism-Leninism, has been thoroughly assimilated by the Chinese Communists—the Hegelian-Marxist faith in a redemptive historic process and the Leninist faith that the Communist Party is itself the sole agent of historic redemption. Chinese Communist literature is genuinely imbued with this faith, however doubtful may be the party's credentials as the party of the proletariat. However immersed they may have been in a peasant environment, the leaders of the party never for a moment doubted that they were the chosen instruments of History, destined to lead China on the road to an industrialized socialism. While the concept "socialism" has undergone strange transformations since Stalin chose to proclaim its existence in the Soviet Union, and while it may yet undergo even stranger metamorphoses in China, this faith has definitely precluded the possibility of the party becoming "a peasant party" and wedded it —for good or ill—to the ideal of the industrialized power state. It also undoubtedly sustained the party's spirits during its darker days.

Third, as has been stated, the party is the agent of historical redemption; thus, the Leninist theory and practice of party organization has remained a hard unchanging core in the midst of change. The basic Leninist formula of a tightly organized elite which strives toward power by identifying itself with the dynamism engendered by the immediate needs and discontents of the masses[29] has, without a doubt, played a large role in accounting for the success of Chinese Communism. The experience of China has simply demonstrated that a mass basis can be provided by the peasantry and other strata of society, and that the industrial proletariat need play no role in this formula.

Fourth, totalitarianism is a tendency inherent in the Leninist conception of the party. As the sole agent of a unified historic process, the party must be the ultimate arbiter in every sphere of human life. This tendency inherent in Marxism-Leninism has, of course, been reinforced to the ultimate degree by the concrete example of the Soviet Union itself. A reading of the writings of Mao Tse-tung and of "The Documents on the Correction of Tendencies" would suggest, I think, that this totalitarian tendency is part of the vital core of Chinese Communism inhibited only by the force of external circumstances and softened until recently by the party's sparing use of force. This is true in spite of the fact that the Chinese Communist Party has not yet claimed to have attained socialism. By stressing "the hegemony of the proletariat" even in this presocialist era, it is able to preserve for itself the right of ultimate decision in every sphere of human experience. Thus, Mao Tse-tung's own writings on literature demonstrate the extent to which he has arrogated to himself the position of arbiter in that sphere. Totalitarianism will, I think, be inhibited in a Communist China only by limits imposed by external circumstances.

Finally, the Leninist doctrine of imperialism, which so strongly attracted the founders of the Chinese Communist Party in the days of the May Fourth movement, still plays a vital role in Chinese Communism. It has been suggested at the beginning of this study that it was this element above all which first seemed to give Marxism-Leninism its burning relevance to the situation in which the Chinese intelligentsia found itself involved. Quite apart from the truth or falsehood of Lenin's interpretation of imperialism, the fact that he *had* a theory of imperialism (derived largely, to be sure, from others), and the fact that he turned his attention to the hatreds and resentments aroused by nineteenth- and twentieth-century western imperialism, and had included them as a factor in his calculations, differentiated him sharply from both the liberals and the Marxists of the West who continued in their complacent belief that all the central problems of mankind would be solved in the West and by the West. This political insight may itself have been more a function of his Russian background than of his Marxism; it may itself have reflected his own ambiguous relationship to what he regarded as the smug self-centered West. Whatever the case, however, this political insight made it possible for him to establish a rapport with the politically articulate intelligentsia of Asia. The Leninist theory of imperialism thus became the binding link between Marxism-Leninism and Asiatic resentments. So widespread has been the acceptance of the Leninist theory of imperialism in China, for instance, even in circles far removed from the Communist Party, that wherever imperialism was discussed the Leninist interpretation came to be taken for granted.

Whether living experience will ever teach the Chinese Communists to doubt the Leninist theory that imperialism is a phenomenon peculiar to a certain stage of "capitalism" is a question which only the future and their own interests can decide.

In sum, then, while Chinese Communism did conclusively demonstrate *in fact* the utter lack of any necessary, organic relation between Communist parties and the industrial proletariat, the movement still retains certain fundamental elements of Marxist-Leninist tradition.

Notes

1. "Ch'ing-Kang-shan Ch'ien-wei Chung-yang ti pao-kao" (A Report of the Chingkan-

shan Front Committee to the Central Committee), p. 516.

2. *Ibid.*, p. 542.

3. *Ibid.*, p. 516.

4. *Ibid.*, p. 516.

5. Edgar Snow, *Red Star Over China* (New York, 1938), p. 180.

6. George Lukacs, *Lenin, Eine Studie über den Zusammenhang seiner Gedanken* (Lenin, a Study of the Structure of his Thought), p. 23.

7. *Ibid.*, p. 24.

8. *Shao-shan Pao-kao* (Report of Chou En-lai), p. 7.

9. Trotsky, *Problems of the Chinese Revolution*, p. 158.

10. *International Press Correspondence*, vol. X, no. 51, p. 1063 (November 13, 1930).

11. Trotsky, *Problems of the Chinese Revolution*, p. 239.

12. Nym Wales, *Inside Red China* (New York, 1939), p. 221.

13. Lenin, "Thèses sur la question agraire" (Theses on the Agrarian Question), *Oeuvres complètes*, XXV, 319.

14. See *Soviety v Kitae* (Soviets in China), pp. 425-432.

15. "Wei kung-hui hui-yüan wen-t'i kei ko-Su-chü kung-hui hsin" (A Letter to Union Branches in All the Soviet Areas Concerning the Problem of Union Members), *Hung-ch'i Chou-pao*, no. 52, p. 53 (November 15, 1932).

16. See, for example, chapters vi and xxvii of Marx's *Capital*, vol. I.

17. "Wei kung-hui hui-yüan wen-t'i kei ko-Su-chü kung-hui hsin," p. 35.

18. *Ibid.*, p. 36.

19. *Ibid.*, p. 35.

20. *Ibid.*, p. 36.

21. *Soviety v Kitae* (Soviets in China), p. 92.

22. *Ibid.*, p. 106.

23. Lenin, "Sur les questions coloniales et nationales," *Oeuvres complètes,* XXV, 420.

24. Stalin, "The Revolution in China and the Tasks of the Communist International," *Communist International*, vol. V (June 30, 1927).

25. *Soviety v Kitae*, p. 95.

26. *Tragedy of the Chinese Revolution*, p. 404.

27. *Inside Red China*, p. 335.

28. See Chapter VIII, note 39.

29. The recent history of Eastern Europe would suggest that the latter part of this formula is not necessarily an essential, permanent element. The Communist Party has in these countries shown its complete willingness to attain power by such means as the control of the Ministry of the Interior. In China, however, the original formula was applied in full.

IV. MAO'S FEUD WITH THE CCP CENTRAL COMMITTEE

26. THE BOLSHEVIK RECONSTRUCTION OF THE PARTY

JOHN E. RUE

In 1931 Mao reached the height of his power in the soviet areas. Three years later he was in prison, as the first phase of his struggle with the 28 Bolsheviks, who represented the Comintern line in China, reached a denouement. The story of these years is one of intrigue and conflict between the interests of the international Communist movement and those of the Chinese Communists.

As 1930 drew to a close, Li Li-san fell and the 28 Bolsheviks rose to power in the CCP. In the process the old CCP cadres outside the soviet areas were almost all destroyed. Concurrently, the revolt at Fu-t'ien split the party in the central soviet districts. In Moscow, Lominadze and Syrtsov circulated a memorandum among the members of the CPSU Central Committee suggesting that Stalin be deposed from his position as general secretary. This perfectly legal plea was labeled the product of a conspiracy, and Lominadze and Syrtsov were imprisoned. The unsuccessful rebellion among the Stalinists opposed to the forced pace

From John E. Rue, *Mao Tse-tung in Opposition, 1927-1935* (Stanford University Press, © 1966), pp. 238-65, 336-38. Reprinted by permission.

of super-industrialization and disheartened by the miseries of the collectivized peasantry soon led the true believers and police agents in the Comintern to tighten their control of the apparatus. This increasing stress on theoretical conformity and the cult of Stalin's personality was to culminate in the bloody purge of Old Bolsheviks six years later.

THE FALL OF LI LI-SAN

Pavel Mif and his protégés appeared in Shanghai in the early summer of 1930. Li Li-san did nothing to oppose them until they attacked his June 11 resolution. Then he placed Wang Ming on probation for six months, officially reprimanded Po Ku (Ch'in Pang-hsien), Wang Chia-hsiang, and Ho Tzu-shu, and for several weeks refused to talk to Mif.[1] Mif sent off an urgent letter to Moscow demanding that Li be reproved for his disrespect, but did not immediately get the response he wanted. Lominadze, who was at the time in Stalin's good graces, undoubtedly made the next move—Ch'ü Ch'iu-pai and Chou En-lai, both of whom had been on good terms with Lominadze in 1927, were sent back to Shanghai to review Li Li-san's policies and actions. With them were the Chinese labor leaders Mif had ejected from the Comintern several months earlier. When this unwelcome group appeared in Shanghai, they brought with them a Comintern directive dated July 23 that they used to support Li in his contest with Mif. The directive was ambiguous enough to permit Ho Meng-hsiung, a labor leader opposed to Li who read the new directive without permission from the Politburo, to use it as a basis for *attacking* Li. But with the assistance of Chou and Ch'ü, Li was able to expel Ho from his post as a Central Committee alternate before the Third Plenum convened in September.[2]

When the Plenum met, Chou and Ch'ü insisted that Li was open to criticism only for tactical errors. They directed their main attack at Ho and his followers in the labor union faction. These comrades, Chou and Ch'ü declared, were right deviationists who did not believe in the new revolutionary wave. They underestimated the significance of the soviet areas and the Red Army and failed to recognize the value of armed insurrections.[3] By attacking Ho, Chou and Chü managed to associate Mif with a right deviation. Mif also attacked Ho, but he wanted the Plenum to condemn the left aspects of Li Li-san's line as well. Chou and Ch'ü, however, refused to admit that Li had developed a line of his own contrary to that of the Comintern. Li was reelected to the Politburo along with three of his supporters, Hsiang Chung-fa, Li Wei-han, and Ho Ch'ang, and Ch'ü Ch'iu-pai and Chou En-lai.[4] Fourteen members of the Central Committee and twenty-two others attended the Plenum. Since between nine and seventeen members of the Central Committee had died or been expelled since the Sixth Congress, seven new members of the Central Committee,

eight new alternates, and two new members of the Supervisory Committee (which supervised purges) were elected. This brought the total number of comrades in the central organs to twenty-three full members of the Central Committee and eight alternates, and three full members of the Supervisory Committee and two alternates.[5] I have attempted to identify as many members of the new Central Committee as possible, since it was this group of old Communists who led the resistance to Mif and his 28 Bolsheviks in the next three months. Of the thirty-five who may have been members, twenty-six were in Shanghai, four in Moscow, four in the soviet areas, and one in prison in Nanking. Of those in Shanghai only one, Shen Tse-min, was a member of the Mif faction. Six were Li Li-sanists: Li himself, Hsiang Chung-fa, Li Wei-han, Ho Ch'ang, Kuan Hsiang-ying, and Li Ch'iu-shih. Five had just returned from Moscow, where they opposed Mif: Ch'ü Ch'iu-pai and Chou En-lai, who had previously been labeled left putschists; and Teng Chun-hsia, Yü Fei, and Hsü Hsi-ken, who had been identified with the right-wing labor faction. Also labeled as rightists were Lo Chang-lung, Wang K'e-ch'üan, Wang Feng-fei, Kuo Miao-ken, Ts'ai Po-chen, Ch'en Yu, Wang Chung-i, and P'eng Tse-hsiang. There were six other old Communists in Shanghai whose political tendencies at the time I have not been able to discover: Hsiang Ying, Jen Pi-shih, K'ang Sheng, Lo I-nung (Lo I-yüan?), Yang Pao-an and Liu Shao-ch'i. None of these six comrades were specifically condemned as Li Li-sanists or rightists by the Fourth Plenum. Mao, Chu Teh, Tseng Shan, and possibly Fang Chih-min may have been elected or reelected to the Central Committee at the Third Plenum, for they were placed on the Central Bureau for the Soviet Areas immediately afterward. They remained aloof from the dispute. Of the four possible members in Moscow—Chang Kuo-t'ao, Ts'ai Ho-shen, Huang P'ing, and Lin Yü-nan—the first three opposed both Mif and Li. The man in Nanking, Yün Tai-ying, had been captured while on a dangerous mission for Li Li-san, who had hoped it would lead to Yün's demise. The mission had partially fulfilled its purpose, and Yün was in prison.*

In the face of this broad coalition of old cadres in Shanghai, Mif could not reassert the authority of the Comintern and impose a new leadership on the CCP without assistance from Moscow. He called for help. His appeal was answered on November 16, when a letter arrived from the ECCI condemning both the Li Li-san line and the line adopted by the Third Plenum. Li left for Moscow forthwith. On arrival he was interrogated by a committee of the Far Eastern Department of the Comintern, headed by Otto Kuusinen. The committee then drew up a report on his errors for the Presidium of the ECCI. Li had gone to Moscow with the expectation that here would be some old friends around to assist and defend him, but instead found himself entangled in the Lominadze-Syrtsov affair, with none to be-friend him. Lominadze and Syrtsov had circulated their memorandum among the members of the CPSU Central Committee at about the time Li's interrogation began. They were

* In addition to the 32 men named, it is extremely likely that a few Whampoa cadets and military men associated with Chou En-lai were also elected members or alternate members of the Central Committee. Liu Po-ch'eng, Yeh Chien-ying, Kung Ho-ch'ung, and Kung Ch'u, none of whom were in Shanghai, are among the possibilities. Hsiao's list of those removed from the Central Committee after the Fourth Plenum substantiates this. (Hsiao, pp. 125-49.)

expelled from that body for their audacity on December 2. Since in most of the Communist world those who are guilty must be guilty of the currently fashionable sin, this event altered the course of Li's trial: his line was suddenly condemned as one aspect of the plot against Stalin.

The report of the Far Eastern Department charged that Li had been playing with insurrections again: he had tried to involve the Soviet Union and Outer Mongolia in a general world war by provoking the imperialists to intervene in China. It charged that his orientation toward labor had led him to underestimate the Red Army and the rural bases, and to demand wrongly that the first all-China soviet government and the first regular Red Army be organized in a city. Finally, it reprimanded him for his disrespect to Mif. The report also charged Chou and Ch'ü with having compromised with Li even though they had recognized the contradiction between his line and the Comintern's. Ch'ü was especially treacherous, for he had promised in Moscow to support the Comintern and had then thrown his support to Li in Shanghai. Li and Chü, the report said, had been under the influence of Lominadze since 1927. According to the CCP journal *Bolshevik*, Comrades "Pi" (Piatnitsky?) and Magyar testified before the Presidium of the ECCI that Lominadze's influence on Li was visible in Li's rich peasant policy of distributing land according to labor power and refusing to allot land to coolies and hired farm hands, as in certain aspects of his labor policy. Chang Kuo-t'ao was called on to contribute his judgment and disagreed. He asserted that Li had initially formulated his peasant and labor policies under the influence of Borodin and Ch'en Tu-hsiu, and had come under the influence of Lominadze only after the fundamental aspects of his line had been worked out. Therefore, Chang urged, the fight against Li Li-sanism must be a two-front struggle in which the right deviation was treated as the main danger.[6]

The Presidium not only condemned Li, it also condemned Ch'ü for his two-faced double-dealing, his factionalism, and his "wily oriental diplomacy." It asserted that his views on the agrarian and peasant questions were associated not only with those of Borodin, Ch'en Tu-hsiu, and Lominadze, but with those of T'an P'ing-shan as well. If that statement had any historical truth at all, it presumably meant that Ch'ü had at one time or another agreed with each one of the four and was therefore ex post facto guilty of their deviations—right opportunism, left putschism, Trotskyism, and refusal to obey Comintern directives.[7] These conclusions laid the basis for Ch'ü's expulsion from the CCP Politburo in the following month. When the hearings ended, Li was directed to stay in the Soviet Union and study at Lenin University in order to rectify his mistakes. He did not return to China until 1945.

THE RECONSTRUCTION OF THE CENTRAL COMMITTEE

While Li was being tried in Moscow, the coalition of Ch'ü, Chou, and Hsiang repulsed the first attempt of Shen Tse-min and Wang Ming to gain control of the Politburo. Their obduracy could not last, however, and they were soon compelled to confess their errors and reinstate the members of Mif's faction Li had demoted. They also readmitted Ho Meng-hsiung to the Central Committee.[8] Ho, who was not aware of recent events in Moscow, made the fateful error of call-

ing for an emergency conference to reconstitute the party's leading organs, as Lominadze had four years earlier. Unlike Ho, Mif knew that Lominadze had become an outcast, so he and his protégés demanded a regular plenum of the Central Committee to officially expel Li from the Politburo, reconstitute that body, and take adequate measures to overcome the effects of Li Li-san's line. With no one left in Moscow with enough power to restrain them, they got their way, and early in January 1931 the Fourth Plenum convened under Mif's guidance.

At this Plenum the Central Committee was reduced from thirty to sixteen full members and alternates.[9] Although we do not know how many members the Committee had when the Plenum convened, we are fairly sure that there were not many more than 32, so some of the 39 men who attended the Plenum's opening sessions were not Committee members. For some reason, Lo Chang-lung and Ho Meng-hsiung appeared at one of these sessions still demanding an emergency conference. Li Li-san and Chü Ch'iu-pai were expelled from the Central Committee early in the course of the Plenum, as were the men most closely identified with Li Li-san. Those known to have been expelled are Li Wei-han, Ho Ch'ang, Kuan Hsiang-ying, and Li Ch'iu-shih. Ho Meng-hsiung, Lo Chang-lung, Wang K'e-ch'üan, Hsü Hsi-ken, Yü Fei, Kuo Miao-ken, Ts'ai Po-chen, Ch'en Yu, P'eng Tse-hsiang, and others left the Plenum or the party, or were reprimanded for their anti-Comintern activities, before the end of the month. After making groveling confessions, Chou En-lai and Hsiang Chung-fa were reinstated to membership on the Politburo. Mif's protégés Wang Ming, Po Ku, Chang Wen-t'ien (also known as Lo Fu and Szu Mei), and Shen Tse-min dominated it.[10]

After a bitter debate accompanied by name-calling and threats of violence, Ho Meng-hsiung and Lo Chang-lung left the meeting with some of the expelled Li Li-sanists. At subsequent meetings of the Labor Federation and the Kiangsu and Shanghai party committees they continued to call for an emergency conference and accused the 28 Bolsheviks of turning the CCP into "Stalin's China section."[11]

On January 17, a mixed group of leaders of the labor union and Li Li-san factions called a meeting in a Shanghai hotel to reconstitute the party leadership in their own way, beyond Mif's control. Seeking as broad a base as possible, they invited expelled rightists and Trotskyites to attend.* Someone informed the British police, who raided the meeting and arrested 25 persons, among them Ho Meng-hsiung, Lin Yü-nan, Li Ch'iu-shih, and Wang Ming's enemy Hu Yeh-p'ing. All were turned over to the KMT and shot in Lung-hua prison on February 7.[12] According to sources hostile to the 28 Bolsheviks, it was Wang who had informed the British police, in a personal vendetta against Hu Yeh-p'ing, who had published an accurate account of the toadying, unprincipled methods Wang had used in his climb to first place

* While Lo Chang-lung was campaigning against "Stalin's China section," Ch'en Tu-hsiu called a conference in Shanghai of all opposition groups, evidently hoping to win the majority of the old Chinese party leaders over to the Trotskyite opposition. This conference set up a nine-man Central Executive Committee that included Ch'en Tu-hsiu, P'eng Shu-chih, Kao Yü-han, Liu Jen-ch'ing, and Ts'ai Chen-te. Wang Chung-i, who may have attended this conference, also maintained contacts with the group advocating an emergency conference. This laid the basis for the new Politburo's accusation that the Ho Meng-hsiung and Lo Chang-lung opposition was in collusion with Trotskyites and expelled rightists. (Brandt, Schwartz, and Fairbank, p. 36; Hsiao, p. 143.)

among the 28 Bolsheviks. Hu, the husband of the prominent writer Ting Ling, was the leader of the Shanghai rickshaw-pullers' union, a friend of Chou En-lai, and a minor poet to boot.[13] Rumors surrounding his betrayal therefore alienated many old Communists and left-wing writers, artists, and labor leaders, as well as contributing to a general state of confusion and suspicion in the party.

Early in February Wang Ming published The Two Lines, his version of the inner-party struggle against Li Li-san, Ch'ü Ch'iu-pai, and the right wing. Wang's main theoretical point in this pamphlet was that all the old cadres in the CCP—Li Li-sanists, rightist, and compromisers—had failed to grasp the fact that Chinese capitalists were counterrevolutionary. These cadres had labeled capitalists and their political representatives a "third group" or an "intermediate camp." Concentrating the main attack on imperialists and feudal remnants, the old cadres had been blind to the error of forming tactical alliances with capitalists and bourgeois reformers. By this line of analysis Wang opened the way to a united front from below.* He denied that Communists could form alliances for any purpose whatsoever with any party, army, or organization against the imperialists or the landlords. Henceforth any Communist who tried to do so or who quietly supported others who tried to do so was a right deviationist or a two-faced, double-dealing compromiser.[14] If applied retrospectively, this formula was general enough to embrace everyone in the CCP except the 28 Bolsheviks, for they alone had been out of China throughout the period when all party members in the country had worked within the KMT. More important, the new line precluded

* See note a, p. 118, for an explanation of the various forms of the united front.

any coalition with any other political party or army against the Japanese, who were soon to invade Manchuria and attempt to drive the Nationalist armies out of Shanghai.

Having placed the 28 Bolsheviks in the Politburo, Mif returned to Moscow to assume command of the Chinese section of the Far Eastern Department of the Comintern. From this position he would be able to give his protégés strong support against anyone willing to attack or resist their regime. At the same time, Chang Kuo-t'ao returned from Moscow to Shanghai, and soon moved to oust the new Politburo before the 28 Bolsheviks could consolidate their control. Early in March, he attempted to replace the Politburo by a new standing committee led by himself, with Hsiang Chung-fa as secretary-general and Chou En-lai as the third man.[15] His attempt failed. At a secret meeting in April the Politburo agreed to split up and move to the soviet areas. Jen Pi-shih set off for Ho Lung's soviet in northwestern Hunan. Shen Tse-min and Chang Kuo-t'ao went to the O-yü-wan soviet in western Anhwei. Chou En-lai, Po Ku, and Chang Wen-t'ien agreed to go to the central soviet districts. This left Liu Shao-ch'i, Hsiang Chung-fa, and Wang Ming in charge of a small Central Bureau in Shanghai.[16]

Then another disaster befell the new Politburo. The KMT police in Hankow captured Ku Shun-chang, a young Communist whom Li Li-san had raised out of the depths of the Shanghai slums to a position of leadership during the general strikes of 1926-27. Angered by the anti-Li Li-san line of the new Politburo and despising those who had opportunistically fallen in with it, he gave the KMT police the underground addresses of Ch'ü Ch'iu-pai, Chou En-lai, Li Wei-han, Hsiang Chung-fa, and others in Shang-

hai. He also identified Yün Tai-ying who was still in prison, as a Communist. Yün was immediately shot. The homes of the Shanghai Communists were raided. Hsiang Chung-fa was captured, and executed on June 24.[17] The others were not at home when the police arrived and so escaped. According to Li Ang, when the Communists discovered Ku's betrayal they took revenge by killing some hundred members of his family, who had served as unwitting hostages against his defection since he had entered the secret service of the CCP. The Ku family had connections throughout the Shanghai labor movement, and by this dreadful act the CCP broke almost every tie it still possessed with the proletariat of Shanghai.*

After Hsiang Chung-fa's death, Wang Ming became the acting secretary-general, Chang Wen-t'ien took charge of the Orgburo, Shen Tse-min (who had already arrived in O-yü-wan soviet area) was appointed head of the Propaganda Bureau, Meng Ch'ing-shu (Wang Ming's wife) took over the Women's Bureau, Po Ku worked with the Youth Corps, and Chou En-lai (the only remaining old leader) continued to head the Military Affairs Committee.[18] This group, or part of it, may have attempted to reach the central soviet districts in the summer of 1931, but the KMT was then in the midst of its third annihilation campaign and had thrown up a blockade that was very difficult to get through. By midsummer

---

* Li Ang [66], pp. 115-16. Li Ang's figures may be exaggerated. According to Dr. Li T'ien-min, who has interviewed the men who were in charge of the Shanghai and Hankow police at the time, only about two dozen people were killed. Four were members of Ku's immediate family and the others people who were living in the same house. (Personal communication—Dr. Li was a visiting scholar at the Hoover Institution in 1965.)

the Comintern had endorsed the decisions of the Fourth Plenum and supported the 28 Bolsheviks in their reconstruction of the party. The Comintern's directives, stressing that the right deviation was the main danger, called for a provisional all-China soviet government to be established in the safest soviet base area, and spelled out details for handling the land problem in the soviet areas. On the basis of these directives, the Politburo circulated a letter to all the soviet areas in September calling for the consolidation of a soviet base and an armed attack on the major cities. It condemned the Red Army for clinging to guerilla warfare and demanded that it organize as a regular army. It called for a new land policy whereby rich peasants should get infertile land and poor peasants the most fertile land, thus countermanding Mao's policy of equal distribution. On the national scene, it called for a major effort to precipitate what it saw as the "imminent collapse" of the KMT regime.[19]

One more reorganization of the Politburo took place before it went to Jui-ching to direct the First All-China Soviet Congress. Sometime in September, Wang Ming and his wife left Shanghai for Moscow (possibly passing through Jui-ching on their way) and Po Ku took charge of the Politburo. In the same month the Japanese launched their attack on Manchuria. Chinese nationalists inside and outside the Nanking government called for unity against the new threat. The new CCP Politburo now had the opportunity to join in the rising sentiment against the invaders and maneuver for leadership within a united front. Instead of taking advantage of this opportunity, the Politburo refused to form any kind of alliance and called for the defeat of both the KMT and the Japanese. Having thus isolated itself from all

other anti-imperialist groups in China and having destroyed its base in Shanghai as well, the Politburo set out to apply in the soviet areas two closely related organizational policies: the fight against the right deviation and the "reform and replenishment of the leading bodies at all levels."[20]

THE ATTACK ON THE MAOISTS: THE CHARGES ARE ENTERED

Mao was identified as the leader of the right deviationists in the soviet areas even before the Politburo arrived there. It prepared for a confrontation by attacking all the policies that he had advocated and removing his supporters from office. This process, however, took quite a long time—there were only 28 Bolsheviks and Mao had many supporters. All the charges Mao attributes to the leaders of the "third left line" in RSQHP were not made until the party conference held in the southern Kiangsi base in November 1931, shortly before the First All-China Soviet Congress. The new Politburo's prolonged struggle against the old cadres in Shanghai delayed its coming. Mao had plenty of time to unravel the story of its activities in Shanghai and prepare for its arrival. Hsü Meng-ch'iu, Hsü T'e-li, and Ch'en Hui-ch'ing (Teng Fa's wife), whose political leanings at the time are not clear, had arrived in January with accounts of events in Shanghai through the previous October. When Hsiang Ying arrived in March to take charge of the Central Party Bureau in the soviet areas, he related his version of the Fourth Plenum. Several other small groups of comrades arrived at Mao's headquarters before the main body of the new Politburo. Po Ku, Chang Wen-t'ien (Lo Fu), Wang Chia-hsiang, and Chou En-lai arrived in the late summer or early autumn.* By that time Mao and Chu had successfully fought three campaigns against the KMT armies, wiped out most of the A-B Corps, executed the leaders of the Fu-t'ien rebels, consolidated the power of their faction in Fukien, and managed the elections of delegates to the First Soviet Congress in the areas within reach of their own First Front Red army. They had confidence in themselves, their army, their policies, and their formidable political machine. The coming confrontation with the Politburo would require them either to alter their politics, surrender control of their army, and give up their hard-won political powers, or else to fight the Politburo and thereby flout Comintern discipline.

While Mao was making his preparations for this confrontation, the new Politburo members were making theirs. They reviewed the record of Mao's conduct of party affairs in the soviet districts. They heard Hsiang Ying's report on Mao's attitudes after Hsiang had replaced Mao as chairman of the Central Bureau, and learned that in purging the A-B Corps Mao had executed several Whampoa cadets and a few Li Li-sanists. In November, after drawing up a set of resolutions, they co-opted enough members to ensure themselves a working majority and convened a party conference. The major aim of the conference was to set the line and guide the work

of the party fraction—i.e., the new Politburo's fraction—at the First All-China Soviet Congress. The essential purpose of the resolutions the Politburo sponsored at the party conference was to attack the Maoists in the Red Army and soviet governments and set the stage for replacing them at the coming All-China Soviet Congress.[21]

The November 1931 Party Conference

The Political Resolution of the November 1931 Party Conference echoed the Politburo's September letter. It charged that the party's local leaders had avoided adopting a strong "class and mass line" and rebuked them for failing to establish links with other base areas. It attacked the guerrilla tactics of the Fourth Red Army. It charged that the land programs adopted by the Kiangsi and Fukien governments established in February 1930 were contaminated by both left and right opportunism, and specifically attacked Mao's February 7 land law on the grounds that equal distribution to all persons was a rich peasant line. It claimed that both the soviet government and the trade union apparatus were filled with "class alien" elements and that the program of mass education against counterrevolutionaries carried on by the party apparatus was motivated by "narrow empiricism."[22] The Conference's "Resolution on Party Reconstruction" directed several of these charges against Mao himself, finding him guilty of narrow empiricism, "opportunistic pragmatism," and a "general ideological poverty." It reasserted the dogma that the agrarian revolution must be led by the proletariat.[23] In other words, it was the clear intent of the Conference that Mao's machine should

* Interview with Lieberman, cited in McLane, p. 38; Wales, *Red Dust*, pp. 63-64. Wang Ming may not have traveled to the Kiangsi base in 1931. If he did, he left almost immediately and may not have attended the First All-China Soviet Congress. He reportedly delivered a speech to a Moscow meeting of the Profintern at the end of 1931. The text of the speech is in *Krasnyi internatsional profsiouzov*, Nos. 1-2 (1932), pp. 67-71, cited in McLane, p. 38n96. See also North, *Moscow*, p. 158; Mao, HC, III, 968; SW, IV, 185; Hsiao, p. 162.

be replaced by new cadres loyal to the 28 Bolsheviks. The "Resolution on the Red Army" rejected the idea that guerrilla warfare should be the mainstay of the army. The immediate aim of the Red Army, it declared, should be to organize revolutionary bases by taking urban areas in one or several provinces. This revived one of Li Li-san's basic ideas. The army should expand, adopt regular forms of warfare, and overcome the conservative notion of guerrillaism that had dominated its councils before 1931.[24] Guerrillaism in this context refers specifically to the Maoist tactics adopted at the Second Mao-ping Conference and the Lou-fang Conference—"luring the enemy to penetrate deep" into the base area.

Thus *all* charges Mao admits were brought against him by the 28 Bolsheviks were made immediately before the First All-China Soviet Congress, which convened on November 7.

The First All-China Soviet Congress

When the Congress convened, the 28 Bolsheviks did not have enough support in the soviet areas to overcome the Maoists; Mao was elected chairman of the Central Executive Committee of the all-China soviet government. He also managed to retain his position as chief political commissar of the First Front Red Army. Hsiang Ying, who had displaced Mao on the Central Bureau in March, was elected vice-chairman of the CEC (under Mao) and commissar for labor. Chang Kuo-t'ao, who was then in the O-yü-wan soviet, was elected second vice-chairman and commissar for justice. Chu Teh became first commissar for war. Ch'ü Ch'iu-pai, who had been expelled from the Central Committee and Politburo at the Fourth Plenum and who

was still in hiding in Shanghai, was elected commissar for education. This post was actually filled by Hsü T'e-li, Mao's old teacher, until Ch'ü arrived in the soviet areas more than a year later. Chang Ting-ch'eng, who had been one of Mao's students in the Peasant Department Institute in Canton, was elected commissar for land. Teng Fa, who had been one of the leaders of the Fukien soviet before the arrival of the Politburo, became head of the police. Teng Tzu-hui, one of Mao's old friends, was elected commissar of finance. Ho Shu-heng, who had founded the Hunan Provincial Party with Mao, was elected chief of the Workers' and Peasants' Inspection. Chou I-li, whose provenance is unknown, took charge of the Interior Department.* Wang Chia-hsiang was the only one of the 28 Bolsheviks elected to any government position. He became commissar for foreign affairs, an honorary post whose sole functions were to conduct relations with the Comintern and make foreign visitors comfortable, should any arrive. Chou En-lai received no position in the government, although he ranked fourth on the CEC. Wang Ming and Shen Tse-min, neither of whom was present, were elected to the CEC, ranking thirteenth and twentieth on the list. Po Ku and Chang Wen-t'ien, who were there, were not elected to anything. To make his sympathies as clear as possible, Mao saw to it that the rightists Hsü Hsi-ken and Ch'en Yu and the Li Li-sanist Kuan Hsiang-ying, whom the Bolsheviks had expelled from the Central Committee, were elected to the CEC. Hsü outranked Wang Ming and Kuan outranked Shen. Ch'en Yu ranked below the three Bolsheviks elected to the committee, but even he ranked above several members

* Chou I-li disappeared before the Second All-China Soviet Congress in January 1934.

of the new government, including Teng Tzu-hui, Ho Shu-heng, and Chou I-li.

The struggle at the November Party Conference had led almost inevitably to a deadlock. The Maoists had won control of the new soviet government and retained control of the First Front Red Army, but the 28 Bolsheviks still controlled the Politburo. The stage was set for a prolonged struggle between the Maoists and the party faction, or, as Mao delicately phrased it in RSQHP, the prolonged struggle against the third left line (of the Politburo).

In spite of the fact that the Maoists won control of the government, the delegates to the First Congress adopted the soviet constitution and, with minor alterations, the land law, labor law, and resolutions on the Red Army introduced by the Politburo. The alterations in the land law were obviously the work of the Maoist faction. In the final text, the interests of the middle peasants were more carefully protected than in the Politburo draft. If a majority of the middle peasants voted to exempt themselves from the land redistribution, they were not required to participate in it, regardless of the wishes of poor peasants and hired farm hands. The final version of the law also protected the interests of the rich peasants by providing that only their excess houses and farm implements should be confiscated, which was a more lenient provision than the Politburo's. This provision was important, since under the new law the rich peasants were to receive the less fertile land and were given the option of having it distributed to them on the basis of their labor power, which included houses, tools, and draft animals. If they could keep more tools and draft animals to cultivate the larger areas of poorer land, the old system of equal distribution (with everyone receiving equal portions of all grades of land) could still be approximated.[25]

An appendix spelling out the privileges of soldiers was added to the Politburo's draft resolution on the Red Army.[26] The Politburo's resolutions on economic policy and the Workers' and Peasants' Inspection may or may not have been passed by the Congress. At any rate, no final versions of these laws have yet come to light.

The Maoist faction won another victory, a great one, when in the last days of the Congress the Ning-tu Uprising occurred and 20,000 officers and men in the KMT's 28th Route Army revolted and came over to the Communists. This provided an excellent example of what might be done if the GCP did not impose on itself the limitations of the policy of a united front from below. The Congress ended in general rejoicing. Delegates from other soviet areas left for their home bases, and Po Ku, Chang Wen-t'ien, and most of the other Politburo members left for Shanghai. Mao, Hsiang Ying, and Chou En-lai remained in the new soviet capital at Jui-ching. The long trial of strength between the Maoists and the Comintern-Stalinist faction had begun.

The Conflict Deepens

One of the first clashes came at an enlarged conference of the Kiangsi Provincial Committee convened immediately after the Congress to discuss and vote on its decisions. The Maoists were very strong in this Committee. They had just completed an egalitarian distribution whereby rich peasants, small landlords, and poor peasants had received equal amounts of all grades of land, and they objected to being called on to reallocate the land to the advantage of the poor peasants, the disadvantage of the rich peasants, and the complete deprivation of the landlords. At the same time as they were asked to thus antagonize the landlords and rich peasants, they were also asked to send more men into the Red Army and to subordinate the previously independent guerrilla units to the regular chain of command, leaving reformed areas relatively undefended. These tasks were not only difficult; many comrades believed they were based on a faulty analysis of local conditions. Mao's reasoning in "Oppose Bookism" had bitten deeply into the consciousness of at least a few of the ruling clique in Kiangsi. Many believed that the Comintern and its agents knew all too little about class relations in Kiangsi and that their directives were completely unsuitable. But the reconstituted Central Bureau of the Politburo, now dominated by the 28 Bolsheviks, asserted that the class basis of the Kiangsi party was very weak. It included all too few genuine proletarians. Its class consciousness was unsteady. Many members, including the leaders, still persisted in the backward, peasant mentality that had characterized the Maoists ever since they had first formed their own faction in the Chingkang Mountains. Although the Kiangsi Committee accepted the decisions of the Soviet Congress, it did so in such a spirit that the Central Bureau issued a sharp reproof for the Committee's display of pragmatism, narrow empiricism, and bureaucratic routinism, and the inadequate reorientation of its work along the lines prescribed by the Comintern.[27]

Early in 1932, a controversy developed between Mao and Chou En-lai over military strategy and the centralization of the Red Army. Mao continued to advocate mobile guerrilla tactics and the strategy of luring the enemy deep into the base area, where small, scattered enemy units would confront much larger contingents of Red troops. The basic strategy adopted by the Red Army under the political leadership of Chou En-lai after 1932 was to hold the base, fight positional warfare, and carry the fight into enemy territory rather than allow enemy troops to penetrate Red territory. Guerrilla tactics were considered useful, but only behind the enemy lines. Although Mao and Chou assisted each other in planning an assault on Kanchow in January 1932, it was an unhappy and unfortunate collaboration: as a result of their tactical disagreements the Red Army failed to capture the city, which was strategically necessary to the control of all southern Kiangsi. After this unsuccessful attempt a Red Army expansion drive got under way and continued intermittently until September 1932.[28] Maoists in the soviet administration immediately found a reason why the army should not be expanded: peasants were busy in the fields and would fight better when they had nothing to do at home. This argument, of course, reveals a "peasant mentality" at odds with the Comintern's attitude at that time. Local army recruiters in the soviet administrations dragged their feet and slowed down the army expansion drive in June and July, so at the Ning-tu Conference in August Chou took the offensive and forced Mao off the Military Committee of the Central Bureau.[29] From that time onward Mao devoted himself to work in the government, although Chou did not publicly replace him as chief political commissar of the Red Armies until May 1933.

Throughout this debate over centralization and expansion of the Red Army Mao also took issue with the Politburo

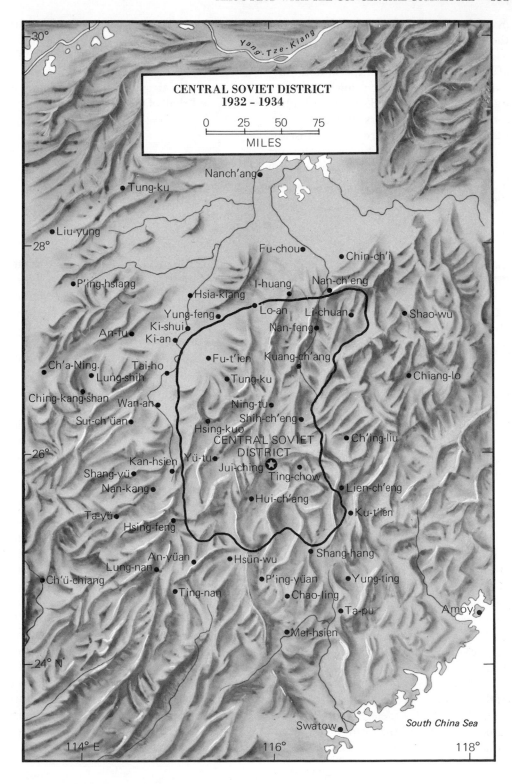

CENTRAL SOVIET DISTRICT
1932 – 1934

0   25   50   75

MILES

over the form of the united front. After the Japanese attack on Shanghai in January 1932 he advocated the formation of a coalition government, a united army made up of all existing armies willing to fight the Japanese, and a new volunteer army of armed workers and peasants.[30] Perhaps under pressure from Moscow, the Politburo insisted that all reformist groups were enemies and that all the imperialists were about to unite to attack the Soviet Union. Under these circumstances the Red Army had to be expanded as rapidly as possible in order to achieve victory in one or several provinces before the imperialist attack on the Soviet Union commenced. Only in this way would it be possible for the CCP to come to the defense of the Soviet Union and participate in the final attack on world capitalism. This, the Politburo's view, was a sublime, utopian, apocalyptic vision of the future role of the CCP. The only difficulty with this strategy, according to a recent Communist historian, was that it was based on a complete misunderstanding of the world situation and of the balance of political forces in China. The Maoist policy, however difficult its implementation, would have been much more useful to the CCP in the long run.[31]

As the debate in the inner circle became more furious, Mao, Chu Teh, and Hsiang Ying on April 5, 1932, issued a declaration of war against the Japanese government in the name of the central government of the Chinese soviet republic. The party issued no statement of encouragement. Instead, from that date until August 1, 1935, the soviet government (sometimes in association with the Red Army) and the Politburo issued separate policy statements on the war against Japan and the form of the united front.[32] In other words, the issue was not settled until Mao took over the central party organs at Tsunyi. In the meantime the soviet government followed Mao's line and the 28 Bolsheviks, bound to Moscow by ties of interest and power, followed that of the Comintern.

LEARNING FROM THE MISTAKES OF THE CCP

By 1932 the Comintern line could be summed up under three simple headings: a struggle on two fronts with the right deviation as the main danger in every section of the Comintern, a united front with the masses against all rival elites of whatever political persuasion, and a subordination of the struggle for power of all Communist parties to the essential task of protecting the Soviet Union—the stern fatherland of the proletariat. In the Maoist reconstruction of history, this was the third left line. As the leader of the 28 Bolsheviks, Wang Ming was assigned the task of applying this line to the Chinese revolution and analyzing deviations in the CCP. He wrote his first major analysis, *The Two Lines*, immediately after the Fourth Plenum. In March 1932 he republished it in Moscow with a new title, *Struggle for the More Complete Bolshevization of the CCP*, adding in a long appendix an analysis of the deviations of leaders in the soviet areas.

RSQHP is a reply to this appendix from the perspective of 1945. Point by point, Mao attacks Wang's theses on five major problems: the intermediate camp or third group, proletarian as opposed to peasant consciousness, the consequences of the Fourth Plenum's line on old and new cadres (the reform of party organs), the capture of large cities, and the struggle on two fronts within the party.

The Intermediate Camp

In both the first edition and the Appendix of *The Two Lines*, Wang criticized the Li Li-sanists and others for failing to realize that all capitalist bourgeois reformers were counterrevolutionary. He insisted that in the stage the Chinese revolution was then in the party should not differentiate between various groups of capitalists and should struggle equally against all imperialists and their agents in China. The party must therefore attack both landlords and rich peasants in the village and all strata of the bourgeoisie in the cities, for both capitalists and feudal remnants were allied with counterrevolutionary imperialism.

In RSQHP Mao charged that this line had led to the failure to find and use temporary allies. At the time it was being followed, he said, some capitalists and bourgeois reformers had been willing to cooperate with the Communists against the KMT, the CCP's main political and military enemy. This had been especially true after the Japanese invasion of Manchuria.[33] The failure to obtain allies, Mao charged, arose out of the blind inattention of the 28 Bolsheviks to the real situation in China. Their line exaggerated the importance of capitalism in the Chinese economy, and therefore led to insistence on a struggle directed mainly against Chinese capitalists.[34] By exaggerating the necessity of fighting capitalism, the 28 Bolsheviks had overlooked the immediate targets—imperialism and feudalism. Denying the existence of the "third group" or "intermediate camp," they failed to devise workable agrarian policies of their own, and also rejected the provisions for dealing with rich peasants in Mao's February 7 land law. In the face of the Japanese invasion of

Manchuria, they had refused to recognize that one imperialist power was more dangerous to China than others. They had refused to form a tactical alliance with the Fukien rebels in 1933 simply because the rebels, though willing to cooperate with the Communists against the KMT and the Japanese, were essentially Chinese capitalists and bourgeois reformers. In the eyes of the 28 Bolsheviks, capitalists and bourgeois reformers were an inseparable part of world imperialism in the "third period," and were therefore the "most dangerous enemies" of the CCP.[35]

Proletarian as Opposed to Peasant Consciousness

In considering the problem of the uneven development of the Chinese revolution, Wang denounced the idea that the peasantry has an unusual revolutionary character in colonial and semicolonial countries, as well as the idea that the peasants could play an independent revolutionary role.[36] He laid heavy emphasis on the leading role of the proletariat and censured CCP members who made light of their role in the Chinese revolution by overstressing that of the peasantry.[37] Mao had been warned against belittling the proletariat when he had been removed from all his party posts in November 1927. Wang reiterated the warning in his pamphlet.

RSQHP pointed out that Wang had erroneously objected to Mao's theory of the "unusual revolutionary character of the peasantry," as well as to his practice of inner-party struggle in defending it.[38] As a result, Wang attacked Mao as a representative of "peasant consciousness" in the party. "Peasant consciousness" had entered the vocabulary of the CCP when Li Li-san had borrowed the term from Stalin's denunciation of A. P. Smirnov for his defense of the interests of the Russian peasants. It was used by the Southwest Kiangsi leaders in their attack on Mao's views immediately before the Fu-t'ien incident; it was used by the A-B Corps; and it was later repeated by the 28 Bolsheviks. Such repetition is excellent testimony to Mao's consistent defense of the revolutionary virtues of the peasantry.

The Reform of Party Organs

In *The Two Lines* Wang claimed that only after the complete reorganization of the party leadership at all levels, the reformation of the Red Army, and the transformation of all party work in the soviet areas would it be possible to defeat the KMT's Fourth Campaign (June 1932-March 1933).[39] RSQHP, on the other hand, held that only the persisting influence of Mao's strategic thinking in the Red Army command had made that defeat possible. The reorganization of the party leadership in the soviet areas (of mid-1933), accomplished when the 28 Bolsheviks gained control of both the party and the army there, had resulted in the utter defeat of the Red Army and the evacuation of the soviet areas at the end of the KMT's Fifth Campaign (October 1933-October 1934).[40] Mao maintained that when positional warfare had replaced his guerrilla strategy, defeat had become inevitable.

The Capture of Large Cities

Wang's attitude toward the capture of large cities changed between the appearance of the first edition of *The Two Lines* and the Moscow edition published one year later. In the first edition the Red Army's capture of Ch'angsha in July 1930 was cited as the point at which Li

Li-san turned from right opportunism to putschism. In the Moscow edition Wang admitted that attacking Ch'angsha might have been a mistake at the time, but argued that the failure to hold it did not warrant the conclusion that "key cities should not be taken anyway." He urged that the Red Army be built into a regular army big enough to capture and hold large cities.[41] It was this line that Chou En-lai adopted and employed to expel Mao from the Political Commissariat of the Red Army at the Ning-tu Conference.

According to RSQHP, the Maoists were of the opinion that the principal difference between Li Li-san and the 28 Bolsheviks lay in the fact that although Li desired the help of the Red Army in taking large cities, in the last phase of his line (June-September 1930) he continued to depend heavily on urban workers' uprisings, which the Red Army was to assist, but not to initiate. The 28 Bolsheviks, on the other hand, wanted to use the Red Army to seize the industrial centers directly, with little or no help from the organized workers' movement or the urban CCP organizations.[42] This was a late development in the Bolshevik line; it came only in 1932. The Comintern officials Mif, Magyar, and Kuusinen, under the direction of the CPSU Central Committee, undoubtedly helped Wang work it out after his return to Moscow in 1931. Mao opposed both versions of Wang's views on the taking of large cities.

The Struggle on Two Fronts Within the Party

In the 1931 edition of his pamphlet, Wang implied that the left aspects of the Li Li-san line were attributable to Lominadze's influence and its right aspects to the influence of Borodin and Ch'en

Tu-hsiu. In the 1932 edition Wang stressed that the right deviation had been the main danger under Li's regime and continued to be so even after the collapse of the Li Li-san line. Wang's critique of the rightists in the party was directed chiefly against "certain people" in the soviet areas who, misinterpreting the policy of the Central Committee, perceived the policy of consolidating the base areas as a "retreat line." These people did not hope to capture large cities at all and refused to believe that the conditions would soon develop under which urban centers could be taken. Finally, when the enemy attacked they resorted to "retreat," "flight," or "escape" toward the center of the base areas.

In his counterattack on Wang's ideas in 1945, Mao wrote that while Wang *had* criticized the Li Li-san line's left aspects, in the main he had attacked its right aspects.[43] Mao did not mention that Wang criticized the left aspects of Li-Li-sanism in 1931, or that the struggle against its right aspects really began only after Wang's return to Moscow and the publication there of the 1932 Appendix. According to Mao, the 28 Bolsheviks attempted to discredit all those who doubted the wisdom or practicability of their line, or who executed it half-heartedly. Such people they labeled "right opportunists," "two-faced persons," and advocates of the "rich peasant line" or the "compromising line." They were attacked not as comrades, but as criminals and enemies. After the Politburo moved to the central soviet districts in 1932, all of these errors were identified with the proponents of the "Lo Ming line."[44] The position of the Maoist faction was undermined in the assault on the Lo Ming line, and Mao himself was placed on probation for persisting in his errors.

THE ATTACK ON THE MAOISTS: THE SECOND PHASE

In late 1932 or early 1933, Po Ku, Chang Wen-t'ien, Wang Chia-hsiang, and the other members of the Politburo who had previously been in Shanghai arrived in Jui-ching. They were accompanied by a Comintern military adviser, a German known as Li T'e,* With his assistance they began their struggle to replace the right-wing Maoists in the party and army with men more willing to submit to orders, place their trust in Comintern analyses, and take the protection of the Soviet Union as the pivot around which all strategic planning of civil and class warfare in China must revolve. The program the Central Committee was then advocating bore a remarkable resemblance to the Li Li-san line. In accordance with Wang Ming's analysis, the Committee concluded that the mistakes that had been made at Ch'angsha did not warrant the deduction that large cities were not to be taken. The Red Army should be expanded to that end, as Wang had recommended.[45] After the Twelfth Plenum of the ECCI had confirmed Wang's judgment in September 1932, the CCP and the soviet government had begun preparing in the soviet areas for an all-out offensive against the cities.[46] Economic mobilization conferences were called immediately. In early 1933 a land investigation drive was started and preparations begun to elect delegates to the second All-China Soviet Congress.[47]

* In March 1964, an article appeared in the East German daily *Neues Deutschland* in which the author, one Otto Braun, identified himself as Li T'e. He also used the aliases "Wagner" (by his own testimony) and "Albert" (according to Hsiao, p. 331).

The Lo Ming Line

A year after Chou En-lai had deposed Mao from his position as chief political commissar of the Red Army, the Politburo arrived to renew the attack on Mao and his supporters. The emergence of the Lo Ming line provided an occasion for a reorganization of the military leadership. Lo Ming was one of the old commanders in the Fukien base who continued to follow the military strategy Chu and Mao had devised on Ching-kang-shan even in 1933. In February of that year, with the backing of the Comintern, the Politburo had ordered the Red Army expanded to a million men, the incorporation of all local militia into the regular army, and a general mobilization of all economic resources.[48] Lo Ming opposed this "Bolshevik forward and offensive line," and in face of the almost complete identity of the new official line with that of Li Li-san, a number of Maoists supported him.

Rather naturally, those who resisted the new line were strongest in guerrilla areas that had never become firmly consolidated bases. Party and army units in the Kiangsi-Fukien and Kiangsi-Kwangtung border regions, and in border hsien in Kiangsi—such as Nan-feng, Kuan-ch'ang, I-huang, Lo-an, Yung-feng, Chi-shui, T'ai-ho, Hui-ch'ang, Hsün-wu and An-yüan—all contributed their quota of Lo Ming partisans.[49] According to an article printed in *Struggle* in July 1933, T'an Ch'en-lin, who had been one of the members of Mao's Front Committee in the Ching-kang Mountains, was then a follower of the Lo Ming line. At that time he was in charge of the party units in the Red Army in Fukien. He is now vice-minister of rural work in the People's Government. According to the same article, four men in the army and party leadership in Kiangsi also supported the Lo Ming line. These were Mao Tse-t'an, Mao Tse-tung's brother; Ku Po, who had helped Mao engineer the Fu-t'ien incident; Hsieh Wei-chün, who had also worked closely with Mao at the time of the incident; and Teng Hsiao-p'ing, who was supporting the Chu-Mao line among the troops on the Kwangtung border. Ku Po and Hsieh Wei-chün disappear from history at about this time. Mao Tse-t'an survived for a time, but was left behind when the Long March began and was captured and executed with Ch'ü Ch'iu-pai in March 1935. Teng is now secretary-general of the CCP. Other men attacked for supporting the Lo Ming line were Teng Tzu-hui, Hsiao Ching-kuang, Ch'en T'an-ch'iu, Yü Tse-hung, Li Shao-chiu, and Yang Wen-chung.[50] The first three survived, Teng and Ch'en to become members of the Central Committee in 1945 and Hsiao to be elected an alternate. Yü Tse-hung, Li Shao-chiu, and Yang Wen-chung disappeared. That those who survived attack as adherents of the Lo Ming line were promoted to high positions after Mao took over the party clearly indicates that they were his supporters.

The Land Investigation Drive

While the campaign against the Lo Ming line led to a purge of Communists working in the Red Army and the other military organizations of the soviet government, the need for money to pay for the expansion of the Red Army led to a change in peasant policy and to a new land investigation drive. The Politburo prepared for this drive in May by calling an enlarged meeting of party cadres in Jui-ching. Kung Ch'u has reported that Chou En-lai opened the meeting by announcing that the party had decided to alter its peasant policy. Henceforth the CCP was to eliminate the landlords entirely, attack the rich peasants, neutralize the middle peasants, and ally itself only with the poor peasants and landless laborers. Landlords were to be herded into camps and all their property confiscated. Rich peasants were to be penalized by extra taxes that would be used to enlarge the army and thus contribute to the protection of the Soviet Union. Kung Ch'u and Ho Ch'ang, who was an old Li Li-sanist, spoke in opposition to these new measures. Chou then announced that the new policy was supported by the Comintern. Kung and Ho continued to argue against it, supported by a majority of those present. They argued that the Russian policy of dividing the peasants into rich, middle, and poor was not valid in China. Some of the "poor" peasants of Russia were richer even than some Chinese landlords. Chou again invoked Comintern authority and finally achieved a reluctant majority. When the meeting was over, Hsiang Ying took Kung home to dinner and told him that under the circumstances it was unwise for him to defend his position so vociferously. Kung replied that the CCP still operated under democratic centralism and that he had every right to voice his dissent until a decision had been reached. But Kung realized at this time that in fact the system had changed—the majority of elected party representatives had been coerced by the Comintern rather than allowed to make decisions on the basis of free debate.*

On June 1, Mao launched the land investigation drive. In his view the drive was necessary to support the war effort,

but was not to be allowed to alienate a large proportion of the peasants and thereby narrow the base of popular support in the soviet areas. It was to correct inequities in the previous land distributions, not initiate a new policy altogether.[51] The Central Bureau directive to party cadres in the soviet government issued one day later attributed the failure of the soviet government to solve the land problem in the past to Mao's incorrect, egalitarian line.[52] Conflict between the adherents of the two lines was soon apparent. Kung Ch'u was recalled to Jui-ching in August, and Chou En-lai, in the presence of Li Teh, Po Ku, and Chu Teh, suspended Kung's membership in the CCP for six months.[53] Many of the lower-level cadres who still supported Mao and his land policy suffered similar fates before the end of the drive that autumn.

The situation had become very tense by November, when the KMT armies were again closing in on the central soviet district, in their Fifth Encirclement Campaign. The Red Army had suffered heavy losses, and a scarcity of salt had caused a great deal of illness. Then the outbreak of the Fukien revolt suddenly gave the Red Army a chance to reach the coast through the territory of a friendly government.

The Fukien Revolt

On November 20, 1933, the KMT's Nineteenth Route Army, commanded by Ch'en Ming-Shu, revolted in Fukien. The following day the rebels called a "provincial conference of delegates of the Chinese people" in Fuchow. Hoping to negotiate an agreement, delegates from the Nineteenth Route Army had contacted Communist representatives in

---

* Kung returned to his post an unhappy man. In December 1934, as the Long March began, he deserted from the Red Army.

Shanghai before the revolt. The Shanghai Communists asked Moscow for advice and were instructed to cooperate with the rebels on a military but not a party basis. They might work with the rebels against both the Japanese and the Nanking government of Chiang Kai-shek, but were to continue to criticize the political line of the Third Party and left KMT members of the rebel government. On October 26, 1933, a military alliance was concluded between the central soviet government and the Red Army on the one hand, and the Fukien provincial government and the Nineteenth Route Army on the other. Although the content of the agreement probably did not go beyond Moscow's instructions, the fact that a political agent representing the Chinese soviet government had signed the agreement in that government's name undoubtedly did.[54]

Throughout the Fukien revolt the Central Bureau attacked the Fukien rebels as sham democrats and simple military conspirators who were akin to the European Social Democrats. In contrast, telegrams from Chu and Mao expressed cautious hope that the Fukien rebels and the Red Army could work out a genuine basis for cooperation and that the rebel leaders would grant freedom to the people of Fukien. The soviet government and the CCP Central Committee issued no joint statements about either the revolt or the anti-Japanese united front in Fukien.[55] As the Second All-China Soviet Congress convened in Jui-ching, the revolt in Fukien was put down by troops loyal to Nanking. By January 20 it had collapsed. After the opportunity for the CCP to form a united front with a friendly army had passed, Mao joined the Politburo in denouncing the rebels.

The Second All-China Soviet Congress

In spite of the continuing attacks on the Maoist faction in the party, the Red Army, and the soviet government from 1931 to 1934, Mao was reelected as chairman of the soviet government in January 1934. The 28 Bolsheviks intended him to serve only as a figurehead, however, playing the role of Kalinin to Po Ku's Stalin. To this end they rearranged the power structure of the all-China soviet government. At the First Congress Mao had been elected chairman of both the Central Executive Committee and the Council of People's Commissars. No one had shared his power, not even his two vice-chairmen, for Chang Kuo-t'ao was not present in the central soviet areas and Hsiang Ying was, at least by reputation, a weak and incapable man. After the change in 1934, however, the Central Executive Committee was led by a 17-member Presidium that had the power to elect the chairman from among its own members. The 28 Bolsheviks probably had a majority of the Presidium on their side and therefore could afford to elect Mao: they could always depose him if he proved uncooperative. Meanwhile, Chang Wen-t'ien became chairman of the Council of People's Commissars, with no deputies or presidium to control him. Chang became the equivalent of the premier of the government, with almost unlimited power, while Mao held the honorary and essentially powerless post of chairman of the Central Executive Committee.[56] If Mao was playing Kalinin, Chang was Molotov.

At the Second All-China Soviet Congress, Mao delivered a report on the activities of the Central Executive Committee and the Council of People's Commissars. If the usual Communist practice was followed, the text of this speech had previously been approved by the Fifth Plenum of the Central Committee, held immediately before the Second Congress. Only the part of this report dealing with economic policy is found in HC.[57] After a short floor discussion of his official report, Mao made some concluding remarks. About one quarter of the text of these remarks, the part that seems to express his own views, is included in HC. His remarks on the attitudes of the party and government toward the Fukien rebellion are not included, but his attack on the 28 Bolsheviks' bureaucratic methods of leadership is, as is his defense of the work of his own supporters, some of whom had been purged in the drive against the Lo Ming line.[58] He first stressed the fact on which all were in agreement: that the work of mobilizing the masses for revolutionary war was the CCP's central task. But, he stated, before the masses could be effectively mobilized the party and government must provide for them the minimum necessities of life. He pointed with pride to the way the comrades in Chang-kang and Tsai-ki hsiang had solved urgent problems facing the people, and he condemned the work of the comrades in Ting-chow for failing to do the same.[59]

Ting-chow, Fukien, was one of the largest cities then held by the Communists. It is highly probable that the 28 Bolsheviks dominated its soviet government. Chang-kang and Tsai-ki may have been strongholds of the Maoist-faction: the evidence is incomplete, but the available facts point toward that conclusion. Chang-kang was in Hsing-kuo, Kiangsi, and Tsai-ki in Shang-hang, Fukien. Both Hsing-kuo and Shang-hang were model hsien created by their respective soviet governments shortly after the First All-China Soviet Congress in 1931, in the period before the 28 Bolsheviks gained control of the leading organs of the soviet governments. As discussed above, Mao's investigation at the end of October 1930 had uncovered small nests of A-B Corpsmen in the hsiang and ch'ü soviets of Hsing-kuo.[60] In the aftermath of the Fu-t'ien incident, Mao's faction had wiped out all local opposition and achieved firm control over this area. Shang-hang had a similar history; there the alleged A-B Corps had been obliterated slightly later than in Hsing-kuo.[61] In defending himself, Lo Ming had specifically mentioned Shang-hang as an area in which he thought the Chu-Mao guerrilla tactics should continue to be used in fighting the enemy. One of Lo Ming's closest associates and fellow purgees, Yang Wen-chung, had also been active in Shang-hang in 1933.[62]

In his concluding remarks, Mao defended and praised the Communists working in Hsing-kuo and Shang-hang. He also praised the Communists who had been successfully utilizing guerrilla tactics against the encircling KMT troops and were therefore doubtful of the applicability to their particular areas of the Central Committee's forward line.[63]

It is not possible to show that Mao's henchmen had been dominant in *all* the areas he singled out for praise, or that members of his faction had been persecuted with particular vigor in some of the places he condemned, but the evidence points in that direction. Those who attended the congress, however, knew the areas in which each faction had been dominant. Certainly they understood the import of where Mao's praise and blame fell.

The Nadir of Mao's Fortunes

As the summer of 1934 approached, the Politburo continued along its suicidal course. The land investigation drive, which had been halted in September or October 1933, recommenced. A new recruitment drive began. And the Bolsheviks and the Maoists began to destroy one another in a fight for their very existence. Mao was put on probation: he was excluded from party meetings and either imprisoned or kept under house arrest at Yü-tu, a hsien capital some 60 miles west of the Communist capital of Juiching. According to Kung Ch'u, the order to place Mao on probation originated in Moscow and resulted from his actions during the Fukien rebellion. The Moscow order followed the adoption of a new line by the Thirteenth Plenum of the ECCI in December 1933 that called on all Communists to support the fight against fascism—the united front from below. The new line emphasized in particular the struggle against Social Democrats, who were known at the time as "social fascists."[64]

Thus from sometime in July 1934 until the beginning of the Long March in October Mao was stripped of power, on probation, and probably imprisoned. He had arrived at this sorry state thanks to the combined efforts of Po Ku in Juiching and Wang Ming in Moscow. Mao's description of the organizational procedures of the party's leaders in 1934 is graphic, bitter, and accurate. Very few anti-Communists have written more revealing descriptions of the struggles at party meetings during the first year of the great purges. Irrespective of circumstances, he said in RSQHP, the exponents of the third left line

invariably attached . . . damaging labels to all comrades in the party who, finding the erroneous line impracticable, expressed doubts about it, disagreed with it, resented it, supported it only lukewarmly, or executed it only halfheartedly. Labels like "right opportunism," "line of the rich peasants," "Lo Ming's line," "line of conciliation," and "double-dealing" [were used, for the leftists] waged "relentless struggles" against [their opponents] as if . . . they were criminals and enemies. Instead of regarding the veteran cadres as valuable assets to the party, the sectarians persecuted, punished, and deposed large numbers of these veterans in the central and local organizations. . . . Large numbers of good comrades were wrongly indicted and unjustly punished; this led to the most lamentable losses inside the party.[65]

Amends should be made, he said. "Comrades who upon investigation are proved to have died as victims of a miscarriage of justice should be absolved from false accusations, reinstated as party members, and forever remembered by all comrades."[66]

He went on to recall the memory of four comrades who had died at the hands of the KMT. Three had been captured in January 1931, in the raid supposedly engineered by Wang Ming to destroy the group in the CCP attempting to organize opposition to the 28 Bolsheviks. These were Li Ch'iu-shih, who had worked in the CCP's Propaganda Department in 1927-28, Lin Yü-nan, director of the Wuhan Labor Union Secretariat and secretary-general of the All-China Federation of Trade Unions in 1927-28, and Ho Meng-hsiung, leader of the Kiangsu Provincial Committee and a secretary to its Peasant Department in 1927. The other was Ch'ü Ch'iu-pai, who was left behind at the beginning of the Long March. Ch'ü had been the major opponent of the 28 Bolsheviks before their seizure of power. The Fourth Plenum had permanently ended his successful career, although he survived and continued to work in the party for four years more.[67] In choosing to revive the memory of these men and posthumously reinstate them as party members, Mao challenged the legitimacy of the power and authority of the 28 Bolsheviks, and thereby of the Comintern apparatus that had supported their pretensions. He intimated that the Bolsheviks had seized power by double-dealing, by betraying comrades to the enemy police even before the first Russian Communist had been shot for meeting secretly with Trotsky. It is no wonder Mao wrote that the Bolsheviks' struggles in the Chinese party had "violated the fundamental principle of democratic centralism, eliminated the democratic spirit of criticism and self-criticism, turned party discipline into mechanical regulation, fostered tendencies toward blind obedience and parrotry, and thus jeopardized and obstructed the development of vigorous and creative Marxism."[68]

LEARNING FROM THE MISTAKES OF THE CPSU

By the time the Red Armies set out on the Long March, Mao had every reason to feel a deep repugnance for Stalinist methods of controlling non-Soviet parties. In 1931, when Mao was at the height of his power, after he had overcome his opponents in southwestern Kiangsi and successfully led the Red Armies against the first three KMT campaigns of encirclement and annihilation, the 28 Bolsheviks had begun their struggle against his ideas on political and military strategy. By 1934, with the support of the Comintern, they had removed him and his most active supporters from all influential positions in the party, army, and government. They had rejected and condemned his agrarian and military policies and replaced them with policies modeled after the practice of the Soviet government and the CPSU. In implementing their "further bolshevization of

the CCP" they had adopted the terroristic policies of the Soviet political police and anticipated in the small soviet districts of South China the great purges in the Soviet Union.

When the Maoist faction took control of the Party Secretariat and the Revolutionary Military Council at the Tsun-yi Conference in January 1935, its only justification was that the strategy of the 28 Bolsheviks had proved itself a dismal failure.[69] The statement of Mao's strategic formulae in terms of Marxist categories still lay in the future. But the protection of the Soviet Union would no longer be the primary purpose of the CCP and the Chinese Red Army. Instead of attempting to copy the Russian Bolshevik model, the party, under Mao, set out to create for itself a strategy based on the requirements of the Chinese revolution.

Notes

For complete titles of citations, see John E. Rue, *Mao Tse-tung in Opposition, 1927-1935* (Stanford University Press, 1966), Notes and Bibliography.

1. "Central [Politburo] Resolution Rescinding the Punishment of the Four Comrades Ch'en Shao-yü, Ch'in Pang-hsien, Wang Chia-ch'iang, and Ho Tzu-shu," *Party Reconstruction*, No. 1 (Jan. 25, 1931), [23], pp. 29-30, in BIC.
2. "Central [Politburo] Resolution Concerning the Question of Comrade Ho Meng-hsiung," *Party Reconstruction*, No. 1 (Jan. 25, 1931), [24], pp. 30-31, in BIC.
3. Schwartz, *Chinese Communism*, p. 154.
4. Brandt, Schwartz, and Fairbank, p. 36.
5. Hsiao, pp. 59, 73.
6. "Discussion of the Li-san line by the Presidium of the ECCI," Dec. 1930, *Bolshevik*, IV, No. 3 (May 10, 1931), [62], 66-75, in BIC.
7. *Ibid.*, pp. 43-47.
8. "Minutes of the Enlarged Politburo Meeting," Nov. 22, 1930, in Hsiao, pp. 93-95.
9. *Ibid.*, p. 155.

10. North, *Moscow*, p. 158n41; Brandt, Schwartz, and Fairbank, p. 36.

11. "Open Fire on the Rightist Faction," *Party Reconstruction*, No. 1 (Jan. 1931), [54], pp. 23-24.

12. Schwartz, *Chinese Communism*, p. 166; Hsiao, p. 130.

13. Li Ang, *Red Stage* [66], English trans., Chap. 12; Isaacs, 1st ed., p. 407.

14. Ch'en Shao-yü (Wang Ming), *The Two Lines* [100], Shanghai edition.

15. North, *Moscow*, p. 158.

16. Hsiao, pp. 161-62.

17. "Order of the Council of People's Commissars of the Soviet Provisional Central Government to Arrest the Deserter of the Revolution Ku Shun-chang," Dec. 10, 1931, *Red Flag Weekly*, No. 27 (Dec. 17, 1931), [33].

18. Brandt, Schwartz, and Fairbank, p. 36.

19. "A Directive Letter of the Central to the Soviet Areas," Sept. 1, 1931, [28], in SSC.

20. Mao, SW, IV, 182; HC, III, 961.

21. Mao, SW, IV, 185; HC, III, 968-69.

22. Hsiao, p. 165.

23. "Resolution on the Question of Party Reconstruction of the First Party Congress of the [Central] Soviet Areas," Nov. 1931, [39], in SSC.

24. "Resolution on the Problem of the Red Army Adopted by the First Party Congress of the [Central] Soviet Areas," Oct. 1931, [37], in SSC.

25. See Hsiao, pp. 178-79, for another interpretation of the effects of the final draft on the rich peasants' interests.

26. "Draft Resolution of the First National Soviet Congress on the Question of the Red Army," *Draft Resolutions Introduced by the CCP Central Committee to the First National Soviet Congress* (Political Department, Third Army Corps, Chinese Workers' and Peasants' Red Army, n.d. [1931?]) [40], in SSC.

27. "Letter from the CCP Central Bureau of the Soviet Areas to the CCP Kiangsi Provincial Committee," Jan. 19, 1932, in *Documents of or Concerning the Enlarged Conference of the Provincial Committee of the Kiangsi Soviet Area* (n.p. [Jui-ching?]: Kiangsi Provincial Committee, Feb. 7, 1932) [29], in SSC.

28. Hsiao, p. 214.

29. *Ibid.*, pp. 210-11, 214; Mao, SW, IV, 185.

30. Ho Kan-chih, *A History of the Modern Chinese Revolution* (Peking: Foreign Languages Press, 1959) [53], pp. 156-61.

31. *Ibid.*

32. McLane, pp. 266-71, gives a complete list of the declarations on these subjects appearing in Russian and Comintern sources between those dates.

33. Mao, SW, IV, 181; HC, III, 965.

34. *Ibid.*

35. Mao, SW, IV, 191; HC, III, 974.

36. *Ibid.*

37. See Hsiao, pp. 204-5, for his summary of Wang's points on this issue.

38. Mao, SW, IV, 192; HC, III, 974.

39. Hsiao, pp. 205-6.

40. Mao, SW, IV, 185-86; HC, III, 968-69.

41. Hsiao, p. 206.

42. Mao, SW, IV, 195-96; HC, III, 978.

43. Mao, SW, IV, 181; HC, III, 964.

44. Mao, SW, IV, 206; HC, III, 986-87; Hsiao, pp. 206-7.

45. Wang Ming, *The Two Lines* [100], 2d ed., Appendix, Chap. 1, Sect. B-2.

46. The full text of the resolution confirming Wang's line was translated into Chinese and published in *Struggle* (Shanghai), No. 31 (Dec. 31, 1932), leaves 2-8, cited in Hsiao, p. 233. This *Struggle*, officially the organ of the CCP, continued to be published in Shanghai until May 1934. Another journal called *Struggle*, officially the organ of the Central Bureau of the Soviet Areas, was published in Kiangsi from Feb. 1933 to Sept. 1934.

47. Mao "Smashing the KMT Fifth 'Campaign' and the Task of Soviet Economic Reconstruction," in Hsiao, pp. 221-22; SW, I, 129-37. For Mao's line on the investigation drive of 1933, see SW, I, 138-40; for the investigations he made in 1933 see NTTC, pp. 96-133.

48. "Urgent Tasks of the Party in the Decisive Fight Against the Enemy's Fourth 'Campaign'" (Central Bureau, CCP, Feb. 8, 1933), *Struggle* (Kiangsi), No. 2 (Feb. 4—probably a misprint of Feb. 14—1933), [31], pp. 1-3, in SSC.

49. Jen Pi-shih, "What is the Forward and Offensive Line?" dated Feb. 19, 1933, *Struggle* (Kiangsi), No. 3 (Feb. 23, 1933), [61], pp. 15-18, in SSC.

50. Kung [63], pp. 242, 245, 267, 272; Hsiao, pp. 234, 239-47 (for a summary of the articles in the Kiangsi *Struggle*); Isaacs, 2d rev. ed., pp. 347-48, for information on Teng Hsiao-p'ing; Mao, NTTC, p. 71, for information on one of his trips with Ku Po and Hsieh Wei-chün, on Nov. 18, 1930.

51. "Instruction No. 11 of the Council of People's Commissars of the Provisional Central Government of the Chinese Soviet Republic—Launching an Extensive and Intensive Land Investigation Drive," dated June 1, 1933, *Red China*, No. 87 (June 20, 1933), [34], p. 5, in SSC.

52. "Resolution of the Central Bureau on the Land Investigation Drive," June 2, 1933, *Red China*, No. 87 (June 20, 1933), [32], p. 2, in SSC.

53. Kung [63], pp. 378-81.

54. Lei Hsiao-ch'en, *Thirty Years of Turmoil in China* (Hong Kong: Asia Press, 1955, 2 vols.) [65], I, 212-16.

55. McLane, p. 271; Hsiao, pp. 248-60; Snow, RSOC, 1st ed., pp. 381-82. The comments of Mao and others on the Fukien revolt in these chapters were completely rewritten in the second edition.

56. "Proclamation of the Central Executive Committee of the Chinese Soviet Republic,

No. 1," dated Feb. 5, 1934, *Red China*, Feb. 12, 1934, [35], p. 1.

57. Mao, SW, I, 141-46; HC, I, 125-30.

58. Mao, SW, I, 147-52; HC, I, 131-36.

59. Mao, SW, I, 148-49; HC, I, 132-33.

60. Mao, NTTC, pp. 7-62.

61. Smedley, *China's Red Army Marches*, p. 269.

62. Hsiao, p. 236.

63. Mao, SW, I, 151-52; HC, I, 135.

64. Kung [63], pp. 395-400; "Fascism, Danger of War, and the Tasks of the Communist Parties in the Various Nations—Resolution of the ECCI 13th Plenum on the Report of Comrad Kuusinen," in Hsiao, pp. 223-24.

65. Mao, SW, IV, 206-7; HC, III, 986-87.

66. Mao, SW, IV, 207; HC, III, 987.

67. Mao, SW, IV, 240, 340, 341; HC, III, 999-1000; Isaacs, 1st ed., p. 407; Li Ang [66], p. 112.

68. Mao, SW, IV, 206; HC, III, 986.

69. Mao, SW, IV, 188; HC, III, 971.

V. THE UNITED FRONT

27. THE SIAN COUP D'ETAT

CHIANG KAI-SHEK

December 12 [1936] At 5:30 a.m., when I was dressing after my exercise, I heard gun firing just in front of the gate of my Headquarters. I sent one of my body-guards to see what was the matter, but as he did not come back to report I sent two others out and then heard gun firing again which then continued incessantly. Thereupon I felt that the North-eastern troops had revolted. On this visit to Shensi I had only my personal body-guards and twenty uniformed soldiers. The soldiers who had been put on guard duty outside my Headquarters were Chang's bodyguards. Presently Lieutenant Mao sent a messenger to report that a mutiny had broken out and that they had already reached the second gate, but that from telephone communication with the barracks behind the mountain he learned that there was nothing untoward in evidence. I asked where Lieutenant Mao was and was told that he was at the front compound near the bridge directing the bodyguard. The messenger said that Mao begged me first to proceed to the mountain at the back of my quarters. I asked what the mutinous troops looked like, and was told

From Chiang Kai-shek, *A Fortnight in Sian: Extracts From A Diary* (The China Publishing Company, Shanghai, 1937), pp. 58-70, 82-84, 105, 107.

that they had on fur caps and belonged to the North-eastern troops.

Accompanied by Tso Pei-chi, one of my own guard officers, and Chiang Hsiao-chung, an A.D.C., I started for the mountain at the back of the house. After crossing the Fei-Hung Bridge we found the eastern side door securely locked and the key could nowhere be found. We then scaled the wall which was only about ten feet high and not difficult to get over. But just outside the wall there was a deep moat, the bottom of which was about thirty feet below the top of the wall. As it was still dark, I missed my footing and fell into the moat. I felt a bad pain and was unable to rise. About three minutes later I managed to stand up and walked with difficulty. After having walked several tens of paces we reached a small temple, where some of my bodyguards were on duty. They helped me to climb the mountain.

At that time I was under the impression that the mutiny was local, that only a section of the troops at Lintung had mutinied, possibly at the instigation of the Communist bandits, and that it was not a preconceived plot planned by Hanching. I also thought that if the whole of the North-eastern army were in revolt, my Headquarters would have been completely surrounded. The absence of mutinous troops outside the wall further convinced me that the mutiny was local. I believed that if we could cross the hill and wait for daybreak, the trouble would be over. On the eastern side of this hill there was no path, but we considered it was not safe to go west, as we might meet the mutinous troops on that side. So we proceeded east. There were precipitous cliffs on which we fumbled about for a hold as we climbed.

After about a half an hour we reached the mountain top and sat down on a piece of level ground for a short rest. I sent a bodyguard to a cliff before us to reconnoitre. Presently gun firing was heard on all sides. Bullets whizzed by quite close to my body. Some of the bodyguards were hit and dropped dead. I then realized that I was surrounded, that the mutiny was not local and that the whole of the North-eastern troops took part in it. So I decided not to take shelter, but to go back to my Headquarters and see what could be done. I walked down the mountain as quickly as I could. Halfway down the mountain I fell into a cave which was overgrown with thorny shrubs and in which there was barely enough space to admit me. I felt exhausted. Twice I struggled to my feet but fell down again. I was compelled to remain there for a rest and to wait further developments.

As the day gradually dawned, I could see from the cave that the Lishan Mountain was surrounded by a large number of troops. Then I heard the detonation of machine-guns and hand grenades near my Headquarters. I knew that my faithful bodyguards at the Headquarters continued their resistance and that the rebels were using artillery to attack them. It was about nine o'clock, after which time no more firing could be heard. The rebels sought for me. Twice they passed the cave in which I took cover, but failed to discover me.

About twenty or thirty feet from my refuge I heard someone hotly arguing with the rebels. It was Chiang Hsiao-chung's voice. The rebels made a more thorough search. I heard one of the mutinous soldiers above the cave saying: "Here is a man in civilian dress; probably he is the Generalissimo." Another soldier said; "Let us first fire a shot." Still another said: "Don't do that." I then raised my voice and said: "I am the Generalissimo. Don't be disrespectful. If you regard me as your prisoner, kill me, but don't subject me to indignities." The mutineers said: "We don't dare." They fired three shots into the air and shouted: "The Generalissimo is here!"

Sun Ming-chiu, a Battalion Commander,* then approached me. He knelt before me with tears in his eyes and requested me to go down the mountain. Then I knew that the soldiers attacking the Headquarters belonged to the 2nd Battalion of Chang's Bodyguards. Sun accompanied me down the mountain. When we reached my Headquarters I intended to go in for a rest. I saw through the doorway that things were in great disorder and the ground was strewn with dead bodies. Sun asked me to go by motor-car to Sian. He said that my room was already in a state of confusion, and that he had received orders from his superiors to invite me to Sian. I ordered Sun to find the Deputy Commander (Chang Hsueh-liang), who he said was in Sian waiting for me. He added: "We don't dare to mutiny against our superior officers; we wish to make a personal representation that Your Excellency will kindly grant our request." To this I

---

* Battalion Commander of Chang Hsueh-liang's Bodyguard Division.

shouted in anger: "Hold your tongue, you rebels! If you want to kill me, kill me right now!" Sun and the Commander of the 2nd Brigade of the 105th Division saluted once again and requested me to board the car for the city. As I wanted to see Chang Hsueh-liang and find out from him what all this meant, I entered the car.

Sun Ming-chiu and the Brigade Commander helped me into the car. Tan Hai, the most trusted A.D.C. of Chang Hsueh-liang, sat with the chauffeur. The car went straight to Sian. When nearing Tungkwan (the East City Gate), I saw Chang's personal car, and the Brigade Commander told me that the Deputy Commander was coming. When the car approached us, Chang was not in it, but he had sent an officer who had been instructed where I was to be taken. My destination was to be the New City Building, which is the Pacification Commissioner's Headquarters at Sian, occupied by Yang Hu-chen. A feeling of doubt arose in my mind. As I understood it was the North-eastern Army which revolted and besieged my Headquarters why should I be sent to Yang's place? By that time the car reached the East Gate. I was further surprised at seeing the guards wearing armlets of the 17th Army (Yang's Army). I then thought that as Yang did not attend my dinner of the previous night, he must have been detained by Chang. I also believed that the high officers of the Central Government at Sian must have met with the same fate, and that the armlets of the 17th Army worn by the soldiers had possibly been taken from Yang's soldiers after being disarmed by Chang's men and were used to conceal their identity. Yang is an old comrade of our Party and has been in long association with the Revolutionary Movement. It was my strong conviction that he took no part in the revolt. We reached the New City Building at ten o'clock.

When I entered the building I did not see Yang. After a while Sung Wen-mei, Commander of the Special Service Battalion of the Pacification Commissioner's Headquarters, entered my room. To him Sun Ming-chiu handed over the guard duty. Sung told me that Chang Hsueh-liang said he wished me to rest for a while and that he would soon come. I ordered him to send for Chang who appeared half an hour later. He was very respectful to me, but I did not return his courtesies. Chang stood with his hands at his sides.

I asked him: "Did you know beforehand about today's revolt?"

He answered in the negative.

I continued: "If you have no previous knowledge of the affair, you should see that I return immediately to Nanking or Loyang. Then it may not be difficult to settle this affair."

Chang answered: "I did not know anything of the actual developments, but I wish to lay my views before Your Excellency, the Generalissimo."

I retorted: "Do you still call me the Generalissimo? If you still recognize me as your superior, you should send me to Loyang; otherwise you are a rebel. Since I am in the hands of a rebel you had better shoot me dead. There is nothing else to say."

Chang replied: "If Your Excellency accepts my suggestions, I shall obey your orders."

I rebuked him by saying: "Which are you, my subordinate or my enemy? If my subordinate, you should obey my orders. If you are my enemy you should kill me without delay. You should choose either of these two steps, but say nothing more for I will not listen to you."

Chang then explained that in taking this action his motive was revolutionary, but not mutinous.

I then shouted in indignation: "Why do you still disclaim any previous knowledge of the mutiny?"

Chang answered: "Even if we are enemies, there is still the possibility for us to enter into negotiations."

I was almost overcome with anger and retorted: "Can there be any talk between enemies? What type of man do you take me to be? Can the rebels and my enemies compel me to surrender by force?"

Chang was somewhat taken aback and added: "I am not alone responsible for this affair. There are many other people who are in the movement, which should be referred to the people for their verdict. Should the people be in sympathy with this movement, then it will prove that I am representing the common will of the people and Your Excellency will realize that my action is not wrong. Then you may retire from office and let me do the work. If the people are not in sympathy with this movement, then I shall admit my own fault and Your Excellency may resume your work. I believe I have not in any way disobeyed your teachings. Please, don't be angry, and consider the matter carefully."

When I heard "the people's verdict" I realized that it was a malicious plot to kill me by using the mob as their excuse. I shouted: "You are crazy. Do you think that the people are in sympathy with your mutiny? Even the so-called 'Popular Front' will not give you their support. You claim that your motives are revolutionary. Can a mutiny be called a revolution? Chen Chiung-ming* also claimed

* Chen Chiung-ming (Civil Governor of Canton and Commander-in-Chief of the Revolutionary Army) mutinied against Dr. Sun Yat-sen at Canton in 1922.

to be a revolutionist, but who in the world could believe him? Since you are a rebel, how can you even expect to command the obedience of your men who surround this house?' How can you be a man yourself? How can you be sure that your men will not follow your example and do as you are doing to me? Remember that four years ago the people wanted to get hold of you and punish you, but I took the blame for you I do not know how many times. Because I took a generous protective attitude towards you, you were able to go abroad. From now on, in spite of the size of the world, where will you find a place for yourself? Living, there will be no place to put your feet; dead, there will be no place to bury your bones. You still do not realize your predicament, but I do. I am really afraid for you."

On hearing this Chang's face suddenly changed colour. He said: "Are you still so obstinate?"

I retorted: "What do you mean by 'obstinate'? I am your superior, and you are a rebel. According to military discipline and the law of the land, you, as a rebel, deserve not only reprimand but also punishment. My head may be cut off, my body may be mutilated, but I must preserve the honour of the Chinese race, and must uphold law and order. I am now in the hands of you rebels. If I allow the honour of the 400,000,000 people whom I represent to be degraded by accepting any demands in order to save my own life we should lose our national existence. Do you think that by using force you can compel me to surrender to you rebels? To-day you have lethal weapons; I have none, but instead I am armed with the principles of righteousness. These are my weapons of defence. With these I must defend the honour of the people whom I represent and must be a faithful follower of our late Leader (Dr. Sun Yat-sen). I shall do nothing to betray the trust imposed on me by the martyrs of the Revolution. I shall not bring shame and dishonour to this world, to the memory of my parents, and to the nation. You, young man, do you think you can make me submissive by force? You mistake my firm stand on the principles of law and order for obstinacy. If you are a brave man, kill me; if not, confess your sins and let me go. If you do neither, you will be in a dangerous position. Why don't you kill me now?"

When he heard this, he was downcast and remained silent. After a while he asked: "Why don't you give more thought to this matter? I am going."

Then I gestured with my hand and said: "Get out!"

He assumed a more respectful manner and asked me whether I would wish to remove to his home. I answered: "I shall never enter the enemy's camp."

He then said that if I lived with him I would be safe.

I retorted: "I need none of your protection."

He then stood up and sat down several times, and watched for any change of my countenance.

I closed my eyes and paid him no attention.

During the following half hour he repeatedly said that he would go; finally he sat down again and ordered the servant to bring food to my room and asked me to eat. I said: "I have already reached the age of fifty, and, since I am the cause of so much worry to the nation what face have I to eat the food won by their sweat and blood, to say nothing of touching the food provided by an enemy?"

I refused to eat. Chang stood by me for a long time. I asked him where was Mr. Shao,* the Chairman of the Shensi Provincial Government.

He answered that Mr. Shao was also in the Headquarters of the Pacification Commissioner. He added that the high military officers of the Central Government were all safe, except Chien Ta-chun, who was wounded by a gun shot in a struggle with the mutinous soldiers. He informed me that it was merely a superficial wound near his ear.

I ordered him to send for Mr. Shao. He sent a guard to look for Mr. Shao, but he himself remained beside me.

A few minutes later, Mr. Shao Li-tzu came and inquired after my health.

Chang then withdrew from my presence.

I asked Mr. Shao: "Have you come from the Office of the Provincial Government?"

Mr. Shao answered, "I came from the Office of the Commander of the Pacification Commissioner's Bodyguards. General Chien was also there, but he is wounded. He was shot through the chest and bled profusely. He has been removed to another place for medical attention."

Although Chang had left my room, Battalion Commander Sung was still waiting at the door. Twice I told him to go away and to close the door, but Sung failed to do so. I then stood up to shut the door myself. Sung entered the room and asked me to pardon him. He said that he was ordered to wait on me and that he did not think it safe to close the door. I knew that he kept a watch over me, but I paid him no more attention.

I told Mr. Shao briefly what I had said to Chang, and then drew up a telegram to my wife. I handed the telegram to Battalion Commander Sung and

---

* Shao Li-tzu.

asked him to take it to Chang for despatch.

At that time, I knew that I would be a martyr of the Revolution and that I must leave my last words to my family.

When Mr. Shao saw that in my heart I had definitely determined to sacrifice my life he was greatly moved.

He said: "I believe it is impossible for you to go back to Loyang, but I think Chang will have no courage to harm you. But if the case is allowed to drag on for some time, I am afraid that other complications will arise. As Your Excellency's personal safety is closely bound up with the safety of the nation, it is advisable for you to take great care of yourself. I remember that in 1927 and 1931 twice you tendered your resignation, but owing to the fact that your services were urgently needed by the Party and the Government, you reentered the political arena after a short time of retirement. How does that compare with present circumstances?"

I told him that the trouble was that I trusted others too much and neglected to take necessary precautions. "For this reason," I continued, "a great injury has been done to the country. After my return to Nanking I shall tender my resignation again and ask the Central Government to punish me. But I shall never resign my post in Sian under the duress of my subordinates. Even if they want me to issue an order, or to grant certain conditions, I will die rather than do so. If I yielded on any point for my personal safety, I would forfeit the confidence placed in me by four hundred million people."

Mr. Shao remained silent.

As I was thinly clad he told me to put on more clothing.

I told him I needed no more clothing. Battalion Commander Sung then of-fered me a fur-lined gown, but I refused to accept it. The attendants served breakfast and biscuits, but I told them to take the food away. I was on the point of exhaustion and lay down to sleep. Mr. Shao left me after telling me to take care of my health. . . .

December 14. . . . I very carefully thought over Chang's request that I move to another place, but could not find any explanation. Could it be that he was afraid that, should I stay long in the New City, in the sphere of influence of Yang, I might get into close touch with the latter, and Chang would not be able to do with me as he liked?

After changing my residence Chang came to see me. I asked him, since I had complied with his request in this matter, whether he and his confederates had decided to send me back. If not, they should decide upon this question. Chang suddenly said that the matter was not so simple. Since many people had participated in the matter he said everything had to be decided by them jointly. Besides, they had already sent out a circular telegram including eight proposals, and I must agree to some of them so that the coup might not become meaningless. If, said he, no results whatever were achieved, the crowd would not agree to sending me back.

The so-called eight proposals were:

1. Reorganize the Nanking Government so that members of other parties and cliques might come in and help save the nation;
2. Stop all civil wars;
3. Release immediately the patriotic leaders who had been arrested in Shanghai;
4. Pardon all political offenders;
5. Guarantee the people's liberty of assembly;

6. Give a free hand to the people to carry out patriotic movements;
7. Carry out the Leader's [Dr. Sun Yat-sen's] will faithfully;
8. Call a National Salvation Conference immediately.

I strongly rebuked him for going back on his own promise which he made before my change of residence, and did not allow him to go on with his speech. I also said that whatever proposals they might have, and however good the proposals might sound, their conduct in effecting the coup was absolutely wrong, and nobody could believe in their sincerity nor support their proposals.

Chang further explained the reasons for their eight proposals and wanted me to consider them. I said I had determined to sacrifice my life rather than sign any document while under duress, and had thought over the situation very carefully. At the former place of confinement I had already told him about it; why should he still be unable to understand my posi-

tion? He should know that although he is able to make a captive of my body, he could never break my will power. I could not possibly yield on any of these points, nor even listen to their proposals until I am back in Nanking. There was no use for them to talk further.

December 25. In the morning T. V. came and told me that Chang had decided to send me back to Nanking, . . .

At the time of departure, Chang insisted upon accompanying me to Nanking. I told him several times to stay, as there would be no one to command the Northeastern Army when he left. Besides, it might not be convenient for him to go to Nanking at present.

He said that he had asked Yang to look after his troops, as well as instructed his subordinates to obey Yang's orders. So we left by plane, and arrived at Loyang at 5:20 p.m. In the evening we stayed at the Branch Academy of the Military Cadets.

28. THE NATIONALIST-COMMUNIST WARTIME ENTENTE

Shortly after the return of the Generalissimo from Sian, the Third Plenary Session of the Fifth Central Executive Committee of the Kuomintang was held in Nanking. On February 10, 1937, five

From *United States Relations with China: With Special Reference to the Period 1944-1949* (U.S. Government Printing Office, Washington, D.C., 1949), pp. 48-49, 523-525.

days before the session opened, the Central Committee of the Chinese Communist Party addressed a telegram to the session which recommended a program including the suspension of civil war and the concentration of the national strength against external aggression, a guarantee of civil rights, the calling of a "national salvation" conference, the preparation for armed resistance and improvement in living conditions of the people. If these points were approved, the Communist Party declared itself prepared to make certain alterations in the policies that had characterized its activities:

1. to stop the program of armed uprisings throughout the country for the overthrow of the National Government in Nanking;

2. to change the Chinese Soviet Government into the Government of the Special Region of the Republic of China and the Red Army into the National Revolutionary Army under the direct leadership of the Military Affairs Commission in Nanking;

3. to enforce the democratic system of universal suffrage within the special regions under the regime of the Government of the Special Regions;

4. to put an end to the policy of expropriating the land of the landlords and to execute the common program of the anti-Japanese united front.[1]

The question of reconciliation with the Communists was dealt with at length by the Third Plenary Session in a resolution passed on February 21, 1937. The resolution reviewed the original leniency of Sun Yat-sen in admitting Communists to the Kuomintang in 1924 and their "subsequent treasonable and rebellious activities" up to the time of the session, when the "Communist bandits, reduced to straits in the Northwest, have begun to announce alleged willingness to surrender." The resolution stated that the Kuomintang would give the Communists a chance to "reform" on four conditions:

1. Abolition of the separate army and its incorporation into the united command of the nation's armed forces.

2. Dissolution of the so-called "Chi-

nese Soviet Republic" and similar organizations and unification of the government power in the hands of the National Government.

3. Absolute cessation of Communist propaganda and acceptance of the Three People's Principles.

4. Stoppage of the class struggle.[2]

These points corresponded closely to the changes in policy the Communist Party had declared itself willing to make. After having laid down the conditions on which the Communists would be permitted to "start life anew", the session in its closing manifesto blamed the Communists for terroristic activities since 1927, "thus undermining the nation's strength which otherwise would have been employed in resisting the invader." The cardinal policy of the Kuomintang was declared to be the eradication of the Communist scourge. However, the achievement of unity through peaceful means was to be the guiding principle, although the Chinese people were warned against the fallacious theories of the class struggle.[3]

These documents established the basic conditions for the entente. During the ensuing months negotiations between the parties continued. Chou En-lai held discussions with the Generalissimo and other Kuomintang officials at Kuling, summer capital of China. Other meetings were held within Chinese Communist territory.

Many of the conditions of the entente were implemented during the course of the negotiations. The civil war ceased. The Communist policies of land confiscation were suspended, and Communist propaganda was preparing the people for the united front. The Kuomintang was making active preparations for increased democratization, including the calling of a People's National Congress for November 1937 to inaugurate a new constitution.[4] Many, though by no means all, of the political prisoners held by the Kuomintang were released.

MANIFESTO ON UNITY BY THE CENTRAL COMMITTEE OF THE CHINESE COMMUNIST PARTY, SEPTEMBER 22, 1937[5]

Beloved Compatriots—The Central Executive Committee of the Communist Party of China respectfully and sincerely issues the following Manifesto to all fathers, brothers and sisters throughout the country or:

At the present juncture when the country is facing extreme danger and the fate of the nation is in the balance, in order to save the country from extinction, we have, on the basis of peace and national unity and joint resistance against foreign aggression, reached an understanding with the Kuomintang of China, and are determined to participate in the concerted effort for overcoming the national emergency. This has a profound significance on the future of the great Chinese nation. For we all know that, when the national existence is endangered, only through internal unity can the aggression of imperialistic Japan be overcome. The foundation of national solidarity is now already laid, and the campaign of national emancipation launched. The Central Executive Committee of the Communist Party of China congratulates itself on the brilliant future of the nation. However, in order to transform this future into the realization of a New China, independent, free and happy, all descendants of Huangti (the first Chinese Emperor) must patiently and unceasingly participate in the concerted struggle.

The Central Executive Committee of the Communist Party of China avails itself of this opportunity to propose the following general objectives for the common struggle of the entire people or:

(1) Struggle for the independence, liberty and emancipation of the Chinese nation by promptly and swiftly preparing and launching the national revolutionary campaign of resistance with a view to recovering the lost territories and restoring the integrity of territorial sovereign rights.

(2) Enforce democracy based on the people's rights and convoke the National People's Congress in order to enact the Constitution and decide upon the plans of national salvation.

(3) Improve the well-being and enrich the livelihood of the Chinese people by relieving famines and other calamities, stabilizing the people's livelihood, consolidating national defense and economy, removing the sufferings of the people and bettering their living conditions.

These are the urgent requirements of China, for which the struggle is aimed. We believe that they will receive the wholehearted support of the entire people. The Communist Party of China is ready to cooperate fully with their compatriots for the attainment of these objectives.

The Communist Party of China fully realizes that this programme is likely to meet with numerous difficulties. The first obstacle will come from Japanese Imperialism. In order to deprive the enemy of all pretext for aggression and dispel doubts on the part of friends, the Central Executive Committee of the Communist Party of China solemnly declares the following in connection with national emancipation:

(1) The San Min Chu-I (Three People's Principles) enunciated by Dr. Sun Yat-sen is the paramount need of China to-day. This Party is ready to strive for its enforcement.

(2) This Party abandons its policy of overthrowing the Kuomintang of China by force and the movement of sovietization and discontinues its policy of forcible confiscation of land from landowners.

(3) This Party abolishes the present Soviet Government and will enforce democracy based on the people's rights in order to unify the national political machinery.

(4) This Party abolishes the Red Army, reorganizes it into the National Revolutionary Army, places it under the direct control of the Military Affairs Commission of the

National Government, and awaits orders for mobilization to share the responsibility of resisting foreign invasion at the front.

Beloved compatriots, the sincerity, honesty and faithfulness of the attitude of this Party have already been manifested before the entire people in both words and action, and have received the approval of the people. In order to secure closer unity with the Kuomintang of China, consolidate national peace and unity, and carry out this sacred revolutionary war, we have decided immediately to translate into action those parts of our words which have not yet been enforced, such as the abolition and reorganization of the Red Army in the Soviet Area, in order to facilitate unified command for resisting the enemy.

The enemy have penetrated into our country; the moment is critical. Compatriots, let our 400 million people rise and unite. Our nation, with its long history, cannot be conquered. Rise and struggle for the consolidation of national unity and overthrow of Japanese oppression. Victory will be ours. Long live the victory for resisting Japan. Long live the independence, liberty and welfare of new China.

STATEMENT BY GENERALISSIMO CHIANG KAI-SHEK ON KUOMINTANG-COMMUNIST UNITY, SEPTEMBER 23, 1937[6]

The aim of the Nationalist Revolution is to seek freedom and equality for China. Dr. Sun Yat-sen said that the San Min Chu I are fundamental principles of national salvation. He earnestly hoped that all our people would strive with one heart to save the state from its perils. Unfortunately, during the past ten years not all of our countrymen have had a sincere and unwavering faith in the Three Principles of the People, nor have they fully realized the magnitude of the crisis confronting our country. The course of the Revolution in its efforts at national reconstruction has been blocked by many obstacles. The result has been waste in our national resources, widespread suffering among the people, increasing humiliations from outside, and growing dangers to the state.

During the past few years the National Government has been calling ceaselessly upon the nation to achieve genuine internal solidarity, and to face unitedly the national crisis. Those who have in the past doubted the Three Principles of the People have now realized the paramount importance of our national interests, and have buried their differences for the sake of internal unity. The Chinese people today fully realize that they must survive together or perish together, and that the interests of the nation must take precedence over the interests of individuals or groups.

The Manifesto recently issued by the Chinese Communist Party is an outstanding instance of the triumph of national sentiment over every other consideration. The various decisions embodied in the Manifesto, such as the abandonment of a policy of violence, the cessation of Communist propaganda, the abolition of the Chinese Soviet Government, and the disbandment of the Red Army are all essential conditions for mobilizing our national strength in order that we may meet the menace from without and guarantee our own national existence.

These decisions agree with the spirit of the Manifesto and resolutions adopted by the Third Plenary Session of the Kuomintang. The Communist Party's Manifesto declares that the Chinese Communists are willing to strive to carry out the Three Principles. This is ample proof that China today has only one objective in its war efforts.

In our revolution we are struggling not for personal ambitions or opinions, but for the realization of the Three Principles of the People. Especially during this period of national crisis, when the fate of China lies in the balance, we ought not to argue over the past, but should try as a nation to make a new start. We should earnestly strive to unite, so that as a united nation we may safeguard the continued existence of the Republic.

If a citizen believes in the Three Principles and works actively for the salvation of the state, the Government should not concern itself with his past, but should give him opportunity to prove his loyalty in service to the Republic. Likewise, the Government will gladly accept the services of any political organization provided it is sincerely working for the nation's salvation, and is willing under the banner of our national revolution to join with us in our struggle against aggression.

The Chinese Communist Party, by surrendering its prejudices, has clearly recognized the vital importance of our national independence and welfare. I sincerely hope that all members of the Communist Party will faithfully and unitedly put into practice the various decisions reached, and under the unified military command that is directing our resistance, will offer their services to the state, fighting shoulder to shoulder with the rest of the nation for the successful completion of the Nationalist Revolution.

In conclusion, I may say that the foundation of the Chinese state rests firmly on the Three Principles first expounded by Dr. Sun Yat-sen. This foundation is one that cannot be shaken or changed. Now that the entire nation is awakened and solidly united, it will boldly follow the unswerving policy of the Government, and will mobilize the entire resources to resist the tyrannical Japanese and save the state from its imminent peril.

Enlightened people the world over now realize that China is fighting not merely for her own survival, but also for world peace and for international faith and justice.

Notes

1. Text in *New China* (Yenan, Mar. 15, 1937).

2. *The China Year Book, 1938*, pp. 532, 470; *China Handbook, 1937-1945*, p. 66.

3. *China Handbook, 1937-1945*, p. 66.

4. Because of the war and repeated postponements this Congress did not meet until November 1946.

5. Lawrence K. Rosinger, *China's Wartime Politics, 1937-1944* (Princeton, Princeton University Press, 1944), pp. 96-97.

6. Chiang Kai-shek, *Resistance and Reconstruction; Messages During China's Six Years of War, 1937-1943* (New York and London, Harper & Brothers, 1943), pp. 20-21. In this volume the date is erroneously given as Sept. 24, 1937. (*The Chinese Year Book, 1938-1939*, p. 340.)

VI. INTERNATIONAL DEVELOPMENTS, 1930-45

29. THE NON-RECOGNITION DOCTRINE

SECRETARY STIMSON TO THE AMBASSADOR IN JAPAN (FORBES)

Washington, January 7, 1932—noon.

Please deliver to the Foreign Office on behalf of your Government as soon as possible the following note:

"With the recent military operations about Chinchow, the last remaining administrative authority of the Government of the Chinese Republic in South Manchuria, as it existed prior to September 18th, 1931, has been destroyed. The American Government continues confident that the work of the neutral commission recently authorized by the Council of the League of Nations will facilitate an ultimate solution of the difficulties now existing between China and Japan. But in view of the present situation and of its own rights and obligations

From *United States Relations with China: With Special Reference to the Period 1944-1949* (U.S. Government Printing Office, 1949), *pp. 446-447*.

therein, the American Government deems it to be its duty to notify both the Imperial Japanese Government and the Government of the Chinese Republic that it cannot admit the legality of any situation *de facto* nor does it intend to recognize any treaty or agreement entered into between those Governments, or agents thereof, which may impair the treaty rights of the United States or its citizens in China, including those which relate to the sovereignty, the independence, or the territorial and administrative integrity of the Republic of China, or to the international policy relative to China, commonly known as the open door policy; and that it does not intend to recognize any situation, treaty or agreement which may be brought about by means contrary to the covenants and obligations of the Pact of Paris of August 27, 1928, to which Treaty both China and Japan, as well as the United States, are parties."

State that an identical note is being sent to the Chinese government.

STIMSON

30. Findings and Recommendations of the League

Assembly on the Lytton Report, February 24, 1933

Section II

The provisions of this section constitute the recommendations of the Assembly under Article 15, paragraph 4, of the Covenant.

Having defined the principles, conditions and considerations applicable to the settlement of the dispute,

THE ASSEMBLY RECOMMENDS
AS FOLLOWS:

1. Whereas the sovereignty over Manchuria belongs to China,

A. Considering that the presence of Japanese troops outside the zone of the South Manchuria Railway and their operations outside this zone are incompatible with the legal principles which should govern the settlement of the dispute, and that it is necessary to establish as soon as possible a situation consistent with these principles,

The Assembly recommends the evacuation of these troops. In view of the special circumstances of the case, the first object of the negotiations recommended

From the *Assembly Report of February 24th, 1933 on the Sino-Japanese Dispute,* issued by the Secretariat of the League of Nations.

hereinafter should be to organise this evacuation and to determine the methods, stages and time-limits thereof.

B. Having regard to the local conditions special to Manchuria, the particular rights and interests possessed by Japan therein, and the rights and interests of third States,

The Assembly recommends the establishment in Manchuria, within a reasonable period, of an organisation under the sovereignty of, and compatible with the administrative integrity of, China. This organisation should provide a wide measure of autonomy, should be in harmony with local conditions and should take account of the multilateral treaties in force, the particular rights and interests of Japan, the rights and interests of third States, and, in general, the principles and conditions reproduced in Section 1 (c) above; the determination of the respective powers of and relations between the Chinese Central Government and the local authorities, should be made the subject of a Declaration by the Chinese Government having the force of an international undertaking.

2. Whereas, in addition to the questions dealt with in the two recommendations 1A and 1B, the report of the Commission of Enquiry mentions in the prin-

ciples and conditions for a settlement of the dispute set out in Section 1 (c) above certain other questions affecting the good understanding between China and Japan, on which peace in the Far East depends,

The Assembly recommends the parties to settle these questions on the basis of the said principles and conditions.

3. Whereas the negotiations necessary for giving effect to the foregoing recommendations should be carried on by means of a suitable organ,

The Assembly recommends the opening of negotiations between the two parties in accordance with the method specified hereinafter.

Each of the parties is invited to inform the Secretary-General whether it accepts, so far as it is concerned, the recommendations of the Assembly, subject to the sole condition that the other party also accepts them.

The negotiations between the parties should take place with the assistance of a Committee set up by the Assembly as follows: The Assembly hereby invites the Governments of Belgium, Great Britain, Canada, Czechoslovakia, France, Germany, the Irish Free State, Italy, The Netherlands, Portugal, Spain and Turkey each to appoint a member to the Committee as soon as the Secretary-General shall have informed them that the two parties accept the Assembly's recommendations. The Secretary-General shall also notify the Governments of the United States of America and of the Union of Soviet Socialist Republics of this acceptance and invite each of them to appoint a member of the Committee should it so desire. Within one month after having been informed of the acceptance of the two parties, the Secretary-General shall take all suitable steps for the opening of negotiations.

In order to enable the Members of the League, after the opening of negotiations, to judge whether each of the parties is acting in conformity with the Assembly's recommendations:

(*a*) The Commitee will, whenever it thinks fit, report on the state of the negotiations, and particularly on the negotiations with regard to the carrying out of the recommendations 1A and B above; as regards recommendation 1A, the Committee will in any case report within three months of the opening of negotiations. These reports shall be communicated by the Secretary-General to the Members of the League and to the non-member States represented on the Committee;

(*b*) The Committee may submit to the Assembly all questions relating to the interpretation of Section II of Part IV of the present report. The Assembly shall give this interpretation in the same conditions as those in which the present report is adopted, in conformity with Article 15, paragraph 10, of the Covenant.

Section III

In view of the special circumstances of the case, the recommendations made do not provide for a mere return to the *status quo* existing before September, 1931. They likewise exclude the maintenance and recognition of the existing regime in Manchuria, such maintenance and recognition being incompatible with the fundamental principles of existing international obligations and with the good understanding between the two countries on which peace in the Far East depends.

It follows that, in adopting the present report, the Members of the League intend to abstain, particularly as regards the existing regime in Manchuria, from any act which might prejudice or delay the carrying out of the recommendations of the said report. They will continue not to recognise this regime either *de jure* or *de facto*. They intend to abstain from taking any isolated action with regard to the situation in Manchuria and to continue to concert their action among themselves as well as with the interested States not Members of the League. As regards the Members of the League who are signatories of the Nine-Power Treaty, it may be recalled that, in accordance with the provisions of that Treaty: "Whenever a situation arises which, in the opinion of any one of them, involves the application of the stipulations of the present Treaty and renders desirable discussion of such application, there shall be full and frank communication between the Contracting Powers concerned."

In order to facilitate as far as possible the establishment in the Far East of a situation in conformity with the recommendations of the present report, the Secretary-General is instructed to communicate a copy of this report to the States non-members of the League who are signatories of, or have acceded to, the Pact of Paris or of the Nine-Power Treaty, informing them of the Assembly's hope that they will associate themselves with the views expressed in the report, and that they will, if necessary, concert their action and their attitude with the Members of the League.

31. Treaty Between the United States and China for the Relinquishment of Extraterritorial Rights in China and the Regulation of Related Matters, Signed at Washington, January 11, 1943, With Accompanying Exchange of Notes

The United States of America and the Republic of China, desirous of emphasizing the friendly relations which have long prevailed between their two peoples and of manifesting their common desire as equal and sovereign States that the high principles in the regulation of

From *United States Relations with China: With Special Reference to the Period 1944-1949* (U.S. Government Printing Office, 1949), pp. 514-19.

human affairs to which they are committed shall be made broadly effective, have resolved to conclude a treaty for the purpose of adjusting certain matters in the relations of the two countries, and have appointed as their Plenipotentiaries:

The President of the United States of America,

Mr. Cordell Hull, Secretary of State of the United States of America, and

The President of the National Government of the Republic of China,

Dr. Wei Tao-ming, Ambassador Extraordinary and Plenipotentiary of the Republic of China to the United States of America;

Who, having communicated to each other their full powers found to be in due form, have agreed upon the following articles:

Article I

All those provisions of treaties or agreements in force between the United States of America and the Republic of China which authorize the Government of the United States of America or its representatives to exercise jurisdiction over nationals of the United States of America in the territory of the Republic of China are hereby abrogated. Nationals of the United States of America in such territory shall be subject to the jurisdiction of the Government of the Republic of China in accordance with the principles of international law and practice.

Article II

The Government of the United States of America considers that the Final Protocol concluded at Peking on September 7, 1901, between the Chinese Government and other governments, including the Government of the United States of America, should be terminated and agrees that the rights accorded to the Government of the United States of America under that Protocol and under agreements supplementary thereto shall cease.

The Government of the United States of America will cooperate with the Government of the Republic of China for the reaching of any necessary agreements with other governments concerned for the transfer to the Government of the Republic of China of the administration and control of the Diplomatic Quarter at Peiping, including the official assets and the official obligations of the Diplomatic Quarter, it being mutually understood that the Government of the Republic of China in taking over administration and control of the Diplomatic Quarter will make provision for the assumption and discharge of the official obligations and liabilities of the Diplomatic Quarter and for the recognition and protection of all legitimate rights therein.

The Government of the Republic of China hereby accords to the Government of the United States of America a continued right to use for official purposes the land which has been allocated to the Government of the United States of America in the Diplomatic Quarter in Peiping, on parts of which are located buildings belonging to the Government of the United States of America.

Article III

The Government of the United States of America considers that the International Settlements at Shanghai and Amoy should revert to the administration and control of the Government of the Republic of China and agrees that the rights accorded to the Government of the United States of America in relation to those Settlements shall cease.

The Government of the United States of America will cooperate with the Government of the Republic of China for the reaching of any necessary agreements with other governments concerned for the transfer to the Government of the Republic of China of the administration and control of the International Settlements at Shanghai and Amoy, including the official assets and the official obligations of those Settlements, it being mutually understood that the Government of the Republic of China in taking over administration and control of those Settlements will make provision for the assumption and discharge of the official obligations and liabilities of those Settlements and for the recognition and protection of all legitimate rights therein.

Article IV

In order to obviate any questions as to existing rights in respect of or as to existing titles to real property in territory of the Republic of China possessed by nationals (including corporations or associations), or by the Government of the United States of America, particularly questions which might arise from the abrogation of the provisions of treaties or agreements as stipulated in Article I, it is agreed that such existing rights or titles shall be indefeasible and shall not be questioned upon any ground except upon proof, established through due process of law, of fraud or of fraudulent or other dishonest practices in the acquisition of such rights or titles, it being understood that no right or title shall be rendered invalid by virtue of any subsequent change in the official procedure through which it was acquired. It is also agreed that these rights or titles shall be subject to the laws and regulations of the Republic of China concerning taxation, national defense, and the right of eminent domain, and that no such rights or titles may be alienated to the government or nationals (including corporations or associations) of any third country without the express consent of the Government of the Republic of China.

It is also agreed that if it should be the desire of the Government of the Republic of China to replace, by new deeds of ownership, existing leases in perpetuity or other documentary evidence relating to real property held by nationals, or by the Government, of the United States of America, the replacement shall be made by the Chinese authorities without charges of any sort and the new deeds of ownership shall fully protect the holders of such leases or other documentary evidence and their legal heirs and assigns without diminution of their prior rights and interests, including the right of alienation.

It is further agreed that nationals or the Government of the United States of America shall not be required or asked by the Chinese authorities to make any payments of fees in connection with land transfers for or with relation to any period prior to the effective date of this treaty.

Article V

The Government of the United States of America having long accorded rights to nationals of the Republic of China within the territory of the United States of America to travel, reside and carry on trade throughout the whole extent of that territory, the Government of the Republic of China agrees to accord similar rights to nationals of the United States of America within the territory of the Republic of China. Each of the two Governments will endeavor to have accorded in territory under its jurisdiction to nationals of the other country, in regard to all legal proceedings, and to matters relating to the administration of justice, and to the levying of taxes or requirements in connection therewith, treatment not less favorable than that accorded to its own nationals.

Article VI

The Government of the United States of America and the Government of the Republic of China mutually agree that the consular officers of each country, duly provided with exequaturs, shall be permitted to reside in such ports, places and cities as may be agreed upon. The consular officers of each country shall have the right to interview, to communicate with, and to advise nationals of their country within their consular districts; they shall be informed immediately whenever nationals of their country are under detention or arrest or in prison or are awaiting trial in their consular districts and they shall, upon notification to the appropriate authorities, be permitted to visit any such nationals; and, in general, the consular officers of each country shall be accorded the rights, privileges, and immunities enjoyed by consular officers under modern international usage.

It is likewise agreed that the nationals of each country, in the territory of the other country, shall have the right at all times to communicate with the consular officers of their country. Communications to their consular officers from nationals of each country who are under detention or arrest or in prison or are awaiting trial in the territory of the other country shall be forwarded to such consular officers by the local authorities.

Article VII

The Government of the United States of America and the Government of the Republic of China mutually agree that they will enter into negotiations for the conclusion of a comprehensive modern treaty of friendship, commerce, naviga-

tion and consular rights, upon the request of either Government or in any case within six months after the cessation of the hostilities in the war against the common enemies in which they are now engaged. The treaty to be thus negotiated will be based upon the principles of international law and practice as reflected in modern international procedures and in the modern treaties which the Government of the United States of America and the Government of the Republic of China respectively have in recent years concluded with other governments.

Pending the conclusion of a comprehensive treaty of the character referred to in the preceding paragraph, if any questions affecting the rights in territory of the Republic of China of nationals (including corporations or associations), or of the Government, of the United States of America should arise in future and if these questions are not covered by the present treaty, or by the provisions of existing treaties, conventions, or agreements between the Government of the United States of America and the Government of the Republic of China not abrogated by or inconsistent with this treaty, such questions shall be discussed by representatives of the two Governments and shall be decided in accordance with generally accepted principles of international law and with modern international practice.

Article VIII

The present treaty shall come into force on the day of the exchange of ratifications.

The present treaty shall be ratified, and the ratifications shall be exchanged at Washington as soon as possible.

Signed and sealed in the English and

Chinese languages, both equally authentic, in duplicate, at Washington, this eleventh day of January, one thousand nine hundred forty-three, corresponding to the eleventh day of the first month of the thirty-second year of the Republic of China.

CORDELL HULL

WEI TAO-MING

SECRETARY HULL TO
THE CHINESE AMBASSADOR
(WEI TAO-MING)

Washington, January 11, 1943

Excellency:

In connection with the treaty signed today between the Government of the United States of America and the Government of the Republic of China in which the Government of the United States of America relinquishes its extra-territorial and related special rights in China, I have the honor to acknowledge the receipt of your note of today's date reading as follows:

"Excellency: Under instruction of my Government, I have the honor to state that in connection with the treaty signed today by the Government of the Republic of China and the Government of the United States of America, in which the Government of the United States of America relinquishes its extraterritorial and related special rights in China, it is the understanding of the Government of the Republic of China that the rights of the Government of the United States of America and of its nationals in regard to the systems of treaty ports and of special courts in the International Settlements at Shanghai and Amoy and in regard to the employment of foreign pilots in the ports of the territory of China are also relinquished. In the light of the abolition of treaty ports as such, it is understood that all coastal ports in the territory of the Republic of China which are normally open to American overseas merchant shipping will remain open to such shipping after the coming into effect of the present treaty and the accompanying exchange of notes.

It is mutually agreed that the merchant vessels of each country shall be permitted freely to come to the ports, places, and waters of the other country which are or may be open to overseas merchant shipping, and that the treatment accorded to such vessels in such ports, and waters shall be no less favorable than that accorded to national vessels and shall be as favorable as that accorded to the vessels of any third country.

It is mutually understood that the Government of the United States of America relinquishes the special rights which vessels of the United States of America have been accorded with regard to the coasting trade and inland navigation in the waters of the Republic of China and that the Government of the Republic of China is prepared to take over any American properties that may have been engaged for those purposes and to pay adequate compensation therefor. Should either country accord the rights of inland navigation or coasting trade to vessels of any third country such rights would similarly be accorded to the vessels of the other country. The coasting trade and inland navigation of each country are excepted from the requirement of national treatment and are to be regulated according to the laws of each country in relation thereto. It is agreed, however, that vessels of either country shall enjoy within the territory of the other country with respect to the coasting trade and inland navigation treatment as favorable as that accorded to the vessels of any third country.

It is mutually understood that the Government of the United States of America relinquishes the special rights which naval vessels of the United States of America have been accorded in the waters of the Republic of China and that the Government of the Republic of China and the Government of the United States of America shall extend to each other the mutual courtesy of visits by their warships in accordance with international usage and comity.

It is mutually understood that questions which are not covered by the present treaty and exchange of notes and which affect the sovereignty of the Republic of China shall be discussed by representatives of the two Governments and shall be decided in accordance with generally accepted principles of international law and with modern international practice.

With reference to Article IV of the treaty, the Government of the Republic of China hereby declares that the restriction on the right of alienation of existing rights or titles to real property referred to in that article will be applied by the Chinese authorities in an equitable manner and that if and when the Chinese Government declines to give assent to a proposed transfer the Chinese Government will, in a spirit of justice and with a view to precluding loss on the part of American nationals whose interests are affected, undertake, if the American party in interest so desires, to take over the right or title in question and to pay adequate compensation therefor.

It is mutually understood that the or-ders, decrees, judgments, decisions and other acts of the United States Court for China and of the Consular Courts of the United States of America in China shall be considered as *res judicata* and shall, when necessary, be enforced by the Chinese authorities. It is further understood that any cases pending before the United States Court for China and the Consular Courts of the United States of America in China at the time of the coming into effect of this treaty shall, if the plaintiff or petitioner so desires, be remitted to the appropriate courts of the Government of the Republic of China which shall proceed as expeditiously as possible with their disposition and in so doing shall in so far as practicable apply the laws of the United States of America.

It is understood that these agreements and understandings if confirmed by Your Excellency's Government shall be considered as forming an integral part of the treaty signed today and shall be considered as effective upon the date of the entrance into force of that treaty.

I shall be much obliged if Your Excellency will confirm the foregoing.

I avail myself of this opportunity to renew to Your Excellency the assurances of my highest consideration."

I have the honor to confirm that the agreements and understandings which have been reached in connection with the treaty signed today by the Government of the United States of America and the Government of the Republic of China are as set forth in the above note from Your Excellency.

I avail myself [etc.]

CORDELL HULL

32. STATEMENT ON CONFERENCE OF PRESIDENT ROOSEVELT, GENERALISSIMO CHIANG KAI-SHEK, AND PRIME MINISTER CHURCHILL, CAIRO, DECEMBER 1, 1943

The several military missions have agreed upon future military operations against Japan. The Three Great Allies expressed their resolve to bring unrelenting pressure against their brutal enemies by sea, land, and air. This pressure is already rising.

The Three Great Allies are fighting this war to restrain and punish the aggression of Japan. They covet no gain for themselves and have no thought of territorial expansion. It is their purpose that Japan shall be stripped of all the islands in the Pacific which she has seized or occupied since the beginning of the first

From the *Department of State Bulletin*, Dec. 4, 1943, p. 393.

World War in 1914, and that all the territories Japan has stolen from the Chinese, such as Manchuria, Formosa, and the Pescadores, shall be restored to the Republic of China. Japan will also be expelled from all other territories which she has taken by violence and greed. The aforesaid three great powers, mindful of the enslavement of the people of Korea, are determined that in due course Korea shall become free and independent.

With these objects in view the three Allies, in harmony with those of the United Nations at war with Japan, will continue to persevere in the serious and prolonged operations necessary to procure the unconditional surrender of Japan.

33. THE YALTA AGREEMENT, FEBRUARY 11, 1945

TEXT OF THE AGREEMENT

On behalf of the United States, Great Britain and the U.S.S.R. on February 11, 1945, Roosevelt, Churchill and Stalin signed at Yalta an agreement containing the political conditions upon which the

From *United States Relations with China: With Special Reference to the Period 1944-1949* (U.S. Government Printing Office, 1949), pp. 113-14.

Soviet Union would enter the war against Japan.[1] This agreement reads as follows:

"The leaders of the three Great Powers —the Soviet Union, the United States of America and Great Britain—have agreed that in two or three months after Germany has surrendered and the war in Europe has terminated the Soviet Union shall enter into the war against Japan on the side of the Allies on condition that:

"1. The status quo in Outer-Mongolia (The Mongolian People's Republic) shall be preserved;[2]

"2. The former rights of Russia violated by the treacherous attack of Japan in 1904 shall be restored, viz:

"(a) the southern part of Sakhalin as well as all the islands adjacent to it shall be returned to the Soviet Union,

"(b) the commercial port of Dairen shall be internationalized, the preeminent interests of the Soviet Union in this port being safeguarded[3] and the lease of Port Arthur as a naval base of the U.S.S.R. restored,[4]

"(c) the Chinese-Eastern Railroad and the South-Manchurian Railroad which provides an outlet to Dairen shall be jointly operated by the establishment of a joint Soviet-Chinese Company it being understood that the preeminent interests of the Soviet Union shall be safeguarded[5] and that China shall retain full sovereignty in Manchuria;

"3. The Kuril islands shall be handed over to the Soviet Union.

"It is understood, that the agreement concerning Outer-Mongolia and the ports and railroads referred to above will require concurrence of Generalissimo Chiang Kai-shek. The President will take measures in order to obtain this concurrence on advice from Marshal Stalin.

"The Heads of the three Great Powers have agreed that these claims of the Soviet Union shall be unquestionably fulfilled after Japan has been defeated.

"For its part the Soviet Union expresses its readiness to conclude with the National Government of China a pact of friendship and alliance between the U.S.S.R. and China in order to render assistance to China with its armed forces for the purpose of liberating China from the Japanese yoke."

Notes

1. As background to the Yalta Agreement, see chapter I concerning the Cairo Declaration and chapter II on the conversations of Vice President Henry A. Wallace with Generalissimo Chiang Kai-shek in Chungking during June 1944, in which the latter requested the assistance of the United States in bringing about an improvement in Sino-Soviet relations. A summary of these conversations, prepared by a member of the Vice Presidential party, is published as annex 43. At the first formal meeting of the Tehran Conference Marshal Stalin declared that the Soviet Union would enter the war against Japan "once Germany was finally defeated." The question of making Dairen a "free port under international guaranty" and Soviet use of the Manchurian railways were discussed informally during the Tehran Conference.

2. The Soviet Union as a result of the insertion of "(The Mongolian People's Republic)" later claimed this provision meant independence. The Chinese position was based on the Sino-Soviet Treaty of 1924 which had recognized Chinese sovereignty in Outer Mongolia. For the outcome of the discussion on this point see p. 117.

3. A controversy was later to arise over this wording, the origin and authorship of which are still obscure. Mr. Harriman, the American Ambassador at Moscow, who was a participant in the discussions, subsequently stated that "there is no reason from the discussions leading up to the Yalta agreements to presume that the safeguarding of the 'preeminent interests of the Soviet Union' should go beyond Soviet interests in the free *transit* of exports and imports to and from [sic] the Soviet Union. . . ." (Italics in the original.)

4. Mr. Harriman has commented on this provision as follows: "I believe President Roosevelt looked upon the lease of Port Arthur for a naval base as an arrangement similar to privileges which the United States has negotiated with other countries for the mutual security of two friendly nations."

5. As regards this provision Mr. Harrriman has also stated his conviction that President Roosevelt had in mind only transit traffic and not any general Russian interest in Manchuria.

34. The Sino-Soviet Treaty of Friendship and Alliance, August 14, 1945

The President of the National Government of the Republic of China, and the Presidium of the Supreme Soviet of the U.S.S.R.,

Desirous of strengthening the friendly relations that have always existed between China and the U.S.S.R., through an alliance and good neighborly postwar collaboration,

Determined to assist each other in the struggle against aggression on the part of enemies of the United Nations in this world war, and to collaborate in the common war against Japan until her unconditional surrender,

Expressing their unswerving aspiration to cooperate in the cause of maintaining peace and security for the benefit of the peoples of both countries and of all the peace-loving nations,

Acting upon the principles enunciated in the joint declaration of the United Nations of January 1, 1942, in the four power Declaration signed in Moscow on October 30, 1943, and in the Charter of the International Organization of the United Nations,

Have decided to conclude the present Treaty to this effect and appointed as their plenipotentiaries:

The President of the National Government of the Republic of China;

His Excellency Dr. Wang Shih-chieh,

From *United States Relations with China: With Special Reference to the Period 1944-1949* (U.S. Government Printing Office, 1949), pp. 585-87.

Minister for Foreign Affairs of the Republic of China,

The Presidium of the Supreme Soviet of the U.S.S.R.;

His Excellency Mr. V. M. Molotov, the People's Commissar of Foreign Affairs of the U.S.S.R.,

Who, after exchanging their Full Powers, found in good and due form, have agreed as follows:

Article I

The High Contracting Parties undertake in association with the other United Nations to wage war against Japan until final victory is won. The High Contracting Parties undertake mutually to render to one another all necessary military and other assistance and support in this war.

Article II

The High Contracting Parties undertake not to enter into separate negotiations with Japan and not to conclude, without mutual consent, any armistice or peace treaty either with the present Japanese Government or with any other government or authority set up in Japan which do not renounce all aggressive intentions.

Article III

The High Contracting Parties undertake after the termination of the war against Japan to take jointly all measures in their power to render impossible a repetition of aggression and violation of the peace by Japan.

In the event of one of the High Contracting Parties becoming involved in hostilities with Japan in consequence of an attack by the latter against the said Contracting Party, the other High Contracting Party shall at once give to the Contracting Party so involved in hostilities all the military and other support and assistance with the means in its power.

This article shall remain in force until such time as the organization "The United Nations" may on request of the two High Contracting Parties be charged with the responsibility for preventing further aggression by Japan.

Article IV

Each High Contracting Party undertakes not to conclude any alliance and not to take any part in any coalition directed against the other High Contracting Party.

Article V

The High Contracting Parties, having regard to the interests of the security and economic development of each of them, agree to work together in close and friendly collaboration after the coming of peace and to act according to the principles of mutual respect for their sovereignty and territorial integrity and of non-interference in the internal affairs of the other contracting party.

Article VI

The High Contracting Parties agree to render each other every possible eco-nomic assistance in the post-war period with a view to facilitating and accelerating reconstruction in both countries and to contributing to the cause of world prosperity.

Article VII

Nothing in this treaty shall be so construed as may affect the rights or obligations of the High Contracting Parties as members of the organization "The United Nations".

Article VIII

The present Treaty shall be ratified in the shortest possible time. The exchange of the instruments of ratification shall take place as soon as possible in Chungking.

The Treaty comes into force immediately upon its ratification and shall remain in force for a term of thirty years.

If neither of the High Contracting Parties has given notice, a year before the expiration of the term, of its desire to terminate the Treaty, it shall remain valid for an unlimited time, each of the High Contracting Parties being able to terminate its operation by giving notice to that effect one year in advance.

In faith whereof the Plenipotentiaries have signed the present Treaty and affixed their seals to it.

Done in Moscow, the Fourteenth August, 1945, corresponding to the Fourteenth day of the Eighth month of the Thirty-fourth year of the Chinese Republic, in two copies, each one in the Russian and Chinese languages, both texts being equally authoritative.

THE PLENIPOTENTIARY OF THE SUPREME SOVIET OF THE U.S.S.R.

THE PLENIPOTENTIARY OF THE PRESIDENT OF THE NATIONAL GOVERNMENT OF THE REPUBLIC OF CHINA.

PART FIVE

THE RISE OF THE CHINESE PEOPLE'S REPUBLIC

INTRODUCTION

The triumph of Chinese communism in 1949 was preceded by four years of civil war, during the early phase of which the United States was deeply involved. Hope for a united, democratic China led to the dispatch of General George C. Marshall to Chungking in December 1945. Selection 35 consists of documents relating to his instructions, his initial success in arranging the cease-fire, the convocation of the Political Consultative Conference, the agreement on Nationalist-Communist military integration, and finally his report in 1947 on the failure of his mediatory mission. Selection 36 is an analysis made in early 1949 by General David Barr, commander of the United States Army Advisory Group in China, of the causes of the Nationalist military defeat, which makes sober reading.

Emerging victorious from civil war, Mao Tse-tung faced the tremendous task of building a new state. Here we see the strong influence of his works at Yenan a decade or so earlier. His *New Democracy*, written in 1940, is a creative adaptation of Marxism-Leninism to the Chinese situation, and it provided a theoretical framework for the transition

From the *Department of State Bulletin*, Feb. 10, 1946, p. 201.

from a semi-feudal, semi-colonial society to a socialist one. He called for the alliance of the four classes (workers, peasants, petty bourgeois, and national bourgeois), state domination of large industries and public utilities, collectivization of the agriculture, and development of a national, scientific mass culture (Selection 37). In 1942 Mao launched the Cheng-feng Movement (Intra-party Struggle) to combat the cadres' three unhealthy tendencies of subjectivism, sectarianism, and formalism (Selection 38). In a similar vein, Liu Shao-ch'i lectured to party members on how to be a good communist (Selection 39). It is clear that the Maoists stressed the importance of winning back the deviants rather than liquidating them, as in the Soviet Union.

One of Mao's basic writings is *On Contradiction* (1937), in which he expounds the dialectical views of the constant struggle of the opposites. He speaks of the "Universality of Contradiction" and the "Particularity of Contradiction," with the former denoting the struggle between new and old, rich and poor, city and village, socialism and capitalism, etc., and the latter, the contradiction between imperialism and all oppressed classes in Chinese society, between feudalism and the great masses of people, and between the various reactionary groups, etc. Twenty years later he elaborated his views in another essay, Mao wrote "The Correct Handling of Contradictions Among the People" (1957) to stress the differences between the antagonistic and non-antagonistic contradictions. The former are those between "ourselves and the enemy" and could be resolved only through hard and mortal struggle, while the latter exist "among the people themselves" and could therefore be resolved peacefully (Selection 40). In sum, "the law of contradiction in things, that is, the law of the unity of opposites, is the fundamental law of nature and of society and therefore also the fundamental law of thought."

The first decade of the People's Republic was marked by impressive accomplishments in various fields, and these "Ten Glorious Years" gave the Chinese Communists a sense of euphoria about the future. Nowhere was this confidence more evident than in 1958 when they launched the Great Leap Forward Movement and introduced the commune. There was a feeling that ideologically China had surpassed the Soviet Union in the race toward true communism, and that industrially she could overtake Britain in fifteen years, i.e. by 1972. But the Great Leap had disastrous consequences, and the commune had to be modified a year later. Selection 41 studies the economic repercussions of the Great Leap, and Selection 42 traces the origins of the commune—not to the Paris commune of 1871 or to the Soviet experience after the Bolshevik Revolution, but to the ancient Chinese idea of *Ta-t'ung* and K'ang Yu-wei's *Book of Universal Commonwealth* (*Ta-t'ung shu*) written in 1887.

Mao's military genius is reflected in many of his writings. Selection 43 consists of quotations from his views on people's war which had proved to be so effective in the civil war. Here he speaks of political power as growing out of a gun barrel, calls imperialism and reactionaries "paper tigers," stresses the spirit of man over sharpness of weapon, urges the establishment of rural bases and the use of villages to surround the cities, and discusses other important tactics of people's war. The international applicability of these ideas was promoted by Lin Piao in his celebrated work of 1965, *Long Live the Victory of the People's War* (Selection 44). This important document, which reveals Communist China's world-view and international strategy, should receive the careful attention of all students of contemporary affairs.

Nothing in the twenty-year history of the People's Republic was more cataclysmic than the Cultural Revolution of 1965-69, which shattered party unity and threw the country into unprecedented turmoil. The various aspects of this upheaval are examined in Selections 45 and 46, while the self-criticism, confession, and self-examination of its chief victim, Liu Shao-ch'i, constitute Selection 47.

The precarious nature of Sino-Soviet relations is a vitally important issue today. The CCP announcement on the centenary of Lenin's birth in 1970 unmistakably underscores the wide ideological gap between the two Communist giants and the great difficulty of reconciliation (Selection 48).

The book concludes with a highly perceptive article, *The People's Middle Kingdom*, by Professor John K. Fairbank (Selection 49). His sense of history and words of wisdom should benefit all of us in our search for a better understanding of China.

I. THE CIVIL WAR

35. THE AMERICAN MEDIATION: THE MISSION OF

GENERAL GEORGE C. MARSHALL, 1945-1947

PRESIDENT TRUMAN TO THE SPECIAL REPRESENTATIVE OF THE PRESIDENT TO CHINA (MARSHALL)

Washington, December 15, 1945

My dear General Marshall: On the eve of your departure for China I want to repeat to you my appreciation of your willingness to undertake this difficult mission.

I have the utmost confidence in your ability to handle the task before you but, to guide you in so far as you may find it helpful, I will give you some of the thoughts, ideas, and objectives which Secretary Byrnes and I have in mind with regard to your mission.

I attach several documents which I desire should be considered as part of this letter. One is a statement of U.S. policy towards China which was, I understand, prepared after consultation with you and with officials of the Department. The second is a memorandum from the Secretary of State to the War Department in regard to China. And the third is a copy of my press release on policy in China. I understand that these docu-

From *United States Relations with China, With Special Reference to the Period 1944-1949* (Washington, D.C., Government Printing Office, 1949), pp. 605-619, 686-694.

ments have been shown to you and received your approval.

The fact that I have asked you to go to China is the clearest evidence of my very real concern with regard to the situation there. Secretary Byrnes and I are both anxious that the unification of China by peaceful, democratic methods be achieved as soon as possible. It is my desire that you, as my Special Representative, bring to bear in an appropriate and practicable manner the influence of the United States to this end.

Specifically, I desire that you endeavor to persuade the Chinese Government to call a national conference of representatives of the major political elements to bring about the unification of China and, concurrently, to effect a cessation of hostilities, particularly in north China.

It is my understanding that there is now in session in Chungking a Peoples' Consultative Council made up of representatives of the various political elements, including the Chinese Communists. The meeting of this Council should furnish you with a convenient opportunity for discussions with the various political leaders.

Upon the success of your efforts, as outlined above, will depend largely, of course, the success of our plans for evacuating Japanese troops from China, particularly north China, and for the subsequent withdrawal of our own armed forces from China. I am particularly desirous that both be accomplished as soon as possible.

In your conversations with Chiang Kai-shek and other Chinese leaders you are authorized to speak with the utmost frankness. Particularly, you may state, in connection with the Chinese desire for credits, technical assistance in the economic field, and military assistance (I have in mind the proposed U.S. military advisory group which I have approved in principle), that a China disunited and torn by civil strife could not be considered realistically as a proper place for American assistance along the lines enumerated.

I am anxious that you keep Secretary Byrnes and me currently informed of the progress of your negotiations and of obstacles you may encounter. You will have our full support and we shall endeavor at all times to be as helpful to you as possible.

Sincerely yours,

Harry Truman

[Enclosure]

Memorandum by Secretary Byrnes

[Washington,] December 9, 1945

For the War Department

The President and the Secretary of State are both anxious that the unification of China by peaceful democratic methods be achieved as soon as possible.

At a public hearing before the Foreign Relations Committee of the Senate on December 7, the Secretary of State said:

"During the war the immediate goal of the United States in China was to promote a military union of the several political factions in order to bring their combined power to bear upon our common enemy, Japan. Our longer-range goal, then as now, and a goal of at least equal importance, is the development of a strong, united, and democratic China.

"To achieve this longer-range goal, it is essential that the Central Government of China as well as the various dissident elements approach the settlement of their differences with a genuine willingness to compromise. We believe, as we have long believed and consistently demonstrated, that the government of Generalissimo Chiang Kai-shek affords the most satisfactory base for a developing democracy. But we also believe that it must be broadened to include the representatives of those large and well organized groups who are now without any voice in the government of China.

"This problem is not any easy one. It requires tact and discretion, patience and restraint. It will not be solved by the Chinese leaders themselves. To the extent that our influence is a factor, success will depend upon our capacity to exercise that influence in the light of shifting conditions in such a way as to encourage concessions by the Central Government, by the so-called Communists, and by the other factions."

The President has asked General Marshall to go to China as his Special Representative for the purpose of bringing to bear in an appropriate and practicable manner the influence of the United States for the achievement of the ends set forth above. Specifically, General Marshall will endeavor to influence the Chinese Government to call a national conference of representatives of the major political elements to bring about the unification of China and, concurrently, effect a cessation of hostilities, particularly in north China.

In response to General Wedemeyer's recent messages, the State Department requests the War Department to arrange for directions to him stipulating that:

(1) He may put into effect the arrangements to assist the Chinese National Government in transporting Chinese troops to Manchurian ports, including the logistical support of such troops;

(2) He may also proceed to put into effect the stepped-up arrangements for the evacuation of Japanese troops from the China theater;

(3) Pending the outcome of General Marshall's discussions with Chinese leaders in Chungking for the purpose of arranging a national conference of representatives of the major political elements and for a cessation of hostilities, further transportation of Chinese troops to north China, except as north China ports may be necessary for the movement of troops and supplies into Manchuria, will be held in abeyance;

(4) Arrangements for transportation of Chinese troops into north China may be immediately perfected, but not communicated to the Chinese Government. Such arrangements will be executed when General Marshall determines either (a) that the movement of Chinese troops to north China can be carried out consistently with his negotiations, or (b) that the negotiations between the Chinese groups have failed or show no prospect of success and that the circumstances are such as to make the movement necessary to effectuate the surrender terms and to secure the long-term interests of the United States in the maintenance of international peace.

STATEMENT BY PRESIDENT TRUMAN ON UNITED STATES POLICY TOWARD CHINA, DECEMBER 15, 1945

The Government of the United States holds that peace and prosperity of the world in this new and unexplored era ahead depend upon the ability of the sovereign nations to combine for collective security in the United Nations organization.

It is the firm belief of this Government that a strong, united and democratic China is of the utmost importance to the success of this United Nations organization and for world peace. A China disorganized and divided either by foreign aggression, such as that undertaken by the Japanese, or by violent internal strife, is an undermining influence to world stability and peace, now and in the future. The United States Government has long subscribed to the principle that the management of internal affairs is the responsibility of the peoples of the sovereign nations. Events of this century, however, would indicate that a breach of peace anywhere in the world threatens the peace of the entire world. It is thus in the most vital interest of the United States and all the United Nations that the people of China overlook no opportunity to adjust their internal differences promptly by means of peaceful negotiation.

The Government of the United States believes it essential:

(1) That a cessation of hostilities be arranged between the armies of the National Government and the Chinese Communists and other dissident Chinese armed forces for the purpose of completing the return of all China to effective Chinese control, including the immediate evacuation of the Japanese forces.

(2) That a national conference of representatives of major political elements be arranged to develop an early solution to the present internal strife—a solution which will bring about the unification of China.

The United States and the other United Nations have recognized the present National Government of the Republic of China as the only legal government in China. It is the proper instrument to achieve the objective of a unified China.

The United States and the United Kingdom by the Cairo Declaration in 1943 and the Union of Soviet Socialist Republics by adhering to the Potsdam Declaration of last July and by the Sino-Soviet Treaty and Agreements of August 1945, are all committed to the liberation of China, including the return of Manchuria to Chinese control. These agreements were made with the National Government of the Republic of China.

In continuation of the constant and close collaboration with the National Government of the Republic of China in the prosecution of this war, in consonance with the Potsdam Declaration, and to remove possibility of Japanese influence remaining in China, the United States has assumed a definite obligation in the disarmament and evacuation of the Japanese troops. Accordingly the United States has been assisting and will continue to assist the National Government of the Republic of China in effecting the disarmament and evacuation of Japanese troops in the liberated areas. The United States Marines are in North China for that purpose.

The United States recognizes and will continue to recognize the National Government of China and cooperate with it in international affairs and specifically in eliminating Japanese influence from China. The United States is convinced that a prompt arrangement for a cessation of hostilities is essential to the effective achievement of this end. United States support will not extend to United States military intervention to influence the course of any Chinese internal strife.

The United States has already been compelled to pay a great price to restore the peace which was first broken by Japanese aggression in Manchuria. The maintenance of peace in the Pacific may be jeopardized, if not frustrated, unless Japanese influence in China is wholly removed and unless China takes her place as a unified, democratic and peaceful nation. This is the purpose of the maintenance for the time being of United States military and naval forces in China.

The United States is cognizant that the present National Government of China is a "one-party government" and believes that peace, unity and democratic reform in China will be furthered if the basis of this Government is broadened to include other political elements in the country. Hence, the United States strongly advocates that the national conference of representatives of major political elements in the country agree upon arrangements which would give those elements a fair and effective representation in the Chinese National Government. It is recognized that this would require modification of the one-party "political tutelage" established as an interim arrangement in the progress of the nation toward democracy by the father of the Chinese Republic, Doctor Sun Yat-sen.

The existence of autonomous armies such as that of the Communist army is inconsistent with, and actually makes impossible, political unity in China. With the institution of a broadly representative government, autonomous armies should be eliminated as such and all armed forces in China integrated effectively into the Chinese National Army.

In line with its often expressed views regarding self-determination, the United States Government considers that the detailed steps necessary to the achievement of political unity in China must be worked out by the Chinese themselves and that intervention by any foreign government in these matters would be inappropriate. The United States Government feels, however, that China has a clear responsibility to the other United Nations to eliminate armed conflict within its territory as constituting a threat to world stability and peace—a responsibility which is shared by the National Government and all Chinese political and military groups.

As China moves toward peace and unity along the lines described above, the United States would be prepared to assist the National Government in every reasonable way to rehabilitate the country, improve the agrarian and industrial economy, and establish a military organization capable of discharging China's national and international responsibilities for the maintenance of peace and order. In furtherance of such assistance, it would be prepared to give favorable consideration to Chinese requests for credits and loans under reasonable conditions for projects which would contribute toward the development of a healthy economy throughout China and healthy trade relations between China and the United States.

PRESS RELEASE ON ORDER FOR CESSATION OF HOSTILITIES, JANUARY 10, 1946

We, General Chang Chun, Representative of the National Government, and General Chou En-lai, Representative of the Chinese Communist Party, have recommended to Generalissimo Chiang Kai-shek and Chairman Mao Tse-tung and have been authorized by them to announce that the following order has been issued to all units, regular, militia, irregular and guerrilla, of the National Armies of the Republic of China and of the Communist-led troops of the Republic of China:

"All units, regular, militia, irregular and guerrilla, of the National Armies of the Republic of China and of Communist-led troops of the Republic of China are ordered to carry out the following directive:

a. All hostilities will cease immediately.

b. Except in certain specific cases, all movements of forces in China will cease. There also may be the movements necessary for demobilization, redisposition, supply, administration and local security.

c. Destruction of and interference with all lines of communications will cease and you will clear at once obstructions placed against or interfering with such lines of communications.

d. An Executive Headquarters will be established immediately in Peiping for the purpose of carrying out the agreements for cessation of hostilities. This Headquarters will consist of three Commissioners; one representing the Chinese National Government, one representing the Chinese Communist Party, and one to represent the United States of America. The necessary instructions and orders unanimously agreed upon by the three Commissioners, will be issued in the name of the President of the Republic of China, through the Executive Headquarters."

As a matter of public interest we are further authorized to announce that the following stipulations regarding the above Cessation of Hostilities Order were agreed upon and made a matter of record in the minutes of the conferences.

1. Paragraph *b*, Cessation of Hostilities Order, does not prejudice military movements south of the Yangtze River for the continued execution of the plan of military reorganization of the National Government.

2. Paragraph *b*, Cessation of Hostilities Order, does not prejudice military

movements of forces of the National Army into or within Manchuria which are for the purpose of restoring Chinese sovereignty.

3. Lines of communications, mentioned in paragraph *b*, Cessation of Hostilities Order, includes post communications.

4. It is further agreed that movements of the forces of the National Army under the foregoing stipulations shall be reported daily to the Executive Headquarters.

We are also authorized to announce that the agreements, recommendations, and directives of the Executive Headquarters will deal only with the immediate problems raised by the cessation of hostilities.

American participation within the Headquarters will be solely for the purpose of assisting the Chinese members in implementing the Cessation of Hostilities Order.

The Executive Headquarters will include an Operations Section, composed of the number of officers and men required to supervise adequately in the field of the various details.

It is agreed that separate and independent signal communications systems may be established for each Commissioner in order to insure rapid and unhampered communications.

The Headquarters will be located initially at Peiping.

Chang Chun
Chou En Lai

RESOLUTION ON GOVERNMENT ORGANIZATION ADOPTED BY THE POLITICAL CONSULTATIVE CONFERENCE, JANUARY 1946

I. Concerning the State Council: Pending the convocation of the National Assembly, the Kuomintang, as a prelimi-nary measure preparatory to the actual inauguration of constitutionalism, will revise the Organic Law of the National Government in order to expand the State Council. The following are the salient points of the revision under contemplation:

1. There will be forty (40) State Councillors, of whom the Presidents of the Executive, Legislative, Judicial, Examination, and Control Yuan will be ex-officio members.

2. The State Councillors will be chosen by the President of the National Government from among the Kuomintang members as well as non-members of the Kuomintang.

3. The State Council is the supreme organ of the Government in charge of national affairs.

4. The State Council will be competent to discuss and decide on:

A. Legislative principles.

B. Administrative policy.

C. Important military measures.

D. Financial schemes and the budget.

E. The appointment and dismissal of Ministers of State with or without portfolios, and the appointment of members of the Legislative and Control Yuan.

F. Matters submitted by the President of the National Government for consideration.

G. Proposals submitted by three or more State Councillors.

5. If the President of the National Government is of opinion that any decision of the State Council is difficult to be carried out, he may submit it for reconsideration. In case three-fifths of the State Councillors, upon reconsideration, uphold the original decision, it shall be carried out accordingly.

6. General resolutions before the State Council are to be passed by a majority vote of the State Councillors present. If

a resolution before the State Council should involve changes in administrative policy, it must be passed by a two-thirds vote of the State Councillors present. Whether a given resolution involves changes in administrative policy or not is to be decided by a majority vote of the State Councillors present.

7. The State Council meets every two weeks. The President of the National Government may call emergency meetings, if necessary.

II. Concerning the Executive Yuan.

1. All Ministers of the Executive Yuan are ipso facto Ministers of State. There may be three to five Ministers of State without portfolios.

2. Members of all political parties as well as individuals with no party affiliations may become Ministers of State with or without portfolios.

III. Concerning miscellaneous matters.

1. Whether the membership of the People's Political Council should be increased and its powers raised, pending the inauguration of the Constitution, will be left to the Government to decide in the light of the circumstances of the time.

2. All Government employees, whether of the Central Government or of the local Governments, should be selected on the basis of merit. No discriminations on account of party affiliations should be allowed.

Note: A. The appointment of State Councillors by the President of the National Government will be made on the nomination of the different parties concerned. In case he does not consent to the candidature of any given individual, the party concerned may nominate another one for the office.

B. When the President of the National Government nominates any individual with no party affiliations as State Coun-

cillor whose candidature is opposed by one-third of the other nominees, he must reconsider the matter and make a different nomination.

C. Half of the State Councillors will be Kuomintang members and the other half will be members of other political parties and prominent social leaders. The exact number of members of other political parties and prominent social leaders who are to serve as State Councillors will form the subject of separate discussions.

D. Of the existing Ministers under the Executive Yuan and the proposed Ministers of State without portfolios, seven or eight will be appointed from among non-Kuomintang members.

E. The number of Ministries to be assigned to non-Kuomintang members will form the subject of separate discussions after the PCC has closed.

RESOLUTION ON PROGRAM FOR PEACEFUL NATIONAL RECONSTRUCTION ADOPTED BY THE POLITICAL CONSULTATIVE CONFERENCE, JANUARY 1946

Now that the war of resistance against Japan has ended and peaceful reconstruction should begin, the National Government has invited representatives of the different political parties and prominent social leaders to the Political Consultative Conference to discuss national problems with the double objective of putting an end to the period of political tutelage and inaugurating constitutionalism at an early date. The present program is drawn up to serve as a guide for the Government, pending the actual inauguration of constitutionalism. Representatives of the different political parties and prominent social leaders will be invited to take part in the Government.

It is to be hoped that one and all will give first consideration to the needs of the nation and the demands of the people, and that they will cooperate wholeheartedly and work for the realization of the program, whose main features are as follows:

I. General Principles

1. The principles of the San Min Chu I will be regarded as the highest guiding principles for national reconstruction.

2. All forces of the nation will unite under the guidance of President Chiang Kai-shek in order to construct a new China, unified, free, and democratic.

3. It is recognized that the democratization of politics, the nationalization of troops, and the equality and legality of all political parties, as advocated by President Chiang, are necessary paths leading to peaceful national reconstruction.

4. Political disputes must be settled by political means in order to maintain peaceful national development.

II. The Rights of the People

1. The freedoms of person, thought, religion, belief, speech, the press, assembly, association, residence, removal, and correspondence should be guaranteed to the people. Any existing laws that contravene these freedoms should be either revised or repealed.

2. Any organization or individual other than judicial organs and the police should be strictly forbidden to arrest, try, and punish the people. Anyone who violates this rule shall be punished. The Habeas Corpus Law which has already been promulgated by the Government should be put into practical operation by Government decree at an early date.

3. The political, social, educational, and economic equality of women should be guaranteed.

III. Political Problems

1. All national measures of the moment should take into consideration the proper interests of the people of all localities, classes, and professions, and allow for their equitable development.

2. In order to increase administrative efficiency, the different grades of administrative machinery should be revamped, their rights and duties should be unified and clearly delimited, all unnecessary Governmental agencies should be abolished, the administrative procedure should be simplified, and the principle of individual responsibility each for his own section of the work should be introduced.

3. A sound system of civil service should be established: competent individuals should be protected; Government employees should be appointed not on the basis of personal or party allegiance, but on that of ability and past experience; no one should be allowed to hold concurrent jobs or to be drawn into Government service through the exertion of purely personal influence.

4. The unity and independence of the judicial power should be guaranteed, precluding it from political interference. The personnel in the courts of law should be increased, their salaries and positions should be raised, the judicial procedure should be simplified, and prisons should be reformed.

5. The supervisory system should be strictly enforced; corruption should be severely punished; facilities should be given to the people to accuse corrupt officials.

6. Local self-government should be actively pushed forth, and popular elec-

tions beginning from the lower administrative units and gradually ascending to the highest unit should be carried out. Provincial, District, and Municipal Councils should be established throughout the country at an early date, and District Magistrates should be elected by the people.

In frontier provinces and districts where minority peoples live, the number of Provincial or District Councillors to be elected by these minority peoples should be fixed according to the proportion they occupy in their respective provinces or districts.

7. All national administrative matters which have to be carried out in the territory of a district which has attained complete self-government must be carried out under the supervision and control of the National Government.

8. The powers of the Central and local Governments should be regulated on the basis of the principle of "a fair distribution of powers". The local Governments may take such measures as are adapted to the special circumstances of the localities concerned, but the regulations issued by the Provincial and District Governments must not contravene the laws and decrees of the Central Government.

IV. Military Affairs

1. The army belongs to the State. It is the duty of the soldier to protect the country and love the people and to insure the unity both of military organization and of military command.

2. All military establishments should be adapted to the needs of national defense. The military system should be reformed in accordance with democratic institutions and the circumstances of the nation. The army and political parties should be separated from each other;

military and civil authority should be vested in different hands; military education should be improved; equipment should be adequate; a sound personnel and finance system should be introduced. All these should be done in order to create a modernized national army.

3. The system of conscription should be improved and made to apply fairly and throughout the whole country. Some form of the volunteer system should be maintained and improved upon in order to meet the needs of a fully equipped army.

4. All troops of the country should be reorganized into a lesser number of units in accordance with the provisions of the "Military Reorganization Plan".

5. Preparations for the rehabilitation and employment of disbanded and retired officers and men should be made. The livelihood of disabled officers and men should be guaranteed. The families of fallen officers and men should be provided for.

6. A time limit should be set for the repatriation of the Japanese troops who have surrendered. Adequate measures should be put into operation at an early date for the disbandment of puppet troops and the liquidation of roving armed bands.

V. Foreign Relations

1. The Atlantic Charter, the Cairo Declaration, the Moscow Four-Power Declaration, and the United Nations Organization Charter should be observed. China will take an active part in the UNO in order to preserve world peace.

2. All remnants of Japanese influence in China should be extirpated according to the provisions of the Potsdam Declaration. The problem of Japan should be solved in cooperation with other Allied

Nations in order to prevent the resurgence of Japanese Fascist-militarist forces and to guarantee the security of the Far East.

3. Friendly relations with the United States, the Soviet Union, the United Kingdom, France, and other democratic countries should be promoted; treaty obligations should be observed; and economic and cultural cooperation should be undertaken in order to work for the prosperity and progress of the world in conjunction with other countries.

4. Commercial treaties, based on the principles of equality and reciprocity, should be concluded at an early date with other nations when necessary, and the position of Chinese residents overseas should be ameliorated.

VI. Economics and Finance

1. A plan of economic reconstruction should be formulated in accordance with the teachings of Dr. Sun Yat-sen's "Industrial Planning", and the cooperation of foreign capital and technique should be welcome.

2. Any enterprise which partakes of the nature of a monopoly or which cannot be undertaken by private initiative should be classified as a state enterprise; the people should be encouraged to undertake all other enterprises. Such should be the principles for the first stage of economic reconstruction, which must be effectively carried out. All existing measures should be examined and improved upon in the light of this principle.

3. In order to hasten the process of China's industrialization the Government should convene a National Economic Conference, to which will be invited social leaders interested in the problem of economic reconstruction. In this way the Government will be able to sound out popular opinion and decide upon the measures to be taken.

4. The development of "official capitalism" should be forestalled. Government officials should be strictly forbidden to take advantage of their official position to indulge in speculation and cornering, evade taxes, smuggle, embezzle public funds, and illegally make use of the means of transportation.

5. Active preparations must be made for the construction of additional railroads and highways, harbors and bays, irrigation and other projects. Subsidies should be granted to those who construct houses, schools, hospitals, and other public buildings.

6. Farm rents and interest rates must be effectively reduced. The rights of the lessee must be protected, and the payment of farm rents must be guaranteed. More and larger loans to farmers must be made available, and usury should be strictly prohibited. All these must be done in order to better the peasants' lot. The land law must be put into operation so as to attain the objective of "He who tills the soil also owns it."

7. Active measures should be taken to help the people increase their productive power by afforestation and the growth of grass, the conservation of water and soil, the development of animal husbandry, the reorganization and further development of agricultural cooperation, the expansion of agricultural experimentation and research, and the ultilization of modern equipment and methods to kill locusts and other insects.

8. Labor laws must be put into operation. The conditions of labor must be improved; the bonus system should be put on trial; unemployment and disablement insurances should be started; child and female labor should be given adequate protection; more workers' schools should

be established in order to raise the cultural level of the working population.

9. Laws governing industrial association should be made at an early date, so that those engaged in industrial undertakings may form their own associations. Laws concerning factory management should be examined and revised on the assumption that there prevails a spirit of conciliation between capital and labor.

10. Financial accounts should be made public. The budget system and annual accounts system should be strictly adopted. Public expenditure should be curtailed, and revenues and expenditures should be balanced. Central Government finance and local finance should be sharply differentiated. The currency should be deflated and the monetary system should be stabilized. The raising of both domestic and foreign loans and the use to which they will be put should be made public and subject to popular supervision.

11. The system of taxation should be reformed. All illegal taxes and extortions should be completely abolished. The various offices for the collection of taxes should be amalgamated, and the procedure of collection should be simplified. Progressive taxes should be imposed on assets and incomes. National banks should be entrusted with special economic tasks in order to help develop industry and agriculture. Assets which have escaped to foreign countries or have been frozen should be commandeered to be used for the balancing of the budget.

VII. Education and Culture

1. The freedom of learning should be guaranteed. Religious beliefs and political ideologies should not be allowed to interfere with school and college administration.

2. Scientific research and artistic creation should be encouraged in order to raise the national cultural level.

3. Compulsory education and social education should be made nation-wide; illiteracy should be actively wiped out. Professional education should be expanded in order to increase the professional ability of the people; normal education should be further developed in order to educate more qualified teachers for compulsory education. The contents of the teaching material in the various grades of schools should be revised in the light of the democratic and scientific spirit.

4. The proportion of the national budget to be devoted to education and cultural enterprises should be increased. The salaries and retirement annuities of teachers in the various grades of schools should be reasonably increased. Poor students should be subsidized, so that they can go to school and continue their studies. Endowments should be made for scientific research and creative literary and artistic work.

5. Privately endowed schools and cultural work among the people should be encouraged and subsidized.

6. In order to promote national health encouragement and assistance should be given to all forms of child welfare, public health installations should be made nation-wide, and physical exercise should be actively encouraged.

7. The wartime censorships of the press, motion pictures, the drama, letters, and telegrams should be abolished. Assistance should be given to the development of businesses in connection with publications, newspapers, news agencies, the drama, and motion pictures. All news agents and cultural enterprises operated by the Government should serve the interests of the entire nation.

VIII. Rehabilitation and Relief

1. Social order in the liberated areas should be restored at an early date. The people must be relieved of all oppressions and sufferings which were heaped on them in the period of enemy occupation. The tendency for prices to rise in the liberated areas must be curbed. All corrupt practices of officials who were sent to the occupied territories to take over from the enemy should be severely punished.

2. Railroads and highways should be quickly repaired. Inland and coastal shipping should be quickly restored. Those people who have migrated to the interior in wartime must be helped by the government to return to their native districts. Homes and jobs should be found for them, if necessary.

3. Good use must be made of the UNRRA supplies in order to relieve the war refugees; medical supplies must be distributed to them in order to cure and prevent diseases; seeds and fertilizers must be given them in order to restore farming. The authorities in charge of this work will be assisted by popular agencies and organizations in the discharge of their duties.

4. Factories and mines in the liberated areas must be quickly made operative; the property rights of the original owners must be protected; work must be resumed at an early date, so that employment may be found for those without useful occupations. Enemy and puppet property should be properly disposed of in order to enable those factories and individuals who have made significant contributions to the war of resistance in the interior to take part in its exploitation.

5. The Yellow River must be quickly put under control. Other irrigation projects which have been damaged or allowed to lapse in the course of the war must be made good at an early date.

6. The Government's decrees to stop conscription and exempt the people from the payment of agricultural taxes for one year must be carried out to the letter by the different grades of Government. No conscription or agricultural taxes under a different guise should be allowed.

IX. Chinese Residents Overseas

1. Chinese residents overseas who have become destitute as a result of enemy oppression will be helped by the Government to reestablish their former business; those members of their families who may be living in China will receive proper relief.

2. Assistance will be given to Chinese residents overseas who have returned to China in the last few years in the course of the war, so that they may go back to their former place of residence. Facilities will be provided for them for the recovery of their property and the reestablishment of their business.

3. All educational and cultural enterprises of Chinese residents overseas will be restored and active assistance will be given them by the Government. Encouragement and assistance will be given to the children of Chinese residents overseas to come back to China for education.

Annex

1. In those recovered areas where the local government is under dispute the status quo shall be maintained until a settlement is made according to Articles 6, 7, and 8 of Chapter III on Political Problems in this program by the National Government after its reorganization.

2. A Committee for the Protection of the People's Liberties will be formed, composed of representatives of the local Council, the Lawyers' Association, and popular organizations. Financial assistance will be given to it by the Government.

3. Revisions will be made, in the light of the usual practices in democratic countries, in the Citizen's Oath-Taking and the examination of candidates for public offices.

4. Membership of the Supreme Economic Council of the Executive Yuan should be increased by the addition of economic experts representing the people at large and of experienced industrialists.

5. It is recommended that the Government put an end to the policy of control over nitrate and sulphur.

6. (a) Those workers originally employed in factories which have been removed to the interior in the course of the war, who now find themselves unemployed due to the closing up of the factories as a result of the war, should be granted a certain amount of financial assistance by the Government.

(b) Those factories which have made significant contributions to the manufacture of military material in the course of the war should continue to receive Government patronage by the latter's purchase of their ready-made articles and as much of their material as possible.

7. The press law should be revised. The Regulations Governing the Registration and Control of Newspapers, Magazines, and News Services in Times of Emergency; Provisional Regulations Governing Newspapers, News Agencies, Magazines, Motion Pictures, and Broadcasts in Liberated Areas; Regulations Governing the Censorship of the Drama and Motion Pictures; Regulations Governing the Censorship of Letters and Telegrams, and other regulations of a similar nature should be repealed. Amusement taxes and stamp taxes on motion pictures, drama, and concert tickets should be lightened.

RESOLUTION ON MILITARY PROBLEMS ADOPTED BY THE POLITICAL CONSULTATIVE CONFERENCE, JANUARY 1946

I. Fundamental principles for the creation of a national army.

1. The army belongs to the State. It is the duty of the soldier to protect the country and love the people.

2. The army shall be established in response to the necessities of national defense. Its quality and equipment shall be improved in the light of the progress made in general education, science, and industry.

3. The military system shall be reformed in the light of the democratic institutions and actual conditions prevailing at the time.

4. The system of conscription shall be reformed and applied fairly and universally. Some form of the volunteer system shall be preserved and reforms shall be introduced in order to meet the requirements of a fully equipped army.

5. Military education shall be conducted in the light of the foregoing principles, and shall forever be dissociated from party affiliations and personal allegiance.

II. Fundamental principles for the reorganization of the army.

1. Separation of army and party.

A. All political parties shall be forbidden to carry on party activities, whether open or secret, in the army. So shall be all cliques based on personal relations or of a territorial nature.

B. All soldiers on active service who owe allegiance to any political party may not take part in the party activities of the district in which they are stationed, when they are on duty.

C. No party or individual may make use of the army as an instrument of political rivalry.

D. No illegal organizations and activities may be allowed in the army.

2. Separation of civil and military authorities.

A. No soldier on active service in the army may serve concurrently as civil officials.

B. The country shall be divided into military districts, which shall be made not to coincide with administrative districts as far as possible.

C. The army shall be strictly forbidden to interfere in political affairs.

III. Methods aiming at the civilian control of the army.

1. When the preliminary measures for the reorganization of the army have been completed, the National Military Council shall be reorganized into a Ministry of National Defense under the Executive Yuan.

2. The Minister of National Defense shall not necessarily be a soldier.

3. The number of troops and military expenditure shall be decided upon by the Executive Yuan and passed by the Legislative Yuan.

4. All troops shall be under the unified control of the Ministry of National Defense.

5. A Military Committee shall be established within the Ministry of National Defense to be charged with the double duty of drawing up schemes for the creation of a national army and of seeing to it that the schemes are faithfully carried out. Members of the Committee shall be drawn from various circles.

IV. Practical methods for the reorganization of the army.

1. The three-man military commission shall proceed according to schedule and agree upon practical methods for the reorganization of the Communist troops at an early date. The reorganization must be completed as soon as possible.

2. The Government troops should be reorganized, according to the plan laid down by the Ministry of War, into ninety (90) divisions. The reorganization should be completed within six (6) months.

3. When the reorganizations envisaged in paragraphs 1 and 2 have been completed, all troops of the country should be again reorganized into fifty (50) or sixty (60) divisions.

4. A commission for the supervision of the reorganization plan shall be established within the National Military Council. Members of the commission shall be drawn from various circles.

AGREEMENT ON THE NATIONAL ASSEMBLY BY SUB-COMMITTEE OF THE POLITICAL CONSULTATIVE CONFERENCE

Based on the resolution on this subject introduced by the Government representatives, the following agreement on the National Assembly was reached in the PCC Sub-Committee dealing with this problem by the various delegations:

1. That the National Assembly shall be convened on May 5, 1946.

2. That the power of the National Assembly is to adopt the Constitution.

3. That the Constitution shall be adopted by a vote of three-fourths of the delegates present.

4. That the 1,200 geographical and vocational delegates, who have been or are going to be elected according to the electoral law of the National Assembly, shall be retained.

5. That the geographical and vocational delegates for the Northeast provinces and Taiwan shall be increased by 150.

6. That 700 seats shall be added to the National Assembly and they shall be apportioned among the various parties and social leaders. The ratio of apportionment shall be decided later.

7. That the total number of delegates to the National Assembly shall be 2,050.

8. That the organ to enforce the Constitution shall be elected six months after the Constitution is adopted.

STATEMENT BY PRESIDENT TRUMAN ON UNITED STATES POLICY TOWARD CHINA, DECEMBER 18, 1946

Last December I made a statement of this Government's views regarding China. We believed then and do now that a united and democratic China is of the utmost importance to world peace, that a broadening of the base of the National Government to make it representative of the Chinese people will further China's progress toward this goal, and that China has a clear responsibility to the other United Nations to eliminate armed conflict within its territory as constituting a threat to world stability and peace. It was made clear at Moscow last year that these views are shared by our Allies, Great Britain and the Soviet Union. On December 27th, Mr. Byrnes, Mr. Molotov and Mr. Bevin issued a statement which said, in part:

"The three Foreign Secretaries exchanged views with regard to the situation in China. They were in agreement as to the need for a unified and democratic China under the National Government for broad participation by democratic elements in all branches of the National Government, and for a cessation of civil strife. They affirmed their adherence to the policy of non-interference in the internal affairs of China."

The policies of this Government were also made clear in my statement of last December. We recognized the National Government of the Republic of China as the legal government. We undertook to assist the Chinese Government in reoccupation of the liberated areas and in disarming and repatriating the Japanese invaders. And finally, as China moved toward peace and unity along the lines mentioned, we were prepared to assist the Chinese economically and in other ways.

I asked General Marshall to go to China as my representative. We had agreed upon my statement of the United States Government's views and policies regarding China as his directive. He knew full well in undertaking the mission that halting civil strife, broadening the base of the Chinese Government and bringing about a united, democratic China were tasks for the Chinese themselves. He went as a great American to make his outstanding abilities available to the Chinese.

During the war, the United States entered into an agreement with the Chinese Government regarding the training and equipment of a special force of 39 divisions. That training ended V-J Day and the transfer of the equipment had been largely completed when General Marshall arrived.

The United States, the United Kingdom and the Union of Soviet Socialist Republics all committed themselves to the liberation of China, including the return of Manchuria to Chinese control. Our Government had agreed to assist the Chinese Government in the reoccupation of areas liberated from the Japanese, including Manchuria, because of China's lack of shipping and transport planes. Three armies were moved by air and eleven by sea, to central China, Formosa, north China and Manchuria. Most of these moves had been made or started when General Marshall arrived.

The disarming and evacuation of Japanese progressed slowly—too slowly. We regarded our commitment to assist the Chinese in this program as of overwhelming importance to the future peace of China and the whole Far East. Surrendered but undefeated Japanese armies and hordes of administrators, technicians, and Japanese merchants, totalling about 3,000,000 persons, had to be removed under the most difficult conditions. At the request of the Chinese Government we had retained a considerable number of American troops in China, and immediately after V-J Day we landed a corps of Marines in north China. The principal task of these forces was to assist in the evacuation of Japanese. Only some 200,-000 had been returned to Japan by the time General Marshall arrived.

General Marshall also faced a most unpropitious internal situation on his arrival in China. Communications throughout the country were badly disrupted due to destruction during the war and the civil conflicts which had broken out since. This disruption was preventing the restoration of Chinese economy, the distribution of relief supplies, and was rendering the evacuation of Japanese a slow and difficult process. The wartime destruction of factories and plants, the war-induced inflation in China, the Japanese action in shutting down the economy of occupied

China immediately after V-J Day, and finally the destruction of communications combined to paralyze the economic life of the country, spreading untold hardship to millions, robbing the victory over the Japanese of significance to most Chinese and seriously aggravating all the tensions and discontents that existed in China.

Progress toward solution of China's internal difficulties by the Chinese themselves was essential to the rapid and effective completion of most of the programs in which we had already pledged our assistance to the Chinese Government. General Marshall's experience and wisdom were available to the Chinese in their efforts to reach such solutions.

Events moved rapidly upon General Marshall's arrival. With all parties availing themselves of his impartial advice, agreement for a country-wide truce was reached and announced on January 10th. A feature of this agreement was the establishment of a unique organization, the Executive Headquarters in Peiping. It was realized that due to poor communications and the bitter feelings on local fronts, generalized orders to cease fire and withdraw might have little chance of being carried out unless some authoritative executive agency, trusted by both sides, could function in any local situation.

The Headquarters operated under the leaders of three commissioners—one American who served as chairman, one Chinese Government representative, and one representative of the Chinese Communist Party. Mr. Walter S. Robertson, Chargé d'Affaires of the American Embassy in China, served as chairman until his return to this country in the fall. In order to carry out its function in the field, Executive Headquarters formed a large number of truce teams, each headed by one American officer, one Chinese Government officer, and one Chinese Communist officer. They proceeded to all danger spots where fighting was going on or seemed impending and saw to the implementation of the truce terms, often under conditions imposing exceptional hardships and requiring courageous action. The degree of cooperation attained between Government and Communist officers in the Headquarters and on the truce teams was a welcome proof that despite two decades of fighting, these two Chinese groups could work together.

Events moved forward with equal promise on the political front. On January 10th, the Political Consultative Conference began its sessions with representatives of the Kuomintang or Government Party, the Communist Party and several minor political parties participating. Within three weeks of direct discussion these groups had come to a series of statesmanlike agreements on outstanding political and military problems. The agreements provided for an interim government of a coalition type with representation of all parties, for revision of the Draft Constitution along democratic lines prior to its discussion and adoption by a National Assembly and for reduction of the Government and Communist armies and their eventual amalgamation into a small modernized truly national army responsible to a civilian government.

In March, General Marshall returned to this country. He reported on the important step the Chinese had made toward peace and unity in arriving at these agreements. He also pointed out that these agreements could not be satisfactorily implemented and given substance unless China's economic disintegration were checked and particularly unless the transportation system could be put in working order. Political unity could not be built on economic chaos. This Government had already authorized certain minor credits to the Chinese Government in an effort to meet emergency rehabilitation needs as it was doing for other war devastated countries throughout the world. A total of approximately $66,000,-000 was involved in six specific projects, chiefly for the purchase of raw cotton, and for ships and railroad repair material. But these emergency measures were inadequate. Following the important forward step made by the Chinese in the agreements as reported by General Marshall, the Export-Import Bank earmarked a total of $500,000,000 for possible additional credits on a project by project basis to Chinese Government agencies and private enterprises. Agreement to extend actual credits for such projects would obviously have to be based upon this Government's policy as announced December 15, 1945. So far, this $500,000,000 remains earmarked, but unexpended.

While comprehensive large scale aid has been delayed, this Government has completed its wartime lend-lease commitments to China. Lend-lease assistance was extended to China to assist her in fighting the Japanese, and later to fulfill our promise to assist in re-occupying the country from the Japanese. Assistance took the form of goods and equipment and of services. Almost half the total made available to China consisted of services, such as those involved in air and water transportation of troops. According to the latest figures reported, lend-lease assistance to China up to V-J Day totalled approximately $870,000,000. From V-J Day to the end of February, shortly after General Marshall's arrival, the total was approximately $600,000,000 —mostly in transportation costs. Thereafter, the program was reduced to the fulfillment of outstanding commitments, much of which was later suspended.

A considerable quantity of civilian goods has also been made available by our agreement with China for the disposal of surplus property which enabled us to liquidate a sizable indebtedness and to dispose of large quantities of surplus material. During the war the Chinese Government furnished Chinese currency to the United States Army for use in building its installations, feeding the troops, and other expenses. By the end of the war this indebtedness amounted to something like 150,000,000,-000 Chinese dollars. Progressive currency inflation in China rendered it impossible to determine the exact value of the sum in United States currency.

China agreed to buy all surplus property owned by the United States in China and on seventeen Pacific Islands and bases with certain exceptions. Six months of negotiations preceded the agreement finally signed in August. It was imperative that this matter be concluded in the Pacific as had already been done in Europe, especially in view of the rapid deterioration of the material in open storage under tropical conditions and the urgent need for the partial alleviation of the acute economic distress of the Chinese people which it was hoped this transaction would permit. Aircraft, all non-demilitarized combat material, and fixed installations outside of China were excluded. Thus, no weapons which could be used in fighting a civil war were made available through this agreement.

The Chinese Government cancelled all but 30,000,000 United States dollars of our indebtedness for the Chinese currency, and promised to make available the equivalent of 35,000,000 United States dollars for use in paying United States governmental expenses in China

and acquiring and improving buildings and properties for our diplomatic and consular establishments. An additional sum of 20,000,000 United States dollars is also designated for the fulfillment of a cultural and educational program.

Before General Marshall arrived in China for the second time, in April, there was evidence that the truce agreement was being disregarded. The sincere and unflagging efforts of Executive Headquarters and its truce teams have succeeded in many instances in preventing or ending local engagements and thus saved thousands of lives. But fresh outbreaks of civil strife continued to occur, reaching a crisis of violence in Manchuria with the capture of Changchun by the Communists and where the presence of truce teams had not been fully agreed to by the National Government.

A change in the course of events in the political field was equally disappointing. Negotiations between the Government and the Communists have been resumed again and again, but they have as often broken down. Although hope for final success has never disappeared completely, the agreements made in January and February have not been implemented, and the various Chinese groups have not since that time been able to achieve the degree of agreement reached at the Political Consultative Conference.

There has been encouraging progress in other fields, particularly the elimination of Japanese from China. The Chinese Government was responsible under an Allied agreement for the disarmament of all Japanese military personnel and for the repatriation of all Japanese civilians and military personnel from China, Formosa and French Indo-China north of the sixteenth degree of latitude. Our Government agreed to assist the Chinese in this task. The scope of the job was tremendous. There were about 3,000,000 Japanese, nearly one-half of them Army or Navy personnel to be evacuated. Water and rail transportation had been destroyed or was immobilized. Port facilities were badly damaged and overcrowded with relief and other supplies. The Japanese had to be disarmed, concentrated and then transported to the nearest available port. In some instances this involved long distances. At the ports they had to be individually searched and put through a health inspection. All had to be inoculated. Segregation camps had to be established at the ports to cope with the incidence of epidemic diseases such as Asiatic cholera. Finally, 3,000,-000 persons had to be moved by ship to Japan.

American forces helped in the disarmament of Japanese units. Executive Headquarters and its truce teams were able to make the complicated arrangements necessary to transfer Japanese across lines and through areas involved in civil conflict on their way to ports of embarkation. American units also participated in the inspections at the port, while American medical units supervised all inoculation and other medical work. Finally, American and Japanese ships under the control of General MacArthur in Japan, and a number of United States Navy ships under the Seventh Fleet transported this enormous number of persons to reception ports in Japan.

At the end of last year, approximately 200,000 Japanese had been repatriated. They were leaving Chinese ports at a rate of about 2,500 a day. By March of this year, rapidly increased efforts on the part of the American forces and the Chinese authorities involved had increased this rate to more than 20,000 a day. By November, 2,986,438 Japanese had been evacuated and the program was con-sidered completed. Except for indeterminate numbers in certain parts of Manchuria, only war criminals and technicians retained on an emergency basis by the Chinese Government remain. That this tremendous undertaking has been accomplished despite conflict, disrupted communications and other difficulties will remain an outstanding example of successful American-Chinese cooperation toward a common goal.

Much has been said of the presence of United States armed forces in China during the past year. Last fall these forces were relatively large. They had to be. No one could prophesy in advance how well the Japanese forces in China would observe the surrender terms. We had to provide forces adequate to assist the Chinese in the event of trouble. When it became obvious that the armed Japanese would not be a problem beyond the capabilities of the Chinese Armies to handle, redeployment was begun at once.

The chief responsibility of our forces was that of assisting in evacuation of Japanese. This task was prolonged by local circumstances. Provision of American personnel for the Executive Headquarters and its truce teams has required a fairly large number of men, particularly since the all important network of radio and other communications was provided entirely by the United States. The Executive Headquarters is located at Peiping, a hundred miles from the sea and in an area where there was the possibility of local fighting. Hence, another responsibility was to protect the line of supply to and from Headquarters. Another duty our forces undertook immediately upon the Japanese surrender was to provide the necessary protection so that coal from the great mines northeast of Tientsin could reach the sea for shipment to supply the cities and railroads of central China. This coal was essential to prevent the collapse of this industrial area. Our Marines were withdrawn from this duty last September. Other units of our forces were engaged in searching for the bodies or graves of American soldiers who had died fighting the Japanese in China. Still others were required to guard United States installations and stores of equipment, and to process these for return to this country or sale as surplus property.

At peak strength a year ago we had some 113,000 soldiers, sailors and marines in China. Today this number is being reduced to less than 12,000, including some 2,000 directly concerned with the operations of Executive Headquarters and will be further reduced to the number required to supply and secure the American personnel of Executive Headquarters and the air field and stores at Tsingtao.

Thus during the past year we have successfully assisted in the repatriation of the Japanese and have subsequently been able to bring most of our own troops home. We have afforded appropriate assistance in the reoccupation of the country from the Japanese. We have undertaken some emergency measures of economic assistance to prevent the collapse of China's economy and have liquidated our own wartime financial account with China.

It is a matter of deep regret that China has not yet been able to achieve unity by peaceful methods. Because he knows how serious the problem is, and how important it is to reach a solution, General Marshall has remained at his post even though active negotiations have been broken off by the Communist Party. We are ready to help China as she moves toward peace and genuine democratic government.

The views expressed a year ago by this Government are valid today. The plan for political unification agreed to last February is sound. The plan for military unification of last February has been made difficult of implementation by the progress of the fighting since last April, but the general principles involved are fundamentally sound.

China is a sovereign nation. We recognize that fact and we recognize the National Government of China. We continue to hope that the Government will find a peaceful solution. We are pledged not to interfere in the internal affairs of China. Our position is clear. While avoiding involvement in their civil strife, we will persevere with our policy of helping the Chinese people to bring about peace and economic recovery in their country.

As ways and means are presented for constructive aid to China, we will give them careful and sympathetic consideration. An example of such aid is the recent agricultural mission to China under Dean Hutchison of the University of California sent at the request of the Chinese Government. A joint Chinese-American Agricultural Collaboration Commission was formed which included the Hutchison mission. It spent over four months studying rural problems. Its recommendations are now available to the Chinese Government, and so also is any feasible aid we can give in implementing those recommendations. When conditions in China improve, we are prepared to consider aid in carrying out other projects, unrelated to civil strife, which would encourage economic reconstruction and reform in China and which, in so doing, would promote a general revival of commercial relations between American and Chinese businessmen.

We believe that our hopes for China are identical with what the Chinese people themselves most earnestly desire. We shall therefore continue our positive and realistic policy toward China which is based on full respect for her national sovereignty and on our traditional friendship for the Chinese people and is designed to promote international peace.

PERSONAL STATEMENT BY THE SPECIAL REPRESENTATIVE OF THE PRESIDENT (MARSHALL), JANUARY 7, 1947

The President has recently given a summary of the developments in China during the past year and the position of the American Government toward China. Circumstances now dictate that I should supplement this with impressions gained at first hand.

In this intricate and confused situation, I shall merely endeavor here to touch on some of the more important considerations—as they appeared to me—during my connection with the negotiations to bring about peace in China and a stable democratic form of government.

In the first place, the greatest obstacle to peace has been the complete, almost overwhelming suspicion with which the Chinese Communist Party and the Kuomintang regard each other.

On the one hand, the leaders of the Government are strongly opposed to a communistic form of government. On the other, the Communists frankly state that they are Marxists and intend to work toward establishing a communistic form of government in China, though first advancing through the medium of a democratic form of government of the American or British type.

The leaders of the Government are convinced in their minds that the Communist-expressed desire to participate in a government of the type endorsed by the Political Consultative Conference last January had for its purpose only a destructive intention. The Communists felt, I believe, that the government was insincere in its apparent acceptance of the PCC resolutions for the formation of the new government and intended by coercion of military force and the action of secret police to obliterate the Communist Party. Combined with this mutual deep distrust was the conspicuous error by both parties of ignoring the effect of the fears and suspicions of the other party in estimating the reason for proposals or opposition regarding the settlement of various matters under negotiation. They each sought only to take counsel of their own fears. They both, therefore, to that extent took a rather lopsided view of each situation and were susceptible to every evil suggestion or possibility. This complication was exaggerated to an explosive degree by the confused reports of fighting on the distant and tremendous fronts of hostile military contact. Patrol clashes were deliberately magnified into large offensive actions. The distortion of the facts was utilized by both sides to heap condemnation on the other. It was only through the reports of American officers in the field teams from Executive Headquarters that I could get even a partial idea of what was actually happening and the incidents were too numerous and the distances too great for the American personnel to cover all of the ground. I must comment here on the superb courage of the officers of our Army and Marines in struggling against almost insurmountable and maddening obstacles to bring some measure of peace to China.

I think the most important factors involved in the recent breakdown of negotiations are these: On the side of the

National Government, which is in effect the Kuomintang, there is a dominant group of reactionaries who have been opposed, in my opinion, to almost every effort I have made to influence the formation of a genuine coalition government. This has usually been under the cover of political or party action, but since the Party was the Government, this action, though subtle or indirect, has been devastating in its effect. They were quite frank in publicly stating their belief that cooperation by the Chinese Communist Party in the government was inconceivable and that only a policy of force could definitely settle the issue. This group includes military as well as political leaders.

On the side of the Chinese Communist Party there are, I believe, liberals as well as radicals, though this view is vigorously opposed by many who believe that the Chinese Communist Party discipline is too rigidly enforced to admit of such differences of viewpoint. Nevertheless, it has appeared to me that there is a definite liberal group among the Communists, especially of young men who have turned to the Communists in disgust at the corruption evident in the local governments—men who would put the interest of the Chinese people above ruthless measures to establish a Communist ideology in the immediate future. The dyed-in-the-wool Communists do not hesitate at the most drastic measures to gain their end as, for instance, the destruction of communications in order to wreck the economy of China and produce a situation that would facilitate the overthrow or collapse of the Government, without any regard to the immediate suffering of the people involved. They completely distrust the leaders of the Kuomintang and appear convinced that every Government proposal is de-

signed to crush the Chinese Communist Party. I must say that the quite evidently inspired mob actions of last February and March, some within a few blocks of where I was then engaged in completing negotiations, gave the Communists good excuse for such suspicions.

However, a very harmful and immensely provocative phase of the Chinese Communist Party procedure has been in the character of its propaganda. I wish to state to the American people that in the deliberate misrepresentation and abuse of the action, policies and purposes of our Government this propaganda has been without regard for the truth, without any regard whatsoever for the facts and has given plain evidence of a determined purpose to mislead the Chinese people and the world and to arouse a bitter hatred of Americans. It has been difficult to remain silent in the midst of such public abuse and wholesale disregard of facts, but a denial would merely lead to the necessity of daily denials; an intolerable course of action for an American official. In the interest of fairness, I must state that the Nationalist Government publicity agency has made numerous misrepresentations, though not of the vicious nature of the Communist propaganda. Incidentally, the Communist statements regarding the Anping incident which resulted in the death of three Marines and the wounding of twelve others were almost pure fabrication, deliberately representing a carefully arranged ambuscade of a Marine convoy with supplies for the maintenance of Executive Headquarters and some UNRRA supplies, as a defence against a Marine assault. The investigation of this incident was a tortuous procedure of delays and maneuvers to disguise the true and privately admitted facts of the case.

Sincere efforts to achieve settlement

have been frustrated time and again by extremist elements of both sides. The agreements reached by the Political Consultative Conference a year ago were a liberal and forward-looking charter which then offered China a basis for peace and reconstruction. However, irreconcilable groups within the Kuomintang, interested in the preservation of their own feudal control of China, evidently had no real intention of implementing them. Though I speak as a soldier, I must here also deplore the dominating influence of the military. Their dominance accentuates the weakness of civil government in China. At the same time, in pondering the situation in China, one must have clearly in mind not the workings of small Communist groups or committees to which we are accustomed in America, but rather of millions of people and an army of more than a million men.

I have never been in a position to be certain of the development of attitudes in the innermost Chinese Communist circles. Most certainly, the course which the Chinese Communist Party has pursued in recent months indicated an unwillingness to make a fair compromise. It has been impossible even to get them to sit down at a conference table with Government representatives to discuss given issues. Now the Communists have broken off negotiations by their last offer which demanded the dissolution of the National Assembly and a return to the military positions of January 13th which the Government could not be expected to accept.

Between this dominant reactionary group in the Government and the irreconcilable Communists who, I must state, did not so appear last February, lies the problem of how peace and well-being are to be brought to the long-suffering and presently inarticulate mass of the people of China. The reactionaries in the Government have evidently counted on substantial American support regardless of their actions. The Communists by their unwillingness to compromise in the national interest are evidently counting on an economic collapse to bring about the fall of the Government, accelerated by extensive guerrilla action against the long lines of rail communications—regardless of the cost in suffering to the Chinese people.

The salvation of the situation, as I see it, would be the assumption of leadership by the liberals in the Government and in the minority parties, a splendid group of men, but who as yet lack the political power to exercise a controlling influence. Successful action on their part under the leadership of Generalissimo Chiang Kai-shek would, I believe, lead to unity through good government.

In fact, the National Assembly has adopted a democratic constitution which in all major respects is in accordance with the principles laid down by the all-party Political Consultative Conference of last January. It is unfortunate that the Communists did not see fit to participate in the Assembly since the constitution that has been adopted seems to include every major point that they wanted.

Soon the Government in China will undergo major reorganization pending the coming into force of the constitution following elections to be completed before Christmas Day 1947. Now that the form for a democratic China has been laid down by the newly adopted constitution, practical measures will be the test. It remains to be seen to what extent the Government will give substance to the form by a genuine welcome of all groups actively to share in the responsibility of government.

The first step will be the reorganization of the State Council and the executive branch of Government to carry on administration pending the enforcement of the constitution. The manner in which this is done and the amount of representation accorded to liberals and to non-Kuomintang members will be significant. It is also to be hoped that during this interim period the door will remain open for Communists or other groups to participate if they see fit to assume their share of responsibility for the future of China.

It has been stated officially and categorically that the period of political tutelage under the Kuomintang is at an end. If the termination of one-party rule is to be a reality, the Kuomintang should cease to receive financial support from the Government.

I have spoken very frankly because in no other way can I hope to bring the people of the United States to even a partial understanding of this complex problem. I have expressed all these views privately in the course of negotiations; they are well known, I think, to most of the individuals concerned. I express them now publicly, as it is my duty, to present my estimate of the situation and its possibilities to the American people who have a deep interest in the development of conditions in the Far East promising an enduring peace in the Pacific.

36. The Nationalist Military Defeat

MAJOR GENERAL DAVID BARR

REPORT OF OPERATIONAL ADVICE GIVEN TO THE GENERALISSIMO, THE MINISTER OF NATIONAL DEFENSE AND THE CHIEF OF THE SUPREME STAFF BY MAJOR GENERAL DAVID BARR, SUBMITTED EARLY IN 1949.

An early estimate of the situation, prior to the first formal meeting of the select combined group, convinced me of the futility of continuing to hold isolated Manchurian cities which were totally dependent upon air for both civilian and military supply. The combined airlift capacity of Chinese civilian and military transports fell far short of the enormous tonnage requirements. The cost of airlift replacement, maintenance and fuel—in a country bereft of gold credits—could only result in economic disaster, while

From *United States Relations with China: With Special Reference to the Period 1944-1949* (U.S. Government Printing Office, Washington D.C., 1949), pp. 325-339.

making only ineffectual contributions to the supply effort.

Early in March, [1948], therefore, when the Communists had withdrawn their main forces from the vicinity of Changchun and Mukden, after their winter offensive, I strongly urged the Generalissimo to take advantage of this opportunity to make a progressive withdrawal from Manchuria. He was aghast at this proposal, stating that no circumstances would induce him to consider such a plan. Hopeful of a compromise, I suggested the withdrawal into Mukden of the Changchun, Kirin and Ssuping-chieh garrisons. To this the Generalissimo replied that political considerations precluded the abandonment of Changchun, the ancient capital of Manchuria, but that he would consider a plan for withdrawing the Kirin garrison into Changchun. The Kirin garrison was accordingly withdrawn at a later date.

In my next conference with the Generalissimo, and after his reiterated determination not to consider a withdrawal from Manchuria, I proposed that an early offensive be launched to open rail communications between Chinchow and Mukden. The Generalissimo enthusiastically concurred, and instructed his staff to prepare a plan in consultation with my assistants.

At a meeting at the Minstry of National Defense War Room on 8 March 1948 General Lo indicated that a general plan for the opening of a corridor to Mukden had been prepared and approved by the Generalissimo. . . . On 5 May 1948, a coordinated attack from Mukden and Chinchow would be mounted to open a corridor along the railroad between those two points.

The lack of a broad strategic plan for operations was so obviously missing that I inquired if such a plan existed. I was told that the Chinese Armed Forces were then operating under a "Six Months' Plan" and that a "Two Year Plan" had been prepared but was not yet approved by the Generalissimo. . . .

A meeting was held at the Ministry of National Defense War Room on 17 March 1948. In discussing the coming offensive to open a corridor to Mukden, the Chinese stated that it would take six months to repair the railroad between Chinchow and Hsinmin.

On being questioned as to the amount of destruction the Nationalists were able to achieve prior to the evacuation of Kirin, the Chinese were vague. I pointed out that a large amount of the arms and ammunition in the hands of the Communists was captured Nationalist equipment and that the practice of permitting such material to fall into the hands of the Communists was prolonging the war. Although I stressed this point many times after that, it was of little avail. The Chinese seemed inherently unable to destroy anything of value.

At a meeting with the Generalissimo on 24 March, I discussed with him the following subjects, among others:

(1) The food situation in Mukden and our ability to assist by immediate delivery of 12 United States C–46's out of a total of 20 available in Japan for turnover to the Chinese.

(2) That United States ammunition from the Pacific, destined for Mukden, had not yet been moved to that city although it had arrived in Shanghai.

(3) The necessity of a definite and detailed plan for the opening of a line of communication to Mukden. In this connection, the Generalissimo again assured me that he intended to hold Mukden at all cost.

(4) The Generalissimo stressed the need for .45 caliber ammunition for use

in the large number of submachine guns being used in the Nationalist Army.

In connection with paragraphs (1) and (4) above, I was able to forward a memorandum to the Generalissimo on 29 March informing him that 1 million rounds of .45 caliber ammunition were being made available to him and that the transfer of 16 to 20 United States C—46's had been approved.

A meeting was held at the Ministry of National Defense War Room on 16 April. . . . Following the above meeting, I called on General Yu Ta-wei, Minister of Communications, and learned that his office had received no instructions regarding the reconstruction of the Chinchow-Hsinmin railroad. He stated, however, that he had been informed of the plan and was going ahead with his preparations.

On the 29th of April, at a conference with the Supreme G-3, he again assured my staff that the Mukden attack would be launched on 5 May. He stated that the Generalissimo had ordered the attack to jump off not later than the 5th day of May. . . .

Having been notified that General Chiang, Deputy Chief of Staff of the Mukden Headquarters was in Nanking, I arranged a conference with him at the Ministry on 4 May 1948. General Chiang led off with a lengthy description of recent Communist movements from the north towards the Mukden area, of their excellent state of supply and training and of the assistance they were receiving from Russia. It was obvious that he was leading up to the news that the proposed Nationalist attack to open the corridor to Chinchow would not be mounted.

He stated that the morale of the Mukden forces was high and that they wanted to fight and defeat the Communists. When asked "why not then fight now before it is too late?", General Chiang answered that reinforcements from North China were necessary. He stated that a strong defense of the Mukden-Chinchow areas should be made at that time and a coordinated attack to open a corridor be made later. He advised to sit tight until the Communist intentions became clear and then take action. This was undoubtedly the policy Wei Li-huang would pursue in spite of all orders to the contrary from the Generalissimo and the Supreme Staff. The opportunity to take the initiative away from the Communists had been lost. It was extremely doubtful if a later attempt to open a corridor would be successful.

I attended the conference mentioned above, on the afternoon of the 5th of May at the Generalissimo's home. Present were the Generalissimo and Madame Chiang Kai-shek, the three Mukden Generals mentioned above and several members of the Supreme General Staff. After a lengthy discourse by the Mukden Generals as to the reasons the long awaited Manchurian operations could not then be staged, the Generalissimo asked for my opinions. I told him that I had heard nothing but reasons why the attack could not be mounted. That at a later date I was convinced the same excuses would be given plus those that would develop during the interim. I recommended that the attack be mounted then and that if this could not be accomplished then Manchuria should be evacuated while an opportunity still offered itself. I pointed out that Communist strength in Manchuria was increasing and that if success was uncertain at this time, it was definitely impossible later. I further pointed out that Chang-chun and Mukden could not be indefinitely supplied by air. The Generalissimo stated that because General Fu Tso-yi could not spare two armies from North China at that time to reinforce the Chinchow garrison, a reinforcement being considered necessary to the success of the operation, he had decided to postpone the attack to 1 August 1948. He further stated that the troops then available in Manchuria would be the only ones that could be counted upon and enjoined the Mukden commanders to use the time available for the intensive training of these troops. (I would like to point out at this time that the Generalissimo had directed General Wei Li-huang as early as the preceding winter to prepare plans and ready himself for an attack early in May to open a corridor from Mukden to Chinchow. That the Supreme G-3 and members of his division had made six separate trips to Mukden in an effort to press preparations for this attack. That both myself and my staff had continuously urged the Chinese towards this effort since early February. The General Wei Li-huang was able to get away with such complete disobedience of orders without punishment or even censure, as far as I know, points out one reason why the Nationalists are losing the present war.)

On 6 May 1948, the Supreme G-3 had a conference with the three visiting Mukden Generals. General Chao had told him that the Communists had learned of the proposed Nationalist attempt to open the corridor and were moving troops to intercept the attack. He insisted that more time was needed to train and organize more troops. His main theme was to *defend* Mukden and Chinchow thus containing large masses of Manchurian Communists which in turn meant the salvation of North China. The G-3 disagreed and pointed out that another such opportunity to wrest the initiative from the Communists and defeat them would not occur again.

At a meeting on 29th May I asked whether there was any intention or thought being given to a withdrawal from Manchuria and was given a negative answer. I stated that if Chinchow fell as a result of inaction at Mukden, then Mukden was surely lost and that this should be made clear to Wei Li-huang. The Chief of Staff informed me that an agreement was reached at the Generalissimo's headquarters that if Wei Li-huang failed to assist the Chinchow garrison, he would be severely punished. . . .

Decision was made by the Generalissimo to defend isolated Tsinan to the last. (Such decisions have been costly to the Nationalists in troops and supplies.) I pointed out again to the Generalissimo and to the Supreme Staff the futility of attempting to hold cities from within restricted perimeters by purely defensive measures against overpowering enemy forces. Tsinan at this time was isolated from Hsuchow by Communist forces at Yenchow and Taian. Although in considerable strength in this area the main Communist force was still on the Honan plains, southeast of Kaifeng. An opportunity existed to do one of two things. By offensive action north from Hsuchow and south from Tsinan, the Nationalist forces were capable of destroying the Communists and reopening the corridor between Hsuchow and Tsinan. The Nationalists were also capable at this time of evacuating Tsinan and withdrawing into Hsuchow. Having no confidence in the will to fight of the Tsinan garrison after their ineffective attempt to recapture Weihsien, and having heard reports of the questionable loyalty of some of the senior commanders, I recommended that the city be evacuated, and the troops be withdrawn to Hsuchow. Again, as in the case of Changchun, I was told that because of political reasons, Tsinan, the capital of Shantung Province, must be defended.

On July 2, 1948, at the invitation of the American Military Attaché, Brig. Gen. Robert H. Soule, I flew over Kaifeng and the area to the southeast thereof where heavy fighting was reported to be in progress. Reports of destruction in Kaifeng by the Chinese Air Force bombing and fire were proven untrue. With the exception of a few bomb craters outside the city walls, no effects of the bombing could be seen. We circled at low altitude all over the reported battle area southeast of the city, but with the exception of a few burning houses in scattered villages, a few mortar shell bursts, some marching troops and two fighter planes flying higher than we were, there was little evidence of the reported clash of half a million men. . . .

On 24 September 1948 I learned that Tsinan had been captured by the Communists. The unexpectedly early fall of the city was the result of a defection to the Communists of an entire Nationalist division which had been entrusted with the defense of the western approaches to the city. This division, former puppet troops, had been suspected and should have previously been relieved.

At a meeting with the Generalissimo on the 29th of September, the following matters, among others, were discussed:

The Generalissimo expressed deep disappointment over the outcome of the battle of Tsinan and stated that its fall was unexpected. He said that it was necessary for a study to be made on Chinese strategy, tactics, training and organization of field units in order that the mistakes committed at Tsinan would not be repeated. He said that the old strategy of holding strong points or key cities at all cost would have to go.

The Generalissimo said that my reasoning was very sound and expressed the hope that I would attend the weekly military operational conference held each Wednesday in the Ministry of Defense War Room. He asked that I give his operational officers the benefit of my experience and advice. I stated that I would be glad to comply with his request.

[In view of Communist activity around Chinchow the Generalissimo had ordered General Wei in Mukden to take aggressive offensive action to relieve the pressure further south. General Barr made the following comment on a meeting held October 1 in the Ministry of National Defense War Room:]

I pointed out that the situation in Chinchow was extremely critical, that five days had passed since General Wei Li-huang had received orders to attack to the west and that there had been no indication of such an attack getting under way. I recommended that the Mukden troops break out to the west of their position at once, ready or not.

At a luncheon meeting on 7 October 1948 the following matters were discussed and recommendations made:

General Ho Ying-chin announced that it had been determined to organize, train and equip an additional 28 strategic reserve divisions (three regiments in each) over and above the nine presently being organized and trained. I pointed out that little progress had been made in the original plan to form nine divisions and asked how he expected to handle 28 more. He replied that there were that many in the south and west that had been depleted in combat, were partially equipped, and could be brought up to strength and equipped with United States aid supplies supplemented by Chinese production. He stated that his representatives would confer shortly with Brigadier General Laurence Keiser, my Ground Division Senior Adviser, on the plan. This was another example of Chinese grandiose planning without thought or regard to the possibility of its implementation.

General Ho stated that the Generalissimo was in Peiping. (The Generalissimo did not return to Nanking until after the fall of Mukden and Chinchow. He directed this operation from Peiping without the assistance of his Supreme Staff whom he failed to keep informed as to what was taking place. In spite of this unorthodox procedure, the plans made and orders given were sound and had they been obeyed, the results would probably have been favorable.)

At a meeting in the Ministry of National Defense War Room on 13 October 1948, the following matters were discussed:

General Wei Li-huang had used only 11 divisions in his breakout to the west instead of 15 as ordered. He had been directed to employ his 52d Army to reinforce his operations. The attack had commenced on 9 October, 13 days after receipt of orders to attack immediately. Progress had been very slow to date. . . .

In a visit to G-3 on the morning of 28 October 1948, my staff learned of the defeat of General Wei Li-huang's forces west of Mukden on 27 October. I recommended that the 11 Nationalist divisions then in the Chinsi-Hulutao area, be evacuated by sea at once or make a determined effort to fight their way south into north China before the main Communist strength could return to prevent it. I further recommended that the troops in Yinkow, and all that could reach Yinkow from Mukden, also be evacuated by sea at once. I could not refrain from pointing out that if Wei Li-huang had

moved southwest promptly after receiving his orders on the 25th of September, instead of delaying until the 9th of October, and then had moved with speed in the attack, he would have saved Chinchow and could have brought all his strength into North China. General Ho admitted that I was correct, but stated that his hands were tied and that the Generalissimo had directed the entire operations alone from Peiping without reference to him or to the Supreme Staff. In this, of course, the Generalissimo was wrong, but the orders he issued to General Wei Li-huang for the conduct of operations in Manchuria were sound. Had they been carried out with determination and speed there was every chance of success. Chinchow, though sorely pressed, held out against the Communists long enough to enable the Mukden and the Hulutao-Chinsi forces to converge to their rescue had they moved promptly and fought with sufficient determination to get there in time. The Nationalist troops, in Manchuria, were the finest soldiers the Government had. The large majority of the units were United States equipped and many soldiers and junior officers still remained who had received United States training during the war with Japan. I am convinced that had these troops had proper leadership from the top the Communists would have suffered a major defeat. The Generalissimo placed General Tu Yu-ming, an officer of little worth, in charge of field operations, properly relegating to General Wei Li-huang over-all supervision from Mukden where he could do little harm. But Tu Yu-ming also fought the battle from Mukden, placing the burden of active command in the field to General Liao Yao-hsiang, Commanding General of the 9th Army Group. Liao was a good general but was killed early in the action. Without top leadership and in the confusion that followed the Communists were able to segment the Nationalist forces and destroy them piecemeal. General Wei Li-huang and General Tu Yu-ming deserted the troops and were safely in Hulutao at the end. The efforts of the troops in the Chinsi-Hulutao area to relieve Chinchow were also futile. Instead of mounting an all-out attack with full force initially, which could have swept aside the Communists who were weakened by withdrawals sent against Wei Li-huang, the attack was developed slowly with troops being thrown in piecemeal. The attack soon bogged down with the troops showing little will to fight. *The loss of Manchuria and some 300,000 of its best troops was a stunning blow to the Government. To me, the loss of the troops was the most serious result. It spelled the beginning of the end. There could be no hope for North China with an additional 360,000 Communist troops now free to move against its north flank.**

[Following the loss of forces in Manchuria the center of activity shifted to Hsuchow.]

At a meeting in the Ministry of National Defense War Room on the 25th of November 1948, the following matters were discussed:

The Supreme G-2 and G-3 briefed the assembly on the current military situation. The strength of the Hsuchow garrison was given as 270,000. Regarding supplies, it was stated that ammunition was sufficient but a food shortage existed. I strongly recommended that Hsuchow be evacuated at once and that its troops move south against the rear of the Communists forces below Shusien. The G-2 reported that the Mukden-Chinchow railroad had been restored. It had taken

* [Italics added—Ed.]

the Communists just 25 days to restore this line, a project the Nationalists had insisted would take 6 months when discussions were under way concerning the proposed Nationalist 5 May attack which never materialized. . . .

[Despite belated efforts of the forces in the Hsuchow area to withdraw to more easily defensible positions these forces were surrounded and destroyed by the Communists as were units moving to their relief. As it became apparent that the remaining military forces of the Government were powerless to stop the Communist armies and that their defeat was inevitable, steps were taken to decrease the size of JUSMAG, for American military personnel associated with it did not have the diplomatic immunity accorded attachés. With the certainty that Nanking would fall in the immediate future and with the disorganized condition of the Chinese armies, its period of usefulness had passed and orders were issued for its removal from China. On December 18 in a telegram to the Department of the Army General Barr stated in part: "Marked by the stigma of defeat and the loss of face resulting from the forced evacuation of China, north of the Yangtze, it is extremely doubtful if the National Government could muster the necessary popular support to mobilize sufficient manpower in this area (South China) with which to rebuild its forces even if time permitted. Only a policy of unlimited United States aid including the immediate employment of United States armed forces to block the southern advance of the Communists, which I emphatically do not recommend, would enable the Nationalist Government to maintain a foothold in southern China against a determined Communist advance. . . . The complete defeat of the Nationalist Army . . . is inevitable."]

[General Barr summarized his views of the causes for the Government's defeat as follows:]

Many pages could be written covering the reasons for the failure of Nationalist strategy. I believe that the Government committed its first politico-military blunder when it concentrated its efforts after V–J Day on the purely military reoccupation of the former Japanese areas, giving little consideration to long established regional sentiments or to creation of efficient local administrations which could attract wide popular support in the liberated areas. *Moreover, the Nationalist Army was burdened with an unsound strategy which was conceived by a politically influenced and militarily inept high command. Instead of being content with consolidating North China, the Army was given the concurrent mission of seizing control of Manchuria, a task beyond its logistic capabilities. The Government, attempting to do too much with too little, found its armies scattered along thousands of miles of railroads, the possession of which was vital in view of the fact that these armies were supplied from bases in central China.** In order to hold the railroads, it was also necessary to hold the large cities through which they passed. As time went on, the troops degenerated from field armies, capable of offensive combat, to garrison and lines of communication troops with an inevitable loss of offensive spirit. Communist military strength, popular support, and tactical skill were seriously under-estimated from the start. It became increasingly difficult to maintain effective control over the large sections of predominantly Communist countryside through which the lines of communication passed. Lack of Nationalist forces qualified to take the field against the Communists

* [Italics added—Ed.]

enabled the latter to become increasingly strong. The Nationalists, with their limited resources, steadily lost ground against an opponent who not only shaped his strategy around available human and material resources, but also capitalized skillfully on the Government's strategic and tactical blunders and economic vulnerability.

Initially, the Communists were content to fight a type of guerrilla warfare, limiting their activities to raids on lines of communication and supply installations. The success of their operations, which were purely offensive, instilled in them the offensive attitude so necessary to success in war. On the other hand, the Nationalist strategy of defense of the areas they held, developed in them the 'wall psychology' which has been so disastrous to their armies. As the Communists grew stronger and more confident, they were able, by concentrations of superior strength, to surround, attack, and destroy Nationalist units in the field and Nationalist held cities. It is typical of the Nationalists, in the defense of an area or a city, to dig in or retire within the city walls, and there to fight to the end, hoping for relief which never comes because it cannot be spared from elsewhere. The Chinese have resisted advice that, in the defense of an area or a city, from attack by modern methods of warfare, it is necessary to take up positions away from the walls where fire and maneuver is possible. Further, they have been unable to be convinced of the necessity for withdrawing from cities and prepared areas when faced with overpowering opposition and certain isolation and defeat, while the opportunity still existed for them to do so. In some cases their reasons for failure to withdraw and save their forces were political, but in most cases, they were convinced that by defensive action alone, they could, through attrition, if nothing else, defeat the enemy. Because of this mistaken concept and because of their inability to realize that discretion is usually the better part of valor, large numbers of Nationalist troops were lost to the Government.

It must be understood that all through the structure and machinery of the Nationalist Government there are interlocking ties of interest peculiar to the Chinese—family, financial, political. No man, no matter how efficient, can hope for a position of authority on account of being the man best qualified for the job; he simply must have other backing. In too many cases, this backing was the support and loyalty of the Generalissimo for his old army comrades which kept them in positions of high responsibility regardless of their qualifications. A direct result of this practice is the unsound strategy and faulty tactics so obviously displayed in the fight against the Communists.

Cooperation among and coordination of effort between the Armed Forces leaves much to be desired. The Ground Forces, being the old and dominant arm, is the source from which the large majority of top military positions are filled. These officers, mostly old and loyal contemporaries of the Generalissimo, have little or no knowledge of the newer arms: the Air Force and the Navy. The Chinese Air Force, consisting of $8\frac{1}{3}$ groups, is far in excess of what a country bereft of gold credits can support. Although it has among its personnel over five thousand United States trained pilots, it accomplished little, other than air-lifting troops and operating its transports for personal gains. There was an ever present reluc-

tance to take a chance on losing equipment or personnel, which was clearly reflected in their constant refusal to operate at other than high altitudes. There was an ingrained resentment in the Chinese Air Force against killing Chinese Communists who had no air support. All of these factors are important and unfortunate because the Chinese Air Force, unopposed, could have rendered invaluable support in ground operations had its capabilities been properly employed. From a military viewpoint, the case of the Navy is not so important since its employment, right or wrong, could have had little effect on the final outcome; all operations were land based. From an economic viewpoint, the Navy could have been of inestimable value in suppressing smugglers in Hong Kong-Canton waters had it been willing to suppress and not participate. It was completely relieved of this mission in March 1948, and reputedly millions of dollars in customs revenue continue to be lost to the Government.

It might be expected that the Communists, being Chinese themselves, would also suffer from these faulty Nationalist traits and characteristics, and to a certain extent they do, but they have wisely subordinated them and made their ideology of Communism almost a fetish. By means of total mobilization in the areas they control, propaganda, and the use of political commissars within their armed forces, they maintain loyalty to the established order. Their leaders are men of proven ability who invariably out-general the Nationalist commanders. The morale and fighting spirit of the troops is very high because they are winning.

II. THEORETICAL FOUNDATION OF
THE NEW STATE

37. ON NEW DEMOCRACY

(1940)

MAO TSE-TUNG

1. WHITHER CHINA?

Since the War of Resistance began, people throughout the country have felt that at last they can see the way forward, and instead of knitting their brows and casting down their eyes in despair, are now cheerful and hopeful. Recently, however, the air has been once more filled with the dust and din of compromise and anti-communism and the people have again been thrown into confusion. Among the first to be affected are the cultural workers and young students, who are more susceptible than others. Again the questions are being asked: What is to be done? Whither China? On the occasion of the publication of *Chinese Culture*,[1] it may therefore be useful to explain the trends of Chinese politics and Chinese culture. . . .

2. TO BUILD A NEW CHINA

For many years we Communists have struggled for China's political and economic revolution and also for her cultu-

From Mao Tse-tung, *On New Democracy* (Foreign Languages Press, Peking, 1964), pp. 1-22, 44-46, 59-64, 67.

ral revolution; our aim is to build a new society and a new state for the Chinese nation. This new society and new state will have new politics, a new economy and also a new culture. In other words, we want to change a politically oppressed and economically exploited China into a politically free and economically prosperous China, and also to change a China which has been kept ignorant and backward under the sway of the old culture into a China which will be enlightened and progressive under the sway of a new culture. In short, we want to build a new China. To build a new culture of the Chinese nation is our aim in the cultural sphere.

3. CHINA'S HISTORICAL FEATURE

We want to build a new culture of the Chinese nation, but what kind of culture is it?

Any given culture as an ideological form reflects the politics and economy of a given society, and in turn has a tremendous influence and effect upon them; economy is the base of society and politics the concentrated expression of this economy.[2] This is our fundamental view on the relation of culture to politics and economy and on the relation between politics and economy. Hence, primarily given forms of politics and economy determine a given form of culture, and secondarily the latter in turn influences and affects the former. "It is not the consciousness of men that determines their being," says Marx, "but, on the contrary, their social being that determines their consciousness."[3] Again he says: "The philosophers have *interpreted* the world in various ways; the point however is to *change* it."[4] These scientific formulations for the first time in human history gave the correct solution to the problem of the relation between consciousness and being, and constituted the fundamental viewpoint of the dynamic revolutionary theory of knowledge as the reflection of reality which was later profoundly expounded by Lenin. This fundamental viewpoint must be borne in mind in our discussion of China's cultural problems.

It is then quite clear that the reactionary elements of the old culture of the Chinese nation which we wish to eliminate cannot be separated from its old politics and old economy, while its new culture which we want to build cannot be separated from its new politics and new economy. The old politics and old economy of the Chinese nation form the basis of its old culture, and its new politics and new economy will form the basis of its new culture.

What are the old politics and old economy of the Chinese nation? And what is the old culture of the Chinese nation?

From the Chou and Ch'in Dynasties onwards, China was a feudal society, with feudal politics and a feudal economy. The predominant culture which was a reflection of these politics and economy was feudal.

Since the invasion of capitalism from abroad and the gradual growth of capitalist elements at home, China has changed by degrees into a colonial, semi-colonial and semi-feudal society. In China today, society is colonial in the Japanese-occupied areas, and basically semi-colonial in the areas under Kuomintang rule, while in both areas society is predominantly feudal and semi-feudal. This, then, is the character of present-day Chinese society and the general situation in present-day China. In such a society colonial, semi-colonial and semi-feudal politics and economy are predominant, and being a reflection of them, the predominant culture is also colonial, semi-colonial and semi-feudal.

Our revolution is directed against these predominant forms of politics, economy and culture. What we want to eliminate is the old colonial, semi-colonial and semi-feudal politics and economy, and the old culture which serves them. What we want to build is their direct opposite, the new politics, the new economy and the new culture of the Chinese nation.

What, then, are the new politics and new economy of the Chinese nation? And what is the new culture of the Chinese nation?

In the historical course of the Chinese revolution there must be two steps, first, the democratic revolution, and second, the socialist revolution: these are two revolutionary stages different in character. The democracy in question belongs no longer to the old category, it is no longer the old democracy; it belongs to the new category, it is New Democracy.

Thus we can say that the new politics of the Chinese nation are the politics of New Democracy; the new economy of the Chinese nation, the economy of New Democracy; and the new culture of the

Chinese nation, the culture of New Democracy.

This is the historical feature of the Chinese revolution at the present time. All parties and individuals taking part in the revolution who fail to understand this historical feature will not be able to direct it and lead it to victory, but will be discarded by the people and left to lament their fate in the wilderness.

4. THE CHINESE REVOLUTION AS PART OF THE WORLD REVOLUTION

The historical feature of the Chinese revolution consists in two steps, democracy and socialism; the first step is no longer democracy in a general sense, but democracy of the Chinese type, a new and special type—New Democracy. How, then, has this historical feature come into existence? Has it been in existence for the past hundred years, or is it of only recent birth?

If we make a study of the development of China and of the world we shall see that this historical feature did not emerge as a consequence of the Opium War, but began to take shape only after the first imperialist world war and the October Revolution in Russia. Let us now study the process of its formation.

Evidently, the colonial, semi-colonial and semi-feudal character of present-day Chinese society requires two steps in the Chinese revolution. The first step is to change a colonial, semi-colonial and semi-feudail society into an independent, democratic society. The second is to push the revolution further and build a socialist society. The Chinese revolution at present is taking the first step.

The preparatory period for taking the first step began with the Opium War in 1840 when China began to change from a feudal into a semi-colonial and semi-feudal society. Then the movement of the T'aip'ing Heavenly Kingdom,[5] the Sino-French War,[6] the Sino-Japanese War,[7] the Reformist Movement of 1898,[8] the Revolution of 1911,[9] the May 4 Movement, the Northern Expedition, the War of the Agrarian Revolution and the present Anti-Japanese War, all of which followed the Opium War and covered a whole century, represent in a sense the first step taken by the Chinese people on different occasions and in various degrees, the step to fight against imperialism and feudalism, to strive to build an independent, democratic society and to complete the first revolution. The Revolution of 1911 was the beginning of that revolution in a fuller sense. In its social character that revolution is bourgeois-democratic and not proletarian-socialist. It is not yet completed, and great efforts are still required because its enemies remain very powerful. When Dr. Sun Yatsen said: "The revolution is not yet completed, all my comrades must strive on," he was referring to the bourgeois-democratic revolution.

A change, however, occurred in the Chinese bourgeois-democratic revolution after the outbreak of the first imperialist world war in 1914 and the founding of a socialist state on one-sixth of the globe in consequence of the October Revolution in Russia in 1917.

Before these events, the Chinese bourgeois-democratic revolution belonged to the category of the old bourgeois-democratic world revolution, and was part of it.

After these events, the Chinese bourgeois-democratic revolution changes its character and comes within the category of the new bourgeois-democratic revolution and, so far as the revolutionary front is concerned, forms part of the proletarian-socialist world revolution.

Why? Because the first imperialist

world war and the first victorious socialist revolution, the October Revolution, have changed the course of world history and marked a new historical era.

This is an era in which the capitalist front has collapsed in one part—one-sixth —of the world and fully revealed its decadence in other parts; those parts still under capitalism cannot get along without depending more than ever on the colonies and semi-colonies; a socialist state has come into being and has declared itself willing to help the liberation movement of all colonies and semi-colonies; the proletariat of the capitalist countries is increasingly freeing itself from the social-imperialist influence of the Social-Democratic Parties and has also declared itself in support of the liberation movement of the colonies and semi-colonies. In this era, any revolution that takes place in a colony or semi-colony against imperialism, that is, against the international bourgeoisie and international capitalism, belongs no longer to the old category of bourgeois-democratic world revolution, but to a new category, and is no longer part of the old bourgeois or capitalist world revolution, but part of the new world revolution, the proletarian-socialist world revolution. Such revolutionary colonies and semi-colonies should no longer be regarded as allies of the counter-revolutionary front of world capitalism: they have become allies of the revolutionary front of world socialism.

Although in its social character the first stage or step of such a revolution in a colonial and semi-colonial country is still basically bourgeois-democratic, and although the task imposed on it by objective conditions is to clear the path for the development of capitalism, it is no longer a revolution of the old type led by the bourgeoisie and aimed at establishing a capitalist society and a state under bourgeois dictatorship, but one of the new type led by the proletariat and aimed at establishing in the first stage a new-democratic society and a state under the joint dictatorship of all revolutionary classes. Thus this revolution will clear an even wider path for the development of socialism. In the course of its progress such a revolution, owing to changes in the situation of its enemies and to changes of alignment within its own front, passes through several further stages; but its basic character remains unchanged.

This revolution attacks the very foundation of imperialism, and for this reason is disapproved and opposed by imperialism. But it is approved by socialism and supported by a socialist state and the international socialist proletariat.

Therefore, such a revolution inevitably becomes part of the proletarian-socialist world revolution.

The correct formulation that the Chinese revolution is part of the world revolution was made as long ago as 1924-27 during China's First Great Revolution. It was made by the Chinese Communists and approved by all those taking part in the anti-imperialist and anti-feudal struggle of the time. However, the theoretical implication of this formulation was not then fully expounded, and consequently the whole question was only vaguely understood.

The "world revolution" referred to here is no longer the old world revolution or the old bourgeois world revolution, for that ended long ago, but a new world revolution, the socialist world revolution. Similarly, the "part" is not a part of the old bourgeois revolution but of the new socialist revolution. This is a tremendous change unparalleled in the history of China and of the world.

This correct formulation made by the Chinese Communists is based on Stalin's theory.

As early as 1918, Stalin wrote in an article commemorating the first anniversary of the October Revolution:

The great world-wide significance of the October Revolution chiefly consists in the fact that:

(1) It has widened the scope of the national question and converted it from the particular question of combating national oppression in Europe into the general question of emancipating the oppressed peoples, colonies and semi-colonies from imperialism.

(2) It has opened up wide possibilities for their emancipation and the right paths towards it, has thereby greatly facilitated the cause of the emancipation of the oppressed peoples of the West and the East, and has drawn them into the common current of the victorious struggle against imperialism.

(3) It has thereby erected a bridge between the socialist West and the enslaved East, having created a new front of revolutions against world imperialism, extending from the proletarians of the West, through the Russian revolution, to the oppressed peoples of the East.[10]

Since writing this article, Stalin has again and again expounded the theory that revolutions in colonies and semi-colonies have departed from the old category and become part of the proletarian-socialist revolution. The article that gives the clearest and most precise explanation was published on June 30, 1925, and in it Stalin carried on a controversy with the Yugoslav nationalists of that time. It contains the following passage:

Comrade Semich refers to a passage in Stalin's pamphlet *Marxism and the National Question*, written at the end of 1912. It is stated there that "the national struggle under the conditions of *rising* capitalism is a struggle of the bourgeois classes among themselves." By this he is evidently trying to hint that his own formula defining the social meaning of the national movement in present historical conditions is correct. But Stalin's pamphlet was written before the imperialist war, at a time when the national question in the eyes of Marxists had not yet assumed world significance, and when the basic demand of the Marxists, the right to self-determination, was judged to be not a part of the proletarian revolution, but a part of the bourgeois-democratic revolution. It would be absurd to ignore the fact that the international situation has radically changed since that time, that the war on the one hand and the October Revolution in Russia on the other have converted the national question from a part of the bourgeois-democratic revolution into a part of the proletarian-socialist revolution. As early as October, 1916, Lenin in his article "The Discussion on Self-Determination Summed Up," said that the fundamental point of the national question, the right of self-determination, had ceased to form part of the general democratic movement and that it had become converted into a component part of the general proletarian-socialist revolution. I will not mention later works of Lenin and of other representatives of Russian Communism on the national question. In view of all this, what interpretation can be placed on Comrade Semich's reference to a certain passage in a pamphlet by Stalin written in the period of the bourgeois-democratic revolution in Russia, now that, as a result of the new historical situation, we have entered a new era, the era of the world *proletarian* revolution? The only interpretation that can be placed on it is that Comrade Semich is quoting without reference to space and time and without reference to the actual historical situation, and that he is thereby violating the most elementary demands of dialectics and failing to take account of the fact that what is correct in one historical situation may prove incorrect in another historical situation.[11]

Thus it can be seen that there are two kinds of world revolution, the first belonging to the bourgeois and capitalist category. The era of this kind of world revolution is long past, having come to an end as early as 1914 when the first imperialist world war broke out, and especially in 1917 when the October Revolution occurred in Russia. Since then, the second kind, namely, the proletarian-socialist world revolution, has started. The main force in this revolution is the proletariat of the capitalist countries and it has as its allies the oppressed peoples of the colonies and semi-colonies. No matter what classes, parties or individuals in the oppressed nations join the revolution, and no matter whether or not they are conscious of this fact and fully understand it, so long as they oppose imperialism, their revolution becomes part of the proletarian-socialist world revolution and they themselves become allies of this revolution.

Today the Chinese revolution assumes an even greater significance. This is a time when the world is being plunged more and more deeply into the Second World War by the economic and political crises of capitalism; when the Soviet Union has reached the period of transition from socialism to communism, and is now capable of leading and helping the proletariat and oppressed nations of the world in their fight against imperialist war and capitalist reaction; when the proletariat of the capitalist countries is preparing to overthrow capitalism and establish socialism; and when China's proletariat, peasantry, intelligentsia and other sections of the petty bourgeoisie have become a mighty independent political force under the leadership of the Chinese Communist Party. At such a juncture, are we not right in claiming that the Chinese revolution has assumed

a greater significance in the world? I think we are. The Chinese revolution has certainly become a very important part of the world revolution.

The first stage of the Chinese revolution, which contains many subdivisions, belongs, so far as its social character is concerned, to a new type of bourgeois-democratic revolution which is not yet a proletarian-socialist revolution in itself, but it has long been part of the proletarian-socialist world revolution and is now even an important part of it and a powerful ally. The first step or stage of this revolution is certainly not, and cannot be, the establishment of a capitalist society under the dictatorship of the Chinese bourgeoisie, but will be the establishment of a new-democratic society under the joint dictatorship of all Chinese revolutionary classes headed by the Chinese proletariat. Then, the revolution will develop into the second stage to establish a socialist society in China.

This is the fundamental feature, the content with all its dramatic details, of the Chinese revolution of today, the whole process of the revolution in the last twenty years since the May 4 Movement of 1919.

5. NEW-DEMOCRATIC POLITICS

The new historical feature of the Chinese revolution is its division into two historical stages, the first stage being a new-democratic revolution. In what way does this new feature actually show itself in the political and economic relations within China? We shall now answer this question.

Before the May 4 Movement of 1919, which occurred after the first imperialist world war of 1914 and the October Revolution in Russia in 1917, the political leaders in the Chinese bourgeois-democratic revolution were the Chinese petty bourgeoisie and bourgeoisie, represented by their intellectuals. At that time the Chinese proletariat had not yet appeared on the political scene as an awakened and independent class force, but took part in the revolution only as a follower of the petty bourgeoisie and the bourgeoisie. The proletariat at the time of the Revolution of 1911, for instance, was a class of this kind.

After the May 4 Movement, although the Chinese national bourgeoisie continued to take part in the revolution, the political leaders of China's bourgeois-democratic revolution no longer belonged to the bourgeoisie, but to the proletariat. By that time the Chinese proletariat, because of its own growth and the influence of the Russian Revolution, had rapidly become an awakened and independent political force. It was the Chinese Communist Party which proposed the slogan "Down with imperialism" together with a thorough-going programme of a complete bourgeois-democratic revolution, and it was the Chinese Communist Party alone which carried out the agrarian revolution.

The Chinese national bourgeoisie, because it belongs to a colonial and semi-colonial country and lives under imperialist oppression, retains, even in the era of imperialism, at certain periods and to a certain degree, a revolutionary quality as expressed in its opposition to foreign imperialism and the home governments of bureaucrats and warlords (instances of the latter can be found in the Revolution of 1911 and in the Northern Expedition), and can ally itself with the proletariat and the petty bourgeoisie to oppose those enemies whom it wants to oppose. This is the difference between the Chinese bourgeoisie and the bourgeoisie of old tsarist Russia. Since tsarist Russia was already a militarist and feudalist imperialist power which carried on aggression against other countries, her bourgeoisie was in no way revolutionary. In tsarist Russia the task of the proletariat was to oppose the bourgeoisie, not to unite with it. On the other hand, because China is a colony and a semi-colony suffering from aggression by others, her national bourgeoisie has at certain periods and to a certain degree a revolutionary quality. Thus in China the task of the proletariat is to take into account the revolutionary quality of the national bourgeoisie and form with it a united front against imperialism and the bureaucratic and warlord regime.

At the same time, however, because the Chinese national bourgeoisie is a bourgeois class in a colony and semi-colony, it is extremely flabby, economically and politically, and, besides its revolutionary quality, it also shows a characteristic proneness to compromise with the enemy of the revolution. Even when it takes part in the revolution, it is unwilling to break completely with imperialism and, being deeply involved in exploitation by land rent in rural areas, it is neither willing nor able to overthrow imperialism completely, much less feudalism. So neither of the two basic problems or tasks of China's bourgeois-democratic revolution can be solved or accomplished by the Chinese national bourgeoisie. In the long period from 1927 to 1937, the big bourgeoisie in China with the Kuomintang as its representative, has all along sought the protection of the imperialists and formed an alliance with the feudal forces to oppose the revolutionary people. The Chinese national bourgeoisie also sided with the counter-revolution in 1927 and for a time afterwards. During the present Anti-Japanese War, a section of the big bourgeoisie, with Wang Ching-wei as its representative, has again capitulated to the enemy—a further betrayal on the part of the big bourgeoisie. This is another difference between the Chinese bourgeoisie and the bourgeoisie in the history of European and American countries, especially France. When it was still in a revolutionary era, the bourgeoisie in those countries, especially in France, was comparatively thorough in carrying out the revolution, while the bourgeoisie in China lacks even that relative thoroughness.

The dual character of the Chinese bourgeoisie, its tendency to serve two masters, is revealed on the one hand by its possible participation in the revolution and on the other by its proneness to compromise with the enemies of the revolution. The bourgeoisie in European and American history shares this dual character. When confronted by a formidable enemy, it unites with the workers and peasants to oppose him; but when the workers and peasants are awakened, it turns to unite with the enemy to oppose them. This is the general rule governing the bourgeoisie in every country of the world, but the trait is even more pronounced in the Chinese bourgeoisie.

It is quite evident that whoever in China can lead the people to overthrow the imperialist and feudal forces will win the people's confidence, because these forces, especially imperialism, are the mortal enemies of the people. Today, whoever can lead the people to drive out Japanese imperialism and carry out democratic policies will be the saviour of the people. History has proved that the Chinese bourgeoisie is incapable of fulfilling this responsibility, which consequently falls upon the shoulders of the proletariat.

Therefore, in all circumstances, the proletariat, the peasantry, the intelligentsia and other sections of the petty bourgeoisie in China are the basic forces which decide China's fate. These classes, some already awakened and others on the point of awakening, will necessarily become the basic components of the state structure and the structure of political power of the democratic republic of China, with the proletariat as the leading force. The democratic republic of China which we now want to establish can only be a democratic republic under the joint dictatorship of all anti-imperialist and anti-feudal people led by the proletariat, that is, a new-democratic republic, or a republic of the genuinely revolutionary new Three People's Principles with the three cardinal policies.

While different from the old European-American form of capitalist republic under bourgeois dictatorship which is now out of date, this new-democratic republic is also different from the socialist republic of the type of the U.S.S.R., the republic of the dictatorship of the proletariat. The socialist republic is already flourishing in the Soviet Union, and will be established in all the capitalist countries and undoubtedly become the dominant form in the structure of state and political power in all industrially advanced countries but, during a given historical period, they are not yet suitable for the revolutions in colonial and semi-colonial countries. Therefore a third form of state must be adopted by the revolutions in colonial and semi-colonial countries during a given historical period, namely, the new-democratic republic. This is the form for a given historical period and therefore a transitional form, but it is the necessary form to which there is no alternative.

The multifarious types of state system

in the world can be reduced to three basic kinds according to the class character of their political power: (1) republics under bourgeois dictatorship; (2) republics under the dictatorship of the proletariat; and (3) republics under the joint dictatorship of several revolutionary classes.

The first kind includes the old democratic states. Today, after the outbreak of the second imperialist war, there is no longer even a trace of democracy in many of the capitalist countries, which have come under or are coming under the bloody militarist dictatorship of the bourgeoisie. Certain countries under the joint dictatorship of the landlords and the bourgeoisie can be classed with this kind.

The second kind exists in the Soviet Union and conditions for its birth are ripening in all capitalist countries. In the future it will become the dominant form throughout the world for a certain period.

The third kind is the transitional form of state to be adopted in revolutions in colonial and semi-colonial countries. Of course, revolutions in different colonial and semi-colonial countries necessarily have certain different characteristics, but these are only minor differences within a general framework of uniformity. So long as they are revolutions in colonies or semi-colonies, the form of state and political power will of necessity be basically the same, a new-democratic state under the joint dictatorship of several anti-imperialist classes. In China today the new-democratic state ought to assume the form of the anti-Japanese united front. It is anti-Japanese and anti-imperialist, a coalition of several revolutionary classes, a united front. But unfortunately, after having resisted Japan for such a long time, the introduction of

democratic government has, generally speaking, not yet started in most parts of the country except in the anti-Japanese democratic bases under the leadership of the Communist Party, and Japanese imperialism has taken advantage of this fundamental weakness to invade large stretches of our country. If this situation remains unchanged, the future of our nation will be gravely imperilled.

What is under discussion here is the state system. After several decades of wrangling since the end of the Ching Dynasty, this question is still not clarified. Actually it is simply the question of the status of various social classes in the state. The bourgeoisie, as a rule, conceals the status of classes and uses the term "citizenship" to cover up the fact of its one-class dictatorship. We must point out clearly that such concealment does no good at all to the revolutionary people. The term "citizenship" may be used provided that it excludes the counter-revolutionaries and collaborators. A dictatorship of all the revolutionary classes over the counter-revolutionaries and collaborators is the kind of state we want today.

The so-called democratic system in modern nations is usually monopolized by the bourgeoisie and has simply become an instrument for oppressing the common people. As to the Principle of Democracy of the Kuomintang, it stands for something to be shared by all the common people and not to be monopolized by a few.

This is a solemn declaration in the Manifesto of the First National Congress of the Kuomintang held in 1924 during the period of the Kuomintang-Communist co-operation. For sixteen years the Kuomintang has betrayed this declaration and consequently created the grave national crisis of today. This is a gross blunder committed by the Kuomintang and we hope that after the baptism of fire in the War of Resistance to Japanese Aggression it will correct the blunder.

As to the question of political structure, it concerns the structural form of political power, the form adopted by certain social classes in organizing their political power to protect themselves against their enemies. Without a suitable organ of political power there would be nothing to represent the state. In China we can adopt a system of people's congresses—the national people's congress, the provincial people's congress, the county people's congress, the district people's congress, down to the township people's congress and let these congresses at various levels elect the organs of government. But a system of really universal and equal suffrage, irrespective of sex, creed, property or education, must be introduced so that each revolutionary class can be equitably represented according to its status in the state, the people's will properly expressed, the revolutionary struggles properly directed and the spirit of New Democracy properly embodied. This is the system of democratic centralism. Only a government of democratic centralism can fully express the will of all the revolutionary people and most effectively fight the enemies of the revolution. The spirit of the phrase "not to be monopolized by a few" must be embodied in the government and the army apparatus; without a genuinely democratic system this aim can never be attained, and there will be a discrepancy between the political structure and the state system.

The state system—joint dictatorship of all revolutionary classes. The political structure—democratic centralism. This is new-democratic government; this is a republic of New Democracy, the republic of the anti-Japanese united front, the re-public of the new Three People's Principles with the three cardinal policies, and the republic of China true to its name. Today we have a Republic of China in name but not in reality, and our immediate task is to make a reality of the name.

Such are the internal political relations which a revolutionary China, a China in the midst of the War of Resistance to Japanese Aggression, ought to and must establish, for this is the only correct orientation for our present work of national reconstruction.

6. NEW-DEMOCRATIC ECONOMY

We must establish in China a republic politically and economically new-democratic.

In this republic big banks and big industrial and commercial enterprises shall be state-owned.

Enterprises such a banks, railways and airlines, whether Chinese-owned or foreign-owned, which are monopolistic in character or too big for private management, shall be operated by the state so that private capital cannot control the livelihood of the people: this is the main principle of the restriction of capital.

This is another solemn statement in the Manifesto of the First National Congress of the Kuomintang during the period of the Kuomintang-Communist co-operation, and is the correct objective for the economic structure of the new-democratic republic. The state-owned enterprises in the new-democratic republic under the leadership of the proletariat will be socialist in character and constitute the leading force in the national economy as a whole, but the republic will neither confiscate other forms of capitalist private property nor forbid the development of capitalist production that "cannot control the livelihood of the people," for China's economy is still very backward.

The republic will by certain necessary measures confiscate the land of landlords and distribute it to those peasants having no land or only a little land, carry out Dr. Sun Yatsen's slogan of "land to the tillers," abolish feudal relations in the rural areas, and turn the land into the private property of the peasants. In the rural areas, the economic activities of rich peasants will be tolerated. This is the line of equalization of landownership. The correct slogan for this line is land to the tillers. In this stage, socialist agriculture is in general not yet to be established, though various types of co-operatives developed on the basis of land to the tillers will contain elements of socialism.

China's economy must develop along the path of restriction of capital and equalization of landownership; it must not be "monopolized by a few"; we must never permit the few capitalists and landlords to control the livelihood of the people, or establish a capitalist society of the European-American type, or allow the old semi-feudal society to remain. Whoever dares to go against this line will certainly not succeed, and will only be dashing his head against a wall.

Such are the internal economic relations which a revolutionary China, an anti-Japanese China, must and inevitably will establish.

This is new-democratic economy.

And new-democratic politics is the concentrated expression of such new-democratic economy.

. . .

11. NEW-DEMOCRATIC CULTURE

We have explained above the historical features of Chinese politics in the new period and the question of the new-democratic republic. We can now proceed to the question of culture.

A given culture is the ideological reflection of the politics and economy of a given society. There is in China an imperialist culture which is a reflection of the political and economic control or partial control of imperialism over China. This culture is promoted and fostered not only by the cultural organizations run directly by the imperialists over China, but also their shameless Chinese toadies. All culture which breeds slave ideology belongs to this category. There is also in China a semi-feudal culture which is a reflection of semi-feudal politics and economy and has as its exponents all those who, while opposing the new culture and new ideologies, advocate the worship of Confucius, the study of the Confucian canon, the old ethical code and the old ideologies. Imperialist culture and semi-feudal culture are affectionate brothers, who have formed a reactionary alliance to oppose China's new culture. This reactionary culture serves imperialism and the feudal class, and must be swept away. Unless it is swept away, no new culture of any kind can be built up. The new culture and the reactionary culture are locked in a life-and-death struggle: there is no construction without destruction, no release without restraint and no movement without rest.

As to the new culture, it is the ideological reflection of new politics and new economy, and is in their service.

As we have already stated in Section 3, Chinese society has gradually changed in character since the emergence of capitalist economy in China: it is no longer an entirely feudal but a semi-feudal society, though feudal economy still predominates. Compared with feudal economy, capitalist economy is a new economy. The new political forces which have emerged and grown simultaneously with this capitalist new economy are the political forces of the bourgeoisie, the petty bourgeoisie and the proletariat. And what ideologically reflects these new economic and political forces and is in their service, is the new culture. Without capitalist economy, without the bourgeoisie, the petty bourgeoisie and the proletariat, and without the political forces of these classes, the new ideology or new culture could not have emerged.

All the new political, new economic and new cultural forces are revolutionary forces in China and are opposed to the old politics, old economy and old culture. The old things are composed of two parts: one is China's own semi-feudal politics, economy and culture and the other is imperialist politics, economy and culture, with the latter leading the alliance. All these are evil and should be completely destroyed. The struggle between the new and the old in Chinese society is a struggle between the new forces of the people—the various revolutionary classes—and the old forces of imperialism and the feudal class. It is a struggle between revolution and counter-revolution. This struggle has lasted a full hundred years if dated from the Opium War, and nearly thirty years if dated from the Revolution of 1911.

But as has been said before, revolutions also can be classified into old and new, and what is new in one historical period becomes old in another. The century of China's bourgeois-democratic revolution can be divided into two main stages—a first stage of eighty years and a second of twenty years. Each has a basic historical feature: China's bourgeois-democratic revolution in the first eighty years belongs to the old category, while that in the next twenty years, owing to the change in the international and domestic political situation, belongs to the new category. Old democracy is the feature of the first eighty years, New Democracy the feature of the last twenty years. This distinction holds good in culture as well as in politics.

How does this distinction show itself in culture? This is the topic we shall take up next.

. . .

15. A NATIONAL, SCIENTIFIC AND MASS CULTURE

The new-democratic culture is national. It opposes imperialist oppression and upholds the dignity and independence of the Chinese nation. It belongs to our own nation, and bears the stamp of our national characteristics. It unites with the socialist and new-democratic cultures of all other nations and establishes with them the relations whereby they can absorb something from each other and help each other to develop, and form together the new world culture but, being a revolutionary national culture, it can never unite with the reactionary imperialist culture of any nation. China should assimilate from foreign progressive cultures in large quantities what she needs for her own culture and we did not sufficiently do so in the past. We must assimilate whatever we find useful today, not only from contemporary foreign socialist or new-democratic cultures, but also from the older cultures of foreign countries, such as those of the capitalist countries in their age of enlightenment. However, we can benefit only if we treat these foreign materials as we do our food, which should be chewed in the mouth, submitted to the working of the stomach and intestines, mixed with saliva, gastric juices and intestinal secretions, and then separated into nutriment to be absorbed and waste matter to be discarded; we should never swallow anything whole or absorb it uncritically. So-called wholesale Westernization[12] is wrong. China has suffered a great deal from the mechanical absorption of things foreign. Likewise, in applying Marxism to China, Chinese communists must fully and properly unite its universal truth with the specific practice of the Chinese revolution, that is to say, the truth of Marxism must be integrated with the national characteristics and given a definite national form before it can be useful; it must not be applied subjectively as a mere formula. Formula-Marxists are only fooling with Marxism and the Chinese revolution, and there is no place for them in the ranks of the Chinese revolution. China's culture should have its own form, which is national. National in form, new-democratic in content—such is our new culture today.

The new-democratic culture is scientific. Opposed to all feudal and superstitious ideas, it stands for seeking truth from facts, for objective truth and for the unity between theory and practice. In this respect, the scientific thought of the Chinese proletariat can, to fight imperialism, feudalism and superstition, form a united front with the still progressive bourgeois materialists and natural scientists, but it can never do so with any reactionary idealism. Communists may form an anti-imperialist and anti-feudal united front for political action with certain idealists and even with religious people, but without implying any approval of their idealism or religious doctrines. A splendid old culture was created during the long period of China's feudal society. To chart the process of development of this old culture, to throw away its feudal dross and to assimilate its dem-

ocratic essence is a necessary condition for the development of our new national culture and for the increase of our national self-confidence, but we must not swallow anything and everything uncritically. In the culture of the past we must separate all the dross of the feudal ruling class from the fine popular elements which are relatively democratic and revolutionary in character. As China's present new politics and new economy have developed out of her old politics and old economy, and China's new culture has also developed out of her old culture, we must respect our own history and not snap the thread of historical continuity. However, this respect for history means only giving history its proper place among the sciences, showing due regard for its dialectical development, but not praising the ancient at the expense of the modern, or recommending any harmful feudal element. As to the people and the student youth, the essential thing is to direct them not to look backward, but to look forward.

The new-democratic culture belongs to the people, hence it is democratic. It should serve the toiling masses of workers and peasants who make up over 90 per cent of the nation's population, so that it may gradually become a culture of their own. There should be a difference in degree between the knowledge imparted to the revolutionary cadres and that imparted to the broad revolutionary masses, but they must also be linked; and similarly the raising of cultural standards must be distinguished from popularization but they too must be linked. Revolutionary culture is a powerful revolutionary weapon for the people. Ideologically it prepares the way for the revolution before its outbreak and becomes a necessary and important sector in the general front when the revolution breaks out. Revolutionary cultural workers are the commanders of various ranks on this sector. From the saying: "Without a revolutionary theory, there can be no revolutionary movement,"[13] we can see how important the revolutionary cultural movement is to the revolution in practice. The cultural movement and revolutionary practice both have a mass character. Therefore all progressive cultural workers should have their own cultural army in the Anti-Japanese War, and this army is the broad mass of the people. A revolutionary cultural worker who keeps aloof from the people is merely a general without an army, and without enough fire-power to destroy the enemy. To attain such an aim, Chinese writing must be reformed under certain conditions, and our spoken language must be brought close to that of the people, for it must be borne in mind that revolutionary culture has its inexhaustible source in the people.

National, scientific and mass culture is the anti-imperialist, anti-feudal culture of the people, the new-democratic and the new Chinese national culture.

When the new-democratic politics, new-democratic economy and new-democratic culture are combined we shall have a republic of New Democracy, a republic of China in name and in fact, the new China we want to build.

New China is within sight of every one of us; let us hail her!

New China is like a ship whose mast is appearing above the horizon; let us acclaim her!

Let us welcome with both hands the new China that is ours!

Notes

1. A magazine founded in January 1940 in Yenan; its first number featured this article.

2. See Lenin, "The Trade Unions, the Present Situation and the Mistakes of Comrade Trotsky" (*Selected Works,* Eng. ed., New York, 1943, Vol. IX, pp. 17, 54).

3. Marx, "Preface to a Contribution to the Critique of Political Economy" (*Selected Works,* Eng. ed., New York, n.d., Vol. I, p. 356).

4. Marx, *Theses on Feuerbach,* xi (*op. cit.,* p. 473).

5. The revolutionary war waged by the Chinese peasants under the leadership of Hung Hsiu-ch'uan, Yang Hsiu-ch'ing and others in the middle of the nineteenth century against the feudal rule and national oppression of the Manchus. The T'aip'ing Heavenly Kingdom was established in 1851 after a successful uprising staged in Chintien village, Kweiping, Kwangsi; the revolutionary forces then marched through Hunan, Hupeh, Kiangsi and Anhwei and in 1853 took Nanking, which became the capital of the Kingdom. Though the T'aip'ing forces reached as far north as the vicinity of Tientsin, they did not establish consolidated bases in the areas under their occupation and, after the establishment of the headquarters of the government in Nanking, their leading group committed many political and military blunders. Finally the Kingdom fell in 1864 under the combined attacks of the Manchu and the British, French and American armed forces.

6. In 1884 the French invaded Vietnam, Kwangsi, Fukien, Taiwan and Chekiang. The Chinese troops, led by Feng Tzu-ts'ai, Liu Yung-fu and others, put up stubborn resistance. In spite of the victories of the Chinese troops, the Manchu regime signed the Treaty of Tientsin with the French government, recognizing its occupation of Vietnam and allowing French influence to penetrate southern China.

7. This war broke out as a result of Japan's aggression upon Korea and provocation against China's ground and sea forces. The Chinese forces fought heroically, but the unpreparedness and irresolution of the corrupt and incompetent Manchu government brought about the ultimate defeat. A humiliating treaty was concluded at Shimonoseki (Bakan), whereby the Manchu government agreed to cede Taiwan and the Penghu Islands to Japan, to pay an indemnity of 200,000,000 taels of silver (a tael being about 1.33 ounces), to allow the Japanese to establish factories in China, to open Shasi, Chungking, Soochow and Hang-

chow as treaty ports, and to let Korea become a vassal state of Japan.

8. Led by K'ang Yu-wei, Liang Ch'i-ch'ao, T'an Szu-t'ung and others, this reformist movement stood for the interests of a section of the liberal bourgeoisie and the enlightened landlords. Although backed by Emperor Kuang Hsu, it had no mass basis and ended in tragic failure.

9. The revolution, sparked off by an armed uprising on October 10 in Wuchang, capital of Hupeh Province, overthrew the autocratic rule of the Manchu Dynasty and was rounded off with the inauguration of the Chinese Republic with Dr. Sun Yat-sen as Provincial President on New Year's Day, 1912. The revolution owed its success to the alliance of the bourgeoisie with the peasants, the workers and the urban petty bourgeoisie, but finally failed because its leading groups did not confer any real benefits on the peasants, compromised with the imperialist and feudal forces and let political power slip into the hands of Yuan Shih-k'ai, founder of the clique of the Northern warlords.

10. Stalin, *Works,* Eng. ed., Moscow, 1953, Vol. IV, pp. 169-70.

11. Stalin, "The National Question Once Again" (*Marxism and the National and Colonial Question,* Eng. ed., London, 1947, pp. 225-26).

12. A view held by a number of "Westernized" Chinese bourgeois intellectuals who adhered to outmoded bourgeois individualism and recommended servile imitation of the European and American examples.

13. Lenin, *What Is to Be Done?* Eng. ed., Moscow, 1947, p. 35.

38. RECTIFY THE PARTY'S STYLE OF WORK

(FEBRUARY 1, 1942)

MAO TSE-TUNG

The Party School opens today and I wish it every success.

I would like to say something about the problem of our Party's style of work.

Why must there be a revolutionary party? There must be a revolutionary party because the world contains enemies who oppress the people and the people want to throw off enemy oppression. In the era of capitalism and imperialism, just such a revolutionary party as the Communist Party is needed. Without such a party it is simply impossible for the people to throw off enemy oppression. We are Communists, we want to lead the people in overthrowing the enemy, and so we must keep our ranks in good order, we must march in step, our troops must be picked troops and our weapons good weapons. Without these conditions the enemy cannot be overthrown.

From *Selected Works of Mao Tse-tung* (Foreign Languages Press, Peking, 1967), Vol. III, pp. 35-51. This speech was delivered by Comrade Mao Tse-tung at the opening of the Party School of the Central Committee of the Communist Party of China.

What is the problem now facing our Party? The general line of the Party is correct and presents no problem, and the Party's work has been fruitful. The Party has several hundred thousand members who are leading the people in extremely hard and bitter struggles against the enemy. This is plain to everybody and beyond all doubt.

Then is there or is there not any problem still facing our Party? I say there is and, in a certain sense, the problem is quite serious.

What is the problem? It is the fact that there is something in the minds of a number of our comrades which strikes one as not quite right, not quite proper.

In other words, there is still something wrong with our style of study, with our style in the Party's internal and external relations and with our style of writing. By something wrong with the style of study we mean the malady of subjectivism. By something wrong with our style in Party relations we mean the malady of sectarianism. By something wrong with the style of writing we mean the malady of stereotyped Party writing.[1] All these are wrong, they are ill winds, but they are not like the wintry north winds that sweep across the whole sky. Subjectivism, sectarianism and stereotyped Party writing are no longer the dominant styles, but merely gusts of contrary wind, ill winds from the air-raid tunnels. (*Laughter.*) It is bad, however, that such winds should still be blowing in the Party. We must seal off the passages which produce them. Our whole Party should undertake the job of sealing off these passages, and so should the Party School. These three ill winds, subjectivism, sectarianism and stereotyped Party writing, have their historical origins. Although no longer dominant in the whole Party, they still constantly

create trouble and assail us. Therefore, it is necessary to resist them and to study, analyse and elucidate them.

Fight subjectivism in order to rectify the style of study, fight sectarianism in order to rectify the style in Party relations, and fight Party stereotypes in order to rectify the style of writing—such is the task before us.

To accomplish the task of overthrowing the enemy, we must accomplish the task of rectifying these styles within the Party. The style of study and the style of writing are also the Party's style of work. Once our Party's style of work is put completely right, the people all over the country will learn from our example. Those outside the Party who have the same kind of bad style will, if they are good and honest people, learn from our example and correct their mistakes, and thus the whole nation will be influenced. So long as our Communist ranks are in good order and march in step, so long as our troops are picked troops and our weapons are good weapons, any enemy, however powerful, can be overthrown.

Let me speak now about subjectivism.

Subjectivism is an improper style of study; it is opposed to Marxism-Leninism and is incompatible with the Communist Party. What we want is the Marxist-Leninist style of study. What we call style of study means not just style of study in the schools but in the whole Party. It is a question of the method of thinking of comrades in our leading bodies, of all cadres and Party members, a question of our attitude towards Marxism-Leninism, of the attitude of all Party comrades in their work. As such, it is a question of extraordinary, indeed of primary, importance.

Certain muddled ideas find currency among many people. There are, for instance, muddled ideas about what is a theorist, what is an intellectual and what is meant by linking theory and practice.

Let us first ask, is the theoretical level of our Party high or low? Recently more Marxist-Leninist works have been translated and more people have been reading them. That is a very good thing. But can we therefore say that the theoretical level of our Party has been greatly raised? True, the level is now somewhat higher than before. But our theoretical front is very much out of harmony with the rich content of the Chinese revolutionary movement, and a comparison of the two shows that the theoretical side is lagging far behind. Generally speaking, our theory cannot as yet keep pace with our revolutionary practice, let alone lead the way as it should. We have not yet raised our rich and varied practice to the proper theoretical plane. We have not yet examined all the problems of revolutionary practice—or even the important ones— and raised them to a theoretical plane. Just think, how many of us have created theories worthy of the name on China's economics, politics, military affairs or culture, theories which can be regarded as scientific and comprehensive, and not crude and sketchy? Especially in the field of economic theory: Chinese capitalism has had a century of development since the Opium War, and yet not a single theoretical work has been produced which accords with the realities of China's economic development and is genuinely scientific. Can we say that in the study of China's economic problems, for instance, the theoretical level is already high? Can we say that our Party already has economic theorists worthy of the name? Certainly not. We have read a great many Marxist-Leninist books, but can we claim, then, that we have theorists? We cannot. For Marxism-Leninism is the theory created by Marx,

Engels, Lenin and Stalin on the basis of practice, their general conclusion drawn from historical and revolutionary reality. If we merely read their works but do not proceed to study the realities of China's history and revolution in the light of their theory or do not make any effort to think through China's revolutionary practice carefully in terms of theory, we should not be so presumptuous as to call ourselves Marxist theorists. Our achievements on the theoretical front will be very poor indeed if, as members of the Communist Party of China, we close our eyes to China's problems and can only memorize isolated conclusions or principles from Marxist writings. If all a person can do is to commit Marxist economics or philosophy to memory, reciting glibly from Chapter I to Chapter X, but is utterly unable to apply them, can he be considered a Marxist theorist? No! He cannot. What kind of theorists do we want? We want theorists who can, in accordance with the Marxist-Leninist stand, viewpoint and method, correctly interpret the practical problems arising in the course of history and revolution and give scientific explanations and theoretical elucidations of China's economic, political, military, cultural and other problems. Such are the theorists we want. To be a theorist of this kind, a person must have a true grasp of the essence of Marxism-Leninism, of the Marxist-Leninist stand, viewpoint and method and of the theories of Lenin and Stalin on the colonial revolution and the Chinese revolution, and he must be able to apply them in a penetrating and scientific analysis of China's practical problems and discover the laws of development of these problems. Such are the theorists we really need.

The Central Committee of our Party has now made a decision calling upon our comrades to learn how to apply the Marxist-Leninist stand, viewpoint and method in the serious study of China's history, and of China's economics, politics, military affairs and culture, and to analyse every problem concretely on the basis of detailed material and then draw theoretical conclusions. This is the responsibility we must shoulder.

Our comrades in the Party School should not regard Marxist theory as lifeless dogma. It is necessary to master Marxist theory and apply it, master it for the sole purpose of applying it. If you can apply the Marxist-Leninist viewpoint in elucidating one or two practical problems, you should be commended and credited with some achievement. The more problems you elucidate and the more comprehensively and profoundly you do so, the greater will be your achievement. Our Party School should also lay down the rule to grade students good or poor according to how they look at China's problems after they have studied Marxism-Leninism, according to whether or not they see the problems clearly and whether or not they see them at all.

Next let us talk about the question of the "intellectuals." Since China is a semicolonial, semi-feudal country and her culture is not well developed, intellectuals are particularly treasured. On this question of the intellectuals, the Central Committee of the Party made the decision[2] over two years ago that we should win over the great numbers of intellectuals and, insofar as they are revolutionary and willing to take part in the resistance to Japan, welcome them one and all. It is entirely right for us to esteem intellectuals, for without revolutionary intellectuals the revolution cannot triumph. But we all know there are many intellectuals who fancy themselves very

learned and assume airs of erudition without realizing that such airs are bad and harmful and hinder their own progress. They ought to be aware of the truth that actually many so-called intellectuals are, relatively speaking, most ignorant and the workers and peasants sometimes know more than they do. Here some will say, "Ha! You are turning things upside down and talking nonsense." (*Laughter.*) But, comrades, don't get excited; there is some sense in what I am saying.

What is knowledge? Ever since class society came into being the world has had only two kinds of knowledge, knowledge of the struggle for production and knowledge of the class struggle. Natural science and social science are the crystallizations of these two kinds of knowledge, and philosophy is the generalization and summation of the knowledge of nature and the knowledge of society. Is there any other kind of knowledge? No. Now let us take a look at certain students, those brought up in schools that are completely cut off from the practical activities of society. What about them? A person goes from a primary school of this kind all the way through to a university of the same kind, graduates and is reckoned to have a stock of learning. But all he has is book-learning; he has not yet taken part in any practical activities or applied what he has learned to any field of life. Can such a person be regarded as a completely developed intellectual? Hardly so, in my opinion, because his knowledge is still incomplete. What then is relatively complete knowledge? All relatively complete knowledge is formed in two stages: the first stage is perceptual knowledge, the second is rational knowledge, the latter being the development of the former to a higher stage. What sort of knowledge is the students' book-learning? Even supposing all their knowledge is truth, it is still not knowledge acquired through their own personal experience, but consists of theories set down by their predecessors in summarizing experience of the struggle for production and of the class struggle. It is entirely necessary that students should acquire this kind of knowledge, but it must be understood that as far as they are concerned such knowledge is in a sense still one-sided, something which has been verified by others but not yet by themselves. What is most important is to be good at applying this knowledge in life and in practice. Therefore, I advise those who have only book-learning but as yet no contact with reality, and also those with little practical experience, to realize their own shortcomings and become a little more modest.

How can those who have only book-learning be turned into intellectuals in the true sense? The only way is to get them to take part in practical work and become practical workers, to get those engaged in theoretical work to study important practical problems. In this way our aim can be attained.

What I have said will probably make some people angry. They will say, "According to your explanation, even Marx would not be regarded as an intellectual." I say they are wrong. Marx took part in the practice of the revolutionary movement and also created revolutionary theory. Beginning with the commodity, the simplest element of capitalism, he made a thorough study of the economic structure of capitalist society. Millions of people saw and handled commodities every day but were so used to them that they took no notice. Marx alone studied commodities scientifically. He carried out a tremendous work of research into their actual development and derived a thoroughly scientific theory from what

existed universally. He studied nature, history and proletarian revolution and created dialectical materialism, historical materialism and the theory of proletarian revolution. Thus Marx became a most completely developed intellectual, representing the acme of human wisdom; he was fundamentally different from those who have only book-learning. Marx undertook detailed investigations and studies in the course of practical struggles, formed generalizations and then verified his conclusions by testing them in practical struggles—this is what we call theoretical work. Our Party needs a large number of comrades who will learn how to do such work. In our Party there are many comrades who can learn to do this kind of theoretical research; most of them are intelligent and promising and we should value them. But they must follow correct principles and not repeat the mistake of the past. They must discard dogmatism and not confine themselves to ready-made phrases in books.

There is only one kind of true theory in this world, theory that is drawn from objective reality and then verified by objective reality; nothing else is worthy of the name of theory in our sense. Stalin said that theory becomes aimless when it is not connected with practice.[3] Aimless theory is useless and false and should be discarded. We should point the finger of scorn at those who are fond of aimless theorizing. Marxism-Leninism is the most correct, scientific and revolutionary truth, born out of and verified by objective reality, but many who study Marxism-Leninism take it as lifeless dogma, thus impeding the development of theory and harming themselves as well as other comrades.

On the other hand, our comrades who are engaged in practical work will also come to grief if they misuse their experience. True, these people are often rich in experience, which is very valuable, but it is very dangerous if they rest content with their own experience. They must realize that their knowledge is mostly perceptual and partial and that they lack rational and comprehensive knowledge; in other words, they lack theory and their knowledge, too, is relatively incomplete. Without comparatively complete knowledge it is impossible to do revolutionary work well.

Thus, there are two kinds of incomplete knowledge, one is ready-made knowledge found in books and the other is knowledge that is mostly perceptual and partial; both are one-sided. Only an integration of the two can yield knowledge that is sound and relatively complete.

In order to study theory, however, our cadres of working-class and peasant origin must first acquire an elementary education. Without it they cannot learn Marxist-Leninist theory. Having acquired it, they can study Marxism-Leninism at any time. In my childhood I never attended a Marxist-Leninist school and was taught only such things as, "The Master said: 'How pleasant it is to learn and constantly review what one has learned.' "4 Though this teaching material was antiquated, it did me some good because from it I learned to read. Nowadays we no longer study the Confucian classics but such new subjects as modern Chinese, history, geography and elementary natural science, which, once learned, are useful everywhere. The Central Committee of our Party now emphatically requires that our cadres of working-class and peasant origin should obtain an elementary education because they can then take up any branch of study —politics, military science or economics. Otherwise, for all their rich experience they will never be able to study theory.

It follows that to combat subjectivism we must enable people of each of these two types to develop in whichever direction they are deficient and to merge with the other type. Those with book-learning must develop in the direction of practice; it is only in this way that they will stop being content with books and avoid committing dogmatist errors. Those experienced in work must take up the study of theory and must read seriously; only then will they be able to systematize and synthesize their experience and raise it to the level of theory, only then will they not mistake their partial experience for universal truth and not commit empiricist errors. Dogmatism and empiricism alike are subjectivism, each originating from an opposite pole.

Hence there are two kinds of subjectivism in our Party, dogmatism and empiricism. Each sees only a part and not the whole. If people are not on guard, do not realize that such one-sidedness is a short-coming and do not strive to overcome it, they are liable to go astray.

However, of the two kinds of subjectivism, dogmatism is still the greater danger in our Party. For dogmatists can easily assume a Marxist guise to bluff, capture and make servitors of cadres of working-class and peasant origin who cannot easily see through them; they can also bluff and ensnare the naive youth. If we overcome dogmatism, cadres with book-learning will readily join with those who have experience and will take to the study of practical things, and then many good cadres who integrate theory with experience, as well as some real theorists, will emerge. If we overcome dogmatism, the comrades with practical experience will have good teachers to help them raise their experience to the level of theory and so avoid empiricist errors.

Besides muddled ideas about the "theorist" and the "intellectual", there is a muddled idea among many comrades about "linking theory and practice", a phrase they have on their lips every day. They talk constantly about "linking", but actually they mean "separating", because they make no effort at linking. How is Marxist-Leninist theory to be linked with the practice of the Chinese revolution? To use a common expression, it is by "shooting the arrow at the target". As the arrow is to the target, so is Marxism-Leninism to the Chinese revolution. Some comrades, however, are "shooting without a target", shooting at random, and such people are liable to harm the revolution. Others merely stroke the arrow fondly, exclaiming, "What a fine arrow! What a fine arrow!" but never want to shoot it. These people are only connoisseurs of curios and have virtually nothing to do with the revolution. The arrow of Marxism-Leninism must be used to shoot at the target of the Chinese revolution. Unless this point is made clear, the theoretical level of our Party can never be raised and the Chinese revolution can never be victorious.

Our comrades must understand that we study Marxism-Leninism not for display, nor because there is any mystery about it, but solely because it is the science which leads the revolutionary cause of the proletariat to victory. Even now, there are not a few people who still regard odd quotations from Marxist-Leninist works as a ready-made panacea which, once acquired, can easily cure all maladies. These people show childish ignorance, and we should enlighten them. It is precisely such ignorant people who take Marxism-Leninism as a religious dogma. To them we should say bluntly, "Your dogma is worthless." Marx, Engels, Lenin and Stalin have re-

peatedly stated that our theory is not a dogma but a guide to action. But such people prefer to forget this statement which is of the greatest, indeed the utmost, importance. Chinese Communists can be regarded as linking theory with practice only when they become good at applying the Marxist-Leninist stand, viewpoint and method and the teachings of Lenin and Stalin concerning the Chinese revolution and when, furthermore, through serious research into the realities of China's history and revolution, they do creative theoretical work to meet China's needs in different spheres. Merely talking about linking theory and practice without actually doing anything about it is of no use, even if one goes on talking for a hundred years. To oppose the subjectivist, one-sided approach to problems, we must demolish dogmatist subjectiveness and one-sidedness.

So much for today about combating subjectivism in order to rectify the style of study throughout the Party.

Let me now speak about the question of sectarianism.

Having been steeled for twenty years, our Party is no longer dominated by sectarianism. Remnants of sectarianism, however, are still found both in the Party's internal relations and in its external relations. Sectarian tendencies in internal relations lead to exclusiveness towards comrades inside the Party and hinder inner-Party unity and solidarity, while sectarian tendencies in external relations lead to exclusiveness towards people outside the Party and hinder the Party in its task of uniting the whole people. Only by uprooting this evil in both its aspects can the Party advance unimpeded in its great task of achieving unity among all Party comrades and among all the people of our country.

What are the remnants of inner-Party

sectarianism? They are mainly as follows:

First, the assertion of "independence". Some comrades see only the interests of the part and not the whole; they always put undue stress on that part of the work for which they themselves are responsible and always wish to subordinate the interests of the whole to the interests of their own part. They do not understand the Party's system of democratic centralism; they do not realize that the Communist Party not only needs democracy but needs centralization even more. They forget the system of democratic centralism in which the minority is subordinate to the majority, the lower level to the higher level, the part to the whole and the entire membership to the Central Committee. Chang Kuo-tao[5] asserted his "independence" of the Central Committee of the Party and as a result "asserted" himself into betraying the Party and became a Kuomintang agent. Although the sectarianism we are now discussing is not of this extremely serious kind, it must still be guarded against and we must do away completely with all manifestations of disunity. We should encourage comrades to take the interests of the whole into account. Every Party member, every branch of work, every statement and every action must proceed from the interests of the whole Party; it is absolutely impermissible to violate this principle.

Those who assert this kind of "independence" are usually wedded to the doctrine of "me first" and are generally wrong on the question of the relationship between the individual and the Party. Although in words they profess respect for the Party, in practice they put themselves first and the Party second. What are these people after? They are after fame and position and want to be in the limelight. Whenever they are put in charge of a branch of work, they assert their "indepedence". With this aim, they draw some people in, push others out and resort to boasting, flattery and touting among the comrades, thus importing the vulgar style of the bourgeois political parties into the Communist Party. It is their dishonesty that causes them to come to grief. I believe we should do things honestly, for without an honest attitude it is absolutely impossible to accomplish anything in this world. Which are the honest people? Marx, Engels, Lenin and Stalin are honest, men of science are honest. Which are the dishonest people? Trotsky, Bukharin, Chen Tu-hsiu and Chang Kuotao are extremely dishonest; and those who assert "independence" out of personal or sectional interest are dishonest too. All sly people, all those who do not have a scientific attitude in their work, fancy themselves resourceful and clever, but in fact they are most stupid and will come to no good. Students in our Party School must pay attention to this problem. We must build a centralized, unified Party and make a clean sweep of all unprincipled factional struggles. We must combat individualism and sectarianism so as to enable our whole Party to march in step and fight for one common goal.

Cadres from the outside and those from the locality must unite and combat sectarian tendencies. Very careful attention must be given to the relations between outside and local cadres because many anti-Japanese base areas were established only after the arrival of the Eighth Route Army or the New Fourth Army and much of the local work developed only after the arrival of outside cadres. Our comrades must understand that in these conditions it is possible for our base areas to be consolidated and for our Party to take root there only when the two kinds of cadres unite as one and when a large number of local cadres develop and are promoted; otherwise it is impossible. Both the outside and the local cadres have their strong and weak points, and to make any progress they must overcome their own weak points by learning from each other's strong points. The outside cadres are generally not up to the local cadres in familiarity with local conditions and links with the masses. Take me for instance. Although I have been in northern Shensi five or six years, I am far behind the local comrades in understanding local conditions and in links with the people here. Our comrades going to the anti-Japanese base areas in Shansi, Hopei, Shantung and other provinces must pay attention to this. Moreover, even within the same base area, owing to the fact that some districts develop earlier and others later, there is a difference between the local cadres of a district and those from outside it. Cadres who come from a more developed to a less developed district are also outside cadres in relation to that locality, and they, too, should pay great attention to fostering and helping local cadres. Generally speaking, in places where outside cadres are in charge, it is they who should bear the main responsibility if their relations with the local cadres are not good. And the chief comrades in charge should bear greater responsibility. The attention paid to this problem in some places is still very inadequate. Some people look down on the local cadres and ridicule them, saying, "What do these locals know? Clodhoppers!" Such people utterly fail to understand the importance of local cadres; they know neither the latter's strong points nor their own weaknesses and

adopt an incorrect, sectarian attitude. All outside cadres must cherish the local cadres and give them constant help and must not be permitted to ridicule or attack them. Of course, the local cadres on their part must learn from the strong points of the outside cadres and rid themselves of inappropriate, narrow views so that they and the outside cadres become as one, with no distinction between "them" and "us", and thus avoid sectarian tendencies.

The same applies to the relationship between cadres in army service and other cadres working in the locality. They must be completely united and must oppose sectarian tendencies. The army cadres must help the local cadres, and vice versa. If there is friction between them, each should make allowance for the other and carry out proper self-criticism. Generally speaking, in places where army cadres are actually in positions of leadership, it is they who should bear the main responsibility if their relations with the local cadres are not good. Only when the army cadres understand their own responsibility and are modest in their attitude towards the local cadres can the conditions be created for the smooth progress of our war effort and our work of construction in the base areas.

The same applies to the relationship among different army units, different localities and different departments. We must oppose the tendency towards selfish departmentalism by which the interests of one's own unit are looked after to the exclusion of those others. Whoever is indifferent to the difficulties of others, refuses to transfer cadres to other units on request, or releases only the inferior ones, "using the neighbour's field as an outlet for his overflow", and does not give the slightest consideration to other departments, localities or people—such a person is a selfish departmentalist who has entirely lost the spirit of communism. Lack of consideration for the whole and complete indifference to other departments, localities and people are characteristics of a selfish departmentalist. We must intensify our efforts to educate such persons and to make them understand that selfish departmentalism is a sectarian tendency which will become very dangerous, if allowed to develop.

Another problem is the relationship between old and new cadres. Since the beginning of the War of Resistance, our Party has grown enormously, and large numbers of new cadres have emerged; that is a very good thing. In his report to the Eighteenth Congress of the Communist Party of the Soviet Union (B.), Comrade Stalin said, ". . . there are never enough old cadres, there are far less than required, and they are already partly going out of commission owing to the operation of the laws of nature." Here he was discussing the cadres' situation and not only the laws of nature. If our Party does not have a great many new cadres working in unity and co-operation with the old cadres, our cause will come to a stop. All old cadres, therefore, should welcome the new ones with the utmost enthusiasm and show them the warmest solicitude. True, new cadres have their shortcomings. They have not been long in the revolution and lack experience, and unavoidably some have brought with them vestiges of the unwholesome ideology of the old society, remnants of the ideology of petty-bourgeois individualism. But such shortcomings can be gradually eliminated through education and tempering in the revolution. The strong point of the new cadres, as Stalin has said, is that they are acutely sensitive to what is new and are therefore enthusiastic and active to a high de-

gree—the very qualities which some of the old cadres lack.[6] Cadres, new and old, should respect each other, learn from each other and overcome their own shortcomings by learning from each other's strong points, so as to unite as one in the common cause and guard against sectarian tendencies. Generally speaking, in places where the old cadres are mainly in charge, it is they who should bear the chief responsibility if relations with the new cadres are not good.

All the above—relations between the part and the whole, relations between the individual and the Party, relations between outside and local cadres, relations between army cadres and other cadres working in the locality, relations between this and that army unit, between this and that locality, between this and that department and relations between old and new cadres—are relations within the Party. In all these relations it is necessary to enhance the spirit of communism and guard against sectarian tendencies, so that the ranks of our Party will be in good order, march in step and therefore fight well. This is a very important problem which we must solve thoroughly in rectifying the Party's style of work. Sectarianism is an expression of subjectivism in organizational relations; if we want to get rid of subjectivism and promote the Marxist-Leninist spirit of seeking truth from facts, we must sweep the remnants of sectarianism out of the Party and proceed from the principle that the Party's interests are above personal or sectional interests, so that the Party can attain complete solidarity and unity.

The remnants of sectarianism must be eliminated from the Party's external as well as its internal relations. The reason is this: we cannot defeat the enemy by merely uniting the comrades throughout the Party, we can defeat the enemy only by uniting the people throughout the country. For twenty years the Communist Party of China has done great and arduous work in the cause of uniting the people of the whole country, and the achievements in this work since the outbreak of the War of Resistance are even greater than in the past. This does not mean, however, that all our comrades already have a correct style in dealing with the masses and are free from sectarian tendencies. No. In fact, sectarian tendencies still exist among a number of comrades, and in some cases to a very serious degree. Many of our comrades tend to be overbearing in their relations with non-Party people, look down upon them, despise or refuse to respect them or appreciate their strong points. This is indeed a sectarian tendency. After reading a few Marxist books, such comrades become more arrogant instead of more modest, and invariably dismiss others as no good without realizing that in fact their own knowledge is only half-baked. Our comrades must realize the truth that Communist Party members are at all times a minority as compared with non-Party people. Supposing one out of every hundred persons were a Communist, then there would be 4,500,000 Communists among China's population of 450,000,000. Yet, even if our membership reached this huge figure, Communists would still form only one per cent of the whole population, while 99 per cent would be non-Party people. What reason can we then have for not co-operating with non-Party people? As regards all those who wish to co-operate with us or might co-operate with us, we have only the duty of co-operating and absolutely no right to shut them out. But some Party members do not understand this and look down upon, or even shut out, those who wish to co-operate with us. There are no grounds whatsoever for doing so. Have Marx, Engels, Lenin and Stalin given us any grounds? They have not. On the contrary, they have always earnestly enjoined us to form close ties with the masses and not divorce ourselves from them. Or has the Central Committee of the Communist Party of China given us any grounds? No. Among all its resolutions there is not a single one that says we may divorce ourselves from the masses and so isolate ourselves. On the contrary, the Central Committee has always told us to form close ties with the masses and not to divorce ourselves from them. Thus any action divorcing us from the masses has no justification at all and is simply the mischievous result of the sectarian ideas some of our comrades have themselves concocted. As such sectarianism remains very serious among some of our comrades and still obstructs the application of the Party line, we should carry out extensive education within the Party to meet this problem. Above all, we should make our cadres really understand how serious the problem is and how utterly impossible it is to overthrow the enemy and attain the goal of the revolution unless Party members unite with the non-Party cadres and with non-Party people.

All sectarian ideas are subjectivist and are incompatible with the real needs of the revolution; hence the struggle against sectarianism and the struggle against subjectivism should go on simultaneously.

There is no time today to talk about the question of stereotyped Party writing; I shall discuss it at another meeting. Stereotyped Party writing is a vehicle for filth, a form of expression for subjectivism and sectarianism. It does people harm and damages the revolution, and we must get rid of it completely.

To combat subjectivism we must propagate materialism and dialectics. However, there are many comrades in our

Party who lay no stress on the propaganda either of materialism or of dialectics. Some tolerate subjectivist propaganda and regard it with equanimity. They think they believe in Marxism, but make no effort to propagate materialism and do not give it a thought or express any opinion when they hear or read subjectivist stuff. This is not the attitude of a Communist. It allows many of our comrades to be poisoned by subjectivist ideas, which numb their sensitivity. We should therefore launch a campaign of enlightenment within the Party to free the minds of our comrades from the fog of subjectivism and dogmatism and should call upon them to boycott subjectivism, sectarianism and stereotyped Party writing. Such evils are like Japanese goods, for only our enemy wishes us to preserve them and continue to befuddle ourselves with them; so we should advocate a boycott against them, just as we boycott Japanese goods.[7] We should boycott all the wares of subjectivism, sectarianism and stereotyped Party writing, make their sale difficult, and not allow their purveyors to ply their trade by exploiting the low theoretical level in the Party. Our comrades must develop a good nose for this purpose; they should take a sniff at everything and distinguish the good from the bad before they decide whether to welcome it or boycott it. Communists must always go into the whys and wherefores of anything, use their own heads and carefully think over whether or not it corresponds to reality and is really well founded; on no account should they follow blindly and encourage slavishness.

Finally, in opposing subjectivism, sectarianism and stereotyped Party writing we must have in mind two purposes: first, "learn from past mistakes to avoid future ones", and second, "cure the sickness to save the patient." The mistakes of the past must be exposed without sparing anyone's sensibilities; it is necessary to analyse and criticize what was bad in the past with a scientific attitude so that work in the future will be done more carefully and done better. This is what is meant by "learn from past mistakes to avoid future ones". But our aim in exposing errors and criticizing shortcomings, like that of a doctor curing a sickness, is solely to save the patient and not to doctor him to death. A person with appendicitis is saved when the surgeon removes his appendix. So long as a person who has made mistakes does not hide his sickness for fear of treatment or persist in his mistakes until he is beyond cure, so long as he honestly and sincerely wishes to be cured and to mend his ways, we should welcome him and cure his sickness so that he can become a good comrade. We can never succeed if we just let ourselves go, and lash out at him. In treating an ideological or a political malady, one must never be rough and rash but must adopt the approach of "curing the sickness to save the patient", which is the only correct and effective method.

I have taken this occasion of the opening of the Party School to speak at length, and I hope comrades will think over what I have said. (*Enthusiastic applause.*)

Notes

1. Stereotyped writing, or the "eight-legged essay," was the special form of essay prescribed in the imperial examinations under China's feudal dynasties from the 15th to the 19th centuries; it consisted in juggling with words, concentrated only on form and was devoid of content. Structurally the main body of the essay had eight parts—presentation, amplification, preliminary exposition, initial argument, inceptive paragraphs, middle paragraphs, rear paragraphs and concluding paragraphs, and the fifth to eighth parts each had to have two "legs," *i.e.*, two antithetical paragraphs, hence

the name "eight-legged essay." The "eight-legged essay" became a byword in China denoting stereotyped formalism and triteness. Thus "stereotyped Party writing" characterizes the writings of certain people in the revolutionary ranks who piled up revolutionary phrases and terms higgledy-piggledy instead of analysing the facts. Like the "eight-legged essay," their writings were nothing but verbiage.

2. This was the decision of recruiting intellectuals adopted by the Central Committee of the Communist Party of China in December 1939, which is printed under the title "Recruit Large Numbers of Intellectuals" in the *Selected Works of Mao Tse-tung*, Vol. II.

3. See J. V. Stalin, "The Foundations of Leninism," *Problems of Leninism,* Eng. ed., FLPH, Moscow, 1954, p. 31.

4. This is the opening sentence of the *Confucian Analects,* a record of the dialogues of Confucius and his disciples.

5. Chang Kuo-tao was a renegade from the Chinese revolution. In early life, speculating on the revolution, he joined the Chinese Communist Party. In the Party he made many mistakes resulting in serious crimes. The most notorious of these was his opposition, in 1935, to the Red Army's northward march and his defeatism and liquidationism in advocating withdrawal by the Red Army to the minority-nationality areas on the Szechuan-Sikang borders; what is more, he openly carried out traitorous activities against the Party and the Central Committee, established his own bogus central committee, disrupted the unity of the Party and the Red Army, and caused heavy losses to the Fourth Front Army of the Red Army. But thanks to patient education by Comrade Mao Tse-tung and the Central Committee, the Fourth Front Army and its numerous cadres soon returned to the correct leadership of the Central Committee of the Party and played a glorious role in subsequent struggles. Chang Kuo-tao, however, proved incorrigible and in the spring of 1938 he slipped out of the Shensi-Kansu-Ningsia Border Region and joined the Kuomintang secret police.

6. See J. V. Stalin, "Report to the Eighteenth Congress of the C.P.S.U. (B.) on the Work of the Central Committee," *Problems of Leninism,* Eng. ed., FLPH, Moscow, 1954, pp. 784-86.

7. Boycotting Japanese goods was a method of struggle frequently used by the Chinese people against Japanese imperialist aggression in the first half of the 20th century, as in the patriotic May 4th Movement of 1919, after the September 18th Incident of 1931, and during the War of Resistance Against Japan.

39. SELECTIONS FROM HOW TO BE A GOOD COMMUNIST

LIU SHAO-CH'I

A PARTY MEMBER'S PERSONAL INTERESTS MUST BE UNCONDITIONALLY SUBORDINATED TO THE INTERESTS OF THE PARTY

Personal interests must be subordinated to the Party's interests, the interests of

From Liu Shao-ch'i, *How To Be A Good Communist* (Foreign Languages Press, Peking, 1965), pp. 45-55.

the local Party organization to those of the entire Party, the interests of the part to those of the whole, and temporary to long-term interests. This is a Marxist-Leninist principle which must be followed by every Communist.

A Communist must be clear about the correct relationship between personal and Party interests.

The Communist Party is the political

party of the proletariat and has no interests of its own other than those of the emancipation of the proletariat. The final emancipation of the proletariat will also inevitably be the final emancipation of all mankind. Unless the proletariat emancipates all working people and all nations—unless it emancipates mankind as a whole—it cannot fully emancipate itself. The cause of the emancipation of the proletariat is identical with and inseparable from the cause of the emancipation of all working people, all oppressed nations and all mankind. Therefore, the interests of the Communist Party are the emancipation of the proletariat and of all mankind, are communism and social progress. When a Party member's personal interests are subordinated to those of the Party, they are subordinated to the interests of the emancipation of the class and the nation, and those of communism and social progress.

Comrade Mao Tse-tung has said:

At no time and in no circumstances should a Communist place his personal interests first; he should subordinate them to the interests of the nation and of the masses of the people. Hence, selfishness, slacking, corruption, striving for the limelight, etc. are most contemptible, while selflessness, working with all one's energy, whole-hearted devotion to public duty, and quiet hard work are the qualities that command respect.[1]

The test of a Party member's loyalty to the Party, the revolution and the cause of communism is whether or not he can subordinate his personal interests absolutely and unconditionally to the interests of the Party, whatever the circumstances.

At all times and on all questions, a Party member should give first consideration to the interests of the Party as a whole, and put them in the forefront and place personal matters and interests second. The supremacy of the Party's interests is the highest principle that must govern the thinking and actions of the members of our Party. In accordance with this principle, every Party member must completely identify his personal interests with those of the Party both in his thinking and in his actions. He must be able to yield to the interests of the Party without any hesitation or reluctance and sacrifice his personal interests whenever the two are at variance. Unhesitating readiness to sacrifice personal interests, and even one's life, for the Party and the proletariat and for the emancipation of the nation and of all mankind—this is one expression of what we usually describe as "Party spirit", "Party sense" or "sense of organization". It is the highest expression of communist morality, of the principled nature of the party of the proletariat, and of the purest proletarian class consciousness.

Members of our Party should not have personal aims which are independent of the Party's interests. Their personal aims must harmonize with the Party's interests. If the aim they set themselves is to study Marxist-Leninist theory, to develop their ability in work, to establish revolutionary organizations and to lead the masses in successful revolutionary struggles—if their aim is to do more for the Party—then this personal aim harmonizes with the interests of the Party. The Party needs many such members and cadres. Apart from this aim, Party members should have no independent personal motives such as attaining position or fame, or playing the individual hero, otherwise they will depart from the interests of the Party and may even become careerists within the Party.

If a Party member thinks only of the communist interests and aims of the Party, is really selfless and has no personal aims and considerations divorced from those of the Party, and if he ceaselessly raises the level of his political consciousness through revolutionary practice and through the study of Marxism-Leninism, then the following ensues.

First, he has a high communist morality. Taking a clear-cut, firm proletarian stand, he is able to show loyalty to and love for all comrades, all revolutionaries and working people, help them unreservedly and act towards them as his equals, and he will never allow himself to hurt a single one of them for his own interests. He is able to feel for others, place himself in their position, and be considerate of them. On the other hand, he is able to wage resolute struggle against the pernicious enemies of mankind and persevere in the fight for the interests of the Party, the proletariat, and the emancipation of the nation and all mankind. He is "the first to worry and the last to enjoy himself".[2] Whether in the Party or among the people, he is the first to suffer hardship and the last to enjoy comfort; he compares himself with others not with respect to material enjoyment but to the amount of work done for the revolution and the spirit of hard endurance in struggle. In times of adversity he steps forward boldly, and in times of difficulty he does his duty to the full. He has such revolutionary firmness and integrity that "neither riches nor honours can corrupt him, neither poverty nor lowly condition can make him swerve from principle, neither threats nor force can bend him".[3]

Second, he has the greatest revolutionary courage. Having no selfish motives, he has nothing to fear. Having done nothing to give himself a guilty conscience, he can lay bare and courageously correct his mistakes and shortcomings, which are like "an eclipse of the sun or the moon".[4] Because he has the courage of righteous conviction, he never fears the truth, courageously upholds it, spreads it and fights for it. Even if it is temporarily to his disadvantage and if, in upholding the truth, he suffers blows of all kinds, is opposed or censured by most other people and so finds himself in temporary (and honourable) isolation, even to the point where he may have to give up his life, he will still breast the waves to uphold the truth and will never drift with the tide.

Third, he learns how best to grasp the theory and method of Marxism-Leninism. He is able to apply them in keenly observing problems and in knowing and changing reality. Because he takes a clear-cut, firm proletarian stand and is tempered in Marxism-Leninism, he is free from personal apprehensions and self-interest, so that there is no impediment to his observation of things or distortion of his understanding of the truth. He seeks the truth from the facts, and he tests all theories and distinguishes what is true from what is false in revolutionary practice. He does not take a dogmatist or empiricist approach to Marxism-Leninism but integrates the universal truth of Marxism-Leninism with concrete revolutionary practice.

Fourth, he is the most sincere, most candid and happiest of men. Because he has no private axe to grind, nothing to conceal from the Party and nothing he cannot tell others, he has no problems of personal gain or loss and no personal anxieties other than for the interests of the Party and the revolution. Even when he is working on his own without supervision and is therefore in a position to do something bad, he is just as "watchful over himself when he is alone"[5] and does not do anything harmful. His work bears examination and he is not afraid of having it checked. He does not fear criticism and at the same time is able to criticize others with courage and sincerity.

Fifth, he has the greatest self-respect and self-esteem. For the sake of the Party and the revolution he can be most forbearing and tolerant towards comrades and can suffer wrong in the general interest, even enduring misunderstanding and humiliation without bitterness if the occasion so demands. No personal aims lead him to flatter anyone or to desire flattery from others. When it comes to personal matters, he knows how to conduct himself and has no need to humble himself in order to get help from others. He knows how to take good care of himself in the interests of the Party and the revolution and how to strengthen both his grasp of theory and his practical effectiveness. But when it is necessary to swallow humiliation and bear a heavy load for some important purpose in the cause of the Party and the revolution, he can take on the most difficult and vital tasks without the slightest reluctance, never passing the difficulties to others.

A member of the Communist Party should possess the finest and highest human virtues and take a clear-cut and firm Party and proletarian stand (that is, possess Party spirit and class spirit). Ours is a fine morality precisely because it is proletarian and communist. It is founded not on the protection of the interests of individuals or of the exploiting few, but on those of the proletariat and the great mass of working people, of the cause of the final emancipation of all mankind, the liberation of the whole world from the calamities of capitalism, and the building of a happy and beautiful communist world—it is a morality founded on the Marxist-Leninist theory of scientific communism. As we Commu-

nists see it, nothing can be more worthless or indefensible than to sacrifice oneself in the interests of an individual or a small minority. But it is the worthiest and justest thing in the world to sacrifice oneself for the Party, for the proletariat, for the emancipation of the nation and of all mankind, for social progress and for the highest interests of the overwhelming majority of the people. Indeed, countless members of the Communist Party have looked death calmly in the face and made the ultimate sacrifice without the slightest hesitation. Most Communists consider it a matter of course to die for the sake of the cause, to lay down their life for justice, when that is necessary. This does not stem from any revolutionary fanaticism or hunger for fame but from their scientific understanding of social development and their deep political consciousness. There is no morality in class society to compare with this high communist morality. The universal morality which supposedly transcends class is sheer deceptive nonsense and is in fact a morality designed to protect the interests of the exploiting few. Such a concept of morality is always idealist. It is only we Communists who build our morality on the scientific basis of historical materialism, and publicly proclaim its purpose to be the protection of the interests of the proletariat in the struggle for the emancipation of itself and of all mankind.

The Communist Party represents the general and long-range interests of the proletariat and all mankind in their struggle for emancipation; the Party's interests are the concentrated expression of this cause. One must never regard the Communist Party as a narrow clique, like a guild pursuing the interests of its members. Anyone who does so is no Communist.

A Party member has interests of his own, which may be inconsistent with or even run counter to the interests of the Party in certain circumstances. Should this happen, it is incumbent on him to sacrifice his personal interests and unconditionally subordinate them to the interests of the Party; under no pretence or excuse may he sacrifice the Party's interests by clinging to his own. At all times and in all circumstances, he should fight heart and soul for the Party's interests and for the Party's development, regarding every success and victory won by the Party and the proletariat as his very own. Every Party member should strive to increase his effectiveness and ability in the service of the people. But this must be done in the fight for the advancement, success and victory of the Party's cause, and there must be no striving for individual development divorced from the fight to advance the Party's cause. The facts prove that only by complete devotion in the fight for the advancement, success and victory of the Party's cause can a Party member heighten his effectiveness and ability, and that he cannot possibly make progress or heighten his ability in any other way. Hence a Party member can and must completely merge his personal interests with those of the Party.

Members of our Party are no ordinary people but the awakened vanguard fighters of the proletariat. They must consciously represent the class interests and class ideology of the proletariat. Therefore, their personal interests must never project beyond those of the Party and the proletariat. It is all the more necessary for each cadre and leader of the Party to be a living embodiment of the general interests of the Party and the proletariat, and to merge his personal interests completely in their general interests and aims. In present-day China, it is the proletariat that best represents the interests of national liberation, and therefore our Party members must be worthy champions of the interests of the nation as a whole.

Members of our Party must subordinate personal to Party interests and are required to sacrifice them to Party interests if necessary. But this by no means implies that our Party does not recognize, or brushes aside, the personal interests of its members or that it wants to wipe out their individuality. Party members do have their personal problems to attend to, and, moreover, they should develop themselves according to their individual inclinations and aptitudes. Therefore, so long as the interests of the Party are not violated, a Party member can have his private and family life, and develop his individual inclinations and aptitudes. At the same time, the Party will use every possibility to help members develop their individual inclinations and aptitudes in conformity with its interests, furnish them with suitable work and working conditions and commend and reward them. As far as possible, the Party will attend to and safeguard its members' essential interests; for example, it will give them the opportunity to study and to acquire an education, it will help them cope with health and family problems and, when necessary, it will even give up some of its work in order to preserve comrades working under the rule of reaction. But all this has no other purpose than the over-all interests of the Party. For the fulfilment of its tasks the Party must ensure that members have the conditions necessary for life, work and education so that they can perform their tasks with enthusiasm and without worry. Comrades in responsible Party positions must bear all this in mind when they deal with Party members' problems.

To sum up, on his side, every Party member should completely submit himself to the interests of the Party and self-sacrificingly devote himself to the public duty. He should forgo all personal aims and private considerations which conflict with the Party's interests. He should not think of himself all the time, make endless personal demands on the Party or blame the Party for not promoting or rewarding him. Whatever the circumstances, he should study hard, try to make progress, be courageous in struggle and make ceaseless efforts to raise the level of his political consciousness and his understanding of Marxism-Leninism, so as to be able to contribute more to the Party and the revolution. On their side, all Party organizations and comrades in responsible positions, in dealing with the problems of Party members, should see how they work, live and study, and enable them to work better for the Party, ceaselessly develop themselves and raise their level in the course of the revolutionary struggle of the proletariat. In particular, attention should be paid to comrades who are really selfless and who serve the people well. Only so, through combined attention and effort by both sides can the interests of the Party be well served.

Notes

1. "The Role of the Chinese Communist Party in the National War," *Selected Works of Mao Tse-tung,* Vol. II.

2. See *Yueh Yang Lou Chi,* by Fan Chung-yen of Sung Dynasty (989-1052 A.D.).

3. From *Mencius,* Book III, "Teng Wen Kung," Part I.

4. See *Confucian Analects,* Book XIX, "Tzu Chang", Chapter 21. "The faults of the superior man are like the eclipses of the sun and moon. When they appear, all men see them; when he corrects them, all men look up to him."

5. From the Confucian "Doctrine of the Mean" in the *Book of Rites:* "There is nothing more visible than what is secret, and nothing more manifest than what is minute. Therefore the superior man is watchful over himself when he is alone."

40. THE CORRECT HANDLING OF

CONTRADICTIONS AMONG THE PEOPLE

MAO TSE-TUNG

We are confronted by two types of social contradictions—those between ourselves and the enemy and those among the people themselves. The two are totally different in their nature.

From *Quotations From Chairman Mao Tse-tung* (Foreign Languages Press, 1966), pp. 45-57.

On the Correct Handling of Contradictions Among the People (February 27, 1957), 1st pocket ed., p. 2.

To understand these two different types of contradictions correctly, we must first be clear on what is meant by "the people" and what is meant by "the enemy". . . . At the present stage, the period of building socialism, the classes, strata and social groups which favour, support and work for the cause of socialist construction all come within the category of the people, while the social forces and groups which resist the socialist revolution and are hostile to or sabotage socialist construction are all enemies of the people.

Ibid., pp. 2-3.

In the conditions prevailing in China today, the contradictions among the people comprise the contradictions within the working class, the contradictions within the peasantry, the contradictions within the intelligentsia, the contradictions between the working class and the peasantry, the contradictions between the workers and peasants on the one hand and the intellectuals on the other, the contradictions between the working class and other sections of the working people on the one hand and the national bourgeoisie on the other, the contradictions within the national bourgeoisie, and so on. Our People's Government is one that genuinely represents the people's interests, it is a government that serves the people. Nevertheless, there are still certain contradictions between the government and the people. These include contradictions among the interests of the state, the interests of the collective and the interests of the individual; between democracy and centralism; between the leadership and the led; and the contradiction arising from the bureaucratic style of work of certain government workers in their relations with the masses. All these are also contradictions among the people. Generally speaking, the people's basic identity of interests

underlies the contradictions among the people.

Ibid., pp. 3-4.

The contradictions between ourselves and the enemy are antagonistic contradictions. Within the ranks of the people, the contradictions among the working people are non-antagonistic, while those between the exploited and the exploiting classes have a non-antagonistic aspect in addition to an antagonistic aspect.

Ibid., p. 3.

In the political life of our people, how should right be distinguished from wrong in one's words and actions? On the basis of the principles of our Constitution, the will of the overwhelming majority of our people and the common political positions which have been proclaimed on various occasions by our political parties and groups, we consider that, broadly speaking, the criteria should be as follows:

(1) Words and actions should help to unite, and not divide, the people of our various nationalities.

(2) They should be beneficial, and not harmful, to socialist transformation and socialist construction.

(3) They should help to consolidate, and not undermine or weaken, the people's democratic dictatorship.

(4) They should help to consolidate, and not undermine or weaken, democratic centralism.

(5) They should help to strengthen, and not discard or weaken, the leadership of the Communist Party.

(6) They should be beneficial, and not harmful, to international socialist

unity and the unity of the peace-loving people of the world.

Of these six criteria, the most important are the socialist path and the leadership of the Party.

Ibid., pp. 57-58.

The question of suppressing counter-revolutionaries is one of a struggle between ourselves and the enemy, a contradiction between ourselves and the enemy. Among the people, there are some who see this question in a somewhat different light. Two kinds of persons hold views different from ours. Those with a Rightest way of thinking make no distinction between ourselves and the enemy and take the enemy for our own people. They regard as friends the very persons whom the broad masses regard as enemies. Those with a "Left" way of thinking magnify contradictions between ourselves and the enemy to such an extent that they take certain contradictions among the people for contradictions with the enemy and regard as counter-revolutionaries persons who are not really counter-revolutionaries. Both these views are wrong. Neither can lead to the correct handling of the question of suppressing counter-revolutionaries or to a correct assessment of this work.

Ibid., p. 25.

Qualitatively different contradictions can only be resolved by qualitatively different methods. For instance, the contradiction between the proletariat and the bourgeoisie is resolved by the method of socialist revolution; the contradiction between the great masses of the people and the feudal system is resolved by the method of democratic revolution; the

contradiction between the colonies and imperialism is resolved by the method of national revolutionary war; the contradiction between the working class and the peasant class in socialist society is resolved by the method of collectivization and mechanization in agriculture; contradiction within the Communist Party is resolved by the method of criticism and self-criticism; the contradiction between society and nature is resolved by the method of developing the productive forces. . . . The principle of using different methods to resolve different contradictions is one which Marxist-Leninists must strictly observe.

"On Contradiction" (August 1937), *Selected Works*, Vol. I, pp. 321-22.

Since they are different in nature, the contradictions between ourselves and the enemy and the contradictions among the people must be resolved by different methods. To put it briefly, the former are a matter of drawing a clear distinction between ourselves and the enemy, and the latter a matter of drawing a clear distinction between right and wrong. It is, of course, true that the distinction between ourselves and the enemy is also a matter of right and wrong. For example, the question of who is in the right, we or the domestic and foreign reactionaries, the imperialists, the feudalists and bureaucrat-capitalists, is also a matter of right and wrong, but it is in a different category from questions of right and wrong among the people.

On the Correct Handling of Contradictions Among the People (February 27, 1957), 1st pocket ed., pp. 5-6.

The only way to settle questions of an ideological nature or controversial issues among the people is by the democratic method, the method of discussion, of criticism, of persuasion and education, and not by the method of coercion or repression.

Ibid., p. 11.

To be able to carry on their production and studies effectively and to arrange their lives properly, the people want their government and those in charge of production and of cultural and educational organizations to issue appropriate orders of an obligatory nature. It is common sense that the maintenance of public order would be impossible without such administrative regulations. Administrative orders and the method of persuasion and education complement each other in resolving contradictions among the people. Even administrative regulations for the maintenance of public order must be accompanied by persuasion and education, for in many cases regulations alone will not work.

Ibid., pp. 11-12.

Inevitably, the bourgeoisie and petty bourgeoisie will give expression to their own ideologies. Inevitably, they will stubbornly express themselves on political and ideological questions by every possible means. You cannot expect them to do otherwise. We should not use the method of suppression and prevent them from expressing themselves, but should allow them to do so and at the same time argue with them and direct appropriate criticism at them. We must undoubtedly criticize wrong ideas of every description. It certainly would not be right to refrain from criticism, look on while

wrong ideas spread unchecked and allow them to monopolize the field. Mistakes must be criticized and poisonous weeds fought wherever they crop up. However, such criticism should not be dogmatic, and the metaphysical method should not be used, but efforts should be made to apply the dialectical method. What is needed is scientific analysis and convincing argument.

Ibid., pp. 55-56.

To criticize the people's shortcomings is necessary, . . . but in doing so we must truly take the stand of the people and speak out of whole-hearted eagerness to protect and educate them. To treat comrades like enemies is to go over to the stand of the enemy.

"Talks at the Yenan Forum on Literature and Art" (May 1942), *Selected Works*, Vol. III, p. 92.

Contradiction and struggle are universal and absolute, but the methods of resolving contradictions, that is, the forms of struggle, differ according to the differences in the nature of the contradictions. Some contradictions are characterized by open antagonism, others are not. In accordance with the concrete development of things, some contradictions which were originally non-antagonistic develop into antagonistic ones, while others which were originally antagonistic develop into non-antagonistic ones.

"On Contradiction" (August 1937), *Selected Works, Vol.* I, p. 344.

In ordinary circumstances, contradictions among the people are not antagonistic. But if they are not handled properly, or if we relax our vigilance and lower our guard, antagonism may arise. In a socialist country, a development of this kind is usually only a localized and temporary phenomenon. The reason is that the system of exploitation of man by man has been abolished and the interests of the people are basically the same.

On the Correct Handling of Contradictions Among the People (February 27, 1957), 1st pocket ed., p. 14.

In our country, the contradiction between the working class and the national bourgeoisie belongs to the category of contradictions among the people. By and large, the class struggle between the two is a class struggle within the ranks of the people, because the Chinese national bourgeoisie has a dual character. In the period of the bourgeois-democratic revolution, it had both a revolutionary and a conciliationist side to its character. In the period of the socialist revolution, exploitation of the working class for profit constitutes one side of the character of the national bourgeoisie, while its support of the Constitution and its willingness to accept socialist transformation constitute the other. The national bour-

geoisie differs from the imperialists, the landlords and the bureaucrat-capitalists. The contradiction between the national bourgeoisie and the working class is one between the exploiter and the exploited, and is by nature antagonistic. But in the concrete conditions of China, this antagonistic class contradiction can, if properly handled, be transformed into a non-antagonistic one and be resolved by peaceful methods. However, it will change into a contradiction between ourselves and the enemy if we do not handle it properly and do not follow the policy of uniting with, criticizing and educating the national bourgeoisie, or if the national bourgeoisie does not accept this policy of ours.

Ibid., pp. 4-5.

It [the counter-revolutionary rebellion in Hungary in 1956] was a case of reactionaries inside a socialist country, in league with the imperialists, attempting to achieve their conspiratorial aims by taking advantage of contradictions among the people to foment dissension and stir up disorder. This lesson of the Hungarian events merits attention.

Ibid., p. 15.

III. THE GREAT LEAP AND THE COMMUNE

41. ECONOMIC AFTERMATH OF THE GREAT LEAP

IN COMMUNIST CHINA

KANG CHAO

In 1958 the Chinese Communist leadership launched the so-called Great Leap movement with the aim of increasing production on all economic fronts at an unprecedentedly high rate. As a result, the nation plunged rapidly into a deep economic quagmire.

Under the new program, production targets for many commodities were repeatedly adjusted upward, and maximum pressure was applied on production units to achieve assigned output quotas by whatever means necessary. Another salient feature of the Great Leap movement was a greater emphasis on indigenous methods of production and labor-intensive investment projects. This policy, officially called "walking with two legs," represented a sharp departure from previous development strategy which had stressed only modern production techniques and large-scale investment projects. The technical dualism introduced in 1958 was based on the assumption that native and small plants require less capital and a shorter construction period and that such plants can

From *Asian Survey*, Vol. IV, No. 5 (May 1964), pp. 851-58. Reprinted by permission. The author is Associate Professor of Economics, University of Wisconsin, Madison, Wis.

make use of local resources and labor that might otherwise be unemployed. These arguments were even more persuasive because of the discontinuation of Soviet loans which led to restraints on the importation of modern equipment for the ambitious economic development plans. Theoretically, the technical dualism envisaged by the Great Leap program is not inherently unreasonable. In a country like Communist China, the rate of economic growth could be maximized, assuming a fixed amount of investment, by developing labor-intensive production. Misallocation of resources would occur only if this strategy were carried too far and conducted in a chaotic fashion.

The Great Leap movement, lasting about two years, was abandoned in 1960 after the country had been afflicted by a prolonged and serious agrarian crisis. The economic situation made continued industrial expansion impossible. The most obvious consequence of the Great Leap was the enormous waste involved. Indigenous production methods often proved either too costly in comparison with their counterparts in the modern sector or capable of producing only low quality goods. A large number of the backyard furnaces hastily built in 1958 dissolved into piles of mud and brick after a few rains. Others were given up by the local authorities because of prohibitively high operation costs. Only a small portion of the indigenous blast furnaces survived and then only after some renovation. Similar situations prevailed in other industries, such as the small coal pits utilizing primitive methods of production that had been opened in 1958.

Another serious form of wastage was created as a result of inter-industry imbalance. Because the Great Leap movement was improvised rather than well planned in terms of inter-industry coordination, and because bottlenecks came sooner in some industries than in others as the movement proceeded, the economy was completely off-balance toward the end of 1958 and during 1959. Stocks piled up in those industries which had overproduced, while production capacities could not be fully utilized in other fields due to material shortages.

Resource misallocation due to industrial imbalance may be only temporary since the Communist leadership can avoid further waste of this type by altering or discontinuing the program. However, from official statements and non-official disclosures, we know that in addition to the waste of resources incurred in the Great Leap movement, there were more profound shocks to the economy, some of which lasted for a considerable period after the movement was discontinued and which could be corrected only through serious readjustments.

Unfortunately, it is very difficult to make a full assessment of these more fundamental factors even today, four years after the Great Leap movement was abandoned. However, certain preliminary evaluations can be made. The

Great Leap followed immediately after nation-wide decentralization in industry, commerce, finance and other areas in the economy. It was also at this time that the commune system was introduced. All these drastic institutional changes in mainland China have had profound effects. Moreover, some of the damaging effects became noticeable only after 1959 when extremely unfavorable weather conditions and other natural calamities were also devastating the country. Since 1960, the Communist authorities in China have withheld all economic information so that an outside observer is unable to evaluate these developments in quantitative terms.

Clearly, one far-reaching result of the Great Leap movement was the statistical confusion that ensued, creating new difficulties for future planning. Since the founding of the State Statistical Bureau in 1952, the Chinese Communists had striven to establish a workable statistical system over the whole nation to facilitate economic planning. The avowed objective of the State Statistical Bureau was to collect reliable and comprehensive data by standardizing statistical schedules, methods of computation, and definitions of terms and designations. Undoubtedly, the statistical system was greatly improved during the first five year plan period. However, these efforts were partially nullified in 1958 and 1959 by decentralization and the Great Leap.[1] Under the decentralization policy, more than 80% of the centrally controlled enterprises were transferred to provincial jurisdiction. Local party cadres, who had been given greater responsibility and independence in handling production statistics, did not always follow the rules set by the State Statistical Bureau. Standard statistical schedules, computation methods, and commodity designations were frequently changed by the local governments to suit their own needs and purposes.

The Great Leap movement, on the other hand, created additional burdens for the State Statistical Bureau. Under the "walking with two legs" policy, more than 700,000 tiny industrial units emerged throughout the country in 1958.[2] These native industries utilizing indigenous methods produced non-standardized goods. The lack of well-trained accountants and statisticians to provide regular statistical reports was common. In some small-sized industries, there were not even instruments to measure output.[3] More serious was the tendency among production units to exaggerate output because of the intense pressure to fulfill targets. Local cadres, hoping that the glowing reports would stimulate other units to accomplish spectacular results, were unwilling to check on, and in some cases connived in, the statistical exaggerations made by individual enterprises.

The statistical confusion reached its climax in 1959 when the central government openly admitted surprisingly large errors in some of the 1958 figures, and consequently adjusted the planned targets for 1959. However, this confession merely exposed the chaotic situation; it did not change it. Several years were required for the Communist planners to remove fully the statistical confusion created. Meanwhile, massive statistical errors increased the difficulties of economic planning. Communist planners have been deprived of reliable current production data from which to work out consistent plans for the future. To formulate the so-called material balance tables, moreover, the planners need fairly accurate technical coefficients indicating how much of one commodity will be required as material input in producing one unit of another commodity. However, with the technical dualism that rapidly developed in 1958-1959, most technical coefficients or input-output ratios had so greatly diverged between modern and native industries that national averages became less meaningful. As a result, it became more difficult for the planners to maintain inter-industry balance even when production figures were well controlled.

Quality control: One universal phenomenon in the Great Leap era was the drastic decline in the quality of commodities. A number of factors were responsible. Shortages of raw materials existed in varying degree in practically all manufacturing plants during this period. As a remedy, producers were asked to use inferior materials, poor substitutes, or scrap materials, which would inevitably lower the quality of finished products. At the same time, a larger number of new workers were recruited by industries from the countryside and were immediately put to work without having received sufficient training in production techniques. Deterioration in quality was also attributed to the fact that in many plants the normal process of production and technical requirements were not strictly observed.[4] But, more important was the tendency for some producers to deliberately lower quality as the only possible means of fulfilling the unreasonably high output quotas. The deterioration in the quality of products reached such an alarming level that six nation-wide conferences were held by various industrial ministries in June 1959 to correct the situation.

Except for a few cases, this problem

may have been a temporary one without any long-lasting impact on the economy. One might expect the quality of production to return to normal when the production drive was discontinued, shortages of materials were relieved, normal production processes and technical requirements were carefully observed, and regular quality control was reinstated.

One probable exception, however, is machine production in which the quality of output may have been affected for a number of years. Machines of inferior quality tend to make poor products. Some plants in Communist China have reported that they constantly have difficulty in stabilizing the quality of their products because they are using non-standard machinery built in the Great Leap period.[5]

Still worse is the problem of quality in water conservation projects. The inferior quality of ordinary goods at most makes them defective or useless articles. Even the injurious effects of defective medicines can be prevented by not using them. But the poor quality of water conservation projects can be far more serious and their damaging effects can hardly be prevented, once construction has been completed. In 1958, more than 100 million people were mobilized to construct dams, reservoirs, and other irrigation projects. Most of these were small projects hurriedly approved without adequate advance surveys or proper designs. During that period, even for large-scale, well-planned projects, normal construction procedures were altered under the pressure of speeding up the work. Precautionary measures were often labeled "superstition" and were abandoned. As hydraulic engineers know, unsatisfactorily designed and poorly constructed flood-control projects may make the control of floods more difficult and

the results of floods more disastrous. Improperly built water reservoirs may raise the underground water level in the neighboring area above its critical point resulting in the land becoming too alkaline. Similarly, irrigation systems with inadequate drainage may also cause alkalinization or salinization.[6] In fact, some hydraulic engineering experts had warned the Communist cadres before and during the Great Leap about the dangers of building water conservation projects without careful planning, survey and design. Since 1959, articles have appeared in leading Communist journals and newspapers condemning the heavy damage in agricultural production caused by re-alkalinization and other man-made disasters. Today, certain observers on both sides of the bamboo curtain are inclined to believe that the abnormal weather conditions in the past few years would have been less disastrous if the Chinese Communists had not built so many indigenous and defective water conservation projects during the Great Leap period.

Lack of maintenance: Under heavy pressure to increase output during the Great Leap, all industrial enterprises over-used or abused their machinery and equipment. Regular maintenance and check-ups were reduced to a minimum in order to gain more time for operation.[7] Some machines were operated at such a high speed as to exceed the technically permissible limit. It was also very common in the transportation system that vehicles were overloaded and kept running with little or no normal maintenance.

Repair and maintenance departments in large enterprises were converted into manufacturing workshops. This was partly because an illusion had been created that maintenance services could be abandoned without affecting the conditions of the machinery. Since workers in the repair and maintenance departments knew more than the newly recruited workers about the equipment and production skills, those departments were frequently converted into production units as a very convenient way to increase production. These conversions were euphemistically termed the promotion of repair and maintenance departments. In this period, a great number of independent repair shops in the cities were also encouraged to become production units by local authorities.[8]

The impact of reduced maintenance and repair activities was extensively felt only after a period of time; conversely, it will also take time to reverse the trend. Unfortunately for the Communists, the corrective measures taken after 1959 were modified by another factor, that is, a shortage of spare parts. Great Leap targets assigned to machine-producing enterprises were assigned only on the basis of major machine parts; the output of accessories and attachments was usually not taken into account. Hence, individual enterprises naturally concentrated all their efforts on increasing the production of the essential machine parts at the expense of the output of appurtenances and accessories.[9] Consequently, in many large enterprises, workshops producing spare parts and accessories were converted into units manufacturing machines proper. One Communist source has reported that almost all iron and steel enterprises established in 1958 lack inspecting devices, spare parts, and other necessary accessories.[10]

A very serious impact was first felt in the transportation system in the latter part of 1959 when official reports disclosed that thousands of motor vehicles could hardly be kept in normal opera-tional condition due to the above mentioned difficulties.[11] Within approximately one year, similar problems arose, with varying intensity, in other industries.[12] As a result, beginning in 1961, the Communist leadership launched a new campaign urging all production and transportation units to place a higher priority on maintenance than on production.[13] They were ordered to restore their repair departments or to establish new ones, and were also instructed to observe strictly the normal maintenance schedules and regular check-ups of equipment. In 1961 and 1962, a coordinated plan was mapped out among three machine industry ministries to produce more parts and accessories.[14] All parts-producing units which had changed their production lines during the Great Leap period were ordered to shift back to their original line, or to be re-equipped with new lathes or machines for the production of spare parts.

Diversification of production: Another undesirable result of the Great Leap movement was an unnecessary diversification of production in most large enterprises. One of the main features of industrial development in Communist China prior to 1958 was the emphasis on specialization. Most state enterprises were so designed as to specialize in one or several products, and each was subject to the direct control of the industrial ministry concerned. However, this principle was somewhat negated in 1958 by more diversified production or what the Chinese Communists called "multiple-lines of business."

Diversification of production is not necessarily bad if carried out properly. Indeed, it is quite common in large enterprises in the Western world. There is some saving in cost if a manufacturer produces several commodities which are joint products of the same materials or are related to each other in the production processes or in the requirements of machinery, laboratory equipment, and technical personnel. This type of diversification, which may be called horizontal diversification, provides some protection for the producer against the risk of a sudden decline in the market demand for the commodity in which he might otherwise have specialized. However, except for certain giant industries such as the iron and steel complexes, it is less common to find vertical diversification—i.e., the production of all kinds of raw materials required in making industrial end-products. This type of diversification may not provide any appreciable cost-saving, and even little or no protection for the firm in case of a sudden decline in demand for the end-product.

Industries in Communist China pursued vertical diversification after 1958. This was a consequence of the failure by most plants to obtain sufficient quantities of materials needed for production during the Great Leap period. As a result, factories were inclined, under the decentralized administration, to establish a number of subsidiary units, known as satellite plants, around each main plant in order to supply materials needed by the main plant. Thus, railway bureaus began to run cement plants and steel mills in order to make their own cement and rails. Cement mills began to establish paper mills to supply paper bags. Paper mills began to produce sulphuric acid and caustic soda in their satellite plants. This development was further encouraged by a speech of Mao Tse-tung in September 1958, in which he applauded the operation of multiple businesses as an ingenious idea to make plants self-sufficient and to overcome the shortage of raw materials.[15] In about one

year, thousands of complex industries had been formed, each trying to produce whatever materials were in short supply.

Since the satellite plants were quite different from the main plant in capital and technical requirements, there was little cost saving. In fact, a great number of satellite plants were hurriedly built to meet exigent needs without any serious consideration being given to the geographical distribution of natural resources and other relevant conditions. Consequently, production costs in such plants were abnormally high. Of course, cost considerations had been relegated to secondary importance during the Great Leap period and it seemed justified for an enterprise to fulfill its assigned target even at a high expense. It was only when the Great Leap was over that the Communist planners began to worry about the disequilibrium caused by the undesirable diversification in industries. It has subsequently been suggested that the principle of industrial specialization should be restored, that waste in satellite plants should be eliminated, and that diversification should be confined only to those industries where cost savings may be induced by diversified production.[16]

Labor Morale: Finally, the Great Leap caused a demoralization among workers, managerial and technical personnel that has also had a long-lasting effect. A large number of new workers were recruited into industry in 1958. They differed from the old workers in that most of them were so-called contract workers, hired on a contract basis for a specified period of time.[17] They lacked a feeling of security. Most important, they were not entitled to all of the benefits enjoyed by the old workers such as free medical care, compensation for injury and disability, retirement pensions, and special allowances for dependents. On the other hand, the number of work accidents greatly increased during the Great Leap period due to the relaxation of safety measures under the pressure of the production drive.[18] Demoralization among workers became even worse when the Communist authorities began to repatriate superfluous workers to the countryside in late 1959.

The factors that impaired the morale of managerial and technical personnel were different. Under the slogans "politics takes command" and "reliance on the mass line," the administrative system within an enterprise underwent considerable disruption. Technicians and engineers were humiliated by the existence of a situation under which experts had to listen to non-experts in technical matters, scientific laws were replaced by political demands, and production fell into the hands of a group of "fanatics."

Several years after the Great Leap era, the situation has still not returned to normal in many enterprises. The Communist leadership has recently repeated the necessity to overcome management chaos in those enterprises in which there is no one person responsible for any specific job or assignment.[19] Emphasis is again being placed upon a managerial system in which the entire factory is subordinate to the unified leadership of a general manager, and each staff member is responsible only for those tasks assigned to his post. Workers have been instructed to respect the professional opinion of the engineers and technicians and to observe strictly the normal order and technical requirements in each production process.

The above problems represent some consequences of the Great Leap movement on the subsequent economic development of mainland China. However, one should not describe the Great Leap as a total failure. It is undeniable that output increased remarkably in that period even after official claims have been subjected to an intensive and skeptical scrutiny. More important from a long-run point of view perhaps is the fact that the Great Leap movement, like most blunders made by men, has had its educational effect. Chinese Communist planners must have learned a lesson from it and, presumably, they will try to avoid the same mistakes in the future.

Notes

1. For a detailed discussion, see Choh-ming Li, *The Statistical System of Communist China* (Univ. of Calif. Press, 1962), Ch. VII.

2. *Ching-chi yen-chiu* (Economic Research), No. 10 (1959), 21.

3. *Chi-hua yu tung-chi* (Planning and Statistics), No. 1 (1959), 31.

4. *Ibid.*, No. 11 (1959), 12.

5. *Ibid.*

6. *Jen-min jih pao* (People's Daily), June 26, 1962.

7. *Jen-min shou-tse* (People's Handbook), 1962, p. 233; *Ta-kung-pao* (Impartial Daily), May 7, 1962; and *Jen-min jih-pao*, May 26, 1961.

8. *Jen-min shou-tse*, 1961, p. 238.

9. *Chi-hua yu tung-chi*, No. 9 (1959), 17.

10. *Ibid.*

11. *Ibid.*, No. 4 (1959), 6 and *Ta-kung-pao*, Feb. 26, 1961.

12. *Jen-min shou-tse*, 1962, p. 243.

13. *Ibid.*, 1961, p. 238; *Jen-min jih-pao*, May 26, 1961 and May 3, 1962; and *Ta-king-pao*, May 7, 1962.

14. *Jen-min jih-pao*, May 3, 1962.

15. *Jen-min shou-tse*, 1960, p. 400.

16. *Hung-chi* (Red Flag), No. 9 (1959), 18; *Ching-chi yen-chiu*, No. 6 (1959), 11; *Chi hua yu tung chi*, No. 9 (1959), 6 and No. 15 (1959), 12; and *Ta-kung-pao*, Nov. 21, 1963.

17. *Chi-hua yu tung-chi*, No. 9 (1959), 20.

18. *Kung-jen jih-pao* (Worker's Daily), July 16, 1959.

19. *Jen-min shou-tse*, 1962, p. 250.

42. THE IDEOLOGICAL SOURCE OF THE PEOPLE'S COMMUNES IN COMMUNIST CHINA

WEN-SHUN CHI

Marx and Engels both said little about the form of organization that would replace capitalist society; nor did they describe the practical measures that would need to be taken to achieve the ultimate goal—the communist society. Any blueprint of the new society was actually discouraged as being utopian. Nor was Lenin in favor of making such an attempt. But since 1958 the Chinese Communists have sponsored a specific organizational form which they believe is the shape of the future. The people's commune, they claim, is the best form of organization for the attainment of socialism, and for the subsequent transition to communism. It will, they argue, develop into the basic unit of communist society.[1] Enthusiastically, the Chinese Communists see the people's communes as "the morning sun above the broad horizon of East Asia."[2]

Since their establishment, the people's communes have attracted world-wide attention. Reactions have ranged, according to the ideology of the beholder, from applause to apprehension. Because

From *Pacific Coast Philology*, Vol. II, (April 1967), pp. 62-78. The author is Senior Tutor at the Center for Chinese Studies, University of California, Berkeley. Reprinted by permission of Philological Association of the Pacific Coast.

this organizational form did not originate in Marx, Engels, or Lenin, it is necessary to search elsewhere for its source. This article is an attempt to trace the ideological source of the people's commune as a social system.

Historically, only two types of communes in the Marxist sense have actually existed. The first was the Paris Commune of 1871, which lasted a mere 73 days from its rise on March 17 to its final suppression on May 28. In Marx's description: "It was essentially a working-class government, the product of the struggle of the producing against the appropriating class, the political form at last discovered under which to work out the economic emancipation of labour."[3] The Paris Commune was thus unlike the people's communes which are essentially rural organizations. A few urban communes were organized in China, but only on a tentative, experimental basis, and have been discontinued.

The second instance was the peasant communes which sprang up spontaneously in the Soviet Union during the early post-revolutionary period. These Soviet communes had a short life and were given up as premature when "Stalin in 1930 decided that they were a form for the distant future, not the socialist present."[4] Khrushchev quickly voiced the strong Russian opposition to the Chinese people's communes, arguing that the Soviet fiasco demonstrated their unworkability.[5]

As both these historical attempts ended in failure, we can assume that the Chinese Communists did not derive encouragement from them. In addition, most of the Western countries, and particularly England and America, have seen attempts to set up idealistic communal societies as utopian experiments on a small scale. None have survived or had any real success. Thus there is little basis to suggest that these experiments have served as the ideological source of the Chinese people's communes.

If the West does not provide the ideological roots of the Chinese communes, it seems reasonable to search for such sources in the East. Mao Tse-tung, in a famous article, *On the People's Democratic Dictatorship*, delivered just after Communist control of the mainland had been consummated, noted that "K'ang Yu-wei wrote the *Book of World Communism*,[6] but he did not and could not find the way to world communism." The Chinese title of K'ang's book is *Ta-t'ung Shu* (*Book of Ta-t'ung*). K'ang has a theory of evolution which he derived from the *Spring and Autumn Annals* that history is divided into three stages, the Age of Disorder, the Age of Order, and the Age of Great Peace. The last stage is the ideal world of the future, which is equivalent to *ta-t'ung* as opposed to *hsiao-k'ang*—literally meaning small security and referring to the first two stages. Both terms—*ta-t'ung* and *hsiao-k'ang*—are taken from the chapter *Li-yun* (Evolution of Rites) of *Li Chi* (Book of Rites). *Ta-t'ung* is generally translated as "great unity," "great harmony," or "great community." It seems clear that there is an identity in Mao's

thinking between this old concept of *ta-t'ung* and the modern ideal of world communism. For instance, the official English translation of *On the People's Democratic Dictatorship* has Mao saying: "But the problem with the working class, the working people and the Communists, is not one of being overthrown, but one of working hard to create the conditions for classes, state power, and political parties to wither away in the most natural manner and for mankind to enter the era of world communism." The original Chinese version, however, reads ". . . to enter the era of *ta-t'ung*." This leads us to believe that the *ta-t'ung* concept plays a key role in the thought of Mao, who is undoubtedly the chief architect for the system of people's communes.

The life of Mao reveals that he was strongly influenced by the writings of K'ang Yu-wei at an age when young minds are receptive to new ideas. "At sixteen, Mao attended elementary school about 50 *li* from his home town to study . . . K'ang Yu-wei and his disciple Liang Ch'i-ch'ao were the two men who were held in great esteem in the heart of the young man, Mao Tse-tung."[7] Here, for the first time, Mao really left the home environment and, at the impressionable age of sixteen began to have access to new knowledge of the outside world. We can assume that his impressions were profound and lasting. According to another biographer, Mao "read and re-read the writings of K'ang Yu-wei and Liang Ch'i-ch'ao to such an extent that he could remember almost all of their works by heart. During that time he worshipped them extraordinarily."[8]

K'ang and Liang, master and disciple, were usually linked together because they were the dominant figures in the

Hundred Days of Reform in 1898. By the time that the young Mao was an avid student of their ideas, their published works were already extensive. The *Ta-t'ung Shu* itself had not, however, yet been included among these published works. The book is supposed to have been largely written in 1884-1885 and completed in 1902. The first publication, in 1927, was only partial; the whole being published in 1935, eight years after K'ang's death. K'ang refused to publish it because he felt that the premature introduction of the concept of *ta-t'ung* would do more harm than good. Liang relates that K'ang kept the book secret, and that when he was studying with K'ang at Canton around 1892, only two of the master's disciples, Liang being one of them, were allowed access to it. Fascinated by the scope and force of this concept, Liang enthusiastically urged its propagation. Though K'ang did not agree, he could not restrain Liang and his other disciples from doing so in an informal way.[9] It is clear, then, that the young Mao could not have read the actual book which was later published as *Ta-t'ung Shu*. But it seems likely that the *ta-t'ung* concept did become known and talked of among K'ang's admirers. When the book was itself finally published, it had a powerful and startling impact as that of "a great flood and wild beast." Whether Mao learned of K'ang's work in his youth or not until a later time is not after all important. What is important is that it is evident that the *ta-t'ung* concept did catch and mould Mao's attention and imagination. In addition, it has been speculated by scholars that Mao has borrowed heavily his ideas for communes from *Ta-t'ung Shu*.[10]

In a comparatively recent work, a historian in mainland China asserts that "[the thought of *ta-t'ung*] on one hand

has a great vision; on the other hand, seriously lacks a realistic fighting spirit."[11] This is tantamount to saying that K'ang's idea is fine, but that he does not, and cannot, know how to realize it. In addition, it implies that the vision should be taken up and realized by practical people. This appraisal of K'ang's concept should not be viewed as the opinion of an individual scholar, as would be the case in the free countries of the West. Instead, it must be regarded as the reflection of current official thinking in Communist China—for otherwise the writer would have been accused long ago of incorrect thinking.

Implicitly, Mao has hinted that he himself is the person who is able to show the way to *ta-t'ung* (world communism). One notes, for instance, the concluding lines of Mao's well-known *tz'u* (prose-poem) *On Snow:*

> The great emperors of Ch'in and Han
> Lacking literary brilliance,
> Those of T'ang and Sung
> Having but few romantic inclinations,
> And the prodigious Gengis Khan
> Knowing only how to bend his bow
> And shoot at vultures.
> All are past and gone!
> For men of vision
> We must seek among the present
>   generation.[12]

The suggestion seems to be that only in the present age will be found the truly great men, with Mao among them, or with Mao as the great man. From all we know of Mao, it does seem that he has the ambition and self-confidence to play this role.

I. EMERGENCE AND BACKGROUND OF THE PEOPLE'S COMMUNES

Historically the birth of the people's commune, as officially claimed, was a spontaneous growth among the people. It is reported in a Communist theoretical magazine that as early as the spring of 1958 many small agricultural producers' co-operatives in Honan Province spontaneously merged into a few large ones. At the same time, Party Committees at different levels in the province instituted on a trial basis some large co-operatives of several thousand households each. These included the 9,369 household Weihsing (Sputnik) Co-operative in Chayashan, Suiping County, which was formed in April out of twenty-seven small co-operatives. After the wheat harvest, this experiment became a mass movement when the people learned of Mao's instructions in August that it would be highly beneficial to organize people's communes. An upsurge in the formation of people's communes rapidly spread throughout the whole province.[13] At the end of the year, it was officially estimated that more than 99% of the peasant population of the entire country participated in the people's communes of their own volition and by their own enthusiastic requests.[14]

According to Chinese Communist accounts, the objective conditions which gave rise to the people's communes had both economic and political foundations. "The people's communes are the result of the march of events. . . . The basis for the development of the people's communes is mainly the all-round, continuous leap forward in China's agricultural production and the ever-increasing political consciousness of the 500 million peasants."[15] These can be summarized according to the official explanations as follows:

(A) Economic—Agricultural production has increased from one up to more than ten-fold as a result of the unprecedented farm capital construction and the application of improved farming techniques. Concurrent with agricultural improvement, small and middle-sized enterprises have rapidly developed in villages. But it is difficult for the old, small scale co-operatives to meet the needs of the development of the productive forces. The large production projects in prospect, such as water conservation, forestry, mechanization and hydro-electrification, etc., could not be realized until the small co-operatives were amalgamated into large communes.

(B) Political—The Chinese Communists stress the slogan that politics takes command. Therefore, it is held that the political wakening of the masses plays a decisive role in the development of the people's communes. What made the agricultural products increase by a hundred and even a thousand percent? What made the application of advanced farming techniques possible? These elements are all attributable to the ever-increasing political awareness of the masses. Political awakening or awareness refers specifically to two important movements: the correction of the rightist bourgeois ideology, and overcoming of the conservative ideas in agricultural production, which are replaced by socialist ideology and "leap forwardism." Thus, the editorial of the *People's Daily* of the September 3, 1958 issue states:

The rapid growth of the people's communes definitely does not stem solely from economic causes. The keenness shown by the mass of peasants towards the people's communes speak first of all of their greatly increased socialist and communist consciousness. Through the 1947 debate among the rural population on the socialist and capitalist roads of development in the countryside, the Communist Party smashed the attack launched by the bourgeois rightists, landlords, rich peasants, and counter-reactionaries, and overcame the capitalist trend among the well-to-do middle peasants. Later, through the rectification campaign [*cheng-feng*], it fundamentally changed the relation between the cadres and the masses and eliminated the rightist conservative ideas in agricultural production.

This argument gives the impression that the official Communist explanation of the growth of the people's communes places more emphasis on political agitation rather than economic interpretation of history. Further, both the debate and the rectification campaign are instruments of the Party. The use of them to explain the changes makes the theory of spontaneous growth of the people's communes even less convincing.

II. CHARACTERISTICS OF THE PEOPLE'S COMMUNES

The chief characteristics of the people's communes, as given by Mao in two Chinese characters are *ta* (large) and *kung* (public). A free, as well as an official, translation of these two characters renders the meanings as "bigger size" and "more socialist nature."[16] Mao's terms are first quoted by Wu Chih-p'u in his article "From Agricultural Producers' Co-operatives to People's Communes"[17] and by the editorial of the *People's Daily* on September 3, 1958, and also extensively quoted in other articles in connection with the people's communes. However, a later search of Mao's writings fails to locate the primary source. The two Chinese characters *ta* and *kung*, like other Chinese characters, can be used as different parts of speech without metamorphosis of their forms. *Ta* could mean big, great, bigness, greatness, and *kung*, public, common, publicness. The famous chapter of Li-yün in *Li Chi* has the statement

that "When the great course was pursued, the world was common for all."[18] The two key words in the sentence are *ta*, meaning great, in *ta-tao*, great course; the *kung* in *wei-kung*, meaning for all. The selection of *ta* and *kung*, to characterize the people's communes is not coincidental and its philosophical source is evidently borrowed from this famous treatise.

(A) "Largeness"
(1) In the commune

The first characteristic of the people's communes emphasizes expansion of organization, and a wider scope of activities than the agricultural co-operatives. The largeness in size is obvious because communes are formed by a merging of several co-operatives. The main activity of the agricultural co-operatives, is, as the name suggests, limited to agriculture, while the people's communes cover a wide range of activities, including agriculture, forestry, animal husbandry, side occupations, and fishery; furthermore, small scale industry, agriculture, trade, education, local government, and military affairs are channeled into a single entity. In other words, a commune is an organizational form characterized by the integration of town government and commune administration and the integration of government authority with the organization in charge of production.

(2) In the *Ta-t'ung Shu*

In this respect, a comparison between communes and the organizational form in the *Ta-t'ung Shu* will reveal certain striking similarities. We do not attempt to make any detailed comparison here; general outlines will satisfy our purpose. The plan of the *Ta-t'ung Shu* is as follows: The globe is to be divided into one hundred degrees longitudinally and latitudinally, thus forming ten thousand "degree units." The land area of the globe covers 5,238 "degree units," each "degree unit" being 10,000 square miles. Every inhabitable unit is an administrative unit and has its own local government. There are 3,000 or so such local governments on the globe, above which is the global government. The people in each of the "degree units" lead a communal type of life. This unit is evidently large in size and much larger than Mao's communes, but the nature of their structures is quite similar. Just as with the people's communes, the "degree unit" government covers a wide range of activities, and integrates government authority with the organization in charge of production. Each "degree unit" government has a multiplicity of departments looking after the welfare of people from cradle to grave. Such departments consist of: (1) People's Department, including Maternity Hospital (*jen-pen yüan*), *Nursery* (*yu-ying yüan*), Children's Home (*tz'u-yu yüan*), Old People's Home (*yang-lao yüan*), Poor Man's Home (*hsü-p'in yüan*), House of Eternal Peace (*k'ao-chung yüan*), etc.; (2) Agriculture Department, including forestry, husbandry, and fishery; (3) Mining Department; (4) Industry Department; (5) Commerce Department; (6) Finance Department; (7) Reclamation Department; (8) Water Control Department; (9) Communication Department; (10) Public Health Department; (11) Education Department; (12) Moral Training Department; (13) Wisdom Department (in charge of inventions); (14) Recreation Department (music, museum, zoo, botanical garden); (15) Interdepartment Assembly; (16) Parliament of two chambers; (17) Public Bulletin Office.[19] Though the organization is huge, there are no judicial or military institutions be-

cause such offices are not necessary in the ideal world. This plan gives us a remarkable picture of resemblance between the people's communes and the "degree unit" government: both cover a wide variety of activities and serve as both administrative and productive organs.

(B) *"Publicness"*
(1) In the Commune

The second characteristic of the people's communes is that they are of a socialist nature. The Chinese character used, as shown above, is *kung*, which basically means public, and is an antonym of *szu*, meaning selfish or private. The significance of "more socialist nature" has two aspects: the ownership system, and the distribution system. So far as the ownership system is concerned, the people's commune enhances the collective system (*chi-t'i so-you chih*) of the old agricultural co-operatives and raises, to a certain degree, to the system by the whole people (*ch'üan-min so-yu chih*). The people's communes are eliminating step by step the last remnants of private ownership of means of production. Hence privately held plots of land, privately owned scattered trees and draught animals are slowly in the process of vanishing. Though at present the ownership system is still a collective ownership system, it has a higher degree of the system of ownership by the whole people. Thus, it is claimed by Communist authorities that the people's communes are the best organizational form for effecting the transformation from collective ownership to ownership by the whole people.

The distribution system is still following the principle of "to each according to his work." The principle "to each according to his needs" cannot be realized until the time of communism when products are adequately plentiful. However, at present some communes have instituted the partial supply system. They provide their members with free rice or free meals. Communes with better economic conditions are experimenting with the system of supplying free either seven or ten of the basic life requirements. The seven basic requirements consist of meals, housing, childbirth, education, medical treatment, marriage and funeral expenses; while the ten basic requirements include meals, clothing, childbirth, funeral expenses, marriage expenses, education, housing, fuel for winter, haircuts, and the theatre. In addition, a certain amount of petty cash is paid to members, depending on their type of work.

(2) In the *Ta-t'ung Shu*

The ownership system in K'ang's *Ta-t'ung Shu* is simple and clear-cut. Everything belongs to the public; private property is non-existent. The distribution system retains the wage system according to the principle "to each according to his work," with basic requirements very well provided for by the public, as will be discussed later. The social economy is divided into three main branches, agriculture, industry, and commerce.

(a) Agriculture

All land of the world belongs to the public; no buying or selling of land is permissible. The various kinds of quantities of agricultural products to be produced in different suitable localities and their distribution for consumption in different areas for the needs of the people are to be planned in advance and executed by the central (globe) and local authorities (degree-unit). In the agricultural sectors, the wage system is

to be retained. Agricultural workers, including officials, are paid according to ten levels based on one's ability and experience. Housing is free. Luxurious living quarters on the farms are provided for by the public. The officials in charge of agriculture live in the same quality houses as farmers, so as to have equality. Food and clothing are not free, but are purchasable by their own wages from the public dining halls and stores. The work is light and pleasant, and comforts are plentiful. One has an immense amount of leisure time for enjoying life, improving one's knowledge, and cultivating one's virtues—in short, to reap the benefits of a full physical and spiritual life. The few hours of work a day that will be done by these happy people of the *ta-t'ung* society is comparable to the hobbies of scholars, hermits, great men and heroes in the old society who use their leisure to garden, fish or raise pets. Ease and pleasantness of work results from the use of all sorts of labor-saving machines. Moreover, agriculture includes forestry, fishery, mining, etc., and all farmers, fishermen, herdsmen and miners are generally graduates of respective professional schools. They are intellectuals, not laborers, and definitely are not to be regarded as "working-stiffs" as in our society.[20]

(b) Industry

In the *ta-t'ung* stage, all industries belong to the public, and no private industry is permissible. The types of articles, the suitable sites for their manufacture, and their distribution to various areas for use are planned in advance and carried out by the central and local authorities. All workers are graduates of appropriate technical schools. On the one hand, they are intellectuals rather than laborers; and on the other hand, the industrial workers are treated as any other kind of workers, for instance, the farmers. Their pay is divided into numerous categories according to the quality of and diligence in their work. As in agriculture, the wage system is to be retained, and the workers enjoy extremely comfortable living quarters free of charge, but pay for their own food and clothing. The work is light and pleasant because the invention of machines will lessen the tedium of the work involved. Ample facilities for recreation and education, especially for spiritual cultivation are generously provided. Both farmers and workers can be promoted to be government officials in charge of agriculture and industry.[21]

(c) Commerce

Commerce in the *ta-t'ung* period is to be operated by the public according to a central plan. Farmers will produce raw materials, while workers manufacture them into necessary and useful articles to be distributed and sold to the consuming public. There is to be only one store in each city or town; the size of a store can be as big as a present-day city. Myriads of articles will be available, as complete and rich as a present-day world exhibition. Furthermore, merchandise will sell cheaply because there are no parasitic merchants making profits. All workers of the various levels in the sector of commerce are business school graduates. The same rules governing the treatment of farmers and industrial workers hold true for workers in commerce.[22]

In short, people working in any one of the three sectors have, as a rule, one or two hours of light work to perform daily, and will have available countless comforts. The facilities for enjoying life, for the development and employment of all bodily and mental faculties will be available in equal measure to everybody and in ever increasing fulness. Incidentally, K'ang's ideal coincides with that of Marx of an undifferentiated society in which the differences between industry and agriculture, city and village, mental and manual labor are all abolished. This is also the ideal of the people's communes.

(d) Health, Education and Welfare

As to the accommodations for people from birth to death, K'ang's blueprint is as follows:

(i) Public nurture: Women are entitled to enter the public maternity hospitals (literally "the roots of people institute") as soon as they have conceived. The hospitals are located in favorable places, with the most ideal climate and magnificent scenery, and patients will be attended by well-trained doctors and given great care. Mothers will remain there until the babies no longer need breast feeding. Then the babies are to be sent to public nurseries for care and training.

(ii) Public education: Children at six will enter elementary school, attend middle school from eleven to fifteen years of age, and from sixteen to twenty attend college. In these twenty years, all will enjoy free care and education. After graduation, the young people start working in the society.

(iii) Public welfare: There will be public hospitals to care for the sick and infirm by giving free consultation and treatment. One will go to the Old Men's Home when he retires at sixty, or to the Poor Man's Home if he is unemployed and unable to support himself because of laziness. When one dies, the individual's body will be sent to the House of Eternal Peace (*k'ao-chung yüan*) where his friends and relatives can have a final visit before the dead man's cremation.[23] The blueprint of K'ang, in Western terminology, amounts to taking care of the individual from cradle to grave. In Mencius' famous wording, it is called "to nourish the living and bury the dead."[24] K'ang's ideas originate from and are contained in the chapter of Li-yün.

As far as the second characteristic— more socialist nature—is concerned, a definite similarity between K'ang and the people's communes can be seen. The public mess halls, kindergartens, nurseries, sewing groups, barber shops, public baths, happy homes for the aged, agricultural middle schools and "red and expert" schools, etc., as described in the "Resolution on the Establishment of People's Communes in the Rural Areas" are very similar to those institutions K'ang dreamt of in his *Ta-t'ung Shu* which are described above. The provision set by some communes to supply either seven or ten basic requirements plus small petty cash is again very similar to K'ang's dream of the accommodations of the workers in agriculture, industry, and commerce. The only difference is that K'ang is more fanatical and utopian, and the measures of the people's communes are more practical and realistic.

III. THE FAMILY IN COMMUNE AND TA-T'UNG SHU

One of the most frequent and vociferous accusations, by both Chinese and Westerners, against the people's communes is their destruction of the traditional extended family system. The Chinese Communists seldom argue with individuals or reply specifically to Western critics. However, on this point, the Chi-

nese Party in its "Resolution on Some Questions Concerning the People's Communes" specifically ridiculed the former United States Secretary of State J. F. Dulles:

At present there is a bunch of fools who desperately attack our people's communes, one of whom is Mr. Dulles of the United States. This Dulles, who knows nothing about China but pretends to be a China expert, insanely opposes the people's communes. The thing which especially makes him sad, we are told, is that we have destroyed the most ideal and excellent family system handed down for thousands of years.

The Communists did admit that they have, in a sense, destroyed the family system, but they have their own explanations.

It is common practice in Communist China to quote from Marxist writings as a theoretical foundation for their movements or activities. In his article entitled "The Collectivization and Socialization of Housekeeping,"[25] Hu Sheng quotes the following two passages from Engels:

It will then become evident that the first premise for the emancipation of women is the reintroduction of the entire female sex into public industry; and that this again demands that the quality possessed by the individual family of being the economic unit of society be abolished.[26]

With the passage of the means of production into common property, the individual family ceases to be the economic unit of society. Private housekeeping is transformed into a social industry. The care and education of the children becomes a public matter.[27]

Hu also quotes a similar passage from Lenin's *A Great Beginning* which we need not, to save space, repeat here. The important points of these passages are: (1) women are to go into public industry; (2) housekeeping is transformed into a social industry; (3) care and education of children becomes a public matter; (4) the family ceases to be the economic unit of society. On the whole, the destruction of family is the basic and most important factor. Not only have the people's communes attempted to realize these points, but K'ang in his *Ta-t'ung Shu* has advocated the same changes in an even more radical tone.

Hu Sheng, author of the *Red Flag* article, admitted to the destruction of the family system by the Chinese Communists, but was quick to add that what was destroyed is the family as a mere unit of individual production, which in reality is nothing but a miserable limbo for the laboring people. Women especially are the victims of this prison. To emancipate them, millions of Chinese women are being freed from household drudgery so they may participate in public life and industrial production. The method of effecting the change is through socialization of household labor, which will, on the basis of socialistic collective production, gradually realize socialistic collectivization in other aspects of life for both men and women. The establishment of public mess halls, nurseries, and kindergartens, etc., are only the primary steps of collectivization. People need good medicinal care and public hygiene, culture and education, and a high level of entertainment and recreation, in order to attain a better life. These requirements, it is argued, cannot be furnished within the scope of the old traditional and so-called "feudalistic" family system. The family system as it existed for thousands of years has caused people to be narrow-minded,

and has bred selfish ideas in their minds. This old way of life is incompatible with the socialist and collective mode of large scale production. Not only does it obstruct the development of socialist production by the waste of labor power; it also checks the gradual raising of people's living standards, and harms the establishment of socialistic and communistic ideology.

K'ang, who condemned the family system more than sixty years ago, has a much bolder plan for the future. For him, evils arising from the family system are many. The most obvious and notorious may be summarized:

In the first place, the traditional family system, among other ills, breeds selfishness. It is desired that each individual glorify his own family through attaining wealth and prosperity; but desiring and achieving the fruits of desire are not always closely related. Hence, everyone tries desperately to achieve his own selfish aim but does so at the expense of good virtues. Cunning and falsehood, robberies and murders thus become prevalent. Therefore, people growing up under such a family system tend to be morally deficient and evil. Secondly, the majority of children cannot be born and raised in ideal situations and locations, and thus are unable to enjoy good medical care and receive twenty years of free education as planned by K'ang. Because they have not received full benefit of K'ang's society, they are inferior physically and intellectually when they grow up. Thirdly, for K'ang, evil characters and physical shortcomings are hereditary, and can affect virtuous human nature and the physical development of posterity. Eugenically speaking, it has a deleterious effect for mankind. Lastly, the psychology of selfishness checks the growth of public spirit. Only a hand-f individuals would really be willing to stimulate and support public works, such as hospitals, road construction, and building bridges, etc. Thus, the family system in many respects is harmful to society.

Since the family is the source of nearly all evils, the logical conclusion for realizing an ideal society is the abolition of the family system as an institution. K'ang argues that abolition would be a natural result if the government were responsible for care in the birth, rearing, and educating children, and for attending to sickness and death (funeral) of adults. If parents had little or nothing to do with their own children and if husbands and wives co-habit according to contracts for predetermined periods of time (from one month up to one year, subject to renewal of contract),[28] then parents and children would not meet often, and would hardly even know each other. Under such circumstances how could families exist? Liang, his great disciple, once said, "*Ta-t'ung Shu* consists of hundreds of thousands of words . . . the crucial point is to abolish the family."[29]

As for the emancipation of women, K'ang strongly condemned the inequality of sexes, complaining that it is the most savage thing in history, because millions of women who are exactly like other male human beings have been under oppression in a multitude of cruel ways in all the length and breadth of China and for thousands of years. Both the scope and duration of the crime is heinous. Among the mistreatments of women, K'ang especially points to their being slaves in the kitchen for a lifetime, their being deprived of rights to work as equals of men in society and public life, and their disqualification from serving the government in the capacity of offi-

cials. In K'ang's ideal society, all these inequalities would not exist. If we compare this program with that of the Chinese Communists to put women to work like men in the communes and to serve as commune officials, to free them from the chores of housework labor, especially from the kitchen and care of children, we cannot say the similarity is only coincidental.

As we have said, K'ang's practical measure for the realization of *Ta-t'ung* is through the abolition of the family system, aiming first for the abolition of marriage. Sixty years after the abolition of the marriage system and the change to contractual co-habitation, there would be no families, no private relationships of husbands and wives, or of parents and children. Even if there were private property, there would be nobody left to inherit it. When all land, industry, and business belongs to the public, the *Ta-t'ung* period will have arrived.[30]

IV. MILITARY ORGANIZATIONAL FORMS IN COMMUNE AND TA-T'UNG SHU

Finally, there is another tie between K'ang's blueprint for utopia and the program of the people's communes. There is a famous slogan of three "-izations" contained in the "Resolution on the Establishment of People's Communes," viz: organizations to be militarized, activities to be martialized, and lives to be collectivized. Although it is forceful and parallel in Chinese, it sounds awkward in the English translation. The theme is: "the people have taken to organizing themselves along military lines, working with militancy, and leading a collective life." As for the collectivization of life, both K'ang's and the commune structure are obviously similar. "Working with militancy" is only an attitude towards work, teaching people to work hard and diligently as though in war. It overlaps somewhat with militarized organizations. To organize along military lines is parenthetically mentioned in K'ang's book. K'ang hates wars, and armies are distasteful to him; in the *ta-t'ung* era there would be no war and therefore no army or navy.[31] However, he emphasized that the students in middle schools[32] and colleges[33] should live together and be organized like an army, and that the same principle should apply to the farm workers.[34] Though he did not emphasize this point explicitly in connection with workers in industry and commerce, I gather he implies that the same principle holds true in those two sectors.

V. THE PEOPLE'S COMMUNES AND MARXISM

It is generally believed that the roots of the ideas of communism reach back far in history and, further, that the ideal of a higher society has been preached by many thinkers in the East and West. Milovan Djilas once remarked, "I consider it superfluous to criticize Communism as an idea. The ideas of equality and brotherhood among men, which have existed in varying forms since human society began—and which contemporary Communism accepts in word—are principle to which fighters for progress and freedom will always aspire."[35] In China, the roots reach back to *Li Chi*, from which the term *ta-t'ung* is taken. This term has been popularized by K'ang in his *Ta-t'ung Shu*. We have shown in considerable length the similarities between the *ta-t'ung* utopia and the people's communes. However, the Chinese Communists speak of people's communes in Marxist terms and the communes appear in China wearing a Marxist garment. Then what is the relationship between Marxism and the people's communes?

The establishment of the people's communes is one phase of the Chinese Communist revolution. To answer the question of the relationship between the people's communes and Marxism, it is necessary to examine the relationship between Marxism and the Chinese revolution in general, and between Marxism and the people's communes in particular. First, what does Mao think of Marxism? It is to be noted that Marxism, for Mao, means the Marxism elaborated by Engels, Lenin, and Stalin. The term Marxism-Leninism is frequently used in his writings, and also the phrase, Ma-Lieh-En-Szu—abbreviated transliterations for Marx, Lenin, Engels, and Stalin. Concerning Mao's understanding and evaluation of Marx, the best source can be found in the literature of the Rectification Movement in 1941-1942 when Mao expounded what he considered the true understanding of Marxism.

For Mao, "Marxism-Leninism . . . is a science which will lead the proletarian revolution to victory."[36] He warned that "Marx, Engels, Lenin, and Stalin have repeatedly said that their theory is not a dogma but a guide to action."[37] Mao ridiculed those who study Marxism theories or writings without putting them into application. For example:

One cannot be considered as a theoretician, even if he has read ten thousand copies of books written by Marx, Lenin, Engels, and Stalin, and can recite by heart every sentence.[38]

He warned those "ignorant and foolish" people who take Marxism-Leninism as religious doctrines:

Your dogmas are useless and are, to be frank, even less useful than dog's manure. We can see that dog's manure can fertilize fields and human excrement can feed dogs. Dogmas can neither fertilize land nor feed dogs. What's the use of them (laughter)?[39]

Thus, the combination of theory and practice in learning Marxism is stressed. But most important of all, the aim of learning Marxism is to use it as a tool for carrying out the Chinese revolution. Here are Mao's most important instructions:

This is the attitude of "shooting one's arrow at the target." The "target" is the Chinese revolution, and the "arrow" Marxism-Leninism. The reason why the Chinese Communists have sought for the "arrow" is purely for the purpose of hitting the "target" of the Chinese revolution and the revolution of the East, otherwise the "arrow" is nothing but a curio to be played with, and entirely useless.[40]

From the above quotations, it is obvious that Mao does not approve of the study of Marxism only as a doctrine, but insists on using it as a tool. It is not how much one knows about Marxism that counts, but the extent that one can apply it to the Chinese revolution. To master the theory of Marxism is useless until one can use it as a sharpened tool. In other words, for Mao it is a means rather than an end.

How does Mao use this Marxian tool to carry on his revolution? That is to say, what parts of Marxism does Mao employ in his revolutionary career? He begins with the theory of revolution. Mao says in the opening paragraph of *Problems of War and Strategy,* "The seizure of power by armed force, the settlement of the issues by war, is the central task and the highest form of revolution. This Marxist-Leninist principle of revolution holds good universally,

for China and for all other countries."[41] He also quotes Stalin with perfect approval that "In China it is armed revolution against armed counter-revolution. This is one of the characteristics and one of the advantages of the Chinese revolution."[42] Such frameworks of analysis give him the theoretical foundation for organizing armed rebellion, and for brushing aside all theories of peaceful or legal methods, of gradual socialism or parliamentarism.

The next theory of Marx which Mao makes use of is the theory of class struggle, which states that all history is the history of class struggle; and further, that contending classes are narrowed to two, whose conflicts are inherent in the economic system and therefore inevitable. With some modifications, Mao applies this to the peasantry of China by asserting that the recorded history of China is a history of class struggle between the landlord and the peasant classes. Following Lenin's classic analysis in his *Agrarian Question in Russia* (1908) of peasants into rich peasants, poor peasants, and middle peasants, Mao divided the Chinese peasantry essentially in the same manner, but with more sub-divisions. By applying it, Mao succeeded in organizing the peasants into a massive force for first combating the landlords and finally conquering the whole mainland. In practical tactics, he sometimes united the poor and middle peasants, and neutralized the rich peasants in order to combat the landlords. At other times, he united the poor and middle peasants to fight the rich peasants and landlords. The method of peasant classification plays an important role in carrying out Mao's revolutionary goals at different stages, not only in land reform but also in the people's communes.

According to Marx, class struggle

necessarily leads to the dictatorship of the proletariat. Lenin originates the theory of revolutionary democratic dictatorship of the proletariat and the peasantry. Mao modifies it to people's democratic dictatorship. By definition, people's dictatorship means the combination of democracy among the people and dictatorship over the reactionaries. Thus, reactionaries are deprived of their democratic rights, such as the right of speech, and the right of publication, etc. In actual practice, democracy does not exist at all. Not only are all opposition forces or opposition ideas to be crushed, but any idea deviating from Mao's thought, even among the Communists, is considered a crime. Proletariat dictatorship finally turns into a personal dictatorship. With totalitarian power in his hands, Mao hopes to be able to carry out the revolution and socialist construction according to his own plan without the interruptions and obstructions of forces inside and outside the party. The state power—dictatorial power—is crucial and dear to him. Before the revolution, the central task is to obtain it; and after the victory of the revolution, to keep it is the central task. The editorial of the June 1, 1966 issue of the *People's Daily* under the title "Sweep Clean All Wicked Ghosts and Evil Devils" has this to say:

The fundamental question of revolution is the question of state power. Among all fields of superstructure, ideology, religion, art, law, and state power, the very center is state power. One who has state power has everything; he who has not, has lost everything. Therefore, no matter how many problems have to be tackled after the conquest of power, the proletariat must never forget the state power.

In the case of establishing the people's communes, one can imagine how much dictatorial state power is needed to or-

ganize millions of peasants who had lived in an unorganized life for thousands of years before 1949, and to meet opposition forces at the same time within the party.

Another theory Mao has borrowed from Marxism which has direct bearing on the establishment of the people's communes is the theory of uninterrupted revolution. *Red Flag* in its editorial argues:

The fact that the broad masses of working people, without any hesitation, accept this form of organization, the people's communes . . . also because the Chinese people have grasped the guiding ideology of the Communist Party's Central Committee and Comrade Mao Tse-tung on uninterrupted revolution. The working people want no pause in the course of the revolution and they see that the more rapidly the revolution advances, the more benefit they will derive.[43]

In his Work Report before the Second Conference of the Eighth Communist Party Congress on May 5, 1958, Liu Shao-ch'i elaborated the theory of uninterrupted revolution in roughly the following manner.

Uninterrupted revolution should be the militant slogan of the proletariat, as repeatedly pointed out by Marx, Engels, and Lenin. It is necessary to raise new revolutionary tasks at proper times in order to keep the revolutionary fervor of the masses high and to prevent the Party and State functionaries from being haughty and corruptive because of the achievements they have obtained. The principle of uninterrupted revolution has always been applied by the Central Committee and by Mao to lead the Chinese revolution. For example in March 1949, on the eve of the victory of the democratic revolution, the Party clearly outlined the task of transforming China from a state of new democracy to a state of socialism. Right after the completion of the land reform following the establishment of the People's Republic, the Party in December 1951 pointed out the road for realizing collectivization through co-operative movement, and further in 1953 the Party extensively propagated the socialist reform of agriculture, handicraft and private commerce and industry. After the basic victory of the socialist revolution of the ownership of means of production, the Party again raised and realized the socialist revolution on ideological and political fronts. Thus, these steps enable the revolution to advance from one stage to another and from one victory to another. Therefore, according to the theory of uninterrupted revolution, the switchover from agriculture producers' co-operatives to people's communes is of vital importance for speeding up socialist construction and the transition to communism.

Irrespective of Liu's explanation, we have observed from actual developments that the people's communes suffered a setback in the three trying years of 1959 to 1962 and have retreated a certain degree in recent years. For instance, the public mess hall, one of the characteristic features of the people's communes, is no longer in existence. After a recovery period of a couple of years, we have seen the emergence of the so-called proletariat cultural revolution beginning from 1965, which may be considered as another phase of the uninterrupted revolution. What is going to happen next is anybody's guess.

All evidence suggests that Ta-t'ung Shu supplies a detailed blue-print for an ideal society for Mao which was not available in Marxist writings. This means that the ideals of a perfect society embodied in the people's communes are borrowed by Mao from the Ta-t'ung Shu, and were not entirely of his own creation; but this does not mean that Mao inherits the Chinese tradition. K'ang does not have the slightest hint in his book of achieving this dream through violent force or bloody revolution, or to maintain the structure of his utopia by coercive or brutal measures. He is a romantic thinker, starting from a religious sympathy or kindness, which he calls, after Mencius, the feeling of being unable to bear to see the sufferings of others. He does not attempt to employ any means, especially brutal methods, contrary to his goals to achieve his aim. This is the spirit of *wang-tao* (benevolent or peaceful way), the basic spirit of Confucianism or Chinese tradition, in contrast with *pa-tao* (militant or drastic way). Moreover, Mao's acceptance of Marxism is for political expediency, taking it as a means as he himself expounded. Obviously the attraction of Marxism in China cannot be explained in the framework of the Marxist system, for the victory of communism has little to do with the breakdown of capitalism as Marx originally argued. Thus, *Ta-t'ung Shu* serves as a strong ideological hint to the establishment of the people's communes; and Marxism has been used as a tool to carry on the Chinese revolution, of which the people's communes is only one phase.

Notes

1. Resolution of the Central Committee of the Chinese Communist Party on the Establishment of People's Communes in the Rural Areas, August 29, 1958.

2. Resolution on Some Questions Concerning the People's Communes, Adopted by the Central Committee of the Chinese Communist Party on December 10, 1958.

3. Marx & Engels, "The Civil War in France", *Selected Works I* (Moscow, Foreign Language Publishing House, 1958), p. 522.

4. Robert G. Wesson, *Soviet Communes* (New Brunswick, N.J. Rutgers University Press, 1963), p. 4.

5. In an eight-hour discussion with U.S. Senator Hubert Humphrey on December 1, 1958, Khrushchev expressed his strong disapproval, *Life*, XLVI, No. 2 (January 12, 1959), p. 86. Anna Louis Strong regards Khrushchev "as one of the first anti-commune propagandists." *The Rise of the Chinese People's Communes—And Six Years After* (Peking, New World Press, 1964), p. 3.

6. 1858-1927. His book is translated by L. G. Thompson as *Ta-t'ung Shu: The One-World Philosophy of K'ang Yu-wei* (London, George Allen & Unwin, 1958).

7. Li Jui, *Mao Tse-tung T'ung-chih te Ch'u-ch'i Ko-ming Huo-tung* (Early Year's Revolutionary Activities of Comrade Mao Tse-tung, (Peking, Chung-kuo Ch'ing-nien Ch'u-pan She [Chinese Youth Publishing House] 1957), pp. 8-9.

8. Hsiao San, *Mao Tse-tung te Ch'ing-nien Shih-tai* (The Youth Years of Mao Tse-tung), (Hong Kong, Hsin-Min-chu Ch'u-pan She [New Democracy Publishing House] 1949), p. 30.

9. Liang Ch'i-ch'ao, *Ch'ing-tai Hsüeh-shu Kai-lun* (General Discussion of Ch'ing Dynasty Scholarship) (Shanghai, Commercial Press, ed. 1947), pp. 136-138.

10. Chalmers Johnson, "Building a Communist Nation in China," Robert A. Scalapino, ed., *The Communist Revolution in Asia* (Englewood Cliffs, N.J., Prentice-Hall, 1965), p. 57. Reference is made to a letter written by Huang Yen-fu to the editor of the New York Times dated Dec. 30, 1958 (January 11, 1959), p. 10, E.

11. *Li Chi, K'ang Yu-wei T'an Szu-t'ung Szu-hsiang Yen-chiu* (The Study of the Thought of K'ang Yu-wei and T'an Szu-t'ung) (Shanghai, Jen-min Ch'u-pan She [People's Publishing House] 1958), p. 122.

12. Ch'en, *Mao and the Chinese Revolution* (London, Oxford University Press, 1965), p. 340. Translated by Michael Bullock and Jerome Ch'en.

13. Wu Chih-p'u, "Yu Nung-yeh Sheng-ch'an Ho-tso She Tao Jen-min Kung-she" (From Agricultural Producer's Co-operatives to People's Communes) *Red Flag* No. 8 (September 16, 1958), pp. 7-8.

14. See note 2.

15. See note 1.

16. *People's Communes in China* (Peking, Foreign Language Press, 1958), p. 18.

17. See note 13.

18. Translation mine. There are a number of different translations.

19. K'ang Yu-wei, *Ta-T'ung Shu* (Shanghai, Chung-hua Bookstore, 1935), pp. 383-388; pp. 393-396.

20. *Ibid.*, pp. 362-371.

21. *Ibid.*, pp. 371-375.

22. *Ibid.*, pp. 375-379.

23. *Ibid.*, pp. 290-291.

24. *The Book of Mencius,* Book 1, Chapter III. Section 3.

25. Chia-wu Lao-tung te Chi-t'i-hua, She-hui-hua, *Red Flag* No. 7 (September 1, 1958), p. 26.

26. Marx & Engels, "Origin of Family, Private Property and State", *Selected Works* II, p. 233.

27. *Ibid.* p. 234.

28. *Ta-t'ung Shu*, p. 252.

29. *General Discussion of Ch'ing Dynasty Scholarship*, p. 135.

30. *Ta-t'ung Shu*, p. 380.

31. *Ibid.*, p. 396.

32. *Ibid.*, p. 327.

33. *Ibid.*, p. 332.

34. *Ibid.*, p. 368.

35. *The New Class* (New York, Frederick A. Praeger, 1957), p. vii.

36. "Cheng-tun Tang Te Tso-feng" (Rectify the Party's Work Style) *Mao Tse-tung Hsüan-chi* (*Selected Works of Mao Tse-tung*) III. (Peking, People's House, 1955), p. 822.

37. *Ibid.*, p. 822.

38. "Cheng-tun Hsüeh-feng, Tang-feng, Wen-feng" (Rectify the Learning Style, Party Style, and Literature Style) *Cheng-feng Wen-hsien* (Documents on Rectification Movement) (Hongkong, Hsin Min-chu Ch'u-pan She [New Democracy Publishing House] 1949), p. 10. This passage has been deleted from Mao's *Selected Works.*

39. Ibid., p. 17. Also deleted from *Selected Works.*

40. "Kai-tsao Wo-men te Hsüeh-hsi" (To Reform Our Study) *Documents on Rectification Movement*, p. 50. The last clause of the quotation, from "otherwise . . . to useless", has been deleted from *Selected Works.*

41. *Selected Works* II, p. 529.

42. *Ibid.*, p. 531. Original: "On the Prospects of the Revolution in China."

43. No. 7 (Sept. 1, 1958), p. 14.

IV. PEOPLE'S WAR AND ITS

INTERNATIONAL SIGNIFICANCE

43. CHAIRMAN MAO ON PEOPLE'S WAR

POLITICAL POWER GROWS OUT OF THE BARREL OF A GUN

The seizure of power by armed force, the settlement of the issue by war, is the central task and the highest form of revolution. This Marxist-Leninist principle of revolution holds good universally, for China and for all other countries.

"Problems of War and Strategy"
(November 6, 1938), *Selected Works*, Vol. II, p. 219.

Every Communist must grasp the truth, "Political power grows out of the barrel of a gun."

Ibid., p. 224.

According to the Marxist theory of the state, the army is the chief component of state power. Whoever wants to seize and retain state power must have a strong army. Some people ridicule us as advocates of the "omnipotence of war". Yes, we are advocates of the omnipotence of revolutionary war; that is good, not bad, it is Marxist. The guns of the Russian Communist Party created socialism. We shall create a democratic republic. Experience in the class struggle in the

From *Chairman Mao Tse-tung on People's War* (Foreign Languages Press, 1967), pp. 3-22, 29-37.

era of imperialism teaches us that it is only by the power of the gun that the working class and the labouring masses can defeat the armed bourgeoisie and landlords; in this sense we may say that only with guns can the whole world be transformed.

Ibid., p. 225.

Without armed struggle neither the proletariat, nor the people, nor the Communist Party would have any standing at all in China and it would be impossible for the revolution to triumph. In these years [the eighteen years since the founding of the Party] the development, consolidation and bolshevization of our Party have proceeded in the midst of revolutionary wars; without armed struggle the Communist Party would assuredly not be what it is today. Comrades throughout the Party must never forget this experience for which we have paid in blood.

"Introducing *The Communist*"
(October 4, 1939), *Selected Works*, Vol. II, p. 292.

IMPERIALISM AND ALL REACTIONARIES ARE PAPER TIGERS

All reactionaries are paper tigers. In appearance, the reactionaries are terrifying, but in reality they are not so powerful. From a long-term point of view, it is not the reactionaries but the people who are really powerful.

"Talk with the American Correspondent Anna Louise Strong" (August 1946), *Selected Works*, Vol. IV, p. 100.

Just as there is not a single thing in the world without a dual nature (this is the law of the unity of opposites), so imperialism and all reactionaries have a dual nature—they are real tigers and paper tigers at the same time. In past history, before they won state power and for some time afterwards, the slaveowning class, the feudal landlord class and the bourgeoisie were vigorous, revolutionary and progressive; they were real tigers. But with the lapse of time, because their opposites—the slave class, the peasant class and the proletariat—grew in strength step by step, struggled against them more and more fiercely, these ruling classes changed step by step into the reverse, changed into reactionaries, changed into backward people, changed into paper tigers. And eventually they were overthrown, or will be overthrown, by the people. The reactionary, backward, decaying classes retained this dual nature even in their last life-and-death struggles against the people. On the one hand, they were real tigers; they devoured people by the millions and tens of millions. The cause of the people's struggle went through a period of difficulties and hardships, and along the path there were many twists and turns. To destroy the rule of imperialism, feudalism and bureaucrat-capitalism in China took the Chinese people more than a hundred years and cost them tens of millions of lives before the victory in 1949. Look! Were these not living tigers, iron tigers, real tigers? But in the end they changed into paper tigers, dead tigers, bean-curd tigers. These are historical facts. Have people not seen or heard about these facts? There have indeed been thousands and tens of thousands of them! Thousands and tens of thousands! Hence, imperialism and all reactionaries, looked at in essence, from a long-term point of view, from a strategic point of view, must be seen for what they are—paper tigers. On this we should build our strategic thinking. On the other hand, they are also living tigers, iron tigers, real tigers which can devour people. On this we should build our tactical thinking.

Speech at the Wuchang Meeting of the Political Bureau of the Central Committee of the Communist Party of China (December 1, 1958), quoted in the explanatory note to "Talk with the American Correspondent Anna Louise Strong," *Selected Works*, Vol. IV, pp. 98-99.

Make trouble, fail, make trouble again, fail again . . . till their doom; that is the logic of the imperialists and all reactionaries the world over in dealing with the people's cause, and they will never go against this logic. This is a Marxist law. When we say "imperialism is ferocious," we mean that its nature will never change, that the imperialists will never lay down their butcher knives, that they will never become Buddhas, till their doom.

Fight, fail, fight again, fail again, fight again . . . till their victory; that is the logic of the people, and they too will never go against this logic. This is another Marxist law. The Russian people's revolution followed this law, and so has the Chinese people's revolution.

"Cast Away Illusions, Prepare for Struggle" (August 14, 1949), *Selected Works*, Vol. IV, p. 428.

People of the world, unite and defeat the U.S. aggressors and all their running dogs! People of the world, be courageous, dare to fight, defy difficulties and advance wave upon wave. Then the whole world will belong to the people. Monsters of all kinds shall be destroyed.

"Statement Supporting the People of the Congo (L.) Against U.S. Aggression" (November 28, 1964), *People of the World, Unite and Defeat the U.S. Aggressors and All Their Lackeys,* 2nd ed., p. 14.

PEOPLE, NOT THINGS, ARE THE FACTOR DETERMINING VICTORY OR DEFEAT IN WAR

The people, and the people alone, are the motive force in the making of world history.

"On Coalition Government" (April 24, 1945), *Selected Works,* Vol. III, p. 257.

Weapons are an important factor in war, but not the decisive factor; it is people, not things, that are decisive. The contest of strength is not only a contest of military and economic power, but also a contest of human power and morale. Military and economic power is necessarily wielded by people.

"On Protracted War" (May 1938), *Selected Works,* Vol. II, pp. 143-144.

The richest source of power to wage war lies in the masses of the people. It is mainly because of the unorganized state of the Chinese masses that Japan dares to bully us. When this defect is remedied, then the Japanese aggressor, like a mad bull crashing into a ring of flames, will be surrounded by hundreds of millions of our people standing up-

right, the mere sound of their voices will strike terror into him, and he will be burned to death.

Ibid., p. 186

Take the case of China. We have only millet plus rifles to rely on, but history will finally prove that our millet plus rifles is more powerful than Chiang Kai-shek's aeroplanes plus tanks. Although the Chinese people still face many difficulties and will long suffer hardships from the joint attacks of U.S. imperialism and the Chinese reactionaries, the day will come when these reactionaries are defeated and we are victorious. The reason is simply this: the reactionaries represent reaction, we represent progress.

"Talk with the American Correspondent Anna Louise Strong" (August 1946), *Selected Works,* Vol. IV, p. 101.

REVOLUTIONARY WAR IS A WAR OF THE MASSES

The revolutionary war is a war of the masses; it can be waged only by mobilizing the masses and relying on them.

"Be Concerned with the Well-being of the Masses, Pay Attention to Methods of Work" (January 27, 1934), *Selected Works,* Vol. I, p. 147.

What is a true bastion of iron? It is the masses, the millions upon millions of people who genuinely and sincerely support the revolution. That is the real iron bastion which it is impossible, and absolutely impossible, for any force on earth to smash. The counter-revolution cannot smash us; on the contrary, we shall smash it. Rallying millions upon millions of people round the revolutionary government and expanding our revolutionary war, we shall wipe out all counter-revolution and take over the whole of China.

Ibid., p. 150.

Considering the revolutionary war as a whole, the operations of the people's guerrillas and those of the main forces of the Red Army complement each other like a man's right arm and left arm, and if we had only the main forces of the Red Army without the people's guerrillas, we would be like a warrior with only one arm.

"Problems of Strategy in China's Revolutionary War" (December 1936), *Selected Works*, Vol. I, p. 238.

This army is powerful because it has the people's self-defence corps and the militia—the vast armed organizations of the masses—fighting in co-ordination with it. In the Liberated Areas of China all men and women, from youth to middle age, are organized in the people's anti-Japanese self-defence corps on a voluntary and democratic basis and without giving up their work in production. The cream of the self-defence corps, except for those who join the army or the guerrilla units, is brought into the militia. Without the co-operation of these armed forces of the masses it would be impossible to defeat the enemy.

"On Coalition Government" (April 24, 1945), *Selected Works*, Vol. III, p. 265.

This army is powerful because of its division into two parts, the main forces and the regional forces, with the former available for operations in any region whenever necessary and the latter concentrating on defending their own locali-

ties and attacking the enemy there in co-operation with the local militia and the self-defence corps. This division of labour has won the whole-hearted support of the people. Without this correct division of labour—if, for example, attention were paid only to the role of the main forces while that of the regional forces were neglected—it would likewise be impossible to defeat the enemy in the conditions obtaining in China's Liberated Areas. Under the regional forces, numerous armed working teams have been organized, which are well trained and hence better qualified for military, political and mass work; they penetrate into the rearmost areas behind the enemy lines, strike at the enemy and arouse the masses to anti-Japanese struggle, thus giving support to the frontal military operations of the various Liberated Areas. In all this they have achieved great success.

Ibid., pp. 265-66.

The imperialists are bullying us in such a way that we will have to deal with them seriously. Not only must we have a powerful regular army, we must also organize contingents of the people's militia on a big scale. This will make it difficult for the imperialists to move a single inch in our country in the event of invasion.

Interview with a Hsinhua News Agency correspondent (September 29, 1958).

ESTABLISH RURAL BASES AND USE THE VILLAGES TO SURROUND THE CITIES

Armed struggle by the Chinese Communist Party takes the form of peasant war under proletarian leadership.

"Introducing *The Communist*" (October 4, 1939), *Selected Works*, Vol. II, p. 291.

The anti-Japanese war is essentially a peasant war.

"On New Democracy" (January 1940), *Selected Works,* Vol. II, p. 366.

Since China's key cities have long been occupied by the powerful imperialists and their reactionary Chinese allies, it is imperative for the revolutionary ranks to turn the backward villages into advanced, consolidated base areas, into great military, political, economic and cultural bastions of the revolution from which to fight their vicious enemies who are using the cities for atacks on the rural districts, and in this way gradually to achieve the complete victory of the revolution through protracted fighting; it is imperative for them to do so if they do not wish to compromise with imperialism and its lackeys but are determined to fight on, and if they intend to build up and temper their forces, and avoid decisive battles with a powerful enemy while their own strength is inadequate.

"The Chinese Revolution and the Chinese Communist Party" (December 1939), *Selected Works,* Vol. II, pp. 316-17.

What, then, are these base areas? They are the strategic bases on which the guerrilla forces rely in performing their strategic tasks and achieving the object of preserving and expanding themselves and destroying and driving out the enemy. Without such strategic bases, there will be nothing to depend on in carrying out any of our strategic tasks or achieving the aim of the war.

"Problems of Strategy in Guerrilla War Against Japan" (May 1938), *Selected Works,* Vol. II, p. 93.

The protracted revolutionary struggle in the revolutionary base areas consists mainly in peasant guerrilla warfare led by the Chinese Communist Party. Therefore, it is wrong to ignore the necessity of using rural districts as revolutionary base areas, to neglect painstaking work among the peasants, and to neglect guerrilla warfare.

"The Chinese Revolution and the Chinese Communist Party" (December 1939), *Selected Works,* Vol. II, p. 317.*

And stressing the work in the rural base areas does not mean abandoning our work in the cities and in the other vast rural areas which are still under the enemy's rule; on the contrary, without the work in the cities and in these other rural areas, our own rural base areas would be isolated and the revolution would suffer defeat. Moreover, the final objective of the revolution is the capture of the cities, the enemy's main bases, and this objective cannot be achieved without adequate work in the cities.

Ibid.

From 1927 to the present the centre of gravity of our work has been in the villages—gethering strength in the villages, using the villages in order to surround the cities and then taking the cities.

"Report to the Second Plenary Session of the Seventh Central Committee of the Communist Party of China" (March 5, 1949), *Selected Works,* Vol. IV, p. 363.

THE STRATEGY AND TACTICS OF PEOPLE'S WAR

You fight in your way and we fight in ours; we fight when we can win and move away when we can't.

Quoted from Comrade Lin Piao's article
Long Live the Victory of People's War!
(September 1965), p. 36.

NOTE:

Comrade Mao Tse-tung has provided a masterly summary of the strategy and tactics of people's war: You fight in your way and we fight in ours; we fight when we can win and move away when we can't.

In other words, you rely on modern weapons and we rely on highly conscious revolutionary people; you give full play to your superiority and we give full play to ours; you have your way of fighting and we have ours. When you want to fight us, we don't let you and you can't even find us. But when we want to fight you, we make sure that you can't get away and we hit you squarely on the chin and wipe you out. When we are able to wipe you out, we do so with a vengeance; when we can't, we see to it that you don't wipe us out. It is opportunism if one won't fight when one can win. It is adventurism if one insists on fighting when one can't win. Fighting is the pivot of all our strategy and tactics. It is because of the necessity of fighting that we admit the necessity of moving away. The sole purpose of moving away is to fight and bring about the final and complete destruction of the enemy. This strategy and these tactics can be applied only when one relies on the broad masses of the people, and such application brings the superiority of people's war into full play. However superior he may be in technical equipment and whatever tricks he may resort to, the enemy will find himself in the passive position of having to receive blows, and the initiative will always be in our hands.

Lin Piao: *Long Live the Victory of People's War!* (September 1965), pp. 36-37.

Our strategy is "pit one against ten" and our tactics are "pit ten against one" —this is one of our fundamental principles for gaining mastery over the enemy.

"Problems of Strategy in China's Revolutionary War (December 1936), *Selected Works*, Vol. I, p. 237.

Ours are guerrilla tactics. They consist mainly of the following points:

"Divide our forces to arouse the masses, concentrate our forces to deal with the enemy."

"The enemy advances, we retreat; the enemy camps, we harass; the enemy tires, we attack; the enemy retreats, we pursue."

"To extend stable base areas, employ the policy of advancing in waves; when pursued by a powerful enemy, employ the policy of circling around."

"Arouse the largest numbers of the masses in the shortest possible time and by the best possible methods."

These tactics are just like casting a net; at any moment we should be able to cast it or draw it in. We cast it wide to win over the masses and draw it in to deal with the enemy.

"A Single Spark Can Start a Prairie Fire" (January 5, 1930), *Selected Works*, Vol. I, p. 124.

Our principles of operation are:

(1) Attack dispersed, isolated enemy forces first; attack concentrated, strong enemy forces later.

(2) Take small and medium cities and extensive rural areas first; take big cities later.

(3) Make wiping out the enemy's effective strength our main objective; do not make holding or seizing a city or place our main objective. Holding or seizing a city or place is the out-

come of wiping out the enemy's effective strength, and often a city or place can be held or seized for good only after it has changed hands a number of times.

(4) In every battle, concentrate an absolutely superior force (two, three, four and sometimes even five or six times the enemy's strength), encircle the enemy forces completely, strive to wipe them out thoroughly and do not let any escape from the net. In special circumstances, use the method of dealing the enemy crushing blows, that is, concentrate all our strength to make a frontal attack and an attack on one or both of his flanks, with the aim of wiping out one part and routing another so that our army can swiftly move its troops to smash other enemy forces. Strive to avoid battles of attrition in which we lose more than we gain or only break even. In this way, although inferior as a whole (in terms of numbers), we shall be absolutely superior in every part and every specific campaign, and this ensures victory in the campaign. As time goes on, we shall become superior as a whole and eventually wipe out all the enemy.

(5) Fight no battle unprepared, fight no battle you are not sure of winning; make every effort to be well prepared for each battle, make every effort to ensure victory in the given set of conditions as between the enemy and ourselves.

(6) Give full play to our style of fighting—courage in battle, no fear of sacrifice, no fear of fatigue, and continuous fighting (that is, fighting successive battles in a short time without rest).

(7) Strive to wipe out the enemy when he is on the move. At the same time, pay attention to the tactics of positional attack and capture enemy fortified points and cities.

(8) With regard to attacking cities, resolutely seize all enemy fortified points and cities which are weakly defended. At opportune moments, seize all enemy fortified points and cities defended with moderate strength, provided circumstances permit. As for all strongly defended enemy fortified points and cities, wait till conditions are ripe and then take them.

(9) Replenish our strength with all the arms and most of the personnel captured from the enemy. Our army's main sources of manpower and *matériel* are at the front.

(10) Make good use of the intervals between campaigns to rest, train and consolidate our troops. Periods of rest, training and consolidation should not in general be very long, and the enemy should so far as possible be permitted no breathing space.

These are the main methods the People's Liberation Army has employed in defeating Chiang Kai-shek. They are the result of the tempering of the People's Liberation Army in long years of fighting against domestic and foreign enemies and are completely suited to our present situation. . . . our strategy and tactics are based on a people's war; no army opposed to the people can use our strategy and tactics.

"The Present Situation and Our Tasks"
(December 25, 1947), *Selected Military Writings*, 2nd ed., pp. 349-50.

44. LONG LIVE THE VICTORY OF PEOPLE'S WAR

(SEPTEMBER 3, 1965)

LIN PIAO

CARRY OUT THE STRATEGY AND TACTICS OF PEOPLE'S WAR

Engels said, "The emancipation of the proletariat, in its turn, will have its specific expression in military affairs and create its specific, new military method."[1] Engels' profound prediction has been fulfilled in the revolutionary wars waged by the Chinese people under the leadership of the Chinese Communist Party. In the course of protracted armed struggle, we have created a whole range of strategy and tactics of people's war by which we have been able to utilize our strong points to attack the enemy at his weak points.

During the War of Resistance Against Japan, on the basis of his comprehensive analysis of the enemy and ourselves, Comrade Mao Tse-tung laid down the following strategic principle for the Communist-led Eighth Route and New Fourth Armies: "Guerrilla warfare is basic, but lose no chance for mobile warfare under favourable conditions."[2] He raised guerrilla warfare to the level of

From Lin Piao, *Long Live the Victory of People's War!* (Foreign Languages Press, Peking, 1967), pp. 31-52. In Commemoration of the Twentieth Anniversary of Victory in the Chinese People's War of Resistance Against Japan.

strategy, because, if they are to defeat a formidable enemy, revolutionary armed forces should not fight with a reckless disregard for the consequences when there is a great disparity between their own strength and the enemy's. If they do, they will suffer serious losses and bring heavy setbacks to the revolution. Guerrilla warfare is the only way to mobilize and apply the whole strength of the people against the enemy, the only way to expand our forces in the course of the war, deplete and weaken the enemy, gradually change the balance of forces between the enemy and ourselves, switch from guerrilla to mobile warfare, and finally defeat the enemy.

In the initial period of the Second Revolutionary Civil War, Comrade Mao Tse-tung enumerated the basic tactics of guerrilla warfare as follows:

The enemy advances, we retreat; the enemy camps, we harass; the enemy tires, we attack; the enemy retreats, we pursue.[3]

Guerrilla war tactics were further developed during the War of Resistance Against Japan. In the base areas behind the enemy lines, everybody joined in the fighting—the troops and the civilian population, men and women, old and young; every single village fought. Various ingenious methods of fighting were devised, including "sparrow warfare",[4] land-mine warfare, tunnel warfare, sabotage warfare, and guerrilla warfare on lakes and rivers.

In the later period of the War of Resistance Against Japan and during the Third Revolutionary Civil War, we switched our strategy from that of guerrilla warfare as the primary form of fighting to that of mobile warfare in the light of the changes in the balance of forces between the enemy and ourselves. By the middle, and especially the later, period of the Third Revolutionary Civil War, our operations had developed into large-scale mobile warfare, including the storming of big cities.

War of annihilation is the fundamental guiding principle of our military operations. This guiding principle should be put into effect regardless of whether mobile or guerrilla warfare is the primary form of fighting. It is true that in guerrilla warfare much should be done to disrupt and harass the enemy, but it is still necessary actively to advocate and fight battles of annihilation whenever conditions are favourable. In mobile warfare superior forces must be concentrated in every battle so that the enemy forces can be wiped out one by one. Comrade Mao Tse-tung has pointed out:

A battle in which the enemy is routed is not basically decisive in a contest with a foe of great strength. A battle of annihilation, on the other hand, produces a great and immediate impact on any enemy. Injuring all of man's ten fingers is not as effective as chopping off one, and routing ten enemy divisions is not as effective as annihilating one of them.[5]

Battles of annihilation are the most effective way of hitting the enemy; each time one of his brigades or regiments is wiped out, he will have one brigade or one regiment less, and the enemy forces will be demoralized and will disintegrate. By fighting battles of annihilation, our army is able to take prisoners of war or capture weapons from the enemy in every battle, and the morale of our army rises, our army units get bigger, our weapons become better, and our combat effectiveness continually increases.

In his celebrated ten cardinal military principles Comrade Mao Tse-tung pointed out:

In every battle, concentrate an absolutely superior force (two, three, four and sometimes even five or six times the enemy's strength), encircle the enemy forces completely, strive to wipe them out thoroughly and do not let any escape from the net. In special circumstances, use the method of dealing crushing blows to the enemy, that is, concentrate all our strength to make a frontal attack and also to attack one or both of his flanks, with the aim of wiping out one part and routing another so that our army can swiftly move its troops to smash other enemy forces. Strive to avoid battles of attrition in which we lose more than we gain or only break even. In this way, although we are inferior as a whole (in terms of numbers), we are absolutely superior in every part and every specific campaign, and this ensures victory in the campaign. As time goes on, we shall become superior as a whole and eventually wipe out all the enemy.[6]

At the same time, he said that we should first attack dispersed or isolated enemy forces and only attack concentrated and strong enemy forces later; that we should strive to wipe out the enemy through mobile warfare; that we should fight no battle unprepared and fight no battle we are not sure of winning; and that in any battle we fight we should develop our army's strong points and its excellent style of fighting. These are the major principles of fighting a war of annihilation.

In order to annihilate the enemy, we must adopt the policy of luring him in deep and abandon some cities and districts of our own accord in a planned way, so as to let him in. It is only after letting the enemy in that the people can take part in the war in various ways and that the power of a people's war can be fully exerted. It is only after letting the enemy in that he can be compelled to divide up his forces, take on heavy burdens and commit mistakes. In other words, we must let the enemy become elated, stretch out all his ten fingers and become hopelessly bogged down. Thus, we can concentrate superior forces to destroy the enemy forces one by one, to eat them up mouthful by mouthful. Only by wiping out the enemy's effective strength can cities and localities be finally held or seized. We are firmly against dividing up our forces to defend all positions and putting up resistance at every place for fear that our territory might be lost and our pots and pans smashed, since this can neither wipe out the enemy forces nor hold cities or localities.

Comrade Mao Tse-tung has provided a masterly summary of the strategy and tactics of people's war: You fight in your way and we fight in ours; we fight when we can win and move away when we can't.

In other words, you rely on modern weapons and we rely on highly conscious revolutionary people; you give full play to your superiority and we give full play to ours; you have your way of fighting and we have ours. When you want to fight us, we don't let you and you can't even find us. But when we want to fight you, we make sure that you can't get away and we hit you squarely on the chin and wipe you out. When we are able to wipe you out, we do so with a vengeance; when we can't, we see to it that you don't wipe us out. It is opportunism if one won't fight when one can win. It is adventurism if one insists on fighting when one can't win. Fighting is the pivot of all our strategy and tactics. It is because of the necessity of fighting that we admit the necessity of moving away. The sole purpose of moving away is to fight and bring about the final and complete destruction of the enemy. This strategy and these tactics can be applied only when one relies on the broad masses of the people, and such application brings the superiority of people's war into full play. However superior he may be in technical equipment and whatever tricks he may resort to, the enemy will find himself in the passive position of having to receive blows, and the initiative will always be in our hands.

We grew from a small and weak to a large and strong force and finally defeated formidable enemies at home and abroad because we carried out the strategy and tactics of people's war. During the eight years of the War of Resistance Against Japan, the people's army led by the Chinese Communist Party fought more than 125,000 engagements with the enemy and put out of action more than 1,700,000 Japanese and puppet troops. In the three years of the War of Liberation, we put 8,000,000 of the Kuomintang's reactionary troops out of action and won the great victory of the people's revolution.

ADHERE TO THE POLICY OF SELF-RELIANCE

The Chinese people's War of Resistance Against Japan was an important part of the Anti-Fascist World War. The victory of the Anti-Fascist War as a whole was the result of the common struggle of the people of the world. By its participation in the war against Japan at the final stage, the Soviet army under the leadership of the Communist Party of the Soviet Union headed by Stalin played a significant part in bringing about the defeat of Japanese imperialism. Great contributions were made by the peoples of Korea, Vietnam, Mongolia, Laos, Cambodia, Indonesia, Burma, India, Pakistan, Malaya, the Philippines, Thailand and certain other Asian countries. The people of the Americas, Oceania, Europe and Africa also made their contribution.

Under extremely difficult circumstances, the Japanese Communists and the revolutionary forces of the Japanese people kept up their valiant and staunch struggle, and played their part in the defeat of Japanese fascism.

The common victory was won by all the peoples, who gave one another support and encouragement. Yet each country was, above all, liberated as a result of its own people's efforts.

The Chinese people enjoyed the support of other peoples in winning both the War of Resistance Against Japan and the People's Liberation War, and yet victory was mainly the result of the Chinese people's own efforts. Certain people assert that China's victory in the War of Resistance was due entirely to foreign assistance. This absurd assertion is in tune with that of the Japanese militarists.

The liberation of the masses is accomplished by the masses themselves—this is a basic principle of Marxism-Leninism. Revolution or people's war in any country is the business of the masses in that country and should be carried out primarily by their own efforts; there is no other way.

During the War of Resistance Against Japan, our Party maintained that China should rely mainly on her own strength while at the same time trying to get as much foreign assistance as possible. We firmly opposed the Kuomintang ruling clique's policy of exclusive reliance on foreign aid. In the eyes of the Kuomintang and Chiang Kai-shek, China's industry and agriculture were no good, her weapons and equipment were no good, nothing in China was any good, so that if she wanted to defeat Japan, she had to depend on other countries, and particularly on the U.S.-British imperialists. This was completely slavish thinking. Our policy was diametrically opposed to that of the Kuomintang. Our Party held that it was possible to exploit the contradictions between U.S.-British imperialism and Japanese imperialism, but that no reliance could be placed on the former. In fact, the U.S.-British imperialists repeatedly plotted to bring about a "Far Eastern Munich" in order to arrive at a compromise with Japanese imperialism at China's expense, and for a considerable period of time they provided the Japanese aggressors with war *matériel*. In helping China during that period, the U.S. imperialists harboured the sinister design of turning China into a colony of their own.

Comrade Mao Tse-tung said, "China has to rely mainly on her own efforts in the War of Resistance."[7] He added, "We hope for foreign aid but cannot be dependent on it; we depend on our own efforts, on the creative power of the whole army and the entire people."[8]

Self-reliance was especially important for the people's armed forces and the Liberated Areas led by our Party.

The Kuomintang government gave the Eighth Route and New Fourth Armies some small allowances in the initial stage of the anti-Japanese war, but gave them not a single penny later. The Liberated Areas faced great difficulties as a result of the Japanese imperialists' savage attacks and brutal "mopping-up" campaigns, of the Kuomintang's military encirclement and economic blockade and of natural calamities. The difficulties were particularly great in the years 1941 and 1942, when we were very short of food and clothing.

What were we to do? Comrade Mao Tse-tung asked: How has mankind managed to keep alive from time immemorial? Has it not been by men using their hands to provide for themselves? Why should we, their latter-day descendants, be devoid of this tiny bit of wisdom? Why can't we use our own hands?

The Central Committee of the Party and Comrade Mao Tse-tung put forward the policies of "ample food and clothing through self-reliance" and "develop the economy and ensure supplies", and the army and the people of the Liberated Areas accordingly launched an extensive production campaign, with the main emphasis on agriculture.

Difficulties are not invincible monsters. If everyone co-operates and fights them, they will be overcome. The Kuomintang reactionaries thought that it could starve us to death by cutting off allowances and imposing an economic blockade, but in fact it helped us by stimulating us to rely on our own efforts to surmount our difficulties. While launching the great campaign for pro-

duction, we applied the policy of "better troops and simpler administration" and economized in the use of manpower and material resources; thus we not only surmounted the severe material difficulties and successfully met the crisis, but lightened the people's burden, improved their livelihood and laid the material foundations for victory in the anti-Japanese war.

The problem of military equipment was solved mainly by relying on the capture of arms from the enemy, though we did turn out some weapons too. Chiang Kai-shek, the Japanese imperialists and the U.S. imperialists have all been our "chiefs of transportation corps". The arsenals of the imperialists always provide the oppressed peoples and nations with arms.

The people's armed forces led by our Party independently waged people's war on a large scale and won great victories without any material aid from outside, both during the more than eight years of the anti-Japanese war and during the more than three years of the People's War of Liberation.

Comrade Mao Tse-tung has said that our fundamental policy should rest on the foundation of our own strength. Only by relying on our own efforts can we in all circumstances remain invincible.

The peoples of the world invariably support each other in their struggles against imperialism and its lackeys. Those countries which have won victory are duty bound to support and aid the peoples who have not yet done so. Nevertheless, foreign aid can only play a supplementary role.

In order to make a revolution and to fight a people's war and be victorious, it is imperative to adhere to the policy of self-reliance, rely on the strength of the masses in one's own country and prepare to carry on the fight independently even when all material aid from outside is cut off. If one does not operate by one's own efforts, does not independently ponder and solve the problems of the revolution in one's own country and does not rely on the strength of the masses, but leans wholly on foreign aid—even though this be aid from socialist countries which persist in revolution—no victory can be won, or be consolidated even if it is won.

THE INTERNATIONAL SIGNIFICANCE OF COMRADE MAO TSE-TUNG'S THEORY OF PEOPLE'S WAR

The Chinese revolution is a continuation of the great October Revolution. The road of the October Revolution is the common road for all people's revolutions. The Chinese revolution and the October Revolution have in common the following basic characteristics: (1) Both were led by the working class with a Marxist-Leninist party as its nucleus. (2) Both were based on the worker-peasant alliance. (3) In both cases state power was seized through violent revolution and the dictatorship of the proletariat was established. (4) In both cases the socialist system was built after victory in the revolution. (5) Both were component parts of the proletarian world revolution.

Naturally, the Chinese revolution had its own peculiar characteristics. The October Revolution took place in imperialist Russia, but the Chinese revolution broke out in a semi-colonial and semi-feudal country. The former was a proletarian socialist revolution, while the latter developed into a socialist revolution after the complete victory of the new-democratic revolution. The October Revolution began with armed uprisings in the cities and then spread to the countryside, while the Chinese revolution won nation-wide victory through the encirclement of the cities from the rural areas and the final capture of the cities.

Comrade Mao Tse-tung's great merit lies in the fact that he has succeeded in integrating the universal truth of Marxism-Leninism with the concrete practice of the Chinese revolution and has enriched and developed Marxism-Leninism by his masterly generalization and summation of the experience gained during the Chinese people's protracted revolutionary struggle.

Comrade Mao Tse-tung's theory of people's war has been proved by the long practice of the Chinese revolution to be in accord with the objective laws of such wars and to be invincible. It has not only been valid for China, it is a great contribution to the revolutionary struggles of the oppressed nations and peoples throughout the world.

The people's war led by the Chinese Communist Party, comprising the War of Resistance and the Revolutionary Civil Wars, lasted for twenty-two years. It constitutes the most drawn-out and most complex people's war led by the proletariat in modern history, and it has been the richest in experience.

In the last analysis, the Marxist-Leninist theory of proletarian revolution is the theory of the seizure of state power by revolutionary violence, the theory of countering war against the people by people's war. As Marx so aptly put it, *"Force is the midwife of every old society pregnant with a new one."*[9]

It was on the basis of the lessons derived from the people's wars in China that Comrade Mao Tse-tung, using the simplest and the most vivid language, advanced the famous thesis that *"political power grows out of the barrel of a gun"*.[10]

He clearly pointed out:

The seizure of power by armed force, the settlement of the issue by war, is the central task and the highest form of revolution. This Marxist-Leninist principle of revolution holds good universally, for China and for all other countries.[11]

War is the product of imperialism and the system of exploitation of man by man. Lenin said that *"war is always and everywhere begun by the exploiters themselves, by the ruling and oppressing classes"*.[12] So long as imperialism and the system of exploitation of man by man exist, the imperialists and reactionaries will invariably rely on armed force to maintain their reactionary rule and impose war on the oppressed nations and peoples. This is an objective law independent of man's will.

In the world today, all the imperialists headed by the United States and their lackeys, without exception, are strengthening their state machinery, and especially their armed forces. U.S. imperialism, in particular, is carrying out armed aggression and suppression everywhere.

What should the oppressed nations and the oppressed people do in the face of wars of aggression and armed suppression by the imperialists and their lackeys? Should they submit and remain slaves in perpetuity? Or should they rise in resistance and fight for their liberation?

Comrade Mao Tse-tung answered this question in vivid terms. He said that after long investigation and study the Chinese people discovered that all the imperialists and their lackeys *"have swords in their hands and are out to kill. The people have come to understand this and so act after the same fashion"*.[13] This is called doing unto them what they do unto us.

In the last analysis, whether one dares to wage a tit-for-tat struggle against armed aggression and suppression by the imperialists and their lackeys, whether ones dares to fight a people's war against them, means whether one dares to embark on revolution. This is the most effective touchstone for distinguishing genuine revolutionaries and Marxist-Leninists from fake ones.

In view of the fact that some people were afflicted with fear of the imperialists and reactionaries, Comrade Mao Tse-tung put forward his famous thesis that "the imperialists and all reactionaries are paper tigers". He said:

> All reactionaries are paper tigers. In appearance, the reactionaries are terrifying, but in reality they are not so powerful. From a long-term point of view, it is not the reactionaries but the people who are really powerful.[14]

The history of people's war in China and other countries provides conclusive evidence that the growth of the people's revolutionary forces from weak and small beginnings into strong and large forces is a universal law of development of class struggle, a universal law of development of people's war. A people's war inevitably meets with many difficulties, with many ups and downs and setbacks in the course of its development, but no force can alter its general trend towards inevitable triumph.

Comrade Mao-Tse-tung points out that we must despise the enemy strategically and take full account of him tactically.

To despise the enemy strategically is an elementary requirement for a revolutionary. Without the courage to despise the enemy and without daring to win, it will be simply impossible to make revolution and wage a people's war, let alone to achieve victory.

It is also very important for revolutionaries to take full account of the enemy tactically. It is likewise impossible to win victory in a people's war without taking full account of the enemy tactically, and without examining the concrete conditions, without being prudent and giving great attention to the study of the art of struggle, and without adopting appropriate forms of struggle in the concrete practice of the revolution in each country and with regard to each concrete problem of struggle.

Dialectical and historical materialism teaches us that what is important primarily is not that which at the given moment seems to be durable and yet is already beginning to die away, but that which is arising and developing, even though at the given moment it may not appear to be durable, for only that which is arising and developing is invincible.

Why can the apparently weak newborn forces always triumph over the decadent forces which appear so powerful? The reason is that truth is on their side and that the masses are on their side, while the reactionary classes are always divorced from the masses and set themselves against the masses.

This has been borne out by the victory of the Chinese revolution, by the history of all revolutions, the whole history of class struggle and the entire history of mankind.

The imperialists are extremely afraid of Comrade Mao Tse-tung's thesis that *"imperialism and all reactionaries are paper tigers"*, and the revisionists are extremely hostile to it. They all oppose and attack this thesis and the philistines follow suit by ridiculing it. But all this cannot in the least diminish its importance. The light of truth cannot be dimmed by anybody.

Comrade Mao-Tse-tung's theory of people's war solves not only the problem of daring to fight a people's war, but also that of how to wage it.

Comrade Mao Tse-tung is a great statesman and military scientist, proficient at directing war in accordance with its laws. By the line and policies, the strategy and tactics he formulated for the people's war, he led the Chinese people in steering the ship of the people's war past all hidden reefs to the shores of victory in most complicated and difficult conditions.

It must be emphasized that Comrade Mao Tse-tung's theory of the establishment of rural revolutionary base areas and the encirclement of the cities from the countryside is of outstanding and universal practical importance for the present revolutionary struggles of all the oppressed nations and peoples, and particularly for the revolutionary struggles of the oppressed nations and peoples in Asia, Africa and Latin America against imperialism and its lackeys.

Many countries and peoples in Asia, Africa and Latin America are now being subjected to aggression and enslavement on a serious scale by the imperialists headed by the United States and their lackeys. The basic political and economic conditions in many of these countries have many similarities to those that prevailed in old China. As in China, the peasant question is extremely important in these regions. The peasants constitute the main force of the national-democratic revolution against the imperialists and their lackeys. In committing aggression against these countries, the imperialists usually begin by seizing the big cities and the main lines of communication, but they are unable to bring the vast countryside completely under their control. The countryside, and the countryside alone, can provide the broad areas in which the revolutionaries can manoeuvre freely. The countryside, and the countryside alone, can provide the revolutionary bases from which the revolutionaries can go forward to final victory. Precisely for this reason, Comrade Mao Tse-tung's theory of establishing revolutionary base areas in the rural districts and encircling the cities from the countryside is attracting more and more attention among the people in these regions.

Taking the entire globe, if North America and Western Europe can be called "the cities of the world", then Asia, Africa and Latin America constitute "the rural areas of the world". Since World War II, the proletarian revolutionary movement has for various reasons been temporarily held back in the North American and West European capitalist countries, while the people's revolutionary movement in Asia, Africa and Latin America has been growing vigorously. In a sense, the contemporary world revolution also presents a picture of the encirclement of cities by the rural areas. In the final analysis, the whole cause of world revolution hinges on the revolutionary struggles of the Asian, African and Latin American peoples who make up the overwhelming majority of the world's population. The socialist countries should regard it as their internationalist duty to support the people's revolutionary struggles in Asia, Africa and Latin America.

The October Revolution opened up a new era in the revolution of the oppressed nations. The victory of the October Revolution built a bridge between the socialist revolution of the proletariat of the West and the national-democratic revolution of the colonial and semi-colonial countries of the East. The Chinese revolution has successfully solved the problem of how to link up the national-democratic with the socialist revolution in the colonial and semi-colonial countries.

Comrade Mao Tse-tung has pointed out that, in the epoch since the October Revolution, anti-imperialist revolution in any colonial or semi-colonial country is no longer part of the old bourgeois, or capitalist world revolution, but is part of the new world revolution, the proletarian-socialist world revolution.

Comrade Mao Tse-tung has formulated a complete theory of the new-democratic revolution. He indicated that this revolution, which is different from all others, can only be, nay must be, a revolution against imperialism, feudalism and bureaucrat-capitalism waged by the broad masses of the people under the leadership of the proletariat.

This means that the revolution can only be, nay must be, led by the proletariat and the genuinely revolutionary party armed with Marxism-Leninism, and by no other class or party.

This means that the revolution embraces in its ranks not only the workers, peasants and the urban petty bourgeoisie, but also the national bourgeoisie and other patriotic and anti-imperialist democrats.

This means that the revolution is directed against imperialism, feudalism and bureaucrat-capitalism.

The new-democratic revolution leads to socialism, and not to capitalism.

Comrade Mao-Tse-tung's theory of the new-democratic revolution is the Marxist-Leninist theory of revolution by stages as well as the Marxist-Leninist theory of uninterrupted revolution.

Comrade Mao Tse-tung made a correct distinction between the two revolutionary stages, i.e., the national-democratic and the socialist revolutions; at the same time he correctly and closely linked the two. The national-democratic revolution is the necessary preparation for the socialist revolution, and the socialist revolution is the inevitable sequel to the national-democratic revolution. There is no Great Wall between the two revolutionary stages. But the socialist revolution is only possible after the completion of the national-democratic revolution. The more thorough the national-democratic revolution, the better the conditions for the socialist revolution.

The experience of the Chinese revolution shows that the tasks of the national-democratic revolution can be fulfilled only through long and tortuous struggles. In this stage of revolution, imperialism and its lackeys are the principal enemy. In the struggle against imperialism and its lackeys, it is necessary to rally all anti-imperialist patriotic forces, including the national bourgeoisie and all patriotic personages. All those patriotic personages from among the bourgeoisie and other exploiting classes who join the anti-imperialist struggle play a progressive historical role; they are not tolerated by imperialism but welcomed by the proletariat.

It is very harmful to confuse the two stages, that is, the national-democratic and the socialist revolutions. Comrade Mao Tse-tung criticized the wrong idea of "accomplishing both at one stroke", and pointed out that this utopian idea could only weaken the struggle against imperialism and its lackeys, the most urgent task at that time. The Kuomintang reactionaries and the Trotskyites they hired during the War of Resistance deliberately confused these two stages of the Chinese revolution, proclaiming the "theory of a single revolution" and preaching so-called "socialism" without any Communist Party. With this pre-

posterous theory they attempted to swallow up the Communist Party, wipe out any revolution and prevent the advance of the national-democratic revolution, and they used it as a pretext for their non-resistance and capitulation to imperialism. This reactionary theory was buried long ago by the history of the Chinese revolution.

The Khrushchov revisionists are now actively preaching that socialism can be built without the proletariat and without a genuinely revolutionary party armed with the advanced proletarian ideology, and they have cast the fundamental tenets of Marxism-Leninism to the four winds. The revisionists' purpose is solely to divert the oppressed nations from their struggle against imperialism and sabotage their national-democratic revolution, all in the service of imperialism.

The Chinese revolution provides a successful lesson for making a thoroughgoing national-democratic revolution under the leadership of the proletariat; it likewise provides a successful lesson for the timely transition from the national-democratic revolution to the socialist revolution under the leadership of the proletariat.

Mao Tse-tung's thought has been the guide to the victory of the Chinese revolution. It has integrated the universal truth of Marxism-Leninism with the concrete practice of the Chinese revolution and creatively developed Marxism-Leninism, thus adding new weapons to the arsenal of Marxism-Leninism.

Ours is the epoch in which world capitalism and imperialism are heading for their doom and socialism and communism are marching to victory. Comrade Mao Tse-tung's theory of people's war is not only a product of the Chinese revolution, but has also the characteristics of our epoch. The new experience gained in the people's revolutionary struggles in various countries since World War II has provided continuous evidence that Mao Tse-tung's thought is a common asset of the revolutionary people of the whole world. This is the great international significance of the thought of Mao Tse-tung.

Notes

1. Frederick Engels, "Possibilities and Perspectives of the War of the Holy Alliance Against France in 1852", *Collected Works of Marx and Engels*, Russ. ed., Vol. VII, p. 509.

2. Mao Tse-tung, "On Protracted War", *Selected Works*, FLP, Peking, 1965, Vol. II, p. 116.

3. Mao Tse-tung, "A Single Spark Can Start a Prairie Fire", *Selected Works*, FLP, Peking, 1965, Vol. I, p. 124.

4. Sparrow warfare is a popular method of fighting created by the Communist-led anti-Japanese guerrilla units and militia behind the enemy lines. It was called sparrow warfare first, because it was used diffusely, like the flight of sparrows in the sky; and second, because it was used flexibly by guerrillas or militiamen, operating in threes or fives, appearing and disappearing unexpectedly and wounding, killing, depleting and wearing out the enemy forces.

5. Mao Tse-tung, "Problems of Strategy in China's Revolutionary War", *Selected Works*, FLP, Peking, 1965, Vol. I, p. 248.

6. Mao Tse-tung, "The Present Situation and Our Tasks", *Selected Works*, FLP, Peking, 1961, Vol. IV, p. 161.

7. Mao Tse-tung, "Interview with Three Correspondents from the Central News Agency, the *Sao Tang Pao* and the *Hsin Min Pao*", *Selected Works*, FLP, Peking, 1965, Vol. II, p. 270.

8. Mao Tse-tung, "We Must Learn to Do Economic Work", *Selected Works*, FLP, Peking, 1965, Vol. III, p. 241.

9. Karl Marx, *Capital*, Foreign Languages Publishing House, Moscow, 1954, Vol. I, p. 751.

10. Mao Tse-tung, "Problems of War and Strategy", *Selected Works*, FLP, Peking, 1965, Vol. II, p. 224.

11. *Ibid.*, p. 219.

12. V. I. Lenin, "The Revolutionary Army and the Revolutionary Government", *Collected Works*, Russ. ed., Vol. VIII, p. 529.

13. Mao Tse-tung, "The Situation and Our Policy After the Victory in the War of Resistance Against Japan", *Selected Works*, FLP, Peking, 1961, Vol. IV, pp. 14-15.

14. Mao Tse-tung, "Talk with the American Correspondent Anna Louise Strong", *Selected Works*, FLP, Peking, 1961, Vol. IV, p. 100.

V. THE GREAT PROLETARIAN
CULTURAL REVOLUTION

45. THE BACKGROUND AND DEVELOPMENT OF
"THE PROLETARIAN CULTURAL REVOLUTION"

GENE T. HSIAO*

The Chinese Communist Party is now forty-six years old. Its successful seizure of power in 1949 and many of its subsequent achievements have frequently been attributed to the "solidarity" of its leadership by outside observers. From the time when Mao Tse-tung obtained *de facto* leadership of the Party at the Tsunyi Conference in 1935, no one seri-

* This article is based on an address to a faculty seminar of the Comparative Study of Communist Societies on July 14, 1966. Subsequent research has brought the discussion up to early May 1967 through interviews with informed sources in Japan and Hong Kong and the discovery of new documentary evidence there, including some Red Guard newspapers thus far not publicly available.

I am grateful to the Center for Chinese Studies, University of California, and the Project for their support of my study, and I am especially thankful to the Chancellor's Program Committee for International Studies and the Institute of International Studies for their research grant, which made my field research possible. In addition, I also wish to thank all those in Japan and Hong Kong who assisted me in this study.

From *Asian Survey*, Vol. VII, No. 6 (June 1967), pp. 389-404. Reprinted by permission. The author is professor of government, Southern Illinois University.

ously questioned his authority and the unity of the Party leadership.

"The great proletarian cultural revolution," however, has not only exposed the existence of a powerful opposition to Mao's authority, but has also revealed an almost complete shakeup of the Party's ruling elite, from the Central Committee down to the primary level. In recent months, Mao has had to call in the People's Liberation Army (PLA) to oppose the very Party apparatus of which he remains the head; to strike down what he terms "a handful of Party persons who are in power and taking the capitalist road"; to organize the Red Guards and various other types of "revolutionary rebels" to attack and replace local Party and state administrations, including the management of production units; to halt the activities of the Chinese Communist Youth League, which was traditionally a strong arm and a reserve force of the Party; to reorganize time and again the editorial boards of leading Party organs and other mass media; to start the issuance of numerous wall posters and Red Guard newspapers; to arrest and punish, mostly by the Red Guards, Party and state officials who had served him for decades; and more recently, to openly declare "a struggle for the seizure of power" throughout the country.

Does all this mean that Mao has lost control, or is on the verge of collapse? Who is his real opposition? Is it created by Mao himself; by a group of persons conspiring to overthrow his reign; by objective circumstances within and surrounding the Party; or by a combination of all these and other factors? What, really, is the cause of the revolution? How was it started and developed? And what will be its impact on the future of China?

Opinions as to the cause of the revolution have varied from person to person, time to time, and place to place. There are five general views. One is that the revolution is essentially over the succession to the aging Mao Tse-tung, a struggle for power between Lin Piao and Liu Shao-ch'i. The second contends that the real issue is the course China ought to take in her domestic and foreign policies. The third recognizes the domestic issues as an important contributing cause but holds that the Vietnam War and the Sino-Soviet split have played a decisive role. The fourth considers the revolution a continuation of Chinese tradition, as evidenced in the cult of Mao's personality and his demand for personal loyalty and absolute allegiance. The fifth holds that Mao has lost touch with reality and is "insane."

The last view has failed to provide any positive supporting evidence; the other four all seem to contain some truth. However, the purpose of this article is not to endorse or repudiate the views of others. Each writer is entitled to his own opinion. Moreover, since the revolution is still going on, and since there are still many unknown facts, it remains impos-

sible to prove that any single issue is *the* cause of the revolution. Nor can we predict with certainty the impact of the revolution on the future of China. Like other great political events of history, the revolution appears to be not a simple accident breaking out by chance, but an accumulation of incidents involving a host of complex issues.

Officially, the revolution began with the publication of Yao Wen-yuan's "Comment on the Newly Composed Historical Play 'Hai Jui Dismissed from Office,'" which appeared in the November 10, 1965 issue of the Shanghai *Wen-hui Pao*[1] under Mao's personal direction through the Shanghai Municipal Party Committee.[2] One may wonder why a contemporary revolution from the top had to start by criticizing a historical play dealing with the remote Ming Dynasty (1368-1644), and why it had to start in the port of Shanghai instead of the national capital, since the play's author, Wu Han, was a Deputy Mayor of Peking and the play itself was first staged there in February 1961. Moreover, Wu was not a CCP member, but a representative of the Chinese Democratic League. He developed the play from one of his early works, "Hai Jui Scolds the Emperor," which had appeared long before in the June 16, 1959 issue of *Jen-min Jih-pao*— the leading daily official organ of the Party Central Committee. Then why was it that after more than six years, Wu was suddenly selected by Mao as the first target of the revolution?

To seek a tentative answer for these and related questions, one has to look into the background of the revolution, its beginning and development. On the basis of the documents thus far available to us, there can be no doubt that the revolution is essentially a power struggle between the Maoist group and Liu Shao-ch'i's faction, and that the basic crisis seems to have started with Khrushchev's de-Stalinization program and developed through the sequence of events in the succeeding years. Due to the complexity and ramifications of the revolution, the following discussion must necessarily confine itself to certain important subjects: (1) de-Stalinization and its impact on Mao and the CCP; (2) the Hundred Flowers movement and the Anti-rightist campaign; (3) the commune system and Mao's abdication as State Chairman; (4) the fifth rectification and Mao's "flight" to Shanghai; (5) the beginning of an open power struggle; (6) the development of the power struggle; and (7) conclusions.

DE-STALINIZATION AND ITS IMPACT ON MAO AND THE CCP

The first powerful challenge to Mao's ideological and political authority after 1935 did not come from within the CCP. It came indirectly from Khrushchev's "secret" report to the Twentieth Congress of the Soviet Communist Party dated February 25, 1956, in which he accused Stalin of three major "crimes": (1) the cult of personality, (2) the abuse of criminal justice, and (3) the mismanagement of the economy.[3] While the report has never been published in China, its impact on Mao and the CCP was profound and far-reaching. On the one hand, it seriously undermined the foundation of Mao's theoretical works on which his ideological leadership was based and of which his own personality cult was a part. On the other hand, the report constituted an indirect rebuttal of the CCP's earlier practices in government and law, which had been primarily modeled after the Stalinist pattern.

In reaction, the CCP convened its long overdue Eighth National Congress in September of the same year, at which [time] a reorganization of the Party power structure and other important events took place. In the ideological realm, a provision of the 1949 Party Constitution accepting Mao's thought as the guide line of CCP work was omitted in the new 1956 Party Constitution. Related to this major concession was the re-allocation of power within the CCP center. Previously, according to the 1945 Party Constitution, the Chairman of the CC* served concurrently as Chairman of the Central Politburo and the Central Secretariat. There was no mention of the CC's Vice Chairmanship and its function. In consequence, the Chairmanship of the CC was an all-powerful dictatorship. At this point, however, the Eighth Congress formally elected four Vice Chairmen of the CC and created a Standing Committee of the Politburo.[4] While the Chairman of the CC remained concurrently Chairman of its Politburo, he was no longer Chairman of the Central Secretariat. Instead, the Congress elected a General Secretary, Teng Hsiao-p'ing, to handle the daily work of the Central Secretariat. These six—the Chairman, four Vice Chairmen, and General Secretary—formed the original membership of the new collective ruling elite—the Politburo's Standing Committee,[5] which constitutionally speaking does not have a designated Chairman. Lin Shao-ch'i, as first Vice Chairman of the CC, was given part of the Chairman's power to conduct "certain important conferences."

Ten years later, Mao himself interpreted this arrangement—the delegation of his power to Liu and Teng—in the following words:

In light of the problems that occurred within the Soviet Union and considering the

* Central Committee.

security of our own country, I decided to divide the Standing Committee of the Politburo into the first and second lines . . . by withdrawing myself into the second and by placing Liu Shao-ch'i and Teng Hsiao-p'ing in the first. Liu, as Vice Chairman, could conduct certain important conferences and Teng could attend to the daily work [of the CC] . . . When I retreated into the second line by not conducting the daily work and by letting others execute it, my purpose was to cultivate their prestige so that when I have to see God, the country can avoid great chaos . . .[6]

This, Mao implied, was the seed of the present revolution. But a seed cannot grow without soil, and the first soil that supported its growth was the commune system, which came after the Hundred Flowers Movement and the resultant Anti-rightist Campaign.

THE HUNDRED FLOWERS MOVEMENT AND THE ANTI-RIGHTIST CAMPAIGN

One of the many charges which the Maoists have hurled at Liu Shao-ch'i in the present revolution is his role in the Hundred Flowers Movement.[7] Quoting Liu's speeches to local Party organizations in the period from March to May 1957, a Red Guard newspaper accused Liu of having: (1) denied the existence of antagonistic contradictions in a socialist society, (2) favored material incentives instead of "politics take command," (3) preferred flexible to inflexible economic planning, (4) advocated a limited free market in order to compete with state enterprises, (5) supported urban workers' livelihood at a higher level than rural peasants', and (6) defended the constitutional rights of the peasants to withdraw from agricultural cooperatives, of the workers to strike, and of the

students to stage demonstrations. All this, in the opinion of one Maoist source, provided the rightists with a reactionary theoretical basis to attack the Party and paved the way for the spread of "capitalist" thinking in the succeeding years.[8]

The Hundred Flowers Movement was Mao's plan to cope with internal popular uneasiness which had built up in the previous seven years of CCP rule and become manifest after de-Stalinization, especially after the Hungarian Revolution when, in Mao's own words, "tens of thousands of persons went out to the street to oppose the People's Government."[9] But when criticism of the Party reached an intolerable level, the movement ended up in a disastrous "anti-rightist" campaign. Many of the critics were sent to corrective labor camps; those who survived the purge had to sign a "socialist self-reform pact" to pledge their allegiance to the Party.[10] In addition, the Party announced three programs: (1) the participation of leadership personnel, both civilian and military, in physical labor; (2) the launching of a rectification and socialist education movement in industrial enterprises and among the rural populace; and (3) the enforcement of a policy requiring all intellectuals to be both "red and expert" with "red" as the prerequisite to "expert."[11]

These stern measures had a profound impact on later events. But the issue here is what significance is there in the Red Guard charges against Liu Shao-ch'i? Examination of the official documents of both the Hundred Flowers Movement and the Anti-Rightist Campaign discloses no evidence to support the allegation that Liu leaned to the "right." Since the rightists' response to the Hundred Flowers Movement was an assault on the Party as a whole, there is also no reason to believe that Liu did not back up the

Party's anti-rightist policy. In fact, it was Teng Hsiao-p'ing, now accused of being Liu's chief accomplice, who delivered the "Report on the Rectification Movement" of September 23, 1957. Then, how do we explain this somewhat paradoxical situation?

In my opinion, the Red Guard charges do not prove Liu's "pro-rightist" attitude, but reflect the difference between Mao and Liu on matters concerning political and econmic policies. Politically, Liu was inclined to the establishment of a stable order. In his "political report" to the Eighth National Congress of the CCP, he pronounced the end of "revolutionary legality," and assured the people of legal guarantees to their freedoms provided by the 1954 State Constitution.[12] It was also under his leadership as Chairman of the Standing Committee of the National People's Congress that P'eng Chen, then concurrently serving as Secretary General of the Standing Committee, announced on three occasions the readiness of the government to promulgate criminal and civil codes.[13] From the Western point of view, the provisions of these never-published codes might have been harsh. Nevertheless, if adopted they could have become elements of stability. Mao, on the other hand, has always believed in mass movements, as evidenced in his numerous writings.

Economically, Liu tended to place emphasis on the development of industry, whereas Mao gave priority to the collectivization of agriculture. For example, in 1951 Liu remarked: "Without the development of industry and the achievement of industrialization, there is no possibility of realizing agricultural collectivization at all." Mao, on the other hand, noted: "In the area of agriculture, under the conditions of our country we must achieve *cooperativization* first before we

can use large machines."[14] Mao's preference for agricultural collectivization became more conspicuous after the founding of the commune system.

THE COMMUNES AND MAO'S ABDICATION OF THE STATE CHAIRMANSHIP

The Eighth National Congress of the CCP had produced a relatively conservative reform program in most areas of socio-economic life. Now all the harsh measures of the 1957 rectification not only reversed the Congress' basic spirit, but were followed by the creation of a radical commune system. Who was the initial sponsor of this system? Was it really a spontaneous movement, as Anna Louise Strong has suggested? Or was it a planned move? Circumstantial evidence strongly suggests that Mao was at least the leading promoter.

It is well known that the first commune appeared in Honan province in April 1958. After four months of experimentation, the Politburo formally adopted it as a system to replace the advanced agricultural cooperatives. But soon the Sixth Plenum of the CC/CCP found the original version of the commune system unsound.[15] Consequently, the Plenum simultaneously adopted two momentous decisions on December 10, 1958: one amending the commune system; the other accepting Mao's "proposal" that he not be a candidate for the next term as State Chairman.[16] While the proposal's contents are still not public, the CC Plenum's acceptance deserves attention. The following is a translation of the key portion:

In the opinion of this Central Plenum, it is entirely a positive proposal. Because [by allowing] Comrade Mao Tse-tung not to assume the duty of State Chairman but to be Chairman of the Party Center only, it will better enable him to concentrate his energy to handle the problems of Party and state programs, policies, and lines; it will also make it possible for him to spare more of his time to do the theoretical work of Marx-ism-Leninism without impeding him from continuously displaying the role of his lead-ership in state work. . . . In the future when certain special circumstances arise, which require him to resume such work, it will be still possible to nominate him to as-sume the State Chairmanship according to the people's opinion and the Party's decision[17]

Reading between the lines, and con-sidering the timing of the CC Plenum's two decisions, it is obvious that Mao's abdication as State Chairman was re-lated to the radical commune program. It also indicates that the general mood of the CC Plenum was closer to the rela-tively pragmatic approach of the Eighth National Congress. Peking wall posters now report that in the Central Work Conference of October 1966, Mao said: "I was extremely discontented with that decision, but I could do nothing about it."[18] Whether or not the report is accu-rate, the existing evidence suggests that Mao gave up his State Chairmanship *not entirely* by his own choice. At the same time, it would be a grave mistake to in-terpret the incident either as a total loss of power on Mao's part, or as a sign of Mao's intention to make Liu Shao-ch'i his eventual heir. In the former case, the Chinese power structure is such that the final policy-making body is the Party, not the state. If Mao had totally lost his power, he could not have retained the Party Chairmanship. In the latter case, if Mao simply wanted to make Liu his heir-apparent, why should he choose that particular moment to make such a decision? Moreover, the history of the

CCP and its foreign counterparts has shown that one does not have to become the Chief of State first in order to even-tually become the Party boss.

Thus, the key to Mao's abdication seems to lie in his relationship with Liu, the composition of the entire Chinese power structure, and the type of power elements Mao is able to control effec-tively. We shall analyze these problems later. For the moment, we have to follow the events that came after the commune system and Mao's abdication of the State Chairmanship.

THE FIFTH RECTIFICATION AND MAO'S "FLIGHT" TO SHANGHAI

In the wake of these internal changes, Peking's relationship with Moscow dete-riorated rapidly. In June 1959, the Soviet Union breached its October 1957 defense agreement to supply China with a sam-ple of an atomic bomb and related data. A year later, it further tore up several hundred contracts with China and with-drew all its specialist personnel. Con-fronted by natural and man-made dis-asters, the CCP indeed faced the gravest situation since coming to power in 1949. Severe food shortages occurred, and peasant discontent became widespread. All this naturally affected the intellec-tuals and the morale of the PLA, which has its roots in the countryside.

In the Eighth CC Plenum of August 1959, Defense Minister P'eng Te-huai disagreed with the Party's commune and "red and expert" policies, which, in his opinion, had undermined the PLA's pro-fessional capability. But Mao was in-transigent. In consequence, P'eng was accused of being "right opportunist" and sent to work in a rural commune. Lin Piao, who succeeded P'eng as Defense Minister, promptly introduced a program for the "creative study and application of Mao Tse-tung's thought" and "bringing politics into the forefront." Both slogans have since become the catchwords of the Party—a resurgence of the cult of Mao.

The intellectual community, on the other hand, reacted unfavorably to the situation. Many prominent writers began to criticize Mao's misrule. Among them were Wu Han, Teng T'o and Liao Mo-sha, all important members of the Peking municipal authority. Using four periodicals and newspapers controlled by the powerful Peking Municipal Party Committee, they wrote, among others, three series of articles: on the story of a Ming dynasty official, Hai Jui; "Evening Chats at Yenshan"; and "Notes from Three-Family Village."[19] By employing a traditional Chinese method, *ying-she* (using precedents to reflect on the current scene), they indirectly attacked the increasing cult of Mao, the mismanagement of the economy, and the abuse of justice. They demanded: return to peasants of land illegally annexed under the commune system; rehabilitation of unfairly dismissed officials, notably P'eng Te-huai; and reversal of cases of wrongly imprisoned persons. Although most of these charges and demands can be justified within the CCP regime's own political and legal framework,[20] Mao's reply was to launch another rectification.

At the Tenth Plenum of the CC in September 1962, Mao returned to an active role in the day-to-day business of the Standing Committee (by abolishing the differentiation between the "first" and "second" lines of participation),[21] and urged a sharpening of the class struggle to cope with growing "bourgeois" influences.[22] This resulted in two mass movements: one was later termed the fifth rectification (since 1949) of un-

orthodox tendencies in the art and literary field; and the other, the socialist education movement in the rural areas. In both cases, the root of the problems appears to lie in Mao's commune policy, which created peasant misery, damaged the economy, and consequently induced the intellectuals' criticism.[23]

As the movements developed, Mao's line once again met with "rightist" resistance.[24] According to Ch'en Po-ta, Chief of the General Cultural Revolutionary Committee, in 1962 Teng Hsiao-p'ing suggested "to contract with individual households for the production" of certain products. In the following year, the question of the "first and second" lines was again brought up for discussion. "The Chairman retreated into the second line. This was an organization (Party) measure. Teng thought he had the decisive power in his hands. The dominant line of the entire Party is Chairman Mao's correct line. But Liu and Teng carried out their erroneous line by taking advantage of the time when Chariman Mao was taking a rest."[25] This means that in 1963–4 Liu and Teng again took charge of the CC's daily work. But before the end of 1964, Mao found something wrong with Liu-Teng's agricultural policy.[26] In January 1965, therefore, he called a national work conference of the Politburo to push his line of agricultural policy by issuing twenty-three articles for the socialist education movements in rural villages in order to "purify politics, ideology, organization, and economics."[27] However, by this time Mao "found Peking already under P'eng Chen's complete control." There was not even room for him "to put in a needle."[28] Whether or not someone in Peking really plotted against Mao's life is open to doubt. But indications are that Mao at least believed that his freedom of political activity was threatened in Peking.[29] In the summer of that year he left Peking for Shanghai, which was traditionally Chou En-lai's regional Party base.

THE BEGINNING OF AN OPEN POWER STRUGGLE

The reason for Mao's selection of Wu Han and his play as the official starting point of the revolution now becomes clear and logical. In the first place, Wu was a leading intellectual member of the Peking municipal authority and in his writings was closely associated with Teng T'o and Liao Mo-sha, the so-called "Trio." An attack on Wu would inevitably lead to his associates and then to their superior, P'eng Chen, Mayor of Peking and First Secretary of the Peking Municipal Party Committee. Secondly, once P'eng Chen was proved to be a leader of this "counter-revolutionary and revisionist" group, it would further lead to Liu Shao-ch'i, who had been P'eng Chen's political guardian for decades. Thirdly, the issues which Wu and his associates had used to criticize Mao are similar to those which Khrushchev had used to denounce Stalin, namely, the cult of personality, the mismanagement of the economy, and the abuse of justice. Rebuttal of these criticisms was not only necessary in order to remove their influences, but would also provide Mao with a convenient weapon to attack Liu's faction as Soviet revisionists, a label which enjoys tremendous popularity in mainland China.

Following Yao Wen-yuan's November 1965 criticism of Wu Han's play, Ch'i Pen-yu, a newly important member of the Maoist faction, demanded the study of history for the sake of the proletarian revolution.[30] Obviously, without realizing the seriousness of Yao's criticism

and the reason and power behind it, Teng T'o sent a telegram to the Shanghai Municipal Party Committee asking for an explanation. On December 13, he even called in students of higher-education schools in Peking to discuss Wu Han's play and defend his point of view. But the pressure was mounting. Wu Han finally made a self-criticism of his play on December 30, acknowledging his failure to apply Mao's theory of class struggle.[31] However, it was too late to avert his fate. An editorial note of *Jen-min Jih-pao* accompanying his self-criticism called for further debate of the case in order to get at the "truth."

The 1966 New Year's Day issue of *Jen-min Jih-pao* contained two messages from the Party. One was a call for more effective implementation of the Party's agricultural policy and the sharpening of class struggle; the other, an address to writers of the nation by Chou Yang, Deputy Director of the Party's Department of Propaganda, to intensify the fifth rectification. In the wake of these messages—which, as on earlier occasion, foreshadowed important impending events—more criticisms appeared dealing with Wu Han's play and the question of dynastic justice and legality. However, no mention was yet made of his associates, Teng T'o and Liao Mo-sha. In fact, on March 10, Sung Shih, Deputy Director of the Department of University Education under the Peking Municipal Party Committee, called a meeting of more than one thousand political instructors and commissars from Peking universities to try to offset the activities against the Trio. But sixteen days later on March 26, two incidents took place. Apparently confident of his power status within the Party, Chief of State Liu Shao-ch'i left Peking with his wife and Foreign Minister Ch'en Yi for a state visit to Pakistan and Afghanistan. In the afternoon of that same day, P'eng Chen delivered a speech of welcome to the visiting General Secretary of the Japanese Communist Party, Kenji Miyamoto, and immediately disappeared from the public scene.

Liu's departure provided the Maoist faction with an excellent opportunity to extract self-confessions (published in the April 16 issues of *Peking Jih-pao* and *Ch'ien-hsien*) from the Peking Municipal Party Committee, admitting guilt in the Trio's case. With this evidence, the PLA promptly—for the first time in the history of the People's Republic—interfered directly in a political struggle. Noting the existence of an "anti-Party black line" in the literary world and arguing its inevitable effect upon the effectiveness of the military, the PLA's official organ, *Chieh-fang-chün Pao,* in an editorial of April 18, 1966, flatly charged that the "enemies" were using unorthodox art and literature to corrode the PLA with the intention of destroying it. The editorial further alleged that this "black line" was basically a continuation of the "national defense literature" sponsored by Chou Yang and other Party literary workers in 1936 in support of the Party's policy to set up an "All-China United People's Government of National Defense."[32] Disregarding the fact that this policy was the basis from which Mao in 1935 developed the notion of "a people's republic,"[33] which served as the foundation of all his later works on the theory of the state, the PLA now identified Mao with Lu Hsün, supposedly a literary worker for the proletariat. Most other literary figures of the "national defense literature" period were linked with Wang Ming and Chou Yang—as rightists.

On the following day (April 19)—the next after the PLA's "declaration of war against the literary world"—Liu Shao-ch'i

returned to China. There was no publicized reception for him in Peking. He reemerged on the public scene, nine days after his return, to welcome a visiting Albanian delegation. In a 4000-word speech at the dinner party of April 28 for the Albanians, Liu made no reference whatsoever to Mao's name, Mao's thought, or the cultural revolution. In sharp contrast to this highly unusual phenomenon, Chou En-lai, in a 5000-word address at a welcome rally for the Albanians on the afternoon of April 30, made eleven references to the name and thought of Mao Tse-tung.

P'eng Chen's disappearance from the public scene after his March 26 speech of welcome to Miyamoto was an indication of the mounting tension in the struggle. He was not arrested until December 3, 1966. What happened during the interim? This leads us to the events after Liu's return to Peking.

THE DEVELOPMENT OF THE POWER STRUGGLE

The period from May to July 1966 was marked by tension and confusion, as well as an alleged move by Liu to "impeach" Mao. A sensational Yugoslav "eyewitness" report from Peking, widely translated in various Japanese and non-mainland Chinese newspapers,[34] asserted that in the beginning of June, Mao sent Lin Piao's troops into Peking to take over the leading mass media and to force the reorganization of the Peking Municipal Party Committee. In reaction, Liu's faction moved to impeach Mao by planning to call a plenum of the CC/CCP. On July 17, Lin's force took over the railway between Tientsin and Peking, and on the following day moved additional troops into the capital to subdue the pro-Liu garrison and public security forces and to arrest Liu's ally, Chief of General Staff Lo Jui-ch'ing, who had not appeared in public since November 1965.[35] At this point, according to the same report, Teng Hsiao-p'ing changed his mind. Instead of supporting Liu, he accepted Mao's instruction not to convene the CC plenum scheduled for July 21 by Liu's faction. After Mao had the Peking situation completely under his control, he returned on July 28 and called the Eleventh Plenum of the CC four days later.

The validity of this Yugoslav account is highly questionable. According to Liu Shao-ch'i's October self-criticism,[36] and an official Red Guard newspaper of Peking University,[37] the date of Mao's return to Peking was July 18, instead of July 28. Moreover, a reliable Japanese source indicates that Lo Jui-ch'ing was not arrested until December 23, 1966. Such being the case, Liu's "plot" to impeach Mao at the allegedly abortive CC Plenum of July 21 can hardly be true. However, during this crucial period from May to July, Lin Piao did openly threaten to use force. Earlier in May, Yao Wen-yuan—Mao's spokesman in Shanghai—implicitly charged that the real intention of Liu's group was to replace Chou En-lai with P'eng Chen as the Premier and to rehabilitate ex-Defense Minister P'eng Te-huai and thus to restore his "revisionist" line against Lin Piao's program.[38] On June 4, the Party Center announced the reorganization of the Peking Municipal Committee and two days later the official organ of the PLA issued a statement which threatened to use force if necessary in order to carry out Mao's line.[39]

In the midst of these developments, Mao instructed Nieh Yuan-tzu, a teaching assistant of philosophy at Peking University, to write wall posters criticizing the University's President, Lu P'ing,

and others.[40] But Nieh's wall poster, being the first of the kind in the power struggle (later praised by Mao as the "Manifesto of the Peking People's Commune in the 1960's")[41] met with great resistance from the pro-Liu faction. In fact, many of the wall posters, and some of the Red Guards that emerged simultaneously under Mao's direction, came under the control of pro-Liu students. At the same time, Liu himself, still in charge of the "first line" of the Party Center, sent out so-called "work teams" consisting of Party cadres instead of "Maoist masses" to conduct the cultural revolution in educational institutions, with his wife, Wang Kuang-mei, at the head of the Ch'ing-hua University team. A week after Mao's return to Peking (July 24), he abolished all Liu's work teams and called a Central Work Conference which decided to convene the Eleventh Plenum of the CC on August 1, the birthday of the PLA.[42]

Backed by the army, Mao demoted Liu from the second to the eighth position in the Party, while T'ao Chu was raised from a regional Party chief to fourth place on the CC, and Teng Hsiao-p'ing remained in his previous position. Lin Piao became the second in command, and Chou En-lai the third. This arrangement, however, was temporary. On August 5, when the Plenum was still in session, Mao personally wrote "My First Wall Poster, Bombing the [Liu-Teng] Headquarters!"[43] It called the attention of all "comrades" to the importance of Nieh Yuan-tzu's wall posters; implicitly attacked the "Liu-Teng line" as a reactionary bourgeois line; identified this line with "White Terror,"[44] and related the "mistakes" of the Liu-Teng line to the "rightist" tendencies in the 1962 Tenth Plenum of the CC and in the preliminary drafting of the "Twenty Three Articles" for the socialist education movement in 1964. Following this, the Eleventh Plenum (on August 8) adopted sixteen articles as a theoretical and practical basis for the revolution. The decision called for permanent "cultural revolutionary committees" at all administrative levels, and the application of Mao's mass line, class line, and theory of contradictions. But it cautioned against legal punishment of the rightists before the end of the revolution, except for "active counter-revolutionaries." However, as the Maoist Red Guards' action became more and more violent and the resistance stronger and stronger, Mao in October convened the momentous Central Work Conference. In Lin Piao's words, this was a continuation of the Eleventh CC Plenum.

At the Conference, Mao reviewed the past and made two other important points to his audience: (1) the intention of his Red Guards was not to overthrow those criticized but to teach them; (2) Liu and Teng were not the only persons to blame, "The Party Center also has the responsibility" for all the mistakes made in Party lines.[45] While Mao's address left sufficient room for a compromise, it also expressly named Liu and Teng as the principal culprits. Thus, Lin Piao, Ch'en Po-ta, Chiang Ch'ing, and other supporters of Mao all accused Liu and Teng of being leaders of the reactionary bourgeois line.[46] Relatively quiet at this stormy session were Chou En-lai and T'ao Chu.[47] However, the pressure on Liu was extremely high and he made a self-criticism. He admitted mistakes, among others, in the execution of the agricultural cooperative policy in 1951 and 1955, his "right-leaning" in 1962 and 1964, and his replacement of Mao's mass line by work teams in the summer of 1966. In reviewing the causes of all these and other mistakes, he further admitted his failure to understand "the profound significance of the cultural revolution," to completely change his "bourgeois world outlook," and to learn and appreciate "the meaning of Chairman Mao's thought."[48]

Whether or not initiated by Liu's faction, the so-called "Black Wind of December" came soon after the conference. Wall posters called: "Long Live Liu Shao-ch'i!" Students criticized Lin Piao for his lack of theoretical achievements and his outright flattering of Mao Tse-tung.[49] Violence and armed clashes occurred in many places, including Peking.[50] To warn the resisting forces, four top members of Liu's faction (P'eng Chen, Lo Jui-ch'ing, Lu Ting-i, and Yang Shang-kung) were subjected to open mass humiliation and trials in January 1967. Liu and his wife were also forced to face personally the Red Guards' criticism. This worsened the situation. More violence occurred in the country. In response, Mao declared an open "struggle for the seizure of power" and announced a program of suppression of counter-revolutionaries under the "temporary power organizations"—the revolutionary committees consisting of representatives of the masses, cadres, and military personnel.[51]

CONCLUSIONS

The Chinese Communist power structure contains five elements: the ideology, the Party, the state, the economy, and the army. The ideology is the guide line of the Party, which supervises the state. The economy, in a totalitarian system, cannot develop without the Party and the state. Nor can it decide the *immediate* outcome of a power struggle. Consequently, it is the army—a traditional element of Chinese politics—that is the decisive element in the present power struggle.

A little over ten years ago when Mao accepted objective circumstances and retreated into the "second line" by not attending the daily work of the CC, and later in 1958 when he decided to resign from the State Chairmanship, he was certainly confident that his power status would not be impaired and his line altered. The reason for this is not difficult to see. First, he had the control of the army and retained the supreme authority of ideology. Secondly, all the men in charge of the "first line" of the Party, the state, and the economy (Liu Shao-ch'i, Teng Hsiao-p'ing, Chou En-lai, and Ch'en Yün respectively) had been his faithful servants for decades. Thirdly, under the arrangement of the new power center, the four leaders mentioned above were not expected to form an alliance against Mao or his line, but to work independently, check on one another, and coordinate their activities through the "second line"—Mao himself. Fourthly, Mao's relationship with Liu had for long been very intimate. As Chang Kuo-t'ao has pointed out, they discussed almost everything, official or private, with each other. So when Mao needed a man to take charge of the daily executive work and perhaps eventually to become his successor, Liu seemed the ideal candidate because of his personal relationship with Mao and his prestige and strength in the Party.

But the events in the past ten years have not been to Mao's liking. Faced with the harsh realities of the economy, Liu, Teng, and Ch'en Yün came closer to one another in their views. During the dark years from 1959 to 1961, they allowed the operation of a limited free market, the restitution of small plots to peasants, and the contracting of certain production with individual peasant households—all this being called, in Chinese jargon, the system of *san-tzu i-pao*. Although it was largely due to this relatively pragamtic line that the economy began to recover in 1962, in Mao's view it violated his policy—complete socialization of the economy. Thus, he abolished the "first line" in 1962 and urged a sharpening of the class struggle. However, in the following two years, he had "to take a rest," as Ch'en Po-ta termed it. This put Liu and Teng back in charge of the daily work again. Late in 1964, when Mao instructed Liu and others to draft the "Twenty Three Articles," he found they had all deviated from his policy and therefore become "revisionists." Consequently, there came the revolution and the power struggle.

Apparently, the majority of the CC members still share Liu's relatively pragmatic approach to the economy. Because of this, Mao is unable to convene the long overdue Ninth National Congress of the CCP and the National People's Congress to discuss issues and if need be, to impeach Liu and other undesirable members of the CC/CCP, including P'eng Chen. On the other hand, Mao is in control of the situation and may eventually win the struggle with the continued support of the majority of the PLA. But, though the army can win a battle, it cannot run a party and a state, let alone the economy. Thus, the question comes back to the problem of the loyalty of the cadres (the bureaucracy). Mao is undoubtedly aware of this,[52] and knows that Liu's strength lies precisely among the cadres. Viewed from this angle, and in light of Mao's October 1966 address to the Central Work Conference, the possibility of an eventual compromise still cannot be ruled out. It seems more likely however (at least to this writer) that Liu will lose his power but be spared —to live out his days like another Wang Ming.

Notes

1. Yao was then Editor-in-Chief of the Shanghai *Chieh-fang jih-pao,* and his comment was reprinted in *Jen-min Jih-pao* (hereinafter cited as JMJP), Peking, November 30, 1965, pp. 5-6.
2. See the editorial of *Hung-ch'i,* No. 9, 1966, pp. 31-34.
3. An English translation of the report is reprinted in Alex Inkeles and Kent Geiger, *Soviet Society* (Boston, 1961), pp. 263-295.
4. The four Vice Chairmen were Liu Shao-ch'i, Chou En-lai, Chu Te, and Ch'en Yün.
5. In the Fifth Plenum of the Eighth CC/CCP (May, 1958), Lin Piao was elected as Fifth Vice Chairman of the CC and thus brought the membership of the Standing Committee to seven.
6. Address to the Central Work Conference of October 1966, *Yomiuri* (in Japanese), Tokyo, January 7, p. 3. Hereinafter cited as Mao's October 1966 Adress.
7. For a reference to these charges, see "One Hundred Examples of Liu Shao-ch'i's Statements Against Mao Tse-tung's Thought," *Ching-kang-shan,* Peking, February 1, 1967, p. 6.
8. "The Real Rightist Face of China's No. 1 Counter-Revolutionary Revisionist Liu Shao-ch'i in the 1957 Anti-Rightist Struggle," *Tung-fang-hung,* Peking, January 4, 1967, pp. 4, 2.
9. Mao Tse-tung, "On the Correct Handling of Contradictions Among the People," in the 1958 *Jen-min Shou-ts'e* (hereinafter cited as JMST) (Peking), pp. 9, 10.
10. Those who led the ceremony to pledge such allegiance to the Party were President of the Chinese Academy of Sciences Kuo Mo-jo, ex-President of the Supreme People's Court Shen Chün-ju, and then Minister of Public Health Li Te-ch'üan. See *Kuang-min Jih-pao* (hereinafter cited as KMJP), Peking, March 17, 1958, p. 1.
11. For reference to these measures, see the following documents and reports: CC/CCP Directive of May 10, 1957; CC/CCP Directive of August 8, 1957; CC/CCP Directive of September 12, 1957; all in the 1958 JMST, pp.

43-45. A summary of the debate on the policy of "red and expert" by Chiang Nan-hsiang, President of Ch'ing-hua University, is in KMJP, January 5, 1958, p. 1.
12. In the 1957 JMST, pp. 9-26, especially p. 21.
13. See P'eng Chen's three reports on the work of the NPC's Standing Committee, dated July 16, 1955, June 16, 1956, and June 28, 1957 respectively.
14. Both statements are in *Ching-kang-shan,* *supra* note 7. For further reference to similar statements of Mao and Liu's "political report" to the Eighth National Congress of the CCP, *supra* note 12, at pp. 14-17; Mao's essay "On the Question of Agricultural Cooperation," 1955, any edition.
15. For reference to the original version of the commune system, see The Department of Marxism-Leninism, Chinese People's University, *Lun Jen-min Kung-she Yü Kung-ch'an Chu-I* (On the People's Commune and Communism) (Peking, 1958).
16. Both decisions are in the 1959 JMST, Vol. 1, pp. 39-45.
17. In *idem,* p. 39.
18. *Central Daily News,* Taipei, January 6, 1967, p. 1, quoting a Japanese dispatch from Peking.
19. These series of articles are now all reprinted in Hong Kong, Taipei, and Tokyo.
20. For example, in contrast to the advanced agricultural producers cooperatives, the commune system has never been officially adopted by the National People's Congress or its Standing Committee.
21. See Mao's October 1966 address.
22. "Communiqué of the Tenth Plenum of the Eighth CC/CCP," JMJP, September 29, 1962, p. 1.
23. At the 1962 "West Chamber Conference" discussing economic policy, Ch'en Yün was quoted as saying that as a result of Mao's "Great Leap Forward" policy, agricultural production dropped sharply, the general populace did not have enough food to eat, and the area of good land was "reduced by several hundred million *mou.*" In *Tung-fang-hung,* Peking, January 27, 1967, p. 4.
24. See the editorial of *Hung-ch'i,* No. 11, 1966, pp. 19-21.
25. See Ch'en Po-ta's October 25, 1966 address to the Central Work Conference, in *Koming Kung-jen Pao,* Peking, January 12, 1967, p. 3.

26. In Mao's October 1966 address.

27. The text of these articles is published in the Japanese journal, *Sekai,* Tokyo, February, 1967, pp. 123-129.

28. In Mao's October 1966 address.

29. For a discussion of this matter, see Nakajima Mineo, "The Truth of Mao Tse-tung's Escape from Peking," *Chuo Koron,* Tokyo, March 1967, pp. 118-143.

30. In *Hung-ch'i,* No. 13, 1965, pp. 14-22.

31. "On My Own Criticism of 'Hai Hui Dismissed from Office,'" JMJP, December 30, 1965, pp. 5-6.

32. Inasmuch as the revolution takes on the form of an ideological dispute, it is important to note that the policy of setting up an "All-China United People's Government of National Defense" was first enunciated by Wang Ming in line with a 1935 resolution of the Comintern to organize a "people's front." See "Resolution of the Seventh Comintern Congress on Facism, Working-Class Unity, and the Tasks of the Comintern (August 20, 1935)," in Jane Degras, *The Communist International 1919-1943 Documents,* Vol. 3 (London, 1965), p. 364; Wang Ming's statement in *idem,* pp. 356-357. For reference to the original documents on the question of "national defense literature," see a rare collection, *Kuo-fang Wen-hsüeh Lun-chan* (Debate on National Defense Literature) (Shanghai, 1936).

33. Mao Tse-tung "On the Tactics of Fighting Japanese Imperialism," *Selected Works* (in Chinese) (Peking, 1966), pp. 137, 151-155.

34. See, for example, *Central Daily News,* Taipei, December 29, 1966, p. 1.

35. Liu's alliance with Lo Jui-ch'ing, who used to be considered Mao's faithful aide, is confirmed by a document published six years before the present revolution. See Commission for the Investigation and Study of Chinese Communist Personnel Data, *Fei-wei Chung-yao Jen-shih Tiao-ch'a* (Study of Important Chinese Communist Personnel) (Taipei, 1959), p. 354.

36. The text of Liu's self-criticism is in *Mainichi,* Tokyo (Japanese edition), January 28 and 29, p. 2 Hereinafter cited as Liu's October 1966 Self-Criticism.

37. *Hsin-pei-ta* (Peking), January 24, 1967, p. 4.

38. Yao Wen-yuan, "Comment on 'Three-Family Village,'" JMJP, May 11, 1966, pp. 1, 3-4; reprinted from *Wen-hui Pao,* Shanghai, May 10, 1966.

39. In KMJP, June 6, 1966, pp. 1, 3-4; reprinted from *Chieh-fang-chün Pao* of the same date.

40. See Mao's October 1966 address. Neih's wall poster first appeared on May 25 and was then published in JMJP, June 2, 1966, upon Mao's personal instruction. See K'ang Sheng's Speech at the People's Great Hall, September 8, 1966, in *Current Background,* No. 819, Hong Kong, March 10, 1967, p. 23.

41. See the editorial of *Hung-ch'i,* No. 3, 1967, p. 17.

42. In Liu's October 1966 Self-Criticism.

43. The text of this poster came from a private source. Its key part was quoted by Lin Piao in his October 25, 1966 address to the Central Work Conference and published in *Ko-ming Kung-jen Pao,* Peking, January 12, 1967, p. 3.

44. In the Chinese context, "White Terror" was a term used early in the Kiangsi Soviet period to identify it with the Nationalist suppression of the Communists.

45. In Mao's October 1966 address.

46. For references, see Lin Piao's address to the Central Work Conference of October 1966, in *Yomiuri,* January 10, 1967, p. 6; *Ko-ming Kung-jen Pao,* Peking, January 12, 1967, p. 3.

47. T'ao was subsequently denounced by the Maoist faction for his "double-crossing" dealings with both Mao and Liu. For reference to a list of his "guilt," see *Hsin-pei-ta,* Peking, January 24, 1967, p. 4.

48. In Liu's October 1966 Self-Criticism.

49. In *Ching-kang-shan,* Peking, December 22, 1966, p. 4.

50. For reference, *Hsin-pei-ta,* Peking, January 24, 1967, p. 3.

51. See the editorial of *Hung-ch'i,* No. 3, 1967, pp. 13-18.

52. See "Must Correctly Treat the Cadres," editorial, *Hung-Ch'i,* No. 4, 1967, pp. 5-11.

46. THE ROOT OF CHINA'S CULTURAL REVOLUTION:

THE FEUD BETWEEN MAO TSE-TUNG AND LIU SHAO-CH'I

CHU-YÜAN CHENG

Under the cloak of the Great Proletarian Cultural Revolution, the intraparty struggle in Communist China is now entering its third year. In view of the continued intensification of the Maoist group's campaign to overthrow Liu Shao-ch'i, Chairman of the People's Republic of China, a final showdown between the two powerful factions in the top hierarchy of the Chinese Communist Party seems inevitable. What are the basic causes of the changed relationship between Mao and Liu, or, to phrase it more precisely, what are the underlying reasons for Mao's shift of favor from Liu Shao-ch'i to Defense Minister Lin Piao? The answer to this question will help to explain the origin of the Cultural Revolution.

During the two decades after World War II, Liu Shao-ch'i was regarded as Chairman Mao's right-hand man, an enthusiastic supporter and devoted preacher of Mao's doctrine. Until the summer of 1966 he had always been referred to in official statements as Mao's

From *Orbis*, Vol. XI, No. 4 (Winter 1968), pp. 1160-78. Reprinted by permission. The author is with the Center for Chinese Studies, The University of Michigan.

"closest comrade-in-arms"—a term now used exclusively to describe Lin Piao. Today, however, available post-1945 records and new revelations published in Red Guard newspapers during the past year make it evident that Liu and Mao have been at variance for at least half the period of their association in positions of authority. Although Liu, like Marshal P'eng Teh-huai, former Defense Minister, probably had no intention of ousting Mao, his faith in Mao's leadership wavered, and since 1956 he has been reluctant to promote Mao's personality cult. In recent years, while he continued to support Mao as the Party's supreme leader, he put forward a series of policies conflicting with Maoist philosophy. His behavior thus seriously challenged Mao's megalomania and led to his demotion in 1966 from his esteemed position as Mao's chosen successor. The issue of succession has developed into a titanic power struggle which underlies the current Cultural Revolution.

THE PERSONALITY CULT FACTOR

At the heart of the struggle is the question of the personality cult of Mao Tse-tung. Even before his conquest of the Chinese mainland, Mao had regarded himself as a hero without precedent in Chinese history and the ablest communist theoretician since Marx and Lenin. His egotism was fully displayed in his masterpiece, a poem on snow, written in 1945, in which, after critically reviewing the great heroes in Chinese history, he concluded:

To find men truly great and noble-hearted,
We must look here in the present.[1]

Liu Shao-ch'i fully understood Mao's mentality and temperament. He won Mao's favor when, in 1945, as Secretary of the Chinese Communist Party (CCP) Central Committee, he incorporated the "Thoughts of Mao Tse-tung" in the Party Constitution, as its guiding doctrine. Under his initiation and manipulation, the new constitution adopted by the Seventh Party Congress on June 11, 1945 specifically and prominently stipulated: "The CCP guides its entire program according to the 'Thoughts of Mao Tse-tung'—the teachings that unite the theories of Marxism-Leninism with the practices of Chinese revolution." In Liu's report delivered to this Congress on May 14, he hailed Mao as "not only the greatest revolutionary and statesman in Chinese history, but also the greatest theoretician and scientist who dauntlessly led the entire Party and the entire Chinese people to wage struggles that shook the world, and whose theoretical attainments and moral courage were of the highest."[2] He proposed that the Party Constitution state that it be the duty of every party member to study Mao's "Thoughts." Liu's effort not only helped to establish Mao as an unchallenged leader, but also promoted Mao's personality cult. To reward him, Mao selected him as the Acting

Chairman of the CCP when he himself went to Chungking for peace talks with the Nationalist Government in August 1945.

During the period 1945 to 1954 Liu's continuous loyalty to Mao and his enthusiastic promotion of "Thoughts" showed no signs of change. With Mao's support, he steadily advanced his influence in the Party's Central Committee, the trade unions and the Communist Youth League. In 1954 he became Chairman of the National People's Congress, Communist China's highest law-making body.

Liu's Developing Opposition

The turning point in the Mao-Liu relationship came in 1956. Perhaps under the influence of the de-Stalinization campaign instituted at the Twentieth Congress of the Communist Party of the Soviet Union (CPSU), or perhaps due to Liu's growing discontent with Mao's paternalism, the Eighth Party Congress of the CCP, held in September of that year, demonstrated a remarkable change in attitude toward the personality cult. The "Thoughts of Mao Tse-tung" were deleted from the 1956 Party Constitution. Liu Shao-ch'i, on behalf of the Central Committee, delivered a Political Report to the Congress in which he gave credit to Mao's "correct leadership," in very general terms, but his former zeal in extolling Mao and the "Thoughts" was apparently abating. Instead, he openly pointed out the many drawbacks in the party system, particularly its failure to achieve proper collective leadership. He demanded that "party organization at all levels without exception should adhere to the Party's principle of collective leadership and broaden democratic life within the Party."[3] He further insisted that in order to achieve collective leadership and party unity in deed and not in name alone, "every leader must examine and consider opinions contrary to his own."[4] Compared with his earlier remarks, such statements definitely reflect Liu's changing attitude toward Mao's leadership.

In 1957 official reports disclosed that Liu opposed Mao's "Hundred Flowers Movement"—a new pattern initiated to encourage Chinese intellectuals to speak freely—and that, in response to the pressures exerted by Liu and P'eng Chen, who was both Secretary General of the National People's Congress and Mayor of Peking, Mao had to launch the "anti-rightist" campaign to suppress dissent among the intellectuals.[5]

The institution of the communes and the Great Leap Forward in 1958 marked a new stage in the Mao-Liu relationship. Ostensibly, Liu continued to support Mao's radical line, but in several individual cases he departed from Mao's position. After he replaced Mao as Chairman of the Chinese People's Republic (CPR) in 1959, his attitude toward Mao's leadership changed conspicuously. In an article celebrating the tenth anniversary of the CPR, Liu stressed that "The ten year victory of the Chinese people is the victory of Marxism-Leninism and the victory of the leadership of the Chinese Communist Party."[6] No particular credit went to Mao Tse-tung or his "Thoughts."

Liu's changing attitude toward Mao's works had considerable effect on the top party and army hierarchy. The secret journal of the Army, *Kung-tso Tung-hsün* (*The Works Bulletin*), which was circulated among high-ranking army officers and which became available in the United States in 1963, revealed the prevalence of anti-Maoism in the Army during the post-1959 period. Some military

leaders excluded the study of Chairman Mao's works from their programs and denied the systematic nature of the "Thoughts." Some even stated openly that the classical writings of Marx, Engels, Lenin and Stalin are theoretical, while other writings (implying Mao's) are not.[7] Marshal Lo Jung-huan, a former member of the CCP Politburo and Mao's top aide in supervising the Army, disclosed that the man who actively opposed the study of Mao's works was General Tan Chen, former director of the Army's General Political Department. Lo also divulged that "In the past, some persons said that Chairman Mao's works dealt only with practical matters, having no theoretical significance."[8]

In 1961, after Marshal Lin Piao launched a campaign for the Army to study Mao's writings, Liu Shao-ch'i presented his view that the Party needed to initiate a new campaign for studying (1) basic theories of Marxism-Leninism about socialist revolution and construction; (2) the theoretical and practical problems of socialism in China as expounded by Comrade Mao Tse-tung on the basis of Marxist-Leninist principles; (3) the general line and other policies formulated by the Party Central Committee; and (4) experiences of the Soviet Union and other fraternal countries in economic construction.[9] Liu had thus identified Mao's works as only one item among a number worth studying.

In 1962, when Liu printed a revision of his own *How to Be a Good Communist* —a collection of lectures originally delivered in 1939 in Yenan—he deliberately avoided mentioning the "Thoughts of Mao Tse-tung." Instead he re-emphasized that "All Party members should learn from the thinking of Marx and Lenin and strive to be their worthy pupils."[10] In a speech in May 1963 he again referred to the "necessity of learning from the theories of Marx, Engels, Lenin and Stalin," without mentioning Mao's works. In 1964, he allegedly remarked in a letter to a prominent party leader, "We should not regard Mao Tse-tung's works and speeches as dogmas, just as we should not regard Marxist-Leninist theories as dogmas."[11]

Liu's open statements since 1956 have consistently indicated that although he admits the practical value of Mao's works, he denies their universal application. According to Liu, their ingenuity and creativity cannot be compared with that of Marx and Lenin. Nor can Mao's works he regarded as "the acme of Marxism-Leninism," as they have been extolled within the last three years by Lin Piao, Ch'en Po-ta and other Maoist leaders. Until June 1966, even though many top officials had joined the chorus of sycophancy directed by Lin Piao toward Mao and his "Thoughts," Liu was reported to have asserted that "Marxism-Leninism will certainly continue to develop and it cannot stop at the stage of the Thoughts of Mao Tse-tung. . . . Those people who take such a view that 'TMTT' is the acme of Marxism-Leninism are erroneous and mechanomorphic."[12]

Lin Piao's Advance

In contrast to Liu's reluctance to heap praise upon Mao, Lin Piao has exploited every means of winning favor. Ever since the day he replaced P'eng Teh-huai as Defense Minister, his main strategy has been to ingratiate himself through intensive propagation of Mao's "Thoughts." Immediately after he was named Minister of Defense, he published an article entitled "Raise High the Red Banner of the Party's General Line and the Military Thoughts of Mao Tse-tung."[13] Of the forty or more articles marking the CPR's tenth anniversary, Lin's was the only one mentioning Mao's thoughts in the title.

Then at an enlarged session of the Military Committee of the CCP in October 1960, one year after he had gained full control of the army leadership, Lin launched a campaign for intensive study of the "Thoughts." This conference was regarded as a historical event in the Army. According to the Army's secret journal, the main function of the meeting was to criticize the "bourgeois military line" advocated by P'eng Teh-huai and Huang K'e-ch'eng (former Chief of the General Staff of the Army) and to accept Lin Piao's new program for strengthening the military's political and ideological efforts. Lin praised Mao as "a great contemporary Marxist-Leninist" and made the following statement: "Mao Tse-tung's Thoughts (TMTT) developed and improved Marxism-Leninism through concrete practice in the Chinese revolution. . . . Mao Tse-tung's Thoughts are the guiding force of the Chinese people's revolution and of socialist construction, a powerful ideological weapon against imperialism, revisionism and dogmatism." He called on the Army to "raise high the Red Flag of the TMTT, to become thoroughly acquainted with it, and to insist on its supremacy in the conduct of all affairs." It was also disclosed by the Army secret journal that the draft of the resolution of this conference was revised by Mao himself,[14] signifying Mao's strong desire for a revival of his personality cult in the Army and in the Party.

The tone of Lin Piao's remarks in 1960 amplified the words of Liu Shao-ch'i in the 1945 Party Congress, and just as Liu had won Mao's favor then, Lin now became the favorite. Since the 1960 army conference Lin Piao has been openly praised as the man who "has creatively applied the TMTT"—the highest encomium one can possibly acquire in contemporary China. The slogan "give prominence to politics" or "put politics to the fore"—a means of propagating "Thoughts" advocated by Lin—soon became the fundamental guideline of the regime's propaganda. Another of Lin's slogans, "Read the works of Chairman Mao, follow his teaching and act according to his instructions," has become the most popular catchword in recent years.

Beneficiaries and Victims of the Purge

That the personality cult issue has been at the core of the power struggle is borne out by a review of the background of those major figures who have been promoted with Lin Piao during the current purge. Without exception, those who increased their authority and power had been closely associated with Lin in the adulation of Mao's "Thoughts." Chou En-lai was credited by Marshal Lo Jung-huan as the man who defined "Thoughts" as Marxism-Leninism, in an epoch in which the collapse of the imperialist system is being accelerated while the victory of socialism is constantly advancing.[15] Ch'en Po-ta, who leads the present Cultural Revolution, has vigorously praised "Thoughts" for the past two decades, and in 1958 glorified it as "the decisive factor in every aspect of the revolutionary struggle and socialist construction." In 1966 Ch'en coined a new title for Mao: "Our great leader, great teacher, supreme commander and great helmsman." Since August 1966 Ch'en has been promoted from an alternate member of the CCP Politburo to a full member in the Standing Committee and now ranks fifth in the top party hierarchy.

In contrast to these rising stars, the victims of the purge have been singled out for the commonly alleged "crime" of opposition to or contempt for Mao's "Thoughts." Some are accused of "waving the Red Flag to oppose the Red Flag" or "opposing 'TMTT' under the cloak of 'TMTT.'" The "crime" committed by Teng Hsiao-p'ing, the Party Secretary General, was this statement he was reported to have made in a speech at a party conference: "The personality cult has been reflected in our Party life and social life. The 20th Soviet Party Congress has the great merit of teaching us how dangerous is the glorification of the individual. Our task is, therefore, to oppose any excessive veneration of an individual."[16] Chou Yang, the outspoken former Deputy Director of the CCP Propaganda Department and a veteran leader of left-wing writers after the 1930's, was called a "leader of the black threat in literature and arts who has been an opponent of 'TMTT' for 30 years." Chou was also identified as the man who hindered the large-scale publication of Mao's works. It was alleged that under his guidance, in 1962 for instance, only about 50,000 sets of the Selected Works of Mao Tse-Tung were printed, while 140,000 sets of The Dream of the Red Chamber were published in the same year.[17]

The "crime" committed by Lo Jui-ch'ing, former Chief of the General Staff of the Army (1959-1966) and one of the major victims in the early stage of the Cultural Revolution, was his open opposition to the cult of personality. Yang Ch'eng-wu, the man who succeeded Lo as Acting Chief of Staff, revealed recently that after the Twentieth Congress of the CPSU in 1956 Lo had stated specifically that he was opposed to "mentioning personal genius again." According to Yang, "Lo apparently used the same technique adopted by Khrushchev against Stalin to oppose our great leader Chairman Mao." In 1960, when Lin Piao suggested that the Army regard Mao's works as its supreme guiding doctrine, Lo refused the proposal, stating that such a practice "does not conform with our State system."[18]

The same accusation was pinned on other purged leaders. Lu Ting-i, Director of the CCP Propaganda Department for two decades, was impeached for ridiculing as "oversimplification," "vulgarization" and "pragmatism" the campaign to apply Mao's works to the conduct of all affairs. Li Ching-ch'uan, a former full member of the CCP Politburo and the First Secretary of the CCP Southwest Bureau, was charged for warning his subordinates against saying that "TMTT is the peak of Marxism-Leninism in the current era."[19] Both Lu and Li have been continuously humiliated by the Maoist group since August 1966.

Nothing is more revealing of the central issue than this editorial in the Army's mouthpiece, *Chieh-fang Chun-pao* (*Liberation Army Daily*), which was published immediately after the purge of P'eng Chen:

The attitude towards Mao Tse-tung's Thoughts, whether to accept it or resist it, to support it or oppose it, to love it warmly or be hostile to it, this is the touchstone to test and the watershed between true revolution and counterrevolution, between Marxism-Leninism and revisionism. He who wants to make revolution must accept Mao Tse-tung's Thoughts and act in accordance with it. A counterrevolutionary will inevitably disparage, distort, resist, attack, and oppose Mao Tse-tung's Thoughts.[20]

Intensified Veneration of Mao

One conspicuous feature of the current Cultural Revolution is that millions of copies of classical books have been burned and the publication of most periodicals has been suspended in order to concentrate all available facilities on printing Mao's works. According to an official report, ten million sets of the *Selected Works of Mao Tse-tung* were published during the first sixteen years of communist control. Under the new campaign the regime had printed fifteen million sets by the end of 1966, and another eighty-six million sets in 1967.[21] Such extensive circulation of a single publication is unprecedented in China. Today the nation's broadcasting network spends more than two-thirds of its air time reading from the book *Quotations from Chairman Mao Tse-tung*. The Red Guards are required "to take as their highest obligation the study, dissemination, application and defense of 'TMTT.'"

It seems plausible that Mao, having regarded himself as a great theoretician in line with Marx, Engels, Lenin and Stalin, was particularly sensitive to the posthumous purge of Stalin in 1956. The de-Stalinization issue in the Soviet Union affected him deeply and became the basic cause of the Sino-Soviet rupture. His frustration and latent fears were compounded by developments in China soon afterward. The 1957 Hundred Flowers Movement in which thousands of Chinese intellectuals openly condemned the CCP, and the 1959 intraparty debate when Marshal P'eng Teh-huai attacked Mao's radical programs, greatly dismayed him. So that there might be no posthumous purge in his case, Mao evidently decided to eliminate any person of influence in China who put forth opinions contrary to his own. Mao's megalomania makes him particularly vulnerable to sycophants and hostile to those reluctant to venerate him. There was no evidence that either P'eng Teh-huai or Liu Shao-ch'i harbored intentions of grasping Mao's power; rather, they hoped to influence Mao toward endorsing more pragmatic policies.

DIVERGENCE ON POLICIES

Liu Shao-ch'i and Mao differ on at least three major aspects of CCP policy in domestic affairs.

Class Struggle

First, their concepts of class struggle are different. According to Mao, throughout the historical period of proletarian revolution and proletarian dictatorship, throughout the historical transition from capitalism to communism, there is always class struggle between the proletariat and the bourgeoisie as well as between the socialist and capitalist systems. Mao conceives that even after its elimination the bourgeois class still retains its influence on society; that the customs of the old society remain, and that there is a spontaneous tendency toward capitalism among the peasants and small producers. This class struggle inevitably finds expression within the Party. Pressure from foreign imperialism and the existence of bourgeois influence at home constitute the source of revisionist ideas within the Party.[22] In 1957 Mao warned that "The class struggle is by no means over." In September 1962, at the Tenth Plenary Session of the CCP Central Committee, he called for the whole Party "never to forget class struggle." Under his initiative, a nationwide socialist education campaign was launched for the purpose of repressing the spread of any viewpoints on economic and ideological matters similar to Khrushchev's "revisionism."

But in the opinion of Liu Shao-ch'i,

Teng Hsiao-p'ing, and certain other party leaders, class struggle cannot be carried on indefinitely; after the elimination of capitalists in the urban areas and landlords and rich peasants in the rural districts, it should be regarded as basically concluded. In his 1956 Political Report to the CCP Eighth Party Congress Liu pointed out that with the "exception of a few localities, the feudal landlords have been eliminated as a class. The rich peasant class is also being eliminated. Landlords and rich peasants who used to exploit the peasants are being reformed. They are making a fresh start in life and becoming people who live by their own work. The national bourgeois elements are in the process of being transformed from exploiters into working people." According to Liu, "The task confronting the Party now is to build China into a great socialist country as quickly as possible."[23] Such counter-appraisals of class struggle bear great consequences on almost every front.

Economic Affairs

The second vital difference in viewpoint between Liu and Mao was expressed in the guidelines and policies they advocated for the development of the national economy, especially the crucial problem of agricultural collectivization. Mao foresaw a spontaneous tendency for the peasantry to develop toward capitalism in the countryside: "If the position is not held by socialism," he said, "capitalism will definitely occupy it." Therefore, he thought it urgent to complete the process of collectivization as soon as possible. In early 1955, when collectivization caused widespread peasant resistance, the majority of leaders in the CCP Central Committee recommended a slowdown in the program, and, with the approval of Liu Shao-ch'i, 200,000 agricultural cooperatives were dissolved. Mao moved against the tide and called a meeting of the secretaries of the provincial, municipal and district party committees on July 31, 1955. He severely attacked those party leaders who suggested a deceleration for "tottering along like a woman with bound feet, always complaining that others are going too fast."[24] Overriding the decision of the CCP Central Committee, he demanded a 30 per cent increase in the number of agricultural cooperatives to be set up that year. Mao's radical policy in 1955 eventually culminated in the hasty establishment of people's communes in 1958.

In opposition to Mao's view, Liu Shao-ch'i, in a 1951 All-China Propaganda Work Conference, condemned for their "utopian agricultural socialism" those people in the Party who suggested that socialization of agriculture could be achieved simply through the establishment of cooperatives. He emphasized that "if there is no adequate development of modern industry, no agricultural collectivization can be achieved."[25]

Major differences of equal significance are apparent with respect to the guideline concerning industrialization. Because of his "guerrilla war" fixation, Mao inclines to apply the basic features of guerrilla war to economic affairs. For example, he regards China's immense population as a great asset. According to Mao, "Under the leadership of the Communist Party, as long as there are people, every kind of miracle can be performed." In his view, through a continued process of indoctrination it is possible to inspire the people to discard material incentive and tighten their belts in order for the regime to achieve a high rate of economic growth. Following this line of thinking, Mao has always given priority

to politics and is convinced that industrialization can be carried out through large-scale mass movements and labor-intensive techniques. The Great Leap Forward initiated by him in 1958-1959 was the direct result of Maoist thought on industrializing China.

According to Liu Shao-ch'i, Ch'en Yun and many other top party leaders in charge of economic affairs, industrialization can be achieved only by using rational economic methods. Material incentive and profit realization are indispensable in running an economy regardless of the social structure supporting it. Liu was quoted as saying "A factory must make money, otherwise it must be closed." He also asserted that "The enthusiasm of a socialist people's democracy lies in the people's concern for their own economic life. They must be concerned with wages, living accommodations, food, transportation and such matters, and only through the solution of these problems can the political life be attractive." Liu opposed the mass-line in economic construction and believed that industrialization and modernization must rely on the talents of experts, among whom should be factory directors, engineers and technicians. The whole set of guidelines, policies and measures advocated by Liu thus constituted the antithesis of Mao's concept.[26]

The failure of the communes and the collapse of the Great Leap Forward in 1960 forced Mao to accept the moderate line advocated by Liu Shao-ch'i, Teng Hsiao-p'ing and Ch'en Yun. Following the Ninth Plenary Session of the CCP in January 1961, a series of new economic policies was introduced, featuring a shift of priority from heavy industry to agriculture, suspension of the Great Leap, and a radical revision of the commune system. This wholesale retrenchment signified a concession by Mao and marked a major deflation of his prestige. During this period, Liu and Teng were in charge of the Central Committee. In order to promote peasant incentive, they approved such measures as allowing commune directors to assign production tasks to each individual peasant household.[27] In many places, farmlands were returned to individuals, a step signaling the revival of individual economy and the *de facto* dissolution of the commune system which Mao once regarded as the ladder to the communist paradise.

Attitude toward Intellectuals

The third policy difference between Mao and Liu stems from their attitudes toward intellectuals. In 1956 Mao accepted Chou En-lai's proposal to adopt a moderate line toward the nonparty intellectuals with the intention of stimulating literature, art and science.[28] At a February 1957 Supreme State Conference, Mao delivered his historical speech "On the Correct Handling of Contradictions Among the People," in which he personally invited intellectuals to criticize the Party and the government as a means of rectifying the growing tendency toward bureaucracy. This led to the short-lived Hundred Flowers Movement, the period when thousands of scholars, writers and scientists frankly criticized the regime. The soft line was bitterly opposed by Liu Shao-ch'i and P'eng Chen, however, and was soon turned into an "anti-rightist campaign." All who had denounced the regime were dismissed and subjected to thought reform. Mao's popularity suffered because of this incident, and his appeal to the Chinese intellectuals diminished considerably. Then, in late 1961, at the onset of an economic crisis, the regime once again advocated a Hun-

dred Flowers Movement to solicit the opinions of the intellectuals. But now it was Liu and P'eng rather than Mao who supported the new relaxation. Throughout 1961 and 1962 numerous "Forums of Higher Intellectuals" were held to "seek the opinion of higher intellectuals, consolidate their unity, develop their activism and muster their working enthusiasm."

It was in this atmosphere that many leading scholars and writers in the fields of philosophy, history, literature and the arts openly expressed "unorthodox"—or anti-Maoist—views. Yang Hsien-chen, a top party ideologist and former President of the CCP High Party Academy, advocated his theory of "two-combine-one," an approach to "class reconciliation," as an echo of Liu Shao-ch'i's view that China was free of class conflicts and in opposition to Mao's dictum that class struggle must be carried to the end. In 1961, Wu Han, a scholar specializing in Ming history and a former Vice Mayor of Peking, published a historical play entitled *Dismissal of Hai Jui*. The play dealt with a benevolent mandarin of the sixteenth century who fearlessly opposed the court for the sake of the people, and was thereafter dismissed by the emperor. In the same year, Wu's play was staged and received wide acclaim. In November 1965, Wu Han was accused by the Maoist group of making "veiled criticisms of contemporary people by dramatizing historical figures and events," and of using Hai Jui as a symbol to praise Marshal P'eng Teh-huai, who had openly criticized Chairman Mao's radical line and had been dismissed in August 1959.

During 1961-1962, many well-known writers published a series of articles on historical subjects related to current problems. Most of them made concerted attacks on the party leadership and particularly on Chairman Mao by rejecting his commune system and ridiculing his Great Leap.[29] Among the most prominent writers were Teng T'o, a leading journalist, the former Editor-in-Chief of the party organ, *People's Daily,* and a close aide of Mayor P'eng Chen; Liao Mo-sha, former head of the United Front Department of the Peking CCP Committee, and Wu Han, the famous historian. The growing tendency to deviate from Maoism in history, literature and the arts signaled that the conflict between Mao Tse-tung and Liu Shao-ch'i had extended to the sphere of culture.

Effect on the Party

Events leading to the outbreak of the current struggle indicate that views opposing Mao's radical policies and utopian blueprint sprang up continuously within the Party following the collapse of the Great Leap. P'eng Teh-huai's opposition had great impact on the Army and the Party. The moderate line of Liu Shao-ch'i and Teng Hsiao-p'ing received increasing support both within and outside the Party. In May 1963, Mao claimed that many party cadres "shut their eyes to the activities of bad elements and ogres of all kinds and in many cases failed to differentiate the enemy from their own, and went so far as to collaborate with the enemy and become corrupted and demoralized." He warned that if the situation continued, "the whole of China would change its color before long."[30] On at least three occasions—in September 1962, the summer of 1964, and September 1965—he strove to reverse the tide through the customary rectification campaign but found these efforts ineffective. According to the Red Guards' newspaper, the Standing Committee of the CCP Politburo has since

1958, at Mao's suggestion, been divided into two units, with Liu and Teng in charge of day-to-day decision-making, and Mao responsible only for major policy decisions. But apparently, after 1960, Liu and Teng made many important decisions without consulting Mao. At the October 26, 1966 Central Committee meeting, Mao complained: "Liu Shao-ch'i and Teng Hsiao-p'ing treated me as if I were their dead parent at a funeral."[31] To recover his absolute authority, Mao sought the collaboration of Lin Piao, who still showed loyalty to him. Lin seized this opportunity to consolidate his own position. Thus began the fierce power struggle with Mao and Lin on one side and Liu and Teng on the other.

THE STRUGGLE FOR SUCCESSION

Despite the growing antipathy between them, Liu Shao-ch'i's position as Mao's heir-apparent remained unchanged until late 1961. According to Marshal Viscount Bernard Montgomery, Mao personally told him in 1961 that Liu would be his successor.[32] The decision to demote Liu may have been made in 1963.

In late 1962, a recently published party document reveals, Liu attempted to reverse the Party's decision on P'eng Teh-huai's case and restore the Marshal's honor and position. Liu was quoted as asserting that the report P'eng Teh-huai had sent to the Party Central Committee in August 1959, which attacked Mao's general line, the Great Leap and the communes, had been borne out by the facts, and that the purge Mao organized against P'eng was "unfair and had been carried too far." Supported and encouraged by Liu and other leaders, P'eng in June 1962 had written a new report of 80,000 words to the Central Committee demanding a reversal of the verdict in his case.[33] Liu's efforts in behalf of P'eng may have been the last straw that induced Mao to discard Liu as his successor.

In 1963, probably at Mao's initiative, the regime launched a nationwide "Emulate the People's Liberation Army (PLA) Campaign." The Army, under the control of Lin Piao, was lauded as a dedicated, indoctrinated force safeguarding the revolution and serving as its "model." The rising power of the Army had reached into almost every field. To compete with the party apparatus headed by Liu Shao-ch'i and Teng Hsiao-p'ing, a new system of political departments, modeled after the PLA, was introduced in 1964 into industry, communication, trade and finance units, as well as educational and scientific research organizations. Each ministry has set up a political department to intensify the day-by-day study of Mao's "Thoughts," to combat "bourgeois ideology" and "revisionism," and to promote a high level of production. The real purpose of the system, however, appears to be the creation of an army-backed control network parallel to the party network existing in the administration and party apparatus. Many of the directors of the political departments are veteran military men.

In addition, regional army commanders have been appointed as party secretaries of the CCP Central Committee's six regional bureaus. In the early 1950's the Party deputized political commissars as watchdogs over the PLA. Now army generals have become secretaries of the Party. In the State Council, military leaders have been made ministers or vice ministers. All these changes in organization and personnel clearly signify the steady expansion of the Army's power. Without Mao's support, such a develop-ment would have encountered great resistance.

In early 1965, Lin Piao was elevated to the rank of First Vice Premier, a position occupied by Ch'en Yun for many years.[34] P'eng Chen, one of Liu Shao-ch'i's close associates, was removed as Secretary General of the National People's Congress, a key position he had held continuously since 1954 in addition to his capacity as Mayor of Peking.

To consolidate Lin Piao's position as Mao's new successor, the Mao-Lin group had next to eliminate opponents within the Army and to control public opinion as well as the CCP Central and Provincial Committees. This made necessary the purge of General Lo Jui-ch'ing, the nation's top policeman who became Chief of Staff of the Army in 1959, and who had been regarded as Lin Piao's chief rival in the Army. In the summer of 1966, P'eng Chen, the powerful Mayor of Peking, and Lu Ting-i and Chou Yang, two prominent leaders who had controlled the CCP propaganda machine and cultural affairs for more than three decades, were victimized. Hundreds of editors of local party newspapers, writers, and several dozens of presidents and vice presidents of the nation's top universities and colleges also were ousted. After the Eleventh Plenary Session of the CCP Central Committee held in early August 1966, the spearhead was pointed directly at Liu Shao-ch'i. He not only lost his position as First Vice Chairman of the CCP Central Committee but his rank in the Standing Committee of the Politburo descended from number two to number eight. Since then the struggle for power has dominated all domestic developments. Ch'en Po-ta, the man who is in charge of the Cultural Revolution, frankly admitted in a January 18, 1967 speech:

From the very beginning, the Great Cultural Revolution has been a struggle for the seizure of power. The Cultural Revolution marked its inception by the struggle with P'eng Chen, Lu Ting-i, Lo Jui-ch'ing, and Yang Shang-kung [a member of the CCP Central Secretariat]. This is a struggle for power.[35]

Ch'en's admission leaves no doubt about the main function of the Cultural Revolution. It also implies that so long as Liu Shao-ch'i remains in power, the struggle will continue.

THE FEUD'S SIGNIFICANCE

Thus, the feud between Mao Tse-tung and Liu Shao-ch'i can be traced back for more than a decade. In the earlier stages their dissension arose mainly from Mao's megalomania, his intention to perpetuate his personality cult, and his paternalism in leadership. Since the collapse of the Great Leap in 1960, a divergence of opinion on the basic issues of national policy has intensified the feud. When Mao decided to substitute Lin Piao for Liu Shao-ch'i as his successor, the power contest divided the "comrades-in-arms" into two groups of antagonists.

In historical perspective, Mao's megalomania and paternalism cannot be separated from the crucial role he has played over a period of three decades in the Chinese Communist Party. It was under his leadership that the CCP achieved its signal triumph over the Kuomintang in 1949. Since then, he has developed a mentality which leads him to consider anyone who opposes him as one who opposes the Party. His ambition has been not only to establish himself as an unchallengeable leader in the CCP but also to elevate his doctrine—his "Thoughts"—to the status of sacrosanct dogma. Before the death of Stalin in 1953, Mao's personality cult and paternalism coincided with the political atmosphere in the Soviet Union, where Stalin pursued the same goal. Khrushchev's de-Stalinization drive in 1956 disposed the leaders in the CCP to challenge Mao's ambition. The deletion of the "Thoughts of Mao Tse-tung" from the 1956 Party Constitution indicated the shift of the wind. Leaders like Liu Shao-ch'i, Teng Hsiao-ping and others, while harboring no intention to lay claim to Mao's supreme leadership, hoped to deemphasize his personality cult. They wanted to put Mao's doctrine in proper historical perspective and make it acceptable to other communists in the world. They credited Mao's contribution because it integrated Marxism-Leninism with China's special conditions, but they denied it as a theory of universal truth. They also declined to echo Lin Piao's slogan that "the 'TMTT' is the acme of Marxism-Leninism," believing that such an assertion would imply the decay rather than the further advancement of Marxism-Leninism and would cause dissension among communist leaders in foreign countries. The reluctance of Liu and Teng to propagate Mao's doctrine to excess lies at the root of their demotion in the party hierarchy.

Mao's strong paternalism has also been a cause of friction with colleagues and immediate subordinates. Available evidence indicates that on many occasions he ignored the formal decisions of the CCP Central Committee and made his own decisions through organizations outside that body. In some cases he directly summoned secretaries of the provincial and local party committees to implement his policy, and in other cases he called the Supreme State Conference to approve his program.[36] During the past decade, he put aside the basic Party

Constitution under which the Party Congress should meet every five years to select a new Central Committee, Politburo, Chairman and Vice Chairman. It has been twelve years since the last Party Congress was convened. Also, during the past decade, about one-third of the members of the Central Committee have been inactive for one reason or another. The highest organ of the CCP is thus partially paralyzed. In the course of the current Cultural Revolution Mao has again resorted to devices outside the legitimate party apparatus and procedures to assert his power. The "Cultural Revolution Group" led by Ch'en Po-ta, his secretary, and Chiang Ch'ing, his wife, and the Red Guards organization are Mao's contrivances, bypassing the party apparatus and operating, it would seem, against the collective leadership system which Mao himself vigorously advocated in the 1930's and 1940's.

Even if Mao, by means of army support, eventually succeeds in expelling Liu Shao-ch'i, he and his new successor will face a weakened party machine and an erosion of discipline as a result of the current power struggle and the Red Guards' rampage. When half of the leaders in the Party's Politburo are accused of anti-Maoism, the validity of Mao's "Thoughts" must be questioned among the party cadres and the people. Without a strong and united Party, the perpetuation of Mao's personality cult, and particularly the emphasis given to his "Thoughts," could hardly be maintained. Judging from developments in mainland China during past months, Liu Shao-ch'i's influence is still profound. Even if Liu is removed as Chairman of the CPR, the moderate line he advocated during the post-1961 period would persist in party councils and perhaps gain strength. In the years ahead, the new leaders in Communist China may adopt "Liuism"

without Liu Shao-ch'i, just as the new Soviet leaders adopted "Khrushchevism" without Khrushchev.

Notes

1. Andrew Boyd, *Mao Tse-tung, Nineteen Poems* (Peking: Foreign Language Press, 1958), p. 22.
2. Liu Shao-ch'i, *On the Party* (Peking: Foreign Language Press, 1951), p. 33.
3. Liu Shao-ch'i, *The Political Report of the Central Committee of the CCP to the Eighth National Congress* (Peking: Foreign Language Press, 1956), pp. 93-94. Teng Hsiao-p'ing, in his "Report on the Revision of Party Constitution," expressed the same views. Teng regretted that there had been an eleven-year gap between the Seventh and Eighth Congress. *Jen-min Shou-ts'e 1957 (People's Handbook 1957)*, p. 31.
4. *Ibid.*
5. According to Chien Wei-ch'ang, Vice President of Tsinghua University, Liu and P'eng opposed the Hundred Flowers Movement (*Jen-min Jih-pao [People's Daily]*, July 17, 1957—hereafter referred to as *JMJP*). Hsu Liang-ying, a Communist Party cadre, also disclosed that Liu and P'eng forced Mao to suspend the movement and to launch the "anti-rightist campaign" (*JMJP*, August 3, 1957).
6. Liu Shao-ch'i, "The Victory of Marxism-Leninism in China," *JMJP*, October 1, 1959.
7. *The Works Bulletin*, No. 3, 1961, p. 10.
8. *Ibid.*, No. 8, 1961, p. 18.
9. *JMJP*, July 1, 1961.
10. Liu Shao-ch'i, *How to Be a Good Communist* (Peking: Foreign Language Press, 1962), p. 12.
11. Quoted from an article entitled "Thoroughly Criticize and Repudiate China's Khrushchev," *Chieh-fang Chun-pao (Liberation Army Daily)*, October 12, 1967.
12. *Ching-kang-shan (Ching-Kang Mountain)*, published by the Red Guards in Tsinghua University, February 1, 1967, p. 6.
13. *JMJP*, September 30, 1959.
14. *The Works Bulletin*, No. 2, 1961, p. 4.
15. *Ibid.*, No. 8, 1961, p. 18.
16. *Ching-kang-shan*, February 1, 1967, p. 6.
17. *JMJP*, July 15, 1966, p. 3.
18. Yang Ch'eng-wu, "Establish the Absolute Authority of the Great Supreme Commander, Chairman Mao and TMTT in a Big Way," *JMJP*, November 2, 1967.
19. Article by Proletarian Revolutionaries of

CCP Southwest Bureau, broadcast by Ch'engtu Radio Station, October 26, 1967.

20. June 7, 1966.

21. *Peking Review*, January 3, 1968, p. 14.

22. Mao Tse-tung, "On the Correct Handling of Contradictions Among the People," February 27, 1957, published in *People's China*, No. 13, 1957, pp. 3-26.

23. Liu Shao-ch'i, *Political Report, op. cit.*, pp. 15-16.

24. Mao Tse-tung, "On Agricultural Co-operation," published in *People's China*, November 1955, pp. 3-17.

25. *Ching-kang-shan*, February 1, 1967, p. 6.

26. "Two Diametrically Opposed Lines in Building the Economy," written jointly by the editorial boards of *Wen Hui Pao, Liberation Daily* and *Party Branch Life*, all published in Shanghai; reprinted in *JMJP*, August 25, 1967.

27. *Ts'ai-mao Hung-ch'i* (*Red Flag in Financial and Commercial Fronts*), published by a rebel group of financial and commercial circles in Peking, February 23, 1967, p. 4.

28. In January 1956, the CCP Central Committee met to discuss the question of the intellectuals. On behalf of the Committee, Chou En-lai delivered an extended speech admitting major shortcomings in treating Chinese intellectuals and proposing remedies. For details see Chu-yuan Cheng, *Scientific and Engineering Man-power in Communist China 1949-1963*, National Science Foundation, 1966, pp. 158-159.

29. See Chu-yuan Cheng, "Power Struggle in Communist China," *Asian Survey*, September 1966, pp. 469-483.

30. *Liberation Army Daily*, editorial, June 6, 1966.

31. Quoted from *China Topics* (London), March 10, 1967.

32. The *Sunday Times* (London), October 22, 1961.

33. Wen Hung-chun, Tso Hung-ping and Hsin Pei-wen, "Defend Yenan—A Vivid Example of Opposing the Party Through Novels," *JMJP*, November 12, 1967; also see editorial, "From the Defeat of P'eng Teh-huai to the Bankruptcy of China's Khrushchev," *Hung-ch'i* (*Red Flag*), No. 13, 1967, pp. 23-24.

34. *Jen-min Shou-ts'e* 1966.

35. Ch'en Po-ta's speech, "Problems of Seizing Power," *Tung-fang-hung* (*The East is Red*), a Red Guard's newspaper published by the coordinate office of Red Guards in the Peking area, February 18, 1967, p. 1.

36. For instance, on July 31, 1955 Mao called a Conference of Secretaries of Provincial and Local Party Committees to adopt his accelerated program of agricultural cooperation. On February 27, 1957 Mao called a Supreme State Conference to implement his Hundred Flowers Movement. Both programs had failed to get major support from the CCP Central Committee. See Chu-yuan Cheng, *Communist China: Its Situation and Prospect* (Hong Kong: Freedom Press, 1959), pp. 28-29.

47. THE RECANTATION OF LIU SHAO-CH'I

SELF-CRITICISM
(October 23, 1966)

Comrades!

I persist in observing Chairman Mao's and Comrade Lin Piao's directives. Fur-

From *Collected Works of Liu Shao-ch'i, 1958-1967* (Union Research Institute, Hong Kong, 1968), pp. 357-377. Reprinted by permission.

thermore, I agree with Comrade Chen Po-ta's report. I have read the reports of various group meetings and feel that in the directive given to a number of local and central departments concerning the great proletarian cultural revolution, I committed deviations and mistakes of varying degrees. Many comrades have already submitted self-criticisms, for which I am most remorseful. Why? Because their acts during the first stage of the great proletarian cultural revolution were related with my mistakes. For over 50 days after June 1, 1966, while I was directing the great cultural revolution, I committed blunders causing a wrong line and direction. While other comrades, such as those of the Peking departments of the Central Committee and those in charge of the departments of the State Council responsible for the direction of the cultural revolution, the work teams sent by the new Peking Municipal Party Committee and concerned local comrades are also to blame in varying degrees, I should bear the greatest responsibility.

During a certain period prior to July 18 when Chairman Mao was absent from Peking, the Central Committee's daily work was pivoted around me. I made decisions affecting the conduct of the cultural revolution in all quarters of Peking and made reports to the Central Committee meetings. At this time, I sanctioned others' wrong decisions and made erroneous decisions myself like the dispatch of work teams at the request of various departments of the Central Committee and the Central Committee of the Communist Youth League. At that time, they positively urged me to send work personnel to various quarters. Apart from those dispatched to schools upon the request of the new Peking Municipal Party Committee, work teams were sent to government organs. As soon as they reached their assigned posts, the work teams immediately adopted various methods to suppress the masses, such as prohibiting demonstrations and parades in streets and wall posters and restricting the masses' activities to their own units. Another example includes the approval of the mistaken method used by the work team of Peking University, whereby stu-

dent's revolutionary actions were looked upon as counter-revolutionary activities. Worse still, this was carried out as a basic working method throughout the country.

Most schools in Peking launched so-called "struggles to oust cadres." In many schools, work teams went so far as to direct students to struggle against students, encircle and attack revolutionary students, suppress dissenting views, and accuse, without authorization, certain students belonging to counter-revolutionary, rightist or pseudo-"Left" factions. This caused panic among many students.

I had asked Wang Kuang-mei about a series of campaigns at Tsinghua University in which she participated. The mistake committed there was a typical example of following a mistaken line. Regarding the dissolution of the Peking Municipal Party Committee and the Communist Youth League, it would have been better if I had approved their self-criticisms and then permitted them to resume participating in the cultural revolution. That would have been the correct way of dealing with the matter. However, my approval of the view to resume their active participation was given too early. It was a mistake to transfer the authority to the preparatory committees of the cultural revolution organizations immediately after the withdrawal of work teams.

At that time, requests came from many quarters for work teams. The requests became more urgent after newspapers published the report that a work team had been sent to Peking University. At that time, if we had not considered the requests for work teams or had not sent work teams to schools and government organs, in what other way could we have acted? There would have been people who thought that we did not fully comprehend the great cultural revolution, when the masses had already risen.

The present situation shows that it is a great revolution with a rousing spirit and a new stage of the proletarian revolution. However, most comrades and I did not understand that such was the situation. Furthermore, we did not have any experience in handling such a situation. Our only way was to learn from the mass movement, and we should not have dispatched work teams to act in the place of the masses or set up a great cultural revolution structure to give guidance to the masses. Even if the masses had demanded the dispatch of work teams, the only thing we could have done was to send a small number of liaison men and try to understand the actual situation. We should not have expressed our own views on the mass movement. The masses would not have been satisfied merely with the dispatch of liaison men. However, at that time, we should not have done anything more than to handle the situation by sending some liaison men. At the time, some comrades discovered that the work teams were in conflict with the masses, and taking up this issue, proposed that the dispatch of work teams was unnecessary.

For instance, Comrade Chen Po-ta made such a proposal. He understood Chairman Mao's thinking. Had we also understood Chairman Mao's thought, we would have suspended these activities, and would not have pursued a mistaken line and direction.

At that time, the direction of work teams and certain work aroused doubts in some localities. Some Party leaders were also doubtful, believing that in carrying out revolution for the masses, the work teams would have to put up many restrictions causing discontent among the masses. Precisely at this critical moment when I was directing the Central Work Meetings, I committed the above-mentioned mistakes. Work teams carried on their activities for 50 days. My mistakes aggravated the teams' blunders. In some places, new teams had to be sent to replace those who failed in their missions. Most comrades of the work teams did not have sufficient understanding. Unwilling to learn from the masses, they insisted that the masses tread the path they had laid out for them. Such a method is counter to a mass movement. In fact they took the stand of reactionary bourgeoisie, throttling the lofty movement of the great proletarian cultural revolution. If I did not realize at that moment that such conditions were abnormal and detrimental to the interests of the Party and the society, then I must have committed right-inclined opportunism. Although it was no more than 50 days, the damage done was enormous. Up to now the results of such damage have not been reckoned. It accounts for the acuteness of opposition among the masses in certain places.

The blunders I committed were not matters of chance. In my past history I made mistakes against principle and Party line. They are as follows:

On February 1, 1946, after the Political Consultative Conference was closed, I issued a directive to the Central Committee, stating that the conference marked a new stage on the road to the realization of peace. It was a mistaken view with an illusion of peace. Of course, what I said concerning army training, rent reduction and production was correct. I also committed a policy mistake in directing the war in the northeast at the beginning of 1946. I did not give sufficient support for Comrade Lin Piao's direction of the war.

In the summer of 1947, I presided at meetings on land reform. At that time I failed to find a systematic and overall solution to the problem of the division of landlord's land. The "Left" tendency discovered then was not promptly rectified. For instance, too many people were killed, and middle peasants' interests were infringed upon.

In the spring of 1949, I talked about many things that had happened during the period of Tientsin cadres' urban work. I proposed that certain excessively violent ways against bourgeois industries and commerce should be checked, and also the elimination of urban feudal leaders. Nevertheless, in a number of speeches, I committed the mistake of "Left" inclined naiveté.

In July, 1951, I wrongly criticized the Shansi Provincial Party Committee, pointing out that they should not have developed the mutual-aid teams into higher level agricultural cooperatives.

In 1955, Comrade Teng Tzu-hui proposed to reduce the size of the 200,000 cooperatives or dissolve them. The Central Committee meeting over which I presided failed to raise objection, thereby giving virtual approval to his plan. Consequently, at subsequent rural work meetings of the Central Committee, Teng reduced the size of or dissolved the 200,000 cooperatives.

In 1962 I committed the mistake of being right inclined. In 1964 I was superficially "Left" inclined, but actually right inclined. In the great proletarian cultural revolution, I committed a blunder with the Party line; this was related with my previous mistakes.

At a Central Work Conference, convened in January, 1962, I delivered a written report but not a speech. In 1958, although in my written statements and verbal reports I acknowledged the great achievements attained after the Three Red Banners were put into effect, there were still a number of mistakes. Our achievements were primary; mistakes and defects in our work, secondary. These defects and mistakes have been corrected for the most part or are being rectified.

A still greater event took place at the Central Work Conference over which I presided from February 21 to 26, 1962. When the financial policy was being discussed, a deficit was found. Again, I committed a mistake in my judgement of the difficulties. I thought such a deficit was normal during extraordinary times. The conference therefore approved Comrade Chen Yun's speech directed towards the State Council. We let the provincial first-grade Party member cadres discuss this question and express dissenting opinions. At the conference, someone proposed independent working style; others basically opposed the Three Red Banners and criticized the activists as being worthless persons and deliberately suppressed the key projects of the three-line construction; investments that should have been cancelled were not cancelled.

I had too much confidence in Comrade Chen Yun and thus listened to him alone. Ideologically, the two of us shared various common views. For this reason, I recommended Comrade Chen Yun to the Central Committee and Chairman Mao as the Head of the Financial Group of the Central Committee. As Chairman Mao was not in Peking then, I went to him and delivered a report. Afterwards I learned that Chairman Mao was not at all in agreement with my appraisal of the situation. At that time, Teng Hsiaoping dwelled on the advantages of Anhwei's "responsibility farm," to which I made no objection.

Hence, at the Ninth Plenum, Teng advocated the contracting of farm production to each household and proposed the so-called "three reconciliations and one reduction."

This was counter to the General Line; it was formed on the basis of a wrong estimate of the domestic and international situations. I heard directly about the system of contracting farm production to each household, but I did not stop him from advocating it. It was my mistake. At the same time, I felt the urgency of the current situation, so I requested the Chairman to come back to the north. In the summer of 1962, I committed myself to the right-inclined line at the Peitaiho Conference. On the Chairman's return to Peking, he set out to draft the resolution on the intensification of collective economy and commerce and brought up the contradictions of class struggle at the Peitaiho Conference. At the Tenth Plenary Session of the Central Committee two resolutions were adopted, and a communique was issued. All these began to correct my mistakes and changed the situation fundamentally and completely.

In 1964, I committed the same mistakes that I did in 1962, that is " 'Left' in appearance but right in substance." On April 1, 1964, Chairman Mao personally formulated the "First Ten Articles." In September, 1964, some leading comrades of the Central Committee drew up the "Second Ten Articles" and published them on November 14. At that time, I had no knowledge of how the "Second Ten Articles" came to be drawn up. I learned only recently. It was Peng Chen who wrote a report to Chairman Mao six months after the "First Ten Articles" were formulated. The "Second Ten Articles" were drawn up on the basis of the spirit of that report. It was after September, 1964, that I found the "Second

Ten Articles" to be harmful because they hampered the efforts to arouse the masses.

In 1964, I called on various provinces to send delegates to Peking for talks. I emphasized that cadres at various levels should take steps to stabilize the rural areas. What I said was quite correct, but because I had emphasized the words too strongly, certain problems became absolutely settled and unchangeable. This amounted to a mistake on my part. In addition, I said that the "Four Clearances" Campaign was not intensive and thorough enough, and it had failed. Owing to an over-estimate of the effect of class struggle, I committed a blunder in my statement of the reasons for the improvement of industrial and agricultural production. In addition, I said that to make it effective the "Four Clearances" Campaign should only be launched in a mass movement. When I said so, I thought that the investigative meetings that Chairman Mao wanted to hold would be insufficient. In reality this negated Chairman Mao's thought. It was a very grave mistake on my part, casting very bad influences.

At that time I had too much confidence in Wang Kuang-mei's experience summary. I wanted to popularize the Peking experience in other parts of the country. This gave many comrades a bad impression. As a matter of fact, Wang Kuang-mei's experience had already proved wrong. At the Central Committee meeting in 1964 I had not realized my own mistakes. I was confused with the contradictions between the "Four Clearances" and "Four Non-Clearances" and the contradictions within and without the Party. I had only read the Twenty-Three Articles once, but I could not explain the substance of them.

That was not Marxism-Leninism. I forgot then all about the set of theories that our Party resorted to in class struggle over the past few decades. This accounted for my mistake of being " 'Left' in appearance but right in substance." My mistakes were later corrected when Chairman Mao personally presided over a meeting at which the Twenty-Three Articles were adopted. The Twenty-Three articles were laid down to rectify Party authorities who followed the bourgeois steps and to campaign against a very few bad people. The most outstanding historical mistakes that I committed were those of right inclination in 1962 and 1964. This time I again committed very serious mistakes of right-opportunism, which were pointed out to me and corrected by our Party's and the people's great Chairman Mao on his return to Peking.

On July 24, after deciding to withdraw the work teams, a work-team meeting was held. On August 1, the 11th Plenary Session of the Eighth Central Committee was convened, at which the Sixteen Articles were adopted. During the latter part of the Plenum the question of our mistakes was brought up for discussion which was followed by the election of members of the Standing Committee of the Central Committee. At the Plenum Comrade Lin Piao was unanimously recommended as Chairman Mao's first assistant and successor. Comrade Lin Piao is better than I in every respect; so are other comrades in the Party. I am determined to abide by a Party member's discipline and do nothing before anybody that amounts to "agreement by mouth but disagreement at heart."

The reasons that accounted for my mistakes are as follows:

1. I did not understand that the great cultural revolution marked a new stage of more intensive and extensive development in the socialist revolution, nor did I understand how the cultural revolution could be carried out. To fulfil all the tasks laid down in the Sixteen Articles, we must, however we tackle them, follow the mass line, go more extensively and intensively into the masses and mobilize them to conduct self-education, carry out self-liberation, and promote more urgently the proletarian rebel spirit. However, I distrusted the masses and could not make up my mind whether we should mobilize the masses to conduct self-education and self-liberation. On the contrary, I believed completely in the functions of work teams, wanting to monopolize the mass movement. I was griped by the fear of confusion, great democracy, rebellion by the masses against us, and uprisings of counter-revolutionaries.

2. I misjudged the situation regarding the proletarian cultural revolution and wrongly regarded the normal inevitable defects in a mass movement as anti-Party, anti-socialist, and anti-proletarian dictatorship adverse currents. Hence I made a wrong judgement, because I took the bourgeois reactionary stand and became a bourgeois dictator.

3. Ideologically, I could not completely change my bourgeois world outlook, thus retaining many idealistic and metaphysical viewpoints. Hence I vacillated in my stand when I looked at problems and when I deliberated on how to deal with them. Sometimes I took the bourgeois stand. At the office I assumed bureaucratic mannerisms and dealt with my colleagues as a boss with his subordinates.

4. The most fundamental problem was that I did not learn to grasp Chairman Mao's thought. While waging a struggle,

I could not correctly apply Chairman Mao's thought. I could not go deep into the midst of the masses to learn from them, nor did I make reports to Chairman Mao. In fact, I often countered Chairman Mao's thought and could not listen to my comrade's correct views. On the contrary, I could easily accept incorrect ideas.

These I understand to be my own mistakes. Naturally, I have not mentioned enough of my mistakes. I am determined to learn Chairman Mao's thought and to learn from Comrade Lin Piao and I have made up my mind to do things in the interest of the Party and the people.

CONFESSION
(Summer 1967)

Comrades of the Revolutionary Rebels of Chungnanhai,

On the Xth of X month 1967 you issued an urgent order that Liu Shao-ch'i should present a written self-examination before the Xth of X month specifically replying to the eight questions posed in Ch'i Pen-yu's essay. My answer is as follows:

1. In March 1936 I went to Tientsin as a representative of the Party Central Committee (at that time the Party's Northern Bureau was there). The Head of the Organisation Department of the Northern Bureau at that time, Comrade K'e Ch'ing-shih raised a question with me: he said that there were a number of comrades in Peking prison and that most

Liu Shao-ch'i made this confession in response to eight questions asked by Ch'i Pen-yu in *People's Daily* of April 1, 1967. While the exact date of the confession is not known at the moment, it first appeared on wall posters in early August 1967. The text is taken from *Union Research Service*, LI, No. 10 (May 3, 1968), pp. 235-238.

of them had already served their sentences but that without going through certain formalities they could not be released: he asked me whether or not I could go through the formalities, and at that time I questioned him in return: "What is your opinion?" K'e replied that one could have the comrades in prison go through the formalities, so I immediately *wrote a letter* about this (the words "wrote a letter" were put in by counterrevolutionary revisionist, Wang Kuang-mei, and below whenever my words are in italics they were written by Wang Kuang-mei herself) reporting it to the Party Central Committee of Shen Pei and asking the Central Committee for a decision. But it wasn't long before I received the Central Committee's answer, namely that the affair should be handled by Comrade K'e Ch'ing-shih. *At that time the everyday work of the Party Central Committee was handled by Chang Wen-t'ien (whose first names are also Lo Fu). According to Chang Wen-t'ien's version he did not at that time report to Chairman Mao and did not discuss the matter at a meeting but made the reply of his own accord.* At that time I knew that Comrade Yin Chien was in prison but I did not know the others nor did I know how many there were. Neither did I know how this was afterwards handled. After Comrade Yin Chien came out of prison it was the spring of 1937 and I met him once in the house of K'e Ch'ing-shih. Not long afterwards Comrade Yin Chien died from an illness. I did not bother to find out what specific formalities they went through and it was only recently when I read a rebel newspaper that I knew they had published an "anticommunist notice." With regard to this matter I accept a certain responsibility.

2. After the victory in the Anti-Japa-

nese War, in January 1946 our Party made a ceasefire agreement with the K.M.T. Afterwards the old Political Consultative Conference was assembled and it proposed a "programme for peaceful national construction." In the ceasefire order of our Party of the 20 January was a reference to the "new phase of peace and democracy." On the first of February, in accordance with the opinions of the Central Committee's discussion, I wrote a directive about the "new phase of peace and democracy." This directive contains errors.

3. After liberation I made every effort to advocate the socialist transformation of capitalist industry and commerce. I did not oppose this. In 1951 I approved an article sent from Shansi about agricultural co-operatives: this approval was wrong. At a meeting of the Central Committee I listened to a report on the question of co-operatives by Teng Tzu-hui and I did not refute his mistaken opinions. Thereupon he promoted them widely and cut back 200,000 co-operatives. Afterwards Chairman Mao criticised the errors of Teng Tzu-hui and published a very important essay on agricultural co-operatives thus bringing a high tide of agricultural co-operatives.

4. At the 8th Party Congress in 1956, I presented to the Congress a political report on behalf of the Party Central Committee. It spoke about the class struggle within the country. For example, it said "the struggle between limiting and opposing limitation has been the main form of the internal class struggle in recent years and reflects our country's main class contradictions—the struggle to carry out the three antis and five antis. This is because there are quite a large number of bourgeois elements who are carrying out illegal activities harmful to the country's and the people's livelihood. One

cannot but determinedly take steps to put an end to this." But in another part of this report it says "the contradiction between our country's bourgeoisie and the proletariat has already been resolved," and this proposition is wrong. The resolution of the 8th Party Congress on the work report also says "now this socialist transformation has already won a decisive victory. This shows that the contradictions between our country's socialist proletariat and the bourgeoisie have already basically been resolved." "The history of the system of class exploitation which has gone on for several thousand years has already basically come to an end and the socialist system has basically been set up in our country. . . . The basic internal contradiction in our country . . . is the contradiction between a progressive socialist system and the production forces of a backward society." Chairman Mao at the time expressed his opposition to these sentences in the resolution but there was no time to revise them and it was passed in this form and has still not been refuted today. Apart from this, in the political report and the resolution of the 8th Party Congress there was no mention of Mao Tsetung's thought as the guiding ideology for the whole Party and as the guiding principle for the whole Party and the whole country, and this was wrong. *A step backward had been taken from the position of the 7th Party Congress.*

5. During the three years of difficulty I did not attack the Three Red Flags. At one Central Committee meeting when I heard Teng Tsu-hui say that the Anhwei field of responsibility had many good points, I did not refute him and *he went everywhere talking nonsense.* The Three Reconciliations and One Reduction was put forward by an individual comrade in a rough draft and was not brought up at

a Central Committee meeting. At the time I still did not know that this point of view had appeared. Afterwards, it was removed from that comrade's safe.

6. In 1962 when *How to be a Good Communist* was reprinted, this was endorsed and revised for me by someone else. I saw that it was published in *Red Flag* and *People's Daily*. I ought to take the main responsibility.

7. In the summer of 1964 I made speeches in several cities, in some of which were tendencies which were "Left" in form but "right" in fact. In my self-examination of the 23rd of October last year I gave a detailed explanation. There is no need to do so again. The "peach garden" experience was at the time comparatively good. It was not an example of "Left" in form and "right" in substance.

8. In the proletarian cultural revolution, as to why I have advocated and promoted the bourgeois reactionary line, I myself am also not clear about this. Nor have I read any essay which can fully explain why I have made errors of line. After the 11th Plenum of the 8th Party Congress criticised my errors, there were also others who committed errors of a similar nature, but they also do not know why. I am going to endeavour to study Chairman Mao's works and carefully peruse other books which Chairman Mao directs me to read as well as the relevant essays in newspapers, in order to be able to get this question fully clear from the ideological viewpoint, and moreover sincerely to hold a self-examination among the revolutionary masses. Only then shall I be able to reply as to why I committed errors of line in this Proletarian Cultural Revolution and how to correct this error.

With greetings, proletarian cultural revolution greetings, long live the in-vincible great thought of Mao Tse-tung! Long live the great leader, great teacher, great commander, great helmsman Mao Tse-tung.

Ch'i Pen-yu's eight questions as translated from *People's Daily* of April 1, 1967.

1. Why, on the eve of the outbreak of the Anti-Japanese War, did you personally propagate the philosophy of saving one's own skin, of capitulationism and of betrayal; why did you direct other people to become turncoats and to surrender to the Kuomintang; why did you betray the Communist Party and openly publish an "anti-communist notice" and swear to oppose the Communist Party?

2. Why, after the victory in the Anti-Japanese War, did you put forward the capitalist line of the "new phase of peace and democracy?"

3. Why, after liberation, did you make every effort to oppose the socialist transformation of capitalist industry and commerce? Why did you oppose agricultural co-operatives and cut them back?

4. Why, after the completion of the three great socialist transformations, did you do your best to propagate the theory of the extinction of the class struggle, actively promote a class co-operation and do away with class struggle?

5. Why, in the period of the three years of hardship, did you join in the chorus with freaks and monsters within the country and poisonously attack the Three Red Flags, and promote the revisionist line of the Three Freedoms and One Contract and the Three Reconciliations and One Reduction?

6. Why, in 1962, did you once again publish that great poisonous weed *How to be a Good Communist,* which is a book opposed to revolution, to class struggle, to seizing political power, to the dictatorship of the proletariat, to Marxism-Leninism, to Mao Tse-tung's thought and which propagates the bourgeois world view and a reactionary bourgeois idealist philosophy?

7. Why, in the socialist education movement, did you promote and advocate the line which in form was "Left" but in reality "right" opportunism, and why did you sabotage the socialist education movement?

8. Why, during the proletarian cultural revolution have you colluded with another very big person in authority within the Party going the capitalist road and advocated and promoted the bourgeois reactionary line?

SELF-EXAMINATION
(July 9, 1967)

To Fighters of the New August 1 Combat Regiment of Peking Building Construction Industry Institute,
To All Revolutionary Teachers, Students and Staff Members of Peking Building Construction Industry Institute,

On the evening of July 4, Comrade Wang Tung-hsing, director of the General Office of the CCP Central Committee, informed me that the Party Central Committee wanted me to write an examination for the fighters of the New August 1 Combat Regiment of the Building Construction Industry Institute. My examination is as follows:

I

Toward the end of July 1966, our great teacher, great leader, great supreme commander and great helmsman Chairman Mao called on all responsible comrades of the Central Committee and responsible comrades who came to Peking from various areas to take a personal part in the great proletarian cultural revolution going on in various schools in Peking. The object was to acquire perceptual knowledge.

In response to this call by Chairman Mao, on August 1 last year I went to Comrade Li Hsueh-feng's office and discussed with the comrades of the new Peking Municipal Party Committee the

question of which school I should go to. After the discussion, it was unanimously decided that I should go to the Building Construction Industry Institute. Comrade Li Hsueh-feng also decided to go along. Since the Building Material Industry Ministry was led by the State Building Construction Commission, so Comrade Ku Mu also went to your Institute to participate in the great cultural revolution. At the time, I asked the Cultural Revolution Group of the Central Committee to send some people to participate, and it sent Comrade Ch'i Pen-yu. At the time, the several of us did not have the idea of creating experiences and popularizing them in the whole country.

On the evening of August 2, I came to your Institute to attend your rally. The above-mentioned comrades also came along. In addition, we had Liu Lan-t'ao and several other comrades who came to Peking from other areas. They decided to participate only then and there. I had no knowledge in advance.

I attended your August 2 rally mainly for the purpose of hearing some different opinions among you. And finally I spoke a few words.

On the evening of August 3, Comrades Li Hsueh-feng, Ku Mu, and Ch'i Pen-yu and I again came to your Institute. We talked first with the representatives of the "August 1 Regiment" and then with the representatives of the "Revolutionary Regiment." Our main purpose was also to hear their opinions. Finally, I talked to the representatives of the "August 1 Regiment" and the "Revolutionary Regiment" separately about several opinions of mine.

On the evening of August 4, while in Chungnanhai I had a talk with the responsible comrades of the work team. In the main I asked them a few questions and finally I said something.

Liu Shao-ch'i, identified as China's Khrushchov, made this reported self-examination at the Peking Building Construction Industry Institute on July 9, 1967. The text is taken from *Survey of China Mainland Press*, No. 4037 (October 9, 1967), pp. 1-7.

On August 5, Chairman Mao's big-character poster bombarding the head-quarters came out. It was then that I knew I had made grave mistakes in this great proletarian cultural revolution. At that time I already felt that I could no longer interfere with the affairs of the Building Construction Industry Institute. On the afternoon that day, I told Comrade Li Hsueh-feng over the phone that I would not go to the Building Construction Industry Institute again and would not interfere with its affairs. I had no knowledge about Comrade Li Hsueh-feng's speech on August 5 or of a later speech by Wu Hsing-feng at the Building Construction Industry Institute. After August 5, several students of the Institute wrote to me, and I also received several brief bulletins. But I did not reply. Some of these I sent to Comrade Li Hsueh-feng, and some I handled myself.

The above is a brief account of my participation in the great proletarian cultural revolution at the Peking Building Construction Industry Institute.

II

On June 1 last year (1966), after the publication in the whole country, which was approved by Chairman Mao himself, of the first Marxist-Leninist big-character poster by Comrade Nieh Yuan-tzu and six other comrades of Peking University, the great proletarian cultural revolution movement in Peking and in other parts of the nation was unfolded with great fanfare. However, in the 50 days and more after June 1, last year, I made a mistake in line and in orientation while guiding the great proletarian cultural revolution. I should bear the main responsibility for this mistake, although other comrades—such as other leading comrades of the Central Committee who were in Peking, the leading comrades of certain ministries and commissions of the State Council, the leading comrades of the new Peking Municipal Party Committee, the leading comrades of certain work teams, and certain leading comrades of other localities—also had a certain responsibility. I began to understand this mistake I myself had made only after Chairman Mao's big-character poster bombarding the headquarters came out on August 5. Before that, I did not know that I had committed such a grave error.

For some time prior to July 18 last year, the daily work of the Party Central Committee was in my charge in the absence of Chairman Mao. The conditions of the great cultural revolution in various respects in Peking were regularly reported at meetings of the Central Committee over which I presided. These meetings made some wrong decisions, approved or agreed to some wrong suggestions.

For instance:

—Sending out a large number of work teams to various universities, middle schools and some State organs in Peking.

—Devising some measures for restricting the revolutionary actions of the masses, such as drawing a line of distinction between people inside and outside an organization, forbidding the masses to demonstrate in the streets, prohibiting pasting big-character posters in the streets.

—Distributing Brief Bulletin No. 9 on the cultural revolution in Peking University to Party committees in various localities, describing the revolutionary actions of the revolutionary teachers and students as counter-revolutionary incidents.

—Distributing reports and discussion summaries which some bureaus of the Central Committee submitted to the

Central Committee concerning the great proletarian cultural revolution, and so on.

In many schools in Peking, the so-called struggle for "eliminating interference" was conducted. In the Building Construction Industry Institute, the so-called struggle for "eliminating interference" became a struggle for "catching swimming fish." But I had no knowledge of it beforehand, nor did I hear anything about "catching swimming fish" at meetings of the Central Committee. Such a struggle gave rise to the phenomenon where in many schools, under the leadership of the work teams, students struggled against each other, freedom of the person was restricted and other illegal acts were committed, revolutionaries were encircled and attacked, dissent was suppressed, and even some students were branded as "counter-revolutionaries," "rightists," "sham Leftists," "swimming fish," etc. As a result, in this period the general orientation of the struggle was shifted, and many schools were engulfed by an atmosphere of white terror. Such an atmosphere of terror was reactionary; it was an atmosphere of white terror.

When the work teams first went to various schools, they were generally welcomed by the masses. Very soon, however, differences of opinion arose among the masses. Some criticized and doubted the leadership of the work teams or the opinions of certain of their members. Others criticized and doubted the opinions of certain leaders of the Party. When the majority of the work teams did a lot of things that should have been done by the mass movement and placed many restrictions on it, this naturally gave rise to discontent and doubts among the masses. Even if some speeches were too drastic, they were revolutionary speeches which demonstrated the speakers' courage to think, to speak, to struggle, and to rebel. Of course, there were a small number of rightist speeches. This, to be sure, was a normal thing. Adequate time should be allowed for all kinds of opinions to be fully expressed, fully debated and made clear.

But precisely at this critical moment, one after another, those erroneous decisions mentioned above were made at meetings of the Central Committee held to hear reports-meetings at which I presided. In the 50 days and more after the work teams were sent out, I gave consistent support to the work teams. This, then, added to the possibility of the work teams making mistakes, and added to the gravity of the mistakes which were made. The majority of the responsible members of the work teams neither understood the great proletarian cultural revolution nor properly learned from the masses. At the very outset they asked the broad masses who had been aroused to act according to the plans and steps which we and the work teams conceived on the basis of our subjective wishes. This ran counter to the law governing the development of the revolutionary mass movement, and many serious incidents occurred. In fact, we took the reactionary bourgeois stand, practiced bourgeois dictatorship, suppressed the great cultural revolution which was then vigorously developing, confused the right and the wrong, the white and the black, thereby inflating the arrogance of the bourgeoisie and demoralizing the proletariat.

Even at this moment I still did not wake up, not knowing that the creation of such a situation was extremely abnormal, extremely unfavorable to the great proletarian cultural revolution, and extremely unfavorable to the cause of the Party and the socialist cause. This was a mistake having to do with the Right opportunist line. In a short span of 50 days and more, the damage and influence caused by the mistake of this kind were tremendous. Up to now, the consequences have not been entirely eliminated; in some places they have even been aggravated, bringing about serious feeling of opposition between the masses.

This mistake of mine runs counter to Mao Tse-tung's thought and to the theories, lines, principles and policies concerning the great proletarian cultural revolution as set forth in the circular of May 16, 1966.

III

It was Chairman Mao and the Party Central Committee which asked me to take charge of the daily routine of the Party Central Committee in case Chairman Mao was not in Peking. Owing to the fact that prior to August 5 last year I still did not understand my mistake in line and orientation made in the great proletarian cultural revolution, so in several speeches at the Building Construction Industry Institute I did not take the initiative to admit my responsibility, and I did not formally stand out and straightforwardly tell all the teachers and students of the Institute that I should bear the main responsibility for the various mistakes made in the initial period of the great cultural revolution in the Institute in order to lessen the responsibility of the other leading comrades of the Central Committee who were then in Peking, of the new Peking Municipal Party Committee, of the Building Material Industry Ministry and of the work teams.

At that time I just said in a generalized way that the work team had made mistakes in your Institute. The responsibility for the mistakes could not be borne entirely by the work team; the Party Central Committee and the new Peking Municipal Party Committee were also responsible . . . You were clear about the mistakes made by the work team in your Institute, and you might discuss them. You might also discuss the mistakes of the Party Central Committee and the new Peking Municipal Party Committee. One should be responsible for one's mistakes. Here, I did not say that I should bear the main responsibility, nor did I say that at that time the daily work of the Party Central Committee was in my charge in the absence of Chairman Mao. As a result, as to who should bear the main responsibility for the mistakes made at that time, it was far from clear. At that time, what I said was incorrect.

I attended your all-Institute debate on August 2, and heard two kinds of different opinion. Besides, the students handed me a slip, proposing a third different opinion. Although these different opinions included some questions of principle and orientation, yet I believed that basically they were still different opinions within the ranks of the people and should be discussed and debated in a normal way, so that the right could be distinguished from the wrong, what was correct could be upheld, what was wrong could be corrected, and it might be possible to unite one and all. This was because the great proletarian cultural revolution had to rely on the revolutionary students, revolutionary teachers, and revolutionary staff members to unite with all people who could be united with before it could be successful. The great cultural revolution in a school should be undertaken mainly by the students. I believed that unity which was achieved on the basis of a desire for unity and after adequate discussions and debates—in the course of which the right was distinguished from the wrong, the truth was upheld and the mistakes were corrected —was precisely what we needed at that time. We could not say that such unity was "combining two into one." Here, of course, I should make an examination. At the time, I did not elaborate sufficiently or correctly enough on this question.

After hearing the opinions of various quarters on August 2 and 3 last year and again hearing the speeches by leading comrades of the work team on August 4, there gradually formed in my mind the following impression: The orientation of struggle adhered to by the "August 1 Combat Regiment" was a correct one; they were firmly opposed to the erroneous leadership of the original Party Committee of the Institute and the work team, and their proletarian revolutionary rebel spirit was good. On the other hand, the "Revolutionary Regiment," though they too said that the leadership of the Institute Party Committee and the work team had shortcomings and made mistakes, basically protected both, because members of the "Revolutionary Regiment" were the hoodwinked. They pointed the spearhead of their struggle not at the Party Committee or the work team, but mainly at the "August 1 Regiment." For this reason, the general orientation of their struggle was fundamentally wrong. My view on this was basically identical with the views of the new Peking Municipal Party Committee. Yet I did not in time tell this view of mine to the teachers, students and staff members of the Institute. Only in my talk with comrades of the work team on August 4 did I mention this briefly—and then not in a very general manner.

Besides this, during my contacts with various quarters I also found that the Party and League organizations at the Building Construction Industry Institute were still controlled by the same set of men. They had not held any re-election, nor did they cease to carry out activities. For this reason, the activities of the Party and League organizations were often aimed at maintaining the old order and at opposing the revolutionary rebel spirit and the revolutionary rebel actions. Hence, I once suggested re-election of the Party and League organizations. If it proved impossible to hold an election for the time being, temporary convenors might be elected. On the whole, Party and League members should not hold secret meetings. When meetings were held, people outside the Party and the League—in a number doubling their own —should be invited to attend. The aim of this suggestion of mine was to prevent the great cultural revolution at the time from being controlled by the original Party and League organizations, which tried only to obstruct the development of the movement. Was my suggestion adopted? If the answer was affirmative, did it cause the majority of the cadres in the Institute to be attacked? I do not know. If the majority of the cadres were attacked because of the adoption of my suggestion, then I should take the main responsibility.

In my several speeches I also touched on the following problems:

1. Some people rose to make trouble and to rebel against our Party Committee and work team. We should not be afraid; we should support them in rising to make trouble and to rebel, even if a small number of bad people also participated. This was because the overwhelming majority of them were good people and supported the Chinese Communist

Party, socialism and Chairman Mao. Bad people were only a minority. If we were afraid that some people rose to make trouble and prevented them from rebeling against us, then we would surely make mistakes in orientation. However, in explaining this question, I talked too much, and I said this: "Don't be afraid that bad people go on to the stage, for this may do us some good. You can kill a snake only when it comes out of the cave." These words were wrong and should be refuted.

2. In several speeches I emphasized the need to unite with the majority and unite with all people who could be united with. I did not explain that all people with whom unity is possible should be united and a great revolutionary alliance and revolutionary "three-way combination" should be realized with the proletarian revolutionaries as the core and under the premise of the sameness of general orientation. Without taking the proletarian revolutionaries as the core and without the premise of the sameness of general orientation, it would be impossible to realize a great revolutionary alliance and revolutionary "three-way combination." Even if they were realized, they could not be consolidated.

3. In my several speeches I quoted from Marx: "The proletariat can liberate itself only by liberating the whole mankind." As to the question of what people should be included in the liberation of the whole mankind, I first of all pointed that they included the workers, peasants and other working people, students, and intellectuals. They constituted the bulk of humanity. However, they also included landlords, rich peasants, counter-revolutionaries, bad people, rightists and capitalists who had not been sentenced to death, and also included the wives and children of those who had been sentenced to death. All of them need to be reformed. And to reform these people, a great deal of work had to be done. As a result, when dealing with the transformation of the remnants of these exploiting classes, I talked too much and paid too much attention to them. This aroused the feeling on the part of people that I had stood matter on its end. This was wrong.

As for the mistakes which I had made at the Peking Building Construction Industry Institute and their bad influence, I ask the comrades to freely expose and criticize them.

As regards my erroneous guiding ideas and their evil influence in the early period of the great proletarian cultural revolution, I ask the comrades to freely expose and criticize them.

As regards my other speeches and actions, I also ask the comrades to freely expose and thoroughly criticize those which do not conform to the great thought of Mao Tse-tung.

Finally, I extend my apology to the revolutionary teachers, students and staff members who have been suppressed and harmed by the erroneous line which I represent! Those revolutionary teachers, students and staff members and the broad masses of members of the work teams who were hoodwinked by the erroneous line and who made mistakes under varying degrees in the initial period of the great proletarian cultural revolution bear little responsibility. The main responsibility rests with me. They too are the victims of the erroneous line, and I also want to extend my apology to them!

I hope that while exposing and criticizing me, our comrades will form a great revolutionary alliance and revolutionary "three-way combination" with the proletarian revolutionaries as the core, and build Peking Building Construction Industry Institute into a red great school for Mao Tse-tung's thought.

Carry through the great proletarian cultural revolution to the end!

Long live the proletarian revolutionary rebel spirit!

Long live the great, glorious and correct Chinese Communist Party!

Long live the great and invincible thought of Mao Tse-tung!

Long live the great teacher, great leader, great supreme commander and great helmsman Chairman Mao! A long, long life to him!

VI. PROSPECT OF SINO-SOVIET RELATIONS

48. LENINISM OR SOCIAL-IMPERIALISM?

In Commemoration of the Centenary of the

Birth of the Great Lenin

EDITORIAL DEPARTMENTS OF
RENMIN RIBAO, HONGQI,
AND JIEFANGJUN BAO

I. THE BANNER OF LENINISM IS INVINCIBLE

The centenary of the birth of the great Lenin falls on April 22 this year.

Throughout the world, the Marxist-Leninists, the proletariat and the revolutionary people are commemorating this date of historic significance with the highest respect for the great Lenin.

After the death of Marx and Engels, Lenin was the great leader of the international communist movement and the great teacher of the proletariat and oppressed people of the world.

In 1871, the year after Lenin was born, the uprising of the Paris Commune occurred; this was the first attempt of the proletariat to overthrow the bourgeoisie. The world was entering the era of imperialism and proletarian revolution late in the nineteenth and early in the twentieth centuries when Lenin began his revolutionary activities. In his struggles against imperialism and opportunism of every kind, and especially

From *Peking Review,* No. 17, April 24, 1970, pp. 5-15.

against the revisionism of the Second International, Lenin inherited, defended and developed Marxism and brought it to a new and higher stage, the stage of Leninism. As Stalin put it, "Leninism is Marxism of the era of imperialism and of the proletarian revolution."[1]

Lenin analyzed the contradictions of imperialism, revealed the law governing it and solved a series of major questions of the proletarian revolution in the era of imperialism and settled the question of socialism "achieving victory first in one or several countries."[2] He expounded the thesis that the proletariat must assume leadership in the bourgeois-democratic revolution and led the Russian proletariat in staging a general rehearsal in the revolution of 1905. Under his leadership the Great October Socialist Revolution brought about the fundamental change from the old world of capitalism to the new world of socialism, opening up a new era in the history of mankind.

Lenin's theoretical and practical contributions to the cause of the proletarian revolution were extremely great.

After the death of Lenin, Stalin inherited and defended the cause of Leninism in his struggles against domestic and foreign class enemies and against the Right and "Left" opportunists in the Party. He led the Soviet people in continuing the advance along the socialist road and in winning great victories. During World War II the Soviet people under the command of Stalin became the main force in defeating fascist aggression and made magnificient contributions which will live for ever in the history of mankind.

We Chinese Communists and the Chinese people will never forget that it was precisely in Leninism that we found our road to liberation. Comrade Mao Tsetung says: "The salvoes of the October Revolution brought us Marxism-Leninism." "They [the Chinese—*Tr.*] found Marxism-Leninism, the universally applicable truth, and the face of China began to change."[3] He points out: "The Chinese people have always considered the Chinese revolution a continuation of the Great October Socialist Revolution."[4]

Applying the theory of Marxism-Leninism, Comrade Mao Tse-tung creatively solved the fundamental problems of the Chinese revolution and led the Chinese people in waging the most protracted, fierce, arduous and complicated revolutionary struggles and revolutionary wars ever known in the history of the world proletarian revolution and in winning victory in the people's revolution in China, this large country in the East. This is the greatest victory in the world proletarian revolution since the October Revolution.

We are now living in a great new era of world revolution. The international situation has undergone world-shaking changes since Lenin's time. The development of world history as a whole has proved that Lenin's revolutionary teachings are correct and that the banner of Leninism is invincible.

But history has its twists and turns. Just as Bernstein-Kautsky revisionism emerged after the death of Engels, so did Khrushchov-Breshnev revisionism after the death of Stalin.

Eleven years after Khrushchov came to power, a split occurred within the revisionist clique and he was replaced by Brezhnev. More than five years have elapsed since Brezhnev took office. And now it is this Brezhnev who is conducting the "commemoration" of the centenary of Lenin's birth in the Soviet Union.

Lenin once said: "It has always been the case in history that after the death of revolutionary leaders who were popular among the oppressed classes, their enemies have attempted to appropriate their names so as to deceive the oppressed classes."[5]

This is exactly what the renegade Brezhnev and his ilk are doing to the great Lenin. In their so-called Theses on the Centenary of the Birth of Vladimir Ilyich Lenin, they have the impudence to distort the great image of Lenin, the revolutionary teacher of the proletariat, and pass off their revisionist rubbish as Leninism. They pretend to "commemorate" Lenin, but in reality they are appropriating the name of Lenin to press forward with their social-imperialism, social-fascism and social-militarism. What an outrageous insult to Lenin!

Today our fighting tasks are thoroughly to expose the betrayal of Leninism by the Soviet revisionist renegades, to lay bare the class nature of Soviet revisionist social-imperialism, point out the historical law that social-imperialism, like capitalist imperialism, will meet its inevitable doom, and further promote the great struggle of the people of the world against U.S. imperialism, Soviet revisionism and all reaction. Here is the tremendous significance of our commemoration of the centenary of the birth of the great Lenin.

II. THE FUNDAMENTAL QUESTION OF LENINISM IS THE DICTATORSHIP OF THE PROLETARIAT

In his struggles against opportunism and revisionism, Lenin repeatedly pointed out that the fundamental question in the proletarian revolution is that of using violence to seize political power, smash the bourgeois state machine and establish the dictatorship of the proletariat.

He said: "The latter [the bourgeois state—Tr.] *cannot* be superseded by the proletarian state (the dictatorship of the proletariat) in the process of 'withering away'; as a general rule, this can happen only by means of a violent revolution."[6]

He added that Marx's theory of the dictatorship of the proletariat "is inseparably bound up with all he taught on the revolutionary role of the proletariat in history. The culmination of this role is the proletarian dictatorship."[7]

The victory of the October Revolution led by Lenin was a victory for the Marxist theory of the proletarian revolution and the dictatorship of the proletariat. The road of the October Revolution is the road of the proletariat achieving the dictatorship of the proletariat through violent revolution.

Around the time of the October Revolution, Lenin summed up the new revolutionary practice and further developed the Marxist theory of the dictatorship of the proletariat. He pointed out that the socialist revolution covers "a whole epoch of intensified class conflicts"[8] and that "until this epoch has terminated, the exploiters inevitably cherish the hope of restoration, and this *hope* is converted into *attempts* at restoration."[9] Therefore, he maintained that the dictatorship of the proletariat "is necessary . . . not only for the *proletariat* which has overthrown the bourgeoisie, but for the entire *historical period* between capitalism and 'classless society,' communism."[10]

Today, as we commemorate the centenary of Lenin's birth, it is of vital practical significance to study anew these brilliant ideas of Lenin's.

As is well known, it is precisely on the fundamental question of the proletarian revolution and the dictatorship of the proletariat that the Soviet revisionist renegade clique has betrayed Leninism and the October Revolution.

Far back, when Khrushchov began to reveal his revisionist features, Comrade Mao Tsetung acutely pointed out: "I think there are two 'swords': One is Lenin and the other Stalin. The sword of Stalin has now been abandoned by the Russians." "As for the sword of Lenin, has it too now been abandoned to a certain extent by some leaders of the Soviet Union? In my view, it has been abandoned to a considerable extent. Is the October Revolution still valid? Can it still be the example for all countries? Khrushchov's report at the 20th Congress of the C.P.S.U. says it is possible to gain political power by the parliamentary road, that is to say, it is no longer necessary for all countries to learn from the October Revolution. Once this gate is opened, Leninism by and large is thrown out."[11]

III. COUNTER-REVOLUTIONARY COUP D'ETAT BY THE KHRUSCHOV-BREZHNEV RENEGADE CLIQUE

How was it possible for the restoration of capitalism to take place in the Soviet Union, the first socialist state in the world, and how was it possible for the Soviet Union to become social-imperialist? If we examine this question from the standpoint of Marxism-Leninism, and especially in the light of Comrade Mao Tse-tung's theory of continuing the revolution under the dictatorship of the proletariat, we shall be able to understand that this was mainly a product of the class struggle in the Soviet Union, the result of the usurpation of Party and government leadership by a handful of Party persons in power taking the capitalist road there, in other words, the result of the usurpation of the political power of the proletariat by the Soviet bourgeoisie. At the same time, it was the result of the policy of "peaceful evolution" which world imperialism, in trying to save itself from its doom, has pushed in the Soviet Union through the medium of the Soviet revisionist renegade clique.

Comrade Mao Tse-tung points out: "Socialist society covers a considerably long historical period. In the historical period of socialism, there are still classes, class contradictions and class struggle, there is the struggle between the socialist road and the capitalist road, and there is the danger of capitalist restoration."[12]

In socialist society the class struggle still focuses on the question of political power. Comrade Mao Tse-tung points out: "Those representatives of the bourgeoisie who have sneaked into the Party, the government, the army and various spheres of culture are a bunch of counter-revolutionary revisionists. Once conditions are ripe, they will seize political power and turn the dictatorship of the proletariat into a dictatorship of the bourgeoisie."[13]

Classes and class struggle continued to exist in the Soviet Union long after the October Revolution, although the bourgeoisie had been overthrown. Stalin cleared out quite a gang of counter-revolutionary representatives of the bourgeoisie who had wormed their way into the Party—Trotsky, Zinoviev, Kamenev, Radek, Bukharin, Rykov and the like. This showed that sharp class struggle was going on all the time and that there was always the danger of capitalist restoration.

Being the first state of the dictatorship of the proletariat, the Soviet Union lacked experience in consolidating this dictatorship and preventing the restoration of capitalism. In these circumstances and after Stalin's death, Khrushchov, a capitalist roader in power hiding in the Soviet Communist Party, came out with a surprise attack in his "secret report" viciously slandering Stalin and by every kind of treacherous manoeuvre usurped Party and government power in the Soviet Union. This was a counter-revolutionary coup d'etat which turned the dictatorship of the proletariat into the dictatorship of the bourgeoisie and which overthrew socialism and restored capitalism.

Brezhnev was Khrushchov's accomplice in the counter-revolutionary coup d'etat and later replaced him. Brezhnev's rise to power is, in essence, the continuation of Khrushchov's counter-revolutionary coup. Brezhnev is Khrushchov the Second.

Comrade Mao Tse-tung points out:

"The rise to power of revisionism means the rise to power of the bourgeoisie."[14] "The Soviet Union today is under the dictatorship of the bourgeoisie, a dictatorship of the big bourgeoisie, a dictatorship of the German fascist type, a dictatorship of the Hitler type."[15]

This brilliant thesis of Comrade Mao Tse-tung's most penetratingly reveals the class essence and social roots of Soviet revisionist social-imperialism and its fascist nature.

Since the Soviet revisionist renegade clique usurped Party and government power in the Soviet Union, the Soviet bourgeois privileged stratum has greatly expanded its political and economic power and has occupied the ruling position in the Party, the government, and the army as well as in the economic and cultural fields. And from this stratum there has emerged a bureaucrat monopoly capitalist class, namely, a new type of big bourgeoisie which dominates the whole state machine and controls all the social wealth.

Utilizing the state power under its control, this new-type bureaucrat monopoly capitalist class has turned socialist ownership into ownership by capitalist roaders and turned the socialist economy into a capitalist economy and a state monopoly capitalist economy. In the name of the "state," it unscrupulously plunders the state treasury and embezzles at will the fruits of the labour of the Soviet people in every possible way. Indulging in luxury and debauchery, it rides roughshod over the people.

This new-type bureaucrat monopoly capitalist class is a bourgeoisie that has turned the hope of restoration into *attempts* at restoration. It has suppressed the heroic sons and daughters of the October Revolution, is lording it over the people of different nationalities in the Soviet Union and has set up its own small counter-revolutionary tsarist court. Therefore, it is reactionary in the extreme and mortally hates and fears the people.

Like all other reactionary and decadent classes, this new-type bureaucrat monopoly capitalist class is riddled with internal contradictions. In their desperate efforts to keep the power they have usurped, the members of this class are both working hand in glove with each other and scheming and struggling against one another. The greater their difficulties, the fiercer their strife, open and secret.

In order to extort maximum profits and maintain its reactionary rule, this new-type bureaucrat monopoly capitalist class not only exploits and oppresses the people of its own country, but it necessarily engages in rabid expansion and aggression, joins the company of world imperialism in redividing the world and pursues the most vicious social-imperialist policies.

This new-type bureaucrat monopoly capitalist class constitutes the class basis of Soviet revisionist social-imperialism. At present the general representative of this class is Brezhnev. He has frantically pushed and developed Khrushchov revisionism and is completing the evolution from capitalist restoration to social-imperialism, which was already begun when Khrushchov was in power.

Since Brezhnev took office, he has pushed the so-called new economic system in an all-round way and established the capitalist principle of profit in a legal form, thus intensifying the exploitation of the working people by the oligarchy of bureaucrat monopolists. He and his like extort exorbitant taxes in total disregard of the lives of the people, follow Hitler's policy of "guns instead of butter" and accelerate the militarization of the national economy to meet the needs of social-imperialism for arms expansion and war preparation.

The perverse acts of the Soviet revisionist renegade clique have caused immense damage to the social productive forces and brought about grave consequences: the decline of industry, the deterioration of agriculture, the reduction in livestock, inflation, shortages of supplies, the unusual scarcity of commodities on state markets and the increasing impoverishment of the working people. The Soviet revisionist renegades have not only squandered a vast amount of the wealth accumulated by the Soviet people through decades of hard work, but have also humbly begged for loans from West Germany, a country defeated in World War II, and are even selling out the country's natural resources and inviting Japanese monopoly capital into Siberia. The economy of the Soviet Union is already in the grip of an inextricable crisis. As friends of the Soviet people, we the Chinese people, along with the people of the world, are extremely indignant with the Soviet revisionist renegades who have brought so much damage and disgrace to the homeland of Leninism; we feel deep sympathy for the broad masses of the Soviet people who are suffering enormously from the all-round restoration of the capitalist system.

The Soviet revisionist renegade clique once said that the dictatorship of the proletariat "has ceased to be indispensable in the U.S.S.R." and that the Soviet Union "has . . . become a state of the entire people."[16] But now they are slapping their own faces and asserting that the "state of the entire people continues the cause of the proletarian dictatorship"[17] and that "the state of the whole people" and "the state of proletarian dictatorship" are "of one and the same type."[18] They are also making a hullabaloo about "strengthening party leadership," "strengthening discipline," "strengthening centralism" and so on. "A state of the entire people" and at the same time a "proletarian dictatorship"— they lump together these two diametrically opposed concepts for no other purpose than to deceive the masses and camouflage the dictatorship of the big bourgeoisie. By "party leadership" they actually mean political control over the broad masses of the party members and the people by the handful of social-fascist oligarchs. By "discipline" they mean suppression of all who are dissatisfied with their rule. And by "centralism" they mean further centralizing the political, economic and military power in the hands of their gang. In short, they are putting all these signboards up for the purpose of strengthening their fascist dictatorship and preparing for wars of aggression.

Beset with difficulties at home and abroad, the Soviet revisionist renegade clique is resorting more and more openly to counter-revolutionary violence to buttress its reactionary rule which betrays Lenin and the October Revolution. In the Soviet Union of today, special agents and spies run amuck and reactionary laws and decrees multiply. Revolution is a crime, and people are everywhere being jailed on false charges; counter-revolution is a merit, and renegades congratulate each other on their promotion. Large numbers of revolutionaries and innocent people have been thrown into concentration camps and "mental hospitals." The Soviet revisionist clique even sends tanks and armoured cars brutally to suppress the people's resistance.

Lenin pointed out: "Nowhere in the world is there such an oppression of the majority of the country's population as there is in Russia," and nationalities other than Russians were regarded "as *inorodtsi* (aliens)."[19] National oppression "turned the nationalities without any rights into great reservoirs of fierce hatred for the monarchs."[20] Now the Soviet revisionist new tsars have restored the old tsar's policy of national oppression, adopted such cruel measures as discrimination, forced migration, splitting and imprisonment to oppress and persecute the minority nationalities and turned the Soviet Union back into the "prison of nations."[21]

The Soviet revisionist renegade clique exercises comprehensive bourgeois dictatorship throughout the ideological sphere. It wantonly suppresses and destroys the proletariat's socialist ideology and culture while opening the floodgates to the rotten bourgeois ideology and culture. It vociferously preaches militarism, national chauvinism and racism and turns literature and art into tools for pushing social-imperialism.

In denouncing the dark rule of the tsarist system, Lenin indicated that police tyranny, savage persecution and demoralization had reached such an extent that "the very stones cry out"![22] One can just as well compare the rule of the Soviet revisionist renegade clique with the tsarist system castigated by Lenin.

In staging the counter-revolutionary coup d'etat, the Khrushchov-Brezhnev renegade clique played a role which no imperialist or reactionary was in a position to play. As Stalin said, "The easiest way to capture a fortress is from within."[23] The fortress of socialism, which had withstood the 14-nation armed intervention, the Whiteguard rebellion, the attack by several million Hitlerite troops and imperialist sabotage, subversion, blockade and encirclement of every kind, was finally captured from within by this handful of renegades. The Khrushchov-Brezhnev clique are the biggest renegades in the history of the international communist movement. They are criminals indicted by history for their towering crimes.

IV. SOCIALISM IN WORDS, IMPERIALISM IN DEEDS

Lenin denounced the renegades of the Second International as "socialism in words, imperialism in deeds, *the growth of opportunism into imperialism*."[24]

The Soviet revisionist renegade clique, too, has grown from revisionism into social-imperialism. The difference lies in the fact that the social-imperialists of the Second International such as Kautsky did not hold state power; they only served the imperialists of their own countries to earn a few crumbs from the super-profits plundered from the people of other countries. The Soviet revisionist social-imperialists, however, directly plunder and enslave the people of other countries by means of the state power they have usurped.

The historical lesson is: Once its political power is usurped by a revisionist clique, a socialist state will either turn into social-imperialism, as in the case of the Soviet Union, or be reduced to a dependency or a colony, as in the case of Czechoslovakia and the Mongolian People's Republic. Now one can see clearly that the essence of the Khrushchov-Brezhnev renegade clique's rise to power lies in the transformation of the socialist state created by Lenin and Stalin into a hegemonic social-imperialist power.

The Soviet revisionist renegade clique

talks glibly about Leninism, socialism and proletarian internationalism, but it acts in an out-and-out imperialist way.

It talks glibly about practising "internationalism" towards its so-called fraternal countries, but in fact it imposes fetter upon fetter, such as the "Warsaw Treaty Organization" and the "Council for Mutual Economic Assistance," on a number of East European countries and the Mongolian People's Republic, thereby confining them within its barbed-wire "socialist community" and freely ransacking them. It uses its over-lord position to press its "international division of labour," "specialization in production" and "economic integration," to force these countries to adapt their national economies to the Soviet revisionist needs and turn them into its markets, subsidiary processing workshops, orchards, vegetable gardens and ranches, all so that outrageous super-economic exploitation can be carried on.

It has adopted the most despotic and vicious method to keep these countries under strict control and stationed massive numbers of troops there, and it has even openly dispatched hundreds of thousands of troops to trample Czechoslovakia underfoot and install a puppet regime at bayonet point. Like the old tsars denounced by Lenin, this gang of renegades bases its relations with its neighbours entirely "on the feudal principle of privilege."[25]

The Soviet revisionist renegade clique talks glibly about its "aid" to countries in Asia, Africa and Latin America, but in fact, under the guise of "aid," it is trying hard to bring a number of these countries into its sphere of influence in contending with U.S. imperialism for the intermediate zone. Through the export of war materiel and capital and through unequal trade, Soviet revisionism is plundering their natural resources, interfering in their internal affairs and looking for chances to grab military bases.

Lenin pointed out: "To the numerous 'old' motives of colonial policy, finance capital has added the struggle for the sources of raw materials, for the export of capital, for 'spheres of influence,' . . . for economic territory in general."[26] Soviet revisionist social-imperialism is moving along precisely this orbit of capitalist imperialism.

The Soviet revisionist renegade clique talks glibly about its "full support" for the revolutionary struggles in other countries, but in fact it is collaborating with all the most reactionary forces in the world to undermine the revolutionary struggles of various peoples. It wildly vilifies the revolutionary masses in the capitalist countries as "extremists" and "mobs" and tries to split and disintegrate the people's movements there. It has supplied money and guns to the reactionaries of Indonesia, India and other countries and thus directly helped them massacre revolutionaries, and is scheming night and day to put out the flames of the people's armed struggles in Asia, Africa and Latin America, and suppress the national-liberation movements. Like U.S. imperialism, it is acting as a world gendarme.

The Soviet revisionist renegade clique talks glibly about its approval of "struggle against imperialism," mouthing a few phrases scolding the United States now and then, but in fact, Soviet revisionism and U.S. imperialism are both the biggest imperialisms vainly attempting to dominate the world. There is absolutely nothing in common between the Soviet revisionists' so-called opposition to the United States and the struggles of the people of the various countries against U.S. imperialism. In order to redivide the world, Soviet revisionism and U.S. imperialism are contending and colluding with each other at the same time. What Soviet revisionism has done on a series of major issues, such as the questions of Germany, the Middle East, Southeast Asia, Japan and nuclear weapons, is evidence of its crimes in contending and colluding with U.S. imperialism. Both of them are playing imperialist power politics at the expense of the interests of the people of all countries. Whatever compromises may be reached between Soviet revisionism and U.S. imperialism are merely temporary agreements between gangsters.

Lenin pointed out: "Contemporary militarism is the result of capitalism."[27] Contemporary war "arises out of the very nature of imperialism."[28]

Since Brezhnev came to power, the Soviet revisionist renegade clique has gone farther and farther down the road of militarism. It has taken over Khrushchov's military strategic principle of nuclear blackmail and energetically developed missile-nuclear weapons, and at the same time redoubled its efforts to expand conventional armaments, comprehensively strengthening its ground, naval and air forces, and carried out the imperialist "gunboat policy" throughout the world.

On the question of war, formerly Khrushchov hypocritically advocated a world "without weapons, without armed forces and without wars" to cover up actual arms expansion and war preparation. Today, Brezhnev and company have somewhat changed their tune. They have gone all out to stir up war fanaticism, clamouring that the present international situation is "fraught with the danger of a new world war,"[29] brazenly threatening to "forestall the opponent" and bragging about their "stra-

tegic missiles" being "capable of destroying any target at any place."[30] They have been increasing military expenditures still more frantically, stepping up their mobilization and preparation for wars of aggression and plotting to unleash a blitzkrieg of the Hitler type.

The Soviet revisionist renegade clique has occupied Czechoslovakia by surprise attack, encroached upon Chinese territories such as Chenpao Island and the Tiehliekti area and made nuclear threats against our country. All this fully reveals the aggressive and adventurous nature of Soviet revisionist social-imperialism. Like the U.S. imperialists, the handful of oligarchs of Soviet revisionist social-imperialism have become another arch-criminal preparing to start a world war.

V. THE "BREZHNEV DOCTRINE" IS AN OUTRIGHT DOCTRINE OF HEGEMONY

In order to press on with its social-imperialist policy of expansion and aggression, the Brezhnev renegade clique has developed Khrushchov revisionism and concocted an assortment of fascist "theories" called the "Brezhnev doctrine."

Now let us examine what stuff this "Brezhnev doctrine" is made of.

First, the theory of "limited sovereignty." Brezhnev and company say that safeguarding their so-called interests of socialism means safeguarding "supreme sovereignty."[31] They flagrantly declare that Soviet revisionism has the right to determine the destiny of another country "including the destiny of its sovereignty"[32]

What "interests of socialism"! It is you who have subverted the socialist system in the Soviet Union and pushed your revisionist line of restoring capitalism in a number of East European countries and the Mongolian People's Republic. What you call the "interests of socialism" are actually the interests of Soviet revisionist social-imperialism, the interests of colonialism. You have imposed your all-highest "supreme sovereignty" on the people of other countries, which means that the sovereignty of other countries is "limited," whereas your own power of dominating other countries is "unlimited." In other words, you have the right to order other countries about, whereas they have no right to oppose you; you have the right to ravage other countries, but they have no right to resist you. Hitler once raved about "the right to rule."[33] Dulles and his ilk also preached that the concepts of national sovereignty "have become obsolete"[34] and that "single state sovereignty" should give place to "joint sovereignty."[35] So it is clear that Brezhnev's theory of "limited sovereignty" is nothing but an echo of imperialist ravings.

Secondly, the theory of "international dictatorship." Brezhnev and company assert that they have the right to "render military aid to a fraternal country to do away with the threat to the socialist system."[36] They declare: "Lenin had foreseen" that historical development would "transform the dictatorship of the proletariat from a national into an international one, capable of decisively influencing the entire world politics."[37]

This bunch of renegades has completely distorted Lenin's ideas.

In his article "Preliminary Draft of Theses on the National and Colonial Questions," Lenin wrote of "transforming the dictatorship of the proletariat from a national one (i.e., existing in one country and incapable of determining world politics) into an international one (i.e., a dictatorship of the proletariat covering at least several advanced countries and capable of exercising decisive

influence upon the whole of world politics)."[38] Lenin meant here to uphold proletarian internationalism and propagate proletarian world revolution. But the Soviet revisionist renegade clique has emasculated the proletarian revolutionary spirit embodied in this passage of Lenin's and concocted the theory of "international dictatorship" as the "theoretical basis" for military intervention in or military occupation of a number of East European countries and the Mongolian People's Republic. The "international dictatorship" you refer to simply means the subjection of other countries to the new tsars' rule and enslavement. Do you think that by putting up the signboard of "aid to a fraternal country" you are entitled to use your military force to bully another country, or send your troops to overrun another country as you please? Flying the flag of "unified armed forces," you invaded Czechoslovakia. What difference is there between this and the invasion of China by the allied forces of eight powers in 1900, the 14-nation armed intervention in the Soviet Union and the "16-nation" aggression organized by U.S. imperialism against Korea!

Thirdly, the theory of "socialist community." Brezhnev and company shout that "the community of socialist states is an inseparable whole"[39] and that the "united action"[40] of the socialist community" must be strengthened.

A "socialist community" indeed! It is nothing but a synonym for a colonial empire with you as the metropolitan state. The relationship between genuine socialist countries, big or small, should be built on the basis of Marxism-Leninism, on the basis of the principles of complete equality, respect for territorial integrity, respect for state sovereignty and independence and of non-interference in each other's internal affairs, and on the basis of the proletarian internationalist principle of mutual support and mutual assistance. But you have trampled other countries underfoot and made them your subordinates and dependencies. By "united action" you mean to unify under your control the politics, economies and military affairs of other countries. By "inseparable" you mean to forbid other countries to free themselves from your control and enslavement. Are you not brazenly trying to enslave the people of other countries?

Fourthly, the theory of "international division of labour." Brezhnev and company have greatly developed this nonsense spread by Khrushchov long ago. They have not only applied "international division of labour" to a number of East European countries and the Mongolian People's Republic as mentioned above, but have extended it to other countries in Asia, Africa and Latin America. They allege that the Asian, African and Latin American countries cannot "secure the establishment of an independent national economy."[41] unless they "cooperate" with Soviet revisionism. "This co-operation enables the Soviet Union to make better use of the international division of labour. We shall be able to purchase in these countries increasing quantities of their traditional export commodities—cotton, wool, skins and hides, dressed non-ferrous ores, vegetable oil, fruit, coffee, cocoa beans, tea and other raw materials, and a variety of manufactured goods."[42]

What a list of "traditional export commodities"!

It is a pity that this list is not complete. To it must be added petroleum, rubber, meat, vegetables, rice, jute, cane sugar, etc.

In the eyes of the handful of Soviet revisionist oligarchs, the people of the Asian, African and Latin American countries are destined to provide them with these "traditional export commodities" from generation to generation. What kind of "theory" is this? The colonialists and imperialists have long advocated that it is they who are to determine what each country is to produce in the light of its natural conditions, and they have forcibly turned Asian, African and Latin American countries into sources of raw materials and kept them in a state of backwardness so that industrial capitalist countries can carry on the most savage colonial exploitation at their convenience. The Soviet revisionist clique has taken over this colonial policy from imperialism. Its theory of "international division of labour" boils down to "industrial Soviet Union, agricultural Asia, Africa and Latin America" or "industrial Soviet Union, subsidiary processing workshop Asia, Africa and Latin America."

Mutual and complementary exchange of goods and mutual assistance on the basis of equality and mutual benefit between genuine socialist countries and Asian, African and Latin American countries are conducted for the purpose of promoting the growth of an independent national economy in these countries keeping the initiative in their own hands. However, the theory of "international division of labour" is preached by the handful of Soviet revisionist oligarchs for the sole purpose of infiltrating, controlling and plundering the Asian, African and Latin American countries, broadening their own spheres of influence and putting these countries under the new yoke of Soviet revisionist colonialism.

Fifthly, the theory that "our interests are involved." Brezhnev and company clamour that "the Soviet Union which, as a major world power, has extensive international contacts, cannot regard passively events that, though they might be territorially remote, nevertheless have a bearing on our security and the security of our friends."[43] They arrogantly declare: "Ships of the Soviet Navy" will "sail . . . wherever it is required by the interests of our country's security"![44]

Can a country regard all parts of the world as areas involving its interests and lay its hands on the whole globe because it is a "major power"? Can a country send its gunboats everywhere to carry out intimidation and aggression because it "has extensive international contacts"? This theory that "our interests are involved" is a typical argument used by the imperialists for their global policy of aggression. When the old tsars engaged in foreign expansion, they did it under the banner of "Russian interests." The U.S. imperialists too have time and again shouted that the United States bears responsibility "not only for our own security but for the security of all free nations," and that it will "defend freedom wherever necessary."[45] How strikingly similar are the utterances of the Soviet revisionists to those of the old tsars and the U.S. imperialists!

The Soviet revisionist renegade clique which has long gone bankrupt ideologically, theoretically and politically cannot produce anything presentable at all; it can only pick up some trash from imperialism and, after refurbishing, come out with "Brezhnevism." This "Brezhnevism" is imperialism with a "socialist" label, it is outright hegemonism, naked neo-colonialism.

VI. THE SOVIET REVISIONISTS' DREAM OF A VAST EMPIRE

In exposing tsarist Russia's policy of aggression a hundred years ago, Marx pointed out: "Its methods, its tactics, its manoeuvres may change, but the guiding star of this policy—world hegemony—will never change."[46]

Tsar Nicholas I once arrogantly shouted: "The Russian flag should not be taken down wherever it is hoisted."[47] Tsars of several generations cherished the fond dream, as Engels said, of setting up a vast "Slav empire" extending from the Elbe to China, from the Adriatic Sea to the Arctic Ocean. They even intended to extend the boundaries of this vast empire to India and Hawaii. To attain this goal, they "are as treacherous as they are talented."[48]

The Soviet revisionist new tsars have completely taken over the old tsars' expansionist tradition, branding their faces with the indelible stigma of the Romanov dynasty. They are dreaming the very dream the old tsars failed to make true and they are far more ambitious than their predecessors in their designs for aggression. They have turned a number of East European countries and the Mongolian People's Republic into their colonies and dependencies. They vainly attempt to occupy more Chinese territory, openly copying the old tsars' policy towards China and clamouring that China's northern frontier "was marked by the Great Wall."[49] They have stretched their arms out to Southeast Asia, the Middle East, Africa and even Latin America and sent their fleets to the Mediterranean, the Indian Ocean, the Pacific and the Atlantic in their attempt to set up a vast Soviet revisionist empire spanning Europe, Asia, Africa and Latin America.

The "Slav empire" of the old tsars vanished like a bubble long ago and tsardom itself was toppled by the Great October Revolution led by Lenin in 1917. The reign of the old tsars ended in thin air. Today too, in the era when imperialism is heading for total collapse, the new tsars' mad attempt to build a bigger empire dominating the whole world is nothing but a dream.

Stalin said: "Lenin called imperialism 'moribund capitalism.' Why? Because imperialism carries the contradictions of capitalism to their last bounds, to the extreme limit, beyond which revolution begins."[50]

Since Soviet revisionism has embarked on the beaten track of imperialism, it is inevitably governed by the law of imperialism, and afflicted with all the contradictions inherent in imperialism.

Comrade Mao Tse-tung points out: "The United States is a paper tiger. Don't believe in the United States. One thrust and it's punctured. Revisionist Soviet Union is a paper tiger too."[51]

In carrying out rabid expansion and aggression, Soviet revisionist social-imperialism is bound to go to the opposite of what it expects and create the conditions for its own downfall. Soviet revisionism treats the other countries of the "socialist community" as its fiefs, but it can never succeed in perpetuating its colonial rule over the people of these countries, nor can it alleviate its contradictions with these countries. East Europe today is just like a powder keg which is sure to go off. The intrusion of the Soviet revisionist tanks into Prague does not in the least indicate the strength of Soviet revisionist social-imperialism, on the contrary it marks the beginning of the collapse of the Soviet revisionist colonial empire. With its feet deep in the Czechoslovak quagmire, Soviet revisionist social-imperialism cannot extricate itself.

By its expansion and plunder in Asia, Africa and Latin America, Soviet revisionism has set itself against the people of these regions. It has so overreached itself and become so burdened that it is swollen all over like a man suffering from dropsy. Even the U.S. imperialist press says: "We've discovered that they [the Russians] blunder as badly as we do—if not worse."[52]

With Soviet revisionist social-imperialism joining the company of world imperialism, the contradictions among the imperialists have become more acute. Social-imperialism and imperialism are locked in a fierce rivalry to broaden their respective spheres of influence. The strife between social-imperialism and imperialism, which are encircled ring upon ring by the world's people, must inevitably accelerate the destruction of the entire imperialist system.

At home the rule of Soviet revisionist social-imperialism also rests on a volcano. During the period of the Stolypin reaction, Lenin wrote that the upsurge of the struggle of the Russian working class "may be rapid, or it may be slow," "but in any case it is leading to a revolution."[53] In the Soviet Union today the conflict and antagonism between the new-type bureaucrat monopoly capitalist class on the one hand and the enslaved proletariat, labouring peasants and revolutionary intellectuals on the other are becoming increasingly acute. Class struggle develops independently of man's will and must lead to revolution sooner or later.

The Soviet Union was originally a union of multi-national socialist states. Such a union can be built, consolidated and developed only under socialist conditions and on the basis of equality and voluntary affiliation. The Soviet Union, as Stalin indicated, "had before it the unsuccessful experiments of multi-national states in bourgeois countries. It had before it the experiment of old Austria-Hungary, which ended in failure." Nevertheless, the union of Soviet multi-national states was "bound to stand every and any test," because "real fraternal cooperation among the peoples has been established" by the socialist system "within the system of a single federated state."54 Now the Soviet revisionist renegade clique has subverted the socialist system, exercised a bourgeois dictatorship and substituted national oppression for national equality and the jungle law of the bourgeoise for mutual help and fraternity among the nationalities. Now that the proletarian basis, the socialist basis, of the original union has been discarded, will not the huge multi-national "union" under the rule of the bourgeoisie of a new type one day undergo the same crisis and end in failure, as the Austro-Hungarian empire did in the past?

To extricate itself from its impasse at home and abroad, Soviet revisionist social-imperialism, like U.S. imperialism, feverishly engages in missile-nuclear blackmail and seeks a way out through military adventures and large-scale war of agression. But will war bring a new lease of life to imperialism and social-imperialism in their death throes? No. Just the opposite. History irrefutably proves that, far from saving imperialism from its impending doom, war can only hasten its extinction.

Chairman Mao points out: "With regard to the question of world war, there are but two possibilities: One is that the war will give rise to revolution and the other is that revolution will prevent the war."55

Chairman Mao also says: "People of the world, unite and oppose the war of aggression launched by any imperialism or social-imperialism, especially one in which atom bombs are used as weapons! If such a war breaks out, the people of the world should use revolutionary war to eliminate the war of aggression, and preparations should be made right now!"56

This great call made by Chairman Mao on the basis of the present international situation indicates the orientation of struggle for the proletariat and the revolutionary people throughout the world. The people of the world must maintain high vigilance, make every preparation and be ready at all times to deal resolute crushing blows to any aggressor who dares to unleash war!

In recent years, the Soviet revisionist renegade clique, inheriting the old tricks of the old tsars, has been backing and engineering, half openly, half secretly, a new "Movement for Pan-Slavism" and publicizing the "sacredness of the national spirit" of the Russians in a futile attempt to poison the minds of the Soviet labouring masses and younger generation with this reactionary trend of thought and induce the Soviet people to serve as tools for the policies of aggression and war of the handful of Soviet revisionist oligarchs. In all sincerity, we would like to remind the fraternal Soviet people never to be taken in by "Pan-Slavism."

What is "Pan-Slavism"?

In exposing the old tsars, Marx and Engels pointed out incisively: "Pan-Slavism is an invention of the St. Petersburg Cabinet."57 Engels said that the old tsars used this swindle in preparation for war "as the last sheet anchor of Russian tsarism and Russian reaction." Therefore, "Pan-Slavism is the Russians' worst enemy as well as ours."58

Like Hitler's "Aryan master race," the "Pan-Slavism" of the Soviet revisionist new tsars is exceedingly reactionary racism. They publicize these reactionary ideas only to serve expansion abroad by the handful of reactionary rulers of their "superior race." For the broad masses of the people, this only spells catastrophe.

Lenin once pointed out: "The oppression of 'subject peoples' is a double-edged weapon. It cuts both ways—against the 'subject peoples' and against the Russian people."[59] It is precisely under the smokescreen of "Pan-Slavism" that the handful of Soviet revisionist oligarchs are now working against time both to plot wars of aggression and to step up their attacks on the Soviet people, including the Russian people.

The interests of the proletariat and the broad masses in the Soviet Union are diametrically opposed to those of the Soviet revisionist new tsars but are in accord with the interests of the revolutionary people the world over. If the Soviet revisionist new tsars launch a large-scale war of aggression, then, in accordance with Lenin's principle in dealing with imperialist wars of aggression, the proletariat and the revolutionary people of the Soviet Union will surely refuse to serve as cannon-fodder for the unjust war unleashed by Soviet revisionist social-imperialism. They will carry forward the cause of the heroic sons and daughters of the Great October Revolution and fight to overthrow the new tsars and re-establish the dictatorship of the proletariat.

Two hundred years ago, eulogizing the "achievements" of the wars of aggression of Tsarina Catherine II, a Russian poet wrote: "Advance, and the whole universe is thine!"[60] Now the Soviet revisionist new tsars have mounted the horse of the old tsars and "advanced." They are dashing about recklessly, unable to rein in and completely forgetting that their ancestors were thrown from this same horse and that thus the Russian empire of the Romanov dynasty came to an end. It is certain that the new tsars will come to no better end than the old tsars. They will surely be thrown from their horse and dashed to pieces.

VII. PEOPLE OF THE WORLD, UNITE AND FIGHT TO OVERTHROW U.S. IMPERIALISM, SOVIET REVISIONISM AND ALL REACTION

Comrade Mao Tse-tung points out: "The Soviet Union was the first socialist state and the Communist Party of the Soviet Union was created by Lenin. Although the leadership of the Soviet Party and state has now been usurped by revisionists, I would advise comrades to remain firm in the conviction that the masses of the Soviet people and of Party members and cadres are good, that they desire revolution and that revisionist rule will not last long."[61]

The Chinese people cherish deep feelings for the people of the Soviet Union. During the Great October Revolution led by Lenin, Chinese laborers in Russia fought shoulder to shoulder with the Russian proletarians. The people of our two countries have supported each other, helped each other and forged a close friendship in the course of protracted revolutionary struggles. The handful of Soviet revisionist oligarchs are perversely trying to sow dissension and undermine the relations between the Chinese and Soviet peoples, but in the end they will be lifting a rock only to drop it on their own feet.

The Soviet people are a great people with a glorious revolutionary tradition who were educated by Lenin and Stalin. They will under no circumstances allow the new tsars to sit on their backs for long. Though the fruits of the October Revolution have been thrown away by the Soviet revisionist renegades, the principles of the October Revolution are eternal. Under the great banner of Leninism, the mighty current of people's revolution is bound to break through the ice of revisionist rule, and the spring of socialism will surely return to the land of the Soviet Union!

Comrade Mao Tse-tung points out: "Whether in China or in other countries of the world, to sum up, over 90 per cent of the population will eventually support Marxism-Leninism. There are still many people in the world who have not yet awakened because of the deceptions of the social-democrats, revisionists, imperialists and the reactionaries of various countries. But anyhow they will gradually awaken and support Marxism-Leninism. The truth of Marxism-Leninism is irresistible. The masses of the people will eventually rise in revolution. The world revolution is bound to triumph."[62]

In commemorating the centenary of the birth of the great Lenin, we are happy to see that, under the guidance of Marxism-Leninism-Mao Tse-tung Thought, the cause of the world proletarian revolution is advancing from victory to victory. The genuine Marxist-Leninist forces are steadily growing throughout the world. The liberation struggles of the oppressed nations and people are vigorously forging ahead. All countries and people subjected to aggression, control, intervention or bullying by U.S. imperialism and Soviet revisionism are forming the broadest united front. A new historical period of struggle against U.S. imperialism and Soviet revisionism has begun. The death-knell is tolling for imperialism and social-imperialism.

Invincible Marxism-Leninism-Mao Tse-tung Thought is the powerful weapon of the proletariat for knowing and changing the world, the powerful weapon for propelling history forward. Marxism-Leninism-Mao Tse-tung Thought, integrated with the revolutionary masses in their hundreds of millions and with the concrete practice of people's revolution in all countries, will certainly bring forth inexhaustible revolutionary strength to smash the entire old world to smithereens!

Long live great Marxism!

Long live great Leninism!

Long live great Mao Tse-tung Thought!

Notes

1. Stalin, "The Foundations of Leninism," *Collected Works*, Chinese ed., Vol. 6, p. 63.

2. Lenin, "The Military Programme of the Proletarian Revolution," *Collected Works*, Chinese ed., Vol. 23, p. 75.

3. Mao Tse-tung, "On the People's Democratic Dictatorship," *Selected Works of Mao Tsetung*, Chinese ed., Vol. 4, p. 1476 and p. 1475.

4. Chairman Mao's speech of April 17, 1957.

5. Lenin, "Imperialism and the Split in Socialism," *Collected Works*, Chinese ed., Vol. 23, p. 117.

6. Lenin, "The State and Revolution," *Selected Works*, Chinese ed., Vol. 3, p. 179.

7. *Ibid.*, p. 184.

8. Lenin, "The Socialist Revolution and the Right of Nations to Self-Determination," *Collected Works*, Chinese ed., Vol. 22, p. 138.

9. Lenin, "The Proletarian Revolution and the Renegade Kautsky," *Collected Works*, Chinese ed., Vol. 28, p. 235.

10. Lenin, "The State and Revolution," *Selected Works*, Chinese ed., Vol. 3, p. 192.

11. Chairman Mao's Speech at the Second Plenary Session of the Eighth Central Committee of the Communist Party of China, November 15, 1956.

12. Chairman Mao's Speeches at the Working Conference of the Central Committee at Peitaiho in August 1962 and at the Tenth Plenary Session of the Eighth Central Committee of the Party in September of the same year.

13. "Circular" of the Central Committee of the Communist Party of China, May 16, 1966.

14. A talk of Chairman Mao's in August 1964.

15. A talk of Chairman Mao's on May 11, 1964.

16. "Programme of the C.P.S.U." adopted at the Soviet revisionist "22nd Congress."

17. Soviet revisionist Theses on the Centenary of the Birth of Vladimir Ilyich Lenin.

18. Soviet revisionist *Pravda*, March 5, 1970.

19. Lenin, "Socialism and War," *Collected Works*, Chinese ed., Vol. 21, p. 285.

20. Lenin, "Speech at the First All-Russia Congress of the Navy," *Collected Works*, Chinese ed., Vol. 26, p. 322.

21. Lenin, "The Revolutionary Proletariat and the Right of Nations to Self-Determination," *Collected Works*, Chinese ed., Vol. 21, p. 392.

22. Lenin, "Review of Home Affairs," *Collected Works*, Chinese ed., Vol. 5, p. 258.

23. *History of the Communist Party of the Soviet Union (Bolsheviks), Short Course*, Chinese ed., People's Publishing House, p. 471.

24. Lenin, "The Tasks of the Third International," *Collected Works*, Chinese ed., Vol. 29, p. 458.

25. Lenin, "On the National Pride of the Great Russians," *Collected Works*, Chinese ed., Vol. 21, p. 85.

26. Lenin, "Imperialism, the Highest Stage of Capitalism," *Collected Works*, Chinese ed., Vol. 22, p. 293.

27. Lenin, "Bellicose Militarism and the Anti-Militarist Tactics of Social-Democracy," *Collected Works*, Chinese ed., Vol. 15, p. 166.

28. Lenin, "Eighth Congress of the R.C.P. (B)," *Collected Works*, Chinese ed., Vol. 29, p. 168.

29. Soviet revisionist *Uchitelskaya Gazeta*, February 5, 1970.

30. A.A. Grechko, Soviet revisionist Minister of Defence. See Soviet revisionist *Kommunist*, No. 3, 1969.

31. Soviet revisionist *International Affairs*, No. 11, 1968.

32. Soviet revisionist *Krasnaya Zvezda*, February 14, 1969.

33. *The Nuremberg Trial*, Vol. II.

34. *Foreign Affairs* (U.S.), October 1957.

35. P.C. Jessup, *A Modern Law of Nations*.

36. L.I. Brezhnev's speech at the Polish revisionist "5th Congress," November 12, 1968.

37. K.T. Mazurov's report at the October Revolution "anniversary meeting" in Moscow, November 6, 1968.

38. Lenin, "Preliminary Draft of Theses on the National and Colonial Questions," *Selected Works*, Chinese ed., Vol. 4, p. 292.

39. Soviet revisionist *Izvestia*, July 2, 1968.

40. "The Fundamental Document" of the sinister Moscow meeting in June 1969.

41. L.I. Brezhnev's speech at the sinister Moscow meeting, June 7, 1969.

42. A.N. Kosygin's report at the Soviet revisionist "23rd Congress," April 5, 1966.

43. A.A. Gromyko's report at the "session of the Supreme Soviet of the U.S.S.R.," July 10, 1969.

44. Speech of S.G. Gorshkov, the Soviet revisionist naval commander-in-chief, on Soviet Navy Day, 1969.

45. Former U.S. President Johnson's speeches, June 3 and June 20, 1964.

46. Marx, "Speech at the Meeting of Poles in London on January 22, 1867," *Marx and Engels Collected Works*, Chinese ed., Vol. 16, p. 226.

47. G.I. Nevelskoi, *The Exploits of Russian Naval Officers in the Russian Far East*, p. 124.

48. Engels, "Foreign Policy of Russian Tsardom," *Marx and Engels Collected Works*, Chinese ed., Vol. 22, p. 17.

49. "Statement of the Government of the U.S.S.R.," June 13, 1969.

50. Stalin, "The Foundations of Leninism," *Collected Works*, Chinese ed., Vol. 6, p. 65.

51. A talk of Chairman Mao's on January 30, 1964.

52. *U.S. News & World Report*, January 5, 1970.

53. Lenin, "The Beginning of Demonstrations," *Collected Works*, Chinese ed., Vol. 16, p. 357.

54. Stalin, "On the Draft Constitution of the U.S.S.R.," *Problems of Leninism*, Chinese ed., People's Publishing House, 1964, pp. 649-50.

55. Comrade Lin Piao, "Report to the Ninth National Congress of the Communist Party of China."

56. "Usher in the Great 1970's"—1970 New Year's Day editorial of *Renmin Ribao, Hongqi* and *Jiefangjun Bao, Renmin Ribao*, January 1, 1970.

57. Marx and Engels, "Socialist Democratic Alliance and the International Worker-Association," *Marx and Engels Collected Works*, Chinese ed., Vol. 18, p. 492.

58. Engels' Letter to Karl Kautsky, February 7, 1882, *Marx and Engels on Art*, Chinese ed., People's Literature Publishing House, 1963, Vol. 3, p. 361.

59. Lenin, "National Equality," *Collected Works*, Chinese ed., Vol. 20, p. 233.

60. G.R. Dershavin, "To the Capture of Warsaw."

61. Chairman Mao's Speech at the Working Conference (Enlarged) of the Central Committee of the Communist Party of China, January 30, 1962.

62. *Ibid.*

VII. HISTORICAL PERSPECTIVE

49. THE PEOPLE'S MIDDLE KINGDOM

JOHN K. FAIRBANK

I

"Communist China"—how far Communist? How far Chinese? And what is the difference anyway? How are we to evaluate the impact that decades of war and violence and revolutionary zeal have had upon the China of today? Do Peking's leaders use the terminology of Marxism-Leninism-Maoism but express sentiments inherited from the Middle Kingdom? Are they unconsciously in the grip of their past, even when most explicitly condemning it? Certainly there is a resonance between China today and earlier periods. But how great is the actual continuity?

American expectations of Chinese behavior have groped along two lines—the approach by way of Moscow, the Soviet example, and the approach by way of history, Chinese tradition. The two overlap considerably, but both are faulted by discontinuity. China today is not just another Russia. It is very different indeed. Nor is the People's Republic just another imperial dynasty. Times have changed.

History can only help to synthesize these two approaches and suggest the degree of overlap. Chinese traditions, the Soviet example and the accidental

From *Foreign Affairs*, July 1966, pp. 574-86. Reprinted by permission.

conjunctions of events can all be given meaning in a chronological perspective. But history is invoked by all parties—by our Marxist adversaries, so addicted to their "world history," and by our own policy-makers, particularly when we have to be aggressive. Even the stoutest pragmatists can hardly leave it alone. Yet it is an art, not a science, a game any number can play except historians, who feel too ignorant to play with self-confidence.

The first difficulty for all China-pundits is the very high level of generality at which the game is played. Surely "Chinese history" offers "lessons" as diverse as the experience of a quarter of mankind during 3,000 years. But we are all entangled in the old Chinese custom of viewing the Chinese realm, *t'ien-hsia* or "all under Heaven," as a unit of discourse. We still characterize dynastic periods—Han, T'ang, Sung, Ming, Ch'ing, etc.—as homogeneous slices of experience even when each lasted two or three hundred years. It is like a tenth-grade course on "Europe since the Fall of Rome." At such a level of generality, platitude is unavoidable. Statesmen who need an analytic scalpel are handed a sledgehammer.

Our second problem is the subjective factor. Appraising the impact of Communism on China is like studying the life of a man who got religion. He lives in the same house, with many of the same habits, and looks much the same. His conversion is greater subjectively, as judged by what he says, than objectively, as visible in his conduct. Yet his life has presumably taken a sharp turn and will never be the same again.

The degree of change in recent decades in China cannot be measured quantitatively but only by drawing a qualitative picture of a traditional model. This may then be compared with a similarly abstract contemporary model. Changes of "content" will by definition be greater than changes of "pattern."

II

China as seen in the middle of the nineteenth century was most remarkable for its great cultural self-consciousness, a sense of its own history and superiority. This ethos or self-image was held and perpetuated by the ruling class, best described as literati. The ruling stratum included nearly all people of substance and status, preëminently the holders of degrees gained through the official examinations or, in about one-third of the cases, through purchase. From these degree-holders or "gentry" were selected the actual officials, who totalled some twenty to forty thousand, depending on how one counts, in any case a remarkably small number considering that they governed a country of three or four hundred million people. The literate ruling class included on its lower level a large penumbra of landlords and merchants, since men of wealth could buy degree status by their contributions to government. At its top level, it included the aristocracy created by the dynasty and the dynasty itself with the emperor at its apex.

Mobility into and out of this ruling stratum gave it strength and durability.

The government's philosophy was to preserve itself by recruiting the able. The ruler's chief task was to find men of talent. Unusual talent could rise.

This old Chinese government was hard for Westerners to understand because it really operated at two levels, one official and the other informal. On the official level the emperor and his bureaucracy kept a monopoly of all the symbols of authority, and sat on top of all large-scale activities. The government not only dominated education through the examination system; it had long since broken up the Buddhist church and kept Taoism and Buddhism decentralized in isolated units across the countryside. The secular faith of Confucianism was expounded under official auspices in the Confucian temples. The officials kept all large merchant enterprises under their control by the simple device of squeezing the merchants, and absorbing them into the official class when they got big enough. All large-scale public works were, of course, governmental. The emperor patronized the arts and had the greatest collections of both art and literature. He censored literature with a heavy hand to suppress anti-Manchu works. The emperor as a high priest conducted sacrifices to the forces of nature at the temples of heaven and of agriculture at Peking. He was also the high exemplar of the religion of filial piety so stressed in the Confucian classics. His prerogatives covered everything and made him potentially the strongest monarch who had ever lived.

Yet this formal government by its small size was necessarily very superficial. It sat on top of the society without a rival, but it did not penetrate villages. They were the scene of an informal or unofficial kind of government, headed by the gentry degree-holders in each locality. This local élite coöperated with the few local magistrates to maintain the social order. They were examination-oriented, always eager to encourage talent that might rise to power. Meantime, they stood for stability and felt an obligation to keep city walls, moats, bridges, roads and temples in repair, to encourage private schooling within the family clan, and even in time of need to organize public relief and raise militia to maintain order.

This local-gentry tradition has only begun to be studied. It included a good deal of local initiative and clan spirit, if not indeed public spirit. Gentry scholars compiled thousands of local histories or gazetteers and family genealogies. They had a secular faith in the Confucian social order. They denounced all improper conduct, heterodoxy and the subversiveness of missionaries with their doctrines of egalitarianism. Gentry and officialdom were at one in supporting the "three bonds" that held Chinese society together—the subordination of children to parents, of wives to husbands, and of subjects to rulers. They did not believe in individualism or equality as abstract principles, but stressed the duties of all good men functioning in their proper niches in the social hierarchy.

The main object of government at both the official and unofficial levels was to perpetuate itself and the social order by living off the peasants and, at the same time, maintaining their welfare. The peasantry being illiterate were politically passive, since political action in this bureaucratic society was through the written word if at all. The peasant village happily never saw an official and dealt with his taxgatherers only periodically. Though illiterate, the villagers of course had a rich culture of folklore and custom, religious faith and superstition,

and complex interpersonal relations within and between families. Our picture of this folk society is still seen largely through Confucian glasses. It was, of course, pre-modern and cut off from the outside world. The peasant economy used a highly developed manpower technology that had accumulated over millennia. In good crop years life went on with much stability and many satisfactions; the Confucian ideals of social order had thoroughly permeated the society. Even bandits could follow the norms long since mirrored in some of the vernacular novels. Secret societies had their own ancient traditions. Both Buddhism and Taoism had a message for the old wives, and everyone knew that talent, assiduity, frugality and loyalty to family and friends could help one get along.

This traditional society was mature within the limits of its pre-modern technology and so had a high degree of homeostasis or capacity to maintain a steady equilibrium. It was therefore ill-suited to modernization. The Jesuits pictured it to the European Enlightenment as an example of social harmony guided by ethics. But the law, for example, as Western merchants discovered at Canton, was administered purely as a tool of state and society, not to protect individual rights. It penalized a multitude of infractions of the social order, but obliged the magistrate to add in extra-legal considerations in each case. The letter of the law was obscure or contradictory, and held in low esteem in comparison with ethical principles. Going to law was also bad news for all concerned because of official exactions. Litigation was thus a *pis aller,* and the law was no help to economic growth.

Much more could be said about our traditional model. Sinologues East and

West, ever since Ennin visited T'ang China from Japan in 838-847 and Marco Polo served there under the Mongols in 1275-1292, have never ceased trying to describe the curiously different Chinese way, a topic as enduring in Western culture as utopianism and the limits of state authority. One's main impression in retrospect today, I think, is of the strong Chinese feeling for "the social order," not "individualism," as the basis of welfare and the good life.

III

Down through the seventeenth and eighteenth centuries, China's evolution continued along established lines. The Ch'ing dynasty rounded out its frontiers across Inner Asia by subjugating the Western Mongols, Sinkiang and Tibet. The Manchu rulers at Peking further perfected their control over domestic administration with all its checks and balances. China was at peace within, and the population apparently grew by leaps and bounds. Meanwhile, the Europeans moved into the successive phases of their modern revolution, both in science and technology and in national political development. The commercial and industrial revolutions began to overrun the earth. China, at the end of the line, was soon beleaguered.

By the late nineteenth century, the inadequacies of the traditional Chinese model were very plain to see. There was no ideal of progress, no sanction for economic gain and growth, no independence for the merchant or legal protection of his enterprise against official exactions. China was not able to transplant modern industry as Japan was doing, and consequently could not build adequate military power. Her great society fell behind. Westerners became en-

trenched in the centers of foreign trade, the treaty ports, and continued to dominate the processes of modernization.

Most obviously, this was a political problem. The Ch'ing dynasty failed to assert its central control over the economic and social processes that modernization encouraged. Partly it lacked the resources and skills, partly the idea, which the Japanese leaders had got from abroad. In the last analysis the Ch'ing leadership lacked the desire to remake China's traditional society on a foreign model. This was an innate disability, due to China's long history of superiority in her East Asian world. Sitting at the feet of the barbarians was more than Chinese pride could take.

At the same time, however, China's political weakness in the late nineteenth century was an accident of history, due to the declining vigor of the dynasty and the rise of rebellions borne on the back of population pressure. The Taipings and other rebels of the 1850s and '60s almost finished off the Peking régime. It made its peace with the foreigners in order to survive and conquer the rebels. Thereafter it had to accept the foreigners as partners in modernization. But unlike the Japanese, the Ch'ing leadership never really accepted the idea of mastering the foreign-invented processes of modernization and so controlling China's fate, as the Communists are now attempting to do. Instead, unable like Japan to modernize the state and abolish foreign privilege, China fell victim to foreign exploitation in the eventual age of imperialism at the turn of the century.

Traditional China collapsed over a long period with many bangs and whimpers. The emperor's supremacy over all men was tarnished by the post-Opium War treaties of the 1840s and denied by the second settlement of 1858-60. Yet tribute missions continued to come to Peking until 1908. The transition was gradual. China did not send ministers abroad until the 1870s, and then only grudgingly. She entered the family of nations only part way. Thus her imperial claims to supremacy in East Asia were maintained side by side with the unequal treaties that put China in a semi-colonial position vis-à-vis the West. This mixed order lasted 50 years.

The imperial institution, keystone of the old social order, finally came under attack from Chinese nationalism. Since the Manchus' incapacity to meet the modern challenge had led to China's humiliation, the revolutionaries of the 1900s, by a non sequitur, denounced the monarchy as the source of China's weakness. In 1911-12 they threw out bath, bathtub, baby and all. Abolishing the monarchy had the effect of decapitating the society and created a serious vacuum of leadership.

Meanwhile the teachings of Confucius had equally suffered attrition. New learning from the West undermined the old faith. Missionaries gained few converts but their preachings of egalitarianism, individualism, science and democracy were lent credence by the superior firepower of foreign gunboats. By the time the peripheral states that had normally been tributary to the Chinese court had become Western colonies, it was plain that the old order was doomed. In 1905 the examinations were abolished in favor of a school system that, however, developed only slowly. As the gentry class disintegrated, new classes began to arise. Meanwhile the economy had been oriented more toward foreign trade through the new treaty ports, urbanization had grown with new factories and communications, and learning from

abroad, especially from Japan, had become the accepted panacea. By the end of World War I, China had lost not only her secular faith of Confucianism, but also the formal government headed by the emperor with his broad prerogatives, and even the informal leadership of the local-gentry élite. The swollen numbers of the peasantry were living precariously. Talent had some new outlets but few established channels. Warlords in regional bases were wrecking the processes of government. Foreign influences were everywhere and the great tradition was in the melting pot.

IV

The humiliating weakness and confusion of the warlord era gave the Westerners of the last generation a stereotype of China as "a heap of loose sand" or "a mere geographical expression." It also impelled patriotic youth to support a revival of central power. A new nationalism swept China in the 1920s. The overriding consideration was how to achieve national self-respect. Western influences were providing a stimulus for individualism, for the emancipation of women to control their own marriages and become educated, for the study of science and adoption of technology to achieve "progress." There was a recognition of Western superiority in many ways. All sorts of ideas flooded in and were taken up. But the over-riding and deep-down concern was for the national glory. One could not be Chinese without having a dedicated conviction of the innate worth and superiority of Chinese culture. A strong state to provide a home for it was the first essential.

This new nationalism converged with or overlapped the traditional urge to reunify the state after the collapse of a dynasty. The 40 years from the end of the Ch'ing in 1912 to the Communist takeover of 1949 is about the standard length of a dynastic interregnum in earlier instances. There had been comparable periods of disorder at the end of the T'ang, the Sung and the (Mongol) Yuan dynasties. The consolidation of Ch'ing power took 40 years from the seizure of Peking in 1644 to the last suppression of rebels in 1683. In every such period, there eventually arose a universal demand for a return to peace and order under central authority. By the end of World War II in China, this had become a widespread longing.

The rebuilding of central power was, of course, not merely a Communist achievement but began with the Kuomintang. Sun Yat-sen based his revolution on the foreign edge of China, using the funds of overseas Chinese merchants in Malaya and Hawaii, recruiting the patriotism and eloquence of students abroad in Japan and Europe, mounting his ten putsches from around the edge of China with arms smuggled in to secret societies allied with him. Yet he found that the democratic West could give him all the equipment and methods of modernization except the essential one of organizing power in postdynastic China. He found constitutions of little use, warlord armies unreliable no matter how good their weapons, and parliamentary parties as friable as the politicians who joined them, without constituencies and without loyalty to any common authority. By 1919 Sun was convinced that his revolution, if it was to make any comeback at all, must be led by a reorganized party. He found a model for this in Leninism, and Soviet delegates helped him organize the Kuomintang in the early 1920s at the same time that they helped the Chinese Communist Party come into being in 1921.

The competition between the Kuomintang and the Chinese Communists in the 1920s, which has almost monopolized the attention of historians, was never as close a race as some have liked to think. There was no real competition at first between Sun Yat-sen's many thousands of middle-aged revolutionaries and the few dozens or hundreds of young Communist students. By 1927 the Nationalist reunification had succeeded up to a point and the social revolution of the Communists was deferred. Apparently China was ready for the former but not for the latter. The new student class and the merchants in the cities were most aware of the foreign "imperialist" presence and most moved by the new nationalism, whereas the crisis in peasant life and the breakup of the old family system in the villages were not yet in the forefront of concern.

The first move in rebuilding a central government was the establishment of a party dictatorship and a party army to support it. This was achieved under the national government at Canton in the early 1920s, in Sun Yat-sen's last years. Many of the Cantonese and other leaders in his group accepted Lenin's theory of imperialism and were united by antiforeignism but abjured the class struggle within the nation. Out of Canton, as head of the Northern Expedition to unify China, came Chiang Kai-shek. It is now evident that his rise was due not merely to a talent for political-military manipulation, but also to his devotion to the primary cause of the day, national reunification. For this he saw the indoctrinated party army as the essential tool, acting on behalf of the Kuomintang dictatorship. China's nominal reunification under the Nanking government in 1928 thus marked the first great institutional step of substituting party dictatorship for dynastic rule.

This transition, with all its modern potentialities, now permitted the state for the first time to penetrate the villages. Twentieth-century China had inherited a polity that was highly authoritarian but superficial. Modern totalitarianism has been achieved by expanding the old authoritarianism down into the body social—politicizing, activating and manipulating a populace that was formerly inert in politics and parochial in its interests. Among so vast a public, this has been a slow process. In addition to the practical concerns of livelihood that induce modernization, it has been motivated by national pride. One result of mass participation has been dilution of quality and lowering of standards in the first instance. If we compare the upbuilding of China's new order with the old structure sketched above, we will be struck by the simultaneous revival of old patterns and creation of new content to fit into them.

V

The transition from dynastic to party rule, at least in theory, had taken only 16 years, from 1912 to 1928. It shows considerable continuity in the midst of discontinuity. Dynasties and parties have in common, first, a definable and ongoing group of power holders, whether it is a harem-produced swarm of princes or a central committee thrown up by the intra-party political struggle. Secondly, this ongoing group selects, not without much interplay of pressures, the top executive and assists him in running the government. The top man, Chinese-style, has to be both a sage and a hero, enunciating the ideology, making the final decisions and ruling in person, not just

reigning. He must be a model of propriety and the patron of art and letters, even a poet, as well as the arbiter of disputes and maintainer of morale. His ideological pronouncements are important because his rule is still very personal, by moral teaching more than by legal process. Personal loyalty still plays a role.

Finally, the structure of government is still similar. The military are quite separate from the civil administration but both are headed by the One Man. Meanwhile there is a third, separate echelon of supervisory personnel. In the old days it included palace eunuchs as well as dynastic family members and the whole establishment of the Censorate, both at the capital and in the provinces. Both Chiang and Mao have sat on the ancient tripod of civil bureaucracy, army and supervisory agencies, which now include secret police and informers as well as the party apparatus.

Discontinuity, of course, is most evident in the substitution of Marxism-Leninism-Maoism for imperial Confucianism, of a dialectic doctrine of struggle instead of harmony. Yet we should not overlook the pattern of orthodoxy so evident in both cases: the faith in a true teaching revealed in classical works, the role of the One Man or Leader as their expositor, the recruitment of talent as tested by the orthodox teaching, and the constant indoctrination of the entire government apparatus as a means of giving it unity and keeping it under control. Talent is still recruited and examined, a bureaucratic career still requires qualities of loyalty, obedience and finesse in personal relations, and heterodoxy is still condemned and attacked.

One principal change comes from the expansion of politics. Every village now participates in the political life that was formerly reserved for the ruling class. Peasant passivity has given way to activism by all citizens. Where a dynasty used to claim it ruled the Middle Kingdom with the Mandate of Heaven, now the "people" are said to make their own destiny through their chosen (?) instrument, the Chinese Communist Party. One of Mao's departures from Marxism-Leninism is to assert that the Party leads China's regeneration not only on behalf of the proletariat but also on behalf of a coalition of major classes—in effect, the whole people.

Without attempting further to describe it, one can only conclude from the outside that the content of the new orthodoxy is a far cry indeed from the comparatively static doctrines of Confucian self-discipline within an immutable social order inherited from the golden age of antique sages. Having supplanted the forces of nature or "Heaven," the "people" are now viewed as the vital makers of history, brimming with creative capacities. The Maoist leadership with its insight can liberate these long latent "productive forces." The new China is science-minded, "people"-minded, dynamic and convinced of its own creativity.

Yet this new order still subordinates the individual. Chinese youth escaped the family only to come under the small group, the production team, the party and the nation. From the first Mao has warred against individualism as the germ of bourgeois thinking. Civil liberties piously listed in state documents are reserved for the "people" not for those viewed by authority as "enemies of the people." An accused has few judicial rights—how can his petty interest outweigh that of all the rest of the Chinese people? Law still lacks any sanctity or even a codified and publicized content

and reliable procedure. People's courts and procurators steer by political considerations as well as by Mao's normative pronouncements and administrative regulations. The authoritarianism of the traditional state left little sanction for individualism, and the Communists do not propose to supply any now.

Just here, however, history perhaps has a message for us. The old China, in daily life below the official level, was humane in many senses of the term. The ideal "superior man" (*chün-tzu*), whose learned and proper conduct entitled him to public prestige and leadership, was not merely a servant of state authority. When not in office he pursued self-cultivation (*hsiu-shen*), calligraphy and poetry, even philosophic meditation. The old Chinese compulsion to train oneself in literacy and other accomplishments was not purely repressive self-discipline but created one's capacity for friendship and personal enjoyment. Confucian humanism had a long tradition, albeit within a collectivist social order, and peasants who today join in politics, as only the "superior man" used to do, may sometimes also aspire on a mass scale to the self-cultivation that was once the hallmark of the gentry élite. The historical adage that revolutions after their excesses swing back toward past norms has received some support from Soviet revisionism, and Peking's fulminations against it make it seem a bit more probable for China in due time.

Continuity is thus a matter of degree. So much remains of the old landscape and its many problems: the Yellow River still flows 500 miles across the North China Plain, silting its bed above the level of the fields. There are still the precarious rainfall in the Northwest and the danger of drought and famine, the weaknesses of a capital-poor and labor-intensive farm economy, the need to keep up morale and "nourish honesty" (*yang-lien*) as of old among so far-flung a bureaucracy. Chairman Mao's vision of betterment must still be achieved inside a society that has a deeply ingrained inheritance, more profoundly imbedded than either we or even Chairman Mao, from our opposite sides, may realize. It is represented, for instance, in the Chinese ideographic writing system, which it seems cannot be changed into a more flexible alphabetic or other purely phonetic system.

Even the most iconoclastic new leaders, facing these problems, will be tempted to revive traditional ways of meeting them, like the well-worn device of mutual responsibility that sets neighbor spying on neighbor within a street committee. Whatever the leaders may hope, the people by their responses, less creative than the leadership, may revive old ways under new names. Certain continuities like pride of culture may well up in a resurgent nationalism that no man can control. It is in this context that we must view Peking's recent series of remarkable disasters in foreign relations.

It is a truism that the Long March generation now in power have been spiritually in combat all their lives and are psychologically struggle-prone. By 1949 their heaven-storming militancy had picked the United States, the biggest thing in sight, as their implacable foe. By 1960 they had added the Soviet Union. This imprudent and irrational course has been justified by Mao and explained by outside observers partly on ideological grounds. Mao's doctrinaire extremism has not only challenged the Chinese people to superhuman efforts, it also keeps the Leninist faith intact.

But the vehemence of Peking's denunciations of the two outside worlds that now encircle the embattled People's Middle Kingdom (*Jen-min Chung-kuo*) seems more than "ideological" in the usual sense of the term. Such impassioned scorn, such assertive righteousness, also echo the dynastic founders of ages past.

Founding a dynasty required a man larger than life, and several great dynasties were put together by individuals with some touch of paranoia. The unifiers of the Ch'in in 221 B. C. and the Sui in 589 A. D. pulled the empire together in fevered bursts of energy. The founder of the Ming who threw out the Mongols in 1368 also had illusions of grandeur, cut off heads, liked to have errant ministers ceremoniously beaten in court, built vast walls and palaces, and got all East Asia to send him tribute missions. This fanaticism was in the minority tradition of emperors who conquer by the sword and organize manpower to build great public works—a Great Wall, a Grand Canal—rather than in the majority tradition of those who consolidate and rule through the bureaucracy. Dynastic founders were often great blueprint artists who reorganized Chinese society according to dogmatic plans and visionary doctrines. They were usually followed by consolidators who tidied up the régime and eventually let the people relax.

Mao's hostile extremism today toward an outside world that he only vaguely discerns must be seen as a function or offshoot of his extremism within his own country. Remaking China, remolding all of its people, building a modern state power, are an all-absorbing task. No one else in world history has ever tackled such a big job, for no other country has ever been so big and so materially backward. Mao's considerable achievement